D1631205
TRENTINO-ALTO ADIGE
Pages 166–175
THE VENETO AND FRIULI
Pages 138–165
VENICE
Pages 84–137
EMILIA-ROMAGNA
Pages 254–269
UMBRIA
Pages 348–363
LE MARCHE
Pages 364–373
ABRUZZO, MOLISE AND PUGLIA
Pages 500–513
Ancona
Pescara
L'Aquila
ROMA
ROME AND LAZIO
Campobasso
Foggia
Bari
SOUTHERN ITALY
Napoli
Salerno
Potenza
Taranto
BASILICATA AND CALABRIA
Pages 514–521
NAPLES AND CAMPANIA
Pages 482–499
Catanzaro
Messina
Reggio di Calabria
Palermo
Catania
Agrigento
SICILY
Pages 522–543

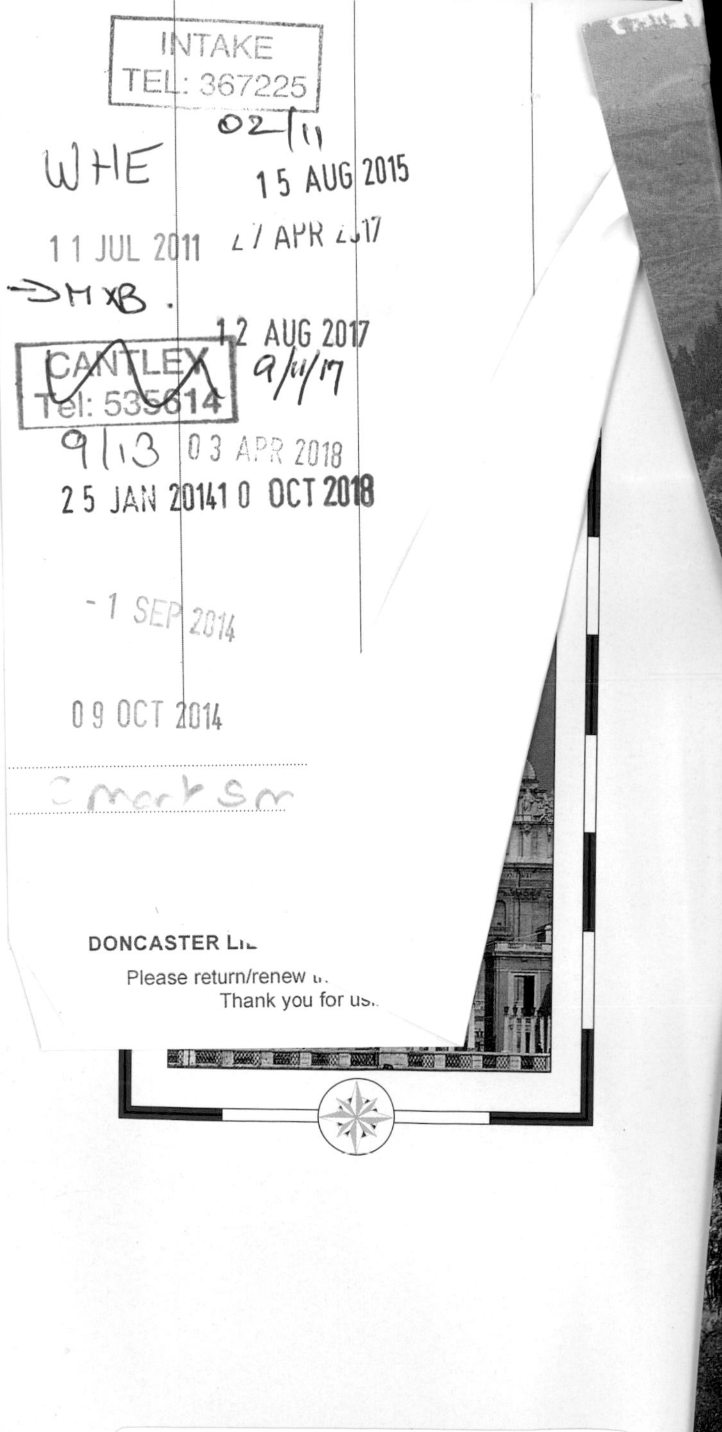

INTAKE
TEL: 367225
CANTLEX
Tel: 535614
11 JUL 2011
25 JAN 2014
- 1 SEP 2014
09 OCT 2014
15 AUG 2015
12 AUG 2017
03 APR 2018
10 OCT 2018
DONCASTER LI
Please return/renew
Thank you for us

DONCASTER LIBRARY
30122 03210934 6

EYEWITNESS TRAVEL

# ITALY

LONDON, NEW YORK,
MELBOURNE, MUNICH AND DELHI
www.dk.com

PROJECT EDITOR Fiona Wild
ART EDITORS Vanessa Courtier, Annette Jacobs
EDITORS Francesca Machiavelli, Sophie Martin,
Helen Townsend, Nicky Tyrrell
DESIGNERS Jo Doran, Anthea Forlee,
Paul Jackson, Marisa Renzullo

MAIN CONTRIBUTORS
Ros Belford, Susie Boulton, Christopher Catling,
Sam Cole, Paul Duncan, Olivia Ercoli, Andrew Gumbel,
Tim Jepson, Ferdie McDonald, Jane Shaw

MAPS
Lovell Johns Ltd, Dorling Kindersley Cartography

PHOTOGRAPHER
John Heseltine

ILLUSTRATORS
Stephen Conlin, Donati Giudici Associati srl, Stephen Gyapay,
Roger Hutchins, Maltings Partnership, Simon Roulstone,
Paul Weston, John Woodcock

Reproduced by Colourscan (Singapore)
Printed and bound by South China Printing Co. Ltd., China

First published in Great Britain in 1996
by Dorling Kindersley Limited
80 Strand, London WC2R 0RL

**Reprinted with revisions 1997, 1999, 2000, 2001, 2002, 2003, 2004, 2005, 2006, 2007, 2008, 2009, 2010, 2011**



A CIP CATALOGUE RECORD IS AVAILABLE FROM THE BRITISH LIBRARY.

ISBN 978-1-40534-701-3

Floors are referred to throughout in accordance with European usage; ie the "first floor" is the floor above ground level.

*Front cover main image:*
*Abbey of Montecorona, Umbertide, Umbria*

**The information in this DK Eyewitness Travel Guide is checked annually.**

Every effort has been made to ensure that this book is as up-to-date as possible at the time of going to press. Some details, however, such as telephone numbers, opening hours, prices, gallery hanging arrangements and travel information are liable to change. The publishers cannot accept responsibility for any consequences arising from the use of this book, nor for any material on third party websites, and cannot guarantee that any website address in this book will be a suitable source of travel information.

We value the views and suggestions of our readers very highly. Please write to: Publisher, DK Eyewitness Travel Guides, Dorling Kindersley, 80 Strand, London WC2R 0RL, Great Britain.

◁ **Fertile wine-growing region around Panzano in Chianti, Tuscany**

# CONTENTS

***David* by Bernini, Rome**

## INTRODUCING ITALY



## NORTHEAST ITALY



## NORTHWEST ITALY

A traditional small shop in Volterra, Tuscany

Gondolas weaving through the maze of canals in Venice

Basilica of San Francesco in Assisi, started in 1228

# HOW TO USE THIS GUIDE

This guide helps you get the most from your visit to Italy, providing expert recommendations as well as detailed practical information. *Introducing Italy* maps the whole country and sets it in its historical and cultural context. The 15 regional chapters, plus *Rome, Florence* and *Venice*, describe important sights with the help of maps and images. Each section is introduced with features on regional architecture and food specialities. *Travellers' Needs* gives details of hotels and restaurants and the *Survival Guide* contains practical information on everything from transport to personal safety.

## ROME

The centre of Rome has been divided into five sightseeing areas. Each area has its own chapter, which opens with a list of the sights described. All the sights are numbered and plotted on an Area Map. The detailed information for each sight is presented in numerical order, making it easy to locate within the chapter.

**All pages** relating to Rome have red thumb tabs.

**A locator map** shows where you are in relation to other areas of the city centre.

**1 Area Map**
*For easy reference, the sights are numbered and located on a map. The sights are also shown on the* Street Finder *on pages 447–57.*

**Sights at a Glance** lists the chapter's sights by category: Churches, Museums and Galleries, Historic Buildings, Streets and Piazzas.

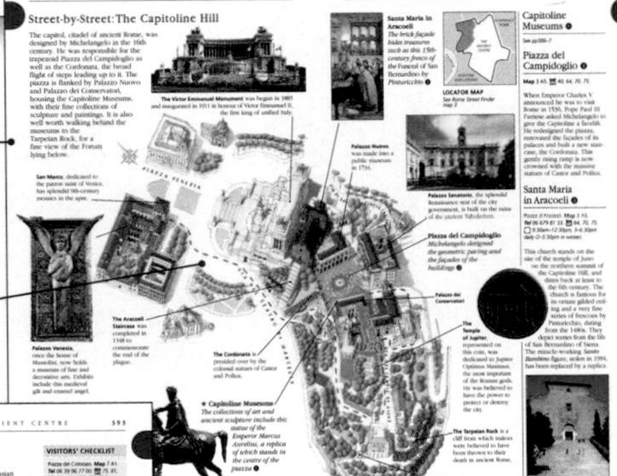

**2 Street-by-Street Map**
*This gives a bird's-eye view of the heart of each sightseeing area.*

**A suggested route** for a walk is shown in red.

**Stars** indicate the sights that no visitor should miss.

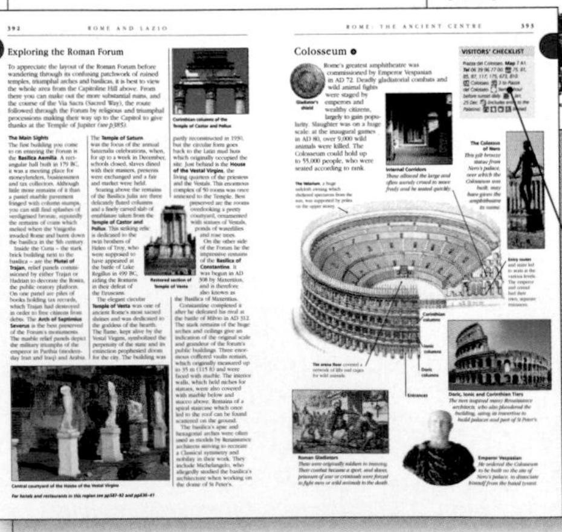

**3 Detailed information**
*All the sights in Rome are described individually. Addresses and practical information are provided. The key to the symbols used in the information block is shown on the back flap.*

## 1 Introduction

*The landscape, history and character of each region is described here, showing how the area has developed over the centuries and what it offers to the visitor today.*

## ITALY AREA BY AREA

Apart from Rome, Florence and Venice, Italy has been divided into 15 areas, each of which has a separate chapter. The most interesting towns and places to visit have been numbered on a *Regional Map*.

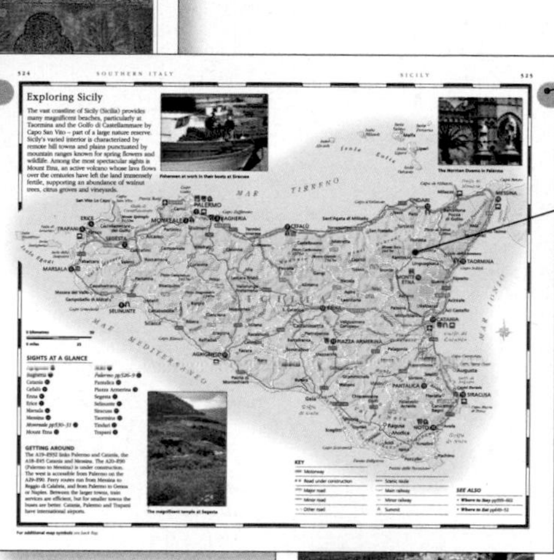

**Each area** of Italy can be identified quickly by its colour coding, shown on the inside front cover.

## 2 Regional Map

*This shows the main road network and gives an illustrated overview of the whole region. All entries are numbered and there are also useful tips on getting around the region by car and train.*

## 3 Detailed information

*All the important towns and other places to visit are described individually. They are listed in order, following the numbering given on the* Regional Map. *Within each entry, information is given on the most important sights. The name of the provincial capital is given for smaller towns at the top of each entry.*

**Story boxes** explore specific subjects further.

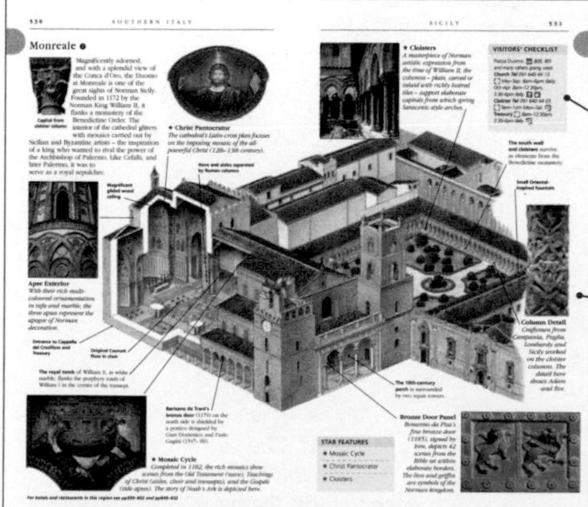

**For all the top sights**, a Visitors' Checklist provides the practical information you need to plan your visit.

## 4 Italy's top sights

*These are given two or more full pages. Historic buildings are dissected to reveal their interiors; museums and galleries have colour-coded floorplans to help you locate the most interesting exhibits.*

# INTRODUCING ITALY

# DISCOVERING ITALY

Italy offers a remarkable kaleidoscope of regions and experiences for all visitors. Extending over 1,000 km (620 miles) from top to toe, it stretches from far northern reaches that take in the Alps and the industrialized Po plain, all the way down to sun-soaked Mediterranean shores and islands of the south. Its incomparable artistic and cultural heritage centres on the Renaissance, but there are also myriad natural wonders. The following four pages are designed to help visitors pinpoint the highlights of each fascinating region.

Emperor Augustus, Turin

## VENICE

- **Magical Piazza San Marco**
- **Rialto fresh produce market**
- **Romantic gondola cruises**

Enchanting Venice, city-on-water par excellence, simply demands to be visited. But remember that it does get damp and foggy and can be outrageously expensive. Moreover there is hardly a low season, meaning that the main sights such as **Piazza San Marco** *(see pp108–9)* and the **Rialto** bridge and markets *(see p97)*, as well as the many art galleries and museums, can get crowded. In contrast, leisurely days can be spent wandering through the labyrinthine alleyways and happening upon out-of-the-way churches adorned with exquisite works of art.

Starting with the fascinating **Grand Canal** *(see pp88–91)*, *vaporetti* convey passengers around town and across the lagoon to distinctive outlying islands such as **Murano** and **Burano** *(see p121)*. A romantic gondola trip is a great way to discover the mystical backstreets and quieter canals.

## VENETO & FRIULI

- **Romeo and Juliet's Verona**
- **Padua's splendid Cappella degli Scrovegni**
- **The ruins of Aquileia**

Nymphaeum statue, Veneto

The northeast of Italy has undergone large-scale industrial development since World War II, but its splendid heritage of history and art merits exploring. A drive through the vine-clad hills is rewarded by stately villas, charming towns and family-run wineries that produce high-grade vintages. The bustling Veneto cities of **Verona** *(see pp142–7)*, the setting for the tragic story of Romeo and Juliet, and Padua with its impressive **Cappella degli Scrovegni** *(see pp156–7)*, make for memorable visits.

Santa Maria della Salute on the banks of the Grand Canal, Venice

Vine-clad hills typical of the Veneto countryside

Further east is low-key Friuli and the melancholy remains of former Roman city **Aquileia** *(see p164)*, razed to the ground in glee by notorious Attila the Hun in AD 452. Delightful **Cividale di Friuli** *(see p163)* is set at the foothills of the beautiful Julian Alps.

## TRENTINO-ALTO ADIGE

- **Skiing in the Dolomite mountain range**
- **Enchanting medieval castles**
- **The "Ice Man" in Bolzano**

An impeccable combination of traditional alpine pastoral culture and Germanic heritage is the trademark of these erstwhile Austrian domains. Ancient timber farmhouses and medieval castles and monasteries grace the slopes of the imposing **Dolomites** *(see pp82–3)*, in dramatic contrast to the modern resorts that serve the winter crowds who flock here to ski and snowboard. In summer-time nature enthusiasts and climbers take to paths through flourishing orchards and across meadows of wild-

◁ View over Florence of the richly decorated 15th-century Duomo and Campanile

Corniglia, one of the Cinque Terre in Liguria

flowers, en route to high-altitude mountain huts.

For rainy days, the pretty town of **Bolzano** *(see p172)* hosts the 5,000-year-old mummy of Ötzi the "Ice Man" in a state-of-the-art museum.

## LOMBARDY

- **Fashion capital Milan**
- **The glorious lakes by ferry**
- **Bergamo and Mantova**

Milan, home to Versace, Gucci and Armani, boasts elegant architecture such as the Gothic **Duomo** *(see p193)* and a wealth of art treasures, headed by Leonardo da Vinci's *Last Supper (see p192)*. It is also home to **La Scala** *(see p193)*, the country's leading opera house. Nearby are Italy's famous lakes – **Como** and **Maggiore** *(see pp190–91)* – adorned with villas and served by leisurely ferries.

**Bergamo** *(see p201)* merits a visit, as do **Pavia** *(see p203)* and **Mantova** *(see p207)*, each with exquisite Renaissance monasteries and palaces.

Window shopping in Via Montenapoleone, Milan

## VALLE D'AOSTA & PIEDMONT

- **Turin and the Shroud**
- **Olympic skiing**
- **Parco Nazionale del Gran Paradiso**

The Piedmont capital **Turin** *(see pp220–25)* is synonymous with the Fiat automobile plant and the remarkable Holy Shroud; it also hosted the 2006 Winter Olympics. It is renowned for its fine food and the Langhe hills produce some of Italy's best red wines, such as Barbera and Nebbiolo. Cheeses are also noteworthy, as well as rice in waterlogged fields near **Vercelli** *(see p228)*.

A little further afield, the imposing western Alps rise to giddy heights, peaking with glacier-bound **Mont Blanc** *(see p214)*, astride the French-Italian border.

The wild alpine valleys of **Parco Nazionale del Gran Paradiso** *(see pp216–7)* are home to vast numbers of wildlife, predominantly ibex and chamois.

## LIGURIA

- **Cinque Terre**
- **Italian Riviera resorts**
- **The thriving city of Genoa**

Tourists flock to the delightful hamlets of the dramatic **Cinque Terre** coast *(see p241)*, to roam along the dizzy pathways that cut across terraced hillsides. The Italian Riviera enjoys a balmy climate and is famous for its flower and fresh food markets, **San Remo** *(see p235)* in particular. The Ligurian Sea also attracts yachting enthusiasts, whose craft call in to the many picturesque village marinas.

The region's capital, **Genoa** *(see pp236–9)*, also has much to offer the visitor, from pasta with pesto sauce to the house of Christopher Columbus, and from a regenerated waterfront to one of Europe's largest aquariums.

Mosaic from Sant'Apollinare Nuovo basilica, Ravenna

## EMILIA-ROMAGNA

- **Beach life at Rimini**
- **Historic Bologna**
- **Ravenna and its mosaics**

Centrally located with an extension to the Adriatic coast, Emilia-Romagna takes in a large slice of the Apennine mountains, providing opportunities for a wide range of outdoor activities. A visit should include **Bologna** *(see p262–5)*, the impressive beach resort of **Rimini** *(see p266)*, with its extensive seafront, and the marvellous Byzantine mosaics in the churches of **Ravenna** *(see pp266–9)*.

Food plays an important part in life here and it is probably the region's gastronomy that attract most people. Tortellini pasta, cured Parma ham, Parmesan cheese and fragrant balsamic vinegar from **Modena** *(see p260)* are known the world over.

## FLORENCE & TUSCANY

- **Renaissance art in Florence**
- **Pisa and the Leaning Tower**
- **Chianti vineyards**

Justifiably popular, if overcrowded, Florence is home to Renaissance art, perfect Italian gardens, magnificent squares and splendid sights such as the **Duomo** *(see pp280–81)* and the **Uffizi** *(see pp286–9)*.

Nearby are Pisa, famous for its **Leaning Tower** *(see p326)*, **Lucca** *(see pp320–23)* and **Siena** *(see pp338–43)*, just a few of the attractive towns dotted around the area.

The Tuscan countryside with its rolling hills, pencil-thin cypress trees and bright poppy fields in spring is a dream for artists and visitors alike. A host of vineyards in the renowned Chianti region *(see pp250–51)* invite passers-by for a tasting.

The quintessential Tuscan countryside

## UMBRIA

- **Assisi and St Francis**
- **Art town of Perugia**
- **Spectacular scenery of the Monti Sibillini**

Quieter than Tuscany, this inspirational region has a lot to offer in terms of both nature and Romanesque art. **Assisi** *(see pp354–5)* is high on the sight-seeing list for its beautiful position and 13th-century Basilica, associated with the peregrinations of St Francis. Other memorable towns include medieval **Perugia** *(see pp352–3)*, **Orvieto** *(see p358)* with its glorious Duomo and peaceful **Spoleto** *(see p360)*. The **Monti Sibillini** *(see p362)* put on unrivalled displays of wildflowers in summer, while the densely wooded hills encourage wildlife, including boars and songbirds.

Tiered exterior of Rome's ancient Colosseum

## LE MARCHE

- **The republic of San Marino**
- **The Adriatic's beach resorts**
- **Renaissance Urbino**

This low-key region on the Adriatic coast has a wealth of surprises in store and is also home to Europe's oldest republic – **San Marino** *(see p368)*. Its resorts and beaches are busy in midsummer as the lively nightlife attracts young crowds. The port towns of **Ancona** *(see p372)* and **Pesaro** *(see p368)* have animated fish markets, vital for the region's seafood cuisine. Set in the hilly interior, **Urbino** *(see pp370–71)* is simply glorious – its Palazzo Ducale a triumph of 15th-century architecture.

## ROME & LAZIO

- **The ancient Roman Colosseum and Forum**
- **Vatican City and St Peter's**
- **Etruscan sites**

The nation's capital city has an overwhelming array of memorable sights ranging from Roman to Renaissance to Baroque. The ancient **Forum** *(see p390–92)* and **Colosseum** *(see p393)* are a must.

The independent Vatican City state is a highlight of any visit, with its wealth of art treasures, the **Sistine Chapel** *(see pp424–6)* and the magnificent **St Peter's** *(see pp418–9)*.

Out-of-town sights include the atmospheric ancient Etruscan sites of **Cerveteri** *(see p466)* and **Tarquinia** *(see p466)*, as well as renowned villas at **Tivoli** *(see p468)* and **Viterbo** *(see pp464–5)*.

The historic cathedral of Amalfi in Campania

## NAPLES & CAMPANIA

- **The ruins of Pompeii**
- **The trendy island of Capri**
- **Gorgeous Amalfi Coast**

A region of contrasts, Campania has several of Italy's top sights. **Naples** *(see pp486–93)* spells excellent pizzas, wonderful museums and enchanting churches, although it can be maddeningly chaotic. **Pompeii** *(see pp494–5)*, the

Roman town that was laid waste by the mighty volcano Vesuvius in AD 79, is fascinating, although many relics found here are housed at the **Museo Archeologico Nazionale** *(see pp490–91)* in Naples.

A ferry trip to the legendary island of **Capri** *(see pp498–9)*, beloved of the Romans, is recommended, and should take in the limestone rock formations and marine caves.

Last but definitely not least is the divine and immensely popular **Amalfi Coast** *(see p497)* with terraced hillsides planted with fragrant lemon trees, high above sparkling bays and beaches.

Unusual *Trulli* houses in Alberobello, Puglia

## ABRUZZO, MOLISE & PUGLIA

- **Gargano beaches**
- ***Trulli* houses in Alberobello**
- **Parco Nazionale d'Abruzzo**

Something for everyone can be had in these southern regions. There are beaches galore on the **Gargano peninsula** *(see p508)*, curious *trulli* houses at **Alberobello** *(see p511)*, ancient sights at **Trani** *(see p509)*, **L'Aquila** *(see p504)*, and **Lecce** *(see pp512–13)* – famed for its decorative Baroque architecture.

In contrast, wolves and bears inhabit the wild reaches of the rugged Gran Sasso in the **Parco Nazionale d'Abruzzo** *(see pp506–7)*, where high altitude trekking is popular. Age-old pastoral life and traditional dress persists in the mountain village of **Scanno** *(see p505)*.

Temple of Concord in the Valley of Temples, Sicily

## BASILICATA & CALABRIA

- **The "stone town" of Matera**
- **The Riace bronze statues**
- **Unspoiled fishing villages**

Italy's far south receives few visitors. The handful of attractions commence with **Matera** *(see pp518–19)*, the UNESCO World Heritage site that came to fame as the location for the controversial film *Passion of Christ* (2004). Here, over the ages, primitive stone dwellings were shaped into the rocky hill-sides, making an astonishing sight.

A pair of awesome 5th-century BC statues known as the Riace Bronzes are worth a trip to **Reggio di Calabria** *(see p521)*, on the Straits of Messina. Down on the coast, the pretty fishing village of **Tropea** *(see p520)* promises fine views and good beaches.

## SICILY

- **Active volcanoes**
- **Charming Cefalù and Taormina**
- **Monumental Greek ruins**

Mediterranean in essence, Sicily has a remarkable range of landscapes. Towering **Mount Etna** *(see p539)* dominates, the mountainous interior offers excellent walking amid brilliant wildflowers, while a string of stunning beaches attract sunlovers.

Visitors will be enchanted by the Byzantine marvels at **Monreale's cathedral** *(see pp530–31)*, pretty **Cefalù** *(see p535)* as well as Classical Greek ruins at **Taormina** *(see p538)*, **Selinunte** *(see p534)* and **Agrigento** *(see p535)*.

## SARDINIA

- **Jet-set beach resorts**
- **Prehistoric nuraghe**
- **Charming Alghero**

Sardinia is an island of contrasts. Gorgeous turquoise water laps the exclusive **Costa Smeralda** *(see p548)*, and sleek yachts call in at its scenic bays. **Cala Gonone** *(see p550)* is a little quieter, and charming **Alghero** *(see p548)* on the western coast has a distinctly Spanish flavour.

The wild and rocky interior is frequented by reticent shepherds, and enigmatic **nuraghe** *(see p549)* can be found all over the island.

The beautiful turquoise waters of the Costa Smeralda, Sardinia

# Putting Italy on the Map

Italy sits at the heart of the Mediterranean, shielded from the rest of Europe by the vast sweep of the Alps. The Po, its longest river, arcs across the industrial north, while the Apennine mountains split the boot-shaped peninsula down its length. Italy, with a population of 58 million governed from Rome, covers 301,268 sq km (116,320 sq miles) and includes Sicily and Sardinia.

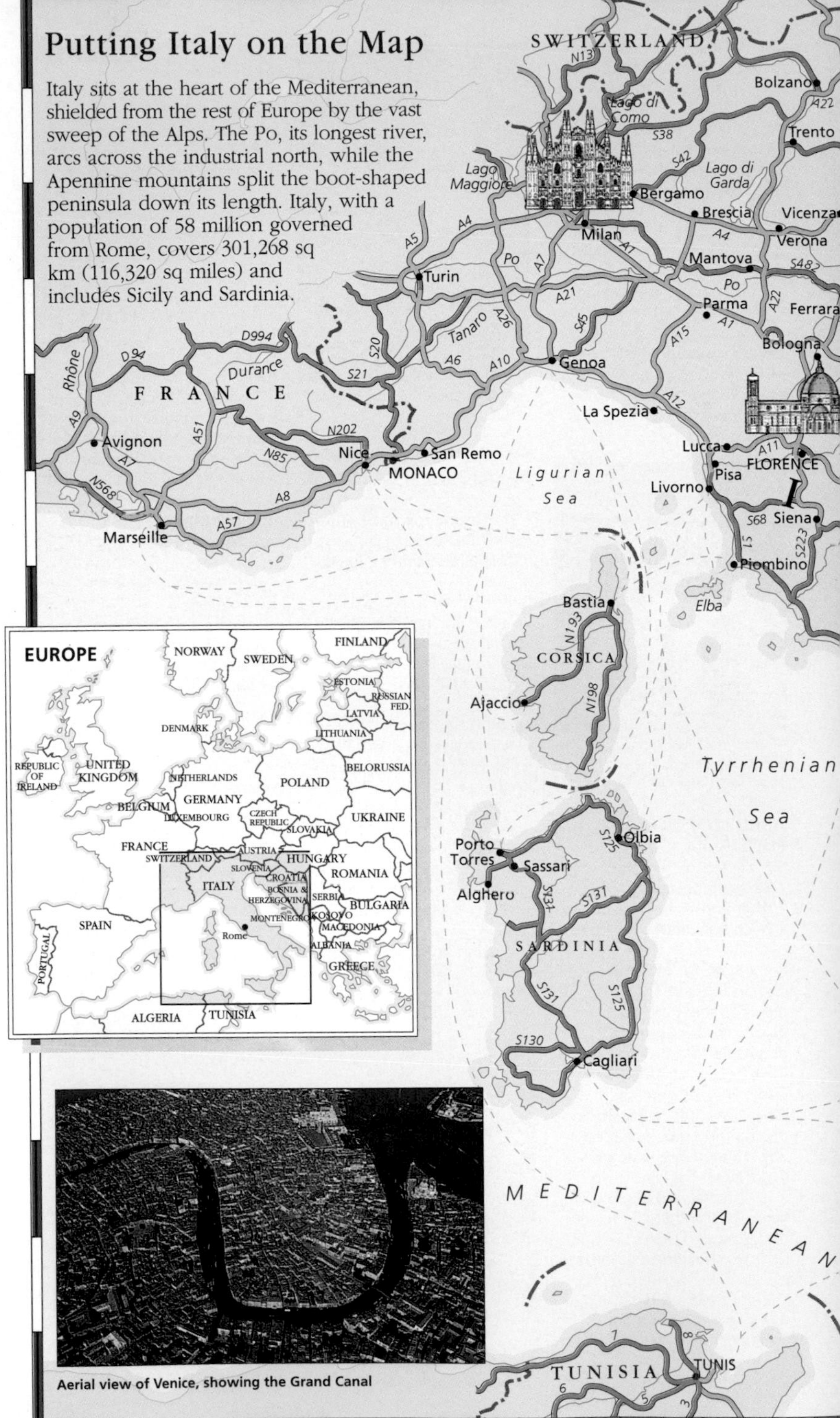


Aerial view of Venice, showing the Grand Canal

Satellite photograph of southern Europe and the Mediterranean

# Northern Italy

Airline connections link the rest of Europe with Milan, Turin, Bologna, Pisa, Florence, Verona and Venice. Major roads and railways also provide excellent links to cities all over Europe. Transport services are very efficient, with motorways and railways along both coasts, and across the area's main east-to-west axis at the foot of the Alps. Milan, Verona and Bologna are the key transport hubs, while Florence forms the focus of links to the south.

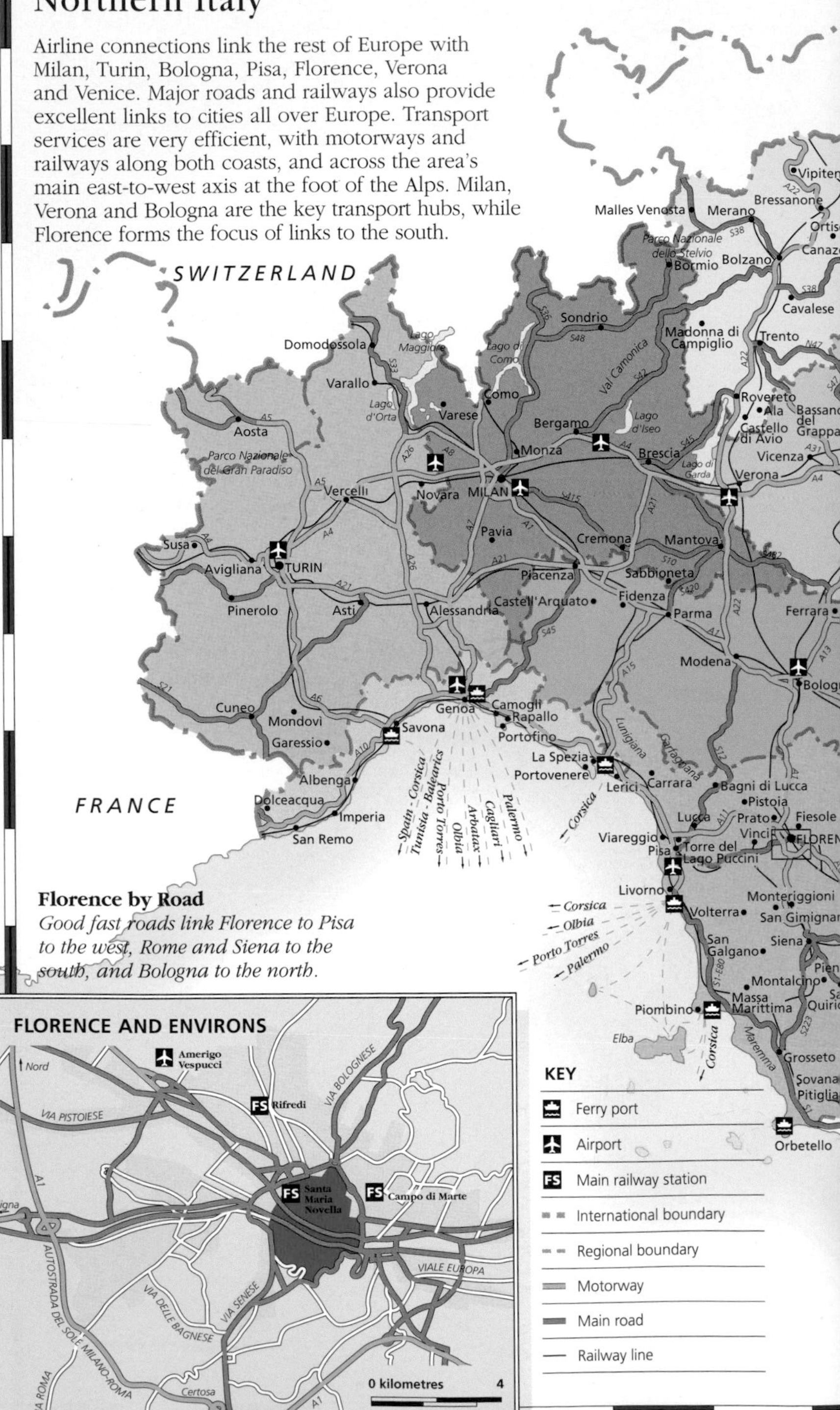


**Florence by Road**

*Good fast roads link Florence to Pisa to the west, Rome and Siena to the south, and Bologna to the north.*

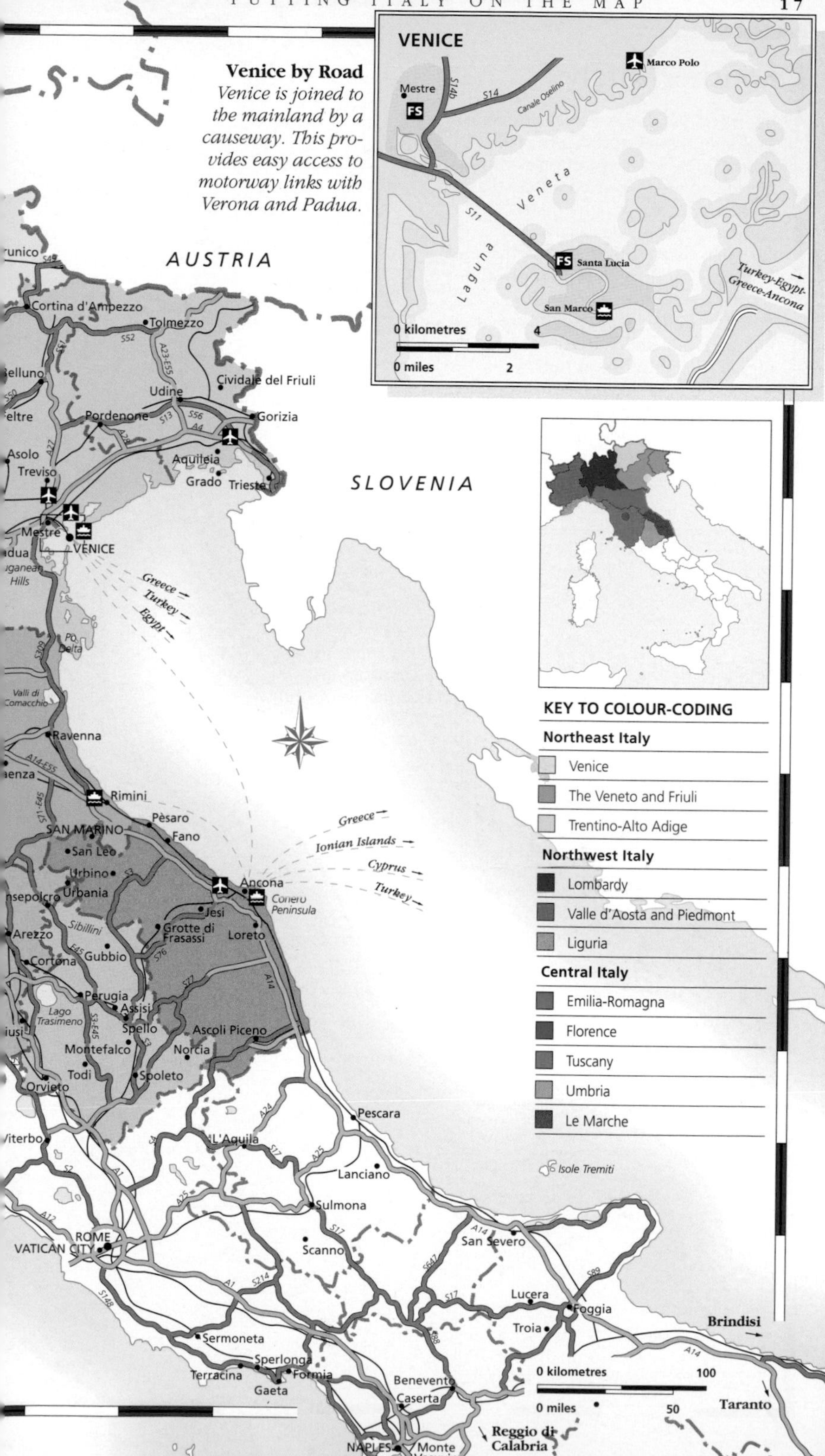
Venice by Road
Venice is joined to the mainland by a causeway. This provides easy access to motorway links with Verona and Padua.
VENICE
Mestre
Marco Polo
S14b
S14
Canale Oselino
Laguna Veneta
S11
Santa Lucia
San Marco
Turkey-Egypt-Greece-Ancona
0 kilometres 4
0 miles 2
AUSTRIA
SLOVENIA
Cortina d'Ampezzo
Tolmezzo
Belluno
Cividale del Friuli
Udine
Pordenone
Gorizia
Feltre
Asolo
Treviso
Aquileia
Grado
Trieste
Mestre
VENICE
Euganean Hills
Greece
Turkey
Egypt
Po Delta
Valli di Comacchio
Ravenna
Rimini
Pèsaro
SAN MARINO
Fano
San Leo
Urbino
Urbania
Ancona
Conero Peninsula
Greece
Ionian Islands
Cyprus
Turkey
Jesi
Grotte di Frasassi
Loreto
Sibillini
Arezzo
Gubbio
Cortona
Perugia
Lago Trasimeno
Assisi
Spello
Ascoli Piceno
Montefalco
Norcia
Todi
Spoleto
Orvieto
Pescara
Viterbo
L'Aquila
Lanciano
Sulmona
ROME
VATICAN CITY
Scanno
San Severo
Lucera
Foggia
Troia
Brindisi
Sermoneta
Sperlonga
Terracina
Formia
Gaeta
Benevento
Caserta
NAPLES
Monte Vesuvio
Reggio di Calabria
Taranto
0 kilometres 100
0 miles 50
Isole Tremiti
KEY TO COLOUR-CODING
Northeast Italy
Venice
The Veneto and Friuli
Trentino-Alto Adige
Northwest Italy
Lombardy
Valle d'Aosta and Piedmont
Liguria
Central Italy
Emilia-Romagna
Florence
Tuscany
Umbria
Le Marche

## Southern Italy

International airline services operate to Rome, Naples and Palermo in southern Italy. Transport links within the region are generally slower than in the north, particularly inland and on the islands of Sicily and Sardinia, where buses are often a faster option than trains. Mainland coastal road and rail links are good, however, especially those linking Rome and Naples, the region's main transport hubs, which are connected by a high-speed train service. Two trans-Apennine motorways offer the quickest cross-country routes.

### Sicily and Sardinia

*Ferries operate to Sicily from Naples, Villa San Giovanni and Reggio di Calabria. Onward connections include boats to Malta and Tunisia. Ferries run to Sardinia from several mainland ports, notably Civitavecchia, Genoa and Livorno.*

**KEY**

- Ferry port
- Airport
- International boundary
- Regional boundary
- Motorway
- Main road
- Railway line

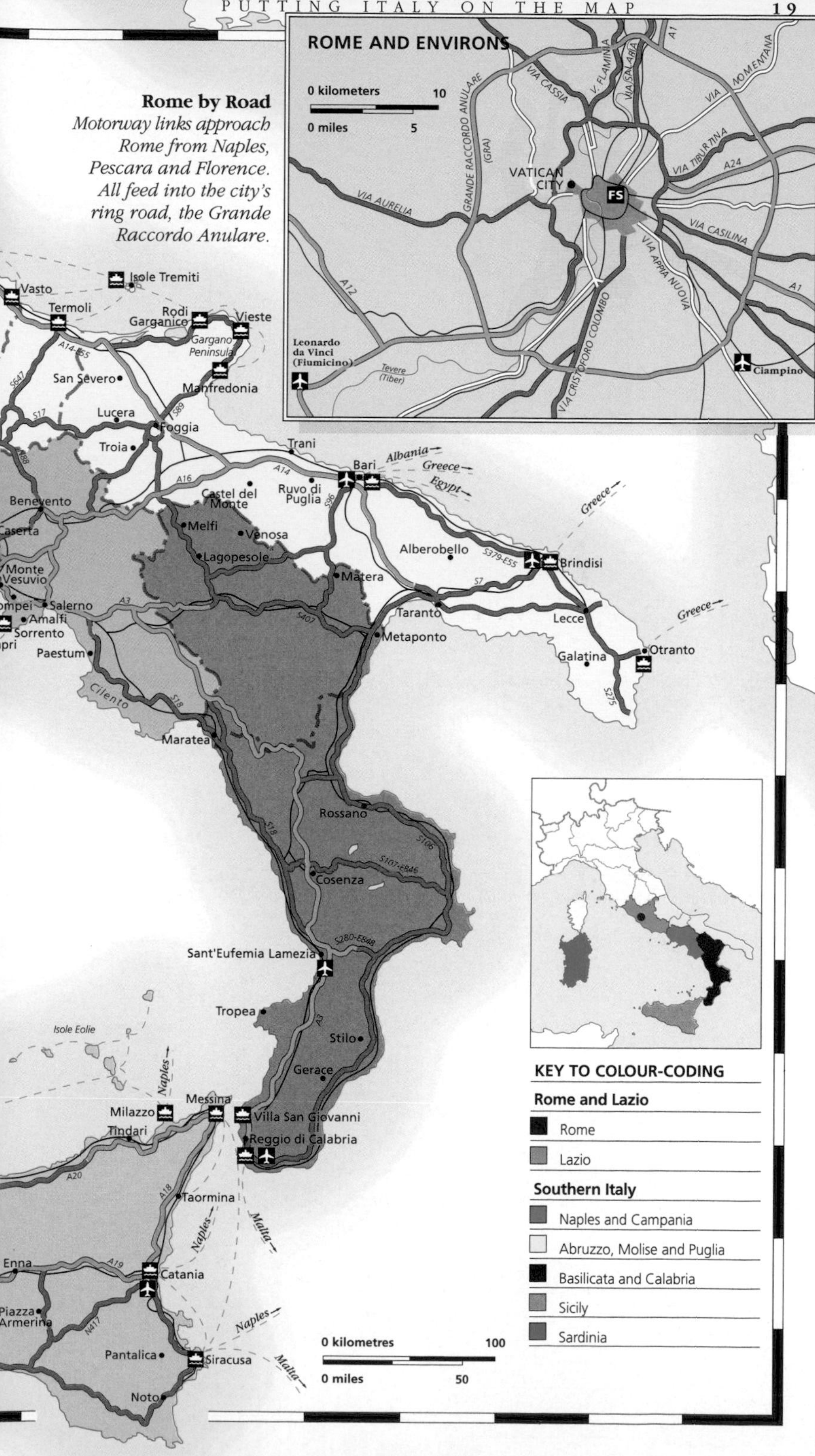


## Rome by Road

*Motorway links approach Rome from Naples, Pescara and Florence. All feed into the city's ring road, the Grande Raccordo Anulare.*

PRIMA DEL MEZZODÌ
AGRA
GOA
TOBOLSK
ISPAHAN
MOSKOW
COSTANTINOPOLI
CAPO DI BUONA SPERANZA
ROMA
DECLINAZIONE AUSTRALE
DOPO IL MEZZODÌ
LIMA
QVEBEC
BUENOS-AIRES
RIO DE IANEIRO
PICO DI TANERIFFE
LISBONA
MADRID
PARIGI
23 DIC. 1829
PALAZZO DEL GOVERNATORE

# A PORTRAIT OF ITALY

*Italy has drawn people in search of culture and romance for many centuries. Few countries can compete with its Classical origins, its art, architecture, musical and literary traditions, its scenery or food and wine. The ambiguity of its modern image is also fascinating: since World War II Italy has climbed into the top ten world economies, yet at its heart it retains many of the customs, traditions and regional allegiances of its agricultural heritage.*

Wedding Ferrari in typical Italian style

Italy has no single cultural identity. From the northern snow-capped peaks of the Alps, to the rugged southern shores of Sicily, lies a plethora of distinctive regions and peoples. Politically, Italy is a young country: it did not exist as a unified nation state until 1870, and its 20 regions have maintained their cultural individuality. Visitors to Italy are often pleasantly surprised by the diversity of its dialects, cuisines and architecture. There is also a larger regional division. People speak of two distinct Italies: the rich industrial north and the poorer agricultural south, known as *Il Mezzogiorno* or Land of the Midday Sun. The frontier separating the two is indeterminate, lying somewhere between Rome and Naples.

The north is directly responsible for Italy's place among the world's top industrial nations. It has been the powerhouse behind the Italian economic miracle, its success achieved by internationally renowned names such as FIAT, Prada, Ferragamo, Pirelli, Olivetti, Zanussi, Alessi and Armani. In contrast, the south, once a cradle of high culture and civilization, has been dogged by unemployment and

A secluded villa surrounded by cypress trees on a Tuscan hilltop

◁ Three sundials covering the façade of Palazzo del Governatore, on Piazza Garibaldi, Parma

organized crime. Some of its areas rank among the most depressed in Europe, although many southern towns did benefit from an injection of Millennium funds.

A conversation in the open air

The historic divide between north and south is a powerful factor in contemporary politics. The federalist party, the Northern League, owes its popularity to this split. Those in favour of separation complain that the south is a drain on resources: Milan is seen as efficient and rich, while Naples is viewed as chaotic, dirty and corrupt.

History and geography have both contributed to the division. The north is closer in both location and spirit to Germany and France while the south has suffered a succession of invasions from foreign powers: Carthaginians and Greeks in ancient times, Saracens and Normans in the Middle Ages and until the middle of the 19th century, the Bourbons from Spain held sway.

## TRADITION

Distinctive variations in Italy's regions have much to do with the mountainous landscape and inaccessible valleys. Tuscan and Ligurian hill-towns, for instance, have quite different silhouettes, and the farmhouses in Puglia, the famous *trulli,* are unlike those found in the landscape of Emilia-Romagna.

In southern Italy the landscape, architecture, dialects, food, and even the appearance of the people, have closer affinities with the Eastern Mediterranean and North Africa than with Europe. In the far south, study of the local dialects has revealed traces of ancient Greek and old Albanian, preserved in tightly knit communities isolated by the rugged geography. Christianity and pagan ritual are closely linked; sometimes the Virgin is portrayed as a thinly disguised Demeter, the Earth goddess.

Throughout Italy, ancient techniques of husbandry endure and many livelihoods are closely connected to the land and the seasons. Main crops include sugar beet, maize, wheat, olives and grapes; colourful Easter celebrations *(see p66)* pay tribute to the bounty of the soil. Although some of the north's postwar economic prosperity can be attributed to industry (especially car production in and around Turin), much of it has grown from the expansion of family-owned artisan businesses and the export of hand-made goods abroad. This is recognized as a distinct sector of the economy. The internationally successful retail clothes chain Prada is a good example. The "Made in Italy" label,

Café-goers relaxing in Marina di Pisa, Tuscany

Medieval skyscrapers emerging from the Tuscan landscape of San Gimignano

found on goods such as clothes, shoes and leather bags, guarantees a high standard.

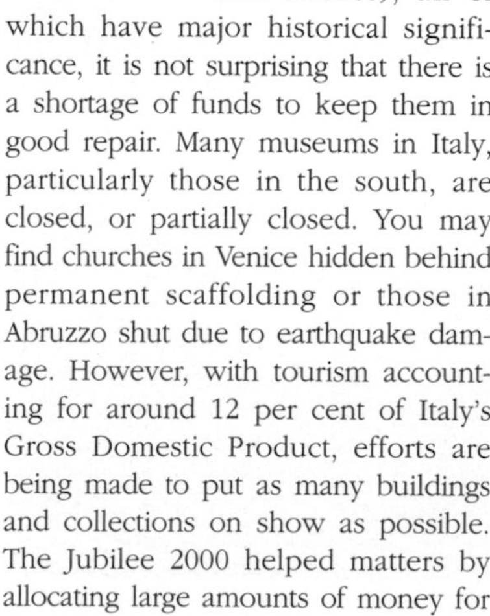

Sophia Loren

## CULTURE AND ARTS

The arts in Italy have had a long and glorious history and Italians are very proud of this. Given the fact that Italy has more than 100,000 monuments (archaeological sites, cathedrals, churches, houses and statues), all of which have major historical significance, it is not surprising that there is a shortage of funds to keep them in good repair. Many museums in Italy, particularly those in the south, are closed, or partially closed. You may find churches in Venice hidden behind permanent scaffolding or those in Abruzzo shut due to earthquake damage. However, with tourism accounting for around 12 per cent of Italy's Gross Domestic Product, efforts are being made to put as many buildings and collections on show as possible. The Jubilee 2000 helped matters by allocating large amounts of money for the restoration of buildings and sites belonging to the Catholic Church.

The performing arts are also underfunded, yet there are some spectacular cultural festivals. Almost every town of any size has its own opera house and La Scala opera house in Milan stages world-class productions.

Cinema is another flourishing art form in Italy and has been so since its invention. The sets at Cinecittà, on the

Bernini's 17th-century Fontana del Tritone, Rome

Roadside stall near Positano, Campania

outskirts of Rome, have been used by many famous directors such as Fellini, Pasolini, de Sica, Visconti and many others. Italian films such as *La Vita è Bella* and *The Son's Room* have found critical acclaim and box-office success both in Italy and abroad. In Italy the arts belong to everyone: opera is attended by people from all backgrounds, regardless of social status, as are cinemas and galleries.

Italian chic, Armani style

## SOCIAL CUSTOMS AND POLITICS

Italian society is still highly traditional, and Italians can be very formal. Between the generations degrees of familiarity exist: reserve *ciao* (hello or goodbye) for friends your age or younger, and greet older people with *piacere* (pleased to meet you), *buon giorno* (good day) or *buona sera* (good evening) and on parting, say *arrivederci* (goodbye). Strangers are met with a handshake, but family and friends receive a kiss.

Italian chic decrees that the clothes you wear should give the impression of wealth. If Italians wear similar outfits, it is because they are conformists in fashion as in other aspects of daily life.

Italian politics, in contrast, are not so well regulated. Governments in the postwar era were characterized by short-lived coalitions, dominated by the Christian Democrats. In 1993 Italy experienced a political crisis when an organized network of corruption was exposed, disgracing a huge number of politicians and businessmen. Although the investigations failed to eradicate corruption, they led to the formation of two large coalitions, centre-left and centre-right. Silvio Berlusconi, leader of the Forza Italia party, became prime minister in 1994 but lasted only a short while as he, too, was accused of corruption. In 1998 Massimo D'Alema became Italy's first left-wing Prime Minister. Recent years have seen an alternation of centre-right and centre-left governments, some of them short-lived.

## MODERN LIFE

Food and football are the great constants; Italians live for both. Much time is spent on preparing food and eating. The Italian diet, particularly in the

Statue of Emperor Domitian in the Vatican Gardens

**The solution to heavy traffic in Rome: motorbikes and scooters**

south, is among the healthiest in the world. Football is a national passion and inspires massive public interest and media attention, not least as a way of expressing regional loyalties.

As far as religion is concerned, the number of practising Catholics has been in decline for some years. Although Rome lies at the centre of world Catholicism, today many Italians are uninterested in religion, but still attend mass in number on saints' days or feast days. As a consequence of immigration, other religions are now on the increase.

**Strolling through one of Bologna's many porticoes**

The emphasis on conformity and a commitment to the institution of the family remain key factors in Italian society despite the country's low birth rate. Grandparents, children and grandchildren often still live in family units, although this is becoming less common. All children are pampered, but the most cherished ones are, usually, male. Women's Liberation fought a powerful campaign in the 1970s and did much to change attitudes to women in the workplace, particularly in metropolitan areas. However, the idea that men should help with housework and the care of the children is still a fairly foreign notion among the older generation.

With the miracle of its postwar economic recovery, where industry and technology were united with design, Italy has become a success story. Although the economy was dented by the worldwide recessions of recent years, the exposure of corruption in many walks of public life and political upheaval, Italy appears unchanged to foreign visitors. Its ability to keep its regional identities and traditional values allows it to ride out any changes relatively unscathed.

# Medieval and Early Renaissance Art

The story of early Italian art, from the 13th century until the late 15th century, illuminates one of the richest periods in European art history. For the first time since Classical antiquity, painters and sculptors created a convincing pictorial space in which figures, modelled "in the round", were given life. Ethereal buildings were replaced by those firmly rooted in the real world, reproducing what artists actually saw. This revolution in art included the reintroduction of the fresco technique, giving artists huge surfaces for telling pictorial stories.

**c.1305 Giotto di Bondone**, *The Meeting at the Golden Gate* (Cappella degli Scrovegni, Padua) Giotto broke away from the ornate Byzantine style to visualize naturalness and human emotions. His way of working would later be dubbed the Florentine style.

**1235 Bonaventura Berlinghieri**, *St Francis Altarpiece* (San Francesco, Pescia)

**1285 Duccio di Buoninsegna**, *Rucellai Madonna,* panel (Uffizi, Florence). Duccio dominated the Sienese painting style which combined bold linear movements with a new human intimacy.

**1339 Ambrogio Lorenzetti**, *Good Government Enthroned* (Sala dei Nove, Palazzo Pubblico, Siena)

| 1220 | 1240 | 1260 | 1280 | 1300 | 1320 |
|---|---|---|---|---|---|
| MIDDLE AGES | | | | FORERUNNERS TO RENAISSANCE | |
| 1220 | 1240 | 1260 | 1280 | 1300 | 1320 |

**c.1259 Nicola Pisano**, Pulpit (Baptistry, Pisa cathedral)

**c.1265 Coppo di Marcovaldo**, *Madonna and Child* (Santa Monica dei Servi, Orvieto)

**c.1280 Cimabue**, *Madonna Enthroned with Angels and Prophets,* also known as *Santa Trinità Madonna* (Uffizi, Florence)

**c.1291 Pietro Cavallini**, *Last Judgment,* detail (Santa Cecilia, Trastevere, Rome)

**c.1316–18 Simone Martini**, *Vision of St Martin* (Lower Church of San Francesco, Assisi)

**c.1297 Giovanni Pisano**, Pulpit (Sant'Andrea, Pistoia)

**c.1336 Andrea Pisano**, *Baptism of St John the Baptist,* panel on the South Doors (Baptistry, Florence cathedral)

**c.1425–52 Lorenzo Ghiberti**, *Gates of Paradise,* panel on the East Doors. (Baptistry, Florence cathedral). These elaborate doors mark a transition from the Gothic style to the Early Renaissance style, in Florence.

**c.1435 Donatello**, *David* (Museo del Bargello, Florence)

**1357 Andrea Orcagna**, *Enthroned Christ with Madonna and Saints* (Strozzi Altarpiece, Santa Maria Novella, Florence)

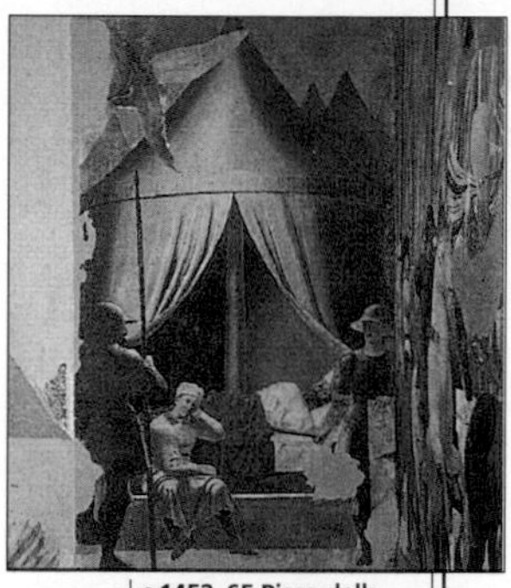

**c.1452–65 Piero della Francesca**, detail of *The Dream of Constantine* (San Francesco, Arezzo)

**c.1410 Nanni di Banco**, *Four Crowned Martyrs* (Orsanmichele, Florence)

**c.1456 Paolo Uccello**, *Battle of San Romano* (Uffizi, Florence)

| 1360 | 1380 | 1400 | 1420 | 1440 | 1460 |
|---|---|---|---|---|---|

EARLY RENAISSANCE

| 1360 | 1380 | 1400 | 1420 | 1440 | 1460 |
|---|---|---|---|---|---|

**1423 Gentile da Fabriano**, *Adoration of the Magi* (Uffizi, Florence)

**c.1440 Fra Angelico**, *Annunciation* (San Marco, Florence)

**c.1350 Francesco Traini**, *Triumph of Death* (Campo Santo, Pisa)

**c.1463 Piero della Francesca**, *Resurrection* (Pinacoteca, Sansepolcro)

**c.1465 Fra Filippo Lippi**, *Madonna with Child and Angels* (Uffizi, Florence)

**c.1465–74 Andrea Mantegna**, *Arrival of Cardinal Francesco Gonzaga* (Palazzo Ducale, Mantova)

**c.1425–8 Masaccio**, *The Tribute Money* (Cappella Brancacci, Florence)

**c.1470 Andrea del Verrocchio**, *David* (Bargello, Florence)

## FRESCO TECHNIQUE

Fresco, meaning "fresh", refers to the technique of painting onto a thin layer of damp, freshly laid plaster. Pigments are drawn into the plaster by surface tension and the colour becomes fixed as the plaster dries. The pigments react with the lime in the plaster to produce strong, rich colours, such as those in Masaccio's *The Tribute Money*.

***The Tribute Money* by Masaccio (Cappella Brancacci, Florence)**

# High Renaissance Art

The High Renaissance in the late 15th century was marked by an increasing sense of realism in many religious works and the technical mastery of such renowned artists as Michelangelo, Leonardo da Vinci and Raphael. The different schools of Renaissance painting, while drawing on Classical models, produced varying styles: Florentine painting was noted for its cool clarity, while sensuous colour and warm light characterized many Venetian works. By the mid-16th century, however, these styles shifted to the fanciful, contorted imagery of Mannerism.

**c.1480 Andrea Mantegna**, *Dead Christ* (Brera, Milan)

**1481–2** Sistine Chapel wall frescoes painted by various artists.

**c.1481–2 Pietro Perugino**, *Christ Delivering the Keys of the Kingdom to St Peter,* wall fresco (Sistine Chapel, Rome)

**c.1483–88 Andrea del Verrocchio**, completed by Alessandro Leopardi, *Equestrian Monument of Bartolomeo Colleoni* (Campo dei Santi Giovanni e Paolo, Venice)

**c.1487 Giovanni Bellini**, *San Giobbe Altarpiece* (Accademia, Venice)

**c.1495 Leonardo da Vinci**, *Last Supper* (Santa Maria delle Grazie, Milan)

**c.1503–1505 Leonardo da Vinci**, *Mona Lisa* (Louvre, Paris)

**1505 Raphael**, *Madonna of the Goldfinch* (Uffizi, Florence)

**1508–12 Michelangelo**, *Sistine Chapel ceiling* (The Vatican, Rome). Over 200 preliminary drawings were made for this incredible vision of God's power and humanity's spiritual awakening.

**1519–26 Titian**, *Madonna of the Pesaro Family* (Santa Maria Gloriosa dei Frari, Venice)

1480 | 1500 | 1520

HIGH RENAISSANCE

1480 | 1500 | 1520

**1485 Leonardo da Vinci**, *Virgin of the Rocks* (Louvre, Paris)

**c.1485 Sandro Botticelli**, *Birth of Venus* (Uffizi, Florence)

**c.1486 Leonardo da Vinci**, *Uomo Vitruviano* (Accademia, Venice)

**1499–1504 Luca Signorelli**, *Damned Consigned to Hell* (Cappella Nuova, Orvieto cathedral)

**1501–1504 Michelangelo**, *David* (Galleria dell'Accademia, Florence)

**1505 Giovanni Bellini**, *Madonna and Child with Four Saints* (San Zaccaria altarpiece, Accademia, Venice)

**c.1508 Giorgione**, *Tempesta* (Accademia, Venice)

**1509 Raphael**, *School of Athens* (Stanza della Segnatura, The Vatican, Rome). The scale, magnificence and harmony of this fresco represent the ideals of the High Renaissance. These ideals sought to express superhuman rather than human values.

**1512–14 Raphael**, *Angel Delivering St Peter from Prison,* detail from the *Liberation of St Peter from Prison* (Stanza di Eliodoro, The Vatican, Rome)

**1516 Michelang**, *Dying Slave* (Louvre, Paris)

**1517 Sodoma**, *Marriage of Alexander an Roxana* (Villa Farnesina, Ro

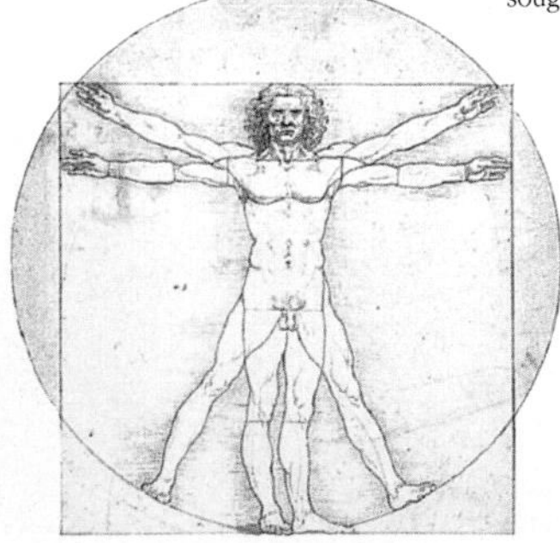

**1523 Rosso Fiorentino**, *Moses Defends the Daughters of Jethro* (Uffizi, Florence)

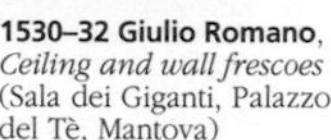

**1530–32 Giulio Romano**, *Ceiling and wall frescoes* (Sala dei Giganti, Palazzo del Tè, Mantova)

**c.1532 Michelangelo**, *"Blockhead" Captive* (Galleria dell' Accademia, Florence)

**1534–5 Paris Bordone**, *Fisherman Delivering the Ring* (Accademia, Venice)

**c.1540–42 Titian**, *David and Goliath* (Santa Maria della Salute, Venice)

**c.1550 Moretto**, *Ecce Homo with Angel* (Pinacoteca Tosio Martinengo, Brescia)

**c.1562–6 Jacopo Tintoretto**, *Finding of the Body of St Mark* (Brera, Milan)

1540 1560

MANNERISM

1540 1560

**1534–41 Michelangelo**, *Last Judgment,* wall fresco (Sistine Chapel, Rome)

**c.1546 Titian**, *Portrait of Pope Paul III Farnese with his Nephews,* (Museo di Capodimonte, Naples)

**c.1534–40 Parmigianino**, *Madonna and Angels or Madonna with the Long Neck* (Uffizi, Florence). Attenuated proportions and contrasting colours make this a fine example of the Mannerist style.

**1538 Titian**, *Venus of Urbino* (Uffizi, Florence)

**c.1540 Agnolo Bronzino**, *Portrait of Lucrezia Panciatichi* (Uffizi, Florence). Elongated features, such as Lucrezia's fingers, are typical of the exaggerated Mannerist style.

**1556 Veronese**, *Triumph of Mordecai* (San Sebastiano, Venice)

**c.1526–30 Correggio**, *Assumption of the Virgin* (Dome of Parma cathedral). Neither a Mannerist nor a High Renaissance painter, Correggio was a master of illusion, skilled at making ascending figures float convincingly, as seen in the fresco above.

# Italian Architecture

Corinthian capital

The buildings of Italy span almost 3,000 years, drawing influences from a wide variety of sources. Etruscan and Roman buildings borrowed heavily from ancient Greece, while in later centuries Norman, Arabic and Byzantine styles coloured Italy's Romanesque and Gothic architecture. Classical ideals infused the country's Renaissance buildings, later giving way to the inspired innovations of the Baroque period.

**Orvieto's Duomo** *displays the ornate and intricate decoration, notably sculpture, common to many Gothic cathedrals. Building stretched from the 13th to the early 17th centuries.*

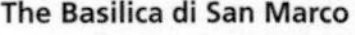

The Basilica di San Marco

**The Basilica di San Marco** *(AD 832–1094) in Venice combines Classical, Romanesque and Gothic architecture, but its key inspiration was Byzantine* (see pp110–11).

| 200 | 400 | 600 | 800 | 1000 |
|---|---|---|---|---|
| CLASSICAL | | BYZANTINE | | ROMANESQU |
| 200 | 400 | 600 | 800 | 1000 |

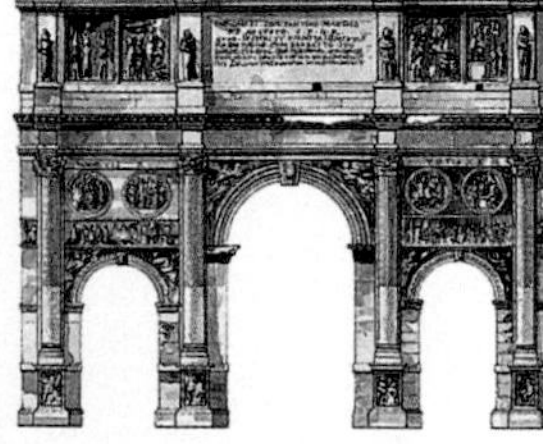

**Triumphal arches** *such as Rome's Arch of Constantine (AD 313) were a uniquely Roman invention. Built to celebrate military victories, they were adorned with reliefs depicting episodes from successful campaigns* (see p380).

**The round-arched** Romanesque style emerged from the Dark Ages in structures such as the Duomo in Modena. The churches usually had simple interiors that derived from Roman basilicas.

**The building of domes** over square or rectangular spaces was a major development of the Byzantine era.

## ETRUSCAN ARCHITECTURE

Virtually the only architectural memorials to the Etruscans are their necropolises (c.6th century BC), found primarily in Tuscany, Lazio and Umbria. Little else survives, probably because most day-to-day buildings were made from wood. The Etruscans' close cultural and trading ties with Greece, however, suggest their architecture would have borrowed heavily from Greek models. Rome, in turn, looked to Etruscan architecture for inspiration, and most early Roman public buildings were probably Etruscan in style.

Model of Etruscan temple with Classical Greek portico

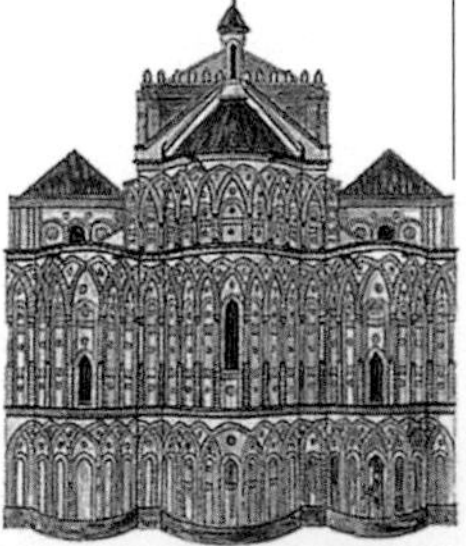

**The cathedral of Monreale** *in Sicily, built in the 12th century, contains Norman elements blended with exotic Arabic and Byzantine decoration* (see pp530–31).

**Bramante's** *Tempietto at San Pietro in Montorio, Rome (built 1502–10) was a Renaissance tribute to the precise, Classical temples of ancient Rome* (see p380).

**Baroque façades,** *such as this one added to Syracuse's Duomo between 1728 and 1754, were often grafted onto older churches.*

**Industrial innovations** *in glass and metal were applied in new buildings, like Mengoni's imposing Galleria Vittorio Emanuele II (1865) in Milan* (see p194).

**The Mole Antonelliana** (1863–89), in Turin, topped by a soaring granite spire, was for a time the tallest building in the world *(p224).*

**The Classical ideals** of Rome and ancient Greece were reintroduced into Italian architecture during the Renaissance.

**Papal patronage** and the vigour of the Counter-Reformation fuelled the Baroque, a period of architectural splendour, invention and exuberance.

**Torre Velasca's** 26-floor tower in Milan (1950s) pioneered the use of reinforced concrete.

| 0 | 1400 | 1600 | 1800 | 2000 |
|---|---|---|---|---|
| | RENAISSANCE | BAROQUE | 19TH CENTURY | 20TH CENTURY |
| 0 | 1400 | 1600 | 1800 | 2000 |

**Siena's Duomo** (1136 –1382), an imposing Romanesque-Gothic cathedral, went through 200 years of architectural transformation *(see pp342–3).*

**Santa Maria Novella** in Florence has a Renaissance façade (1456–70) by Alberti and a Gothic interior.

**Gian Lorenzo Bernini** (1598–1680), architect of St Peter's Square, was a dominant figure in Roman Baroque.

**Andrea Palladio** (1508–80) built Neo-Classical villas and palazzi. His style was imitated in Europe for over two centuries *(see p80).*

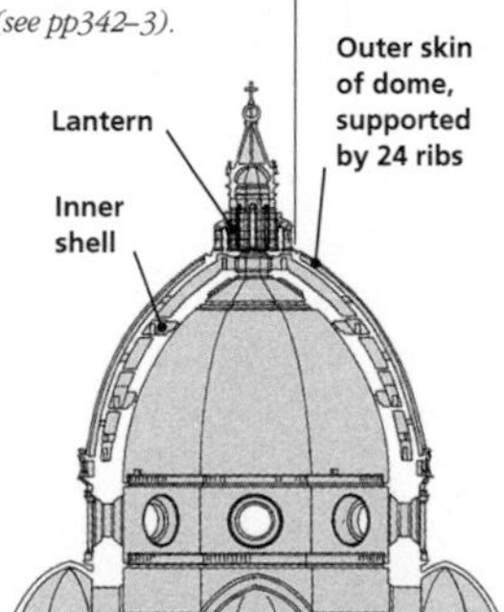


**Brunelleschi's dome** *for the Duomo in Florence, completed in 1436, was a masterpiece of Renaissance design and ingenious engineering* (see p253).

**The Gesù** *in Rome was designed for the Jesuits by Vignola in 1568. With its powerful façade and lavish decoration it was the prototype for countless other Baroque churches* (see p381).

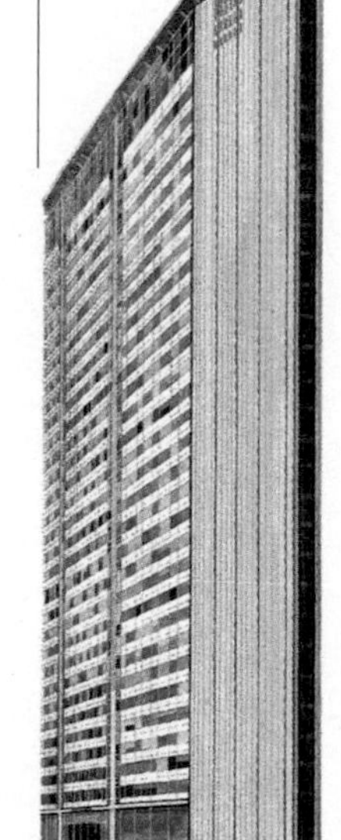

**The Pirelli building** *in Milan, designed by Ponti and Nervi (late 1950s), is a great example of modern Italian architecture* (see p185).

# Saints and Symbols in Italian Art

Saints and symbols are especially important in Italian art. They form part of an established visual language used by artists to narrate stories of the Bible and the Catholic church to church-goers. Paintings of the saints were the focus for prayer and each offered assistance in a particular aspect of daily life. Patron saints protected specific cities, or trades, and individuals who bore their name. Saints' days and religious festivals still play an important part in Italian life.

## THE EVANGELISTS

The four evangelists, Matthew, Mark, Luke and John are each represented by a winged creature, standing for a divine mission.

**Eagle (St John)**

**St Dominic** is usually portrayed wearing the habit of his order. The lily is another of his attributes.

**St Cosmas and St Damian** are always shown together, dressed in physicians' clothing.

**St Mark the Evangelist** often holds his book of the Gospels.

**St John** carries a book of the Gospel bearing his name.

**St Thomas Aquinas** is usually shown with a star, barely visible in this painting on his Dominican habit.

**St Lawrence** carries a palm leaf as well as the gridiron on which he was roasted.

**Virgin Enthroned with the Child and Saints** *(c.1450) was painted on dry plaster by the Dominican friar, Fra Angelico. It is on display at the Museo di San Marco, Florence* (see p276).

**The Virgin**, usually shown in blue robes, is depicted as Mater Amabilis – the "Mother Worthy of Love".

**St Peter Martyr**, here with a palm leaf, is sometimes depicted with a head wound, carrying a sword.

## SYMBOLS

In order to identify different saints or martyrs they were given "attributes" or symbols – particular objects to carry, or clothing to wear. These were items that played a particular role in their life story. Martyrs were known by their instruments of torture or death. Symbolism also appears in the sky, animals, flowers, colours and numbers.

**The lamb** *symbolizes Christ, the Lamb of God, or in early Christian art, the sinner.*

**The skull** *is a "memento mori" to remind us of death and impermanence.*

**Winged man (St Matthew)**

**Winged lion (St Mark)**

**Winged ox (St Luke)**

**Giovanni Bellini's painting of *Madonna and Child with Four Saints*** **(see p119)**

**St Peter the Apostle**, the "rock" on which the Christian church was founded, carries the keys to heaven.

**The Madonna**, with the Christ Child, is an emblem of perfect motherly love.

**St Catherine of Alexandria** is shown here with a piece of the wheel on which she was martyred.

**St Jerome** is always portrayed as an old man, often a hermit, whose life was devoted to scholarship.

**Detail from Madonna and Child with Four Saints**, *by Giovanni Bellini. The painting was produced for an altarpiece at San Zaccaria, Venice in 1505, where it is still on display.*

**The angel**, a messenger of God to man, is portrayed in this scene as a musician of Heaven.

**St Lucy** is depicted here holding her own eyes in a dish. She became the patron saint of the blind and symbolizes light.

**The lily**, *flower of the Virgin, is the symbol of purity, resurrection, peace and chastity.*

**The cockle shell** *most often represents pilgrimage. It is a particular attribute of St Roch.*

**The palm** *represents, in Christian art, a martyr's triumph over death.*

# Writers, Poets and Dramatists

Italy has produced many writers (in Latin and Italian) who have won worldwide acclaim. Each of them provides an illuminating insight into the country's turbulent past: the Classical poets Virgil, Horace and Ovid give vivid accounts of the concerns and values of ancient Rome; medieval Florence and Tuscany are brought to life in the poetry of Dante and Petrarch and the salacious tales of Boccaccio. In less than a century these three great writers created a new literary language to rank with any in Europe. Italy's modern literature still commands international attention – Umberto Eco has to his credit one of the most widely read books of the 20th century.

**Primo Levi** *(1919–87) gave an astonishing account of his survival of the Jewish Holocaust and World War II's aftermath in* The Truce *and* If This Is A Man.

**Dario Fo** (born 1926) won the Nobel prize for Literature in 1997.

**Umberto Eco** *(born 1932), a professor at the University of Bologna, wrote the novel* The Name Of The Rose, *which explored his passion for the Middle Ages. The book was made into a film (above) in 1986.*

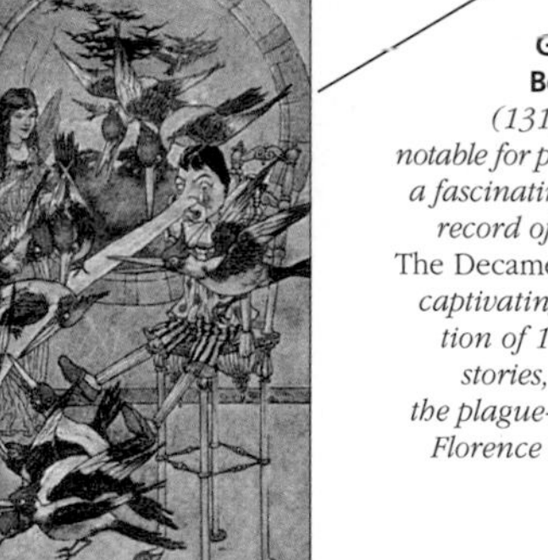

**Pinocchio**, *written by Carlo Collodi (1826–90) in 1883, is one of the world's best known children's stories. "Collodi" was Carlo Lorenzini's pseudonym, taken after his mother's birthplace in Tuscany.*

**Giovanni Boccaccio** *(1313–75) is notable for providing a fascinating social record of his era.* The Decameron, *his captivating collection of 100 short stories, is set in the plague-stricken Florence of 1348.*

**Dante's** (1265–1321) Divine Comedy *(c.1308–21), is a journey through Hell, Purgatory and Paradise. It includes horrific accounts of the torments suffered by the damned.*

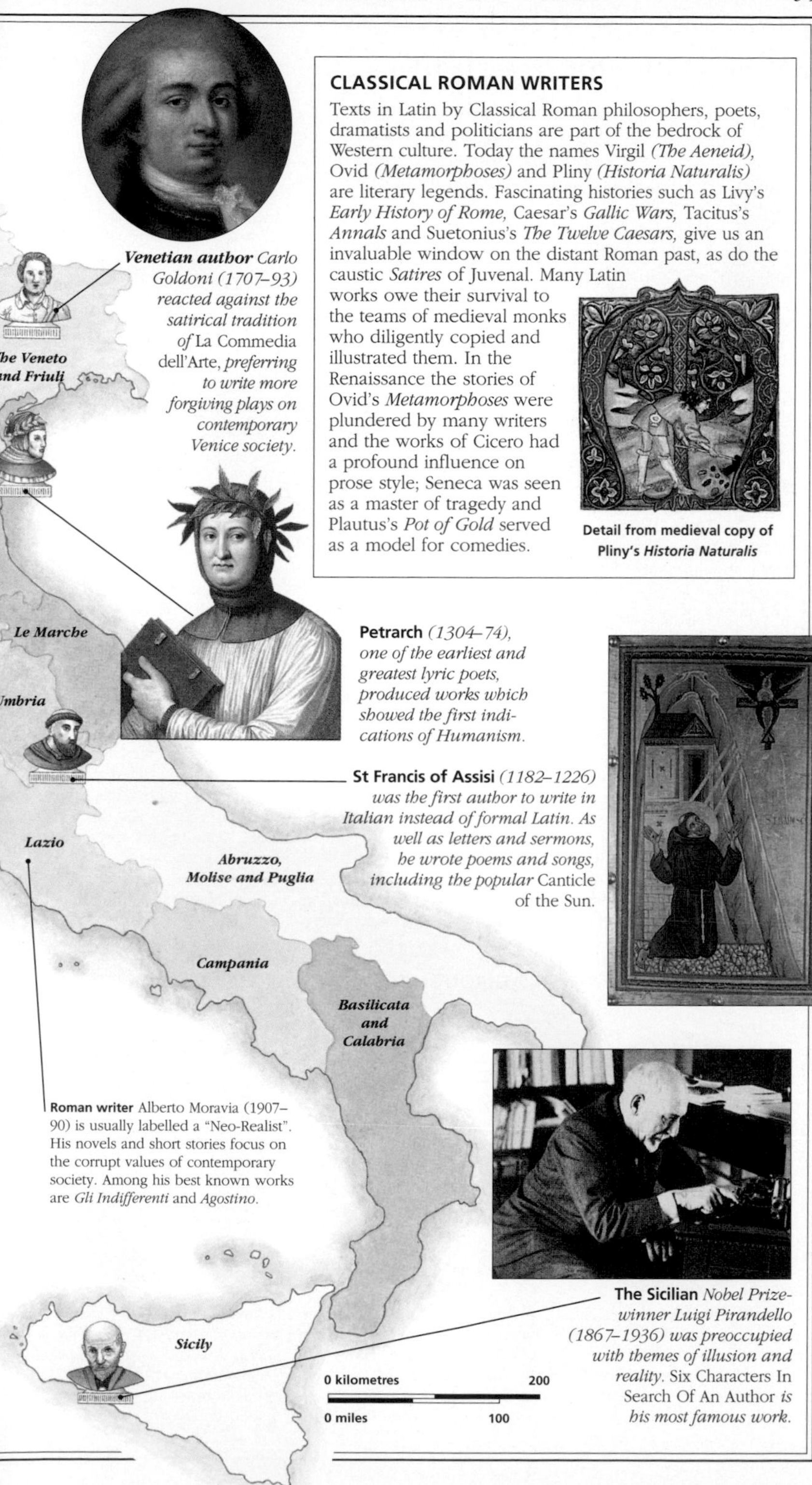


## CLASSICAL ROMAN WRITERS

Texts in Latin by Classical Roman philosophers, poets, dramatists and politicians are part of the bedrock of Western culture. Today the names Virgil *(The Aeneid)*, Ovid *(Metamorphoses)* and Pliny *(Historia Naturalis)* are literary legends. Fascinating histories such as Livy's *Early History of Rome*, Caesar's *Gallic Wars*, Tacitus's *Annals* and Suetonius's *The Twelve Caesars*, give us an invaluable window on the distant Roman past, as do the caustic *Satires* of Juvenal. Many Latin works owe their survival to the teams of medieval monks who diligently copied and illustrated them. In the Renaissance the stories of Ovid's *Metamorphoses* were plundered by many writers and the works of Cicero had a profound influence on prose style; Seneca was seen as a master of tragedy and Plautus's *Pot of Gold* served as a model for comedies.

**Detail from medieval copy of Pliny's *Historia Naturalis***

***Venetian author*** *Carlo Goldoni (1707–93) reacted against the satirical tradition of* La Commedia dell'Arte, *preferring to write more forgiving plays on contemporary Venice society.*

**Petrarch** *(1304–74), one of the earliest and greatest lyric poets, produced works which showed the first indications of Humanism.*

**St Francis of Assisi** *(1182–1226) was the first author to write in Italian instead of formal Latin. As well as letters and sermons, he wrote poems and songs, including the popular* Canticle of the Sun.

**Roman writer** Alberto Moravia (1907–90) is usually labelled a "Neo-Realist". His novels and short stories focus on the corrupt values of contemporary society. Among his best known works are *Gli Indifferenti* and *Agostino*.

**The Sicilian** *Nobel Prize-winner Luigi Pirandello (1867–1936) was preoccupied with themes of illusion and reality.* Six Characters In Search Of An Author *is his most famous work.*

# Music and Opera in Italy

Before Italy's unification, particularly during the 17th and 18th centuries, each major city had its own traditions of music-making. Rome, as the papal city, had musical traditions less hedonistic than elsewhere, and avoided opera. Florence had its day at the turn of the 16th century, with its celebrated *camerata* (groups set on reviving the traditions of Ancient Greek spectacle). Venice fostered church music on a grand scale, and Naples, during the 18th century, was renowned for comic opera. In the 19th century, Milan became the undisputed centre of Italian opera, centred on La Scala.

Stradivarius violin

## THE MEDIEVAL AND RENAISSANCE PERIODS

Through Boccaccio *(see p34)*, among others, it is known that singing, dancing and poetry often went hand in hand in medieval and Renaissance Italy. Italy concentrated on music as part of a spectacle rather than as a pure art form.

Important contributors to the music of these periods include Guido d'Arezzo (c.995–1050), a monk who perfected musical notation, and Francesco Landini (1325–97), one of the first known composers whose songs displayed a distinct concern for lyricism. The next 150 years were to be characterized by the *Ars Perfecta* style, culminating with composer Giovanni Palestrina (1525–94). His vocal style subjected dissonance to strict control, and it was employed for most church music. Madrigals (vocal settings of poems by Petrarch and other poets) were also popular.

The early 17th century saw Italian composers such as Carlo Gesualdo (c.1561–1613) and Claudio Monteverdi challenge these traditions by introducing more declamation and more of the unexpected.

La Pietà, Venice, where Vivaldi performed

## THE BAROQUE ERA

Claudio Monteverdi's music straddled the transition from the Renaissance period to 17th-century Baroque. The word "baroque" means highly ornamented, even bizarre, and embellishment was rife. Monteverdi's madrigals began as standard pieces for four voices but ended up as mini-operas. This was due to the popularity of an individual instrumental style and the development of the *basso continuo* (a supporting organ, harpsichord or lute that unleashed the possibility for solos and duets). At this point, the beginnings of the string orchestra were in place.

A new fashion for declamation meant that various emotional states were being represented with sighs and sobs rather than just description. Monteverdi's *Vespers* followed others' in exploiting the stereophonic possibilities of San Marco in Venice by contrasting different forces

## MAJOR ITALIAN COMPOSERS THROUGH THE AGES

**Claudio Monteverdi** *(1567–1643) was best known for his* Vespers *of 1610. Both his madrigals and operas are considered major landmarks in the development of music.*

**Antonio Vivaldi** *(1678–1741) wrote over 600 concertos, many of which are for the violin.* The Four Seasons, *a set of concertos, is among the best-selling classical music of all time.*

**Gioacchino Rossini** *(1792–1868) was most famous for his comic operas, like* The Barber of Seville. *The romantic, expressive side of his more serious works was often overlooked.*

Luciano Pavarotti performed in the most modern surroundings

in different parts of the building. In the 1680s, Arcangelo Corelli (1653–1713) turned to classicism. Corelli was famous for the *concerto grosso,* a style that contrasted the solo string group with the full ensemble. He was followed by Antonio Vivaldi (1678–1741), who concentrated his efforts on developing the solo form of the *concerto grosso.* He used wind and plucked instruments as well as violins.

## THE EMERGENCE OF OPERA

Opera first emerged during the wedding celebrations of Italy's wealthy 16th-century families. Monteverdi was the first composer to establish his work firmly in the opera repertoire. During the 17th century, Alessandro Scarlatti (1660–1725) formulated a model which consisted of an orchestral overture followed by a sequence of narrative, set as *recitative,* and interrupted by *da capo* (three-part) arias. Themes for the weightier *opera seria* were largely drawn from mythology, while the lighter *opera buffa* had stock scenes that sometimes owed a large debt to the traditions of *Commedia dell'Arte.* Famous for his comic operas, such as *The Barber of Seville,* was the composer Gioacchino Rossini. Among other contributors, Vincenzo Bellini (1801–35) and Gaetano Donizetti (1797–1848) developed *bel canto* singing, a style stressing fine tone and ornamentation.

The two most prominent opera composers of the latter half of the 19th century were Giuseppe Verdi and Giacomo Puccini (1858–1924). Verdi often turned to the works of Shakespeare as well as to contemporary subjects in order to form a basis for his work, while many composers, like Puccini, turned to the new trend of *verismo* (slices of realism) – *La Bohème* is one of the most refined examples of this style.

**Giuseppe Verdi** *(1813–1901), whose first works were for La Scala, was the most important opera composer of the 19th century. His most celebrated works include* Rigoletto *and* Aida.

**Puccini's *Tosca,* first staged in 1900**

## THE 20TH CENTURY

In the early 20th century, Puccini's *La Fanciulla del West* (The Girl of the West) brought cowboys into opera, *Turandot* looked towards the Orient and *Tosca* brought torture and murder. Some composers have attempted to emulate French and German music, and only a few Italian pieces, such as those by Ottorino Respighi (1879–1936), have been regularly performed. The most important name in post-war Italian music was Luciano Berio (1925–2003), who developed Music Theatre, an art form lying somewhere between drama and opera. In later years, however, Berio continued the tradition of Grand Opera with his elaborate production of *Un Re in Ascolto.* But it is Luciano Pavarotti (1935–2007) who must be credited with renewing an international interest in opera. In the 1990s, his televised performances with "Three Tenors" co-stars José Carreras and Placido Domingo secured a massive world audience for opera. Another star of opera and classical music is internationally renowned conductor Riccardo Muti, former director of La Scala.

**The illuminated interior of Rome's Teatro dell'Opera**

# Italian Design

Italy has had phenomenal success evolving stylish, desirable forms for everyday objects. Its 20th-century achievements can be credited to a handful of forward-thinking industrial giants, such as Olivetti, willing to entrust important product decisions to a group of inspired designers, like Ettore Sottsass. The design genius was to rethink the function of consumer objects, apply new technology, and then make the result look seductive.

**The streamlined** *aesthetic of Italian design extends even to pasta; this Marille version was created by car designer Giorgio Giugiaro for Voiello in 1983.*

**Sleek, sculptural** *Alessi cutlery (1988), designed by Ettore Sottsass, combines maximum utility with elegance and aesthetic integrity.*

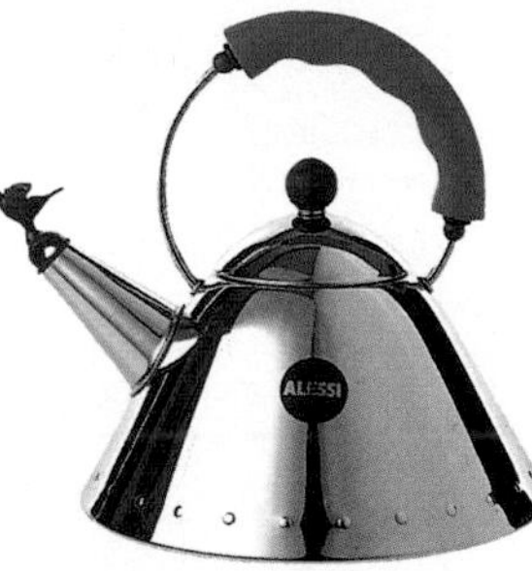


**The Alessi kettle** *(1985), designed by Michael Graves, achieved such popularity in its first year of production that over 100,000 were sold.*

**One of the best** *known coffeemakers is Bialetti's Moka Express. Although designed in 1930, it is still enormously popular today.*

**Christophe Pilet's** *chair, designed for Giulio Cappellini's collection of contemporary furniture, expresses the idea of the living style of the 1990s.*

**The folding Cumano** *table, designed by Achille Castiglione for Zanotta in 1979, is still revered as a "designer object".*

**The Patty Difusa** *chair, with unusual wooden arms that curve into legs, was designed by William Sawaya for Sawaya & Moroni in Milan.*

**Pininfarina's streamlined** *form for the Ferrari Testarossa (1986) pushes car design almost into the realms of sculpture.*

**Light in weight**, *and compact in shape, Olivetti's Valentine typewriter revolutionized the role of the desk typewriter. Designed by Ettore Sottsass in 1969, its portability allowed the user to work anywhere.*

B*abc*

**Italian printer** *Giambattista Bodoni (1740–1813) designed the sophisticated typeface that bears his name and is still popular 200 years after its creation.*

**Milan's Giorgio Armani** *is best known for his updating of classic items such as the jacket, creating a flattering, smart and comfortable, "deconstructed" look.*

**Prada, the Milan-based** *fashion house headed by Miuccia Prada, features minimalist, cutting-edge designs and the use of innovative fabrics.*

**The Artemide** *company is renowned for combining metal and glass in many of their designs, especially lamps and lighting fixtures.*

**Florence has a long** *reputation as a producer of high quality crafts, particularly fashion accessories such as handbags, shoes, belts, jewellery and briefcases.*

**Gucci's** *classic items, including bags and shoes, are a revered totem for the fashion-conscious.*

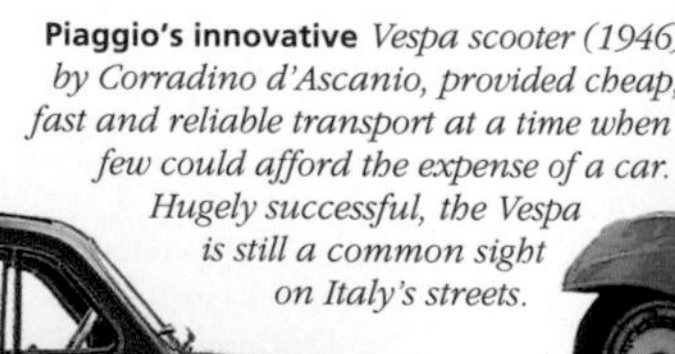

**Piaggio's innovative** *Vespa scooter (1946), by Corradino d'Ascanio, provided cheap, fast and reliable transport at a time when few could afford the expense of a car. Hugely successful, the Vespa is still a common sight on Italy's streets.*

**The FIAT 500** *(1957), like the Vespa, became a symbol of mobility and democratization, an expression of Italy's rapid postwar recovery.*

# Scientists, Inventors and Explorers

Italy has fostered a long tradition of important scientific thought and discovery, fuelled in the Renaissance by such men as Galileo, who searched for a new understanding of the universe. Meanwhile, explorers such as Columbus had set off to find new worlds, a move heralded in the 13th century by Marco Polo. The spirit of scientific enquiry continued up to the 20th century, with the invention of radio and pioneering work in the field of nuclear physics.

**Guglielmo Marconi** *invented the first practical system for sending radio signals. In 1901, he succeeded in picking up a signal that had been sent to England from Newfoundland.*

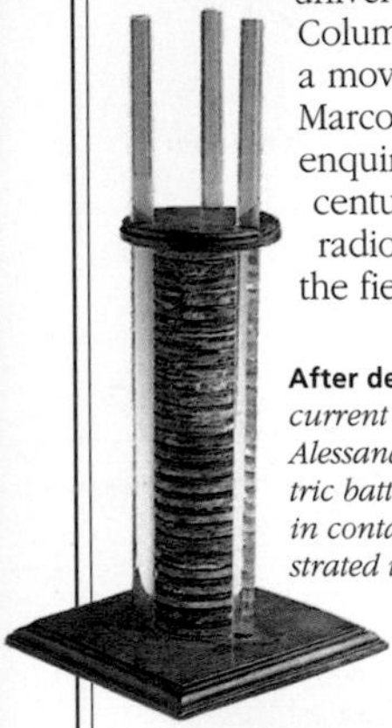

Trentino Alto Adig

Lombardy

Valle d'Aosta and Piedmont

The Vene and Fri

Liguria

Tuscany

**After deducing** *that an electric current made frogs' legs move, Alessandro Volta invented the electric battery, a "pile" of metal discs in contact with acid. He demonstrated it to Napoleon in 1801.*

**Genoese-born** *Christopher Columbus sailed west from Spain in 1492. He reached the Indies in three months, navigating with such aids as an astrolabe.*

**The explorer** *Amerigo Vespucci established that the New World was a separate land mass. A pamphlet wrongly described him as its discoverer, and so, in 1507, America acquired its name.*

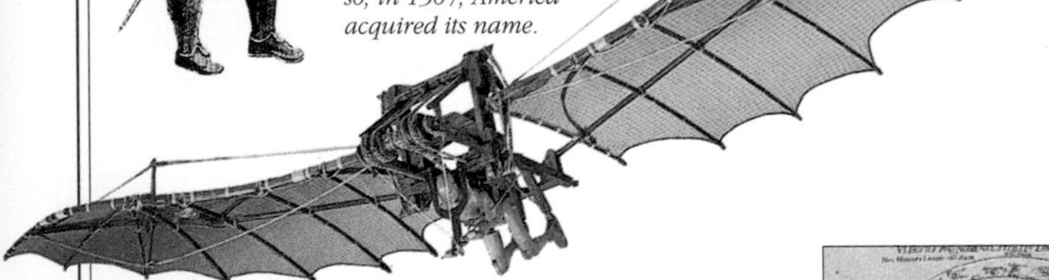

**Leonardo da Vinci** *was the ultimate Renaissance man, accomplished in both arts and sciences. He conceived his first design for a flying machine in c.1488, more than 400 years before the first aeroplane took off. This model is based on one of his technical drawings.*

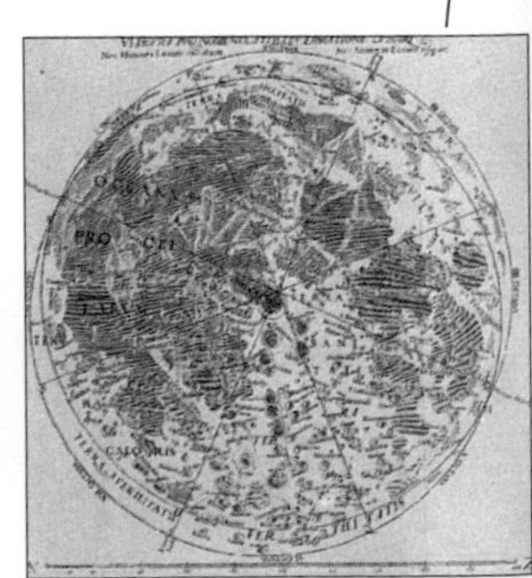

**The telescope** *enabled astronomers to produce accurate lunar maps. Domenico Cassini, astronomy professor at Bologna University, refined the instrument. In 1665 he traced the meridian line in the church of San Petronio.*

0 kilometres 200

0 miles 100

**Padua University**, founded in 1222, was a centre of scientific learning in the Renaissance. Galileo, inventor of the telescope, taught physics here, and the lectern he used is still on view.

**The Venetian Marco Polo** *set off for the east as a youth in 1271. He stayed at the court of the Mongol emperor, Kublai Khan, for nearly two decades before returning home. He is seen here arriving at Hormuz in the Persian Gulf from India.*

**Galileo Galilei** *proved that the earth revolved around the sun, overturning Church doctrine. He was convicted of heresy in 1633. Here he shows the rings of Saturn to Venetian senators.*

**Winner of** *the Nobel Prize for Physics in 1938, Enrico Fermi directed the first controlled nuclear chain reaction. He built the world's first nuclear reactor for producing power at the University of Chicago.*

**Pliny the Elder** wrote his catalogue of human knowledge, *Natural History*, in AD 77. He died when Vesuvius erupted two years later, but his book retained its authority for 1,500 years.

**Spectacles were invented** *in Italy in the 13th century. They are first recorded in Venice, still an important centre for glasswork today.*

**The mathematician Archimedes** *was born in c.287 BC in Syracuse, Sicily, then a Greek colony. Legend has it that he discovered the principle of specific gravity while in the bath.*

TEMPLA DOMVM EXPOSITIS: VICOS FORA MOENIA PONTES:
VIRGINEAM TRIVII QVOD REPARARIS AQVAM.
PRISCA LICET NAVTIS STATVAS DARE COMMODA PORTVS:
ET VATICANVM CINGERE SIXTE IVGVM:
PLVS TAMEN VRBS DEBET: NAM QVAE SQVALORE LATEBAT:
CERNITVR IN CELEBRI BIBLIOTHECA LOCO.

# THE HISTORY OF ITALY

The concept of Italy as a geographic entity goes back to the time of the Etruscans, but Italy's history is one of discord and division. Prior to the 19th century, the only time the peninsula was united was under the Romans, who by the 2nd century BC had subdued the other Italian tribes. Rome became the capital of a huge empire, introducing its language, laws and calendar to most of Europe before succumbing to Germanic invaders in the 5th century AD. Another important legacy of the Roman empire was Christianity and the position of the pope as head of the Catholic church. The medieval papacy summoned the Franks to drive out the Lombards and, in AD 800, crowned the Frankish king Charlemagne Holy Roman Emperor. Unfortunately, what seemed to be the dawn of a new age turned out to be anything but. For five centuries popes and emperors fought to decide which of them should be in charge of their nebulous empire.

Julius Caesar

Meanwhile, a succession of foreign invaders – Normans, Angevins and Aragonese – took advantage of the situation to conquer Sicily and the south. The north, in contrast, saw a growth of independent city states, the most powerful being Venice, fabulously wealthy through trade with the East. Other cities, such as Genoa, Florence, Milan, Pisa and Siena, also had their days of glory. Northern Italy became the most prosperous and cultured region in western Europe and it was the artists and scholars of 15th-century Florence who inspired the Renaissance. Small, fragmented states, however, could not compete with great powers. In the 16th century Italy's petty kingdoms fell prey to a foreign invader, this time to Spain, and the north subsequently came under the control of Austria.

One small kingdom that remained independent was Piedmont, but during a war between Austria and France it fell to Napoleon in 1796. In the 19th century, however, it was Piedmont that became the focus for a movement towards a united Italy, a goal that was achieved in 1870, thanks largely to the heroic military exploits of Garibaldi. In the 1920s, the Fascists seized power and, in 1946, the monarchy was abandoned for today's republic.

16th-century map of Italy, of the kind used by Venetian and Genoese sailors

◁ Fresco by Melozzo da Forlì of the court of Sixtus IV (1471–84), a powerful and worldly Renaissance pope

# The Age of the Etruscans

The Etruscans were Italy's first major civilization. The frescoes, jewellery and pottery found in their tombs are evidence of a highly artistic, cultured people. Their origin is a mystery, as is their language, but from the 9th century BC they spread through central Italy, their chief rivals being the Greeks in the south. Etruria was never a unified state, just a loose confederation of cities. In the 6th century Etruscan kings ruled Rome, the city that would ultimately eclipse them.

**ITALY IN 650 BC**

*Etruscan kingdoms*

*Greek colonies*

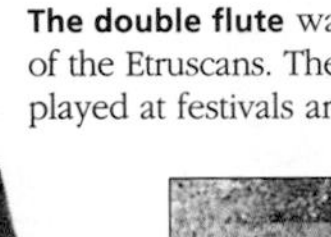

**The double flute** was a speciality of the Etruscans. The instrument was played at festivals and funerals alike.

**Terracotta Winged Horses**
*This beautiful relief of yoked horses (4th century BC) decorated the façade of the Ara della Regina temple at Tarquinia.*

**Bronze Sheep's Liver**
*The inscriptions served as a guide for telling the future from animals' entrails.*

**Terracotta Cremation Urn**
*The lid of the urn shows the deceased holding a writing tablet. The Etruscans introduced the alphabet to Italy.*

**TOMB OF THE LEOPARDS**
Feasts and revelry are common themes in the frescoes that decorate Etruscan tombs. These musicians are from a tomb fresco (c.500 BC) at Tarquinia *(see p466)*.

## TIMELINE

**9th century BC** Pre-urban communities established along river valleys in Etruria

**753 BC** Legendary date of foundation of Rome by Romulus

**c.700 BC** Growth of cities in Etruria; earliest Etruscan inscriptions

**616 BC** Etruscans become rulers of Rome under Tarquino the Older

900 BC | 800 BC | 700 BC

**c.900 BC** First traces of Iron Age in Italy; Villanovan period

**c.800 BC** Greeks settle in Sicily and south of Italy

**715–673 BC** Reign of the wise Numa Pompilius, second king of Rome

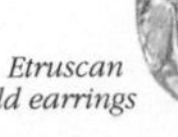

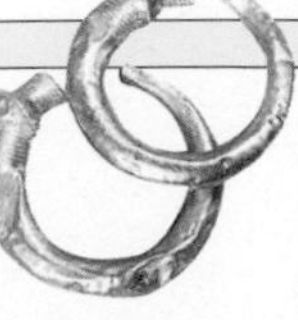

*Etruscan gold earrings*

**A Boxing Match**
*Athletic competitions were held at funerals. This vase, which dates from about 500 BC, was made in Etruria, but imitates the Greek black-figure style of pottery.*

**The musicians** and the dancer in the tomb painting are painted with a realism that indicates the influence of Greek art.

**The lyre** was made from a tortoise shell and played with a plectrum.

**Apollo of Veii**
*This magnificent statue of Apollo (c.500 BC) shows the stylized facial features characteristic of Etruscan art.*

**Bronze Mirror**
*Wealthy Etruscans lived in great luxury. The women used polished bronze mirrors with engraved backs. This one shows Helen of Troy and the goddess Aphrodite.*

## WHERE TO SEE ETRUSCAN ITALY

**Rock tombs** *like these at Sovana* (p336) *are common in the volcanic tufa of central Italy.*

Tuscany, Lazio and Umbria are rich in Etruscan remains, especially tombs. There are huge necropolises in Lazio at Cerveteri and Tarquinia *(p466)*. The latter also has an important museum. Other museums with major collections of Etruscan art and artifacts include Villa Giulia *(p440)* and the Vatican's Museo Gregoriano *(p422)* in Rome, the Museo Archeologico in Florence *(p277),* the Museo Nazionale in Chiusi *(p332)* and the Museo Guarnacci in Volterra *(p334)*.

**Temple of Neptune**
*This fine temple at Paestum (5th century BC) is a legacy of Greek colonization of the south.*

600 BC | 500 BC | 400 BC

**509 BC** Last Etruscan king, Tarquinius Superbus, expelled from Rome; establishment of Roman Republic

**499 BC** Battle of Lake Regillus; Romans defeat alliance of Latins and Etruscans

**474 BC** Etruscan fleet defeated by Greeks off Cumae; blow to Etruscan naval power

**450 BC** Roman law codified in the Twelve Tables

*Mixing bowl, imported from Greece*

**c.400 BC** Gauls start to settle along valley of the Po

**396 BC** Veii, a major Etruscan city in present-day Lazio, falls to Rome

**390 BC** Gauls sack Rome; Capitol saved thanks to alarm sounded by cackling geese

*Relief of Capitoline geese, found in the Roman Forum*

# From Republic to Empire

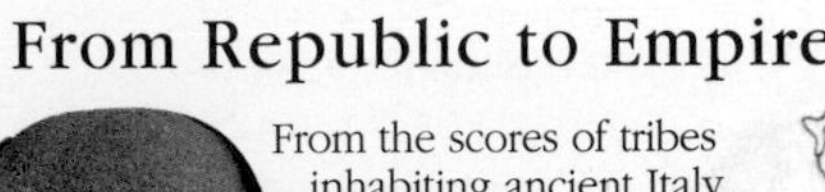

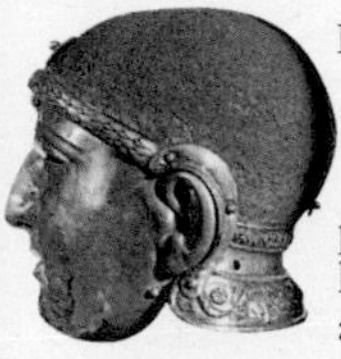

Roman mask and helmet (1st century BC)

From the scores of tribes inhabiting ancient Italy, one people, the Romans, emerged to conquer the peninsula and impose their language, customs and laws on the rest. Rome's success was due to superb skill in military and civil organization. The state was a republic ruled by two consuls, elected each year, but as the extent of Rome's conquests grew, power passed to generals such as Julius Caesar. The Republic became unworkable and Caesar's heirs became the first Roman emperors.

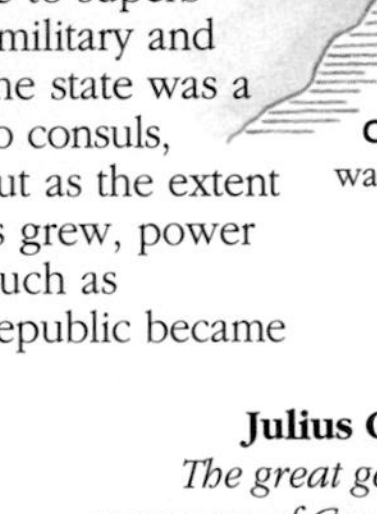

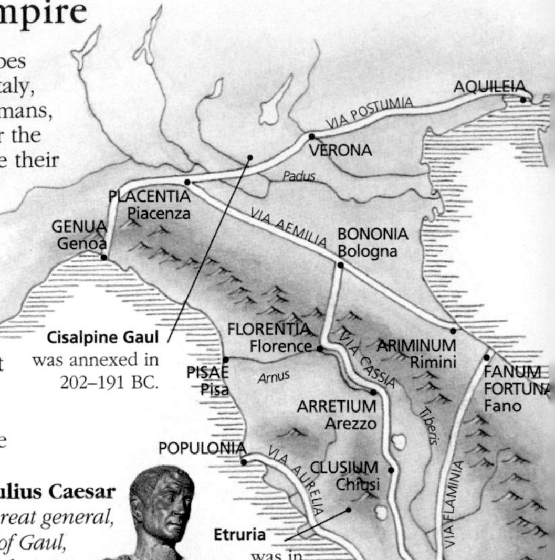

**Cisalpine Gaul** was annexed in 202–191 BC.

**Etruria** was in Roman hands by 265 BC.

**Julius Caesar**
*The great general, conqueror of Gaul, returned to Italy in 49 BC to defeat Pompey. His rise to absolute power marked the end of the Republic.*

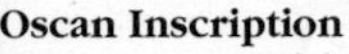

**Oscan Inscription**
*The languages of the peoples conquered by Rome lived on for centuries before being replaced by Latin. The Oscans lived in what is now Campania.*

**War Elephant**
*In 218 BC the great Carthaginian general Hannibal brought 37 elephants across the Alps – to spread alarm in the Roman ranks.*

**Roman Aqueduct**
*The Romans' talent for engineering found its most spectacular expression in huge aqueducts. These could be up to 80 km (50 miles) long, though for most of that distance the water ran underground.*

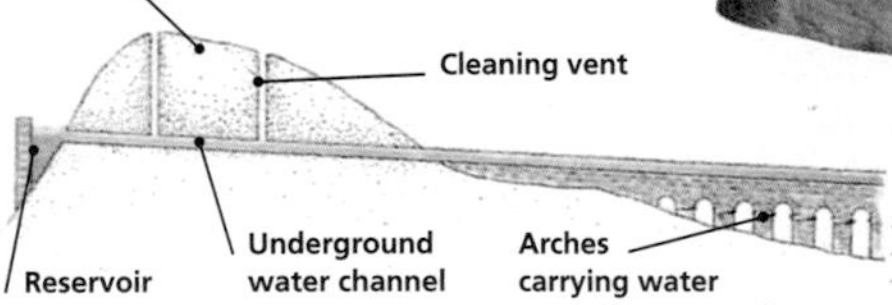

## TIMELINE

*Via Appia*

**312 BC** Building of Via Appia and Aqua Appia aqueduct

**308 BC** Etruscan city of Tarquinii falls to Rome

**300 BC**

**287–212 BC** Life of Archimedes, the great Greek mathematician of Syracuse

**275 BC** Greek King Pyrrhus defeated by Romans at Beneventum

**265 BC** Romans capture last Etruscan city

**264–241 BC** First Punic War (between Rome and Carthage)

**250 BC**

**237 BC** Romans occupy Corsica and Sardinia

**218 BC** Second Punic War; Hannibal crosses the Alps

**216 BC** Roman defeat at Battle of Cannae

**200 BC**

**191 BC** Gaulish territory south of the Alps falls to Rome

*Hannibal, Carthaginian leader in the Second Punic War*

**Cicero Addresses the Senate**
*State business was debated in the Senate. The great orator Cicero (106–43 BC) argued for the Republic and against tyranny.*

**Roman Legionary**
*This bronze shows a legionary in standard kit of helmet, breastplate, leather kilt with iron plates, greaves on his shins, and sandals.*

RFINIUM
LERIA
CAPUA
VIA APPIA
BRUNDISIUM
Brindisi
TARENTUM
Taranto
RHEGIUM
Reggio di Calabria

**The Via Appia** was extended from Capua to Brindisi in 190 BC.

**Sicily** became the first Roman province in 241 BC.

## WHERE TO SEE ITALY FROM THE REPUBLICAN ERA

Republican structures are very rare, most having been rebuilt under the Empire. In Rome itself, two notable exceptions are the 2nd-century BC Temples of the Forum Boarium *(p433)*. However, the legacy of the age to modern Italy is not hard to appreciate. Countless roads, such as the Via Appia Antica *(p441)*, and towns were planned originally by Roman engineers. Two striking examples of towns with original Roman street plans are Lucca *(pp320–21)* and Como *(p191)*.

**These huge basalt blocks** *at Tharros in Sardinia* (p551) *were part of a Roman road.*

## ROMAN ROADS

After conquering other tribes, the Romans imposed their authority by building roads along which legions could march rapidly to deal with any trouble. They also built towns. Many, such as Ariminum (Rimini), were "colonies", settlements for Roman citizens – often veteran legionaries.

**Aerial View of Bologna**
*Roman street plans are still visible in city centres today. The route of the old Via Aemilia cuts straight through the centre of Bologna.*

**168 BC** End of Third Macedonian War; Romans now masters of Greece

**150 BC**

**146 BC** End of Third Punic War; Carthage destroyed

**104 BC** Slave revolt in Sicily



*Milestone from the Via Aemilia*

**100 BC**

**89 BC** Social War: Rome's Italian allies granted citizenship

**80 BC** Building starts on the first Roman amphitheatre, at Pompeii

**73–71 BC** Slave revolt led by Spartacus

**50 BC**

**49 BC** Caesar crosses the Rubicon and drives Pompey from Rome

**45 BC** Introduction of 12-month Julian calendar

**44 BC** Murder of Julius Caesar; end of Roman Republic

**31 BC** Octavian defeats Mark Antony at Battle of Actium

**30 BC** Suicide of Mark Antony and Cleopatra in Egypt

# The Golden Age of Rome

From the age of Augustus to the reign of Trajan, Rome's power grew until her empire stretched from Britain to the Red Sea. Despite the extravagance of emperors such as Nero, taxes and booty from military campaigns continually refilled the Imperial coffers. Under the wiser rule of Trajan, Hadrian and Marcus Aurelius in the 2nd century AD, Roman citizens enjoyed wealth and comfort, with most of the work performed by slaves. Entertainment included visits to the baths, the theatre and the games. The town of Pompeii, buried when Vesuvius erupted in AD 79, preserves many fascinating details of everyday life.

**ROMAN EMPIRE IN AD 117**

*Maximum extent of the Empire*

**Mosaic of Gladiators**
*Bloodthirsty gladiatorial combats were very popular. The gladiators were mostly slaves captured in war.*

**Frescoes of festoons and medallions**

**Trajan's Column**
*The carvings record Trajan's successful campaigns in Dacia (present-day Romania) in the first decade of the 2nd century AD.*

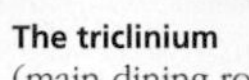

**The triclinium** (main dining room) had a beautiful frieze of cupids.

**Roman Shops**
*Buildings in towns were lined with small shops open to the street, like this pharmacy. The front was closed with wooden panels and locked at night.*

**HOUSE OF THE VETTII**

This reconstruction shows one of Pompeii's finest houses *(see pp494–5)*. The Vettii were not aristocrats, but freedmen, former slaves, who had made a fortune through trade. The rooms were richly decorated with frescoes and sculptures.

**TIMELINE**

**9 BC** Dedication of Ara Pacis *(see p410)* in Rome to celebrate peace after wars in Gaul and Spain

**AD 17** Tiberius fixes boundary of Empire along the Rhine and Danube

*Bronze cooking pots from kitchen at Pompeii*

**AD 79** Eruption of Vesuvius destroys Pompeii and Herculaneum

50 BC | AD 1 | AD 50

**27 BC** Augustus takes title Princeps, in effect becoming the first Roman emperor

**AD 37–41** Reign of Caligula

**AD 43** Roman conquest of Britain in reign of Claudius

**AD 67** Traditional date for martyrdom of St Peter and St Paul in Rome

**AD 68** Deposition and suicide of Nero

**AD 80** Inaugural games in Colosseum

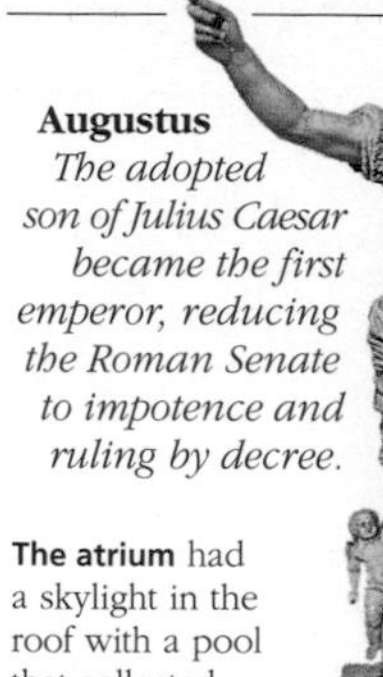

**Augustus**
*The adopted son of Julius Caesar became the first emperor, reducing the Roman Senate to impotence and ruling by decree.*

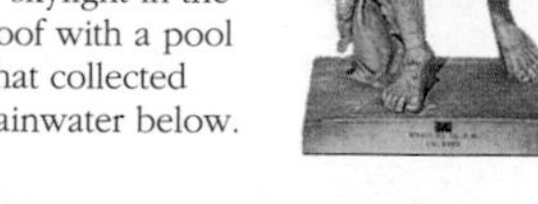

**The atrium** had a skylight in the roof with a pool that collected rainwater below.

**Front entrance**

## WHERE TO SEE IMPERIAL ROME

The best places to discover how people lived are Pompeii *(pp494–5)* and Herculaneum. Artifacts and works of art from these sites are held at the Museo Archeologico in Naples *(pp490–91)*, while local museums all over Italy contain statues and other remains. Famous sights in Rome include the Pantheon *(p404)* and the Colosseum *(p393)*. Hadrian's Villa, at Tivoli *(p468)*, and Ostia *(p467)* are also fascinating to visit, but the whole country preserves traces of Rome's glory – from the Arch of Augustus in Aosta *(p215)* to Villa del Casale *(p537)* in Sicily.

**The Forum** (pp390–91), *with its temples and law courts, was the centre of daily life in ancient Rome.*

**Reception room**

**Mosaic of a Banquet**
*The Romans ate reclining on low couches. A popular accompaniment for many dishes was* garum, *a salty sauce made of dried fish.*

**Peristyle or colonnade**

**The internal garden** was a feature borrowed by the Romans from the Greeks.

**Household Shrine**
*Religious rites were practised both in public and in private. This shrine from the House of the Vettii was dedicated to the* lares, *the household gods.*

**AD 97** Roman Empire reaches largest extent in reign of Trajan

**AD 161–180** Reign of Marcus Aurelius

**AD 193–211** Reign of Septimius Severus

**AD 212** Roman citizenship extended to include people from all parts of the Empire

**AD 100** | **AD 150** | **AD 200**

**ate 1st century D** Amphitheatre f Verona built

**AD 125** Pantheon rebuilt by Hadrian

**AD 134** Hadrian's Villa at Tivoli completed

*Emperor Septimius Severus*

**AD 216** Baths of Caracalla completed in Rome

# The Splitting of the Empire

**Glass flask with Christian symbol (4th century AD)**

A decisive turning point in the history of the Roman Empire came with Emperor Constantine's conversion to Christianity in AD 312 and his decision to build a new capital at Constantinople (Byzantium). By the 5th century the Empire was split into two. Rome and the Western Empire could not stem the tide of Germanic invaders migrating southwards and Italy fell first to the Goths and later to the Lombards. The Eastern Empire retained nominal control over parts of Italy from its stronghold at Ravenna, which became the richest, most powerful city of the age, while the great palaces and arenas of Rome were reduced to ruins.

**ITALY IN AD 600**

- *Byzantine territories*
- *Lombard territories*

**The Donation of Constantine**
*A medieval legend, encouraged by the papacy, tells how Constantine granted Pope Sylvester temporal power over Rome.*

**Belisarius** (500–565) was a general who won much of Italy back from the Goths.

**Justinian** reigned from 527 to 565. He was a great lawgiver and one of the most powerful Byzantine emperors.

**Theodolinda of the Lombards**
*The 6th-century queen converted her people to orthodox Catholicism. Here, gold is melted for the church she built at Monza* (see p201).

## TIMELINE

- **270** Aurelian Wall built to protect Rome from Germanic invaders
- **303–5** Persecution of Christians throughout the Empire in the reign of Diocletian
- **312** Constantine defeats rival Maxentius at Battle of the Milvian Bridge
- **313** Edict of Milan grants freedom of worship to Christians
- **c.320** Building of first St Peter's in Rome
- **324** Christianity becomes state religion
- 300
- **404** Ravenna becomes seat of western emperor
- 400
- **410** Sack of Rome by Alaric the Visigoth
- **476** End of Western Empire
- **488** Italy invaded by the Theodoric the Ostrogoth
- 500
- **535** Belisarius lands in Sicily; reconquest of most of Italy by Byzantine Empire
- **547** Church San Vit in Rave
- **564** Lombards invade Italy, establishing their capital at Pavia

*Gold coin of Theodoric*

**Charlemagne**
*The King of the Franks was invited by the pope to crush the Lombards. In return, he was crowned Holy Roman Emperor in AD 800.*

**Saracens Besieging Messina** *(843)*
*In the 9th century Sicily was conquered by Muslims from Africa. Saracen raiders even reached Rome, where Pope Leo IV built a new wall to defend the Vatican.*

**The emperor** holds a large gold paten, the dish in which the bread is placed for Mass.

**Maximian, Archbishop of Ravenna**

**Priests**

## THE COURT OF JUSTINIAN

Byzantine churches were decorated with glorious mosaics of coloured glass and gold leaf. This one from the apse of the church of San Vitale in Ravenna *(see p268)*, completed in 547, depicts members of the Imperial court.

## WHERE TO SEE EARLY CHRISTIAN AND BYZANTINE ITALY

Though the fall of the Roman Empire led to war, famine and depopulation, the continuity of the Christian religion has preserved many monuments of the late Empire and Byzantine period. Rome has the catacombs *(p442)* and great basilicas, such as Santa Maria Maggiore *(p413)*. In Ravenna, the administrative capital of the Byzantine Empire, are the churches of San Vitale and Sant'Apollinare *(pp268–9)* with their magnificent mosaics. Sicily and the south also preserve many Byzantine churches, while the finest example of late Byzantine architecture is San Marco in Venice *(pp110–11)*.

**Stilo** *in Calabria has a beautiful Byzantine church, the Cattolica* (p520), *dating from the 10th century.*

**Santa Costanza** *in Rome* (p441) *was built in the 4th century as the mausoleum of Constantine's daughter. Late Roman mosaics decorate the vaults.*

**595** Lombards
ɔntrol two
ɩirds of Italy

**600**

*Gregory the Great (reigned 590–604)*

**599** Pope Gregory negotiates peace between the Lombards and the Byzantine Empire

**752** Lombard King Aistulf takes Byzantine stronghold of Ravenna

**700**

**754** Pope appeals to Franks for help; King Pepin invades Italy and defeats Lombards

**774** Charlemagne conquers Italy and takes Lombard crown

**800** Charlemagne crowned Holy Roman Emperor in St Peter's

**800**

**878** Saracens capture city of Syracuse from Byzantine Empire and gain control of Sicily

**900**

*6th-century Lombard gold helmet in the Bargello museum, Florence* (see p283)

# The Rise of Venice

Enrico Dandolo, Doge of Venice (c.1120–1205)

Medieval Italy saw waves of foreign invaders joining in the struggle for power between popes and emperors. In the confusion, many northern cities asserted their independence from feudal overlords. The most powerful was Venice, governed by its doge and Great Council, which grew rich through trade with the East and by shipping Crusaders to fight the Saracens in the Holy Land. Its maritime rivals on the west coast were Genoa and Pisa.

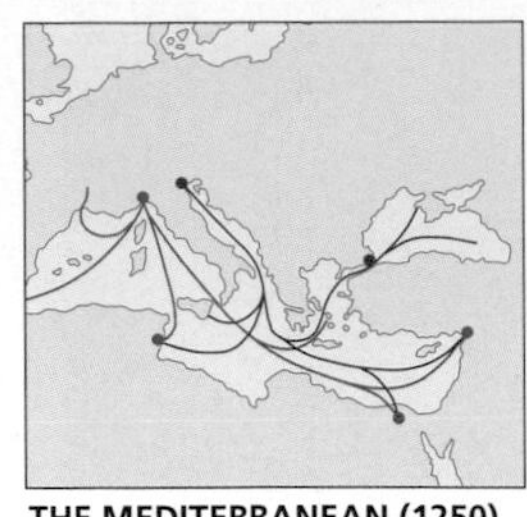

**THE MEDITERRANEAN (1250)**

— *Genoese trade routes*

— *Venetian trade routes*

**Matilda of Tuscany**

*Matilda, Countess of Tuscany (1046–1115) supported the radical Pope Gregory VII against the Emperor Henry IV. When she died, she left her lands to the church.*

**Venetian Galley**

*The galleys used by Venice, both as warships and for carrying cargo, were similar to ancient Greek vessels.*

## MARCO POLO'S DEPARTURE FOR CHINA

Venice traded in Chinese silks and spices imported via the Middle East, but no Venetian had been to China before Marco Polo's father Nicolò. Marco Polo set off with his father in 1271, returning 25 years later with fantastic tales of his time at the court of Kublai Khan.

## TIMELINE

**1000** Doge of Venice, Pietro Orseolo II, defeats Dalmatian pirates in Adriatic

**11th century** School of Law at Bologna develops into Europe's first university

*Medieval students*

**1139** Naples incorporated into Kingdom of Sicily

1000 | 1050 | 1100

**1030** Norman knight Rainulf granted county of Aversa by Duke of Naples

**1061** Normans Robert Guiscard and Roger de Hauteville capture Messina from the Arabs

**1063** San Marco in Venice rebuilt

**1073–85** Pope Gregory VII reforms church and papacy

**1076** Salerno, last Lombard city, falls to Normans

**1084** Normans sack Rome

**1115** Death of Countess Matilda

**1130** Ro II crown king of Sicily

**St Francis of Assisi** *(1181–1226)*
*In* The Dream of Pope Innocent III *by Giotto, painted around 1290–1295, St Francis holds up the tottering edifice of the Roman church. The Franciscans' rule of poverty brought about a religious revival in reaction to the wealth of the church.*

### WHERE TO SEE EARLY MEDIEVAL ITALY

Of the many churches built in this period, especially fine examples are Venice's San Marco *(p110)*, Sant'Antonio *(p158)* in Padua and the Duomo in Pisa *(p324)*. The Leaning Tower *(p326)* also dates back to the 12th century. Medieval castles include Frederick II's Castel del Monte in Puglia *(p509)* and Castello dell'Imperatore in Prato.

**Castello dell' Imperatore**, *Prato, was built about 1240.*

**Monastery of Sant'Apollonia**

**Today's Riva degli Schiavoni**

**Nicolò Polo**, his brother Maffeo and son Marco prepare to embark. They sailed first to Acre in the Levant.

**Fourth Crusade**
*Discord between the leaders of the crusade and Pope Innocent III culminated in the sacking of Constantinople in 1204.*

**Frederick II** *(1194–1250)*
*The emperor kept a court of poets and scholars in Sicily. He won Jerusalem from the Arabs by diplomacy, but was constantly at war with the pope and the cities of Lombardy.*

**1155** Frederick Barbarossa crowned Holy Roman Emperor

**1198** Frederick II becomes king of Sicily

**1204** Sacking of Constantinople

**1209** Franciscan Order founded

**1216** Dominican Order founded

**1250** Death of Frederick II

**1260** Urban IV invites Charles of Anjou to rule Naples and Sicily

**1265** Birth of Dante

1150 | 1200 | 1250

*Frederick Barbarossa dressed as a Crusader*

**1220** Frederick II crowned Holy Roman Emperor

**1228** Gregory IX excommunicates Frederick II; struggle between Guelphs (the papal party) and Ghibellines (supporters of the emperor)

**1237** Lombard League defeat Frederick at Battle of Cortenuova

**1271** Marco Polo sets off on journey to China

# The Late Middle Ages

Old feuds between pope and emperor thrived throughout the 14th century, kept alive by two warring factions – the Guelphs, who backed the papacy, and the Ghibellines, who favoured Imperial power. The cities of Lombardy and Tuscany used the political confusion to grow in strength. It was against this turbulent backdrop that a great new age in painting was inspired by artists such as Duccio and Giotto. Also at this time the Florentine poets Dante and Petrarch laid the foundations of Italian literature.

**Sienese bishop's staff**

**ITALY IN 1350**

- Papal States
- Holy Roman Empire
- Angevin Kingdom of Naples

## MEDIEVAL TOWN SQUARE

Throughout central Italy, the town square was an expression of civic pride and independence. Towns, such as Perugia *(see pp352–3)*, tried to overshadow their rivals in the splendour of their town halls. The centre of Perugia has changed little since the 14th century when the town's main rival was Siena.

**The campanile or bell tower**

**A griffin, symbol of Perugia**

**The main chamber** of the town hall, the Sala dei Notari, is decorated with the coats of arms of Perugia's mayors.

**The Fontana Maggiore** was begun in 1275 and includes panels by Nicola Pisano. Prominently placed, it is an emblem of the town's wealth.

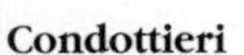

**Condottieri**
*Cities paid* condottieri, *leaders of bands of mercenaries, to fight their wars. Siena hired Guidoriccio da Fogliano, seen here in a fresco by Simone Martini (1330).*

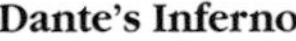

**Dante's Inferno**
*One of the harshest punishments in Dante's vision of hell is reserved for corrupt popes, such as Boniface VIII (reigned 1294–1303), who are placed upside down in fiery pits.*

## TIMELINE

**1282** Sicilian Vespers; uprising against French rule in Palermo; 2,000 French soldiers killed

**1282** Peter of Aragon lands at Trapani, conquers Sicily and is crowned king in Palermo

**1275**

**1296** Work begins on the Duomo in Florence

**1298** Marco Polo returns from China to Venice

*The poet and scholar Petrarch*

**1300**

**1304** Birth of Petrarch

**1309–43** Reign of Robert the Wise of Naples

**1309** Clement V moves papacy to Avignon

**1310** Work begins on Palazzo Ducale in Venice

**1313** Birth of Boccaccio

**1321** Dante completes *La Divina Commedia* and dies the same year

**1325**

**1337** Death of Giotto

**The Black Death**
*Bubonic plague reached Italy in 1347, carried on Genoese ships from the Black Sea. It killed over a third of the population, reducing the remainder to a state of superstitious terror.*

### WHERE TO SEE LATE MEDIEVAL ITALY

Many central Italian cities and towns have public buildings from the 13th and 14th centuries; among the most impressive are Palazzo Vecchio *(p291)* in Florence and Siena's Palazzo Pubblico *(p340)*. Smaller towns that preserve much of their medieval character include Volterra *(p334)* and the walled Monteriggioni *(p334)* in Tuscany, Gubbio *(p352)* and Todi *(p359)* in Umbria and Viterbo *(pp464–5)* in Lazio. The Duomo in Orvieto *(pp358–9)* is a fine example of a late 13th-century Gothic cathedral.

**Piazza dei Priori** *in Volterra* (p324) *is one of the most beautiful medieval squares in Italy.*

**The cathedral** was started in 1350 and used to include an outside pulpit in the square.

**Construction of Alessandria**
*Almost all towns were ringed with strong walls. This fresco (1407) by Spinello Aretino is a valuable record of medieval building techniques.*

**Return of Pope Gregory XI to Rome** *(1378)*
*For 70 years the popes had lived in Avignon, protected by the French kings, while nobles and republicans fought for control of Rome.*

**1339** Simon Boccanegra becomes first doge of Genoa; Giovanna I Queen of Naples

**1347–9** Black Death

*Medieval doctor*

**1378–1415** Period of Schism, with rival popes and antipopes in Rome and Avignon

**1380** Genoese fleet surrenders to Venetians at Chioggia

**1350** | **1375** | **1400**

**1347** Cola di Rienzo tries to re-establish Roman Republic

**1354** Cola di Rienzo killed in Rome

**1378** Gregory XI returns from Avignon to Rome

**1385** Gian Galeazzo Visconti becomes ruler of Milan

**1406** Pisa annexed by Florence

# The Renaissance

**Leonardo da Vinci (1452–1519)**

Fifteenth-century Italy saw a flowering of the arts and scholarship unmatched in Europe since the days of Greece and Rome. Architects turned from the Gothic to Classical models for inspiration, while painting, with its new understanding of perspective and anatomy, produced a generation of artists that included such giants as Leonardo da Vinci, Raphael and Michelangelo. The patronage for this cultural "rebirth" came from the wealthy families that ruled the city states of the north, led by the Medici of Florence. In spite of intense rivalry, they oversaw a period of uneasy stability out of which the Renaissance grew.

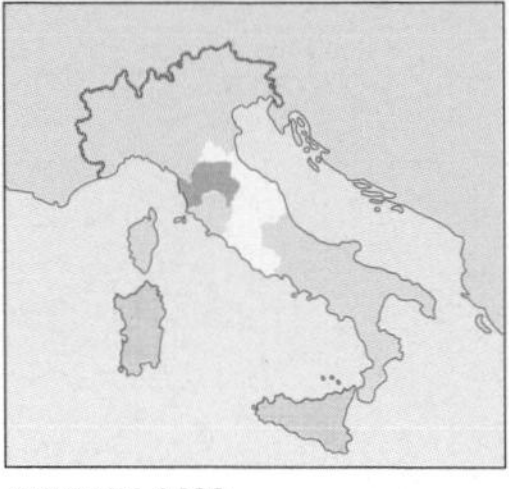

**ITALY IN 1492**

- *Republic of Florence*
- *Papal States*
- *Aragonese possessions*

**Handing over the Keys of St Peter**
*Perugino's fresco in the Sistine Chapel* (see p426) *links the authority of the pope to the New Testament and, through the Classical buildings in the background, to ancient Rome.*

**Execution of Savonarola** *(1498)*
*Having assumed the leadership of Florence in 1494, the fanatical monk was hanged, then burned for heresy in Piazza della Signoria.*

**Galeazzo Maria Sforza** was the son of Milan's ruler.

**Piero de' Medici**, Lorenzo's father, was given the nickname "the Gouty".

**Self-portrait of the artist**

## TIMELINE

**1420** Martin V re-establishes papacy in Rome

**1425**

**1434** Cosimo de' Medici comes to power in Florence

**1435** Publication of *On Painting* by Alberti, which contains the first system for the use of linear perspective

**1436** Brunelleschi completes dome of Florence cathedral

**1442** Naples captured by Alfonso of Aragon

**1444** Federico da Montefeltro becomes Duke of Urbino

**1450**

**1452** Birth of Leonardo da Vinci

**1453** Fall of Constantinople

**1458–64** War between Houses of Aragon and Anjou over Kingdom of Naples

**1469** Lorenzo the Magnificent becomes ruler of Florence

*Cosimo de' Medici*

*Filippo Brunelleschi*

**The Battle of Pavia** *(1525)*
*The French King Francis I was captured at this battle against the army of the Habsburg Emperor Charles V, who won control of Italy.*

## THE PROCESSION OF THE MAGI

Benozzo Gozzoli's fresco (1459) in the Palazzo Medici-Riccardi, Florence, depicts members of the Medici family and other contemporary notables. It contains many references to a great church council held in Florence in 1439.

**Lorenzo de' Medici** (the Magnificent) was depicted as one of the three kings travelling to Bethlehem.

### WHERE TO SEE RENAISSANCE ITALY

Many cities were flourishing centres of the arts in the 15th century. None can rival Florence *(pp270–313)* with its great palazzi and the Uffizi gallery *(pp286–89)*, but Venice *(pp84–137)*, Urbino *(pp370–71)* and Mantova *(p207)* all preserve great treasures. In Rome, do not miss the Vatican's Sistine Chapel and Raphael Rooms *(pp424–27)*.

*The* **Spedale degli Innocenti** *by Brunelleschi in Florence* (p277) *shows the Classical symmetry and restraint of Renaissance architecture.*

**Humanism**
*Carpaccio's painting of St Augustine is thought to show Cardinal Bessarion (c.1395–1472), one of the scholars who revived interest in Classical philosophy, especially Plato.*

**Pope Julius II**
*During his reign (1503–13), the worldly Julius made the papacy a major power in European politics. Raphael's portrait shows him as a shrewd old statesman.*

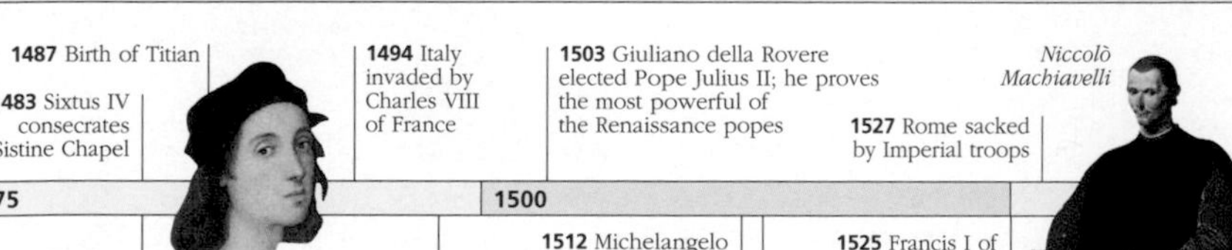

**1475** Birth of Michelangelo

**1483** Sixtus IV consecrates Sistine Chapel

**1483** Birth of Raphael

*Raphael*

**1487** Birth of Titian

**1494** Italy invaded by Charles VIII of France

**1498** Savonarola executed; Machiavelli secretary to ruling Council in Florence

**1500**

**1503** Giuliano della Rovere elected Pope Julius II; he proves the most powerful of the Renaissance popes

**1512** Michelangelo completes Sistine Chapel ceiling

**1513** Giovanni de' Medici crowned Pope Leo X

**1525** Francis I of France captured at Battle of Pavia

**1527** Rome sacked by Imperial troops

*Niccolò Machiavelli*

**1532** Machiavelli's book *The Prince* is published, five years after his death

# The Counter-Reformation

After the Sack of Rome in 1527, Italy was at the mercy of Charles V, Holy Roman Emperor and King of Spain. Pope Clement VII, who had opposed Charles, crowned him emperor in Bologna. In response to the growing threat from Protestantism, a series of reforms, known as the Counter-Reformation and backed by the Inquisition, imposed rigid orthodoxy. New religious orders, such as the Jesuits, were set up to take the battle for men's souls far overseas. The missionary spirit of the age inspired the dramatic forms of the Baroque.

Gian Lorenzo Bernini

**ITALY IN 1550**

Spanish possessions

States allied with Spain

**Emperor Charles V and Pope Clement VII**
*The two former enemies settled their differences and the future destiny of Italy in the Treaty of Barcelona (1529).*

## BAROQUE STUCCO DECORATION

This stucco relief by Giacomo Serpotta (c.1690) in the Oratory of Santa Zita in Palermo is a magnificent example of Late Baroque exuberance. The subject is a favourite of the period, the Battle of Lepanto, a great naval triumph for the combined forces of Christendom against the Turks (1571).

**The Virgin Mary** intervenes on the side of the Christians.

**The centre** of the ingenious creation is, in effect, a framed painting in perspective.

**Baroque Architecture**
*Guarino Guarini's decoration of the dome of the Chapel of the Holy Shroud in Turin* (see p221) *was completed in 1694.*

**The young boy** rests his hand on a helmet, symbol of the victorious Christians.

## TIMELINE

**1530–37** Alessandro de' Medici ruler of Florence

**1542** Inquisition established in Rome

**1545–63** Council of Trent sets out agenda of Counter-Reformation

*Andrea Palladio*

**1580** Death of architect Palladio

**1589** Palestrina publishes setting of the Latin Hymnal

**1600** Philosopher Giordano Bruno burned for heresy in Rome

1550

1575

**1529** Charles V crowned Holy Roman Emperor in San Petronio, Bologna

**1540** Founding of Jesuit Order

**1541** Michelangelo completes *Last Judgment* in Sistine Chapel

**1560** San Carlo Borromeo appointed Bishop of Milan

**1564** Birth of Galileo

**1571** Victory over Turkish fleet at Battle of Lepanto

*Giovanni Pierluigi da Palestrina*

**Trial of Galileo**
*The great astronomer was often in trouble with the Inquisition. He was summoned to Rome in 1633 and forced to deny that the Earth and planets moved round the sun.*

**Lepanto** was the last major sea battle in which Venetian galleys played an important role.

**Cherubs, a favourite motif in Baroque decoration**

**St Ignatius Loyola**
*The Spanish saint was the founder of the Jesuits – sanctioned by the pope in Rome in 1540.*

**The turban, symbol of the defeated Turks**

**Revolt of Masaniello** *(1647)*
*High taxes made Spanish rule in Naples unpopular. A proposed tax on fruit sparked off this failed revolt.*

## WHERE TO SEE BAROQUE ITALY

**The Ecstasy of St Teresa** *by Bernini* (p412) *has the dynamic theatricality characteristic of the best Baroque sculpture.*

The Baroque is strongly associated with Rome and in particular with its great public spaces such as Piazza Navona *(pp398–9)* and the many churches by Borromini and Bernini. Other cities and towns with striking Baroque architecture include Lecce *(pp512–13)* in Puglia, Palermo *(pp526–29)*, Noto *(p543)* and Syracuse *(pp542–3)* in Sicily, and Turin *(pp220–21)*.

**1626** New St Peter's consecrated in Rome

**1631** Duchy of Urbino absorbed by Papal States

**1669** Venice loses island of Crete to the Turks

**1694** Andrea Pozzo completes ceiling fresco for the church of Sant'Ignazio in Rome

**1678** Birth of Vivaldi

**1625** | **1650** | **1675**

**1633** Galileo condemned by papal authorities

**1642** *L'Incoronazione di Poppea* by Monteverdi

**1647** Revolt in Naples in response to tax on fruit

**1669** Major eruption of Mount Etna

**1693** Eastern Sicily ruined by earthquake that kills 5 per cent of the island's population

**1674** Revolt against Spanish rule in Messina

# The Grand Tour

The Romantic poet Shelley, visitor to Italy

The treaty of Aix-la-Chapelle in 1748 marked the start of 50 years of peace. It was about this time that Italy, with its great art treasures and Classical ruins, including the newly excavated Pompeii, became Europe's first great tourist destination. Young English "milords" visited Rome, Florence and Venice as part of a new type of pilgrimage, the Grand Tour; while artists and poets sought inspiration in Rome's glorious past. In 1800, Napoleon, who conquered and briefly united Italy, threatened to destroy the old order, but in 1815 the status quo was restored.

**Charles III's Fleet at Naples** *(1753)*
*Ruler of Naples from 1734 to 1759, when he became King of Spain, Charles attempted genuine political reforms.*

**Goethe in the Roman Campagna**
*Goethe toured Italy in the 1780s. Great poets who followed his example included the Romantics Keats, Shelley and Byron.*

**Farnese Hercules** (see p491)

**The Dying Galatian** (see p386)

## GALLERY OF VIEWS OF ANCIENT ROME BY PANNINI

Giovanni Pannini (1691–1765) painted views of Roman ruins for foreigners. This painting is a capriccio, an imaginary scene incorporating many well-known views and Classical statues.

**Venetian Carnival**
*The colourful folklore of Carnival attracted many tourists, but Venice's days of greatness were over. In 1797, the proud maritime republic was ceded to Austria by Napoleon.*

## TIMELINE

1700 | 1720 | 1740

**1707** Birth of playwright Carlo Goldoni

**1713** Treaty of Utrecht gives Naples and Sardinia to Austria and Sicily to Piedmont

**1718** Piedmont and Sardinia united under House of Savoy; Sicily passes to Austria

**1725** *The Four Seasons* by Vivaldi

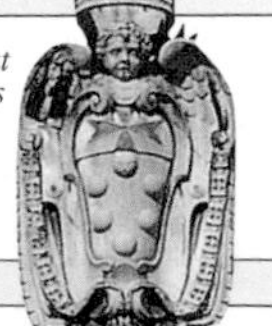

*Medici coat of arms*

**1735** Peace of Vienna confirms Charles III as King of the Two Sicilies (Naples and Sicily)

**1737** End of Medici dynasty in Florence; Grand Duchy of Tuscany passes to Austrian House of Lorraine

**1748** First excavations at Pompeii

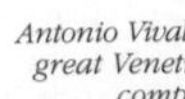

*Antonio Vivaldi, great Venetian composer*

**View of the Roman Forum by Piranesi**
*The popular series of etchings* Vedute di Roma *(Views of Rome) by Giovanni Battista Piranesi (1720–78) inspired a new interest in excavating the ruins of ancient Rome.*

## WHERE TO SEE 18TH-CENTURY ITALY

The 18th century produced two of Rome's best-loved tourist attractions: the Spanish Steps *(p409)* and the Trevi Fountain *(p410)*. It was also the age of the first purpose-built museums, including the Vatican's Museo Pio-Clementino *(p421)*. The Neo-Classical sculpture of Antonio Canova (1757–1822) was immensely popular during this period. His tomb is in Santa Maria Gloriosa dei Frari in Venice *(pp98–9)*. Of Neo-Classical buildings, the most imposing is a vast monument to enlightened despotism: the Palazzo Reale at Caserta *(p496)*.

**Pauline Borghese**, *Napoleon's sister, was the model for Antonio Canova's* Venus *(1805) in the Villa Borghese collection in Rome* (p439).

**The Colosseum** was as popular a subject in the 18th century as it is on today's picture postcards.

**The Laocoön** *(see p417)*

**View of the Pantheon** *(see p404)*

**Napoleon**
*When Napoleon conquered Italy in 1800, he was seen by many as a liberator. The enchantment wore off as he took priceless works of art back to Paris.*

**Congress of Vienna** *(1815)*
*The conference decided that Austria should keep Lombardy and Venice, thereby sowing the seeds of the Italian unification movement.*

*La Scala Opera House, Milan* (see p187)

**1778** La Scala opened in Milan

**1797** Venice given to Austria by Treaty of Campo Formio; France controls rest of northern Italy

**1800–1801** Napoleon conquers Italy

**1808** Murat becomes King of Naples

**1809** Pope Pius VII exiled from Rome

**1760** | **1780** | **1800**

**1773** Pope dissolves Jesuit Order

**1780** Joseph II succeeds to Austrian throne; minor reforms in Lombardy

**1806** Joseph Bonaparte becomes King of Naples

**1768** Corsica sold by Genoa to France

**1765–90** Reign of Leopold Grand Duke of Tuscany, who introduces enlightened reforms

**1796–7** Napoleon's first campaign in northern Italy

**1815** Congress of Vienna restores status quo in Italy, though Austria keeps Venice

# The Risorgimento

The word "Risorgimento" (resurgence) describes the five decades of struggle for liberation from foreign rule, culminating in the unification of Italy in 1870. In 1848, patriots rose up against the Austrians in Milan and Venice, the Bourbons in Sicily and the pope in Rome, where a republic was declared. Garibaldi valiantly defended the republic, but all the uprisings were too localized. By 1859, the movement was better organized with Vittorio Emanuele II at its head. Two years saw the conquest of all but Venice and Rome, both of which fell within a decade.

**Vittorio Emanuele**

**ITALY IN 1861**

*Kingdom of Italy*

**Giuseppe Mazzini** *(1805–72)*
*An exile for much of his life, Mazzini fought alongside Garibaldi to unite Italy as a republic, rather than a kingdom.*

**The guns** were rusty, old converted flintlocks.

**The red shirt** was the badge of the Garibaldini.

**Italian Railways**
*The short railway line from Naples to Portici was opened in 1839. Politically fragmented, Italy was slow to create an effective rail network.*

**Revolt of Messina**
*When, in 1848, Messina revolted, Ferdinand II subjected the town to a savage bombardment, earning himself the nickname King Bomba.*

## TIMELINE

1820 | 1830 | 1840 | 1850

**1820s** Carbonari secret society active in Papal States

**1831** Insurrection in Romagna and Le Marche against papal rule

**1831** Mazzini founds *Giovine Italia* (Young Italy) movement

**1840** First major railway links established

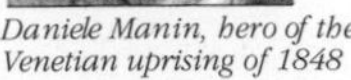

*Daniele Manin, hero of the Venetian uprising of 1848*

**1847** Economic crisis

**1848** Revolutions throughout Italy

**1849** Accession of Vittorio Emanuele II as ruler of Piedmont

**1849** Republic of Rome crushed by French troo

**1852** Cavour becomes prir minister of Piedmont

**Battle of Solferino** *(1859)*
*With the help of a French army led by Napoleon III, the Piedmontese won Milan and Lombardy from the Austrians.*

**Two old paddle steamers** brought the Thousand from Quarto near Genoa.

**The skiffs** were lent by other ships moored in Marsala harbour.

## GARIBALDI AND THE THOUSAND

Giuseppe Garibaldi (1807–82) was a leader of courage and genius. In 1860, he landed at Marsala with 1,000 volunteers. The garrison at Palermo surrendered, Sicily fell and he went on to conquer Naples, thus presenting Vittorio Emanuele with half a kingdom.

### WHERE TO SEE RISORGIMENTO ITALY

Almost every town in Italy honours the heroes of the Risorgimento with a Via Garibaldi, a Via Cavour, a Piazza Vittorio, a Via Mazzini and a Via XX Settembre (the date of the fall of Rome in 1870). Many cities also have Risorgimento museums. One of the best is in Turin *(p223)*.

**The Victor Emmanuel Monument** (p384) *is a prominent, but largely unloved, Roman landmark.*

**Count Camillo di Cavour** *(1810–61)*
*Cavour's diplomacy as prime minister of Piedmont ensured that the House of Savoy became rulers of the new Italy. He also coined the word "Risorgimento".*

**Giuseppe Verdi** *(1813–1901)*
*Composers such as Verdi, Donizetti and Rossini made the 19th century the great era of Italian opera. Verdi's early operas inspired the Risorgimento.*

**859** Battles of Magenta and Solferino; iedmont acquires Lombardy from Austria nd duchies of Parma, Modena and Tuscany

**1860** Garibaldi and the Thousand capture Kingdom of the Two Sicilies

**1861** Kingdom of Italy proclaimed with capital at Turin

**1866** Italy wins Venice from Austria

*Pope Pius IX, who remained a virtual prisoner in the Vatican when Rome became capital of Italy*

**1870** Rome falls to royalist troops and is made capital of new kingdom; Vatican announces doctrine of papal infallibility

**1878** Death of Vittorio Emanuele; accession of King Umberto I

**1882** Deaths of Garibaldi and Pope Pius IX

**1890** Italian colony of Eritrea established by royal decree

**1893** Troops sent to suppress insurrection in Sicily

1860 | 1870 | 1880 | 1890

# Modern Italy

Fascism under Mussolini (1922–43) promised the Italians greatness, but delivered only humiliation. In spite of this, Italy has become one of Europe's leading economies with a standard of living undreamt of at the turn of the 20th century. This has been achieved in the face of great obstacles. Since 1946, the Republic has passed through many crises: a series of unstable coalitions, the terrorist outrages in the 1970s and, in the 1990s, corruption scandals involving numerous government ministers and officials.

**1900** Assassination of King Umberto I

**1908** Earthquake destroys many towns and villages in Calabria and eastern Sicily; Messina almost completely razed to the ground; over 150,000 die

**1909** In his *Futurist Manifesto,* Filippo Marinetti condemns all traditional art as too static. His idea of a new dynamic art is expressed in works such as Umberto Boccioni's bronze *Unique Forms of Continuity in Space*

**1911–12** Italy conquers Libya

**1915** Italy enters World War I

**1917** Defeat at Caporetto on Italy's northeastern border; Italian troops, such as these Alpini, retreat to defensive positions

**1918** Austrian advance halted at the river Piave, just north of Venice

**1920s** Postwar years see continued emigration to the United States. Here, emigrants cheer as they reach New York aboard the *Giulio Cesare*

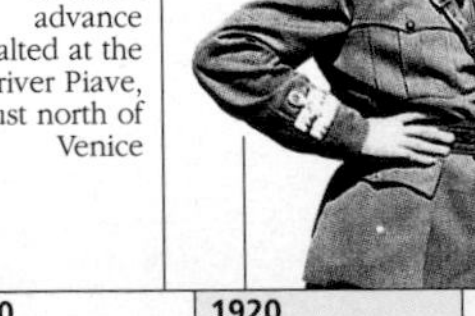

**1922** Fascists march on Rome; Mussolini invited to form government

**1936** FIAT produces first "Topolino" car

**1936** Italy conquers Abyssinia; pact with Germany, forming anti-Communist "Axis"

**1940** Italy enters World War II

**1943** Allies land in Sicily; Italy signs armistice and new Badoglio government declares war on Germany

**1943** Mussolini imprisoned, then freed by Germans

**1946** Referendum in which Italy votes to become a republic; Christian Democrat party forms first of a long series of coalition governments

**1957** Treaty of Rome; Italy one of the six founder members of the European Economic Community

**1960** *La Dolce Vita,* Federico Fellini's film satire on Rome's decadent café society, is released



**1960** Olympic Games held in Rome

1900 | 1910 | 1920 | 1930 | 1940 | 1950

1900 | 1910 | 1920 | 1930 | 1940 | 1950

**1978** Ex-prime minister Aldo Moro kidnapped and assassinated by the Red Brigades

**1966** River Arno bursts its banks, flooding Florence and damaging many priceless works of art

**1983** Bettino Craxi, Italy's first Socialist prime minister, forms government

**1992** Scandals expose widespread corruption in the postwar political system

**1992** Judge Giovanni Falcone killed by Mafia in Sicily

**1994** TV magnate Silvio Berlusconi becomes prime minister after forming political party "Forza Italia". Alleged financial irregularities force him to resign later that year

**1996** Fire destroys La Fenice theatre in Venice

**1997** Earthquake in Assisi seriously damages the Basilica di San Francesco, destroying Giotto's frescoes

**2000** Rome celebrates the Holy Year known as the Jubilee

**2002** Euro is adopted

**2006** Italy wins World Cup in Germany

**2008** Silvio Berlusconi wins third term as prime minister

**2015** Milan hosts the Universal Exposition

| 1970 | 1980 | 1990 | 2000 | 2010 | 2020 |
|---|---|---|---|---|---|

| 1970 | 1980 | 1990 | 2000 | 2010 | 2020 |
|---|---|---|---|---|---|

**1969** Bomb outrage in Milan at Piazza Fontana; 13 killed and many injured

**1978** Election of Pope John Paul II

**1982** Italian football team wins World Cup in Spain

**1990** World Cup staged in Italy

**1997** Dario Fo wins the Nobel prize for literature

**1999** Roberto Benigni wins 3 Oscars for his film *La Vita è Bella*, including best actor and best foreign language film

**2001** Silvio Berlusconi is voted back into power

**2005** Election of Pope Benedict XVI

**2006** Romano Prodi sworn in as prime minister

## ITALIAN CINEMA SINCE WORLD WAR II

The social problems of late 1940s Italy inspired a wave of cinema known as Neo-Realism. Leading exponents included Roberto Rossellini, who made *Roma Città Aperta* (1945), Vittorio de Sica, the director of *Bicycle Thieves* (1948), Pier Paolo Pasolini and Luchino Visconti. Since that time, the major Italian directors have cultivated their own personal styles.

**Vittorio de Sica (1901–74)**

Visconti's later films, such as *Death in Venice* (1971), show formal beauty and decadence, while Federico Fellini's *La Dolce Vita* (1960) and *Roma* (1972) depict life as a grotesque carnival.

Italy has also produced some commercially successful films, such as Sergio Leone's late 1960s westerns and the Oscar-winning *Cinema Paradiso* and *La Vita è Bella*.

# ITALY THROUGH THE YEAR

Throughout Italy, the variety of local character and colour is astonishing. This is mainly due to the survival of regionalism, particularly in the southern parts of the country. Old traditions, customs and lifestyles are still greatly respected and there is a deep attachment to the land, which is reflected in a healthy interest in the food and produce, as well as a perseverance of seasonal religious and secular events. Annual festivals, whether in rural or urban areas, range from wine-tasting and gastronomic celebrations to elaborate commemorations of every patron saint imaginable.

## SPRING

The Italian spring begins early, particularly in the south. City streets and main sights are rarely overcrowded (except at Easter in Rome). The weather, however, can be unpredictable and wet in the central and northern parts of the country. Spring specialities, such as asparagus, spinach and rocket, begin to feature on restaurant menus. This is a season of great celebration; festivals and fairs abound, especially in Sicily, and the Easter papal address always draws massive crowds to St Peter's.

Tuscan asparagus

### MARCH

**Mostra Vini Spumanti**, *(mid-Mar)*, Madonna di Campiglio, Trentino-Alto Adige. Fair celebrating sparkling wine.
**Sa Sartiglia**, Oristano, Sardinia. Three-day carnival ending on Shrove Tuesday.

Procession of the Grieving Madonna on the isle of Procida

**Su e zo per i ponti** *(Sun, varies)*, Venice. A lively race through the city's streets, up and down the bridges.

### APRIL

**Procession of the Grieving Madonna** *(Good Friday)*, Procida, Campania. A colourful religious procession throughout the island.
**Holy Week** *(Easter Week)*. Numerous Easter celebrations from Palm Sunday to Easter Sunday, throughout the country.
**Papal Address** *(Easter Sunday)*, Rome. The pope makes his Easter address from the Vatican.
**Dance of the Devils and Death** *(Easter Sunday)*, Prizzi, Sicily. Dance recital symbolizing the attempts of evil to vanquish the forces of God.
**Scoppio del Carro** *(Easter Sunday)*, Florence. Firework display is lit by a mechanical dove in front of the Duomo.
**Festa della Madonna che Scappa in Piazza** *(Easter Sunday)*, Sulmona, Abruzzo. Re-enactment of a meeting between the Virgin and the Risen Christ.
**Festa degli Aquiloni** *(first Sun after Easter)*, San Miniato, Tuscany. Kite lovers perform aerial acrobatics at this festival.
**Festa di San Marco** *(25 Apr)*, Venice. St Mark, the patron saint of Venice, is commemorated by a gondola race across St Mark's Basin.
**Mostra Mercato Internazionale dell'Artigianato** *(last week)*, Florence. An important European exhibition of arts and crafts.

Spring strawberries

Scoppio del Carro (Explosion of the Carriage) festival in Florence

**Sagra Musicale Lucchese** *(Apr–Jul)*, Lucca, Tuscany. Festival of sacred music held in Romanesque churches.

### MAY

**Festa di Sant'Efisio** *(1 May)*, Cagliari, Sardinia. Paraders in traditional Sardinian costume.
**Festa di San Nicola** *(7–9 May)*, Bari, Puglia. A statue of St Nicholas is taken to the sea.
**Festa dei Ceri** *(15 May)*, Gubbio, Umbria. Festival, including a race with four teams carrying large candles.
**Festa di San Domenico Abate** *(first Thu)*, Cocullo, Abruzzo. Includes a procession with a statue of St Dominic covered with live snakes.
**Festa della Mela** *(late May)*, Ora (Auer), Trentino-Alto Adige. An annual "Festival of the Apple".
**Greek Drama in Theatre** *(May–Jun)*, Syracuse, Sicily. Festival of Greek drama.
**Maggio Musicale** *(May–Jun)*, Florence. This is the city's biggest arts festival, including music, drama and dance.

Street carpeted with flowers for the Infiorata in Genzano

## SUMMER

Summer brings the crowds to Italy, particularly the cities. Italians, however, flee and head for the coast, usually in August. The queues for tourist attractions can be long and hotels are often fully booked. Festivals vary; religious events are interspersed with those of the arts and local folklore.

## JUNE

**Festa della Fragola** *(1 Jun)*, Borgo San Martino, Piedmont. Musical and folkloric performances in celebration of the strawberry.
**Biennale** *(Jun–Sep)*, Venice. The world's biggest exhibition of contemporary art takes place during odd-numbered years only.
**Infiorata** *(Corpus Christi day)*, Genzano, Lazio. A procession through streets carpeted with flowers.
**Festa di San Giovanni** *(mid-Jun–mid-Jul)*, Turin, Piedmont. Festival in honour of the city's patron saint, John.
**Calcio Storico** *(24 Jun and two other days in Jun)*, Florence. Football in 16th-century costumes; fireworks.
**Festa di Sant'Andrea** *(27 Jun)*, Amalfi, Campania. Fireworks and processions.
**Festival dei Due Mondi** *(late Jun–early Jul)*, Spoleto, Umbria. International festival of drama, music and dance.
**Gioco del Ponte** *(last Sun)*, Pisa. "The Bridge Parade" of marchers in antique armour.
**Estate Romana** *(late Jun–mid-Sep)*, Rome. Open-air cinema, performances, ballet and concerts.

## JULY

**Corsa del Palio** *(2 Jul)*, Siena. Tuscany's most famous event *(see p331)* presents a medieval flag-waving exhibition and horse race.
**Festa della Madonna della Bruna** *(first Sun)*, Matera, Basilicata. A lively procession of clergymen and knights in costume.
**Festa dei Noiantri** *(last two weeks of Jul)*, Rome. A colourful festival in the streets of Trastevere.
**Festa della Santa Maria del Carmine** *(16 Jul)*, Naples. Featuring the illumination of the city's bell tower.
**Umbria Jazz** *(Jul)*, Perugia. World-famous jazz artists perform.
**International Film Festival** *(Jul–Aug)*, Taormina, Sicily.

Musician from Florence's Calcio

The Sienese Palio in action

**Opera Festival** *(Jul–Aug)*, Verona, Veneto. Renowned opera festival *(see p137)* overlapping with the **Shakespeare Festival**, providing music, drama, opera and dance.

## AUGUST

**Medieval Palio** *(first week-end Aug)* Feltre, Veneto. Parades and archery competitions, medieval-style.
**Festa del Mare** *(15 Aug)*, Diano Marina, Liguria. This "Festival of the Sea" boasts a spectacular firework display.
**Festa dei Candelieri** *(14 Aug)*, Sassari, Sardinia. "Festival of the Candle", dating from the 16th century.
**Corsa del Palio** *(16 Aug)*, Siena, Tuscany. See July entry.
**Venice Film Festival** *(late Aug–early Sep)*. International festival on the Lido.
**Rossini Festival** *(Aug–Sep)*, Pesaro, Le Marche. A celebration of the composer's work, in his birthplace.
**Settimane Musicali di Stresa** *(late Aug–end Sep)*, Stresa, Lombardy. Four weeks of concerts and recitals.

Sun, sand and sea – essential ingredients of a Tuscan beach holiday

## AUTUMN

Autumn is a slow, gentle season in Italy but that doesn't mean there are fewer festivals and fairs. In addition to the various religious events at this time of year, gastronomic festivals are especially popular, commemorating such delectables as chestnuts, local cheeses, sausages and mushrooms. Autumn is the season of the *vendemmia*, the grape harvest, which is often used as an excuse for village festivities at which the latest local wines flow freely.

The climate *(see pp72–3)* in late autumn is often cold and wet in the north. The south, however, can be quite warm right through October.

Advertisement for the September Palio in Asti, Piedmont

## SEPTEMBER

**Festa di San Sebastiano e Santa Lucia** *(1–3 Sep)*, Sassari, Sardinia. Includes a contest where competitors improvise short poems.
**Procession of the Macchina di Santa Rosa** *(3 Sep)*, Viterbo, Lazio. Commemoration of the saint's body being transported to the Church of Santa Rosa in 1258.
**Giostra del Saracino** *(first Sun)*, Arezzo, Umbria. Joust of the Saracen and knights, dating from the 13th century.
**Regata Storica** *(first Sun)*, Venice. A procession of historic boats followed by a colourful gondola race.
**Human chess game** *(second week)*, Marostica, near

The widely cultivated olive tree

Vicenza. A popular costumed game held in the main square every even year.
**Rassegna del Chianti Classico** *(second week)*, Chianti, Tuscany. Celebration of the local wines.
**La Notte Bianca** *(mid-Sep)*, Rome. Concerts, events and free admission to some museums during the night.
**The Miracle of San Gennaro** *(19 Sep)*, Naples. Re-enactment of the liquefaction of the saint's blood, in a lively mass at the Duomo.
**Palio** *(third Sun)*, Asti, Piedmont. Includes a costumed medieval procession and bareback horse racing.

## OCTOBER

**Amici della Musica** *(Oct–Apr)*, Florence, Tuscany. The "Friends of Music" concert season begins.
**Fiera del Tartufo** *(first Sun)*, Alba, Piedmont. A variety of events centred around the locally grown white truffle.
**Festa di San Francesco** *(4 Oct)*, Assisi, Umbria. Feast in honour of the saint.
**Wine festivals** *(first week)*, Castelli Romani, Lazio.
**Sagra del Tordo** *(last Sun)* Montalcino, Tuscany. Celebration of the thrush; costumed archery contests.
**Festa dell'Uva** *(dates vary)*, Bolzano, Trentino-Alto Adige. Grape festival with live music and a costumed procession featuring allegoric carts.
**International Festival of Cinema** *(dates vary)*, Rome. A week of screenings, high-profile events and celebrity spotting in the capital.

A roast chestnut stall in autumn

## NOVEMBER

**Festa dei Popoli** *(Nov)*, Florence, Tuscany. Film festival showing documentary films in their original languages with Italian subtitles.
**Festa della Salute** *(21 Nov)*, Venice. Cherished by Venetian locals, this feast gives thanks to the Virgin Mary in memory of a 1630 plague.

The human chess game in the town square of Marostica

## WINTER

There are fairs, markets and religious events up and down the country at this time of year. Neapolitan Christmas cribs are famous and nearly every church has one. The Christmas holiday itself is low key; more is made of other religious events such as the liquefaction of San Gennaro's blood in Naples and the Carnevale in Venice.

Rome during one of its rare snowfalls

## DECEMBER

**Festa di Sant'Ambrogio** *(early Dec)*, Milan. The official opening of La Scala Opera season *(see p193)*.
**Festa della Madonna di Loreto** *(10 Dec)*, Loreto, Le Marche. Celebration of the Virgin's Holy House.
**Mercato della Befana** *(mid-Dec–6 Jan)*, Rome. Well-known Christmas fair held in Piazza Navona.
**The Miracle of San Gennaro** *(16 Dec)*, Naples. See September.
**Christmas fair** *(mid-Dec)*, Naples. Fair selling crib figures and decorations.
**Fiaccole di Natale** *(Christmas Eve)*, Abbadia di San Salvatore, Tuscany. Features carols and processions in memory of the first shepherds.
**Midnight Mass** *(24 Dec)*, at churches all over the country.
**Christmas Day** *(25 Dec)*, St Peter's Square, Rome. Public blessing by the pope.

La Befana at Piazza Navona, Rome

## JANUARY

**Capodanno** *(1 Jan)*, all over the country. New Year's Day is celebrated with fireworks and volleys from hunters firing into the air to scare off ghosts and spirits of the old year and welcome in the new.
**La Befana** *(6 Jan)*, through out Italy. Children's holiday with presents and sweets.
**Pitti Immagine Uomo, Pitti Immagine Donna, Pitti Immagine Bimbo**, Fortezza da Basso, Florence. Month of international fashion shows for women, men and children.
**Festa di San Sebastiano** *(20 Jan)*, Dolceacqua, Liguria. A laurel tree covered with colourful communion hosts is carried through town.

Carnevale, Viareggio

**Festa d'o'Cippo di Sant'Antonio** *(17 Jan)*, Naples. A procession for St Anthony, protector of animals.
**Carnevale** *(a month-long event finishing Shrove Tue)*, Viareggio, Tuscany. A carnival famous for its lively, topically themed floats.
**Fair of St Orsa** *(30–31 Jan)*, Aosta, Valle d'Aosta. Exhibition of traditional arts and crafts.

## FEBRUARY

**Carnevale** *(last ten days before Lent, finishing Shrove Tuesday)*, Venice. Pre-Lent festival meaning "farewell to meat". Events are organized, but anyone can buy a mask and watch the array of gorgeous costumes on show.
**Sagra delle Mandorle in Fiore** *(first or second week)*, Agrigento, Sicily. Annual almond blossom celebration.
**Bacanal del Gnoco** *(dates vary)*, Verona. Traditional masked procession with both international and local allegorical floats. Masked balls are held in the town's squares.
**Carnevale** *(dates vary)*, Mamoiada, Sardinia. Processions include *mamuthones* wearing sinister black masks.

### PUBLIC HOLIDAYS

**New Year's Day** (1 Jan)
**Epiphany** (6 Jan)
**Easter Sunday & Monday**
**Liberation Day** (25 Apr)
**Labour Day** (1 May)
**Republic Day** (2 Jun)
**Ferragosto** (15 Aug)
**All Saints' Day** (1 Nov)
**Immaculate Conception** (8 Dec)
**Christmas Day** (25 Dec)
**Santo Stefano** (26 Dec)

Carnevale revellers in Venice

# The Sporting Year

World Cup mania

Football is by far the most important sport in Italy, uniting the country when the national team *(Azzurri)* plays. Other sports throughout the year also attract a large following, so fans are never at a loss for varied activities. For most big sporting events, tickets can be obtained for cash at club outlets such as the venue itself. Agencies provide hard-to-get tickets at often higher prices. Beware of the inevitable touts at popular events as their expensive tickets may not be valid.

**Calcio Fiorentino**, *one of Italy's few indigenous sports, is said to be the medieval precursor of modern football.*

**Coppa Italia football final**

**Memorial d'Aloia rowing competition, held in Umbria**

**The professional water polo** *season takes place from March through to July. The Canottieri Napoli team play consistently well through the championship.*

**The Giro d'Italia** *cycling race takes place over many stages. Mario Cipollini won a record number of stages.*

| January | February | March | April | May | June |
|---|---|---|---|---|---|

**Indoor Athletics Championships**

**Rome Marathon**

**International Showjumping, Rome**

**Rugby** *is becoming increasingly popular. Italy takes part in the Six Nations Championship in February and March, along with England, Scotland, Wales, Ireland and France.*

**The Rome Masters**, *previously known as the Italian Open, takes place in Rome during May. The event is one of the most prestigious clay court tennis competitions in the world.*

**The Italian leg** *of the Circuito Mondiale in Mugello. Valentino Rossi has dominated the MotoGP World Championship for over a decade*

**The Italian Outdoor European Swimming Championships** *are held every year in July. The Olympic gold medal winner Massimiliano Rosolino, pictured here, celebrates a victory.*

**Italy has some of the best** *ski resorts in Europe, and in 2006 Turin hosted the Winter Olympics. Above is Alberto Tomba, once a champion of the slopes.*

**The Italian Grand Prix**, *held annually at Monza, is Italy's round of the international Formula One World Championship. Giancarlo Fisichella is one of Italy's most successful drivers.*

**Trofeo dei Templi rowing competition, Sicily**

**The San Remo Car Rally**, *held each year in October, was made famous by driver Micky Biason and the Lancia Delta Integrale.*

| | August | September | October | November | December |
|---|---|---|---|---|---|

**iena Palio (see p341), eld on July and 6 August**

**Italy won the World Cup in 2006**

**The Italian football** *season runs from September through to May. It culminates with the Coppa Italia final, which is equivalent to the British FA Cup. Italy's football obsession, however, reaches fever pitch when the World Cup takes place every four years.*

**The Outdoor Athletics Championship** *has become very popular. One of Italy's foremost athletes was Stefano Baldini (now retired), winner of an Olympic gold medal in 2004.*

**KEY TO SPORTING SEASONS**

- Football
- Water polo
- Rugby
- Basketball
- Volleyball
- Skiing

# The Climate of Italy

The Italian peninsula has a varied climate falling into three distinct geographical regions. Cold Alpine winters and warm, wet summers characterize the northern regions. In the extensive Po Valley, arid summers contrast with freezing, damp winters. The rest of Italy has a pleasant climate with long, hot summers and mild winters. Cooler weather along the backbone of the Apennines can bring snow during the winter months.

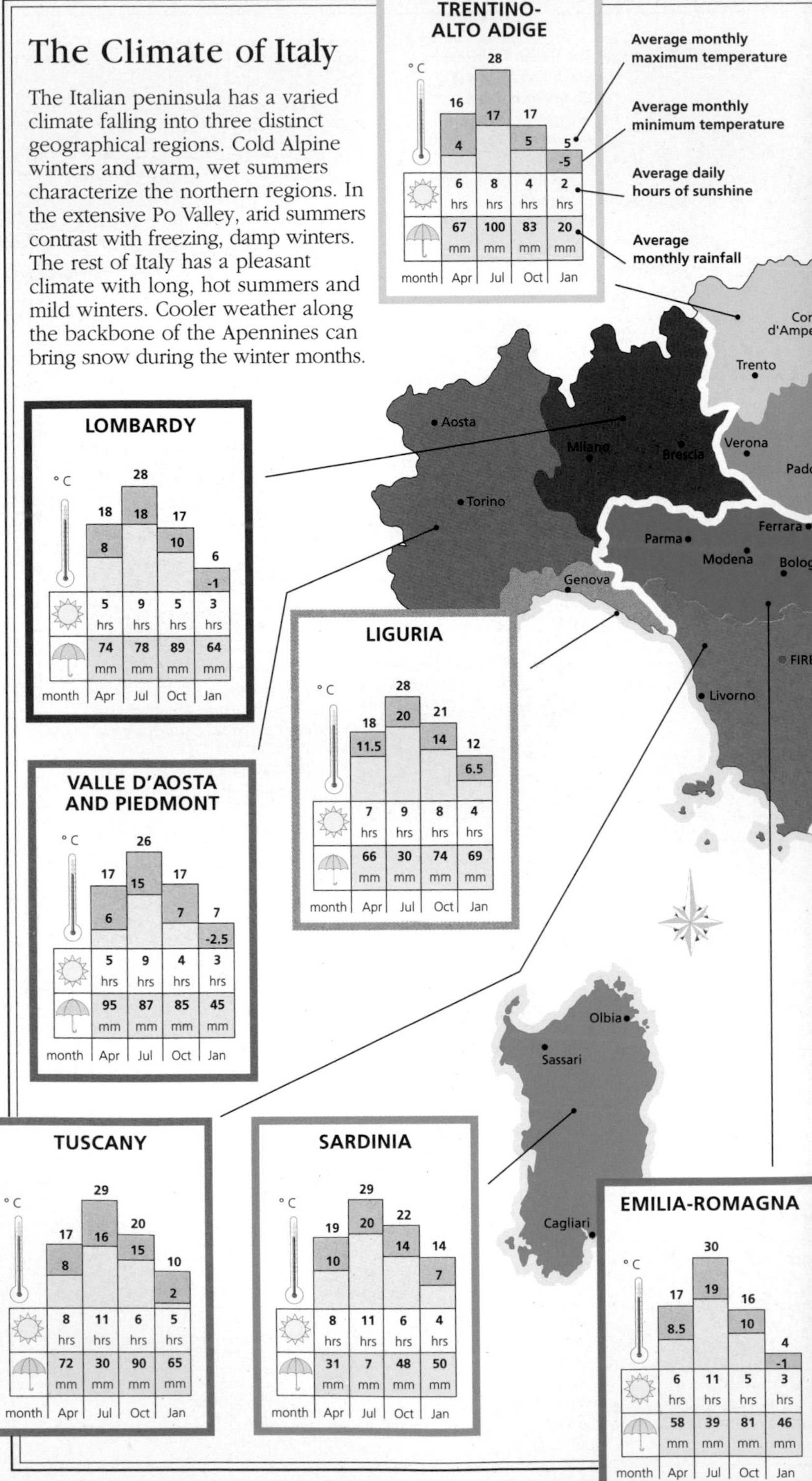


**TRENTINO-ALTO ADIGE**

| month | Apr | Jul | Oct | Jan |
|---|---|---|---|---|
| max °C | 16 | 28 | 17 | 5 |
| min °C | 4 | 17 | 5 | -5 |
| sunshine | 6 hrs | 8 hrs | 4 hrs | 2 hrs |
| rainfall | 67 mm | 100 mm | 83 mm | 20 mm |

**LOMBARDY**

| month | Apr | Jul | Oct | Jan |
|---|---|---|---|---|
| max °C | 18 | 28 | 17 | 6 |
| min °C | 8 | 18 | 10 | -1 |
| sunshine | 5 hrs | 9 hrs | 5 hrs | 3 hrs |
| rainfall | 74 mm | 78 mm | 89 mm | 64 mm |

**LIGURIA**

| month | Apr | Jul | Oct | Jan |
|---|---|---|---|---|
| max °C | 18 | 28 | 21 | 12 |
| min °C | 11.5 | 20 | 14 | 6.5 |
| sunshine | 7 hrs | 9 hrs | 8 hrs | 4 hrs |
| rainfall | 66 mm | 30 mm | 74 mm | 69 mm |

**VALLE D'AOSTA AND PIEDMONT**

| month | Apr | Jul | Oct | Jan |
|---|---|---|---|---|
| max °C | 17 | 26 | 17 | 7 |
| min °C | 6 | 15 | 7 | -2.5 |
| sunshine | 5 hrs | 9 hrs | 4 hrs | 3 hrs |
| rainfall | 95 mm | 87 mm | 85 mm | 45 mm |

**TUSCANY**

| month | Apr | Jul | Oct | Jan |
|---|---|---|---|---|
| max °C | 17 | 29 | 20 | 10 |
| min °C | 8 | 16 | 15 | 2 |
| sunshine | 8 hrs | 11 hrs | 6 hrs | 5 hrs |
| rainfall | 72 mm | 30 mm | 90 mm | 65 mm |

**SARDINIA**

| month | Apr | Jul | Oct | Jan |
|---|---|---|---|---|
| max °C | 19 | 29 | 22 | 14 |
| min °C | 10 | 20 | 14 | 7 |
| sunshine | 8 hrs | 11 hrs | 6 hrs | 4 hrs |
| rainfall | 31 mm | 7 mm | 48 mm | 50 mm |

**EMILIA-ROMAGNA**

| month | Apr | Jul | Oct | Jan |
|---|---|---|---|---|
| max °C | 17 | 30 | 16 | 4 |
| min °C | 8.5 | 19 | 10 | -1 |
| sunshine | 6 hrs | 11 hrs | 5 hrs | 3 hrs |
| rainfall | 58 mm | 39 mm | 81 mm | 46 mm |

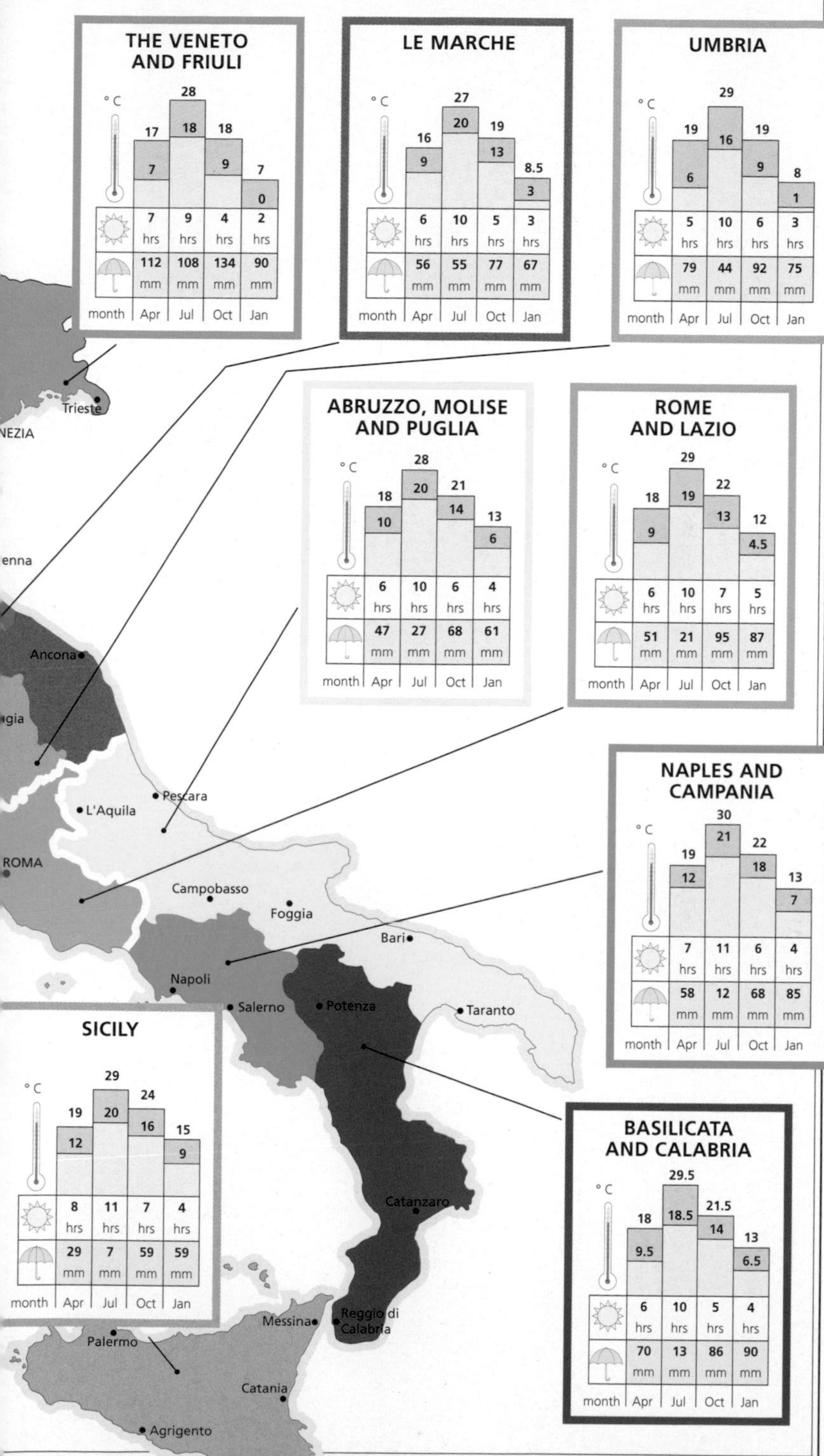
THE VENETO AND FRIULI
°C
17 7 | 28 18 | 18 9 | 7 0
7 hrs | 9 hrs | 4 hrs | 2 hrs
112 mm | 108 mm | 134 mm | 90 mm
month | Apr | Jul | Oct | Jan
LE MARCHE
°C
16 9 | 27 20 | 19 13 | 8.5 3
6 hrs | 10 hrs | 5 hrs | 3 hrs
56 mm | 55 mm | 77 mm | 67 mm
month | Apr | Jul | Oct | Jan
UMBRIA
°C
19 6 | 29 16 | 19 9 | 8 1
5 hrs | 10 hrs | 6 hrs | 3 hrs
79 mm | 44 mm | 92 mm | 75 mm
month | Apr | Jul | Oct | Jan
ABRUZZO, MOLISE AND PUGLIA
°C
18 10 | 28 20 | 21 14 | 13 6
6 hrs | 10 hrs | 6 hrs | 4 hrs
47 mm | 27 mm | 68 mm | 61 mm
month | Apr | Jul | Oct | Jan
ROME AND LAZIO
°C
18 9 | 29 19 | 22 13 | 12 4.5
6 hrs | 10 hrs | 7 hrs | 5 hrs
51 mm | 21 mm | 95 mm | 87 mm
month | Apr | Jul | Oct | Jan
NAPLES AND CAMPANIA
°C
19 12 | 30 21 | 22 18 | 13 7
7 hrs | 11 hrs | 6 hrs | 4 hrs
58 mm | 12 mm | 68 mm | 85 mm
month | Apr | Jul | Oct | Jan
SICILY
°C
19 12 | 29 20 | 24 16 | 15 9
8 hrs | 11 hrs | 7 hrs | 4 hrs
29 mm | 7 mm | 59 mm | 59 mm
month | Apr | Jul | Oct | Jan
BASILICATA AND CALABRIA
°C
18 9.5 | 29.5 18.5 | 21.5 14 | 13 6.5
6 hrs | 10 hrs | 5 hrs | 4 hrs
70 mm | 13 mm | 86 mm | 90 mm
month | Apr | Jul | Oct | Jan
Trieste
Ancona
Pescara
L'Aquila
ROMA
Campobasso
Foggia
Bari
Napoli
Salerno
Potenza
Taranto
Catanzaro
Messina
Reggio di Calabria
Palermo
Catania
Agrigento

# NORTHEAST ITALY

# Northeast Italy at a Glance

The sheer variety to be found in northeast Italy makes it a fascinating area to explore. The majestic Dolomites dominate the north, straddling Trentino-Alto Adige and the Veneto, and are dotted with medieval castles and modern skiing resorts. On the plain, the cities of Verona, Vicenza and Padua are all noted for outstanding architecture and museums, while the rural hinterland boasts beautiful villas. The incomparable and spectacular city of Venice, with its magnificent monuments, rises from the lagoon. Further east, in Friuli, there are important Roman remains. This map pinpoints some of the highlights.

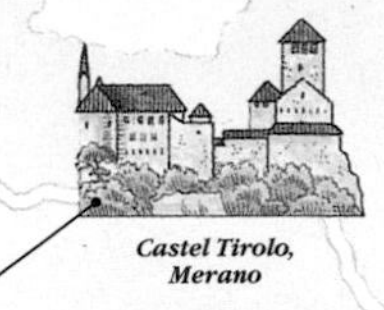

Castel Tirolo, Merano

**Alto Adige** *is a dramatic region of snow-covered mountain valleys scattered with forbidding castles and onion-domed churches in the Tyrolean style* (see pp170–71).

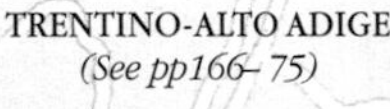

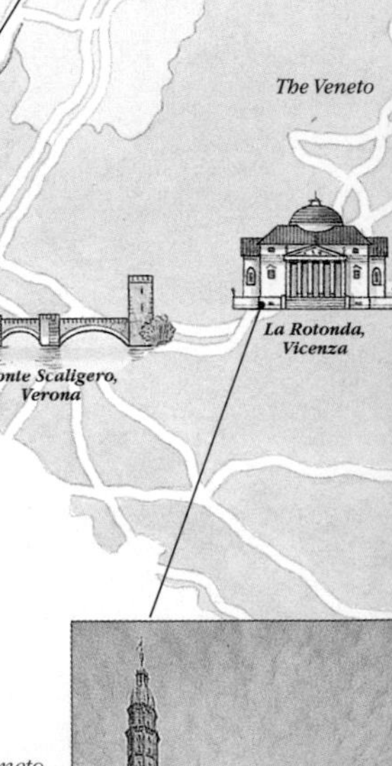


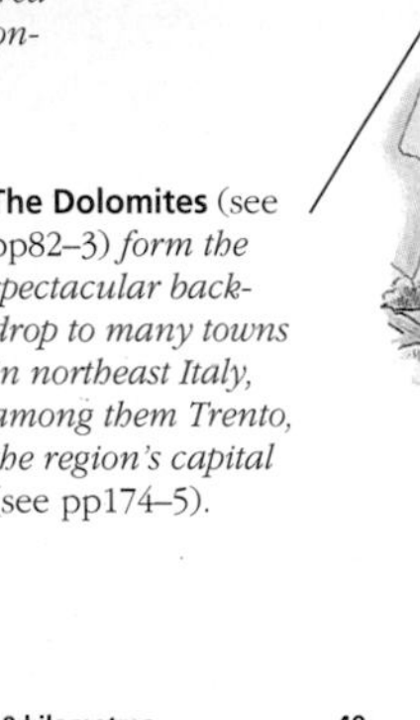

**The Dolomites** (see pp82–3) *form the spectacular backdrop to many towns in northeast Italy, among them Trento, the region's capital* (see pp174–5).

**Verona** *is one of the loveliest cities in the Veneto, boasting the Castelvecchio and a Roman arena now used for performances of opera* (see pp142–7).

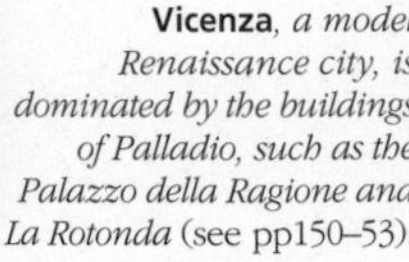

**Vicenza**, *a model Renaissance city, is dominated by the buildings of Palladio, such as the Palazzo della Ragione and La Rotonda* (see pp150–53).

◁ **Dusk over the atmospheric city of Verona**

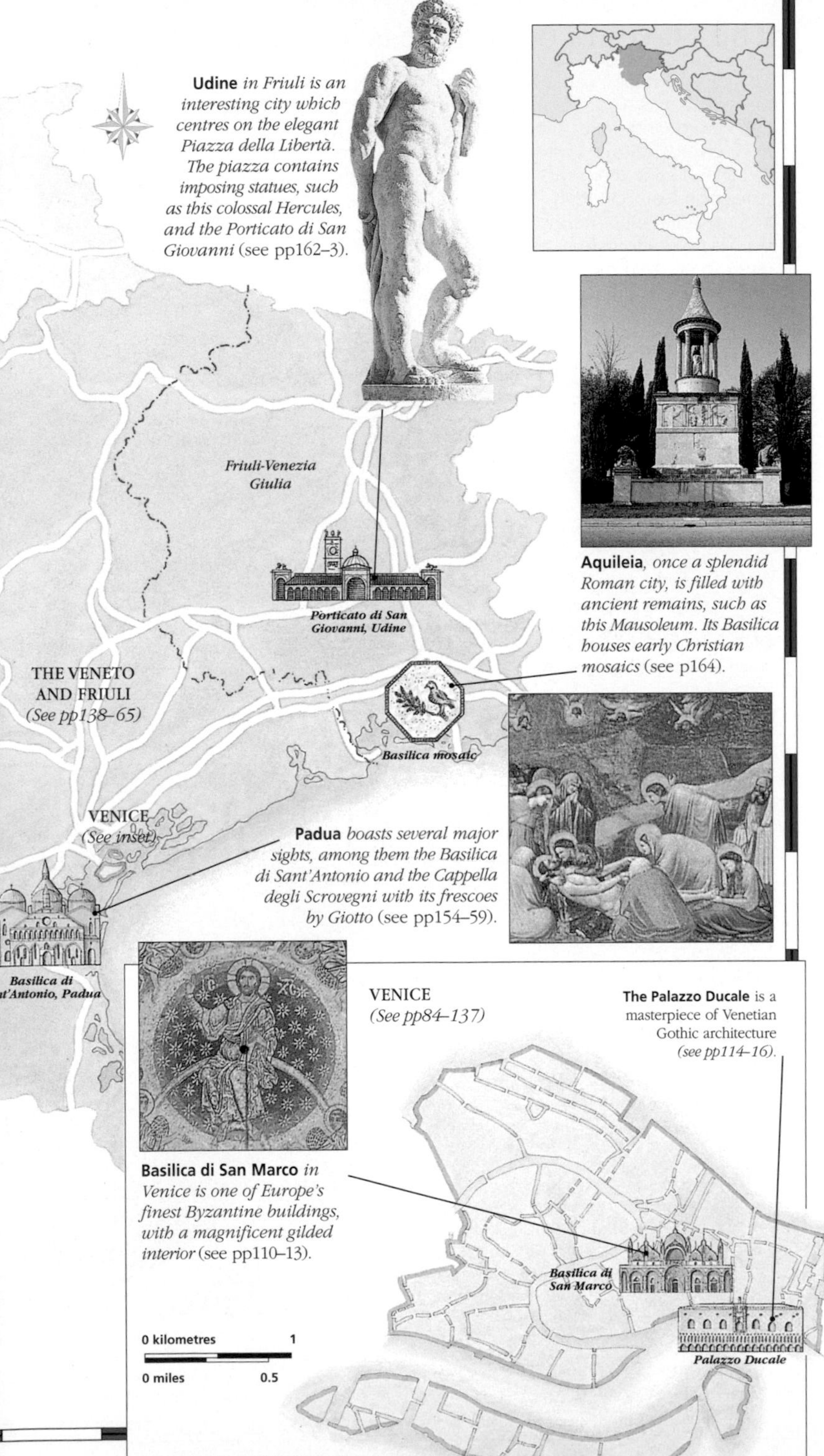


**Udine** *in Friuli is an interesting city which centres on the elegant Piazza della Libertà. The piazza contains imposing statues, such as this colossal Hercules, and the Porticato di San Giovanni* (see pp162–3).

**Aquileia**, *once a splendid Roman city, is filled with ancient remains, such as this Mausoleum. Its Basilica houses early Christian mosaics* (see p164).

**Padua** *boasts several major sights, among them the Basilica di Sant'Antonio and the Cappella degli Scrovegni with its frescoes by Giotto* (see pp154–59).

**The Palazzo Ducale** is a masterpiece of Venetian Gothic architecture *(see pp114–16).*

**Basilica di San Marco** *in Venice is one of Europe's finest Byzantine buildings, with a magnificent gilded interior* (see pp110–13).

# The Flavours of Northeast Italy

This diverse region is the least Italian area of Italy. Bordering on Balkan and Austro-Hungarian territory, its food reflecting its rich culture and landscape. Venice's traditional trading links have given a Middle-Eastern flavour to some dishes, such as sweet and sour *saor* sauce, and spices like nutmeg, saffron and cinnamon feature widely. While pasta is eaten, many dishes are accompanied with the more typical polenta, made from yellow maize flour, and risotto is also a favourite. Butter tends to be used more than olive oil. From hearty, rib-sticking fare to the most delicate and sophisticated of dishes, this is a region full of gastronomic surprises.

**Saffron**

**Delicate, sweet fried pastries in a Trieste bakery**

## THE VENETO & VENICE

The Veneto is now one of Italy's main rice-growing regions. Rice was introduced from Spain by the Arabs, and is the staple ingredient for many versatile local dishes. Creamy risottos come in many guises including *di mare* (with seafood), in which cuttlefish ink gives the dish a dramatic, dark appearance. The Veneto's favourite pasta is *bigoli*, a thick spaghetti.

Vegetables are plentiful, including courgettes (zucchini), asparagus, bitter red radicchio (endive) from Treviso and variegated radicchio from Castelfranco.

Venetian specialities include *cichetti* and *antipasti* – snacks and starters such as marinaded sardines, fried artichokes (*articiochi* in Venetian dialect), and seafood in bite-size portions, especially mussels *(peoci)*. Venetian crab *(granceola)* is highly prized, and the local fish soup *(sopa de pesse)* is deliciously hearty. Finely sliced raw beef *(carpaccio)*, had its origins here, created by Giuseppe Cipriani at Venice's Harry's Bar. Delicious, traditional *tiramisù* is also said to originate from Venice, and sorbets are common too. It was the Venetians who introduced cane sugar to Europe and their sweet tooth is still evident in the rich candied fruit, sultanas and pine nuts acquired from the Turks and Byzantines.

**Selection of Venetian *antipasti*, the perfect appetizer**

### REGIONAL DISHES AND SPECIALITIES

*Antipasto di frutti di mare* (a mixed seafood appetizer) is a special favourite in Venice, where the ingredients come fresh from the Adriatic. From lovely Lake Garda, *anguilla del pescatore* (stewed eel), *lavarelli al vino bianco* (lake fish in white wine) and *carpione* (a type of lake trout) are all fishy delights. Another fish speciality of the region is *baccalà alla veneziana*, made with dried salt cod. Pork and salamis feature throughout the area but in Friuli goose is often used as an alternative to pork, with succulent cured meat offerings such as *salame d'oca* (goose salami). Game is also found on the menu, together with sauerkraut and filling goulash, while desserts often have an Austrian flavour, too, such as *apfel strudel*. But the region is also proud of claiming as its own the voluptuous, classic Italian dessert *tiramisù*.

**Asparagus**

**Sarde in Saor** *Venetian speciality of fried sardines in a sweet and sour onion marinade, with pine nuts.*

Delivering fresh vegetables on the waterways of Venice

## FRIULI-VENEZIA GIULIA

A culinary crossroads, this region marks the meeting point of Slavic, Germanic and Latin traditions and was once the poorest of the northern Italian regions. Varieties of Hungarian goulash and Austrian strudels often appear on local menus. The area produces fine sweet ham and prosciutto (including the fabled, succulent San Daniele). Goose is a staple dish, as is Istrian lamb, grazed in the open air on local herbs and grasses that impart a delicious flavour.

Trieste is famous for its Viennese pastries and sweet *gnocchi*, prune dumplings sprinkled with sugar and cinnamon. Friuli's dairy speciality is Montasio, a hard cheese made from cow's milk.

Fresh radicchio and peppers piled high in a Treviso market

## TRENTINO & ALTO ADIGE

Strong Austrian influences from the Alto Adige combine with hearty fare from the mountainous region of Trentino as well as more southern Italian flavours. Staple dishes include cured meats such as *speck* (smoked ham) and salamis, as well as warming soups including the classic minestrone. Bread dumplings – *canederli* in Italian but *knödel* in Alto Adige – feature more than pasta. Trentino risottos include sweet and savoury variations. Especially good are those made with *finferli* mushrooms, highly prized and similar to Tuscan *porcini* (ceps) in flavour and quality. Alpine trout is flavoursome and game dishes, especially venison and rabbit, are popular in season, often served with polenta. The Trentino apple is crisp and delicious.

### ON THE MENU

**Carpaccio** (Venice & the Veneto) Wafer-thin slices of raw beef in extra virgin olive oil with rocket leaves and slivers of Parmesan cheese.

**Fegato alla Veneziana** Calf's liver served on a bed of onions.

**Jota** (Friuli-Venezia Giulia) A soup of barley and sauerkraut. This cheap and filling dish is often mixed with *brovada* – turnips that have been steeped in a wooden cask of grape pressings.

**Strangolapreti** (Trentino-Alto Adige) Dumplings (*gnocchi*) made with bread, spinach or potatoes, coated with butter and cheese. Literally means "priest stranglers"!

**Risi e bisi** *Soft and moist risotto mixing rice with fresh peas, sometimes with ham and Parmesan cheese.*

**Polenta** *Cornmeal porridge served plain as a side dish, often with rabbit, or* con pancetta *(with bacon).*

**Tiramisù** *A rich pudding of mascarpone, sponge fingers, coffee and marsala. The name means "pick me up".*

# Understanding Architecture in Venice and the Veneto

Trade contact with the East led medieval Venice to develop its own exotic style – known as Venetian Gothic – blending Byzantine domes and Islamic minarets with European Gothic pointed arches and quatrefoils. In the 16th century, Palladio introduced his interpretations of Classical architecture through a series of churches, public buildings and rural villas in Venice and the Veneto. The 17th century brought the Baroque style, though its exuberance was tempered by Palladio-influenced restraint.

**Andrea Palladio (1508–80)**

## THE ARCHITECTURE OF VENICE: BYZANTINE TO BAROQUE

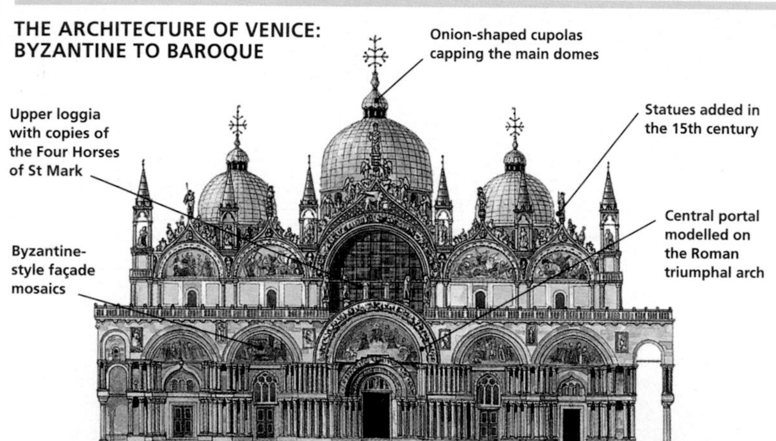


**The Basilica di San Marco**, *western Europe's finest Byzantine church (completed 11th century), was given lavish treatment to make it a dazzling shrine for the relics of St Mark, the Evangelist, and a fitting symbol of Venetian aspirations* (see pp110–13).

## THE GENIUS OF PALLADIO

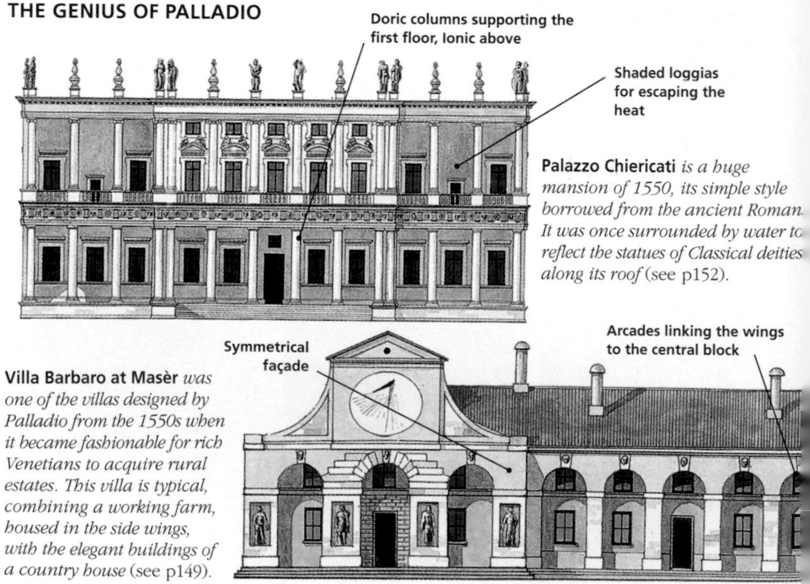


**Palazzo Chiericati** *is a huge mansion of 1550, its simple style borrowed from the ancient Roman. It was once surrounded by water to reflect the statues of Classical deities along its roof* (see p152).

**Villa Barbaro at Masèr** *was one of the villas designed by Palladio from the 1550s when it became fashionable for rich Venetians to acquire rural estates. This villa is typical, combining a working farm, housed in the side wings, with the elegant buildings of a country house* (see p149).

## WHERE TO SEE THE ARCHITECTURE

A vaporetto trip along the Grand Canal in Venice *(see pp88–91)* is a splendid way of getting an overview of Venetian architecture. Ca' d'Oro, Ca' Rezzonico and Ca' Pesaro may also be visited as they contain museums and a visit to the Basilica di San Marco and the Palazzo Ducale is a must. There are numerous examples of Palladio's architecture in the Veneto, but the star is the Villa Barbaro *(see p149)*. Several of his villas line the Brenta Canal *(see p160)*, and the town of Vicenza *(see pp150–53)* is full of his buildings, including La Rotonda, his famous villa.

**Typical Venetian Gothic window**

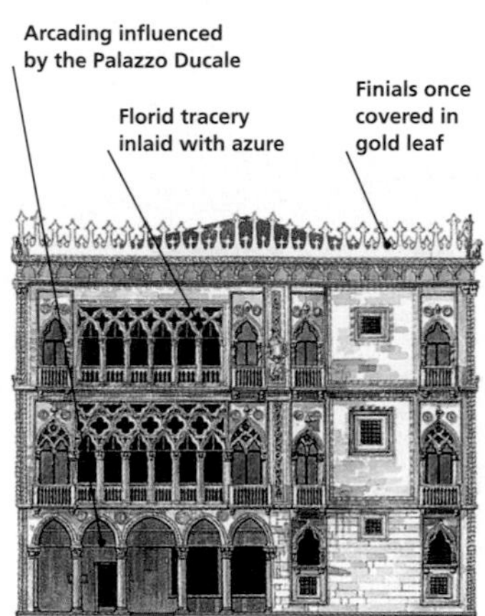


**Ca d'Oro**, *the 15th-century "House of Gold", reveals Moorish influence in its roof finials and sinuous pointed arches* (see p94).

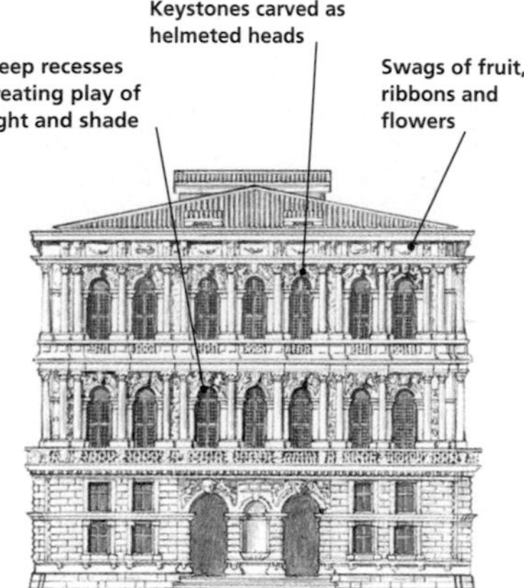


**The 17th-century Ca' Pesaro** *typifies the Venetian Baroque style – Classical columns and rich, but subtle ornamentation* (see p89).

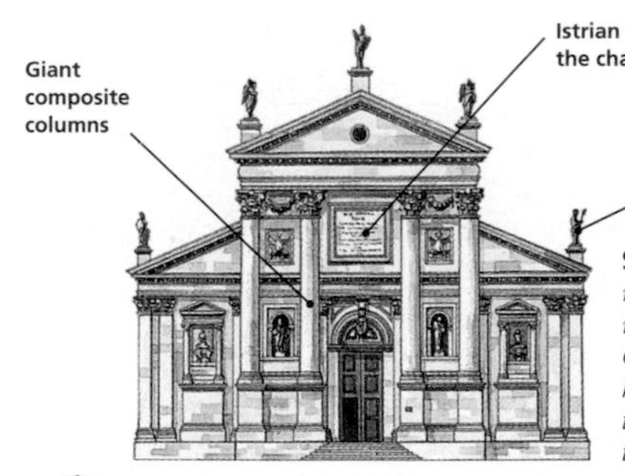


**San Giorgio Maggiore**, *built in 1559–80, is marvellously sited at the entrance to the Venetian inner harbour. It broke from the prevailing Gothic style, introducing the clean simplicity and harmonious proportions of Classical architecture to Venice, and more resembles an ancient Roman temple than a Christian church* (see pp120–21).

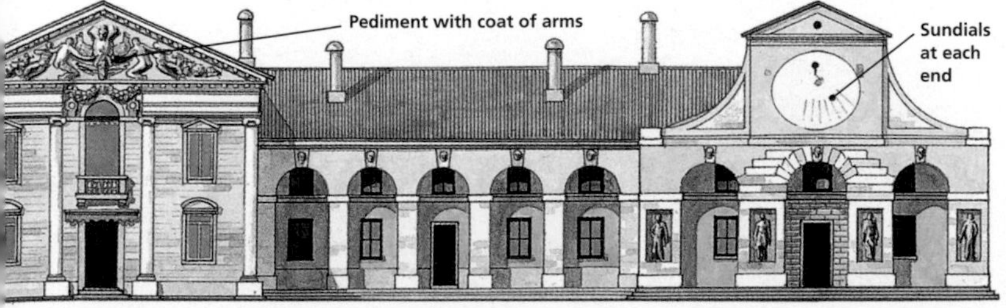

# The Dolomites

The Dolomites are the most distinctive and beautiful mountains in Italy. They were formed of mineralized coral which was laid down beneath the sea during the Triassic era, and uplifted when the European and African continental plates dramatically collided 60 million years ago. Unlike the glacier-eroded saddles and ridges of the main body of the Alps, the pale rocks here have been carved by the corrosive effects of ice, sun and rain, sculpting the cliffs, spires and "organ pipes" that we see today. The eastern and western ranges of the Dolomites have slightly different characteristics; the eastern section is the more awe-inspiring, especially the Catinaccio (or Rosengarten) range which is particularly beautiful, turning rose pink at sunset.

Onion dome, a common local feature

**STRADA DELLE DOLOMITI**

One of the most spectacular routes through the Dolomites links Bolzano *(see p172)* with Cortina d'Ampezzo *(see p161)*. It follows the lie of the land, passing some of the greatest peaks, and the most majestic landscape.

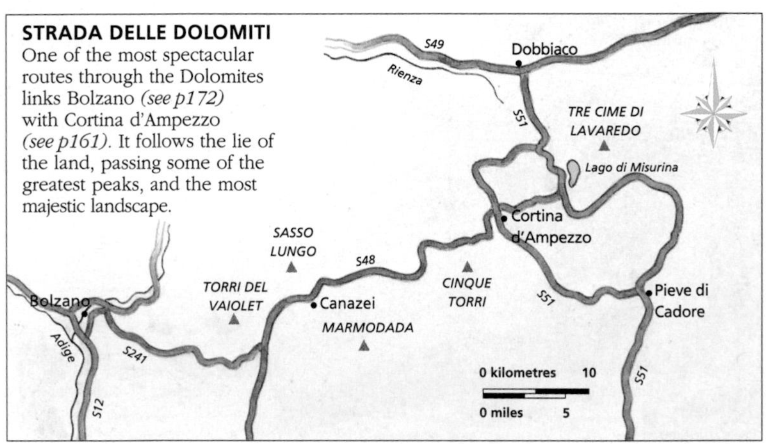


**DISTINCTIVE PEAKS OF THE DOLOMITES**

The peaks of the Dolomites include several with distinctive shapes and some of the highest mountains in the range. Many are easily identifiable and have been individually named.

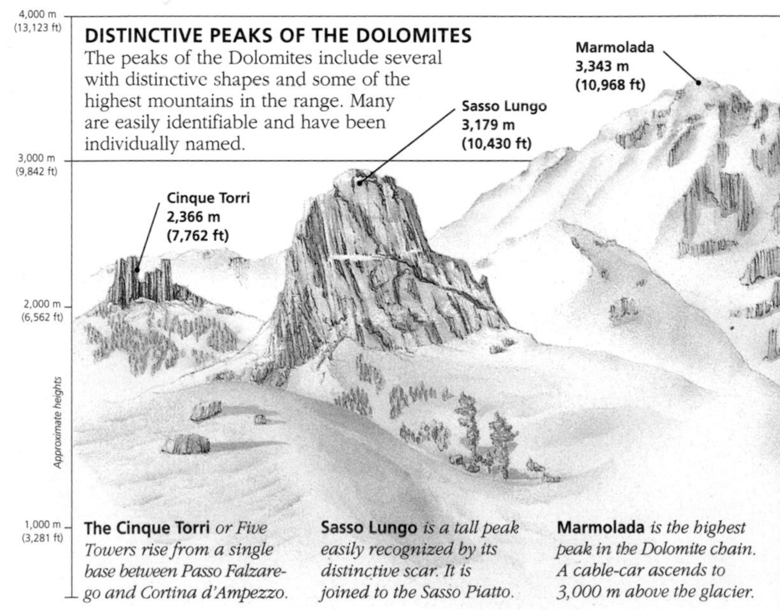


**The Cinque Torri** *or Five Towers rise from a single base between Passo Falzarego and Cortina d'Ampezzo.*

**Sasso Lungo** *is a tall peak easily recognized by its distinctive scar. It is joined to the Sasso Piatto.*

**Marmolada** *is the highest peak in the Dolomite chain. A cable-car ascends to 3,000 m above the glacier.*

**Lago di Misurina** *is a large and beautiful lake lying beside the resort of Misurina. The crystal clear waters reflect the surrounding mountains, mirroring various peaks such as the distinctive and dramatic Sorapiss, in shimmering colours.*

**Outdoor activities** *in this area of dramatic landscapes include skiing in winter, and walking and rambling along the footpaths, and to picnic sites, in summer. Chair-lifts from the main resorts provide easy access up into the mountains themselves, transporting you into some breathtaking scenery.*

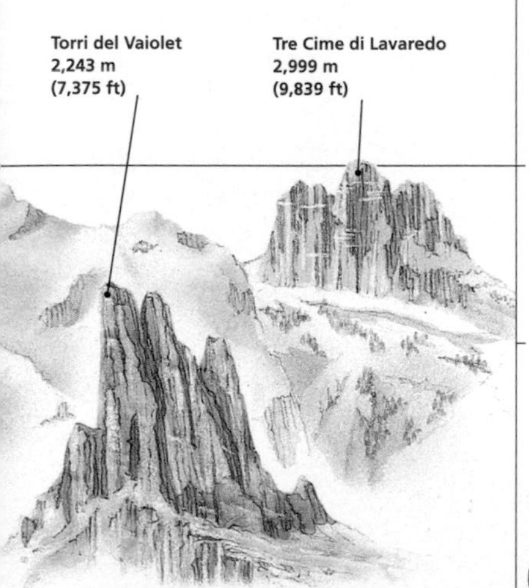


**The Torri del Vaiolet** *is part of the beautiful Catinaccio range, known for its colour.*

**Tre Cime di Lavaredo** *or Drei Zinnen dominate the valleys north of the Lago di Misurina.*

## NATURE IN THE DOLOMITES

Forests and meadows support a breathtaking richness of wildlife in the region. Alpine plants, which flower between June and September, have evolved their miniature form to survive the harsh winds.

### The Flora

**Gentian roots** *are used to make a bitter local liqueur.*

**The orange mountain lily** *thrives on sun-baked slopes.*

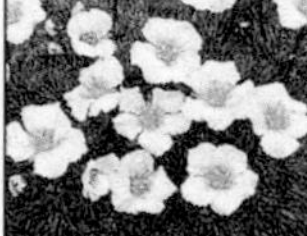

**The pretty** *burser's saxifrage grows in clusters on rocks.*

**Devil's claw** *has distinctive pink flower heads.*

### The Fauna

**The ptarmigan** *changes its plumage from mottled brown in summer to snow white in winter for effective camouflage. It feeds on mountain berries and young plant shoots.*

**The chamois**, *a shy mountain antelope prized for its soft skin, is protected in the national parks, where hunting is forbidden.*

**Roe deer** *are very common as their natural predators – wolves and lynx – are decreasing in number. An appetite for tree saplings causes problems for foresters.*

# VENICE

*Lying in the extreme northeast of Italy, Venice, gateway to the Orient, became an independent Byzantine province in the 10th century. Exclusive trading links with the East and victory in the Crusade of 1204 brought wealth and power, which were only gradually eroded by European and Turkish rivals. Today, Venice's ties are with the local Veneto region which stretches from the flat river plains to the Dolomites.*

Venice is one of the few cities in the world that can be truly described as unique. It survives against all the odds, built on a series of low mud banks amid the tidal waters of the Adriatic, and regularly subject to floods. During the Middle Ages, under the leadership of successive doges, Venice expanded its power and influence throughout the Mediterranean to Constantinople (modern Istanbul). The immense wealth of the city was celebrated in art and architecture throughout the city. The riches of St Mark's alone bear witness to Venice's position as a world power from the 12th to 14th centuries. After slowly losing ground to the new states of Europe, however, it fell to Napoleon in 1797. Finally, Venice joined the Kingdom of Italy in 1866, so bringing unity to the country for the first time in its history.

Today, Venice has found a new role. Her palazzi have become museums, shops, hotels and apartments and her convents have been turned into centres for art restoration. Yet little of the essential fabric of Venice has altered in 200 years. The city's sounds are still those of footsteps and the cries of boatmen. The only engines are those of barges delivering supplies or waterbuses ferrying passengers between stops. The same well-worn streets are still trodden. More than 14 million visitors a year succumb to the magic of this improbable place whose "streets are full of water" and where the glories of the past are evident at every turn.

**A busy street on the island of Burano, with its distinctive, brightly painted houses**

◁ **Gondola prows, with their characteristic *ferri*, and Santa Maria della Salute in the background**

# Exploring Venice

Venice is divided into six ancient administrative districts or *sestieri*: Cannaregio, Castello, San Marco, Dorsoduro, San Polo and Santa Croce. You can walk to most places in Venice itself, and take a ride on a waterbus to any of the islands. The Venice Card *(see p682)* covers all transport as well as admission to most museums, such as Ca' Rezzonico, the Palazzo Ducale and Museo Correr.

## SIGHTS AT A GLANCE

### Churches

*Basilica di San Marco pp110–11* 18
Madonna dell'Orto 1
San Giacomo dell'Orio 6
San Giorgio Maggiore 31
San Giovanni Grisostomo 3
San Giovanni in Bragora 29
Santi Giovanni e Paolo 24
Santa Maria Formosa 26
*Santa Maria Gloriosa dei Frari pp98–9* 8
Santa Maria dei Miracoli 4
Santa Maria della Salute 17
San Nicolò dei Mendicoli 13
San Pantalon 11
San Polo 7
San Rocco 10
San Sebastiano 14
Santo Stefano 23
San Zaccaria 27

### Buildings and Monuments

Arsenale 30
Campanile 21
*Palazzo Ducale pp114–16* 19
Rialto 5
Scuola di San Giorgio degli Schiavoni 28
Statue of Colleoni 25
Torre dell'Orologio 20

### Museums and Galleries

*Accademia pp106–7* 15
Ca' d'Oro 2
Ca' Rezzonico 12
Museo Correr 22
Peggy Guggenheim Collection 16
*Scuola Grande di San Rocco pp100–101* 9

### Lagoon

Burano 33
Murano 32
*Torcello pp122–3* 34

0 metres 500
0 yards 500

### KEY

- Street-by-Street: San Polo *pp96–7*
- Street-by-Street: Dorsoduro *pp102–3*
- Street-by-Street: Piazza San Marco *pp108–9*
- International airport
- FS Railway station
- Ferry boarding point
- *Vaporetto* boarding point
- *Traghetto* crossing *(see p682)*
- Gondola mooring
- Tourist information

Santa Maria della Salute, at the mouth of the Grand Canal

For additional map symbols *see back flap*

## SEE ALSO


- ***Street Finder*** pp126–35
- ***Where to Stay*** pp558–61
- ***Where to Eat*** pp606–9


## GETTING AROUND

The only road into Venice is the S11 from Mestre, which carries you over the causeway to the Tronchetto and Piazzale Roma where there are car parks and bus stops. Rail travellers arrive at Santa Lucia station on the Grand Canal. In the city, public transport is by *vaporetto*, or waterbus – the No.1 is best for sightseeing as it travels the length of the Grand Canal *(see pp136–7)*.

# The Grand Canal: Santa Lucia to the Rialto

The best way to view the Grand Canal as it winds through the heart of the city is from a *vaporetto*, or waterbus. Several lines travel the length of the canal *(see p683)*. The palaces lining the waterway were built over a span of five centuries and present a panoramic survey of the city's history, almost all bearing the name of some once-great Venetian family.

**San Marcuola**
*The church was rebuilt in the 18th century, but the planned new façade overlooking the canal was never completed.*

**San Geremia** houses the relics of St Lucy, once kept in the church of Santa Lucia where the railway station now stands.

**Palazzo Labia**
*Between 1745–50, Giambattista Tiepolo decorated the ballroom with scenes from the life of Cleopatra.*

Canale di Cannaregio

Palazzo Corner-Contarini

San Marcuola

Riva di Biasio

Ferrovia

FS

Ponte degli Scalzi

**Fondaco dei Turchi**
*A warehouse for Turkish traders in the 17th–19th centuries, this is now the Natural History Museum.*

**San Simeone Piccolo**
*This 18th-century domed church is based on the Pantheon in Rome.*

### THE GONDOLAS OF VENICE

The gondola has been a part of Venice since the 11th century. With its slim hull and flat underside, the craft is perfectly adapted to negotiating narrow, shallow canals. There is a slight leftward curve to the prow, which counteracts the force of the oar, preventing the gondola from going round in circles.

In 1562 it was decreed that all gondolas should be black to stop people making an ostentatious show of their wealth. For special occasions they are decorated with flowers. Today, gondola rides are expensive and usually taken by tourists *(see p683)*. However, *traghetti* (gondola ferries) are a cheap, convenient way of crossing the Grand Canal.

**Gondolas tied up by steps**

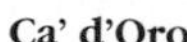

**Ca' d'Oro**

*The delicate Gothic tracery of the façade makes this a striking landmark. Its art collection* (see p94) *includes Bernini's model for a fountain (c.1648).*

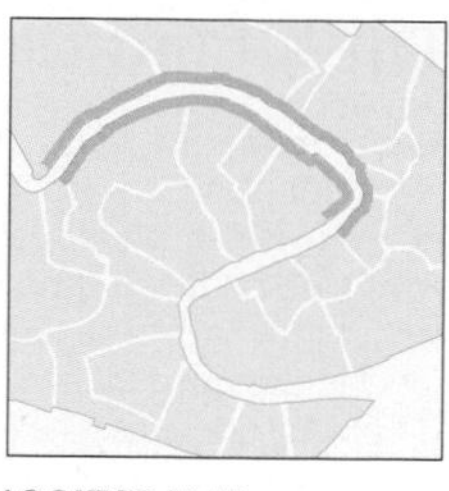

**LOCATOR MAP**

*See Venice Street Finder maps 1, 2, 3*

**Palazzo Vendramin Calergi**

*This is one of the finest early Renaissance palaces in Venice. The German composer Richard Wagner (left) died here in 1883.*

**Palazzo Sagredo**

*Graceful Veneto-Byzantine and Gothic arches are both featured on the waterfront façade.*

**The Pescheria** has been the site of a busy fish market for six centuries.

**Palazzo Michiel dalle Colonne** takes its name from its distinctive colonnade.

**The Rialto Bridge** *(see p97)* spans the canal in the commercial heart of the city.

San Stae

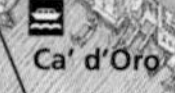


Rialto Mercato

Rialto

**San Stae**

*The façade of this Baroque church is richly adorned with statues. It is a popular concert venue.*

**Ca' Pesaro**

*The huge, stately Baroque palace today houses a gallery of modern art and the Oriental Museum.*

# The Grand Canal: the Rialto to San Marco

After passing the Rialto, the canal doubles back on itself along a stretch known as La Volta (the bend). It then widens out and the views become more spectacular approaching San Marco. Façades may have faded and foundations frayed with the tides, yet the canal remains, in the words of the French ambassador in 1495, "the most beautiful street in the world".

**Palazzo Mocenigo**
*Lord Byron stayed in this huge 18th-century palace in 1818.*

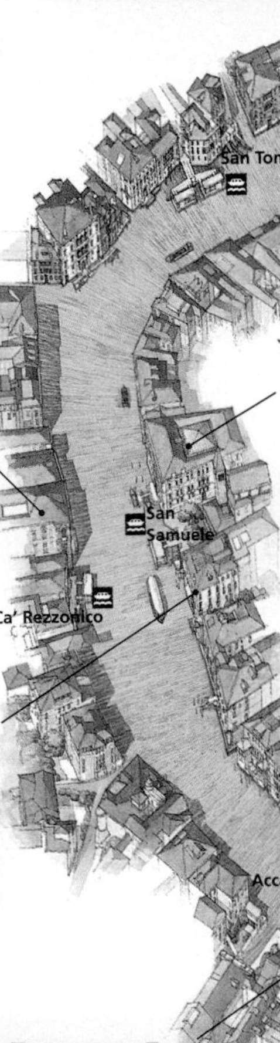

**Palazzo Garzoni** is a renovated Gothic palace, now part of the university.

**Ca' Rezzonico**
*Now a museum of 18th-century Venice* (see p103)*, the palace was the last home of the poet Robert Browning, seen here with his son Pen.*

**Palazzo Grassi**
*This elegant palazzo dates from the 1730s. Bought by French tycoon François-Henri Pinault in 2005, it is now used for art exhibitions.*

**Palazzo Capello Malipiero**
*The palace was rebuilt in 1622. Beside it stands the 12th-century campanile of San Samuele.*

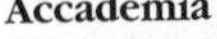

**Accademia**
*The world's greatest collection of Venetian paintings is housed here in the former Scuola della Carità* (see pp106–7)*, which has a Baroque façade by Giorgio Massari.*

**Palazzo Barbaro**
*Novelist Henry James wrote* The Aspern Papers *here in 1888.*

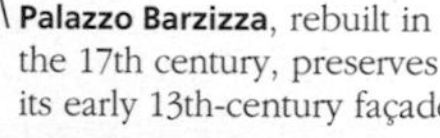


**The Riva del Vin** is the quay where wine *(vin)* used to be unloaded. It is one of the few spots where you can sit and relax on the banks of the Grand Canal.

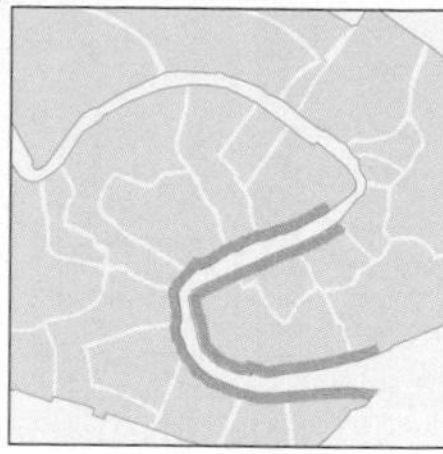

**LOCATOR MAP**

*See Venice Street Finder maps 6, 7*

**Palazzo Barzizza**, rebuilt in the 17th century, preserves its early 13th-century façade.

**Peggy Guggenheim Collection**
*A one-storey palazzo houses Guggenheim's great modern art collection* (see pp104–5).

**Santa Maria della Salute**
*The vast weight of this Baroque church is supported by over one million timber piles* (see p105).

**Palazzo Gritti-Pisani**
*The former home of the Gritti family is now the luxury Gritti Palace Hotel* (see p560).

**Harry's Bar**, founded in 1931 by Giuseppe Cipriani, is famous for its cocktails.

**Palazzo Dario**
*Beautiful coloured marbles give the 1487 palace a highly individual façade. Legend has it the building is cursed.*

**The Punta della Dogana** customs house, built in the 17th century, now contains the François Pinault Foundation of contemporary art. It is crowned by a golden globe topped by a weathervane.

**Travelling slowly along the Grand Canal by gondola ▷**

Madonna dell'Orto, with 15th-century façade statues of St Christopher and the Apostles

# Madonna dell'Orto ❶

Campo Madonna dell'Orto. **Map** 2 F2. ***Tel*** *041 275 04 62.* *Madonna dell'Orto.* *10am–5pm Mon–Sat.* *1 Jan, 25 Dec.*

This lovely Gothic church, founded in the mid-14th century, was dedicated to St Christopher, patron saint of travellers, to protect the boatmen who ferried passengers to the islands in the northern lagoon. A 15th-century statue of the saint, restored by the Venice in Peril fund, stands above the main portal. The dedication was changed and the church reconstructed in the early 15th century, after the discovery, in a nearby vegetable garden *(orto)*, of a statue of the Virgin Mary said to have miraculous powers.

The interior, faced almost entirely in brick, is large and uncluttered. On the right is a magnificent painting by Cima da Conegliano, *St John the Baptist and Other Saints* (c.1493). The vacant space in the chapel opposite belongs to Giovanni Bellini's *Madonna with Child* (c.1478), stolen in 1993 for the third time.

The church's greatest remaining treasures are the works of art by Tintoretto, who was a parishioner of the church. His tomb, which is marked with a plaque, lies with that of his children, in the chapel to the right of the chancel. The most dramatic of his works are the towering masterpieces that decorate the chancel (1562–4). On the right wall is the *Last Judgment*, whose turbulent content caused John Ruskin's wife, Effie, to flee the church in horror. In *The Adoration of the Golden Calf* on the left wall, the figure carrying the calf, fourth from the left, is believed to be a portrait of the artist. Inside the chapel of San Mauro, off the end of the right nave, stands a statue of the Madonna by Giovanni de' Santi. It was restored by the Venice in Peril fund, and inspired the rededication of the church.

# Ca' d'Oro ❷

Calle Ca' d'Oro. **Map** 3 A4. ***Tel*** *041 523 87 90.* *Ca' d'Oro.* *8:15am–7:15pm daily (to 2pm Mon).*

In 1420 Marino Contarini, a wealthy patrician, commissioned the construction of what he hoped would be the city's most magnificent palace *(see p81)*. The building's intricate carving was entrusted to a team of Venetian and Lombard craftsmen, while the façade was beautifully adorned with the most elaborate and expensive decorative finishes of the day, including gold leaf, vermilion and ultramarine.

**Tullio Lombardo's *Double Portrait***

**The magnificent Gothic façade of the Ca' d'Oro, or House of Gold**

Over the years the palace was extensively remodelled, and by the 18th century was in a state of semi-dereliction. In 1846 it was bought by the Russian Prince Troubetzkoy for the famous ballerina Maria Taglioni. Under her direction the palace suffered barbaric restoration, losing, among other things, its staircase and much of its original stonework. It was finally rescued by Baron Giorgio Franchetti, a wealthy patron of the arts, who bequeathed both the building and his private art collection to the state in 1915.

Pride of place on the first of the gallery's two floors goes to Andrea Mantegna's *St Sebastian* (1506), the artist's last work, which occupies a special alcove of its own. Elsewhere, the floor's main exhibits are ranged around the *portego* (gallery). This is largely dominated by the vivid 15th-century *Double Portrait* (c.1493) by the sculptor Tullio Lombardo; Sansovino's lunette of the *Madonna and Child* (c.1530); and several bronze reliefs by the Paduan Andrea Briosco, "Il Riccio" (1470–1532). Rooms leading off the *portego* to the right contain numerous bronzes and medallions, with some examples by Pisanello and Gentile Bellini. Paintings here also include the famous *Madonna of the Beautiful Eyes*, attributed to Giovanni Bellini, a *Madonna and Child*, attributed to Alvise Vivarini (both late 15th century), and Carpaccio's *Annunciation* and *Death of the Virgin* (both c.1504). A room to the left of the *portego* contains non-Venetian paintings, notably a *Flagellation* by Luca Signorelli (c.1480). A lovely staircase leads to the second floor, which opens with a room hung with tapestries. It has bronzes by Alessandro Vittoria and paintings by

Titian and Van Dyck. The *portego* displays frescoes (c.1532) by Pordenone from the cloister of Santo Stefano, while an anteroom contains damaged frescoes by Titian taken from the Fondaco dei Tedeschi.

**Giovanni Bellini's 1513 altarpiece in San Giovanni Grisostomo**

## San Giovanni Grisostomo ❸

Campo San Giovanni Grisostomo. **Map** 3 B5. ***Tel*** *041 523 52 93.* *Rialto.* *8:15am–12:15pm, 3–7:30pm daily.* *during mass.*

This pretty terracotta-coloured church is located near to the Rialto. Built between 1479 and 1504, it is a lovely Renaissance design, the last work of Mauro Coducci.

The interior is built on a Greek-cross plan. The light meter illuminates Giovanni Bellini's *St Jerome with Saints Christopher and Augustine* (1513) above the first altar on the right. This was most probably Bellini's last painting, executed when he was in his eighties.

Over the high altar hangs Sebastiano del Piombo's *St John Chrysostom and Six Saints* (1509–11).

## Santa Maria dei Miracoli ❹

Campo dei Miracoli. **Map** 3 B5. ***Tel*** *041 275 04 62.* *Rialto, Fondamente Nuove.* *10am–5pm Mon–Sat.* *1 Jan, 25 Dec.*

An exquisite masterpiece of early Renaissance architecture, the Miracoli is the church where many Venetians like to get married. Tucked away in a maze of alleys and waterways in eastern Cannaregio, it is small and somewhat elusive.

Santa Maria dei Miracoli is decorated in various shades of marble, with some fine bas reliefs and sculpture. It was built in 1481–9 by the architect Pietro Lombardo and his sons to enshrine *The Virgin and Child* (1408), a painting believed to have miraculous powers. The picture, by Nicoló di Pietro, can still be seen above the altar.

The interior of the church is embellished by pink, white and grey marble, at its best when lit up by rays of pale sunshine. It is crowned by a barrel-vaulted ceiling (1528) which has 50 portraits of saints and prophets. The balustrade, between the nave and the chancel, is decorated by Tullio Lombardo's carved figures of St Francis, Archangel Gabriel, the Virgin and St Clare.

The screen around the high altar and the medallions of the Evangelists in the cupola spandrels are also Lombardo's work. Above the main door, the choir gallery was used by the nuns from the neighbouring convent, who entered the church through an overhead gallery. Santa Maria dei Miracoli has undergone a major restoration programme, which was funded by the American Save Venice organization.

**Decorative column from inside Santa Maria dei Miracoli**

### SANTA MARIA DEI MIRACOLI

*This beautifully proportioned façade is composed of decorated panels and multicoloured polished marble.*

# Street-by-Street: San Polo

The Rialto bridge and markets make this area a magnet for visitors. Traditionally the city's commercial quarter, it was here that bankers, brokers and merchants conducted their affairs. Streets are no longer lined with stalls selling spices and fine fabrics, but the food markets and pasta shops are unmissable. Away from the bridge, streets quickly become less crowded, leading to tiny squares and quiet churches.

**The Rialto Markets** have existed for centuries, and are renowned for their produce. The Pescheria sells fresh fish and seafood.

**The 17th-century** church of San Cassiano houses a carved altar (1696) and a *Crucifixion* by Tintoretto (1568).

**Sant'Aponal** has a façade decorated with worn Gothic reliefs. The church was founded in the 11th century, but is now deconsecrated.

**The Frari**

**San Silvestro**

**San Giovanni Elemosinario** is an inconspicuous church that was rebuilt in the early 16th century, although its campanile dates from the end of the 14th century. Inside it are interesting frescoes by Pordenone.

**KEY**

— — — Suggested route

0 metres 75

0 yards 75

**STAR SIGHT**

★ Rialto

*For hotels and restaurants in this region see pp558–61 and pp606–9*

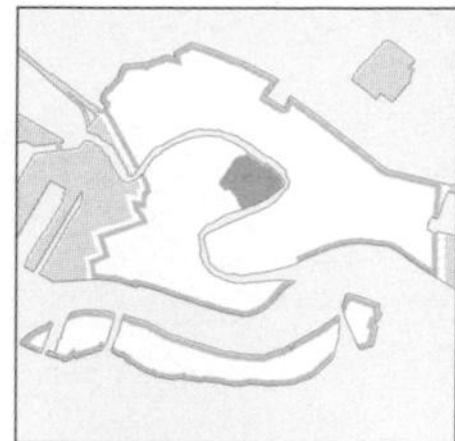

**LOCATOR MAP**
*See Venice Street Finder maps 2, 3, 6, 7*

**San Giacomo di Rialto's** clock face (1410), which has sadly been a poor time-keeper over the years, adorns one of Venice's oldest churches.

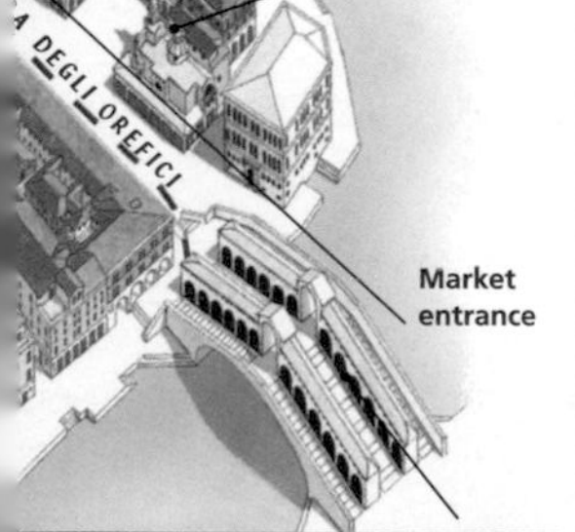


**Market entrance**

★ **Rialto**
*One of Venice's most famous sights, the bridge offers fine views of the Grand Canal, and marks the heart of the city* ❺

**The lively Erberia, selling fresh fruit and vegetables**

## Rialto ❺

Ponte di Rialto. **Map** 7 A1. *Rialto.*

The Rialto takes its name from *rivo alto* (high bank) and was one of the first areas of Venice to be inhabited. A banking and then market district, it remains one of the city's busiest and most bustling areas. Locals and visitors alike jostle among the colourful stalls of the Erberia (fruit and vegetable market) and Pescheria (fish market).

Stone bridges were built in Venice as early as the 12th century, but it was not until 1588, after the collapse, decay or sabotage of earlier wooden structures, that a solid stone bridge was designed for the Rialto. Completed in 1591, the new bridge remained the only means of crossing the Grand Canal until 1854, when the Accademia bridge was built.

Few visitors leave Venice without crossing the famous bridge. It is a wonderful place to watch and photograph the constant activity of boats on the Grand Canal below.

## San Giacomo dell'Orio ❻

Campo San Giacomo dell'Orio. **Map** 2 E5. ***Tel*** *041 275 04 62.* *Riva di Biasio or San Stae.* *10am–5pm Mon–Sat.* *1 Jan, 25 Dec.*

This church is a focal point of a quiet quarter of Santa Croce. The name "dell'Orio" may derive from a laurel tree *(alloro)* that once stood near the church. San Giacomo was founded in the 9th century, rebuilt in 1225 and thereafter repeatedly modified, resulting in a mixture of styles. The campanile, basilica ground plan and Byzantine columns survive from the 13th century. The ship's keel roof and the columns are Gothic, and the apses are Renaissance.

The sacristy contains a beautiful ceiling by Veronese in addition to some interesting altar paintings.

## San Polo ❼

Campo San Polo. **Map** 6 F1. ***Tel*** *041 275 04 62.* *San Silvestro.* *10am–5pm Mon–Sat.* *1 Jan, 25 Dec.*

Founded in the 9th century, rebuilt in the 15th and revamped in the early 19th in Neo-Classical style, this church is worth visiting for the lovely Gothic portal and the Romanesque lions at the foot of the 14th-century campanile – one holds a serpent between its paws, the other a human head.

Inside, follow the signs for the *Via Crucis del Tiepolo* – 14 pictures of the Stations of the Cross (1749) by the painter Giandomenico Tiepolo: many include vivid portraits of Venetian life. The church also has paintings by Veronese, Palma il Giovane (the Younger) and a dramatic *Last Supper* by Tintoretto.

**A Romanesque lion at the base of San Polo's 14th-century campanile**

# Santa Maria Gloriosa dei Frari ❽

More commonly known as the Frari (a corruption of Frati, meaning brothers), this vast Gothic church dwarfs the eastern area of San Polo. The first church on the site was built by Franciscan friars in 1250–1338, but was replaced by a larger building completed in the mid-15th century. The airy interior is striking for its sheer size and for the quality of its works of art, including masterpieces by Titian and Giovanni Bellini, a statue by Donatello and several grandiose tombs.

**The campanile** is 83 m (262 ft) high, the tallest in the city after that of San Marco.

**Foscari Monument**
*Doge Foscari died in 1457, after a long and eventful 34-year reign.*

**★ Assumption of the Virgin**
*Titian's glowing and spectacular work (1518) draws the eye through the monk's choir, to the altar, and heavenwards.*

**Rood Screen**
*(1475)*
*Pietro Lombardo and Bartolomeo Bon carved the rood screen and its decorative marble figures.*

**The *Madonna di Ca' Pesaro*** (1526) shows Titian's mastery of light and colour.

**★ Monks' Choir**
*This consists of three-tiered stalls (1468), carved with bas-reliefs of saints and Venetian city scenes.*

**For hotels and restaurants in this region see pp558–61 and pp606–9**

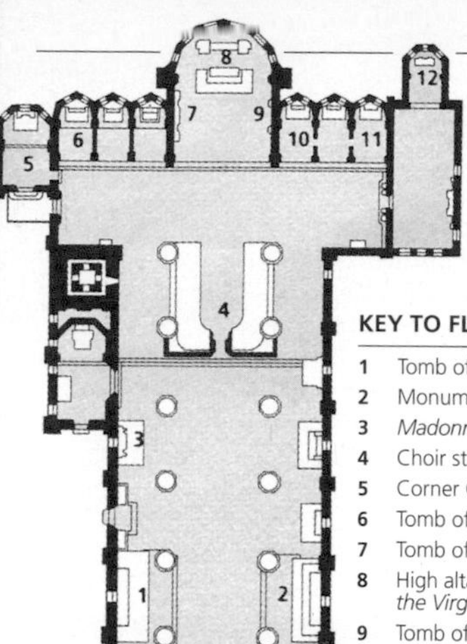


## FLOORPLAN

The Frari's imposing cruciform interior, which is 90 m (295 ft) long, holds 12 sights that should not be missed.

### KEY TO FLOORPLAN

1 Tomb of Canova
2 Monument to Titian
3 *Madonna di Ca' Pesaro* by Titian
4 Choir stalls
5 Corner Chapel
6 Tomb of Monteverdi
7 Tomb of Doge Nicolò Tron
8 High altar with *Assumption of the Virgin* (1518) by Titian
9 Tomb of Doge Francesco Foscari
10 *John the Baptist* (c.1450) by Donatello
11 B Vivarini's altar painting (1474), Bernardo Chapel
12 *Madonna and Child with Saints* (1488) by Bellini

### VISITORS' CHECKLIST

Campo dei Frari. **Map** 6 D1. ***Tel*** *041 275 04 62.* *San Tomà.* *9am–6pm Mon–Sat, 1–6pm Sun & religious hols.* *1 Jan, 25 Dec.* *except for those attending mass.* *frequent.*

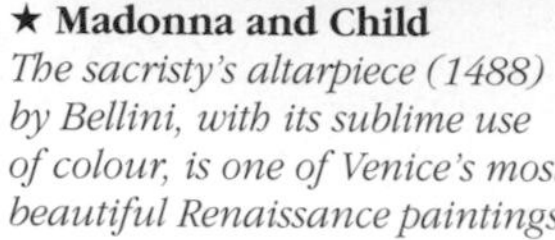

**★ Madonna and Child**
*The sacristy's altarpiece (1488) by Bellini, with its sublime use of colour, is one of Venice's most beautiful Renaissance paintings.*

**The former monastery**, which houses the State Archives, has two cloisters, one in the style of Sansovino, another designed by Palladio.

**Entrance**

**Tomb of Canova**
*Canova designed, but never constructed, a Neo-Classical marble pyramid like this as a monument for Titian. After Canova's death in 1822, the sculptor's pupils used a similar design for their master's tomb.*

### STAR FEATURES

★ Monks' Choir

★ Assumption of the Virgin by Titian

★ Madonna and Child by Bellini

# Scuola Grande di San Rocco ❾

Restored main entrance to the Scuola di San Rocco

Founded in honour of San Rocco (St Roch), a saint who dedicated his life to helping the sick, the Scuola started out as a charitable confraternity. Construction began in 1515 under Bartolomeo Bon and was continued by Scarpagnino until his death in 1549. The work was financed by donations from Venetians keen to invoke San Rocco's protection and the Scuola quickly became one of the wealthiest in Venice. In 1564 its members decided to commission Tintoretto to decorate its walls and ceilings. His earliest paintings, the first of over 50 works he eventually left in the Scuola, fill the small Sala dell'Albergo off the Upper Hall. His later paintings occupy the Ground Floor Hall, immediately within the entrance.

Tintoretto's magnificent *Crucifixion*, painted in 1565 for the Sala dell'Albergo in the Scuola di San Rocco

## GROUND FLOOR HALL

The ground floor cycle was executed in 1583–7, when Tintoretto was in his sixties, and consists of eight large paintings illustrating, among others, the life of Mary. The series starts with an *Annunciation* and ends with an *Assumption*.

The tranquil scenes of *The Flight into Egypt, St Mary Magdalene* and *St Mary of Egypt* are remarkable for their serenity. This is portrayed most lucidly by the repentant hermit's isolated spiritual contemplation in *St Mary of Egypt*. In all three paintings, the landscapes are rendered with rapid strokes, and are an important part of the composition.

Detail from *The Flight into Egypt* (1582–7) by Tintoretto

## UPPER HALL AND SALA DELL'ALBERGO

Scarpagnino's great staircase (1544–6), with its upper flight decorated with two vast paintings commemorating the plague of 1630, leads to the Upper Hall. Here, biblical subjects decorate the ceiling and walls, painted by Tintoretto from 1575–81.

The ceiling paintings portray scenes from the Old Testament. The three large and dynamic square paintings in the centre show episodes from the Book of Exodus: *Moses Strikes Water from the Rock, The Miracle of the Bronze Serpent* and *The Fall of Manna in the Desert*. These all allude to the charitable aims of the Scuola in alleviating thirst, sickness and hunger respectively. All three paintings are crowded compositions displaying much violent movement.

The vast wall paintings in the hall feature episodes from the New Testament, linking with the ceiling paintings. Two of the most striking paintings are *The Temptation of Christ*, which shows a handsome young Satan offering Christ two loaves of bread, and *The Adoration of the Shepherds*. Like *The Temptation of Christ, The Adoration* is composed in two halves, with a female figure, shepherds and an ox below, and the Holy Family and onlookers above.

The beautiful carvings below the paintings were added in the 17th century by sculptor Francesco Pianta. The figures are allegorical and include (near the altar) a caricature of Tintoretto with his palette and brushes, representing Painting.

The easel painting *Christ Carrying the Cross*, also in the

*For hotels and restaurants in this region see pp558–61 and pp606–9*

**Detail from *The Temptation of Christ* (1578–81) by Tintoretto**

Upper Hall, was once attributed to Giorgione, though many believe it to be by Titian.

Near the entrance to the Sala dell'Albergo, is the *Annunciation* by Titian. The Sala dell'Albergo itself holds the most breathtaking of his works – the *Crucifixion*

### VISITORS' CHECKLIST

Campo San Rocco.
**Map** 6 D1. ***Tel*** *041 523 48 64.*
*San Tomà.*
*9:30am–5:30pm daily.*
*1 Jan, Easter, 25 Dec.*
**www**.scuolagrandesanrocco.it

(1565). Henry James remarked of this painting: "No single picture contains more of human life; there is everything in it, including the most exquisite beauty." Tintoretto began the cycle of paintings in this room in 1564, when he won the commission with the ceiling painting *San Rocco in Glory*. On the wall opposite the *Crucifixion* are paintings of episodes from the Passion: *Christ before Pilate, The Crowning with Thorns* and *The Ascent to Calvary*.

### KEY TO PAINTINGS

**GROUND FLOOR HALL 1** The Annunciation; **2** The Adoration of the Three Kings; **3** The Flight into Egypt; **4** The Massacre of the Innocents; **5** St Mary Magdalene; **6** St Mary of Egypt; **7** The Presentation in the Temple; **8** The Assumption.

**UPPER HALL WALLS 9** San Rocco; **10** St Sebastian; **11** The Adoration of the Shepherds; **12** The Baptism of Christ; **13** The Resurrection; **14** The Agony in the Garden; **15** The Last Supper; **16** The Vision of San Rocco; **17** The Miracle of the Loaves and Fishes; **18** The Resurrection of Lazarus; **19** The Ascension; 20 Christ Heals the Paralytic; **21** The Temptation of Christ.

**UPPER HALL CEILING 22** Moses Saved from the Waters; **23** The Pillar of Fire; **24** Samuel and Saul; **25** Jacob's Ladder; **26** Elijah on a Chariot of Fire; **27** Elijah Fed by the Angels; **28** Daniel Saved by the Angels; **29** The Passover; **30** The Fall of Manna; **31** The Sacrifice of Isaac; **32** The Miracle of the Bronze Serpent; **33** Jonah Emerges from the Whale; **34** Moses Strikes Water from the Rock; **35** Adam and Eve; **36** Three Children in the Furnace; **37** God Appears to Moses; **38** Samson Brings out Water from the Jawbone of an Ass; **39** The Vision of the Prophet Ezekiel; **40** The Vision of Jeremiah; **41** Elisha Distributes Bread; **42** Abraham and Melchizedeck.

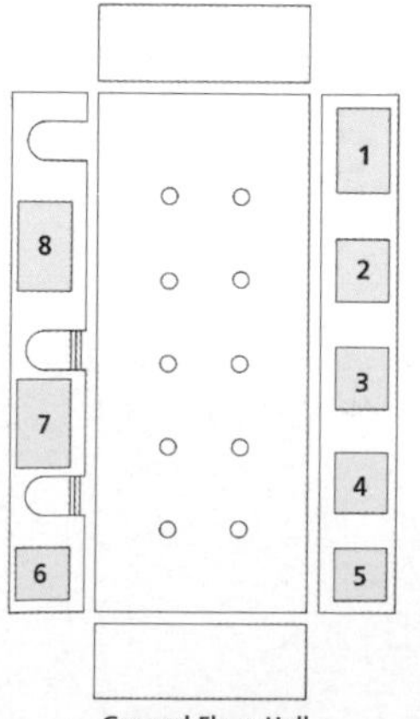


**Ground Floor Hall**

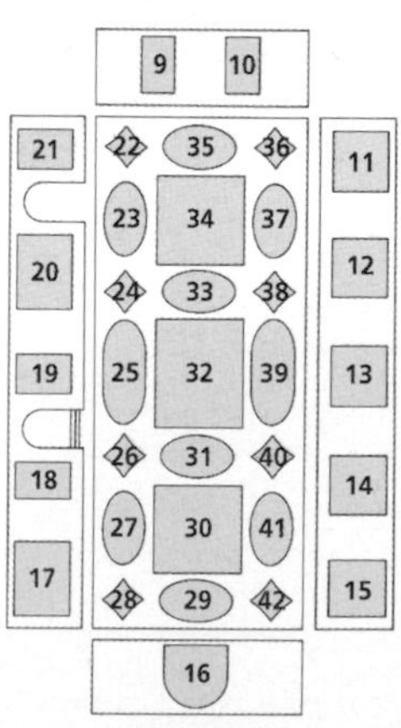


**Upper Hall**

## San Rocco ❿

Campo San Rocco.
**Map** 6 D1. ***Tel*** *041 523 48 64.*
*San Tomà.* *9:30am–5:30pm daily.*

On the same square as the celebrated Scuola Grande di San Rocco is the church of the same name. Designed by the sculptor and architect, Bartolomeo Bon, in 1489 and largely rebuilt in 1725, the exterior suffers from a mixture of styles. The façade was added in 1765–71. Inside, the chancel is decorated with a series of paintings by Tintoretto depicting scenes from the life of San Rocco.

## San Pantalon ⓫

Campo San Pantalon. **Map** 6 D2.
***Tel*** *041 523 58 93.* *San Tomà, Piazzale Roma.* *Mon–Sat.*

**Fumiani's epic ceiling painting (1680–1740) in San Pantalon**

The overwhelming feature of this late 17th-century church is its vast painted ceiling, dark, awe-inspiring and remarkable for its illusionistic effect of height. The ceiling comprises a total of 40 scenes, and admirers claim that this is the world's largest work of art on canvas.

The scenes show the martyrdom and apotheosis of the physician St Pantalon. The artist, Gian Antonio Fumiani, took 24 years (1680–1704) to achieve the masterpiece, before allegedly falling to his death from the scaffolding.

# Street-by-Street: Dorsoduro

**Santa Margherita**

Built up on a strata of solid subsoil is the *sestiere* of Dorsoduro – the name means "hard backbone". It has as its focal point the lively Campo Santa Margherita, the largest open space in this part of Venice. The square bustles with activity, particularly in the morning when the market stalls are open, and in the evening when it is the haunt of students from nearby Ca' Foscari, now part of Venice university. The surrounding streets contain some architectural stunners, notably Ca' Rezzonico and the Scuola Grande dei Carmini, which has decorations by Tiepolo. Of the area's waterways, the delightful Rio San Barnaba is best appreciated from the Ponte dei Pugni, near the barge selling fruit and vegetables – itself a time-honoured Venetian sight. Alongside the Rio Terrà Canal there are some lively cafés and a fascinating shop selling masks for Carnevale.

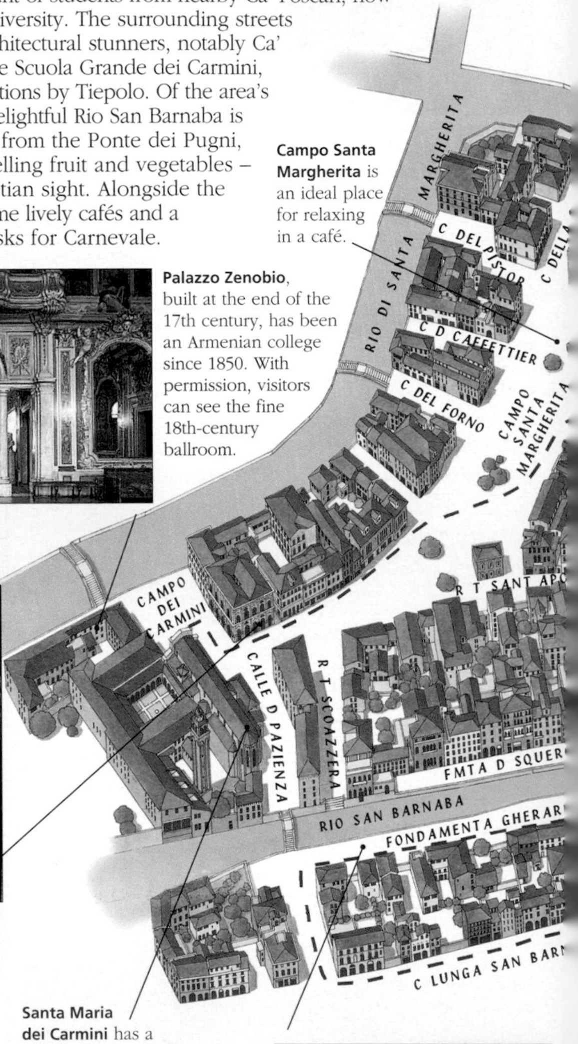

**Campo Santa Margherita** is an ideal place for relaxing in a café.

**Palazzo Zenobio**, built at the end of the 17th century, has been an Armenian college since 1850. With permission, visitors can see the fine 18th-century ballroom.

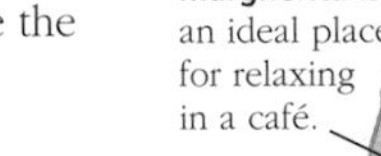

**Scuola Grande dei Carmini** contains nine ceiling panels (1739–44) in the hall on the upper floor, painted by Tiepolo for the Carmelite confraternity.

**Santa Maria dei Carmini** has a Gothic side porch carved with Byzantine reliefs.

**KEY**

 Suggested route

0 metres 50

0 yards 50

**Fondamenta Gherardini** runs beside the Rio San Barnaba, one of the prettiest canals in the *sestiere.*

*For hotels and restaurants in this region see pp558–61 and pp606–9*

**★ Ca' Rezzonico**
*The ballroom covers the width of the palazzo once owned by Browning* ⓬

**LOCATOR MAP**
*See Venice Street Finder maps 5, 6*

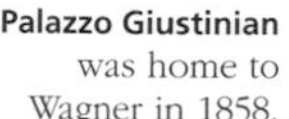

**Palazzo Giustinian** was home to Wagner in 1858.

**Ca' Foscari** was completed in 1437 for Doge Francesco Foscari.

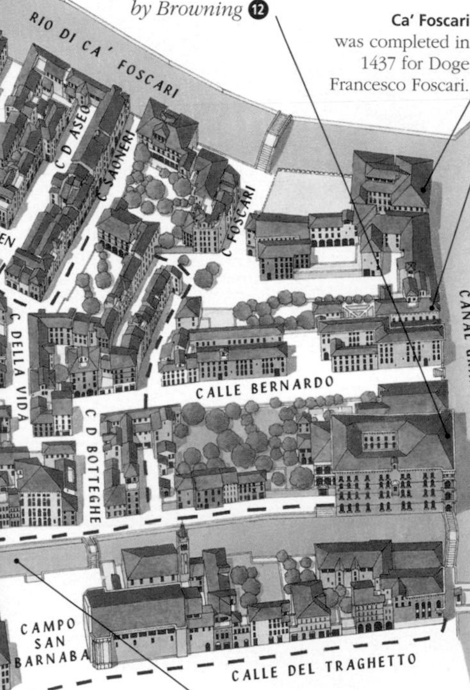


**Ponte dei Pugni** was a traditional scene of fist fights between rival factions. They were finally banned in 1705 for being too violent.

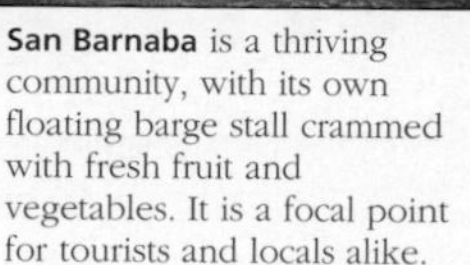

**San Barnaba** is a thriving community, with its own floating barge stall crammed with fresh fruit and vegetables. It is a focal point for tourists and locals alike.

**STAR SIGHT**

★ Ca' Rezzonico

**Tiepolo's *New World* fresco, part of a series in Ca' Rezzonico**

## Ca' Rezzonico ⓬

Fondamenta Rezzonico 3136. **Map** 6 E3. ***Tel*** *041 241 01 00.* *Ca' Rezzonico.* *10am–6pm Wed–Mon (Nov–Mar: to 5pm. Last adm: 1 hr before closing).* *1 Jan, 1 May, 25 Dec.*

This palazzo houses the museum of 18th-century Venice, its rooms furnished with frescoes, paintings and period pieces taken from other palaces or museums. Building began with Longhena (architect of La Salute, *see p105*) in 1667, but the funds of the Bon family, who commissioned it, ran dry before the second floor was started. In 1712 the unfinished palace was bought by the Rezzonico family of Genoa, who spent a large portion of their fortune on its completion.

The Rezzonico family sold it on, in 1888, to the famous poet Robert Browning and his son, Pen. The outstanding attraction in the palace today is Giorgio Massari's ballroom, which occupies the entire breadth of the building. It is adorned with gilded chandeliers, carved furniture by Andrea Brustolon and a ceiling with *trompe l'oeil* frescoes. Other rooms have frescoes by Giambattista Tiepolo, including his lively *Nuptial Allegory* (1758), and one by his son, Giandomenico, originally in his villa at Zianigo. There are paintings by Longhi, Guardi, and – rare in Venice – Canaletto. On the top floor is a reconstructed 18th-century apothecary's shop and the Pinacoteca Martini.

Nave of San Nicolò dei Mendicoli, one of the oldest churches in Venice

## San Nicolò dei Mendicoli ⓭

Campo San Nicolò. **Map** 5 A3. ***Tel*** *041 275 03 82.* *San Basilio.* *10am–noon, 3–5pm Mon–Sat.*

Contrasting with the remote and rundown area which surrounds it, this church still remains one of the most charming in Venice. Founded in the 7th century, it has been rebuilt extensively over the years. The little porch on the north flank is 15th century and once sheltered the beggars, or *mendicanti*, who gave the church its name.

Thanks to the Venice in Peril fund, in the 1970s the church underwent one of the most comprehensive restoration programmes since the floods of 1966. Flooding had become such a problem that the priest often ferried himself around the church in a small wicker boat. The floor, which was 30 cm (1 ft) below the level of the canals, was rebuilt and raised slightly to prevent further flood damage. The roofs and lower walls were reconstructed, and paintings and statues restored.

The interior is delightfully embellished, particularly the nave with its 16th-century gilded wooden statues. These include the figure of San Nicolò himself. On the upper walls is a series of paintings of the life of Christ (c.1553) by Alvise dal Friso and other pupils of Veronese.

Outside, a small column supports a stone lion, in a humbler echo of the Column of San Marco in the Piazzetta.

## San Sebastiano ⓮

Campo San Sebastiano. **Map** 5 C3. ***Tel*** *041 275 04 62.* *San Basilio.* *10am–5pm Mon–Sat.* *1 Jan, 25 Dec.*

This church has one of the most homogeneous interiors in the whole of Venice. The splendour was created by Veronese who, from 1555 to 1560 and again in the 1570s, was commissioned to decorate the sacristy ceiling, the nave ceiling, the frieze, the east end of the choir, the high altar, the doors of the organ panels and the chancel.

The paintings feature radiant colours and rich costumes. Those on the sacristy ceiling depict the *Coronation of the Virgin* and the *Four Evangelists*.

Of the other paintings, the finest are the three that tell the story of Esther, Queen of Xerxes I of Persia, famous for securing the deliverance of the Jewish people.

Veronese is buried here. His tomb is situated in front of the beautifully paved chapel to the left of the chancel.

## Accademia ⓯

*See pp106–7.*

## Peggy Guggenheim Collection ⓰

Palazzo Venier dei Leoni. **Map** 6 F4. ***Tel*** *041 240 54 11.* *Accademia.* *10am–6pm Wed–Mon.* *25 Dec.*

Intended as a four-storey palace, the 18th-century Palazzo Venier dei Leoni in fact never rose beyond the ground floor – hence its nickname, *Il Palazzo*

The truncated palazzo housing the Peggy Guggenheim Collection

*Nonfinito* (The Unfinished Palace). In 1949 the building was bought as a home by the American millionairess Peggy Guggenheim (1898–1979), a collector, dealer and patron of the arts.

A perspicacious and high-spirited woman, she initially befriended, and then furthered the careers of, many innovative abstract and Surrealist artists. One was Max Ernst, who became her second husband. The collection consists of 200 fine paintings and sculptures, each representing the 20th century's most influential modern art movements. The dining room has notable Cubist works of art, including *The Poet* by Pablo Picasso, and an entire room is devoted to Jackson Pollock, who was "discovered" by Guggenheim. Other artists represented are Braque, Chagall, de Chirico, Dalí, Duchamp, Léger, Kandinsky, Klee, Mondrian, Miró, Malevich, Rothko, Bacon and Magritte, whose Surreal *Empire of Light* (1953–4) shows a night scene of a darkened house in a wooded setting with a bright day sky above. The sculpture collection, which includes Constantin Brancusi's elegant *Maiastra* (1912), is laid out in the house and garden.

***Maiastra* by Constantin Brancusi**

Perhaps the most provocative piece is Marino Marini's *Angelo della Città* (Angel of the Citadel, 1948), located on the terrace overlooking the Grand Canal. This shows a prominently displayed man sitting on a horse, erect in all respects. Embarrassed onlookers avert their gaze to enjoy views of the Grand Canal.

The Guggenheim, one of the most visited sights in Venice, is the best place in the city to see modern art. Light-filled rooms and the large modern canvases provide a striking contrast to the Renaissance paintings that usually form the highlights in most Venetian churches and museums. A bonus for English speakers is the team of assistants, who are often visiting arts graduates from English-speaking countries.

The garden has been paved and features an array of sculptures. Peggy Guggenheim's ashes are also preserved here, near the place where her pet dogs were buried. A shop and restaurant are housed in buildings off the garden. Call for information on temporary exhibits.

**The Baroque church of Santa Maria della Salute, at the mouth of the Grand Canal**

## Santa Maria della Salute ⓱

Campo della Salute. **Map** 7 A4. ***Tel*** *041 274 39 28.* *Salute.* *9am–noon, 3–5:30pm daily.* *the sacristy may be closed in the morning during religious holidays.* *to sacristy.*

This great Baroque church standing at the entrance of the Grand Canal is one of the most imposing architectural landmarks of Venice. Henry James likened it to "some great lady on the threshold of her salon".

**Interior of the Salute with the octagonal space at its core**

Santa Maria della Salute was built in thanksgiving for the city's deliverance from the plague epidemic of 1630, hence the name *Salute*, which means health and salvation.

Each November, in celebration, worshippers light candles and approach across a bridge of boats spanning the mouth of the Grand Canal for the occasion.

Baldassare Longhena started the church in 1630 at the age of 32, and worked on it for the rest of his life. It was not completed until 1687, five years after his death.

The interior is comparatively sober. It consists of a large octagonal space below the cupola and six chapels radiating from the ambulatory. The large domed chancel and grandiose high altar dominate the view from the main door.

The altar's sculptural group by Giusto Le Corte represents the Virgin and Child giving protection to Venice from the plague. The best of the paintings are in the sacristy to the left of the altar: Titian's early altarpiece of *St Mark Enthroned with Saints Cosmas, Damian, Roch and Sebastian* (1511–12) and his dramatic ceiling paintings of *Cain and Abel, The Sacrifice of Abraham and Isaac* and *David and Goliath* (1540–9). *The Wedding at Cana* (1551) on the wall opposite the entrance is a major work by Jacopo Tintoretto.

# Accademia ⓯

The art collection in the Accademia offers a complete spectrum of the Venetian school, from the Byzantine era through the Renaissance to the Baroque and later. The basis of the collection was the Accademia di Belle Arti founded in 1750 by the painter Giovanni Battista Piazzetta. In 1807 Napoleon moved the collection to these premises, enriching it with artworks removed from churches and monasteries. The Accademia is currently undergoing extensive restoration, which may result in changes to the floorplan.

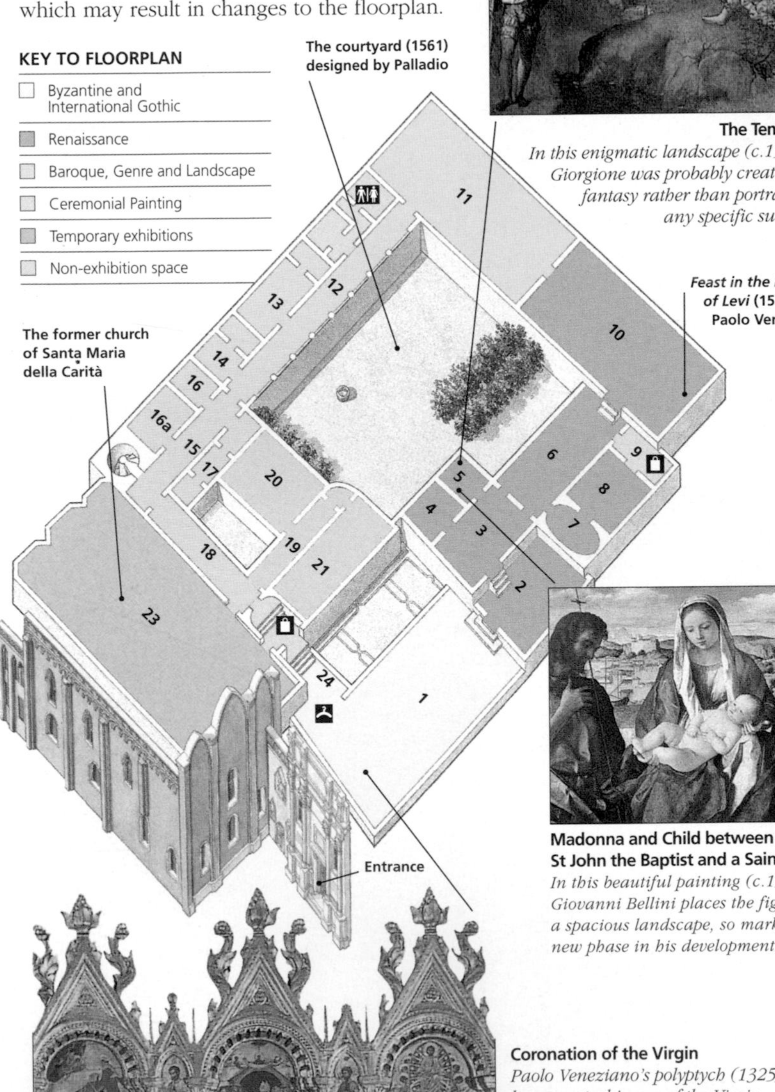


**The Tempest**
*In this enigmatic landscape (c.1507), Giorgione was probably creating a fantasy rather than portraying any specific subject.*

**Madonna and Child between St John the Baptist and a Saint**
*In this beautiful painting (c.1504), Giovanni Bellini places the figures in a spacious landscape, so marking a new phase in his development.*

**Coronation of the Virgin**
*Paolo Veneziano's polyptych (1325) has a central image of the Virgin surrounded by a panoply of religious scenes. This detail shows episodes from the Life of St Francis.*

***Healing of the Madman*** **(c.1496) by Vittore Carpaccio**

## VISITORS' CHECKLIST

Campo della Carità. **Map** 6 E3. ***Tel*** *041 522 22 47.* Accademia. *8:15am–7:15pm daily (to 2pm Mon) (last adm: 45 mins before closing).* *1 Jan, 1 May, 25 Dec.* **www**.gallerieaccademia.org

## BYZANTINE AND INTERNATIONAL GOTHIC

Room 1 shows the influence of Byzantine art on the early Venetian painters. In Paolo Veneziano's glowing *Coronation of the Virgin* (1325), the linear rhythms are unmistakably Gothic, but the gold background and central panel are distinctly Byzantine.

In contrast, *The Coronation of the Virgin* (1448) by Michele Giambono reveals a delicate naturalism, typical of the International Gothic style.

## RENAISSANCE

The Renaissance came late to Venice, but by the second quarter of the 15th century it had transformed the city into a thriving art centre rivalling Florence and Rome. Central to Venetian art in the 15th century was the *Sacra Conversazione*, in which the Madonna is portrayed with various saints in a harmonious composition. Giovanni Bellini's altarpiece for San Giobbe (c.1487) in room 2 is one of the finest examples of this subject.

In contrast, the High Renaissance exuberance of Paolo Veronese is exemplified in the monumental *Feast in the House of Levi* (1573). The painting occupies a whole wall in room 10. Tintoretto's huge masterpiece *The Miracle of St Mark Freeing a Slave* (1548) is also on display here.

## BAROQUE, GENRE AND LANDSCAPE

Venice lacked native Baroque painters, but a few non-Venetians kept the Venetian school alive in the 17th century. The most notable was the Genoese Bernardo Strozzi (1581–1644). The artist was a great admirer of the work of Veronese, as can be seen in his *Feast at the House of Simon* (1629) in room 11.

Also represented in this room is Giambattista Tiepolo, the greatest Venetian painter of the 18th century.

The long corridor (12) and the rooms that lead from it are largely devoted to light-hearted landscape and genre paintings from the 18th century. Among them are pastoral scenes by Francesco Zuccarelli, works by Marco Ricci, scenes of Venetian society by Pietro Longhi and a view of Venice by Canaletto (1763). This is a fine example of his sense of perspective.

## CEREMONIAL PAINTING

Rooms 20 and 21 return to the Renaissance, featuring two great cycles of paintings from the late 16th century. The detail in these large-scale anecdotal canvases provides a fascinating glimpse of the life, customs and appearance of Venice at the time.

Room 20 houses *The Stories of the Cross* by Venice's leading artists. In room 21, minutely detailed *Scenes from the Legend of St Ursula* (1490s) by Carpaccio mix reality and imagination by linking episodes from the life of the saint to the settings and costumes of 15th-century Venice.

***Feast in the House of Levi*** **(1573) by Paolo Veronese**

# Street-by-Street: Piazza San Marco

Throughout its long history Piazza San Marco has witnessed pageants, processions, political activities and countless Carnival festivities. Visitors flock here in their thousands for two of the city's most important historic sights – the Basilica and the Palazzo Ducale. These magnificent buildings complement lesser sights, such as the Campanile, Museo Correr and Torre dell'Orologio, not to mention the gardens of the Giardinetti Reali, open-air orchestras, elegant cafés – notably Quadri and Florian's – and numerous smart shops.

**Lion of St Mark**

**Torre dell'Orologio**
*The clock tower, with hidden clockwork figures, dates from the Renaissance* 20

**Traditionally Gondolas** have moored in the Bacino Orseolo, which is named after Doge Orseolo.

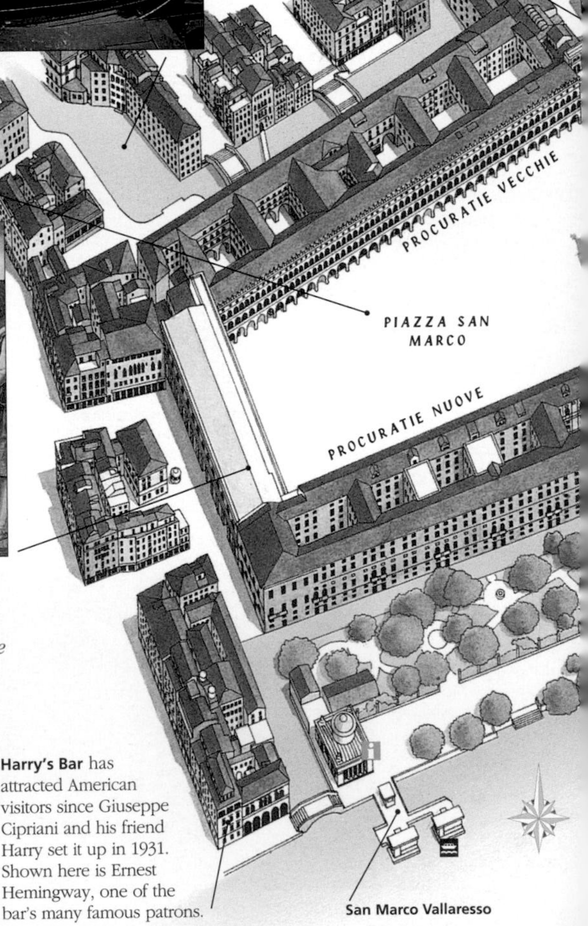

**The Piazza** was described by Napoleon as the "most elegant drawing room in Europe".

**Museo Correr**
*Giovanni Bellini's* Pietà *(1455–60) is one of many masterpieces hanging in the galleries of the Correr* 22

**Harry's Bar** has attracted American visitors since Giuseppe Cipriani and his friend Harry set it up in 1931. Shown here is Ernest Hemingway, one of the bar's many famous patrons.

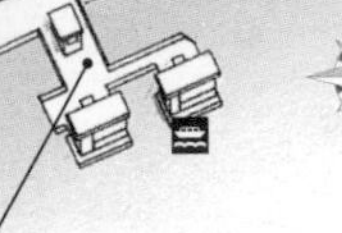

**San Marco Vallaresso**

*For hotels and restaurants in this region see pp558–61 and pp606–9*

**★ Basilica di San Marco**
*This 13th-century façade mosaic shows the body of St Mark being carried into the basilica* ⓲

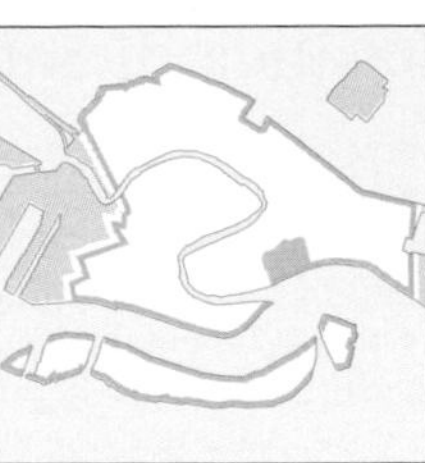

**LOCATOR MAP**
*See Venice Street Finder map 7*

**The Campanile**
*The present Campanile replaced one that collapsed in 1902* ㉑

**The Bridge of Sighs** (1600) was built as a passageway between the Palazzo Ducale and the prison. It reputedly took its name from the sighs of prisoners being led to trial.

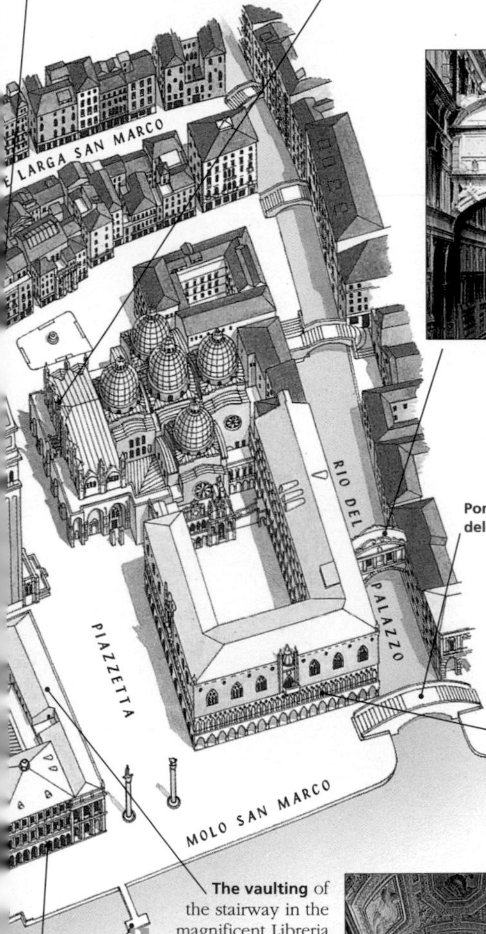

LARGA SAN MARCO

RIO DEL PALAZZO

PIAZZETTA

MOLO SAN MARCO

**Ponte della Paglia**

**★ Palazzo Ducale**
*Once home to Venice's rulers, and to the offices of State, the Doges' Palace is a triumph of Gothic architecture* ⓳

**The vaulting** of the stairway in the magnificent Libreria Sansoviniana (1588) is decorated with frescoes and gilded stucco. The national library of St Mark is housed here.

**San Marco Giardinetti**

**The Zecca**, designed by Sansovino and started in 1537, was the city mint until 1870, and gave its name to the *zecchino* or Venetian ducat.

**0 metres** 75

**0 yards** 75

**STAR SIGHTS**

★ Basilica di San Marco

★ Palazzo Ducale

# Basilica di San Marco ⓲

Venice's famous Basilica blends the architectural and decorative styles of East and West to create one of the greatest buildings in Europe. The exterior owes its almost Oriental splendour to countless treasures from the Republic's overseas empire. Among these are copies of the famous bronze horses, brought from Constantinople in 1204, and a wealth of columns, bas-reliefs and coloured marbles studded across the main façade. Mosaics from different epochs adorn the five doorways, while the main portal is framed by some of Italy's loveliest Romanesque carving (1240–65).

**St Mark and Angels**
*The statues crowning the central arch are additions from the early 15th century.*

**The Pentecost Dome**, showing the Descent of the Holy Ghost as a dove, was probably the first dome to be decorated with mosaics.

**The elegant arches** echo those of the lower floor, forming a repeat pattern.

**★ Horses of St Mark**
*The four horses are replicas of the gilded bronze originals, now protected inside the Basilica's museum.*

**STAR FEATURES**

★ Façade Mosaics

★ Horses of St Mark

**Romanesque carvings** adorn the arches of the main portal.

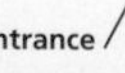

**Entrance**

**★ Façade Mosaics**
*A 17th-century mosaic shows the body of St Mark being taken from Alexandria, reputedly smuggled past Muslim guards under slices of pork.*

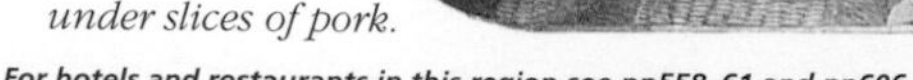

*For hotels and restaurants in this region see pp558–61 and pp606–9*

**Ciborium**

*The fine alabaster columns of the altar canopy, or baldacchino, are adorned with scenes from the New Testament.*

**The Ascension Dome** features a magnificent 13th-century mosaic of Christ surrounded by angels, the 12 Apostles and the Virgin Mary.

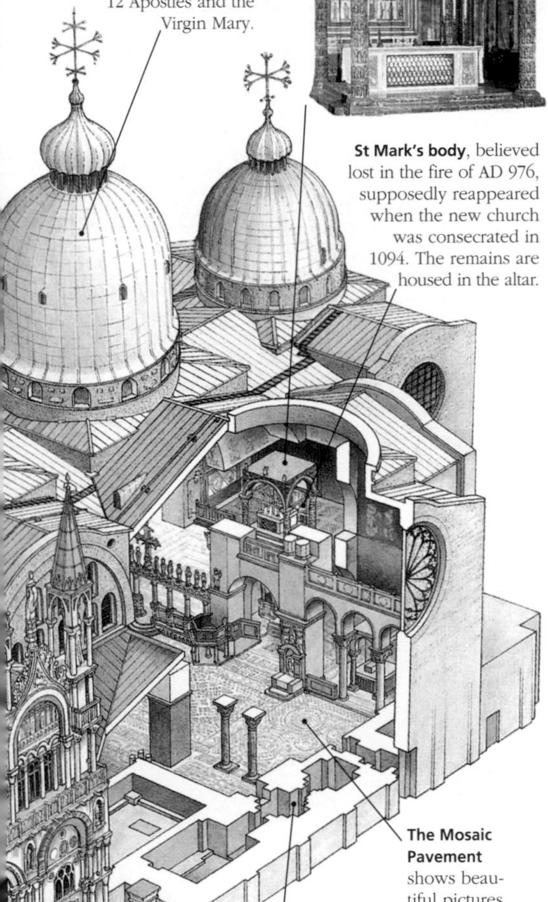

**St Mark's body**, believed lost in the fire of AD 976, supposedly reappeared when the new church was consecrated in 1094. The remains are housed in the altar.

**The Mosaic Pavement** shows beautiful pictures of birds and beasts, some of which are allegorical.

**St Mark's Treasury**

**The Tetrarchs**

*This charming sculptured group in porphyry (4th-century Egyptian) is thought to represent Diocletian, Maximian, Valerian and Constantine. Collectively they were the Tetrarchs, appointed by Diocletian to help rule the Roman Empire.*

## VISITORS' CHECKLIST

Piazza San Marco. **Map** 7 B2. ***Tel*** *041 270 83 11.* San Marco. **Basilica, Museum, Treasury** *9:45am–5pm Mon–Sat, 2–4pm Sun & hols.* *sightseeing limited during services.* **Pala d'Oro** *9:45am–5pm daily (Oct–Mar: to 4pm).* *Treasury.* **www**.basilicasanmarco.it

## THE BUILDING OF ST MARK'S

Built on a Greek cross plan and crowned with five huge domes, this is the third church to stand on the site. The first, which enshrined the body of St Mark in the 9th century, was destroyed by fire. The second was pulled down in favour of a church reflecting Venice's growing power. The present design was inspired by the Church of the Apostles in Constantinople and was completed and decorated over the centuries. From 1075, all ships returning from abroad had, by law, to bring back a precious gift to adorn "the House of St Mark". The mosaics inside are mostly 12th–13th century and cover 4,240 sq m (45,622 sq ft). Some were later replaced by such artists as Titian and Tintoretto. Until 1807 St Mark's was the doge's private chapel, used for ceremonies of State, after which it succeeded San Pietro di Castello as the cathedral of Venice.

**13th-century carving of a grape harvester on the main portal**

## Exploring the Basilica

St Mark's magnificent interior is clad with dazzling mosaics, which begin in the *narthex,* or atrium of the Basilica, and culminate in the glittering panels of the Pentecost and Ascension domes. The Genesis Cupola in the atrium has a stunning Creation of the World described in concentric circles. The *pavimento* or floor is also patterned with mosaics in marble and glass. Steps from the atrium lead to the Museo Marciano, home to the Basilica's famous horses. Other treasures include the jewel-encrusted Pala d'Oro, behind the high altar, the Nicopeia icon and the precious hoards of silver, gold and glassware in the Treasury.

**Madonna di Nicopeia**
*This Byzantine icon, looted in 1204, is one of Venice's most revered images.*

**The Porta dei Fiori** or Gate of Flowers is decorated with 13th-century reliefs.

**Cappella dei Mascoli**

**North side aisle**

**★ Pentecost Dome**
*Showing the Apostles touched by tongues of flame, the Pentecost Dome was lavishly decorated in the 12th century.*

**Atrium**

**Steps to Museo Marciano**

**Cappella Zen**

**Baptistry**

**★ Ascension Dome**
*A mosaic of Christ in Glory decorates the enormous central dome. This masterpiece was created by 13th-century Venetian craftsmen, who were strongly influenced by the art and architecture of Byzantium.*

**★ Treasury**
*A repository for precious artifacts from both Italy and Constantinople, the treasury houses objects such as this 11th-century silver-gilt coffer.*

**★ Pala d'Oro**
*The altarpiece, created in the 10th century by medieval goldsmiths, is made up of 250 panels such as this one.*

**The sacristy door** has fine bronze panels by Sansovino which include portraits of himself with Titian and Aretino.

**The Altar of the Sacrament** is decorated with mosaics of the parables and miracles of Christ dating from the late 12th or early 13th century.

**The columns** of the inner façade are thought to be fragments of the first basilica.

**South side aisle**

### STAR FEATURES

- ★ Treasury
- ★ Ascension and Pentecost Domes
- ★ Pala d'Oro

## MOSAICS

Clothing the domes, walls and floor of the Basilica are over 4,000 sq m (43,000 sq ft) of gleaming golden mosaics. The earliest, dating from the 12th century, were the work of mosaicists from the East. Their delicate techniques were soon adopted by Venetian craftsmen, who gradually took over the Basilica's decoration, combining Byzantine inspiration with Western influences. During the 16th century, many sketches by Tintoretto, Titian, Veronese, and other leading artists were reproduced in mosaic.

Among the most dazzling mosaics – many of which have been heavily restored – are those in the 13th-century central Ascension Dome and the 12th-century Pentecost Dome over the nave.

## PALA D'ORO

Beyond the Cappella di San Clemente lies the entrance to the most valuable treasure of San Marco: the Pala d'Oro. This jewel-spangled altarpiece, situated behind the high altar, consists of 250 enamel paintings on gold foil, enclosed within a gilded silver Gothic frame. Originally commissioned in Byzantium in AD 976, the altarpiece was further embellished over the centuries. Napoleon stole some of the precious stones in 1797, but the screen still gleams with pearls, rubies, sapphires and amethysts.

## MUSEO MARCIANO

Steps from the atrium, signposted Loggia dei Cavalli, take you up to the church museum, where the gallery offers a splendid view into the basilica. The gilded bronze horses, housed in a room at the far end of the museum, were stolen from the top of the Hippodrome (ancient racecourse) in Constantinople (modern Istanbul) in 1204 but their origin, either Roman or Hellenistic, remains a mystery. Also on show are mosaics, medieval manuscripts and antique tapestries.

## BAPTISTRY AND CHAPELS

The baptistry (closed to the public) was added by Doge Andrea Dandolo (1343–54), who is buried here, with Sansovino, who designed the font. The adjoining Cappella Zen (also closed to the public) became a funeral chapel for Cardinal Zen in 1504 in return for a bequest to the State. The left transept of the Cappella dei Mascoli is decorated with scenes from the life of Mary, while the third chapel in the same transept houses the icon of the Madonna of Nicopeia. Looted in 1204, it was once carried into battle at the head of the Byzantine army.

Noah and the Flood, atrium mosaics from the 13th century

# Palazzo Ducale 19

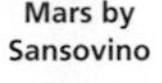

The Palazzo Ducale (Doges' Palace) was the official residence of each Venetian ruler (doge) and was founded in the 9th century. The present palace owes its external appearance to the building work of the 14th and early 15th centuries. To create their airy Gothic masterpiece, the Venetians broke with tradition by perching the bulk of the palace (built in pink Veronese marble) on top of an apparent fretwork of loggias and arcades (built from white Istrian stone).

Mars by Sansovino

**★ Giants' Staircase**
*This 15th-century staircase is crowned by Sansovino's statues of Mars and Neptune, symbols of Venice's power.*

**★ Porta della Carta**
*This 15th-century Gothic gate was once the main entrance to the palace. From it, a vaulted passageway leads to the Arco Foscari and the internal courtyard.*

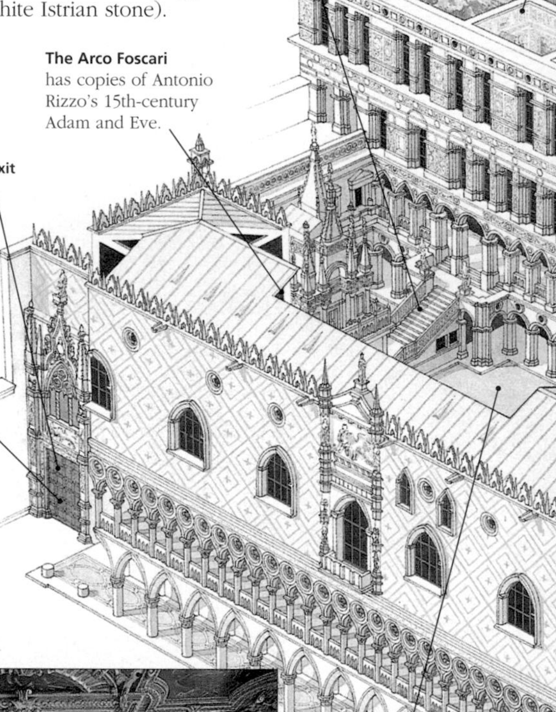

**★ Sala del Maggior Consiglio**
*This vast hall was used as a meeting place for members of Venice's Great Council. Tintoretto's huge* Paradise *(1590) fills the end wall.*

*For hotels and restaurants in this region see pp558–61 and pp606–9*

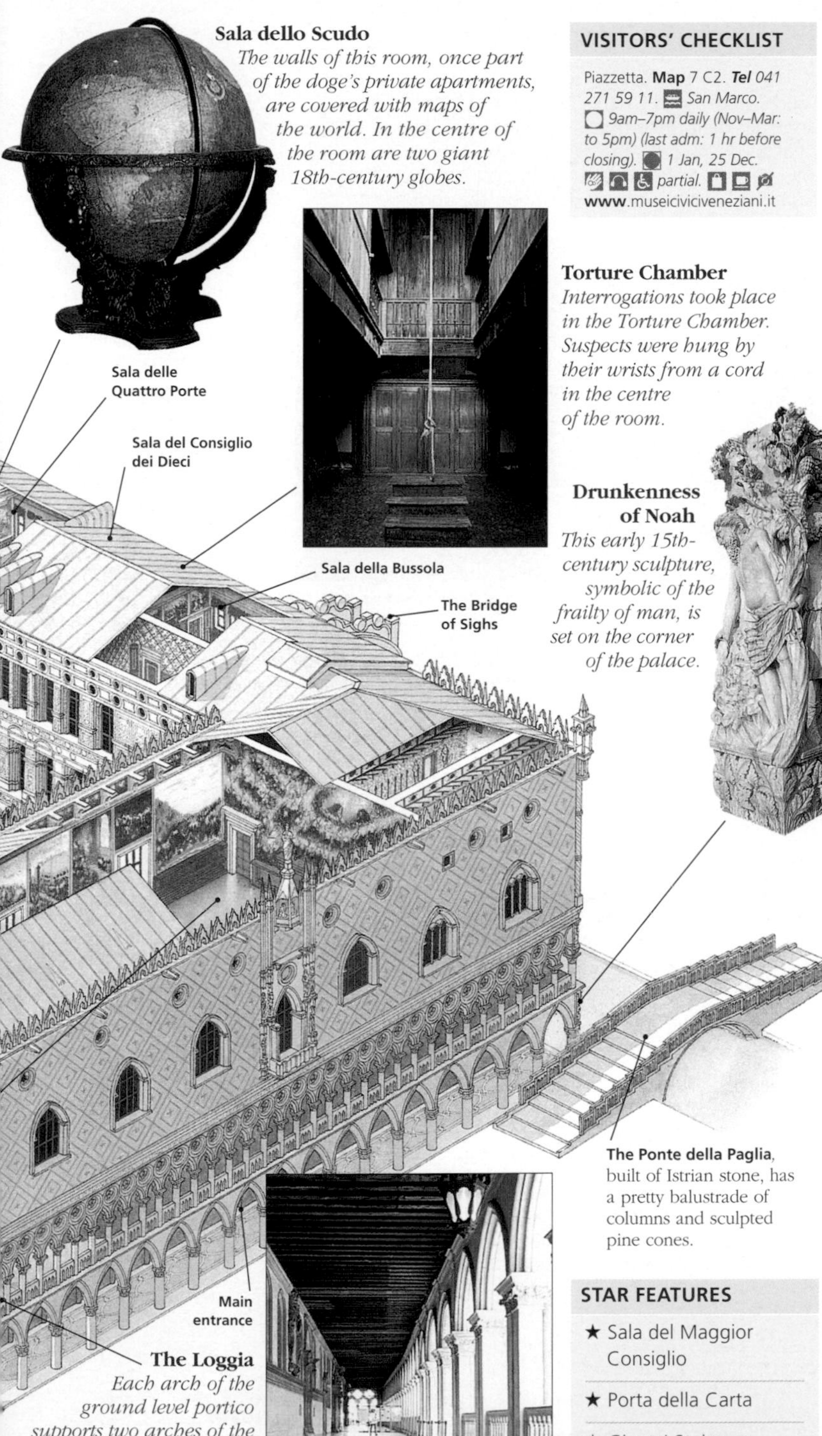


**Sala dello Scudo**
*The walls of this room, once part of the doge's private apartments, are covered with maps of the world. In the centre of the room are two giant 18th-century globes.*

**Torture Chamber**
*Interrogations took place in the Torture Chamber. Suspects were hung by their wrists from a cord in the centre of the room.*

**Drunkenness of Noah**
*This early 15th-century sculpture, symbolic of the frailty of man, is set on the corner of the palace.*

**The Ponte della Paglia**, built of Istrian stone, has a pretty balustrade of columns and sculpted pine cones.

**The Loggia**
*Each arch of the ground level portico supports two arches of the loggia, which commands fine views of the lagoon.*

## VISITORS' CHECKLIST

Piazzetta. **Map** 7 C2. ***Tel*** *041 271 59 11.* *San Marco.* *9am–7pm daily (Nov–Mar: to 5pm) (last adm: 1 hr before closing).* *1 Jan, 25 Dec.* *partial.* **www**.museicivicivenezian.it

## STAR FEATURES

★ Sala del Maggior Consiglio

★ Porta della Carta

★ Giants' Staircase

# Exploring the Palazzo Ducale

A tour of the Palazzo Ducale takes visitors through a succession of richly decorated chambers and halls, arranged over three floors, culminating with the Bridge of Sighs which links the palace to the prisons. Casanova was once imprisoned here and made a daring escape from the Palazzo through a hole in the roof.

**Jacopo and Domenico Tintoretto's *Paradise*, one of the world's largest paintings, in the Sala del Maggior Consiglio**

## SCALA D'ORO AND COURTYARD

A passage from the Porta del Frumento opens into the palace courtyard. The ticket office and palace entrance are to the left. At the top of Antonio Rizzo's 15th-century Giants' Staircase, the new doge would be crowned with the *zogia* or dogal cap. The Scala d'Oro (golden staircase), designed by Jacopo Sansovino, leads to the palace's upper floors. It takes its name, however, from the elaborate gilt stucco vault created by Alessandro Vittoria (1554–8).

## SALA DELLE QUATTRO PORTE TO THE SALA DEL SENATO

The second flight of the Scala d'Oro leads to the Sala delle Quattro Porte, with a ceiling designed by Palladio and frescoed by Tintoretto. The end walls of the next room, the Anticollegio, are decorated with mythological scenes by Tintoretto, while Veronese's masterly *Rape of Europa* (1580), opposite the window, is one of the palace's most dramatic works. The adjoining Sala del Collegio was where the doge and his counsellors met to receive ambassadors and discuss matters of State. Embellishing the magnificent ceiling are 11 paintings by Veronese. In the next room, the Sala del Senato, the doge and some 200 senators discussed foreign affairs. The paintings are by Tintoretto and pupils.

## SALA DEL CONSIGLIO DEI DIECI TO THE ARMERIA

The Sala del Consiglio dei Dieci was the meeting room of the powerful Council of Ten, founded in 1310 to protect State security. Two fine works by Veronese adorn the ceiling: *Age and Youth* and *Juno Offering the Ducal Crown to Venice* (both 1553–4). In the Sala della Bussola, offenders awaited their fate in front of the Council of Ten. The room's *bocca di leone* (lion's mouth), was used to post secret denunciations and was just one of several in the palace. The wooden door here leads to the State Inquisitors' Room and thence to the torture chamber and prisons. The Armoury – one of the finest such collections anywhere in Europe – occupies the following rooms.

***Dialectic* (c.1577) by Veronese in the Palazzo Ducale's Sala del Collegio**

## SALA DEL MAGGIOR CONSIGLIO

The Scala dei Censori leads to the second floor and past the Sala del Guariento and Antonio Rizzo's statues of Adam and Eve (1480s) to the magnificent Sala del Maggior Consiglio. A vast chamber, it was used as a meeting place for the Great Council and for grand State banquets. By the mid-16th century the Great Council had around 2,000 members. Any Venetian of high birth over 25 was entitled to a seat unless he married a commoner.

**A *bocca di leone* for denunciations**

Tintoretto's huge *Paradise* (1587–90) occupies the eastern wall. Measuring 7.45 by 24.65 m (25 by 81 ft), it is one of the largest paintings in the world. The itinerary then continues in more sombre vein, crossing the Bridge of Sighs to enter the dank world of the prisons.

*For hotels and restaurants in this region see pp558–61 and pp606–9*

## Torre dell'Orologio ⓴

Piazza San Marco. **Map** 7 B2. ***Tel*** *041 520 90 70.* San Marco. *10am–4pm (must be pre-booked).*

This richly decorated clock tower on the north side of the piazza was built in the late 15th century. Mauro Coducci is thought to have worked on the design. With its display of the phases of the moon and the signs of the zodiac, the gilt-and-blue enamel clock face was designed with seafarers in mind. According to legend, once the clock was completed, the two inventors of the complex mechanism had their eyes gouged out to prevent them from ever creating a replica.

On the upper level, the winged lion of St Mark stands against a star-spangled blue backdrop. At the very top the two huge bronze figures, known as the *Mori*, or Moors, strike the bell on the hour.

**The clock face of the Torre dell'Orologio**

## Campanile ㉑

Piazza San Marco. **Map** 7 B2. ***Tel*** *041 522 40 64.* San Marco. *Nov–Mar: 9:30am–3:45pm daily (to 4:45pm Sat & Sun); Apr–Oct: 9am–7:30pm daily.*

From the top of St Mark's campanile, high above the piazza, visitors can enjoy views of the city, the lagoon and, visibility permitting, the peaks of the Alps. It was from here that Galileo demonstrated his telescope to Doge Leonardo Donà in 1609. To do so he would have climbed the internal ramp. Access today is via a lift.

The first tower, completed in 1173, was built as a lighthouse to assist navigators in the lagoon. It took on a less benevolent role in the Middle Ages, when offenders were imprisoned – and in some cases left to die – in a cage hung near its summit. With the exception of several 16th-century renovations, the tower survived unharmed until July 1902 when, with little warning, it collapsed. The only casualties were the Loggetta at the foot of the tower and the custodian's cat. Donations flooded in, and in 1903 the foundation stone was laid for a new campanile *"dov'era e com'era"* ("where it was and as it was"). The new tower was opened on 25 April (the Feast of St Mark) 1912. Due to small structural shifts, work has begun to reinforce the foundations and should be completed by 2012.

## Museo Correr ㉒

Procuratie Nuove. Entrance in Ala Napoleonica. **Map** 7 B2. ***Tel*** *041 240 52 11.* San Marco. *Apr–Oct: 9am–7pm; Nov–Mar: 9am–5pm (last adm: 1hr before closing).* *1 Jan, 25 Dec.* *(includes adm to Libreria Sansoviniana and Museo Archeologico).*

Teodoro Correr bequeathed his extensive collection of works of art to Venice in 1830, thus forming the core of the city's fine civic museum.

Its first rooms form a suitably Neo-Classical backdrop for early statues by Antonio Canova (1757–1822). The rest of the floor covers the history of the Venetian Republic, with maps, coins, armour and a host of doge-related exhibits. The second floor contains a picture collection second only to that of the Accademia.

***Young Man in a Red Hat* (c.1490) by Carpaccio in the Museo Correr**

The paintings, hung chronologically, trace the evolution of Venetian painting, and show the influence that Ferrarese, Paduan and Flemish artists had on the Venetian school.

The gallery's most famous works are by Carpaccio: *Portrait of a Young Man in a Red Hat* (c.1490), and *Two Venetian Ladies* (c.1507). The latter is traditionally, but probably incorrectly, known as *The Courtesans* because of the ladies' low-cut dresses. The Museo del Risorgimento on the same floor looks at the history of Venice until unification with Italy in 1866.

**The ceiling of Santo Stefano, built in the form of a ship's keel**

## Santo Stefano ㉓

Campo Santo Stefano. **Map** 6 F2. ***Tel*** *041 275 04 62.* Accademia *or Sant'Angelo.* *10am–5pm Mon–Sat.* *1 Jan, 25 Dec.*

Deconsecrated six times on account of the blood spilled within its walls, Santo Stefano – one of Venice's most beautiful churches – is now remarkably serene. Built in the 14th century, and altered in the 15th, the church has a carved portal by Bartolomeo Bon, and a campanile with a typical Venetian tilt. The interior has a splendid ship's keel ceiling, carved tie-beams, and the sacristy crammed with valuable paintings.

# Santi Giovanni e Paolo 24

Known more colloquially as San Zanipolo, Santi Giovanni e Paolo vies with the Frari *(see pp98–9)* as the city's greatest Gothic church. Built by the Dominicans in the 14th century, it is striking for its vast scale and architectural austerity. Known as the Pantheon of Venice, it houses monuments to no fewer than 25 doges. Among these are several fine works of art, executed by the Lombardi family and other leading sculptors.

**The Nave**
*The cross-vaulted interior is tied by wooden beams and supported by stone columns.*

**The bronze statue** is a monument to Doge Sebastiano Venier, who was Commander of the Fleet at Lepanto.

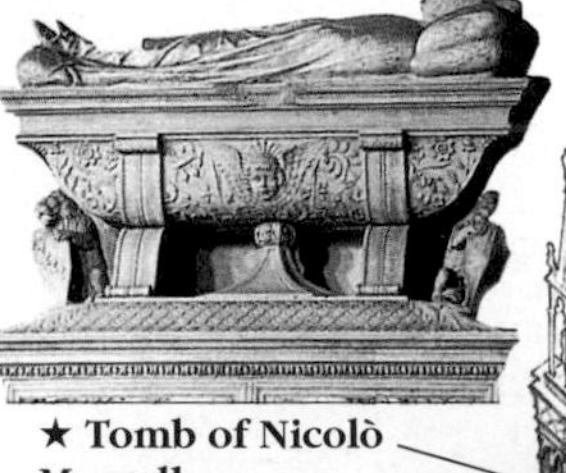

**★ Tomb of Nicolò Marcello**
*This magnificent Renaissance monument to Doge Nicolò Marcello (died 1474) was sculpted by Pietro Lombardo.*

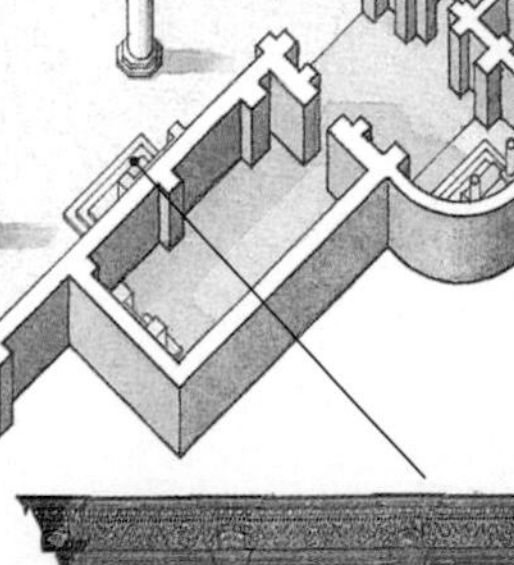

**The doorway**, which is decorated with Byzantine reliefs and carvings by Bartolomeo Bon, is one of Venice's earliest Renaissance architectural works.

Entrance

**★ Tomb of Pietro Mocenigo**
*Pietro Lombardo's superb tomb (1481) commemorates the doge's military pursuits when he was Grand Captain of the Venetian forces.*

**★ Polyptych by Bellini**
*This painting (c.1465) shows St Vincent Ferrer, a Spanish cleric, flanked by St Sebastian and St Christopher.*

## VISITORS' CHECKLIST

Campo Santi Giovanni e Paolo (also signposted San Zanipolo). **Map** 3 C5. ***Tel*** *041 523 59 13.* *Fondamente Nuove, Ospedale Civile.* *9am–6pm daily (from 1pm Sun & religious hols).* *Sun am (for mass).*

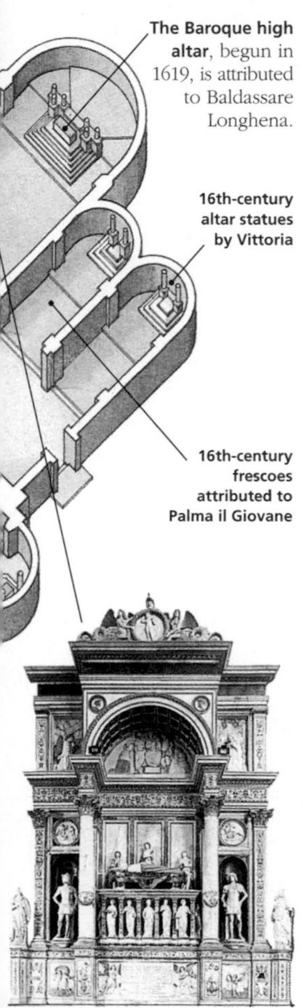


**★ Tomb of Andrea Vendramin**
*Lombardo's masterpiece (1476–8) takes the form of a Roman triumphal arch.*

## STAR FEATURES

★ Doges' Tombs

★ Polyptych by Bellini

# Statue of Colleoni ㉕

Campo Santi Giovanni e Paolo. **Map** 3 C5. *Ospedale Civile.*

Bartolomeo Colleoni, the famous *condottiere* or commander of mercenaries, left his fortune to the Republic on condition that his statue was placed in front of San Marco. A prominent statue in the piazza would have broken with precedent, so the Senate cunningly had Colleoni raised before the Scuola di San Marco instead of the basilica. A touchstone of early Renaissance sculpture, the equestrian statue of the proud warrior (1481–8) is by the Florentine Andrea Verrocchio, but was cast in bronze after his death by Alessandro Leopardi. The statue has a strong sense of power and movement which arguably ranks it alongside the works of Donatello.

# Santa Maria Formosa ㉖

Campo Santa Maria Formosa. **Map** 7 C1. ***Tel*** *041 275 04 62.* *Rialto.* *10am–5pm Mon–Sat.* *1 Jan, 25 Dec.*

Designed by Mauro Coducci in 1492, this church is most unusual in having two main façades – one overlooks the *campo,* the other the canal. The bell tower or campanile, added in 1688, is noted for the grotesque face at its base.

Two paintings stand out in the interior: a triptych (1473) by Bartolomeo Vivarini and Palma il Vecchio's *St Barbara* (c.1510).

# San Zaccaria ㉗

Campo San Zaccaria. **Map** 8 D2. ***Tel*** *041 522 12 57.* *San Zaccaria.* *10am–noon, 4–6pm Mon–Sat, 4–6pm Sun & public hols.* *chapels and crypt.*

Set in a quiet square just a stone's throw from the Riva degli Schiavoni, the church of San Zaccaria is a successful blend of Flamboyant Gothic and Classical Renaissance styles. Founded in the 9th century, its façade was later rebuilt by Antonio Gambello in Gothic style. When Gambello died in 1481, Mauro Coducci completed the upper section, adding many of its Renaissance panels.

The interior's artistic highlight is Giovanni Bellini's serene and sumptuously coloured *Madonna and Child with Saints* (1505) in the north aisle. A door off the right nave leads to the Chapel of St Athanasius, which in turn leads to the Chapel of San Tarasio. The chapel contains vault frescoes (1442) by Andrea del Castagno, and polyptychs (1443– 4) by Antonio Vivarini and Giovanni d'Alemagna.

**Palma il Vecchio's *St Barbara* (c.1510) in Santa Maria Formosa**

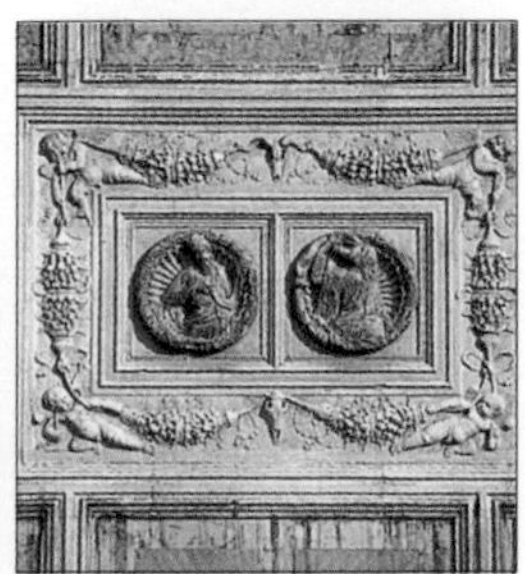
**A Renaissance panel by Coducci on the façade of San Zaccaria**

# Scuola di San Giorgio degli Schiavoni 28

Fondamenta Furlani. **Map** 8 E1. ***Tel*** *041 522 88 28.* *San Zaccaria.* *9:15am–6pm Mon; 9:15am–1pm, 2:45–6pm Tue–Sun (Sun am only).* *1 Jan, 1 May, 25 Dec and other religious hols.*

Within this small gem are some of the finest paintings of Vittore Carpaccio. They were commissioned by the Schiavoni, or Dalmatian Slav community in Venice.

The Scuola was established in 1451 and rebuilt in 1551. It has changed very little since. The exquisite frieze, executed between 1502 and 1508, shows scenes from the lives of patron saints: St George, St Tryphone and St Jerome. Each episode of the narrative cycle is remarkable for its vivid colouring, minute detail and historic record of Venetian life. Outstanding among them are *St George Slaying the Dragon* and *St Jerome Leading the Tamed Lion to the Monastery*.

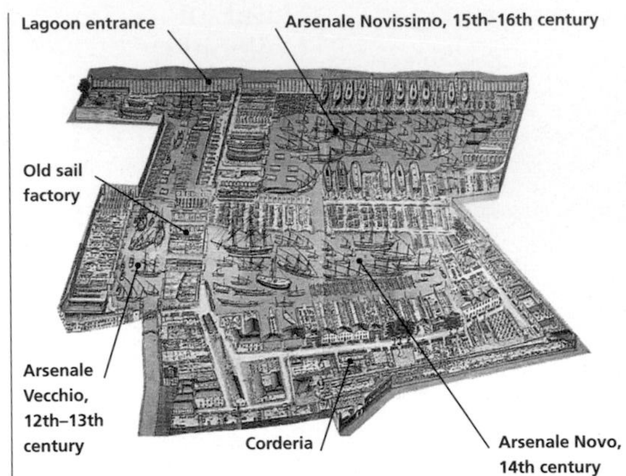


**18th-century engraving of the Arsenale**

# San Giovanni in Bragora 29

Campo Bandiera e Moro. **Map** 8 E2. ***Tel*** *041 520 59 06.* *Arsenale.* *9am–noon Mon–Sat.*

The existing church is essentially Gothic (1475–9), and the interior contains major works of art that demonstrate the transition from Gothic to early Renaissance. Bartolomeo Vivarini's altarpiece *Madonna and Child with Saints* (1478) is unmistakably Gothic. Contrasting with this is Cima da Conegliano's large-scale *Baptism of Christ* (1492–5), which adorns the main altar.

# Arsenale 30

**Map** 8 F1. *Arsenale.* **Museo Storico Navale** Campo San Biagio. **Map** 8 F3. ***Tel*** *041 520 02 76.* *8:45am–1:30pm Mon–Fri; 8:45am–1pm Sat.* *public hols.*

The Arsenale was founded in the 12th century and by the 16th had become the greatest naval shipyard in the world, capable of constructing a whole galley in 24 hours, using an assembly-line system. Surrounded by crenellated walls, it was like a city within a city. Today the site is largely disused. Its impressive 15th-century gateway, twin towers and guardian lions can be viewed from the *campo* or bridge outside. The gateway was built by Antonio Gambello and is often cited as Venice's first Renaissance construction.

Around the corner, in Campo San Biagio, the **Museo Storico Navale** charts Venetian naval history from the heyday of the Arsenale to the present. Exhibits include friezes from famous galleys of the past and a replica of the *Bucintoro*, the Doge's ceremonial barge.

# San Giorgio Maggiore 31

**Map** 8 D4. ***Tel*** *041 522 78 27.* *San Giorgio.* *9:30am–12:30pm, 2:30–6pm daily (to 5pm in winter).* *(Campanile).* **Fondazione Cini** ***Tel*** *041 271 02 29.* *by appt Mon–Fri; 10am–4pm Sat & Sun (to 5pm May–Sep).*

Appearing like a stage set across the water from the Piazzetta is the little island

***St George Slaying the Dragon*** **(1502–8) by Carpaccio, in the Scuola di San Giorgio degli Schiavoni**

of San Giorgio Maggiore. The church and monastery, constructed between 1559–80, are among Andrea Palladio's greatest architectural achievements. The church's temple front and the spacious interior with its perfect proportions and cool beauty are typically Palladian *(see pp80–81)*. These qualities are echoed by the church of Il Redentore on the nearby island of Giudecca, built by Palladio in 1577–92.

On the chancel walls of San Giorgio Maggiore, are two fine paintings by Tintoretto: *The Last Supper* and *Gathering of the Manna* (both 1594). In the Chapel of the Dead is his last work, *The Deposition* (1592–4), finished by his son Domenico.

The top of the campanile affords superb views of the city and lagoon. You can see the monastery cloisters below, now part of the **Fondazione Cini**, a cultural centre that is used to host international exhibitions.

Palladio's San Giorgio Maggiore

## Murano 32

LN, 41 and 42 from Fondamente Nuove; DM from Ferrovia and Piazzale Roma.

Much like Venice, Murano comprises a cluster of small islands, connected by bridges. It has been the centre of the glassmaking industry since 1291, when the furnaces were moved here from the city because of the risk of fire and the disagreeable effects of smoke. Some of the houses on the water date from this period.

The colonnaded exterior of Murano's Basilica dei Santi Maria e Donato

### Museo Vetrario

Palazzo Giustinian, Fondamenta Giustinian. **Tel** *041 73 95 86.* *10am–6pm (Nov–Mar: to 5pm) Thu–Tue.* *1 Jan, 1 May, 25 Dec.*

In the 15th and 16th centuries Murano was the principal glass-producing centre in Europe and today, most tourists visit for glass alone. The Museo Vetrario in the Palazzo Giustinian houses a fine collection of antique pieces. The prize exhibit is the dark blue Barovier wedding cup (1470–80), with enamel work by Angelo Barovier.

### Basilica dei Santi Maria e Donato

Fondamenta Giustinian. **Tel** *041 73 90 56.* *8:30am–6pm daily.*

With its lovely colonnaded apse, this basilica is the architectural highlight of the island. Despite some heavy-handed restoration undertaken in the 19th century, this 12th-century church still retains much of its original beauty. Visitors should note the Gothic ship's keel roof, the apse with its mosaic Madonna and the beautiful medieval mosaic floor, which dates from 1140.

## Burano 33

*LN from Fondamente Nuove; LN from San Zaccaria via Lido and Punta Sabbioni.*

Burano is the most colourful of the lagoon islands and can be distinguished from a distance by the tilting tower of its church. In contrast with the haunting Torcello, the island is densely populated, its waterways fringed with brightly painted houses.

The main thoroughfare is Via Baldassare Galuppi, named after the Burano-born composer. It features traditional lace and linen stalls and open-air trattorias serving fresh fish.

### Museo dei Merletto

Piazza Baldassare Galuppi. **Tel** *041 73 00 34.* *Apr–Oct: 10am–5pm Wed–Mon; Nov–Mar: 10am–4pm.* *1 Jan, 1 May, 25 Dec.*

Venetian glass goblet

The people of Burano are fishermen and lacemakers by tradition. You can still see fishermen scraping their boats or mending nets, but today lacemakers are rare. In the 16th century the local lace was the most sought-after in Europe – it was so delicate it became known as *punto in aria* ("points in the air"). After a slump in the 18th century, the industry revived and a lacemaking school was set up here in 1872. Authentic Burano lace is hard to find, but you can watch it being made at the school, now a museum, which also displays fine examples of antique lace.

Brightly painted street in Burano

# Torcello 34

Established between the 5th and 6th centuries, the island of Torcello boasts the oldest building in the lagoon – the cathedral of Santa Maria dell'Assunta. Founded in AD 639, it contains some splendid ancient mosaics. The adjoining church of Santa Fosca, of pure Byzantine design, is another mark of Torcello's former glory – before being eclipsed by Venice it had a population of 20,000.

**★ Apse Mosaic**
*The 13th-century Madonna, set against a gold background, is one of the most beautiful mosaics in Venice.*

**★ Doomsday Mosaics**
*The highly decorative 12th-century mosaic of the* Last Judgment *covers the west wall.*

**Pulpit**
*The present basilica dates from 1008, but includes earlier features. The pulpit contains 7th-century fragments.*

**The Roman sarcophagus** below the altar is said to contain the relics of St Heliodorus.

**★ Iconostasis**
*The exquisite Byzantine marble panels of the rood screen are carved with peacocks, lions and flowers.*

**Nave Columns**
*Two rows of slender marble columns, 18 in all, separate the three naves. Their finely carved capitals date from the 11th century.*

*For hotels and restaurants in this region see pp558–61 and pp606–9*

**Torcello's Last Canals**
*Silted canals and malaria hastened Torcello's decline. One of the remaining waterways runs from the* vaporetto *stop to the basilica.*

## VISITORS' CHECKLIST

*LN from Fondamente Nuove then T from Burano.* **Santa Maria & Campanile** ***Tel*** *041 296 06 30.* *10:30am–6pm daily (Nov–Feb: 10am–5pm). Campanile closes 30 mins earlier.* *cathedral only.* *campanile only.* **Santa Fosca** *for masses only.* **Museo dell'Estuario** ***Tel*** *041 73 07 61.* *10:30am–5:30pm Tue–Sun (Nov–Feb: 10am–5pm).* *public hols.*

**The altar** was rebuilt in 1939 and stands below a 15th-century wood relief of *Santa Fosca Sleeping*.

**The central dome** and cross sections are supported by columns of Greek marble with Corinthian capitals.

**Santa Fosca**
*Built in the 11th and 12th centuries on a Greek-cross plan, the church has a serene Byzantine interior with a central pentagonal apse.*

**The Portico** of Santa Fosca, with its elegant stilted arches, is built on three sides of the church, and probably dates from the 12th century.

***Vaporetto* boarding point** →

**The Museo dell'Estuario** houses many old church treasures.

## STAR FEATURES

★ Iconostasis

★ Doomsday Mosaics

★ Apse Mosaics

**Attila's Throne**
*It was said that the 5th-century king of the Huns used this marble seat as his throne.*

# Shopping in Venice

The attractive shop windows that line the narrow streets of Venice are an irresistible attraction for any visitor. Myriad fashion brands are available in gleaming ultra-modern stores, but the city also has a strong artisan tradition. Expert craftspeople in tiny workshops open to the public create delightful and highly original objects in glass, wood, leather and papier-mâché. Skilled hands transform coloured glass rods into playful miniature animals and exquisite flowers, while plaster moulds turn out shapes destined to become ornate masks. Interior-design establishments also abound, and sleek kitchenware and fabrics make unusual purchases. Beautiful boutiques offering antique furniture and accessories are concentrated in the city centre.

## WHERE TO SHOP

The glittering Mercerie, which runs from Piazza San Marco to the Rialto, has been Venice's main shopping street since the Middle Ages and, along with the fashion avenue Calle Larga XXII Marzo, is still a draw for the crowds. The zigzagging Frezzeria is full of unusual shops, while across the Grand Canal, the narrow streets from the Rialto southwest towards Campo San Polo are lined with a variety of less expensive stores. The bustling Lista di Spagna, near the station, and the Strada Nova towards the Rialto cater for the everyday needs of the locals.

The islands of Murano and Burano are the places to buy traditional glass and lace.

## FOOD AND MARKETS

One of the delights of Venice is exploring the city's food markets and shops. Fruit and vegetable stalls sprawl to the west of the Rialto Bridge and along the Grand Canal. The Pescheria, or fish market, occupies the furthest section. The neighbouring streets are full of gourmet food shops. Wine, olive oil, vinegar and grappa in decorative bottles, as well as dried pasta in many shapes, colours and flavours are all good purchases.

**Aliani**'s cheese shop offers a mouthwatering selection of picnic fare, while **Drogheria Mascari** has a fine range of dried fruit, coffee and alcohol. **Rizzo**, on the other side of the bridge, is a master pasta-maker.

## GLASS

The island of Murano is a good place to watch expert glass-blowing. However, for contemporary glass creations head back to Venice, around San Marco – try **Venini**'s showroom for stunning platters and huge vases, and **L'Isola** for Carlo Moretti's tumblers in rich colours.

The art of bead-making is alive and flourishing thanks to sisters **Marina e Susanna Sent**'s simple, irresistible necklaces. At **Antichità Claudia Zaggia**, customers can sort through an astonishing range of beautiful antique beads and create their own necklaces.

## CLOTHING AND ACCESSORIES

**Promod**, near San Marco, has reasonably priced fun gear for the young set. Nearby is **Benetton**'s megastore, with its trademark bright clothes, while, opposite, **Max Mara** has superlative womenswear. Other leading names in fashion – **Armani**, **Roberto Cavalli**, **Missoni** and **Gucci** – also have stylish shops around Piazza San Marco.

Just off San Lio, **Giovanna Zanella** can be found at her cobbler's bench crafting zany shoes and sandals. Her amazing range even includes gondola decorations.

## MASKS AND COSTUMES

Mass-produced Carnival masks can be found all over the city, but a genuine one makes for a wonderful souvenir. With its striking designs, **Papier Mâché** has revived traditional mask-making. Near Campo San Polo, **Tragicomica** sells masks and costumes, as well as Commedia dell'Arte figures. You will also find these at **Leon d'Oro**, where they make string puppets too. At the end of Calle Larga XXII Marzo is **La Ricerca**, a showcase for the De Marchi brothers' remarkable leather masks. Dorsoduro also has several outstanding workshops: **Mondonovo**, just off Campo Santa Margherita, has a marvellous selection of masks, some of which featured in the Kubrick film *Eyes Wide Shut*.

## JEWELLERY

**Nardi**, located in the arcades of Piazza San Marco, crafts an exquisite brooch with a moor's head, among other things. A short distance away are the sparkling premises of **Bulgari**, while **Cartier**, with its beautiful collection of watches, can be found along the nearby Mercerie. Shops on the Rialto Bridge sell cheaper designs; this is a good place to find bracelets and chains, the prices of which are determined by the weight of the gold. Over the bridge, under the arcades of the ancient goldsmiths' district, is **Attombri** – two brothers who design unusual jewellery from antique Murano glass beads.

## FABRICS AND INTERIOR DESIGN

Venice is famed for fine silks and velvets and sumptuous brocades, many of which are still sold at **Trois**, close to the Gritti Palace hotel. On the Grand Canal, at Sant'Angelo, **Rubelli** is fabric heaven, with a wide range of designs and rich upholstery. More down-to-earth but good-quality household linen and brilliantly coloured bath accessories are sold at **TSL**, which has several stores around town.

For original kitchen items, the choice at **Epicentro** is hard to beat; or head to **Marchiol**, hidden away in a Castello backstreet, for modern light fittings and lamps.

## BOOKS AND GIFTS

At the Giardinetti Reali, on the San Marco waterfront, the **Venice Pavilion Bookshop** annexe of the Tourist Board has an exhaustive collection of books dealing with many aspects of the city. The **Libreria Mondadori** bookstore offers a decent English-language section, while **Mare di Carta** offers nautical books and magazines.

**Alberto Valese-Ebru** uses a distinctive marbling technique on fabrics as well as paper. Nearby, **Paolo Olbi** has a wide range of papers and artistic books for sale.

On the opposite side of the Grand Canal, at San Tomà, **Daniela Porto** has lovely old printed maps and frames, perfect as gifts, and **Signor Blum** on Campo San Barnaba has charming hand-made carved and painted wooden objects and toys.

## DIRECTORY

### FOOD AND MARKETS

**Aliani (Casa del Parmigiano)**
Erberia Rialto, San Polo 214/8. **Map** 3 A5.
***Tel*** *041 520 6525.*

**Drogheria Mascari**
Ruga Rialto, Calle dei Spezeri, San Polo 381.
**Map** 3 A5.
***Tel*** *041 522 9762.*

**Rizzo**
Salizzada S. Giovanni Grisostomo, Cannaregio 5778. **Map** 3 B5.
***Tel*** *041 522 2824.*

### GLASS

**Antichità Claudia Zaggia**
Calle Toletta, Dorsoduro 1195. **Map** 6 D3.
***Tel*** *041 522 31 59.*

**L'Isola – Carlo Moretti**
Campo San Moisè, San Marco 1468.
**Map** 7 A3.
***Tel*** *041 523 1973.*

**Marina e Susanna Sent**
Campo S. Vio, Dorsoduro 669. **Map** 6 F4.
***Tel*** *041 520 81 36.*

**Venini**
Piazzetta dei Leoncini, San Marco 314.
**Map** 7 B2.
***Tel*** *041 522 4045.*

### CLOTHING AND ACCESSORIES

**Armani**
Calle Goldoni, San Marco 4412.
**Map** 7 A2.
***Tel*** *041 523 4758.*

**Benetton**
Via II Aprile, San Marco 5051. **Map** 7 B2.
***Tel*** *041 296 0493.*

**Giovanna Zanella**
Calle Carminati, Castello 5641. **Map** 7 B1.
***Tel*** *041 523 5500.*

**Gucci**
Calle Larga XXII Marzo, San Marco 2102.
**Map** 7 A3.
***Tel*** *041 241 3968.*

**Max Mara**
Campo San Salvador, San Marco 5033.
**Map** 7 A1.
***Tel*** *041 522 6688.*

**Missoni**
Calle Vallaresso, San Marco 1312. **Map** 7 B3.
***Tel*** *041 520 5733.*

**Promod**
Campo S. Bartolomeo, San Marco 5377. **Map** 7 B1.
***Tel*** *041 241 0668.*

**Roberto Cavalli**
Calle Villaresso, San Marco 1314. **Map** 7 B3.
***Tel*** *041 520 5733.*

### MASKS AND COSTUMES

**Leon d'Oro**
Frezzeria, San Marco 1770.
**Map** 7 A2.
***Tel*** *041 520 3375.*

**Mondonovo**
Rio Terrà Canal, Dorsoduro 3063.
**Map** 6 D3.
***Tel*** *041 528 7344.*

**Papier Mâché**
Calle Lunga Santa Maria Formosa, Castello 5175.
**Map** 7 C1.
***Tel*** *041 522 9995.*

**La Ricerca**
Ponte delle Ostreghe, San Marco 2431.
**Map** 7 A3.
***Tel*** *041 522 8250.*

**Tragicomica**
Calle dei Nomboli, San Polo 2800.
**Map** 6 F1.
***Tel*** *041 721 102.*

### JEWELLERY

**Attombri**
Sottoportego degli Orefici, San Polo 74.
**Map** 3 A5.
***Tel*** *041 521 2524.*

**Bulgari**
Calle Larga XXII Marzo, San Marco 2282.
**Map** 7 A3.
***Tel*** *041 241 0553.*

**Cartier**
Mercerie San Zulian, San Marco 606.
**Map** 7 B2.
***Tel*** *041 522 2071.*

**Nardi**
Procuratie Nuove, Piazza San Marco, San Marco 69/71. **Map** 7 B2.
***Tel*** *041 522 5733.*

### FABRICS AND INTERIOR DESIGN

**Epicentro**
Frezzeria, San Marco 1728/A. **Map** 7 B2.
***Tel*** *041 523 34 92.*

**Marchiol**
Ruga Giuffa, Castello 4920. **Map** 7 C1.
***Tel*** *041 522 5131.*

**Rubelli**
Campiello del Teatro, San Marco 3877.
**Map** 6 F2.
***Tel*** *041 523 6110.*

**Trois**
Campo San Maurizio, San Marco 2666.
**Map** 6 F3.
***Tel*** *041 522 2905.*

**TSL Tessile San Leonardo**
Rio Terrà San Leonardo, Cannaregio 1318.
**Map** 2 D3.
***Tel*** *041 718 524.*

### BOOKS AND GIFTS

**Alberto Valese-Ebru**
Campiello Santo Stefano, San Marco 3471.
**Map** 6 F3.
***Tel*** *041 523 8830.*

**Daniela Porto**
Rio Terrà dei Nomboli, San Polo 2753.
**Map** 6 E1.
***Tel*** *041 523 1368.*

**Libreria Mondadori**
Salizzada San Moisè, San Marco 1345.
**Map** 7 A3.
***Tel*** *041 522 2193.*

**Mare di Carta**
Fondamenta dei Tolentini, Santa Croce 222.
**Map** 5 C1.
***Tel*** *041 716 304.*

**Paolo Olbi**
Calle della Mandola, San Marco 3653.
**Map** 6 F2.
***Tel*** *041 528 5025.*

**Signor Blum**
Campo San Barnaba, Dorsoduro 2840.
**Map** 6 D3.
***Tel*** *041 522 6367.*

**Venice Pavilion Bookshop**
Palazzetto Selva, Giardinetti Reali, San Marco 2. **Map** 7 B3.
***Tel*** *041 522 5150.*

# VENICE STREET FINDER

All the map references given for sights, hotels and restaurants in Venice refer to this section of the book. The key map below shows which areas of the city are covered by the Street Finder. The first figure of the map reference indicates which map to turn to, and the letter and number which follow are for the grid reference. Standard Italian spelling has been used on all the maps in this book, but when exploring Venice you will find that the names on many street signs are written in Venetian dialect. Mostly this means only a slight variation in spelling (as in the word Sotoportico/Sotoportego below), but some names look totally different. For example, the church of Santi Giovanni e Paolo *(see map 3)*, is frequently signposted as "San Zanipolo". A further map showing the vaporetto routes follows the street maps.

### RECOGNIZING STREET NAMES

The signs for street *(calle)*, canal *(rio)* and square *(campo)* will soon become familiar, but the Venetians have a colourful vocabulary for the maze of alleys which makes up the city. When exploring, the following may help.

FONDAMENTA S.SEVERO

**Fondamenta** is a street that runs alongside a canal, often named after the canal it follows.

RIO TERRA GESUATI

**Rio Terrà** is a filled-in canal. Similar to a *rio terrà* is a *piscina*, which often forms a square.

SOTOPORTEGO E PONTE S.CRISTOFORO

**Sotoportico or Sotoportego** means a covered passageway.

SALIZADA PIO X

**Salizzada** is a main street (formerly a paved street).

RIVA DEI PARTIGIANI

**Riva** is a wide *fondamenta,* often facing the lagoon.

RUGAGIUFFA

**Ruga** is a street lined with shops.

CORTE DEI DO POZZI

**Corte** means a courtyard.

RIO MENUO O DE LA VERONA

**Many streets and canals** in Venice often have more than one name: o means "or".

0 metres 500

0 yards 500

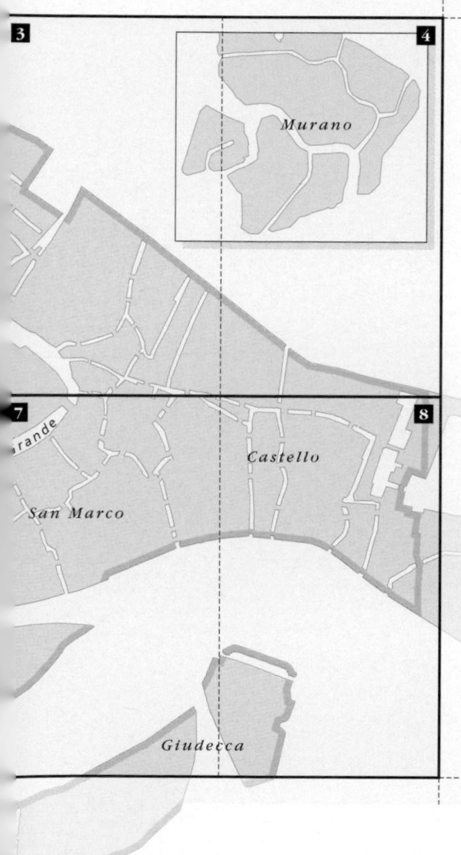


**KEY TO STREET FINDER**

- Major sight
- Place of interest
- Railway station
- Ferry boarding point
- Vaporetto boarding point
- Traghetto crossing
- Gondola mooring
- Bus terminus
- Tourist information
- Hospital with casualty unit
- Parking
- Police station
- Church
- Synagogue
- Post office
- Railway line

**SCALE OF MAP PAGES**

0 metres 150

0 yards 150

**SCALE OF MURANO INSET**

0 metres 300

0 yards 300

Canale delle
Canale Colambola
PONTE DELLA LIBERTA
FONDAMENTA DI SACCA SAN GIROLAMO
SACCA DI SAN GIROLAMO
CALLE LARGA DEI PENITENTI
FONDAMENTA CASE NUOVE
CALLE FERAU
CALLE DEL FORNER
CPLO DELLE COOPERATIVE
Canale di Cannaregio
FONDAMENTA DI SAN GIOBBE
Ponte dei Tre Archi
Ponte dei Tre Archi
CALLE DELLE BECCARIE
CPLO D. BECCARIE
CD. MAGAZEN
CALLE D. CANNE
CALLE D. SCARLATTO
CD. COLORI
CALLE D. TINTOR
CALLE BISCOTELLA
CALLE DELLA CERERIA
Rio di San Giobbe
San Giobbe
CAMPO SAN GIOBBE
Crea
Rio della Crea
Rio della Crea
FONDAMENTA
FMTA SAVORGN
CALLE TINTORIA
CD. PORPORA
CALLE D. MADONNA
CALLE D. STP SCURO
CALLE BUSELLO
CALLE CENDON
CALLE SECONDA D. DO
CALLE PESARO
CALLE DELLA MISE
CALLE PRIULI DETTA DEI CAVALLETTI
CALLE CARMELITANI
Scalzi
FMTA D. SCALZI
Ponte degli Scal
Stazione Ferrovie dello Stato Santa Lucia
FONDAMENTA SANTA LUCIA
Ferrovia
FONDAMENTA SAN SIMEON PICCOLO
CALLE TRAGHETTO DI SANTA LUCIA
CALLE BERGAMASCHI
Can d. Santa Chiara
FONDAMENTA DI SANTA CHIARA
FONDAMENTA DI SANTA CHIARA
C VOLTO
Piazzale Roma
Ponte della Costituzione
FONDAMENTA CROCE
FONDAMENTA DEI TOLENTINI
GIARDINO EX PAPADOPOLI
CORTE CASE NUOVE
CAMPO DELL

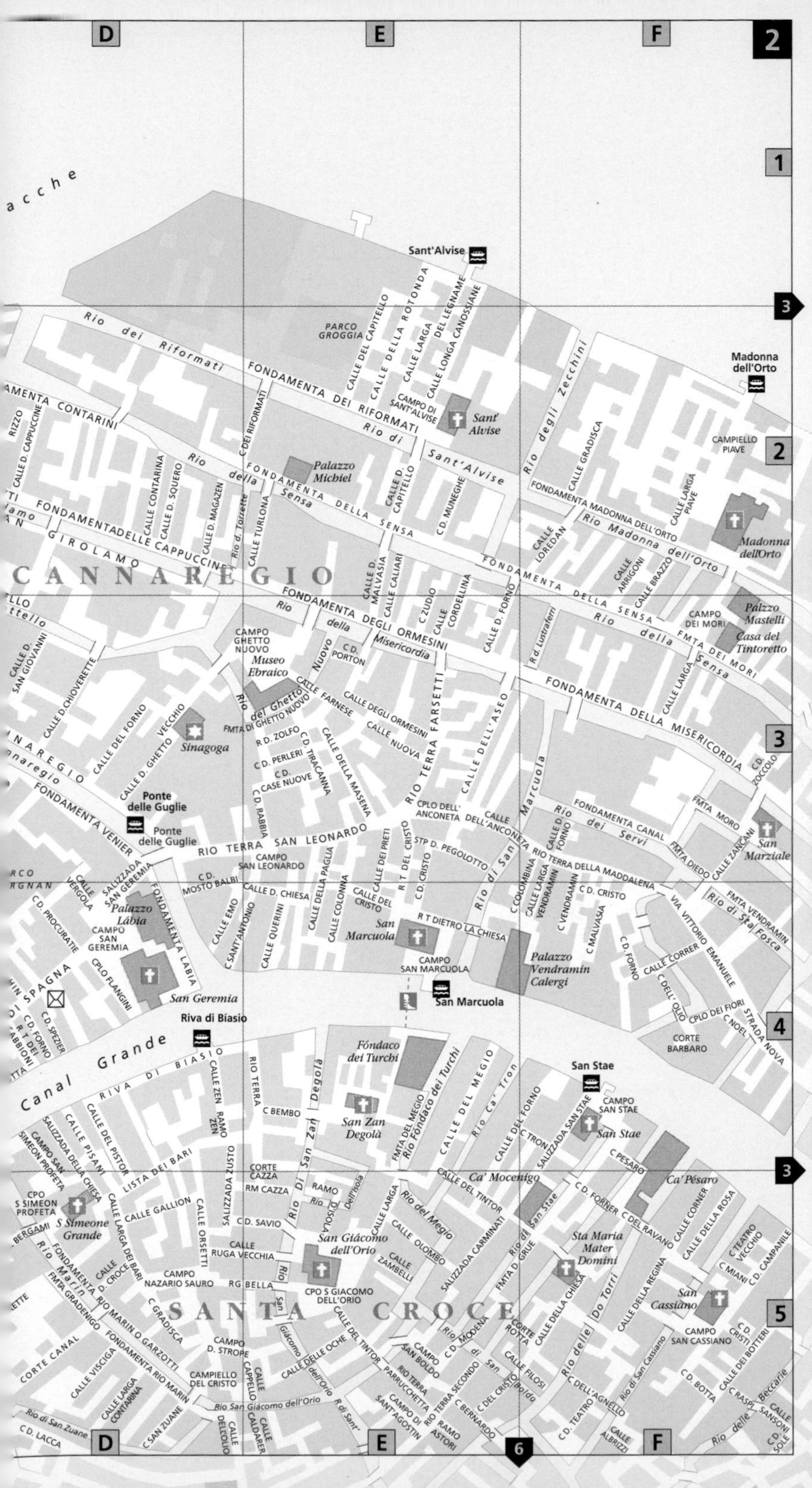

D
E
F
2
1
2
3
4
5
3
3
6
Sant'Alvise
PARCO GROGGIA
CALLE DEL CAPITELLO
CALLE DELLA ROTONDA
CALLE LARGA
DEL LEGNAME
CALLE LONGA CANOSSIANE
CAMPO DI SANT'ALVISE
Sant' Alvise
Rio dei Riformati
FONDAMENTA DEI RIFORMATI
Rio di Sant'Alvise
Madonna dell'Orto
CAMPIELLO PIAVE
Rio degli Zecchini
CALLE GRADISCA
CALLE LARGA PIAVE
FONDAMENTA MADONNA DELL'ORTO
Rio Madonna dell'Orto
Madonna dell'Orto
FONDAMENTA CONTARINI
Rio della Sensa
FONDAMENTA DELLA SENSA
Palazzo Michiel
CALLE D. CAPITELLO
C.D. MUNEGHE
C DEI RIFORMATI
CALLE CONTARINA
CALLE D. SQUERO
CALLE D. MAGAZEN
Rio d. Torrette
CALLE TURLONA
CALLE D. CAPPUCCINE
FONDAMENTA DELLE CAPPUCCINE
GIROLAMO
CANNAREGIO
CALLE LOREDAN
CALLE ARRIGONI
CALLE BRAZZO
FONDAMENTA DELLA SENSA
Rio della Sensa
FMTA DEI MORI
CAMPO DEI MORI
Palzzo Mastelli
Casa del Tintoretto
FONDAMENTA DEGLI ORMESINI
Rio della Misericordia
CALLE D. MALVASIA
CALLE CALIARI
C. ZUDIO
CALLE CORDELLINA
CALLE D. FORNO
Rd. Lustraferri
CAMPO GHETTO NUOVO
Museo Ebraico
Rio del Ghetto Nuovo
C.D. PORTON
CALLE FARNESE
CALLE DEGLI ORMESINI
CALLE NUOVA
RIO TERRA FARSETTI
CALLE DELL'ASEO
FONDAMENTA DELLA MISERICORDIA
CALLE LARGA
C.D. ZOCCOLO
CALLE D. SAN GIOVANNI
CALLE D. CHIOVERETTE
CALLE DEL FORNO
CALLE D. GHETTO VECCHIO
Sinagoga
FMTA DI GHETTO NUOVO
R D. ZOLFO
C.D. PERLERI
C.D. TIRACANNA
C.D. CASE NUOVE
CALLE DELLA MASENA
C.D. RABBIA
Ponte delle Guglie
FONDAMENTA VENIER
RIO TERRA SAN LEONARDO
CAMPO SAN LEONARDO
CPLO DELL' ANCONETA
CALLE DELL'ANCONETA
STP D. PEGOLOTTO
Rio di San Marcuola
FONDAMENTA CANAL
Rio dei Servi
FMTA MORO
FMTA DIEDO
CALLE ZANCANI
San Marziale
RIO TERRA DELLA MADDALENA
C.D. CRISTO
VIA VITTORIO EMANUELE
FMTA VENDRAMIN
Rio di Sta Fosca
SALIZZADA SAN GEREMIA
FONDAMENTA LABIA
C.D. MOSTO BALBI
CALLE D. CHIESA
CALLE DEI PRETI
R T DEL CRISTO
C.D. CRISTO
CALLE DELLA PAGLIA
CALLE COLONNA
CALLE DEL CRISTO
C COLOMBINA
CALLE LARGA VENDRAMIN
C VENDRAMIN
C MALVASIA
C.D. FORNO
CALLE CORRER
C.D. PROCURATIE
CALLE VERGOLA
Palazzo Làbia
CAMPO SAN GEREMIA
CPLO FLANGINI
San Geremia
CALLE EMO
C SANT'ANTONIO
CALLE QUERINI
San Marcuola
R T DIETRO LA CHIESA
CAMPO SAN MARCUOLA
San Marcuola
Palazzo Vendramin Calergi
C DELL' OLIO
CPLO DEI FIORI
C NOEL
STRADA NOVA
CORTE BARBARO
SPAGNA
C.D. SPEZIER
C.D. FORNO
Riva di Biasio
Canal Grande
RIVA DI BIASIO
CALLE ZEN
RAMO ZEN
RIO TERRA
C BEMBO
Rio di San Zan Degolà
Fóndaco dei Turchi
San Zan Degolà
FMTA DEL MEGIO
Rio Fondaco dei Turchi
CALLE DEL MEGIO
Rio Ca' Tron
CALLE DEL FORNO
C TRON
San Stae
CAMPO SAN STAE
SALIZZADA SAN STAE
San Stae
C PESARO
Ca' Pésaro
Ca' Mocenigo
CALLE DEL TINTOR
C.D. FORNER
C DEL RAVANO
CALLE CORNER
CALLE DELLA ROSA
SALIZZADA DELLA CHIESA
CAMPO SAN SIMEON PROFETA
CALLE PISANI
CALLE DEL PISTOR
LISTA DEI BARI
SALIZZADA ZUSTO
CORTE CAZZA
RM CAZZA
RAMO DELL'ISOLA
Rio Dell'Isola
CALLE LARGA
Rio del Megio
Rio di San Stae
CPO S SIMEON PROFETA
S Simeone Grande
CALLE GALLION
CALLE ORSETTI
C.D. SAVIO
CALLE RUGA VECCHIA
San Giácomo dell'Orio
CALLE OLOMBO
CALLE ZAMBELLI
SALIZZADA CARMINATI
FMTA D. GRUE
Sta Maria Mater Domini
C TEATRO VECCHIO
C MIANI
C.D. CAMPANILE
BERGAMI
Rio Marin
FONDAMENTA RIO MARIN
FMTA GRADENIGO
CALLE LARGA DEI BARI
C.D. CROCE
CAMPO NAZARIO SAURO
RG BELLA
Rio di San Giácomo
CPO S GIACOMO DELL'ORIO
SANTA CROCE
CALLE DELLA CHIESA
Rio delle Do Torri
CALLE DELLA REGINA
San Cassiano
CAMPO SAN CASSIANO
C.D. CRISTI
C GRADISCA
FONDAMENTA RIO MARIN O GARZOTTI
CAMPO D. STROPE
CALLE DEL TINTOR
CALLE DELLE OCHE
CAMPO SAN BOLDO
C.D. MODENA
Rio di San Boldo
CORTE ROTTA
CALLE FILOSI
Rio delle
CALLE DEI BOTTERI
CORTE CANAL
CALLE VISCIGA
CALLE LARGA CONTARINA
CAMPIELLO DEL CRISTO
CALLE CAPPELLO
Rio San Giácomo dell'Orio
RIO TERRA PARRUCHETTA
CAMPO DI SANT'AGOSTIN
RIO TERRA SECONDO
RAMO ASTORI
C BERNARDO
C.D. CRISTO
C DELL'AGNELLO
Rio di San Cassiano
C.D. BOTTA
C RASPI
Rio delle Beccarie
CALLE SANSONI
C.D. SOLE
Rio di San Zuane
C.D. LACCA
C SAN ZUANE
CALLE DELL'OLIO
CALLE CALDARER
C.D. TEATRO
CALLE ALBRIZZI

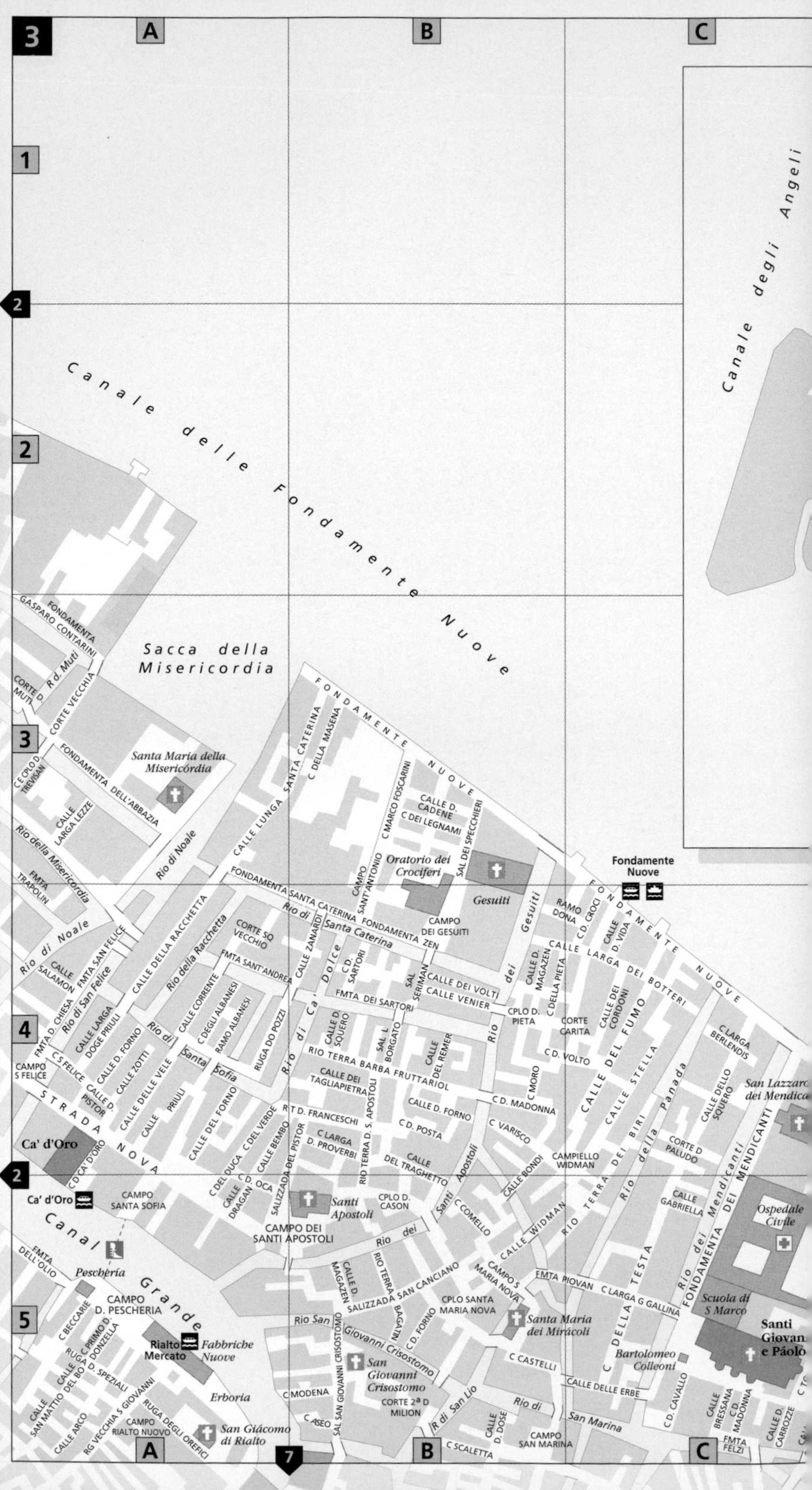

3
A
B
C
1
2
3
4
5
Canale delle Fondamente Nuove
Canale degli Angeli
Sacca della Misericordia
Santa Maria della Misericórdia
Oratorio dei Crociferi
Gesuiti
Fondamente Nuove
Ca' d'Oro
Canal Grande
Pescheria
Rialto Mercato
Fabbriche Nuove
Erboria
San Giácomo di Rialto
Santi Apostoli
CAMPO DEI SANTI APOSTOLI
San Giovanni Crisostomo
Santa Maria dei Miràcoli
Bartolomeo Colleoni
Scuola di S Marco
Santi Giovanni e Pàolo
Ospedale Civile
San Lazzaro dei Mendicanti
FONDAMENTE NUOVE
FONDAMENTA GASPARO CONTARINI
CORTE VECCHIA
FONDAMENTA DELL'ABBAZIA
CALLE LUNGA SANTA CATERINA
FONDAMENTA SANTA CATERINA
CALLE DELLA RACCHETTA
Rio della Misericordia
Rio di Noale
Rio di San Felice
Rio di Santa Caterina
STRADA NOVA
CAMPO SANTA SOFIA
CAMPO D. PESCHERIA
CAMPO DEI GESUITI
CALLE LARGA DEI BOTTERI
CALLE DEL FUMO
CALLE STELLA
RIO TERRA BARBA FRUTTARIOL
RIO TERRA DEI BIRI
Rio della Panada
Rio dei Mendicanti
FONDAMENTA DEI MENDICANTI
SALIZZADA SAN CANCIANO
CAMPIELLO WIDMAN
CALLE WIDMAN
CALLE DELLA TESTA
FMTA PIOVAN
C LARGA G GALLINA
CALLE DELLE ERBE
Rio di San Marina
CAMPO SAN MARINA
C SCALETTA
CORTE 2ª D MILION
CAMPO RIALTO NUOVO
RUGA DEGLI OREFICI

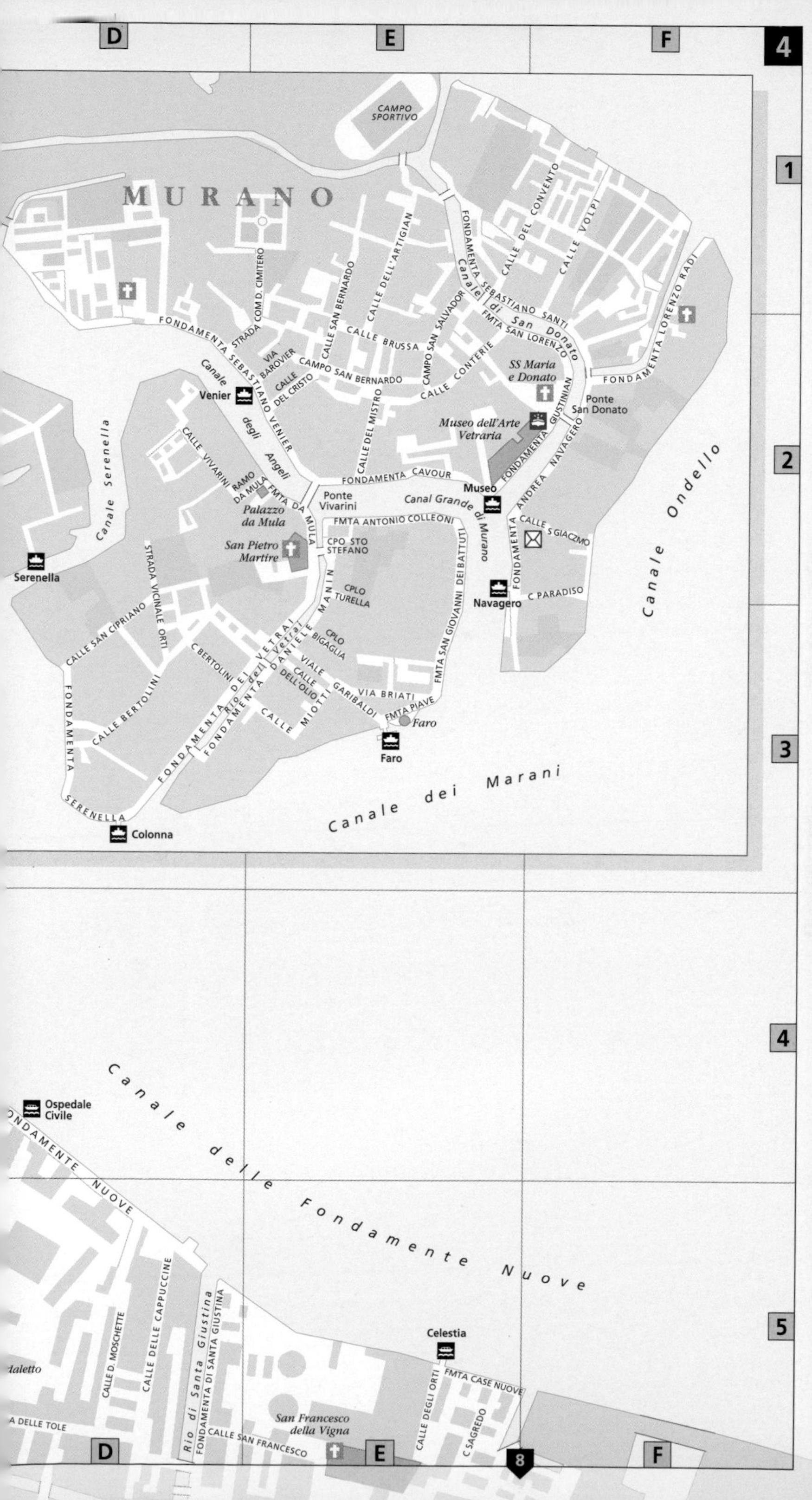
D
E
F
4
1
2
3
4
5
MURANO
CAMPO SPORTIVO
FONDAMENTA SEBASTIANO VENIER
Canale degli Angeli
STRADA COMD. CIMITERO
VIA BAROVIER
CALLE DEL CRISTO
CAMPO SAN BERNARDO
CALLE SAN BERNARDO
CALLE DELL'ARTIGIAN
CALLE BRUSSA
CAMPO SAN SALVADOR
CALLE CONTERIE
CALLE DEL MISTRO
FONDAMENTA SEBASTIANO SANTI
Canale di San Donato
FMTA SAN LORENZO
CALLE DEL CONVENTO
CALLE VOLPI
FONDAMENTA LORENZO RADI
SS Maria e Donato
GUSTINIAN
Ponte San Donato
Museo dell'Arte Vetraria
FONDAMENTA
FONDAMENTA CAVOUR
Museo
Canal Grande di Murano
FONDAMENTA ANDREA NAVAGERO
CALLE S GIACZMO
C PARADISO
Navagero
Canale Ondello
Venier
Canale Serenella
Serenella
CALLE VIVARINI
RAMO DA MULA
FMTA DA MULA
Palazzo da Mula
San Pietro Martire
Ponte Vivarini
FMTA ANTONIO COLLEONI
CPO STO STEFANO
CPLO TURELLA
MANIN
FMTA SAN GIOVANNI DEI BATTUTI
STRADA VICINALE ORTI
CALLE SAN CIPRIANO
C BERTOLINI
CALLE BERTOLINI
FONDAMENTA DEI VETRAI
Rio dei Vetrai
FONDAMENTA DANIELE MANIN
CPLO BIGAGLIA
VIALE GARIBALDI
CALLE DELL'OLIO
CALLE MIOTTI
VIA BRIATI
FMTA PIAVE
Faro
Faro
FONDAMENTA SERENELLA
Colonna
Canale dei Marani
Canale delle Fondamente Nuove
Ospedale Civile
FONDAMENTE NUOVE
CALLE D. MOSCHETTE
CALLE DELLE CAPPUCCINE
Rio di Santa Giustina
FONDAMENTA DI SANTA GIUSTINA
CALLE SAN FRANCESCO
San Francesco della Vigna
Celestia
FMTA CASE NUOVE
CALLE DEGLI ORTI
C SAGREDO
A DELLE TOLE
daletto
8

5
A
B
C
1
2
3
4
5
CAMPO SANT'ANDREA
SANTA CROCE
GIARDINO EX PAPADOPOLI
CORTE DEGLI AMAI
CAMPO DEI TOLENTINI
San Nicolò da Tolentino
PIAZZALE ROMA
Canale di Santa Chiara
Canale Scomenzera
Canale di Santa Maria Maggiore
FONDAMENTA SANT'ANDREA
R T SANT'ANDREA
C NUOVA D. TABACCHI
FONDAMENTA PAPADOPOLI
FONDAMENTA COSSETTI
FMTA CONDULMER
FONDAMENTA DEI TOLENTINI
CAMPAZZO TRE PONTI
FMTA MAGAZEN
FONDAMENTA MINOTTO
Rio del Malcanton
FMTA DEL GAFFARO
FONDAMENTA FABBRICA TABACCHI
Rio delle Burchielle
FONDAMENTA DELLE BURCHIELLE
CALLE DEI PENSIERI
C BERNARDO
FMTA TRE PONTI
Rio Nuovo
FMTA RIO NUOVO
C.D. MISERICORDIA
CALLE CREMONESE
FMTA PAGAN
RIO TERRA DEI PENSIERI
CORTE CORRER
Rio della Cazziola
FMTA CAZZIOLA
C SORIANA
CORTE GALLO
FONDAMENTA
C DELLA SBIACCA
CALLE E CORTE BA
Rio Nuo
DEL RIO NUOV
FMTA DI S M MAGGIORE
FONDAMENTA RIZZI
FMTA DI SANTA MARIA MAGGIORE
FONDAMENTA DELLE PROCURATIE
CALLE LARGA RAGUSEI
CORTE CONTARINI
CALLE NUOVA
CALLE CAPPELLO
C VIOTTI
CALLE D. PROC
C SPORCA
FMTA D. MADONNA
FONDAMENTA DEI CERERI
Rio del Tintor
FONDAMENTA ROSSA
Rio Briati
CALLE RAGUSEI
C CAMERINI
C DELL'OLIO
FONDAMENTA DELL'ARZIERE
Rio dell'Arziere
FMTA RUGHETTA
CALLE DEI GUARDIANI
FONDAMENTA FOSCARINI
Rio di S Marg
Scuola Grande d. Carmini
CAMPO DEI CARMINI
RIO TERRA DEI SECCHI
CALLE DEL CRISTO
BRIATI
Rio dei Carmini
FONDAMENTA DEL SOCCORSO
C.D. PAZIENZA
Santa Maria dei Carmini
C LARGA S MARIA
FONDAMENTA SANTA MARTA
CALLE NUOVA TERESE
C NUOVA
C STRETTA
FONDAMENTA
Collegio Armeno
FONDAMENTA DELLE TERESE
Rio delle Terese
FONDAMENTA TRON
CPLO TRON
C RIELLO
C S LORENZO
CT MAGGIORE
Rio dell'Angelo Raffaele
DORSODURO
C.D. REMORCHIANTI
CAMPO SAN NICOLO
FONDAMENTA BARBARIGO
CALLE MADDALENA
FMTA SAN SEBASTIANO
CORTE DEI VECCHI
Rio di San Sebastiano
Rio
CALLE
San Nicolò dei Mendicoli
FMTA LIZZA
FONDAMENTA DI PESCHERIA
Angelo Raffaele
CALLE DELL'AVOGARIA
Rio dell'Avogaria
DOGOLIN
CPLO D. STENDARDO
Rio di San Nicolò
CORTE LARDONA
CPO ANGELO RAFFAELE
C DIETRO AI MEGAZZINI
FMTA DEI BARI
CALLE BEVILACQUA
CALLE NAVE
C NUOVA
C.D. FRATI
San Sebastiano
FONDAMENTA SAN BASILIO
CALLE BALASTRO
Stazione Marittima
SALIZZADA SAN BASEGIO
CALLE CHIESA
FONDA
BANCHINA DEL PORTO COMMERCIALE
BANCHINA DI SAN BASEGIO
CALLE D. MORTI
C DELLA MASENA
C DEI CARTELLOTTI
FMTA ZATTERE PONTE L
San Basilio
Canale di Fusina
Sacca Fisola
FONDAMENTA BEATA GIULIANA
CALLE DEI FIGHERI
CALLE DEL VAPORETTO
CALLE FISOLA
C MONFALCONE
Canale dei Lavraneri
Mulino Stucky
CALLE DELLA SCUOLA
CALLE DELLA SACCA
FONDAMENTA
CALLE RIMINI
CALLE LARGA DEI LAVRANERI
Rio di San Biagio
CAMPO DELLA CHIESA
C SENIGALLIA
GIUDECCA
FMTA SAN GERARDO SAGREDO
Can Sacca Fisola
San Biagio
CAMPIELLO PRIULI
FMTA DELLE CONVERTITE
Rio delle Convertite

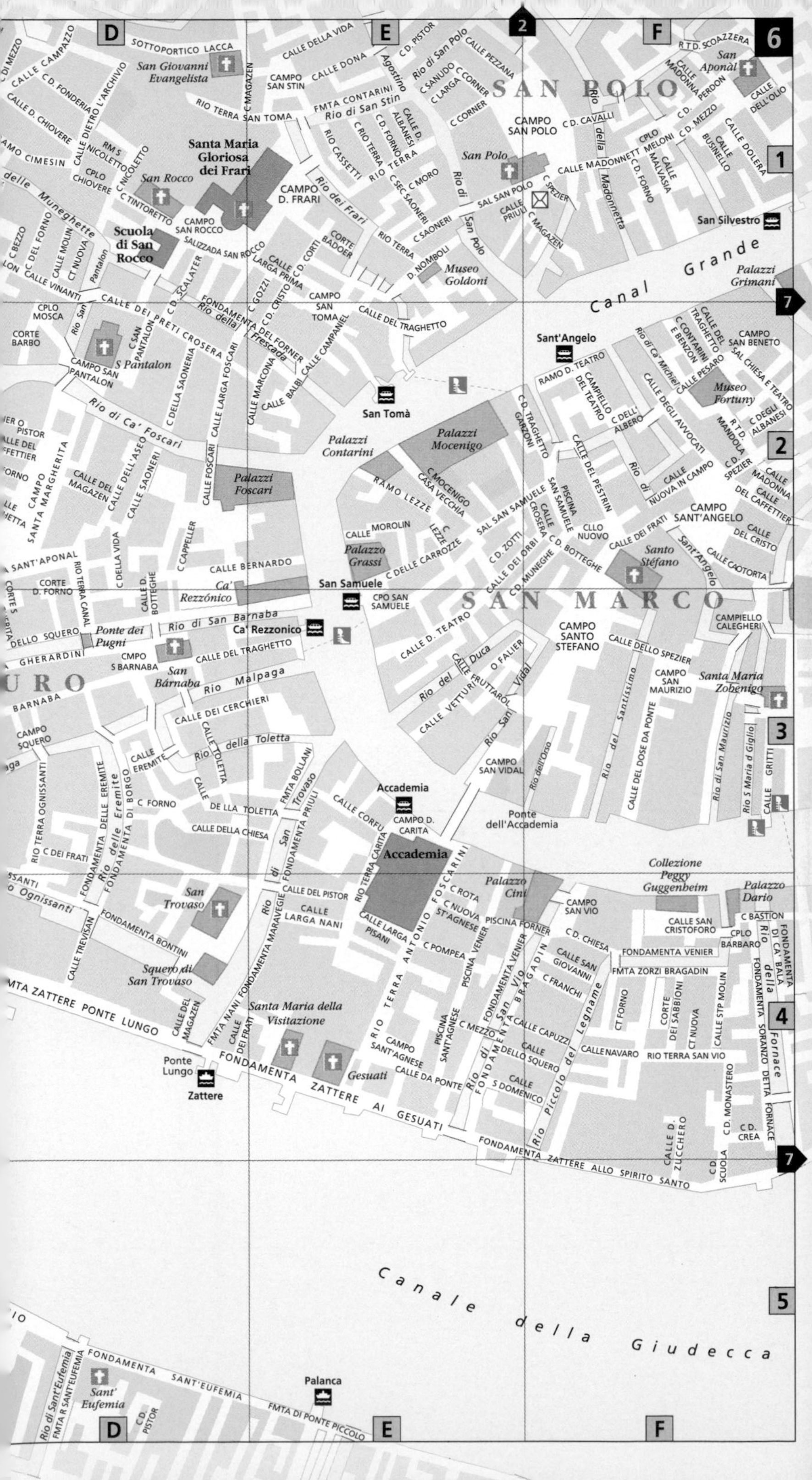
D
E
F
2
6
SOTTOPORTICO LACCA
San Giovanni Evangelista
CALLE DELLA VIDA
C D. PISTOR
Rio di San Polo
CALLE PEZZANA
R T D. SCOAZZERA
San Aponal
CALLE CAMPAZZO
C D. FONDERIA
CALLE DIETRO L'ARCHIVIO
C MAGAZEN
CAMPO SAN STIN
CALLE DONA
Agostino
C SANUDO
C CORNER
C LARGA
SAN POLO
CALLE MADONNA
PERDON
CALLE DELL'OLIO
CALLE D. CHIOVERE
RIO TERRA SAN TOMA
FMTA CONTARINI
Rio di San Stin
C CORNER
CAMPO SAN POLO
C D. CAVALLI
Rio della Madonnetta
C D. MEZZO
CALLE BUSINELLO
CALLE DOLERA
1
Santa Maria Gloriosa dei Frari
CAMPO CIMESIN
RM S NICOLETTO
C NICOLETTO
CPLO CHIOVERE
San Rocco
C TINTORETTO
CAMPO D. FRARI
Rio dei Frari
RIO CASSETTI
C RIO TERRA
C D. FORNO
CALLE D. ALBANESI
RIO TERRA
C SEC SAONERI
C MORO
San Polo
Rio di San Polo
CALLE MADONNETTA
CPLO MELONI
C D. FORNO
CALLE MALVASIA
SAL SAN POLO
CALLE PRIULI
C SPEZIER
C MAGAZEN
San Silvestro
delle Muneghette
C BEZZO
C DEL FORNO
CALLE MOLIN
CT NUOVA
Pantalon
Scuola di San Rocco
CAMPO SAN ROCCO
SALIZZADA SAN ROCCO
CORTE BADOER
C SAONERI
RIO TERRA
D. NOMBOLI
Museo Goldoni
Canal Grande
Palazzi Grimani
7
CALLE VINANTI
CALLE LARGA PRIMA
C D. CORTI
C D. SCALATER
C D. CRISTO
C GOZZI
CAMPO SAN TOMA
CPLO MOSCA
Rio San
CALLE DEI PRETI CROSERA
FONDAMENTA DEL FORNER
Rio della Frescada
CALLE DEL TRAGHETTO
Sant'Angelo
CALLE DEL TRAGHETTO
C CONTARINI E BENZON
Rio di Ca' Michiel
CAMPO SAN BENETO
SAL CHIESA E TEATRO
CORTE BARBO
S Pantalon
C SAN PANTALON
CALLE SAONERIA
CALLE LARGA FOSCARI
CALLE MARCONA
CALLE BALBI
CALLE CAMPANIEL
CAMPO SAN PANTALON
RAMO D. TEATRO
CAMPIELLO DEL TEATRO
CALLE PESARO
Museo Fortuny
CALLE DEGLI AVVOCATI
Rio di Ca' Foscari
San Tomà
C D. TRAGHETTO GARZONI
C DELL' ALBERO
R T D. MANDOLA
C DEGLI ALBANESI
Palazzi Contarini
Palazzi Mocenigo
2
CALLE DEL MAGAZEN
CALLE DELL'ASEO
CALLE SAONERI
CAMPO SANTA MARGHERITA
CALLE FOSCARI
Palazzi Foscari
RAMO LEZZE
C MOCENIGO CASA VECCHIA
CALLE DEL PESTRIN
Rio di
CALLE NUOVA IN CAMPO
C D. SPEZIER
CALLE MADONNA
CALLE DEL CAFFETTIER
CAMPO SANT'ANGELO
SAL SAN SAMUELE
PISCINA SAN SAMUELE
CALLE CROSERA
CLLO NUOVO
CALLE DEI FRATI
CALLE DEL CRISTO
C CAPPELLER
CALLE MOROLIN
C LEZZE
Palazzo Grassi
C DELLE CARROZZE
C D. ZOTTI
CALLE DEI ORBI
C D. MUNEGHE
C D. BOTTEGHE
Santo Stéfano
Sant'Angelo
CALLE CAOTORTA
SANT'APONAL
RIO TERRA CANAL
C DELLA VIDA
CALLE BERNARDO
C D. BOTTEGHE
CORTE D. FORNO
Ca' Rezzónico
San Samuele
CPO SAN SAMUELE
SAN MARCO
CAMPIELLO CALEGHERI
DELLO SQUERO
Ponte dei Pugni
Rio di San Barnaba
Ca' Rezzonico
CALLE D. TEATRO
CAMPO SANTO STEFANO
CALLE DELLO SPEZIER
GHERARDINI
CMPO S BARNABA
CALLE DEL TRAGHETTO
Rio del Duca
CALLE FRUTTAROL
O FALIER
CAMPO SAN MAURIZIO
Santa Maria Zobenigo
San Bárnaba
Rio Malpaga
CALLE VETTURI
Vidal
URO
BARNABA
CALLE DEI CERCHIERI
Rio San
Rio del Santissimo
CALLE DEL DOSE DA PONTE
Rio di San Maurizio
3
CAMPO SQUERO
CALLE EREMITE
Rio della Toletta
CALLE TOLETTA
FMTA BOLLANI
Trovaso
CAMPO SAN VIDAL
Rio dell'Orso
Rio S Maria d Giglio
CALLE GRITTI
RIO TERRA OGNISSANTI
FONDAMENTA DELLE EREMITE
Rio delle Eremite
FONDAMENTA DI BORGO
C FORNO
CALLE DE LLA TOLETTA
FONDAMENTA PRIULI
CALLE CORFU
Accademia
CAMPO D. CARITA
Ponte dell'Accademia
CALLE DELLA CHIESA
Rio di San
C DEI FRATI
RIO TERRA CARITA
Accademia
Collezione Peggy Guggenheim
Palazzo Dario
OGNISSANTI
Rio Ognissanti
San Trovaso
CALLE DEL PISTOR
CALLE LARGA NANI
C ROTA
C NUOVA ST'AGNESE
Palazzo Cini
CAMPO SAN VIO
C BASTION
CALLE SAN CRISTOFORO
FONDAMENTA BONTINI
Rio
FONDAMENTA MARAVEGIE
CALLE LARGA PISANI
C POMPEA
RIO TERRA ANTONIO FOSCARINI
PISCINA FORNER
PISCINA VENIER
C D. CHIESA
FONDAMENTA VENIER
CPLO BARBARO
Rio della Fornace
CALLE TREVISAN
Squero di San Trovaso
FONDAMENTA VENIER
CALLE SAN GIOVANNI
FMTA ZORZI BRAGADIN
C FRANCHI
FONDAMENTA DI CA' BALA
FMTA ZATTERE PONTE LUNGO
CALLE DEL MAGAZEN
FMTA NANI
CALLE DEI FRATI
Santa Maria della Visitazione
RIO TERRA
PISCINA SANT'AGNESE
C MEZZO
San Vio
C CAPUZZI
CT FORNO
CORTE DEI SABBIONI
CT NUOVA
CALLE STP MOLIN
FONDAMENTA SORANZO DETTA FORNACE
4
Ponte Lungo
Zattere
FONDAMENTA ZATTERE AI GESUATI
Gesuati
CAMPO SANT'AGNESE
CALLE DA PONTE
Rio di San Vio
CALLE DELLO SQUERO
CALLE S DOMENICO
Rio Piccolo del Legname
CALLE NAVARO
RIO TERRA SAN VIO
C D. MONASTERO
CALLE D. ZUCCHERO
C D. CREA
FONDAMENTA ZATTERE ALLO SPIRITO SANTO
C D. SCUOLA
7
Canale della Giudecca
5
FONDAMENTA SANT'EUFEMIA
Sant' Eufemia
C D. PISTOR
Rio di Sant'Eufemia
FMTA R SANT'EUFEMIA
Palanca
FMTA DI PONTE PICCOLO
D
E
F

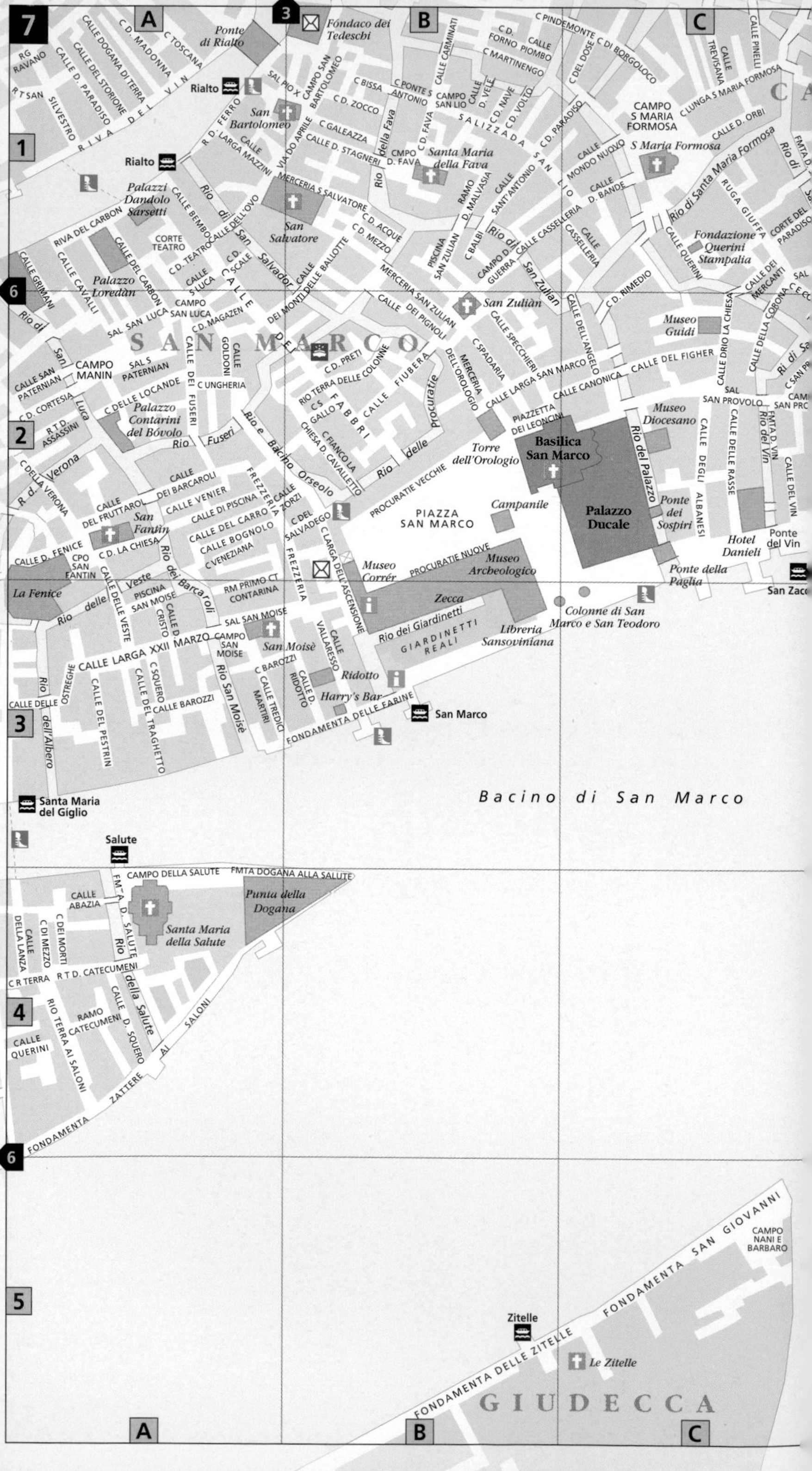

7
A
B
C
1
2
3
4
5
Ponte di Rialto
Fóndaco dei Tedeschi
Rialto
San Bartolomeo
Santa Maria della Fava
CAMPO S MARIA FORMOSA
S Maria Formosa
Palazzi Dandolo Farsetti
San Salvatore
Fondazione Querini Stampalia
Palazzo Loredàn
San Zulìan
Museo Guidi
SAN MARCO
CAMPO MANIN
Palazzo Contarini del Bóvolo
Museo Diocesano
Basilica San Marco
Torre dell'Orologio
Campanile
PIAZZA SAN MARCO
Palazzo Ducale
Ponte dei Sospiri
Hotel Danieli
Ponte del Vin
San Fantin
La Fenice
Museo Corrér
Museo Archeologico
Ponte della Paglia
San Zaccaria
Zecca
Colonne di San Marco e San Teodoro
Libreria Sansoviniana
GIARDINETTI REALI
San Moisè
Ridotto
Harry's Bar
San Marco
Bacino di San Marco
Santa Maria del Giglio
Salute
CAMPO DELLA SALUTE
FMTA DOGANA ALLA SALUTE
Punta della Dogana
Santa Maria della Salute
FONDAMENTA ZATTERE AI SALONI
FONDAMENTA SAN GIOVANNI
CAMPO NANI E BARBARO
Zitelle
Le Zitelle
FONDAMENTA DELLE ZITELLE
GIUDECCA

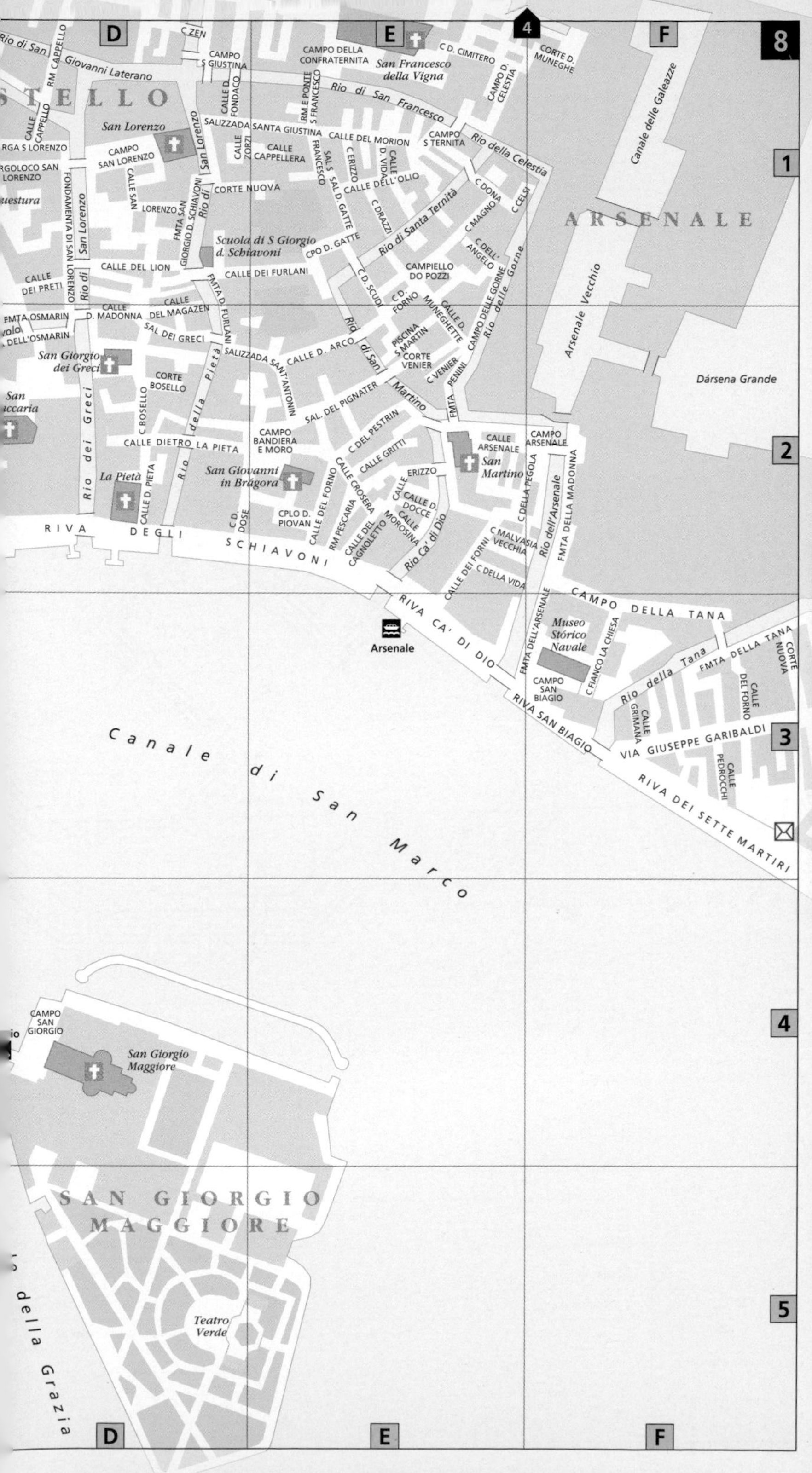
D
E
F
4
1
2
3
4
5
CASTELLO
ARSENALE
Canale delle Galeazze
Arsenale Vecchio
Dársena Grande
San Francesco della Vigna
Campo della Confraternita
Rio di San Francesco
San Lorenzo
Campo San Lorenzo
Rio di San Giovanni Laterano
Salizzada Santa Giustina
Calle del Morion
Rio della Celestia
Corte Nuova
Scuola di S Giorgio d. Schiavoni
Calle del Lion
Calle dei Furlani
Rio di Santa Ternità
Campiello do Pozzi
Rio delle Gorne
Campo delle Gorne
San Giorgio dei Greci
Sal dei Greci
Salizzada Sant'Antonin
Calle d. Arco
Rio di San Martino
Corte Venier
Corte Bosello
San Zaccaria
Rio dei Greci
Rio della Pietà
Calle Dietro la Pietà
La Pietà
Campo Bandiera e Moro
San Giovanni in Brágora
Sal. del Pignater
Calle Crosera
Calle del Forno
San Martino
Calle Arsenale
Campo Arsenale
Rio dell'Arsenale
Fmta della Madonna
Riva degli Schiavoni
Riva Ca' di Dio
Rio Ca' di Dio
Calle dei Forni
Campo della Tana
Museo Stórico Navale
Campo San Biagio
Riva San Biagio
Rio della Tana
Fmta della Tana
Via Giuseppe Garibaldi
Riva dei Sette Martiri
Arsenale
Canale di San Marco
Campo San Giorgio
San Giorgio Maggiore
SAN GIORGIO MAGGIORE
Teatro Verde
della Grazia

# Venice Vaporetto Routes

## The Vaporetto Routes

*The ACTV network runs regular services around the city and out to most of the islands. Some services are circular; others extend their routes during the high season. There are also additional lines during the summer months. More details of the different types of* vaporetti *and how to use them are given on pages 682–3.*

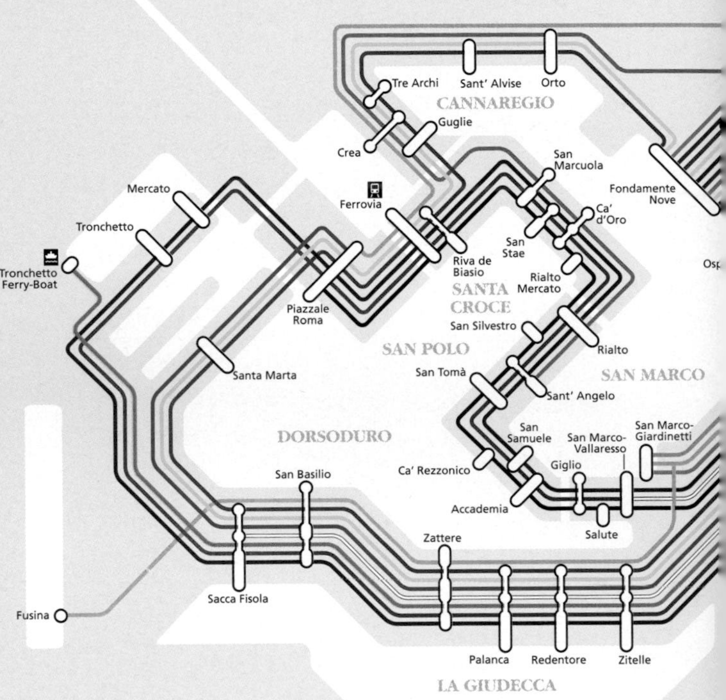


| KEY | | |
|---|---|---|
| Airport | Terminal route B | City centre route 1 |
| Railway station | Terminal route O | City centre route 2 (part sea |
| Car ferry | Terminal route R | City centre route 5 (seasona |
| Waterbus stop | Terminal route C (seasonal) | City centre route 8 (seasona |
| Terminal route A | Terminal route F | City centre route 13 |

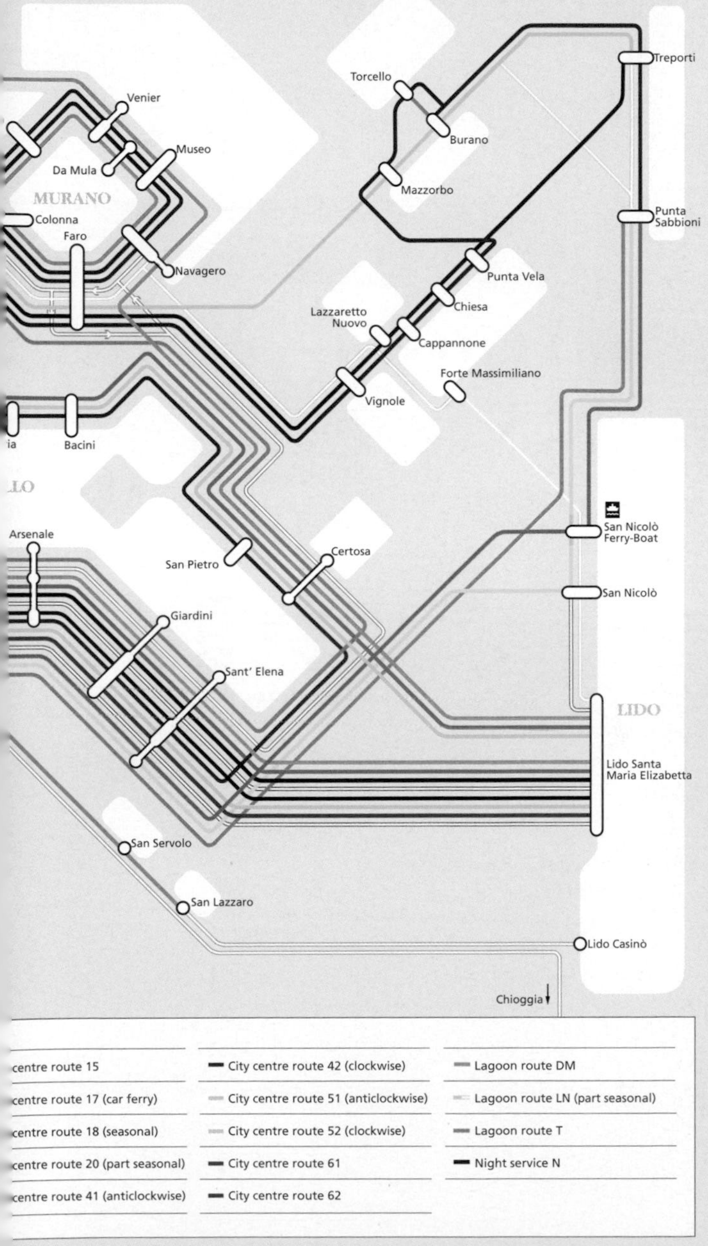
Torcello
Burano
Mazzorbo
Treporti
Punta
Sabbioni
Venier
Museo
Da Mula
MURANO
Colonna
Faro
Navagero
Punta Vela
Chiesa
Lazzaretto
Nuovo
Cappannone
Forte Massimiliano
Vignole
ia
Bacini
LO
San Nicolò
Ferry-Boat
Arsenale
Certosa
San Pietro
San Nicolò
Giardini
Sant' Elena
LIDO
Lido Santa
Maria Elizabetta
San Servolo
San Lazzaro
Lido Casinò
Chioggia
centre route 15
centre route 17 (car ferry)
centre route 18 (seasonal)
centre route 20 (part seasonal)
centre route 41 (anticlockwise)
City centre route 42 (clockwise)
City centre route 51 (anticlockwise)
City centre route 52 (clockwise)
City centre route 61
City centre route 62
Lagoon route DM
Lagoon route LN (part seasonal)
Lagoon route T
Night service N

# THE VENETO AND FRIULI

*The Veneto is a region of tremendous contrasts, encompassing the breathtaking natural beauty of the Dolomites, Lake Garda (Italy's largest lake) and the rolling Euganean Hills, and the man-made delights of magnificent ancient cities such as Verona, Vicenza and Padua. Neighbouring Friuli-Venezia Giulia lines the border with Slovenia to the east, taking in the Carnic Hills in the north, the Roman town of Aquileia and the bustling Adriatic port of Trieste.*

The Romans built frontier posts on this fertile land of silt deposits, and these survive today as the cities of Vicenza, Padua, Verona and Treviso. Strategically placed at the hub of the empire's road network, the cities prospered under Roman rule, but suffered in the wave of Germanic invasions of the 5th century AD.

The region's fortunes revived under the benign rule of the Venetian empire. The medieval cities of the Veneto lay on important trade routes such as the Serenissima, the road connecting the flourishing port cities of Venice and Genoa, and the Brenner Pass, used by commercial travellers crossing the Alps from northern Europe. Wealth from agriculture, commerce and the spoils of war paid for the beautification of these cities through the building of Renaissance palaces and public buildings, many designed by the Veneto's great architect, Andrea Palladio. His palazzi and villas are telling symbols of the leisured existence once enjoyed by the area's aristocrats.

Today the Veneto is a thriving wine exporter, textile producer and agricultural centre, and Friuli is a focus for new technology, while remaining largely agricultural. Both regions are popular tourist destinations, despite lying a little in the shadow of Venice, and boast an abundant and enchanting variety of attractions.

A leisurely *passeggiata* in one of Verona's ancient streets

◁ The Renaissance bridge by Palladio at Bassano del Grappa in the Veneto

# Exploring the Veneto and Friuli

The flat landscape of the Veneto plain is dramatically offset by the spectacular Dolomite mountains which form the northwestern border to the Veneto. Friuli, Italy's most northeasterly region, lies tucked up against Austria to the north and Slovenia to the east. Both the Veneto and Friuli are bordered to the south by the Adriatic, with its beaches and ports, which provide a contrast with the area's gently rolling countryside, the vast stretch of Lake Garda and the many attractive resorts and ancient towns.

View of Verona from the Teatro Romano

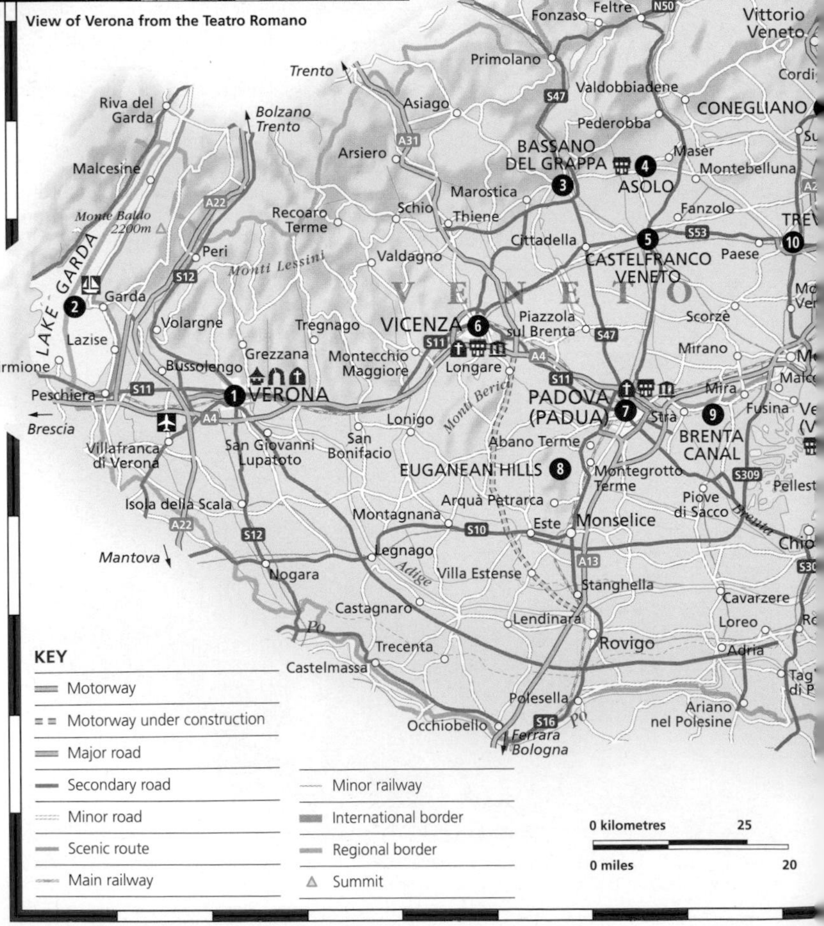

**KEY**

- Motorway
- Motorway under construction
- Major road
- Secondary road
- Minor road
- Scenic route
- Main railway
- Minor railway
- International border
- Regional border
- Summit

0 kilometres 25

0 miles 20

**For additional map symbols** *see back flap*

### *SEE ALSO*


- ***Where to Stay*** pp561–4
- ***Where to Eat*** pp609–13


### GETTING AROUND

An extensive rail network and good bus services make this region easy to explore by public transport, though only buses operate around Lake Garda. Motorways and main roads provide good links between the main cities. The Venice Simplon-Orient-Express train, which operates from London to Venice, offers a novel approach to the area.

*Monte Coglians 2780m*
Kitzbühel Lienz
Timau
Santo Stefano di Cadore
*Monte Oisternig 2052m*
Klagenfurt
*Monte Terza Grande 2585m*
Paluzza
A23
Tarvisio
*Monte Sernio 2190m*
Sauris
*Carnia*
Ampezzo
Chiusaforte
14 TOLMEZZO
*Tagliamento*
*Monte Canin 2587m*
Venzone
FRIULI-VENÉZIA GIULIA
Campone
Gemona del Friuli
S13
Pulfero
Maniago
Maiano
Stregna
17 CIVIDALE DEL FRIULI
Spilimbergo
Fagagna
16 UDINE
*Friuli*
S56
GORIZIA
PORDENONE
15
S13
Codroipo
Mortegliano
18
*Villa Manin*
San Vito al Tagliamento
Palmanova
Ljubljana
S53
A4
Cordovado
Cervignano del Friuli
Monfalcone
Marano Lagunare
19
Sistiana
Portogruaro
AQUILEIA
*Grotta del Gigante*
Grignano
Villa Opicina
*Livenza*
San Giorgio di Livenza
*Tagliamento*
Grado
TRIESTE 20
Basovizza
San Donà di Piave
Lignano Pineta
Bibione
*Golfo di Trieste*
Múggia
Rijeka
Eraclea
Caorle
Eraclea Mare
Cavallino
*Golfo di Venézia*

**The bridge at Cividale del Friuli**

**A mountain chalet in Cortina d'Ampezzo**

### SIGHTS AT A GLANCE

# Verona ❶

Verona is a vibrant trading centre, the second biggest city in the Veneto region (after Venice) and one of the most prosperous in northern Italy. Its ancient centre boasts many magnificent Roman ruins, second only to those of Rome itself, and fine palazzi built of *rosso di Verona*, the local pink-tinged limestone, by the city's medieval rulers. Verona has two main focal points: the massive 1st-century AD Arena, which is still the setting for major events including a large opera festival, and Piazza Erbe with its colourful market. One of the main attractions, however, is the church of San Zeno Maggiore *(see pp146–7)*, which boasts unusual medieval bronze door panels: they are carved with extraordinary scenes, some biblical, others on the life of San Zeno.

**Scaligeri statue in Castelvecchio**

**View of Verona from the Museo Archeologico**

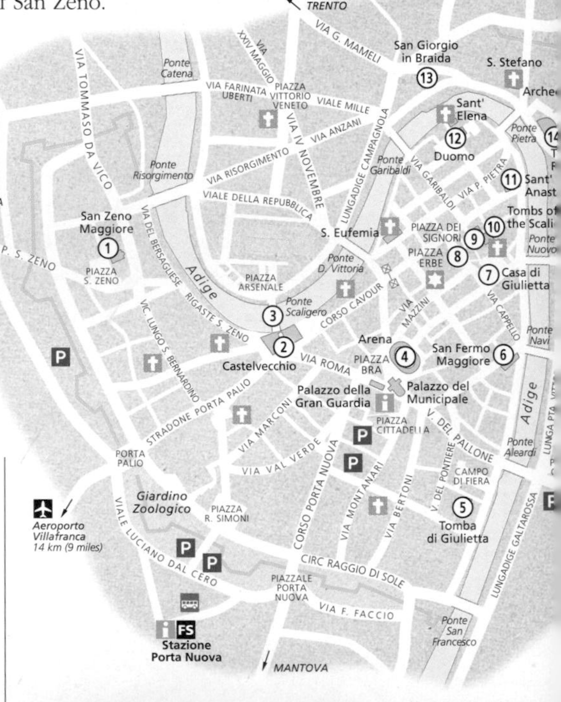


### Verona's Rulers

In 1263 the Scaligeri began their 124-year rule of Verona. They used ruthless tactics in their rise to power, but once established, the Scaligeri family brought peace to the city. They proved to be relatively just and cultured rulers – the poet Dante was welcomed to their court in 1301, and dedicated the final part of his epic *Divine Comedy* to the ruling Cangrande I. Today their legacy remains in their ornate tombs and in Castelvecchio.

In 1387 Verona fell to the Visconti of Milan, and a succession of outsiders – Venice, France and Austria – then ruled the city until the Veneto was united with Italy in 1866.

### Castelvecchio

Corso Castelvecchio 2. ***Tel*** *045 806 26 11.* *8:30am–7:30pm daily (from 1:30pm Mon). Last adm: 1 hr before closing.* *1 Jan, 25 & 26 Dec.*

This impressive castle, built by Cangrande II between 1355 and 1375, houses one of the finest art galleries in the Veneto outside Venice. It is arranged to give striking views of the castle as well as the exhibits within.

The first section contains late Roman and early Christian items – silver plate,

**Verona's enormous Roman Arena seen from Piazza Brà**

*For hotels and restaurants in this region see pp561–4 and pp609–13*

Ponte Scaligero, part of the old defence system of Castelvecchio

5th-century brooches, glass painted with a portrait of Christ the Shepherd in gold, and the carved marble sarcophagus of Saints Sergius and Bacchus (1179).

The section on medieval and early Renaissance art vividly demonstrates the influence of northern art on local painters: the emphasis is on brutal realism as opposed to serene idealism. The late Renaissance works include a fine collection of 15th-century Madonnas.

Jewellery, armour, swords and shield bosses, Veronese's *Deposition* (1565) and a portrait painting attributed to either Titian or Lorenzo Lotto are displayed in other sections.

A walkway offers views of the river Adige, the Ponte Scaligero and the 14th-century equestrian statue of Cangrande I from his tomb *(see p144)*.

### Ponte Scaligero

This medieval bridge was built by Cangrande II between 1354 and 1376. Such is the Veronese affection for the bridge that it was rebuilt after the retreating Germans blew it up in 1945, an operation that involved dredging the river to salvage the masonry. The bridge leads from Castelvecchio to the Arsenal on the north bank, built by the Austrians between 1840 and 1861 and now fronted by public gardens.

### Arena

Piazza Brà. ***Tel*** *045 800 51 51.* *8:30am–7:30pm daily (from 1:30pm Mon). Last adm: 1 hr before closing.* *1 Jan, 25 & 26 Dec; Jun–Aug: from mid-afternoon on performance days.* *partial.*

Completed in AD 30, this is the world's third-largest Roman amphitheatre, after Rome's Colosseum and the amphitheatre at Santa Maria Capua Vetere, near Naples. It could hold almost the entire population of Roman Verona, and visitors came from across the Veneto to watch gladiatorial combats. Since then, the arena has seen executions, fairs, bullfights and opera productions.

## VISITORS' CHECKLIST

*261,000.* *Villafranca 14 km (9 miles) SW.* FS *Piazzale 25 Aprile.* *Via degli Alpini 9 (045 806 86 80).* *daily.* *combined churches ticket.* *Apr: Vinltaly wine fair; Jun–Aug: Estate Teatrale Veronese; Nov: International Horse Fair.* **www**.tourism.verona.it

### San Fermo Maggiore

Stradone San Fermo. ***Tel*** *045 59 28 13.* *daily (Nov–Feb: Tue–Sun).*

San Fermo Maggiore is not one but two churches: this is most clearly seen from the outside, where the apse has pointed Gothic elements rising above a sturdy Romanesque base. The lower church, begun in 1065 by Benedictine monks on the site of an earlier sanctuary, has frescoes on the simple arcades.

The more impressive upper church dates from 1313 and is covered with a splendid ship's keel roof. The interior also boasts much medieval fresco work including a 14th-century section by Stefano da Zevio depicting Musician Angels. Nearby is the Brenzoni mausoleum (c.1440) by Giovanni di Bartolo, and above it a 1426 fresco of the *Annunciation* by Pisanello (1377–1455).

Giardino Giusti
SALITA S. SEPOLCRO
VIA S. NAZARO
VICENZA PADOVA VENEZIA
PIAZZALE PORTA VESCOVO
VIA FRANCESCO TORBIDO
0 metres 500
0 yards 500

## SIGHTS AT A GLANCE

Arena ④
Casa di Giulietta ⑦
Castelvecchio ②
Duomo ⑫
Giardino Giusti ⑯
Museo Archeologico ⑮
Piazza Erbe ⑧
Piazza dei Signori ⑨
Ponte Scaligero ③
Sant'Anastasia ⑪
San Fermo Maggiore ⑥
San Giorgio in Braida ⑬
*San Zeno Maggiore (pp146–7)* ①
Teatro Romano ⑭
Tomba di Giulietta ⑤
Tombs of the Scaligeri ⑩

**Key to Symbols** *see back flap*

The 11th-century apse of the lower church of San Fermo Maggiore

# Exploring Verona

Since the days of the Roman Empire, Piazza Erbe – built on the site of the ancient Roman forum – has been the centre of Verona. Many of the city's fine palazzi, churches and monuments are nearly as ancient, several dating from the medieval period.

The fountain, erected in the 14th century at the centre of Piazza Erbe

### Piazza Erbe

Piazza Erbe is named after the city's old herb market. Today's stalls, shaded by umbrellas, sell everything from herb-flavoured roast suckling pig in bread rolls to succulent fresh-picked fruit and delicious wild mushrooms.

At the northern end of the square is the Baroque **Palazzo Maffei** (1668), surmounted by statues. In front of it rises a column supporting the **Venetian lion** marking Verona's absorption into the Venetian empire (1405). On the west side is the **Casa dei Mercanti**, a largely 17th-century building that dates originally from 1301. Opposite, wall frescoes are still visible above the cafés.

The **fountain** in the middle of the piazza is often overshadowed by the market stalls, though the statue at its centre dates from Roman times. It serves as a reminder that this piazza has been used as a market-place for 2,000 years.

### Piazza dei Signori

**Torre dei Lamberti**
*Tel 045 927 30 27.*
*8:30am–7:30pm daily (Mar–Oct: to 8:30pm).*

In the centre of the square is a 19th-century **statue of Dante**, whose gaze seems fixed on the forbidding **Palazzo del Capitano**, once the home of Verona's military commanders. Beside it is the equally intimidating **Palazzo della Ragione**, the palace of Reason, or law court; both were built in the 14th century. The courtyard of the law court has a handsome external stone staircase, added in 1446–50. Stunning views of the Alps can be enjoyed from atop the 84-m (275-ft) **Torre dei Lamberti**, which rises from the western side of the courtyard.

Behind the statue of Dante is the **Loggia del Consiglio** (1493), the council chamber. The building is topped by statues of Roman worthies born in Verona: they include Pliny the Elder, the natural historian, and Vitruvius, the architectural theorist.

The square is linked to Piazza Erbe by the Arco della Costa, or the Arch of the Rib, named after the whale rib long ago hung beneath it.

The frescoed Renaissance façade of the Loggia del Consiglio on Piazza dei Signori

### Tombs of the Scaligeri

Via Arche Scaligeri.

Beside the entrance to the tiny Romanesque church of **Santa Maria Antica**, once the parish church of the powerful Scaligeri family, lie a profusion of bizarre tombs of the one-time rulers of Verona.

Over the entrance to the church is the impressive tomb of Cangrande I (died 1329), surmounted by an equestrian statue of the ruler, a copy of the original which is now in Castelvecchio *(see p143)*.

The other Scaligeri tombs are next to the church, behind a wrought-iron fence which incorporates the ladder emblem of the family's original name *(della Scala*, meaning "of the steps"). Towering above the fence are the tombs of Mastino II (died 1351) and Cansignorio (died 1375), splendidly decorated with a profusion of tiny Gothic spires. Other members of the Scaligeri family lie within a series of plainer tombs which stand nearer the church wall.

14th-century Scaligeri tomb

### Sant'Anastasia

Piazza Sant'Anastasia. ***Tel*** *045 59 28 13.* *daily.* *Nov–Feb: Mon.*

The huge and lofty church of Sant'Anastasia was begun in 1290. Faded 15th-century frescoes and carved scenes from the life of St Peter Martyr adorn its Gothic portal.

Inside, there are two holy-water stoups, supported on figures of beggars, known as *i gobbi* (the hunchbacks). These figures were carved a century apart: the earlier one (on the left) dates from 1495.

The sacristy, off the north aisle, is home to a fine (but damaged) fresco by Pisanello: *St George and the Princess* (1433–8).

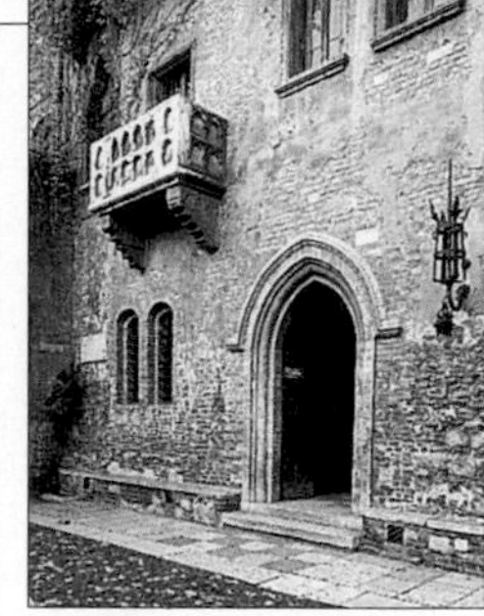

The so-called Casa di Giulietta

### ROMEO AND JULIET

The tragic story of Romeo and Juliet, two young lovers from rival families, was written by Luigi da Porto of Vicenza in the 1520s and has inspired countless dramas, films and ballets.

At the **Casa di Giulietta** (Juliet's house), No. 23 Via Cappello, Romeo is said to have climbed to Juliet's balcony; in reality this is a restored 13th-century inn. Crowds throng to see the simple façade, and stand on the small marble balcony. The run-down **Casa di Romeo** is a few streets away, in Via Arche Scaligeri.

The so-called **Tomba di Giulietta** is displayed in a crypt below the cloister of San Francesco al Corso on Via del Pontiere. The stone sarcophagus lies in an extremely atmospheric setting.

Both the Casa and the Tomba di Giulietta are open daily (on Mondays in the afternoon only). There is an admission charge.

### Duomo

Piazza Duomo. **Tel** *045 59 56 27.* *daily.* *Nov–Feb: Mon.*

Verona's cathedral was begun in 1139 and is fronted by a magnificent Romanesque portal carved by Nicolò, one of the two master masons responsible for the façade of San Zeno *(see pp146–7)*. Here he sculpted the sword-bearing figures of Oliver and Roland, two of Charlemagne's knights, whose exploits were much celebrated in medieval poetry. Alongside them stand evangelists and saints with wide eyes and flowing beards. To the south there is a second Romanesque portal carved with Jonah and the Whale and with comically grotesque caryatids.

The highlight of the interior is Titian's lovely *Assumption* (1535–40), and outside there is a Romanesque cloister in which the excavated ruins of earlier churches are visible. The 8th-century baptistry, or San Giovanni in Fonte (St John of the Spring), was built from Roman masonry; the marble font was carved in 1200.

### Teatro Romano
### Museo Archeologico

Regaste Redentore 2. **Tel** *045 800 03 60.* *1:30–7:30pm Mon (all day if pub hol); 8:30am–7:30pm Tue–Sun. The theatre closes early in the afternoon on performance days.* *1 Jan, 25 & 26 Dec.*

This Roman theatre was built in the 1st century BC; little survives of the stage area, but the semicircular seating area is largely intact. It offers great views over Verona: in the foreground is the only one of three Roman bridges to have survived, though it was rebuilt after World War II.

A lift carries visitors from the Teatro Romano up the cliffs to the monastery above, now an interesting archaeological museum. The exhibits around the tiny cloister and in the old monks' cells include mosaics, pottery and glass. There is also a fine bronze bust of the first Roman emperor, Augustus (63 BC–AD 14), who in 31 BC overcame his opponents, including Mark Antony and Cleopatra, to become the sole ruler of the Roman world.

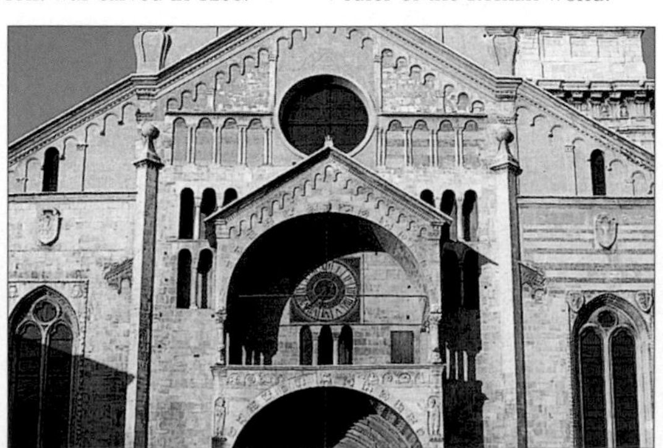

The imposing façade of Verona's Duomo, Santa Maria Matricolare

Statuary and formal hedges in the Renaissance Giardino Giusti

### Giardino Giusti

Via Giardino Giusti 2. **Tel** *045 803 40 29.* *9am–8pm daily (Oct–Mar: to sunset).* *25 Dec.*

This fine Renaissance garden was laid out in 1580. As with other gardens of the period, there is a deliberate juxtaposition of nature and artifice: the formal lower garden of clipped box hedges, gravel walks and potted plants contrasts with wilder, natural woods above.

John Evelyn, the English author and diarist who visited Verona in 1661, thought this the finest garden in Europe.

### San Giorgio in Braida

Lungadige San Giorgio. **Tel** *045 834 02 32.* *daily.* *during mass.*

This lovely domed Renaissance church was begun in about 1530 by Michele Sanmicheli. The altar includes the famous *Martyrdom of St George* (1566) by Veronese, and above the west door is the *Baptism of Christ*, usually attributed to Tintoretto (1518–94).

# Verona: San Zeno Maggiore

Detail from San Zeno's façade

San Zeno, built in 1120–38 to house the shrine of Verona's patron saint, is the most ornate Romanesque church in northern Italy. The façade is adorned with an impressive rose window, marble reliefs, and a graceful porch canopy. The highlight, however, is the fascinating 11th- and 12th-century bronze door panels. A squat tower just north of San Zeno is said to cover the tomb of King Pepin of Italy (777–810).

**Nave Ceiling**
*The nave has a magnificent example of a ship's keel ceiling, so called because it resembles the inside of an upturned boat. This ceiling was constructed in 1386 when the apse was rebuilt.*

**The bell tower**, started in 1045, reached its present height of 72 m (236 ft) in 1173.

**Altarpiece by Mantegna**
*The Madonna's halo in Andrea Mantegna's altarpiece of the Virgin and Child with saints (1457–59) echoes the shape of the church's rose window.*

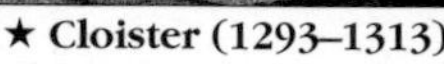

**★ Cloister (1293–1313)**
*The arches are rounded Romanesque on one side, pointed Gothic on another.*

Former washroom

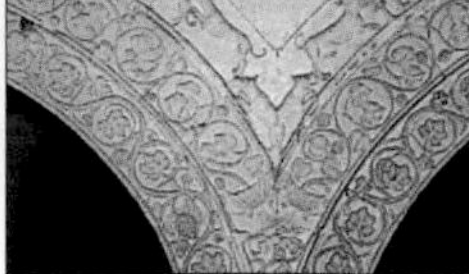

**Crypt**
*The vaulted crypt contains the tomb of San Zeno, appointed eighth bishop of Verona in AD 362, who died in AD 380.*

*For hotels and restaurants in this region see pp561–4 and pp609–13*

**Nave and Main Altar**
*The plan of the church is modelled on an ancient Roman basilica, the Hall of Justice. The main altar is situated in the raised sanctuary where the judge's throne would have stood.*

## VISITORS' CHECKLIST

P. San Zeno. ***Tel*** *045 59 28 13.* *8:30am–6pm Mon–Sat, 1–6pm Sun (Nov–Feb: 10am–1pm, 1:30–5pm Tue–Sat, 1–5pm Sun).* *for mass.* *times vary.* **www**.chieseverona.it

## BRONZE DOOR PANELS

The 48 bronze panels of the west doors are primitive but forceful in their depiction of biblical stories and scenes from the life of San Zeno. Those on the left date from 1030 and survive from an earlier church on the site; those on the right were made after the earthquake in 1137. The panels are the work of three separate craftsmen, and are linked with masks. Huge staring eyes and Ottoman-style hats, armour and architecture feature prominently. Among the scenes, some of which are unclear, are Adam and Eve, Salome dancing for the head of John the Baptist, and a startling Descent into Limbo.

**Descent into Limbo** | **Christ in Glory** | **Human head**

**Striped brickwork** is typical of Romanesque buildings in Verona. Courses of local pink brick are alternated with ivory-coloured tufa.

**The rose window**, dating from the early 12th century, symbolizes the Wheel of Fortune: figures on the rim show the rise and fall of human luck.

**The Romanesque porch** is one of the finest examples of the style in northern Italy. Since 1138 it has shielded biblical bas-reliefs, above the west doors, from the elements.

**Marble side panels**, which were carved in 1140, depict events from the Life of Christ (to the left of the doors) and scenes from the Book of Genesis (to the right).

**★ West Doors**
*Each of the wooden doors has 24 bronze plates nailed on to make the doors look like solid metal. A multi-coloured bas-relief above them depicts San Zeno, flanked by the people of Verona, vanquishing the devil.*

## STAR FEATURES

- ★ Cloister
- ★ West Doors

# Lake Garda ❷

Garda, the largest and easternmost of the Italian lakes, borders three regions: Trentino to the north, Lombardy to the west and south, and the Veneto to the south and east. The low-lying countryside around the southern stretches becomes increasingly dramatic further north, until impressive rocky cliffs, sometimes swathed in pines, hug the shoreline of the northern tip. The numerous sporting facilities, many sights, and splendid scenery of snow-capped mountains help make the lake a favourite summer playground.

## VISITORS' CHECKLIST

Brescia, Verona & Trento. *Viale Marconi 8, Sirmione (030 91 61 14).* FS *Peschiera del Garda, Desenzano del Garda.* *to all towns.* **Il Vittoriale** Gardone. ***Tel*** *0365 29 65 23.* *Tue–Sun (garden daily).* **Rocca Scaligera** Sirmione. ***Tel*** *030 91 64 68.* *Tue–Sun.*

**Eastern tip of Sirmione Peninsula**
*Beyond the town is a path which follows the rim of the peninsula, passing boiling sulphur springs.*

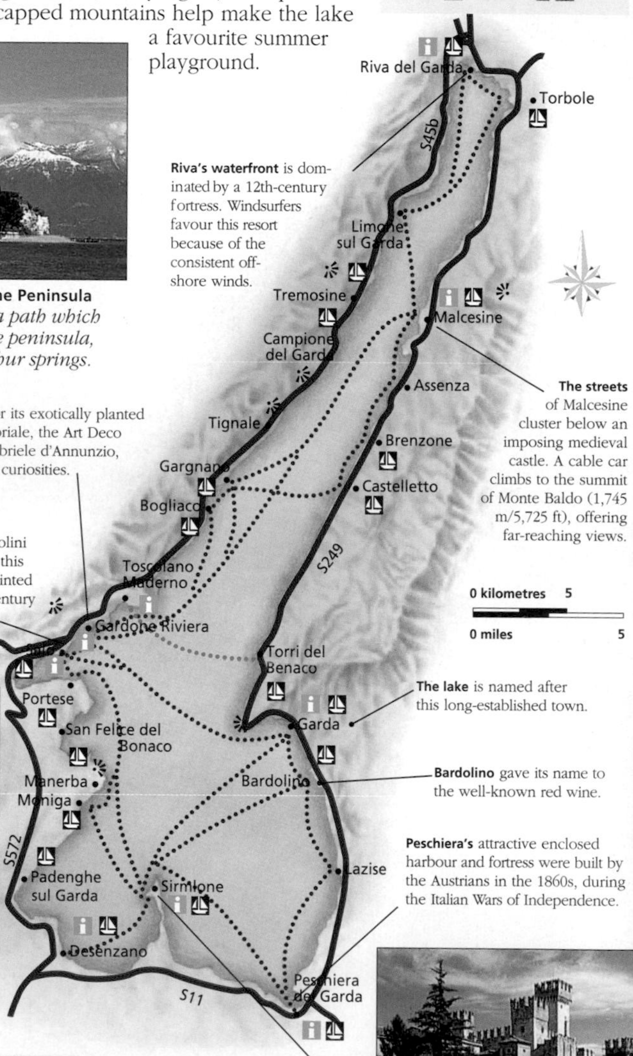

**Riva's waterfront** is dominated by a 12th-century fortress. Windsurfers favour this resort because of the consistent offshore winds.

**Gardone** is noted for its exotically planted park and for Il Vittoriale, the Art Deco villa of the poet Gabriele d'Annunzio, which is filled with curiosities.

**The Republic of Salò** was established here by Mussolini in 1943. The cathedral in this elegant town of pastel-painted houses contains a 14th-century altarpiece by Veneziano.

**The streets** of Malcesine cluster below an imposing medieval castle. A cable car climbs to the summit of Monte Baldo (1,745 m/5,725 ft), offering far-reaching views.

Riva del Garda
Torbole
S45b
Limone sul Garda
Tremosine
Malcesine
Campione del Garda
Assenza
Tignale
Brenzone
Gargnano
Castelletto
Bogliaco
S249
Toscolano Maderno
Gardone Riviera
Salò
Torri del Benaco
Portese
Garda
San Felice del Benaco
Manerba
Moniga
Bardolino
S572
Padenghe sul Garda
Sirmione
Lazise
Desenzano
Peschiera del Garda
S11

0 kilometres 5
0 miles 5

**The lake** is named after this long-established town.

**Bardolino** gave its name to the well-known red wine.

**Peschiera's** attractive enclosed harbour and fortress were built by the Austrians in the 1860s, during the Italian Wars of Independence.

**The hydrofoils,**
*catamarans and steamers which ply the lake offer glimpses of villas and gardens which cannot be seen from the coastal road.*

**KEY**

- Steamer route
- Car ferry
- Sailing club or centre
- Tourist information
- Viewpoint

**Sirmione**
*A fascinating medieval castle, the Rocca Scaligera, dominates the town of Sirmione. At the tip of the peninsula lie Roman ruins.*

*For hotels and restaurants in this region see pp561–4 and pp609–13*

The 16th-century wooden bridge by Palladio at Bassano del Grappa

## Bassano del Grappa ❸

Vicenza. 39,000. FS
Largo Corona d'Italia 35 (0424 52 43 51). Thu & Sat am.

This peaceful town lies at the foot of Monte Grappa. The river Brenta is straddled by the graceful Ponte degli Alpini, which was designed in 1569 by Palladio. It is built of timber to allow it to flex when hit by the spring meltwaters. Bassano is well known for its majolica products (decorated and glazed earthenware), some of which are on display in the **Palazzo Sturm**. The town is also synonymous with the popular Italian after-dinner drink, the clear spirit known as *grappa*. It is produced from the lees *(graspa)* left over from wine production; information about the process is given in the **Museo degli Alpini**.

**Palazzo Sturm**
Via Ferracina. ***Tel*** *0424 52 49 33.*
*Tue–Sun.*

**Museo degli Alpini**
Via Angarano 2. ***Tel*** *0424 50 36 50.*
*Tue–Sun.*

## Asolo ❹

Treviso. 2,000. Piazza Garibaldi 73 (0423 52 90 46). Sat. **www**.asolo.it

Asolo is beautifully sited among the cypress-clad foothills of the Dolomites. This tiny walled town was once ruled by Queen Caterina Cornaro (1454–1510), the Venetian wife of the King of Cyprus, who poisoned her husband so that Venice would gain Cyprus. Cardinal Pietro Bembo, a poet, coined the verb *asolare* to describe the bittersweet life of enforced idleness she endured in exile here. Among others who fell in love with the narrow streets and grand houses was poet Robert Browning, who named a volume of poems *Asolanda* (1889) after Asolo.

**Environs:** At Masèr, 10 km (6 miles) east of the town, stands the magnificent **Villa Barbaro** *(see pp80–81)*. It was designed by Palladio in about 1555, in conjunction with the artist Veronese, and perfectly blends symmetry and light, airy rooms with sumptuous *trompe l'oeil* frescoes.

**Villa Barbaro**
Masèr. ***Tel*** *0423 92 30 04.*
*Mar–Oct: Tue, Sat, Sun & hols; Nov–Feb: Sat, Sun & hols.* *1 Jan, Easter Sun, 25 Dec.*

## Castelfranco Veneto ❺

Treviso. *30,000.* FS
*Via Francesco M Preti 66 (0423 49 14 16).* *Tue am & Fri am.*

Fortified in 1199 by rulers of Treviso as a defence against the neighbouring Paduans, the historic core of this town lies within well-preserved walls. In the **Casa di Giorgione**, said to be the birthplace of the painter Giorgione (1478–1511), about whom little is known, there is a museum devoted to his life. Giorgione innovatively used landscape to create mood, adding figures to intensify the atmosphere – for instance in his broodingly mysterious but evocative most famous work, *The Tempest* *(see p106)*. Another of his few directly attributable works hangs here in the **Duomo**: the *Madonna and Child with Saints Liberal and Francis* (1504).

**Environs:** About 8 km (5 miles) northeast of the town, at the village of Fanzolo, lies the **Villa Emo** (c.1555). Designed by Palladio, it is a typical example of his work: a cube flanked by two symmetrical wings. Inside there are lavish frescoes by Zelotti.

**Casa di Giorgione**
Piazzetta del Duomo. ***Tel*** *0423 72 50 22.* *Tue–Sun.* *pub hols.*

**Villa Emo**
Via Stazione 5, Fanzolo. ***Tel*** *0423 47 63 34.* *May–Oct: daily (pm only Mon–Sat); Nov–Apr: daily.* *1 Jan, 25, 26 & 31 Dec.*

Fresco (c.1561) by Veronese adorning the Villa Barbaro near Asolo

# Street-by-Street: Vicenza ❻

Face at No. 21 Contrà Porti

Vicenza is known as the adoptive city of Andrea Palladio (1508–80), who started out as a stonemason and became the most influential architect of his time. The evolution of his distinctive style is visible all around the city. In the centre is the monumental basilica he adapted to serve as the town hall, nearby is the Teatro Olimpico, and all around are the palaces he built for Vicenza's wealthy citizens.

**Loggia del Capitaniato**
*This covered arcade was designed by Palladio in 1571.*

**Contrà Porti**
is bordered by some of the most elegant palazzi in Vicenza.

**Palazzo Valmarana Braga**
*Palladio's impressive building of 1566 is decorated with giant pilasters and sculpted scenes. It was not completed until 1680, 100 years after the architect's death.*

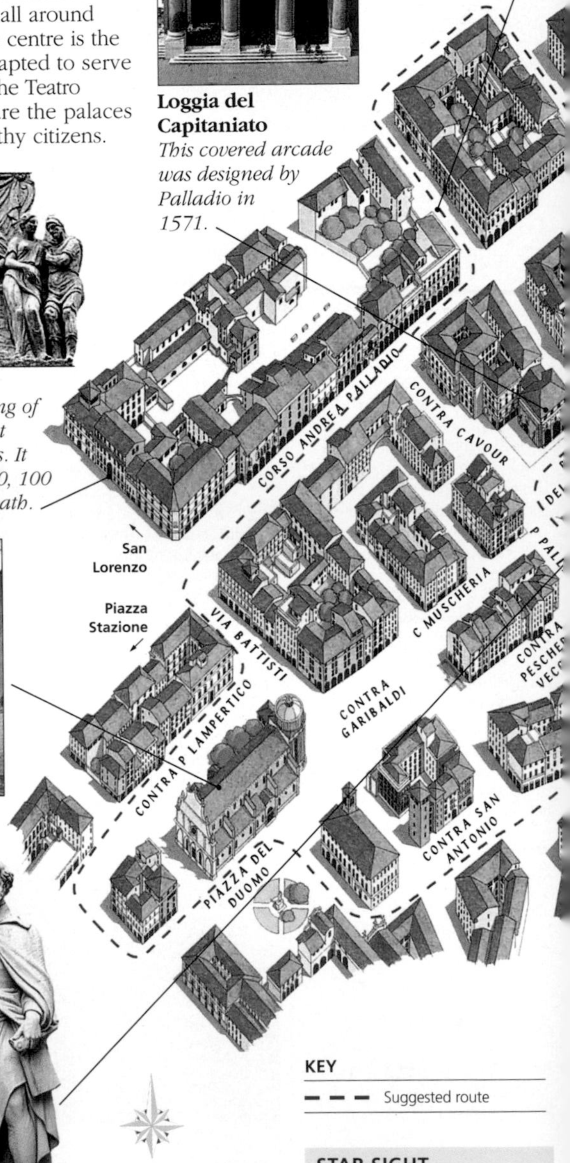

CORSO ANDREA PALLADIO

CONTRA CAVOUR

C MUSCHERIA

VIA BATTISTI

CONTRA GARIBALDI

CONTRA P LAMPERTICO

PIAZZA DEL DUOMO

CONTRA SAN ANTONIO

San Lorenzo

Piazza Stazione

**Duomo**
*Vicenza's cathedral was rebuilt after bomb damage during World War II left only the façade and choir entirely intact.*

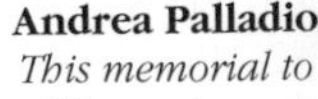

**Andrea Palladio**
*This memorial to Vicenza's most famous citizen is usually surrounded by market stalls.*

0 kilometres 2

0 miles 1

**KEY**

— — — Suggested route

**STAR SIGHT**

★ Piazza dei Signori

**A large hall** is all that remains of the 15th-century Palazzo della Ragione.

**Santa Corona**

**Torre di Piazza**, built in the 12th century, is an impressive 82 m (269 ft) high.

**Teatro Olimpico Museo Civico**

## VISITORS' CHECKLIST

*116,000. FS Piazza Stazione. Piazza dei Signori 8 (0444 54 41 22). Tue & Thu. May–Jun: concert season; Sep–Oct: theatre season; end Jun–early Jul: Concerti in Villa.*
**www**.vicenzae.org

**★ Piazza dei Signori**
*Palladio's elegant buildings flank the Piazza dei Signori, including the majestic two- tier colonnades of the 16th-century "Basilica", built around the old Palazzo della Ragione.*

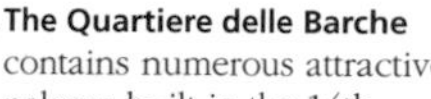

**The Quartiere delle Barche** contains numerous attractive palaces built in the 14th-century Venetian Gothic style.

**Ponte San Michele**
*This elegant stone bridge, built in 1620, provides lovely views of the surrounding town.*

**La Rotonda Monte Berico Villa Valmarana ai Nani**

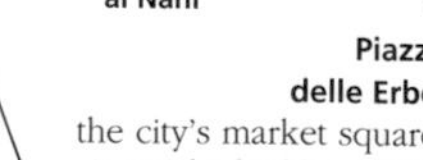

**Piazza delle Erbe**, the city's market square, is overlooked by a 13th-century prison tower.

**Casa Pigafetta**
*This striking 15th-century house was the birthplace of Antonio Pigafetta, who in 1519 set sail round the world with Magellan.*

**The lion of St Mark gazing down on Piazza dei Signori**

### Piazza dei Signori

**Basilica** ***Tel*** *0444 32 36 81.*
*only for exhibitions.*

This square at the heart of Vicenza is dominated by the Palazzo della Ragione, often referred to as the **Basilica**. Its green, copper-clad roof is shaped like an upturned boat with a balustrade bristling with the statues of Greek and Roman gods. The colonnades were designed by Palladio in 1549 as a facing to support the city's 15th-century town hall, which had begun to subside. This was Palladio's first public commission, and a great success. Beside it stands the 12th-century Torre di Piazza.

The **Loggia del Capitaniato**, to the northwest, was built by Palladio in 1571: the Loggia's upper rooms contain the city's council chamber.

### Contrà Porti

Contrà (an abbreviation of *contrada*, or district) is the Vicenza dialect word for street. On one side of the Contrà is a series of pretty Gothic buildings with painted windows and ornate balconies, reminiscent of Venice and a reminder that Vicenza was once part of the Venetian empire.

Several elegant Palladian palazzi stand on this street. Palazzo Porto Barbarano (No. 11), Palazzo Thiene (No. 12) and Palazzo Iseppo da Porto (No. 21) illustrate the sheer variety of Palladio's style – all share Classical elements but each is unique. An intriguing detail is that Palazzo Thiene appears to be of stone, though it is in fact built of cheap, lightweight brick, cleverly rendered to look like masonry.

# Exploring Vicenza

Vicenza, the great Palladian city and one of the wealthiest cities in the Veneto, is celebrated the world over for its splendid and varied architecture; it also offers the visitor elegant shops and cafés to visit.

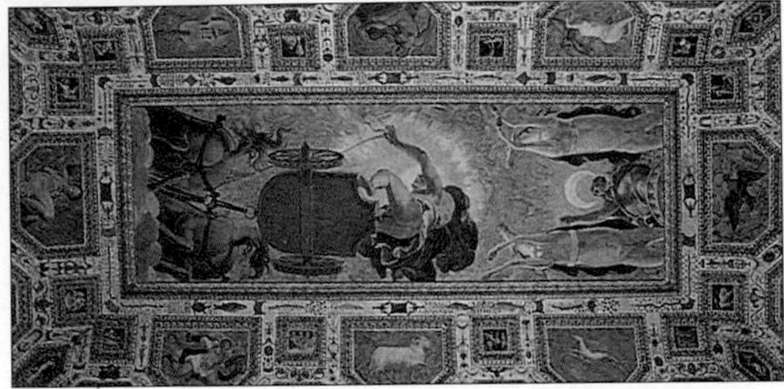

**Brusazorzi's ceiling fresco in the large entrance hall of the Museo Civico**

### Museo Civico

Piazza Matteotti 37–39. ***Tel*** *0444 32 13 48.* *Tue–Sun.* *1 Jan, 25 Dec.*

This museum is housed in **Palazzo Chiericati** *(see p80)* by Palladio, built in 1550. Inside is a fresco by Domenico Brusazorzi of a naked charioteer, representing the Sun, who seems to fly over the entrance hall. The upstairs rooms hold many excellent pictures. Among the Gothic altarpieces from churches in Vicenza is Hans Memling's *Crucifixion* (1468–70), the central panel from a triptych whose side panels are now in New York.

Other rooms contain works by the local artist Bartolomeo Montagna (c.1450–1523).

### Santa Corona

Contrà Santa Corona. ***Tel*** *0444 32 19 24.* *for renovation.*

This great Gothic church was built in 1261 to house a thorn donated by Louis IX of France and said to be from Christ's Crown of Thorns. The Cappella Porto houses the tomb of Luigi da Porto (died 1529), author of the novel *Giulietta e Romeo*, on which Shakespeare based his famous play. Notable paintings include Giovanni Bellini's *Baptism of Christ* (c.1500) and the *Adoration of the Magi* (1573) by Paolo Veronese.

### Teatro Olimpico

Piazza Matteotti 11. ***Tel*** *0444 22 28 00.* *9am–4:30pm Tue–Sun (Jul–Aug: to 7pm).* *during performances, 1 Jan, 25 Dec.*

Europe's oldest surviving indoor theatre is a remarkable structure, largely made of wood and plaster, and painted to look like marble. Palladio began work on the design in 1579, but he died the year after. His pupil Vincenzo Scamozzi took over the project, completing the theatre in time for its opening performance of Sophocles' tragic drama *Oedipus Rex* on 3 March 1585.

**Odeon Frescoes**
*The gods of Mount Olympus, after which the theatre is named, decorate the Odeon, a room used for music recitals.*

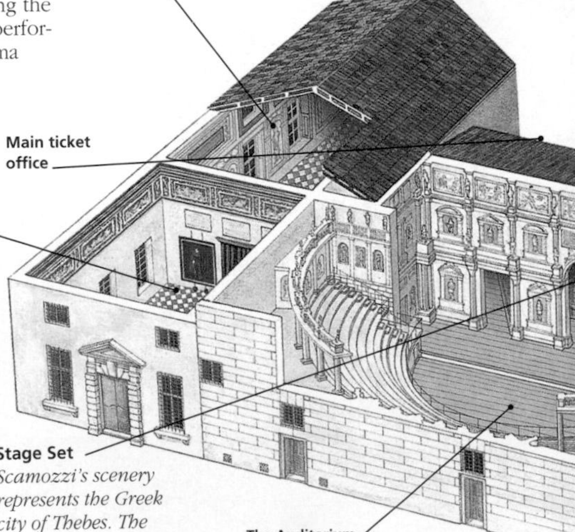

**The Anteodeon** contains frescoes depicting the theatre's opening performance, and oil lamps from the original stage set.

**Main ticket office**

**Stage Set**
*Scamozzi's scenery represents the Greek city of Thebes. The streets are cleverly painted in perspective and rise at a steep angle to give the illusion of great length.*

**The Auditorium** was designed by Palladio to resemble the outdoor theatres of ancient Greece and Rome, such as the Arena at Verona *(see p143)*, with a semi-circle of "stone" benches and a ceiling painted to portray the sky.

### San Lorenzo

Piazza San Lorenzo. *daily.*

The portal of this church is a magnificent example of Gothic stone carving, richly decorated with the figures of the Virgin and Child, and St Francis and St Clare. Inside there are fine tombs, and damaged frescoes. The lovely cloister, north of the church, is an attractive, flower-filled haven of calm.

### Monte Berico

Basilica di Monte Berico. ***Tel*** *0444 32 64 64.* *daily (only pm Sun).*

Monte Berico is the green, cypress-clad hill to the south of Vicenza to which wealthy residents once escaped, in the heat of summer, to enjoy the cooler air and pastoral charms of their country estates. Today, shady *portici*, or colonnades, adorned with shrines, line the wide avenue linking central Vicenza to the basilica on top of the hill. The domed basilica itself, built in the 15th century and enlarged in the 18th, is dedicated to the Virgin who appeared here during the 1426–8 plague to announce that Vicenza would be spared.

The ornate interior contains a moving *Pietà* fresco (1500) by Bartolomeo Montagna, a fossil collection in the cloister, and Veronese's fine painting, *The Supper of St Gregory the Great* (1572), in the refectory.

La Rotonda (1550–52), most famous of all Palladio's works

The Baroque hilltop church, the Basilica di Monte Berico

### Villa Valmarana ai Nani

Via dei Nani 8. ***Tel*** *0444 32 18 03.* *10am–noon, 3–6pm Tue–Sun (8 Nov–7 Mar: 10am–noon, 2–4:30pm Sat & Sun only).*

The wall alongside the Villa Valmarana, built in 1688 by Antonio Muttoni, is topped by figures of dwarfs (*nani*) which give the building its name.

Inside, the walls are covered with frescoes by Tiepolo, in which the gods of Mount Olympus float about on clouds watching scenes from the epics of Homer and Virgil. In the separate Foresteria (guest house), the 18th-century frescoes depicting peasant life and the seasons, painted by Tiepolo's son Giandomenico, are imbued with an earthy realism.

The villa can be reached by an enjoyable, ten-minute walk from the basilica on Monte Berico. Head downhill along Via Massimo d'Azeglio to the high-walled convent on the right where the road ends, then take Via San Bastiano.

### La Rotonda

Via Rotonda 45. ***Tel*** *0444 32 17 93.* **Villa** *mid-Mar–4 Nov: Wed.* **Garden** *Tue–Sun.*

With its perfectly regular, symmetrical forms, this villa, also known as the Villa Capra Valmarana, is the epitome of Palladio's architecture *(see pp80–81)* of which there are several fine examples throughout the Veneto. The design, consisting of a dome rising above a cube, received immediate acclaim for the way it blends perfectly with its surroundings. A pleasant contrast exists between the terracotta roof tiles, the white walls and the green lawns.

The villa, built in 1550–52, has inspired many copies in cities as far away as London, St Petersburg and Delhi. Fans of *Don Giovanni* will enjoy spotting locations used in Joseph Losey's 1979 film.

La Rotonda can be reached by bus from town, or on foot, following the path alongside the Villa Valmarana ai Nani.

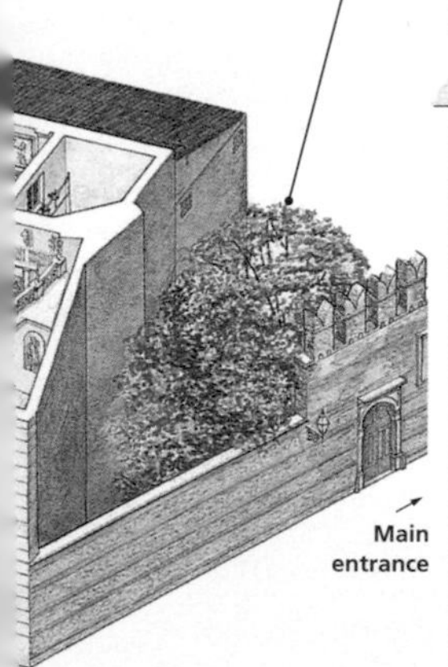

**The façade statues** of stately toga-clad figures are portraits of sponsors who paid for the theatre's construction.

**The courtyard** giving access to the Teatro is decorated with ancient sculptures. These were donated by members of the Olympic Academy, the learned body that built the theatre.

**Main entrance**

# Street-by-Street: Padua ❼

Padua (Padova) is an old university town with an illustrious academic history. Rich in art and architecture, it has two particularly outstanding sights. The magnificent Cappella degli Scrovegni *(see pp156–7)*, north of the city centre, is famous for Giotto's lyrical frescoes. Close to the railway station, it forms part of the complex incorporating the Eremitani church and museums. The Basilica di Sant'Antonio, which forms the focal point in the southern part of the city, is one of the most popular pilgrimage destinations in Italy.

**Palazzo del Capitanio**
*Built between 1599 and 1605 for the head of the city's militia, the tower incorporates an astronomical clock made in 1344.*

**Piazza dei Signori** is bordered by attractive arcades which house small speciality shops, cafés and old-fashioned wine bars.

**Corte Capitaniato**, a 14th-century arts faculty (open for concerts), contains frescoes which include a rare portrait of the poet Petrarch.

**Loggia della Gran Guardia**
*This fine Renaissance building dating from 1523 once housed the Council of Nobles. It is now used as a conference centre.*

**★ Duomo and Baptistry**
*The 12th-century baptistry of the Duomo contains one of the most complete medieval fresco cycles to survive in Italy, painted by Giusto de' Menabuoi in 1378.*

**The Palazzo del Monte di Pietà** has 16th-century arcades and statues enclosing a medieval building.

**KEY**

– – – Suggested route

0 metres 75

0 yards 75

**STAR SIGHT**

★ Duomo and Baptistry

**Caffè Pedrocchi**
*Built like a Classical temple, the Caffè Pedrocchi has been a famous meeting place for students and intellectuals since it opened in 1831.*

## VISITORS' CHECKLIST

*220,000. FS Piazzale della Stazione 13A (049 875 20 77). Piazza Boschetti. Mon–Sat, Piazza delle Erbe. Jun–Sep: Cultural Festival.*
**www.**turismopadova.it

**A bronze statue** of a woman (1973) by Emilio Greco stands at the centre of this largely pedestrianized square.

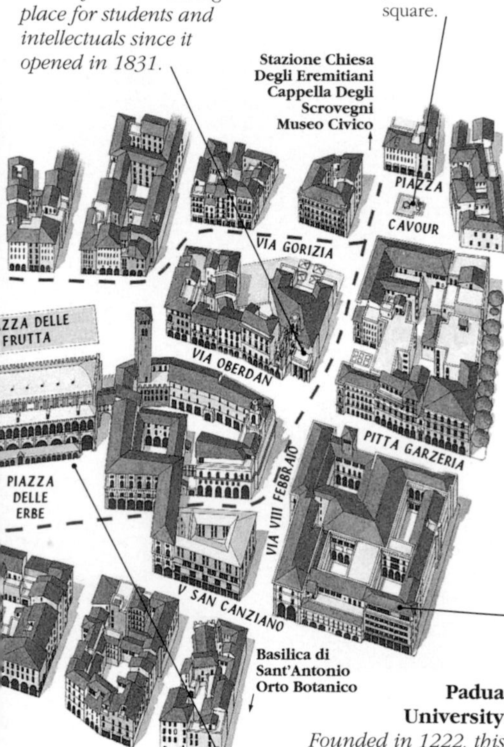


**Padua University**
*Founded in 1222, this is Italy's second oldest university. Elena Piscopia was the first woman graduate, in 1678.*

**lazzo lla Ragione**, e medieval court of justice, ntains magnificent frescoes.

**Piazza delle Erbe**
*There are some excellent views to be had over the market place from the 15th-century loggia which runs alongside the 13th-century Palazzo della Ragione.*

### Duomo and Baptistry

Piazza Duomo. **Baptistry *Tel*** *049 65 69 14. 10am–6pm daily. Easter, 25 Dec.*

The Duomo was built in 1552 to plans partly by Michelangelo, on the site of an earlier, 14th-century cathedral. Beside it stands a domed baptistry (c.1200). The interior is entirely decorated with vibrant frescoes painted by Giusto de' Menabuoi, dating from around 1378. The frescoes depict episodes from the Bible, including scenes of the Creation, the Miracles, the Passion, the Crucifixion and the Resurrection of Christ.

### Palazzo della Ragione

Piazza delle Erbe (entrance via the town hall). ***Tel*** *049 820 50 06. 9am–7pm Tue–Sun (Nov–Feb: to 6pm). 1 Jan, 1 May, 25 & 26 Dec.*

The "Palace of Reason" was built in 1218 to serve as Padua's law court and council chamber. The vast main hall was originally decorated with frescoes by Giotto, but fire destroyed his work in 1420. The Salone is breathtaking in its sheer size. It is the largest undivided medieval hall in Europe, 80 m (260 ft) long, 27 m (90 ft) wide and 27 m (90 ft) high. Frescoes painted in 1420–25 by Nicola Miretto cover its walls: the 333 panels depict the months of the year, with appropriate gods, signs of the zodiac and seasonal activities. A 1466 copy of the huge Gattamelata statue *(see p158)* by Donatello stands at one end of the hall.

### Caffè Pedrocchi

Via VIII Febbraio 15. ***Tel*** *049 878 12 31. daily. Aug.* **Museum** *Tue–Sun.*

Caffè Pedrocchi opened in 1831, and became famous as the café that never closed its doors. Today people come as much to talk, play cards or watch the world go by as to eat or drink. The upstairs rooms, decorated in Moorish, Egyptian and other styles, house a museum documenting modern Italian history.

# Padua: Cappella degli Scrovegni

Enrico Scrovegni built this chapel in 1303, hoping thereby to spare his dead father, a usurer, from the eternal damnation in hell described by the poet Dante in his *Inferno*. The interior of the chapel is entirely covered with beautiful frescoes of scenes from the life of Christ, painted by Giotto between 1303 and 1305. As works of great narrative force, they exerted a powerful influence on the development of European art.

**The Nativity**
*The naturalism of the Virgin's pose marks a departure from Byzantine stylization, as does the use of natural blue for the sky, in place of celestial gold.*

**Expulsion of the Merchants**
*Christ's physical rage, the cowering merchant and the child hiding his face show an animation that is characteristic of Giotto's style.*

**The Coretti**
*Giotto painted the two panels known as the Coretti as an exercise in perspective, creating the illusion of an arch with a room beyond.*

View towards altar

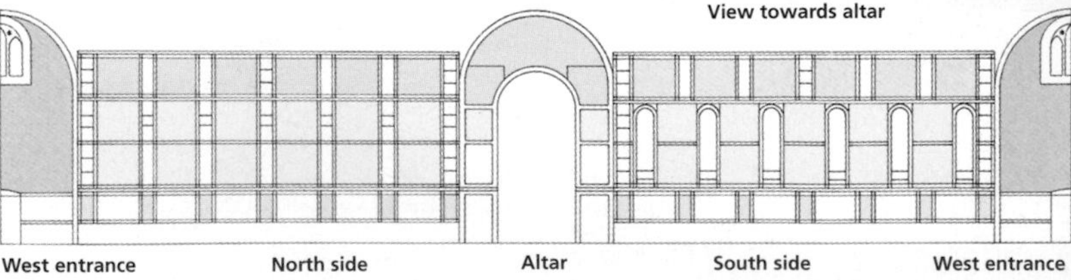


## GALLERY GUIDE

*Due to the Cappella degli Scrovegni's small size, the number of visitors allowed in at any one time is strictly limited. Prior to entering, visitors are required to spend 15 minutes in a decontamination chamber, where multimedia, multilingual information on the chapel is provided. The visit itself is also restricted to 15 minutes. Advance booking is compulsory, either by phone (049 201 00 20) or online (www.cappella degliscrovegni.it), with a credit card payment.*

**KEY**

- Episodes of Joachim and Anna
- Episodes from the Life of Mary
- Episodes from the Life and Death of Christ
- The Virtues and Vices
- The Last Judgment

### The Last Judgment

*This scene fills the entire west wall of the chapel. Its formal composition is closer to Byzantine tradition than some of the other frescoes, with parts probably painted by assistants. A model of the chapel is shown (centre left, at the bottom) being offered to the Virgin by Scrovegni.*

### VISITORS' CHECKLIST

Piazza Eremitani. ***Tel*** *049 201 00 20.* to *Piazzale Boschetti.* *9am–7pm daily (also occasional evenings).* *main public hols. Advance booking compulsory* (*see opposite*).

View towards entrance

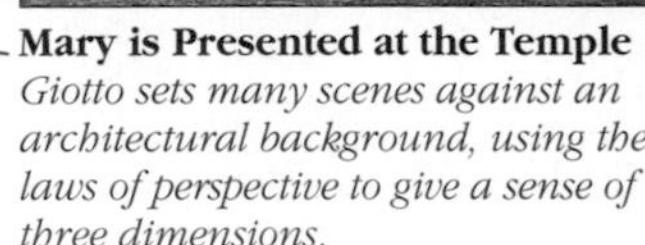

### Mary is Presented at the Temple

*Giotto sets many scenes against an architectural background, using the laws of perspective to give a sense of three dimensions.*

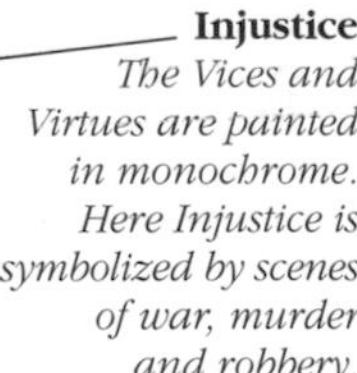

### Injustice

*The Vices and Virtues are painted in monochrome. Here Injustice is symbolized by scenes of war, murder and robbery.*

### Lament over the Dead Christ

*Giotto's figures express their grief in different ways: some huddle together, another gestures wildly.*

### GIOTTO

The Florentine artist Giotto (1266–1337) is regarded as the father of the Renaissance, the great revival in the Classical traditions of Western art. His work, with its sense of pictorial space, naturalism and narrative drama, marks a decisive break with the Byzantine tradition of the preceding 1,000 years. Although he was regarded in his lifetime as a great artist, few of the works attributed to him are fully documented. Some may have been painted by others, but his authorship of the frescoes in the Scrovegni Chapel need not be doubted.

# Exploring Padua

Padua is a city of many attractions, with a rich history: this is reflected in the major museum complex which occupies a group of 14th-century monastic buildings attached to the church of the Eremitani, a reclusive Augustinian order. Next door is the Cappella degli Scrovegni *(see pp156–7)*. Padua is, in addition, the setting for one of Italy's most important churches – the splendid Basilica di Sant'Antonio – and for one of the earliest universities to be founded in Italy.

**15th-century *Angels in Armour* by Guariento, Museo Civico Eremitani**

### Chiesa degli Eremitani and Museo Civico Eremitani

Piazza Eremitani 8. ***Tel*** *049 820 45 51*. **Museum** *Tue–Sun.*

The Eremitani church, built from 1276 to 1306, contains magnificent roof and wall tombs. Among them is that of Marco Benavides (1489–1582), a professor of law at the city university, whose Renaissance tomb was the work of Florentine architect Ammannati (1511–92). Celebrated frescoes (1454–7) by Mantegna, portraying scenes from the lives of St James and St Christopher, were destroyed during a bombing raid in 1944. Two scenes from this magnificent series survive in the Cappella Ovetari, south of the sanctuary: *The Martyrdom of St James* and *The Martyrdom of St Christopher*.

The Museo Civico Eremitani comprises a coin collection (which includes rare Roman medallions and an almost complete set of Venetian coinage), an archaeological section and an art gallery.

The rich archaeological collection contains interesting Roman tombs, fine mosaics and impressive life-size statues. Renaissance bronzes include the comical *Drinking Satyr* by Il Riccio (1470–1532).

The beautiful 14th-century Crucifix from the Cappella degli Scrovegni is in the Quadreria Emo Capodilista, as well as works by Giotto, and 15th- to 18th-century paintings from the Venetian and Flemish schools.

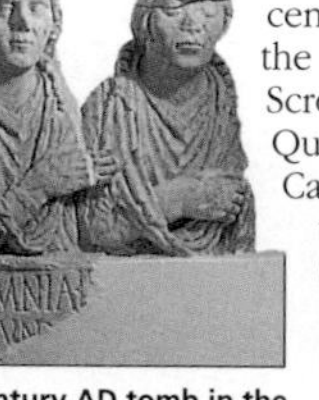


**A 1st-century AD tomb in the archaeological collection**

### Basilica di Sant'Antonio

Piazza del Santo. ***Tel*** *049 878 97 22.*

This exotic church, with its minaret-like spires and Byzantine domes, is also known as Il Santo. It was built from 1232 to house the remains of St Anthony of Padua, a preacher who modelled himself on St Francis of Assisi. Although he was a simple man who rejected worldly wealth, the citizens of Padua built one of the most lavish churches in Christendom to serve as his shrine.

The influence of Byzantine architecture is clearly visible in the basilica's outline: a cone-shaped central dome rises above seven encircling domes; the façade combines Gothic and Romanesque elements.

Inside, the high altar features Donatello's magnificent reliefs (1444–5) on the miracles of St Anthony, and his statues of the Crucifixion, the Virgin and Paduan saints. The tomb of St Anthony, hung with offerings, lies in the north transept; large marble reliefs depicting the saint's life, carved in 1505–77 by various artists, adorn the walls around it. A lively fresco scene of the Crucifixion by Altichiero da Zevio (1380s) adorns the south transept.

**The Basilica di Sant'Antonio, and Donatello's statue of Gattamelata**

### Statue of Gattamelata

Beside the entrance to the basilica stands one of the great works of the Renaissance: a statue of the mercenary soldier Gattamelata. This gritty portrait was created in 1443–52, in honour of a man who during his life did great service to the Venetian Republic. The artist Donatello won fame for the monument, the first equestrian statue made on such a large scale since Roman times.

### Scuola del Santo and Oratorio di San Giorgio

Piazza del Santo 11. **Tel** *049 878 97 22.* *daily.*

Five excellent frescoes, including the earliest documented paintings by Titian, are to be found in these two buildings. The Scuola del Santo contains two scenes from the life of St Anthony, which were painted by Titian in 1511. The works in the San Giorgio oratory are by Altichiero da Zevio and Jacopo Avenzo, who painted them in 1378–84.

### Orto Botanico

Via Orto Botanico 15. **Tel** *049 827 21 19.* *daily (Nov–Mar: Mon–Sat am).*

Padua's botanical garden, one of the oldest in Europe (1545), still retains much of its original appearance. The gardens and hothouses were used to cultivate the first lilac trees (1568), sunflowers (1568) and potatoes (1590) to be grown in Italy.

### Palazzo del Bo

Via VIII Febbraio 2. **Tel** *049 827 30 47.* *for guided tours only.* *Tue, Thu, Sat am, Mon, Wed, Fri pm. Times vary – phone to check.*

The historic main university building originally housed the medical faculty, renowned throughout Europe. Among its famous teachers and students was Gabriele Fallopio (1523–62), after whom the Fallopian tubes are named.

Guided tours include the pulpit Galileo used when he taught physics here from 1592 until 1610 and the wooden anatomy theatre, built in 1594 and now the oldest surviving medical lecture theatre in the world.

The 16th-century anatomy theatre in the old medical faculty of the university's Palazzo del Bo, Padua

The Euganean Hills, formed by ancient volcanic activity

## Euganean Hills ❽

FS *to Terme Euganee, Montegrotto Terme.* *Viale Stazione 60, Montegrotto Terme (049 892 83 11).*

The conical Euganean Hills, remnants of long-extinct volcanoes, rise abruptly out of the surrounding plain. Hot water springs bubble up out of the ground at Abano Terme and Montegrotto Terme where scores of establishments offer thermal treatments, ranging from mud baths to immersion in the hot sulphurated waters. Spa cures originated in Roman times; remains of the original baths and theatre are still visible at Montegrotto Terme.

### Abbazia di Praglia

Via Abbazia di Praglia 16, Bresseo di Teolo. **Tel** *049 999 93 00.* *Tue–Sun (pm only).* *Jan, religious holidays.* **Donations** *welcome.*

The Benedictine monastery at Praglia, 6 km (4 miles) west of Abano Terme, is a peaceful haven in the hills where the monks grow herbs and restore manuscripts. They lead guided tours of parts of the abbey and the church (1490–1548), noted for its beautiful cloister. There are also richly carved stalls in both the choir and the refectory, and paintings and frescoes by Zelotti, a 16th-century painter from Verona, in the dome of the church and the refectory.

### Casa di Petrarca

Via Valleselle 4, Arquà Petrarca. **Tel** *0429 71 82 94.* *Tue–Sun (also Mon if pub hol).* *pub hols.*

The picturesque town of Arquà Petrarca, on the southern edge of the Euganean Hills, is named after Francesco Petrarca (1304–74). This medieval poet, known in English as Petrarch, spent the final years of his life here, in a house frescoed with scenes from his lyrical poems, overlooking a landscape of olive groves and vineyards. He lies buried in a simple sarcophagus in front of the church.

The Casa di Petrarca (part 14th century) in Arquà Petrarca

### Villa Barbarigo

Valsanzibio. **Tel** *049 805 92 24.* *Mar–Nov: 10am–1pm, 2pm–sunset daily.*

This 18th-century villa to the north of Arquà boasts one of the finest Baroque gardens in the Veneto. These were planned by Antonio Barbarigo in 1669, and are a grandiose mix of statuary, fountains, a maze, formal parterres, lakes and avenues of cypress trees.

The 16th-century Villa Foscari at Malcontenta, beside the Brenta Canal

## Brenta Canal ❾

Padua and Venezia. *Venezia Mestre, Dolo, Mira.* *to Mira, Dolo and Strà.* **Canal trips on *Il Burchiello*:** Padua. ***Tel*** *049 820 69 10.* *25 Jan–7 Feb.* **www**.ilburchiello.it

Over the centuries, in order to prevent the Venetian lagoon silting up, the rivers flowing into it were diverted. The river Brenta was canalized in two sections: the older branch, between Padua and Fusina (just west of Venice), dates back to the 1500s and flows for 36 km (22 miles). Its potential as a transport route was quickly realized and fine villas were built along its length. Many of these elegant buildings can still be admired today – the S11 road runs alongside most of the canal's length – and several of them are open to the public.

The 18th-century **Villa Nazionale** at Strà has an extravagant frescoed ceiling by Tiepolo. The **Barchessa Valmarana** at Mira (a pretty village) boasts 18th-century decorations. In the village of Malcontenta is **Villa Foscari**, or Villa Malcontenta, one of Palladio's loveliest villas *(see pp80–81)*. It was built in 1560 and the interior decorated with magnificent frescoes by Zelotti. These villas may also be visited as part of an indulgent 8.5-hour guided tour from Padua, travelling to Venice (or, on alternate days, from Venice to Padua) along the river in a leisurely fashion on board the *Burchiello* motor launch – the cost, however, is fairly prohibitive.

**Barchessa Valmarana**
Via Valmarana 11, Mira. ***Tel*** *041 426 63 87.* *Mar–Oct: 10am–6pm daily; Nov–Feb: Sat & Sun, groups only.*

**Villa Nazionale**
Via Pisani, Strà. ***Tel*** *049 50 20 74.* *Tue–Sun.* *1 Jan, 1 May, 25 Dec.* *Fri–Sun (in Italian)*

**Villa Foscari**
Via dei Turisti, Malcontenta. ***Tel*** *041 547 00 12.* *Tue & Sat am.* *Nov–Mar.*

## Treviso ❿

*81,700.* *Via Sant'Andrea 3 (0422 54 76 32).* *Tue & Sat am.* **www**.turismo.provincia.treviso.it

Despite comparisons with Venice, the lovely fortified city of Treviso has its own very distinctive character.

A good place to start a tour of the streets, some lined with attractive balconied houses, is **Calmaggiore**. The street links the Duomo with the Palazzo dei Trecento, the rebuilt 13th-century town hall. The **Duomo** was founded in the 1100s but rebuilt several times. Inside, Titian's *Annunciation* (1570) vies for attention with the striking *Adoration of the Magi* fresco (1520) by Titian's arch-rival, Il Pordenone. More paintings by Titian and other artists of the Renaissance may be seen in the **Museo Civico**.

The fish market, which dates from medieval times, is held on an island in the middle of Treviso's river Sile; this allows the remains of the day's trading to be flushed away.

The bulky Dominican church of **San Nicolò**, nestling by the 16th-century city wall, contains interesting tombs and frescoes, including, on a wall of the chapter house, the first-ever depiction of spectacles in art. A magnificent tomb (1500) by Antonio Rizzo is framed by a fresco of pageboys (c.1500) by Lorenzo Lotto.

**Museo Civico**
Chiesa di Santa Caterina, Piazza Mario Botteri 1. ***Tel*** *0422 54 48 64.* *for renovation.*

The houses of the medieval town of Treviso overlooking ancient canals

The façade and entrance to the Renaissance Palazzo dei Rettori in Belluno

## Conegliano ⓫

*Treviso. 35,000. FS Via XX Settembre 61 (0438 212 30). Fri.*

Conegliano lies among Prosecco-producing vineyards, and winemakers from all over Italy learn their craft at Conegliano's renowned wine school. Via XX Settembre, the winding and arcaded main street, is lined with fine 15th- to 18th-century palazzi, many in the Venetian Gothic style or decorated with fading frescoes. The **Duomo** contains the town's one great work of art, an altarpiece painted by local artist Cima da Conegliano (1460–1518) depicting the *Virgin and Child with Saints* (1493).

A mythical statue on Conegliano's theatre

Reproductions of Cima's most famous works are on show in the **Casa di Cima**, the artist's birthplace. The detailed landscapes in the background of his paintings were based on the hills around the town; the same views can still be seen from the gardens surrounding the Castelvecchio (old castle).

**Casa di Cima**
Via Cima. ***Tel*** *0438 23 961.*
*Sat & Sun, pm only.*

## Belluno ⓬

*36,000. FS Piazza Duomo 2 (0437 94 00 83). Sat.*

Picturesque Belluno, capital of Belluno province, serves as a bridge between the two different parts of the Veneto, with the flat plains to the south and the Dolomite peaks to the north. Both are encapsulated in the views to be seen from the 12th-century **Porta Rugo** at the southern end of Via Mezzaterra, the main street of the old town. More spectacular still are the views from the bell tower of the 16th-century **Duomo** (subsequently rebuilt). The nearby baptistry houses a font cover with the figure of John the Baptist carved by Andrea Brustolon (1662–1732). Brustolon's works also grace the churches of San Pietro (on Via San Pietro) and Santo Stefano (Piazza Santo Stefano). North of Piazza del Duomo stands the city's most elegant building, the **Palazzo dei Rettori** (1491) – once home to the town's Venetian rulers – and the 12th-century **Torre Civica**, all that now survives of a medieval castle.

The **Museo Civico** contains paintings by Bartolomeo Montagna (1450–1523) and Sebastiano Ricci (1659–1734), and a notable archaeological section. North of the museum is Belluno's finest square, the **Piazza del Mercato**, with its arcaded Renaissance palaces and its fountain of 1410.

South of the town are the ski resorts of the Alpe del Nevegal; in the summer a chair lift operates from Faverghera up the flank of the mountain to a height of 1,600 m (5,250 ft), offering extensive views.

**Museo Civico**
Piazza Duomo 16. ***Tel*** *0437 94 48 36. May–Sep: Tue–Sun; Oct–Apr: daily.*

## Cortina d'Ampezzo ⓭

*Belluno. 6,800. Piazzetta San Francesco 8 (0436 32 31). Tue am & Fri am.* **www**.infodolomiti.it

Italy's top ski resort, much favoured by the smart set from Turin and Milan, is well supplied with restaurants and bars. Cortina is set amid the extremely dramatic scenery of the Dolomites *(see pp82–3)*, which explains part of the resort's attraction: all around, crags and spires thrust their distinctive weather-beaten shapes above the trees.

Cortina benefits from better than average sports facilities, thanks to hosting the 1956 Winter Olympics. In addition to downhill and cross-country skiing, there is also a ski jump and a bobsleigh run for those who favour something more adventurous than usual, as well as an Olympic ice stadium, several swimming pools, tennis courts and riding facilities.

During the summer months, Cortina becomes an excellent base for walkers. Useful information on trails and guided walks is available from the tourist office or, during the summer, from the Guides' office opposite.

Corso Italia in Cortina d'Ampezzo, Italy's most important ski resort

**Traditional copper pans on display in the Museo Carnico in Tolmezzo**

## Tolmezzo ⓮

*10,000.* *Via della Vittoria 4 (0433 448 98).* *Mon am.* **www**.turismofvg.it

Tolmezzo is the capital of the Carnia region, named after the Celtic tribe that inhabited the area around the 4th century BC. The town is surrounded by the high peaks of the Carnic Alps, including the pyramidal Monte Amariana (1,906 m – 6,253 ft) to the east. The best place to begin a tour of the region is the **Museo delle Arti Popolari**, which has displays of local costumes, crafts, textiles and agriculture.

Southwest of the town, a scenic road climbs 14 km (8.5 miles) to the ski resort of **Sella Chianzutan**, a good base for walking in the summer. More resorts line the road, west of Tolmezzo, to **Ampezzo**, at which point a minor road heads north through the gorge of the River Lumiei. Following this road to the Ponte di Buso bridge and the **Lago di Sauris** is an excellent introduction to the majestic Carnic Alps.

Above this point the road is often impassable in winter, but in summer there are flower-filled meadows all along the road up to Sella di Razzo, and then back along the **Pesarina Valley**, via Comeglians and Ravascletto. Returning south, **Zuglio** was once the Roman town of Forum Iulii Carnicum, guarding the road over the pass. Today it is worth a detour for the remains of its Roman basilica, baths and forum.

**Museo delle Arti Popolari**
Via della Vittoria 2. ***Tel*** *0433 432 33.* *Tue–Sun (Aug: daily).* *1 Jan, 25 Dec.*

## Pordenone ⓯

*49,000.* *Piazza XX Settembre (0434 52 03 81).* *Sat am & Wed.* **www**.turismofvg.it

Old Pordenone consists of one long street, the **Corso Vittorio Emanuele**, lined with pretty arcaded houses of pink brick, some with the faded traces of decorative frescoes on their façades. The 13th-century **Palazzo Comunale** forms a striking conclusion to the street with its eccentrically shaped roofline of curves and minaret-like side towers, and its 16th-century clocktower. Opposite is the **Museo d'Arte**, housed in the 17th-century Palazzo Ricchieri, where works by the local artist Il Pordenone (1484 –1539) are on display.

Around the corner stands the **Duomo**, which contains the lovely altar painting of the *Madonna della Misericordia* (1515) by Il Pordenone. The bell tower beside the Duomo is a fine example of Romanesque decorative brickwork.

**Museo d'Arte**
Corso Vittorio Emanuele 51. ***Tel*** *0434 39 23 12.* *for renovation.*

**Lago di Sauris, an artificial lake lying in the Carnic Alps above Tolmezzo**

## Udine ⓰

*99,000.* *Piazza I Maggio 7 (0432 29 59 72).* *Sat.*

Udine is a city of varied and surprising architecture. In the centre lies **Piazza della Libertà**, where the Loggia del Lionello (1448–56), built of pink stone in Venetian Gothic style, stands beside the Art Deco Caffè Contarena. Opposite, the Renaissance symmetry of the Porticato di San Giovanni is interrupted by the Torre dell'Orologio (Clock Tower, 1527) crowned by two bronze Moors who strike the hours. Note also the fountain of 1542, the two 18th-century statues, and the column supporting the Lion of St Mark.

Beyond the **Arco Bollani**, a gateway designed by Palladio in 1556, steps lead up to a 26-m (85-ft) hill which offers sweeping views over the city. On the hill is the 16th-century castle, now the **Musei Civici e Galleria di Storia e Arte Antica**, which houses fine art and archaeology collections.

Southeast of Piazza Matteotti, where a small market is held, at the end of Via Savorgnana, stands the **Oratorio della Purità**, and the **Duomo** with its octagonal bell tower. Both contain important paintings and frescoes by Giambattista Tiepolo (1696–1770). More of Tiepolo's work can be seen in the **Palazzo Arcivescovile**, which the artist decorated with frescoes.

*For hotels and restaurants in this region see pp561–4 and pp609–13*

The arcaded Porticato di San Giovanni on Piazza della Libertà, Udine

**Environs:** Outside Codroipo, 24 km (15 miles) west, rises the imposing **Villa Manin**. A road passes through the villa's grounds, so its massive size can be seen even when the house – once the retreat of Ludovico Manin, the last doge of Venice (1725–1802) – and its magnificent gardens are closed to the public.

**Musei Civici e Galleria di Storia e Arte Antica**
Castello di Udine. ***Tel*** *0432 27 15 91.* *Tue–Sun.* *1 Jan, Easter, 1 May, 25 Dec.*

**Palazzo Arcivescovile**
Piazza Patriarcato 1.
***Tel*** *0432 250 03.* *Wed–Sun.* *1 Jan, Easter, 25 Dec.*

**Villa Manin**
Passariano. ***Tel*** *0432 82 12 11.* *Tue–Sun.* *1 Jan, 25 Dec.* *for exhibitions only.*

## Cividale del Friuli ⓱

*11,000.* *Piazza Paolo Diacono 10 (0432 71 04 60).* *Sat.*
**www**.cividale.net

A gate in the medieval walls of Cividale leads down the main street and straight to the dramatic ravine of the River Natisone, which is spanned by the arch of the **Ponte del Diavolo** (Devil's Bridge).

Above the river's north bank stands the **Tempietto Longobardo** (Lombardic Chapel), a very rare example of an 8th-century church decorated with reliefs of saints, modelled in stucco. The town's history is traced in the excellent **Museo Archeologico Nazionale**, which contains the excavated remains of buildings from a Roman town, and a collection of Lombardic items including jewellery, ivory and weapons.

Next door is the **Duomo**, rebuilt in 1453 after a fire, with its beautiful silver altarpiece (13th century). The **Museo Cristiano**, off the south aisle, contains sculptures from the original church: of particular interest is the altar donated by Ratchis, the Lombardic Duke of Friuli and later King of Italy (737–44), which is finely carved with scenes from the Life of Christ, including a charming Nativity. There is in addition the unusual baptismal font of Patriarch Callisto (737–56): this octagonal structure, with a roof supported by pillars, is decorated with symbols of the Evangelists.

The Lion of Venice above the entrance to Gorizia's castle

**Tempietto Longobardo**
Piazzetta San Biagio. *daily.*

Interior view of the Tempietto Longobardo in Cividale del Friuli

**Museo Archeologico Nazionale**
Palazzo dei Provveditori Veneti, P.za del Duomo 13. ***Tel*** *0432 70 07 00.* *9am–2pm Mon, 8:30am–7:30pm Tue–Sun.* *1 Jan, 25 Dec.*

**Museo Cristiano**
Via Condotti 1. ***Tel*** *0432 73 11 44.* *Wed–Sun.* *pub hols.*

## Gorizia ⓲

*37,000.* *Corso Italia 9 (0481 53 57 64).* *Thu, Fri.*
**www**.turismofvg.it

Gorizia was at the centre of fierce fighting during both world wars and was split in two by the 1947 Treaty of Paris, leaving part in Italy, part in Yugoslavia (now Slovenia).

The town's arcaded streets and pastel-painted houses have been carefully restored following substantial damage during World War II. A visit to the modern Museo Provinciale della Grande Guerra (Museum of the Great War), housed in the basement of the **Museo Provinciale**, provides a fascinating introduction to the realities of war. The museum uses videos, photographs, and life-size mock-ups of trenches, latrines and gun emplacements to show the waste, squalor and heroism of war.

Rooms on the upper floor of the museum house temporary exhibitions and items from the town's art collection, which includes works by local artists.

On a mound nearby rises the castle, encircled by 16th-century fortifications. From here there are extensive views stretching over the town to the mountains beyond.

**Environs:** To the southwest of Gorizia, scenic country roads pass through the foothills of the **Carso**, a limestone plateau stretching down to Trieste. The plateau is dotted with fields enclosed by drystone walls, and gouged with tunnels, caves and underground rivers.

**Museo Provinciale**
Borgo Castello 13. ***Tel*** *0481 53 39 26.* *Tue–Sun.* *25 Dec.*

The attractive harbourside at Grado, along the coast south of Aquileia

## Aquileia ⓳

3,300. Piazza Capitolo 4 (0431 91 087). Tue.

Aquileia, now little more than a village but encircled by the ruins of palatial villas, baths, temples and market buildings, provides a poignant reminder of the lost splendour of the Roman Empire.

It was here that Emperor Augustus received Herod the Great, King of Judea, in 10 BC, and it was here too, in AD 381, that the early Christian church held a major council attended by the learned saints Ambrose and Jerome to settle doctrinal issues. In the 5th century, however, the town was abandoned following several sackings. Fortunately, substantial parts of the early Christian basilica have survived, which contain the town's particular treasure: ornate floor mosaics.

### Basilica

Piazza Capitolo. ***Tel*** *0431 910 67.* *daily.* *during mass.* **Crypt**

The basilica was founded in about AD 313 and much of the original structure still survives, including the magnificent floor mosaics of the nave and **Cripta degli Scavi** below. The designs are a mixture of geometric patterns, biblical stories and scenes from everyday life in ancient Aquileia. There is a lively portrayal of the tale of Jonah, who was swallowed by an extraordinary sea monster: the fishing boats are also surrounded by a rich array of creatures from the deep, including wide-eyed dolphins and squid.

### Museo Archeologico Nazionale

Via Roma 1. ***Tel*** *0431 910 16.* *8:30am–7:30pm daily (to 2pm Mon).*

The mosaics in the basilica demonstrate a tradition of craftsmanship that flourished in the city from the 2nd century AD. Additional examples of mosaics and stone carvings from the Classical era (1st to 3rd centuries) are on display in this museum, together with glass, amber, and a collection of flies, beautifully worked in gold, that formed the adornment of a Roman matron's veil.

### Museo Paleocristiano

Località Monastero. ***Tel*** *0431 911 31.* *8:30am–1:45pm Tue–Sun.* *1 Jan, 1 May, 25 Dec.*

This museum, which stands not far from Aquileia's ancient harbour beside the once-navigable River Natissa, focuses on the development of art during the early Christian era.

**Environs:** South of Udine, **Palmanova** is worth a visit for its remarkable octagonal layout and intact walls. The town was built in 1593 by the Venetians to commemorate the Battle of Lepanto.

**Grado** sits on a group of low islands in the middle of the Adriatic lagoon, attached to the mainland by a narrow causeway. The town grew into a port for Aquileia in the 2nd century and was used as a haven by Aquileia's citizens during the barbarian invasions. Today, Grado is a popular seaside resort. At the centre of the old town is the **Duomo**, which contains 6th-century frescoes in the apse, similar to those on the vaults of San Marco in Venice *(see pp110–13)*. Nearby, in the church of **Santa Maria delle Grazie**, there are more 6th-century mosaics.

### SYMBOLISM IN EARLY CHRISTIAN ART

Christians were persecuted until their religion was granted official status by Constantine the Great in AD 313. Prior to this they had developed a language of secret symbols to express their beliefs, many of which can be seen in the mosaics and marble tomb chests of Aquileia. Many of these and other symbols later found their way into popular bestiaries and folk art.

Part of the 4th-century floor mosaic in the basilica at Aquileia

**The Winged figure of Victory** *holding a laurel wreath was a Classical symbol of triumph, and holiness. Later, it came to represent Christ's resurrection, and more generally, victory over death.*

## Trieste 20

*218,000.* *Piazza Unità d'Italia 4/b (040 347 83 12).* *Tue–Sat.* **www**.turismofvg.it

Trieste is an atmospheric city, tucked up next to Slovenia, with a long, bustling harbour lined with handsome buildings and lapped by the waves of the Adriatic Sea.

### Acquario Marino

Molo Pescheria 2. ***Tel*** *040 30 62 01.* *9am–7pm Tue–Sun (Nov–Mar: to 1:30pm).*

The aquarium, one of Trieste's most popular attractions, contains examples of the fascinating marine life in the Adriatic.

### Castello di San Giusto

P.za Cattedrale 3. ***Tel*** *040 30 93 62.* *daily. Castle: 9am–7pm (Nov–Mar: to 5pm); museums: 9am–1pm.*

Up above the harbour stands a hilltop castle built by Trieste's Venetian governors from 1368. It is set on a terrace that offers sweeping views over the Gulf of Trieste. The castle houses two museums containing Roman mosaics, and a collection of weapons and armour.

### Basilica Paleocristiana

Via Madonna del Mare 11. ***Tel*** *040 436 31.* *10am–noon Thu (by appointment only).*

Beside the castle lie the substantial ruins of the Roman basilica or law court built around AD 100. Note the stone magistrates' bench and throne.

### Duomo

P.za Cattedrale 2. ***Tel*** *040 30 96 66.* *daily.* *Oct–Mar: Sun am.*

In the church of **San Giusto**, the city's Duomo, magistrates' bench and throne of the Roman basilica were reinterpreted to become the seat of the bishop and clergy. Because the building was formed in the 14th century by linking two 5th-century churches that stood side by side, there are two thrones and benches here. The two apses are decorated with very fine 13th-century mosaics in the Venetian style.

The Castello di Miramare on the bay of Trieste

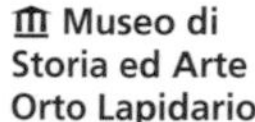

### Museo di Storia ed Arte ed Orto Lapidario

Piazza della Cattedrale 1. ***Tel*** *040 31 05 00.* *Tue–Sun am.* *public hols.*

The important archaeological collection here provides fascinating evidence of Trieste's extensive trade links with the ancient Greek world.

13th-century mosaics in the apse of San Giusto, Trieste's Duomo

**Environs:** From **Villa Opicina**, just north of Trieste, sweeping views may be had over the city, its bay and south down the coast of Slovenia. A little beyond, at Borgo Grotta Gigante, lies the **Grotta del Gigante**, a huge cavern filled with stunning "organ pipe" formations and tall columns of stalagmites.

At Grignano, 8 km (5 miles) northwest of the city, stands the **Castello di Miramare**, a white castle set in lush green gardens beside the sparkling blue Adriatic. It was built by the Habsburg Archduke Maximilian in 1856–60 as his summer retreat, a few years before he was assassinated in Mexico. It is still furnished in contemporary style.

### Grotta del Gigante

Borgo Grotta Gigante 42a. ***Tel*** *040 32 73 12.* *Tue–Sun (Jul & Aug: daily).*

### Castello di Miramare

Viale Miramare, Grignano. ***Tel*** *040 22 41 43.* *daily.* *(castle).*

**The Tortoise** *hiding in his shell represented darkness and ignorance, while the cockerel, who crows at dawn, signified light and enlightenment.*

**ICHTHUS, or fish**, *was an acronym for* Iesous CHristos THeou Uios Soter *– Jesus Christ, Son of God, Saviour, in ancient Greek.*

**Colourful birds**, *such as peacocks, symbolized immortality and the glorious transformation of the soul when it arrives in Heaven.*

# TRENTINO-ALTO ADIGE

*The Italian-speaking Trentino – named after Trento, the regional capital – and the German-speaking Alto Adige or Südtirol (South Tyrol, the region bordering the upper reaches of the River Adige) differ dramatically in culture. However, they do share one feature in common: the majestic Dolomites that form the backdrop to every town and village, covered in snow for three months of every year and carpeted with exquisite Alpine plants for another three.*

The region's mountains have been cut by glaciers into a series of deep, broad valleys. Many of these face south, so it remains unusually warm and sunny, even in winter. Travellers have passed up and down these valleys for generations – as confirmed by the extraordinary discovery, in 1991, of a 5,000-year-old man's body found emerging from the surface of a melting glacier in Alto Adige. The frozen corpse wore leather boots, stuffed with hay for warmth, and was armed with a copper ice pick.

The paths that Neolithic man once trod became major road networks under the Romans, when many of the region's cities were founded. By the Middle Ages, Alto Adige had established its very own distinctive culture under the Counts of Tyrol, whose land (later appropriated by the Habsburgs) straddled both sides of today's Italian/Austrian border. The Tyrolean nobility built the castles that still line the valleys and the mountain passes, in order to protect travellers from brigands.

Another ancient legacy is the tradition of hospitality to be found in the numerous guesthouses along the valleys. Many of these are built in the distinctive Tyrolean style, with beautiful timber balconies for making the most of the winter sun, and overhanging roof eaves to keep snow at a distance. Cosy in winter, with log fires and warming food, and offering marvellous views, they make the ideal base for enjoying the region's mountain footpaths and ski slopes.

**Skiers enjoying the slopes around Monte Spinale, near Madonna di Campiglio, in Trentino**

**◁ A typical view of the Dolomites between Bressanone and Ortisei, in Alto Adige**

# Exploring Trentino-Alto Adige

Trentino-Alto Adige is a region where unspoiled nature is complemented by a wealth of sporting opportunities. The tributary valleys feeding into the Adige valley contain lakes, rivers and streams, and also woodland, vineyards and Alpine pasture full of butterflies, birds and flowers. Southeast of the region rise the distinctive limestone peaks of the Dolomites, while further north the area becomes more mountainous still, enclosed finally by the splendid heights of the Alps.

Via Ponte Aquila in Bressanone

## SIGHTS AT A GLANCE

Bolzano (Bozen) 6
Bressanone (Brixen) 5
Brunico (Bruneck) 4
Canazei 8
Castello di Avio 15
Cavalese 9
Cembra 11
Madonna di Campiglio 12
Malles Venosta (Mals im Vinschgau) 1
Merano (Meran) 2
Ortisei (Sankt Ulrich) 7
Rovereto 14
San Martino di Castrozza 10
Trento 13
Vipiteno (Sterzing) 3

**KEY**

- Motorway
- Major road
- Secondary road
- Minor road
- Scenic route
- Main railway
- Minor railway
- International border
- Regional border
- △ Summit

0 kilometres 2
0 miles 10

**For additional map symbols** *see back flap*

Castel Tirolo above the town of Merano

View of the Dolomites from Madonna di Campiglio

## GETTING AROUND

The region's main artery is the Brenner Pass road: it runs from Austria in the north, following the River Adige from Bolzano to Trento, and southwards on to Verona. Both the motorway and the main road beside it are among the busiest in Europe, and the valley roads can also be congested during the ski season. Winter driving can be hazardous, requiring special tyres and snow chains. An excellent rail and coach network serves the whole area.

### SEE ALSO


- ***Where to Stay*** pp565–7
- ***Where to Eat*** pp613–5

Abbazia di Monte Maria, founded in the 12th century, near Malles Venosta

## Malles Venosta ❶

MALS IM VINSCHGAU

*4,600.* FS *Via San Benedetto 1 (0473 83 11 90). Wed.* **www**.altavenosta-vacanze.it

Malles Venosta sits in high border country, close to Switzerland and Austria, and was a customs point during the Middle Ages. The town has several Gothic churches, whose spires and towers give an appealing skyline, mirroring the jagged peaks that rise all around. The oldest is the tiny church of **San Benedetto**, a 9th-century Carolingian building on Via San Benedetto, with frescoes of its patrons.

**Environs:** The medieval **Castel Coira** (Churburg) rises at Sluderno (Schluderns), 4 km (2.5 miles) southeast of Malles. It contains an excellent collection of weapons and armour.

Clinging to the mountainside above the town of Burgusio (Burgeis), 5 km (3 miles) north of Malles, is the Benedictine **Abbazia di Monte Maria** (Marienberg), founded in the 12th century but enlarged in the 18th and 19th. The church's crypt shelters an outstanding series of 12th-century frescoes.

The glorious medieval town of **Glorenza** lies just 2 km (1.25 miles) south of Malles.

**Castel Coira**
Churburg, Sluderno. ***Tel*** *0473 61 52 41. 20 Mar–Oct: Tue–Sun (& Mon if pub hol). compulsory.*

**Abbazia di Monte Maria**
***Tel*** *0473 83 13 06. May–Oct: Mon–Sat; Nov–Apr: groups by appt only. public hols.*

## Merano ❷

MERAN

*35,000.* FS *Corso della Libertà 45 (0473 27 20 00). Tue, Fri.* **www**.merano.eu

Merano is an attractive spa town popular with Austrians, Germans and Italians. On Corso Libertà, a street of smart shops and hotels, stands the **Kurhaus** or Spa Hall built in 1914, now a concert venue. Furnished in period style, the 15th-century **Castello Principesco** was home to the Habsburg Archduke Sigismund. Inviting gardens line the River Passirio, which winds its way through the town. The Passeggiata Lungo Passirio d'Inverno (Winter Walk) follows the north bank to the Roman bridge, Ponte Romano; the Passeggiata d'Estate (Summer Walk) on the south bank leads to the medieval Ponte Passirio.

The Art Nouveau façade of the Kurhaus in Merano

**Environs:** The romantic 12th-century **Castel Tirolo** lies 4 km (2.5 miles) to the north. It hosts a museum of Tyrolean history.

The grounds of **Castel Trauttmansdorff** house a fascinating botanical garden.

**Castello Principesco**
Via Galilei. ***Tel*** *0473 25 03 29. Tue–Sun & public hols. Jan–Feb.*

**Castel Tirolo**
Via Castello 24, Tirolo. ***Tel*** *0473 22 02 21. mid Mar–Nov: Tue–Sun. Dec–mid-Mar.*

**Castel Trauttmansdorff**
Via S. Valentino 51a. ***Tel*** *0473 23 57 30. 1 Apr–15 Nov: daily.*

## Vipiteno ❸

STERZING

*5,600.* FS *Piazza Città 3 (0472 76 53 25). daily.* **www**.vipiteno.com

Surrounded by mineral-rich valleys, Vipiteno is very Tyrolean in feel. On Via Città Nuova, lined with fine mansions, rise the Gothic **Palazzo Comunale**, containing Renaissance sculpture and paintings, and the Torre dei Dodici, the symbol of the town. Wood carvings in the **Museo Multscher** are by Hans Multscher; the Bavarian sculptor came to Vipiteno in 1456–8 to carve the altar for the parish **church**, which lies just south of the town.

Wrought-iron sig Vipiteno

To the west, the charming **Val di Racines** includes waterfalls and a natural rock bridge.

**Palazzo Comunale**
Via Città Nuova 21. ***Tel*** *0472 72 37 00. Mon–Fri. Fri pm & pub hols.*

**Museo Multscher**
Via della Commenda. ***Tel*** *0472 76 64 64. Apr–Oct: Tue–Sat. public hols.*

The medieval castle dominating the town of Brunico

## Brunico ❹

BRUNECK

13,000. FS Piazza Municipio 7 (0474 55 57 22). Wed. **www**.bruneck.com

This attractive town, overlooked by the imposing form of its medieval **castle**, retains 14th-century fortifications and a network of narrow streets that can only be explored on foot. The church of **St Ursula**, to the northwest of St Ursula's Gate, holds a series of outstanding mid-15th-century altar reliefs of the Nativity. The **Museo Etnografico di Teodone** offers displays of traditional agricultural life and local costumes; this folklore museum also provides an ideal opportunity to visit a 16th-century farmhouse and barn.

St Ursula's Gate sundial, Brunico

**Museo Etnografico di Teodone**
Via Duca Diet 24, Teodone. **Tel** 0474 55 20 87. *Easter–Oct: Tue–Sat, Sun and public hols pm (Aug: also Mon).*

## Bressanone ❺

BRIXEN

18,000. FS
*Via Ratisbona 9 (0472 83 64 01).*
*Mon.* **www**.brixen.org

The narrow medieval alleys of Bressanone cluster around the cathedral and the palace of the prince-bishops who ruled the town for much of its history. The **Duomo**, on Piazza del Duomo, was rebuilt in the 18th century but retains its 12th-century cloister, decorated with superb 15th-century frescoes. The lavish interiors of Palazzo Vescovile, the bishops' Renaissance palace, house the **Museo Diocesano**. It contains precious items from the Middle Ages, as well as the **Museo dei Presepi**, with its collection of wooden crib figures that are carved locally.

**Environs:** At Velturno (Feldthurns), just 8 km (5 miles) southwest, stands the Renaissance **Castello di Velturno**, the summer retreat of the rulers of Bressanone noted for its frescoed rooms. A little over 3 km (2 miles) north of Bressanone lies the **Abbazia di Novacella**, a picturesque group of fortified monastic buildings with an outstanding series of cloister frescoes. Further north up the valley, at **Rio di Pusteria** (Mühlbach), the remains of a 16th-century fortified barrier can be seen to the east of the town. The barrier funnelled ancient travellers through the customs post that divided Tyrol from the Görz district.

High above Rio di Pusteria, to the southeast, looms the massive outline of the **Castello di Rodengo** (Rodeneck). The castle contains wonderful 13th-century frescoes showing battle scenes, the Last Judgment and courtly episodes from the *Iwein* romance by Hartmann von Aue, the medieval poet.

**Museo Diocesano & Museo dei Presepi**
Piazza Palazzo Vescovile 2. **Tel** 0472 83 05 05. *10am–6pm Tue–Sun (Jul–Sep: 7pm–midnight) (Museo dei Presepi: 10am–6pm Tue–Sun).* *24 & 25 Dec.*

**Castello di Velturno**
Velturno. **Tel** 0472 85 55 25. *Mar–Nov: Tue–Sun.* *only.*

**Abbazia di Novacella**
Via Abbazia 1/2b, Varna. **Tel** 0472 83 61 89. *Mon–Sat.* *Mon (Jan–Mar) & pub hols.* *only.*

**Castello di Rodengo**
Rodengo. **Tel** 0472 45 40 56.
*May–mid-Oct: Tue–Sun.*

The cloisters of Bressanone Duomo with their 15th-century frescoes

**The Baroque interior of the church of St Ulrich in Ortisei**

## Bolzano 6

BOZEN

*98,000.* FS *Piazza Walther 8 (0471 30 70 00).* *Sat.* **www**.bolzano-bozen.it

Bolzano, the capital of the Alto Adige, is the gateway between the Italian-speaking Trentino region and the German-speaking Alto Adige, or Südtirol, and has a marked Tyrolean atmosphere. The old centre, **Piazza Walther**, is dominated by the 15th-century Gothic **Duomo**, with its multicoloured mosaic-patterned roof and elaborate spire.

The "wine door" inside the Duomo is carved with figures at work among vines and reflects the importance of wine to the local economy. In the middle of Piazza Walther is a statue of Walther von der Vogelweide, the 13th-century troubadour – born, according to legend, in this area. North of the square, the streets are lined with houses adorned with intricate gables, balconies and oriel windows. The outdoor market, starting at Piazza Grano, forms an inviting array of local produce that continues along the arcaded Via dei Portici. This street continues to the **Museo Civico**, where South Tyrolean history is introduced through domestic interiors, wood carvings and costumes, while the modern **Museo Archeologico** houses Ötzi, the famous 5,000-year-old "Iceman". The **Chiesa dei Domenicani** (Dominican church), on Piazza Domenicani, has 14th-century *Triumph of Death* frescoes and a frescoed cloister.

**The Duomo spire, Bolzano**

**Museo Civico**
Via Cassa di Risparmio 14. ***Tel*** *0471 97 46 25.* *for renovation.*

**Museo Archeologico**
Via Museo 43. ***Tel*** *0471 32 01 00.* *Tue–Sun (Jul, Aug & Dec: daily).* *1 Jan, 1 May, 25 Dec.*

## Ortisei 7

SANKT ULRICH

*4,500.* *Via Rezia 1 (0471 79 63 28).* *Fri.* **www**.valgardena.it

Ortisei is the prosperous main resort for the pretty Val Gardena and Alpe di Siusi region, and a major centre for woodcarving; examples of local craftsmanship may be seen in local shops, in the **Museo della Val Gardena** (which also focuses on local archaeology), and in the church of **St Ulrich**.

To the south is the **Alpe di Siusi** (Seiser Alm) region, noted for its Alpine meadows, balconied farmsteads and onion-domed churches. The best way to explore this beautiful area is by cableway from Ortisei: to the northeast another cable-car runs to 2,518-m (8,260-ft) high Monte Seceda, and walks from here lead into the Odle Dolomites.

**Museo della Val Gardena**
Via Rezia 83. ***Tel*** *0471 79 75 54.* *Jan–Mar: Tue–Fri; mid-May–Oct: Mon–Fri; Jul & Aug: daily.*

## Canazei 8

*1,800.* *Piazza Marconi 5 (0462 60 96 00).* *Sat (Jul–Sep).*

Located at the base of some of the highest and most awe-inspiring groups of peaks, Canazei is a good base for exploring the Dolomites. In summer, chair-lifts climb to viewpoints where the beauty of the encircling mountains can be appreciated to the full. The most popular viewpoints are Pecol and Col dei Rossi, reached by the Belvedere cableway from Via Pareda in Canazei: the cliffs of the Sella group are visible to the north, with Sasso Lungo to the west

**Skiers enjoying views of the Dolomites above Canazei**

*For hotels and restaurants in this region see pp565–7 and pp613–15*

and Marmolada, the highest of the Dolomites at 3,343 m (10,965 ft), to the south.

**Environs:** At **Vigo di Fassa**, 13 km (8 miles) southwest, the **Museo Ladino** focuses on the Ladin-speaking people of some of the valleys. Ladin – a Rhaeto-Romance language – is taught in local schools and the ancient traditions still thrive.

**Museo Ladino**
Strada de Sen Jan 5, Vigo di Fassa. *Tel 0462 76 01 82. Tue–Sat pm (late Jun–mid-Sep & 20 Dec–6 Jan: daily).*

## Cavalese ❾

*3,600. Via Fratelli Bronzetti 60 (0462 24 11 11). last Tue of month (not Jul).* **www**.visitfiemme.it

**The frescoed façade of the Palazzo della Magnifica Comunità**

Cavalese is the chief town in the Val di Fiemme, a pretty region of flower-filled aromatic pastures, delightful wooded valleys and Tyrolean architecture. At the centre of the town stands the **Palazzo della Magnifica Comunità**. Originally built in the 13th century, this was the seat of the medieval governing council which ruled the area as a semi-autonomous region. Today the panelled interiors contain medieval paintings by local artists, and an archaeology collection. Most visitors come for the excellent summer and winter resort facilities, and to climb, by cable-car, to the 2,229 m (7,311 ft) top of **Alpe Cermis**, the mountain that rises to the south of the town.

**Environs:** The church in **Tesero**, the next village east, bears a 15th-century fresco by an unknown painter depicting Sabbath-breakers. The church itself, dating back to 1450, has a flurry of Gothic vaulting, and a modern representation of the Crucifixion painted against a background of the village.

At **Predazzo**, about 13 km (8 miles) east, the **Museo Geologico e Mineralogico** explains the local geology.

**Vines growing on the terraced slopes of the Cembra valley**

**Palazzo della Magnifica Comunità**
Piazza Cesare Battisti 2. *Tel 0462 34 03 65. call to check times.* **www**.mcfiemme.eu

**Museo Geologico e Mineralogico**
Via SS Filippo e Giacomo 1. *Tel 0462 50 03 66. 10am–noon & 5–7pm Mon–Sat (mid-Sep–Feb by appt).*

## San Martino di Castrozza ❿

*470. Via Passo Rolle 165 (0439 76 88 67).* **www**.sanmartino.com

The resort of San Martino occupies one of the most scenic and accessible valleys in the southern Dolomites, making it very popular with walkers and skiers. Cable cars rise to the peak of **Alpe Tognola** (2,163 m, 7,095 ft), southwest of the town, and up the **Cima della Rosetta** (2,609 m, 8,557 ft) to the east. Both offer fabulous views of the Pale di San Martino peaks, a stirring sight as the massive rock peaks, split by glaciers, rise above a sea of green meadows and woodland. San Martino is almost entirely surrounded by forest, which once supplied the Venetian Republic with timber for ships. The forest is now protected, and as a result it is possible to see Alpine flowers, mushrooms, birds and other wildlife with relative ease.

**Piramidi di Segonzano, near Cembra**

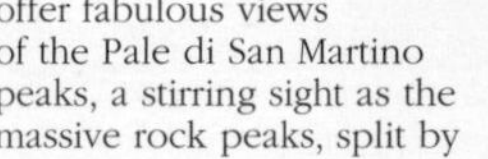

## Cembra ⓫

*2,500. Piazza Toniolli 2 (0461 68 31 10). Wed am.*

The wine-producing town of Cembra nestles on the terraced slopes of a scenic valley of flower-filled villages. Some 6 km (4 miles) east of Cembra stand the **Piramidi di Segonzano**, a rare series of erosion pillars, some over 30 m (100 ft) high, each topped by a rock. The footpath to the pillars is well signposted, with informative noticeboards along the way explaining the formation of the bizarre columns, which are similar in appearance to giant termites' nests. Their setting amid bird-filled woodland makes the steep climb up to the site well worthwhile. A further reward is the fine view, from the top of the hill, along the Cembra valley and westwards as far as the Brenta group of Dolomites.

**Piramidi di Segonzano**
Strada Statale 612 to Cavalese. *daily.*

The impressive falls of the Cascate di Nardis, Madonna di Campiglio

## Madonna di Campiglio ⓬

*1,300.* *Via Pradalago 4 (0465 44 75 01).* *Jul–Aug: Tue & Thu.* **www**.campiglio.to

Madonna di Campiglio is the chief resort in the Val Meledrio. Nestling between the Brenta and Adamello groups of peaks, it makes the perfect base for walking or skiing amid the magnificent mountain terrain. Cableways radiate out from the town in every direction, giving easy access to the peaks.

**Environs:** The church at **Pinzolo**, 14 km (9 miles) south, has a well-preserved fresco depicting a *Dance of Death* (1539). The inevitable march of the figures, both rich and poor, is underlined by a text written in local dialect.

North of Pinzolo, the road west from Carisolo leads to the verdant and popular, yet unspoilt, **Val Genova**. About 4 km (2 miles) along the valley is the spectacular **Cascate di Nardis**, a waterfall that plunges down 90 m (300 ft). The two masses of rock at the bottom are said to be the forms of petrified demons.

## Trento ⓭

*105,000.* FS *Via Manci 2 (0461 21 60 00).* *Thu am.*

Trento, the capital of the region to which it gave its name, is also the most attractive town in Trentino: it has a fine Romanesque cathedral and a richly decorated castle, and streets lined with handsome Renaissance mansions. Trento is noted as the venue for the **Council of Trent** (1545–63), set up by the Catholic Church to consider reforms that might encourage breakaway groups, in particular the German Protestants, to return to the fold. The reforms, which ushered in the period of the Counter-Reformation, were only partly successful.

The **Duomo**, site of some of the Council meetings, was built in robust Romanesque style from the 13th century. It was three centuries before it was completed, in 1515, but the builders maintained architectural harmony by ignoring Gothic and Renaissance styles entirely. The result is a church of unusual integrity, noble and assured. The Duomo stands on **Piazza Duomo**, the city's main square, which was first laid out by the Romans as their central market place or forum. Trento's Roman name, Tridentum, is commemorated in the figure of Neptune who stands holding his trident at the top of the 18th-century fountain, which stands in the middle of the main square.

Inner courtyard of the Magno Palazzo

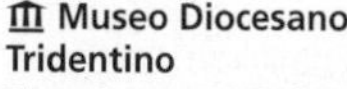

### Museo Diocesano Tridentino

Piazza Duomo 18. ***Tel*** *0461 23 44 19.* *Wed–Mon.* *1 Jan, 25 Dec.*

This museum is housed in the **Palazzo Pretorio**, an imposing medieval building that stands on the eastern side of Piazza Duomo. Its contents include early ivory reliquaries, Flemish tapestries and paintings depicting the Council of Trent.

### Castello del Buonconsiglio

Via Bernardo Clesio 5. ***Tel*** *0461 23 37 70.* *Tue–Sun.* *1 Jan, 25 Dec.*

This large castle, built in the 13th century and later enlarged with additional buildings, is part of the defences of the town. Trento was an important frontier on the main road linking Italy to northern Europe, and thick walls still encircle the town.

The southern section of the castle consists of the magnificent **Magno Palazo** (1530), built for the ruling prince-bishops of Trento, who were given extensive powers by the Holy Roman Emperor to foster loyalty and discourage defection to the pope. The lavish decoration (including frescoes of virile satyrs and nymphs by Gerolamo Romanino, 1531–2) speaks of huge wealth and a luxurious lifestyle. The fine rooms, now the setting for the **Museo Provinciale**, contain paintings, ceramics and 15th-century wood carvings, and prehistoric, Etruscan and Roman items. The **Torre dell'Aquila** (Eagle Tower) nearby contains frescoes painted around 1400. They depict the months

Palazzo Pretorio and the Duomo in Trento's main square

*For hotels and restaurants in this region see pp565–7 and pp613–15*

The commanding form of the Ossario del Castel Dante in Rovereto

of the year in charming detail: the month of January, for instance, has some delightful snowballing scenes.

**Environs:** Immediately to the west of Trento a scenic round-trip along a winding road leads up the north flank of **Monte Bondone** and back, via **Vezzano**, down the western slopes. The views along the route are magnificent, in particular from Vaneze and Vason. East of Trento, Pergine marks the start of the **Val Sugana**, a broad valley with attractive and popular lakes. In the hills north of Lake Levico lies the spa town of **Levico Terme**, distinguished by elegant Neo-Classical buildings set amid beautifully wooded parkland.

## Rovereto ⓮

*33,000.* FS *Corso Rosmini 6 (0464 43 03 63). Tue.*
**www**.visitrovereto.it

Rovereto was at the centre of fierce fighting during World War I, after which the Venetian castle (built in 1416) that dominates the town was transformed into the **Museo Storico della Guerra**, a war museum. The displays include sections devoted to wartime humour, propaganda and spying. Near the entrance to the museum, stairs lead out on to the castle roof for a view of the imposing **Ossario del Castel Dante**.

Some distance away is the **Campana dei Caduti** (Bell of the Fallen), one of the largest bells in Italy, which was cast from melted-down cannons at the end of World War II and mounted in an imposing building above the town; it is rung daily at sunset.

Below the war museum stands the **Museo Civico**, with its collections on archaeology, art, natural history and folklore, while the Mario Botta-designed **Museo di Arte Contemporanea di Trento e Rovereto (MART)** showcases 20th-century Italian art.

**Environs:** A little over 8 km (5 miles) north of Rovereto is **Castel Beseno**, rising on a hill to the east. This enormous castle, by far the largest in the region, was built and rebuilt from the 12th century to the 18th to guard the junction of the three valleys. The ruins are undergoing restoration.

Five kilometres (3 miles) south of Rovereto, the main road passes through a valley littered with massive house-sized boulders created by landslips: these are known as Lavini di Marco or **Ruina Dantesca**, because they are mentioned in Dante's *Inferno* (XII, 4–9). Fossilized dinosaur footprints have been discovered there.

**Museo Storico della Guerra**
Via Castelbarco 7. ***Tel*** *0464 43 81 00. Tue–Sun. 1 Jan, 24, 25, 31 Dec.*

**Museo Civico**
Borgo Santa Caterina 41. ***Tel*** *0464 43 90 55. Tue–Sun. 1 Jan, 5 Aug, 1 Nov, 25 Dec.*

**MART**
Corso Bettini 43. ***Tel*** *0464 43 88 87. Tue–Sun.*

**Castel Beseno**
Besenello. ***Tel*** *0464 83 46 00. Mar–Nov: Tue–Sun (Mon if public hol); Dec–Feb: Sat & Sun.*

Castello di Avio in its lush setting

## Castello di Avio ⓯

Via Castello, Sabbionara d'Avio. ***Tel*** *0464 68 44 53.* FS *to Vo, then 3-km (2-mile) walk. Mar–Sep: 10am–6pm Tue–Sun; Oct–Feb: 10am–5pm Tue–Sun.*

Castles line the Adige valley all the way to the Brenner Pass, but few are as accessible as the Castello di Avio. It was founded in the 11th century, extended in the 13th, and today offers visitors far-reaching views. Among the numerous frescoes with secular themes is a rare series in the Casa delle Guardie (the Sentry House) depicting 13th-century battle scenes.

The extensive walls enclosing Castel Beseno above Rovereto

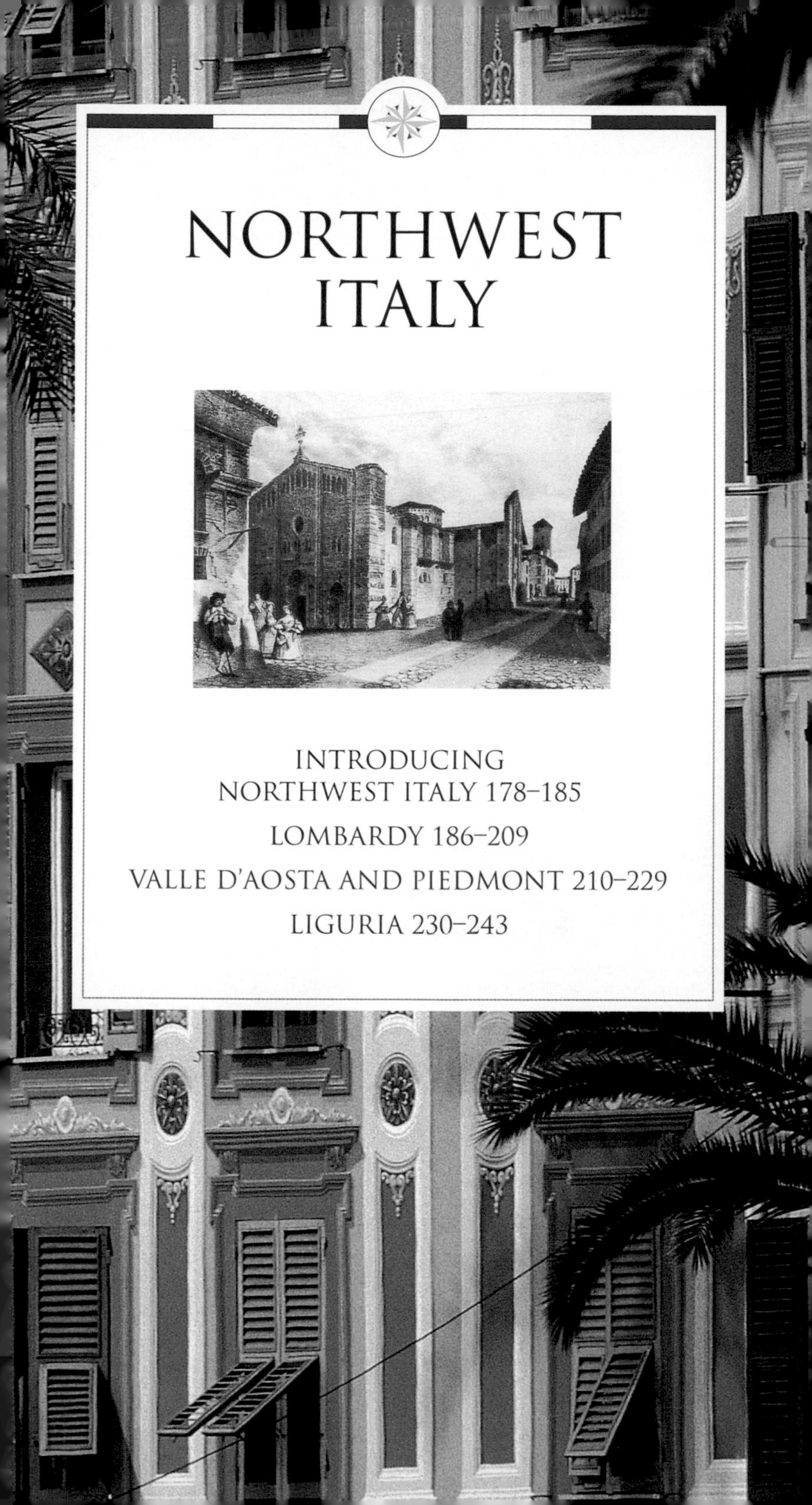

# NORTHWEST ITALY

# Northwest Italy at a Glance

The northwest of Italy is made up of three very different geological characteristics: the jagged Alps, the flat plain, and the undulating shoreline of the Mediterranean. Within this varied landscape, some of it still wild and unspoilt, lie extremely rich and diverse vestiges of the area's substantial cultural heritage. The major sights, in the regions of Valle d'Aosta and Piedmont, Liguria and Lombardy, are shown on this map.

**The Parco Nazionale del Gran Paradiso** *is a beautiful wilderness, and the habitat of rare Alpine fauna and flora* (see pp216–17).

**The capital of Piedmont** *is Turin, an elegant and bustling city of splendid Baroque architecture. Its skyline is dramatically dominated by the Mole Antonelliana* (see p224).

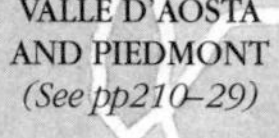


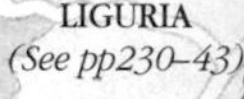

**San Remo** *is a typical Riviera resort, with palm trees and a casino. The onion-domed outline of the Russian church adds an exotic flavour to the town* (see p234).

**The Basilica di Sant'Andrea** *in Vercelli is an important Romanesque building, one of the earliest to use Gothic elements* (see p228).

◁ **Typical shuttered Ligurian façades in Santa Margherita Ligure**

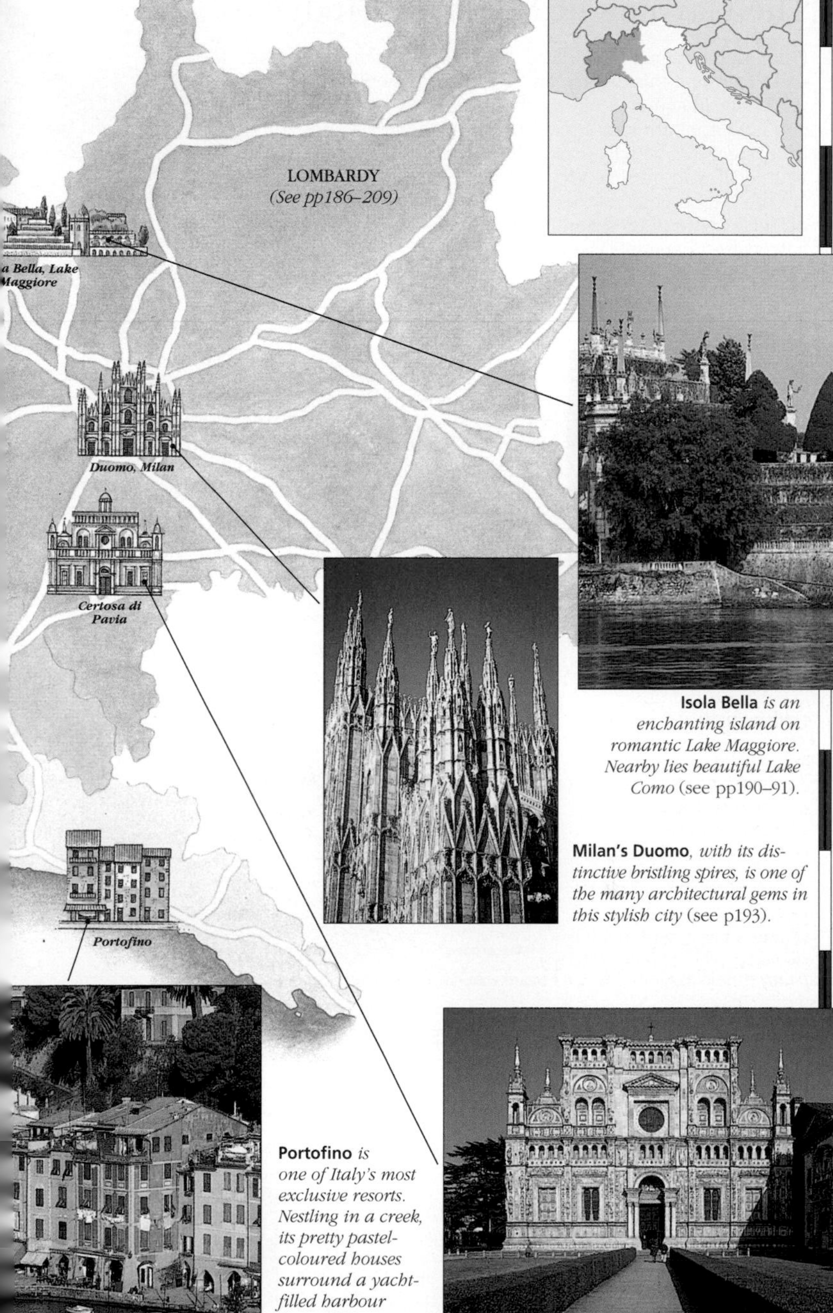


**Isola Bella** *is an enchanting island on romantic Lake Maggiore. Nearby lies beautiful Lake Como* (see pp190–91).

**Milan's Duomo**, *with its distinctive bristling spires, is one of the many architectural gems in this stylish city* (see p193).

**Portofino** *is one of Italy's most exclusive resorts. Nestling in a creek, its pretty pastel-coloured houses surround a yacht-filled harbour* (see p240).

**The Certosa di Pavia**, *a charming Carthusian monastery, includes a richly decorated Gothic church with a magnificent Renaissance façade, and a series of attractive cloisters* (see pp204–5).

# The Flavours of Northwest Italy

From Mediterranean Liguria to the Alps, the Lombardy plain and Piedmont, this diverse area is characterized by its rich yet hearty cuisine. Along with the Veneto, Lombardy and Piedmont are Italy's main rice-growing areas and risotto features widely, especially delicious when made with local wild mushrooms. The white truffles of Alba are the "white gold" of Piedmont, while lush pastures produce some of the country's best meat and many of Italy's finest cheeses. The mild Ligurian climate favours olives and herbs – especially basil, used in pesto sauce. And fish teem in the sparkling Mediterranean.

Fresh basil

A precious haul of aromatic Piedmontese truffles

## LOMBARDY

This is the home of dishes prepared *alla Milanese,* rich in butter, *osso buco* (shin of veal), vegetable soups and boiled meats *(bollito misto).* From veal to beef and from pork to poultry, Lombardy produces some of the country's finest meat, but it is also associated with *cucina povera* (the cuisine of the poor) in which polenta (maize porridge) still features from its days as the staple diet of impoverished countryfolk. The other staple food, the short-grained rice that is used in risotto, grows abundantly in the area around Pavia. Lombardy is one of Italy's largest cheese-making regions, the most famous including Gorgonzola, Mascarpone, Bitto and Grana Padano.

Mouthwatering range of northwest Italy's finest cheeses

## PIEDMONT & VALLE D'AOSTA

The "Slow Food" movement was born in Piedmont in 1986. Its mission is "to defend biodiversity in our food supply, spread taste education and connect producers of excellent food". The movement now has more than 100,000 members in more than 50 countries. Piedmontese flavours are

## REGIONAL DISHES AND SPECIALITIES

Veal is especially popular in Lombardy and Piedmont, and a great favourite with the Milanese is *osso buco.* Another classic Piedmontese dish, *vitello tonnato* is a surprisingly delicious blend of cold roast veal and tuna fish served with a mayonnaise sauce with gherkins and capers. As well as pesto, a traditional dish from Genoa is *buridda alla Genovese* – a delicious fish soup or stew containing mussels, shrimps, octopus, squid and clams. Shavings of truffle in dishes such as risotto and *fagiano tartufato* (pheasant stuffed with white truffle and pork fat) give a taste of sheer luxury and, fortunately, a little of this very expensive delicacy goes a long way. And, for those with a sweet tooth, *panettone* is a soft Christmas cake studded with dried and candied fruit, another Milanese speciality.

Gianduiotti

**Bagna Caôda** *From Piedmont, a warm mix of olive oil, anchovies and garlic into which raw vegetables are dipped.*

Boxes of fresh fish are unloaded onto a Ligurian quayside

robust, rich and earthy, laced with French flair, reflecting a history of French rule and influence.

The paddy fields of Vercelli are the rice capital of Europe and truffle risotto, especially when flavoured using the prized white variety from Alba, is truly memorable fare.

The mountains are famous for cow's milk cheese, especially the semi-soft Fontina from the Valle d'Aosta, cured meats, salamis, terrines and game. Piedmont also produces Italy's greatest red wines, and the prized Barolo and Barbaresco often feature as a marinade in beef dishes.

The Turinese are passionate about chocolate, echoing Turin's tradition of chocolate-making originating in the 17th century. Most famous are the sublime ingot-shaped *gianduiotti,* filled with a rich chocolate-hazelnut cream. The city is also the birthplace of *grissini,* crisp breadsticks that grace every restaurant table. The tradition of the *aperitivo* also originates in Turin. The spread that accompanies a glass of Prosecco or a cocktail in bars throughout the city between 6pm and 8pm is substantial.

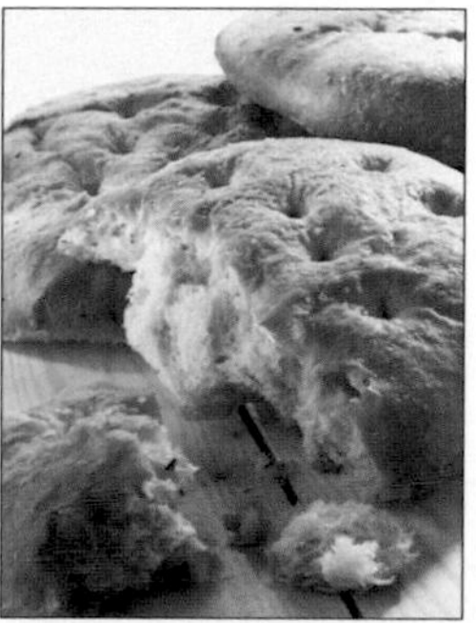
Delicious foccacia bread made with Ligurian olive oil

## LIGURIA

The Mediterranean climate is perfect for growing herbs, fruit and vegetables, nuts and olives. Ligurian olive oil is of the highest quality and is used in the preparation of many dishes. To accompany pasta, pesto is the signature sauce, made from basil, pine nuts, garlic and olive oil, as well as a mix of Pecorino and Parmesan. This use of aromatic herbs is typical of Ligurian cuisine in general.

Not surprisingly, fish and seafood are as common as meat and dairy in this region, where the vast majority of people live on the coast.

### ON THE MENU

**Agnolotti** Piedmont pasta speciality – crescent-shaped ravioli stuffed with meat or vegetables. Served with *ragù* or a creamy sauce.

**Brasato al Barolo** Braised beef cooked gently with vegetables in Barolo wine.

**Lumache** Piedmontese snails, the best of which come from Cherasco, served either in garlic and butter or in a sauce of olive oil, tomatoes and garlic.

**Oca alla Piemontese** Goose preserved in fat.

**Risotto alla Milanese** Rich, saffron-scented dish of rice with white wine, onion and Parmesan cheese.

**Trenette con pesto** *A Ligurian dish of flat noodles with a sauce of basil, garlic, pine nuts and olive oil.*

**Osso Bucco** *Milanese shin of veal, braised slowly in white wine. The bone marrow is considered a delicacy.*

**Zabaione** *A frothy dessert of egg yolks, sugar and Marsala, zabaione is a speciality of the Piedmont region.*

# The Wines of Northwest Italy

Medieval illustration of a grape crusher

Grapes are grown throughout the northwest – from the cliffs of Liguria to the steep mountainsides of Valle d'Aosta. The best wines, however, come from Piedmont, in particular the Langhe hills southwest of Turin, source of two of Italy's finest reds: the rich, powerful, long-lived Barolo and Barbaresco. Both of these are now showing the benefits of modern techniques and a renewed interest in high-quality wine making. Lighter, everyday red wines that go well with the local cuisine include Dolcetto and the popular Barbera. Another Piedmont speciality is sparkling *spumante,* Italians' instinctive choice whenever there is something around to celebrate.

Castiglione Falletto in the heart of Piedmo

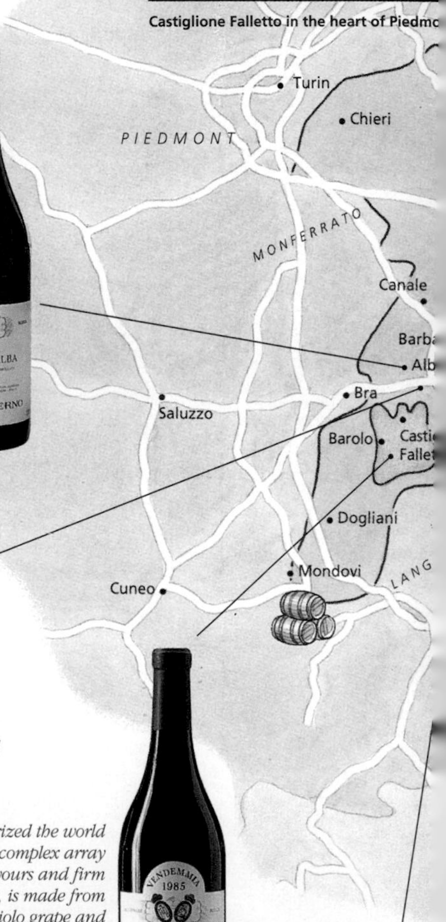

**Barbera d'Alba** *comes from the adaptable Barbera grape, which can grow on almost any slope. Its ubiquitous nature means that the wines it yields can be light and full of fruit, as well as dense, strong and full-flavoured. Good producers include Aldo Conterno, Voerzio, Pio Cesare, Altare, Gaja, Vaira and Vietti.*

Turin
Chieri
PIEDMONT
MONFERRATO
Canale
Bra
Saluzzo
Barolo
Dogliani
Mondovi
Cuneo

**Dolcetto** *is grown in seven different areas. Dolcetto d'Alba has a delicious perfume and deep purple colour. Best drunk within one or two years, it ranges in flavour from fresh and fruity to the rich, concentrated plumminess of some of the top wines, such as those produced by Giuseppe Mascarello.*

**KEY**

- Barolo
- Barbaresco
- Other vineyard areas

0 kilometres 25

0 miles 15

**Barolo**, *prized the world over for its complex array of flavours and firm tannins, is made from the Nebbiolo grape and may take up to 20 years to mature. Vigna Colonnello is a top Barolo from Aldo Conterno, made only in the best years, like 2006, 2005, 2004 and 1993.*

**The white truffle** of Alba is an autumn speciality from the Langhe hills. Highly prized for its earthy scent, it is excellent with Barolo.

**Moscato d'Asti** *is an excellent* aperitivo *or light dessert wine made from the aromatic, fruity Moscato grape. It is light in alcohol with a gently sweet finish and may have a slight sparkle. Ideal for refreshing the palate after a hearty Piedmontese meal, Araldica's versatile Moscato is delicious when served well chilled.*

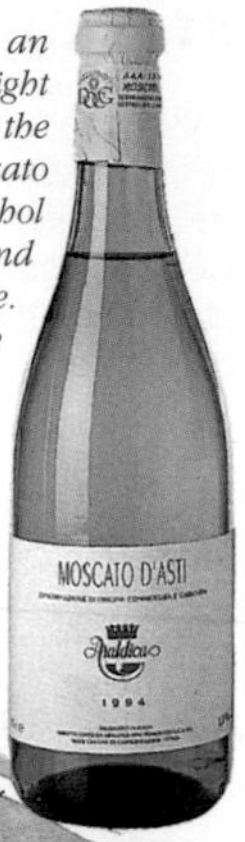

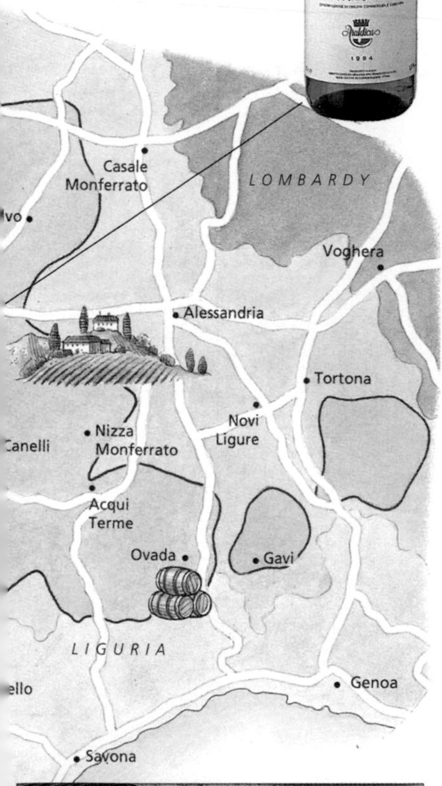

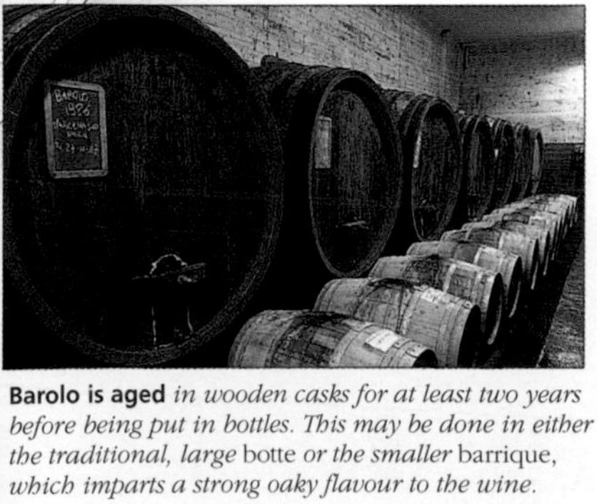

## GRAPES OF THE NORTHWEST

The Nebbiolo grape is used to produce two of Italy's finest red wines, Barolo and Barbaresco, as well as other regional wines in the Valtellina and north of Turin. It is a difficult grape to cultivate and requires a long growing season to soften its high acidity. However, the final results are worth it: in the Langhe region the Nebbiolo offers complex perfumes and a range of flavours, often encased within strong tannins. Easier to handle and lighter, the Dolcetto and Barbera both came from the Monferrato region originally. These reds yield lighter, fruitier wines but, when at their best, no less distinctive than those of the Nebbiolo. Of the white grapes, the Moscato is Piedmont's oldest known variety. Famous for the successful sparkling Asti Spumante, the best grapes are reserved for Moscato d'Asti.

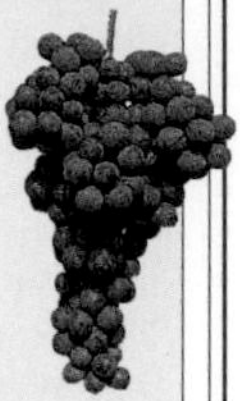

**Nebbiolo grapes**

## HOW TO READ THE LABEL

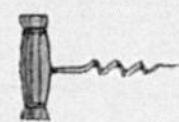

**Good Vintages**

*Barolo and Barbaresco had good years in* 2006, 2005, 2004, 2003, 2000, 1998, 1997.

**Barolo is aged** *in wooden casks for at least two years before being put in bottles. This may be done in either the traditional, large* botte *or the smaller* barrique*, which imparts a strong oaky flavour to the wine.*

# Understanding Architecture in Northwest Italy

Although the buildings of the northwest tend to be solid and imposing – a result partly of the more severe climate – there is no distinctive architectural stamp as there is around Venice, Florence or even in Rome. Instead, a variety of buildings in different styles, many borrowed or reinterpreted from elsewhere, are dotted across the area: enchanting medieval castles, outstanding Romanesque and Gothic buildings, unusual Baroque structures. The northwest is also rich in modern architecture – in terms of both design and materials – influenced by the region's industrial developments and its strong flair for innovative design, which also often draws its inspiration from earlier architectural styles.

**Castello Sforzesco, 1451–66** *(see p192)*

## CHARACTERISTICS OF NORTHWEST ITALIAN ARCHITECTURE

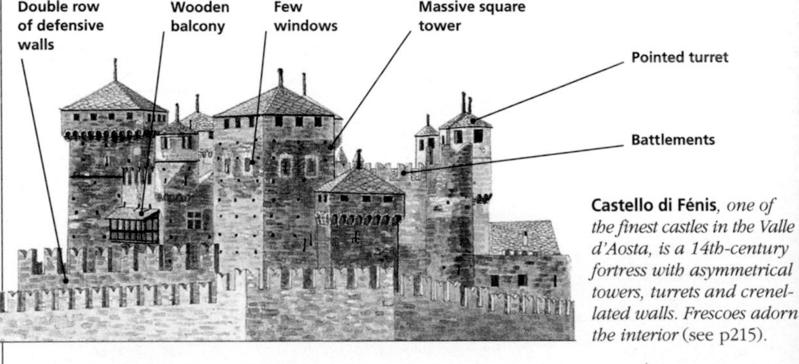


**Castello di Fénis**, *one of the finest castles in the Valle d'Aosta, is a 14th-century fortress with asymmetrical towers, turrets and crenellated walls. Frescoes adorn the interior* (see p215).

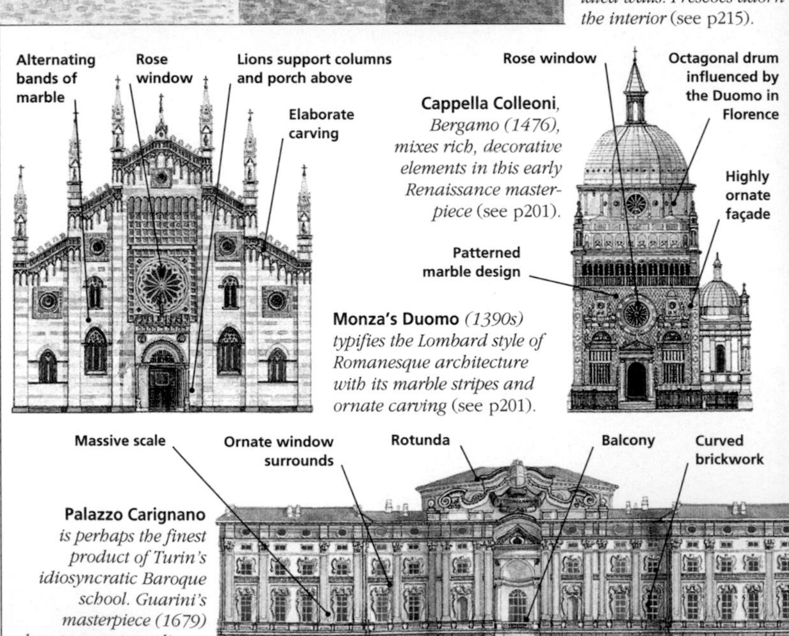


**Cappella Colleoni**, *Bergamo (1476), mixes rich, decorative elements in this early Renaissance masterpiece* (see p201).

**Monza's Duomo** *(1390s) typifies the Lombard style of Romanesque architecture with its marble stripes and ornate carving* (see p201).

**Palazzo Carignano** *is perhaps the finest product of Turin's idiosyncratic Baroque school. Guarini's masterpiece (1679) boasts an extraordinary undulating brick façade and a fine rotunda* (see p223).

## WHERE TO SEE THE ARCHITECTURE

The road to Aosta is flanked by numerous medieval castles *(see p214)* while inspirational Romanesque and Gothic churches are found in Lombardy – at Monza *(p201)*, Pavia *(p203)*, Milan *(pp192–201)*, and Como *(pp190–91)*. The 15th-century Certosa di Pavia *(pp204–5)* is a must, as well as the charming city of Mantua *(p207)*. Turin *(pp220–24)* is famous for its unique Baroque school, and Bergamo for its exuberance. Architecture from the last two centuries is best represented in Milan and Turin, and in Genoa some exciting redevelopment projects are taking place.

**Renzo Piano's mast structure (1992) in Genoa's redeveloped port**

## 19TH–20TH CENTURY ARCHITECTURE

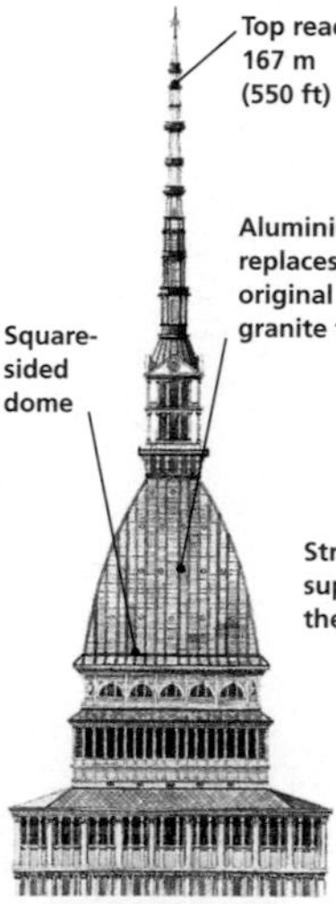

Top reaches 167 m (550 ft)

Aluminium replaces original granite top

Square-sided dome

**The Mole Antonelliana** *(1863–97), designed by Antonelli, was the tallest building in the world when it was built* (see p224).

**Galleria Vittorio Emanuele II** *in Milan, designed by Mengoni in 1865, was the first Italian building to use glass and iron structurally* (see p194).

Central dome

Mosaics

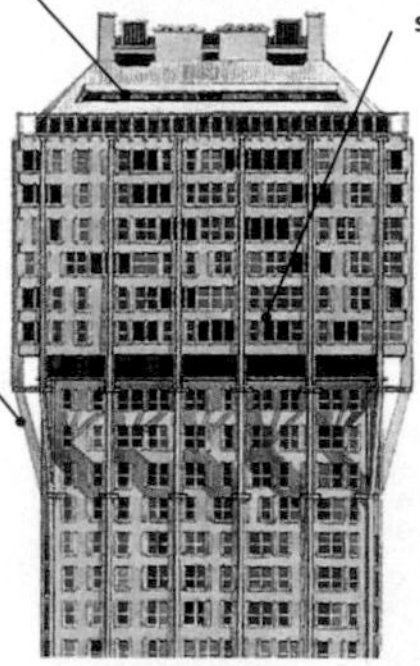

Glass balcony

Overhanging upper storeys

Struts support the top

**Torre Velasca, Milan** *is a 26-floor tower south of the Duomo. The design, from the 1950s, was influenced by medieval castles such as the Castello Sforzesco.*

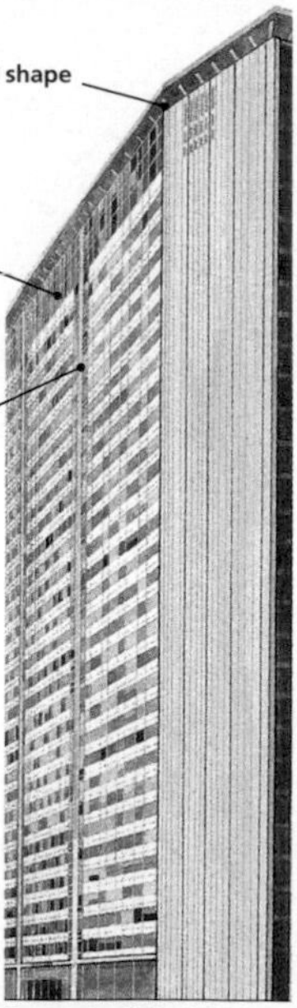

Elliptical shape

Taller windows

Tapering struts

Spiral ramps up to roof

Roof served as test track

Reinforced concrete

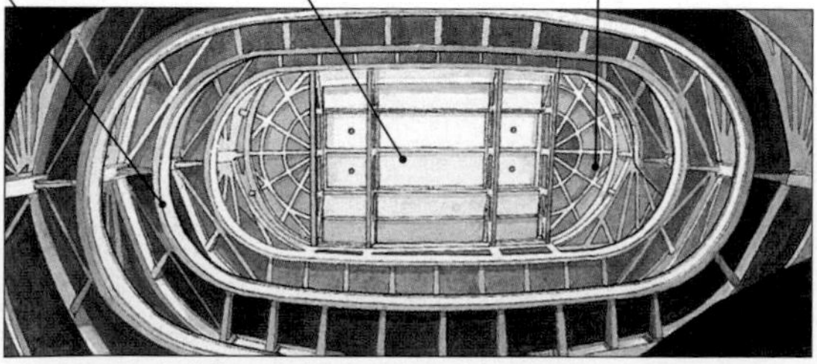

**The Lingotto building, Turin,** *was built in 1915–18 as FIAT's car factory. Made of advanced materials, it was the first large-scale modern building in Italy. The structure of the ramps up to the roof is similar to the interior of Guarini's Baroque dome for San Lorenzo in Turin.*

**Milan's Pirelli building**, *by Ponti and Nervi, is an elegant and innovative skyscraper built in 1959.*

# LOMBARDY

*The region of Lombardy stretches from the Alps, on the border with Switzerland, down through the romantic lakes of Como and Maggiore to the broad, flat plain of the River Po. It is an area of lakeside villas with azalea-filled gardens, of wealthy towns with imposing palazzi and highly decorated churches, and of efficient, modern industry and large-scale agriculture, the financial heart of Italy. At its centre stands Milan, the style-conscious capital of Lombardy.*

The region was named after the Lombards or Longobards, a Germanic tribe that invaded Italy in the 6th century AD. During the Middle Ages, Lombardy was part of the Holy Roman Empire, but not always loyal to its German emperors. The Lombards, who had a talent for banking and commerce, resented any outside interference with their prosperity.

The 12th century saw the rise of the Lega Lombarda, or Lombard League, a band of forceful separatists founded to counter the brutal imperialism of Frederick Barbarossa (their most modern incarnation being the Lega Nord political party). Power was seized by the region's great families, most notably the Visconti and the Sforza of Milan, from the 14th to the early 16th century. These dynasties also became great patrons of the arts, commissioning exquisite palaces, churches and artworks, many of which can still be seen. Bergamo, Mantua and Cremona – not to mention Milan itself – contain a remarkably rich array of art treasures. Here are such pinnacles of European civilization as the charterhouse at Pavia, Leonardo da Vinci's *Last Supper* and the magnificent paintings of the Pinacoteca di Brera in Milan.

Lombardy – famous as the birthplace of Virgil, Monteverdi, Stradivarius and Donizetti – today offers visitors the contrasting pleasures of lyrical lakeside landscapes (resorts on lakes Como and Maggiore have attracted poets, aristocrats and gamblers for centuries) and beautiful, bustling cities.

**Strolling through Milan's enormous Galleria Vittorio Emanuele II**

◁ **The peaceful shores of the beautiful Lake Como, southwest of Bellagio**

# Exploring Lombardy

The enormous plain of the River Po runs through much of Lombardy, providing a landscape that is flat and perfectly suited to the consequent expansion of industry in the region. This is, however, also a region of great contrasts. To the north, in a still unspoilt setting in the foothills of the mountains, lie the lakes Como and Maggiore, as well as the dramatic valleys and peaks of the Parco Nazionale dello Stelvio around Bormio, Sondrio and Val Camonica. Further south, busy industrialized areas give way to huge tracts of agriculture dotted with towns of great beauty such as Cremona, Mantua and Pavia, which offer a rich and splendid array of artistic pleasures.

**A view of Isola Bella on Lake Maggiore**

## SIGHTS AT A GLANCE

Bergamo 5
Brescia 9
*Certosa di Pavia pp204–5* 12
Cremona 13
Lago d'Iseo 8
Lake Como 1
Lake Maggiore 2
Lodi 10
Mantua 15
*Milan (Milano) pp192–201* 3
Monza 4
Parco Nazionale dello Stelvio 6
Pavia 11
Sabbioneta 14
Val Camonica 7

**The colourful façade of the Cappella Colleoni in Bergamo**

**For additional map symbols**
*see back flap*

Livigno
Merano
PARCO NATIONALE DELLO STELVIO
Bormio
6
Santa Caterina Valfurva
Alpi Retiche
Pizzo Verona 3453m
Sondalo
Chiareggio
Grosio
Bolzano
Pizzo Scalino 3323m
S38
Ponte di Legno
Caspoggio
S42
Sondrio
Tirano
Edolo
Adamello 3554m
Aprica
Saviore dell'Adamello
Valbondione
VAL CAMONICA
Parco Nazionale delle Incisioni Rupestri
Capo di Ponte
Breno
7
Clusone
Monte Colombine 2215m
Trento
S42
Lovere
Limone sul Garda
Pisogne
Bovegno
Magasa
Marone
8
S45b
LAGO D'ISEO
Carro
Barghe
Gargnano
Sarnico
Iseo
Nave
Salò
Rovato
Lago di Garda
Chiari
9 BRESCIA
S11
Rezzato
Desenzano del Garda
A4
S11
Lonato
Verona
Ghedi
Orzinuovi
Montichiari
Oglio
Solferino
Manerbio
Leno
Chiese
Verona
S236
Soresina
Goito
Roverbella
Pontevico
Casaloldo
Ostiano
Mincio
S45b
Asola
A22
Castel d'Ario
A21
Cicognolo
S10
15 MANTOVA
13 CREMONA
Piadena
S420
Pianura Padana
S12
Ostiglia
San Daniele Po
Gazzuolo
Po
SABBIONETA
Quistello
Sermide
S482
14
Suzzara
Ferrara
Casalmaggiore
Po
Gonzaga
Poggio Rusco
Po
Viadana
Modena

Passo di Gavia in the Parco Nazionale dello Stelvio on the eastern fringes of Lombardy

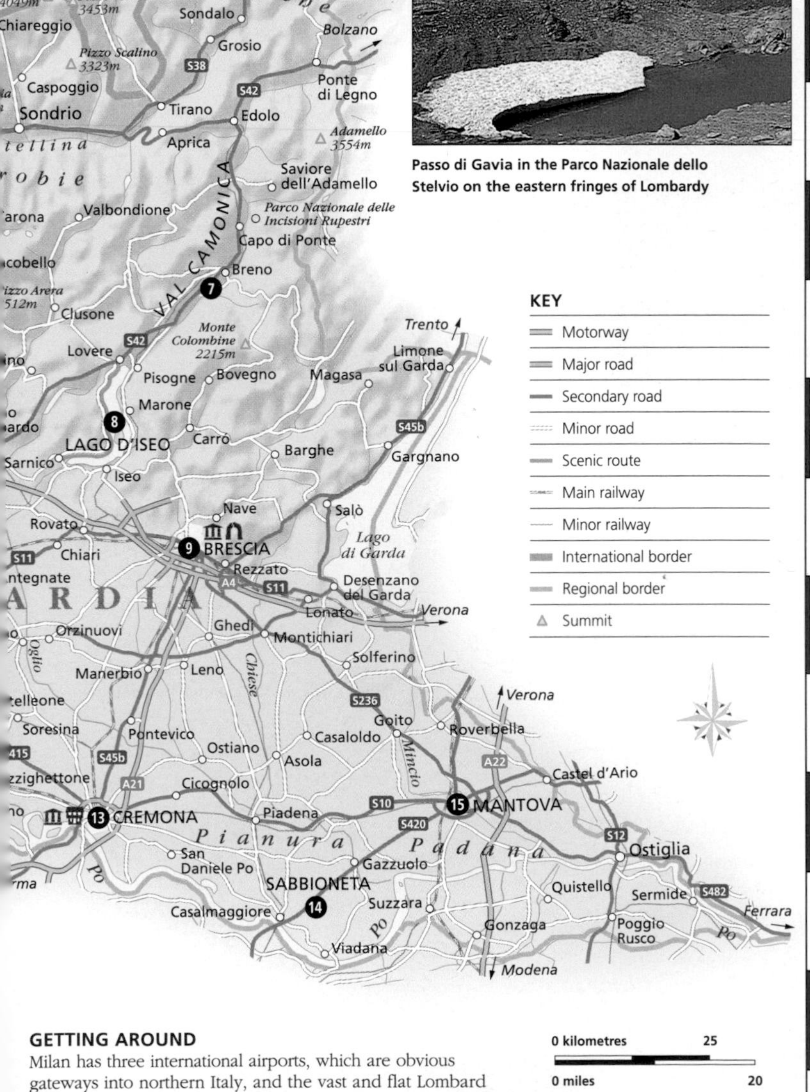

**KEY**

- Motorway
- Major road
- Secondary road
- Minor road
- Scenic route
- Main railway
- Minor railway
- International border
- Regional border
- Summit

## GETTING AROUND

Milan has three international airports, which are obvious gateways into northern Italy, and the vast and flat Lombard plain has its advantages when it comes to transport: roads and railway lines criss-cross it and make trips between the larger towns very easy. The lakes, however, are better visited by car, as only two main towns are served by trains, though there are bus and boat services around the shores. The Parco Nazionale dello Stelvio and the mountains are more remote still, but offer good tourist facilities.

**SEE ALSO**

• ***Where to Stay*** pp567–71

• ***Where to Eat*** pp615–18

# Lake Como ❶

Set in an idyllic landscape of mountains and rugged hillsides, Lake Como has for centuries attracted visitors who come here to go boating, for walks in the hills, or for relaxation and inspiration. The northern stretches, in particular, are shrouded in an almost eerie calm. The long and narrow lake, crafted into a wishbone shape by glacial erosion, offers fine views up to the Alps and down to the towns of Como and Lecco.

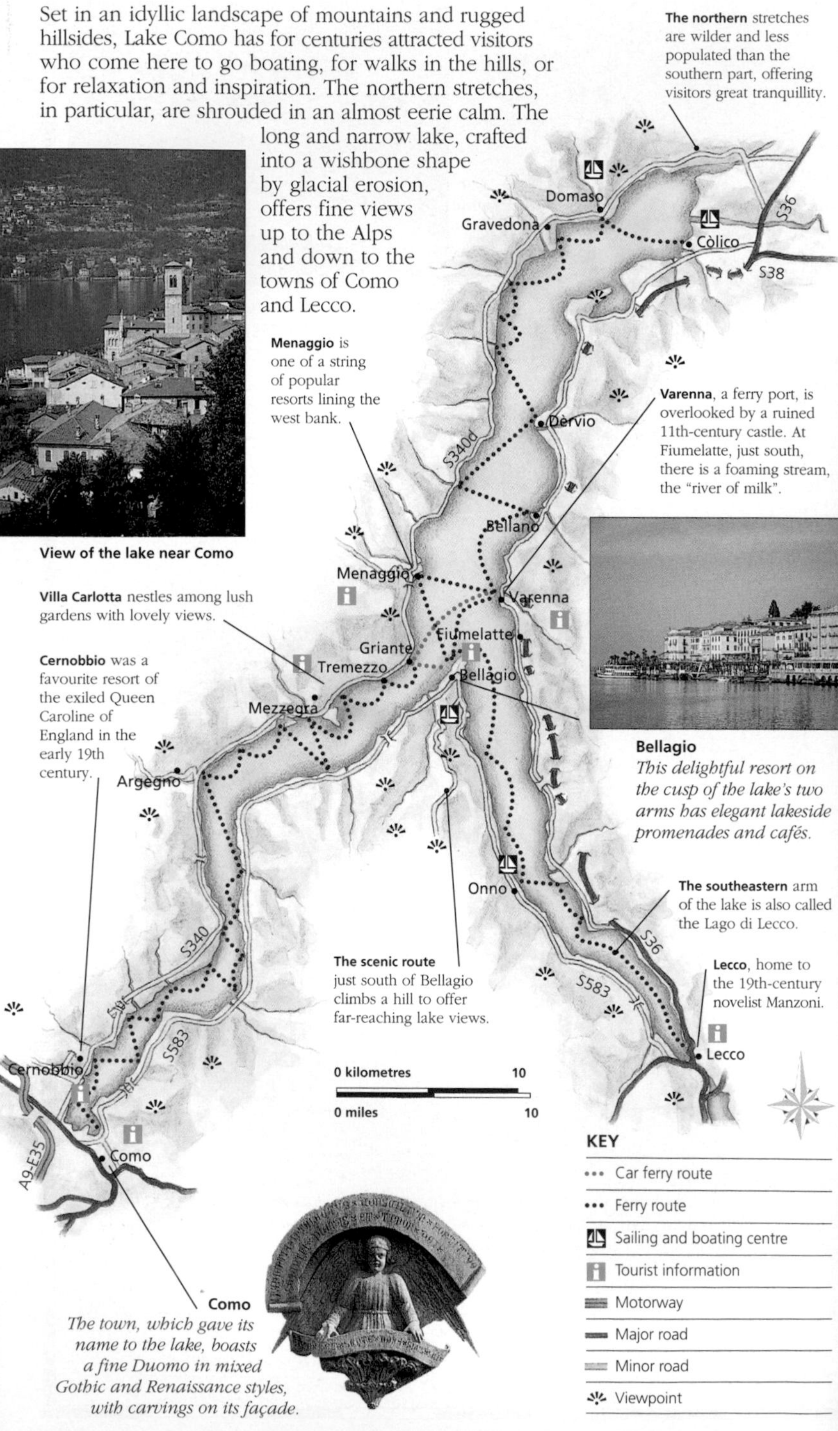


View of the lake near Como

### VISITORS' CHECKLIST

FS *Como, Lecco.* *all towns.* *P.za Cavour 17, Como (031 26 97 12); Via Sauro 6, Lecco (0341 29 57 20).* **www**.lakecomo.org

**Tadoline's copy (1834) of Canova's *Cupid and Psyche* in Villa Carlotta**

**Exploring Lake Como**

In the heart of **Como** lies the elegant Piazza Cavour. Nearby rises the beautiful 14th-century **Duomo**, with its 15th- and 16th-century reliefs and paintings, and fine tombs. The 18th-century dome is by Turin's famous Baroque architect, Juvarra. Next to the Duomo stand the 13th-century Broletto (town hall), charmingly striped in white, pink and grey, and the tall Torre del Comune. At Tremezzo, **Villa Carlotta** is an elegant 18th-century summerhouse known for its gardens. In springtime, all sorts of flowers burst into colour in this pretty setting. The villa houses a collection of sculptures.

**Lecco**, a small industrial town lying to the south of the lake's eastern arm, was home to Alessandro Manzoni (1785–1873). The writer's childhood home, the **Casa Natale di Manzoni**, is devoted to memorabilia of his life and works. A monument in Piazza Manzoni depicts scenes from his most famous novel, *I Promessi Sposi (The Betrothed)* – set in 17th-century Lecco and Milan.

**Villa Carlotta**
Via Regina 2b, Tremezzo. ***Tel** 0344 404 05.* *15 Mar–Oct: 9am–6pm daily (Mar & Oct: 9am–noon, 2–4:30pm).* **www**.villacarlotta.it

**Casa Natale di Manzoni**
Via Guanella 1, Lecco. ***Tel** 0341 48 12 47.* *9:30am–5:30pm Tue–Sun.* *1 Jan, Easter, 1 May, 15 Aug, 25 Dec.*

## Lake Maggiore ❷

Verbania. FS *Stresa, Verbania, Baveno & the islands.* *Piazza Marconi 16, Stresa (0323 301 50).* **www**.distrettolaghi.it

Lake Maggiore, the second largest Italian lake after Lake Garda, is a long expanse of water nestling right against the mountains and stretching into Alpine Switzerland; it is warmer in atmosphere and more romantic than Lake Como. The gently sloping shores are dotted with camellias, azaleas and verbena vegetation – from which the ancient lake derived its Roman name, Verbanus.

A huge copper statue of Cardinal San Carlo Borromeo, the chief patron of the lake, stands in **Arona**, the town where he was born in 1538. It is possible to climb up and look out over the lake through his eyes and ears. Arona also boasts a ruined castle and a chapel, Santa Maria, dedicated to the Borromeo family.

Further up the western coast of the lake is **Stresa**, the chief resort and main jumping-off point for visits to the islands; the town boasts many grand hotels, handsome villas and pleasant gardens. Behind Stresa, a cable car ride away, rises Monte Mottarone, a snow-capped peak offering spectacular panoramic views of the surrounding mountains, including Monte Rosa.

**The statue of Carlo Borromeo in Arona**

The **Borromean islands**, at the centre of the lake near Stresa, are small jewels of natural beauty augmented by artificial grottoes, architectural follies and landscaped gardens. The **Isola Bella** is home to the 17th-century **Palazzo Borromeo** and its splendid gardens, while Isola Madre is largely given over to a botanical garden. The only island inhabited all year round is Isola dei Pescatori, with a population of 50. The private Isola di San Giovanni is the smallest of the isles, with a villa that once belonged to the great conductor Arturo Toscanini (1867–1957).

The lake becomes quieter towards the Swiss border, but continues to be lined with attractive villas. The **Villa Taranto**, on the outskirts of Verbania, houses a fine exotic botanical collection.

About 3 km (2 miles) west of **Cannobio**, a market town near Switzerland, is the dramatic gorge and tumbling waterfall of the Orrido di Sant'Anna, which can be reached by boat.

**Palazzo Borromeo**
Isola Bella. *from Stresa.* ***Tel** 0323 305 56.* *mid-Mar–Oct: daily.* **www**.borromeoturismo.it

**Villa Taranto**
Via Vittorio Veneto III, Verbania, Pallanza. ***Tel** 0323 55 66 67.* *mid-Mar–Oct: daily.*

**Isola Bella's 17th-century Palazzo Borromeo and garden on Lake Maggiore**

# Milan ❸

Detail from the Duomo

Centre of fashion, business and finance, Milan has a bustling, businesslike feel about it. It is smart rather than attractive – a city of wealth as opposed to imagination and the heartland of the Italian economy. Its name is thought to come from a composite of the Latin words *medio* and *planum*, meaning "middle of the plain". It has long been an important trading centre at the junction of transalpine routes, and a prize for powerful dynasties. Today, it is the best place to see Italy at its most cosmopolitan and stylish.

***Portrait of a Young Woman* by Pollaiuolo, Museo Poldi-Pezzoli**

### Castello Sforzesco

Piazza Castello. ***Tel*** *02 88 46 37 00.* **Castello** *daily.* **Musei del Castello** *9am–5:30pm Tue–Sun.* *public hols.* **www**.milanocastello.it

The first castle on this site was built by the Visconti family, but demolished when their reign ended in the mid-15th century. Milan's new ruler, Francesco Sforza, built in its place this Renaissance palace. The castle is based on a series of courtyards, the most beautiful of which, the Cortile della Rocchetta, is a graceful arcaded square designed by Bramante and Filarete. The palace now contains, together with sections on Applied Arts, Archaeology and Coins, the **Musei del Castello**. This fine collection of furniture, antiquities and paintings includes Michelangelo's unfinished sculpture known as the *Rondanini Pietà*. The canvases in the picture collection, dating from the Renaissance to the 18th century, are particularly impressive.

**Michelangelo's *Rondanini Pietà* (c.1564) in the Castello Sforzesco**

### Museo Poldi-Pezzoli

Via Alessandro Manzoni 12. ***Tel*** *02 79 48 89.* *10am–6pm Tue–Sun.* **www**.museopoldipezzoli.it

Giacomo Poldi-Pezzoli was a wealthy nobleman who, on his death in 1879, bequeathed his magnificent art collection to the state. Its most famous painting is the 15th-century Renaissance *Portrait of a Young Woman* by Antonio Pollaiuolo, though there are also works by Piero della Francesca, Botticelli and Mantegna, among others. The applied arts section is richly endowed with fascinating items ranging from rugs and lace to glass, enamels and porcelain, as well as sculpture, jewellery and sundials.

### SIGHTS AT A GLANCE

Castello Sforzesco ①
Civico Museo Archeologico ⑫
Duomo ⑥
Galleria Vittorio Emanuele II ⑤
Museo Poldi-Pezzoli ③
Palazzo Reale (Museo della Reggia) ⑦
Parco Sempione ⑬
Pinacoteca Ambrosiana ⑨
*Pinacoteca di Brera pp198–9* ②
San Lorenzo Maggiore ⑪
San Satiro ⑧
Sant'Ambrogio ⑩
Teatro alla Scala ④

Key to Symbols *see back flap*

### Teatro alla Scala

P.za della Scala. ***Tel*** *02 85 45 62 16.* **Box Office *Tel*** *02 72 00 37 44.* **Museo Teatrale** Largo Ghiringhelli 1 (Piazza Scala). ***Tel*** *02 88 79 24 73.* *9am–noon, 1:30–5pm daily.* **www**.teatroallascala.org

This Neo-Classical theatre opened in 1778 and is one of the world's most prestigious opera houses. It has one of the largest stages in Europe and hosts sumptuous productions. Two hours before each performance 140 tickets go on sale; unsold tickets are discounted. The **Museo Teatrale** houses sets and costumes of past productions, portraits of conductors and theatrical items dating back to Roman times. There is also a good view of the auditorium, with its gilded box galleries, *trompe-l'oeil* effects and huge chandelier.

**The façade of the world-famous Teatro alla Scala**

## VISITORS' CHECKLIST

*1,465,000.* *Malpensa 50 km (31 miles) NW; Linate 8 km (5 miles) E.* FS *Stazione Centrale, P.za Duca d'Aosta.* *P.za Freud.* *P. del Duomo 19 (02 77 40 43 43); Stazione Centrale (02 77 40 43 19).* *daily.* *7 Dec: Sant'Ambrogio.* **www**.provincia.milano.it

### Duomo

Piazza del Duomo. ***Tel*** *02 72 02 26 56.* *daily.* **Baptistry digs** *9am–5pm.* **Treasury** *9:30am–1pm, 2–6pm Mon–Fri, 9:30–11:30am, 2–5pm Sat, 1:30–4pm Sun & public hols.* **Roof** *9am–5:45pm (to 4:15pm Nov–Feb).* *for roof.* **www**.duomomilano.it

Milan's giant cathedral is one of the largest Gothic churches in the world. It was begun in the 14th century under Prince Gian Galeazzo Visconti but not completed until more than 500 years later. The building's most startling feature is the extraordinary roof, with its 135 spires and innumerable statues and gargoyles, and from which, on a clear day, there are views of the Alps. Below, the façade boasts a dazzling assortment of styles from Gothic through to Renaissance and Neo-Classical. The bronze doors are faced with bas-reliefs recounting episodes from the life of the Virgin and of Sant'Ambrogio, and scenes retelling the history of Milan.

Inside, the aisles are divided by 52 giant pillars and lit from all sides by remarkable stained-glass windows. Look out for the Visconti family symbol – a serpent swallowing a man – in the fine tracery of the apse windows. Among the many tombs and statues is a depiction of the flayed San Bartolomeo carrying his own skin.

The treasury, beneath the main altar, contains much medieval gold and silverwork, and the remains of a 4th-century baptistry.

**The Gothic Duomo, crowned with spires**

# Exploring Milan

In addition to the great monuments in Milan, such as the cathedral and the castle, there is a host of varied and interesting museums, churches and civic buildings which provide an enthralling mix of old and new. This chic and busy metropolis offers plenty of opportunities for cultural activities, gastronomic adventures, designer-fashion shopping or just strolling about, Milan-style.

**The glass ceiling and dome covering the Galleria Vittorio Emanuele II**

### Galleria Vittorio Emanuele II

Main entrances on Piazza del Duomo and Piazza della Scala.

This ornate shopping arcade, known as *il Salotto di Milano* (Milan's drawing room), was designed by the architect Giuseppe Mengoni in 1865. The galleria had a tragic start, however, as Mengoni fell to his death from the scaffolding not long before its inauguration in 1877 (a year before the arcade was actually finished). Tourists are nevertheless attracted to its stylish shops and cafés, as well as Savini, one of Milan's historic restaurants.

The galleria itself has a floor plan in the shape of a Latin cross, with an octagonal centre adorned with mosaics representing four continents (Europe, America, Africa and Asia), together with others representing Art, Agriculture, Science and Industry. Its finest feature is its metal and glass roof, crowned with a magnificent central dome. The roof was the first structure in Italy to use metal and glass in a structural way, rather than just decoratively. The floors are decorated with mosaics of the signs of the zodiac; tourists may be seen stepping on the genitals of Taurus the Bull, which is said to bring good luck.

### Palazzo Reale

Piazza del Duomo. **Tel** *02 87 56 72.*
*Museo della Reggia.*

The former royal palace, for centuries home to the Visconti and other rulers of Milan, houses the **Museo della Reggia**. It displays the sumptuous interiors of the building and showcases the four historic phases of the palace including the Neo-Classical era and the Restoration. Palazzo Reale is also a prestigious venue for temporary art exhibitions. The building abutting it to the west (the Arengario) has been transformed into a Modern Art museum, and many Italian art works from the 20th century are displayed here.

### Villa Belgiojoso Bonaparte – Museo dell'Ottocento and Galleria d'Arte Moderna

Villa Belgiojoso Bonaparte, Via Palestro 16. **Tel** *02 76 34 08 09.*
*9am–1pm, 2–5:30pm Tue–Sun.*
**www**.gam-milano.com

Milan's 19th-century and Modern Art collections are housed in a Neo-Classical villa built by Leopold Pollack in 1790 for Count Ludovico Barbiano di Belgiojoso. It was lived in by Napoleon in 1802 and later by Marshal Radetzky. The villa houses 19th-century Italian art, showing all the major art movements, as well as the Grassi and Vismara collect-ions of 19th- and 20th-century Italian and foreign artists and the Marino Marini Museum. Of particular note are works by Giorgio Morandi (1890–1964), Carlo Carrà (1881–1966), as well as by Modigliani (1884–1920) and De Chirico (1888–1978). Non-Italian artists include Van Gogh, Cézanne, Gauguin, Picasso, Matisse, Klee, Mondrian and Kandinsky.

***Still Life* (1920) by Giorgio Morandi in the Galleria d'Arte Moderna**

*For hotels and restaurants in this region see pp567–71 and pp615–18*

*Fruit Basket* (c. 1596) by Caravaggio in the Pinacoteca Ambrosiana

### Pinacoteca Ambrosiana

Piazza Pio XI 2. **Tel** *02 80 69 21.* *10am–5:30pm Tue–Sun.* **www**.ambrosiana.it

The Ambrosiana is home to Cardinal Federico Borromeo's magnificent library of 30,000 manuscripts. These include a 5th-century illustrated *Iliad,* early editions of Dante's *Divine Comedy* (1353) and the *Atlantic Codex* (1478–1519) by Leonardo da Vinci. In order to exhibit as much of the *Atlantic Codex* as possible, the pages on show are changed every three months.

The building also houses an art gallery, bequeathed by Borromeo in 1618. The collection ranges from 14th-century pieces to works of the early 19th century. Among the canvases are *Portrait of a Musician* by Leonardo, the *Madonna of the Canopy* by Botticelli (15th century), a cartoon version of Raphael's Vatican fresco, *The School of Athens* (16th century), and Caravaggio's *Fruit Basket.* There is also a strong collection of Venetian art, with paintings by Giorgione, Titian, Bassano and Tiepolo, and panel paintings by the late 15th-century Lombard painter Bergognone.

### San Satiro

Via Speronari 3. **Tel** *02 87 46 83.* *7:30–11:30am, 3:30–5:30pm daily.*

This church, its full title Santa Maria presso San Satiro, is one of the most beautiful Renaissance buildings in Milan. Built on the site of a 9th-century sanctuary, little of which remains apart from the Cappella della Pietà, beside an 11th-century bell tower.

The interior seems to be in the shape of a Greek cross, but this is an illusion created by *trompe-l'oeil* effects, since space restrictions led Bramante to choose a T-shaped plan. Above the altar is a 13th-century fresco. An octagonal baptistry lies off the right aisle. The church's façade was finished in the 19th century.

### Civico Museo Archeologico

Corso Magenta 15. **Tel** *02 86 45 00 11.* M *1, 2 Cadorna.* *16, 19.* *18, 50, 58.* *9am–1pm, 2–5:30pm Tue–Sun.* *(phone ahead).*

At the entrance to this museum visitors are greeted by a huge stone from the Val Camonica with Bronze Age engravings, and nearby is a model of Roman Milan. The exhibition begins in a hall on the right, containing clay objects and Roman sculpture. At the end of this room is a huge fragment of a torso of Hercules and 3rd-century AD floor mosaics. Also in this room are two of the most important works in the museum: the Parabiago Patera and the Diatreta Cup. The Patera is a gilded silver plate with a relief of the goddess Cybele (4th century AD). The Diatreta Cup, dating from the same period, is a single piece of coloured glass, with finely wrought, intricate decoration.

The courtyard contains the Torre di Ansperto, a Roman tower from the Maximinian walls erected between 1 BC and AD 5. The basement has a collection of Attic red- and black-figure vases and Etruscan relics.

### Parco Sempione

Piazza Castello–Piazza Sempione. M *1 Cadorna, Cairoli, 2 Lanza, Cadorna.* *Ferrovie Nord, Cadorna.* *1, 3, 4, 12, 14, 27, 29, 30.* *43, 57, 61, 70, 94.* *Mar–Apr: 6:30am–9pm; May: 6:30am–10pm; Jun–Sep: 6:30am–11:30pm; Oct: 6:30am–9pm; Nov–Feb: 6:30am–8pm.*

Although it covers an area of about 47 ha (116 acres), this park occupies only a part of the old Visconti ducal garden, enlarged by the Sforza in the 15th century to make a 300-ha (740-acre) hunting reserve.

The present-day layout was designed by Emilio Alemagna between 1890–93.

During World War II the park was used to cultivate wheat, but after a period of reconstruction it was returned to its former splendour.

Among the trees are the monuments to Napoleon III by Francesco Barzaghi, De Chirico's Metaphysical construction *Mysterious Baths,* the sulphur water fountain and the Torre Branca, a tower made of steel tubes in 1932 after a design by Gio Ponti.

View of the Parco Sempione with the Arco della Pace in the background

# Shopping in Milan

In Milan, one of the most affluent cities in Italy, shopping is synonymous with buying designer apparel. High-fashion flagship stores here are invariably smart and stylish, especially in the city centre, and looking is almost as satisfying as making a purchase. However, Milan also has many independent boutiques with a range of styles to suit all tastes. If you are looking for gifts to take home, there are some excellent *pasticcerie* (pastry shops), where you can buy authentic delicacies and traditional local confectionery. Alternatively, a cutting-edge object of design will make for an impressive souvenir of your trip to the city.

## WHERE TO SHOP

All leading fashion designers have shops in the area between Via Montenapoleone, Via della Spiga, Via Manzoni and Via Sant'Andrea, the so-called "fashion quadrilateral".

Those interested in interior design will enjoy Via Durini, while lovers of antiques should head to Brera or the Navigli, where antiques markets are held monthly.

If time is of the essence, call ahead to check opening hours. In Milan generally, non-food shops are closed on Monday mornings, and food shops are closed on Monday afternoons. The largest shops tend to stay open throughout the day, but sometimes a lunch break is taken. Shops are closed on Sundays, except for the run-up to Christmas and during the main fashion shows.

## DESIGNER FASHION

Milan is renowned as a world capital of fashion, and most national and international designers have a flagship store here. As well as the designers that you would expect to find in a fashion centre, such as **Dolce & Gabbana**, **Giorgio Armani**, **Gucci**, **Prada** and **Hugo Boss**, there are many smaller designer stores. For an overview of what's new, check out multibrand boutiques such as **Banner**, which features a selection of the best from a wide array of names. For the latest on what the younger set is wearing, go to **Amedeo D** or to the Corso di Porta Ticinese area.

Up-and-coming designers are gathering in the areas around Corso Garibaldi and Corso Como. As well as of-the-moment clothes and accessories, **10 Corso Como** offers a bookshop, record store, art gallery, café and restaurant, and even a top-class B&B. The **Gianfranco Ferrè** boutique, on the other hand, has a spa attached.

Most designers carry men's as well as women's apparel. Specialist men's stores include **Pal Zileri**, **Ermenegildo Zegna** and **Corneliani**.

## REGULAR CLOTHING

Designer outlets sell samples, seconds and last season's goods at a discount. Among Milan's longest-established outlets are **Salvagente** and **DMagazine**. Many designers also have their own outlets: fans of Max Mara, for example, should head for **Diffusione Tessile**.

Milan's main department stores are **La Rinascente** and **Coin**. The former carries many leading-edge fashion designers, while the latter features smaller fashion labels, handbags, costume jewellery and housewares. There is more to Milan than upmarket, cutting-edge designer fashion, though. For good-value casualwear for the whole family, try **Oviesse**.

Many fashion shoppers also scour the stalls at the Saturday market at Viale Papiniano, at the Piazza Sant'Agostino end, which starts at 8.30am and goes on until 5pm. Corso Vercelli is also recommended.

## ACCESSORIES

Handbags, shoes, hats and jewellery, real or otherwise, are also worth seeking out. Chains such as **Furla** and **Coccinelle** offer a wide array of bags, while those looking for shoes can head to **René Caovilla** for a pair of stylish heels, or purchase comfortable shoes with a twist from **Tod's** and **Hogan**. **Garlando** carries a number of classic styles in a wide array of colours and sizes, while **Ghigodonna** has elegant shoes in larger sizes. **Borsalino** is synonymous with stylish headwear.

The "fashion quadrilateral" also features many jewellers, such as **Federico Buccellati**, **Bulgari** and **Pianegonda**.

## FOOD AND WINE

Gourmands will have a great time in Milan. **Peck** consists of three floors of the best that Italy can offer, in terms of both food and wine. **Giovanni Galli Marroni e Canditi** offers a different take on chocolate-coated delicacies.

For those who like a hands-on approach to their food, **High Tech** is a goldmine for kitchen tools, including all the top names such as Alessi, as well as plates and cutlery.

## DESIGN, BOOKS AND GIFTS

Milan is the cradle of designer furniture. Several top stores are around Piazza San Babila. A stroll down Via Durini will reveal, among others, **Cassina** and **B&B**. For lighting, see **Flos** and **Artemide**. Those interested in 20th-century design could visit **Spazio 900**.

If an item of furniture is not an option, the next best thing might be a book on design or architecture. Visit the bookshop of the **Triennale** or that of the art-catalogue publisher **Skira** for the best on the market.

**Fabriano**, the company that developed the first paper mill in the 1200s, has a store selling handsome writing paper, envelopes and gift items.

## DIRECTORY

### DESIGNER FASHION

**10 Corso Como**
Corso Como 10.
**Tel** *02 2900 2674.*
**Tel** *02 626 163 (B&B).*
**Tel** *02 2901 3581 (bar & restaurant).*
**Tel** *02 653 531 (gallery).*
**www**.10corsocomo.it

**Amedeo D**
Corso Vercelli 23.
**Tel** *02 4800 4048.*
**www**.amedeod.it

**Banner**
Via Sant'Andrea 8.
**Tel** *02 7600 4609.*
**www**.biffi.com

**Corneliani**
Via Montenapoleone 12.
**Tel** *02 777 361.*
**www**.corneliani.com

**Dolce & Gabbana**
Via della Spiga 26 (women).
**Tel** *02 7600 1155.*
Corso Venezia 15 (men).
**Tel** *02 7602 8485.*
Via della Spiga 2 (women's accessories).
**Tel** *02 795 747.*
Corso Venezia 7 (D&G).
**Tel** *02 7600 4091.*
**www**.dolcegabbana.it

**Ermenegildo Zegna**
Via Montenapoleone 27.
**Tel** *02 7600 6437.*
**www**.zegna.com

**Gianfranco Ferrè**
Via Sant'Andrea 15.
**Tel** *02 794 864 or 02 780 406* (spa and beauty parlour).
**www**.gianfrancoferre.com

**Giorgio Armani**
Via Sant'Andrea 9
**Tel** *02 7600 3234.*
Via Manzoni 31 (megastore).
**Tel** *02 7231 8600.*
Via Montenapoleone 2 (Collezioni).
**Tel** *02 7639 0068.*
Via Montenapoleone 10 (Armani Junior).
**Tel** *02 783 196.*
Via Manzoni 37 (Armani Casa).
**Tel** *02 657 2401.*
Corso di Porta Ticinese 60 (Armani Jeans).
**Tel** *02 8324 1924.*
**www**.giorgioarmani.com

**Gucci**
Via Montenapoleone 5–7.
**Tel** *02 771 271.*
Galleria Vittorio Emanuele (accessories).
**Tel** *02 859 7991.*
**www**.gucci.com

**Hugo Boss**
Corso Matteotti 11 (men).
**Tel** *02 7639 4667.*
Corso Matteotti 8 (women).
**Tel** *02 7601 3266.*
**www**.hugoboss.com

**Pal Zileri**
Via Manzoni 20.
**Tel** *02 7639 4680.*
**www**.palzileri.com

**Prada**
Galleria Vittorio Emanuele 63–65.
**Tel** *02 876 979.*
Via Montenapoleone 8 (women).
**Tel** *02 777 1771.*
Via Montenapoleone 6 (men).
**Tel** *02 7602 0273.*
Via della Spiga 18 (accessories).
**Tel** *02 780 465.*
**www**.prada.com

### REGULAR CLOTHING

**Coin**
Piazza Cinque Giornate.
**Tel** *02 5519 2083.*
Corso Vercelli 8.
**Tel** *02 4399 0001.*
Piazza Cantore.
**Tel** *02 5810 4385.*
**www**.coin.it

**Diffusione Tessile**
Galleria San Carlo 6.
**Tel** *02 7600 0829.*

**DMagazine**
Via Montenapoleone 26.
**Tel** *02 7600 6027.*

**Oviesse**
Galleria Passarella 2.
**Tel** *02 7628 1677.*
Corso Garibaldi 72.
**Tel** *02 655 1649.*
Corso Buenos Aires 35.
**Tel** *2040 4801.*
**www**.oviesse.it

**La Rinascente**
Piazza del Duomo.
**Tel** *02 88 521.*
**www**.rinascente.it

**Salvagente**
Via Fratelli Bronzetti 16.
**Tel** *02 7611 0328.*
**www**.salvagentemilano.it

### ACCESSORIES

**Borsalino**
Galleria Vittorio Emanuele.
**Tel** *02 8901 5436.*
**www**.borsalino.com

**Bulgari**
Via Montenapoleone 2.
**Tel** *02 777 001.*
**www**.bulgari.com

**Coccinelle**
Via Manzoni 26.
**Tel** *02 7602 8161.*
Corso Buenos Aires 16.
**Tel** *02 2040 4755.*

**Federico Buccellati**
Via della Spiga 2.
**Tel** *02 7600 3867.*
**www**.federicobuccellati.it

**Furla**
Piazza Liberty 8.
**Tel** *02 782 449.*
Corso Vercelli 11.
**Tel** *02 4801 4189.*
**www**.furla.com

**Garlando**
Via Madonnina 2.
**Tel** *02 874 665.*
**www**.alfonsogarlando.it

**Ghigodonna**
Viale Tunisia 2.
**Tel** *02 2940 8414.*
**www**.ghigocalzature.com

**Hogan**
Via Montenapoleone 23.
**Tel** *02 7601 1174.*
**www**.hogan.com

**Pianegonda**
Via Montenapoleone 6.
**Tel** *02 7600 3038.*
**www**.pianegonda.com

**René Caovilla**
Via Bagutta 28.
**Tel** *02 7631 9049.*
**www**.renecaovilla.com

**Tod's**
Via della Spiga 22.
**Tel** *02 7600 0983.*
Galleria Vittorio Emanuele.
**Tel** *02 877 997.*
**www**.todsgroup.com

### FOOD AND WINE

**Giovanni Galli Marroni e Canditi**
Via Victor Hugo 2.
**Tel** *02 8646 4833.*

**High Tech**
Piazza XXV Aprile 12.
**Tel** *02 624 1101.*

**Peck**
Via Spadari 9.
**Tel** *02 802 3161.*
**www**.peck.it

### DESIGN, BOOKS AND GIFTS

**Artemide**
Corso Monforte 19.
**Tel** *02 7600 6930.*
**www**.artemide.com

**B&B**
Via Durini 14.
**Tel** *02 764 4411.*
**www**.bebitalia.it

**Cassina**
Via Durini 16.
**Tel** *02 7602 0745.*
**www**.cassina.it

**Fabriano**
Via Ponte, Vetero 17.
**Tel** *02 7631 8754.*
**www**.cartierefabriano.it

**Flos**
Corso Monforte 7.
**Tel** *02 794 559.*
**www**.flos.net

**Skira**
Via Torino 61.
**Tel** *02 724 441.*
**www**.skira.it

**Spazio 900**
Viale Campania 51.
**Tel** *02 7012 5737.*
Corso Garibaldi 42.
**Tel** *02 7200 1775.*

**Triennale**
Viale Alemagna 6.
**Tel** *02 7201 8128.*
**www**.triennale.it

# Milan: Pinacoteca di Brera

Milan's finest art collection is held in an imposing 17th-century building, the Palazzo di Brera. This is where, in the 18th century, the Accademia di Belle Arti was founded; the picture collection developed alongside the academy. Inside the Brera hang some of the finest examples of Italian Renaissance and Baroque painting, including works by Piero della Francesca, Mantegna, Canaletto, Bellini, Raphael, Tintoretto, Veronese and Caravaggio. The collection also includes 20th-century works by some of Italy's most famous modern artists.

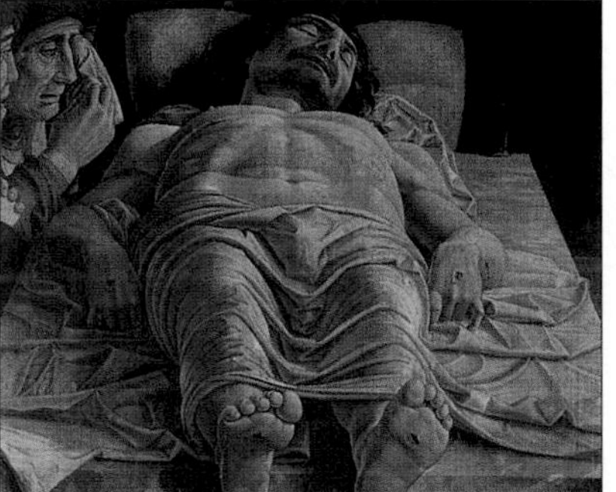

**★ Dead Christ by Mantegna**
*The subtle lighting and dramatic perspective of this lamentation by Mantegna (1430–1506) make it one of his greatest masterpieces.*

**GALLERY GUIDE**
*The collection is displayed in 38 rooms, and was first built up by paintings from churches, later from acquisitions. Not all of it is permanently on view – this is due to restoration work and research.*

**Twin staircases** lead up to the first-floor entrance of the Pinacoteca.

**The Kiss** *(1859)*
*Francesco Hayez's painting is one of the most reproduced works of Italian 19th-century art. Patriotic and sentimental, it became a symbol of the optimism surrounding the unification of Italy.*

**The bronze statue** (1809) by Canova depicts Napoleon as a demi-god with Victory wings in his hand.

**KEY TO FLOORPLAN**

- 15th- to 16th-century Italian painting
- 16th- to 17th-century Dutch and Flemish painting
- 17th-century Italian painting
- 18th- to 19th-century Italian painting
- 20th-century Italian painting and sculpture and Jesi Collection
- Non-exhibition space

**Works by** Rubens and Van Dyck represent some of the non-Italian artists on show.

*For hotels and restaurants in this region see pp567–71 and pp615–18*

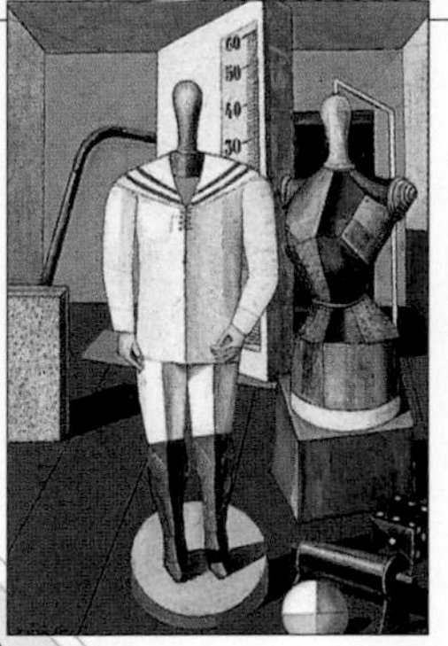

**Mother and Son** *(1917)*
*The metaphysical paintings of Carlo Carrà show a dream world full of strange and obscure symbols.*

## VISITORS' CHECKLIST

Via Brera 28. ***Tel*** *02 72 26 31; 02 89 42 11 46.* *Lanza, Montenapoleone & Duomo.* *61, 97.* *8:30am–7:15pm Tue–Sun (last adm: 45 min before closing).* *1 Jan, 1 May, 25 Dec.* **www**.brera.beniculturali.it

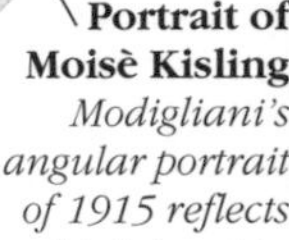

**Portrait of Moisè Kisling**
*Modigliani's angular portrait of 1915 reflects his interest in African sculpture.*

**Twinned columns** support the arcades in the courtyard.

**The stone façade** presents a regular and slightly austere appearance.

**Madonna della Candeletta** *(c.1490)*
*This painting by Carlo Crivelli was the central part of a polyptych. It is richly detailed with much distinctive ornamentation.*

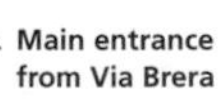

**Main entrance from Via Brera**

**★ Marriage of the Virgin by Raphael**
*This graceful altarpiece was painted in 1504. The circular temple is signed with the artist's name.*

## STAR PAINTINGS

- ★ Dead Christ by Mantegna
- ★ Marriage of the Virgin by Raphael

# Milan: Southwest of the Centre

Some of Milan's finest treasures are to be found in its religious buildings: the ancient monasteries and churches make up some very fine architectural ensembles in themselves, as well as incorporating important ruins and relics dating back to Roman times. It is also in Milan that one of the most famous images in the world is to be found: Leonardo's evocative masterpiece, *The Last Supper*.

**The entrance to Sant'Ambrogio, flanked by unequal bell towers**

### Sant'Ambrogio

Piazza Sant'Ambrogio 15. ***Tel*** *02 86 45 08 95.* **Basilica** *7am–noon, 3–7pm daily.* **Museum** *10am–noon, 3–5pm Tue–Sun.*
**www**.santambrogio-basilica.it

Sant'Ambrogio, or St Ambrose, Milan's patron saint and its bishop in the 4th century, was so eloquent that bees were said to fly into his mouth, attracted by his honey tongue. This is the basilica that he began building in AD 379, though today most of it is 10th-century Romanesque. A gateway leads to the bronze doors of the entrance, flanked by two bell towers. Inside, note the fine rib vaulting and pulpit, and the striking 9th-century altar decorated with gold, silver and gems. In a chapel off the south aisle, fine mosaics line a stunning cupola. Down in the crypt lies the tomb of Sant'Ambrogio himself.

Above the portico, a small museum contains architectural fragments, tapestries and paintings relating to the church.

### San Lorenzo Maggiore

Corso di Porta Ticinese 39. ***Tel*** *02 89 40 41 29. 7:30am–12:30pm, 2:30–6:45pm daily.*
**Cappella Sant'Aquilino** *9am–6:30pm daily. for the Cappella.*
**www**.sanlorenzomaggiore.com

This church contains a vast collection of Roman and early Christian remains. The octagonal basilica was built in the 4th century, above what was probably a Roman amphitheatre, and rebuilt in the 12th and 16th centuries.

In front of the church stands a row of 16 Roman columns and a statue of the Emperor Constantine. Fine 4th-century mosaics adorn the Cappella di Sant'Aquilino, a Romanesque chapel, which also contains two early Christian sarcophagi. Other Roman architectural elements, incorporated into the building of this church, are in a chamber below the chapel.

**San Lorenzo Maggiore viewed from the northeast**

### Santa Maria delle Grazie

Piazza Santa Maria delle Grazie 2. ***Tel*** *02 48 01 42 48.* **Cenacolo** ***Tel*** *02 92 80 03 60 (booking compulsory – up to 60 days in advance). 8:15am–6:45pm Tue–Sun. public hols.*
**www**.cenacolovinciano.org

This beautiful 15th-century Renaissance convent, its lovely apse and calm small cloister designed by Bramante, contains one of the key images of western civilization: the *Cenacolo (The Last Supper)* by Leonardo da Vinci. The image captures the moment at which Christ tells his disciples that one of them will betray him. The Christ figure is unfinished: Leonardo did not consider himself worthy enough to complete it.

The artist also spurned the standard fresco technique of painting on wet plaster, applying tempera to the dry wall instead. The result has deteriorated badly: the paint is flaking off, and restoration has proved difficult. The painting is now protected by a filtering system.

**Leonardo da Vinci's *Last Supper* (1494–7) adorning the refectory wall of Santa Maria delle Grazie**

**THE EDICT OF MILAN**

Milan was colonized by the Romans in 222 BC, and quickly grew to be an important city at the junction of various trading routes. As the Roman Empire grew and then split into two, the emperors began to neglect Rome for the better-placed Mediolanum (literally, city in the middle of the plain). It was here that Emperor Constantine declared his edict of AD 313, in which Christianity was recognized as one of the permitted religions of the empire, ending centuries of persecution. The emperor is said to have converted following a vision, but by the 4th century adopting Christianity was also one way to unite the disparate empire.

Emperor Constantine

## Monza ❹

Monza. 125,000. FS *P.za Carducci 2 (039 32 32 22).* *9am–12:30pm, 3–6pm daily.* *Thu & Sat.*

These days Monza is mostly famous for its international Formula One **Autodromo**, which lies inside a vast park that also has an elegant Rococo hunting lodge, the Villa Reale, and a golf course. At one time, however, Monza was one of the most important towns in Lombardy. Theodolinda, the 6th-century Lombard queen, built its first cathedral and bequeathed her treasure to the town.

In the town centre is the **Duomo**, with its notable green and white 14th-century façade and beautiful 15th-century frescoes portraying Theodolinda's life. Behind the high altar is the small Iron Crown, believed to have belonged to Emperor Constantine: it is prized for the iron strip, said to have been one of the nails from the cross of Christ. More local treasures may be found in the Duomo's **Museo e Tesoro del Duomo**, including a silver hen standing over seven tiny chicks – which symbolize Lombardy and the seven provinces it ruled – and a relic said to be John the Baptist's tooth.

**Autodromo**
Parco di Monza. ***Tel*** *039 248 21.* *daily.* *public hols.*

**Duomo**
Piazza Duomo. ***Tel*** *039 38 94 20.* **Museo e Tesoro del Duomo** *9am–1pm, 2–6pm Tue–Sun.*

Leonello d'Este (c.1440) by Pisanello in the Accademia Carrara, Bergamo

## Bergamo ❺

*118,000.* FS *Via Gombito 13 (035 24 22 26).* *9am–12:30pm, 2–5:30pm daily.* *Mon.* **www**.comune.bergamo.it

Bergamo owes much of its artistic inspiration and architectural splendour to the influence of Venice, which ruled it from the 15th to the late 18th century. The town is divided into two distinct parts: Bergamo Alta, crowning the hill with its cluster of attractive medieval and Renaissance buildings, and the more modern Bergamo Bassa below.

The jewel of the upper town is **Piazza Vecchia**, containing one of the most appealing architectural ensembles in the region. Its buildings include the 12th-century Torre del Comune with its fine clock and curfew bell that rings daily at 10pm, the late 16th-century Biblioteca Civica and the attractive 12th-century Palazzo della Ragione, or law courts, adorned with a statue of the Lion of Venice.

The arcades of the Palazzo della Ragione lead to Piazza del Duomo, the square of the Neo-Classical Duomo. The square is dominated by the **Cappella Colleoni** *(see p184)*, a chapel built in 1476 to house the tomb of Bergamo's famous political leader, Bartolomeo Colleoni. It is flanked by two 14th-century buildings: an octagonal baptistry and the porch leading to the Romanesque basilica of Santa Maria Maggiore. The basilica's austere exterior contrasts with its Baroque interior, which contains the tomb of Bergamo-born composer Gaetano Donizetti (1797–1848).

Detail from the Cappella Colleoni

The collection from the **Galleria dell' Accademia Carrara**, a major picture gallery with works by Venetian masters and local artists, as well as masterpieces from the rest of Italy, is housed temporarily in **Palazzo della Ragione** while the building is being restored. It includes 15th- and 16th-century works by Pisanello, Crivelli, Mantegna, Giovanni Bellini, Botticelli, Titian, Raphael and Perugino, 18th-century canvases by Tiepolo, Guardi and Canaletto, as well as paintings by Holbein, Dürer, Brueghel and Velázquez.

**Palazzo della Ragione**
Città Alta. ***Tel*** *035 39 96 77.* *Jun–Sep: 10am–9pm Tue–Fri, 10am–11pm Sat; Oct–May: 9:30am–5:30pm Tue–Fri, 10am–6pm Sat.*

A leafy pathway through the Parco Nazionale dello Stelvio

## Parco Nazionale dello Stelvio ❻

Trento, Bolzano, Sondrio & Brescia. *from Bormio to Santa Caterina Valfurva & Madonna dei Monti.* *Via de Simoni 42, Bormio (0342 90 08 11).* **www**.stelviopark.it

The Stelvio, Italy's largest national park, is the gateway from Lombardy to the glacier-strewn Dolomite mountains stretching into Trentino-Alto Adige. The glaciers are dotted with more than 50 lakes, and dominated by craggy peaks such as Gran Zebrù, Cevedale and Ortles – the tallest mountain here at 3,905 m (12,811 ft).

For walkers, the area offers excellent hiking, and access to remote areas populated by ibexes, marmots, chamois and eagles. The only real population centre in the Lombardy part of the park is at **Bormio**, which boasts plenty of winter and summer sports facilities, and is a good base from which to explore the area. The town's **Giardino Botanico**, a 1 km (0.6 mile) walk from the centre, displays some of the species of mountain plants found in the region.

**Giardino Botanico Alpino Rezia**
Via Sertorelli, Loc. Rovinaccia, Bormio. ***Tel*** *0342 92 73 70. Jun–mid-Sep: daily.* **www**.stelviopark.it

## Val Camonica ❼

Brescia. FS *Capo di Ponte.* *Via Briscioli, Capo di Ponte (0364 420 80).* **www**.proloco.capo-di-ponte.bs.it

This attractive broad valley formed by a glacier is the setting for an extraordinary series of prehistoric rock carvings. These form an astonishing outdoor mural from the Lago d'Iseo to Capo di Ponte and beyond, and the valley has been declared a cultural protection zone by UNESCO. More than 180,000 engravings from the Neolithic era until early Roman times have been discovered; the best are in the **Parco Nazionale delle Incisioni Rupestri**. Do not miss the Naquane rock, carved with nearly 1,000 figures from the Ice Age. The **Centro Camuno** focuses on the Roman settlement in the valley.

**Centro Camuno di Studi Preistorici**
Via Marconi 7, Capo di Ponte. ***Tel*** *0364 420 91. to tourists.*

**Parco Nazionale delle Incisioni Rupestri**
Capo di Ponte. ***Tel*** *0364 421 40. 8:30am–7:30pm Tue–Sun (Nov–Feb to 5pm). 1 Jan, 1 May, 25 Dec.*

## Lago d'Iseo ❽

Bergamo & Brescia. FS *Iseo.* *Lungolago Marconi 2, Iseo (030 98 02 09).* **www**.lagodiseo.org

This glaciated lake is surrounded by tall mountains and waterfalls and boasts a mini-mountain of its own, in the form of the island of Monte Isola. Along the shores of the lake are a clutch of fishing villages such as Sale Marasino and Iseo itself. From Marone, on the east bank of the lake, a road leads to the village of **Cislano**, about 5 km (3 miles) away. Here, extraordinary spire-like rock formations rise from the ground, each spire topped by a boulder. These distinctive erosion pillars, one

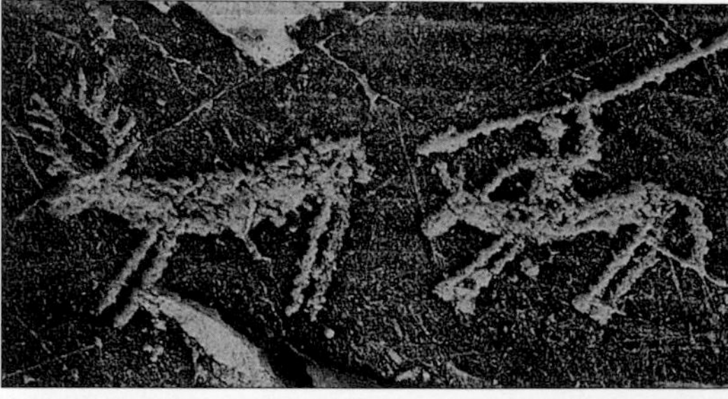
Prehistoric engraving of a mounted hunter and stag in the Val Camonica

The partly Renaissance Ponte Coperto, straddling the River Ticino at Pavia

of the strangest and most beautiful natural wonders in Lombardy, are known locally as the "Fairies of the Forest".

## Brescia ❾

190,000. FS *Via Musei 32 (030 374 94 38).* *Sat.* **www**.provincia.brescia.it

Lombardy's second city after Milan boasts a rich artistic heritage, ranging from Roman temples to the triumphalist Mussolini-era architecture of Piazza Vittoriale. The major sights include the Roman ruins around Piazza del Foro, consisting of the **Tempio Capitolino** – a three-part temple incorporating the **Museo di Santa Giulia**, Brescia's main gallery – and a theatre; the **Pinacoteca Civica Tosio Martinengo**, containing works by Raphael and Lorenzo Lotto; and the **Duomo** on Piazza Paolo VI, with its 11th-century core and white 17th-century exterior. One of the relics in the Duomo is the banner from the *Carroccio,* or sacred ox cart, which served as a symbol for the medieval Lega Lombarda. **Piazza della Loggia**, where the market is held, is named after the Renaissance loggia, built in Palladian style. The 18th-century church of San Nazaro e San Celso on Via Bronzoni contains an altarpiece by Titian.

**Tempio Capitolino**
Via Musei 57a. *11am–4pm Tue–Sun.*

**Museo di Santa Giulia**
Via Musei 81b. ***Tel*** *030 297 78 34.* *daily.*

**Pinacoteca Civica Tosio Martinengo**
Via Martinengo da Barcol. ***Tel*** *030 377 49 99.* *10am–1pm, 2:30–6pm Tue–Sun.* *1 Jan, 1 May, 1 Nov, 25 Dec.*

## Lodi ❿

Lodi. *40,000.* FS *Via Fanfulla 14 (0371 44 27 11).* *Tue, Thu, Sat & Sun.* **www**.turismo.provincia.lodi.it

This is a charming medieval town of pastel-coloured houses, pretty courtyards and gardens. Just off Piazza della Vittoria, the arcaded square on which the 12th-century Duomo stands, is the fine Renaissance church of the **Incoronata**. The magnificent octagonal interior is entirely decorated with wall paintings and gilding, and crowned with a dome. One of the chapels has 15th-century works by Bergognone.

## Pavia ⓫

*81,000.* FS *Palazzo del Broletto, Piazza della Vittoria (0382 07 99 43).* *Wed & Sat.* **www**.turismo.provincia.pv.it

During Pavia's golden age, the city was the Lombards' capital, and later witnessed coronations of Charlemagne and Frederick Barbarossa. Even after it lost its status to Milan in 1359, Pavia remained an important city, and great Romanesque churches, tall towers and other monuments still reflect this.

As well as the Charterhouse (Certosa) *(see pp204–5)*, there is the sandstone **Basilica di San Michele** off Corso Garibaldi. The building was founded in the 7th century but largely rebuilt in the 12th after being struck by lightning. Its façade is decorated with symbols and friezes of fantastic animals, and inside there are intricate carvings on the columns; a chapel to the right of the main altar contains a 7th-century silver crucifix.

In the town centre, around Piazza della Vittoria, are several ancient monuments, such as the medieval **Broletto** (town hall), with its 16th-century façade, and the **Duomo**, originally begun in 1488 and worked on in turn by Amadeo, Leonardo and Bramante. The dome was added in the 1880s. The 11th-century tower that stood next to it collapsed suddenly in 1989. Crossing the river is the **Ponte Coperto**, a Renaissance covered bridge with a consecrated chapel halfway along it. The bridge was rebuilt after World War II.

Pavia is also the site of one of Europe's oldest (1361) and most respected universities, now residing around a series of Neo-Classical courtyards off Strada Nuova. This road continues northwards to the 14th-century castle, now home to the **Museo Civico**.

Northwest of Piazza Castello is the 12th-century church, **San Pietro in Ciel d'Oro**. It no longer boasts the fine gilded ceiling after which it is named, but does still contain a magnificent shrine to St Augustine, whose bones were allegedly brought to Pavia in the 8th century. The body of the philosopher Boëthius (c.480–524) is buried down in the crypt.

The Roman Tempio Capitolino in Brescia

**Museo Civico**
Castello Visconteo, Viale 11 Febbraio. ***Tel*** *0382 338 53.* *10am–5:50pm Tue–Sun.* *public hols.*

# Certosa di Pavia ⓬

The Charterhouse 8 km (5 miles) north of Pavia is the pinnacle of Renaissance architecture in Lombardy, a gloriously decorated Carthusian monastery built over 200 years. Conceived as a monument to Gian Galeazzo Visconti, the Milanese ruler who founded the complex in 1396, this shrine was created by the great 15th-century craftsman Giovanni Antonio Amadeo, among others, who used innovative techniques of relief work and multicoloured decoration. The Certosa is still home to Carthusian monks, who are under a strict vow of silence.

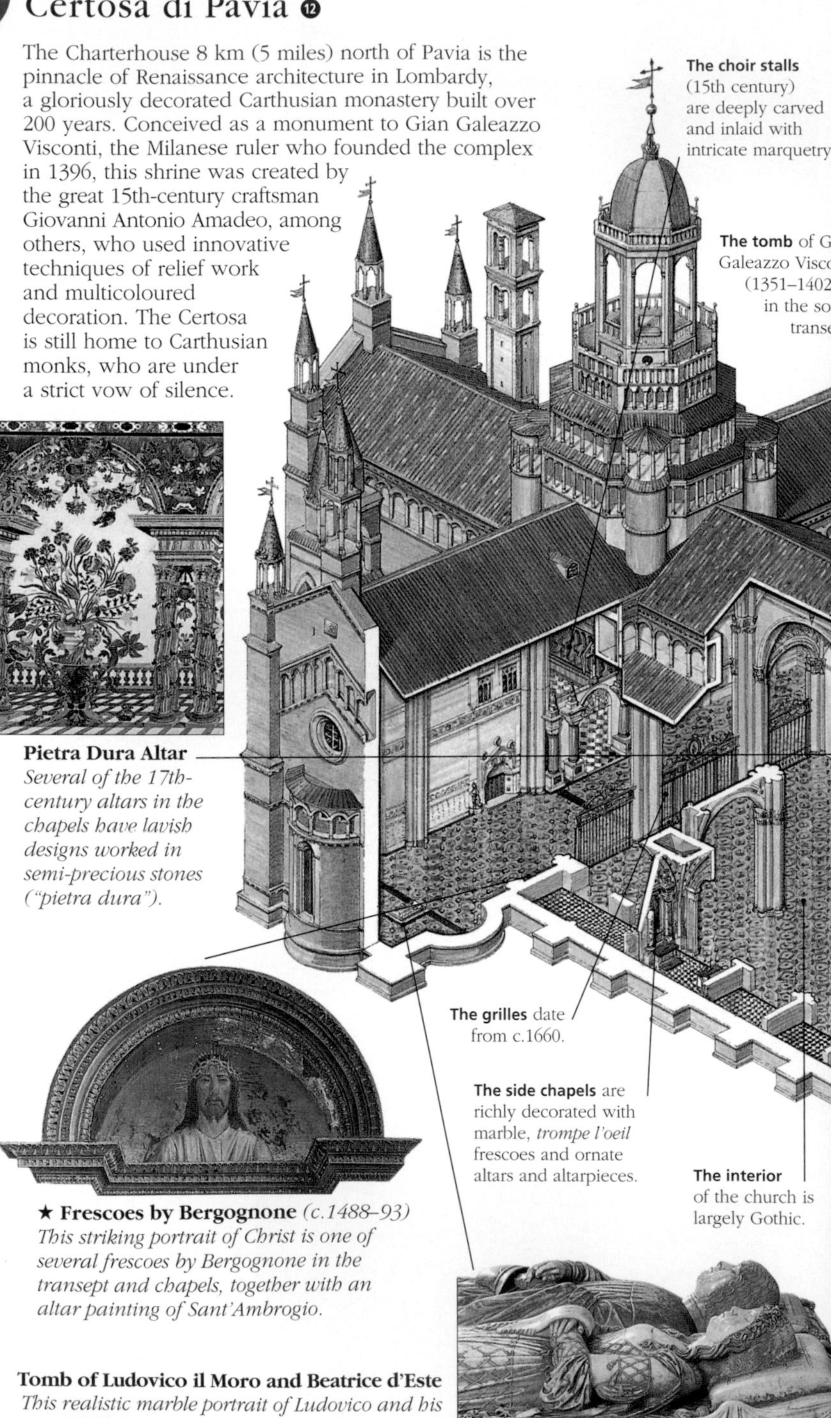

**The choir stalls** (15th century) are deeply carved and inlaid with intricate marquetry.

**The tomb** of Gia Galeazzo Viscon (1351–1402) in the sou transep

**Pietra Dura Altar**
*Several of the 17th-century altars in the chapels have lavish designs worked in semi-precious stones ("pietra dura").*

**The grilles** date from c.1660.

**The side chapels** are richly decorated with marble, *trompe l'oeil* frescoes and ornate altars and altarpieces.

**The interior** of the church is largely Gothic.

**★ Frescoes by Bergognone** *(c.1488–93)*
*This striking portrait of Christ is one of several frescoes by Bergognone in the transept and chapels, together with an altar painting of Sant'Ambrogio.*

**Tomb of Ludovico il Moro and Beatrice d'Este**
*This realistic marble portrait of Ludovico and his child bride was begun by Cristoforo Solari in 1497, some 11 years before Ludovico's death.*

***For hotels and restaurants in this region see pp567–71 and pp615–18***

**Great Cloister**
*This huge cloister is reached through the Small Cloister. It is framed on three sides by the two-storey monks' cells, each backed by a small garden. A hatch beside the door permits food to be delivered without any communication.*

## VISITORS' CHECKLIST

Viale del Monumento, Pavia. ***Tel*** *0382 92 56 13. from Pavia & Milan. FS Certosa. Followed by 1 km (0.5 mile) walk. 9–11am, 2:30–4:30pm Tue–Sun & pub hols (Mar, Oct: to 5pm; Apr, Sep: to 5:30pm; May–Aug: to 6pm). (Last adm: 30 mins before closing.) Donation to guide.*

**Monk's cell**

**The New Sacristy** is painted with colourful ceiling frescoes.

**This delightful**, arcaded Small Cloister, with fine terracotta ornamentation, contains a small garden, planted in formal designs.

**★ Renaissance Façade**
*The 15th-century lower part of the façade is profusely decorated with statues and carvings of Roman emperors, saints (here St Peter), apostles and prophets. The upper part dates from 1500.*

**Main entrance to the Certosa**

**★ Altarpiece by Perugino**
*The six-panel altarpiece was painted in 1499 but now only one panel – that depicting God the Father – is original; it is flanked by two paintings by Bergognone.*

## STAR FEATURES

- ★ Frescoes by Bergognone
- ★ Renaissance Façade
- ★ Altarpiece by Perugino

The Duomo on Piazza del Comune, Cremona

## Cremona ⓭

*76,000.* FS *Piazza del Comune 5 (0372 232 33). Wed & Sat.* **www**.provincia.cremona.it

Cremona, a major agricultural market, is most famous for music, thanks to native sons such as the composer Claudio Monteverdi (1567–1643) and the violin-maker Stradivarius (1644–1737). The town itself is dominated by the beautiful Piazza del Comune.

The main attraction is the exuberant part-Romanesque **Duomo**, and its bell tower – said to be the tallest medieval tower in Italy – known as the **Torrazzo**; the two are linked by a Renaissance loggia. The wonderful façade is dominated by the large 13th-century rose window and by a number of intricate touches, including a small portico with statues of the Virgin and saints. Inside, the Duomo is sumptuously decorated with magnificent early 16th-century frescoes and Flemish tapestries, as well as paintings in the side chapels. The top of the Torrazzo offers sweeping views. Outside the Duomo, note the pulpit where itinerant preachers, including San Bernardino of Siena, addressed the local populace.

Next to the Duomo stands an octagonal 12th-century baptistry, while on the other side of the piazza rise the arcades of the late 13th-century **Loggia dei Militi** where the town's lords once met, now a war memorial.

The **Palazzo del Comune** is the other major building on the square. It was rebuilt in the 1200s and houses the Stradivari family collection of violins.

The **Museo Civico**, in a 16th-century palazzo, contains paintings, wood carvings, the cathedral's treasure, ceramics and a section on archaeology. The building also houses the **Museo Stradivariano**, which displays drawings, models and tools from Stradivarius's workshop.

On the eastern outskirts of the town, on the road to Casalmaggiore, lies the Renaissance church of **San Sigismondo** (closed at lunchtime). It was here that Francesco Sforza married Bianca Visconti in 1441, and the church was subsequently rebuilt (from 1463) in honour of the event. The interior is richly decorated with 16th-century paintings, altarpieces and frescoes by artists of the Cremona school (Campi family, Gatti and Boccaccino).

**Torrazzo**
P. del Comune. ***Tel*** *0372 49 50 29. 10am–1pm, 2:30–6pm Tue–Sun.*

**Palazzo del Comune**
Piazza del Comune. ***Tel*** *0372 205 02. 9am–6pm Tue–Sat; 10am–6pm Sun. public hols.*

**Museo Stradivariano & Museo Civico**
Via Ugolani Dati 4. ***Tel*** *0372 40 77 70. 9am–6pm Tue–Sat; 10am–6pm Sun. public hols.*

## Sabbioneta ⓮

Mantua. *4,600. from Mantua. Piazza d'Armi 1 (0375 520 39). Wed am. apply at tourist office.* **www**.sabbioneta.org

Sabbioneta is the result of a delightful experiment in the theory of Renaissance architecture. It was built by Vespasiano Gonzaga Colonna (1531–91) as an ideal city, and within its hexagonal walls is a perfect gridwork arrangement of streets and buildings designed on a human scale. The finest buildings include the splendid Teatro All'Antica designed by Scamozzi, the Palazzo Ducale and the frescoed Palazzo del Giardino, which may be visited as part of a tour of the town.

### ANTONIO STRADIVARI AND HIS VIOLINS

The city of Cremona has been synonymous with violin-making since the 1530s, when Andrea Amati's instruments became sought after at the royal courts throughout Europe because of their superior tone to the medieval fiddle.

19th-century engraving of Antonio Stradivari

However, it was Antonio Stradivari, known as Stradivarius (1644–1737) – the pupil of Andrea Amati's grandson Niccolò – who raised the level of violin craftsmanship to genius. He used to go walking in the forests of the Dolomites in search of the perfect wood for his instruments. Stradivarius produced more than 1,100 violins in his workshop, of which more than 400 exist to this day. The main stopping-off points on a Stradivarius tour of Cremona are the Museo Stradivariano, the Museo Civico and the great man's tombstone in the public gardens in Piazza Roma.

The ceiling of the Camera degli Sposi, by Mantegna, in the Palazzo Ducale

## Mantua ⓯

*55,000.* FS *Piazza Andrea Mantegna 6 (0376 43 24 32). Thu.* **www**.turismo.mantova.it

Mantua (Mantova in Italian) is a striking place of fine squares and aristocratic architecture, bordered on three sides by lakes formed by the River Mincio. The climate can be humid as a result, but the city makes up for it with its cultural history: it was the birthplace of the poet Virgil and the playground of the Gonzaga dukes for three centuries. It was also the refuge where Shakespeare sent Romeo into exile from Verona, and the setting for Verdi's opera *Rigoletto*. These links are all celebrated in street names, signposts and monuments around the town. The theatrical connections are enhanced by the 18th-century **Teatro Accademico Bibiena**, on Via Accademia, which Mozart's father claimed was the finest he had ever seen.

Mantua is focused on three attractive main squares: Piazza dell'Erbe, Piazza del Broletto, named after the 13th-century building adorned with a statue of the poet Virgil, and the cobbled Piazza Sordello. On one side of Piazza Sordello is the **Duomo**, with an 18th-century façade and fine interior stuccoes by Giulio Romano (c.1492–1546); on another side, the forbidding façade of the Palazzo Bonacolsi, with its tall prison tower. Piazza dell'Erbe is dominated by the **Basilica di Sant'Andrea** (15th century), designed largely by Leon Battista Alberti, the early Renaissance architect and theorist, and now flanked by an arcade of shops. The square is also notable for the appealing 11th-century Rotonda di San Lorenzo, and the part-13th-century Palazzo della Ragione with its 15th-century clock tower.

Detail from the 15th-century clock tower on Piazza dell'Erbe

### Palazzo Ducale

*Piazza Sordello 40.* ***Tel** 0376 22 48 32. 8:30am–7pm (last adm: 6pm) Tue–Sun. 1 Jan, 1 May, 25 Dec. 0376 32 82 53 (by appt).* **Camera degli Sposi** *Book ahead on* ***Tel** 041 241 18 97 or* **www**.ducalemantova.org, **www**.mantovaducale.it

The vast, 500-room home of the Gonzaga family covers the northeastern corner of the town and incorporates Castello San Giorgio (a 14th-century fortress), a basilica, and the palace proper.

The many works of art include an unfinished series of 15th-century frescoes by Pisanello, retelling episodes from the Arthurian legends; a large portrait by Rubens (17th century) of the ducal family in the Salone degli Arcieri; and – most absorbing of all – the frescoes by Mantegna in the **Camera degli Sposi** (1465–74). These portray Lodovico Gonzaga and members of his family and court in all their magnificence *(pp208–9)*. The entire room is decorated with images of people, animals and fantastic landscapes, and completed by a light-hearted *trompe l'oeil* ceiling of figures, *putti* and a blue sky.

### Palazzo Tè

*Viale Tè.* ***Tel** 0376 32 32 66. Mon pm, Tue–Sun. 1 Jan, 1 May, 25 Dec.* **www**.centropalazzote.it

At the other end of town stands the early 16th-century Palazzo Tè, built by Giulio Romano for the Gonzaga family as a base from which they could go horse riding. Here the artworks conspire with the architecture to produce striking effects: in the **Sala dei Giganti**, for instance, the frescoed Titans seem to be tearing down the very pillars of the room. Also remarkable is the **Sala di Amore e Psiche**, decorated with erotic scenes from Apuleius' *Golden Ass* and said to celebrate Federico II's love for his mistress. Other rooms are lavishly painted with horses and signs of the Zodiac.

The 13th-century façade of Palazzo Ducale overlooking Piazza Sordello

15th-century fresco, by Mantegna, from the Camera degli Sposi in the Palazzo Ducale ▷

# VALLE D'AOSTA AND PIEDMONT

*Piedmont and the neighbouring Valle d'Aosta are – apart from Turin and its cultural splendours – essentially countryside. To the north lie the Alps, with ski resorts such as Courmayeur, and the wild stretches of the Parco Nazionale del Gran Paradiso. To the south lie the vineyard-clad hills around Barolo, and seemingly endless fields of grain and rice, used in the local dish, risotto.*

The northwest is also rich in culture. From the 11th century to the 18th, both the verdant Valle d'Aosta and Piedmont were part of the French-speaking principality of Savoy and enjoyed the influences of both sides of the Alpine divide. Even today, French and dialectal variants are still spoken in the remote valleys of Piedmont and in much of the Valle d'Aosta. It was only under Duke Emanuele Filiberto in the 16th century that the region was brought definitively into the Italian sphere of influence; and later it was to play the key role in the Risorgimento *(see pp62–3)*, the ambitious movement that united Italy under a king from Piedmont. The vestiges of this history are to be found in the medieval castles of the Valle d'Aosta and the clusters of chapels known as *sacri monti* (sacred mountains) built into the foothills of the Alps. Piedmont also spawned a school of painting, which is in evidence in the small parish churches and excellent fine art collections in the region. The most impressive architecture in the northwest, however, is undoubtedly to be found in Turin, a much underrated and surprisingly elegant Baroque city which boasts, among other things, one of the best Egyptian museums in the world. Piedmont is also known for its industry – FIAT in Turin, Olivetti in Ivrea, Ferrero in Alba – but it has not forgotten its agricultural roots, and food and drink play an important role in the life of the region: the hills of southern Piedmont produce many of the great Italian red wines.

**Traditional pavement café in the heart of Turin**

◁ **The 13th-century Châtelard castle in the Valle d'Aosta**

# Exploring Valle d'Aosta and Piedmont

The vast flat plain of the Po, covered with the watery expanse of rice fields around Vercelli and Novara, eventually gives way, in the west, to the majestic heights of the Alps. Turin, the largest city in the area and the capital of Piedmont, stands at the edge of the plain, nestling almost in the shadow of the mountains. Further northwest, attractive Alpine valleys headed by dramatic peaks provide the setting for the traditional villages, ancient towns and castles around Aosta. The Parco Nazionale del Gran Paradiso is an unspoilt tract of breathtaking scenery.

Rice fields around Vercelli

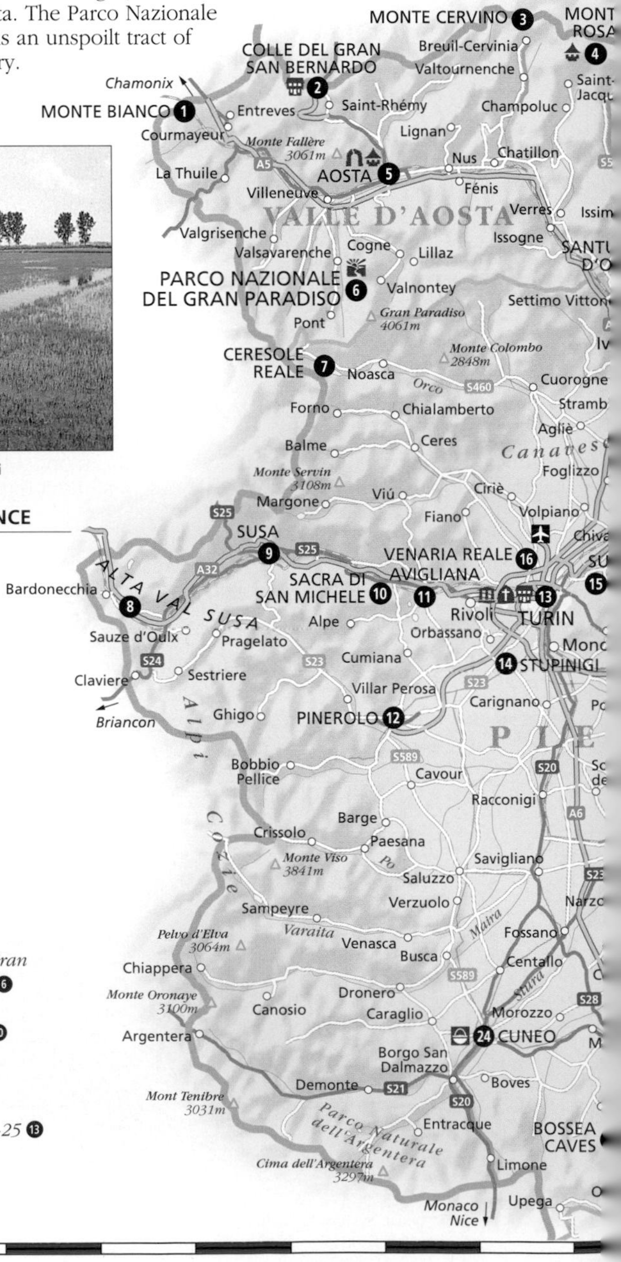

## SIGHTS AT A GLANCE

Alta Val Susa 8
Aosta 5
Asti 23
Avigliana 11
Basilica di Superga 15
Bossea Caves 25
Ceresole Reale 7
Colle del Gran San Bernardo 2
Cuneo 24
Domodossola 18
Garessio 26
Lake Orta 20
Monte Bianco 1
Monte Cervino 3
Monte Rosa 4
Novara 21
*Parco Nazionale del Gran Paradiso pp216–17* 6
Pinerolo 12
Sacra di San Michele 10
Santuario d'Oropa 17
Stupinigi 14
Susa 9
*Turin (Torino) pp220–25* 13
Venaria Reale 16
Varallo 19
Vercelli 22

**For additional map symbols** *see back flap*

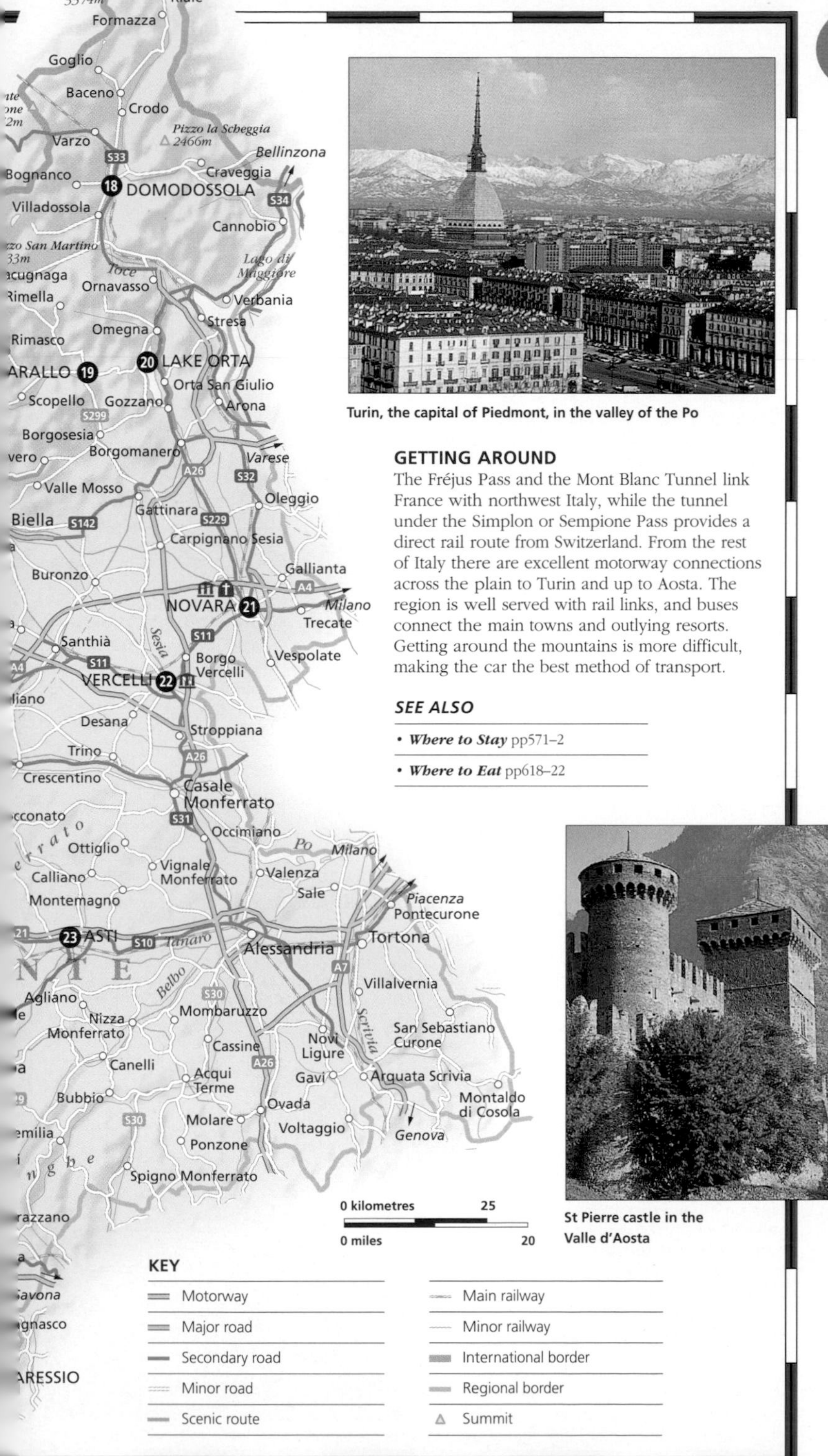


Turin, the capital of Piedmont, in the valley of the Po

## GETTING AROUND

The Fréjus Pass and the Mont Blanc Tunnel link France with northwest Italy, while the tunnel under the Simplon or Sempione Pass provides a direct rail route from Switzerland. From the rest of Italy there are excellent motorway connections across the plain to Turin and up to Aosta. The region is well served with rail links, and buses connect the main towns and outlying resorts. Getting around the mountains is more difficult, making the car the best method of transport.

### *SEE ALSO*


- ***Where to Stay*** pp571–2
- ***Where to Eat*** pp618–22


St Pierre castle in the Valle d'Aosta

## Monte Bianco ❶

Aosta. FS *Pré-St-Didier.* *Courmayeur.* *Piazzale Monte Bianco 13, Courmayeur (0165 84 20 60).* **www**.aiat-monte-bianco.com

Monte Bianco (Mont Blanc), the tallest mountain in the Alps at 4,810 m (15,780 ft), dominates the western Aosta valley and its attractive all-year resort, **Courmayeur**. A series of cable car rides from Entrèves, 5 km (3 miles) further north, leads to Chamonix. Passing its highest point (3,842 m, 12,606 ft) at Aiguille du Midi, it offers a spectacular view. From Pré-St-Didier, below Courmayeur, the **Little St Bernard Pass**, with its small glaciers, forests and ravines, can be explored.

**A St Bernard dog**

## Colle del Gran San Bernardo ❷

Aosta. FS *Aosta.* *Strada Nazionale Gran San Bernardo 13, Etroubles (0165 785 59).* *daily.* **www**.gransanbernardo.net

The Great St Bernard pass is synonymous with the hardy mountain rescue dogs that have been trained locally by Catholic monks since the 11th century. The **Monks' Hospice**, founded around 1050 by St Bernard of Aosta, lies just over the Swiss border (bring your passport), on the shores of a lovely lake; the dogs are still being trained here. The pretty Great St Bernard valley itself includes the town of Etroubles, set in a forest of conifers, the hamlet of St-Oyen with its pretty parish church, and the resort of St-Rhémy-en-Bosses.

**Monks' Hospice**
Colle San Bernardo, Switzerland.
***Tel*** *00 41 277 87 12 36.* *daily.*

## Monte Cervino ❸

Aosta. FS *Breuil-Cervinia.* *Via Guido Rey 17, Breuil-Cervinia (0166 94 91 36).* **www**.montecervino.it

The distinctive triangular peak of Monte Cervino (the Matterhorn) rises to 4,478 m (14,691 ft) and is easily recognizable. Below the mountain lies a scattering of attractive villages like Antey-St-André, Valtournanche (which gave its name to the valley) and the resort of **Breuil-Cervinia**. From Breuil a cable car rises to the Plateau Rosa (3,480 m, 11,418 ft) offering dramatic views of the surrounding mountains. This entire area is a paradise for both skiers and walkers.

## Monte Rosa ❹

Aosta. FS *Verrès.* *St-Jacques.* *Route Varasc, Champoluc/Ayas (0125 30 71 13).* **www**.aiatmonterosa.com

Monte Rosa, Italy's second-highest mountain, overlooks the picturesque Ayas and Gressoney valleys. The rolling lower Ayas valley is dominated by the ruins of the 11th-century **Castello di Graines**. Higher up, the resort of Champoluc has a cable car connection with the striking **Testa Grigia** (3,315 m/10,877 ft). The Gressoney valley is home to the Walser people, who speak a German dialect. At the bottom of the valley, north of Pont-St-Martin, lies **Issime**: the 16th-century church here has a fresco of the Last Judgment on its façade.

**Castello di Graines**
Graines, Strada Statale 506.

### MEDIEVAL CASTLES AND FORTS IN THE VALLE D'AOSTA

The mountains alone provided insufficient protection to the fragmented fiefs that covered the Valle d'Aosta in the Middle Ages. The medieval lords, who ruled ruthlessly over their small domains, built castles to enforce their often fragile power. Of the many built, 70 castles survive in some form to this day. You will pass a number of them if you drive into Italy by the Mont Blanc tunnel; they stretch from Aosta to Pont-St-Martin.

Originally Aosta castles were designed to be defensive and threatening, such as the looming tower of **Montmayer**, perched high on a huge rock by the Valgrisenche valley. Nearby, the equally forbidding dark tower of **Ussel** throws a melancholy, brooding watchfulness over the valley.

**Fénis** and **Verrès** represent an important shift in the function of the feudal castle. Both Fénis, a splendid 14th-century showpiece *(see p184)*, and Verrès were not just important military outposts but also examples of palatial opulence and good living. **Issogne** too furthered this luxurious trend with its elaborate frescoes, loggias and fountains.

Decoration was also important to Vittorio Emanuele II, owner of **Sarre**, who turned the halls of his fortress into a plush hunting lodge. The owners of **Châtelard**, set in some of the highest vineyards in Europe, placed fine wine production alongside military aims.

**The strategically sited 14th-century castle at Verrès**

**The 12th-century cloister, with 40 carved columns of darkened marble, in Sant'Orso**

# Aosta ❺

37,000. FS *Piazza Chanoux.* *(0165 333 52).* *Tue.* **www**.aiataosta.com

Lying on a plain surrounded by dramatic mountains, the town of Aosta provides a remarkable mixture of ancient culture and spectacular scenery. The Romans captured it from the Salassian Gauls in 25 BC, and Aosta is still dotted with fine Roman architecture built in honour of Emperor Augustus – indeed the town was once called *Augusta Praetoria,* its name only evolving into Aosta over the centuries. The medieval town was later fortified by the Challant family and then by the Dukes of Aosta, who added towers to the old Roman walls.

Modern Aosta is a bustling crossroads for local industries and tourists on their way to the mountains. The centre, however, still consists of a delightful grid of large squares and surprising architectural treasures, which justify Aosta's nickname of "Rome of the Alps".

## Roman Ruins

**Roman Theatre**, Via Baillage. *9am–8pm daily (to 7pm Sep, to 6:30pm Oct & Feb, to 5:30pm Nov–Jan).* **Amphitheatre**, Convento di San Giuseppe, Via dell'Anfiteatro. ***Tel*** *0165 26 21 49.* *daily.* **Roman Forum**, Piazza Giovanni XXIII. *daily.*

In Roman times, entry to Aosta was over the **bridge** to the east of the town (beyond the modern bridge) and through the **Arch of Augustus**. This triumphal arch is today marred by a roof added in the 18th century. Ahead stands the **Porta Pretoria**, its double row of stone arches flanked by a medieval tower; the gateway originally stood about 2.5 m (8 ft) higher than at present. Also worth a look is the 20-m (65-ft) high façade of the **Roman Theatre**. The elliptical **Amphitheatre**, a little to the north, is reached through the convent of San Giuseppe. In the old town, next to the cathedral, lies the **Roman Forum**, or market place, with its huge cryptoporticus: the function of this impressive underground gallery remains the subject of speculation.

**Detail of a medieval mosaic on the floor of Aosta's Cattedrale**

## Cattedrale

Piazza Giovanni XXIII. *6:30am–8pm daily (early Sep–Easter: 6:30am–noon, 3–7pm).* **Museo del Tesoro** ***Tel*** *0165 404 13.* *same as the Cathedral.* *during religious services.*

This relatively modest shrine to St John the Baptist was first built in the 12th century, but has been altered many times since. The interior is Gothic, with finely carved 15th-century choir stalls, and floor mosaics. Next door, the **Museo del Tesoro** contains a rich collection of statuettes and reliquaries, and a number of impressive medieval tombs.

## Sant'Orso

Via Sant'Orso. *daily.*

East of the town walls is the architectural highlight of Aosta: a medieval complex of church buildings. Sant'Orso itself has an unusual Gothic façade with a narrow, tall portal. The interior has 11th-century frescoes, a crypt of the same date holding the tomb of St Orso, patron saint of Aosta, and a beautiful **cloister** with columns and capitals carved into highly detailed figures and animals.

**Environs:** The castle at **Fénis** *(see p214),* 12 km (8 miles) east, is one of the few castles in the Aosta valley with a well-preserved interior, including beautiful frescoes and wooden galleries. **Issogne**, 38 km (23 miles) southeast, is the setting for another highly decorated castle, remodelled around 1490. It has many frescoes and decorative motifs, including an octagonal fountain with a centrepiece in the shape of a pomegranate tree.

**Castello di Fénis**
Fénis. ***Tel*** *0165 76 42 63.* *daily.* *Tue (Oct–Feb); 1 Jan, 25 Dec.*

**Castello di Issogne**
Issogne. ***Tel*** *0125 92 93 73.* *daily.* *Wed (winter); 1 Jan, 25 Dec.*

**Some of the impressive ruins standing in the Roman Forum in Aosta**

# Parco Nazionale del Gran Paradiso ❻

A breathtaking wilderness of dramatic mountains and lush meadows, the Gran Paradiso is Italy's foremost national park, created in 1922 from part of a former royal hunting reserve of the House of Savoy. It is mainly a summer resort for walkers due to its unspoiled scenery, rare wildlife and unusual Alpine flowers, though there is also cross-country skiing during the winter months. The king of the park is the ibex, a relative of the goat family all but extinct in the rest of Europe. The park is also prized by naturalists for its chamois, ptarmigan, golden eagles, rare butterflies and marmots.

**Castello di Aymavilles**
*The 18th-century core of this castle is framed by medieval corner towers.*

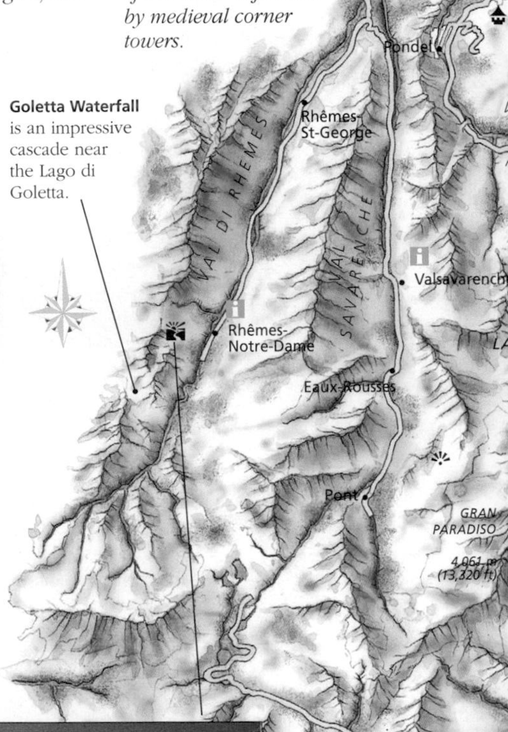


**Goletta Waterfall** is an impressive cascade near the Lago di Goletta.

**Male Ibex**
*The ibex lives largely above the tree line. Groups are often seen around Col Lauson at dawn and dusk, and also around Pont in June.*

**Val di Rhêmes-Notre-Dame**
*This peaceful and broad valley offers magnificent scenery with waterfalls and fast-flowing streams running from the glacier at its head.*

*For hotels and restaurants in this region see pp571–2 and pp618–22*

**Cascata di Lillaz**
*This tall, dramatic waterfall, situated a little to the east of the rustic village of Lillaz, is best observed after the spring snow melt.*

## VISITORS' CHECKLIST

Piemonte and Valle d'Aosta. *Segreteria Turistica, Cheriettes Aymavilles (0165 90 26 93); Centro Visitatori Parco Nazionale del Gran Paradiso, Ceresole Reale, (0124 95 31 66).* FS *Aosta & Pont Canavese.* *from Aosta or Pont Canavese to the different valleys.* **Paradisia Alpine Garden** Valnontey, Cogne. ***Tel*** *0165 74 92 64.* *mid-Jun–mid-Sep: daily.* **www**.grandparadis.it **www**.parks.it

**Cogne** is the main resort and a good base from which to explore the park. Maps of the park's routes and footpaths are available here.

**Lillaz** is sedate and off the beaten track, while Valnontey and Cogne are two of the busiest resorts.

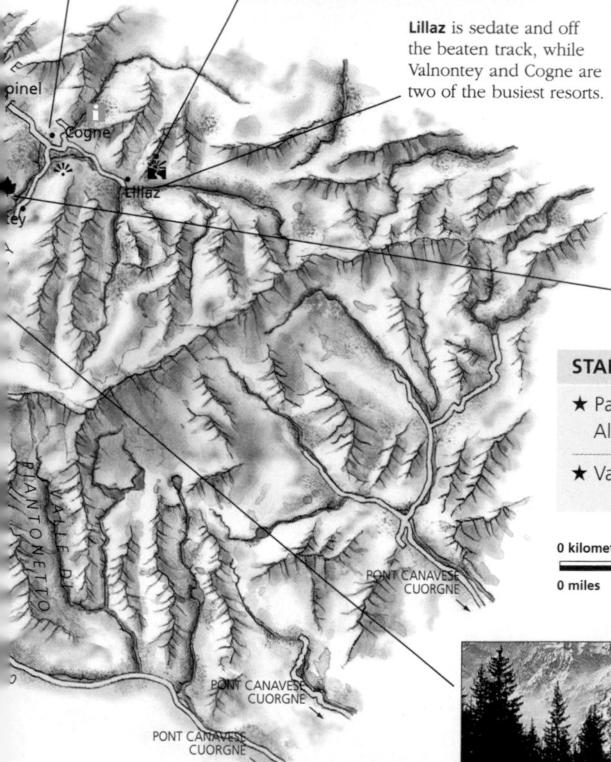

pinel
Cogne
Lillaz
ey
VALLE DI PIANTONETTO
PONT CANAVESE CUORGNE
PONT CANAVESE CUORGNE
PONT CANAVESE CUORGNE

**★ Paradisia Alpine Garden**
*The botanic garden contains a collection of Alpine plants, including the delicate "twinflower".*

## STAR SIGHTS

★ Paradisia Alpine Garden

★ Valnontey

0 kilometres 5
0 miles 5

**★ Valnontey**
*This lovely valley, after which the resort is named, provides dramatic views of glaciers and easy access to various footpaths.*

**KEY**

- Tourist information
- Main road
- Viewpoint

The small resort of Ceresole Reale under winter snow

## Ceresole Reale 7

Turin. to Ceresole Reale. *Palazzo Comunale, Ceresole Reale (0124 95 32 00).* **www**.turismotorino.org

On the southern, Piedmont side of the extensive Parco Nazionale del Gran Paradiso *(see pp216–17)* lies the small resort of Ceresole Reale. The route from Cuorgnè traverses rolling countryside and follows the S460 along a narrow gorge with a cascading stream. At **Noasca**, a spectacular waterfall may be seen high above the houses.

Ceresole Reale lies in a basin surrounded by meadows and forests of larch, and framed by mountains – the Gran Paradiso range to the north, Levanna to the southwest – which are reflected in the clear waters of a spectacular artificial mountain lake, which is actually a dammed reservoir, providing energy to supply Turin with electricity. This nevertheless unspoiled corner of the country is a good base for walking, climbing and hiking, and also offers facilities for skiing during the winter.

## Alta Val Susa 8

Turin. FS *Oulx.* *to Sauze d'Oulx.* *Via Louset, Sestriere (0122 75 54 44).* **www**.vialattea.it

The closest ring of mountain resorts to Turin, and as a consequence popular for weekend excursions, is also known colloquially as the Via Lattea or "milky way". Villages such as **Bardonecchia** and **Sauze d'Oulx** preserve traditional old stone and wood buildings that have been a feature of the region for centuries. The small church in Bardonecchia has, in addition, a fine 15th-century carved choir. In contrast, the super-modern complex at **Sestriere** was purpose-built to accommodate skiers in winter and hikers in summer.

From Bardonecchia a chairlift operates some of the way up **Punta Colomion**, which rises immediately to the south of the resort. The summit, at 2,054 m (6,738 ft), offers fine views, and numerous hiking and walking possibilities.

## Susa 9

Turin. *7,000.* FS *Corso Inghilterra 39 (0122 62 24 70).* *Tue.* **www**.turismotorino.org

This attractive mountain town flourished in Roman times: the **Arch of Augustus**, built in 8 BC, commemorates the alliance between the local Gaulish chieftain and the Emperor Augustus. Other relics from the Roman period include two arches of an aqueduct, sections of an amphitheatre and traces of the old town walls. **Porta Savoia**, an imposing Roman gateway dating from the 4th century, was remodelled in the Middle Ages.

Most of the historic centre of the town is medieval, including the castle of Countess Adelaide and the **Duomo**, both originally 11th century. The Duomo, much altered since then, houses a polyptych (c.1500) attributed to Bergognone, and a precious 14th-century Flemish triptych portraying the *Virgin and Saints*. South of the town lies the Gothic church of **San Francesco**, surrounded by an area of early medieval houses.

The impressive part-Roman gateway, Porta Savoia, in Susa

A street in the traditional village of Bardonecchia, in Alta Val Susa

Carved capitals on the Porta dello Zodiaco at the Sacra di San Michele

## Sacra di San Michele ⑩

Strada Sacra San Michele. ***Tel*** *011 93 91 30.* 🚌 *Jul–Aug: Sun pm from Avigliana & Turin.* 🕘 *9:30am–noon, 2:30–6pm Tue–Sun (Oct–Mar: to 5pm). Phone to arrange group visits.* **www**.sacradisanmichele.com

This somewhat forbidding abbey complex is perched on a ridge halfway up Monte Pirchiriano, at 962 m (3,156 ft). Its monastic community was founded around the year 1000, possibly on the site of a previous sanctuary, though the exterior looks every bit as much a fortress as the spiritual refuge that it was for 600 years.

During its prime, the abbey attracted pilgrims on their way to Rome, and as a result it grew enormously wealthy and powerful, controlling over 100 other abbeys in Italy, France and Spain. It was subsequently looted several times, despite being fortified, before falling into decline and eventually being suppressed in 1662.

The sanctuary is reached by climbing 154 steep steps hewn out of the rock, which offer wonderful views over the surrounding countryside and up to the Alps. At the very top of this stairway, known as the Scalone dei Morti (Stairway of the Dead), is the Romanesque Porta dello Zodiaco, a doorway carved with creatures and symbols relating to the signs of the Zodiac. Beyond the doorway a few more steps lead into the church itself, which dates from the 12th–13th centuries and incorporates traces of an earlier building. The interior houses 15th- and 16th-century paintings and frescoes, and a 16th-century triptych by the Piedmontese artist Defendente Ferrari. The crypt holds the tombs of the early dukes and princes of the House of Savoy-Carignano.

## Avigliana ⑪

Turin. 👥 *11,200.* FS 🚌 ℹ *Piazza del Popolo 2 (334 60 34 334).* 🛒 *Thu.* **www**.comune.avigliana.to.it

On a fine day, this small town perched beside two glacier-fed lakes and encircled by tall mountains looks breathtakingly beautiful. Avigliana is overlooked by a castle, first erected in the mid-10th century but now in ruins, which was once the home of the Counts of Savoy. Until the early 15th century the town was one of their favourite bases.

The medieval houses here are largely unspoiled, particularly in the two main *piazzas,* Santa Maria and Conte Rosso. Other buildings of note are the Casa della Porta Ferrata and the 15th-century Casa dei Savoia, both on Via XX Settembre. The church of San Giovanni (13th–14th century) contains early 16th-century paintings by Defendente Ferrari.

## Pinerolo ⑫

Turin. 👥 *36,000.* FS 🚌 ℹ *Viale Giolitti 7–9 (0121 79 55 89).* 🛒 *Wed & Sat.* **www**.turismotorino.org

Pinerolo lies in an attractive setting beside hills at the confluence of the Lemina and Chisone valleys. The town was the capital of the Acaia family, a branch of the House of Savoy, and in the 14th and 15th centuries it was known for the cultural atmosphere that prevailed here under the family's patronage. However, the town enjoyed none of the stability of Turin: it was occupied by the French five times between the 15th and 18th centuries. During the 17th century the French demolished many of the town's ancient buildings in order to make Pinerolo a defensive stronghold; among the political prisoners allegedly held here was the notorious "Man in the Iron Mask". Today the town is a busy centre of commerce.

A number of monumental buildings do remain, however. The **Duomo**, at the centre of the town, was remodelled in Gothic style in the 15th–16th centuries and has a fine portal and an impressive bell tower. Via Principi d'Acaia climbs up to the 14th-century palace of the Princes of Acaia, and to the 15th-century church of **San Maurizio**, where the Acaia princes are buried; beside it rises a 14th-century bell tower.

The medieval arcades surrounding Piazza Conte Rosso in Avigliana

# Turin ⓭

Mention Turin (Torino) and most people will think of industry and prosperity. It is certainly an economic powerhouse but it is also a town of grace and charm, with superb Baroque architecture and excellent museums, set against the dramatic scenery of the foothills of the Alps. Turin is also, of course, home to the famous Turin Shroud, the FIAT car company and the Juventus football team. The 2006 Winter Olympics were held here.

**Exploring Turin**

Though settled by the Romans (**Porta Palatina** is an impressive 1st-century AD relic), and the seat of a university since the Middle Ages, Turin came into its own only after 1563, when Emanuele Filiberto of Savoy moved his capital here. Three centuries of prosperity ensued. Turin then became the base for Italy's unification movement and, from 1861 to 1865, the capital of the newly united country. Subsequently its main power was economic. In 1899 the Agnelli family created the car company **FIAT** (Fabbrica Italiana Automobili Torino), which grew to be one of the biggest in Europe. After World War II, Turin attracted thousands of poor Italians from the south who came to work in its factories. Though there have been social conflicts and labour disputes as a result, managers and workers unite over football: the Juventus team is owned by the Agnelli family.

**The FIAT car factory logo**

**Statue of Emperor Augustus in front of the Roman Porta Palatina**

### Duomo

Piazza San Giovanni. ***Tel** 011 436 15 40.* *daily.*

The cathedral, which was built in 1491–8 and dedicated to St John the Baptist, is the only example of Renaissance

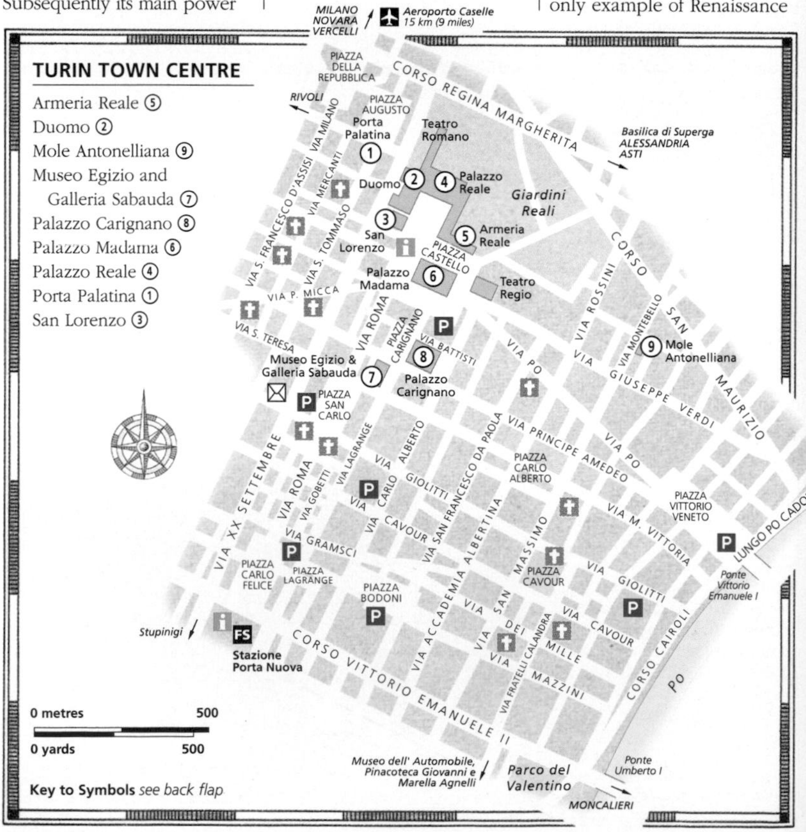

**TURIN TOWN CENTRE**

Armeria Reale ⑤
Duomo ②
Mole Antonelliana ⑨
Museo Egizio and Galleria Sabauda ⑦
Palazzo Carignano ⑧
Palazzo Madama ⑥
Palazzo Reale ④
Porta Palatina ①
San Lorenzo ③

0 metres 500
0 yards 500

**Key to Symbols** *see back flap*

***For hotels and restaurants in this region see pp571–2 and pp618–22***

The 15th-century Duomo, with the Cappella della Sacra Sindone beyond

## VISITORS' CHECKLIST

1,000,000. Caselle 15 km (9 miles) N. FS Porta Nuova, Piazza Carlo-Felice. Porta Susa, Piazza XVIII Dicembre. Corso Vittorio Emanuele II 131. Piazza Castello (011 53 51 81), also at Stazione Porta Nuova. Sat. 24 Jun: Festa di San Giovanni. www.turismotorino.org

architecture in Turin. The sober square bell tower, which pre-dates the rest of the church by 30 years, stands in refreshing contrast to Turin's sumptuous Baroque buildings; its top was designed by Filippo Juvarra in 1720. Inside, the Duomo is heavy with statuary and paintings. On the right side of the church is the **Cappella della Sacra Sindone** (Chapel of the Holy Shroud), which is actually incorporated into the Palazzo Reale *(see p216)*. The chapel is a remarkable feat, designed by Guarino Guarini (1624–83), with an extraordinary mesh-like cupola; the exterior view is equally eccentric.

### Palazzo Madama

Piazza Castello. ***Tel*** *011 443 3501.* *10am–6pm Tue–Sat, 10am–8pm Sun.* www.palazzomadamatorino.it

Turin's main square once contained a medieval castle which incorporated elements of the original Roman city walls. The castle was later enlarged and remodelled, and a new façade by Juvarra was added, at the request of a royal widow, in the 18th century. The Palazzo Madama – as it was renamed – now sits in the centre of the square with a stately, balustraded façade.

The interior, with its grand staircase and first floor, both designed by Juvarra, is home to the **Museo Civico d'Arte Antica**. This extensive collection contains treasures ranging from the Graeco-Roman era to the 19th century. The display includes the famous *Portrait of an Unknown Man* by Antonello da Messina (15th century) among the paintings and sculptures, and reproductions of the Duc de Berry's beautiful *Book of Hours* from c.1420. Other sections contain displays of glass, jewellery, textiles and furniture.

The façade of the Palazzo Madama, designed by Filippo Juvarra in 1718–21

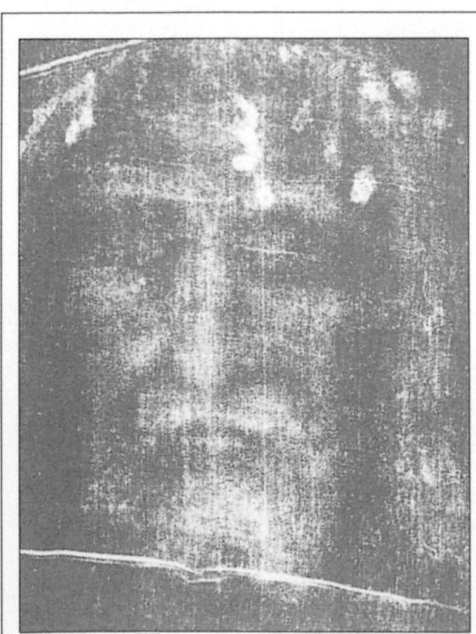
Detail of the mysterious 12th-century Turin Shroud

### THE TURIN SHROUD

The most famous – and most dubious – holy relic of them all is kept in Turin's Duomo. The shroud, said to be the winding-sheet in which the body of Christ was wrapped after His crucifixion, owes its fame to the fact that the shroud bears the imprint of a crucified man with a wound in his side, and bruises from what might have been a crown of thorns.

The shroud is one of the most famous medieval relics. Its early history is unclear, but the House of Savoy was in possession of it around 1450, and had it displayed in Guarini's chapel from 1694. The "original" shroud – which sits in a silver casket inside an iron box within a marble coffer – is not on view, though a replica is, together with a welter of scientific explanations as to the shroud's possible origins. In 1988, however, the myth of the shroud was exploded: a carbon-dating test showed that it dates back no further than the 12th century. The shroud nevertheless remains an object of religious veneration.

# Exploring Turin

The city of Turin is blessed with numerous interesting museums, which are housed in splendid palazzi and civic buildings. The centre itself is relatively small, with broad, straight streets, often bordered with historic cafés and shops, which are pleasant places to stroll along. The city is also famous for its innovative cuisine and boasts some of the country's finest restaurants.

**Granite statue of Ramses II (13th century BC) in the Museo Egizio**

### Museo Egizio

Via Accademia delle Scienze 6. ***Tel*** *011 561 77 76.* *8:30am–7:30pm Tue–Sun (last adm: 6:30pm).* *1 Jan, 25 Dec.* **www**.museitorino.it

Turin owes its magnificent Egyptian Museum – one of the most important in the world – largely to the Piedmont-born Bernardo Drovetti, who was stationed in Egypt as French Consul General at the time of the Napoleonic Wars. It was the booty he brought back that formed the basis of this very fine collection of Egyptian artifacts. On the ground floor, the items on display include monumental sculptures and reconstructed temples; upstairs, there are collections of papyrus and everyday objects. Among the most impressive sculptures are a black granite Ramses II (13th century BC, or 19th dynasty), the slightly earlier Amenophis II, and the basalt figure of Gemenef-Har-Bak, a vizier from the 26th dynasty. The Sala della Nubia contains a reconstruction of the 15th-century BC **Rock Temple of Ellessiya**.

Extraordinary wall and tomb paintings are displayed on the upper floor, together with items of daily use such as the tools used for measuring, weaving, fishing and hunting. The 14th-century BC Tomb of Kha and Merit, complete with the food, tools and ornaments buried with them for the afterlife, is particularly fascinating. The papyrus collection is beautiful and of enormous interest to scholars: these documents have been vital to modern understanding of Egyptian language, customs and history – one document, the *Papiro dei Re* (Royal Papyrus), crucially lists all the pharaohs up to the 17th dynasty, with their dates.

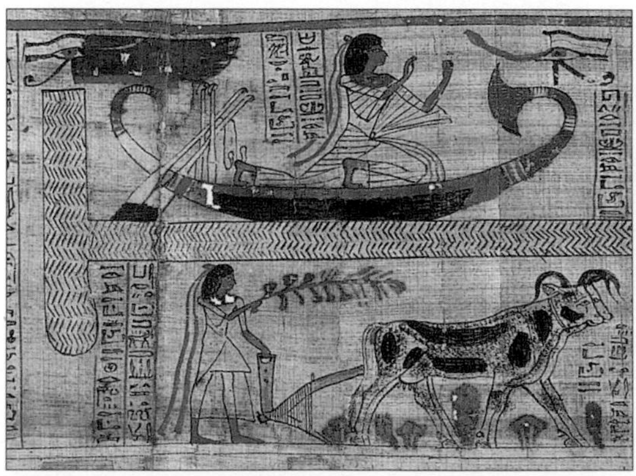

**Detail from an 18th-dynasty papyrus Book of the Dead, Museo Egizio**

**G Ferrari's *St Peter and a Donor* (16th century), Galleria Sabauda**

### Galleria Sabauda

Via Accademia delle Scienze 6. ***Tel*** *011 440 69 03.* *8:30am–2pm Tue, Fri–Sun; 2–7:30pm Wed & Thu.* **www**.museitorino.it

The Palazzo dell'Accademia delle Scienze, the building by Guarini in which the Egyptian Museum is housed, is also home to the House of Savoy's main painting collection. The top two floors are the setting for a stunning array of works by Italian, French, Flemish and Dutch masters.

The collection was originally begun in the mid- to late 1400s, and has been expanded over the centuries. It is grouped in regional schools. The Piedmontese section includes masterpieces by Gaudenzio Ferrari (c.1480–1546) and two early 16th-century paintings by Defendente Ferrari. Among works of particular interest from other Italian schools are Antonio and Piero Pollaiuolo's 15th-century *Tobias and the Archangel Raphael*, and the *Ritratto di*

*Gentiluomo* (portrait of a nobleman) by Bronzino. Bellini, Mantegna, and Veronese are among other Italian artists represented.

The section on Dutch and Flemish art includes important works such as Jan Van Eyck's *St Francis* (15th century) and Rembrandt's *Old Man Sleeping* (17th century), as well as several portraits by Van Dyck, which include a study of Charles I's children, and his *Principe Tommaso di Savoia-Carignano* (1634). Among the French works on display are 17th-century landscape paintings by Claude Lorrain and Poussin.

**Spacious arcades on Turin's Via Roma**

### Palazzo Carignano

Via Accademia delle Scienze 5. ***Tel*** *011 562 11 47.* *9am–7pm Tue–Sat; 9am–1pm Sun.*

**The main façade of Palazzo Carignano by Guarini**

This Baroque palazzo is not only Guarini's masterpiece, it is arguably the finest building in Turin, with its magnificent façade and ornate rotunda. It was built in 1679 for the Carignano family – an offshoot of the main House of Savoy and ancestors of the Italian kings – but came into its own in the 1800s. The first king of Italy, Vittorio Emanuele II, was born here in 1829. After Italy was unified in 1861 by a series of referenda, the former royal residence was used as the first national parliament building.

The palazzo is home to the **Museo Nazionale del Risorgimento**, which through paintings and a collection of artifacts (housed in the rooms where history was made), tells the story of unification. It introduces Mazzini, Cavour and Garibaldi – key figures in the Risorgimento *(see pp62–3)*.

### Via Roma

Running through the historic centre, Turin's main street Via Roma leads from Piazza Castello (north) through Piazza San Carlo to the distinctive arched façade of Stazione Porta Nuova (south). Via Roma is a magnificent concourse lined with stylish shops and shaded arcades, interrupted only by cobbled squares. A grid pattern of side streets branches off either side of Via Roma, revealing additional shopping arcades.

### Piazza San Carlo

The ensemble of Baroque architecture on this square, now a pedestrian zone, has earned it the nickname of "Turin's drawing room". At its southern end are the twin churches of Santa Cristina and San Carlo; both were built in the 1630s, though **Santa Cristina** has a Baroque façade, crowned with statues, which was designed by Juvarra in the early 18th century.

At the centre of the square stands a 19th-century statue of Duke Emanuele Filiberto. The work, by Carlo Marocchetti, has become an emblem of the city. At the corners of the square, frescoes depict the Holy Shroud. The **Galleria San Federico**, in the square's northwestern corner, is a stylish shopping arcade.

Piazza San Carlo is known for its society cafés. In one such establishment, in 1786, Antonio Benedetto Carpano invented the drink known as vermouth, which is still very popular all over Italy today.

### Pinacoteca Giovanni e Marella Agnelli

Lingotto, Via Nizza 230. ***Tel*** *011 006 20 08.* *10am–7pm Tue–Sun (last adm: 6:15pm).* **www**.pinacoteca-agnelli.it

Located on the roof of the former FIAT factory redesigned by architect Renzo Piano, this museum holds paintings by Modigliani and Canaletto, as well as two statues by Canova.

### Parco del Valentino

Corso Massimo D'Azeglio. *daily.* **Borgo Medioevale** Viale Virgilio 107. ***Tel*** *011 443 17 01.* *9am–7pm daily (to 8pm Apr–Oct).* **Orto Botanico** ***Tel*** *011 670 59 85.* *Apr–Sep: Sat & Sun.* **www**.borgomedievaletorino.it

This park contains the **Borgo Medioevale**, a complex of medieval buildings erected for an exhibition in the late 1880s. The edifices show different types of design and construction, based on traditional houses and castles found throughout the region.

The **Orto Botanico**, beside the medieval complex, is an impressive botanical garden in a pleasant setting.

**Looking south across the elegant Piazza San Carlo, "Turin's drawing room"**

# Turin: Symbols of the City

Turin's architecture mirrors the city's transition from monarchic power to industrial power. Witness the ostentation of the Baroque apartments of the Savoy family in Palazzo Reale; and contrast them with the futuristic Mole Antonelliana, a tall structure that heralded the dawn of the modern industrial age. Much of Turin's history in the 20th century has been dominated by the motor car: FIAT is synonymous with Turin. For the curious, the city's extensive motor museum is worth a visit, since it maps out the history of Italian car design.

### Mole Antonelliana

Via Montebello 20. ***Tel*** *011 813 85 60.* **Panoramic lift** *10am–8pm Tue–Sun (to 11pm Sat).* **Museo del Cinema** ***Tel*** *011 813 85 64.* *9am–8pm Tue–Sun (to 11pm Sat) (last adm: 45 mins before closing).* **www**.museocinema.it

This building is the Turin equivalent of the Eiffel Tower in Paris: an unmissably tall landmark that is a signature for the city. It looks like a glorified lightning conductor: indeed in 1954 an electric storm struck down the top 47 m (155 ft), which was later replaced. The 167-m (550-ft) Mole, by Alessandro Antonelli (1798–1888), was meant to be a synagogue, but upon its completion in 1897, the city used it to house the Risorgimento museum. The Mole ("massive structure") – for a time the tallest building in the world – provides panoramic views from its lift and now houses the Cinema Museum.

**The interior of San Lorenzo's dome**

**A lavishly decorated gallery in the 17th-century Palazzo Reale, a royal residence until unification**

### Palazzo Reale

Piazzetta Reale. ***Tel*** *011 436 14 55.* *8:30am–6:30pm Tue–Sun.* *25 Dec.* **www**.piemonte.beniculturali.it

This palace was the seat of the Savoy royal family from 1660 until the unification of Italy in 1861. Behind the austere façade, designed by Amedeo di Castellamonte, lie richly decorated state apartments; the ceilings were painted by Morello, Miel and Seyter in the 17th century. The many splendid furnishings, tapestries and ornaments date from the 17th to the 19th centuries; they include the elaborate Chinese Cabinet, the Alcove Room, the lavishly decorated Throne Room, and the innovative Scala delle Forbici, or Scissor Stairs, created by Juvarra in 1720. Behind the palace are extensive gardens, which extend northwards.

To the left of the main entrance is the church of **San Lorenzo**. This fine Baroque building, begun in 1634, is by architect Guarino Guarini, its ornate interior boasting another of his extraordinary, geometric domes.

**The 19th-century tower, Mole Antonelliana, dominating Turin**

### Armeria Reale

Piazza Castello 191. ***Tel*** *011 54 38 89.* *9am–2pm Tue–Fri, 1–7pm Sat, Sun & hols (last adm: 30 mins before closing).* *1 Jan, 25 Dec.* **www**.artito.arti.beniculturali.it

One wing of the Palazzo Reale, on the northern side of the main square, provides the splendid setting for one of the most extensive and breathtaking collections of arms and armoury in the world.

Opened to the public in 1837, the armoury originally belonged to the House of Savoy. The fine rooms, such as the splendid Galleria Beaumont, designed by Juvarra in 1733, hold treasures ranging from Roman and Etruscan times to the 1800s. The collection has magnificent medieval and Renaissance items from some of the world's greatest armourers and gunsmiths, including a pistol that belonged to Emperor Charles V. One section is devoted largely to Oriental arms and armour.

The Royal Library contains a collection of drawings, including a self-portrait by Leonardo da Vinci on view for special exhibitions only.

**Environs:** About 3 km (2 miles) out of the city centre is the vast **Museo dell'Automobile**. Founded in 1933, it now houses over 150 veteran, vintage and classic cars. The collection includes glorious Bugattis,

Maseratis, Lancias, FIATs and also a number of fine foreign cars. The first petrol-driven car made in Italy (1896) is kept here, as well as the first FIAT (1899) and the 1929 Isotta Fraschini *coupé de ville* used to transport Gloria Swanson in the film *Sunset Boulevard*. Note also that a large number of the sports cars from the 1950s are right-hand drive; this brief trend was in deference to the great British car-makers such as Aston Martin.

There is also a library and a documentation centre which are both open to the public.

Designs from 1949 for the Ferrari 166 MM

**Museo dell'Automobile**
Corso Unità d'Italia 40. **Tel** *011 67 76 66.* *for restoration.*
**www**.museoauto.it

## Stupinigi ⓮

Piazza Principe Amedeo 7, Stupinigi. **Tel** *011 358 12 20.* *63 to Piazza Caio Mario & then 41.* *times vary so call ahead.*
**www**.mauriziano.it

An interior view of the 18th-century Palazzina di Caccia di Stupinigi

In 1729–30 the architect Filippo Juvarra (1676–1736) designed a magnificent hunting lodge at Stupinigi, a beautiful location 9 km (5 miles) south-west of Turin. Known as the Palazzina di Caccia di Stupinigi, the building was created for Duke Vittorio Amedeo II of Savoy and is one of the very finest hunting lodges, built on an impressive scale, reminiscent of the palace of Versailles in France.

The dynamic and complex plan incorporates semicircles and an octagon, with the main block consisting of a dome rising above a circular building from which wings jut out, not unlike the arms of a windmill.

The mass of the central section is lightened by balustrading topped with urns and figures, while the dome is crowned with an 18th-century bronze figure of a stag.

The huge interior includes rooms sumptuously decorated with *trompe l'oeil* paintings and frescoes on a hunting theme – the 18th-century *Triumph of Diana,* for instance, in the main *salone.* About 40 of those rooms house the interesting **Museo d'Arte e di Ammobiliamento**, a museum specializing in 17th- and 18th-century furniture and furnishings. Many of the ornate items on display in these rooms were originally kept in other former royal residences.

Outside there are extensive grounds, which feature an elegant combination of spectacular broad avenues, parkland and colourful formal parterres.

## Basilica di Superga ⓯

Strada Basilica di Superga 73, Comune di Torino. *Sassi.* *daily.* *8 Sep.* **Tombs Tel** *011 899 74 56.* *daily; times vary so call ahead.* *pub hols.* **www**.basilicadisuperga.com

On a hill to the east of Turin, accessible by car or tram, stands the superb Baroque basilica of Superga, built by Juvarra in 1717–31. The commission came from Duke Vittorio Amedeo II, in fulfilment of a vow made to the Virgin Mary in 1706 while the French were besieging the duke and his army in Turin.

The beautiful yellow and white façade is dominated by a large portico designed like a Classical temple, with a 65-m (213-ft) high dome immediately beyond. It is flanked by twin bell towers. The interior is magnificent, decorated in light blue and yellow, and contains numerous fine paintings and carvings.

Underneath the basilica lies the great mausoleum which houses the tombs of the kings, princes and princesses of Savoy from the 18th and 19th centuries. The victims of the 1949 aircrash, including the city's football team, are commemorated on a plaque behind the basilica.

One of the other benefits of visiting the basilica is seeing the views over Turin.

The imposing façade of the 18th-century Baroque Basilica di Superga designed by Filippo Juvarra

The 17th-century Basilica dell'Assunta dominating Sacro Monte, Varallo

## Venaria Reale ⑯

P.za della Repubblica 4. ***Tel*** *011 499 23 33.* FS 🚌 🕐 *daily; times vary, so call ahead.* ♿ **www**.lavenaria.it

This grandiose complex dates from the mid-17th century, when Charles Emanuel II of Savoy decided to build a royal hunting lodge on the site of the existing town of Altessano Superiore. Venaria Reale incorporates the **Reggia di Diana**, a formal palace and garden built between 1660 and 1671, as well as **La Mandria**, the 3,000-hectare park surrounding it.

The historical centre of Venaria was designed by Amadeo di Castellamonte between 1667 and 1690; its focal point is the Piazza dell'Annunziata, with two statues depicting the Angel Gabriel and the Virgin Mary.

## Santuario d'Oropa ⑰

Via Santuario d'Oropa 480, Comune di Biella. ***Tel*** *015 255 512 00.* FS *Biella.* 🚌 *from Biella.* 🕐 *8am–noon daily.* ♿ **Chiesa Antica** 🕐 *8am–noon, 2–7pm daily.* **Chiesa Nuova** 🕐 *summer: 9:30am–5:30pm daily; winter: 9am–4:30pm Tue, Thu & Sat, 9am–5:30pm Sun.* **www**.santuariodioropa.it

Perched above the wool town of Biella stands the tranquil church and hospice complex of Oropa, a series of three squares surrounded by pale buildings with stone-shingled roofs, cut into the hillside. The sanctuary was founded in the 4th century by Sant' Eusebio, Bishop of Vercelli. It was intended as a hospice for the poor, and to honour the "Black Madonna" which he had brought back from the Holy Land. The Madonna, said to be the work of St Luke himself, is the object of some of the most important pilgrimages in the region.

The statue of the Madonna is kept in the restored **Chiesa Antica** (Old Church). Beyond it, at the top of the complex, is the imposing Neo-Classical **Chiesa Nuova** (New Church), which was begun in 1885 but completed only in 1960.

## Domodossola ⑱

Verbania. 👥 *20,000.* FS 🚌 ℹ *Stazione entrance, P.za Matteotti 24 (0324 24 82 65).* 🛒 *Sat.* **www**.prodomodossola.it

At the centre of this pretty mountain town of Roman origin lies the **Piazza Mercato**, or market square, framed by attractive arcades and houses from the 15th and 16th centuries. The Ossola valley, where the town lies, sits in an Alpine landscape of pasture and forest sliced by rivers and streams. Pretty villages north of the town include **Crodo**, with its cold-water mineral spas, and **Baceno**, where the 14th–16th-century church contains fine frescoes and wood carvings.

## Varallo ⑲

Vercelli. 👥 *7,900.* FS 🚌 ℹ *Corso Roma 38 (0163 56 44 04).* 🛒 *Tue.* **www**.atlvalsesiavercelli.it

The small town and tourist resort of Varallo lies halfway up the attractive Sesia valley, and boasts a remarkable church, **Santa Maria delle Grazie**. The late 15th-century church is notable for its beautiful frescoed wall depicting the Life of Christ and *trompe l'oeil* architectural elements; the paintings are the work of Gaudenzio Ferrari (1484–1546).

A long stairway behind the church (and also a cableway) climbs up to the extraordinary **Sacro Monte**, a religious community built at an altitude of about 610 m (2,000 ft). This "Sacred Mount" was founded as a sanctuary of the New Jerusalem in 1486 under the patronage of the Archbishop of Milan, San Carlo Borromeo.

The Basilica dell'Assunta, with a 19th-century façade, is set in a tranquil courtyard with palm trees and a fountain; the interior is a riot of ornate Baroque architecture. Dotted around it are over 40 chapels representing the sacred sites of Jerusalem, with statues and painted figures positioned in front of frescoed backdrops painted by Gaudenzio Ferrari, Tanzio da Varallo and others.

***Christ Condemned*** **(16th century) in a chapel at Varallo's Sacro Monte**

**The interior of the church of San Giulio in the centre of Lake Orta**

## Lake Orta ⓴

Novara. FS *Orta.* *Via Panoramica, Orta San Giulio (0322 90 56 14).* **www**.distrettolaghi.it

Lake Orta is one of Italy's least visited lakes – unjustly, as it is delightfully set among the foothills of the Alps.

The lake's main resort is **Orta San Giulio**, a small town containing handsome palazzi, and houses decorated with wrought-iron balconies. In the lakeside **Piazza Principale** stands the Palazzo della Comunità, a frescoed building of 1582 resting on arcades. A cobbled pathway leads up to the 15th-century church of **Santa Maria Assunta** (rebuilt in the 17th century), with a Romanesque doorway and an interior that is richly decorated with 17th-century frescoes and paintings.

Above Orta San Giulio is the sanctuary of **Sacro Monte**, built from 1591 to 1770 and dedicated to St Francis of Assisi. A winding path, offering lovely views of the lake, climbs to the church. The path is lined by 21 chapels, most of them Baroque, in which frescoes and life-size figure groups by various artists depict scenes from the life of St Francis.

In the centre of the lake rises the picturesque **Isola San Giulio**. The island was said to have been liberated from snakes and monsters by the 4th-century Christian preacher Julius, from whom the island's name derives. The basilica here is notable for its 12th-century black marble pulpit decorated with wild animals and birds, and for the 15th-century frescoes – including one attributed to Gaudenzio Ferrari, of the *Virgin and Child Enthroned.*

## Novara ㉑

*105,000.* FS *Baluardo Quintino Sella 40 (0321 39 40 59).* *Mon, Thu & Sat.* **www**.turismonovara.it

**Fresco detail of a horseman (17th century) by Morazzone in San Gaudenzio, Novara**

Novara has distant origins as the Roman city of Nubliaria – meaning "surrounded in mist". Nowadays its delightful arcaded streets and squares, and historic buildings, exude a quiet affluence. Many of the most important buildings stand around Piazza della Repubblica. They include the beautiful Renaissance courtyard of the **Broletto** (town hall), with its graceful 15th-century red-brick arcades and covered stairway. The buildings now house a small **Museo Civico**, comprising an archaeological section and a picture gallery.

Across the piazza rises the **Duomo**, rebuilt by the architect Alessandro Antonelli in around 1865 in Neo-Classical style, with a huge central doorway. The interior contains dramatic Renaissance paintings of the Vercelli school and Flemish tapestries, as well as the remains of an earlier sanctuary on this site: these include the frescoed 12th-century chapel of San Siro and the 15th-century cloisters. The octagonal **Baptistry** next door dates in part from the 5th century and is painted with medieval frescoed scenes of the terrible Apocalypse.

A few streets away stands the **Basilica di San Gaudenzio**. It is strikingly crowned by an elongated four-tiered dome and spire. designed by Antonelli, and reminiscent of his Mole Antonelliana in Turin *(see p224)*. At the top of the spire, which is 121 m (400 ft) high, is a statue of San Gaudenzio himself. Inside, the late 16th-century church contains a fine collection of Renaissance and Baroque paintings by artists from Piedmont: these include a notable 17th-century battle scene by Tanzio da Varallo, a 16th-century altarpiece by Gaudenzio Ferrari, and a fresco painting by Pier Francesco Morazzone (c.1572–1626).

**View across Lake Orta to the Isola San Giulio**

**Museo Civico**
Via Fratelli Rosselli 20. ***Tel*** *0321 62 30 21.* *times vary so call ahead.* **www**.comune.novara.it

**Baptistry**
Piazza della Repubblica.
***Tel*** *0321 66 16 71.* *ask at the Curia Arcivescovile.*

## Vercelli ㉒

50,000. FS *Viale Garibaldi 90 (0161 58 002).* *Tue & Fri.* **www**.atlvalsesiavercelli.it

Vercelli is the rice capital of Europe, set in a vast plain of paddy fields that provide a sight of shimmering sheets of water stretching far into the distance. Vercelli itself also developed its own school of painting in the 16th century, and has one major architectural treasure, the 13th-century **Basilica di Sant'Andrea**.

The Basilica, standing just across from the railway station, is famous as the first example of Italian architecture to be influenced by the Gothic style of northern France – note the beautiful vaulted nave and the flying buttresses, typical Gothic elements. Overall, however, the Basilica remains a stunning achievement in Romanesque architecture, built from 1219 to 1227 as part of an abbey for the papal legate Cardinal Guala Bicheri. The façade, curiously, changes colour half-way up, the blue-grey of the lower part turning to red and white in the twin towers; these are linked by a double arcade. A carving attributed to Antelami (12th century) adorns the central lunette.

The three-aisled interior is gently illuminated through rose windows. The muted decoration is largely focused on the vaulting, which is supported by tall, slender shafts. Off the north side is the simple 13th-century cloister, beautifully framed by arcades rising from clustered columns.

Vercelli's other important historic buildings are not far away, including the imposing 16th-century **Duomo**, the **Ospedale Maggiore** (13th century), and the church of **San Cristoforo**, with frescoes and a particularly fine Madonna (both c.1529) painted by Gaudenzio Ferrari. The **Museo Borgogna** is the best place to admire the masterpieces of the Vercelli school. The main shopping street, Corso Libertà, has a handful of attractive 15th-century houses and courtyards.

Detail of the carving on the 15th-century porch at the entrance to the Duomo in Asti

**Museo Borgogna**
Via A Borgogna 6. ***Tel*** *0161 25 27 76.* *Tue–Fri pm, Sat am, Sun pm.* *1 Jan, 15 Aug, 1 Nov, 25 Dec.*
 **www**.museoborgogna.it

The 13th-century cloisters of the Basilica di Sant'Andrea in Vercelli

## Asti ㉓

*74,000.* FS *Piazza Alfieri 29 (0141 53 03 57).* *Wed & Sat.* **www**.astiturismo.it

Renowned for its sweet *spumante* (sparkling) wine, Asti is at the centre of Italy's most prestigious wine region *(see pp182–3)* and also a tranquil and noble city of medieval towers, elegant churches and warm red roofs.

Just north of the main railway station lies the Piazza del Campo del Palio, the largest square in Asti and formerly the site of its annual horse race, now in Piazza Alfieri. The race, held towards the end of September to coincide with the local wine fair, rivals the Palio in Siena *(see p341)* for outrageous horsemanship and medieval pageantry.

Beyond this square lies the triangular-shaped **Piazza Alfieri**. A statue here commemorates the local poet and dramatist Vittorio Alfieri (1749–1803), in whose honour both this square and the main street were renamed.

Corso Alfieri runs the entire length of the old city centre. At its eastern end stands the 15th-century church of **San Pietro in Consavia**, with its terracotta decoration, 17th-century frescoes, and attractive cloister. Beside it is the circular Romanesque **baptistry** which dates from the 10th–12th centuries; it was once the church of the knights of the Order of St John of Jerusalem, who had their headquarters here.

West of Piazza Alfieri is the **Collegiata di San Secondo** (13th–15th century), named after Asti's patron saint, which houses a Renaissance polyptych by Gandolfino d'Asti and 15th-century frescoes. The area around the western section of Corso Alfieri contains a few of the medieval towers for which the town was once famous; they include the Torre dei Comentini, the very elegant Torre Troyana

The watery expanses of the rice fields around Vercelli

and, at the far end, the Torre Ropa. This was built on the ruins of a tower in which San Secondo, a Roman soldier, was held. The nearby 14th-century Gothic **Duomo** has a 15th-century porch and, inside, 18th-century frescoes, and two 12th- to 13th-century carvings on the west corner of the transept.

## Cuneo 24

*56,000. FS Via Amedeo II 8a (0171 69 02 17). Tue.*
**www**.cuneoholiday.com

"Cuneo" in Italian means wedge-shaped, and this perfectly describes the sliver of land that the town occupies at the confluence of two rivers, the Gesso and the Stura di Demonte. In early November the town hosts the regional cheese fair, with unusual local cheese varieties.

The town centres on a large square, **Piazza Galimberti**, with its old arcades, where the traders come to hawk their wares every Tuesday. Much of the town was rebuilt in the 18th and 19th centuries, providing Cuneo with wide, tree-lined boulevards, though the impressive viaduct that takes the railway line into town dates from the 1930s. The deconsecrated 13th-century church of **San Francesco** has a fine 15th-century portal.

**The Castello di Casotto in the hills above the resort of Garessio**

The 18th-century church of **Santa Croce** has a concave façade by Francesco Gallo.

Cuneo is a good base for exploring the pretty local valleys, such as the Valle Stura, where rare flowers grow.

## Bossea Caves 25

Località Bossea, Comune Frabosa Soprana. ***Tel*** *0174 34 92 40.*
*FS Mondovì. from Mondovì.*
*daily for guided tours only.*
**www**.grottadibossea.com

Some 25 km (16 miles) south of Mondovì, near the end of a scenic route that follows the valley of the Torrente Corsaglia up into the Maritime Alps, are the caves of Bossea, some of the finest in Italy. The series of caves contains remarkable stalactite columns and shapes that have formed over many hundreds of thousands of years. Guided tours lead through different chambers – some of them surprisingly vast – following the underground rivers and lakes. The skeleton of a prehistoric bear, *Ursus spelaeus*, which was discovered here, is also on display.

Bring a sweater – the temperature rarely rises above 9°C (50°F).

**Market day in the enormous Piazza Galimberti at the centre of Cuneo**

## Garessio 26

*Cuneo. 4,000. FS Piazza Carrara 137 (0174 80 56 70). Fri.*
**www**.garessio.net

One of the prettier resorts of the Maritime Alps, Garessio is no more than a sprinkling of houses spread out over the hills, surrounded by woods of chestnut trees. It is also a popular spa.

According to legend, the waters here have miraculous powers: in about AD 980 an octogenarian nobleman found instant relief from his kidney and circulatory problems by drinking the mineral-rich water. Since then, the waters have been drunk for their remedial properties – linked in particular with the relief of diuretic and digestive problems – and for their refreshing taste.

**Environs:** About 10 km (4 miles) west of Garessio stands the **Castello di Casotto**, the dramatically sited summer palace used by the House of Savoy. The royal family used to come here to enjoy the local mineral water, the attractive scenery and the exceptionally pure air of the hills.

The town of **Ormea**, 12 km (7 miles) southwest, is interesting for its ruined 11th-century castle, its church with late 14th-century Gothic frescoes, and its attractive houses.

**Castello di Casotto**
Garessio. ***Tel*** *0174 80 56 70.*
*by appointment.*

# LIGURIA

*Liguria is a long, thin coastal strip nestling at the foot of vine-covered mountains. Here pastel-coloured houses bask in the Mediterranean sun, while their gardens, flourishing in the mild climate, are a riot of colourful plants. In contrast with resorts like Portofino and even San Remo, the bustling city of Genoa, for centuries a trading port of immense power, is the only major population centre.*

Genoa has a long history as a seafaring power, achieving greatness first as a trading post with ancient Greece and Phoenicia, and later, as the capital of a small commercial empire that at one stage eclipsed even Venice. The great sea admiral Andrea Doria came from Genoa, as did the 15th-century explorer of the Americas, Christopher Columbus.

Genoa's rise began in the 12th century, when it succeeded in beating the Saracen pirates that plagued the Ligurian coast. Thereafter, the maritime republic prospered, profiting from the Crusades to set up trading posts in the Middle East and marshalling its naval might to humble its rivals. The golden age lasted from the 16th to the mid-17th century, and included the glorious reign of Andrea Doria who enriched the city by financing the wars of Genoa's European allies through the offices of the city's bank. Factionalism among the ruling aristocracy, however, and foreign conquest, by the French in 1668 and the Austrians in 1734, led to the region's decline. It was only in the early 19th century, with unification fervour spreading thanks to native son Giuseppe Mazzini and the revolutionary Garibaldi, that Liguria ever recaptured a glimpse of its former prominence. Today, sheltered by the steep slopes that rise from the sea, faded, elegant mansions lie along the coast, particularly in San Remo, where aristocrats came to spend the winter at the end of the 19th century.

Green shutters and rich ochre walls characterize the houses of Portofino

◁ Rugged cliffs tumble into the sea along Liguria's Riviera Levante

# Exploring Liguria

Liguria divides neatly into two parts. The western coastline, known as the Riviera Ponente, is a thin strip of coastal plain stretching across to the French border, while the eastern coastline, or Riviera Levante, is more rugged and picturesque, descending directly into the sea. Between the two lengths of coast lies the region's capital and biggest port, Genoa (Genova). The faded elegance of the tranquil coastal villages contrasts with this cramped and busy port which snakes along the coast, hemmed in between the sea and the mountains rising steeply behind it.

Stag motif of the city of Cervo, above the cathedral doors

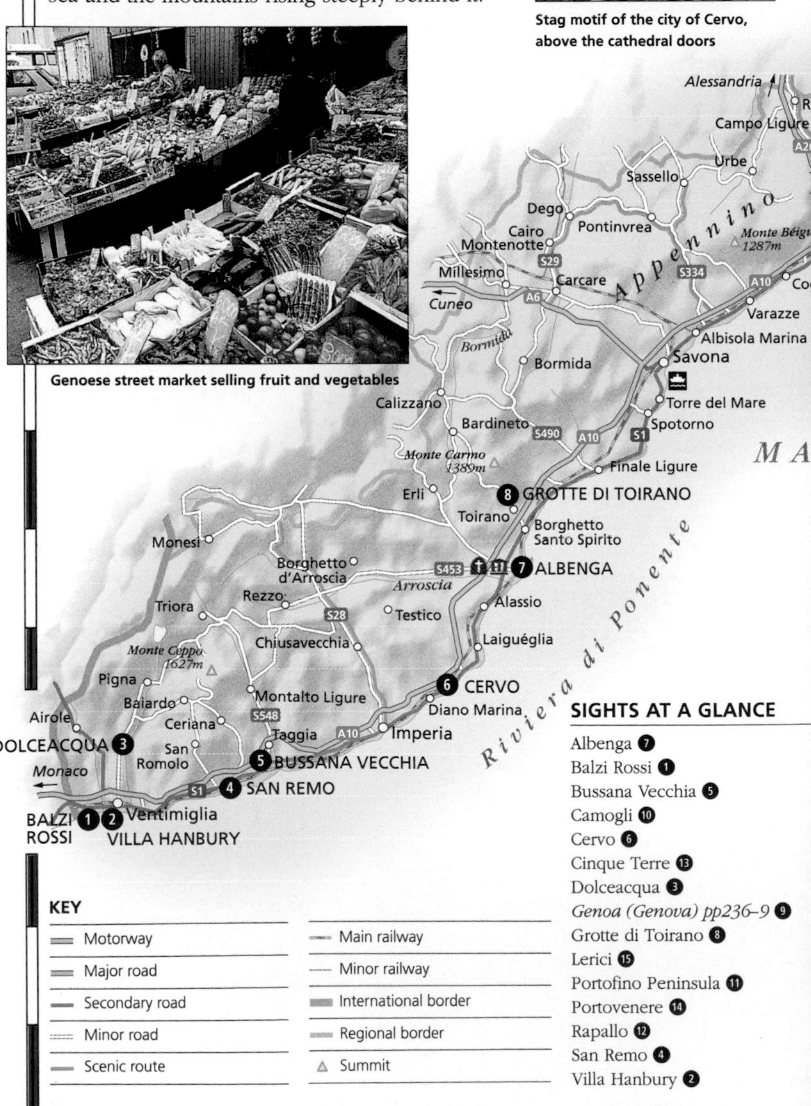


Genoese street market selling fruit and vegetables

## SIGHTS AT A GLANCE

Albenga 7
Balzi Rossi 1
Bussana Vecchia 5
Camogli 10
Cervo 6
Cinque Terre 13
Dolceacqua 3
*Genoa (Genova) pp236–9* 9
Grotte di Toirano 8
Lerici 15
Portofino Peninsula 11
Portovenere 14
Rapallo 12
San Remo 4
Villa Hanbury 2

For additional map symbols *see back flap*

The smart resort of San Remo on the Riviera Ponente, west of Genoa

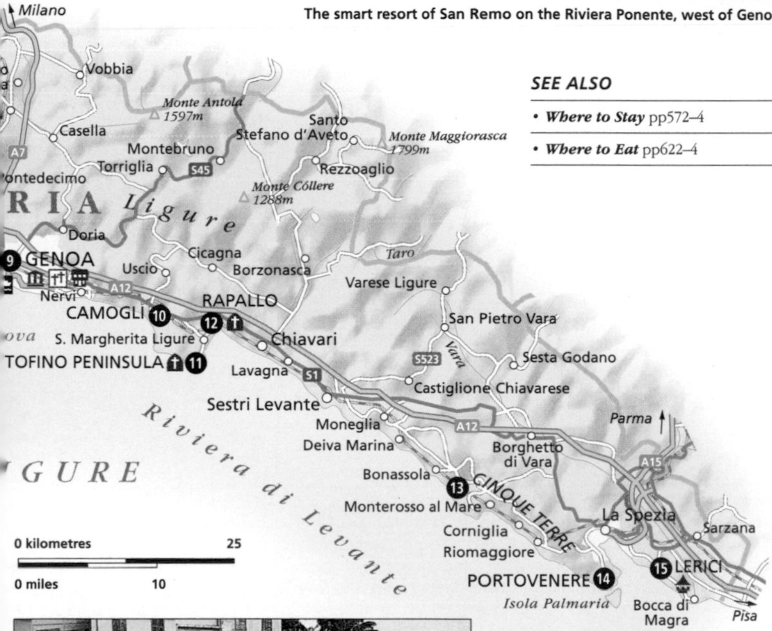

Milano
Vobbia
Monte Antola 1597m
Santo Stefano d'Aveto
Monte Maggiorasca 1799m
Casella
Montebruno
Torriglia
Rezzoaglio
Monte Cóllere 1288m
Doria
GENOA 9
Nervi
Uscio
Cicagna
Borzonasca
Taro
Varese Ligure
CAMOGLI 10
RAPALLO 12
San Pietro Vara
Vara
S. Margherita Ligure
Chiavari
PORTOFINO PENINSULA 11
Lavagna
Sesta Godano
Castiglione Chiavarese
Sestri Levante
Parma
Moneglia
Deiva Marina
Borghetto di Vara
Riviera di Levante
Bonassola
CINQUE TERRE 13
Monterosso al Mare
La Spezia
Sarzana
Corniglia
Riomaggiore
15 LERICI
PORTOVENERE 14
Isola Palmaria
Bocca di Magra
Pisa
0 kilometres 25
0 miles 10

## SEE ALSO


- ***Where to Stay*** pp572–4
- ***Where to Eat*** pp622–4

Houses wedged into the cliffs in Riomaggiore, Cinque Terre

## GETTING AROUND

If you keep to the coast, transport in Liguria is straightforward. The A10–E80 motorway, becoming the A12–E80 at Genoa, and a mainline railway hug the shore from the French border to Tuscany. The main stations along the route are at Ventimiglia, San Remo, Imperia, Savona, Genoa and La Spezia. There are good road and rail links between Genoa and Milan and Turin. Access to inland Liguria is harder because of the mountains. Bus services link many of the coastal towns with the prettiest hill villages. You can explore some of the countryside by car by following the smaller routes, such as the S28 from Imperia towards Garessio in Piedmont, the S334 from Albisola or the S456 from Voltri towards Milan.

The spectacular gardens of the Villa Hanbury near Ventimiglia

## Balzi Rossi ❶

Imperia. FS *Ventimiglia & Menton.* *from Ventimiglia to Ponte San Luigi & then a 10-minute walk.* **www**.archeoge.arti.beniculturali.it

An unassuming promontory is the setting for some of the most important caves in northern Italy. Guided tours lead through the traces of the cave-dwelling civilization of pre-Iron Age Liguria. The caves contain excavated burial sites where the dead were adorned with sea-shells. The **Museo Nazionale dei Balzi Rossi** contains tools, weapons and stone-etched female figures dating from 100,000 years ago. There is also a reproduction of an etching of a horse.

**Museo Nazionale dei Balzi Rossi**
Via Balzi Rossi 9. ***Tel*** *0184 381 13.* *Tue–Sun.* *1 Jan, 1 May, 25 Dec.*

## Villa Hanbury ❷

Corso Monte Carlo 43, Località La Mortola. ***Tel*** *0184 22 92 92.* FS *Ventimiglia.* *from Ventimiglia.* *9:30am–4pm (Mar–mid-Jun: to 5pm; mid-Jun–Sep: to 6pm) daily.* *Wed Nov–Mar.* **www**.amicihanbury.com

In 1867 the English botanist Sir Thomas Hanbury and his brother bought this villa on the Mortola promontory. They took full advantage of the exceptionally mild Ligurian climate to establish a garden of exotic plants along the sloping pathways of the seaside villa.

The collection, gathered by Hanbury on trips to Africa and Asia, has grown to number more than 3,000 varieties of tropical flora including rubber trees, palms and wild cacti.

The garden is now run by the state and is one of the most impressive botanical gardens in Italy. Even winter sees a wealth of colour and vegetation here.

## Dolceacqua ❸

Imperia. *1,800.* FS *Via Doria 10 (0184 20 68 99).* *Thu.* **www**.dolceacqua.it

This pretty village, 8 km (5 miles) north of Ventimiglia, is built on either side of the churning River Nervia, its two halves joined by an arching 33 m (108 ft) medieval stone bridge. The highlight is the ruined 12th- to 15th-century **castle**, inhabited for a while in the 16th century by the powerful Doria family from Genoa. The two square towers at the front dominate the village. The terraced vineyards in the surrounding hills produce grapes for general consumption as well as for a robust red wine known as Rossese or vino di Dolceacqua.

The village of Dolceacqua with its medieval bridge and ruined castle

## San Remo ❹

Imperia. *60,000.* FS *Largo Nuvoloni 1 (0184 590 59).* *Tue & Sat.* **www**.rivieradeifiori.org

The Casinò Municipale in San Remo, completed in 1906

San Remo is a pleasant resort of faded elegance. The composer Tchaikovsky, Alfred Nobel (the father of modern explosives) and the nonsense poet Edward Lear all stayed in the stuccoed mansions of the palm-lined seafront avenue, the Corso Imperatrice. The focus of the town, then as now, is the Casino. A little further down the Corso stands the ornate Russian Orthodox church of San Borilio.

The old town, La Pigna (fir cone), is a huddle of narrow lanes with medieval houses and pastel-coloured shutters. A coach service goes from San Remo to San Romolo, a small village 786 m (2,579 ft) above sea level that offers beautiful views of the area.

An enchanting flower market is held on Corso Garibaldi (6–8am, Jun–Oct), while the Italian Song Festival takes place here in February.

## Bussana Vecchia ❺

Imperia. Off San Remo–Arma di Taggia road.

Bussana Vecchia is a marvellously atmospheric ghost town. In February 1887 an earthquake shook the village,

*For hotels and restaurants in this region see pp572–4 and pp622–4*

reducing its Baroque church and surrounding houses to ruins. (One survivor, Giovanni Torre del Merlo, went on to invent the ice-cream cone.)

The town was rebuilt closer to the sea and since then the original village has been taken over by artists, who have restored some interiors, providing a venue for summer concerts and exhibitions.

## Cervo ❻

Imperia. 1,200. FS *Piazza Santa Caterina 2 (0183 40 81 97).* *Thu.* **www**.rivieradeifiori.it

Cervo is the prettiest of the many old seafront villages just east of Imperia, with a narrow complex of streets and houses rising dramatically up from the shingle beach. At the top of the village stands the concave Baroque façade of **San Giovanni Battista**. Charming chamber orchestra performances are held in front of the church in July and August. The church is also known as the *"dei corallini"*, after the coral fishing which once brought prosperity to the local people. Now Cervo is an unassuming but characteristic Ligurian holiday resort, with unspoilt hotels near the beach.

San Giovanni Battista at Cervo

Spectacular rock formations in the grottoes of Toirano

## Albenga ❼

Savona. 21,000. FS *Piazza del Popolo (0182 55 84 44).* *Wed.* **www**.inforiviera.it

Until the Middle Ages, the Roman port of Albium Ingaunum played an important maritime role. The sea, however, gradually moved further out, leaving the town, now called Albenga, stranded on the Centa River. Most striking now is its Romanesque brick architecture, in particular the three 13th-century towers clustered around the cathedral of **San Michele**. The cathedral's interior was restored to its medieval form in the late 1960s. To the south is an intriguing 5th-century **Baptistry** with a ten-sided exterior and octagonal interior. Inside, the original 5th-century blue and white mosaics of doves represent the 12 apostles. To the north of the cathedral is the small Piazza dei Leoni, named after its three stone lions imported from Rome.

The 5th-century Baptistry at Albenga

In a 14th-century palace on Piazza San Michele is the **Museo Navale Romano**, founded in 1950 following the salvage of a Roman ship that had sunk in the 1st century BC. The museum contains ancient amphorae as well as exhibits salvaged from more recent shipwrecks.

**Baptistry**
Piazza San Michele. ***Tel*** *0182 512 15.* *10am–noon, 3–6pm Tue–Sun.* *1 Jan, Easter, 25 Dec.*

**Museo Navale Romano**
Piazza San Michele 12. ***Tel*** *0182 512 15.* *10am–noon, 3–6pm Tue–Sun.* *1 Jan, Easter, 25 Dec.*

## Grotte di Toirano ❽

Piazzale delle Grotte, Toirano. ***Tel*** *0182 980 62.* *from Albenga to Borghetto Santo Spirito.* FS *to Borghetto Santo Spirito or Loano.* *9:30am–noon, 2–5pm daily.* *mid-Nov–25 Dec.* *times vary (book ahead).* **www**.toiranogrotte.it

Beneath the delightful medieval town of Toirano lies a series of caves containing relics of Paleolithic life dating from 100,000 years ago.

Guided tours through the **Grotta della Basura** (Witch's Cave) reveal remarkable prehistoric human and animal footprints, and a collection of ancient bear bones and teeth in the "bear cemetery".

The **Grotta di Santa Lucia**, which can also be visited by guided tour, reveals the full beauty of the yellow and grey stalactites and stalagmites that have formed here over hundreds of thousands of years.

The **Museo Preistorico della Val Varatella** at the entrance to the Grotta della Basura has a small display of finds from the caves, as well as a model of a prehistoric bear.

**Museo Preistorico della Val Varatella**
Piazzale delle Grotte. ***Tel*** *0182 980 62.* *9am–12:30pm, 2–5pm daily.*

# Street-by-Street: Genoa ❾

There is something refreshingly rough-edged about Genoa (Genova in Italian), Italy's most important commercial port. In contrast to the genteel resorts along the neighbouring coast, the narrow streets of the old town are the haunts of sailors and streetwalkers.

With its natural harbour and the mountains to protect it, Genoa rose to prominence as a sea-based power. During the 16th century Andrea Doria cemented Genoa's importance, and also proved an astute patron of the arts.

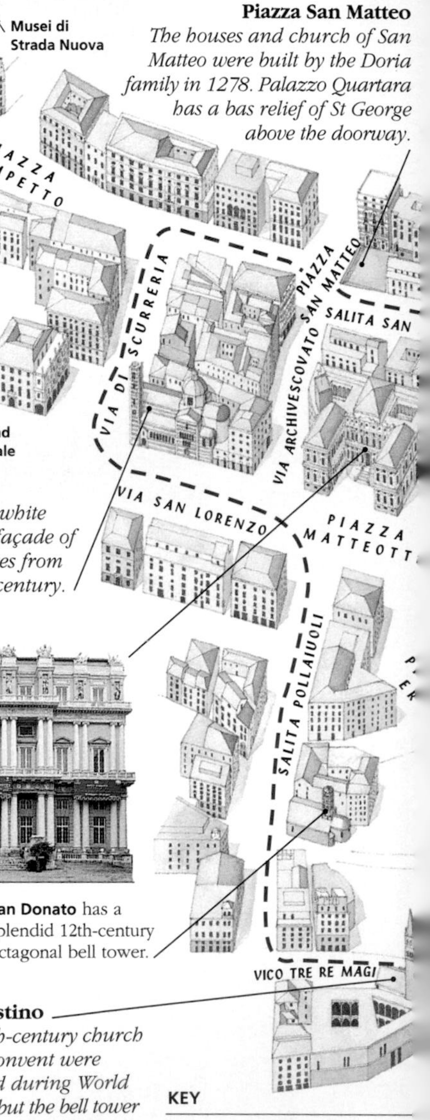

**Piazza San Matteo**
*The houses and church of San Matteo were built by the Doria family in 1278. Palazzo Quartara has a bas relief of St George above the doorway.*

↖ **Musei di Strada Nuova**

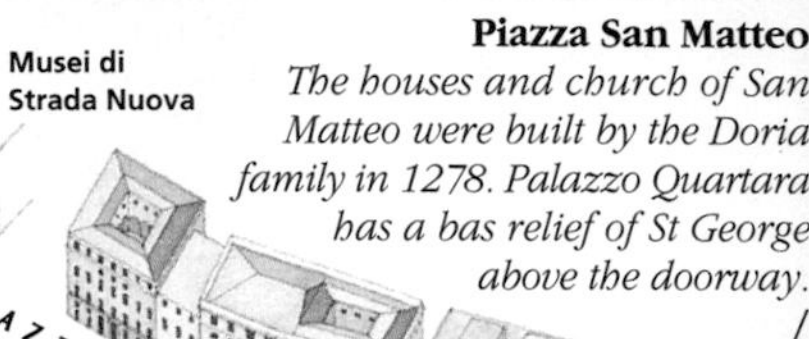


← **The port and Palazzo Reale**

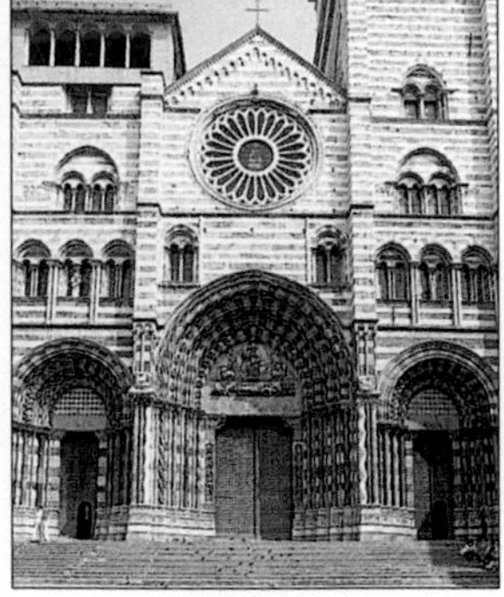

**San Lorenzo**
*The black and white striped Gothic façade of the Duomo dates from the early 13th century.*

**Palazzo Ducale**
*Once the seat of the doges of Genoa, this elegant building with its two fine 16th-century courtyards and arcades now contains a major arts and cultural centre.*

**San Donato** has a splendid 12th-century octagonal bell tower.

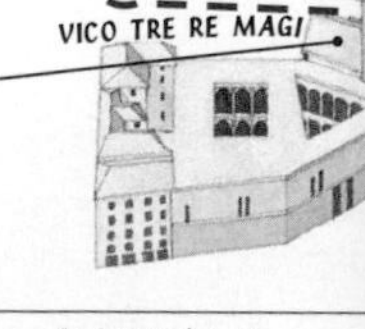

**Sant'Agostino**
*The 13th-century church and convent were bombed during World War II, but the bell tower remains. The cloisters now house sculpture like this fragment from the tomb of Margaret of Brabant by Pisano (1312).*

**KEY**

– – – Suggested route

**0 metres** **100**

**0 yards** **100**

*For hotels and restaurants in this region see pp572–4 and pp622–4*

**Church of Gesù**
*This Baroque church, built between 1589 and 1606, is also known as the church of Santi Ambrogio e Andrea.*

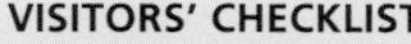

## VISITORS' CHECKLIST

*640,000. Cristoforo Colombo 6 km (4 miles) W. FS Stazione Principe, Piazza Acquaverde. Stazione Marittima, Ponte dei Mille. Aeroporto Cristoforo Colombo (010 601 52 47); Stazione Principe (010 246 26 33). Mon, Wed & Thu. 24 Jun: San Giovanni Battista; Jul: Ballet Festival; Oct: Fiera Nautica.* **www**.apt.genova.it

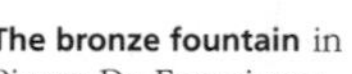


**Piazza De Ferrari** is the site of the Neo-Classical Banco di Roma and the Accademia, as well as the restored Teatro Carlo Felice.

**The bronze fountain** in Piazza De Ferrari was constructed in 1936.

**Porta Soprana**
*The eastern gateway to the city has curved outer walls and stands close to the site of Christopher Columbus's house.*

**Sant'Andrea**
*The 12th-century cloisters standing in a small garden are all that remain of the convent that once stood here.*

**19th-century lion guarding the steps leading to the Duomo**

### San Lorenzo (Duomo)

Piazza San Lorenzo. ***Tel*** *010 254 12 50.* *daily.* **Museo del Tesoro** ***Tel*** *010 254 12 50.* *9am–noon, 3–6pm Mon–Sat.*

The Duomo, with its black and white striped exterior, blends many architectural styles, from the 12th-century Romanesque side portal of San Giovanni to the Baroque touches of some of its side chapels. The three portals at the west end are in French Gothic style.

The most sumptuous of the chapels is dedicated to St John the Baptist, patron saint of the city; it includes a 13th-century sarcophagus that once held the venerated saint's relics.

Steps lead down from the sacristy to the **Museo del Tesoro di San Lorenzo**. It houses such treasures as the Roman green glass dish said to have been used at the Last Supper, and a blue chalcedony plate on which the head of John the Baptist was allegedly served up to Salome.

### The Port

**Aquarium** *Ponte Spinola.* ***Tel*** *010 234 56 78.* *9:30am–7:30pm daily (to 8:30pm Sat, Sun & hols); Jul & Aug: 8:30am–10pm daily. Last adm: 90 mins before closing.* **www**.acquariodigenova.it

The port is the heart of Genoa and the origin of its power as a seafaring city state in the 11th and 12th centuries. A workaday place, it is ringed by busy roads and 1960s buildings.

Among the vestiges of its medieval glory is the **Lanterna** lighthouse (restored in 1543) near the Stazione Marittima. In the old days fires would be lit at the top of the Lanterna to guide ships into port. Today, regeneration of the port is in part due to the Renzo Piano-designed conference centre *(see p185)* and the **Aquarium**, one of the largest in Europe and an ideal place to sample the richness of marine life.

# Exploring Genoa

Visitors are well rewarded when they explore Genoa – a city proud of its history and legends. The palazzi of Via Balbi and Via Garibaldi, and the paintings and sculptures dotted around the city in churches and museums, are among the finest in northwestern Italy. The environs, too, provide scenic and relaxing locations for excursions along the coast or in the steep hills behind.

The courtyard of the University on Via Balbi

### Sant'Agostino

Piazza Sarzano 35. ***Tel*** *010 251 12 63.* *on request only.* **Museo di Architettura e Scultura Ligure** ***Tel*** *010 251 12 63.* *9am–7pm Tue–Fri; 10am–7pm Sat & Sun.* *public hols.*

This Gothic church was begun in 1260, but it was bombed to pieces in World War II. It is now deconsecrated and all that remains of the original building is the fine Gothic bell tower, decorated with coloured tiles. The monastery, of which the church of Sant'Agostino was once a part, was also bombed. What remained were two ruined cloisters – one of which forms the only triangular building in Genoa. The cloisters have been reconstructed and converted into the **Museo di Architettura e Scultura Ligure**. It contains the city's collection of architectural pieces and fragments of sculpture, as well as frescoes – all salvaged from Genoa's other destroyed churches. The finest piece is a magnificent fragment from the tomb of Margaret of Brabant, who died in 1311. She was the wife of Emperor Henry VII who invaded Italy in 1310. Carved by Giovanni Pisano around 1313, the sculptures from her tomb were restored and repositioned in 1987. The figures, whose garments are arranged in simple folds, seem to be helping Margaret to lie down to rest.

### Palazzo Reale

Via Balbi 10. ***Tel*** *010 271 02 36.* *9am–7pm Tue–Sun (to 1:30pm Tue, Wed).* *1 Jan, 25 Apr, 1 May, 15 Aug, 25 Dec.*

This austere-looking residence, used by the Kings of Savoy from the 17th century onwards, has a highly ornate Rococo interior – notably its ballroom and its Hall of Mirrors. Among the paintings is a *Crucifixion* by Van Dyck. The lovely garden, which slopes down towards the old port, includes an intriguing cobblestone mosaic around the central fountain, depicting houses and animals.

Opposite the palace is the old **University** (1634) designed by the architect Bartolomeo Bianco, as was much of Via Balbi. The large building brilliantly overcomes Genoa's hilly topography, and is constructed on four levels.

### Palazzo Bianco

Via Garibaldi 11. ***Tel*** *010 557 21 93.* *9am–7pm Tue–Fri (from 10am Sat & Sun).* **Palazzo Rosso** ***Tel*** *010 557 49 72.* *9am–7pm Tue–Fri (from 10am Sat & Sun).*

The Palazzo Bianco is situated on Genoa's most beautiful street, **Via Garibaldi**, where there are numerous fine 16th-century mansions and palazzi. The Palazzo Bianco contains the city's prime collection of paintings, including the works of many Genoese artists such as Luca Cambiaso, Bernardo Strozzi, Domenico Piola and Giovanni Benedetto

A portrait of Columbus, Villa Doria at Pegli

## CHRISTOPHER COLUMBUS IN GENOA

The name of Cristoforo Colombo, or Christopher Columbus, as English speakers know him, is in evidence all over Genoa. A statue of the explorer of the New World greets you as soon as you emerge in Piazza Acquaverde from Porta Principe railway station; various public buildings bear his name; even the airport is named after him. In the 17th-century Palazzo Belimbau, built on top of the old city walls, is a series of frescoes by the local artist Tavarone celebrating the explorer's life, and you can see three of his letters in the Sala del Sindaco in Palazzo Tursi (the city hall) on Via Garibaldi. It is not certain whether Columbus (c.1451–1506) was born in Genoa, in Savona 15 km (9 miles) to the west, or even outside Italy. However, city registers mention his father, a weaver, and various family homes within the city. The small ivy-clad house adjacent to Porta Soprana may have been Columbus's childhood home, where he first discovered his passion for the sea.

The house where Columbus may have lived

*For hotels and restaurants in this region see pp572–4 and pp622–4*

The romantic gardens at Villa Durazzo-Pallavicini in Pegli

Castiglione. Better-known artists include Filippino Lippi (a lovely *Madonna with Saints*), Van Dyck, Veronese and Rubens. Across the street in the **Palazzo Rosso** are more paintings, including works by Dürer and Caravaggio, as well as ceramics and furniture. Upstairs in the *piano nobile* the rooms are adorned with 17th-century frescoes by Genoese artists such as de Ferrari and Piola.

**Staglieno Cemetery**
Piazzale Resasco, Staglieno. ***Tel*** *010 87 01 84.* *daily.* *pub hols.*

Fine tomb architecture from the huge Staglieno Cemetery

This grandiose cemetery, just over the hills northeast of Genoa along the Bisagno River, is so big (33 ha, 81.5 acres) that it has its own internal bus system. Founded in 1844, its tombs and monuments make up an eerie city of miniature cathedrals, Egyptian temples and Art Nouveau palaces. Its most famous resident is Giuseppe Mazzini, the Genoese revolutionary who died near Pisa in 1872.

**Environs:** Until World War II, **Pegli**, 6 km (4 miles) west of the city centre, was a popular weekend retreat for rich Genoese. Now it forms part of the city, but maintains an air of tranquillity thanks to its parks and two villas, the 19th-century **Villa Durazzo-Pallavicini** and the 16th-century **Villa Doria**. The latter houses a naval history museum celebrating Genoa's glorious past: you can see compasses, astrolabes, globes, model ships and a portrait of Columbus, ascribed to Ghirlandaio, probably dating from 1525. An archaeological museum in the Villa Durazzo-Pallavicini relates the pre-Roman history of the Ligurian coast. The villa's garden is landscaped with romantic grottoes, pavilions and fountains.

**Nervi**, 8 km (5 miles) to the east of the city, is another former resort town, famous for its seafront promenade, the **Passeggiata Anita Garibaldi** (named after Garibaldi's wife). The walk follows a route that has been cut into the rock face, giving panoramic views of the coast. The lush **Parco Municipale** is another feature of Nervi. It once formed the grounds of two aristocratic villas – the Villa Serra and the Villa Gropallo. The former, on Via Capolungo, now houses the **Galleria d'Arte Moderna** featuring modern Italian painting. The **Villa Luxoro** on Via Aurelia is notable for its collection of clocks, fabrics, furniture and lace. The area is also famous as Garibaldi's departure point when he set off for Sicily with his *Mille* (the famous "Thousand" men) to help bring about the unification of Italy. A large monument at Quarto dei Mille, about 3 km (2 miles) back towards the city, marks the place where the volunteers met in May 1860 to follow the intrepid revolutionary *(see pp62–3)*. **Villa Grimaldi** houses an art and sculpture collection showing late 18th- and early 19th-century works by Fattori, Boldi and Messina.

**Galleria d'Arte Moderna**
Villa Serra, Via Capolungo 3, Nervi. ***Tel*** *010 372 60 25.* *Tue–Sun.*

**Villa Doria**
Piazza Bonavino 7, Pegli. ***Tel*** *010 696 98 85.* *daily.* *public hols.*

**Villa Durazzo-Pallavicini**
Via Pallavicini 11, Pegli. ***Tel*** *010 66 68 64.* *9am–7pm Tue–Sun (Oct–Mar: to 5pm).* *pub hols.*

**Villa Grimaldi**
Via Capolungo 9, Nervi. ***Tel*** *010 32 23 96.* *Tue–Sun.*

**Villa Luxoro**
Via Mafalda di Savoia 3, Nervi. ***Tel*** *010 32 26 73.* *Tue–Sat am.* *public hols.*

*Pini* (c.1920) by Rubaldo Merello in the Galleria d'Arte Moderna at Nervi

**Pastel-coloured houses near the pebbly beach at Camogli**

## Camogli ⓾

Genoa. 6,500. FS Via *XX Settembre 33 (0185 77 10 66).* *Wed.* **www**.camogli.it

Built on a pine-wooded slope, Camogli is a fishing village where sea-shells adorn the pastel-painted house walls, and the smell of frying fish wafts out from the small restaurants into the streets. Near the pebble beach and fishing port is the medieval Castello della Dragonara.

Camogli celebrates its famous festival of the Blessing of the Fish on the second Sunday of May when sardines are fried in a huge pan 4 m (13 ft) in diameter. The fish is distributed free to all-comers.

## Portofino Peninsula ⓫

Genoa. *Portofino.* *Via Roma 35 (0185 26 90 24).* **www**.turismoinliguria.it

Portofino is the most exclusive harbour and resort town in Italy, crammed with the yachts of the wealthy. You can reach Portofino by road (cars are not allowed into the village), or boat, from the resort of Santa Margherita Ligure. Above the town are the church of **San Giorgio**, containing relics said to be of the dragon-slayer, and a castle.

On the other side of the peninsula, which you have to reach on foot (a two-hour walk) or by boat, is the **Abbazia di San Fruttuoso**, named after a 3rd-century saint whose followers were ship-wrecked here and, according to legend, protected by three lions. The white abbey buildings, set among pines and olive trees, date mostly from the 11th century, although the imposing Torre dei Doria was added 500 years later. You can take a boat to try to locate the **Cristo degli Abissi**, a bronze statue of Christ that sits on the sea bed near San Fruttuoso, protecting sailors. Further west along the coast is Punta Chiappa, a rocky promontory famous for the changing colours of the surrounding sea.

**Abbazia di San Fruttuoso**
San Fruttuoso. ***Tel*** *0185 77 27 03.* *daily; times vary, so call ahead.* *Nov.*

## Rapallo ⓬

Genoa. *30,000.* FS *Lungomare Vittorio Veneto 7 (0185 23 03 46).* *Thu.* **Cable car *Tel*** *0185 523 41.* **www**.turismoinliguria.it

Historians know Rapallo as the place where two post-World War I treaties were signed, while film buffs might recognize it from the 1954 movie *The Barefoot Contessa*, which was shot here. Rapallo was also a haven for writers such as DH Lawrence and Ezra Pound. Its villas still have a patrician feel to them, as do the riding stables, golf course and tennis courts. The palm-lined esplanade ends in a small 16th-century **castle**, in which art exhibitions are occasionally held. A cable car from the centre of the town leads to the 16th-century **Santuario di Montallegro**, which houses a Byzantine icon said to possess miraculous powers.

**The 16th-century castle jutting into Rapallo harbour**

**Santuario di Montallegro**
Montallegro. ***Tel*** *0185 23 90 00.* *daily.*

**Large yachts moored in Portofino's famous harbour**

The dramatic coastline near Corniglia in the Cinque Terre

## Cinque Terre ⓭

La Spezia. FS *to all towns.* ⛴ *Monterosso, Vernazza.* ℹ *Via Fegina 40, Monterosso (0187 81 70 59) (summer only); Piazza Rio Finale 26, Riomaggiore (0187 92 06 33).* **www**.parconazionale5terre.it

The Cinque Terre are five self-contained villages – Monterosso al Mare, Vernazza, Corniglia, Manarola and Riomaggiore – located on the rocky coastline of the Riviera di Levante. Clinging dramatically to the steep cliffs, these villages are linked only by an ancient footpath known as the Sentiero Azzurro (Blue Path), which offers spectacular views of the rocky coastlines and terraced vineyards that produce the local dry white Cinque Terre wines. The footpath also provides access to secluded beaches.

These days the five villages suffer from some depopulation. The largest, **Monterosso al Mare**, on the northwestern edge of the Cinque Terre, overlooks a wide bay with its own sandy beach. **Vernazza**, further down the coast, has streets linked by steep steps or *arpaie*. **Corniglia**, perched at the pinnacle of rocky terraces, seems untouched by the passage of time, as does **Manarola**, which is linked by the famous Via dell'Amore, or Lovers' Lane, to **Riomaggiore**, a 15-minute walk away.

The best way to visit the villages is by boat (from La Spezia, Lerici or Porto Venere) or by train (La Spezia–Genoa railway line).

## Portovenere ⓮

La Spezia. 👥 *4,600.* 🚌 ⛴ ℹ *Piazza Bastreri (0187 79 06 91).* 🛒 *Mon.* **www**.portovenere.it

Named after the goddess Venus, Portovenere is one of the most romantic villages on the Ligurian coast with its cluster of narrow streets lined with pastel-coloured houses.

In the upper part of the village is the 12th-century church of **San Lorenzo**. A sculpture over the doorway here depicts the martyrdom of the saint who was roasted alive on a grill. On the stone promontory that curls out into the sea is the small, black-and-white 13th-century church of **San Pietro**. From here, or from the 16th-century castle on top of the cliffs on the northwestern side of the village, there are superb views of the Cinque Terre and the small island of Palmaria, about 400 m (435 yds) offshore.

Above the doorway of San Lorenzo in Portovenere

## Lerici ⓯

La Spezia. 👥 *13,000.* 🚌 ⛴ ℹ *Via Biagini 6, Località Venere Azzurra (0187 96 73 46).* 🛒 *Sat am.* **www**.parconazionale5terre.it

This stretch of coast, along the Gulf of La Spezia or Poets' Gulf, was once popular with such literati as Yeats and DH Lawrence. The village of San Terenzo, across the bay from Lerici, was where the poet Shelley spent the last four years of his life. It was from his home, the Casa Magni, that he set out in 1822 on a voyage to meet Leigh Hunt in Livorno. Tragically, he was shipwrecked near Viareggio and drowned.

The popular resort of Lerici sits on the edge of a beautiful bay overlooked by pastel-coloured houses. The forbidding medieval **Castello di Lerici** (13th century), built by the Pisans and later passed to the Genoese, dominates the holiday villas below. Today it houses a museum of geopaleontology and hosts art exhibitions and concerts.

**Castello di Lerici**
Piazza San Giorgio. ***Tel*** *0187 96 91 14.* *Tue–Sun.* *9–26 Dec.* **www**.castellodilerici.it

The harbour of Vernazza in the Cinque Terre

A stunning view of Manarola on the Sentiero Azzurro, Cinque Terre ▷

# CENTRAL ITALY

# Central Italy at a Glance

The central regions of Italy are popular with visitors because they offer a range of beautiful landscapes and towns rich in culture and history, including outstanding churches, towers and palaces. Emilia-Romagna is home to the impressive Po Delta that provides a haven for wildlife. Tuscany is dominated by Florence, one of Italy's most celebrated centres. Umbria and Le Marche offer gentle pastoral countryside and picturesque hilltowns. The major sights of this rewarding area are shown here.

**The Leaning Tower** *of Pisa and the Duomo* (see pp324–6), *splendid examples of 12th- and 13th-century architecture, are decorated with Arabic-inspired, complex geometric patterns.*

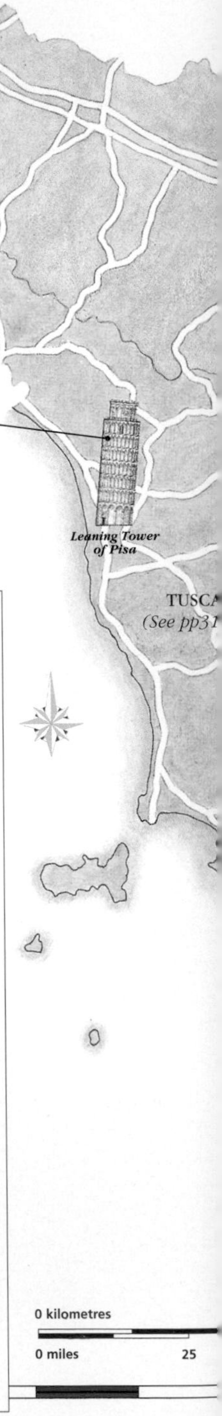

*Leaning Tower of Pisa*

**FLORENCE**
*(See pp270–313)*

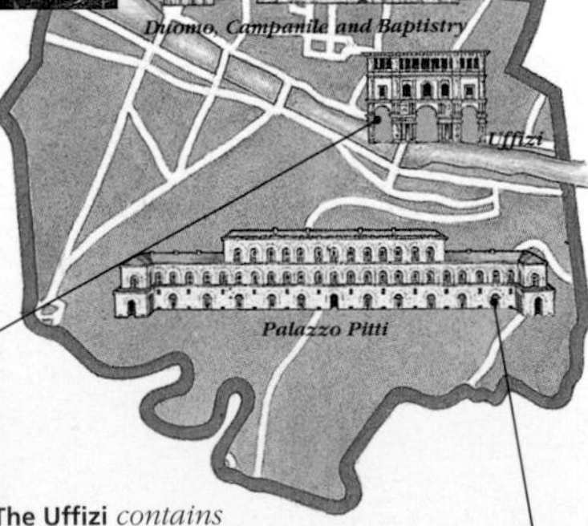


**The Duomo** *and the Baptistry, set in the heart of Florence, dominate the city* (see pp280–82). *The dome dwarfs many surrounding buildings.*

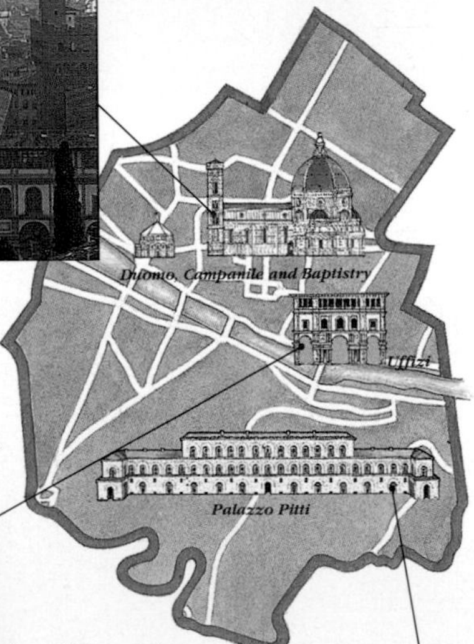

**The Uffizi** *contains a superb collection of Florentine art from Gothic to High Renaissance and beyond* (see pp286–9).

**The Palazzo Pitti**, begun in 1457 for the banker Luca Pitti, became the main residence of the Medici. It now houses their treasures (see pp302–3).

0 kilometres 1
0 miles 0.5

0 kilometres
0 miles 25

◁ **Autumn colour in Tuscany, in the hills of the Val d'Orcia, south of Siena**

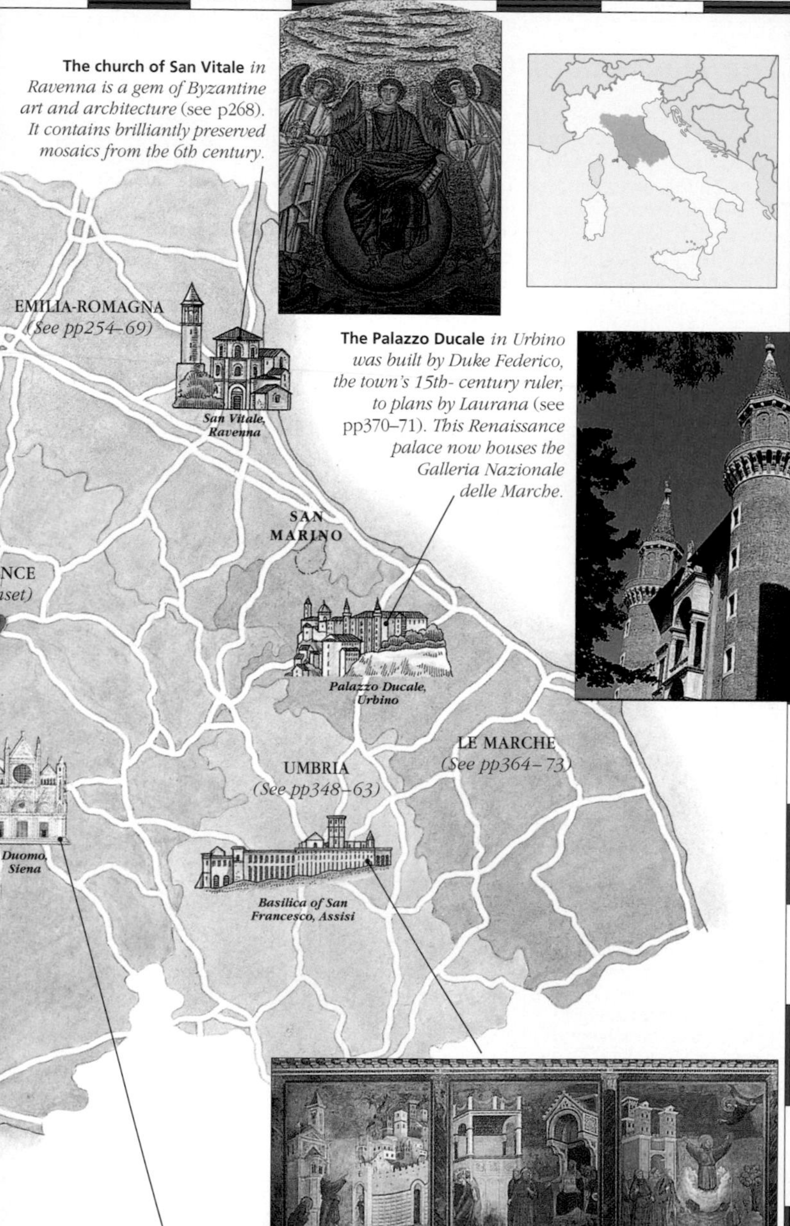


**The church of San Vitale** *in Ravenna is a gem of Byzantine art and architecture* (see p268). *It contains brilliantly preserved mosaics from the 6th century.*

**The Palazzo Ducale** *in Urbino was built by Duke Federico, the town's 15th- century ruler, to plans by Laurana* (see pp370–71). *This Renaissance palace now houses the Galleria Nazionale delle Marche.*

**Siena**, *a medieval town steeped in tradition, centres around the Campo, the large piazza shaped like a scallop shell* (see pp338–43). *The lively horse race, the Corsa del Palio, is held here in July and August.*

**Giotto's fresco cycle** *from the Basilica of San Francesco in Assisi was executed in the 13th century* (see pp354–7). *The church is visited by thousands of pilgrims each year.*

# The Flavours of Central Italy

Emilia-Romagna is Italy's gourmet capital, and home to Parmesan, Parma ham and balsamic vinegar. Bologna has earned the epithet *La Grassa* ("the fat") for rich dishes in which butter, cheese and velvety sauces feature strongly. The lush lands and rolling hills of Tuscany, Umbria and Le Marche tend to offer simpler flavours and more rustic, peasant cuisine. Top-quality pork from the Cinta Senese pig, beef from the Chianina cattle of Tuscany, fabulous *fungi* and Umbrian truffles, superb game, and saffron-scented fish soups from the coast of Le Marche are all gastronomic delights of Central Italy.

Italian tomatoes

Tray of perfect, freshly made tortellini pasta

## EMILIA-ROMAGNA

Not only is this rich, fertile land the home of many of Italy's most classic ingredients, but it has also given the world *bolognese* sauce (*ragù*). The authentic sauce contains some 20 ingredients and is usually served with tagliatelle – never spaghetti. Pasta is an art form here.

Legend has it that tagliatelle was invented in honour of Lucrezia Borgia's golden hair, while tortellini pasta is said to be modelled on the shape of Venus's navel.

The region's pork butchers are the most famous in Italy, making excellent sausages, *salumi* and mortadella, and using every part of the animal including the trotters, which are stuffed to form the local speciality *zamponi*.

Emilia and coastal Romagna were once two provinces, and there is still a culinary distinction between them. While Emilia's gastronomy is liberally laced with butter, cheese and mushrooms, Romagna's keynotes tend to be olive oil, garlic and onions – and fish. The Adriatic in this region teems with life and is an especially good catching ground for turbot (*rombo*) – the "pheasant of the sea".

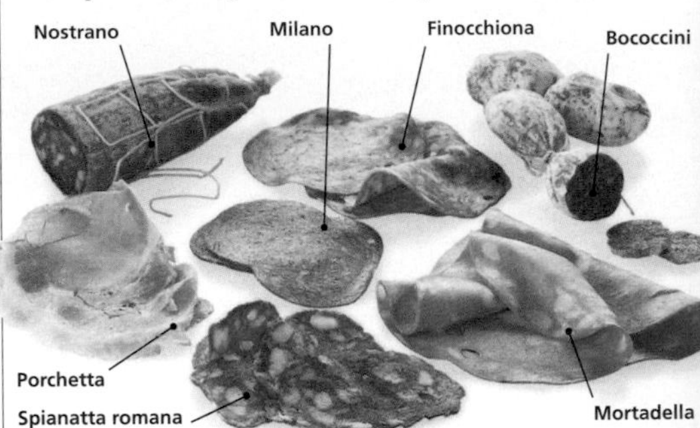


Selection of the finest Italian salumi and other cooked meats

## REGIONAL DISHES AND SPECIALITIES

Tuscan olive oil is outstanding in quality. It has many uses and is an integral part of *crostini*, slices of toasted bread smeared with olive oil on which different toppings are spread, such as chicken livers in *crostini alla Toscana. Salumi* producers are a great feature of the region and *prosciutto di cinghiale* (wild boar ham) is a rich, gamey delicacy. As well as *tagliatelle al ragù* in Bologna, other very popular pastas include tortellini and tortelloni (the latter being larger than the former), often filled with cheese, butter and herbs. *Panforte* is the Italian Christmas speciality cake – a delicious confection of fruits, nuts, honey, sugar and spices. Try also *ricciarelli*, diamond-shaped almond biscuits, and *torta di riso* – a rich, golden cake made with rice.

Crostini alla Toscana

**Cacciucco** *A fish and seafood soup from Livorno, flavoured with herbs and tomatoes and ladled over garlicky toast.*

Just part of a gigantic wheel of Parmigiano-Reggiano, or Parmesan

## TUSCANY

Tuscany is the orchard and vegetable garden of Italy. It is also famous for its red meat, especially from the prized Valdichiana cattle, from south of Arezzo. Pork is also excellent, and the Tuscan passion for hunting ensures that hare, pheasant and wild boar, often served with local chestnuts, feature prominently on menus.

If there is one staple Tuscan ingredient it is fruity olive oil, liberally used in cooking and for seasoning everything from bread to salads, vegetables, stews and soups.

Broths and soups are very popular, often made with beans, especially white cannellini beans. Not for nothing are Tuscans known as *toscani mangiafagioli* (Tuscan bean-eaters).

## UMBRIA & LE MARCHE

Umbria, "the green heart of Italy", is the only area outside Piedmont where truffles are found in such high concentration. Norcia is the capital of the black truffle and shops everywhere sell truffle paste and truffle oils. Norcia is also famous for its pigs, and a favourite dish is *porchetta* – whole roast suckling pig stuffed with herbs. Wild mushrooms are plentiful in season, in particular delicious *porcini* (ceps). Game features too, usually in the form of birds such as pheasant, guinea fowl or pigeon, with the odd songbird thrown in. The rural interior of Le Marche also features *porchetta*; lamb and rabbit are popular, too. The long coastline yields a bounty of fish, often made into fish broths and, a speciality of Ancona, *zuppa di pesce*, fish soup with saffron.

Tuscan market stall piled high with fresh, ripe vegetables

### ON THE MENU

**Baci** From Perugia, these are chocolate-coated hazelnuts, their name literally meaning "kisses" in Italian.

**Bistecca alla Fiorentina** Steak, marinated in herbs, garlic and finest extra virgin olive oil, rapidly grilled over wood coals. The best meat for this is Chianina beef.

**Lepre in dolce e forte** Traditional Tuscan hare stew with red wine, lemon, orange and lime peel, garlic, rosemary, vegetables and cocoa.

**Vincisgrassi** A baked, layered dish from Le Marche of ham, pasta and béchamel sauce, often served sprinkled with truffle shavings.

**Tagliatelle al ragù** *Flat strips of pasta are tossed with the quintessential Italian meat sauce from Bologna.*

**Arista alla Fiorentina** *Pork loin is roasted in the oven with garlic and rosemary, a speciality of Florence.*

**Zuccotto** *A Tuscan speciality of light sponge cake filled with hazelnuts, almonds, chocolate and cream.*

# The Wines of Central Italy

**Roman mosaic of a bird eating grapes**

Vineyards are seen everywhere in Central Italy, from the rolling cypress-fringed hills of Tuscany to the flatter, Lambrusco-producing plains of Emilia-Romagna. The finest red wines are made in the hills of southeastern Tuscany: Chianti Classico, Brunello di Montalcino and Vino Nobile di Montepulciano. Today's innovative mix of modern and traditional techniques is steadily improving the quality of much of the region's wine.

**Chianti Classico** *is the heart of the Chianti zone. Chianti may be light and fruity or dense and long-lived – price is the usual guide. Rocca delle Macie is very reasonably priced.*

**Vernaccia di San Gimignano** *is a Tuscan white wine with a long, distinguished history. Traditionally a golden, often oxidized wine, it is now also produced in a fresher style, for early drinking. Teruzzi e Puthod make consistently good Vernaccia.*

Pisa

Florence

Greve

San Gimignano

Siena

TUSCANY

Montalcino

**Vino Nobile di Montepulciano** *is made from the same grapes as Chianti. It can be of superior quality, hence its claim to be a "noble wine". The vineyards are set around the delightful hilltop village of Montepulciano.*

**Brunello di Montalcino** *is made from Sangiovese, Brunello being its local name. Its firm tannins may need up to ten years to soften before the rich, spicy flavours are revealed. Rosso di Montalcino, on the other hand, can be enjoyed much younger.*

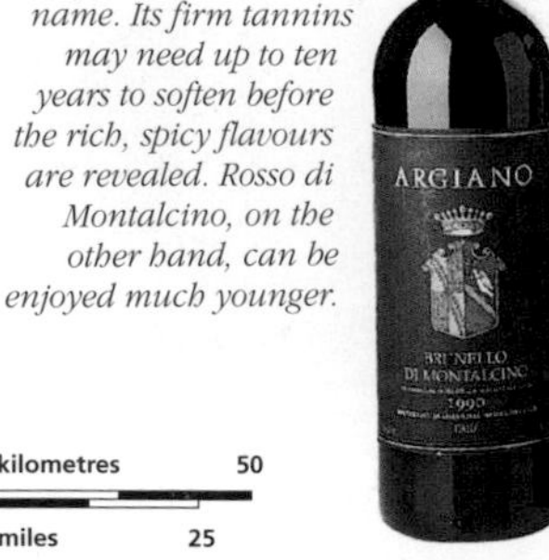


0 kilometres 50

0 miles 25

## SUPER-TUSCANS

During the 1970s innovative wine makers set out to create new, individual wines even though under the existing rules they would be labelled as simple table wine. A trend which started with Antinori's Tignanello (a Sangiovese-Cabernet Sauvignon blend), this approach has reinvigorated Tuscan wine, to produce some exciting variations.

**Sassicaia, a red wine made from the Cabernet Sauvignon grape**

Chianti estate at Badia a Passignano in Tuscany

**Verdicchio** *is a dry white wine from Le Marche with a crisp, slightly salty taste. The single-vineyard Verdicchio, such as Umani Ronchi's CaSal di Serra, is winning much acclaim.*

**Orvieto Classico** *is a popular Umbrian white wine. This fresh, dry* (Secco) *version from the Antinori estate is a good example of a modern-style Orvieto. The wine also comes in a sweeter form, known as* Abboccato.

## GRAPES OF CENTRAL ITALY

The versatile Sangiovese grape dominates wine making in Central Italy. It is the main grape in Chianti, in Vino Nobile di Montepulciano, in Brunello di Montalcino, and in many of the Super-Tuscan wines. Of the established whites, Trebbiano and Malvasia head the list. Imported varieties such as white Chardonnay and red Cabernet Sauvignon are playing an increasing role, often being used to complement and enhance native varieties.

**Sangiovese grapes**

## HOW TO READ THE LABEL

**The DOCG name** is a reliable guide to the origin of the wine.

**Producer's name**

**Year of production**

**The bottler's** name and address are given as a guarantee of the wine's origin.

**Alcoholic content**

## GOOD WINE PRODUCERS

**Chianti**: Antinori, Badia a Coltibuono, Brolio, Castello di Ama, Castello di Rampolla, Fattoria Selvapiana, Felsina Berardenga, Il Palazzino, Isole e Olena, Monte Vertine, Riecine, Rocca delle Macie, Ruffino, Tenuta Fontodi. **Brunello di Montalcino**: Argiano, Altesino, Caparzo, Castelgiocondo, Costanti, Il Poggione, Villa Banfi. **Vino Nobile di Montepulciano**: Avignonesi, Le Casalte, Poliziano. In **Umbria**: Adanti, Lungarotti.

**Good Chianti Vintages**
2008, 2007, 2004, 2003, 2001, 2000, 1999, 1997, 1995, 1993, 1990, 1988.

# Understanding Architecture in Central Italy

Central Italy has countless fine Renaissance buildings, many of them concentrated in and around Florence. Their clear lines, elegant simplicity and harmonious proportions came out of a re-evaluation of the past. Turning their backs on the Gothic style, the architects of the Renaissance returned to Classical Rome for inspiration. Most of the large buildings had been started by the late 15th century, paid for by the Catholic Church or by powerful noble families, such as the Medici of Florence.

**The Palazzo Ducale in Urbino (begun 1465)**

## RELIGIOUS BUILDINGS

**Arched bays** trisect the façade.

**Pope Pius II's coat of arms**

**One of 12 roundels by Luca della Robbia**

**Small circular windows**

**Square plan topped by small dome**

**Symmetrical floorplan** is based on a Greek cross.

**Harmonious proportions**

**Pienza's Duomo** *was built by Bernardo Rossellino in 1459 for Pope Pius II as part of his vision of the ideal Renaissance city* (see p333).

**The Pazzi Chapel** *of Santa Croce in Florence (1433) is one of Brunelleschi's most famous works, decorated with terracotta roundels by Luca della Robbia* (see pp284–5).

**Santa Maria della Consolazione** *in Todi, begun in 1508, owes much to the ideas of the architect Bramante* (see p359).

## TOWN AND COUNTRY HOUSES

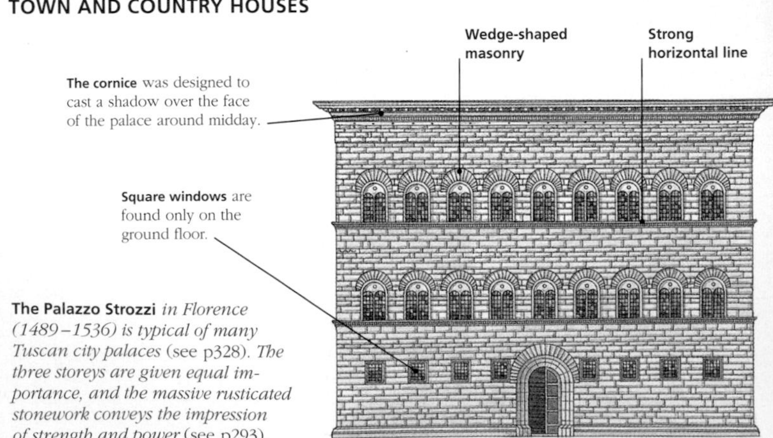


**The Palazzo Strozzi** *in Florence (1489–1536) is typical of many Tuscan city palaces* (see p328). *The three storeys are given equal importance, and the massive rusticated stonework conveys the impression of strength and power* (see p293).

## WHERE TO SEE THE ARCHITECTURE

The simple canons of the Renaissance were interpreted differently away from the hotbed of artistic thought and cultural endeavour of Florence, which has the greatest number of churches and palaces. Alberti's Tempio Malatestiano at Rimini *(see p266)* evokes the sobriety of ancient Roman architecture yet seeks to reinterpret it in his own unique fashion. Urbino's Palazzo Ducale *(pp370–71)* perfects the grace and polish of the era and is a truly noble period residence. On a smaller scale are the planned Renaissance centres of elegant towns such as Ferrara *(p261)*, Pienza *(p333)* and Urbania *(p369)*. All three centres are examples of enlightened patronage, and pay homage to the art of antiquity.

**Vista in the Boboli Gardens, Florence**

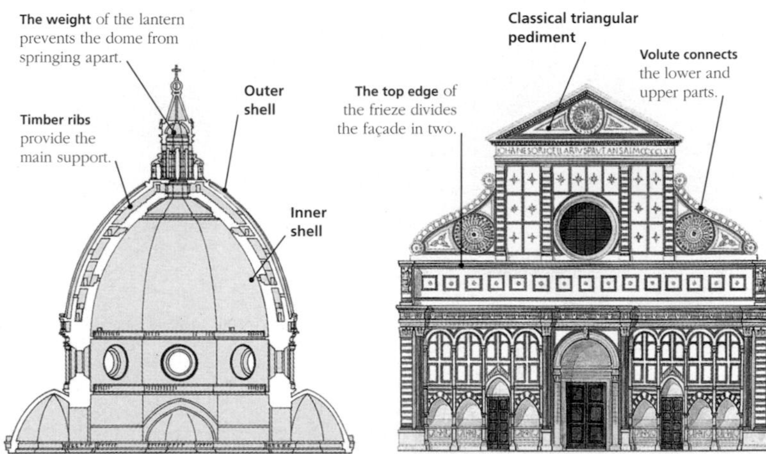



**The Duomo in Florence** *is crowned by the revolutionary dome (1436) by Brunelleschi, which had to be built without scaffolding due to its size. The timber structure is covered by an inner and outer shell* (see pp280–81).

**The façade of Santa Maria Novella** *in Florence (1458–70) was designed by Leon Battista Alberti. He incorporated some of the existing Gothic features into an overall design typical of the Renaissance* (see pp296–7).

**The villa at Poggio a Caiano** *(1480) was redesigned in the Renaissance by Giuliano da Sangallo* (see p328). *The graceful, curved staircase was added around 1802.*

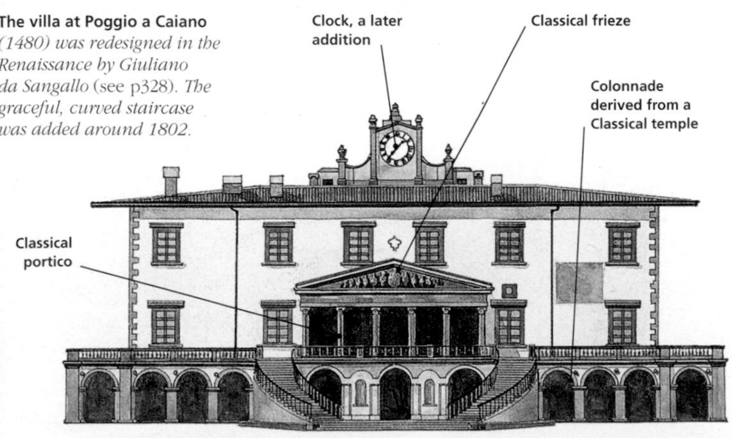

# EMILIA-ROMAGNA

*Emilia-Romagna is the heartland of central Italy, a broad corridor through the hills and plains of the Po Valley that marks the watershed between the cold north of the Alps and the hot Mediterranean south. With its rich agricultural land, historical cities and thriving industry, it is one of the most prosperous areas in Italy.*

Most of the major towns in Emilia-Romagna lie near the Via Aemilia, a Roman road built in 187 BC that linked Rimini on the Adriatic coast with the garrison town of Piacenza. Prior to the Romans, the Etruscans had ruled from their capital, Felsina, located on the site of present-day Bologna. After the fall of Rome, the region's focus moved to Ravenna, which became a principal part of the Byzantine Empire administered from Constantinople.

During the Middle Ages pilgrims heading for Rome continued to use the Via Aemilia. Political power, however, passed to influential noble families – the Malatesta in Rimini, the Bentivoglio in Bologna, the d'Este in Ferrara and Modena, and the Farnese in Parma and Piacenza. Great courts grew up around the families, attracting poets such as Dante and Ariosto, as well as painters, sculptors and architects whose works still grace the medieval centres of these towns. Cobbled together from separate Papal States in 1860, modern Emilia-Romagna was given its present borders in 1947. Emilia, the western part of the region, is traditionally associated with a more northern outlook and a tendency towards the left in politics. Romagna, on the other hand, has witnessed an increase in the support for right-wing parties calling for political independence from Rome.

The entire region has a reputation as a great gastronomic centre. Agriculture has long thrived on the Po's alluvial fringes, earning the Pianura Padana (Po Plain) epithets such as the "bread basket" and "fruit bowl" of Italy. Pigs still outnumber humans in many areas, and some of the country's most famous staples – Parma ham and Parmesan cheese – originate here.

The medieval Palazzo del Comune in Ferrara

◁ The Fontana del Nettuno (Neptune's Fountain) in Bologna

# Exploring Emilia-Romagna

Emilia-Romagna is a chequerboard of fields and plains between the Po river to the north and the forest-covered Apennine mountain slopes to the south. The best place to begin a tour of the region is centrally situated Bologna. Modena, its long-time rival, boasts one of the country's loveliest Romanesque cathedrals. Parma has a more provincial feel and Ferrara, too, has an easy-going air. Castell'Arquato offers a taste of the smaller villages that dot the hills south of the Po.

Piazza Cavalli, Piacenza's central square



### SEE ALSO



- ***Where to Stay*** pp574–6
- ***Where to Eat*** pp624–6

Reed-lined shores along the Po Delta

### SIGHTS AT A GLANCE

## GETTING AROUND

Excellent road and rail links, aided by mostly flat terrain, make this region quick and easy to get around. Bologna is connected by the A1–E35 to Florence and by the A13 to Ferrara and Venice. The busy A1–E35 links Bologna to Milan via Piacenza, Fidenza and Parma. The A15–E31 connects Parma with La Spezia, and the A21–E70 joins Piacenza and Cremona. Fast, frequent train services run along almost parallel routes.

**The beach at Cesenatico, north of Rimini on the Adriatic coast**

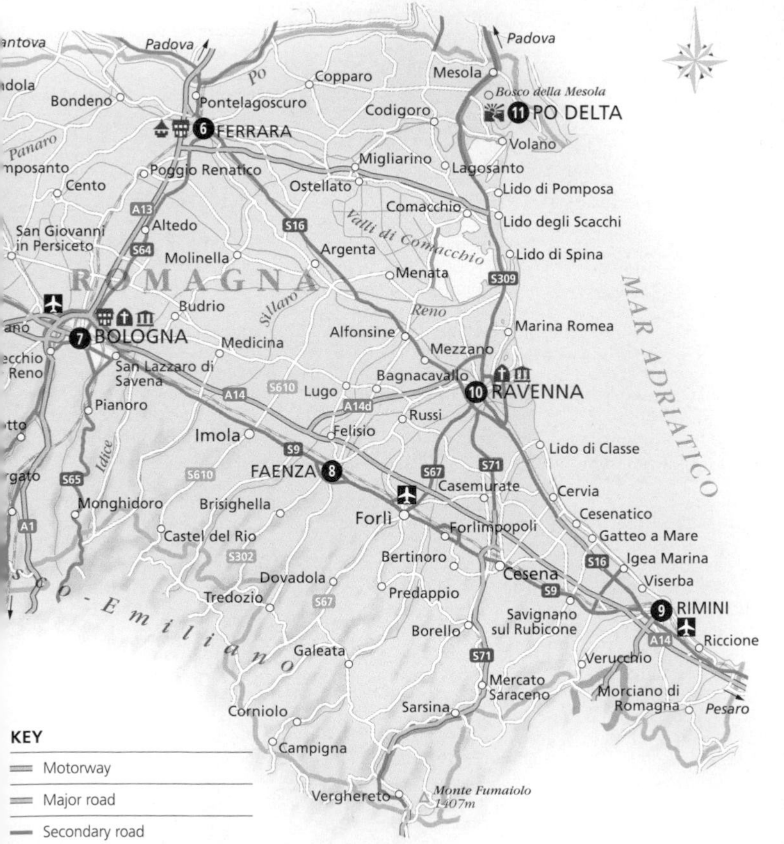

Padova
Po
Copparo
Mesola
Bosco della Mesola
Bondeno
Pontelagoscuro
Codigoro
11 PO DELTA
6 FERRARA
Panaro
Volano
Migliarino
Lagosanto
Poggio Renatico
Cento
Ostellato
Lido di Pomposa
Comacchio
Lido degli Scacchi
A13
Altedo
S16
Valli di Comacchio
San Giovanni in Persiceto
S64
Molinella
Argenta
Lido di Spina
ROMAGNA
Menata
S309
Budrio
Sillaro
Reno
MAR ADRIATICO
Marina Romea
7 BOLOGNA
Medicina
Alfonsine
Mezzano
San Lazzaro di Savena
Bagnacavallo
S610
Lugo
10 RAVENNA
A14
A14d
Russi
Pianoro
Felisio
Imola
Lido di Classe
Idice
S9
8 FAENZA
S67
S71
S610
Casemurate
Cervia
S65
Monghidoro
Brisighella
Forlì
Cesenatico
Forlimpopoli
Gatteo a Mare
A1
Castel del Rio
Bertinoro
S16
Igea Marina
S302
Cesena
Dovadola
Viserba
S9
Predappio
Tredozio
S67
Savignano sul Rubicone
9 RIMINI
Borello
A14
Riccione
Appennino Tosco-Emiliano
Galeata
S71
Verucchio
Mercato Saraceno
Morciano di Romagna
Sarsina
Pesaro
Corniolo
Campigna
Verghereto
Monte Fumaiolo 1407m

**KEY**

- Motorway
- Major road
- Secondary road
- Minor road
- Scenic route
- Main railway
- Minor railway
- International border
- Regional border
- Summit

0 kilometres 25

0 miles 20

The 13th-century Palazzo Pretorio in Castell'Arquato

## Piacenza ❶

105,000. FS Piazza Cavalli 7 (0523 32 93 24). Wed & Sat.

Piacenza traces its history back to Roman times. Located near the Po, it served as a fortified camp protecting the Emilian plain from invasion. The centre is still based on the Roman plan.

Piacenza has a pleasantly understated old centre full of fine medieval and Renaissance buildings. Pride of place goes to two bronze equestrian **statues** in the central Piazza Cavalli, the work of the 17th-century sculptor Francesco Mochi, a pupil of Giambologna. Lauded as masterpieces of Baroque sculpture, the statues represent Alessandro Farnese, a soldier of fortune, and his son, Ranuccio: both were rulers of 16th-century Piacenza.

Behind the statues is the red-brick **Palazzo del Comune**, also known as "Il Gotico", an evocatively battlemented Lombard-Gothic palace begun at the end of the 13th century. It is one of Italy's most beautiful medieval buildings.

The **Duomo**, at the end of Via XX Settembre, has a rather leaden Lombard-Romanesque exterior (begun in 1122), and a 14th-century campanile. The interior features Guercino's painted cupola and medieval frescoes. There are also frescoed saints near the main door, painted to resemble members of the congregation.

The **Museo Civico** offers an eclectic mixture of sculpture and paintings – the star among these is the *Madonna and Child with John the Baptist* by Botticelli (1444–1510). There is also an armoury and archaeology section. The highlight here is the so-called *Fegato di Piacenza*, an Etruscan bronze representation of the sheep livers once used by priests for divination, inscribed with deities' names.

**Museo Civico**
Palazzo Farnese, Piazza Cittadella. ***Tel*** *0523 49 26 58.* *Tue –Sun (Tue–Thu am only).* *public hols.*

## Castell'Arquato ❷

Piacenza. *4,500.* *Piazza Municipio 1 (0523 80 32 15).* *Mon.*

Tucked into the folded hills between Fidenza and Piacenza, Castell'Arquato is one of the prettiest villages in the countryside south of the Po. Day visitors come at the weekends to escape Emilia's larger cities, thronging the restaurants and bars around the beautiful **Piazza Matteotti**. The best medieval building on the piazza is the 13th-century **Palazzo Pretorio**, a Romanesque basilica. The impressive **Rocca Viscontea** (14th century), a former fortress, is on Piazza del Municipio. The village's hilltop site offers good views, particularly over the verdant Arda valley to the east.

## Fidenza ❸

Parma. *23,000.* FS *Piazza Duomo 16 (0524 833 77).* *Wed & Sat.*

Like many towns hugging the line of the Po, Fidenza owed its early prominence to the Via Aemilia (the old Roman road). The town assumed greater importance as a medieval way station for pilgrims en route to Rome. Today Fidenza is visited for its superb **Duomo** on Piazza Duomo (13th century), a composite piece of architecture that embraces Lombard, Gothic and transitional Romanesque elements. The most immediately eye-catching feature is the opulent façade, probably created by the craftsmen who worked with Benedetto Antelami on Parma's Duomo. Inside, the walls are dotted with fragments of medieval frescoes, while the crypt contains the relics of San Donnino, the Duomo's patron.

Detail from façade of Duomo in Fidenza

*For hotels and restaurants in this region see pp574–6 and pp624–6*

Interior of Parma Baptistry

## Parma ❹

175,000. FS Via Melloni 1a (0521 21 88 89). Wed & Sat; Thu (flea market). www.comune.parma.it/

Few Italian towns are as prosperous as Parma, not only a byword for fine food and good living but also a treasure trove of excellent paintings, superlative sculpture and fine medieval buildings. It boasts one of Italy's top opera houses and a panoply of elegant shops and first-rate bars and restaurants.

The Lombard-Romanesque **Duomo** on Piazza Duomo, among the greatest in northern Italy, is renowned for the painting that fills its main cupola, the *Assumption* (1526–30) by Antonio da Correggio. The nave is adorned with the work of Correggio's pupils. The south transept features a carved frieze of *The Deposition* (1178) by Benedetto Antelami, who was also responsible for much of the exquisite **Baptistry** (1196) just south of the cathedral. The reliefs inside and outside the latter – particularly those describing the months of the year – are among the most important of their age in Italy.

East of the Duomo is the church of **San Giovanni Evangelista** (rebuilt 1498–1510) whose dome features a fresco (c.1520) of the *Vision of St John at Patmos* by Correggio. Frescoes by Parmigianino can be seen here and in the 16th-century church of **Madonna della Steccata** on Via Dante.

### Palazzo Pilotta

*Piazzale della Pilotta 15.* **Galleria** ***Tel*** *0521 23 33 09.* *Tue–Sun am.* **Museo** ***Tel*** *0521 23 37 18.* *Tue–Sat am, Sun pm.*

This vast palace was built for the Farnese family during the 1500s and rebuilt after bomb damage from World War II. It comprises several parts, including the **Teatro Farnese** (1628), a copy of Palladio's ravishing theatre in Vicenza, built entirely of wood.

Both Correggio and Parmigianino are represented in the palace's **Galleria Nazionale**, which also houses works by Fra Angelico, El Greco and Bronzino, and two paintings by Ludovico Carracci: the *Apostles at the Sepulchre* and the *Funeral of the Virgin* (both late 16th century).

The **Museo Archeologico Nazionale**, on the lower floor, has exhibits from Velleia, an Etruscan necropolis, and from prehistoric sites in the hills around Parma.

### Camera di Correggio

*Via Melloni.* ***Tel*** *0521 23 33 09.* *Tue–Sun (am only).*

Originally the refectory of the Benedictine convent of San Paolo, this room was frescoed by Correggio in 1518 with mythological scenes.

Campanile and Baptistry in Parma

### THE MAKING OF PARMESAN CHEESE AND PARMA HAM

No cheese is as famous or as vital to Italy's cuisine as Parmesan *(Parmigiano)*. There are two types: the superior Parmigiano-Reggiano and the lower-quality Grana. The cheese is made using techniques that have barely altered in centuries. Partially skimmed milk is added to whey, to promote fermentation, and rennet is used to curdle the milk. The cheese is then salted and shaped. Parmesan is not only used in cooking but is delicious eaten on its own, or with pears – an Italian speciality.

Shop selling Parmesan cheese and Parma ham

Parma ham owes its excellence to techniques perfected over many years and to the special conditions in which it is cured. It is made from pigs fattened on whey left over from the making of Parmesan cheese. The meat has a character that requires little more than salt and pepper to produce the famous *prosciutto crudo*. The breezy hills of Langhirino, south of Parma, are ideal for curing the hams, which are aged for up to ten months. Each ham is branded with the five-pointed crown of the old Duchy of Parma.

*Flora* by Carlo Cignani (1628–1719) in the Galleria Estense in Modena

## Modena 5

175,000. FS *Piazza Grande 14 (059 203 26 60).* *Mon.* **www**.comune.modena.it/infoturismo

To most Italians Modena means fast cars, for both Ferrari and Maserati have factories in its industrial outskirts, and opera, since this is the birthplace of Luciano Pavarotti. Monuments to an earlier age, however, make this one of Emilia's most enticing historic destinations. A thriving colony since Roman times, the city rose to medieval prominence on the back of its broad agricultural hinterland and the arrival in 1598 of the d'Este nobles from Ferrara. This family continued to rule the city until the 18th century.

### Duomo

Corso Duomo. ***Tel*** *059 21 60 78.* *daily.* **Torre Ghirlandina** *Apr–Oct: 9:30am–12:30pm, 3–7pm Sun.* *Aug.*

Modena's superlative **Duomo** rises alongside the old Roman Via Emilia. One of the region's greatest Romanesque buildings, it was founded by Countess Matilda of Tuscany, ruler of Modena in the 11th century. It was designed by Lanfranco and dedicated to San Geminiano, the city's patron saint, whose stone coffin lies under the choir. Its most noticeable feature is the **Torre Ghirlandina**, a perilously leaning tower begun at the same time as the Duomo and completed two centuries later. It once housed the *Secchia*, a wooden bucket whose 1325 theft from Bologna allegedly sparked a war between the two cities. It also inspired Tassoni's 17th-century mock epic poem *La Secchia Rapita* (The Stolen Bucket), and became the symbol of a rivalry between the cities.

The large reliefs on the Duomo's main (west) façade are the work of the 12th-century sculptor Wiligelmus. The highlight of the rather severe interior is a large carved *tribuna* (rood screen) decorated with 12th-century scenes from the Passion.

### Palazzo dei Musei

Largo di Porta Sant'Agostino 337. **Galleria Estense** ***Tel*** *059 439 57 11.* *8:30am–7:30pm Tue–Sun.* *1 Jan, 1 May, 25 Dec.* **Biblioteca Estense** ***Tel*** *059 22 22 48.* *Mon–Sat (am only Fri & Sat).* *pub hols.*

Northwest of the Duomo, and reached through an attractive warren of old streets, is the Palazzo dei Musei. Formerly an arsenal and workhouse, it is now home to the city's best museums and galleries. Its finest section is the **Galleria Estense**, given over to the d'Este private art collection, which was transferred here when the city of Ferrara, the family's former dominion, became part of the Papal States. Most of the paintings are by Emilian and Ferrarese artists (notably Reni and the Carracci) but there are also works by Velázquez, Tintoretto, Bernini and Veronese.

Among the permanent displays in the **Biblioteca Estense**, the d'Este Library, are a 1481 edition of Dante's *Divine Comedy*, and dozens of fascinating maps and diplomatic letters, many dating back centuries. A map dated 1501 was among the first to show the 1492 voyage by Columbus to the New World. The jewel of the collection is the magnificent illuminated Borso d'Este Bible, with gloriously decorated pages containing over 1,200 miniatures by 15th-century artists of the Ferrara school, most notably Taddeo Crivelli and Franco Russi.

The Torre Ghirlandina in Modena

**Environs:** The **Ferrari** factory, 20 km (12 miles) to the south, was founded by Enzo Ferrari in 1945. The FIAT-owned manufacturer now produces around 2,500 cars annually. The **Galleria Ferrari** has a small exhibition featuring memorabilia, classic engines and many vintage cars.

### Galleria Ferrari

Via Dino Ferrari 43, Maranello. ***Tel*** *0536 94 32 04.* *9:30am–6pm daily.* *1 Jan, 25 Dec.*

Ferrari 250 SWB, produced between 1959 and 1962

## Ferrara 6

140,000. FS Castello Estense, Largo Castello (0532 20 93 70). Mon & Fri.

The d'Este Dynasty has left an indelible mark on Ferrara, one of the region's greatest walled towns. The noble family took control of the town under Nicolò II in the late 13th century, holding power until 1598, when the family was forced by the papacy to move to Modena.

Façade of the Duomo in Ferrara

### Castello Estense

Largo Castello. **Tel** *0532 29 92 33.* *Tue–Sun (Mar–May: daily).* *public hols.*

With its towers and battlements, the Este family's dynastic seat (begun 1385) looms over the town centre. Ferrante and Giulio d'Este were incarcerated in its dungeons for plotting to overthrow Alfonso I d'Este. Parisina d'Este, wife of Nicolò III, was executed here for having an affair with Ugo, her illegitimate stepson.

The impressive medieval Castello Estense in Ferrara

### Palazzo del comune

Piazza Municipale.

Bronze statues of Nicolò III and Borso d'Este, one of Nicolò's reputed 27 children, adorn this medieval palace (begun 1243). Both are copies of the 15th-century originals by Leon Battista Alberti.

### Museo della Cattedrale

Via San Romano. **Tel** *0532 76 12 99.* *Tue–Sun.* *6 Jan, Easter, 25 & 26 Dec.*

Ferrara's 12th-century Duomo is a Romanesque-Gothic hybrid designed by Wiligelmus. Fine reliefs on the façade depict scenes from the Last Judgment. The excellent **museum** (in a deconsecrated church opposite the cathedral) contains a fine set of marble reliefs of the *Labours of the Months* (late 1100s), two painted organ shutters (1469) of *St George* and the *Annunciation* by Cosmè Tura, and the *Madonna of the Pomegranate* (1408) by Jacopo della Quercia.

### Palazzo Schifanoia

Via Scandiana 23. **Tel** *0532 641 78.* *Tue–Sun.* *public hols.*

This d'Este summer retreat, begun in 1385, is famous for its Salone dei Mesi (Room of the Months), decorated with beautiful 15th-century murals by Tura and other Ferrarese painters with scenes of the different months.

### Museo Archeologico Nazionale

Palazzo di Ludovico il Moro, Via XX Settembre 122. **Tel** *0532 662 99.* *9am–2pm Tue–Sun.* *1 May, 25 Dec.*

The most interesting exhibits here are artifacts that were excavated from Spina, a Greco-Etruscan trading post near Comacchio on the Po Delta.

### Palazzo dei Diamanti

Corso Ercole d'Este 21. **Tel** *0532 20 58 44.* *Tue –Sun am, Thu pm.* *1 Jan, 1 May, 25 Dec.*

Named after the diamond motifs on its façade, this palace houses a modern art gallery, a museum devoted to the Risorgimento, and the Pinacoteca Nazionale, which contains works from leading exponents of the local Renaissance school.

### THE D'ESTE FAMILY DYNASTY

During their medieval heyday, the d'Este family presided over one of Europe's leading courts, combining the roles of blood-crazed despots with enlightened Renaissance patrons. Nicolò III, for example, had his wife and her lover brutally murdered. Alfonso I (1503–34) married Lucrezia Borgia, descendant of one of Italy's most notorious families, while Ercole I (1407–1505) attempted to poison a nephew who tried to usurp him (and eventually had him executed). At the same time the d'Este court attracted writers like Petrarch, Tasso and Ariosto, and painters such as Mantegna, Titian and Bellini. Ercole I also rebuilt Ferrara, creating one of Europe's finest Renaissance cities.

Portrait of Alfonso I d'Este by Titian (c.1485–1576)

# Street-by-Street: Bologna ❼

Detail of façade from San Petronio

The historic city centre of Bologna is a handsome ensemble of brick buildings and charming porticoed streets. Medieval palaces are clustered around the two central squares, Piazza Maggiore and Piazza del Nettuno, flanked to the south by the churches of San Petronio and San Domenico. The university of Bologna is the oldest in Europe and the venerable Archiginnasio was its first official building. Further afield, the skyline is etched by the Asinelli and Garisenda towers, and by the campanile of Santo Stefano.

**Fontana di Nettuno**
*The famous Neptune fountain (1566) was designed by Tommaso Laureti and decorated with magnificent bronze figures by Giambologna.*

Tourist information

Railway station
↑ Ferrara

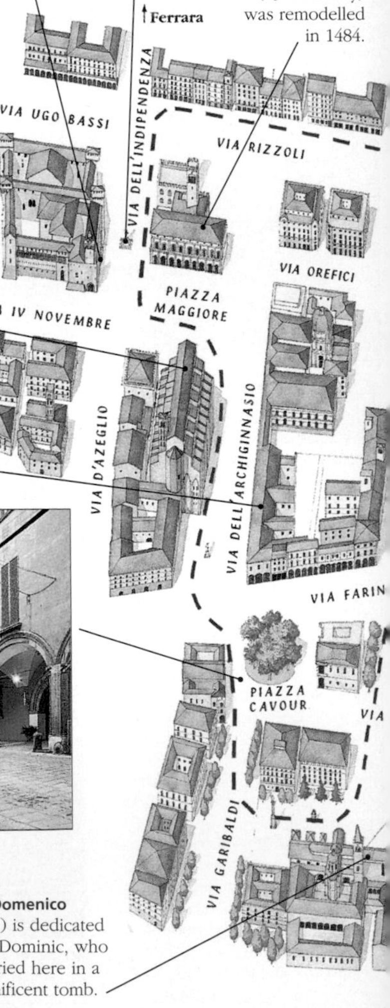

**The Palazzo del Podestà** (13th century) was remodelled in 1484.

Modena ←

VIA UGO BASSI

VIA DELL'INDIPENDENZA

VIA RIZZOLI

VIA OREFICI

PIAZZA MAGGIORE

VIA IV NOVEMBRE

VIA D'AZEGLIO

VIA DELL'ARCHIGINNASIO

VIA FARIN

PIAZZA CAVOUR

VIA

VIA GARIBALDI

**★ San Petronio**
The Martyrdom of St Sebastian *(15th century) in the Cappella di San Sebastiano is by Lorenzo Costa of the Ferrarese School.*

**Archiginnasio**

**Piazza Cavour**
*The flagged medieval streets and shady porticoed buildings found in this pleasant piazza are typical of Bologna's elegant city centre.*

**San Domenico** (1251) is dedicated to St Dominic, who is buried here in a magnificent tomb.

**STAR SIGHT**

★ San Petronio

*For hotels and restaurants in this region see pp574–6 and pp624–6*

## VISITORS' CHECKLIST

*400,000. Marconi 9 km (5 miles) NW. FS Piazza Medaglia d'Oro. Piazza XX Settembre. Airport; Piazza Maggiore 1/A; Stazione Centrale (051 23 96 60). Fri & Sat. Mar–Jun: Bologna Music Festival; Jun–Sep: Bologna Sogna.* **www**.bolognaturismo.info

**San Giacomo Maggiore**
*The* Triumph of Death *fresco by Costa (1483–6) adorns the Cappella Bentivoglio.*

Pinacoteca Nazionale

Museo di Anatomia Umana Normale

VIA ZAMBONI

VIA BENEDETTO XIV

Ravenna

VIA SAN VITALE

STRADA MAGGIORE

ZZA DI RTA NANA

VIA SANTO STEFANO

Firenze

**Torri degli Asinelli e Garisenda**
*The colossal towers are two of the few remaining towers begun by Bologna's important families in the 12th century.*

**Abbazia di Santo Stefano**
*The Fontana di Pilato, or Pilate's fountain, in the courtyard features a basin with Lombard inscriptions from the 8th century.*

**KEY**

Suggested route

### San Giacomo Maggiore

Piazza Rossini. ***Tel*** *051 22 59 70.* *daily.*

This Romanesque-Gothic church, begun in 1267 but altered substantially since, is visited mainly for the Cappella Bentivoglio, a superb family chapel founded by Annibale Bentivoglio in 1445 and consecrated in 1486. Pride of place naturally goes to a portrait with subtle characterization of the patrons by Lorenzo Costa (1460–1535), who was also responsible for the frescoes of the *Apocalypse*, the *Madonna Enthroned* and the *Triumph of Death*. The chapel's altarpiece, depicting the *Virgin and Saints with Two Angel Musicians* (1488), is the work of Francesco Francia. The Bentivoglio family is further glorified in the tomb of Anton Galeazzo Bentivoglio (1435) opposite the chapel. It was among the last works of the noted Sienese sculptor, Jacopo della Quercia. The Oratory of Santa Cecilia features frescoes on the lives of Santa Cecilia and San Valeriano by Costa and Francesco Francia (1504–6).

**The Bentivoglio tomb (1435) by Jacopo della Quercia**

# Exploring Bologna

Monuments to Bologna's rich cultural heritage are scattered across the city, from the leaning towers and the church of San Petronio in the old centre to the Pinacoteca Nazionale in the university district.

### Torri degli Asinelli e Garisenda

Piazza di Porta Ravegnana.
**Torre degli Asinelli** ◯ *daily.*

The famous leaning towers – Torre degli Asinelli and Torre Garisenda – are among the few survivors of the original 200 that once formed the skyline of Bologna. Both were begun in the 12th century, though there were probably earlier towers on the site – Dante mentioned a pair of towers here in his *Inferno*. Torre Garisenda was shortened as a safety measure within only a few years of its construction, and still leans some 3 m (10 ft) from the vertical. At 97 m (318 ft) tall, Torre Asinelli is the fourth highest tower in Italy after those in Cremona, Siena and Venice. Its 500-step ascent offers fine views over the city's rooftops to the hills beyond.

### Abbazia di Santo Stefano

Via Santo Stefano 24. **Tel** *051 22 32 56.* ◯ *9am–noon, 3:30–6:30pm daily.* **www**.abbaziasantostefano.it

Santo Stefano is a curious collection of four medieval churches (originally seven) jumbled together under one roof. The 11th-century church

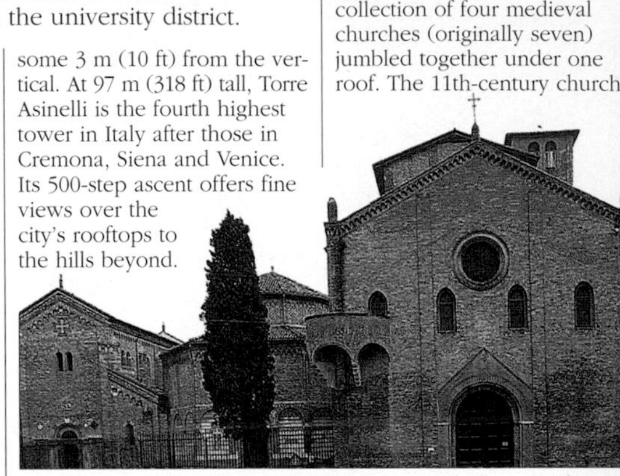

**Exterior of the Abbazia di Santo Stefano**

### SAN PETRONIO

Piazza Maggiore. **Tel** *051 22 21 12.* ◯ *daily.*

Dedicated to the city's 5th-century bishop, this church ranks among the greatest of Italy's brick-built medieval buildings. Founded in 1390, it was originally intended to be larger than St Peter's in Rome, but its size was scaled down when the church authorities diverted funds to the nearby Palazzo Archiginnasio. The resulting financial shortfall left the church decidedly lopsided, with a row of columns on its eastern flank that were intended to support an additional internal aisle. The project's financial profligacy, nonetheless, was said to have been instrumental in turning Martin Luther against Catholicism.

**Gothic Interior**
*The interior is airy, with graceful pillars supporting the roof. Twenty-two chapels, shielded by screens, open off the nave. In 1547 the Council of Trent* (see p174) *was temporarily moved here due to the plague.*

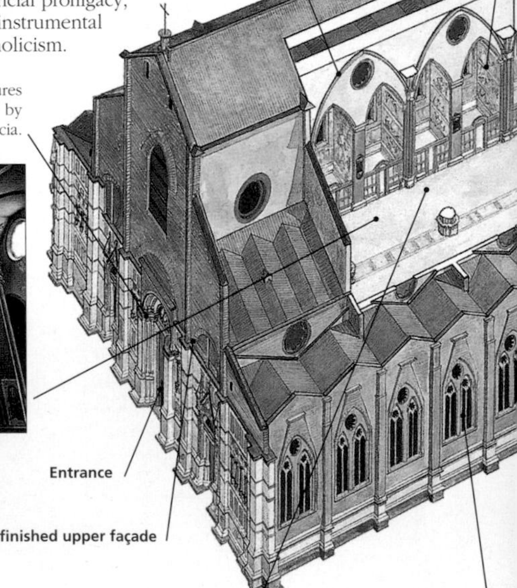

**The altarpiece of** the *Martyrdom of St Sebastian* is from the late Ferrarese School.

**The pink and white interior** adds to the overall light and airy effect.

**The canopied main portal** features beautiful biblical reliefs (1425–38) by Jacopo della Quercia.

**Entrance**

**Unfinished upper façade**

**The meridian line** was traced in 1655 by the astronomer Gian Domenico Cassini. It is 67 m (219 ft) long.

**The stained-glass windows** (1464–6) in this chapel are by Jacob of Ulm.

*For hotels and restaurants in this region see pp574–6 and pp624–6*

of the Crocifisso provides little more than a corridor to polygonal San Sepolcro, the most appealing of the quartet. Also dating from the 11th century, its centrepiece is the tomb of St Petronius, a marvellously overstated affair modelled on the Holy Sepulchre of Jerusalem. The courtyard contains the so-called Fontana di Pilato, an 8th-century basin.

The 5th-century Santi Vitale e Agricola is the oldest church in the city. It was rebuilt in the 8th and 11th centuries. Inside are the sarcophagi of Saints Vitalis and Agricola, martyred in the 4th century. Santa Trinità features a small museum of minor paintings and religious artifacts, including wooden statues of the *Adoration of the Magi* painted by Simone dei Crocifissi (c.1370).

**Choir Stalls**
*The exquisite inlaid choir stalls of the Chapel of the Holy Sacrament were made by Raffaello da Brescia in 1521.*

### Pinacoteca Nazionale

Via delle Belle Arti 56. ***Tel*** *051 421 19 84.* *Tue–Sun.* *1 Jan, 1 May, 16 Aug, 25 Dec.* **www.** pinacotecabologna.it

Bologna's principal art gallery, and one of northern Italy's most important collections, stands on the edge of the city's university district, a bustling area of bars, bookshops and cheap restaurants. The gallery is mainly dedicated to work by Bolognese painters, notably Vitale da Bologna, Guido Reni, Guercino and the Carracci family. Members of the Ferrarese School are also represented, in particular Francesco del Cossa and Ercole de' Roberti. The two highlights are Perugino's *Madonna in Glory* (c.1491) and Raphael's famous *Ecstasy of St Cecilia*, painted around 1515, both artists having worked in Bologna.

***The Ecstasy of St Cecilia*** **(c.1515) by Raphael in Bologna's Pinacoteca Nazionale**

### Museo delle Cere Anatomiche

Via Irnerio 48. ***Tel*** *051 24 42 15/ 051 24 22 17.* *9am–1pm Mon–Fri.* *1 Jan, Easter, 1 May, 25 Dec, pub hols.*

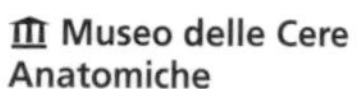

The Museum of Anatomical Waxworks is one of the more memorable of Bologna's smaller museums, featuring occasionally gruesome visceral waxworks and numerous models of organs, limbs and flayed bodies. Sculpted rather than made from casts, they have an artistic as well as scientific appeal. The models were used as medical teaching aids until the 19th century. Exhibits from the 18th century are in Palazzo Poggi, which also contains the Museo Cartageographica.

### San Domenico

Piazza di San Domenico 13. ***Tel*** *051 640 04 11.* *daily.*

Bologna's San Domenico can lay claim to being the most important of Italy's many Dominican churches. Begun in 1221, after St Dominic's death, it was built to house the body of the saint, who died here and lies buried in a tomb known as the Arca di San Domenico. A magnificent composite work, the tomb's statues were executed by Nicola Pisano; the reliefs of scenes from the *Life of St Dominic* were the work of Nicola Pisano and his assistants; the canopy (1473) is attributed to Nicola di Bari; while the figures of the angels and Saints Proculus and Petronius are early works by Michelangelo. The reliquary (1383) behind the sarcophagus contains St Dominic's head.

**Arca di San Domenico in the Basilica di San Domenico**

Fresco of Malatesta and St Sigismund (1451) by Piero della Francesca in the Tempio Malatestiano, Rimini

## Faenza 8

Ravenna. 54,000. FS
*Voltone Molinella 2 (0546 252 31).*
*Tue, Thu & Sat.*

Faenza is synonymous with the **faïence** ceramic-ware to which it gave its name. Renowned across Europe for over 500 years, the pottery, with its distinctive blue and ochre colouring, is still made in countless small factories around the town.

The highlight of Faenza is the **Museo Internazionale delle Ceramiche**, one of the largest ceramic collections in Italy. Its exhibits feature not only examples of local ware, but also pottery from other countries and other periods, including Roman ceramics and medieval majolica. There is also a section devoted to the modern ceramic art of Picasso, Matisse and Chagall.

**Museo Internazionale delle Ceramiche**
Viale Baccarini 19. ***Tel*** *0546 69 73 11.* *Apr–Oct: Tue–Sun; Nov–Mar: Tue–Sun (Tue–Thu am only).* *1 Jan, 1 May, 15 Aug, 25 Dec.*

## Rimini 9

*130,000.* FS *Piazzale Fellini 3 (0541 569 02).* *Wed & Sat.*
**www**.riminiturismo.it

Rimini was once a quaint sea side resort, whose charms were celebrated in the early films of Federico Fellini (1920–93), the director born and raised here. Today it is the largest beach resort in Europe. The seafront, which stretches unbroken for almost 15 km (9 miles), is lined with clubs, bars and restaurants. The crowded beaches are clean and well groomed, though entrance fees are charged at private beaches.

The town's old quarter, by contrast, is pleasantly quiet. Its charming cobbled streets gather around **Piazza Cavour**, dominated by the 14th-century **Palazzo del Podestà**. Rimini's finest building is the **Tempio Malatestiano**, built as a Franciscan church but converted in 1450 by Leon Battista Alberti, the great Florentine architect, into one of Italy's great Renaissance monuments. The work was commissioned by Sigismondo Malatesta (1417– 68), a descendant of Rimini's ruling medieval family, and reputedly one of the most evil and debauched men of his time. Ostensibly designed as a chapel, the Tempio became little more than a monument to Malatesta. Inside are sculptures by Agostino di Duccio and a fresco (1451) by Piero della Francesca of Malatesta kneeling before St Sigismund (1451).

The entwined initials of Malatesta and his fourth wife, Isotta degli Atti, provide a recurring decorative motif, and there are reliefs depicting scenes of bacchanalian excess and oddities such as strangely posed elephants (a Malatesta family emblem). All this led Pope Pius II to condemn the building as "a temple of devil-worshippers", and to burn Malatesta's effigy for acts of "murder, violation, adultery, incest, sacrilege and perjury".

**Environs:** Further along the coast, the resorts become relatively quieter. **Cesenatico**, 18 km (11 miles) north, offers all the usual facilities yet the beaches are less crowded.

**Tempio Malatestiano**
Via IV Novembre. ***Tel*** 0541 511 30. *8:30am–12:30pm, 3:30–7pm daily (9am–1pm, 3:30–7pm Sun).*

## Ravenna 10

*90,000.* FS *Via Salara 8–12 (0544 354 04).* *Wed & Sat; antiques on 3rd weekend of each month.* **www**.turismo.ravenna.it

Most people visit Ravenna for its superb mosaics from the Byzantine period *(see pp268–9)*, but the town itself is a surprisingly pleasant medley of old streets, fine shops and peaceful piazzas.

Façade of the Renaissance Tempio Malatestiano in Rimini

**Piazza del Popolo, Ravenna's central square**

The **Museo Nazionale** has a wide range of icons, paintings and archaeological displays. The best place to take a break from sightseeing is Piazza del Popolo, a lovely ensemble of medieval buildings.

**Museo Nazionale**
Via Fiandrini. ***Tel*** 0544 344 24.
*Tue–Sun.* *1 Jan, 1 May, 25 Dec.*

## Po Delta ⓫

Ferrara. FS *Ferrara Ostellata.* *to Goro or Gorino.* *from Porto Garibaldi, Goro & Gorino.* *Via Mazzini 4, Comacchio (0533 31 41 54).* **Parco Delta del Po*Tel*** *0533 31 40 03.* **www**.parcodeltapo.it

The Po is Italy's longest river. Its vast basin covers some 15 per cent of the country and supports around a third of the nation's population. Although ravaged in many places by industrial pollution, at its finest it offers beautifully subtle land-scapes – rows of poplar trees across misty fields and vistas over the shifting sands of its vast delta, an estuary of marshes, dunes and islands.

The immense **Parco Delta del Po** is a national park stretching for 600 sq km (234 sq miles), all the way to the Veneto. Wetland areas such as the **Valli di Comacchio** north of Ravenna have long been nature reserves, a winter home to thousands of breeding and migrating birds. Ornithologists gather here to see gulls, coots, bean geese and black terns, and far rarer species such as the white egret, hen harrier and pygmy cormorant. **Comacchio**, the nearest settlement, comprises 13 tiny islands connected by bridges. It is one of several fishing villages in the area, and its most famous catch is eels, often caught using methods, like water gates, that date back as far as Roman times.

**Hen harrier, found in the Po Delta**

Other nature reserves include the **Bosco della Mesola**, a tract of ancient woodland planted by the Etruscans and cared for by generations of monks. You can walk or cycle through it, with excellent opportunities for seeing large herds of deer.

For a good look at the entire region, follow the S309 – part of the old Via Romea pilgrimage trail to Rome – that runs north to south through some 100 km (62 miles) of the park. Numerous smaller lanes branch off into the wilderness. There are also boat trips to some of the delta's more remote corners: key departure points include the villages of Ca' Tie-polo, Ca' Vernier and Taglio di Po. Most areas also offer the possibility of hiring bicycles. The 125-km (78-mile) ride along the right bank of the Po is popular with cyclists.

**The peaceful landscape along the banks of the river in the Po Delta**

# A Tour of Ravenna

Mosaic deail from San Vitale

Ravenna rose to power in the 1st century BC under the Emperor Augustus, who built a port and naval base at nearby Classe, currently the site of a major excavation project. As Rome's power declined, Ravenna was made the capital of the Western Empire (AD 402), a role it retained during the Ostrogoth and Byzantine rule in the 5th and 6th centuries. Ravenna is renowned for its early Christian mosaics – the town had converted to Christianity in the 2nd century AD. The mosaics span the years of Roman and Byzantine rule, offering comparisons between Classically inspired designs and later Byzantine motifs.

**The Good Shepherd ②**
*This mosaic adorns the tiny Mausoleo di Galla Placidia. Begun in 430, this exquisite building probably never received the remains of Placidia, wife of a barbarian emperor.*

**San Vitale ①**
*San Vitale's apse mosaics (526–547) show Christ, San Vitale (being handed a martyr's crown), two angels and Bishop Ecclesius, who began the church* (see pp50–51).

**Baptism of Jesus ③**
*The 5th-century Battistero Neoniano (Neonian Baptistry) is named after the bishop who may have commissioned its decoration, including this beautiful mosaic. It was built near the remains of a Roman bathhouse and is Ravenna's oldest monument.*

**Battistero degli Ariani ⑤**
*The cupola of this late 5th-century baptistry has a mosaic showing the Apostles ringed around a centrepiece depicting the Baptism of Christ.*

## VISITORS' CHECKLIST

**San Vitale & Mausoleo di Galla Placidia**, Via Fiandrini. ***Tel*** *0544 54 16 88.* *Apr–Sep: 9am–7pm daily; Nov–Feb: 9:30am–5pm; Mar & Oct: 9am–5:30pm (last adm: 15 mins before closing).* *1 Jan, 25 Dec.* **Battistero Neoniano**, Via Battistero. ***Tel*** *0544 54 16 88.* *& as above, except Nov–Feb: 10am–5pm.* **Sant'Apollinare Nuovo**, Via di Roma. ***Tel*** *0544 54 16 88.* *& as above.* **Tomba di Dante**, Via Dante Alighieri. ***Tel*** *0544 302 52.* *Apr–Sep: 9am–7pm daily; Oct–Mar: 9am–noon, 2–5pm daily (last adm: 15 mins before closing).* *1 Jan, 25 Dec.* **Battistero degli Ariani**, Via degli Ariani. ***Tel*** *0544 344 24.* *8:30am–4:30pm daily (last adm: 15 mins before closing).* *1 Jan, 1 May.* *A combined ticket is available. For reservations (mandatory for Mausoleo di Galla Placidia):* ***Tel*** *800 303 999, 0544 54 16 88.* **www**.turismo.ravenna.it

GHISELLI
VIA ROCCA AL FOSSI
VIA UGO BASSI
VIA DI ROMA
VIA LUIGI RAVA
Stazione 130m (150 yards)
OLO COSTA
Basilica dello San Spirito
PIAZZA MAMELI
FS
⑤ Battistero degli Ariani
VIA LUIGI CARLO FARINI
MANDO DIAZ
VIA G. CARDUCCI
VIA A. MARIANI
Museo Dantesco
Sant'Apollinare Nuovo ⑥
VIA F. NEGRI
VICOLO PORZIOLINO
Tomba di Dante
RIMINI
Palazzo di Teodorico
VIA ALBERONI
LARGO FIRENZE
ACCIMANNI

**Sant'Apollinare Nuovo ⑥**
*This glorious 6th-century church, named after Ravenna's first bishop, is dominated by two rows of mosaics. Both show processions of martyrs and virgins bearing gifts for Christ and the Virgin.*

**Tomba di Dante ④**
*Dante's wanderings around Italy after his exile from Florence eventually brought him to Ravenna, where he died in 1321. A lamp in his sepulchre (1780) is fed by oil given by the city of Florence.*

**KEY**

— — — Suggested route

0 metres 200
0 yards 200

**Key to Symbols** *see back flap*

# FLORENCE

*Florence is a vast and beautiful monument to the Renaissance, the artistic and cultural reawakening of the 15th century. Writers such as Dante, Petrarch and Machiavelli contributed to its proud literary heritage, though it was the paintings and sculptures of artists such as Botticelli, Michelangelo and Donatello that turned the city into one of the world's greatest artistic capitals.*

While the Etruscans had long settled the hills around Fiesole, Florence first sprang to life as a Roman colony in 59 BC. Captured by the Lombards in the 6th century, the city later emerged from the Dark Ages as an independent city state. By the 13th century a burgeoning trade in wool and textiles, backed by a powerful banking sector, had turned the city into one of Italy's leading powers. Political control was wielded first by the guilds, and later by the Florentine Republic. In time, power passed to leading noble families, of which the most influential were the Medici, a hugely wealthy banking dynasty. Florence, and later Tuscany, remained under the family's almost unbroken sway for three centuries. During this time the city was at the cultural and intellectual heart of Europe, its cosmopolitan atmosphere and wealthy patrons providing the impetus for a period of unparalleled artistic growth. Artists, sculptors and architects flocked to the city, filling its streets, churches and palaces with some of the world's greatest Renaissance works. By 1737 the Medici had died out, leaving the city under Austrian (and briefly Napoleonic) control until Italian Unification in 1860. Between 1865 and 1871 Florence was the capital of the new Kingdom of Italy. The historic streets and artistic heritage were ravaged by the Arno floods of November 1966.

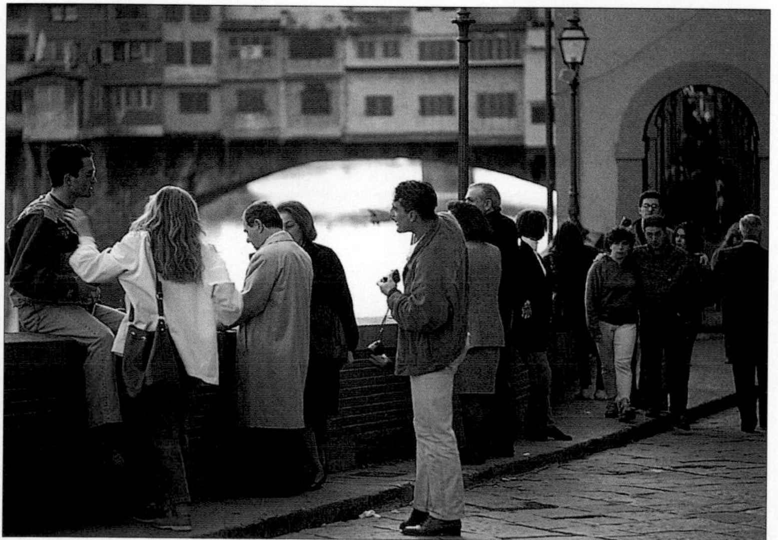

Florentines strolling in front of Ponte Vecchio (1345), the old bridge lined with shops spanning the Arno

◁ The dome of Florence's Duomo, completed in 1436, designed by Brunelleschi

# Exploring Florence

Historic Florence is a surprisingly compact area, and the majority of the sights described on the following pages can easily be reached on foot. Most visitors head for the Duomo, the city's geographical and historical focus, ideally placed to explore the Campanile, Baptistry and Museo dell'Opera del Duomo. To the south is Piazza della Signoria, long the city's political heart, flanked by the Palazzo Vecchio, Florence's town hall, and the Uffizi, one of Italy's leading art galleries. To the east lies the church of Santa Croce, home to frescoes by Giotto and the tombs of some of Florence's greatest men. To the west stands Santa Maria Novella, the city's other great church, also adorned with fresco-filled chapels. Across the Ponte Vecchio and the Arno – the river that bisects the city – is the district of Oltrarno, dominated by Santo Spirito and the vast Pitti Palace, containing galleries with works by great Renaissance artists including Raphael and Titian.

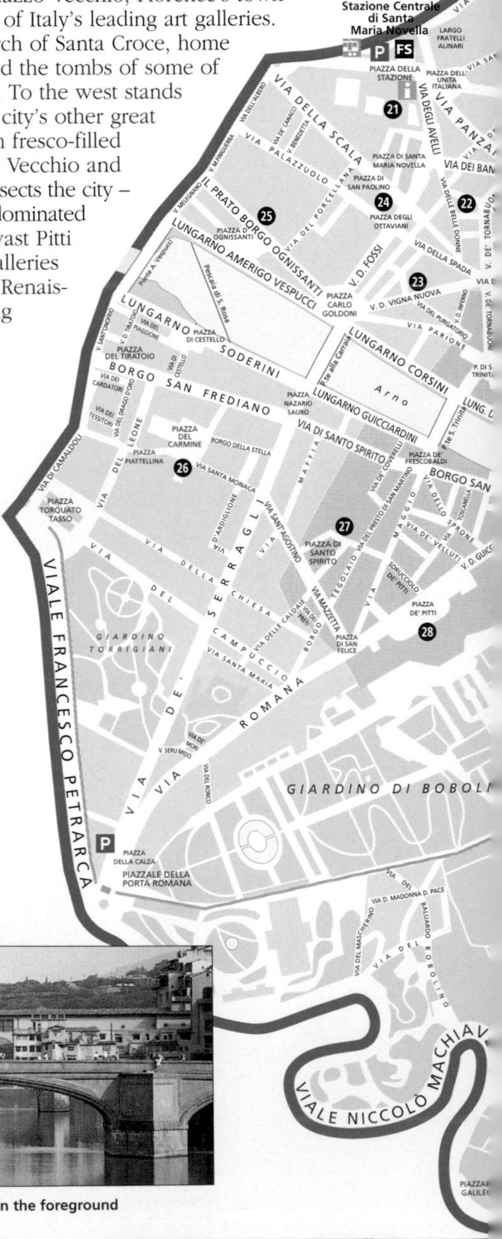

**Bell tower, Palazzo Vecchio**

## GETTING AROUND

Florence has an excellent bus service. A tram linking the city centre to the outskirts is under construction. The compact city centre, a restricted traffic area, is best negotiated on foot.

## KEY

- Street-by-Street: Around San Marco *pp274–5*
- Street-by-Street: Around the Duomo *pp278–9*
- Street-by-Street: Around Piazza della Repubblica *pp292–3*
- Street-by-Street: Around Oltrarno *pp300–1*
- FS Railway station
- P Parking
- i Tourist information
- City walls
- Tram station

**Ponte Vecchio with Ponte Santa Trinità in the foreground**

**For additional map symbols** *see back flap*

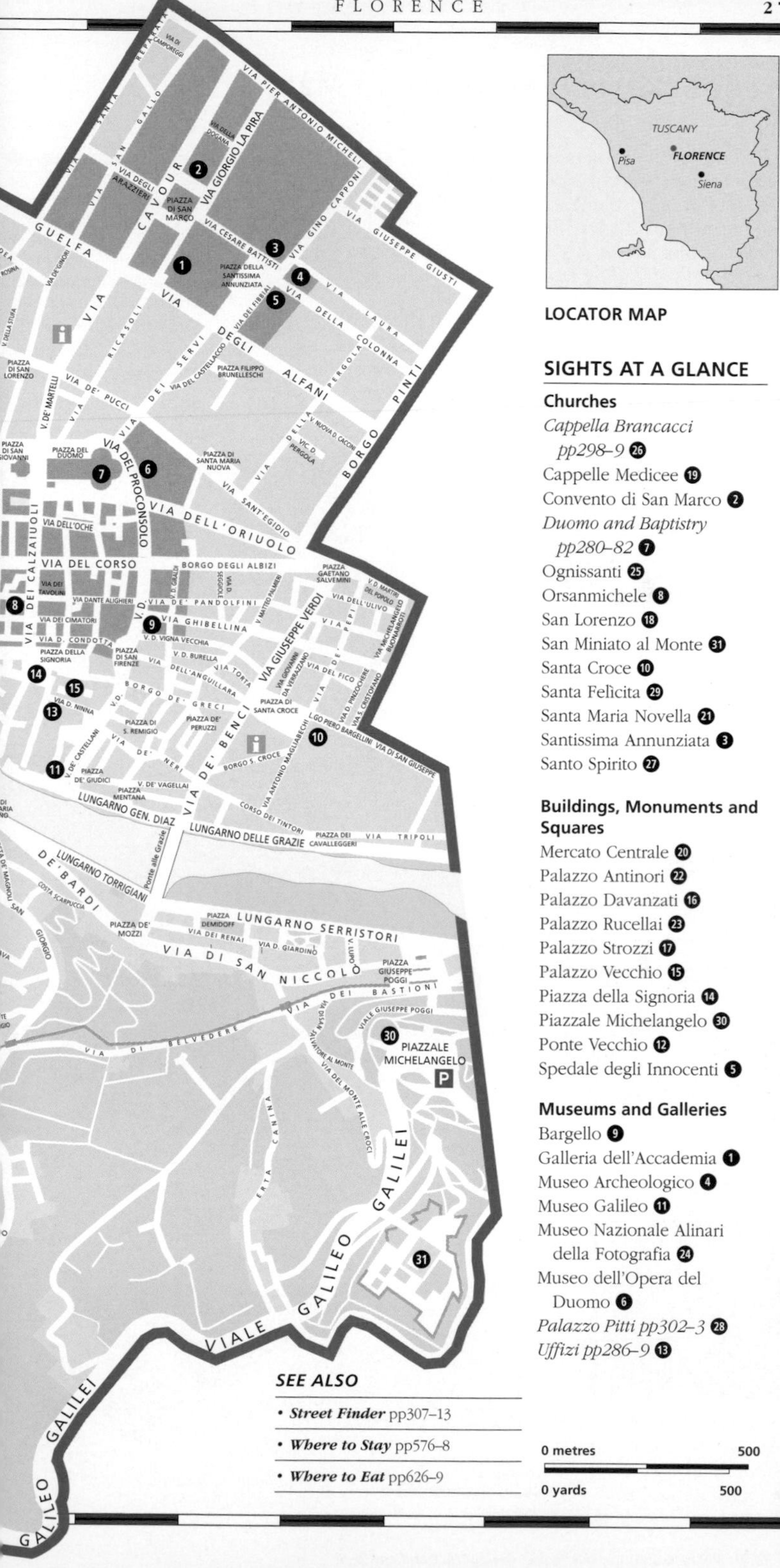


LOCATOR MAP

## SIGHTS AT A GLANCE

### Churches

*Cappella Brancacci pp298–9* 26
Cappelle Medicee 19
Convento di San Marco 2
*Duomo and Baptistry pp280–82* 7
Ognissanti 25
Orsanmichele 8
San Lorenzo 18
San Miniato al Monte 31
Santa Croce 10
Santa Felìcita 29
Santa Maria Novella 21
Santissima Annunziata 3
Santo Spirito 27

### Buildings, Monuments and Squares

Mercato Centrale 20
Palazzo Antinori 22
Palazzo Davanzati 16
Palazzo Rucellai 23
Palazzo Strozzi 17
Palazzo Vecchio 15
Piazza della Signoria 14
Piazzale Michelangelo 30
Ponte Vecchio 12
Spedale degli Innocenti 5

### Museums and Galleries

Bargello 9
Galleria dell'Accademia 1
Museo Archeologico 4
Museo Galileo 11
Museo Nazionale Alinari della Fotografia 24
Museo dell'Opera del Duomo 6
*Palazzo Pitti pp302–3* 28
*Uffizi pp286–9* 13

### SEE ALSO


- ***Street Finder*** pp307–13
- ***Where to Stay*** pp576–8
- ***Where to Eat*** pp626–9


0 metres 500
0 yards 500

# Street-by-Street: Around San Marco

The buildings in this part of Florence once stood on the fringes of the city, serving as stables and barracks. The Medici menagerie of lions, elephants and giraffes was housed here. Today it is a student quarter and the streets are often busy with young people attending the university or the Accademia di Belle Arti, the world's oldest art school, founded in 1563.

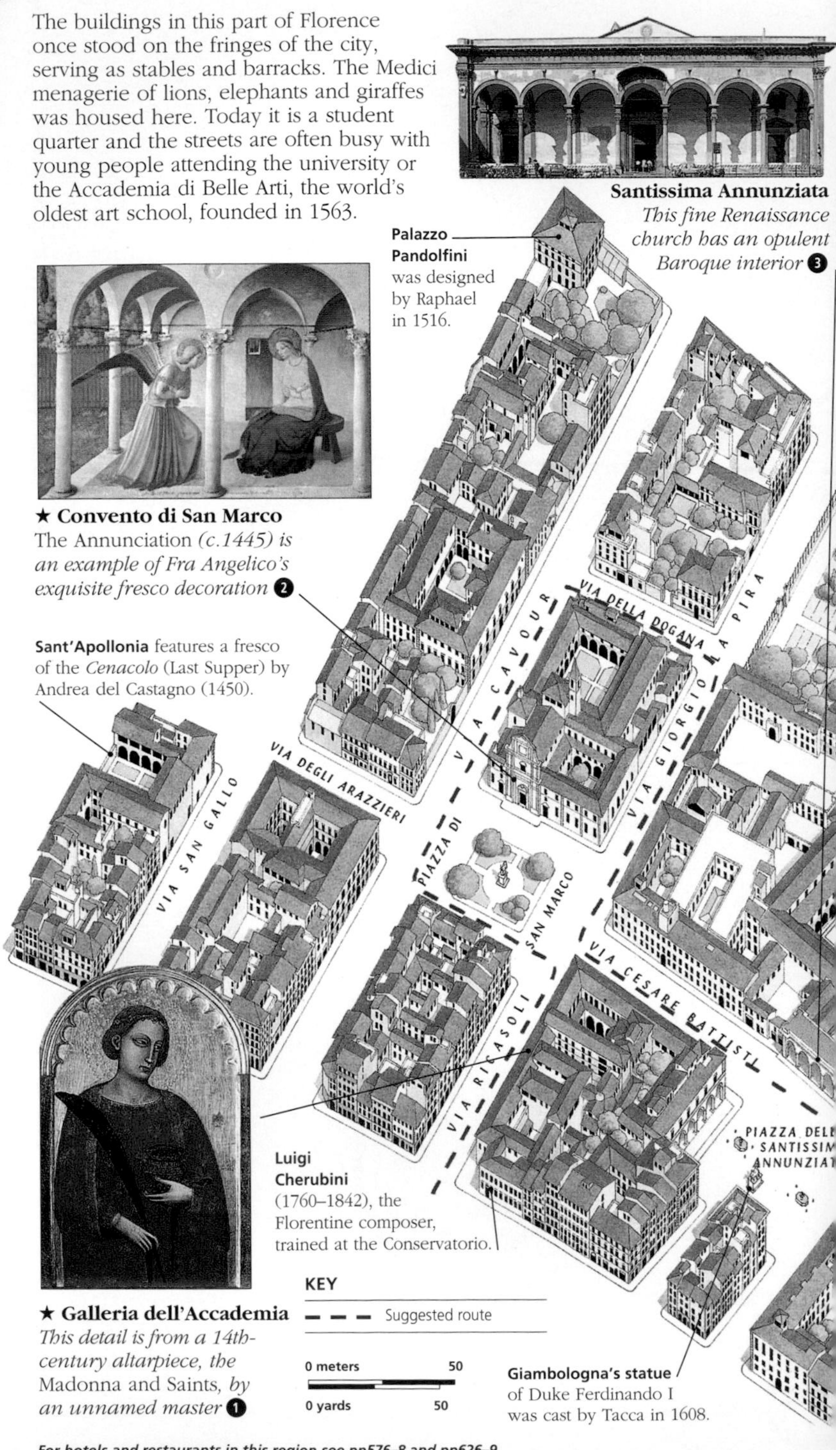


**Santissima Annunziata**
*This fine Renaissance church has an opulent Baroque interior* ❸

**Palazzo Pandolfini** was designed by Raphael in 1516.

**★ Convento di San Marco**
The Annunciation *(c.1445) is an example of Fra Angelico's exquisite fresco decoration* ❷

**Sant'Apollonia** features a fresco of the *Cenacolo* (Last Supper) by Andrea del Castagno (1450).

**Luigi Cherubini** (1760–1842), the Florentine composer, trained at the Conservatorio.

**★ Galleria dell'Accademia**
*This detail is from a 14th-century altarpiece, the* Madonna and Saints, *by an unnamed master* ❶

**KEY**

— — — Suggested route

0 meters 50
0 yards 50

**Giambologna's statue** of Duke Ferdinando I was cast by Tacca in 1608.

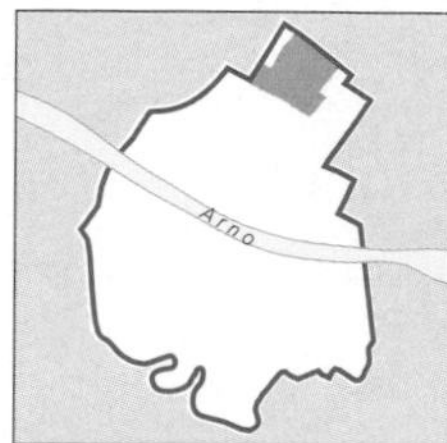


**LOCATOR MAP**
*See Florence Street Finder map 2*

**Spedale degli Innocenti**
*Opened in 1444, the city orphanage by Brunelleschi was decorated with cameos by Andrea della Robbia* ❺

**The Giardino dei Semplici** was opened in 1543.

VIA GINO CAPPONI

**Museo Archeologico**
*Many of the Etruscan objects in the museum were originally in the Medici collections* ❹

**STAR SIGHTS**

★ Galleria dell'Accademia

★ Convento di San Marco

Part of the 15th-century *Cassone Adimari* by Lo Scheggia in the Accademia

## Galleria dell'Accademia ❶

Via Ricasoli 60. **Map** 2 D4. ***Tel*** *055 238 86 09 (information); 055 29 48 83 (reservations).* *8:15am–6:50pm Tue–Sun (occasional extended hours in the summer).* *public hols.*

The Academy of Fine Arts, founded in 1563, was the first school established in Europe specifically to teach the techniques of drawing, painting and sculpture. The art collection displayed here was formed in 1784 to provide material for students to study and copy.

The most famous work is Michelangelo's *David* (1504), a colossal (5.2 m/ 17 ft) nude of the biblical hero who killed the giant Goliath. The sculpture was commissioned by the city for Piazza della Signoria, but it was moved to the Accademia for safe-keeping in 1873. One copy now stands in its original position *(see pp290–91)* and a second is on Piazzale Michelangelo. The *David* established Michelangelo, at the age of 29, as the foremost sculptor of his time.

Michelangelo's other masterpieces in the Accademia include the *Quattro Prigionieri* (the Four Prisoners), sculpted between 1521 and 1523 and intended to adorn the tomb of Pope Julius II. The muscular figures struggling to free themselves from the stone are among the most dramatic of Michelangelo's works. The statues were presented to the Medici family in 1564 by the artist's nephew, Leonardo. They were then moved to the Grotta Grande in the Boboli Gardens, where casts of the originals can now be seen.

The Accademia also contains an important collection of paintings by 15th- and 16th-century Florentine artists, among them Filippino Lippi, Fra Bartolomeo, Bronzino and Ridolfo del Ghirlandaio. The major works include the *Madonna del Mare* (Madonna of the Sea), attributed to Botticelli (1445–1510), and *Venus and Cupid* by Jacopo Pontormo (1494–1556), based on a preparatory drawing by Michelangelo. Also here is an elaborately painted wooden chest, the *Cassone Adimari* (1440– 45) by Lo Scheggia, the step-brother of Masaccio. Originally part of a wealthy bride's trousseau, it is decorated with details of Florentine life, clothing and architecture. A scene of the bridal party appears on the chest in front of the Baptistry.

Michelangelo's *David*

The Salone della Toscana (Tuscany Room) features more modest paintings and sculptures by 19th-century members of the Accademia and plaster models by the sculptor, Lorenzo Bartolini.

The light and airy former library, designed by Michelozzo

## Convento di San Marco ❷

Piazza di San Marco. **Map** 2 D4. ***Tel*** *055 28 76 28 (information).* *7am–noon, 4–8pm.* **Museo di San Marco** ***Tel*** *055 238 86 08; 055 29 48 83 (reservations).* *8:15am–1:50pm (later Sat, Sun).* *1 Jan, 1 May, 25 Dec, 2nd & 4th Mon and 1st, 3rd & 5th Sun of each month.*

The Convent of San Marco was founded in the 13th century and enlarged in 1437 when Dominican monks from nearby Fiesole moved there at the invitation of Cosimo il Vecchio. He paid a considerable sum to have the convent rebuilt by his favourite architect, Michelozzo, whose simple cloisters and cells provide the setting for a remarkable series of devotional frescoes (c.1438–45) by Florentine painter and Dominican friar Fra Angelico. The convent and art collections form the **Museo di San Marco**.

Michelozzo's magnificent **Chiostro di Sant'Antonino** was named after the convent's first prior, Antonino Pierozzi (1389–1459), who later became the Archbishop of Florence. Most of the faded frescoes in this cloister describe scenes from the saint's life by Bernardino Poccetti. The panels in the corner are by Fra Angelico. A door in the right side of the cloister leads to the **Ospizio dei Pellegrini** (Pilgrims' Hospice). Today it houses the museum's free-standing paintings, including two famous masterpieces: Fra Angelico's moving *Deposition* (c.1435–40), an altarpiece painted for the church of Santa Trinità, and the *Madonna dei Linaiuoli*, commissioned by the Linaiuoli (flaxworkers' guild) in 1433.

In the courtyard, right of the convent's former bell, is the vaulted **Sala Capitolare** (Chapter House), decorated with a noted but over-restored *Crucifixion and Saints* (1440) painted by Fra Angelico.

Covering one wall of the small **Refettorio** (refectory) is a fresco of the *Last Supper* (c.1480) by Domenico Ghirlandaio. Stairs from the courtyard lead to the first floor, where you suddenly see Fra Angelico's *Annunciation* (c.1440), thought by many to be among the city's most beautiful Renaissance paintings. Beyond, ranged around three sides of the cloister, are the **Dormitory Cells**. These 44 tiny monastic cells are frescoed with scenes from *The Life of Christ* by Fra Angelico and assistants (1439–45). The cells numbered 1 to 11 are generally attributed to Fra Angelico personally, as is the lovely fresco of the *Madonna and Saints* on the right of the corridor *(see p32)*.

A detail from Fra Angelico's poignant *Deposition* (c. 1440)

Cells 12–14 were once occupied by Savonarola, the zealous Dominican monk who became Prior of San Marco in 1491. Among other deeds, Savonarola incited Florentines to rebel against the Medici and was responsible for the burning of many works of art. Denounced as a heretic, he was burned at the stake in Piazza della Signoria in 1498.

Along the third corridor lies an airy colonnaded hall, formerly a public **library** designed by Michelozzo in 1441 for Cosimo il Vecchio. Beyond it lie two cells (38 and 39) which were used by Cosimo when he went on retreat here. Each is decorated with two frescoes (the other cells have only one), and they are both larger than any of the neighbouring rooms.

Fra Angelico's allegorical fresco, the *Mocking of Christ* (c. 1442), showing Jesus blindfolded and being struck by a Roman guard

***The Birth of the Virgin* (1514) by del Sarto in Santissima Annunziata**

## Santissima Annunziata ❸

Piazza della Santissima Annunziata. **Map** 2 E4. ***Tel*** *055 26 61 81.* *7:30am–12:30pm, 4pm–6:30pm daily.*

Founded by the Servite order in 1250, the church of the Holy Annunciation was later rebuilt by Michelozzo between 1444 and 1481. Its atrium contains frescoes by the Mannerist artists Rosso Fiorentino, Andrea del Sarto and Jacopo Pontormo. Perhaps the finest of its panels are *The Journey of the Magi* (1511) and *The Birth of the Virgin* (1514) by Andrea del Sarto.

The heavily decorated, dark interior has a frescoed ceiling completed by Pietro Giambelli in 1669. Here is one of the city's most revered shrines, a painting of the Virgin Mary begun by a monk in 1252 but miraculously completed by an angel, according to devout Florentines. Newly-wed couples traditionally visit the shrine (on the left as you enter the church) to present a bouquet of flowers to the Virgin and to pray for a long, fruitful and fecund marriage.

A door from the north transept leads to the **Chiostrino dei Morti** (Cloister of the Dead), so called because it was originally used as a burial ground. Today it is best known for del Sarto's beautiful fresco, *The Madonna del Sacco* (1525).

**Etruscan warrior, Museo Archeologico**

The church is situated on the northern flank of **Piazza della Santissima Annunziata**, one of the finest Renaissance squares in Florence. Designed by Brunelleschi, the delicate nine-bay arcade fronts the Spedale degli Innocenti to its right, while at the centre of the square stands a bronze equestrian statue of Duke Ferdinando I. Started by Giambologna, it was finished in 1608 by his assistant Pietro Tacca (who designed the square's bronze fountains).

## Museo Archeologico ❹

Via della Colonna 36. **Map** 2 E4. ***Tel*** *055 235 75.* *8:30am–2pm Tue–Sun (to 7pm Tue & Thu); 2–7pm Mon.* *1 Jan, 1 May, 25 Dec.*

The Archaeological Museum in Florence is in a palazzo built by Giulio Parigi for the Princess Maria Maddalena de' Medici in 1620. It now exhibits an outstanding collection of Etruscan, Greek, Roman and Egyptian artifacts, although parts of the collection are being restored following the flood in 1966. The first floor contains a splendid series of Etruscan bronzes as well as the famous *Chimera* (4th century BC), a mythical lion with a goat's head imposed on its body and a serpent for a tail. Equally impressive is the 1st-century *Arringatore* bronze found near Lake Trasimeno in Umbria. It is inscribed with the name of Aulus Metellus. A large section on the second floor is dedicated to Greek vases, notably the famed François Vase, found in an Etruscan tomb near Chiusi.

## Spedale degli Innocenti ❺

Piazza della Santissima Annunziata 12. **Map** 2 E4. ***Tel*** *055 203 73 08.* *10am–7pm daily.* *1 Jan, Easter, 25 Dec.*

**Part of Brunelleschi's arcaded loggia, Spedale degli Innocenti**

Named after Herod's biblical Massacre of the Innocents, the "Hospital" opened in 1444 as Europe's first orphanage. Part of the building is still used for this purpose. Brunelleschi's arcaded loggia is decorated with glazed terracotta roundels, added by Andrea della Robbia around 1498, showing babies wrapped in swaddling bands. At the left end of the portico you can see the *rota*, a rotating stone cylinder on which anonymous mothers could place their unwanted children and ring the bell for them to be admitted to the orphanage.

Within the building lie two elegant cloisters: the **Chiostro degli Uomini** (Men's Cloister), built between 1422 and 1445 and decorated with *sgraffito* roosters and cherubs, and the smaller Women's Cloister (1438). A small upstairs gallery contains a handful of fine works, including terracottas by della Robbia and pictures by Botticelli, Piero di Cosimo and Domenico Ghirlandaio.

# Street-by-Street: Around the Duomo

Stained glass window from the Duomo

While much of Florence was rebuilt during the Renaissance, the eastern part of the city retains a distinctly medieval feel. With its maze of tiny alleys, it is an area that would still be familiar to Dante (1265–1321), whose birthplace allegedly lay somewhere among these lanes. The poet would recognize the church of Santa Maria de' Cerchi where he first glimpsed Beatrice, as well as the gaunt outlines of the Bargello. He would also be familiar with the Baptistry, one of the city's oldest buildings, though he would not know the Campanile nor the Duomo, whose foundations were laid in the poet's old age.

**★ Duomo and Baptistry**
*The exteriors of the Duomo and Baptistry are richly decorated with marbles and reliefs, such as this detail from the Duomo's façade* ❼

**The Loggia del Bigallo** (1358) is where abandoned children were once left. They were then sent to foster homes if they remained unclaimed.

**Orsanmichele**
*The church's niche carvings depict patron saints of trade guilds, such as this copy of Donatello's* St George ❽

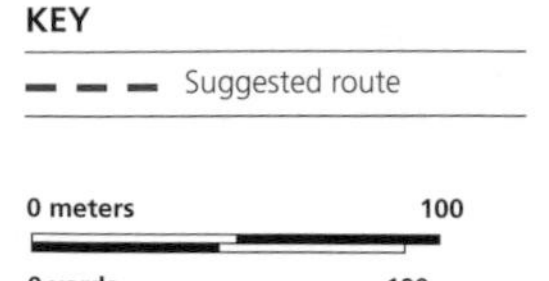


**Via dei Calzaiuoli**, lined with smart shops, is the city's liveliest street.

**Piazza della Signoria**

**Museo dell'Opera del Duomo**
*Works from the Duomo, Campanile and Baptistry are displayed in this museum* ❻

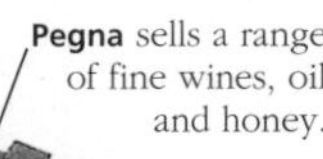

**Pegna** sells a range of fine wines, oil and honey.

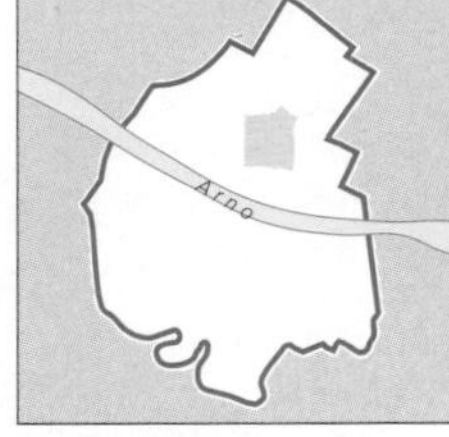


**LOCATOR MAP**
*See Florence Street Finder map 6*

VIA FOLCO PORTINARI

VIA DELL' ORIUOLO

BORGO DEGLI ALBIZI

VIA DE' GIRALDI

VIA DE PANDOLFINI

VIA DEL PROCONSOLO

VIA DEL PRESTO

ALIGHIERI

VIA DELL' ACQUA

PIAZZA DI S. FIRENZE

**Badia Fiorentina**, the abbey church founded in 978, is home to *The Virgin Appearing to St Bernard* (1485) by Filippino Lippi.

**Casa di Dante**, a restored medieval house, is reputedly Dante's birthplace.

**★ Bargello**
*The city's old prison is home to a rich collection of applied arts and sculpture, including this figure of* Mercury *by Giambologna (1564)* ❾

**STAR SIGHTS**

★ Duomo and Baptistry

★ Bargello

**Carving from Luca della Robbia's choir loft in the Museo dell'Opera**

## Museo dell'Opera del Duomo ❻

Piazza del Duomo 9. **Map** 2 D5 (6 E2). ***Tel*** *055 230 28 85.*
*9am–7:30pm daily (to 1:40pm Sun & public hols) (last adm: 40 mins before closing).* *1 Jan, Easter, 25 Dec.*

The Cathedral Works Museum has reopened after extensive remodelling and now a series of rooms is dedicated to the history of the Duomo. The main ground-floor room holds statues from Arnolfo di Cambio's workshop which were once placed in the cathedral's niches. Nearby is Donatello's *St John*. Another room contains 14th- and 15th-century religious paintings and reliquaries.

Michelangelo's *Pietà* has pride of place on the staircase. The hooded figure of Nicodemus is widely believed to be a self-portrait.

The first room on the upper floor contains two choir lofts, dating to the 1430s, by Luca della Robbia and Donatello. Carved in crisp white marble and decorated with coloured glass and mosaic, both depict children playing musical instruments and dancing. Other works by Donatello in this room are his statue of *La Maddalena* (1455) and several Old Testament figures.

The room to the left contains an exhibition of the tablets that used to decorate the bell tower. A lower level houses examples of the tools used by Brunelleschi's workmen and a copy of di Cambio's original cathedral façade.

# Duomo and Baptistry 7

Sir John Hawkwood by Paolo Uccello, in the Duomo

Rising above the heart of the city, the richly-decorated Duomo – Santa Maria del Fiore – and its orange-tiled dome have become Florence's most famous symbols. Typical of the Florentine determination to lead in all things, the cathedral is Europe's fourth largest church, and to this day it still remains the city's tallest building. The Baptistry, with its celebrated bronze doors, may date back to the 4th century, making it one of Florence's oldest buildings. The Campanile, designed by Giotto in 1334, was completed in 1359, 22 years after his death.

**Campanile**
*At 85 m (276 ft), the Campanile is 6 m (20 ft) shorter than the dome. It is clad in white, green and pink Tuscan marble.*

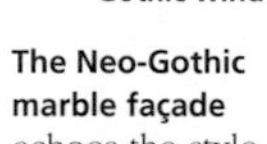

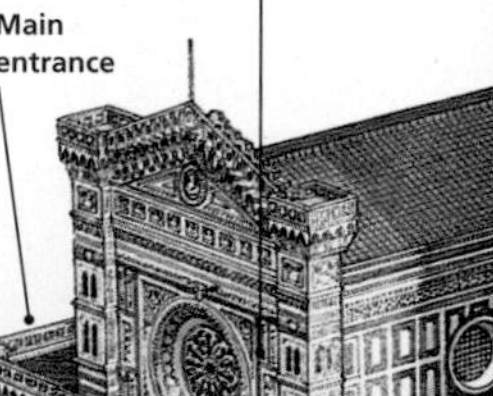

Gothic windows

**The Neo-Gothic marble façade** echoes the style of Giotto's Campanile, but was only added in 1871–87.

Main entrance

**★ Baptistry**
*Colourful 13th-century mosaics illustrating the* Last Judgment *decorate the ceiling above the octagonal font, where many famous Florentines, including Dante, were baptized. The doors are by Andrea Pisano (south) and Lorenzo Ghiberti (north, east).*

North Doors

East Doors
*(See p282)*

South Doors

**Campanile Reliefs**
*Copies of reliefs by Andrea Pisano on the Campanile's first storey depict the Creation of Man, and the Arts and the Industries. The originals are kept in the Museo dell'Opera del Duomo* (see p279).

**The top of the dome** offers spectacular views over the city.

**★ Dome by Brunelleschi**
*Brunelleschi's dome, finished in 1463, was the largest of its time to be built without scaffolding. The outer shell is supported by a thicker inner shell that acts as a platform for it.*

**The *Last Judgment*** frescoes (1572–4) by Vasari were completed by Zuccari.

## VISITORS' CHECKLIST

Piazza del Duomo. **Map** 2 D5 (6 E2). ***Tel*** *055 230 28 85.* *1, 6, 14, 17, 23.* **Cathedral** *10am–5pm Mon–Sat (4:30pm Thu, 4:45pm Sat), 1:30–4:45pm Sun.* **Crypt** *10am–5pm Mon–Sat (4:45pm Sat).* **Baptistry** *noon–7pm Mon–Sat, 8:30am–2pm Sun.* **Dome** *8:30am–7pm Mon–Sat (5:40pm Sat).* **Campanile** *8:30am–7:30pm daily.* **All buildings** *1 Jan, Easter, 15 Aug, 8 Sep, 25 Dec.* **www**.operaduomo.firenze.it

**Bricks were set** between marble ribs in a self-supporting herringbone pattern – a technique Brunelleschi copied from the Pantheon in Rome.

**Chapels at the East End**
*The three apses, crowned by smaller copies of the dome, have five chapels each. The 15th-century stained glass is by Ghiberti.*

**Entrance leading to the dome**

**The marble sanctuary** around the High Altar was created by Baccio Bandinelli in 1555.

**Marble Pavement**
*The colourful, intricately inlaid pavement (16th century) was designed in part by Baccio d'Agnolo and Francesco da Sangallo.*

**Dante Explaining the Divine Comedy** *(1465)*
*This painting by Michelino shows the poet outside Florence against a backdrop of Purgatory, Hell and Paradise.*

## STAR FEATURES

★ Baptistry

★ Dome by Brunelleschi

# The East Doors of the Baptistry

Lorenzo Ghiberti's famous bronze Baptistry doors were commissioned in 1401 to mark the city's deliverance from the plague. Ghiberti was chosen to make a set of new doors after a competition that involved seven leading artists, including Donatello, Jacopo della Quercia and Brunelleschi. The trial panels by Ghiberti and Brunelleschi are so different from Florentine Gothic art of the time, notably in the use of perspective and individuality of figures, that they are often regarded as the first works of the Renaissance.

**Ghiberti's winning panel**

**"GATE OF PARADISE"**

Having spent 21 years working on the North Doors, Ghiberti was commissioned to make the East Doors (1424 –1452). Michelangelo enthusiastically dubbed them the "Gate of Paradise". The original ten relief panels showing scriptural subjects are now exhibited in the Museo dell'Opera del Duomo *(see p279);* those on the Baptistry are copies.

**Abraham and the Sacrifice of Isaac**

*The jagged modelled rocks symbolizing Abraham's pain are carefully arranged to emphasize the sacrificial act.*

**Joseph Sold into Slavery**

*Ghiberti, a master of perspective, formed the architectural elements in shallower relief behind the figures to create the illusion of depth in the scene.*

## KEY TO THE EAST DOORS

| | |
|---|---|
| 1 | 2 |
| 3 | 4 |
| 5 | 6 |
| 7 | 8 |
| 9 | 10 |

**1** Adam and Eve are Expelled from Eden
**2** Cain Murders his Brother, Abel
**3** The Drunkenness of Noah and his Sacrifice
**4** Abraham and the Sacrifice of Isaac
**5** Esau and Jacob
**6** Joseph Sold into Slavery
**7** Moses Receives the Ten Commandments
**8** The Fall of Jericho
**9** The Battle with the Philistines
**10** Solomon and the Queen of Sheba

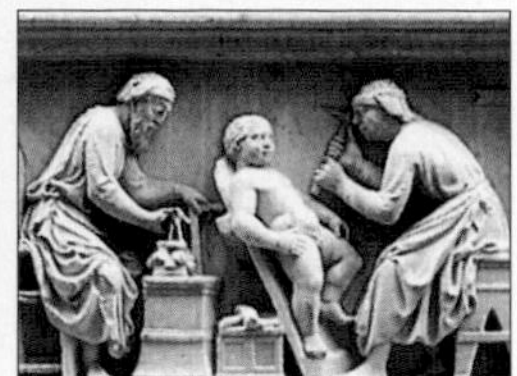
Detail of carvings by Donatello on the wall of Orsanmichele

## Orsanmichele 8

Via dell'Arte della Lana. **Map** 3 C1 (6 D3). ***Tel*** *055 28 49 44.* *10am–5pm Tue–Sun.* *1 Jan, 1 May, 25 Dec.*

Built in 1337 as a grain market, Orsanmichele was later converted into a church which took its name from *Orto di San Michele,* a monastic garden long since vanished. The arcades of the market became windows, which are today bricked in, but the original Gothic tracery can still be seen. The decoration was entrusted to Florence's major *Arti* (guilds). Over 60 years they commissioned sculptures of their patron saints to adorn the 14 exterior niches; however today many of the figures are copies. Among the sculptors were Lorenzo Ghiberti, Donatello and Verrocchio.

The beautifully tranquil interior contains an opulent 14th-century altar by Andrea Orcagna, a *Virgin and Child* by Bernardo Daddi (1348) and a statue of the *Madonna and Child with St Anne* by Francesco da Sangallo (1522).

Brunelleschi's *Sacrifice of Isaac* (1402) in the Bargello

## Bargello 9

Via del Proconsolo 4. **Map** 4 D1 (6 E3). ***Tel*** *055 238 86 06.* *14, A.* *8:15am–1:50pm daily.* *2nd & 4th Mon, 1st, 3rd & 5th Sun of each month; 1 Jan, 1 May, 25 Dec.*

Florence's second-ranking museum after the Uffizi, the Bargello contains a wonderful medley of applied arts and Italy's finest collection of Renaissance sculpture. Begun in 1255, the fortress-like building was initially the town hall (making it the oldest seat of government in the city), but later became a prison and home to the chief of police (the *Bargello*). It also became known for its executions, which took place in the main courtyard until 1786, when the death sentence was abolished by Grand Duke Pietro Leopoldo. Following extensive renovation, the building opened as one of Italy's first national museums in 1865.

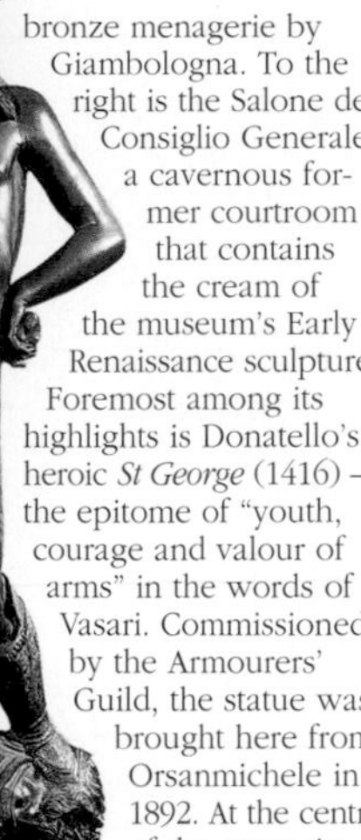
Donatello's *David* (c.1430) in the Bargello

The key exhibits range over three floors, beginning with the Michelangelo Room, superbly redesigned after extensive damage during the 1966 flood. Three contrasting works by Michelangelo lie dotted around the room, the most famous a tipsy-looking *Bacchus* (1497), the sculptor's first large free-standing work. Close by is a powerful bust of *Brutus* (1539–40), the only known portrait bust by Michelangelo, and a beautifully delicate circular relief depicting the *Madonna and Child* (1503–5). Countless works by other sculptors occupy the same room. Among them is an exquisite *Mercury* (1564) by the Mannerist genius, Giambologna, as well as several virtuoso bronzes by the sculptor and goldsmith Benvenuto Cellini (1500–71).

Across the courtyard, full of fragments and the coats of arms of the Bargello's various incumbents, two more rooms contain exterior sculptures removed from sites around the city. The courtyard's external staircase leads to the first floor, which opens with a wonderfully eccentric bronze menagerie by Giambologna. To the right is the Salone del Consiglio Generale, a cavernous former courtroom that contains the cream of the museum's Early Renaissance sculpture.

Foremost among its highlights is Donatello's heroic *St George* (1416) – the epitome of "youth, courage and valour of arms" in the words of Vasari. Commissioned by the Armourers' Guild, the statue was brought here from Orsanmichele in 1892. At the centre of the room, in direct contrast, is Donatello's androgynous *David* (c.1430), famous as the first free-standing nude by a Western artist since antiquity. Among the room's more easily missed works, tucked away on the right wall, are two reliefs depicting *The Sacrifice of Isaac* (1402). Created by Brunelleschi and Lorenzo Ghiberti respectively, both were entries in the competition to design the Baptistry doors.

Beyond the Salone, the Bargello's emphasis shifts to the applied arts, with room after room devoted to rugs, ceramics, silverware and a host of other beautiful *objets d'art*. The most celebrated of these rooms is the Salone del Camino on the second floor, which features the finest collection of small bronzes in Italy. Some are reproductions of antique models, others are small copies of Renaissance statues. Giambologna, Cellini and Antonio del Pollaiuolo are among those represented.

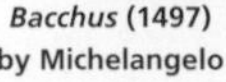
*Bacchus* (1497) by Michelangelo

# Santa Croce ⑩

Work began around 1294 on the Gothic church of Santa Croce, which contains tombs and monuments of famous Florentines, such as Michelangelo, Galileo and Machiavelli, as well as radiant early 14th-century frescoes by Giotto and his pupil Taddeo Gaddi. In the cloister alongside the church stands the Cappella de' Pazzi (Pazzi Chapel), a Renaissance masterpiece designed by Filippo Brunelleschi.

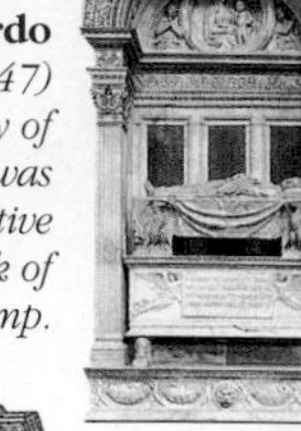

**Tomb of Leonardo Bruni** *(1447)*
*Rossellino's effigy of this great humanist was unusual in its sensitive realism and lack of monumental pomp.*

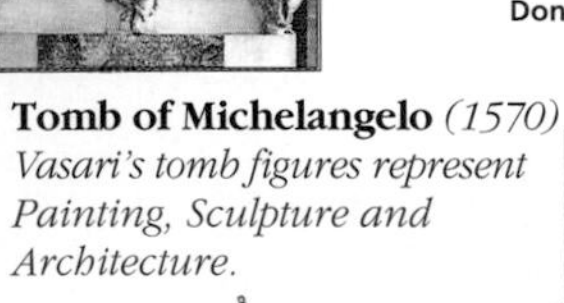

**Tomb of Michelangelo** *(1570)*
*Vasari's tomb figures represent Painting, Sculpture and Architecture.*

Ticket booth and entrance

*Annunciation* by Donatello (15th century)

Tomb of Machiavelli

**The Neo-Gothic façade** by Niccolò Matas was added in 1863.

Tomb of Galileo

Exit

*Tree of Life* by Taddeo Gaddi

Refectory

**Cimabue's Crucifixion**
*Badly damaged in the flood of 1966, this 13th-century masterpiece is among the highlights of the collection, as is Taddeo Gaddi's magnificent* Last Supper *(c.1355–60).*

**★ Cappella de' Pazzi**
*Brunelleschi's domed chapel with Classical proportions was begun in 1443. The roundels (c.1442–52) are by Luca della Robbia.*

*For hotels and restaurants in this region see pp576–8 and pp626–8*

## VISITORS' CHECKLIST

Piazza di Santa Croce. **Map** 4 E1 (6 F4). ***Tel*** *055 246 61 05.* C, 23. **Basilica** *9:30am–5:30pm daily (from 1pm Sun). Ticket office closes at 5pm.* *during mass.* *(includes visit to the Museo.)* **Museo, Cloister & Cappella de' Pazzi** *as above.* *1 Jan, 25 Dec.* *(includes visit to the Basilica.)*

**The Neo-Gothic campanile** was added in 1842, after the original was destroyed in 1512 by lightning.

**The Cappella Baroncelli**, frescoed by Taddeo Gaddi between 1332 and 1338, contains the first true night scene in Western art.

**Sacristy**

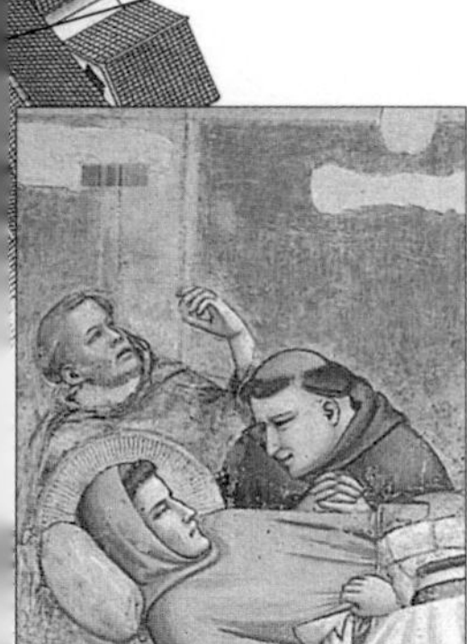

**★ Cappella Bardi Frescoes**
*Giotto frescoed the Bardi and Peruzzi chapels to the right of the high altar between 1315 and 1330. This touching scene from the left-hand wall of the chapel shows* The Death of St Francis *(1317).*

## STAR FEATURES

★ Cappella de' Pazzi

★ Cappella Bardi Frescoes

# Museo Galileo ⓫

Piazza de' Giudici 1. **Map** 4 D1 (6 E4). ***Tel*** *055 26 53 11.* *9:30am–6:30pm Mon–Sat (to 1pm Tue & Sat), 10am–6pm Sun & public hols.* *1 & 6 Jan, 1 May, 8, 25 & 26 Dec.*

This lively and superbly presented museum devotes two floors to various scientific themes, illustrating each with countless fine displays and a panoply of old and beautifully made scientific instruments. It is also something of a shrine to the Pisa-born scientist Galileo Galilei (1564–1642), and features two of his telescopes, as well as large-scale reconstructions of his experiments into motion, velocity and acceleration. These are sometimes demonstrated by the attendants. Other exhibits come from the Accademia del Cimento (Academy for Experimentation), founded in 1657 by Grand Duke Ferdinand II in memory of Galileo.

Some rooms are devoted to astronomical, mathematical and navigational instruments, with galleries concentrating on Galileo, telescopes and optical games. Some of the best exhibits are early maps, globes and astrolabes, the antique microscopes, thermometers and barometers. There are also some fine old clocks, mathematical instruments, calculators, a horrifying collection of 19th-century surgical instruments, and some graphic anatomical models. The museum has installed a large bronze sundial that can be used to read the hour and the date.

**Astrolabe, Museo Galileo**

# Ponte Vecchio ⓬

**Map** 4 D1 (6 E4).

Ponte Vecchio, the oldest surviving bridge in the city, was built in 1345, the last in a succession of bridges and fords on the site that dated back to Roman times. Designed by Giotto's pupil Taddeo Gaddi, it was originally the domain of blacksmiths, butchers and tanners (who used the river for disposing of waste). They were reviled for their noise and stench and were evicted in 1593 by Duke Ferdinando I – replaced by jewellers and goldsmiths. The elevated Corridoio Vasariano runs along the eastern side of the bridge, above the shops. Giorgio Vasari designed the corridor in 1565 to allow the Medici family to move about their residences without having to mix with the public. This was the city's only bridge to escape destruction during World War II and visitors today come as much to admire the views as to browse among the antique shops and specialized jewellery shops. A bust of the famous goldsmith Benvenuto Cellini stands in the middle of the bridge.

**Ponte Vecchio viewed from the Ponte Santa Trinità**

# Uffizi ⓭

The Uffizi, Italy's greatest art gallery, was built in 1560–80 to house offices *(uffici)* for Duke Cosimo I. The architect Vasari used iron as reinforcement, enabling his successor, Buontalenti, to create an almost continuous wall of glass on the upper storey. This was used as a gallery for Francesco I to display the Medici art treasures. In the 19th century the gallery's ancient objects were moved to the archaeological museum and sculpture to the Bargello, leaving a priceless collection of paintings. There are plans to double the entire exhibition space by 2013.

Main staircase

Entrance hall

Entrance

**Bacchus** *(c.1589)*
*Caravaggio's early work depicting the god of wine can be found in the first floor exhibition rooms. The mood of dissipation is echoed in the foreground in the decaying fruit.*

**Corridor ceilings** are frescoed with 1580s "grotesques" inspired by Roman grottoes.

Buontalenti staircase

**Annunciation** *(1333)*
*The Sienese painter Simone Martini was strongly influenced by French Gothic art, and this is one of his masterpieces. The two saints are by Martini's pupil and brother-in-law, Lippo Memmi.*

## GALLERY GUIDE

*Ancient Greek and Roman sculptures are in the second floor corridor around the inner side of the horseshoe-shaped building. The paintings are hung in a series of rooms off the main corridor, in chronological order, to show the development of Florentine art from Gothic to Renaissance and beyond. Many well-known paintings are in rooms 7–18. Due to planned building work until 2012–13 there may be disruptions, such as room closures, artworks moved and changes to opening times.*

**Ognissanti Madonna** *(c.1310)*
*Giotto's grasp of spatial depth and substance in this altarpiece was a milestone in the mastery of perspective.*

### KEY TO FLOORPLAN

- East Corridor
- West Corridor
- Arno Corridor
- Gallery rooms 1–45
- Non-exhibition space

*For hotels and restaurants in this region see pp576–8 and pp626–9*

**The Duke and Duchess of Urbino** *(c.1465–70)*
*Piero della Francesca's portraits of Federico da Montefeltro and his wife Battista Sforza were painted after Battista died aged 26. Her portrait was probably based on her death mask.*

### VISITORS' CHECKLIST

Loggiata degli Uffizi 6. **Map** 4 D1 (6 D4). ***Tel*** *055 238 86 51 (info); 055 29 48 83 (reservations; book in advance to avoid the queues)* B, 23. *8:15am–6:50pm Tue–Sun (occasional extended hours in summer). Last adm: 45 mins before closing.* *1 Jan, 1 May, 25 Dec.* **www**.uffizi.firenze.it

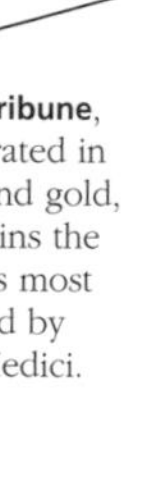

**The Tribune**, decorated in red and gold, contains the works most valued by the Medici.

**The Birth of Venus** *(c.1485)*
*Botticelli shows the goddess of love flanked by Zephyrus, god of the west wind, who blows the risen Venus to shore on a half-shell. The myth may symbolize the birth of beauty through the divine fertilization of matter.*

**The Holy Family** *(1507)*
*Michelangelo's painting, the first to break with the convention of showing Christ on the Virgin's lap, inspired Mannerist artists through its expressive handling of colour and posture.*

**Vasari's Classical Arno façade (begun 1560)**

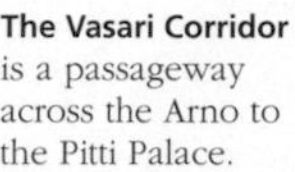

**The Vasari Corridor** is a passageway across the Arno to the Pitti Palace.

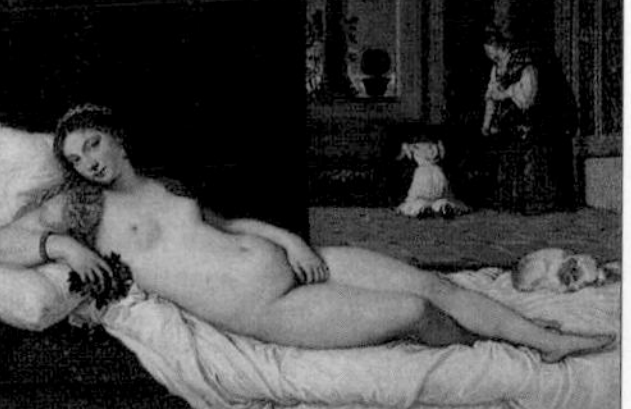

**The Venus of Urbino** *(1538)*
*Titian's sensuous nude, inspired by Giorgione's* Sleeping Venus, *may in fact be a portrait of a courtesan deemed sufficiently beautiful to represent a goddess.*

# Exploring the Uffizi

The Uffizi offers not only the chance to see the world's greatest collection of Italian Renaissance paintings, but also the opportunity to enjoy masterpieces from as far afield as Holland, Spain and Germany. Accumulated over the centuries by the Medici, the collection was first housed in the Uffizi in 1581, and eventually bequeathed to the Florentine people by Anna Maria Lodovica, the last of the Medici.

**_Madonna and Child with Angels_ (1455–66) by Fra Filippo Lippi**

## GOTHIC ART

Past the statues and antiquities of room 1, the Uffizi proper opens in style with three altarpieces of the *Maestà,* or Madonna Enthroned, by Giotto, Duccio and Cimabue, some of Italy's greatest 13th-century painters. Each work marks a stage in the development of Italian painting away from the stilted conventions of Byzantium to the livelier traditions of Gothic and Renaissance art. The shift is best expressed in Giotto's version of the subject (known as the *Ognissanti Madonna*), where new feeling for depth and naturalistic detail is shown in the range of emotion displayed by the saints and angels, and by the carefully evoked three-dimensionality of the Virgin's throne.

Giotto's naturalistic influence can also be seen among the paintings of room 4, which is devoted to the 14th-century Florentine School, an interesting counterpoint to the Sienese paintings of Duccio and his followers in room 3. Among the many fine paintings here are works by Ambrogio and Pietro Lorenzetti, and Simone Martini's *Annunciation*.

Room 6 is devoted to International Gothic, a highly decorative style that represented the height of Gothic expression. It is exemplified by Gentile da Fabriano's exquisite, glittering *Adoration of the Magi* painted in 1423.

## EARLY RENAISSANCE

A new understanding of geometry and perspective during the 15th century increasingly allowed artists to explore the complexities of space and depth. None became more obsessed with these new compositional possibilities than Paolo Uccello (1397–1475), whose picture of *The Battle of San Romano* (1456) in room 7 is one of the gallery's most fevered creations.

Room 7 also contains two panels from 1460 by Piero della Francesca, another artist preoccupied with the art of perspective. The panels, which are among the earliest Renaissance portraits, depict the Duke and Duchess of Urbino on one side and representations of their virtues on the other.

While such works can seem coldly experimental, Fra Filippo Lippi's *Madonna and Child with Angels* (1455–66), in room 8, is a masterpiece of warmth and humanity. Like

**Sandro Botticelli's allegorical painting, _Primavera_ (1480)**

many Renaissance artists, Lippi uses a religious subject to celebrate earthly delights such as landscape and feminine beauty. A similar approach is apparent in the works of Botticelli, whose famous paintings in rooms 10–14 are for many the highlight of the gallery. In *The Birth of Venus,* for example, Venus takes the place of the Virgin, expressing a fascination with Classical mythology common to many Renaissance artists. The same is true of the *Primavera* (1480), which breaks with Christian religious painting by illustrating a pagan rite of spring.

**Detail from *The Annunciation* (1472–5) by Leonardo da Vinci**

## HIGH RENAISSANCE AND MANNERISM

Room 15 features works attributed to the young Leonardo da Vinci, notably a sublime *Annunciation* (1472–5), which reveals hints of his still emerging style, and the *Adoration of the Magi* (1481), which remained unfinished when he left Florence for Milan to paint *The Last Supper* (1495–8).

Room 18, better known as the Tribune, was designed in 1584 by Buontalenti in order to accommodate the best-loved pieces of the Medici collection. Its most famous work is the so-called Medici Venus (1st century BC), a Roman copy of a Greek statue deemed to be the most erotic in the ancient world. The copy proved equally salacious and was removed from Rome's Villa Medici by Cosimo III to keep it from corrupting the city's art students. Other highlights in room 18 include Agnolo Bronzino's portraits of *Cosimo I* and *Eleonora di Toledo*, both painted around 1545, and Pontormo's *Charity* (1530) and the portrait of *Cosimo il Vecchio* (1517).

Rooms 19 to 23 depart from the gallery's Florentine bias, demonstrating how rapidly Renaissance ideas and techniques spread beyond Tuscany. Painters from the German and Flemish schools are well represented, together with painters from Umbria like Perugino, but perhaps the most captivating works are the paintings by Venetian and northern Italian artists such as Mantegna, Carpaccio, Correggio and Bellini.

Room 25, which returns to the Tuscan mainstream, is dominated by Michelangelo's *Holy Family* or Doni Tondo (1456), notable for its vibrant colours and the Virgin's unusually twisted pose. The gallery's only work by Michelangelo, it was to prove immensely influential with the next generation of painters, especially Bronzino (1503–72), Pontormo (1494–1556) and Parmigianino (1503–40). The last of these was responsible for the *Madonna of the Long Neck* (c.1534) in room 29. With its contorted anatomy, unnatural colours and strange composition, this painting is a masterpiece of the style that came to be called Mannerism. Earlier, but no less remarkable masterpieces in rooms 26 and 28 include Raphael's sublime *Madonna of the Goldfinch* (1506) and Titian's notorious *Venus of Urbino* (1538), censured by Mark Twain as the "foulest, the vilest, the obscenest picture the world possesses". Others hold it to be one of the most beautiful nudes ever painted.

***Madonna of the Goldfinch* (1506) by Raphael**

***Madonna of the Long Neck* (c.1534) by Parmigianino**

## LATER PAINTINGS

Visitors, already sated by a surfeit of outstanding paintings, are often tempted to skim through the Uffizi's final rooms. The paintings in rooms 30 to 35 – which are mainly from the Veneto and Emilia-Romagna – are mostly unexceptional, but the gallery's last rooms (41–45) contain important paintings. Rooms 41 and 42 have works by Rubens and Van Dyck. Room 44, dedicated to Rembrandt and northern European painting, features Rembrandt's *Portrait of an Old Man* (1665) and two self-portraits of the artist as a young and old man (painted in 1634 and 1664, respectively). Rooms on the first floor hold works by Caravaggio. These include *Medusa* (1596–8), painted for a Roman cardinal; *Bacchus* (c.1589), one of the artist's earliest works; and the *Sacrifice of Isaac* (c.1590), whose violent subject is belied by the painting's gentle background landscape. These rooms also hold works by Guido Reni.

# Piazza della Signoria ⓮

Savonarola (1452–98)

Piazza della Signoria and Palazzo Vecchio have been at the heart of Florence's political and social life for centuries. The great bell once used to summon citizens to *parlamento* (public meetings) here, and the square has long been a popular promenade for both visitors and Florentines. The piazza's statues (some are copies) commemorate the city's major historical events, though its most famous episode is celebrated by a simple pavement plaque near the loggia: the execution of the religious leader Girolamo Savonarola who was burnt at the stake.

**David**
*This copy of the famous Michelangelo statue symbolizes triumph over tyranny. The original* (see p275) *stood in the piazza until 1873.*

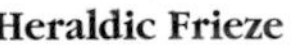

**Heraldic Frieze**
*The crossed keys on this shield represent Medici papal rule.*

**Salone dei Cinquecento** *(1495)*
*This vast chamber contains a statue of Victory by Michelangelo and frescoes by Vasari describing Florentine triumphs over Pisa and Siena.*

**Sala dei Gigli**

**Fontana di Nettuno**, Ammannati's fountain (1575) of the Roman sea god surrounded by water nymphs commemorates Tuscan naval victories.

**The Marzocco** is a copy of the heraldi lion of Florence carved by Donatell in 1420. The origin is in the Bargello *(see p283).*

★ **Palazzo Vecchio** *(completed 1332)*
*This Republican frieze over the palace entrance is inscribed with the words, "Christ is King", implying that no mortal ruler has absolute power.*

★ **The Rape of the Sabine Women by Giambologna**
*(1583) The writhing figures in Giambologna's famous statue were carved from a single block of flawed marble.*

**The Uffizi**

**The Loggia dei Lanzi**
(1382), designed by Orcagna, is named after the Lancers, the bodyguards of Cosimo I who were billeted here.

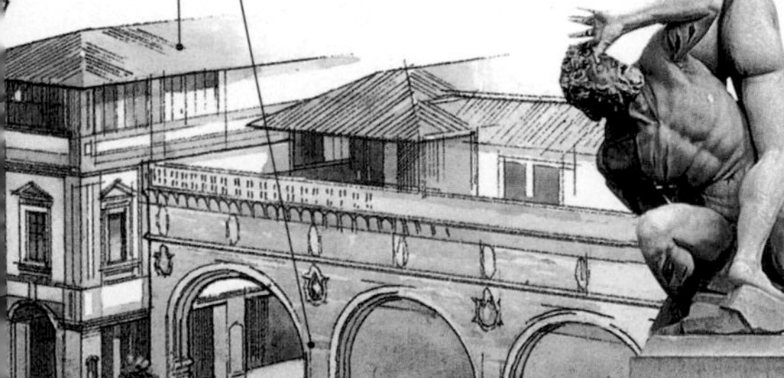

**Roman statues**, possibly of emperors, line the Loggia.

★ **Perseus by Cellini**
*This bronze statue (1554) of Perseus beheading Medusa was intended to warn Cosimo I's enemies of their probable fate.*

**STAR FEATURES**

★ Palazzo Vecchio

★ The Rape of the Sabine Women by Giambologna

★ Perseus by Cellini

## Palazzo Vecchio ⓯

Piazza della Signoria (entrance on via della Ninna). **Map** 4 D1 (6 D3). ***Tel*** *055 276 82 24.* *A, B.* *9am–7pm daily (to 2pm Thu). Last adm: 1 hour before closing.* *1 Jan, Easter, 1 May, 15 Aug, 25 Dec.* ***Secret Itineraries & Children's Museum*** *(by reservation only).* ***Tel*** *055 276 82 24.*

The "Old Palace" still fulfils its original role as town hall. It was completed in 1322 when a huge bell, used to call citizens to meetings or warn of fire, flood or enemy attack, was hauled to the top of the imposing bell tower. While retaining much of its medieval appearance, the interior was remodelled for Duke Cosimo I in 1540. The redecoration was undertaken by Vasari, who incorporated bombastic frescoes (1563–5) of Florentine achievements. Michelangelo's *Victory* statue (1525) graces the Salone dei Cinquecento, which also has a tiny study decorated by Florence's leading Mannerist painters in 1569–1573. Other highlights include the Cappella di Eleonora, painted by Bronzino (1540–45); the loggia, with its views over the city; the Sala dei Gigli (Room of Lilies) with Donatello's *Judith and Holofernes* (c.1455) and frescoes of Roman heroes by Ghirlandaio (1485); as well as the museum for children and the secret rooms and passageways.

**A copy of Verrocchio's Putto fountain in Vasari's courtyard**

# Street-by-Street: Around Piazza della Repubblica

Underlying the street plan of modern Florence is the far older pattern of the ancient Roman city. Nowhere is this more evident than in the grid of narrow streets around Piazza della Repubblica, site of the old Roman forum. This pivotal square housed the city's main food market until the 1860s, when redevelopment tidied up the area, and added the triumphal arch that now stands in today's café-filled square.

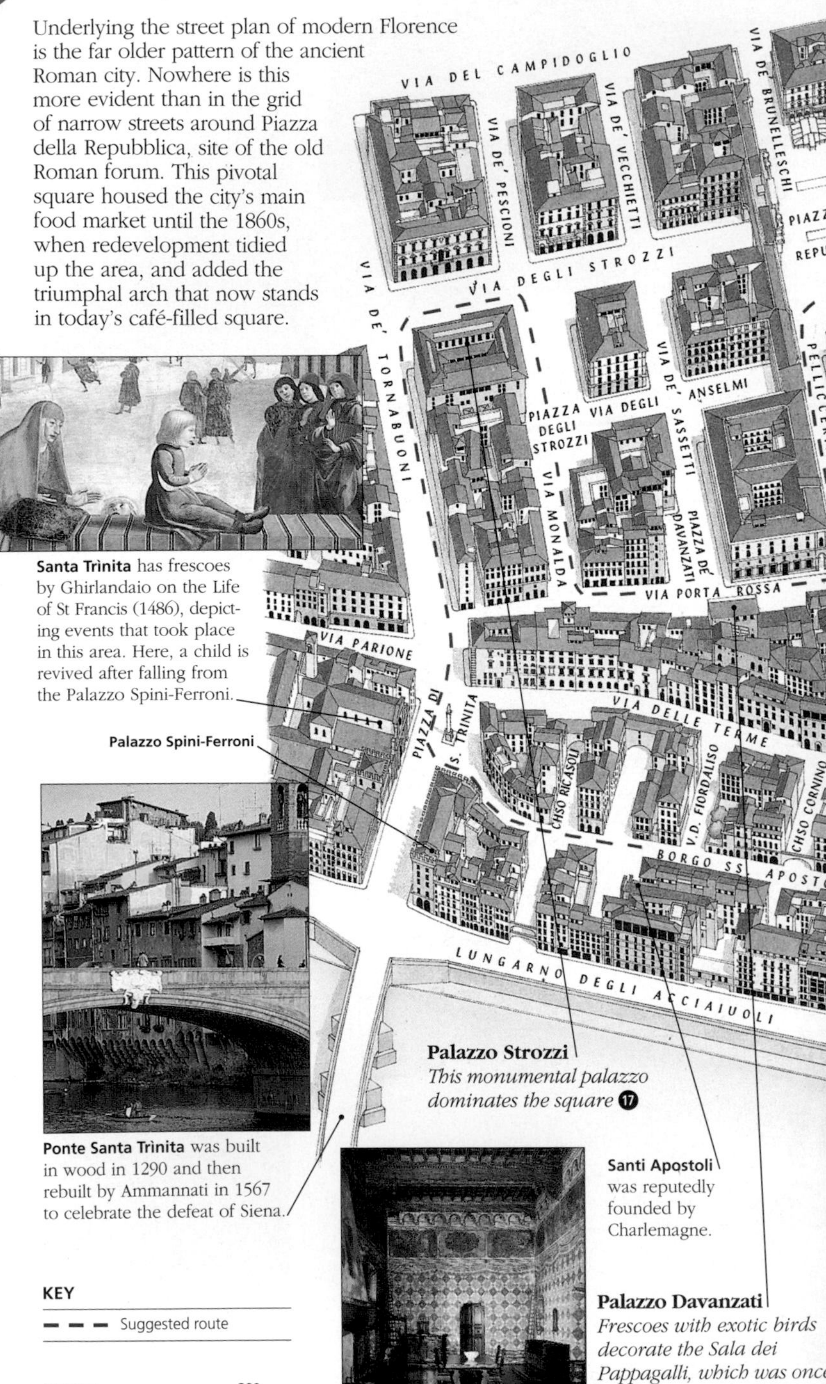


**Santa Trìnita** has frescoes by Ghirlandaio on the Life of St Francis (1486), depicting events that took place in this area. Here, a child is revived after falling from the Palazzo Spini-Ferroni.

**Palazzo Spini-Ferroni**

**Ponte Santa Trìnita** was built in wood in 1290 and then rebuilt by Ammannati in 1567 to celebrate the defeat of Siena.

**Palazzo Strozzi**
*This monumental palazzo dominates the square* ⓱

**Santi Apostoli** was reputedly founded by Charlemagne.

**Palazzo Davanzati**
*Frescoes with exotic birds decorate the Sala dei Pappagalli, which was once the dining room of this 14th-century palazzo* ⓰

**KEY**

— — — Suggested route

0 metres 200

0 yards 200

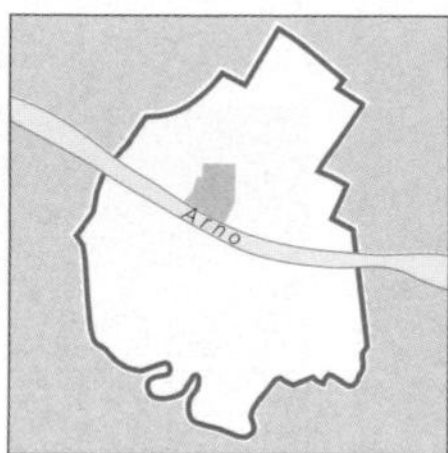


**LOCATOR MAP**
*See Florence Street Finder maps 5, 6*

**Piazza della Repubblica**, which dates from the 19th century, is lined by some of Florence's oldest and best known cafés.

**Mercato Nuovo**, the "New Market" (1547), now deals mainly in souvenirs.

**Palazzo di Parte Guelfa** was the headquarters of the Guelphs, the dominant political party of medieval Florence.

**Ponte Vecchio**
*(See p285)*

VIA POR SANTA MARIA

**Detail of a frieze illustrating a medieval romance in Palazzo Davanzati**

## Palazzo Davanzati ⑯

Via Porta Rossa 13. **Map** 3 C1 (5 C3). ***Tel*** *055 238 86 10.* *8:15am–1:50pm daily.* *1st, 3rd & 5th Mon and 2nd and 4th Sun of the month.* *10am, 11am, noon (2nd floor only).*

This wonderful museum, also known as the Museo dell'Antica Casa Fiorentina, uses original fittings and furniture to recreate a typical well-to-do 14th-century town house. Among the highlights are the Salone Madornale, where large gatherings would have been held, and the Sala dei Pappagalli (Parrots Room), with its frescoes and rich tapestries.

Pelting holes in the vaulted ceiling of the entrance courtyard were for dropping missiles on unwanted visitors. In one corner of the inner courtyard is a well and a pulley system to raise pails of water to each floor – a real luxury since most medieval households had to fetch water from a public fountain.

## Palazzo Strozzi ⑰

Piazza degli Strozzi. **Map** 3 C1 (5 C3). ***Tel*** *055 264 51 55.* *for exhibitions.* **www**.palazzostrozzi.org

Sheer size accounts for the impact of the Palazzo Strozzi, and although it is only three storeys high, each floor exceeds the height of a normal palazzo. It was commissioned by the wealthy banker Filippo Strozzi, who had 15 buildings demolished to make way for the palazzo. He hoped it would rival the Medici palaces elsewhere in the city. Strozzi died in 1491, just two years after the first stone was laid.

Work on the building continued until 1536, with three major architects contributing to its design – Giuliano da Sangallo, Benedetto da Maiano and Simone del Pollaiuolo (also known as Cronaca). The exterior, built of huge rusticated masonry blocks, remains unspoiled. Look out for the original Renaissance torch-holders, lamps and the rings for tethering horses that still adorn the corners and façades. The palace is now primarily used as an exhibition venue. During exhibitions, visitors can also access "La Strozzina", a vaulted gallery space in the basement, where small temporary exhibitions are held.

**Exterior of Palazzo Strozzi, with masonry block rustication**

# San Lorenzo 18

San Lorenzo was the parish church of the Medici family, and in 1419 Brunelleschi was commissioned to rebuild it in the Classical style of the Renaissance. Almost a century later Michelangelo submitted some plans for the façade, and began work on the Medici tombs in the Sagrestia Nuova. He also designed a library, the Biblioteca Mediceo-Laurenziana, to house the family's collection of manuscripts. The lavish family mausoleum, the Cappella dei Principi, was started in 1604.

**Cappella dei Principi**
*The Medici mausoleum, behind the high altar, was begun in 1604 by Matteo Nigetti, and forms part of the Cappelle Medicee.*

**The huge dome** by Buontalenti echoes that of the Duomo *(see pp280–82).*

**The Old Sacristy** was designed by Brunelleschi and decorated by Donatello.

**Campanile**

**Biblioteca Staircase**
*Michelangelo's Mannerist staircase, one of the artist's most innovative designs, was built by Ammannati in 1559.*

**Michelangelo** designed the desks and ceiling of the Biblioteca, where exhibitions of Medici manuscripts are often held.

**The cloister garden** is planted with box hedges, pomegranate and orange trees.

**The Martyrdom of St Lawrence**
*Bronzino's vast Mannerist fresco of 1569 is a bravura, choreographed study of the human form, rather than a reverential response to the agony of the saint.*

**Entrance to church**

**VISITORS' CHECKLIST**

P. San Lorenzo. **Map** 1 C5 (6 D1). *7, 10, 11, 25, 31, 32.* **Basilica** ***Tel*** *055 21 40 42.* *10am–5:30pm Mon–Sat (Mar–Oct: also Sun pm).* **Biblioteca** ***Tel*** *055 21 07 60.* *only to scholars.*

**A simple stone** slab marks the unostentatious grave of Cosimo il Vecchio (1389–1464), founder of the Medici dynasty.

**The Cappelle Medicee** complex comprises the Cappella dei Principi and its crypt, the Sagrestia Nuova *(see p295)*.

**Pulpits by Donatello**
*The bronze pulpits in the nave were Donatello's last works. Completed by his pupils in 1460, the reliefs capture the flinching pain of Christ's Passion and the glory of the Resurrection.*

**St Joseph and Christ in the Workshop**, a striking work showing the young Christ with his father, is by Pietro Annigoni (1910–88), one of the few modern artists whose work is seen in Florence.

**Michelangelo** submitted several designs for the façade of San Lorenzo, but it remains unfinished.

***The Tomb of the Duke of Nemours* (1520–34) by Michelangelo in the Cappelle Medicee's New Sacristy**

## Cappelle Medicee ⓳

Piazza di Madonna degli Aldobrandini. **Map** 1 C5 (6 D1). ***Tel*** *055 238 86 02; 055 29 48 83 (reservations).* *many routes.* *8:15am–1:50pm daily. Last adm: 30 mins before closing.* *1st, 3rd, & 5th Sun of each month, 2nd & 4th Mon, 1 Jan, 1 May, 25 Dec.*

The Medici Chapels divide into three distinct areas. Beyond the entrance hall lies a low-vaulted crypt, a suitably subdued space for the brass-railed tombs of many lesser members of the Medici family. From here steps lead to the octagonal **Cappella dei Principi** (Chapel of Princes), a vast family mausoleum begun by Cosimo I in 1604. The ceiling is garishly frescoed and the walls are smothered in huge swathes of semi-precious *pietre dure* (inlaid stone). Spaced around the walls are the tombs of six Medici Grand Dukes. A corridor leads to Michelangelo's **New Sacristy**, designed as a counterpoint to Brunelleschi's Old Sacristy in San Lorenzo. Three groups of statues, all carved by Michelangelo between 1520 and 1534, stand around the walls: that on the near left hand wall is *The Tomb of the Duke of Urbino* (grandson of Lorenzo the Magnificent). Opposite is *The Tomb of the Duke of Nemours* (Lorenzo's third son). Close to the unfinished *Madonna and Child* (1521) is the simple tomb containing Lorenzo the Magnificent and his murdered brother, Giuliano (died 1478).

## Mercato Centrale ⓴

Piazza del Mercato Centrale. **Map** 1 C4 (5 C1). *7am–2pm Mon–Sat.*

At the heart of the San Lorenzo street market is the bustling Mercato Centrale, Florence's busiest food market. It is housed in a vast two-storey building of cast-iron and glass, built in 1874 by Giuseppe Mengoni.

The ground floor stalls sell meat, poultry, fish, hams, cheeses and olive oils. There are also Tuscan takeaway foods such as *porchetta* (roast suckling pig), *lampredotto* (pig's intestines) and *trippa* (tripe). Fresh fruit, vegetables and flowers are sold on the top floor: look out for wild mushrooms and truffles in the autumn, and broad beans and baby artichokes in early spring.

**Yellow courgette flowers and other vegetables in the Mercato Centrale**

# Santa Maria Novella ㉑

The Church of Santa Maria Novella was built by the Dominicans between 1279 and 1357. The lower Romanesque part of its façade was incorporated into one based on Classical proportions by the pioneering Renaissance architect Leon Battista Alberti in 1456–70. The Gothic interior contains superb frescoes, including Masaccio's powerful *Trinity*. The famous Green Cloister, frescoed with perspective scenes by Paolo Uccello, and the dramatically decorated Spanish Chapel now form a museum.

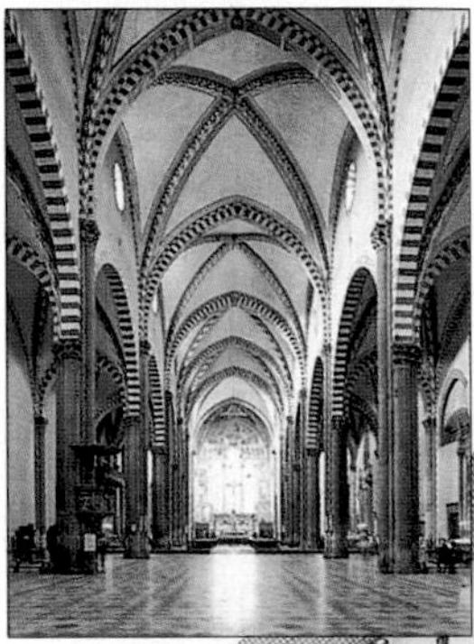

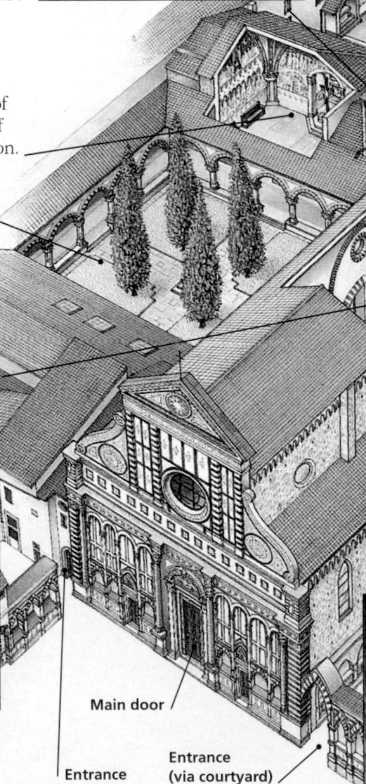

**The arcade arches** are emphasized by grey and white banding.

**Monastic buildings**

**The Nave**

*The piers of the nave are spaced closer together at the altar end. This trick of perspective creates the illusion of an exceptionally long church.*

**Cappellone degli Spagnuoli**, the chapel used by the Spanish courtiers of Eleonora of Toledo, has frescoes of salvation and damnation.

**Chiostro Verde** takes its name from the green base used in Uccello's frescoes, which were sadly damaged by the 1966 floods.

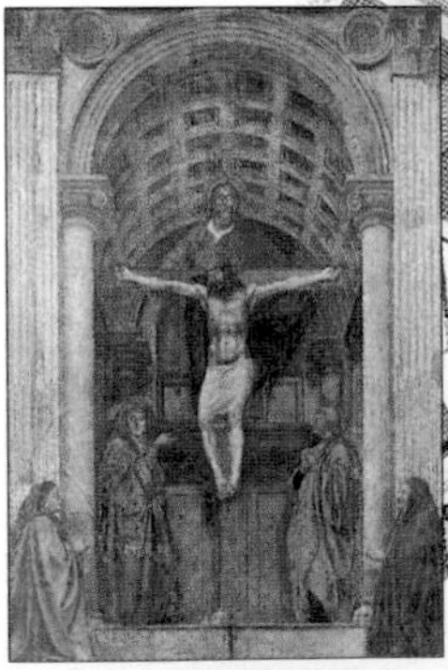

**Trinity by Masaccio**

*This pioneering fresco (c.1428) is renowned as a masterpiece of perspective and portraiture. The kneeling figures flanking the arch are the painting's sponsors, judge Lorenzo Lenzi and his wife.*

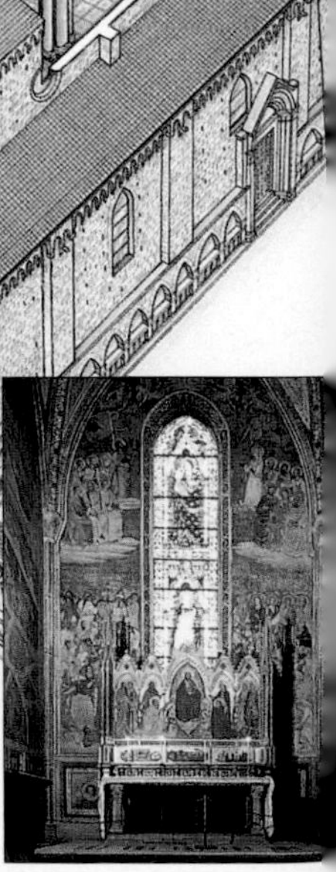

**Main door**

**Entrance to museum**

**Entrance (via courtyard)**

**Cappella Strozzi**

*The 14th-century frescoes by Nardo di Cione and his brother Andrea Orcagna were inspired by Dante's epic poem,* The Divine Comedy.

**VISITORS' CHECKLIST**

Piazza di Santa Maria Novella. **Map** 1 B5 (5 B1). *A, 11, 12, 36, 37.* **Church** ***Tel*** *055 28 21 87.* *9am–5pm daily (from 11am Fri, from 1pm Sun).* **Museo** ***Tel*** *055 28 21 87.* *9am–5pm Mon–Thu & Sat, 9am–2pm Sun. Last adm: 30 mins before closing.* *1 Jan, Easter, 1 May, 15 Aug, 8 & 25 Dec.*

**The Strozzi Tomb** is by Benedetto da Maiano (1493).

**Cappella di Filippo Strozzi** features Filippino Lippi's frescoes of St John raising Drusiana from the dead and St Philip slaying a dragon.

**Cappella Tornabuoni**
*Ghirlandaio's famous fresco cycle,* The Life of John the Baptist *(1485), peoples the biblical episodes with Florentine aristocrats in contemporary dress.*

**Ghirlandaio's *Madonna della Misericordia* (1472) in Ognissanti**

## Palazzo Antinori ㉒

Via de' Tornabuoni. **Map** 1 C5 (5 C2). *to the public.* **Cantinetta Antinori** ***Tel*** *055 29 22 34.* *12:30–2:30pm, 7–10:30pm Mon–Fri.*

Palazzo Antinori was built in 1461–6 and is one of the finest small Renaissance palazzi in Florence. It was acquired by the Antinoris in 1506 and has remained with the family ever since. The dynasty produces a range of wines, oils and liqueurs that can be sampled – along with fine Tuscan dishes – in the Cantinetta Antinori, the wine bar off the main courtyard.

## Palazzo Rucellai ㉓

Via della Vigna Nuova 16. **Map** 1 C5 (5 B2). *to the public.*

Built in 1446–51, this is one of the most ornate Renaissance palaces in the city. It was commissioned by Giovanni Rucellai, whose enormous wealth derived from the import of a rare and costly red dye made from lichen found only on the Spanish island of Majorca. The precious dye was called *oricello,* from which the name Rucellai is derived. Giovanni commissioned several buildings from the architect Leon Battista Alberti, who designed this palace as a virtual textbook illustration of the major Classical orders. The palazzo used to house the Museo Alinari but the collection has now moved to Piazza Santa Maria Novella.

## Museo Nazionale Alinari della Fotografia ㉔

Piazza Santa Maria Novella 14a. **Map** 1 B5 (5 B2). ***Tel*** *055 21 63 10.* *10am–7pm Thu–Tue.* **www**.mnaf.it

The Alinari brothers began taking pictures of Florence in the 1840s. They supplied high-quality postcards and prints to visitors to Florence in the 19th century. The exhibits offer a vivid insight into the social history of Florence at that time. The museum also houses a collection of cameras, documents and objects that illustrate the history of photography.

## Ognissanti ㉕

Borgo Ognissanti 42. **Map** 1 B5 (5 A2). ***Tel*** *055 239 87 00.* *7:45am–12:30pm, 4–6pm Mon–Sat.* *first and last Mon of each month.*

Ognissanti, or All Saints, was the parish church of the Vespucci, one of whose members, the 15th-century navigator Amerigo, gave his name to the New World. The young Amerigo is depicted in Ghirlandaio's fresco of the *Madonna della Misericordia* (1472) in the second chapel on the right between the Virgin and the man in the red cloak.

Ognissanti is also the burial place of Sandro Botticelli. His fresco of *St Augustine* (1480) can be seen on the south wall.

# Cappella Brancacci 26

The Church of Santa Maria del Carmine is famous for the Brancacci Chapel, which contains frescoes on *The Life of St Peter* commissioned by the Florentine merchant Felice Brancacci around 1424. Although the paintings were begun by Masolino in 1425, many of the scenes are by his pupil, Masaccio (who died before completing the cycle) and by Filippino Lippi, who completed the work in 1480. Masaccio's revolutionary use of perspective, his narrative drama and the tragic realism of his figures placed him in the vanguard of Renaissance painting. Many great artists, including Michelangelo, later visited the chapel to study his pioneering work.

**St Peter Healing the Sick**
*Masaccio's realistic portrayal of cripples and beggars was revolutionary in his time.*

**In every scene**, St Peter is distinguished from the crowds as the figure in the orange cloak.

**The grouping** of stylized figures in Masaccio's frescoes reflects his interest in the sculpture of Donatello.

**Masaccio's simple style** allows us to focus on the figures central to the frescoes without distracting detail.

**Expulsion of Adam and Eve**
*Masaccio's ability to express emotion is well illustrated by his harrowing portrait of Adam and Eve being driven out of the Garden of Eden, their faces wracked by misery, shame and the burden of self-knowledge.*

## KEY TO THE FRESCOES: ARTISTS AND SUBJECTS

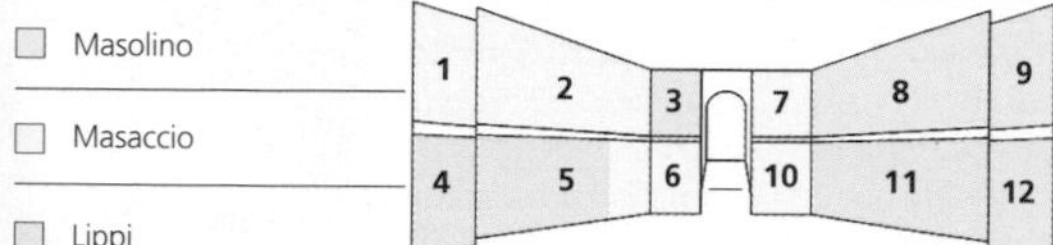


1 Expulsion of Adam and Eve
2 The Tribute Money
3 St Peter Preaching
4 St Peter Visited by St Paul
5 Raising the Emperor's Son; St Peter Enthroned
6 St Peter Healing the Sick
7 St Peter Baptizing the Converts
8 St Peter Healing the Cripple; Raising Tabitha
9 Temptation of Adam and Eve
10 St Peter and St John Giving Alms
11 Crucifixion; Before the Proconsul
12 The Release of St Peter

## VISITORS' CHECKLIST

Piazza del Carmine. **Map** 3 A1 (5 A4). ***Tel*** *055 238 21 95; 055 276 82 24 (reservation required).* *D.* *10am–5pm Mon, Wed–Sat; 1–5pm Sun.* *pub hols.*

**Masolino's *Temptation of Adam and Eve*** is gentle and decorous, in contrast with the emotional force of Masaccio's painting on the opposite wall.

**St Peter** is depicted against a background of Florentine buildings.

**Woman in a Turban**
*The freshness of Masaccio's original colours is seen in this rediscovered roundel, hidden behind the altar for 500 years.*

**Two Figures**
*Masolino's work tends to be more formal, less naturalistic and less animated than that of Masaccio.*

**Before the Proconsul**
*Filippino Lippi was called in to complete the cycle of frescoes in 1480. He added this emotional scene showing the Proconsul sentencing St Peter to death.*

# Street-by-Street: Oltrarno

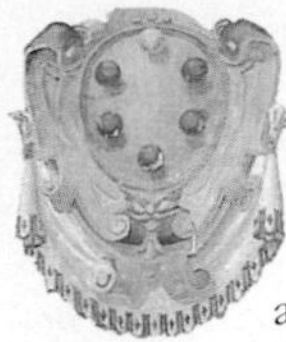

Medici coat of arms

For the most part, the Oltrarno is a homely area of small houses, quiet squares and shops selling antiques, bric-a-brac and foodstuffs. The Via Maggio, a busy thoroughfare, breaks this pattern, but step into the side streets and you escape the bustle to discover a corner of old world Florence. The restaurants serve authentic, reasonably priced food, and the area is full of studios and workshops restoring antique furniture. Among the things to see are Santo Spirito and Palazzo Pitti, one of the city's largest palaces, whose medley of museums contains an art collection second only to that of the Uffizi.

**Santo Spirito**
*Brunelleschi's simple church was completed after the architect's death* ㉗

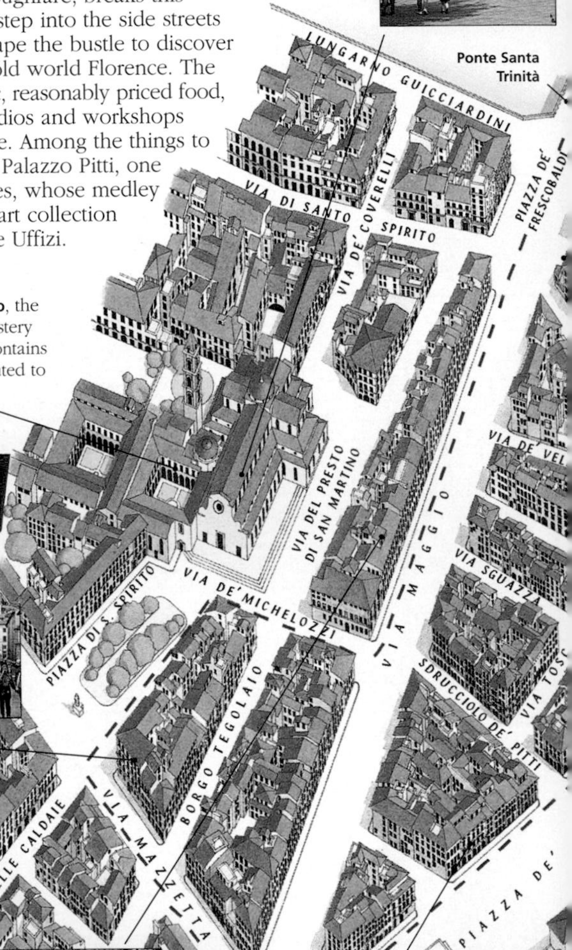

**Cenacolo di Santo Spirito**, the old refectory of a monastery that once stood here, contains a dramatic fresco attributed to Orcagna (c.1360).

**Palazzo Guadagni** (1500) was the first in the city to be built with a roof-top loggia, setting a trend among the aristocracy.

**Palazzo di Bianca Cappello** (1579) is covered in ornate *sgraffito* work and was the home of the mistress of Grand Duke Francesco I.

**Masks and murals** are handmade at this shop, Frieze of Papier Mâché.

Ponte Santa Trinità

LUNGARNO GUICCIARDINI
PIAZZA DE' FRESCOBALDI
VIA DI SANTO SPIRITO
VIA DE' COVERELLI
VIA DEL PRESTO DI SAN MARTINO
VIA MAGGIO
VIA DE' VEL
VIA SGUAZZA
VIA DE' MICHELOZZI
PIAZZA DI S. SPIRITO
SDRUCCIOLO DE' PITTI
VIA TOSC
BORGO TEGOLAIO
VIA MAZZETTA
V. DELLE CALDAIE
PIAZZA DE'
PIAZZA DI S. FELICE

*For hotels and restaurants in this region see pp576–8 and pp626–9*

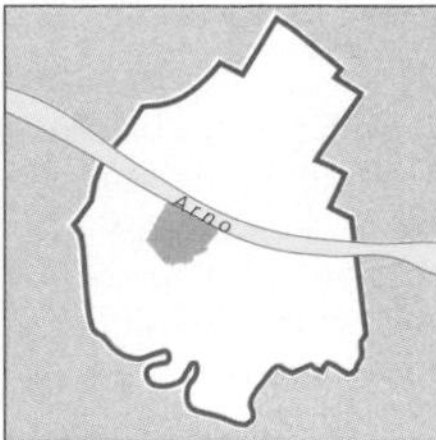

**LOCATOR MAP**
*See Florence Street Finder maps 3, 5*

**The 16th-century fountain** and gargoyle in Piazza de' Frescobaldi were designed by Buontalenti, as was the façade (1593–4) of the nearby church of Santa Trinità.

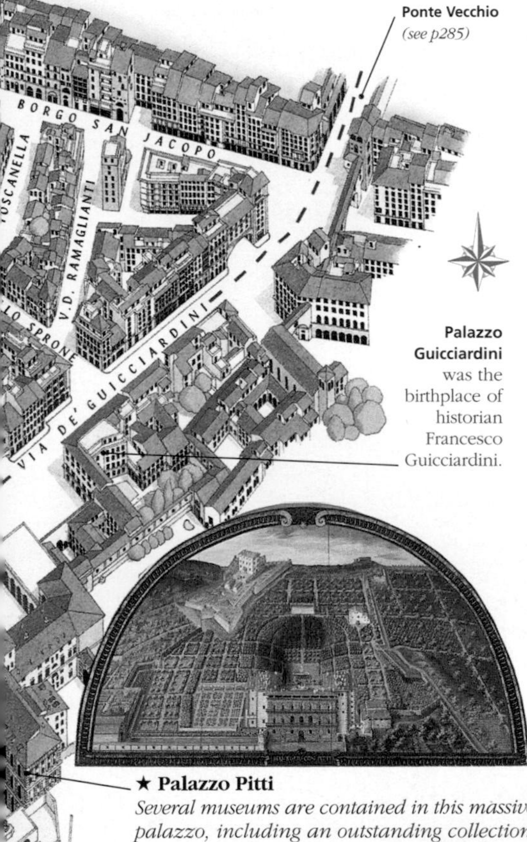


**Ponte Vecchio** *(see p285)*

**Palazzo Guicciardini** was the birthplace of historian Francesco Guicciardini.

**★ Palazzo Pitti**
*Several museums are contained in this massive palazzo, including an outstanding collection of paintings. This painting of Palazzo Pitti was made by Giusto Utens in 1599* ㉘

**KEY**

— — — Suggested route

0 metres 100
0 yards 100

**STAR SIGHT**

★ Palazzo Pitti

## Santo Spirito ㉗

Piazza di Santo Spirito. **Map** 3 B2 (5 B4). D. ***Tel*** *055 21 00 30.* *9:45am–12:30pm, 4–5:30pm Mon–Sat; 4–6:30pm Sun.* *Wed.*

The Augustinian foundation of this church dates from 1250. The present building, dominating the northern end of the pretty Piazza di Santo Spirito, was designed by the architect Brunelleschi in 1435, but not completed until the late 15th century. The unfinished, modest façade was added in the 18th century.

Inside, the harmony of the proportions has been somewhat spoiled by the elaborate Baroque baldacchino and the High Altar, which was finished in 1607 by Giovanni Caccini. The church has 38 side altars, decorated with 15th- and 16th-century Renaissance paintings and sculpture, among them works by Cosimo Rosselli, Domenico Ghirlandaio and Filippino Lippi. The latter painted a magnificent *Madonna and Child* (1466) for the Nerli Chapel in the south transept.

In the north aisle, a door beneath the organ leads to a vestibule with an ornate coffered ceiling. It was designed by Simone del Pollaiuolo, more commonly known as Cronaca, in 1491. The sacristy adjoining the vestibule, in which 12 huge columns are crammed into a tiny space, was designed by Giuliano da Sangallo in 1489.

**Interior of Santo Spirito with colonnaded aisle**

# Palazzo Pitti ㉘

The Palazzo Pitti was originally built for the banker Luca Pitti. The huge scale of the building, begun in 1457 and attributed to Brunelleschi, illustrated Pitti's determination to outrival the Medici family through its display of wealth and power. Ironically, the Medici later purchased the palazzo when building costs bankrupted Pitti's heirs. In 1550 it became the main residence of the Medici, and subsequently all the rulers of the city lived here. Today the richly decorated rooms exhibit countless treasures from the Medici collections.

***The Three Ages of Man* (c.1510), attributed to Giorgione**

## GALLERIA PALATINA

The Palatine Gallery, which forms the heart of the Pitti museum complex, contains countless masterpieces by artists such as Botticelli, Titian, Perugino, Andrea del Sarto, Tintoretto, Veronese, Giorgione and Gentileschi. The works of art, accumulated by the Medici family and the house of Habsburg-Lorraine, are still hung much as the grand dukes wished, regardless of subject or chronology. The gallery consists of 11 main salons, the first five of which are painted with allegorical ceiling frescoes glorifying the Medici. Begun by Pietro da Cortona in 1641, they were completed in 1665 by his pupil Ciro Ferri. Room 1 (Sala di Venere) contains Antonio Canova's statue of the *Venus Italica* (1810), commissioned by Napoleon to replace the *Venus de' Medici* (which was to be taken to Paris). Room 2 (Sala di Apollo) features Titian's *Portrait of a Gentleman* (1540), perhaps the finest of several paintings by the artist in the gallery. Still finer pictures adorn rooms 4 and 5, including some by Perugino, Andrea del Sarto and a host of paintings by Raphael. The most beautiful of the last group are Raphael's High Renaissance *Madonna della Seggiola* or Madonna of the Chair (c.1514–15), and the *Donna Velata* or Veiled Woman (c.1516), whose model was reputedly the artist's mistress. Other paintings in the remaining gallery rooms include Fra Filippo Lippi's lovely *Madonna and Child,* painted in the mid-15th century, and Caravaggio's *The Sleeping Cupid* (1608).

***Judith* (1620–30) by Artemisia Gentileschi**

***Madonna of the Chair* (c.1515) by Raphael**

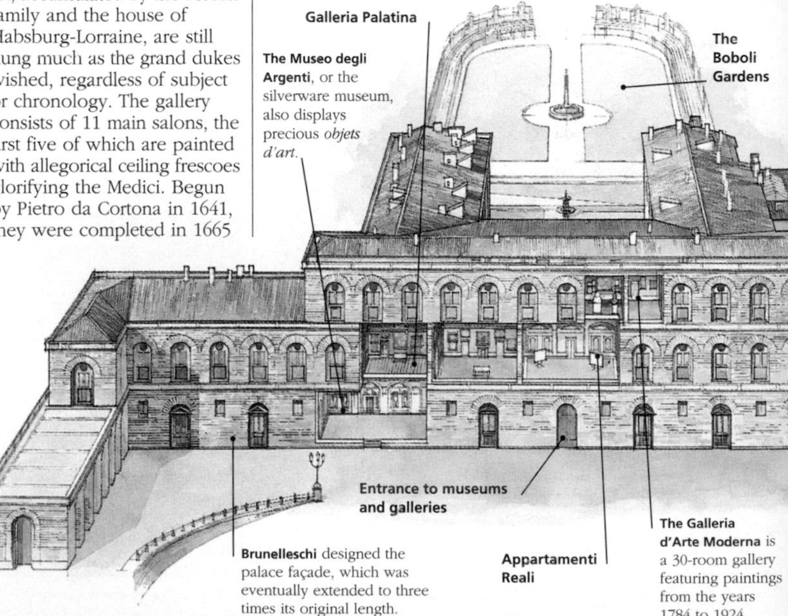

*The Palmieri Rotonda* by Giovanni Fattori (1825–1908)

## APPARTAMENTI REALI

The Royal Apartments on the first floor of the south wing of the palazzo were built in the 17th century. They are decorated with frescoes by various Florentine artists, a series of portraits of the Medici by the Flemish painter Justus Sustermans, who worked at the court between 1619 and 1681, and a group of 18th-century Gobelins tapestries. In the late 18th and early 19th centuries, the apartments were revamped in Neo-Classical style by the Dukes of Lorraine when they succeeded the Medici dynasty as the rulers of Florence.

The apartments are lavishly appointed with ornate gold and white stuccoed ceilings and rich decoration, notably the walls of the Parrot Room, which are covered with an opulent crimson fabric detailed with a bird design. The Tapestry Rooms are hung with 17th- and 18th-century tapestries of French, Belgian and Italian manufacture. The apartments reflect the tastes of three distinct historical periods.

The Throne Room of the Appartamenti Reali

Piazza della Signoria depicted in precious stones

## OTHER COLLECTIONS

The Museo degli Argenti (Silverware Museum) is housed in rooms formerly used by the Medici as summer apartments. The family's lavish taste is reflected in the vast array of precious objects on display. These embrace beautiful examples of Roman glassware, ivory, carpets, crystal, amber, and fine works by Florentine and German goldsmiths. Pride of place goes to 16 *pietre dure* vases (decorated with hard or semi-precious inlaid stones), once owned by Lorenzo the Magnificent.

The Galleria del Costume, which opened in 1983, reflects the changing taste in the courtly fashion of the late 18th century up to the 1920s.

The highlights of the Galleria d'Arte Moderna (Modern Art Gallery) are the wonderful paintings of the *Macchiaioli* (spot-makers), who were a group of Tuscan artists with a style very similar to that of the French Impressionists.

### VISITORS' CHECKLIST

P.za de' Pitti. **Map** 3 C2 (5 B5). *D, 11, 36, 37.* ***Tel*** *055 29 48 83 (info & booking)*
**Galleria Palatina; Royal Apartments** *8:15–6:50 Tue–Sun.* *25 Dec.*
**Boboli Gardens** *8:15–6:30 daily (Mar: to 5:30; Jun–Aug: to 7:30; Nov–Feb: to 4:30).* *1st & last Mon.*
**Other collections** *&* *same as Boboli Gardens.*

## THE BOBOLI GARDENS

A copy of Giambologna's *Oceanus Fountain* (1576)

The Boboli Gardens, a lovely place to escape the rigours of sightseeing, were laid out for the Medici after they bought the Palazzo Pitti in 1549. An excellent example of stylized Renaissance gardening, they were opened to the public in 1766. The more formal parts of the garden, nearest the palazzo, consist of box hedges clipped into symmetrical geometric patterns. These lead to wilder groves of ilex and cypress trees, planted to create a contrast between artifice and nature. Countless statues adorn the gardens, particularly along the Viottolone, an avenue of cypress trees planted in 1637. High above the gardens stands the Forte di Belvedere, designed by Buontalenti in 1590 for the Medici Grand Dukes.

**The Virgin from *The Annunciation* (1528) by Pontormo**

## Santa Felicità ㉙

Piazza di Santa Felicita. **Map** 3 C2 (5 C5). *D.* ***Tel*** *055 21 30 18.* *9am–noon, 3–6pm daily (only am Sun).*

There has been a church on this site since the 4th century. The present structure, begun in the 11th century, was remodelled in 1736–9 by Ferdinando Ruggieri, who retained Vasari's earlier porch (added in 1564) as well as many of the church's original Gothic features.

The Capponi family chapel to the right of the entrance contains two works by Jacopo da Pontormo: *The Deposition* and *The Annunciation* (1525–28). Their strange composition and remarkable colouring make them two of Mannerism's greatest masterpieces.

## Piazzale Michelangelo ㉚

Piazzale Michelangelo. **Map** 4 E3. *12, 13.*

Of all the great Florentine viewpoints – such as the Duomo and Campanile – none offers such a magnificent panorama of the city as Piazzale Michelangelo. Laid out in the 1860s by Giuseppe Poggi, and dotted with copies of Michelangelo's statues, its balconies attract many visitors and the inevitable massed ranks of souvenir sellers. However, this square remains an evocative spot, especially when the sun sets over the Arno and distant Tuscan hills.

## San Miniato al Monte ㉛

Via del Monte alle Croci. **Map** 4 E3. ***Tel*** *055 234 27 31.* *12, 13.* *Apr–Sep: 8am–7pm daily; Oct–Mar: 8am–1pm, 3–7pm daily (only pm Sun).* *public hols.*

San Miniato is one of the most beautiful Romanesque churches in Italy. Begun in 1018, it was built over the shrine of San Miniato (St Minias), a rich Armenian merchant beheaded for his beliefs in the 3rd century. The façade, begun around 1090, has the geometric marble patterning typical of Pisan-Romanesque architecture. The statue on the gable shows an eagle carrying a bale of cloth, the symbol of the powerful Arte di Calimala (guild of wool importers), who financed the church in the Middle Ages. The 13th-century mosaic shows Christ, the Virgin and St Minias. The same protagonists appear in the apse mosaic inside the church, which sits above a crypt supported by columns salvaged from ancient Roman buildings. The floor of the nave is covered with seven mosaic panels of animals and signs of the Zodiac. These mosaics date back to 1207.

**The façade of the church of San Miniato al Monte**

Other highlights include Michelozzo's free-standing Cappella del Crocifisso (1448) and the Renaissance Cappella del Cardinale del Portogallo (1480) with terracotta roundels (1461) on the ceiling by Luca della Robbia. There is a fresco cycle of *Scenes from the Life of St Benedict* by Spinello Aretino in the sacristy, which was completed in 1387.

**Ponte Vecchio and the Arno from the heights of Piazzale Michelangelo**

*For hotels and restaurants in this region see pp576–8 and pp626–9*

# Shopping in Florence

Few cities of comparable size can boast such a profusion and variety of high-quality shops as Florence. As you wander through its medieval streets, you will find all the big names in Italian fashion and jewellery alongside artisan workshops and family-run businesses. The city has translated its reputation as a centre of artistic excellence into a wealth of antiques and fine-art shops. Tuscan tanneries are justifiably renowned, and there is nowhere better than Florence to buy shoes, bags and other leather goods. Those searching for unusual gifts and souvenirs – from handmade stationery to delicious foodstuffs – will also be spoiled for choice.

## WHERE TO SHOP

The centre of Florence is packed with all sorts of shops, from fashion designer flagships to second-hand bookstores. The tiny jewellery shops on the Ponte Vecchio sell both antique items and high-quality new gold pieces. Antiques shops are mostly clustered around Via dei Fossi, Via dei Serragli and Via Maggio. The best bargains can be found in the January and July sales.

## CLOTHING

Most Italian designer names – **Gucci**, **Armani**, **Versace** and **Prada**, for example – are in Via de' Tornabuoni, which is also home to the French designer **Yves Saint-Laurent**. Opposite Palazzo Strozzi is **Louis Vuitton**, with its collections of footware, clothing and luggage. **Dolce & Gabbana** is nearby, as is **Patrizia Peppe**, while **Valentino** is in Via dei Tosinghi. **La Perla**, specializing in sophisticated lingerie, is in Via della Vigna Nuova, but more affordable styles can be found at **Intimissimi**.

Most department stores sell clothing. For mid-range fashion, try **Coin**. The more upmarket **La Rinascente** has designer clothing, lingerie and a great rooftop bar.

For discounts on designer fashion, visit **The Mall** or **Barberino Designer Outlet**, both about 30 minutes away from Florence.

There are fine silks and hand-woven fabrics at **Casa dei Tessuti**.

## SHOES AND LEATHER GOODS

The main meccas for fans of designer Italian shoes are **Ferragamo**, **Gucci** and **Prada**. For more classic styles, head to **Quercioli**, which stocks handmade leather footwear. The mid-priced range is well represented by **Peppe Peluso** and the chain store **Bata**.

The streets around Piazza di Santa Croce are filled with leather shops. Inside the cloisters of the church itself is the **Scuola del Cuoio**, where customers can watch the leather craftsmen at work.

Classic leather bags are sold at **Il Bisonte** and **Beltrami**; for more contemporary styles head to **Coccinelle** and **Furla**.

Bound leather books, leather boxes and leather-covered wooden desk objects are sold at **Scriptorium**.

## JEWELLERY

Florence has always been noted for its gold- and silversmiths. Visit **Torrini**, whose family has produced jewellery for six centuries, and **Pomellato**'s stunning shop for its chunky white gold rings with huge semi-precious gems. **Bulgari** is on the same street, and so is **Parenti**, which has unique antique jewels. Try **Aprosio & Co** for decorative jewellery made from precious metals and tiny glass stones.

## ART AND ANTIQUES

**Romanelli** has bronze statuary and works encrusted in semi-precious stones, and **Ducci** has an exquisite selection of handmade boxes, prints and sculpture in marble and wood. For lovers of Art Nouveau and Art Deco, there is **Galleria Tornabuoni**, while **Ugo Poggi** has a selection of elegant porcelain. **Ugolini** and **Mosaico di Pitti** create tables and framed pictures using the age-old technique of marble inlay.

## BOOKS AND GIFTS

**Feltrinelli International** and **Edison** sell publications in several languages, while **Paperback Exchange** has a wide selection of new and second-hand books in English.

Typical Florentine crafts include bookbinding and handmade marbled paper, used to decorate a variety of objects. These are available at **Il Torchio** and **Il Papiro**.

For terracotta and ceramics, try **Sbigoli Terracotte**; for chandeliers and decorative glass objects head to **La Bottega dei Cristalli**.

Housed in a converted wine cellar, **Signum** sells postcards, posters and prints, while **Mandragora** has a wide range of gifts based on famous artworks in the city.

## FOOD AND MARKETS

Florence's main food market is the covered **Mercato Centrale** (*see p295*), but fruit and vegetable stalls can also be found at the **Mercato di Sant'Ambrogio**. On Tuesday mornings, there is a large market at the **Parco delle Cascine** with food, affordable clothing and shoes.

**Pegna** is a mini-supermarket that stocks fresh foods, as well as a range of gourmet items. The **Bottega dell'Olio** sells extra virgin Tuscan olive oils, spice-flavoured oils and gifts.

**Dolceforte** sells chocolate souvenirs in the shape of the Duomo and the statue of *David*. A huge selection of biscuits and chocolates fills the front half of **Alessi**, while at the back are fine wines, spirits and liqueurs. At **Procacci**, you can stop for a glass of Italian wine while choosing between pots of black or white truffles and other delicacies to buy.

## DIRECTORY

### CLOTHING

**Armani**
Via de' Tornabuoni 48–50r.
**Map** 1 C5 & 5 C2.
***Tel*** *055 21 90 41.*

**Barberino Designer Outlet**
A1 Firenze-Bologna, Exit Barberino di Mugello.
***Tel*** *055 58 42 16.*

**Casa dei Tessuti**
Via dei Pecori 20–24r.
**Map** 1 C5 & 6 D2.
***Tel*** *055 21 59 61.*

**Coin**
Via dei Calzaiuoli 56r.
**Map** 6 D3.
***Tel*** 055 28 05 31.

**Dolce & Gabbana**
Via dei Strozzi 12–18r.
**Map** 1 C5 & 5 C3.
***Tel*** *055 28 10 03.*

**Gucci**
Via de' Tornabuoni 73r.
**Map** 1 C5 & 5 C2.
***Tel*** *055 26 40 11.*

**Intimissimi**
Via dei Calzaiuoli 99r.
**Map** 3 C1 & 6 D3.
***Tel*** *055 230 26 09.*

**Louis Vuitton**
Piazza degli Strozzi 1. **Map** 3 C1. ***Tel*** *055 26 69 81.*

**The Mall**
Via Europa 8, Leccio Reggello.
***Tel*** *055 865 77 75.*

**Patrizia Peppe**
Via degli Strozzi 11/19r.
**Map** 3 C1 & 6 D2.
***Tel*** *055 230 25 18.*

**La Perla**
Via della Vigna Nuova 17–19. **Map** 3 B1 & 5 B3.
***Tel*** *055 21 70 70.*

**Prada**
Via de' Tornabuoni 67r.
**Map** 1 C5 & 5 C2.
***Tel*** *055 28 34 39.*

**La Rinascente**
Piazza della Repubblica 1.
**Map** 1 C5 & 6 D3.
***Tel*** *055 21 91 13.*

**Valentino**
Via dei Tosinghi 52r.
**Map** 1 C5 & 6 D2.
***Tel*** *055 29 31 42.*

**Versace**
Via de' Tornabuoni 13–15r.
**Map** 1 C5 & 5 C2.
***Tel*** *055 28 26 38.*

**Yves Saint-Laurent**
Via de' Tornabuoni 29r.
**Map** 1 C5 & 5 C2.
***Tel*** *055 28 40 40.*

### SHOES AND LEATHER GOODS

**Bata**
Via dei Calzaiuoli 110r.
**Map** 3 C1 & 6 D2.
***Tel*** *055 21 16 24.*

**Beltrami**
Via della Vigna Nuova 70r.
**Map** 1 C5 & 5 C2.
***Tel*** *055 28 77 79.*

**Il Bisonte**
Via del Parione 31r.
**Map** 1 C5 & 5 C3.
***Tel*** *055 21 57 22.*

**Coccinelle**
Via Por Santa Maria 49r.
**Map** 3 C1 & 6 D4.
***Tel*** *055 239 87 82.*

**Ferragamo**
Via de' Tornabuoni 14r.
**Map** 1 C5 & 5 C2.
***Tel*** *055 29 21 23.*

**Furla**
Via de' Calzaiuoli 47r.
**Map** 3 C1 & 6 D3.
***Tel*** *055 23.8 28 83.*

**Peppe Peluso**
Via del Corso 5–6r.
**Map** 3 C1 & 6 D3.
***Tel*** *055 26 82 83.*

**Quercioli**
Via Calzaiuoli 18/20r.
**Map** 3 C1 & 6 D2.
***Tel*** *055 21 39 41.*

**Scriptorium**
Via dei Servi 5–7r.
**Map** 2 D5 & 6 E2.
***Tel*** *055 21 18 04.*

**Scuola del Cuoio**
Piazza di Santa Croce 16.
**Map** 3 C1 & 6 F4.
***Tel*** *055 24 45 33.*

### JEWELLERY

**Aprosio & Co**
Via di Santo Spirito 11.
**Map** 3 B1 & 5 B4.
***Tel*** *055 29 05 34.*

**Bulgari**
Via de' Tornabuoni 61r.
**Map** 1 C5 & 5 C3.
***Tel*** *055 239 67 86.*

**Parenti**
Via de' Tornabuoni 93r.
**Map** 1 C5 & 5 C2.
***Tel*** *055 21 44 38.*

**Pomellato**
Via de' Tornabuoni 89–91r.
**Map** 1 C5 & 5 C2.
***Tel*** *055 28 85 30.*

**Torrini**
Piazza del Duomo 10r.
**Map** 2 D5 & 6 D2.
***Tel*** *055 230 24 01.*

### ART AND ANTIQUES

**Ducci**
Lungarno Corsini 24r.
**Map** 3 B1 & 5 B3.
***Tel*** *055 21 45 50.*

**Galleria Tornabuoni**
Borgo San Jacopo 53r.
**Map** 3 C1 & 5 C4.
***Tel*** *055 28 47 20.*

**Mosaico di Pitti**
Piazza de' Pitti 16–18r.
**Map** 3 B2 & 5 B5.
***Tel*** 055 28 21 27.

**Romanelli**
Lungarno degli Acciaiuoli 74r. **Map** 3 C1 & 5 C4.
***Tel*** *055 239 66 62.*

**Ugo Poggi**
Via degli Strozzi 26r.
**Map** 1 C5 & 5 C3.
***Tel*** *055 21 67 41.*

**Ugolini**
Lungarno degli Acciaiuoli 66–70r. **Map** 3 C1 & 5 C4. ***Tel*** *055 28 49 69.*

### BOOKS AND GIFTS

**La Bottega dei Cristalli**
Via dei Benci 51r.
**Map** 3 C1 & 6 F4.
***Tel*** *055 234 48 91.*

**Edison**
Piazza della Repubblica 27r. **Map** 1 C5 & 6 D3.
***Tel*** *055 21 31 10.*

**Feltrinelli International**
Via Cavour 12–20r. **Map** 2 D4. ***Tel*** *055 21 95 24.*

**Mandragora**
Piazza del Duomo 9r.
**Map** 2 D5 & 6 D2.
***Tel*** *055 29 25 59.*

**Paperback Exchange**
Via delle Oche 4r.
**Map** 2 D5 & 6 E2.
***Tel*** *055 29 34 60.*

**Il Papiro**
Piazza del Duomo 24r.
**Map** 2 D5 & 6 D2.
***Tel*** *055 28 16 28.*

**Sbigoli Terracotte**
Via Sant'Egidio 4r. **Map** 6 F2. ***Tel*** *055 247 97 13.*

**Signum**
Borgo dei Greci 40r.
**Map** 3 C1 & 6 E4.
***Tel*** *055 28 06 21.*

**Il Torchio**
Via de' Bardi 17.
**Map** 3 C2 & 6 D5.
***Tel*** *055 234 28 62.*

### FOOD AND MARKETS

**Alessi**
Via delle Oche 27r.
**Map** 3 C1 & 6 D2.
***Tel*** *055 21 49 66.*

**Bottega dell'Olio**
Piazza del Limbo 2r.
**Map** 3 C1 & 6 D4.
***Tel*** *055 267 04 68.*

**Dolceforte**
Via della Scala 21.
**Map** 1 C5 & 5 B2.
***Tel*** *055 21 91 16.*

**Mercato Centrale**
Via dell'Ariento 10–14.
**Map** 1 C4 & 5 C1.

**Mercato di Sant'Ambrogio**
Piazza Sant'Ambrogio.
**Map** 4 F1.
7am–2pm Mon–Sat.

**Parco delle Cascine**
Piazza Vittorio Veneto.
8am–2pm Tue.

**Pegna**
Via dello Studio 26r.
**Map** 6 E2.
***Tel*** *055 28 27 01.*

**Procacci**
Via de' Tornabuoni 64r.
**Map** 1 C5 & 5 C2.
***Tel*** *055 21 16 56.*

# FLORENCE STREET FINDER

Map references given for sights in the Florence section refer to the maps on the following pages. Where two references are provided, the one in brackets relates to the large-scale maps, 5 and 6. References are also given for Florence hotels *(see pp576–8)* and restaurants *(see pp626–9),* and for useful addresses in the *Travellers' Needs* and *Survival Guide* sections at the back of the book. The map below shows the area of Florence covered by the *Street Finder*. The symbols used for sights and other features on the *Florence Street Finder* maps are listed below. Streets in Florence have double sets of numbers: red numbers are for businesses, and black or blue for domestic residences.

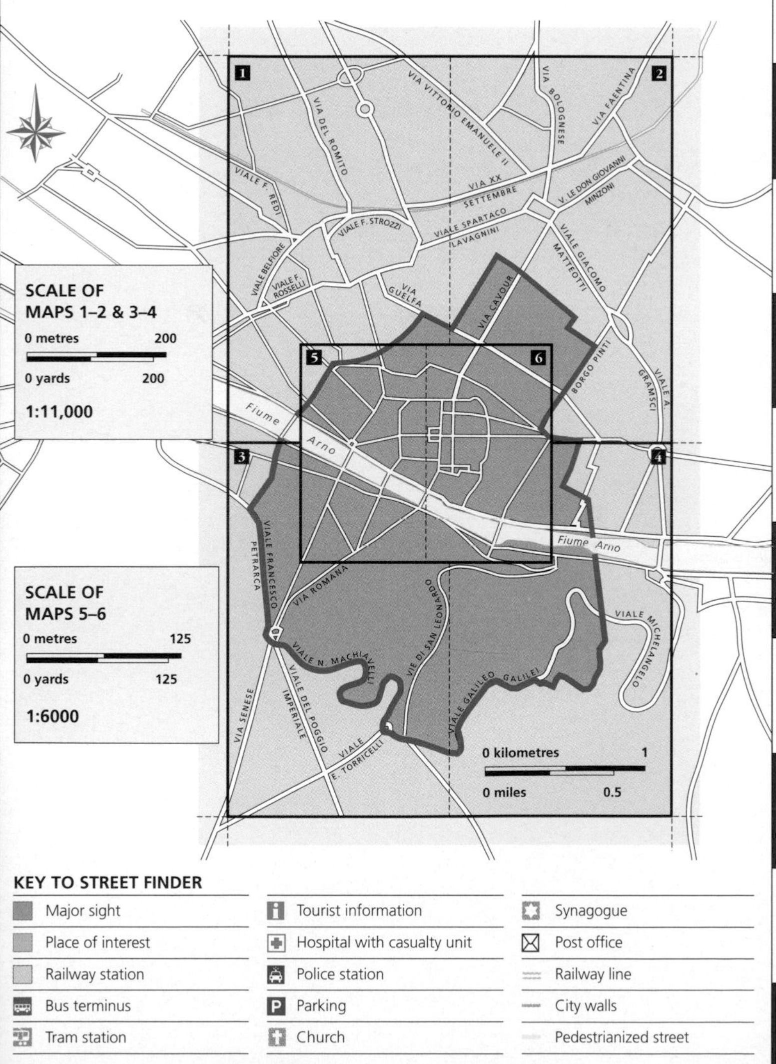

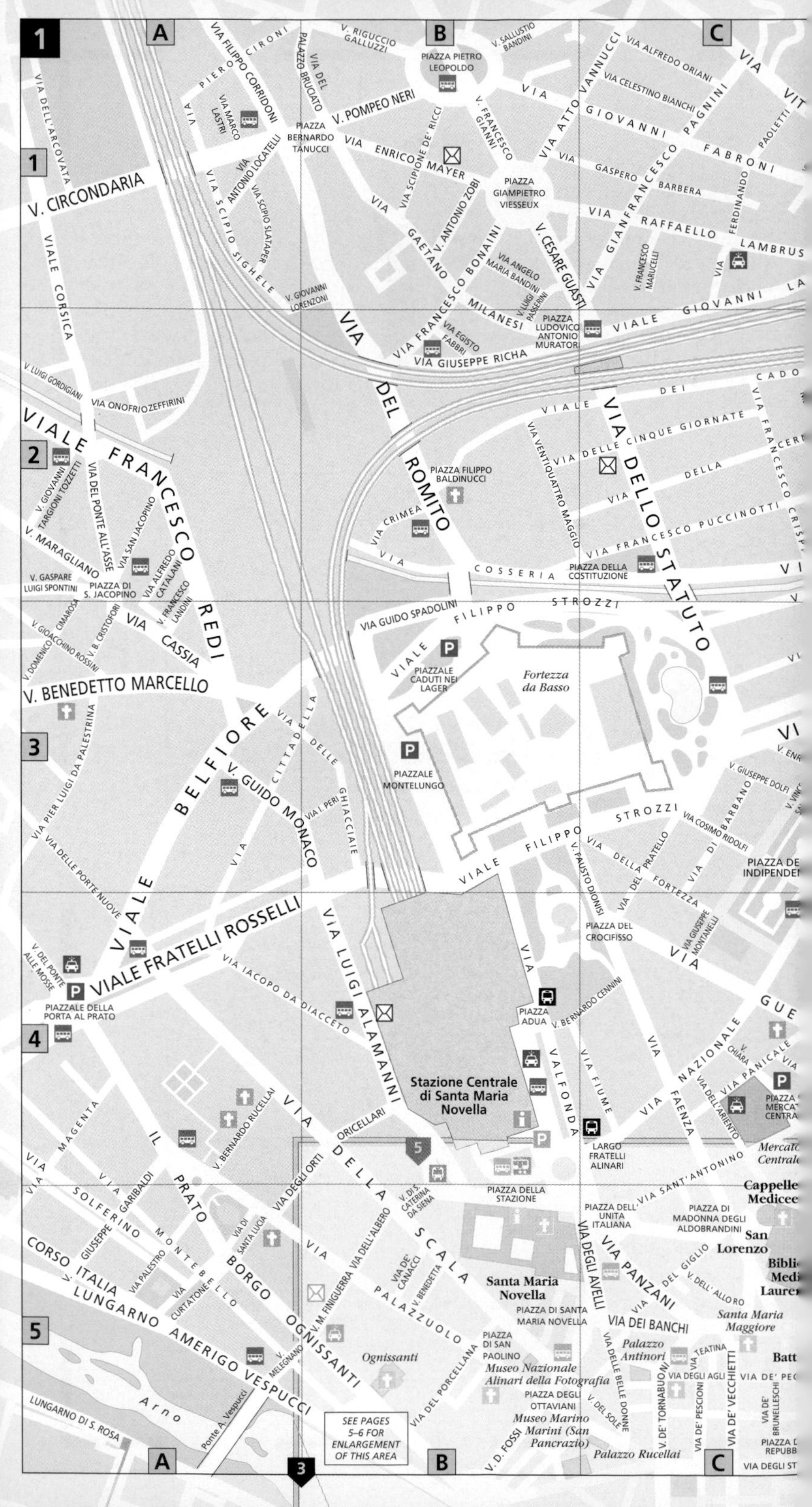
1
A
B
C
1
2
3
4
5
VIA FILIPPO CORRIDONI
V. RIGUCCIO GALLUZZI
VIA DEL PALAZZO BRUCIATO
PIAZZA PIETRO LEOPOLDO
V. SALLUSTIO BANDINI
VIA ATTO VANNUCCI
VIA ALFREDO ORIANI
VIA CELESTINO BIANCHI
VIA GIOVANNI FABRONI
VIA PIERO CIRONI
VIA MARCO LASTRI
V. POMPEO NERI
PIAZZA BERNARDO TANUCCI
VIA ENRICO MAYER
V. FRANCESCO GIANNI
VIA SCIPIONE DE' RICCI
VIA GASPERO BARBERA
VIA GIANFRANCESCO PAGNINI
PAOLETTI
VIA DELL'ARCOVATA
V. CIRCONDARIA
VIA ANTONIO LOCATELLI
VIA SCIPIO SLATAPER
VIA SCIPIO SIGHELE
PIAZZA GIAMPIETRO VIESSEUX
VIA RAFFAELLO LAMBRUSCHINI
VIA FERDINANDO PAOLETTI
VIA GAETANO MILANESI
V. ANTONIO ZOBI
V. CESARE GUASTI
V. FRANCESCO MARUCELLI
VIALE CORSICA
V. GIOVANNI LORENZONI
VIA ANGELO MARIA BANDINI
V. LUIGI PASSERINI
VIA FRANCESCO BONAINI
PIAZZA LUDOVICO ANTONIO MURATORI
VIALE GIOVANNI LAVAGNINI
VIA EGISTO FABBRI
VIA GIUSEPPE RICHA
VIA DEL ROMITO
V. LUIGI GORDIGIANI
VIA ONOFRIO ZEFFIRINI
VIALE DEI CADORINI
VIA DELLO STATUTO
VIA FRANCESCO CRISPI
VIALE FRANCESCO REDI
VIA VENTIQUATTRO MAGGIO
VIA DELLE CINQUE GIORNATE
VIA DELLA CERNAIA
PIAZZA FILIPPO BALDINUCCI
V. GIOVANNI TARGIONI TOZZETTI
VIA DEL PONTE ALL'ASSE
VIA SAN JACOPINO
VIA CRIMEA
VIA FRANCESCO PUCCINOTTI
V. MARAGLIANO
VIA ALFREDO CATALANI
VIA COSSERIA
PIAZZA DELLA COSTITUZIONE
V. GASPARE LUIGI SPONTINI
PIAZZA DI S. JACOPINO
V. FRANCESCO LANDINI
VIA CASSIA
CIMAROSA
V. B. CRISTOFORI
VIALE FILIPPO STROZZI
VIA GUIDO SPADOLINI
V. GIOACCHINO ROSSINI
V. DOMENICO
PIAZZALE CADUTI NEI LAGER
Fortezza da Basso
V. BENEDETTO MARCELLO
VIA PIER LUIGI DA PALESTRINA
VIALE BELFIORE
VIA CITTADELLA
VIA DELLE GHIACCIAIE
V. GUIDO MONACO
VIA I. PERI
PIAZZALE MONTELUNGO
V. ENRICO
V. GIUSEPPE DOLFI
VIA COSIMO RIDOLFI
VIA DI BARBANO
VIA DELLE PORTE NUOVE
V. FAUSTO DIONISI
VIA DEL PRATELLO
VIA DELLA FORTEZZA
PIAZZA DELL'INDIPENDENZA
VIALE FRATELLI ROSSELLI
VIA LUIGI ALAMANNI
PIAZZA DEL CROCIFISSO
VIA GIUSEPPE MONTANELLI
V. DEL PONTE ALLE MOSSE
VIA IACOPO DA DIACCETO
VIA VALFONDA
PIAZZALE DELLA PORTA AL PRATO
PIAZZA ADUA
V. BERNARDO CENNINI
VIA GUELFA
VIA NAZIONALE
V. CHIARA
VIA PANICALE
VIA FIUME
VIA FAENZA
VIA DELL'ARIENTO
PIAZZA DEL MERCATO CENTRALE
Stazione Centrale di Santa Maria Novella
VIA MAGENTA
V. BERNARDO RUCELLAI
VIA DELLA SCALA
VIA ORICELLARI
5
LARGO FRATELLI ALINARI
Mercato Centrale
VIA IL PRATO
VIA SANT'ANTONINO
VIA SOLFERINO
VIA GIUSEPPE GARIBALDI
VIA MONTEBELLO
VIA DEGLI ORTI ORICELLARI
V. DI S. CATERINA DA SIENA
PIAZZA DELLA STAZIONE
Cappelle Medicee
PIAZZA DELL'UNITÀ ITALIANA
PIAZZA DI MADONNA DEGLI ALDOBRANDINI
San Lorenzo
VIA DI SANTA LUCIA
CORSO ITALIA
VIA PALESTRO
BORGO OGNISSANTI
VIA DE' CANACCI
VIA DEGLI AVELLI
VIA PANZANI
VIA DEL GIGLIO
V. DELL'ALLORO
Biblioteca Medicea Laurenziana
V. LUNGARNO AMERIGO VESPUCCI
VIA CURTATONE
V. M. FINIGUERRA
VIA DELL'ALBERO
V. BENEDETTA
VIA PALAZZUOLO
Santa Maria Novella
PIAZZA DI SANTA MARIA NOVELLA
VIA DEI BANCHI
Santa Maria Maggiore
V. MELEGNANO
Ognissanti
PIAZZA DI SAN PAOLINO
Museo Nazionale Alinari della Fotografia
Palazzo Antinori
VIA TEATINA
VIA DEGLI AGLI
Battistero
VIA DE' PECORI
Arno
Ponte A. Vespucci
LUNGARNO DI S. ROSA
VIA DEL PORCELLANA
PIAZZA DEGLI OTTAVIANI
VIA DELLE BELLE DONNE
V. DEL SOLE
Museo Marino Marini (San Pancrazio)
V. D. FOSSI
Palazzo Rucellai
V. DE' TORNABUONI
VIA DE' PESCIONI
VIA DE' VECCHIETTI
VIA DE' BRUNELLESCHI
PIAZZA DELLA REPUBBLICA
VIA DEGLI STROZZI
SEE PAGES 5–6 FOR ENLARGEMENT OF THIS AREA
3

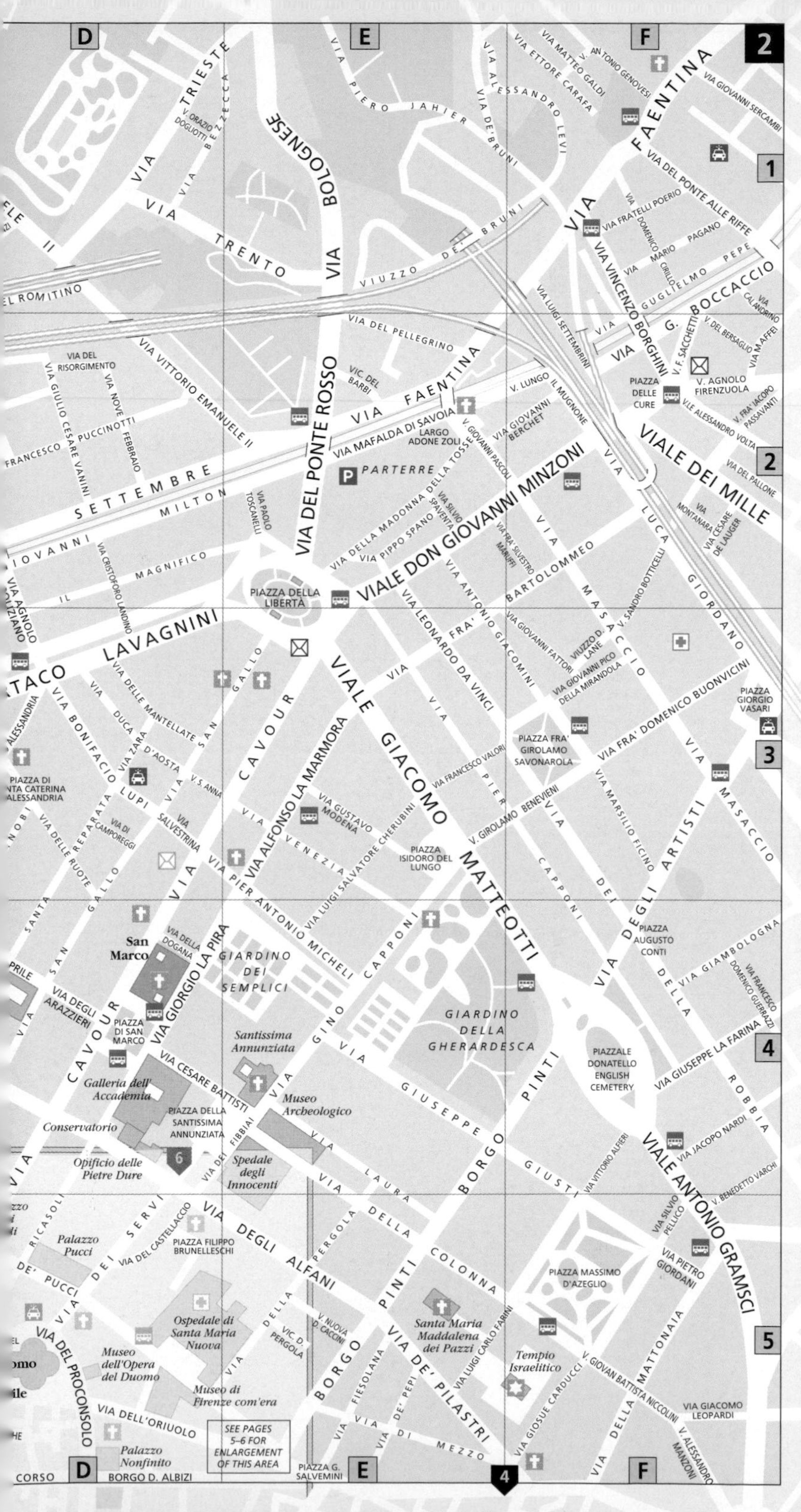

D
E
F
2
1
2
3
4
5
VIA FAENTINA
VIA TRIESTE
VIA BOLOGNESE
VIA TRENTO
VIA DEL PONTE ROSSO
VIALE DON GIOVANNI MINZONI
VIALE GIACOMO MATTEOTTI
VIALE DEI MILLE
VIALE ANTONIO GRAMSCI
VIA G. BOCCACCIO
VIA VINCENZO BORGHINI
VIA MAFALDA DI SAVOIA
VIA VITTORIO EMANUELE II
VIA DEL PELLEGRINO
PARTERRE
LARGO ADONE ZOLI
PIAZZA DELLA LIBERTÀ
PIAZZA DELLE CURE
PIAZZA GIORGIO VASARI
PIAZZA FRA' GIROLAMO SAVONAROLA
PIAZZA ISIDORO DEL LUNGO
PIAZZA AUGUSTO CONTI
PIAZZALE DONATELLO ENGLISH CEMETERY
VIA CAVOUR
VIA SAN GALLO
VIA ALFONSO LA MARMORA
VIA LEONARDO DA VINCI
VIA MASACCIO
VIA DEGLI ARTISTI
VIA FRA' DOMENICO BUONVICINI
VIA GIUSEPPE LA FARINA
VIA GIORGIO LA PIRA
VIA PIER ANTONIO MICHELI
VIA GINO CAPPONI
BORGO PINTI
VIA GIUSEPPE GIUSTI
VIA DEGLI ALFANI
VIA DELLA COLONNA
VIA DE' PILASTRI
VIA DEI SERVI
VIA DEL PROCONSOLO
VIA DELL'ORIUOLO
San Marco
PIAZZA DI SAN MARCO
GIARDINO DEI SEMPLICI
GIARDINO DELLA GHERARDESCA
Santissima Annunziata
Museo Archeologico
Galleria dell' Accademia
PIAZZA DELLA SANTISSIMA ANNUNZIATA
Conservatorio
Opificio delle Pietre Dure
Spedale degli Innocenti
Palazzo Pucci
PIAZZA FILIPPO BRUNELLESCHI
Ospedale di Santa Maria Nuova
Museo dell'Opera del Duomo
Museo di Firenze com'era
Palazzo Nonfinito
PIAZZA MASSIMO D'AZEGLIO
Santa Maria Maddalena dei Pazzi
Tempio Israelitico
PIAZZA G. SALVEMINI
BORGO D. ALBIZI
SEE PAGES 5–6 FOR ENLARGEMENT OF THIS AREA
6
4

3
A
B
C
1
2
3
4
5
SEE PAGES 5–6 FOR ENLARGEMENT OF THIS AREA
LUNGARNO SODERINI
BORGO SAN FREDIANO
LUNGARNO CORSINI
LUNGARNO GUICCIARDINI
LUNGARNO D. ACCIAIUOLI
VIA DI SANTO SPIRITO
BORGO SAN JACOPO
Palazzo Strozzi
Palazzo Corsini
Santa Trinita
Palazzo Spini-Ferroni
Palazzo Bartolini-Salimbeni
Palazzo Davanzati
Santi Apostoli
San Frediano in Cestello
Cappella Brancacci (Santa Maria del Carmine)
Santo Spirito
Cenacolo di Santo Spirito
Santa Felicita
Palazzo Pitti
Museo La Specola
GIARDINO TORRIGIANI
GIARDINO DI BOBOLI
Forte di Belvedere
PIAZZA DELLA CALZA
PIAZZALE DELLA PORTA ROMANA
VIALE FRANCESCO PETRARCA
VIA SENESE
VIALE NICCOLÒ MACHIAVELLI
VIALE DEL POGGIO IMPERIALE
V.LE EVANGELISTICA TORRICELLI
PIAZZALE GALILEO
VIA DI SAN LEONARDO
VIA DEL GELSOMINO
VIA ROMANA
VIA DE' SERRAGLI
VIA MAGGIO
PIAZZA DI SANTO SPIRITO
PIAZZA DE' PITTI
PIAZZA DEL CARMINE
PIAZZA DI VERZAIA
PIAZZA TORQUATO TASSO
VIA DELLA CHIESA
VIA DEL CAMPUCCIO
VIA DANTE DA CASTIGLIONE
VIA DEL BOBOLINO
VIA DELLE CAMPORA
VIA UGO FOSCOLO
VIA LORENZO BELLINI
VIA BENEDETTO CASTELLI
VIALE LORENZO MAGALOTTI
VIA LEONARDO XIMENES

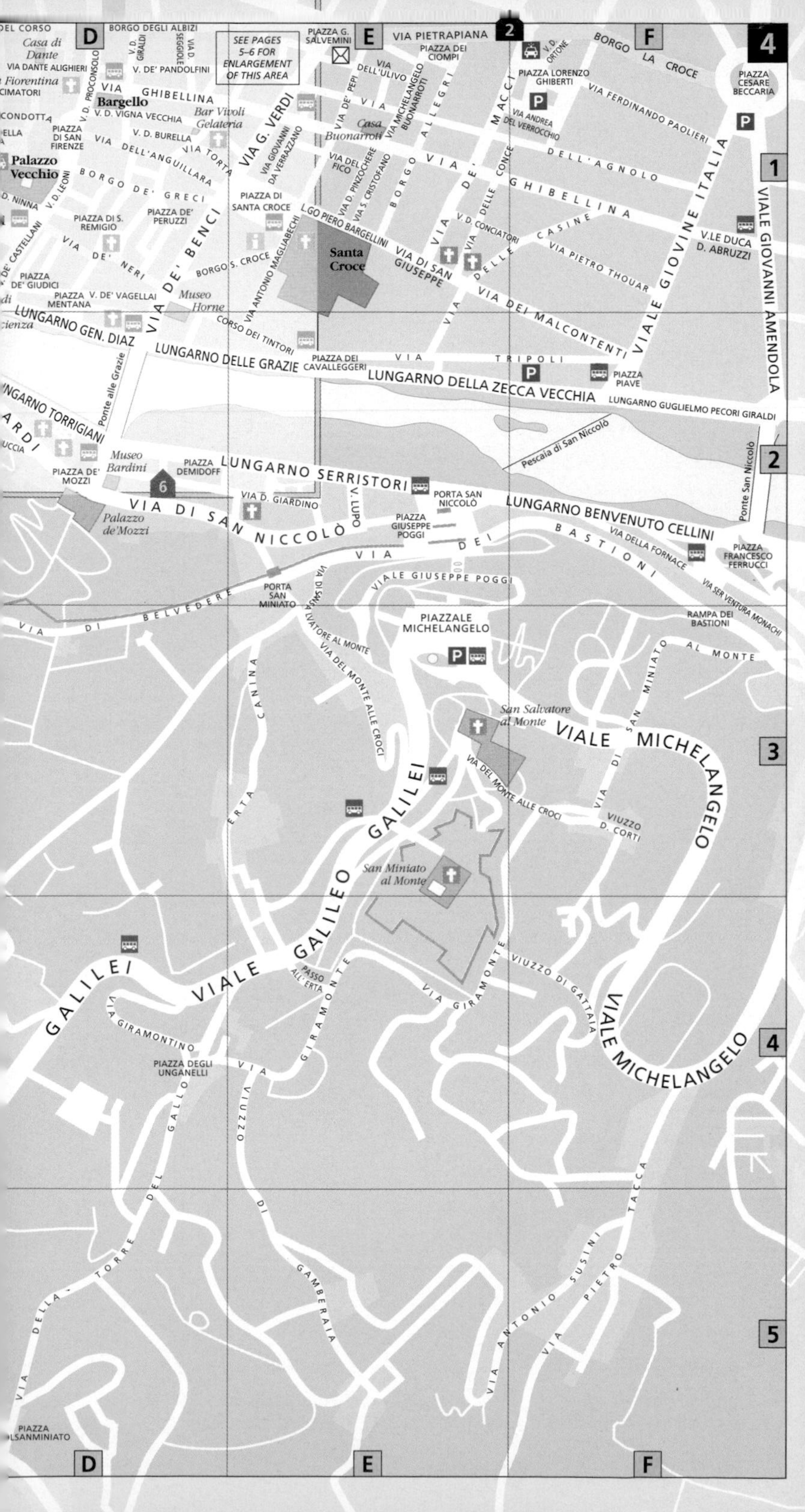
SEE PAGES 5–6 FOR ENLARGEMENT OF THIS AREA
D
E
F
4
2
1
2
3
4
5
6
Casa di Dante
Bargello
Palazzo Vecchio
Bar Vivoli Gelateria
Casa Buonarroti
Santa Croce
Museo Horne
Museo Bardini
Palazzo de'Mozzi
PIAZZALE MICHELANGELO
San Salvatore al Monte
San Miniato al Monte
VIA PIETRAPIANA
BORGO LA CROCE
VIA GHIBELLINA
VIA G. VERDI
VIA DE' BENCI
VIA DELL'AGNOLO
VIALE GIOVINE ITALIA
VIALE GIOVANNI AMENDOLA
VIA DEI MALCONTENTI
VIA TRIPOLI
LUNGARNO DELLE GRAZIE
LUNGARNO DELLA ZECCA VECCHIA
LUNGARNO GEN. DIAZ
LUNGARNO TORRIGIANI
LUNGARNO SERRISTORI
LUNGARNO BENVENUTO CELLINI
LUNGARNO GUGLIELMO PECORI GIRALDI
VIA DI SAN NICCOLÒ
VIA DEI BASTIONI
VIALE GIUSEPPE POGGI
VIA DI BELVEDERE
VIALE MICHELANGELO
VIALE GALILEO GALILEI
VIA DI SAN MINIATO AL MONTE
VIA DEL MONTE ALLE CROCI
VIA GIRAMONTE
VIA DI GAMBERAIA
VIA DELLA TORRE DEL GALLO
VIA ANTONIO SUSINI
VIA PIETRO TACCA
PIAZZA DI SANTA CROCE
PIAZZA LORENZO GHIBERTI
PIAZZA CESARE BECCARIA
PIAZZA DEI CIOMPI
PIAZZA G. SALVEMINI
PIAZZA DEI CAVALLEGGERI
PIAZZA PIAVE
PIAZZA DE' MOZZI
PIAZZA DEMIDOFF
PIAZZA GIUSEPPE POGGI
PIAZZA FRANCESCO FERRUCCI
PORTA SAN NICCOLÒ
PORTA SAN MINIATO
RAMPA DEI BASTIONI
Ponte alle Grazie
Ponte San Niccolò
Pescaia di San Niccolò
PIAZZA DEGLI UNGANELLI
VIUZZO DI GATTAIA
VIUZZO D. CORTI
PASSO ALL'ERTA
ERTA CANINA

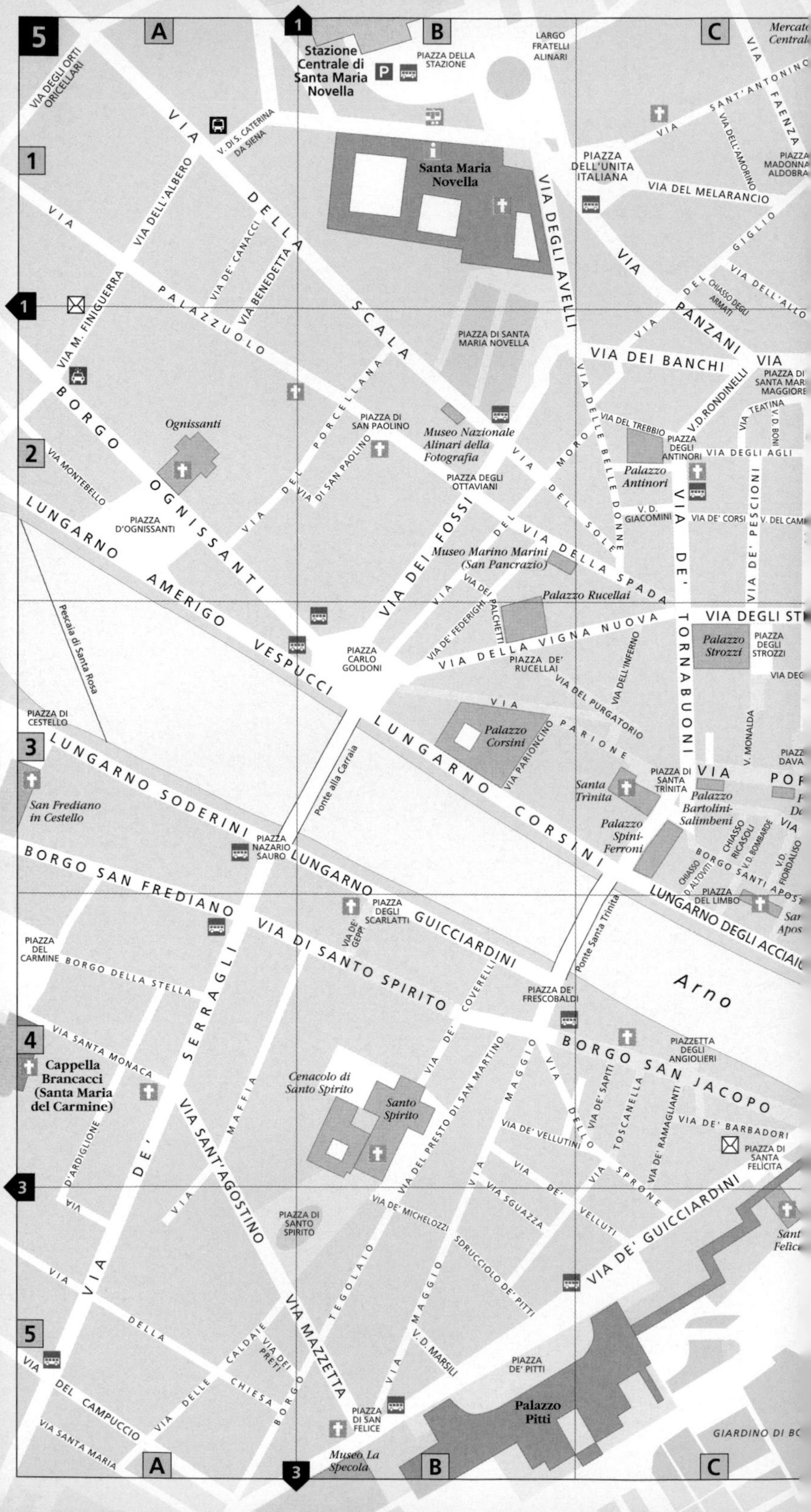

5
Stazione Centrale di Santa Maria Novella
PIAZZA DELLA STAZIONE
LARGO FRATELLI ALINARI
Mercato Centrale
VIA DEGLI ORTI ORICELLARI
VIA DELLA SCALA
V. DI S. CATERINA DA SIENA
Santa Maria Novella
VIA DEGLI AVELLI
PIAZZA DELL'UNITA ITALIANA
VIA SANT'ANTONINO
VIA FAENZA
VIA DELL'AMORINO
PIAZZA MADONNA ALDOBRANDINI
VIA DEL MELARANCIO
VIA DEL GIGLIO
VIA PANZANI
CHIASSO DEGLI ARMATI
VIA DELL'ALLORO
VIA DELL'ALBERO
VIA DE' CANACCI
VIA BENEDETTA
VIA PALAZZUOLO
VIA M. FINIGUERRA
PIAZZA DI SANTA MARIA NOVELLA
VIA DEI BANCHI
PIAZZA DI SANTA MARIA MAGGIORE
VIA D. RONDINELLI
VIA TEATINA
V. D. BONI
BORGO OGNISSANTI
Ognissanti
VIA DEL PORCELLANA
PIAZZA DI SAN PAOLINO
VIA DI SAN PAOLINO
Museo Nazionale Alinari della Fotografia
VIA DEL MORO
VIA DELLE BELLE DONNE
VIA DEL TREBBIO
PIAZZA DEGLI ANTINORI
VIA DEGLI AGLI
Palazzo Antinori
VIA MONTEBELLO
PIAZZA DEGLI OTTAVIANI
VIA DEL SOLE
V. D. GIACOMINI
VIA DE' CORSI
V. DEL CAMPIDOGLIO
VIA DE' PESCIONI
PIAZZA D'OGNISSANTI
LUNGARNO AMERIGO VESPUCCI
VIA DEI FOSSI
Museo Marino Marini (San Pancrazio)
VIA DELLA SPADA
VIA DE' TORNABUONI
VIA DEI PALCHETTI
VIA DE' FEDERIGHI
Palazzo Rucellai
VIA DEGLI STROZZI
Pescaia di Santa Rosa
PIAZZA CARLO GOLDONI
VIA DELLA VIGNA NUOVA
VIA DELL'INFERNO
PIAZZA DE' RUCELLAI
Palazzo Strozzi
PIAZZA DEGLI STROZZI
VIA DEL PURGATORIO
VIA DEL PARIONE
Palazzo Corsini
VIA PARIONCINO
PIAZZA DI CESTELLO
V. MONALDA
LUNGARNO CORSINI
LUNGARNO SODERINI
San Frediano in Cestello
Ponte alla Carraia
Santa Trìnita
PIAZZA DI SANTA TRÌNITA
VIA PORTA ROSSA
Palazzo Bartolini-Salimbeni
Palazzo Spini-Ferroni
CHIASSO RICASOLI
V. D. BOMBARDE
V. D. FIORDALISO
CHIASSO D. ALTOVITI
BORGO SANTI APOSTOLI
PIAZZA NAZARIO SAURO
LUNGARNO GUICCIARDINI
BORGO SAN FREDIANO
PIAZZA DEL LIMBO
LUNGARNO DEGLI ACCIAIUOLI
PIAZZA DEGLI SCARLATTI
VIA DE' GEPPI
PIAZZA DEL CARMINE
BORGO DELLA STELLA
VIA DI SANTO SPIRITO
Ponte Santa Trìnita
Arno
PIAZZA DE' FRESCOBALDI
VIA DE' SERRAGLI
VIA DE' COVERELLI
VIA SANTA MONACA
Cappella Brancacci (Santa Maria del Carmine)
VIA MAFFIA
Cenacolo di Santo Spirito
Santo Spirito
VIA DEL PRESTO DI SAN MARTINO
VIA MAGGIO
VIA DELLO SPRONE
BORGO SAN JACOPO
PIAZZETTA DEGLI ANGIOLIERI
VIA DE' SAPITI
TOSCANELLA
VIA DE' RAMAGLIANTI
VIA DE' BARBADORI
PIAZZA DI SANTA FELÌCITA
VIA DE' VELLUTINI
VIA D'ARDIGLIONE
VIA SANT'AGOSTINO
VIA DE' VELLUTI
VIA SGUAZZA
VIA DE' MICHELOZZI
VIA DE' GUICCIARDINI
PIAZZA DI SANTO SPIRITO
SDRUCCIOLO DE' PITTI
Santa Felìcita
VIA TEGOLAIO
VIA DELLA CHIESA
VIA DELLE CALDAIE
VIA DEI PRETI
VIA MAZZETTA
V. D. MARSILI
PIAZZA DE' PITTI
VIA DEL CAMPUCCIO
BORGO TEGOLAIO
PIAZZA DI SAN FELICE
Palazzo Pitti
GIARDINO DI BOBOLI
VIA SANTA MARIA
Museo La Specola
A
B
C
1
2
3
4
5

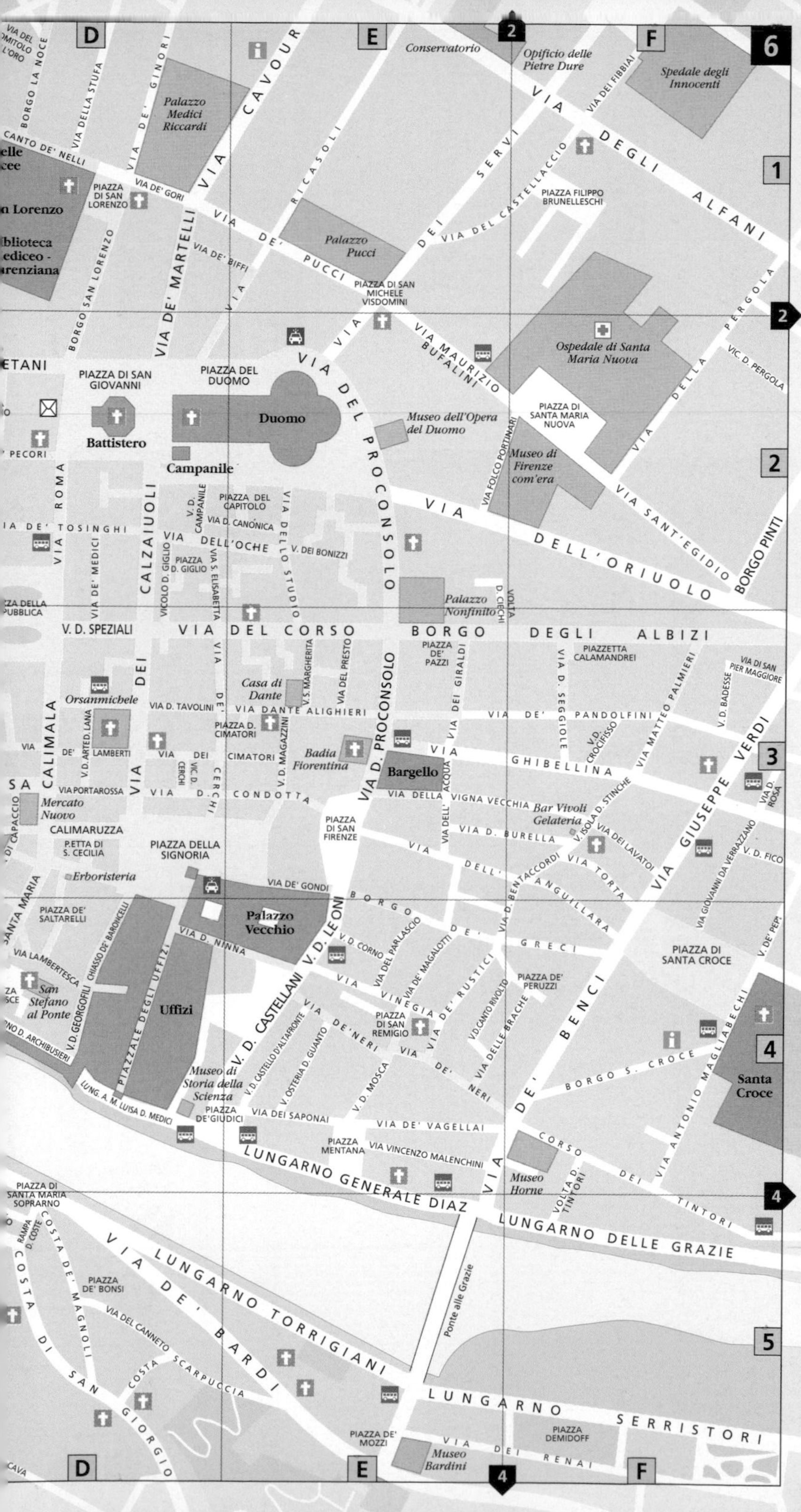

6
Conservatorio
Opificio delle Pietre Dure
Spedale degli Innocenti
Palazzo Medici Riccardi
Via Cavour
Via de' Ginori
Via della Stufa
Borgo la Noce
Canto de' Nelli
Piazza di San Lorenzo
San Lorenzo
Via de' Gori
Via Ricasoli
Via dei Servi
Via degli Alfani
Via dei Fibbiai
Via del Castellaccio
Piazza Filippo Brunelleschi
Palazzo Pucci
Via de' Pucci
Via de' Biffi
Via de' Martelli
Borgo San Lorenzo
Piazza di San Michele Visdomini
Via Maurizio Bufalini
Ospedale di Santa Maria Nuova
Via della Pergola
Vic. d. Pergola
Piazza di San Giovanni
Piazza del Duomo
Battistero
Duomo
Campanile
Via del Proconsolo
Museo dell'Opera del Duomo
Piazza di Santa Maria Nuova
Museo di Firenze com'era
Via Folco Portinari
Via Sant'Egidio
Via dell'Oriuolo
Borgo Pinti
Via Roma
Via de' Tosinghi
Via de' Medici
Via Calzaiuoli
Piazza del Capitolo
V. d. Canonica
Via dell'Oche
V. dei Bonizzi
Via dello Studio
Piazza d. Giglio
Vicolo d. Giglio
Via S. Elisabetta
Palazzo Nonfinito
Volta d. Ciechi
V. d. Speziali
Via del Corso
Borgo degli Albizi
Piazzetta Calamandrei
Piazza de' Pazzi
Via dei Giraldi
Via d. Seggiole
Via Matteo Palmieri
Via di San Pier Maggiore
V. d. Badesse
Orsanmichele
Casa di Dante
Via Dante Alighieri
Via del Presto
V. S. Margherita
Via d. Tavolini
Piazza d. Cimatori
Via dei Cimatori
Via de' Pandolfini
V. d. Crocifisso
Via Giuseppe Verdi
Via Calimala
V. d. Arte d. Lana
Via de' Lamberti
Via dei Cerchi
Badia Fiorentina
Bargello
Via Ghibellina
V. d. Magazzini
Via Portarossa
Via d. Condotta
Via della Vigna Vecchia
Bar Vivoli Gelateria
Via dell'Acqua
V. Isola d. Stinche
Via d. Rosa
Mercato Nuovo
Calimaruzza
Piazza di San Firenze
Via d. Burella
Via dei Lavatoi
P.etta di S. Cecilia
Piazza della Signoria
Via dell'Anguillara
Via Torta
Via Giovanni da Verrazzano
V. d. Fico
Erboristeria
Via de' Gondi
Borgo de' Greci
Via d. Bentaccordi
Piazza de' Saltarelli
Palazzo Vecchio
Via d. Ninna
V. d. Leoni
V. d. Corno
Via del Parlascio
Via de' Magalotti
Piazza di Santa Croce
V. de' Pepi
Via Lambertesca
Chiasso de' Baroncelli
Piazzale degli Uffizi
San Stefano al Ponte
Uffizi
V. d. Castellani
Via Vinegia
Via de' Rustici
Piazza de' Peruzzi
V. d. Canto Rivolto
Via delle Brache
Via de' Benci
Santa Croce
Via Antonio Magliabechi
V. d. Georgofili
Via de' Neri
Piazza di San Remigio
Borgo S. Croce
Lung. A. M. Luisa d. Medici
Museo di Storia della Scienza
V. d. Castello d'Altafronte
V. Osteria d. Guanto
V. d. Mosca
Piazza de' Giudici
Via dei Saponai
Via de' Vagellai
Corso dei Tintori
Piazza Mentana
Via Vincenzo Malenchini
Lungarno Generale Diaz
Museo Horne
Volta d. Tintori
Lungarno delle Grazie
Piazza di Santa Maria Soprarno
Rampa d. Coste
Costa de' Magnoli
Costa di San Giorgio
Via de' Bardi
Lungarno Torrigiani
Piazza de' Bonsi
Via del Canneto
Costa Scarpuccia
Ponte alle Grazie
Lungarno Serristori
Piazza de' Mozzi
Via dei Renai
Piazza Demidoff
Museo Bardini
D
E
F
1
2
3
4
5

# TUSCANY

*Renowned for its art, history and evocative landscape, Tuscany is a region where the past and present merge in pleasant harmony. Hill-towns gaze across the countryside from on high, many encircled by Etruscan walls and slender cypress trees. Handsome palaces testify to the region's wealth while medieval town halls indicate a long-standing tradition of democracy and self-government.*

In the countryside, among the vineyards and olive groves, there are hamlets and farmhouses, as well as fortified villas and castles that symbolize the violence and intercommunal strife that tore Tuscany apart during the Middle Ages. Several imposing castles and villas were built for the Medici family, the great patrons of the Renaissance who supported eminent scientists, such as Galileo.

Northern Tuscany, and the heavily populated plain between Florence and Lucca, is dominated by industry, with intensively cultivated land between the cities and the wild mountainous areas.

The area centred around Livorno and Pisa is now the region's economic hub. Pisa, at the height of its powers, dominated the western Mediterranean from the 11th to the 13th centuries. Its navy opened up extensive trading routes with North Africa, and brought to Italy the benefits of Arabic scientific and artistic achievement. During the 16th century the Arno estuary began to silt up, ending Pisan power.

At the heart of central Tuscany lies Siena, which was involved in a long feud with Florence. Its finest hour came with its victory in the Battle of Montaperti in 1260, but it was devastated by the Black Death in the 14th century and finally suffered a crushing defeat by Florence in the siege of 1554–5.

Northeastern Tuscany, with its mountain peaks and woodland, provided refuge for hermits and saints, while the east was home to Piero della Francesca, the early Renaissance painter whose timeless and serene works are imbued with an almost religious perfection.

**A timeless view and way of life in Casole d'Elsa, near San Gimignano in central Tuscany**

◁ **The complex architecture of Pisa's Duomo (begun in 1063) and the Leaning Tower (begun in 1173)**

# Exploring Tuscany

Tuscan cities such as Florence, Siena and Pisa, together with smaller towns like Lucca, Cortona and Arezzo, contain some of Italy's most famous artistic treasures. Medieval villages such as San Gimignano, with its famous towers, or Pienza, a tiny Renaissance jewel, sit at the heart of the glorious pastoral countryside for which the region is equally renowned. Elsewhere landscapes range from the spectacular mountains of the Alpi Apuane to the gentle hills of Chianti.

## SIGHTS AT A GLANCE

- *Arezzo pp329–31* 14
- Artimino 11
- Bagni di Lucca 3
- Carrara 1
- Chiusi 17
- Cortona 16
- Crete Senesi 21
- Elba 28
- Fiesole 13
- *FLORENCE (see pp270–313)*
- Garfagnana 2
- *Lucca pp320–23* 6
- Maremma 31
- Massa Marittima 27
- Montalcino 20
- Monte Argentario 32
- Montepulciano 18
- Monteriggioni 23
- Pienza 19
- *Pisa pp324–6* 7
- Pistoia 9
- Pitigliano 30
- Prato 10
- San Galgano 26
- *San Gimignano pp344–5* 24
- San Miniato 12
- Sansepolcro 15
- *Siena pp338–43* 22
- Sovana 29
- Torre del Lago Puccini 5
- Viareggio 4
- Vinci 8
- Volterra 25

View of Cortona in eastern Tuscany

**SEE ALSO**


- ***Where to Stay*** pp579–82
- ***Where to Eat*** pp629–32


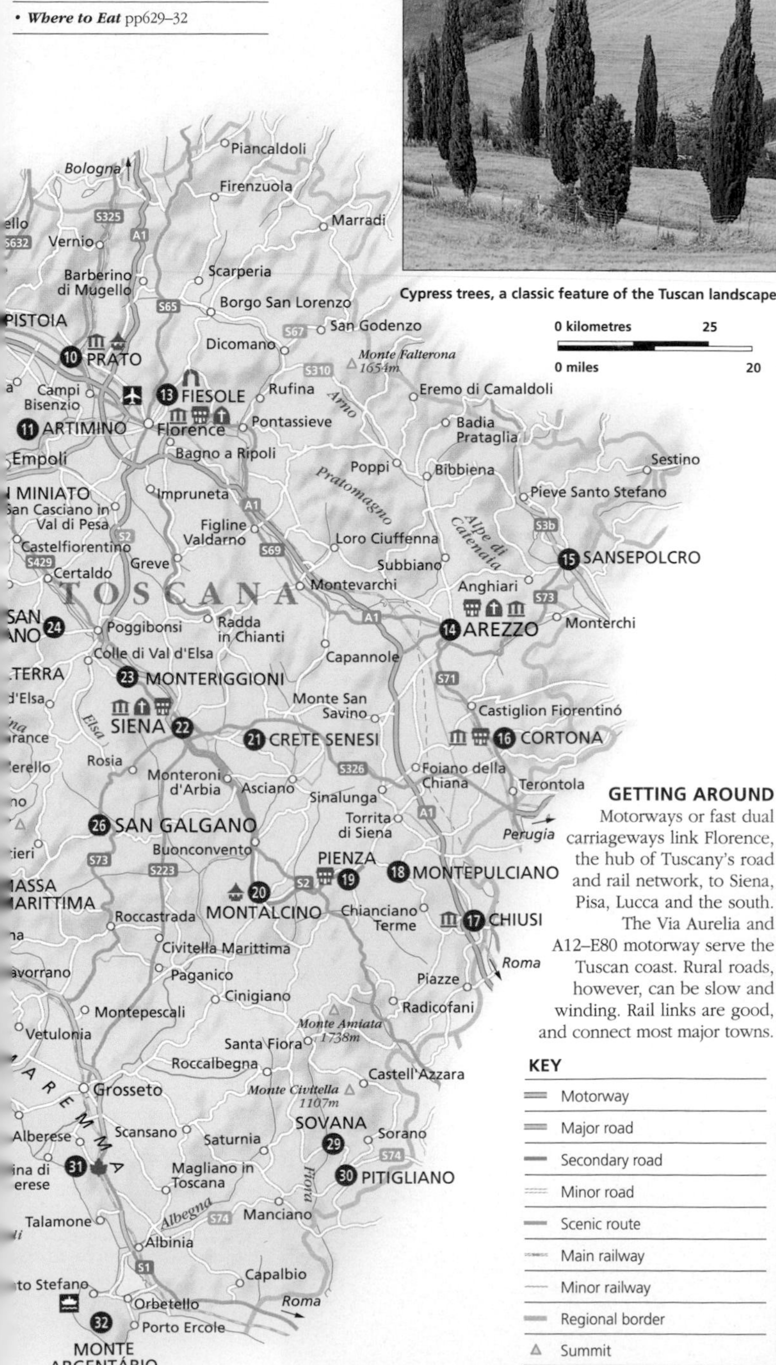

Cypress trees, a classic feature of the Tuscan landscape

0 kilometres 25

0 miles 20

## GETTING AROUND

Motorways or fast dual carriageways link Florence, the hub of Tuscany's road and rail network, to Siena, Pisa, Lucca and the south. The Via Aurelia and A12–E80 motorway serve the Tuscan coast. Rural roads, however, can be slow and winding. Rail links are good, and connect most major towns.

**KEY**

- Motorway
- Major road
- Secondary road
- Minor road
- Scenic route
- Main railway
- Minor railway
- Regional border
- △ Summit

## Carrara ❶

*Massa Carrara. 70,000. FS Piazza Cesare Battisti 1 (0585 64 14 71). Mon.*

Internationally renowned for its marble quarries, Carrara's almost flawless white stone has been prized for centuries by famous sculptors from Michelangelo to Henry Moore (the stone for Michelangelo's *David* came from Carrara). The region's 300 or more quarries date back to Roman times, making this one of the oldest industrial sites in continuous use in the world. Many of the town's marble-sawing mills and workshops welcome visitors, offering them the chance to see the ways in which marble and quartz are worked. These techniques – along with marble artifacts old and new – can be seen at the **Museo Civico del Marmo**.

Local marble is put to good use in the town's **Duomo** in Piazza del Duomo, particularly in the fine Pisan-Romanesque façade with its delicate rose window. The cathedral square also contains Michelangelo's house, used by the sculptor during his visits to select blocks of marble. The town has some lovely corners to explore, in particular the elegant Piazza Alberica. Most visitors head for the stone quarries that are open to the public at nearby **Colonnata** and at **Fantiscritti** (take one of the regular town buses or follow the signs to the "Cave di Marmo"). The latter features a small museum with displays of various marble quarrying techniques.

**A quarry in the marble-bearing hills around Carrara**

**Museo Civico del Marmo**
Viale XX Settembre. **Tel** *0585 84 57 46. Mon–Sat.*

## Garfagnana ❷

*Lucca. FS Castelnuovo di Garfagnana. Piazza delle Erbe, Castelnuovo di Garfagnana (0583 64 10 07).*

A lovely verdant, silent valley wedged between the Orecchiella mountains and the Alpi Apuane, the Garfagnana region can be explored from **Seravezza**, **Barga** or **Castelnuovo di Garfagnana**. While the town of Barga makes the prettiest base, thanks to its tawny stone cathedral and charming streets, Castelnuovo is more convenient for drives and walks in the surrounding mountains. **San Pellegrino in Alpe** in the Orecchiella has a fascinating folklore museum, the **Museo Etnografico**. It is easily seen in conjunction with the **Orto Botanico Pania di Corfino** at the headquarters of the **Parco dell'Orecchiella** at Pania di Corfino, with its collection of local Alpine trees.

To the west is the Parco Naturale delle Alpi Apuane, an area whose spectacular jagged peaks and wooded valleys are criss-crossed by hiking trails and scenic mountain roads.

**Museo Etnografico**
Via del Voltone 15, San Pellegrino in Alpe. **Tel** *0583 64 90 72. Tue–Sun (Jul–Aug: daily).*

**Parco dell'Orecchiella**
Centro Visitatori, Orecchiella. **Tel** *0583 61 90 02. Easter–May, 15–30 Sep Sat & Sun; Jun–Sep: daily; Oct: Sun.*

**Orto Botanico Pania di Corfino**
Parco dell'Orecchiella. **Tel** *0583 64 49 11. May–Sep: Sun (Jul–Aug: daily).*

**The Parco Naturale delle Alpi Apuane on the edge of the Garfagnana**

**One of many seaside cafés lining the waterfront in the popular beach resort of Viareggio**

## Bagni di Lucca ❸

*Lucca. 7,400. Viale Umberto I 97 (0583 80 57 45). Wed, Sat.*

All over Tuscany there are hot springs of volcanic origin, like Bagni di Lucca. The Romans first exploited the springs and built bath complexes where army veterans who settled in the area could relax. More spas came into prominence in the Middle Ages and the Renaissance, and they have continued to be recommended for relieving a variety of ailments, such as arthritis.

Tuscan spas really came into their own in the early 19th century when Bagni di Lucca reached its heyday as one of Europe's most fashionable spas, frequented by emperors, kings and aristocrats. Visitors came not only for thermal cures, but also for the **Casino** (1837), one of Europe's first licensed gambling houses. These days the town is rather sleepy, and its main sights are the 19th-century monuments, including the Neo-Gothic **English Church** (1839) on Via Crawford and the **Cimitero Anglicano** (Protestant Cemetery) on Via Letizia.

**Environs:** Southeast of Bagni di Lucca lies another popular spa town, **Montecatini Terme**. Developed in the 18th century, this town is one of the most interesting with a wide range of spa architecture, from Neo-Classical to Art Nouveau spa establishments.

## Viareggio ❹

*Lucca. 55,000. FS Viale Carducci 10 (0584 96 22 33). Thu.*

Known for its carnival, held in January and early February, this is also the most popular of the resorts on the Versilia coast. Its famous "Liberty" (Art Nouveau) style of architecture can be seen in the grand hotels, villas and cafés built in the 1920s after the resort's original boardwalk and timber chalets went up in flames in 1917. The finest example of the architecture is the **Gran Caffè Margherita** at the end of Passeggiata Margherita, designed by the prolific father of Italian Art Nouveau, Galileo Chini.

## Torre del Lago Puccini ❺

*Lucca. 11,000. FS Viale Kennedy 2 (0584 35 98 93). Fri, & Sun.*

A glorious avenue of lime trees, the Via dei Tigli, connects Viareggio with Torre del Lago Puccini, once the home of the opera composer Giacomo Puccini (1858–1924). He and his wife are buried in their former home, now the **Museo Villa Puccini**, a small museum that features the piano on which the maestro composed many of his works. Equal prominence is given to the villa's original fittings, including the gun room that housed Puccini's hunting rifle. **Lago Massaciuccoli**, a nature reserve for rare and migrant birds, provides a pretty backdrop for open-air performances of Puccini's works.

**Museo Villa Puccini**
Piazzale Belvedere Puccini 226.
***Tel*** *0584 34 14 45. Tue–Sun.*
*Nov, 25 Dec.*

**Near Puccini's lakeside home at Torre del Lago Puccini**

# Street-by-Street: Lucca ❻

Lucca's regular grid of streets still follows the pattern of the former Roman colony founded in 180 BC. Great, solid ramparts, built in the 16th to 17th century, help to shut out traffic, making the city a pleasant place to explore on foot. San Michele in Foro – one of the town's many fine Pisan-Romanesque churches – stands on the site of the Roman forum *(foro)*, the city's main square laid out in ancient times. It is still Lucca's main square today.

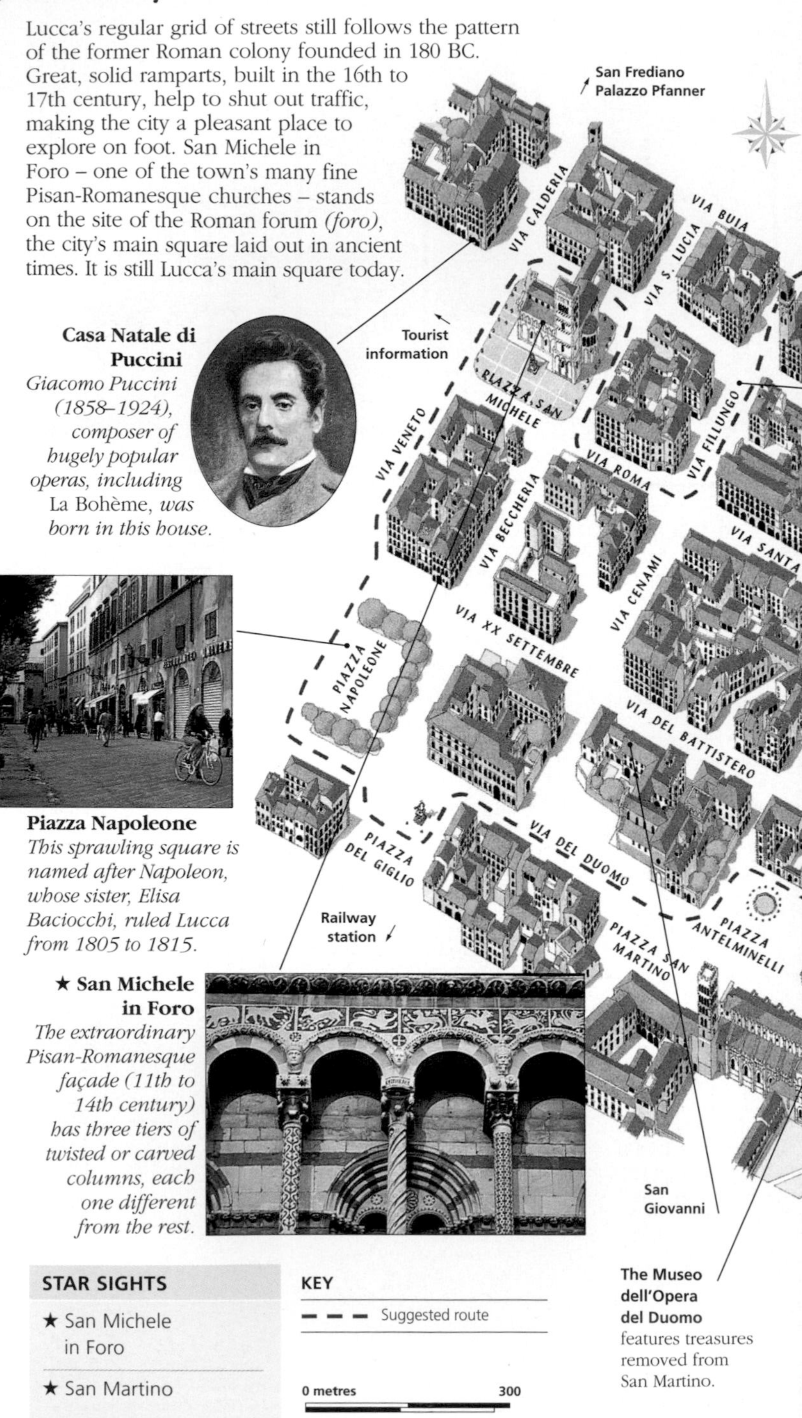


**Casa Natale di Puccini**
*Giacomo Puccini (1858–1924), composer of hugely popular operas, including* La Bohème, *was born in this house.*

**Piazza Napoleone**
*This sprawling square is named after Napoleon, whose sister, Elisa Baciocchi, ruled Lucca from 1805 to 1815.*

**★ San Michele in Foro**
*The extraordinary Pisan-Romanesque façade (11th to 14th century) has three tiers of twisted or carved columns, each one different from the rest.*

**The Museo dell'Opera del Duomo** features treasures removed from San Martino.

**STAR SIGHTS**

★ San Michele in Foro

★ San Martino

**KEY**

– – – Suggested route

0 metres 300

0 yards 300

## VISITORS' CHECKLIST

*100,000.* FS *Piazza Ricasoli.* *Piazzale Verdi.* *Piazza Santa Maria 35 (0583 91 99 31).* *3rd Sun of month (antiques), Wed, Sat.* *12 Jul: Palio della Balestra; Jul–Sep: Estate Musicale; 13 Sep: Luminara di S. Croce; Sep: Lucchese.*
**www**.luccaturismo.it

**In Via Fillungo**, Lucca's main shopping street, several shop fronts are decorated with Art Nouveau details.

**San Martino**
*cca's beautiful 11th-century ıomo is one of the outstand-g examples of the exuberant san-Romanesque style.*

**Apostles from the mosaic on the façade of San Frediano in Lucca**

### San Frediano

Piazza San Frediano. *daily.*

San Frediano's striking façade features a colourful 13th-century mosaic, *The Ascension*, a fine prelude to the church's wonderfully atmospheric interior. Pride of place goes to a splendid Romanesque font on the right, its sides carved with scenes from the Life of Christ and the story of Moses. Note the scene of Moses and his followers (dressed as medieval knights) as they pass through the divided Red Sea. In the second chapel in the north aisle, Aspertini's frescoes (1508–9) tell the story of Lucca's precious relic, the Volto Santo – a carving said to date from the time of the Crucifixion. The fine altarpiece (1422) in the fourth chapel of San Frediano's north aisle is by Jacopo della Quercia.

### San Michele in Foro

Piazza San Michele. *daily.*

Built on the site of the old Roman forum *(foro)*, San Michele's rich mixture of twisted marble columns and Cosmati work (inlaid marble) adorns one of the most exuberant Pisan-Romanesque façades in Tuscany. Built between the 11th and 14th centuries, its decoration is overwhelmingly pagan. Only the huge winged figure of St Michael on the pediment marks this out as a church. The interior has little of interest except for the beautiful painting of *Saints Helena, Jerome, Sebastian and Roch* by Filippino Lippi (1457–1504).

### Casa Natale di Puccini

Corte San Lorenzo 9. ***Tel*** *0583 58 40 28.* *Jun–Oct: 10am–6pm daily; Nov–Dec & Mar–May: 10am–1pm, 3–6pm Tue–Sun.* *1 Jan, 25 Dec.*

The fine 15th-century house in which Giacomo Puccini (1858–1924) was born is now a shrine to the great opera composer. It contains portraits of Puccini, costume designs for his operas and the piano he used when composing his last opera, *Turandot*.

### Via Fillungo

Lucca's principal shopping street winds its way through the heart of the city towards the Anfiteatro Romano. Its northern end has several shops with Art Nouveau ironwork; halfway down lies the deconsecrated church of San Cristoforo, built in the 13th century, with a lovely interior.

**One of the many bars and shops along Via Fillungo**

# Exploring Lucca

Lucca's peaceful narrow lanes wind among the medieval buildings, opening suddenly to reveal churches, tiny piazzas, and many other reminders of the city's long history, including a Roman amphitheatre.

**Medieval buildings mark the outline of Lucca's old Roman amphitheatre**

### Anfiteatro Romano

Piazza del Mercato.

Roman *Luca* was founded in 180 BC, and stones from the ancient Roman amphitheatre have been ransacked over the centuries to build churches and palaces, leaving only a handful of original fragments studded into today's arena-shaped Piazza del Mercato. Slum housing clogged the piazza until 1830, when it was cleared on the orders of Marie Louise, the city's Bourbon ruler of that time. It was then that the amphitheatre's original shape was revealed, a graphic and evocative reminder of Lucca's rich Roman heritage. Low archways at the piazza's cardinal points mark the gates through which beasts and gladiators would once have entered the arena.

### Museo dell'Opera del Duomo

Piazza Antelminelli 5. ***Tel*** *0583 49 05 30.* *daily (Nov–Mar: Mon–Fri am).* *1 Jan, Easter (am), 25 Dec.*

The museum, housed in the former Archbishop's Palace (14th century), displays the treasures of the Duomo of San Martino. These include the

### SAN MARTINO

Piazza San Martino. ***Tel*** *0583 95 70 68.* *daily.* *for sacristy.*

Lucca's cathedral was built after the campanile, hence the façade's cramped and asymmetric appearance. The main portals contain remarkable 13th-century carvings by Nicola Pisano and Guidetto da Como. The Tempietto inside houses a painting by Tintoretto and the Volto Santo, a revered 13th-century effigy once believed to have been carved at the time of the Crucifixion.

**Façade**
*The cathedral façade is decorated with Romanesque sculptures and colonnading (1204).*

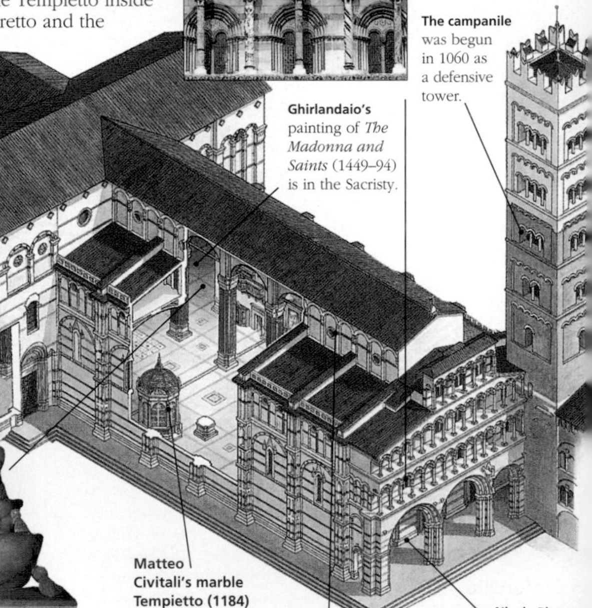

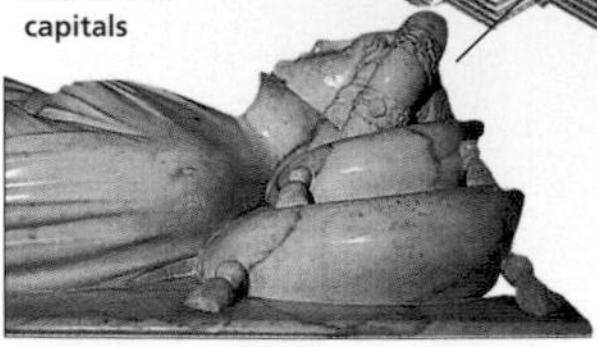

**The campanile** was begun in 1060 as a defensive tower.

**Ghirlandaio's** painting of *The Madonna and Saints* (1449–94) is in the Sacristy.

**Domed chapels encircling the apse**

**Romanesque blind arcades and carved capitals**

**Matteo Civitali's marble Tempietto (1184)**

**Tomb of Ilaria del Carretto**
*This beautiful portrait in marble by Jacopo della Quercia (1405–6) is of the youthful bride of Paolo Guinigi.*

**Circular clerestory** windows, in the nave and above the aisle roof, illuminate the church's unusually tall nave.

**Nicola Pisano** (1200 –78) carved the *Journey of the Magi* and *Deposition* on the left portal.

*For hotels and restaurants in this region see pp579–82 and pp629–32*

Baroque gods and goddesses in the garden of the Palazzo Pfanner

11th-century carved stone head of a king and a rare 12th-century Limoges casket, possibly created for a relic of St Thomas à Becket. The Croce dei Pisani, made by Vincenzo di Michele in 1411, is a sublime masterpiece of the goldsmith's art. It shows Christ on the Tree of Redemption, surrounded by angels, the Virgin, St John and the other Evangelists.

### Palazzo Pfanner

Via degli Asili 33. ***Tel** 340 923 30 85 or 0583 954 029.*
*Mar–Oct: 10am–6pm Thu–Tue; Nov–Feb: by appt.*

This elegant, imposing house (1667) has a beautiful outside staircase. It also boasts one of Tuscany's most delightful formal gardens. Laid out in the 18th century, the garden's central avenue is lined with Baroque statues of the gods and goddesses of ancient Roman mythology. The garden can also be viewed while walking along the ramparts.

The house itself contains an interesting collection of furniture, antiques and medical instruments.

### Ramparts

One of the pleasures of visiting Lucca is strolling along the ramparts – the magnificent city walls, whose tree-lined promenade offers some entrancing views of the city. Work on the ramparts began around 1500, when advances in military technology made the old medieval defences ineffective. On their completion in 1645, the walls were some of the most advanced of their time. One of their most curious features was the open space that lay beyond them, and which survives to this day, cleared to prevent the enemy taking cover in trees and undergrowth. Ironically, the walls never actually had to be defended, and they were eventually converted into a public park in the early 19th century.

Part of the imposing 17th-century ramparts that encircle Lucca

### Santa Maria Forisportam

Piazza di Santa Maria Forisportam.
*daily.*

This church was built at the end of the 12th century, beyond the Roman walls of Lucca. Its name, Forisportam, means "outside the gate". The unfinished marble façade, in Pisan-Romanesque style, has blind arcading. Above the central portal is a relief of the *Coronation of the Virgin* (17th century). The interior was redesigned in the early 16th century, resulting in the nave and transepts being raised. The fourth altar of the south aisle contains a painting of *St Lucy,* and the north transept has an *Assumption,* both by Guercino (1591–1666).

### Museo Nazionale di Villa Guinigi

Via della Quarquonia. ***Tel** 0583 49 60 33. Tue–Sun (Sun till 2pm only). 1 Jan, 1 May, 25 Dec.*

This massive Renaissance villa was built in 1418 for Paolo Guinigi, leading light of the noble family who ruled Lucca in the early 15th century. A familiar landmark of the city is the battlemented tower, the Torre dei Guinigi, with oak trees growing at the top. It offers good views over the city and the Apuan Alps. The garden features traces of a Roman mosaic, together with a pride of Romanesque lions removed from the city's walls.

Romanesque lion in the Museo Nazionale Guinigi

Inside, the museum's first floor is devoted to sculptures and archaeological displays. The highlights are works by Matteo Civitali, Jacopo della Quercia and fine Romanesque reliefs removed from several of Lucca's churches. Most of the paintings in the gallery on the floor above are by minor local artists, with the exception of two works by Fra Bartolomeo (c.1472–1517): *God the Father with Saints Catherine and Mary Magdalene* and the *Madonna della Misericordia.* The floor also has furnishings, church vestments and choir stalls from Lucca's cathedral, inlaid with marquetry views of the city carved in 1529.

# Pisa ❼

Inlaid marble, Duomo façade

For much of the Middle Ages, Pisa's powerful navy ensured its dominance of the western Mediterranean. Trading links with Spain and North Africa in the 12th century brought vast mercantile wealth and formed the basis of a cultural revolution that is still reflected in Pisa's splendid buildings – especially the Duomo, Baptistry and Campanile (Leaning Tower). Pisa's decline began in 1284, with its defeat by Genoa, and was hastened by the silting up of the harbour. The city fell to the Florentines in 1406, but suffered its worst crisis in 1944 when it fell victim to Allied bombing.

The Baptistry, Duomo and Leaning Tower in Pisa's Campo dei Miracoli

### Leaning Tower

*See p326.*
**www**.opapisa.it *(reservations).* *Visits last 30 mins. No children under 8 allowed.*

### Duomo and Baptistry

Piazza Duomo. ***Tel*** *050 83 50 11.* *daily (Duomo: pm only on Sun).* **www**.opapisa.it

Pisa's famous Leaning Tower is now the best-known building in the Campo dei Miracoli (Field of Miracles). Originally, however, it was intended as a campanile to complement the Duomo, which was begun by Buscheto in 1064. Today the Duomo stands as one of the finest Pisan-Romanesque buildings in Tuscany, its wonderful four-tiered façade a medley of creamy colonnades and intricate blind arcades. Buscheto's tomb is in the left arch of the façade. Other important features of the exterior include the Portale di San Ranieri (leading to the south transept) and the bronze doors (1180), decorated with reliefs cast by Bonanno Pisano, the first architect of the Leaning Tower. Inside, the highlights are the carved pulpit (1302–11) by Giovanni Pisano, the *Tomb of Emperor Henry VII* (1315) by Tino da Camaino, and a mosaic of *Christ in Majesty* in the apse, completed by Cimabue in 1302.

A detail from the Duomo pulpit

The circular Baptistry was begun in 1152 along Romanesque lines, and finished a century later (the delay caused by a shortage of money) in a more ornate Gothic style by Nicola and Giovanni Pisano. The former was responsible for the marble pulpit (1260) in the interior, carved with reliefs of the *Nativity,* the *Adoration of the Magi,* the *Presentation,* the *Crucifixion* and the *Last Judgment.* The pillars that support the pulpit feature statues of the Virtues. The inlaid marble font (1246) is by Guido da Como.

### Camposanto

Piazza dei Miracoli. ***Tel*** *050 83 50 11.* *daily.* *1 Jan, 25 Dec.*

The Camposanto (cemetery) is the fourth element in the Campo dei Miracoli's lovely ensemble. Begun in 1278 by Giovanni di Simone, the vast marble arcades of this long, rectangular building are said to enclose soil from the Holy Land. Bombs in World War II all but destroyed its once famous frescoes, leaving only traces of *The Triumph of Death* (1360–80). Nearby is the Orto Botanico, one of Europe's oldest botanical gardens.

A fresco from the *Triumph of Death* cycle in the Camposanto

Santa Maria della Spina alongside the River Arno in Pisa

### Museo dell'Opera del Duomo

Piazza del Duomo 6. ***Tel*** *050 83 10 11.* *daily.*

Housed in the cathedral's 13th-century former Chapter House, this excellent modern museum displays exhibits removed over the years from the Duomo, Baptistry and Camposanto. Among the highlights is an imposing 10th-century hippogriff (half horse, half griffin). Cast in bronze by Moorish craftsmen, this statue was looted by Pisan adventurers during the wars against the Saracens. There are also works by both Nicola and Giovanni Pisano, notably Giovanni's ivory *Virgin and Child* (1300), carved for the Duomo's high altar. Other exhibits include paintings, Roman and Etruscan remains, and ecclesiastical treasures.

10th-century bronze hippogriff

### Museo Nazionale di San Matteo

Lungarno Mediceo, Piazza San Matteo 1. ***Tel*** *050 54 18 65.* *8:30am–7pm Tue–Sun (only am Sun).*

This museum is located on the banks of the Arno in San Matteo, an elegantly fronted medieval convent that in the 1800s also served as a prison. Much of the building has been closed for years – several of the rooms have no numbers and some of the exhibits are poorly labelled. Nevertheless, the museum presents a unique opportunity to examine the complete sweep of Pisan and Florentine art from the 12th to the 17th centuries.

The first rooms are devoted to sculpture and early Tuscan paintings. The best exhibits include a 14th-century polyptych by Francesco Traini of *Scenes from the Life of St Dominic,* Simone Martini's fine polyptych of *The Madonna and Saints* (1321), and a 14th-century statue of the *Madonna del Latte,* attributed to Andrea Pisano, another member of Pisa's talented school of medieval sculptors. The half-length statue, in gilded marble, shows Christ feeding at his mother's breast. In room 6 are some of the highlights of the museum, including Masaccio's *St Paul* (1426), Gentile da Fabriano's radiant 15th-century *Madonna of Humility,* and Donatello's reliquary bust of *San Rossore* (1424–7). Additional rooms contain paintings by Guido Reni, Benozzo Gozzoli, Rosso Fiorentino, and an important picture of *Christ* attributed to Fra Angelico (c.1395–1455).

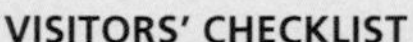

### VISITORS' CHECKLIST

*100,000.* *Galileo Galilei 5 km (3 miles) S.* *Pisa Centrale, Pza della Stazione.* *Pza Sant' Antonio.* *P.za Duomo (050 56 04 64); Pza Vittorio Emanuele 16 (050 422 91).* *Wed & Sat.* *17 Jun: Regata di San Ranieri; last Sun in Jun: Gioco del Ponte.* **www**.pisa.turismo.toscana.it

### Santa Maria della Spina

Lungarno Gambacorti. ***Tel*** *055 321 54 46.* *Tue–Sun.*

The roofline of this tiny church, located just beyond the Ponte Solferino, bristles with spiky Gothic pinnacles, miniature spires and niches sheltering statues of apostles and saints. The decoration reflects the history of the church, which was built between 1230 and 1323 to house a thorn *(spina)* from Christ's Crown of Thorns, the gift of a Pisan merchant. The church was once even closer to the Arno, but was rebuilt on the present site in 1871 to protect it from flooding.

### Piazza dei Cavalieri

The huge building on the north side of this square is the Palazzo dei Cavalieri, home to one of Pisa University's most prestigious colleges: the Scuola Normale Superiore. Designed by Vasari in 1562, the building, which is covered in exuberant black and white *sgraffito* decoration (designs scratched into wet plaster), served as the headquarters of the Cavalieri di Santo Stefano, an order of knights created by Cosimo I in 1561. The imposing statue outside depicts Cosimo I.

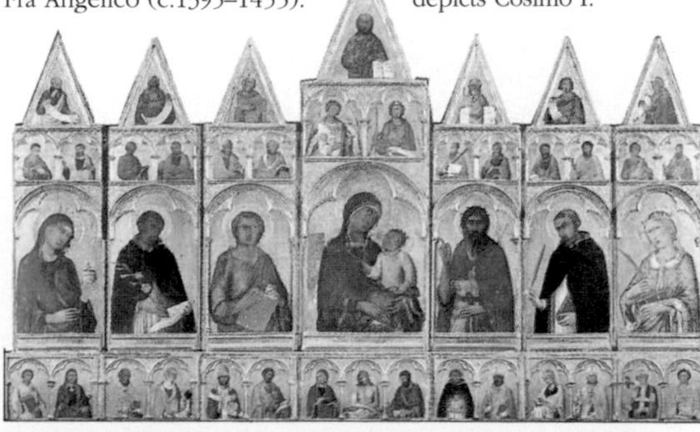

***The Virgin and Child*** **(1321) by Simone Martini in the Museo Nazionale**

# The Leaning Tower of Pisa

Begun in 1173 on sandy silt subsoil, the Leaning Tower (Torre Pendente) started to tilt even before the third storey was finished in 1274. Despite the shallow foundations, construction continued and the structure was completed in 1350. The tower's apparent flouting of the laws of gravity has attracted many visitors over the centuries, including the Pisan scientist Galileo, who climbed to the top to conduct his experiments on the velocity of falling objects. After several engineering interventions that decreased the lean by 38 cm (14 in), the tower is once again safe and open to the public.

Galileo Galilei (1564–1642)

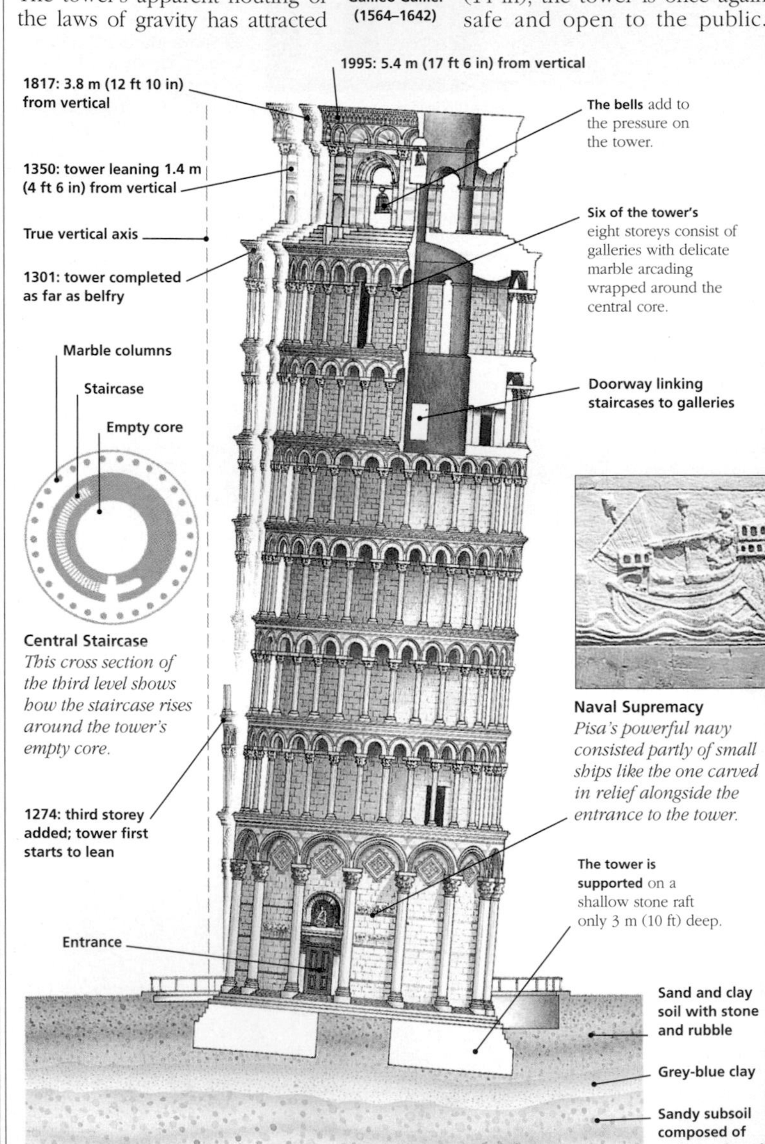


**Central Staircase**
*This cross section of the third level shows how the staircase rises around the tower's empty core.*

**Naval Supremacy**
*Pisa's powerful navy consisted partly of small ships like the one carved in relief alongside the entrance to the tower.*

## Vinci ❽

Florence. 1,500. Wed.

Famous as the birthplace of Leonardo da Vinci (1452–1519), this hilltop town celebrates the genius in the **Museo Leonardiano**, housed in the 13th-century castle. Among the displays are wooden models of Leonardo's machines and inventions, most are based on drawings from his notebooks, copies of which are shown alongside. These include a bicycle, his conception of a car, an armoured tank and even a machine-gun.

**Museo Leonardiano**
Castello dei Conti Guidi.
*Tel 0571 560 55.* *daily.*

**Model bicycle based on designs by Leonardo, Museo Leonardiano**

## Pistoia ❾

93,000. Palazzo dei Vescovi, Piazza del Duomo (0573 216 22). Wed & Sat.

Pistoia's citizens were once known for violence and intrigue, a reputation grounded in the medieval disputes between the city's rival factions, the Bianchi and Neri (Whites and Blacks). Their favoured weapon was a tiny, locally made dagger known as a *pistola*. Long a centre of metalwork, everything from buses to mattress springs are now made here. In the centre, several fine historic buildings are preserved.

**Duomo**
Piazza del Duomo. *daily.*
Piazza del Duomo, Pistoia's main square, is dominated by the Duomo (San Zeno) and its bulky 12th-century campanile, originally built as a watchtower in the city walls. The interior of the Duomo is rich in funerary monuments. The finest of these, in the south aisle, is the tomb of Cino da Pistoia. He was a friend of Dante and fellow poet, and is depicted in a relief (1337) lecturing to a class of young boys.

Nearby is the chapel of St James and its extraordinary silver altar decorated with more than 600 statues and reliefs. Although the earliest of these dates from 1287, the altar was not completed until 1456. One of the craftsmen involved was Brunelleschi, who began his career as a silversmith before turning to architecture. Also in the Piazza del Duomo is the octagonal Baptistry, completed in 1359.

**Detail of frieze (1514–25) by Giovanni della Robbia, Ospedale del Ceppo**

**Ospedale del Ceppo**
Piazza Giovanni XXIII.
This hospital and orphanage, founded in 1277, was named after the *ceppo* (hollowed-out tree trunk) that was used to collect donations for its work. The main façade features coloured terracotta panels (1514–25) by Giovanni della Robbia illustrating the *Seven Works of Mercy*. The portico is by Michelozzo.

**The Pisan-Romanesque façade of Pistoia's Duomo (San Zeno)**

**Cappella del Tau**
Corso Silvano Fedi 70. *Tel 0573 322 04.* *8:30am–1:30pm Mon–Sat.*
The Cappella del Tau (1360) is so called because the monks who built it wore on their cloaks the letter T (*tau* in Greek), symbolizing a crutch and their work with the sick and disabled. Inside there are frescoes by Niccolò di Tommaso on *The Creation* and the *Life of St Anthony Abbot* (1370). Two doors down, the **Palazzo Tau** has work by Marino Marini, Pistoia's best-known 20th-century artist.

***The Fall* (1372) by Niccolò di Tommaso in the Cappella del Tau**

**San Giovanni Fuorcivitas**
Via Cavour. *daily.*
Built in the 12th to 14th centuries, the striking church of San Giovanni Fuorcivitas (literally "St John Outside the City") once stood beyond the city walls. Its north flank is clad in banded marble and there is a Romanesque relief of the Last Supper over the portal. Inside, the holy water stoup, carved in marble with figures of the Virtues, is by Giovanni Pisano (1245–1320). A masterly pulpit, carved in 1270 with scenes from the New Testament, is by Guglielmo da Pisa. Both are among the finest works of this period, when artists were reviving the art of carving.

## Prato ⑩

170,000. Piazza Duomo 8 (0574 241 12). Mon.

While textile factories gird Prato's outskirts, the city centre retains several important churches and museums. The **Duomo** (begun 1211) is flanked by the Pulpit of the Holy Girdle (1434–8), designed by Donatello and Michelozzo, used once a year to display a girdle, reputedly given to Thomas the Apostle before the Assumption of the Virgin. Inside the Duomo is *The Life of John the Baptist* (1452–66) by Fra Filippo Lippi, and a fresco cycle (1392–5) by Agnolo Gaddi.

Other sights include the **Museo Civico**, **Santa Maria delle Carceri**, a Renaissance church in Piazza delle Carceri; the **Castello dell' Imperatore**, a fortress built by Emperor Frederick II in 1237; the **Centro per l'Arte Contemporanea Pecci**; and the **Museo del Tessuto**, which traces the history of Prato's textile industry.

**Museo Civico**
Palazzo Pretorio, Piazza del Comune. ***Tel*** *0574 183 63 02.* *for restoration.*

**Castello dell'Imperatore**
Piazza delle Carceri. *Wed–Mon.*

**Centro per l'Arte Contemporanea Pecci**
Viale della Repubblica 277. ***Tel*** *0574 53 17.* *Wed–Mon.*

**Museo del Tessuto**
Via Santa Chiara 24. ***Tel*** *0574 61 15 03.* *10am–7pm daily.*

***Madonna del Ceppo*** **by Fra Filippo Lippi in Prato's Museo Civico**

**Buontalenti's Villa di Artimino, or "Villa of a Hundred Chimneys"**

## Artimino ⑪

Prato. *400.*

A small fortified hamlet, Artimino is remarkable for the unspoiled Romanesque church of **San Leonardo**. Outside the walls lies the **Villa di Artimino**, designed by Buontalenti in 1594 for Grand Duke Ferdinando I. Also known as the "Villa of a Hundred Chimneys" – after the chimney pots crowding the roofline – it houses the **Museo Archeologico Etrusco**, a collection of archaeological exhibits.

**Environs:** For lovers of Pontormo's paintings, the church of **San Michele** in Carmignano, 5 km (3 miles) north of Artimino, contains *The Visitation* (1530). East of here lies the villa of **Poggio a Caiano**. Built in 1480 by Giuliano da Sangallo for Lorenzo de' Medici *(see p253)*, it was the first Italian villa to be designed in the Renaissance style.

**Villa di Artimino**
Viale Papa Giovanni 23. **Villa *Tel*** *055 875 14 27.* *Tue am by appt.* **Museum *Tel*** *055 871 81 24.* *9:30am–12:30pm daily.*

**Poggio a Caiano**
Piazza Medici. ***Tel*** *055 87 70 12.* *Tue–Sun; also 1st & 4th Mon of month.*

## San Miniato ⑫

Pisa. *3,900.* *Piazza del Bastione (0571 427 45).* *Tue.*

This hilltop town manages to remain aloof from the vast industrial sprawl of the Arno valley. Its key building is the semi-derelict Rocca (castle), built for Frederick II, German Holy Roman Emperor, in the 13th century. Close by stands the **Museo Diocesano**, which is home to a *Crucifixion* (c.1430) attributed to Filippo Lippi, a terracotta bust of Christ attributed to Verrocchio (1435–88), and the *Virgin of the Holy Girdle* by Andrea del Castagno (c.1417–57). Next door, the red-brick Romanesque façade of the **Duomo** dates from the 12th century. Its strange inset majolica plates, evidence of trade with Spain or North Africa, probably represent the North Star and the constellations of Ursa Major and Minor (all three were key points of reference for early navigators).

**Museo Diocesano**
Piazza Duomo. ***Tel*** *0571 40 04 58.* *10am–1pm, 2–5pm Thu–Sun (Apr–Oct: 10am–6pm).*

**Façade of the Duomo in San Miniato**

## Fiesole ⑬

Florence. *15,000.* *Via Portigiani 3 (055 59 87 20).* *Sat.*

Fiesole stands in rolling hilly countryside 8 km (5 miles) north of Florence. Idyllically situated among olive groves, it is a popular retreat from the city thanks to its hilltop position which attracts cool breezes. Founded in the 7th century BC, the original Etruscan colony was a powerful force in central Italy, only

A view over the hills and rooftops of Fiesole from Via di San Francesco

surrendering its supremacy after the foundation of Florence (1st century BC).

The restored **Duomo** of San Romolo in Piazza Mino da Fiesole was begun in 1028. It has a massive bell tower and a bare Romanesque interior. Behind the Duomo, an archaeological area contains the remains of a 1st-century BC **Roman theatre**, traces of **Etruscan walls** from the 4th century BC, and the **Museo Faesulanum**, with a collection of bronzes, ceramics and jewellery dating from the Bronze Age.

Via di San Francesco, a steep lane offering lovely views, leads to the Franciscan friary of **San Francesco** (14th century) and the interesting 9th-century church of **Sant'Alessandro**, with a Neo-Classical façade.

Via Vecchia Fiesolana leads to the hamlet of **San Domenico**, where the 15th-century church of the same name contains a painting of the *Madonna with Angels and Saints* (c.1430) by Fra Angelico and the Chapter House contains a fresco of *The Crucifixion* (c.1430), also by him. Close by, on the Via della Badia dei Roccettini, is the **Badia Fiesolana**, a pretty Romanesque church with a striped marble façade and interior of local grey sandstone, *pietra serena*.

**Museo Faesulanum**
Via Portigiani 1. ***Tel*** *055 596 12 93.*
*daily (Oct–Mar: Wed–Mon).*

## Arezzo ⓮

*92,000.* *Piazza della Repubblica 28 (0575 377 678).* *Sat.*

Arezzo is one of Tuscany's wealthiest cities, its prosperity based on a thriving jewellery industry. Although much of its medieval centre was destroyed during World War II, resulting in extensive rebuilding and many medieval alleys being replaced by broad avenues, the city preserves some outstanding sights: foremost are Piero della Francesca's famous frescoes in the church of **San Francesco** *(see pp330–31)*. Close to the church on Corso Italia, the main street, stands the **Pieve di Santa Maria**, which boasts one of the most ornate Romanesque façades in the region. To its rear stretches the steeply sloping **Piazza Grande**, flanked by an arcade (1573) designed by Vasari, and by the **Palazzo della Fraternità dei Laici** (1377–1552). The latter features a *Madonna* relief by Bernardo Rossellino. The huge **Duomo** to the north is best known for its 16th-century stained glass and a small fresco of *Mary Magdalene* by Piero della Francesca (1416–92). The **Museo Diocesano** features three wooden crucifixes, dating from the 12th and 13th centuries, a bas relief of *The Annunciation* (1434) by Rossellino and paintings by Vasari. More works by Vasari can be seen in the **Casa di Vasari**, a house built by the artist in 1540. Still more frescoes by him are displayed in the **Museo d'Arte Medioevale e Moderna**, a museum that is famed for its excellent collection of majolica pottery.

The **Fortezza Medicea**, a ruined Medici castle built by Antonio da Sangallo during the 16th century, has fine views.

**Museo Diocesano**
Piazzetta Dietro il Duomo 12. ***Tel*** *0575 402 72 29.* *Wed–Sun.*

**Casa di Vasari**
Via XX Settembre 55. ***Tel*** *0575 40 90 50.* *Wed–Mon.*

**Museo d'Arte Medioevale e Moderna**
Via di San Lorentino 8. ***Tel*** *0575 40 90 50.* *Tue–Sun.*

**Fortezza Medicea**
Parco il Prato. ***Tel*** *0575 37 76 78.*
*daily.*

The monthly antiques market held in Arezzo's Piazza Grande

# Arezzo: San Francesco

The 13th-century Church of San Francesco houses one of Italy's greatest fresco cycles, the *Legend of the True Cross* (1452–66), Piero della Francesca's masterpiece. The scenes, on the walls of the choir, are now visible again after a long restoration. They describe the history of the Cross used to crucify Christ, from sprig to Tree of Knowledge, to its use as a bridge during the reign of Solomon, and ultimately its discovery by Helena, mother of Constantine, the first Christian emperor.

**A Group of Onlookers**
*These figures kneel in wonder while Heraclius returns the True Cross to Jerusalem.*

**Excavation of the Cross**
*The town, meant to be Jerusalem, gives a fair representation of 15th-century Arezzo.*

**The Cross** returns to Jerusalem.

**The Defeat of Chosroes** depicts the defeat of a Persian king who had stolen the Cross.

**Judas reveals** where the Cross is hidden.

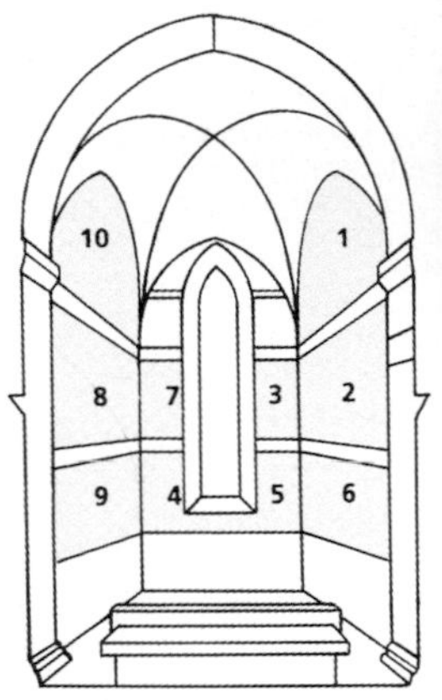


**KEY TO FRESCOES**

**1** The Death of Adam; a sprig from the Tree of Knowledge is planted over his grave; **2** The Queen of Sheba visits Solomon and foresees that a bridge made from the Tree will be used to crucify the greatest king in the world; **3** Solomon, assuming he is the greatest king in the world, orders the bridge to be buried; **4** The Annunciation: Christ's death is foreshadowed in the panel's cruciform structure; **5** Constantine has a vision of the Cross and hears a voice saying "In this sign you shall conquer"; **6** Constantine defeats his rival Maxentius; **7** The Levite Judas is tortured and reveals the location of the True Cross; **8** Three crosses are dug up; Constantine's mother Helena recognizes the True Cross; **9** The Persian king Chosroes is defeated after stealing the Cross; **10** The True Cross is returned to Jerusalem.

**Painted Crucifix**
*The 13th-century Crucifix forms the focal point of the fresco cycle. The figure at the foot of the Cross represents St Francis, to whom the church is dedicated.*

*For hotels and restaurants in this region see pp579–82 and pp629–32*

**The Death of Adam**
*Piero's vivid portrayal of Adam and Eve in old age shows an adept treatment of anatomy. He was one of the first Renaissance artists to paint nude figures.*

## VISITORS' CHECKLIST

P. San Francesco. ***Tel** 0575 35 27 27 (booking mandatory).* 9–6 *Mon–Sat (to 5:30 Sat); 1–5:30pm Sun.* *1 Jan, 25 Dec.*

**The prophets** appear to play no part in the narrative cycle; their presence may be for purely decorative reasons.

**The buildings** in the fresco reflect the newly fashionable styles of Renaissance architecture.

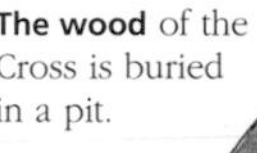

**The wood** of the Cross is buried in a pit.

**Constantine dreams** of the Cross on the eve of battle against rival emperor Maxentius.

**Constantine leads** his cavalry into battle.

**The Queen of Sheba** recognizes the wood of the Cross.

**Solomon's Handshake**
*The handshake between the Queen of Sheba and Solomon, King of Israel, portrays 15th-century hopes for a union between the Orthodox and Western churches.*

**Piero's *The Resurrection* (1463) in Sansepolcro**

## Sansepolcro ⓯

*Arezzo. 16,000. Via Matteotti 8 (0575 74 05 36). Tue, Sat.*

Sansepolcro is the birthplace of Piero della Francesca (1410–92). The town's **Museo Civico** contains two of his masterpieces: *The Resurrection* (1463) and the *Madonna della Misericordia* (1462). It also has a 15th-century *Crucifixion* by Luca Signorelli. In the church of **San Lorenzo** on Via Santa Croce there is a *Deposition* in the Mannerist style by Rosso Fiorentino (1494–1541).

Another renowned painting by Piero della Francesca, the *Madonna del Parto* (1460), can be seen at Via Reglia 1 in Monterchi, 13 km (8 miles) southwest of Sansepolcro.

**Museo Civico**
Via Aggiunti 65. ***Tel*** *0575 73 22 18. daily. public hols.*

## Cortona ⓰

*Arezzo. 23,000. FS Via Nazionale 42 (0575 63 03 52). Sat.*

Cortona was founded by the Etruscans and apart from being one of the oldest hill-towns in Tuscany, it is also one of the most scenic. A major power in the Middle Ages, it was able to hold its own against Siena and Arezzo. Today it is a charming maze of old streets and medieval buildings, like the **Palazzo Comunale** on Piazza della Repubblica. The town's early history is traced in the **Museo dell'Accademia Etrusca**, which contains Etruscan artifacts and a wide variety of Egyptian and Roman remains. The small **Museo Diocesano** features several fine paintings, in particular a *Crucifixion* by the Renaissance artist Pietro Lorenzetti, a *Deposition* (1502) by Luca Signorelli, and a sublime *Annunciation* (c.1434) by Fra Angelico. Signorelli, born in Cortona, is buried in the church of **San Francesco** (built in 1245), which contains an *Annunciation* painted in Baroque style by Pietro da Cortona, another native artist. The **Madonna del Calcinaio** (1485), a gem of Renaissance architecture, is located on the southern outskirts of town.

**The 13th-century Palazzo Comunale in Cortona**

**Museo dell'Accademia Etrusca**
Palazzo Casali, Piazza Signorelli 9. ***Tel*** *0575 63 72 35. daily (except Mon in winter).*

**Museo Diocesano**
Piazza del Duomo 1. ***Tel*** *0575 628 30. daily (Tue–Sun in winter).*

## Chiusi ⓱

*Siena. 10,000. FS Piazza Duomo 1 (0578 22 76 67). Tue.*

Chiusi is now a largely modern town, but in the past it was one of the most powerful cities in the Etruscan league, reaching the height of its influence in the 7th and 6th centuries BC *(see p45)*. Numerous Etruscan tombs lie dotted in the surrounding countryside, the source of the exhibits in the town's **Museo Nazionale Etrusco**. Founded in 1871, the museum is packed with cremation urns, vases decorated with black figures and Bucchero ware, burnished to resemble bronze.

The Romanesque **Duomo** in Piazza del Duomo incorporates recycled Roman pillars and capitals. The wall decorations in the nave, resembling frescoes, were painted by Arturo Viligiardi in 1887. There is a Roman mosaic underneath the high altar. Visits can be made to several Etruscan tombs under the town from the **Museo della Cattedrale**, a museum in the cloister of the Duomo that also features displays of Roman, Lombardic and medieval sculpture.

**Museo Nazionale Etrusco**
Via Porsenna 93. ***Tel*** *0578 201 77. 9am–8pm daily.*

**Museo della Cattedrale**
P. del Duomo. ***Tel*** *0578 22 64 90. daily (Jan–Mar: Tue, Thu, Sat, Sun).*

**Etruscan frieze in the Museo Nazionale Etrusco in Chiusi**

Pienza's Piazza Pio II, designed by Bernardo Rossellino (1459)

## Montepulciano ⑱

Siena. 14,000. Piazza Don Minzoni 1 (0578 75 73 41). Thu. www.prolocomontepulciano.it

This is one of Tuscany's highest hill-towns, its walls and fortifications offering broad views over Umbria and southern Tuscany, and the vineyards providing the Vino Nobile wine that has made its name famous. The streets are brimming with Renaissance palazzi. The main street, the Corso, climbs to the **Duomo** (1592–1630), the setting for one of the masterpieces of the Sienese School, the *Assumption* (1401) by Taddeo di Bartolo. The High Renaissance church, **Tempio di San Biagio** (1518–34), lies off the road to Pienza.

## Pienza ⑲

Siena. 2,300. Piazza Dante Alighieri 18 (0578 74 83 59). Fri.

Pienza is a delightful village whose intimate little centre was almost completely redesigned in the 15th century by Pope Pius II. Born as Aeneas Sylvius Piccolomini in 1405, when the village was known as Corsignano, he became a leading Humanist scholar and philosopher. Elected pope in 1458, he decided to rebuild his birthplace, renaming it Pienza in his own honour. The Florentine architect and sculptor, Bernardo Rossellino, was commissioned to build a cathedral, papal palace and town hall (all completed in the three years from 1459 to 1462), but the grander scheme for a planned model Renaissance town was never realized. Some idea of what might have been, however, can still be gained from the **Palazzo Piccolomini**, the former papal palace, which continued to be inhabited by Pius's descendants until 1968. The rooms open to the public include Pius's bedroom and library, though the highlight of a visit is the superb panorama from the loggia and arcaded courtyard at the palace's rear.

Pleasant walks and more great views can be had from the village walls. The airy **Duomo** *(see p252)* next door contains six altarpieces of the *Madonna and Child*, each commissioned from the leading Sienese painters of the day. Rossellino was forced to build the Duomo on a cramped site with poor foundations, and cracks appeared in the building before it was even completed. Today the church's eastern end suffers from severe subsidence.

**Palazzo Piccolomini**
P.za Pio II. ***Tel*** *0578 74 85 03. 10am-6:30pm Tue–Sun. mid-Feb–early Mar, mid-Nov–mid-Dec.*

## Montalcino ⑳

Siena. 5,100. Costa del Municipio 1 (0577 84 93 31). Fri.

Hilltop Montalcino sits at the heart of vineyards that produce Brunello, one of Italy's finest red wines. It can be sampled in the Enoteca (wine shop) situated in the 14th-century **Fortezza** with its impressive ramparts. The town's timeless streets are a pleasure to wander, and there are some buildings of interest. On the way from the fortress into town is the monastery of Sant' Agostino and its 14th-century church with an attractive rose window and, just beyond, the Palazzo Vescovile. On Piazza del Popolo the slim tower of the Palazzo Communale, constructed in the 13th and 14th centuries, stands tall above the town.

**Fortezza**
Piazzale della Fortezza. ***Tel*** *0577 84 92 11. for ramparts.* **Enoteca** *9am–8pm daily (to 7:30pm Sat, Sun; Nov–Mar: 9am–6pm Tue–Sun).*

The Tempio di San Biagio on the outskirts of Montepulciano

The landscape of the Crete Senesi

## Crete Senesi ㉑

Asciano. FS *Antiche Fonti Lavatoie (0577 71 95 10).*

To the south of Siena and central Tuscany is the area known as the Crete Senesi, which is characterized by round clay hillocks eroded by heavy rain over the centuries. Dubbed the "Tuscan desert", it is almost completely barren. Cypress and pine trees, planted to provide windbreaks along roads and around isolated farm houses, are an important feature in this empty, primeval landscape. Shepherds tend flocks of sheep here; the milk is used to produce the strongly flavoured *pecorino* cheese that is popular throughout Tuscany.

## Siena ㉒

*See pp338–43.*

## Monteriggioni ㉓

Siena. *7,000. Piazza Roma (0577 30 48 34). Jun–Aug.* **www**.monteriggioniturismo.it

Monteriggioni is a gem of a medieval hilltop town. It was built in 1203 and ten years later became a garrison town. It is completely encircled by high walls with 14 heavily fortified towers, built to guard the northern borders of Siena's territory against invasion by Florentine armies.

Dante used Monteriggioni as a simile for the deepest abyss at the heart of his *Inferno*, which compares the town's "ring-shaped citadel… crowned with towers" with giants standing in a moat. The perfectly preserved walls are best viewed from the Colle di Val d'Elsa road. Within the walls, the sleepy town consists of a large piazza, a pretty Romanesque church (on the piazza), a few houses, a couple of craft shops, restaurants, and shops selling many of the locally produced Castello di Monteriggioni wines.

**Environs:** West of Monteriggioni by 3 km (2 miles) lies the former Cistercian Abbey of **Abbadia dell' Isola** (12th century). This Romanesque church was largely rebuilt in the 18th century, after the cupola fell apart. It contains frescoes by Taddeo di Bartolo and Vincenzo Tamagni.

Detail from the pulpit in Volterra's Duomo

## San Gimignano ㉔

*See pp344–5.*

## Volterra ㉕

Pisa. *13,000. Via Giusto Turazza 2 (0588 861 50). Sat.* **www**.comune.volterra.pi.it

Like many Etruscan cities, Volterra is situated on a high plateau, offering fine views over the surrounding hills. In many places the ancient Etruscan walls still survive. The **Museo Guarnacci** contains one of the best collections of Etruscan artifacts in Italy. Of special interest is the group of over 600 cinerary urns, made from alabaster or terracotta, many of which were gathered from local tombs.

The **Palazzo dei Priori**, the medieval seat of government on Piazza dei Priori, is the oldest of its kind in Tuscany. It was begun in 1208 and there are 14th-century frescoes inside. The Pisan-Romanesque **Duomo**, located on Piazza San Giovanni, has a fine 13th-century pulpit with sculptured panels.

Volterra's excellent art gallery and museum, the **Pinacoteca e Museo Civico**, features works by Florentine artists. *Christ in Majesty* (1492) by Ghirlandaio shows Christ hovering above an idealized Tuscan landscape. Luca Signorelli's *Virgin and Child with Saints* (1491) states his debt to Roman art through the reliefs on the base of the Virgin's throne. Painted in the same year, his *Annunciation* is a beautifully balanced composition. Another highlight is Rosso Fiorentino's Mannerist painting, *The Deposition* (1521).

The city is famous for its craftsmen who have been carving elaborate statues and *objets d'art* from locally mined alabaster for 2,500 years.

The beautifully preserved walls of Monteriggioni in central Tuscany

The ruined abbey at San Galgano, surrounded by dense woodland

**Museo Guarnacci**
Via Don Minzoni 15. ***Tel*** *0588 863 47.* *daily.* *1 Jan, 25 Dec.*

**Pinacoteca e Museo Civico**
Via dei Sarti 1. ***Tel*** *0588 875 80.* *daily.* *1 Jan, 25 Dec.*

## San Galgano 26

Siena. *from Siena.*
**Abbey & oratory** *daily.*
**www**.sangalgano.org

The remote Cistercian abbey at San Galgano lies in a superb setting. San Galgano (1148–81) was a brave but dissolute knight who turned to God, renouncing the material world. When he tried to break his sword against a rock as a symbol of his rejection of war, it was swallowed by the stone. This he interpreted as a sign of God's approval. He built a hut on a hill above the abbey (the site of today's beehive-shaped chapel at **Montesiepi**, built c.1185). Here he later died a hermit. Pope Urban III declared him a saint.

The abbey, begun in 1218, is Gothic in style, reflecting the French origins of the Cistercian monks who designed it. They avoided contact with the outside world and divided their lives between prayer and labour. Despite an emphasis on poverty, the monks became wealthy from the sale of wood, and by the middle of the 14th century the abbey was corruptly administered and gradually fell into decline.

In the late 14th century, the English mercenary Sir John Hawkwood sacked the abbey and by 1397 the abbot was its sole occupant. It was eventually dissolved in 1652.

St Galgano's sword stands embedded in a stone just inside the door of the circular **oratory**. The 14th-century stone walls of the side chapel are covered with worn frescoes showing scenes from Galgano's life by Ambrogio Lorenzetti (1344).

## Massa Marittima 27

Grosseto. *9,500.* *Amatur, Via Todini 3–5 (0566 90 27 56).* *Wed.*

Set in the Colline Metallifere (metal-bearing hills) where lead, copper and silver ores were mined as early as Etruscan times, Massa Marittima is far from being a grimy industrial town. Examples of Romanesque architecture survive from the time when the town became an independent republic (1225–1335). The Romanesque-Gothic **Duomo** in Piazza Garibaldi is dedicated to St Cerbone, a 6th-century saint whose story is sculpted in stone above the main portal. Inside the building, the *Maestà* is attributed to Duccio (c.1316).

View across the rooftops of Massa Marittima

The **Museo della Miniera** (museum of mining) is located partially inside a former mine shaft and has exhibits that explain mining techniques, tools and minerals.

The **Museo Archeologico e Museo d'Arte Sacra** has material from Paleolithic to Roman times. Other attractions are the Fortezza Senese and the Torre della Candeliera.

**Museo della Miniera**
Via Corridoni. ***Tel*** *0566 90 22 89.* *Tue–Sun (Jul & Aug: daily).* *compulsory.*

**Museo Archeologico e Museo d'Arte Sacra**
Palazzo del Podestà, P.za Garibaldi. ***Tel*** *0566 90 22 89.* *Tue–Sun.*

Denuded hillocks of clay in the Crete Senesi area southeast of Siena ▷

# Street-by-Street: Siena ㉒

Siena's principal sights cluster in the maze of narrow streets and alleys around the fan-shaped Piazza del Campo. One of Europe's greatest medieval squares, the piazza sits at the heart of the city's 17 *contrade*, a series of parishes whose ancient rivalries are still acted out in the twice-yearly Palio *(see p341)*. Loyalty to the *contrada* of one's birth is fierce, and as you wander the streets you will see the parishes' animal symbols repeated on flags, plaques and carvings. Siena's hilly position also means that city walks offer delightful hidden corners and countless sudden views.

**Unicorn *Contrada***

The Duomo dominating Siena's skyline

**★ Duomo**

*Striped black and white marble pillars, surmounted by a carved frieze of the popes, support the Duomo's vaulted ceiling, painted blue with gold stars to resemble the night sky.*

**Via della Galluzza** leads to the house of St Catherine.

**The Baptistry** has fine frescoes and a font with reliefs by Donatello, Jacopo della Quercia and Ghiberti.

**Each tier** of the Duomo's bell tower has one more window than the floor below.

**Museo dell'Opera del Duomo**

*Duccio's* Maestà, *one of the greatest Sienese paintings, was paraded around Siena's streets on its completion in 1311, and influenced the city's painters for decades to come.*

**KEY**

— — — Suggested route

0 metres 300

0 yards 300

*For hotels and restaurants in this region see pp579–82 and pp629–32*

**Loggia della Mercanzia**
*Built in 1417, the arcade is where Siena's medieval merchants and money dealers carried out their business.*

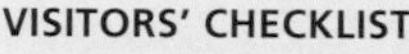

## VISITORS' CHECKLIST

*60,000. FS Piazzale Rosselli. Piazza S. Domenico. Piazza del Campo 56 (0577 28 05 51). Wed. 2 Jul, 16 Aug: Palio; Jul: Settimana Musicale Chigiana (classical music).*
**www**.terresiena.it

**The Logge del Papa**, or Pope's colonnade, was built in honour of Pius II in 1462.

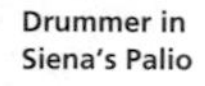

**Drummer in Siena's Palio**

**Tourist information**

**Fonte Gaia**
*These reliefs are 19th-century copies of originals by Jacopo della Quercia.*

**★ Palazzo Pubblico**
*The graceful Gothic town hall was completed in 1342. At 102 m (330 ft), the bell tower, Torre del Mangia, is the second highest medieval tower ever built in Italy.*

**STAR SIGHTS**

★ Duomo

★ Palazzo Pubblico

### Piazza del Campo

Italy's loveliest piazza occupies the site of the old Roman forum, and for much of Siena's early history was the city's principal marketplace. It began to assume its present shape in 1293, when the Council of Nine, Siena's ruling body at the time, began to acquire land with a view to creating a grand civic piazza. The red brick paving was begun in 1327 and completed in 1349, its distinctive nine segments designed to reflect the authority of the Council of Nine and to symbolize the protective folds of the Madonna's cloak. The piazza has been the focus of city life ever since, a setting for executions, bullfights and the twice-yearly drama of the Palio *(see p341)*, a festival centred around a bareback horse race. Cafés, restaurants and fine medieval palazzi now line the Campo's fringes, dominated by the **Palazzo Pubblico** (1297–1342) and **Torre del Mangia**, built in 1348 *(see p340)*. This imposing ensemble tends to overshadow the little **Fonte Gaia** on the piazza's northern edge. The fountain is a 19th-century copy of an original carved by Jacopo della Quercia in 1409–19. Its reliefs depict the *Virtues, Adam and Eve,* and the *Madonna and Child* (the originals are on the rear loggia of the Palazzo Pubblico). The fountain's water is still supplied by a 500-year-old aqueduct.

**The Piazza del Campo and Fonte Gaia from the Torre del Mangia**

# Exploring Siena

Once a capital to rival Florence, Siena is Italy's prettiest medieval town, still endowed with the grandeur of the age in which it was at its peak (1260–1348). Begin an exploration of its historic centre in Piazza del Campo and the surrounding maze of medieval alleys.

Lorenzetti's *Allegory of Good Government* (1338), Palazzo Pubblico

### Palazzo Pubblico

Piazza del Campo 1. *Tel 0577 29 22 26.* **Museo Civico & Torre del Mangia** ◯ *daily.*

Although it continues in its ancient role as Siena's town hall, the Palazzo Pubblico's medieval rooms, some decorated with paintings of the Sienese School, are open to the public. The **Museo Civico** is housed here. The main council chamber, or Sala del Mappamondo, is named after a map of the world painted by Ambrogio Lorenzetti in the early 14th century. One wall is covered by Simone Martini's fresco of the *Maestà* (1315), which depicts the Virgin in Majesty as the Queen of Heaven, attended by the Apostles, saints and angels. Opposite is a fresco (attributed to Simone Martini, but possibly later) of the mercenary *Guidoriccio da Fogliano* (1330). The walls of the chapel alongside are covered with frescoes of the *Life of the Virgin* (1407) by Taddeo di Bartolo, and the choir stalls (1428) are decorated with wooden panels inlaid with biblical scenes. The Sala della Pace contains the famous *Allegory of Good and Bad Government* (1338–40), a pair of frescoes by Ambrogio Lorenzetti. They form one of the most important series of secular paintings from the Middle Ages. In the *Good Government* fresco civic life flourishes, while the *Bad Government*, presided over by a demon, reveals rubbish-strewn streets and ruins.

The Sala del Risorgimento is covered with late 19th-century frescoes illustrating the events leading up to the unification of Italy under King Vittorio Emanuele II.

In the palace courtyard is the entrance to the magnificent **Torre del Mangia**, the palace's huge bell tower. Rising 102 m (330 ft), it is a prominent feature of Siena's skyline. Built by the brothers Muccio and Francesco di Rinaldo between 1338 and 1348, it was named after the first bell-ringer, whose idleness led to the nickname *Mangiaguadagni* (literally "eat the profits"). There are 505 steps to the top of the tower, which has wonderful views.

### Santuario e Casa di Santa Caterina

Costa di Sant'Antonio. *Tel 0577 24 73 93.* ◯ *daily.*

Siena's patron saint, Catherine Benincasa (1347–80), was the daughter of a tradesman. At the age of eight she devoted herself to God and had many visions, as well as later receiving the stigmata (wounds of Christ). Like her namesake, St Catherine of Alexandria, she was believed to have been betrothed to the Christ child in a vision – a scene which inspired many artists. Her eloquence persuaded Pope Gregory XI to return the seat of the papacy to Rome in 1376 after 67 years of exile in Avignon. St Catherine died in Rome and was canonized in 1461.

Today Catherine's house is surrounded by chapels and cloisters. Among them is the Church of the Crucifixion, which was built in 1623 in her orchard to house the late 12th-century Crucifixion, in front of which she received the stigmata in 1375. The house is decorated with paintings of events from her life by artists including her contemporaries Francesco Vanni and Pietro Sorri.

Cloister of Santuario e Casa di Santa Caterina, birthplace of Siena's patron saint

*For hotels and restaurants in this region see pp579–82 and pp629–32*

### Palazzo Piccolomini

Via Banchi di Sotto 52. ***Tel*** *0577 24 71 45.* *Mon–Sat am.* *1–15 Aug.*
Siena's most imposing private palazzo was built for the wealthy Piccolomini family in the 1460s by the Florentine architect and sculptor Bernardo Rossellino. It now contains the Sienese state archives, account books and taxation documents dating back to the 13th century. Some of the leading artists of their day were employed to paint the wooden bindings used to enclose the tax and account records. The paintings, now on display in the Sala di Congresso, often show scenes of Siena itself, bristling with towers, or episodes from the city's past.

Other records include a will attributed to Boccaccio and the council's contract with Jacopo della Quercia for the Fonte Gaia *(see p339)*.

**A detail from Martini's *Blessed Agostino Novello* (c.1330)**

### Pinacoteca Nazionale

Via San Pietro 29. ***Tel*** *0577 28 11 61.* *daily (Sun & Mon am only).*
This fine gallery, which is housed in the 14th-century Palazzo Buonsignori, contains an unsurpassed collection of paintings by artists of the Sienese School. Arranged in chronological order, from the 13th century through to the Mannerist period (1520–1600), highlights include Duccio's *Madonna dei Francescani* (1285) and Simone Martini's masterpiece *The Blessed Agostino Novello and Four of His Miracles* (c.1330). Pietro Lorenzetti's *Two Views*, from the 14th century, are early examples of landscape painting, and Pietro da Domenico's *Adoration of the Shepherds* (1510) shows how the art of Siena remained visibly influenced by its Byzantine roots long after the naturalism of the Renaissance had reached across the rest of Europe.

**The austere exterior of the church of San Domenico (begun 1226)**

### San Domenico

Piazza San Domenico. *daily.*
The preserved head of the city's patroness, St Catherine of Siena (1347–80), can be seen in a gilded tabernacle on the altar of a chapel dedicated to her in the huge, barn-like Gothic church of San Domenico (begun 1226). The chapel itself was built in 1460 for this purpose and is dominated by Sodoma's frescoes (1526), to the right and left of the altar, which show Catherine in states of religious fervour. The church has the only portrait of St Catherine considered authentic, painted by her friend Andrea Vanni.

## THE SIENESE PALIO

The Palio is Tuscany's most celebrated festival and it occurs in the Campo each year on 2 July and 16 August at 7pm. It is a bareback horse race first recorded in 1283, but it may have had its origins in Roman military training. The jockeys represent ten of Siena's 17 *contrade* (districts); the horses are chosen by the drawing of lots and are blessed at the local *contrada* churches. Preceded by days of colourful pageantry, costume processions and heavy betting, the races themselves last only 90 seconds each. Thousands of spectators crowd into the piazza to watch the race, and rivalry between competitors is intense. The winner is rewarded with a silk *palio* (banner). Festivities for the winners can last for weeks.

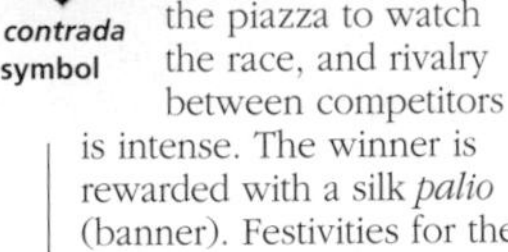

**A *contrada* symbol**

**The Sienese displaying their flag-throwing skills before the Palio**

# Siena: Duomo

A symbol of the Risen Christ on the façade

Siena's Duomo (1136–1382) is one of Italy's greatest cathedrals, a spectacular mixture of sculpture, paintings and Pisan-influenced Romanesque-Gothic architecture. Had 14th-century plans to create a new nave come to fruition, the building would have become the largest church in Christendom. In the event the plan came to nothing, abandoned when the plague of 1348 virtually halved the city's population. Among the Duomo's treasures are sculptural masterpieces by Nicola Pisano, Donatello and Michelangelo, a fine inlaid pavement and a magnificent fresco cycle by Pinturicchio.

**Baptismal Font**
*This Renaissance font by della Quercia, Ghiberti and Donatello stands in the Baptistry.*

**Pulpit Panels**
*Carved in 1265–8 by Nicola Pisano, with help from Arnolfo di Cambio and his son Giovanni, the panels on the octagonal pulpit depict scenes from the* Life of Christ.

**In the nave** black and white marble pillars support the vault.

**Chapel of St John the Baptist**

**The north aisle** contains sculptures by Michelangelo of Saints Peter, Pius, Gregory and Paul (1501–4).

**Inlaid Marble Floor**
The Massacre of the Innocents *is one of a series of scenes in the inlaid marble floor. The marble is usually uncovered during September each year.*

**Piccolomini Library**
*Pinturicchio's frescoes (1509) portray the life of the Piccolomini pope, Pius II. Here he presides at the betrothal of Frederick III to Eleonora of Portugal.*

*For hotels and restaurants in this region see pp579–82 and pp629–32*

**The Museo dell'Opera del Duomo** occupies the side aisle of the unfinished nave, which was roofed over to house the museum.

**The Campanile** was added in 1313.

**Archway leading to the Baptistry**

**Façade gives indication of planned size of nave**

**The unfinished nave**, if completed, would have measured 50 m (162 ft) in length and 30 m (97 ft) in breadth.

**Entrance to Duomo**

**The doors** were built in 1284–97, the rest of the façade a century later.

**Façade Statues**

*Many façade statues have been replaced by copies; the originals are in the Museo dell'Opera del Duomo.*

## VISITORS' CHECKLIST

Piazza del Duomo. ***Tel*** *0577 28 30 48.* *Pollicino.*

**Duomo & Library**

*10:30am–7:30pm Mon–Sat (Jun–Aug: to 8pm; Nov–Feb: to 6:30pm), 1:30–5:30pm Sun (Jun–Aug: to 6pm).*

### Museo dell'Opera del Duomo

Piazza del Duomo 8. ***Tel*** *0577 28 30 48.* *daily.* *1 Jan, 25 Dec.*

Part of this museum is devoted to items removed from the Duomo, including a tondo of a *Madonna and Child,* probably by Donatello, as well as several badly eroded Gothic statues by Giovanni Pisano and Jacopo della Quercia. The highlight is Duccio's huge *Maestà* (1308–11), one of the Sienese School's finest works. It depicts the Madonna and Child on one side, and scenes from the Life of Christ on the other. It was originally placed on the Duomo's high altar, where it replaced the striking *Madonna of the Large Eyes* (1220–30) by an anonymous Sienese painter, also in the museum.

**Statues from the Duomo now on show in the Museo dell'Opera**

### Fortezza Medicea

Viale Maccari. Fortezza *daily.* **Enoteca** ***Tel*** *0577 28 84 97.* *noon–1am Mon–Sat.*

This huge red-brick fortress was built for Cosimo I by Baldassarre Lanci in 1560, following Siena's defeat by the Florentines in the 1554–5 war. After an 18-month siege, during which more than 8,000 Sienese died, the town's banking and wool industries were suppressed by the Florentine masters and all major building work ended.

The fortress now houses the Enoteca Italica, offering visitors the chance both to taste and to buy quality wines from all over Italy. There is also a restaurant on the site.

# Street-by-Street: San Gimignano ㉔

The 13 towers that dominate San Gimignano's majestic skyline were built by noble families in the 12th and 13th centuries, when the town's position – on the main pilgrim route from northern Europe to Rome – brought it great prosperity. The plague of 1348, and the diversion of the pilgrim route, led to its decline as well as its preservation. Today only one of the towers, the Torre Grossa, is open to the public. For a small town, San Gimignano is rich in works of art, good shops and restaurants.

San Gimignano's famous skyline, almost unchanged since the Middle Ages

Sant' Agostino

Tourist information

VIA SAN MATTEO

VIA CAPASSI

VIA DIACCETO

PIAZZA NOMI

PIAZZA DEL DUOMO

PIAZZA DELLA CISTERNA

VIA DELLA COSTERELLA

VIA DI QUERCECCHIO

VIA BERIGNANO

VIA SAN GIOVANNI

**Collegiata**
*This 11th-century church's interior is full of frescoes, including* The Creation *(1367) by Bartolo di Fredi.*

**Palazzo del Popolo**
*The council chamber of the town hall (1288–1323) features a large* Maestà *(1317) by Lippo Memmi.*

**The Annunciation by Ghirlandaio**
*This painting, completed in 1482, is located in a courtyard loggia alongside the Collegiata.*

Bus station

**Via San Giovanni** is lined with shops selling local goods.

### VISITORS' CHECKLIST

*Siena. 7,000. Porta San Giovanni. Piazza del Duomo 1 (0577 94 00 08). Thu. Patron saints' festivals: 31 Jan San Gimignano & 12 Mar Santa Fina; varying dates in Feb: Carnival; 1st Sun in Aug: Fiera di Santa Fina; 29 Aug: Fiera di Sant'Agostino; 8 Sep: Festa della Madonna di Panacole.*
**www**.sangimignano.com

**Among the Piazza del Duomo's** historic buildings is the Palazzo Vecchio del Podestà (1239), whose tower is probably the town's oldest.

**Piazza della Cisterna**
*This square is named after the well at its centre and is the heart of the old town.*

**The Museo Civico** provides access to the tallest of the town's 13 remaining towers.

**KEY**

— — — Suggested route

0 metres 250
0 yards 250

### Museo Civico

Palazzo del Popolo, Piazza del Duomo. ***Tel*** *0577 99 03 12.*
**Museum & tower** *daily.* *1 Jan, 31 Jan, 24 Dec.*

Frescoes in the courtyard of this museum feature the coats of arms of city mayors and magistrates, as well as a 14th-century *Virgin and Child* by Taddeo di Bartolo.

The first room is the Sala di Dante, where an inscription recalls a visit by the poet in 1300. The walls are covered with hunting scenes and a huge *Maestà* fresco (1317) by Lippo Memmi. The floor above has an art collection, which includes excellent works by Pinturicchio, Bartolo di Fredi, Benozzo Gozzoli and Filippino Lippi. The famous *Wedding Scene* frescoes by Memmo di Filippucci (early 14th century) show a couple sharing a bath and going to bed – an unusual record of life in 14th-century Tuscany.

### Collegiata

Piazza del Duomo. *daily.*

This 12th-century Romanesque church contains a feast of frescoes. In the north aisle the frescoes comprise 26 episodes from the Old Testament (1367) by Bartolo di Fredi. The opposite wall features scenes from the *Life of Christ* (1333–41) by Lippo Memmi, while at the back of the church there are scenes from the *Last Judgment* painted by Taddeo di Bartolo. Frescoes (1475) by Ghirlandaio adorn both the tiny Chapel of Santa Fina and the nearby loggia.

**The ceiling of the Collegiata, painted with gold stars**

### Sant'Agostino

Piazza Sant'Agostino. *daily.*

Consecrated in 1298, this church has a simple façade, contrasting markedly with the heavily decorated Rococo interior (c.1740) by Vanvitelli. Above the main altar is the *Coronation of the Virgin* by Piero del Pollaiuolo, dated 1483. The choir is entirely covered in a cycle of frescoes of *The Life of St Augustine* (1465) executed by the Florentine artist Benozzo Gozzoli. In the Cappella di San Bartolo, on the right of the main entrance, is an elaborate marble altar completed by Benedetto da Maiano in 1495.

**Bartolo di Fredi's *Christ*, Sant'Agostino**

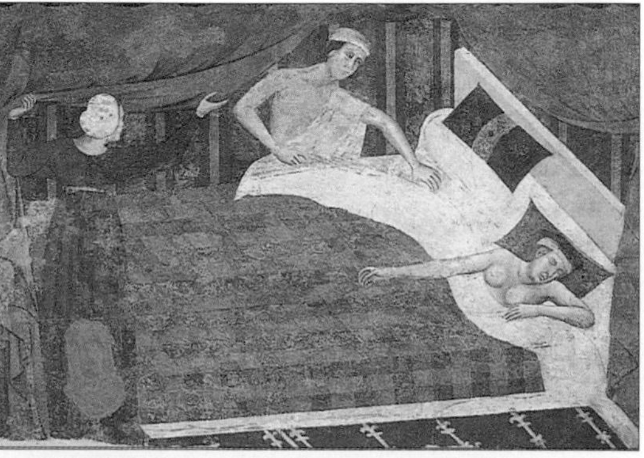

**Fresco from the early 14th-century *Wedding Scene* cycle by Memmo di Filippucci in the Museo Civico**

## Elba 28

*Livorno.* *30,000.* *Portoferraio* *Calata Italia 26 (0565 91 46 71).* *Portoferraio: Fri.*

Elba's most famous resident was Napoleon, who spent nine months here after the fall of Paris in 1814. Today Italy's third largest island is mainly populated by holiday-makers, who come by ferry from Piombino, 10 km (6 miles) away on the mainland. The main town is Portoferraio, with an old port and a modern seafront of hotels and fish restaurants.

The landscape of the island is varied. On the west coast, which tends to be a little quieter, there are sandy beaches suitable for all water sports. The east coast, centred on the town of Porto Azzurro, the island's second port, is more rugged, with high cliffs and stony beaches. Inland, olive groves and vineyards line hillsides, and vegetation covers the mountains. A good way to see the interior is to take the road from Marciana Marina to the old medieval village of Marciana Alta. Close by, a minor road leads to a cable car that runs to Monte Capanne (1,018 m/3,300 ft), a magnificent viewpoint.

**Marciana Marina on Elba**

## Sovana 29

*Grosseto.* *100.* *Piazza Busatti 8 (0564 63 30 99).*

Sovana is one of southern Tuscany's prettiest villages. Its single little street ends in Piazza del Pretorio, home to the ancient church of Santa Maria, which contains frescoes and a 9th-century altar canopy. A lane beyond leads through olive groves to the Romanesque Duomo, filled with reliefs and carvings from an earlier church on the site. Some fine Etruscan tombs lie in the surrounding countryside, many of them clearly signed and easily visited from the village.

**View over Pitigliano and the town's dramatic cliffs and caves**

## Pitigliano 30

*Grosseto.* *4,400.* *Piazza Garibaldi 51 (0564 61 71 11).* *Wed.*

Pitigliano is spectacularly situated high above the cave-riddled cliffs of the Lente valley. Its maze of tiny medieval streets includes a small Jewish ghetto, formed in the 17th century by Jews

## Maremma 31

*Grosseto.* *Maremma Centro Visite, Alberese (0564 40 70 98).* **Marginal Areas** *to entrances from Alberese.* *daily.* **Inner Park Areas** *from Alberese to tour departure point.* *8:30am–1 hr before sunset Wed, Sat, Sun, pub hols.* *only Jun–Sep: walking tours at 7am (4 hrs) & 4pm (3 hrs).* **www**.parcomaremma.it

The Etruscans, followed by the Romans, were the first to cultivate the marshes and low hills of the Maremma. Following the collapse of the Roman Empire, however, the area fell prey to flooding and malaria, twin scourges that left it virtually uninhabited until the 18th century. The land has since been reclaimed, the irrigation canals unblocked and farming developed on the fertile soil. The stunning Parco Naturale della Maremma was set up in 1975 to preserve the area's native flora and fauna, and to prevent development on one of Italy's few pristine stretches of coastline. Entrance to much of the park is restricted to access on foot or by a park bus from Alberese. Other more marginal areas, however, such as the excellent beach at Marina di Alberese and the countryside around Talamone in the south, are easier to see.

**The Ombrone estuary** is a mixture of pines, marsh and dunes and is home to birds such as the flamingo, sea eagle, roller and bee-eater.

*For hotels and restaurants in this region see pp579–82 and pp629–32*

fleeing from Catholic persecution. The **Palazzo Orsini** has its water supply brought in by an impressive aqueduct, built in 1545. It houses the **Museo Zuccarelli** with its small exhibition of work by artist Francesco Zuccarelli (1702– 88), who lived locally. He also painted two of the altarpieces in the medieval **Duomo** in Piazza San Gregorio. The **Museo Etrusco** contains finds from ancient local settlements.

**Museo Zuccarelli**
Palazzo Orsini, Piazza della Fortezza Orsini 4. ***Tel*** *0564 61 60 74.*
*10am–1pm, 3–7pm Tue–Fri (to 5pm in winter).*

**Museo Etrusco**
Piazza della Fortezza Orsini 59. ***Tel*** *0564 61 40 67.* *Call for times.*

## Monte Argentario ㉜

Grosseto. *13,000.* *Piazzale Sant'Andrea, Porto Santo Stefano (0564 81 42 08).* *Tue.*

Monte Argentario was an island until the early 1700s, when the shallow waters separating it from the mainland began to silt up, creating two sandy spits of land, known as *tomboli,* which enclose the Orbetello lagoon. Today the lagoon hosts a beautiful nature reserve. **Orbetello** itself, a lively and relatively unspoilt little town, was linked to the island in 1842, when a dyke was constructed from the mainland. The harbour towns of **Porto Ercole** and **Porto Santo Stefano** are up-market resorts, busy with visitors in summer. Interior roads – notably the Strada Panoramica – offer peaceful drives past rocky coves and bays.

Porto Ercole, Monte Argentario

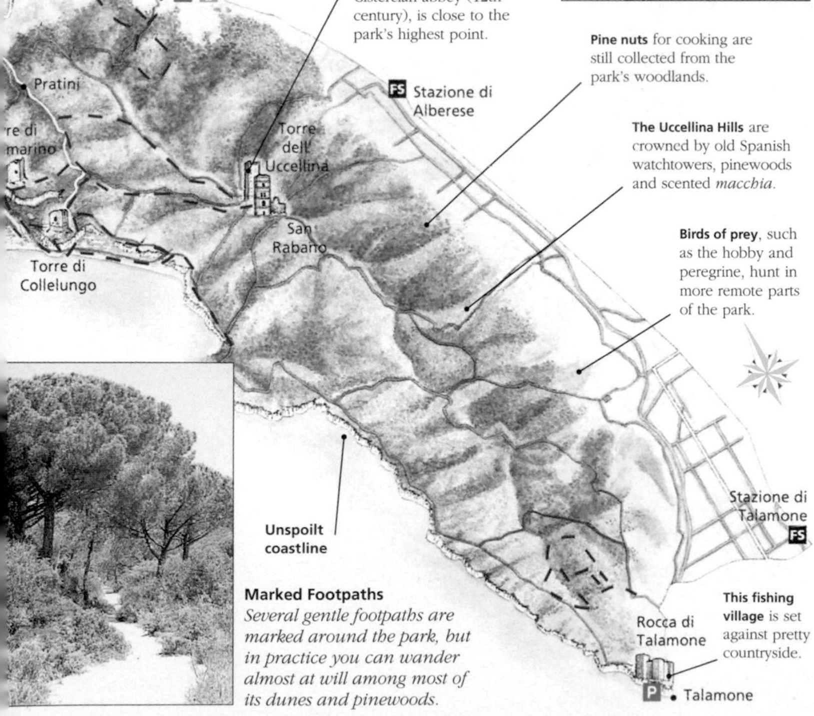

**Entry tickets** are sold at Alberese's park headquarters.

**Wild Boar**
*The most impressive of the Maremma's many wild animals is the indigenous wild boar, a smaller creature than the Eastern European boar found elsewhere in Tuscany.*

**San Rabano**, a ruined Cistercian abbey (12th century), is close to the park's highest point.

**Pine nuts** for cooking are still collected from the park's woodlands.

**The Uccellina Hills** are crowned by old Spanish watchtowers, pinewoods and scented *macchia.*

**Birds of prey**, such as the hobby and peregrine, hunt in more remote parts of the park.

Spergolaia
Alberese
Pratini
Torre di Castelmarino
Torre dell' Uccellina
San Rabano
Torre di Collelungo
Stazione di Alberese
Stazione di Talamone
Rocca di Talamone
Talamone

**Unspoilt coastline**

**Marked Footpaths**
*Several gentle footpaths are marked around the park, but in practice you can wander almost at will among most of its dunes and pinewoods.*

**This fishing village** is set against pretty countryside.

# UMBRIA

*Long dismissed as Tuscany's "gentler sister", Umbria has finally emerged from the shadow of its more famous western neighbour. Forming an expanse of gentle pastoral countryside and high mountain wilderness, the picturesque region has been dubbed the "Green Heart of Italy". Umbria is also well known for the beauty and profusion of its medieval hill-towns.*

The region was inhabited in the 8th century BC by the Umbrians, a peaceable farming tribe, and later colonized by the Etruscans and Romans. In the Middle Ages, the Lombards established a dukedom centred around Spoleto. By the 13th century much of the region was scattered with independent city-states, most of them eventually absorbed by the Papal States, where they remained until Italian unification in 1860.

Today the old towns are Umbria's chief glory. In Perugia, the region's capital, and the smaller centres of Gubbio, Montefalco and Todi, there are numerous Romanesque churches, civic palaces, vivid fresco cycles and endless medieval nooks and crannies. Spoleto, renowned for its summer arts festival, blends grandiose medieval monuments with Roman remains and some of Italy's oldest churches. The surrounding Vale of Spoleto is a chequerboard of agricultural countryside and fascinating traditional villages.

Assisi, the birthplace of St Francis, contains the Basilica di San Francesco, frescoed in part by Giotto. At Orvieto, magnificently situated on its volcanic crag, there are Etruscan remains and one of Italy's finest Romanesque-Gothic cathedrals.

Umbria's oak woods, ice-clear streams and rich soils yield many delicacies. Chief among these are trout and truffles, olive oils to rival those of Tuscany, prized lentils from Castelluccio, cured meats from Norcia and tangy mountain cheeses. A variety of well-regarded wines are produced from the vineyards of Torgiano and Montefalco.

**A shop in Norcia selling a selection of Italy's finest hams, sausages and salamis**

◁ **A street scene in the ancient town of Todi**

# Exploring Umbria

Assisi and Spoleto, Umbria's loveliest towns, are the most convenient and charming bases for exploring the region. Both these medieval gems are unmissable, as is the old centre of Perugia, the region's capital, and the alluring hill-towns of Orvieto, Gubbio, Spello, Montefalco and Todi. Umbria's landscapes are as compelling as its towns, from the eerie wastes of the Piano Grande and the mountain splendour of the Monti Sibillini national park (best reached from Norcia) to the gentler countryside of the Valnerina and the beach-fringed shores of Lake Trasimeno.

## SIGHTS AT A GLANCE

*Assisi pp354–5* 2
Gubbio 1
Lake Trasimeno 4
Montefalco 8
Monti Sibillini 10
Norcia 11
Orvieto 5
Perugia 3
Spello 9
Spoleto 7
Todi 6
Valnerina 12

## SEE ALSO


- ***Where to Stay*** pp582–5
- ***Where to Eat*** pp633–5

**Olive harvest in the Umbrian countryside near Orvieto**

## GETTING AROUND

Excellent road, rail and bus links exist in the region. The A1 from Florence passes Orvieto, which is linked to Todi by the S448. The S75 connects Perugia, Assisi and Spello, then the S3 continues to Trevi, Spoleto and Terni. Rome–Florence trains serve Orvieto, and Rome–Ancona trains serve Spoleto, with branch lines connecting Perugia, Spello and Assisi.

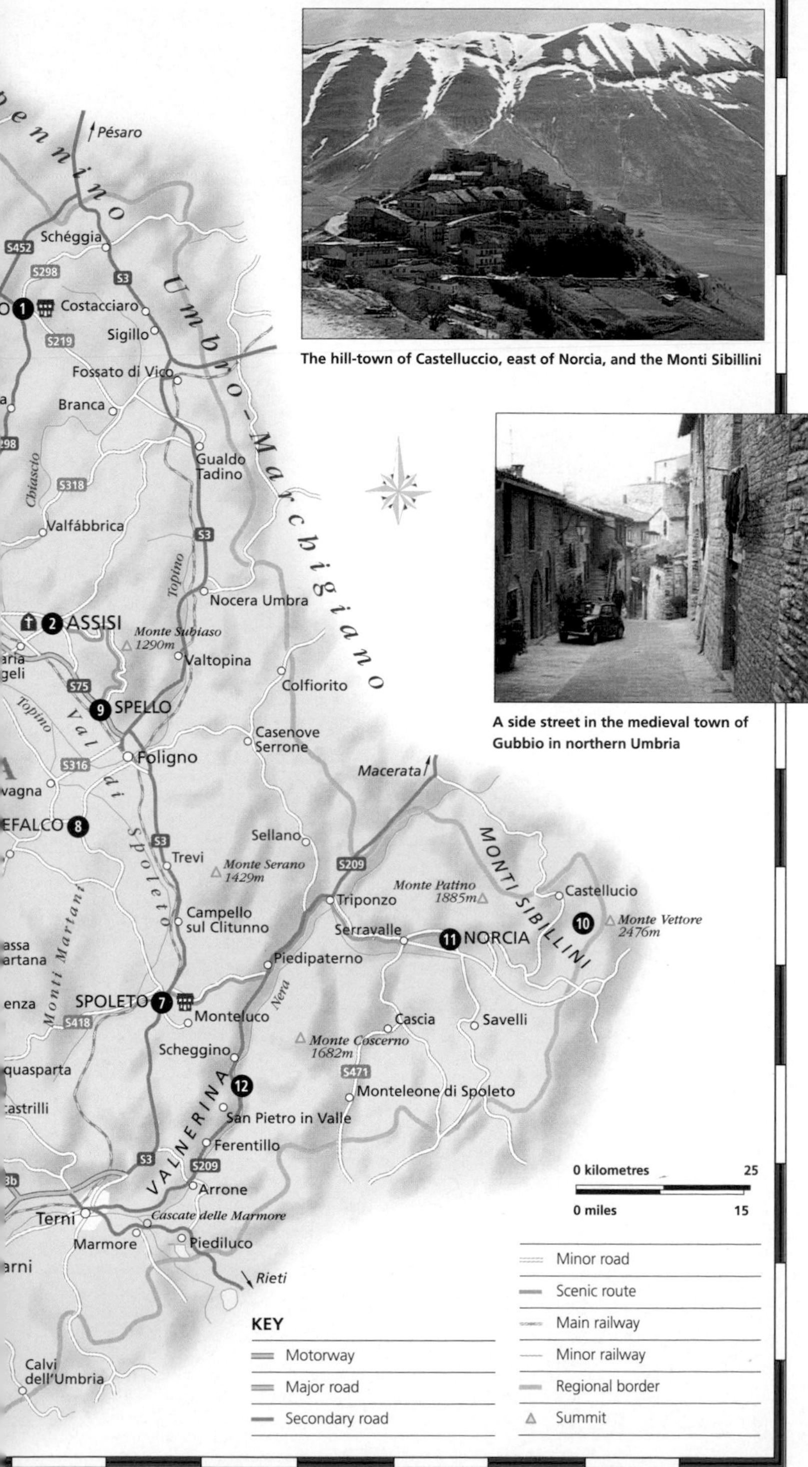


The hill-town of Castelluccio, east of Norcia, and the Monti Sibillini

A side street in the medieval town of Gubbio in northern Umbria

## Gubbio ❶

*Perugia. 33,000. FS Fossato di Vico-Gubbio. Via della Repubblica 15 (075 922 06 93). Tue.*

Gubbio vies with Assisi for the title of Umbria's most medieval town. The beauty of its twisting streets and terracotta-tiled houses is enhanced by the forest-swathed Apennines. Founded by the Umbrians in the 3rd century BC as Tota Ikuvina, it assumed greater prominence in the 1st century AD as a Roman colony (Eugubium). It emerged as an independent commune in the 11th century having spread up the slopes of Monte Ingino. From 1387 to 1508 Gubbio was ruled from Urbino by the Dukes of Montefeltro.

The 13th-century **Duomo** is distinguished by a wagon-vaulted ceiling whose curved arches symbolize hands in prayer. Medieval Via dei Consoli leads to the 13th-century **Palazzo del Bargello** – a stone-faced building formerly the headquarters of the chief of police. Also here is the **Fontana dei Matti** (Fountain of the Mad), named after the tradition that anyone who walks around it three times will go insane.

Macabre legends surround the walled-up **Porte della Morte** (Doors of Death) that can be seen in Via dei Consoli and elsewhere in the town. Reputedly used for the passage of coffins from houses, the doors, once tainted, were sealed and never used again. Their purpose was probably defensive. In the lower town, the church of **San Francesco** (1259–82) is known for 17 faded frescoes showing scenes from the *Life of the Virgin* (1408–13) by Ottaviano Nelli. Opposite is the **Tiratoio** (Weavers' Loggia). Wool was stretched out to dry in its shady arcade. West of here are the ruins of a 1st-century AD Roman amphitheatre.

**The interior of Perugia's San Pietro, rebuilt in the 15th century**

### Palazzo dei Consoli

*Piazza Grande. **Tel** 075 927 42 98. 10am–1pm, 3–6pm daily (Nov–Mar: 10am–1pm, 2–5pm). 1 Jan, 13–15 May, 25 Dec.*

Dominating the skyline of Gubbio is this mighty civic palace, begun in 1332 by Gattapone. Its Salone dell'Arengo houses the Museo Civico, best known for the Eugubine Tablets (250–150 BC). Discovered in 1444, the seven bronze slabs are inscribed with Etruscan and Roman characters, probably a phonetic translation of prayers and rituals from the ancient Umbrian and Etruscan languages. Upstairs a small art gallery contains works by local painters.

**One of the Eugubine Tablets in Gubbio**

### Palazzo Ducale

*Via Federico da Montefeltro. **Tel** 075 927 58 72. 8:30am–7pm Tue–Sun. 1 Jan, 25 Dec.*

Attributed to Francesco di Giorgio Martini, this palace was built in 1470 for the Montefeltro as a copy of the family home in Urbino *(see pp370–71)*. It also has a pretty Renaissance courtyard.

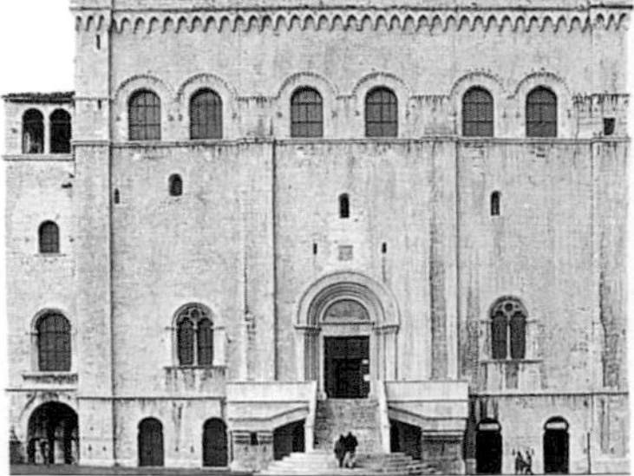

**Façade of the Palazzo dei Consoli in Gubbio**

## Assisi ❷

*See pp354–5.*

## Perugia ❸

*160,000. FS Piazza Matteotti 18 (075 573 64 58). Tue, Sat. **www**.perugia.umbria2000.it*

Perugia's old centre hinges around the pedestrianized Corso Vannucci, named after the local painter Pietro Vannucci (Perugino). At its northern end is Piazza IV Novembre, dominated by the **Fontana Maggiore**, a 13th-century fountain by Nicola and Giovanni Pisano. To the rear rises the 15th-century **Duomo**, its entrance flanked by a statue of Pope Julius III (1555) and a pulpit built for Siena's San Bernardino (1425). Its Cappella del Santo Anello contains the Virgin's "wedding ring", a weighty piece of agate said to change colour according to the character of the person wearing it. The third pillar in the south nave holds a Renaissance painting of the *Madonna delle Grazie* by Gian Nicola di Paolo. The figure is credited with miraculous powers, and mothers bring newly baptized children to kneel before it. Buried in the transepts are Popes Urban IV and Martin IV.

Away from the Corso is the **Oratorio di San Bernardino** (1457–61) on Piazza San Francesco, with a colourful façade by Agostino di Duccio

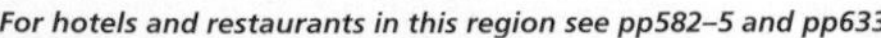

Beyond the old city walls on Borgo XX Giugno stands **San Pietro**, Perugia's most extravagantly decorated church. Founded in the 10th century and rebuilt in 1463, the best feature of the fine interior is the wooden choir (1526).

Piazza Giordano Bruno is home to **San Domenico** (1305–1632), Umbria's largest church, which is known for the Gothic tomb of Benedict XI (c.1304) and decoration by Agostino di Duccio.

### Museo Archeologico Nazionale dell'Umbria

San Domenico, Piazza Giordano Bruno 10. ***Tel*** *075 572 71 41.* *daily.* *1 Jan, 1 May, 25 Dec.*

Housed in the cloisters of San Domenico, this museum exhibits prehistoric, Etruscan and Roman artifacts.

### Palazzo dei Priori

Corso Vannucci 19. ***Tel*** *075 572 85 99.* *daily (Sun: am only).* *1 Jan, 1 May, 25 Dec & 1st Mon each month.* **Collegio del Cambio** *daily.*

The monumental walls and bristling crenellations of this palace mark it as Umbria's finest public building *(see pp54–5)*. Among its fine rooms is the Sala dei Notari (c.1295), the former lawyers' hall, vividly frescoed with scenes from the Old Testament – the work of a follower of Pietro Cavallini. The raised doorway is guarded by a pair of large bronzes made in 1274: a Guelph lion and a griffin, the medieval emblem of Perugia. The Sala di Udienza del Collegio della Mercanzia, built around 1390, was formerly used by the Merchants' Guild. This room is late Gothic in style, with exquisite panelling and 15th-century inlaid wood.

Also in the palace is the **Collegio del Cambio**, Perugia's former money exchange, which was begun in 1452. This room was used by the Bankers' Guild. Its walls are covered with superlative frescoes (1498 –1500) by Perugino, works that are devoted to a mixture of Classical and religious scenes. A glum self-portrait scowls down from the centre of the left wall, while the hand of Perugino's pupil Raphael may be evident in some panels on the right wall.

**Colourful façade of Perugia's Oratorio di San Bernardino**

**Medieval street in Perugia**

**Entrance of Palazzo dei Priori, Perugia**

### Galleria Nazionale dell'Umbria

Palazzo dei Priori, Corso Vannucci 19. ***Tel*** *075 572 10 09.* *Tue–Sun.* *1 Jan, 1 May, 25 Dec.*

Umbria's greatest collection of paintings is displayed here on the third floor of the palace. Most of the works are 13th- to 18th-century paintings by local artists, but the highlights are altarpieces by Piero della Francesca and Fra Angelico.

## Lake Trasimeno ❹

Perugia. FS *Castiglione del Lago.* *Piazza Mazzini 10, Castiglione del Lago (075 965 24 84).* **www**.umbria2000.it

Edged with low hills, this is Italy's fourth-largest lake. Its miles of placid water and reed-lined shores have a tranquil, melancholy beauty.

Drainage of the lake began under the Romans, but today the lake is gently drying up of its own accord. The town of **Castiglione del Lago**, jutting out on a fortified promontory, has an easy-going atmosphere and small sandy beaches. The 16th-century **castle** is used for summer concerts. The church of **Santa Maria Maddalena**, begun in 1836, has a fine *Madonna and Child* (c.1500) by Eusebio di San Giorgio.

Like Castiglione, **Passignano sul Trasimeno** offers boat trips to **Isola Maggiore**. The island's charming village is known for lace-making.

### THE BATTLE OF LAKE TRASIMENO

In 217 BC the Romans suffered one of their worst ever military defeats on the shores of Lake Trasimeno. The Carthaginian general, Hannibal, lured the Romans (who were led by the consul Flaminius) into a masterful ambush close to present-day Ossaia (Place of Bones) and Sanguineto (Place of Blood). Some 16,000 legionaries perished, hacked down on the lake's marshy fringes. Hannibal, by contrast, lost only 1,500 men. Today you can explore the battlefield, which includes over 100 mass graves found near Tuoro sul Trasimeno.

**19th-century engraving of General Hannibal**

# Assisi: Basilica di San Francesco

The burial place of St Francis, this basilica was begun in 1228, two years after the saint's death. Over the next century its Upper and Lower Churches were decorated by the foremost artists of their day, among them Cimabue, Simone Martini, Pietro Lorenzetti and Giotto, whose frescoes on the *Life of St Francis* are some of the most renowned in Italy. The basilica, which dominates Assisi, is one of the great Christian shrines and receives vast numbers of pilgrims throughout the year.

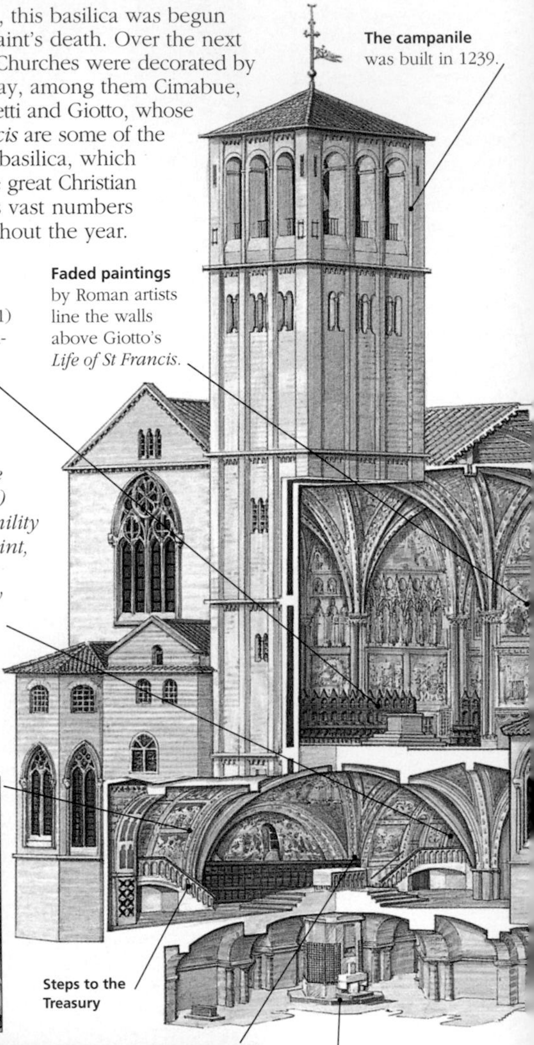

**The campanile** was built in 1239.

**Faded paintings** by Roman artists line the walls above Giotto's *Life of St Francis.*

**The choir** (1501) features a 13th-century stone papal throne.

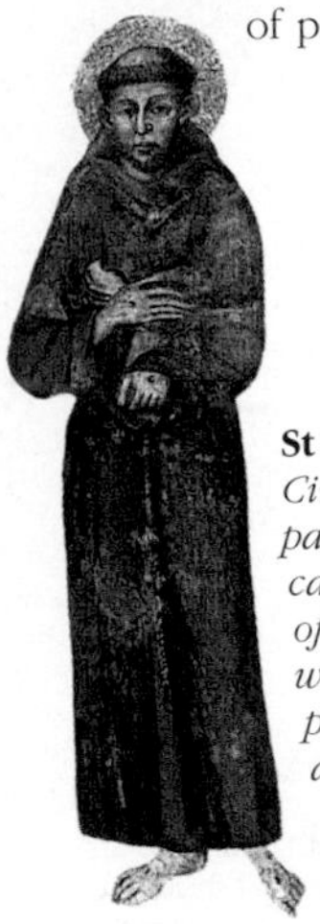

**St Francis**
*Cimabue's simple painting (c.1280) captures the humility of the revered saint, who stood for poverty, chastity and obedience.*

**Steps to the Treasury**

**★ Frescoes by Lorenzetti**
*The bold composition of Pietro Lorenzetti's fresco, entitled* The Deposition *(1323), is based around the truncated Cross, focusing attention on the twisted figure of Christ.*

**Lower Church**
*Side chapels were created here in the 13th century to accommodate the growing number of pilgrims.*

**The crypt** contains the tomb of St Francis.

**STAR FEATURES**

- ★ Frescoes by Lorenzetti
- ★ Frescoes by Giotto
- ★ Cappella di San Martino

**Upper Church**
*The soaring Gothic lines of the 13th-century Upper Church symbolized the heavenly glory of St Francis. This style also influenced later Franciscan churches.*

**★ Frescoes by Giotto**
The Ecstasy of St Francis *is one of 28 panels that make up Giotto's cycle on the* Life of St Francis *(c.1290–95).*

**★ Cappella di San Martino**
*The frescoes in this chapel on the* Life of St Martin *(1315) are by the Sienese painter Simone Martini. This panel shows the* Death of the Saint. *Martini was also responsible for the fine stained glass in the chapel.*

### VISITORS' CHECKLIST

*P. San Francesco.* ***Tel*** *075 819 00 84. 6am–5:45pm daily (Lower Church: from 8:30am). Longer hours Sun & summer.*

# Assisi ❷

*Perugia. 25,000. Piazza del Comune 22 (075 813 86 80). Sat.* **www**.assisi.umbria2000.it

This beautiful medieval town, with its geranium-hung streets, lovely views and fountain-splashed piazzas, is heir to the legacy of St Francis (c.1181–1226), who is buried in the **Basilica di San Francesco**. Sadly the town suffered serious damage during the earthquake of September 1997, but restoration was relatively swift – completed in approximately two years. The tourist office can give information on which sights are open to visitors.

Piazza del Comune, Assisi's main square, is dominated by the columns of the **Tempio di Minerva**, a Roman temple-front from the Augustan age. The Palazzo Comunale, opposite, is home to the **Pinacoteca Comunale**, an art gallery with works by local medieval artists.

Down Corso Mazzini lies the **Basilica di Santa Chiara**, the burial place of St Clare – Francis's companion and the founder of the Poor Clares (an order of nuns). One of its chapels contains the crucifix that is said to have bowed its head and ordered Francis to "Repair God's church". It came from **San Damiano**, a sublime church set amid olive groves south of the Porta Nuova.

The **Duomo (San Rufino)**, built during the 12th and 13th centuries, has a superb Romanesque façade. Inside is a small museum of paintings, and there are archaeological items in the crypt. From the Duomo, Via Maria delle Rose leads to the **Rocca Maggiore** (rebuilt in 1367), an evocative if much-restored castle.

Thirteenth-century **San Pietro**, on Piazza San Pietro, is a simple and carefully restored Romanesque church. The nearby **Oratorio dei Pellegrini**, a 15th-century pilgrims' hospice, contains well-preserved frescoes by Matteo da Gualdo.

**Giotto's fresco, *St Francis Appearing to the Friars at Arles* (c.1295), in the Basilica di San Francesco, Assisi ▷**

## Orvieto 5

Terni. 22,000. FS
Piazza Duomo 24 (0763 34 17 72). Thu & Sat.

Perched on a a 300-m (984-ft) plateau, Orvieto looks down over a vineyard-spotted plain. Visitors flood into the town to admire the **Duomo**, among the greatest of Italy's Romanesque-Gothic cathedrals.

The tiny 14th-century church of **San Lorenzo in Arari** is at the end of Via Scalza. Its walls feature frescoes describing the martyrdom of St Lawrence, who was grilled to death. The altar is made from an Etruscan sacrificial slab. Via Malabranca leads to **San Giovenale** at Orvieto's western tip, a church that is beautifully and almost completely covered in detailed frescoes from the 15th and 16th centuries. It offers broad views over the surrounding countryside. **Sant'Andrea**, in Piazza della Repubblica, is distinguished by a curious 12-sided campanile, part of the original 12th-century building.

View into the Pozzo di San Patrizio in Orvieto

### Museo dell' Opera del Duomo

Piazza Duomo. ***Tel*** *0763 34 35 92.* *Wed–Mon.* **www.**opsm.it

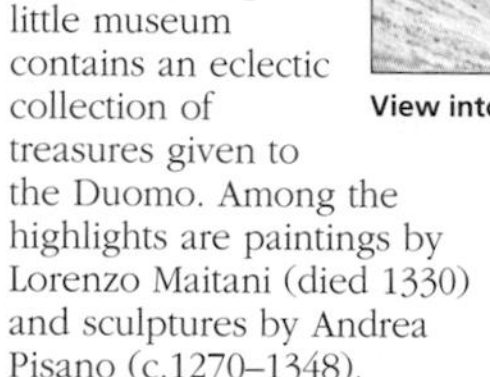

This interesting little museum contains an eclectic collection of treasures given to the Duomo. Among the highlights are paintings by Lorenzo Maitani (died 1330) and sculptures by Andrea Pisano (c.1270–1348).

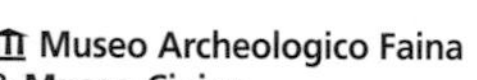

### Museo Archeologico Faina & Museo Civico

Piazza Duomo 29. ***Tel*** *0763 34 15 11.* *daily.* *1 Jan, 24–26 Dec; Nov–Feb: Mon.*

The first of these two museums has a well-known, low-key collection of Etruscan remains including many Greek vases that were found in Etruscan tombs in the area. Museo Civico contains ancient Greek artifacts and Etruscan copies of Greek works.

### Museo d'Arte Moderna "Emilio Greco"

Palazzo Soliano, P.za Duomo. ***Tel*** *0763 34 35 92.* *pm daily (Oct–Mar: Wed–Mon).* *allows entry at Pozzo di San Patrizio.*

This museum is devoted to the modern Sicilian sculptor, Emilio Greco, who made the bronze doors (1964–70) of the Duomo in Orvieto.

### DUOMO OF ORVIETO

Piazza Duomo. ***Tel*** *0763 34 11 67.* *daily.*

Some 300 years in the building, Orvieto's Duomo (begun 1290), with its breathtaking façade, is one of Italy's greatest cathedrals. It was inspired by the Miracle of Bolsena in which real blood from a consecrated host supposedly fell on the altar cloth of a church in nearby Bolsena.

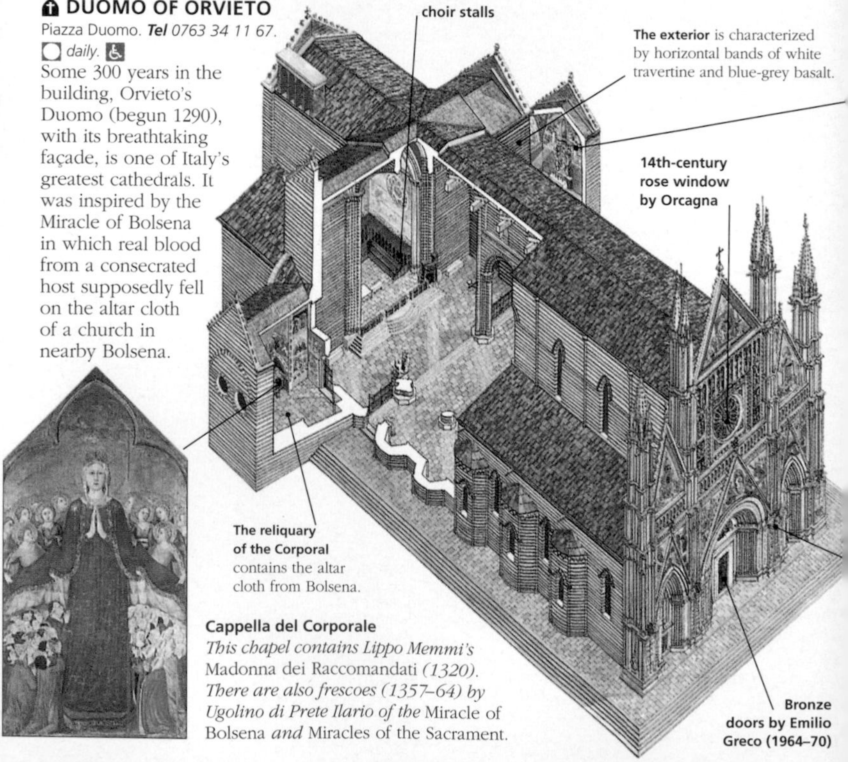

**Carved choir stalls**

**The exterior** is characterized by horizontal bands of white travertine and blue-grey basalt.

**14th-century rose window by Orcagna**

**The reliquary of the Corporal** contains the altar cloth from Bolsena.

**Cappella del Corporale**
*This chapel contains Lippo Memmi's* Madonna dei Raccomandati *(1320). There are also frescoes (1357–64) by Ugolino di Prete Ilario of the* Miracle of Bolsena *and* Miracles of the Sacrament.

**Bronze doors by Emilio Greco (1964–70)**

*For hotels and restaurants in this region see pp582–5 and pp633–5*

### Pozzo di San Patrizio

Viale San Gallo. **Tel** *0763 34 37 68.*
*daily. allows entry at Museo d'Arte Moderna.*

This well was commissioned in 1527 by Pope Clement VII and designed by the Florentine architect Antonio da Sangallo to provide the town with a water supply in case of attack. Two 248-step staircases drop into its dank interior, cleverly arranged as a double helix (spiral) so as not to intersect. The 62-m (203-ft) shaft took ten years to complete.

### Necropoli Etrusca – Crocefisso del Tufo

Strada Statale 71 to Orvieto Scalo, km 1,600. **Tel** *0763 34 36 11.*
*8:30am–7pm (Oct–Mar: to 5pm) daily. 1 Jan, 1 May, 25 Dec.*

This Etruscan necropolis from the 6th century BC has burial chambers built of blocks of tufa. Etruscan letters, thought to be the names of the deceased, are inscribed on the tombs.

**Cappella Nuova**
*Luca Signorelli's great fresco cycle of the* Last Judgment *(1499–1504) features prominently in this chapel. Fra Angelico and Benozzo Gozzoli worked here before Signorelli.*

**The Façade**
*There are detailed carvings (c.1320–30) at the base of its four main pilasters. By Lorenzo Maitani, they depict scenes from the Old and New Testaments, including hell and damnation.*

**View of the hill-town of Todi in southern Umbria**

## Todi ❻

Perugia. *17,000.*
*Piazza del Popolo 38 (075 894 54 16). Sat.*

Looking down over the Tiber valley from its hilltop eyrie, Todi is one of the most strikingly situated of Umbria's famous hill-towns. An ancient Etruscan, and then Roman settlement, it still preserves an uncorrupted medieval air, with several tiny churches, three austere public palaces and many sleepy corners.

Most people are drawn here by the **Piazza del Popolo**, the main square, flanked by the lovely plain-faced **Duomo**. Built in the 13th century on the site of a Roman temple to Apollo, it has a dusky interior and one of Umbria's finest choirs (1521–30). Note Ferraù da Faenza's huge painting (1596) on the rear wall, a less than totally successful copy of Michelangelo's *Last Judgment*, and the altarpiece at the end of the right aisle by Giannicola di Paolo (a follower of Perugino).

Also flanking the piazza are the **Palazzo dei Priori** (1293–1337) and the linked **Palazzo del Capitano** (1290) and **Palazzo del Popolo** (1213). In the Palazzo del Capitano, distinguished by its redoubtable medieval interior, lies the **Museo Etrusco-Romano**. The museum contains a collection of local Etruscan and Roman artifacts. There are altarpieces and sacred objects in the **Pinacoteca Comunale**, also housed in the palace.

A few steps from the piazza rises **San Fortunato** (1292–1462), named after Todi's first bishop, with a florid Gothic doorway (1415–58). The high vaulted plan is based on German Gothic "hall" churches and the "barn" churches of Tuscany, characterized by a low-pitched vault, polygonal apse and naves and aisles of equal height. The choir (1590) is superb, but the church's most famous work is a *Madonna and Child* (1432) by Masolino da Panicale (fourth chapel on the right). The crypt contains the tomb of Jacopone da Todi (c.1228–1306), a noted medieval poet and mystic.

To the right of the church are some shady gardens, from which a path (past the tiny castle) drops through the trees to emerge in front of **Santa Maria della Consolazione** (1508–1607), near the N79. One of central Italy's finest Renaissance churches, and based on a Greek cross, it may have been built to a plan by Bramante. The stark, chill interior is overshadowed by the harmonious exterior.

### Museo Etrusco-Romano and Pinacoteca Comunale

Palazzi Comunali. **Tel** *075 895 61.*
*Tue–Sun.*

**Santa Maria della Consolazione in Todi**

## Spoleto 7

Perugia. 38,000. FS
Piazza della Libertà 7 (0743 21 86 20 or 21 86 21). Tue & Fri.
**www**.spoleto.umbria2000.it

Founded by the Umbrians, Spoleto was one of central Italy's most important Roman colonies, a prominence maintained by the Lombards, who in the 7th century made it the capital of one of their three Italian dukedoms. After a spell as an independent city state, in 1354 Spoleto fell to the papacy.

Spoleto, within its wooded setting, is the loveliest of the Umbrian hill-towns. Its urbane atmosphere is enhanced by its superb monuments and by the Festival dei Due Mondi, one of Europe's leading arts festivals held annually in June and July.

At the southern end of Piazza del Mercato is the **Arco di Druso**, a 1st-century AD Roman arch. It is flanked by the church of **Sant'Ansano**, whose crypt is covered in frescoes that may date from the 6th century. Via Aurelio Saffi, at the piazza's northern end, leads to **Sant'Eufemia**. This utterly simple 10th-century Romanesque church is known for its matroneum (women's gallery), once used to segregate the congregation.

A short way beyond, the fan-shaped Piazza del Duomo opens out to reveal Spoleto's 12th-century **Duomo**, graced with an elegant Romanesque façade. Filling the apse of the Baroque interior is a great fresco cycle. The final work of Fra Lippo Lippi, from 1467–9, it describes episodes from the *Life of the Virgin*. The Cappella Erioli is adorned with Pinturicchio's unfinished *Madonna and Child* (1497).

Ponte delle Torri, Spoleto

The best of the exceptional churches in the lower town is 4th-century **San Salvatore**, located in the main cemetery, a spot suited to the church's eerie sense of antiquity. Nearby stands **San Ponziano**, fronted by a captivating three-tiered Romanesque façade typical of Umbria. It has a 10th-century crypt, supported by odd little columns and decorated with Byzantine frescoes.

Façade of San Pietro in Spoleto

Romanesque **San Gregorio** in Piazza Garibaldi dates from 1069, but its cramped façade and stolid campanile incorporate fragments of Roman buildings. Inside is a raised presbytery and a lovely multi-columned crypt. Well-preserved patches of fresco dot the walls. Some 10,000 Christian martyrs are supposedly buried near the church. They were reputedly slaughtered in the town's Roman **amphitheatre**, traces of which can be seen in the barracks on Via del Anfiteatro.

### Ponte delle Torri

This magnificent 14th-century aqueduct, the "bridge of towers", is 80 m (262 ft) high. Designed by Gattapone (from Gubbio), it is the town's single most famous monument.

### ROMANESQUE CHURCHES IN UMBRIA

Umbria's church-building tradition had its roots in ancient Roman basilicas and in the chapels built over the shrines of its many saints and martyrs. The region's Romanesque façades are usually divided into three tiers, often with three rose windows arranged above a trio of arched portals. The three doors usually correspond to the interior's nave and two aisles, which derive from the simple barn-like plan of Roman basilicas. Inside, the presbytery is often raised in order to allow for the building of a crypt, which usually contained the relics of a saint or martyr. Many of the churches took centuries to build, or were repeatedly modified over time, often acquiring elements of Gothic, Baroque or Renaissance styles.

**San Lorenzo di Arari** *in Orvieto takes its name from an Etruscan altar* (arari). *This 14th-century church has a very simple façade* (see p358).

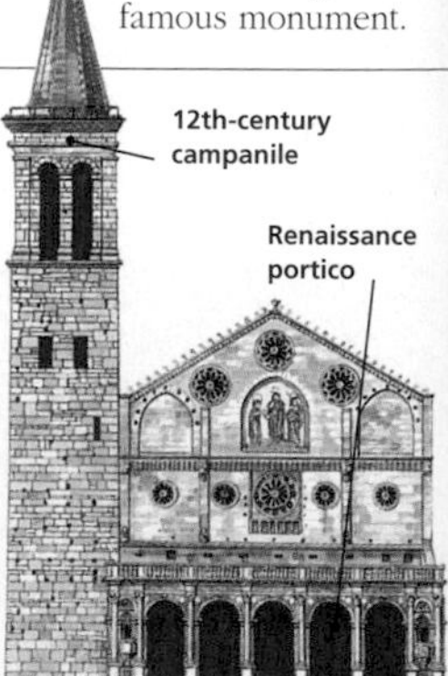


**Spoleto's Duomo** *(1198) has eight rose windows, a mosaic (1207) and a Renaissance portico (1491). The tower was built from old Roman remains.*

From the bridge, there are views of the bastions of the **Rocca Albornoz**, a huge papal fortress built in 1359–64, also by Gattapone. Across the bridge a path leads to the Strada di Monteluco and the church of **San Pietro**, famous for the fascinating 12th-century carvings on its façade.

**Rocca Albornoz**
Piazza San Simone. ***Tel** 0743 464 34.* *daily.* *compulsory.*

**Museo del Tessile e del Costume**
Palazzo Spada, Vicolo Terzo in Corso Mazzini. ***Tel** 0743 459 40.* *Thu–Sun.* *1 Jan, 25 Dec.*
Among the exhibits in this exquisite collection are sacred vestments complete with headgear, ties and gold chains, and a series of 17th-century tapestries that once belonged to Queen Christina of Sweden.

**A panel from Gozzoli's fresco cycle (1452) in Montefalco's Museo Civico**

## Montefalco 8

Perugia. *4,900.* *Mon.*

Montefalco, whose name (Falcon's Mount) draws inspiration from its lofty position and sweeping views, is the best of the fascinating villages in the Vale of Spoleto. Criss-crossed by streets almost too narrow for cars, it takes less than five minutes to walk through the village. Yet you might happily spend a morning here, most of it in the polished **Museo Civico** housed in the former church of San Francesco. Its highlight is Benozzo Gozzoli's *Life of St Francis* (1452), a radiant fresco cycle that borrows heavily from Giotto's cycle in Assisi *(see pp354–7)*. Other painters represented here are Perugino, Tiberio d'Assisi and Nicolò Alunno, all leading medieval Umbrian artists.

The simple Gothic church of **Sant'Agostino** (begun 1279) on Corso Mameli is dotted with frescoes from the 14th–16th centuries. The church also contains three mummies.

In the main square local wines on sale include the rich, red Sagrantino di Montefalco. Just outside the town walls, the church of **Sant'Illuminata** is covered with charming frescoes, the work of the local 16th-century artist Francesco Melanzio. About 2 km (1 mile) beyond, the prettily situated church of **San Fortunato** is decorated with frescoes by Gozzoli and Tiberio d'Assisi.

**Environs:** The village in the Vale of Spoleto with the most spectacular setting is **Trevi**. The churches of **San Martino** (16th century), on Passeggiata di San Martino, and **Madonna delle Lacrime** (1487–1522), south of Trevi on the road into the village, contain paintings by Perugino and Tiberio d'Assisi, among others.

**Museo Civico di San Francesco**
Via Ringhiera Umbra 9. ***Tel** 0742 37 95 98.* *daily (Nov–Feb: Tue–Sun).* *1 Jan, 25 Dec.*

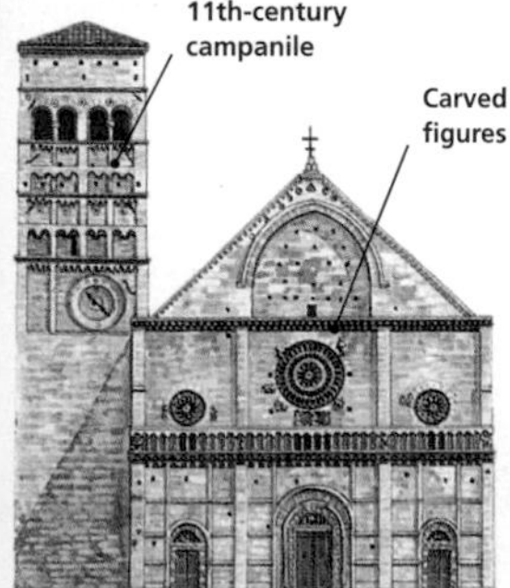

**The Duomo** *(1253) in Assisi is a fine example of the three-tiered façades found across central Italy* (see p355). *It has a pointed arch and a row of arcading.*

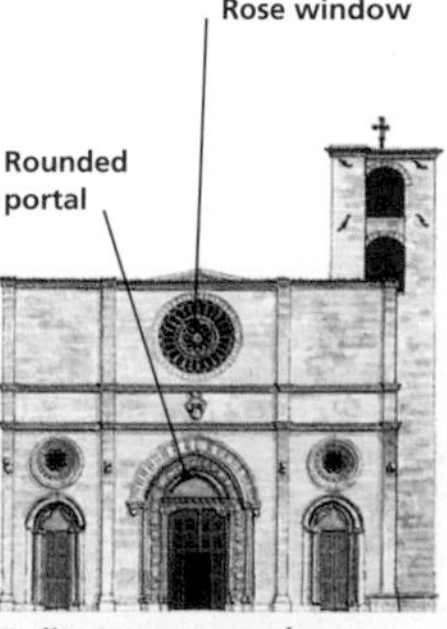

**Todi's Duomo** *was begun in the 12th century, but work on its windows and portals continued until the 17th century* (see p359).

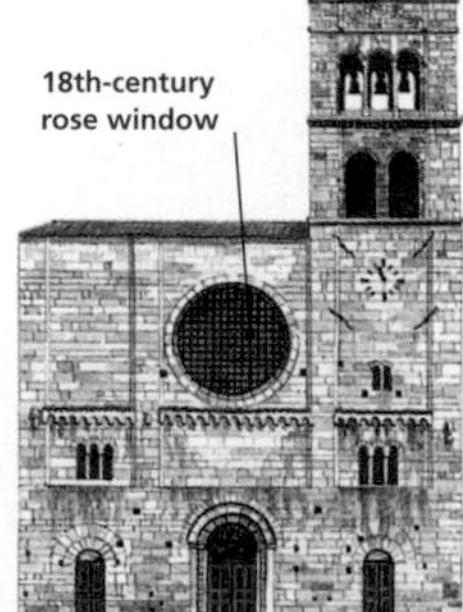

**San Michele** *(c.1195) in Bevagna has a beautiful portal that combines both Romanesque and old Roman fragments* (see p362).

## Spello ❾

Perugia. 8,000. FS
Piazza Matteotti 3 (0742 30 10 09). Wed.

Spello is one of the better known villages in the Vale of Spoleto. It is renowned for a fresco cycle by Pinturicchio in the Cappella Baglioni of the church of **Santa Maria Maggiore** (12th–13th century) on Via Consolare. Executed around 1500, the frescoes depict scenes from the New Testament. Towards the centre of the village is the Gothic church of **Sant'Andrea** (13th century) on Via Cavour. This road becomes Via Garibaldi, which leads to **San Lorenzo**, a Baroque gem of a church dating from the 12th century.

Spello also boasts Roman ruins from the age of Augustus: the **Porta Consolare** at the end of Via Consolare, and the twin-towered **Porta Venere** by Via Torri di Properzio.

The road to Assisi over **Monte Subasio** offers stunning views from the top of the mountain above Spello.

**Environs:** The least known village in the Vale of Spoleto is **Bevagna**. Like Spello, it sprang to life as a way-station on the Via Flaminia (the Roman road that ran through this part of Umbria). The medieval Piazza Silvestri is the setting for two Romanesque churches.

The lofty peaks of the Monti Sibillini in eastern Umbria

**San Silvestro** (1195) is the more atmospheric of the pair, thanks to its shadowy interior and ancient crypt, but **San Michele** (late 12th century) has an elegant portal, famed for the little gargoyles on either side. Both churches are the work of Maestro Binello.

## Monti Sibillini ❿

Macerata. FS *Spoleto.* *Visso.*
*Piazza del Forno 1, Visso (0737 97 27 11).* **www**.sibillini.net

The national park of the Monti Sibillini in eastern Umbria provides the region's wildest and most spectacular scenery. A range 40 km (25 miles) long, the mountains form part of the Apennines, a chain that runs the length of the Italian peninsula. **Monte Vettore** is the loftiest point, and the peninsula's third highest; it stands at 2,476 m (8,123 ft), a great whale-backed peak close to the cave of the mythical sybil that gave the region its name.

Good maps and trails make this a superb walking area, while drivers can follow hairpin roads to some of Italy's most magical landscapes. Chief of these is the **Piano Grande**, a huge upland plain surrounded by a vast amphitheatre of mountains. Bare but for flocks of sheep and bedraggled haystacks, the plain blazes with wild flowers in spring and with lentils later in the year. The only habitation is **Castelluccio**, a beautiful, neglected mountain village now being restored. It can be reached by road from Norcia and Arquata del Tronto.

Pinturicchio's *Annunciation* (c.1500) in Spello's Santa Maria Maggiore

Shop front in Norcia displaying the town's varied meats

## Norcia ⓫

Perugia. *4,700.*
*Piazza San Benedetto (0743 82 81 73).* *Thu.*

The birthplace of St Benedict, Norcia is a robust mountain town and an excellent base for exploring Valnerina and Monti Sibillini. One of Italy's culinary capitals, it is renowned for truffles and for some of Italy's best hams, sausages and salamis. Indeed, the Italian word for a pork butcher's (*norcineria*) derives from the name of the town.

Norcia's main sights are in **Piazza San Benedetto**. On the eastern flank, the church of **San Benedetto** has a 14th-century portal adorned with statues of Benedict and his sister (Santa Scolastica). Legend claims that the church marks the site of Benedict's birth –

*For hotels and restaurants in this region see pp582–5 and pp633–5*

**The 8th-century monastery of San Pietro in Valle, set in the beautiful Valnerina**

indeed there are the remains of a 5th-century building in the crypt. However, the church was more likely to have been built over the site of an old Roman temple, since the forum of the Roman colony of Nursia once occupied this spot.

Left of the church stands the **Palazzo Comunale**, a monument to the town's period as a free commune during the 13th and 14th centuries. On the opposite side of the square rises the **Castellina** (1554), a blunt papal fortress designed by Vignola to help impose order on an unruly mountain district. The **Duomo** (1560), to the left of the Castellina, has been ravaged by earthquakes over the centuries. Indeed, Norcia has been the victim of successive earthquakes and its houses are low and heavily buttressed with thick walls to protect them from further damage. **Sant'Agostino** on Via Anicia features a range of good 16th-century frescoes. A little way beyond, the **Oratorio di Sant'Agostinaccio** in Piazza Palatina contains a superb 17th-century ceiling. Via Umberto shelters the **Edicola** (1354), a strange tabernacle believed to have been carved for a Holy Week procession.

## Valnerina ⓬

*Perugia.* FS *Spoleto, then bus.* *Piazza Garibaldi 1, Cascia (0743 711 47).*

The Valnerina (Little Valley of the River Nera) curves through a broad swathe of eastern Umbria, draining the mountains around Norcia and the Sibillini before emptying into the Tiber. It is edged with craggy, tree-covered slopes and dotted with upland villages and fortified hamlets.

The high spot is **San Pietro in Valle**, an idyllically situated monastery in the hills above the village of Colleponte. Founded in the 8th century, it is one of the few surviving memorials to the Lombards, whose central Italian duchy had its capital in Spoleto. The main body of the monastery church dates from this period, as does the high altar. The nave walls are covered in a wealth of 12th-century frescoes. Some of the best Romanesque carvings in Umbria can be found here.

More popular than the monastery are the **Cascate delle Marmore** near Terni, among Europe's highest waterfalls at 165 m (541 ft). Created by the Romans during drainage work, their waters are now diverted to produce hydroelectric power on all but a few special days. You can view the falls from Marmore village or the S209.

**San Pietro in Valle**
Località Ferentillo, Terni. ***Tel*** *0744 78 03 16.* *daily.*

**Cascate delle Marmore**
7 km (4 miles) along S209 Valnerina, Terni. *sporadically. Ask at tourist information.*

**Piazza San Benedetto and the church of San Benedetto in Norcia**

# LE MARCHE

*Tucked away in a remote corner between the Adriatic Sea and the Apennine mountains, Le Marche (the Marches) is an enchanting rural patchwork of old towns, hill country and long, sandy beaches. In pre-Christian times the area was settled by the Piceni, a tribe eventually assimilated by the Romans.*

In the 4th century BC, exiles from Magna Graecia colonized much of the region. The most notable town was Ancona, also the northernmost point of Greek influence on the Italian peninsula. During the early Middle Ages the region marked the edge of the Holy Roman Empire, giving rise to its present name (*march* meant border area).

The region's historical peak was reached in the 15th century under Federico da Montefeltro, whose court at Urbino became one of Europe's leading cultural centres. Much of Urbino's former grandeur survives, particularly in Federico's magnificent Renaissance Palazzo Ducale, now home to a regional art collection. Ascoli Piceno is almost as enchanting as Urbino, its central Piazza del Popolo among the most evocative old squares in Italy. Smaller towns like San Leo and Urbania and the republic of San Marino also boast fine medieval monuments.

Today probably as many people come to Le Marche for its beaches and towns as for its hilly, unspoilt interior. Especially beautiful are the snowcapped peaks of the Monti Sibillini, situated in magnificent walking and skiing country.

Regional cuisine encompasses the truffles and robust cheeses of the mountains, tender hams and salamis, *olive ascolane* (olives stuffed with meat and herbs) and *brodetto*, fish soup made in several versions up and down the coast. Dry, white Verdicchio is the best known wine, although more unusual names, such as Bianchello del Metauro, are gaining in popularity.

**A field of poppies and olive trees in the heart of Le Marche's countryside**

◁ **Medieval gates and ramparts surrounding the hilltop republic of San Marino**

# Exploring Le Marche

The medieval towns of Urbino and Ascoli Piceno are the highlights of the region, but the rolling hills of the interior contain an abundance of smaller towns and all but undiscovered villages. San Leo, with its dramatic fortress, is one of the best. Most of the countryside is a pretty mixture of woods and remote hills, rising in the west to the majestic Monti Sibillini. Ancona and the attractive town of Pèsaro are the pivotal points of the vast coastline.

**KEY**

- Motorway
- Major road
- Secondary road
- Minor road
- Scenic route
- Main railway
- Minor railway
- International border
- Regional border
- △ Summit

**Rolling countryside between Loreto and Ascoli Piceno**

**View of Ascoli Piceno, one of the prettiest towns in Le Marche**

## SIGHTS AT A GLANCE

Ancona 9
Ascoli Piceno 12
Conero Peninsula 10
Fano 4
Grotte di Frasassi 7
Jesi 8
Loreto 11
Pèsaro 3
San Leo 1
San Marino 2
Urbania 6
*Urbino pp370–71* 5

The rocky reef near Portonovo on the Conero Peninsula

## GETTING AROUND

The A14–E55 provides easy access to the coastal resorts. Dual-carriageway spurs from the A14–E55 lead to Jesi, Urbino and Ascoli Piceno, but north-south roads in the interior can be slow. Bus services are generally good, but in the interior can be infrequent. The railway service along the coast is excellent, with a good service through the heart of the region, though it can be slow.

A market scene in Fano

### *SEE ALSO*

• ***Where to Stay*** pp585–7

• ***Where to Eat*** pp635–6

The bell tower of the Duomo rising above the village of San Leo

## San Leo ❶

Pèsaro. *Piazza Dante Alighieri 14 (0541 91 63 06).* *from Rimini, change at Villanova.*

Few castles are as impressive as the great **fortress** that towers over the village of San Leo. Dante used this crag-top site as a model for the landscapes of *Purgatorio*, while Machiavelli considered the citadel to be the finest piece of military architecture in Italy. Its rocky ramparts once contained the Mons Feretrius, a Roman temple dedicated to Jupiter.

An earlier Roman fortress on the site became a papal prison in the 18th century. Its most famous inmate was the larger-than-life Conte di Cagliostro. A swindler, womanizer, necromancer, quack and alchemist, Cagliostro was imprisoned for heresy in the 1790s. His cell was specially built so that its window faced the village's two churches. It is still visible, together with a small picture gallery, state rooms, and the majestic Renaissance ramparts, built by Francesco di Giorgio Martini for the dukes of Montefeltro in the 15th century.

The captivating village has a quaint cobbled square with a superb 9th-century **Pieve** (parish church). Built partly with stone from the ruined Mons Feretrius, the church was raised over the site of a 6th-century chapel.

Just behind lies the 12th-century **Duomo**, a fine Romanesque building with Corinthian capitals and Roman columns from the Mons Feretrius. The lid of St Leo's sarcophagus is in the crypt. Ancient pagan carvings can be seen on the wall behind the altar.

**Fortress**
Via Leopardi. ***Tel*** *0541 91 63 06.* *daily.* *lunch Oct–Mar.*

## San Marino ❷

*26,000.* *San Marino Città (fr Rimini).* *Contrada Omagnano 20, San Marino (0549 88 29 98).* **www**.visitsanmarino.com

Europe's oldest republic, tiny San Marino was reputedly founded by St Marinus, a 4th-century monk and stonemason forced to flee the religious persecution of the Emperor Diocletian. With him was St Leo, founder of the nearby town of San Leo. Situated on the slopes of Monte Titano, the country has its own mint, stamps, football team – even its own 1,000-strong army. It is also famous for Formula One racing.

Duty-free shop in San Marino

There are no customs formalities in this small country, whose borders are just 12 km (7 miles) apart at the widest point. Sadly, the capital, **San Marino**, is overrun with visitors and souvenir stalls for much of the year. Garibaldi, who sought shelter here after fleeing Venice in 1849, is honoured by a monument in Piazza Garibaldi. **Borgomaggiore**, the largest town, lies at the foot of Monte Titano, with a cable car to the capital above.

## Pèsaro ❸

*85,000.* FS *Piazza della Libertà (0721 693 41).* *Tue & 1st Thu of month.*

Detail of the *Coronation of the Virgin* by Bellini (c 1470) in the Musei Civici

One of the Adriatic's larger seaside resorts, Pèsaro has managed to retain a stylish air. Behind the promenade and the wall of white stucco hotels is a lively, attractive medieval area.

The art gallery of the **Musei Civici** contains Giovanni Bellini's sumptuous polyptych, the *Coronation of the Virgin* (c.1470). The museum also features Renaissance ceramics.

The **Museo Archeologico Oliveriano** presents historical displays from Roman remains to Iron Age artifacts from the necropolis of nearby Novilara.

The best of the town's churches is **Sant'Agostino** on Corso XI Settembre, remarkable for its choir stalls, each a patchwork of inlaid landscapes and narrative scenes.

Pèsaro is also a point of musical pilgrimage. In 1792 the composer Gioacchino Rossini was born here. His home, **Casa Rossini**, contains

*For hotels and restaurants in this region see pp585–7 and pp635–6*

memorabilia, while his piano and some original manuscripts lie in the **Conservatorio Rossini**. His operas are performed in the **Teatro Rossini** in Piazza Lazzarini during the annual August music festival.

**Musei Civici**
P.za Mosca 29. ***Tel*** *0721 38 74 74.* *Tue–Sun.* *1 Jan, 25 Dec.*

**Museo Archeologico Oliveriano**
Via Mazza 97. ***Tel*** *0721 333 44.* *Mon–Sat.*

**Casa Rossini**
Via Rossini 34. ***Tel*** *0721 38 73 57.* *Tue & Wed am, Thu–Sun.*

**Conservatorio Rossini**
Piazza Olivieri 5. ***Tel*** *0721 336 71.* *Mon–Sat, but phone first to arrange.* *public hols.*

## Fano ❹

Pèsaro. *54,000.* *Via Cesare Battisti 10 (0721 80 35 34).* *Wed & Sat.*

Ancient Fano stands out from the string of beach resorts south of Pèsaro, thanks to its fine old centre and historic monuments. Named after Fanum Fortunae, a pagan temple to the goddess Fortuna, it became the terminus of the Via Flaminia (an important consular road from Rome) and the largest Roman colony on the Adriatic coast. The **Arco d'Augusto** (AD 2), on Via Arco d'Augusto, is Fano's most significant ancient monument, having narrowly escaped destruction at the hands of Federico da Montefeltro in 1463. He destroyed its upper section while besieging the town as a papal *condottiere.*

The 16th-century **Fontana della Fortuna**, in Piazza XX Settembre, is dedicated to the goddess Fortuna. The large **Palazzo Malatesta** that rises up to its rear was built around 1420 and enlarged in 1544 for Fano's rulers, the Rimini-based Malatesta family. Inside is the small **Museo Civico** and the **Pinacoteca Malatestiana**, with works by Guercino, Guido Reni and the Venetian artist, Michele Giambono.

**Museo Civico and Pinacoteca Malatestiana**
Piazza XX Settembre.
***Tel*** *0721 82 83 62.* *Tue–Sun.* *1 Jan, 25 & 26 Dec.*

Fontana della Fortuna in Fano

Entrance to the Palazzo Ducale in Urbania

## Urbino ❺

*See pp370–71.*

## Urbania ❻

Pèsaro. *7,200.* *Corso Vittorio Emanuele 21 (0722 31 31 40).* *Thu.*

Urbania, with its elegant arcaded centre, takes its name from Pope Urban VIII (1623–44), who entertained the notion of converting the old medieval village known as Castel Durante into a model Renaissance town.

Its chief attraction is a monument from an earlier age, the huge **Palazzo Ducale**, built by the dukes of Montefeltro as one of several residential alternatives to the Palazzo Ducale in nearby Urbino. It was begun in the 13th century, and then rebuilt in the 15th and 16th centuries. Beautifully situated alongside the Metauro river, it houses a small art gallery, a modest museum, old maps and globes, and the remnants of Duke Federico's famous library.

**Palazzo Ducale**
Palazzo Ducale. ***Tel*** *0722 31 31 51.* *Tue–Sun.* *public hols.*

# Urbino: Palazzo Ducale

Italy's most beautiful Renaissance palace was built for Duke Federico da Montefeltro, ruler of Urbino (1444–82). He was a soldier, but also a man of the arts, and his palace, with its library, paintings and refined architecture, is a tribute to courtly life and to the artistic and intellectual ideals of the Renaissance. The Palazzo Ducale houses the Galleria Nazionale delle Marche.

**★ The Flagellation by Piero della Francesca**
*Dramatic perspective creates an unsettling effect in this 15th-century painting of the scourging of Christ.*

**The palace rising above Urbino**

**Towers attributed to Laurana**

**The simple east side** of the palace was designed by Maso di Bartolomeo before 1460.

**Cortile d'Onore**
*This early Renaissance courtyard was designed by the Dalmatian-born artist Luciano Laurana (1420–79).*

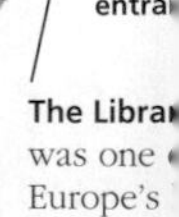

**M entra**

**The Libra** was one Europe's in its day

**Ideal City**
*Attributed to Luciano Laurana, this 15th-century painting of an imaginary Renaissance city is notable for its measured perspective and lack of people.*

*For hotels and restaurants in this region see pp585–7 and pp635–6*

**★ Studiolo**
*The former study of Federico da Montefeltro is decorated with intarsia (inlaid wood), some of it designed by Botticelli.*

**Duke Federico by Pedro Berruguete**
*The duke, shown here with his son in this 15th-century painting, was always portrayed in left profile after an injury to his face.*

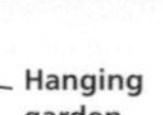
**Hanging garden**

**The rooms** in this wing are known as the Appartamento della Duchessa.

**★ La Muta by Raphael**
The Mute Woman *may be a portrait of Maddalena Doni, a Florentine noblewoman.*

## VISITORS' CHECKLIST

Piazza Duca Federico 13.
***Tel*** *0722 32 26 25.*
*Piazza del Mercatale.*
*8:30am–2pm Mon, 8:30am–7:15pm Tue–Sun. Last adm: 60 mins before closing.*
*1 Jan, 25 Dec.*
**www**.turismo.marche.it

## STAR EXHIBITS

- ★ The Flagellation by Piero della Francesca
- ★ Studiolo
- ★ La Muta by Raphael

# Urbino ❺

Pèsaro. *16,000.* *Piazza Rinascimento* *(0722 26 13).* *Sat.*
**www**.turismo.pesarourbino.it

Amid Urbino's tangle of medieval and Renaissance streets stands the Neo-Classical **Duomo**, on Piazza Federico, built in 1789. Of special interest is the painting of the *Last Supper* by Federico Barocci (c.1535–1612). The **Museo Diocesano** contains a collection of ceramics, glass and religious artifacts.

Urbino's famous son, the painter Raphael (1483–1520), lived in the **Casa Natale di Raffaello**. It has a highly evocative interior, especially the kitchen and courtyard.

In Via Barocci is the medieval **Oratorio di San Giuseppe**, known for its *presepio* (Christmas crib), and the 14th-century **Oratorio di San Giovanni Battista**, whose interior is smothered in 15th-century frescoes of the *Crucifixion* and the *Life of John the Baptist* by Giacomo and Lorenzo Salimbeni.

The 15th-century **Fortezza dell'Albornoz** on Viale Bruno Buozzi is the defensive focus of Urbino's surviving 16th-century walls and bastions.

**Museo Diocesano**
Piazza Pascoli 2. *for restoration; call 0722 2613 for information.*

**Casa Natale di Raffaello**
Via di Raffaello 57. ***Tel*** *0722 32 01 05.* *daily (Sun am only).* *1 Jan, 25 Dec.*

**A street scene in the medieval town of Urbino**

Fresh seafood and fishing boats in the harbour at Ancona

## Grotte di Frasassi ❼

*Ancona.* ***Tel*** *0732 900 90.* *Genga San Vittore Terme.* *daily. Guided tours only (70 mins).* *1 Jan, 10–30 Jan, 4 Dec, 25 Dec.* **www**.frasassi.com

Some of Europe's largest publicly accessible caverns lie in the cave network gouged out by the River Sentino south-west of Jesi. Of the vast network of 18 km (11 miles), an area of about 1,000 m (3,281 ft) is open to the public. The colossal **Grotta del Vento** is large enough to contain Milan cathedral – its ceiling extends to a height of 240 m (787 ft). This cavern has been used for a range of experiments, from sensory deprivation to an exploration of the social consequences of leaving a group of people alone in its depths for long periods.

## Jesi ❽

*Ancona.* *41,000.* *Piazza della Repubblica 11 (0731 53 84 20).* *Wed & Sat.* **www**.comune.jesi.an.it

Perched on a long, rocky ridge, Jesi lies in the heart of the verdant hill country where Verdicchio is produced. A crisp, white wine, Verdicchio is bottled in unique containers – glass models of the terracotta amphorae once used to export the wine to ancient Greece. There are many vineyards in the surrounding countryside.

Housed in the town's 18th-century Palazzo Pianetti is the **Pinacoteca e Musei Civici**, which contains fine late-period paintings by Lorenzo Lotto. Almost as alluring as the gallery's paintings, however, is the great central salon – an orgy of Rococo decoration that once formed the centrepiece of the Palazzo Pianetti. The nearby **Palazzo della Signoria** features an interesting little collection of archaeological finds, while beyond the old town's Renaissance walls stands the 14th-century church of **San Marco**, known for its collection of well-preserved Giottesque frescoes.

**Pinacoteca e Musei Civici**
*Via XV Settembre.* ***Tel*** *0731 53 83 42.* *Tue–Sun.*

**Palazzo della Signoria**
*Piazza Colocci.* ***Tel*** *0731 53 83 45.* *Mon–Sat.* *Mon am & Sat pm.*

## Ancona ❾

*98,000.* *Via Thaon de Revel 4 (071 35 89 91).* *Tue & Fri.* **www**.turismo.marche.it

The capital of Le Marche and its largest port (with ferries to and from Greece and Croatia), Ancona dates back to at least the 5th century BC, when it was settled by Greek exiles from Siracusa. Its name derives from *ankon* (Greek for elbow), a reference to the rocky spur that juts into the sea to form the town's fine natural harbour.

Heavy bombing during World War II destroyed much of the medieval town. The 15th-century **Loggia dei Mercanti** (merchants' exchange) on Via della Loggia survives as a monument to the town's medieval heyday.

Just north of the loggia is the Romanesque church of **Santa Maria della Piazza**, with a lovely façade. The nearby **Pinacoteca Comunale F Podesti e Galleria d'Arte Moderna** includes canvases by Titian and Lorenzo Lotto. In the **Museo Archeologico Nazionale delle Marche** there are displays of Greek, Gallic and Roman art. The **Arco di Traiano**, by the harbour, was erected in AD 115 and is one of Italy's better preserved Roman arches.

An impressive cavern in the cave system of the Grotte di Frasassi

*For hotels and restaurants in this region see pp585–7 and pp635–6*

The beach at the village of Sirolo on the Conero Peninsula

**Pinacoteca Comunale F Podesti e Galleria d'Arte Moderna**
Via Pizzecolli 17. ***Tel*** *071 222 50 41.* *Tue–Sat daily (Sun pm).* *public hols.*

**Museo Archeologico Nazionale delle Marche**
Via Ferretti 1. ***Tel*** *071 20 26 02.* *Tue–Sun.* *1 Jan, 1 May, 15 Aug, 25 Dec.*

## Conero Peninsula 10

Ancona. FS *Ancona.* *from Ancona to Sirolo or Numana.* *Via Thaon de Revel 4, Ancona (071 35 89 91).*

The beautiful cliff-edged Conero Peninsula is the only natural feature to disturb the almost unbroken line of beaches along the coast of Le Marche. Easily accessible from Ancona to the north, it is a semi-wild area known for its scenery, its wines (notably Rosso del Conero) and for a collection of coves, beaches and picturesque little resorts.

The best of these resorts is **Portonovo**, above whose beach stands **Santa Maria di Portonovo**, a pretty 11th-century Romanesque church mentioned by Dante in Canto XXI of *Paradiso*. **Sirolo** and **Numana** are busier and more commercialized, but you can escape the crowds by hiking the flower-swathed slopes of Monte Conero, which stands at 572 m (1,877 ft), or by taking a boat trip to the smaller beaches beyond the resorts.

## Loreto 11

Ancona. *11,000.* FS *Via Solari 3 (071 97 02 76).* *Fri.*

Legend has it that in 1294 the house of the Virgin Mary (**Santa Casa**) miraculously uprooted itself from the Holy Land and was brought by angels to a laurel grove *(loreto)* south of Ancona. Each year several million pilgrims visit the **Santa Casa** in Loreto and its **Basilica**. Begun in 1468, the latter was designed and built in part by Renaissance architects Bramante, Sansovino and Giuliano da Sangallo. Its paintings include works by Luca Signorelli. The **Museo-Pinacoteca** has 16th-century paintings by Lorenzo Lotto.

Santa Casa in Loreto

**Basilica and Santa Casa**
Piazza Santuario. ***Tel*** *071 97 01 04.* *daily.*

**Museo-Pinacoteca**
Palazzo Apostolico. ***Tel*** *071 974 71 98.* *Apr–Oct: Tue–Sun; Nov–Mar: Fri–Sun.*

## Ascoli Piceno 12

*54,000.* *Palazzo Comunale, Piazza Arringo (0736 25 30 45).* *Wed & Sat.*

This alluring town takes its name from the Piceni, a tribe eventually conquered by the Romans in 89 BC. The gridiron plan of Roman Asculum Picenum is visible in the streets today, but it is the town's medieval heritage that attracts most visitors.

The enchanting **Piazza del Popolo** is dominated by the 13th-century **Palazzo dei Capitani del Popolo**, whose façade was designed by Cola dell'Amatrice, and the church of **San Francesco**, a large and faintly austere Gothic ensemble built between 1262 and 1549.

Via del Trivio leads north to a medieval district overlooking the River Tronto. Along Via Cairoli lies the 13th-century Dominican church of **San Pietro Martire**. Opposite is the church of **Santi Vincenzo e Anastasio** (11th century), with an ancient crypt built over a spring said to cure leprosy.

Around Piazza dell'Arringo is the 12th-century **Duomo**, spoiled by a Baroque overlay. Its Cappella del Sacramento contains a polyptych by the 15th-century artist Carlo Crivelli. The **Pinacoteca Civica** has more works by Crivelli and by Guido Reni, Titian and Alemanno. The **Museo Archeologico** contains Roman, Piceni and Lombard artifacts.

**Pinacoteca Civica**
Palazzo Comunale, Piazza Arringo. ***Tel*** *0736 29 82 13.* *Tue–Sun.*

**Museo Archeologico**
Palazzo Panighi, Piazza Arringo. ***Tel*** *0736 25 35 62.* *Tue–Sun.* *1 Jan, 1 May, 25 Dec.*

A view of the medieval town of Ascoli Piceno

# ROME AND LAZIO

# Rome and Lazio at a Glance

The first settlements in the region can be traced back to the early Etruscan civilization in northern Lazio. Rome grew to rule a vast empire and, as the empire began to divide, the region became the centre of the Christian world. Artists and architects flocked to work for the popes and their families, notably in the Renaissance and Baroque periods when some magnificent architectural works were created. The legacy of this uninterrupted history can be seen all over the city and the surrounding area.

**St Peter's**, *with its majestic dome by Michelangelo, is a magnificent and sumptuous 16th-century basilica* (see pp418–19).

**Piazza Navona**, *flanked by cafés, contains three Baroque fountains, including the colossal Fontana dei Quattro Fiumi, one of Bernini's finest works* (see p399).

*St Peter's*

*Fontana dei Quattro Fiumi*

THE VATICAN AND TRASTEVERE
*(See pp414–29)*

*Santa Maria in Trastevere*

**Santa Maria in Trastevere**, *probably the first Christian church in Rome, holds some remarkable mosaics such as this detail from Cavallini's Life of the Virgin which dates from 1291* (see p428).

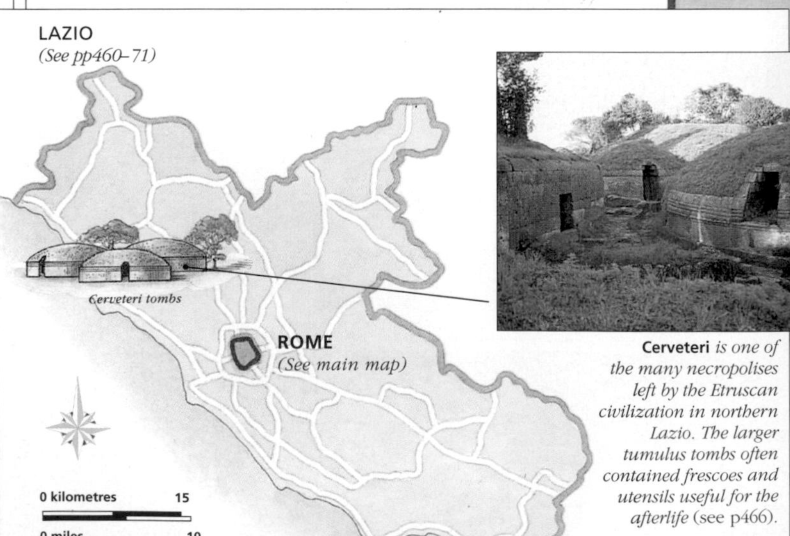


**Cerveteri** *is one of the many necropolises left by the Etruscan civilization in northern Lazio. The larger tumulus tombs often contained frescoes and utensils useful for the afterlife* (see p466).

◁ **Bernini's allegorical Fountain of the Four Rivers at the centre of Piazza Navona**

**The Pantheon**, *built between AD 118–125, is a marvel of Roman engineering with its huge dome hidden behind the Classical portico* (see p404).

***SEE ALSO***

- ***Where to Stay*** pp587–93
- ***Where to Eat*** pp636–43

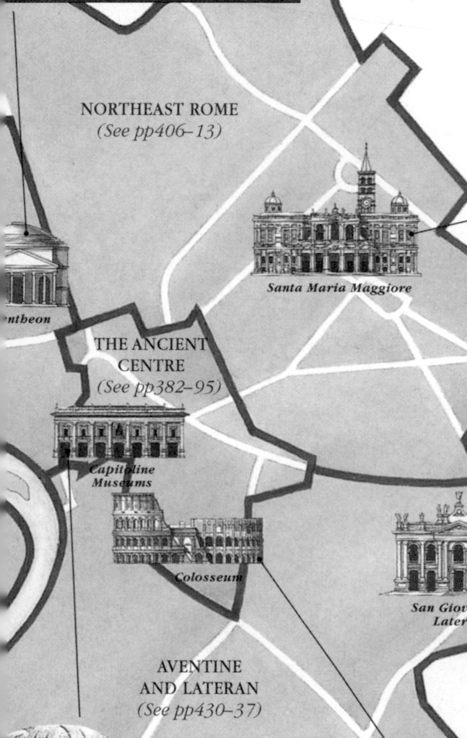

NORTHEAST ROME
*(See pp406–13)*

*Santa Maria Maggiore*

**Santa Maria Maggiore***'s richly decorated interior blends different architectural styles, such as this baldacchino from the 18th century* (see p413).

*Pantheon*

THE ANCIENT CENTRE
*(See pp382–95)*

*Capitoline Museums*

*Colosseum*

*San Giovanni in Laterano*

**San Giovanni in Laterano**, *the Cathedral of Rome, incorporates the elaborate Corsini Chapel built in the 1730s* (see p436).

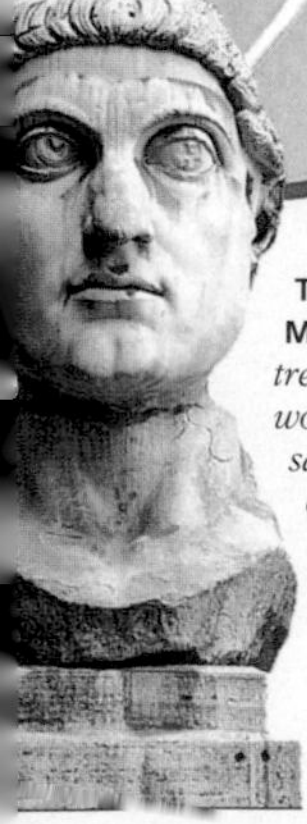

AVENTINE AND LATERAN
*(See pp430–37)*

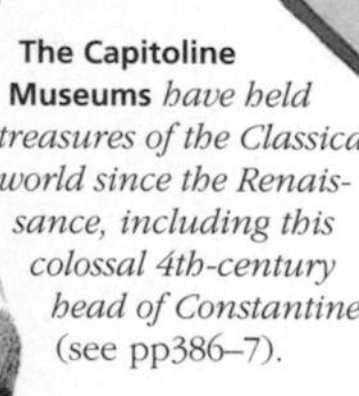

**The Capitoline Museums** *have held treasures of the Classical world since the Renaissance, including this colossal 4th-century head of Constantine* (see pp386–7).

0 metres 750
0 yards 750

**The Colosseum** *was constructed in AD 80 by Emperor Vespasian. His aim was to gain popularity by staging deadly gladiatorial combats and wild animal fights for public viewing* (see p393).

# The Flavours of Rome and Lazio

The countryside of Lazio varies from gently rolling hills to mountains to shimmering coast. Olive groves and vineyards cloak this fertile area, where wild boar roam and many other kinds of game find their way on to the table. But authentic Roman cuisine takes its origins from offal and slow, inventive cooking transforms these traditionally "poor" cuts into flavoursome dishes. Pasta is still the vital ingredient in any meal, and several well-known dishes originate from Rome. Many of the capital's top restaurants are dedicated to fish and seafood and, as home of *la dolce vita*, there is a long tradition of delicious pastries, cakes and ice cream.

**Globe artichokes**

**A stall of Lazio vegetables, fresh from field to market**

Traditional Roman cuisine originated in the Testaccio area, near the old slaughterhouse whose butchers *(vaccinari)* were paid partly in meat, generally offal. The "fifth quarter" *(quinto quarto)* included head, trotters, tail, intestines, brain and other bits of the beast not for the squeamish, but which, when cooked slowly and richly flavoured with herbs and spices, became a culinary delight. These robust dishes, such as the signature dish *coda alla vaccinara* (literally, oxtail in the style of the slaughterhouse butcher) still feature on many menus.

## CUCINA ROMANA

Authentic *cucina romana* also has its roots in Jewish cuisine of the atmospheric Ghetto area, whose origins date back over 400 years. Plump, locally grown globe artichokes are fried whole in olive oil *(carciofi alla giudia)* or served *alla romana*, with oil, garlic and Roman mint. Just as popular are salt cod fillets *(filetti di baccalà)* deep fried, Jewish-style.

Seafood and fish restaurants are among the best in Rome and, while not cheap, many are temples of gastronomy. It was in response to the launch of the first McDonald's

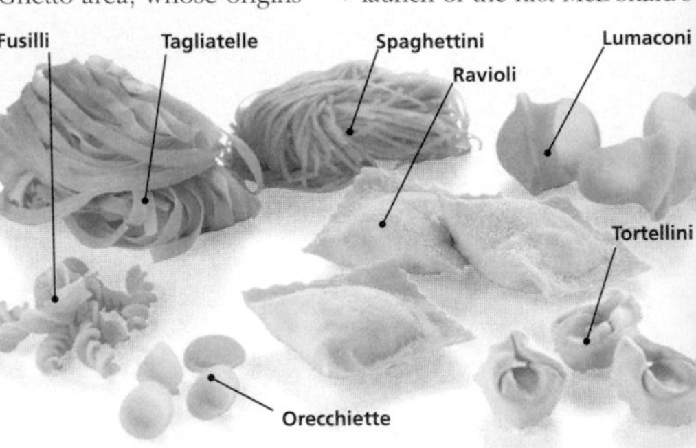


**Just a few of the hundreds of types of pasta available in Italy**

## REGIONAL DISHES AND SPECIALITIES

Crispy fried vegetables, especially artichokes and courgette (zucchini) flowers, are often served as an *antipasto*. For the *primo* course, pasta dishes include *bucatini all'amatriciana* – long, thin pasta tubes in a spicy tomato and bacon sauce, sprinkled with grated Pecorino cheese made from tangy ewe's milk. Veal is a great favourite and delicacies include *rigatoni alla pajata* (pasta with milk-fed veal intestines). Lamb is also very popular, such as *abbacchio al forno* (roasted milk-fed lamb) or *alla cacciatore* ("huntsman's style" with anchovy sauce). Offal is very common in traditional *trattorie*, and delicacies include *cervelle* (calves' brains), *ossobuco* (beef shins with marrow jelly), *pajata* (veal intestines) and *trippa* (tripe).

**Bruschetta**

**Gnocchi alla romana** *Little dumplings, made with semolina flour, are usually served with a tomato or meat* ragù.

Sumptuous Roman pizzas, sizzling hot from the wood-fired oven

in Rome in 1986 that the Slow Food Movement started in Piedmont *(see p174)*, but more typical Roman fast food includes *bruschetta* ("lightly burnt bread" in Roman dialect) rubbed with garlic, sea salt and olive oil and topped with a selection of intense flavours. There's also authentic thin and crispy *pizza romana* from wood-fired ovens, often served *al taglio* – by the slice.

## PASTA, PASTA

Pasta is still the mainstay of the Roman meal, especially spaghetti. *Spaghetti alla carbonara*, made with *pancetta* (cured bacon) or *guanciale* (pig's cheek), egg yolks and cheese, is a classic Roman dish, as is *spaghetti alle vongole*, with garlic and clams. At a conservative estimate, there is one type of pasta for every day of the year, many of which have wonderfully descriptive or poetic names, such as *capelli d'angelo* (angel's hair) or *ziti* (bridegrooms) whose shape is best left to the imagination.

An array of mouthwatering *gelati* in a Roman ice cream parlour

## LA DOLCE VITA

For those with a taste for "the sweet life", nuts, fruits and versatile ricotta cheese are often combined in mouth-wateringly delicious sweets.

Ice cream is an art form in Rome, where some parlours offer over 100 flavours of homemade *gelati*. Types vary from the classic *crema* and *frutta* to *grattachecca* (water ice), from *semifreddo* (a half-frozen sponge pudding, similar to *tiramisù* in consistency) to *granità* (ice shavings flavoured with fruit syrups). Glorious *gelato* is one of the great pleasures here, to be enjoyed at any time of the day – or night.

## ON THE MENU

**Abbacchio alla cacciatore** Baby lamb cooked with anchovies, garlic, Castelli Romani wine, rosemary and olive oil.

**Coda alla vaccinara** Oxtail braised in herbs, tomato and celery.

**Fave al guanciale** Young spring broad (fava) beans simmered in olive oil with pig's cheek and onion.

**Filetti di baccalà** Salt cod fillets in batter – once a Jewish speciality, now a feature of Roman cuisine.

**Spigola alla romana** Sea bass with *porcini* mushrooms (ceps), Roman-style.

**Spaghetti alle vongole** *The classic Italian pasta is here served with a sauce made of baby clams and tomatoes.*

**Saltimbocca alla romana** *Veal slices are rolled with prosciutto and sage. Saltimbocca means "jump in the mouth".*

**Torta di ricotta** *Ricotta cheese is baked in a tart with sugar, lemon, brandy, eggs and cinnamon.*

# Understanding Architecture in Rome and Lazio

The architecture of Imperial Rome, a combination of Etruscan and Classical Greek styles, gradually developed new and uniquely Roman forms based on the arch, the vault and the dome. During the early Christian period simple, rectangular basilicas were built, forms which by the 12th century had been incorporated into the stark Romanesque style. The Renaissance, inspired by the example of Florence, saw a return to Classical ideals of simplicity and harmonious proportions, though it was to be in the flamboyance of the 17th-century Baroque that Rome once again found great architectural expression.

**The extravagant Baroque style of the Fontana di Trevi, Rome**

## FROM ETRUSCAN TO CLASSICAL ROME

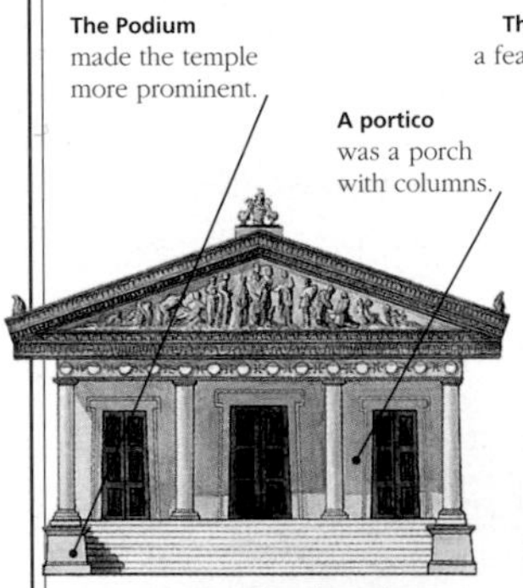


**Etruscan temples**, *based on Greek models, inspired early Roman architecture. A front portico was the only entrance.*

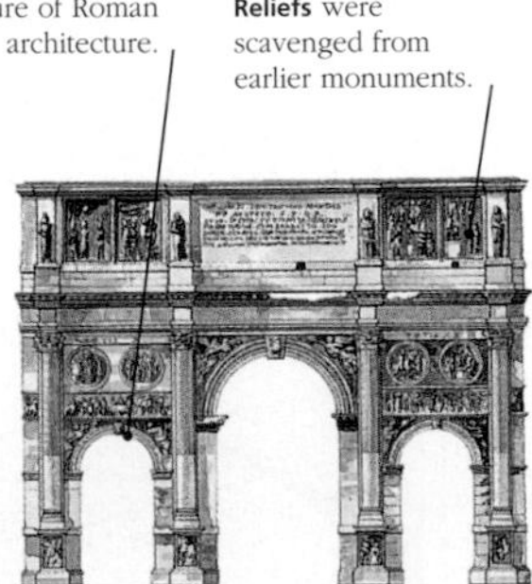


**The Arch of Constantine** *(AD 315) is typical of triumphant Imperial Roman architecture* (see p389). *It stands at a colossal 25 m (82 ft).*

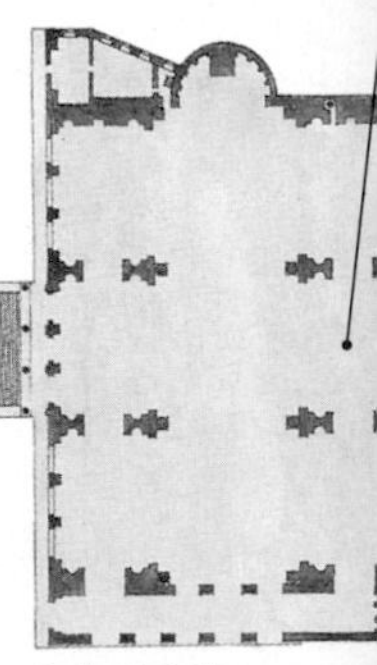


**Early Christian basilicas** *(4th century) were based on a rectangular floorplan.*

## FROM RENAISSANCE TO BAROQUE

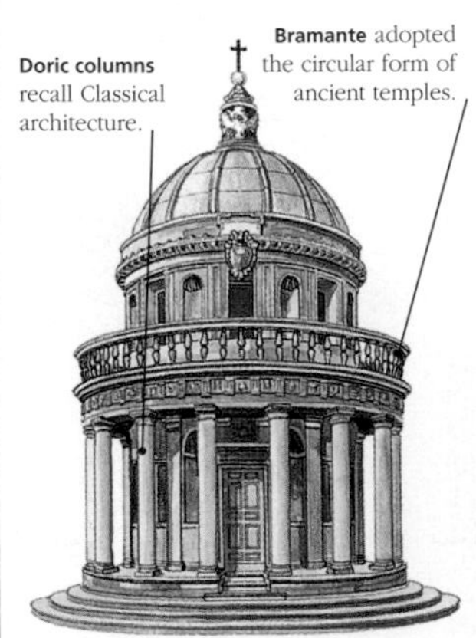


**The Tempietto** *at San Pietro in Montorio, Rome (1502) is a model of Renaissance architecture: simple and perfectly proportioned* (see p429).

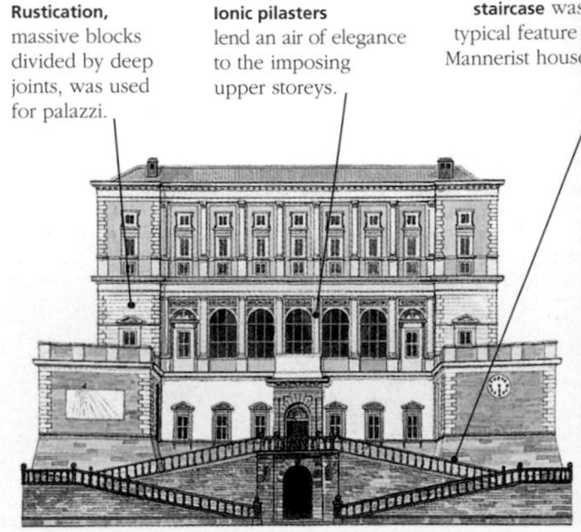


**Palazzo Farnese** *at Caprarola, a pentagonal building completed in 1575* (see p465), *combines some Mannerist tricks of architecture with the strict geometric proportions characteristic of the Renaissance.*

## WHERE TO SEE THE ARCHITECTURE

A walk through the back streets of the centre of Rome will reveal masterpieces of virtually every architectural age. The most ancient treasures are seven obelisks stolen from Egypt. One stands on the back of Bernini's elephant *(see p404)*. Highlights from Ancient Rome include triumphal arches and temples such as the Pantheon *(see p404)*. Romanesque elements survive in the church of San Clemente *(see p435)*, while the Renaissance finds expression in the dome of St Peter's *(see pp418–19)*. Magnificent Baroque treasures dot the entire city, in particular flamboyant fountains that adorn the squares. Outside the city the outstanding sights are the late Renaissance villas such as Caprarola *(see p465)*.

**Part of Bernini's elephant supporting an ancient Egyptian obelisk**

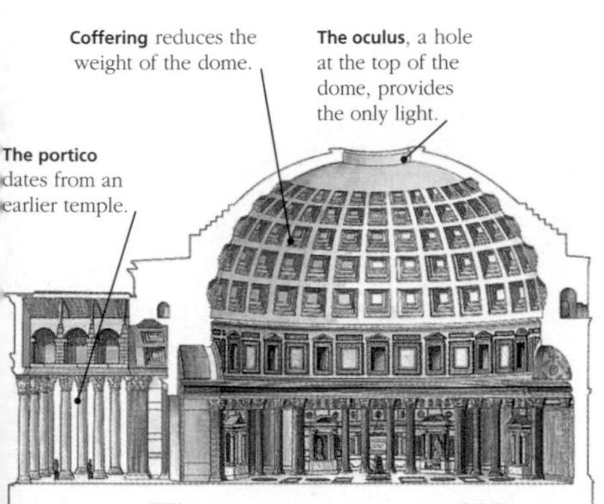


**The Pantheon** (see p404) *is one of the cardinal buildings of late Roman architecture. Completed in AD 125, it reveals how the form of the Greek temple was elaborated upon to create a masterpiece of perfect proportions.*

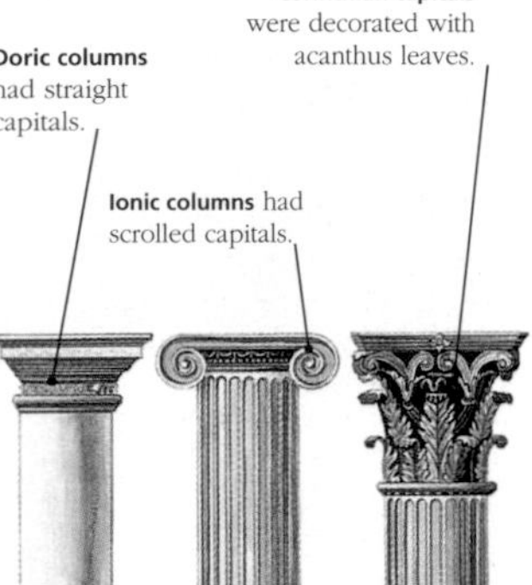


**The orders** *of Classical architecture were building styles based on ancient Greek models, identified by the column capitals.*

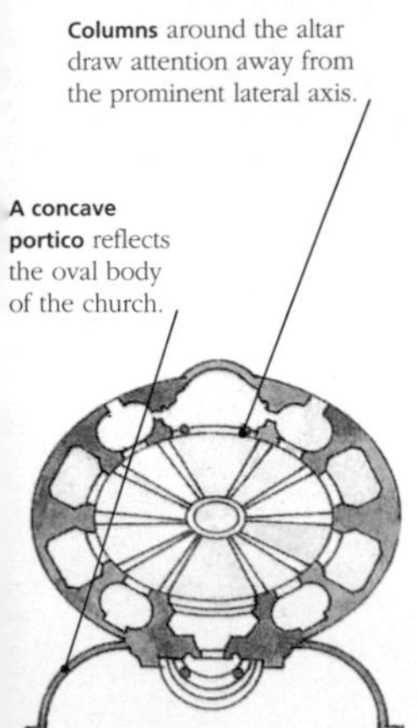


**The oval floorplan** *of the Baroque Sant'Andrea al Quirinale* (see p411) *makes ingenious use of restricted space.*

**The Gesù** *façade (1584) epitomizes Counter-Reformation architecture and has been imitated throughout the Catholic world* (see p403).

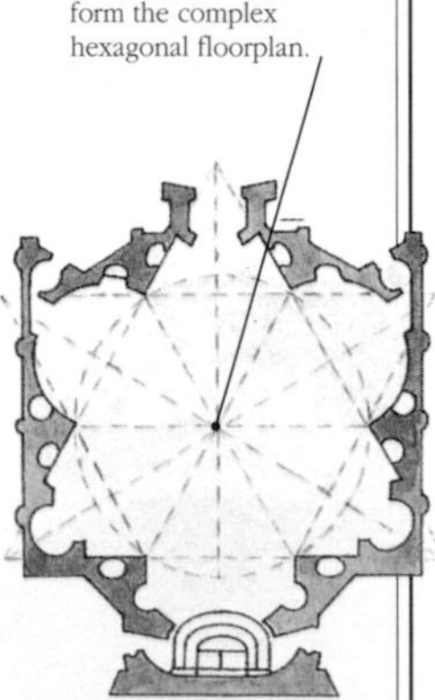


**Sant'Ivo alla Sapienza***'s floorplan (1642) favoured grandiose design over Classical form* (see p400).

# THE ANCIENT CENTRE

The Capitol, the southern summit of the Capitoline Hill, was the symbolic centre of the Roman world and home to the city's three most important temples. These were dedicated to the god Jupiter Optimus Maximus, protector of Rome, Minerva, goddess of wisdom and war, and Juno Moneta, a guardian goddess. Below the Capitol lies the Forum, once the focus of political, social, legal and commercial life; the Imperial Fora, built when Rome's population grew; and the Colosseum, the centre of entertainment. Overlooking the Forum is the Palatine Hill, where Romulus is said to have founded Rome in the 8th century BC, and emperors lived for over 400 years.

**Capitoline Wolf with Romulus and Remus**

## SIGHTS AT A GLANCE

**Churches**
Santa Maria in Aracoeli 3

**Museums and Galleries**
*Capitoline Museums pp386–7* 1

**Historic Piazzas**
Piazza del Campidoglio 2

**Ancient Sites and Buildings**
Arch of Constantine 10
*Colosseum p393* 9
Forum of Augustus 5
Forum of Caesar 7
Mamertine Prison 6
*Palatine pp394–5* 11
*Roman Forum pp390–91* 8
Trajan's Forum and Markets 4

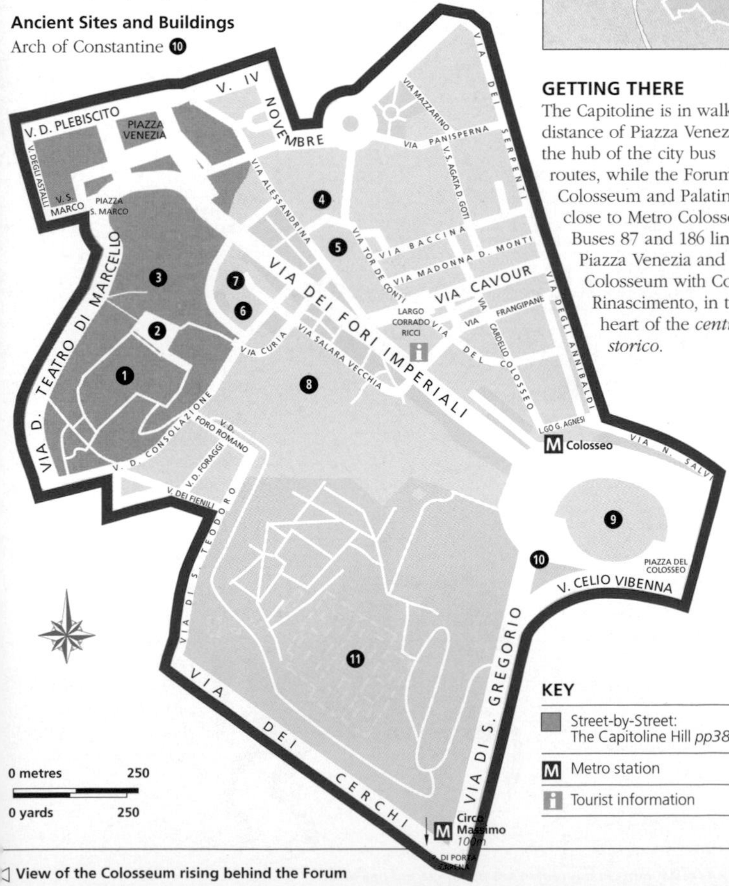

## GETTING THERE

The Capitoline is in walking distance of Piazza Venezia, the hub of the city bus routes, while the Forum, Colosseum and Palatine are close to Metro Colosseo. Buses 87 and 186 link Piazza Venezia and the Colosseum with Corso Rinascimento, in the heart of the *centro storico*.

V. D. PLEBISCITO
PIAZZA VENEZIA
V. DEGLI ASTALLI
V. S. MARCO
PIAZZA S. MARCO
V. IV NOVEMBRE
VIA MAZZARINO
VIA PANISPERNA
V. S. AGATA D. GOTI
VIA DEI SERPENTI
VIA ALESSANDRINA
VIA TOR DE CONTI
VIA BACCINA
VIA MADONNA D. MONTI
VIA CAVOUR
VIA FRANGIPANE
VIA DEI FORI IMPERIALI
LARGO CORRADO RICCI
VIA CARDELLO
VIA DEL COLOSSEO
VIA DEGLI ANNIBALDI
VIA CURIA
VIA SALARA VECCHIA
VIA D. TEATRO DI MARCELLO
V. D. CONSOLAZIONE
V. D. FORO ROMANO
V. D. FORAGGI
V. DEI FIENILI
VIA DI S. TEODORO
LGO G. AGNESI
Colosseo
VIA N. SALVI
PIAZZA DEL COLOSSEO
V. CELIO VIBENNA
VIA DI S. GREGORIO
VIA DEI CERCHI
Circo Massimo 100m
V. DI PORTA CAPENA

0 metres 250
0 yards 250

**KEY**

Street-by-Street: The Capitoline Hill *pp384–5*

Metro station

Tourist information

◁ **View of the Colosseum rising behind the Forum**

# Street-by-Street: The Capitoline Hill

The Capitol, citadel of ancient Rome, was redesigned by Michelangelo in the 16th century. He was responsible for the trapezoid Piazza del Campidoglio as well as the Cordonata, the broad flight of steps leading up to it. The piazza is flanked by Palazzo Nuovo and Palazzo dei Conservatori, housing the Capitoline Museums, with their fine collections of sculpture and paintings. It is also well worth walking behind the museums to the Tarpeian Rock, for a fine view of the Forum lying below.

**The Victor Emmanuel Monument** was begun in 1885 and inaugurated in 1911 in honour of Victor Emmanuel II, the first king of unified Italy.

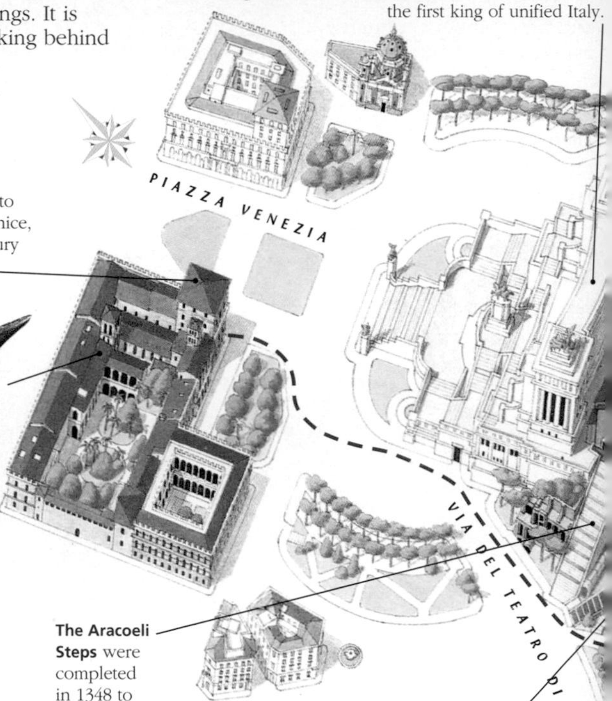

**San Marco**, dedicated to the patron saint of Venice, has splendid 9th-century mosaics in the apse.

**Palazzo Venezia**, once the home of Mussolini, now holds a museum of fine and decorative arts. Exhibits include this medieval gilt and enamel angel.

**The Aracoeli Steps** were completed in 1348 to commemorate the end of the plague.

**The Cordonata** is presided over by the colossal statues of Castor and Pollux.

**★ Capitoline Museums**
*The collections of art and ancient sculpture include this statue of the Emperor Marcus Aurelius, a replica of which stands in the centre of the piazza* ❶

**STAR SIGHT**

★ Capitoline Museums

**KEY**

— — — Suggested route

**0 metres** 75

**0 yards** 75

**Santa Maria in Aracoeli**
*The brick façade hides treasures such as this 15th-century fresco of* The Funeral of San Bernardino *by Pinturicchio* ❸

**LOCATOR MAP**
*See Rome Street Finder map 3*

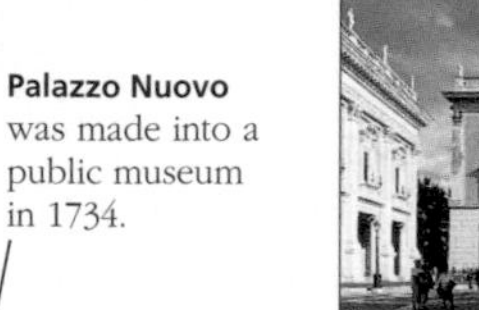

**Palazzo Nuovo** was made into a public museum in 1734.

**Palazzo Senatorio**, the splendid Renaissance seat of the city government, is built on the ruins of the ancient Tabularium.

**Piazza del Campidoglio**
*Michelangelo designed the geometric paving and the façades of the buildings* ❷

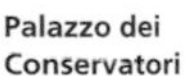

**Palazzo dei Conservatori**

**The Temple of Jupiter**, represented on this coin, was dedicated to Jupiter Optimus Maximus, the most important of the Roman gods. He was believed to have the power to protect or destroy the city.

**The Tarpeian Rock** is a cliff from which traitors were believed to have been thrown to their death in ancient Rome.

**Steps to the Capitoline**

## Capitoline Museums ❶

*See pp386–7.*

## Piazza del Campidoglio ❷

**Map** 3 A5. *40, 64, 70, 75.*

When Emperor Charles V announced he was to visit Rome in 1536, Pope Paul III Farnese asked Michelangelo to give the Capitoline a facelift. He redesigned the piazza, renovated the façades of its palaces and built a new flight of steps, the Cordonata. This gently rising ramp is now crowned with the massive statues of Castor and Pollux.

## Santa Maria in Aracoeli ❸

Piazza d'Aracoeli. **Map** 3 A5.
***Tel*** *06 69 76 38 39.* *64, 70, 75.*
*9am–12:30pm, 3–6:30pm daily (2:30–5:30pm in winter).*

This church stands on the site of the temple of Juno on the northern summit of the Capitoline Hill, and dates back at least to the 6th century. The church is famous for its ornate gilded ceiling and a very fine series of frescoes by Pinturicchio, dating from the 1480s. They depict scenes from the life of San Bernardino of Siena. The miracle-working *Santo Bambino* figure, stolen in 1994, has been replaced by a replica.

**The marble steps and austere façade of Santa Maria in Aracoeli**

# Capitoline Museums: ❶

## Palazzo Nuovo

A collection of Classical sculptures has been kept on the Capitoline Hill since Pope Sixtus IV donated a group of bronze statues to the city in 1471. Paintings as well as sculpture are now housed in two palaces designed by Michelangelo. The Palazzo Nuovo contains a fine selection of Greek and Roman sculptures. Access is via the Palazzo dei Conservatori *(opposite)*.

**LOCATOR MAP**

**Discobolus**
*The twisted torso was part of a Greek statue of a discus thrower. An 18th-century sculptor turned him into a wounded warrior.*

**Mosaic of the Doves**
*This 1st-century AD naturalistic mosaic once decorated the floor of Hadrian's Villa at Tivoli* (see p468).

**Alexander Severus as Hunter**
*In this marble of the 3rd century AD, the emperor's pose is a pastiche of the mythical hero, Perseus, holding up the head of Medusa the Gorgon after he had killed her.*

**Hall of the Philosophers**
*The hall contains Roman copies of portrait busts of Greek politicians, scientists and poets. These adorned the homes of wealthy Romans.*

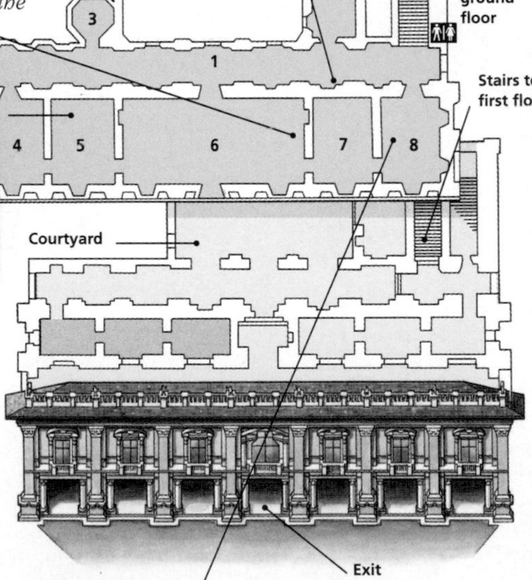


**Dying Galatian**
*Great compassion is conveyed in this Roman copy of a Greek work of the 3rd century BC.*

**KEY TO FLOORPLAN**

- Ground floor
- First floor
- Second floor
- Non-exhibition space

## Palazzo dei Conservatori

The Palazzo dei Conservatori was the seat of the city's magistrates during the late Middle Ages. Its frescoed halls are still used occasionally for political meetings and the ground floor houses the municipal registry office. While much of the palazzo is given over to sculpture, including fragments of a huge sculpture of Constantine, the art galleries on the second floor hold works by Veronese, Tintoretto, Caravaggio, Van Dyck and Titian.

**VISITORS' CHECKLIST**

Musei Capitolini, Piazza del Campidoglio. **Map** 3 A5.
***Tel*** *06 06 08.* *40, 63, 64, 70, 75, 81, 87 and many other routes through Piazza Venezia.*
*9am–8pm Tue–Sun.*
*1 Jan, 1 May, 25 Dec.*
*entrance ticket is valid for both museums.*
**www**.museicapitolini.org

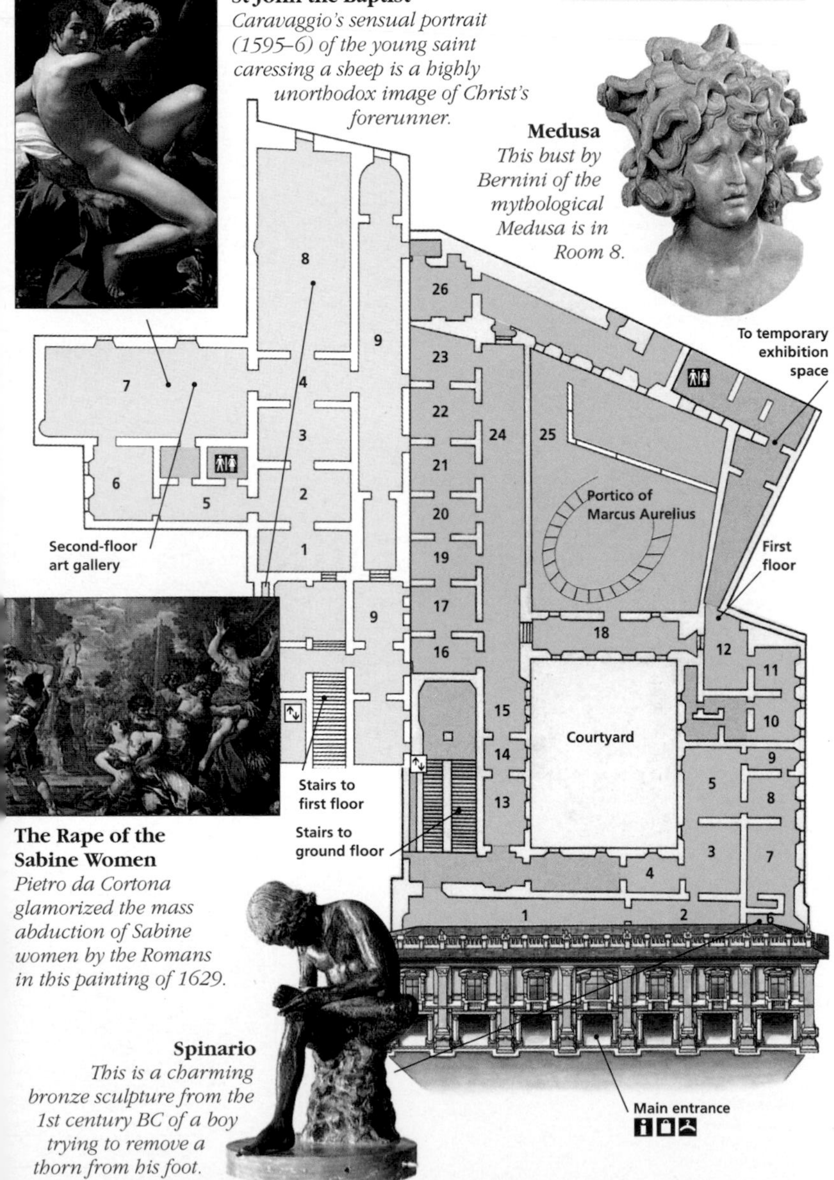


**St John the Baptist**
*Caravaggio's sensual portrait (1595–6) of the young saint caressing a sheep is a highly unorthodox image of Christ's forerunner.*

**Medusa**
*This bust by Bernini of the mythological Medusa is in Room 8.*

**The Rape of the Sabine Women**
*Pietro da Cortona glamorized the mass abduction of Sabine women by the Romans in this painting of 1629.*

**Spinario**
*This is a charming bronze sculpture from the 1st century BC of a boy trying to remove a thorn from his foot.*

## Trajan's Forum and Markets ❹

**Map** 3 B4. **Trajan's Forum**, Via dei Fori Imperiali. *to the public.* **Trajan's Markets**, Via IV Novembre. ***Tel*** *06 69 92 35 21.* *9am–6:45pm daily (last adm: 6pm).*

Trajan began to build his forum in AD 107 to commemorate his final conquest of Dacia (present day Romania) after successful campaigns in AD 101–2 and 105–6. His new forum was the most ambitious yet, with a vast colonnaded open space centring on an equestrian statue of the emperor, a huge basilica, and two big libraries. Dominating the ruins today is **Trajan's Column**, which originally stood between the two libraries.

Trajan's Column

Spiralling up its 30 m (98 ft) high stem are minutely detailed scenes from the Dacian campaigns, beginning with the Romans preparing for war and ending with the Dacians being ousted from their homeland. The subtly modelled reliefs were designed to be seen from viewing platforms on the libraries, and are consequently difficult to interpret from ground level. If you want to examine the scenes in detail there are casts in the Museo della Civiltà Romana *(see p442)*. The **market** complex, which is situated directly behind the forum, was begun slightly earlier. Like the forum it was probably designed by Apollodorus of Damascus, and was the

Via Biberatica, the main street through Trajan's Markets

ancient Roman equivalent of the modern shopping centre. There were around 150 shops selling everything from oriental silks and spices to fruit, fresh fish and flowers. It was also here that the *annone*, or corn dole, was distributed. This was a free ration of corn given to Roman men, a practice which was introduced in the Republic by politicians who wanted to buy votes and prevent unrest during periods of famine.

### RECONSTRUCTION OF TRAJAN'S MARKETS

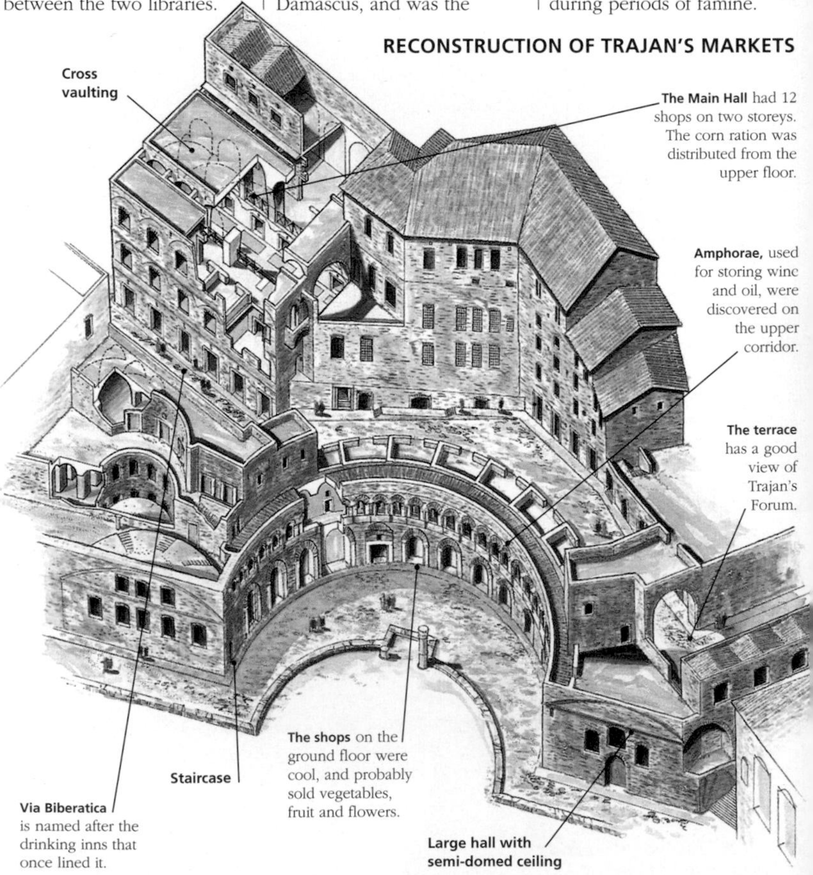

**Cross vaulting**

**The Main Hall** had 12 shops on two storeys. The corn ration was distributed from the upper floor.

**Amphorae,** used for storing wine and oil, were discovered on the upper corridor.

**The terrace** has a good view of Trajan's Forum.

**Via Biberatica** is named after the drinking inns that once lined it.

**Staircase**

**The shops** on the ground floor were cool, and probably sold vegetables, fruit and flowers.

**Large hall with semi-domed ceiling**

## Forum of Augustus ❺

Piazza del Grillo 1. **Map** 3 B5. ***Tel*** *06 06 08.* *87, 186.* *to research scholars by appt.*

The Forum of Augustus, which once stretched from a high wall at the foot of sleazy Suburra to the edge of Caesar's Forum, was built to celebrate Augustus's victory in 41 BC over Brutus and Cassius, the assassins of Julius Caesar. As a consequence the temple in its centre was dedicated to Mars the Avenger. The temple, with its cracked steps and four Corinthian columns, is easily identified. Originally it had a statue of Mars that looked very like Augustus, but in case anyone failed to notice the resemblance, a colossal statue of the emperor himself was placed against the wall of the Suburra quarter.

**19th-century engraving of the Mamertine Prison**

## Mamertine Prison ❻

Clivo Argentario 1. **Map** 3 A5. ***Tel*** *06 679 29 02.* *84, 85, 87, 175, 186.* *for restoration. Call 06 06 08 for information.* **Donation**.

Below the 16th-century church of San Giuseppe dei Falegnami is a dank dungeon in which, according to Christian legend, St Peter and St Paul were imprisoned. They are said to have caused a spring to bubble up into the cell, and to have used the water to baptize two prison guards. The prison was in an old cistern with access to the city's main sewer (the Cloaca Maxima). The lower cell was used for executions, and corpses were thrown into the sewer. However, the inmates, who received no food, often died of starvation.

**Podium of the Temple of Mars the Avenger, Forum of Augustus**

## Forum of Caesar ❼

Via del Carcere Tulliano. **Map** 3 A5. ***Tel*** *06 06 08.* *84, 85, 87, 175, 186, 810, 850.* *to research scholars by appt only.*

The first of Rome's Imperial fora was built by Julius Caesar to relieve congestion in the Roman Forum when Rome's population boomed. He spent a fortune – most of it booty from his recent conquest of Gaul – buying up and demolishing houses on the site. Pride of place went to a temple dedicated in 46 BC to Venus Genetrix (Venus the Ancestor) as Caesar claimed to be descended from the goddess. The temple contained statues of Caesar and Cleopatra as well as of Venus, but all that remains today is a platform and three Corinthian columns. The forum was once enclosed by a double colonnade, under which was sheltered a row of shops. However, this burned down in AD 80 and was rebuilt by Domitian and Trajan. The latter also added the Basilica Argentaria – which became an important financial exchange – as well as shops and a heated public lavatory.

## Roman Forum ❽

*See pp390–91.*

## Colosseum ❾

*See p393.*

## Arch of Constantine ❿

Between Via di San Gregorio and Piazza del Colosseo. **Map** 6 F1. *75, 85, 87, 110, 175, 673, 810.* *3.* *Colosseo.*

This triumphal arch is one of Imperial Rome's last monuments, built in AD 315, a few years before Constantine moved the capital of the Empire to Byzantium. It was built to celebrate Constantine's victory in AD 312 over his co-emperor Maxentius at the Battle of the Milvian Bridge. Constantine attributed the victory to a dream in which he was told to mark his men's shields with *chi-rho*, the first two Greek letters of Christ's name. Christian tradition prefers a version in which the emperor has a vision of the Cross, mid-battle. There is nothing Christian about the arch: most of the reliefs were from earlier pagan monuments.

## Palatine ⓫

*See pp394–5.*

**The north side of the Arch of Constantine**

# Roman Forum ❽

In the early Republic, the Forum was a chaotic place, with food stalls and brothels as well as temples and the Senate House. By the 2nd century BC it was decided that Rome required a more salubrious centre, and the food stores were replaced by business centres and law courts. The Forum remained the ceremonial centre of the city under the Empire, with emperors renovating old buildings and erecting new temples and monuments.

**Arch of Septimius Severus**
*This triumphal arch was erected in AD 203, the 10th anniversary of Emperor Septimius Severus' accession.*

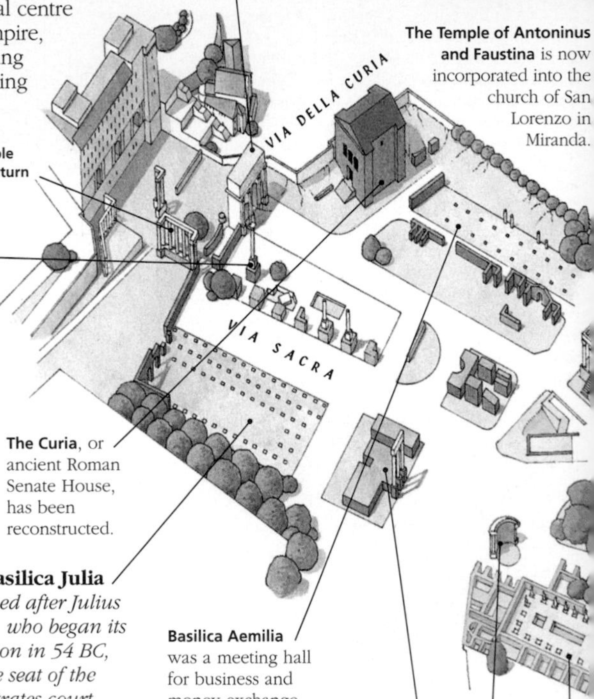

**The Temple of Antoninus and Faustina** is now incorporated into the church of San Lorenzo in Miranda.

VIA DELLA CURIA

VIA SACRA

**Temple of Saturn**

**The Rostra** was the orator's tribune from which speeches were made.

**The Curia**, or ancient Roman Senate House, has been reconstructed.

**Basilica Julia**
*Named after Julius Caesar, who began its construction in 54 BC, this was the seat of the civil magistrates court.*

**Basilica Aemilia** was a meeting hall for business and money exchange.

**Temple of Vesta**

**Temple of Castor and Pollux**
*Although there has been a temple here since the 5th century BC, the columns and elaborate cornice date from AD 6, when the temple was rebuilt.*

**STAR SIGHTS**

- ★ House of the Vestal Virgins
- ★ Basilica of Constantine and Maxentius

0 metres 75

0 yards 75

**★ House of the Vestal Virgins**
*The priestesses who tended the sacred flame in the Temple of Vesta lived here. The house was a large rectangular building around a central garden.*

*For hotels and restaurants in this region see pp587–92 and pp636–41*

**★ Basilica of Constantine and Maxentius**
*The basilica's three vast barrel vaults are all that remain of the Forum's largest building. Like other basilicas, it was used for the administration of justice and conducting business.*

### VISITORS' CHECKLIST

Entrance: Via della Salara Vecchia 5/6. **Map** 3 B5. ***Tel*** *06 39 96 77 00. 85, 87, 117, 175, 186, 810, 850. Colosseo. 3. 8:30am–1 hr before sunset daily. 1 Jan, 1 May, 25 Dec. includes entry to the Colosseum and the Palatine.*

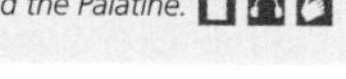

**Arch of Titus**
*This arch was erected by Emperor Domitian in AD 81 to commemorate the sack of Jerusalem by his father Vespasian and brother Titus, 13 years earlier.*

**The Temple of Romulus**, now part of the church of Santi Cosma e Damiano which stands behind it, retains its original 4th-century bronze doors.

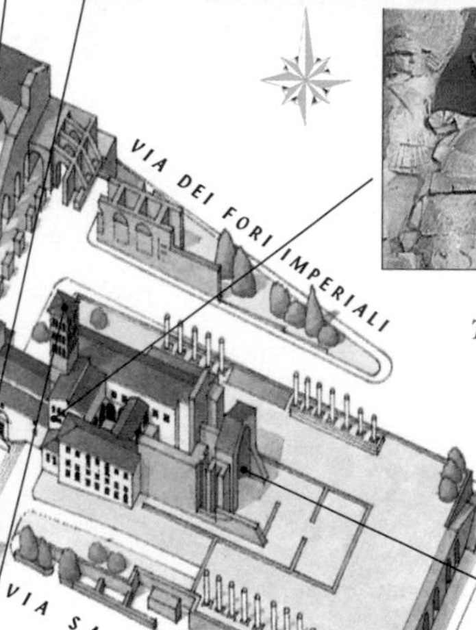


**Antiquarium Forense**
*This small museum contains finds from the Forum. Exhibits range from Iron Age burial urns to this frieze of Aeneas from the Basilica Aemilia.*

**The Temple of Venus and Rome** was built in AD 135, and was largely designed by Hadrian.

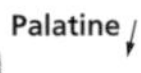


**Santa Francesca Romana**
*The Romanesque bell tower of Santa Francesca Romana towers over one of a number of churches built among the ruins of the Forum.*

### THE VESTAL VIRGINS

The cult of Vesta, the goddess of fire, dates back to at least the 8th century BC. Romulus and Remus were allegedly born of the Vestal priestess Rhea and the god Mars. Six virgins kept the sacred flame of Vesta burning in her circular temple. The girls, who came from noble families, were selected when they were between six and ten years old, and served for 30 years. They had high status and financial security, but were buried alive if they lost their virginity and whipped by the high priest if the sacred flame died out. Although they were permitted to marry after finishing their service, few did so.

**Honorary statue of a Vestal Virgin**

# Exploring the Roman Forum

To appreciate the layout of the Roman Forum before wandering through its confusing patchwork of ruined temples, triumphal arches and basilicas, it is best to view the whole area from the Capitoline Hill above. From there you can make out the more substantial ruins, and the course of the Via Sacra (Sacred Way), the route followed through the Forum by religious and triumphal processions making their way up to the Capitol to give thanks at the Temple of Jupiter *(see p385)*.

**Corinthian columns of the Temple of Castor and Pollux**

**The Main Sights**

The first building you come to on entering the Forum is the **Basilica Aemilia**. A rectangular hall built in 179 BC, it was a meeting place for moneylenders, businessmen and tax collectors. Although little more remains of it than a pastel marble pavement fringed with column stumps, you can still find splashes of verdigrised bronze, reputedly the remains of coins which melted when the Visigoths invaded Rome and burnt down the basilica in the 5th century.

Inside the Curia – the stark brick building next to the basilica – are the **Plutei of Trajan**, relief panels commissioned by either Trajan or Hadrian to decorate the Rostra, the public oratory platform. On one panel are piles of books holding tax records, which Trajan had destroyed in order to free citizens from debts. The **Arch of Septimius Severus** is the best preserved of the Forum's monuments. The marble relief panels depict the military triumphs of the emperor in Parthia (modern-day Iran and Iraq) and Arabia.

The **Temple of Saturn** was the focus of the annual Saturnalia celebrations, when, for up to a week in December, schools closed, slaves dined with their masters, presents were exchanged and a fair and market were held.

Soaring above the remains of the Basilica Julia are three delicately fluted columns and a finely carved slab of entablature taken from the **Temple of Castor and Pollux**. This striking relic is dedicated to the twin brothers of Helen of Troy, who were supposed to have appeared at the battle of Lake Regillus in 499 BC, aiding the Romans in their defeat of the Etruscans.

**Restored section of Temple of Vesta**

The elegant circular **Temple of Vesta** was one of ancient Rome's most sacred shrines and was dedicated to the goddess of the hearth. The flame, kept alive by the Vestal Virgins, symbolized the perpetuity of the state and its extinction prophesied doom for the city. The building was partly reconstructed in 1930, but the circular form goes back to the Latin mud huts which originally occupied the site. Just behind is the **House of the Vestal Virgins**, the living quarters of the priestess and the Vestals. This enormous complex of 50 rooms was once annexed to the Temple. Best preserved are the rooms overlooking a pretty courtyard, ornamented with statues of Vestals, ponds of waterlilies and rose trees.

On the other side of the Forum lie the impressive remains of the **Basilica of Constantine**. It was begun in AD 308 by Maxentius, and is therefore also known as the Basilica of Maxentius. Constantine completed it after he defeated his rival at the battle of Milvio in AD 312. The stark remains of the huge arches and ceilings give an indication of the original scale and grandeur of the forum's public buildings. Three enormous coffered vaults remain, which originally measured up to 35 m (115 ft) and were faced with marble. The interior walls, which held niches for statues, were also covered with marble below and stucco above. Remains of a spiral staircase which once led to the roof can be found scattered on the ground.

The basilica's apse and hexagonal arches were often used as models by Renaissance architects striving to recreate a Classical symmetry and nobility in their work. They include Michelangelo, who allegedly studied the basilica's architecture when working on the dome of St Peter's.

**Central courtyard of the House of the Vestal Virgins**

# Colosseum 9

**Gladiator's shield**

Rome's greatest amphitheatre was commissioned by Emperor Vespasian in AD 72. Deadly gladiatorial combats and wild animal fights were staged by emperors and wealthy citizens, largely to gain popularity. Slaughter was on a huge scale: at the inaugural games in AD 80, over 9,000 wild animals were killed. The Colosseum could hold up to 55,000 people, who were seated according to rank.

## VISITORS' CHECKLIST

Piazza del Colosseo. **Map** 7 A1. ***Tel*** *06 39 96 77 00.* *75, 81, 85, 87, 117, 175, 673, 810.* *Colosseo.* *3 to Piazza del Colosseo.* *8:30am–1 hr before sunset daily.* *1 Jan, 25 Dec.* *includes entry to the Forum and Palatine.* *limited.*

**Internal Corridors**
*These allowed the large and often unruly crowd to move freely and be seated quickly.*

**The Colossus of Nero**
*This gilt bronze statue from Nero's palace, over which the Colosseum was built, may have given the amphitheatre its name.*

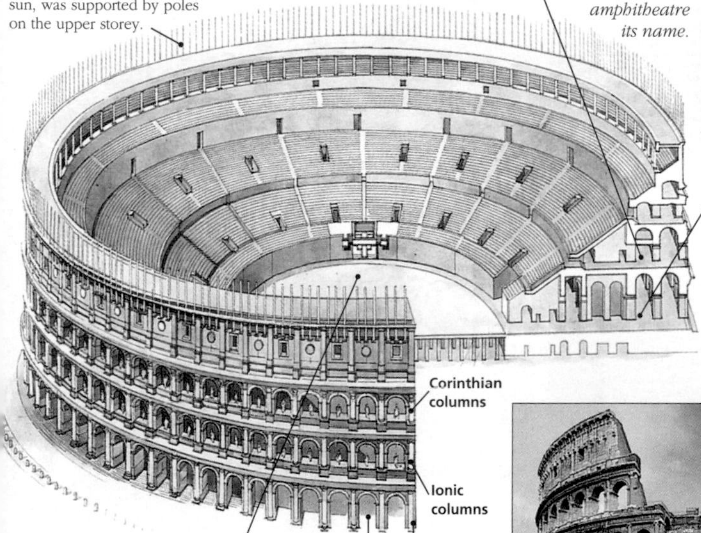

**The Velarium**, a huge sailcloth awning which sheltered spectators from the sun, was supported by poles on the upper storey.

**Entry routes** and stairs led to seats at the various levels. The emperor and consul had their own, separate entrances.

**Corinthian columns**

**Ionic columns**

**Doric columns**

**Entrances**

**The arena floor** covered a network of lifts and cages for wild animals.

**Doric, Ionic and Corinthian Tiers**
*The tiers inspired many Renaissance architects, who also plundered the building, using its travertine to build palaces and part of St Peter's.*

**Roman Gladiators**
*These were originally soldiers in training. Their combat became a sport, and slaves, prisoners of war or criminals were forced to fight men or wild animals to the death.*

**Emperor Vespasian**
*He ordered the Colosseum to be built on the site of Nero's palace, to dissociate himself from the hated tyrant.*

# Palatine ⓫

Statue of the goddess Cybele

The Palatine, once the residence of emperors and aristocrats, is the most pleasant of Rome's ancient sites. The ruins range from the simple house in which Augustus is thought to have lived, to the Domus Flavia and Domus Augustana, the public and private wings of a luxurious palace built by Domitian.

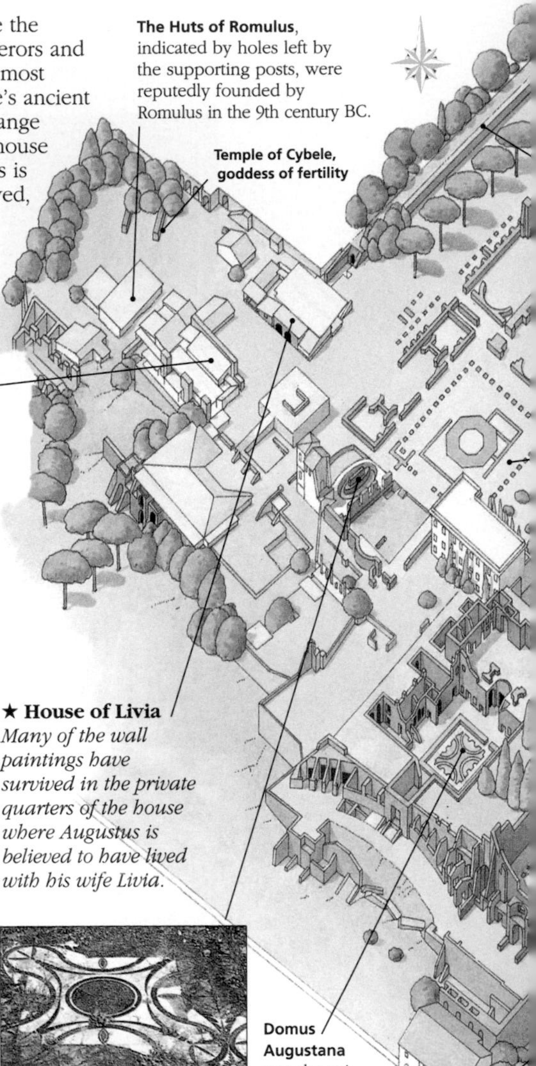

**The Huts of Romulus**, indicated by holes left by the supporting posts, were reputedly founded by Romulus in the 9th century BC.

**Temple of Cybele, goddess of fertility**

**★ House of Augustus**
*This building boasts four rooms with magnificent frescoes.*

**★ House of Livia**
*Many of the wall paintings have survived in the private quarters of the house where Augustus is believed to have lived with his wife Livia.*

**★ Domus Flavia**
*The courtyard of the Domus Flavia was lavishly paved with coloured marble. The Roman poets praised this villa as the most splendid.*

**Domus Augustana** was the private home of the emperors.

**STAR SIGHTS**

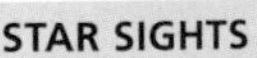

- ★ Domus Flavia
- ★ House of Livia
- ★ House of Augustus

0 metres 75
0 yards 75

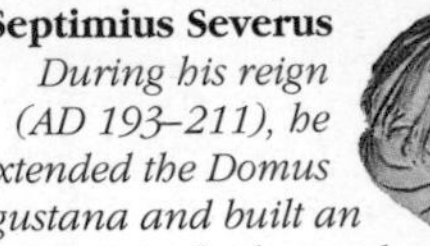

**Emperor Septimius Severus**
*During his reign (AD 193–211), he extended the Domus Augustana and built an impressive bath complex.*

*For hotels and restaurants in this region see pp587–92 and pp636–41*

**Cryptoporticus**
*This underground gallery, elaborately decorated with stuccoed walls, was built by Emperor Nero.*

## VISITORS' CHECKLIST

Via di San Gregorio 30. **Map** 6 F1. ***Tel*** *06 39 96 77 00.* *75, 85, 87, 117, 175, 186, 810, 850.* *Colosseo.* *3.* *8:30am–1 hr before sunset daily.* *1 Jan, 25 Dec.* *includes entry to the Forum, the Colosseum and the Palatine Museum.*

**The courtyard** of the Domus Flavia was lined by Domitian with mirror-like marble, so he could spot would-be assassins.

**The exedra** of the stadium may have housed a balcony.

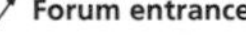

**Forum entrance**

**Stadium**
*Part of the Imperial palace, this enclosure may have been used by the emperors as a private garden.*

**The Palace of Septimius Severus**
*This extension of the Domus Augustana projected beyond the hillside, supported on giant arches.*

## A HISTORY OF THE PALATINE HILL

***Romans of the Decadence*** **by Thomas Couture (1815–79)**

**The Founding of Rome**
According to legend the twins Romulus and Remus were brought up on the Palatine by a wolf. Here Romulus, having killed his brother, is said to have founded the village that was destined to become Rome. Traces of mud huts dating back to the 8th century BC have been found on the hill, lending archaeological support to the legend.

**The Republic**
By the 1st century BC the Palatine was the most desirable address in Rome and home to the leading citizens of the Republic. Its residents, including the erotic poet Catullus and the orator Cicero, were notoriously indulgent, and their villas were magnificent dwellings with doors of ivory, floors of bronze and frescoed walls.

**The Empire**
Augustus was born on the Palatine in 63 BC, and lived there in a modest house after becoming emperor. The hill was therefore an obvious choice of abode for future emperors. Domitian's ambitious house, the Domus Flavia (1st century AD), and its private quarters, the Domus Augustana, remained the official residence of future emperors (who were referred to as *Augustus*) for more than 300 years.

# AROUND PIAZZA NAVONA

The area around Piazza Navona, known as the *centro storico*, has been inhabited for at least 2,000 years. Piazza Navona stands above an ancient stadium; the Pantheon has been a temple since AD 27; and the Theatre of Marcellus in the Ghetto has been converted into exclusive flats. The area's heyday began in the 15th century, when the papacy returned to Rome. Throughout the Renaissance and Baroque eras princes, popes and cardinals settled here, as did the artists and artisans they commissioned to build and adorn lavish palaces, churches and fountains.

Detail of an 18th-century street shrine

## SIGHTS AT A GLANCE

**Churches and Temples**
Chiesa Nuova 6
Gesù 13
La Maddalena 20
San Luigi dei Francesi 3
Santa Maria della Pace 5
Santa Maria sopra Minerva 15
Sant'Ignazio di Loyola 17
Sant'Ivo alla Sapienza 2

**Museums and Galleries**
Palazzo Doria Pamphilj 14
Palazzo Spada 10

**Ancient Sites and Buildings**
Area Sacra di Largo Argentina 12
Pantheon 16

**Historic Buildings**
Palazzo Altemps 4
Palazzo della Cancelleria 7
Palazzo Farnese 9

**Historic Piazzas and Areas**
Campo de' Fiori 8
Ghetto and Tiber Island 11
Piazza Colonna 18
Piazza di Montecitorio 19
Piazza Navona 1

**GETTING THERE**
Corso Vittorio Emanuele II and Corso Rinascimento are main bus arteries, but only minibus 116 runs in the *centro storico*.

**KEY**
Street-by-Street: Around Piazza Navona *pp398–9*
Street-by-Street: Around the Pantheon *pp402–3*
Tourist information

0 metres 250
0 yards 250

◁ **Piazza Navona, with the Fontana del Moro (1653) and the 17th-century church of Sant'Agnese in Agone**

# Street-by-Street: Around Piazza Navona

No other piazza in Rome can rival the theatricality of Piazza Navona. The luxurious cafés are the social centre of the city, and day and night there is always something going on in the pedestrian area around the three flamboyant Baroque fountains. The Baroque is also represented in many of the area's churches. To discover an older Rome, walk along Via del Governo Vecchio to admire the façades of Renaissance buildings, browse in the fascinating antiques shops and lunch in one of the many trattorias.

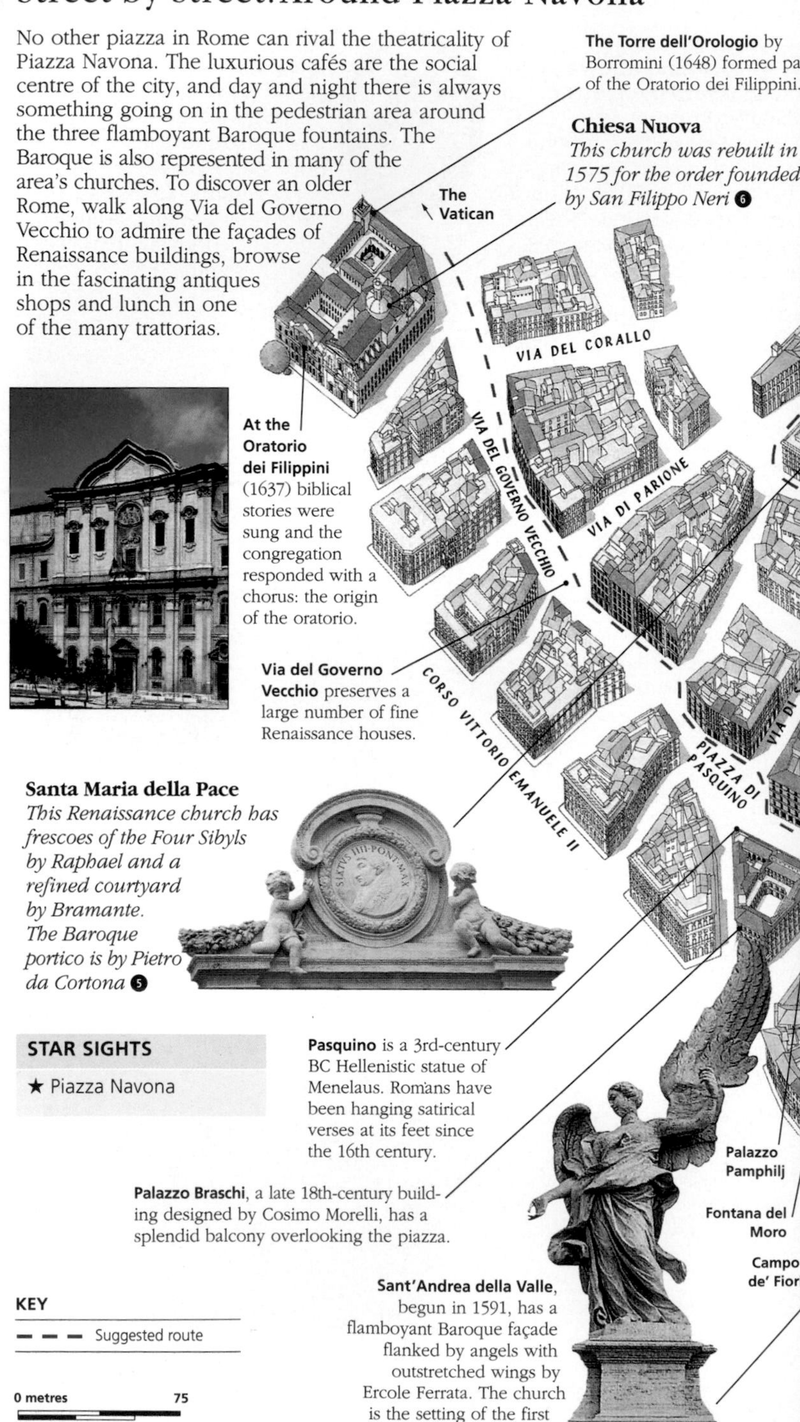


**The Torre dell'Orologio** by Borromini (1648) formed part of the Oratorio dei Filippini.

**Chiesa Nuova**
*This church was rebuilt in 1575 for the order founded by San Filippo Neri* ❻

**At the Oratorio dei Filippini** (1637) biblical stories were sung and the congregation responded with a chorus: the origin of the oratorio.

**Via del Governo Vecchio** preserves a large number of fine Renaissance houses.

**Santa Maria della Pace**
*This Renaissance church has frescoes of the Four Sibyls by Raphael and a refined courtyard by Bramante. The Baroque portico is by Pietro da Cortona* ❺

**STAR SIGHTS**

★ Piazza Navona

**Pasquino** is a 3rd-century BC Hellenistic statue of Menelaus. Romans have been hanging satirical verses at its feet since the 16th century.

**Palazzo Braschi**, a late 18th-century building designed by Cosimo Morelli, has a splendid balcony overlooking the piazza.

**Sant'Andrea della Valle**, begun in 1591, has a flamboyant Baroque façade flanked by angels with outstretched wings by Ercole Ferrata. The church is the setting of the first act of Puccini's *Tosca*.

**KEY**

— — — Suggested route

0 metres 75
0 yards 75

*For hotels and restaurants in this region see pp587–92 and pp636–41*

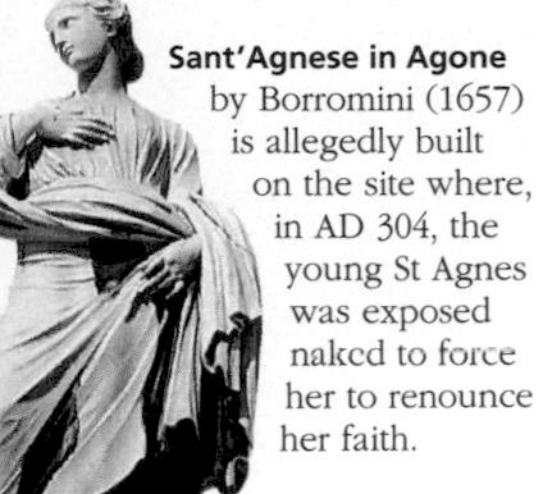

**Sant'Agnese in Agone** by Borromini (1657) is allegedly built on the site where, in AD 304, the young St Agnes was exposed naked to force her to renounce her faith.

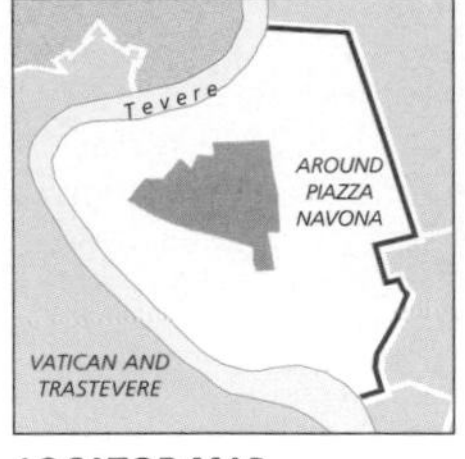


**LOCATOR MAP**
*See Rome Street Finder map 2*

## Piazza Navona ❶

**Map** 2 E4. 🚌 *40, 46, 62, 64, 81, 87, 116, 492, 628.*

Rome's most beautiful Baroque piazza follows the shape of a 1st-century AD stadium built by Domitian, which was used for athletic contests *(agones)*, chariot races and other sports. Traces of the stadium are still visible below the church of Sant'Agnese in Agone, which is dedicated to a virgin martyred on the site for refusing to marry a pagan.

The piazza began to take on its present appearance in the 17th century, when Pope Innocent X, whose family palazzo was on the piazza, commissioned a new church, palace and fountain. The fountain, the Fontana dei Quattro Fiumi, is Bernini's most magnificent, with statues of the four great rivers of the world at that time (the Nile, the Plate, the Ganges and the Danube) sitting on rocks below an obelisk. Bernini also designed the muscle-bound Moor in the Fontana del Moro, though the present statue is a copy. Until the 19th century, the piazza was flooded in August by stopping the fountain outlets. The rich would splash around in carriages, while street urchins paddled. Even today the piazza remains the social centre of the city.

**Fontana dei Quattro Fiumi**

**San Luigi dei Francesi**
*This church, which was completed in 1589, is best known for three paintings by Caravaggio* ❸

**Palazzo Madama**, the seat of the Italian Senate, was originally built for the Medici family in the 16th century, on the site of one of their banks.

**Sant'Ivo alla Sapienza**
*This tiny domed church is one of Borromini's most original creations. He worked on it between 1642 and 1650* ❷

**★ Piazza Navona**
*The piazza is lined with palaces and pavement cafés, and punctuated by flamboyant Baroque fountains* ❶

Largo di Torre Argentina

**Symbolic figure of the River Nile on Bernini's Fontana dei Quattro Fiumi**

## Sant'Ivo alla Sapienza ❷

Corso del Rinascimento 40. **Map** 2 F4. ***Tel*** *06 361 25 62.* *40, 46, 64, 70, 81, 87, 116, 186, 492, 628.* *9am–noon Sun.*

Hidden in the courtyard of Palazzo della Sapienza, seat of the old University of Rome, Sant'Ivo's spiral belfry is nevertheless a distinctive landmark on Rome's skyline. Built by Borromini in 1642–60, the church is astonishingly complex, an ingenious combination of concave and convex surfaces. The work spanned the reigns of three popes, and incorporated in the design are their emblems: Urban VIII's bee, Innocent X's dove and olive branch and the star and hills of Alexander VII.

## San Luigi dei Francesi ❸

Piazza di San Luigi de' Francesi 5. **Map** 2 F4 & 12 D2. ***Tel*** *06 68 82 71.* *70, 81, 87, 116, 186, 492, 628.* *10am–12:30pm, 4–7pm daily.* *Thu pm.*

The French national church in Rome, San Luigi is a 16th-century building, best known for three magnificent canvases by Caravaggio in the Cerasi chapel. Painted between 1597 and 1602, these were Caravaggio's first significant religious works: *The Calling of St Matthew*, *Martyrdom of St Matthew* and *St Matthew and the Angel*. The first version of this last was initially rejected because it depicted the saint as an old man with dirty feet.

**Detail from Caravaggio's *The Calling of St Matthew* (1597–1602) in San Luigi dei Francesi**

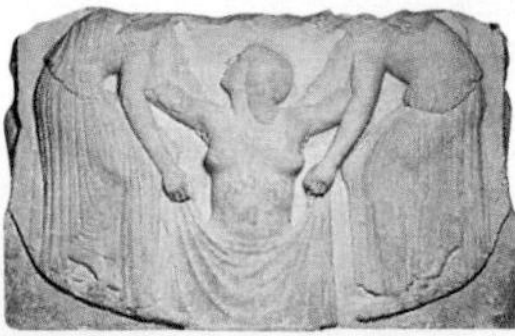

**Side relief of the Ludovisi Throne, on display in the Palazzo Altemps**

## Palazzo Altemps ❹

Via di Sant'Apollinare 46. **Map** 2 E3. ***Tel*** *06 39 96 77 00.* *70, 81, 87, 115, 280, 628.* *9am–7:45pm Tue–Sun.* *1 Jan, 25 Dec.*

An extraordinary collection of Classical sculpture is housed in this branch of the Museo Nazionale Romano *(see p412)*. Restored as a museum during the 1990s, the palazzo was originally built for Girolamo Riario, nephew of Pope Sixtus IV in 1480. In the popular uprising that followed the pope's death in 1484, the building was sacked and Girolamo fled the city. In 1568 Cardinal Marco Sittico Altemps bought the palazzo, it was renovated in the 1570s by Martino Longhi the Elder, who added the obelisk-crowned belvedere and marble unicorn.

The Altemps family were avid collectors; the courtyard and its staircase are lined with ancient sculptures, which complement the Ludovisi sculptures. One of the highlights is the marble statue *Galata's Suicide*, a copy of the bronze original, in the Salone del Camino. Also on the first floor is the Greek, 5th-century BC Ludovisi Throne, a carved relief shows Aphrodite.

**Galata's Suicide in the Palazzo Altemps**

## Santa Maria della Pace ❺

Vicolo del Arco della Pace 5. **Map** 2 E3. ***Tel*** *06 686 11 56.* *46, 62, 64, 70, 81, 87, 116, 492, 628.* *9am–noon Mon, Wed, Sat.*

Named by Pope Sixtus IV to celebrate the peace he hoped to bring to Italy, this church dates from the 1480s and contains a beautiful fresco by Raphael. Bramante's refined cloister was added in 1504, while the façade was designed in 1656 by Pietro da Cortona.

## Chiesa Nuova ❻

Piazza della Chiesa Nuova. **Map** 2 E4. ***Tel*** *06 687 52 89.* *46, 64.* *8am–noon (to 1pm Sun), 4:30–7pm daily.*

San Filippo Neri commissioned this church in 1575 to replace the dilapidated one given to his Order by Pope Gregory XIII. Neri required his followers to humble themselves, and set aristocratic young men to work as labourers on the church. Against his wishes, the nave, apse and dome were richly frescoed after his death by Pietro da Cortona. There are three paintings by Rubens around the altar. The first versions were rejected, so Rubens repainted them on slate, placing the originals above his mother's tomb.

## Palazzo della Cancelleria ❼

Piazza della Cancelleria. **Map** 2 E4. ***Tel*** *06 69 89 34 05.* *46, 62, 64, 70, 81, 87, 116, 492.* *by appt only Tue pm & Sat am.*

A supreme example of the confident delicacy of early Renaissance architecture, this palazzo was begun in 1485, and was allegedly financed by the gambling proceeds of Raffaele Riario, a nephew of Pope Sixtus I. In 1478 Riario was involved in the Pazzi conspiracy against the Medici, and when Giovanni de' Medici became Pope Leo XIII in 1513, he took belated revenge, seizing the palace and turning it into the papal chancellery.

**Tiber Island, with Ponte Cestio, built in 46 BC, linking it to Trastevere**

## Campo de' Fiori 8

**Map** 2 E4. *116 & routes to Corso Vittorio Emanuele II.*

Campo de' Fiori (field of flowers) was one of the liveliest and roughest areas of medieval and Renaissance Rome. Cardinals and nobles mingled with fishmongers and foreigners in the piazza's market; Caravaggio killed his opponent after losing a game of tennis on the square; and the goldsmith Cellini murdered a business rival nearby. Today, the area continues to be a hub of secular activity. The colourful market, trattorias and down-to-earth bars retain the original animated atmosphere.

In the Renaissance the piazza was surrounded by inns, many of which were owned by the 15th-century courtesan Vannozza Catanei, mistress of Pope Alexander VI.

The square was also a place of execution. The statue in its centre is the philosopher Giordano Bruno, burned at the stake for heresy on this spot in 1600 for suggesting the earth moved around the sun.

## Palazzo Farnese 9

Piazza Farnese. **Map** 2 E5. *23, 116, 280 & routes to Corso Vittorio Emanuele II. to the public.*

Originally constructed for Cardinal Alessandro Farnese, who became Pope Paul III in 1534, this palazzo was started by Antonio da Sangallo the Younger, and continued after his death by Michelangelo, who created the cornice on the façade and the courtyard's third storey.

The palace, now the French Embassy, is closed to the public, but when the chandeliers are lit at night you may be able to glimpse the ceiling of the Galleria, an illusionistic masterpiece (1597–1603) by Annibale Carracci based on Ovid's *Metamorphoses*.

**Fruit stalls at Campo de' Fiori's lively morning market**

## Palazzo Spada 10

Piazza Capo di Ferro 13. **Map** 2 E5. ***Tel*** *06 686 11 58. 23, 116, 280 & routes to Largo di Torre Argentina. 8:30am–7:30pm Tue–Sun (last adm: 7pm). 1 Jan, 25 Dec.*

A stucco extravaganza studded with reliefs of illustrious Romans, this palazzo was built in 1550, but bought in 1637 by Cardinal Bernardino Spada. A keen patron of the arts, he commissioned Borromini to create an illusionistic tunnel that appears four times longer than it is. The cardinal's art collection, in the Galleria Spada, includes works by Guercino, Dürer and Artemisia Gentileschi.

## Ghetto and Tiber Island 11

**Map** 2 F5 & 6 D1. *23, 63, 280, 780 and routes to Largo di Torre Argentina.*

The first Jews came to Rome as traders in the 2nd century BC and were greatly appreciated for their financial and medical skills during the Roman Empire. Persecution began in the 16th century, when Pope Paul IV forced all of the Jews to live within a walled enclosure, an area later to form the hub of the present-day Ghetto.

Today Via del Portico d'Ottavia, the district's main street, leads to Rome's central synagogue, passing restaurants and shops selling Roman Jewish food. Ponte Fabricio links the Ghetto with Tiber Island, a centre of healing since 293 BC when a Temple to Aesculapius was founded. The island is now home to a hospital.

# Street-by-Street: Around the Pantheon

The maze of narrow streets around the Pantheon is a mixture of lively restaurants and cafés, and some of Rome's finest sights. This is also the city's financial and political district, home to Parliament, government offices and the stock exchange. The Pantheon itself, with its awe-inspiring domed interior, has long been a symbol of the city.

**Sant'Ignazio di Loyola**
*This church has a superb illusionistic ceiling painted by Andrea Pozzo in 1685* ⑰

**The Temple of Hadrian** now forms the façade of the Stock Exchange.

**Piazza della Minerva** centres on Bernini's outlandish sculpture of an elephant supporting an Egyptian obelisk.

**★ Palazzo Doria Pamphilj**
*Among the masterpieces in the art gallery of this vast family palazzo is this Salomé by Titian painted in 1516* ⑭

**Santa Maria sopra Minerva**
*This is one of Rome's few Gothic churches, with works by Michelangelo, Bernini and Filippino Lippi* ⑮

**★ Pantheon**
*The Pantheon, a temple to "all the gods", is Rome's best-preserved ancient building. It was built in the 1st century AD, probably to a design by Emperor Hadrian* ⑯

**KEY**

– – – Suggested route

**LOCATOR MAP**

*See Rome Street Finder map 3*

**Via della Gatta** is overlooked by this marble statue of a cat *(gatta)* that gives the narrow street its name.

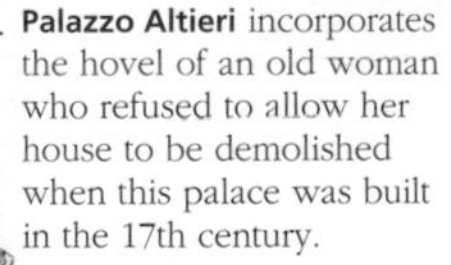

**The Pie' di Marmo**, an ancient marble foot, is probably part of a giant statue from the temple to the Egyptian goddess Isis.

**Palazzo Altieri** incorporates the hovel of an old woman who refused to allow her house to be demolished when this palace was built in the 17th century.

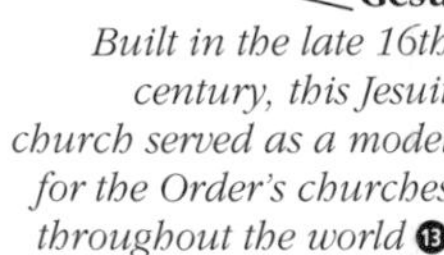

**Gesù**

*Built in the late 16th century, this Jesuit church served as a model for the Order's churches throughout the world* ⓭

**STAR SIGHTS**

★ Pantheon

★ Palazzo Doria Pamphilj

metres 75

yards 75

## Area Sacra di Largo Argentina ⓬

Largo di Torre Argentina. **Map** 2 F5. *40, 46, 62, 64, 70, 81, 87, 186, 492.* *with permit only* (see p664).

The remains of four temples were discovered in the 1920s at the centre of Largo Argentina, now a busy bus terminus and traffic junction. They date from the era of the Republic, and are among the oldest found in Rome. For the purpose of identification, they are known as A, B, C and D. The oldest (temple C) dates from the early 3rd century BC. It was placed on a high platform preceded by an altar and is typical of Italic temple plans as opposed to the Greek model. Temple A is from the 3rd century BC, but in medieval times the small church of San Nicola di Cesarini was built over its podium and the remains of its two apses are still visible. The column stumps to the north belonged to a great portico, known as the Hecatostylum (portico of 100 columns). In Imperial times two marble latrines were built here – the remains of one are visible behind temple A.

Behind temples B and C, near Via di Torre Argentina, are the remains of a great platform of tufa blocks. These have been identified as part of the Curia of Pompey, a rectangular building where the Senate met, and where Julius Caesar was assassinated by Brutus, Cassius and their followers on 15 March 44 BC.

**Area Sacra, with the ruins of circular temple B**

**Baroque *Triumph of Faith over Idolatry* by Pierre Legros, Gesù**

## Gesù ⓭

Piazza del Gesù. **Map** 3 A4. ***Tel*** *06 69 70 01.* *H, 46, 62, 64, 70, 81, 87, 186, 492, 628 & other routes.* *7am–12:30pm (7:30am–1pm Sun), 4–7:45pm daily.*

Built between 1568 and 1584, the Gesù was Rome's first Jesuit church. The Jesuit order was founded in Rome in 1537 by a Basque soldier, Ignatius Loyola, who became a Christian after he was wounded in battle. The order was austere, intellectual and heavily engaged in missionary activity and religious wars.

The much-imitated design of the Gesù typifies Counter-Reformation architecture, with a large nave with side pulpits for preaching to crowds, and a main altar as the centrepiece for the mass. The illusionistic decoration on the nave ceiling and dome was added by Il Baciccia in the 17th century.

The nave depicts the *Triumph of the Name of Jesus* and its message is clear: faithful, Catholic worshippers will be joyfully uplifted to heaven while Protestants and heretics are flung into the fires of hell. The message is reiterated in the Cappella di Sant'Ignazio, a rich display of lapis lazuli, serpentine, silver and gold. The Baroque marble by Legros, *Triumph of Faith over Idolatry*, shows a female "Religion" trampling on the head of the serpent Idolatry, while in Théudon's *Barbarians Adoring the Faith*, an angel aims a kick towards a decrepit old barbarian couple entangled with a snake.

## Palazzo Doria Pamphilj ⓮

Via del Corso 305. **Map** 3 A4. ***Tel*** *06 679 73 23.* *64, 81, 85, 117, 119, 492.* *10am–5pm Mon–Sat.* *1 Jan, Easter, 1 May, 15 Aug, 1 Nov, 25 Dec.* *by appt for private apartments.*

Palazzo Doria Pamphilj is a vast edifice whose oldest parts date from 1435. When the Pamphilj family took over in 1647 they built a new wing, a splendid chapel and a theatre.

The family art collection has over 400 paintings dating from the 15th–18th centuries, including a portrait of Pope Innocent X by Velázquez and works by Titian, Guercino, Caravaggio and Claude Lorrain. The opulent rooms of the private apartments retain many of their original furnishings, including Brussels and Gobelins tapestries, Murano chandeliers and a gilded crib.

**Velázquez's *Pope Innocent X* (1650)**

## Santa Maria sopra Minerva ⓯

Piazza della Minerva 42. **Map** 2 F4. ***Tel*** *06 679 39 26.* *116 & many other routes.* *7am–7pm Mon–Sat, 8am–1pm, 4–7pm Sun.*

One of Rome's rare Gothic buildings, this church was built in the 13th century over what were thought to be the ruins of a Temple of Minerva. It was a stronghold of the Dominicans, who produced some of the Church's most infamous inquisitors, and who tried the scientist Galileo in the adjoining monastery.

Inside, the church has a superb collection of art and sculpture, ranging from 13th-century Cosmatesque tombs to a bust by Bernini. Highlights include Antoniazzo Romano's *Annunciation* featuring Cardinal Juan de Torquemada, uncle of the vicious Spanish Inquisitor, and the Carafa Chapel's frescoes by Filippino Lippi.

In the Aldobrandini Chapel are the tombs of the 16th-century Medici popes, Leo X and his cousin Clement VII, and near the steps of the choir is a stocky *Risen Christ*, begun by Michelangelo.

The church also contains the tombs of many famous Italians, such as St Catherine of Siena who died in 1380 and Fra Angelico, the Dominican friar and painter, who died in 1455. Outside, Bernini's spectacular sculpture of an elephant holds an obelisk on its back.

**Simple vaulted nave of Santa Maria sopra Minerva**

**Interior of the Pantheon, burial place for Italian monarchs**

## Pantheon ⓰

Piazza della Rotonda. **Map** 2 F4. ***Tel*** *06 68 30 02 30.* *116 & many routes* *8:30am–7:30pm daily (9am–6pm Sun).* *1 Jan, 1 May, 25 Dec.*

The Pantheon, the Roman "temple of all the gods", is the most extraordinary and best preserved ancient building in Rome. The first temple on the site was a conventional rectangular affair erected by Agrippa between 27 and 25 BC; the present structure was built and possibly designed by Emperor Hadrian in AD 118.

The temple is fronted by a massive pedimented portico screening what appears to be a cylinder fused to a shallow dome. Only from the inside can the true scale and beauty of this building be appreciated: a vast hemispherical dome equal in radius to the height of the cylinder giving perfectly harmonious proportion to the building. A circular opening, the *oculus*, lets in the only light.

In the 7th century Christians claimed to be plagued by demons as they passed by, and permission was given to make the Pantheon a church. Today it is lined with tombs, ranging from a restrained monument to Raphael to huge marble and porphyry sarcophagi holding the bodies of Italian monarchs.

## Sant'Ignazio di Loyola ⓱

Piazza di Sant'Ignazio. **Map** 2 F4. ***Tel*** *06 679 44 06.* 🚌 *117, 119, 492.* ◯ *7:30am–7pm daily.* ✝

This church was built by Pope Gregory XV in 1626 in honour of St Ignatius of Loyola, founder of the Society of Jesus (Jesuits) and the man who most embodied the zeal of the Counter-Reformation.

Together with the Gesù (*see p403*), Sant'Ignazio forms the nucleus of the Jesuit area of Rome. It is one of the most extravagant Baroque churches and its vast interior is plated with precious stones, marble, stucco and gilt, creating a thrilling sense of theatre. The church has a Latin-cross plan, with an apse and many side chapels. A cupola was planned but never built, as the nuns from a nearby convent objected that it would obscure the view from their roof garden. Instead the space was filled by a perspective painting of a dome on a flat disc.

Even more striking is the illusionistic ceiling created by the Jesuit artist Andrea Pozzo in 1685, a propagandist extravaganza extolling the success of Jesuit missionaries throughout the world. Above four women, representing Asia, Europe, America and Africa, lithe angels and beautiful youths are sucked into a heaven of fluffy clouds.

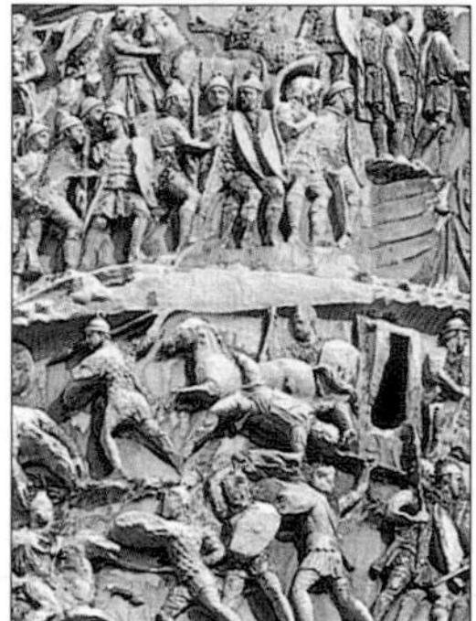

**Detail from the AD 180 Column of Marcus Aurelius, Piazza Colonna**

## Piazza Colonna ⓲

**Map** 3 A3. 🚌 *95, 116, 492.*

Home to Palazzo Chigi, official residence of the prime minister, Piazza Colonna is dominated by and named after the majestic Column of Marcus Aurelius. This was erected after the death of Marcus Aurelius in AD 180 to commemorate his victories over the barbarian tribes of the Danube. It is clearly an imitation of Trajan's Column (*see p388*) with scenes from the emperor's wars spiralling in reliefs up the column. The 80-year lapse between the two works produced a great artistic change: the wars of Marcus Aurelius are rendered with simplified pictures in stronger relief, sacrificing Classical proportions for the sake of clarity and immediacy.

**Baroque illusionistic ceiling by Andrea Pozzo in Sant'Ignazio di Loyola**

## Piazza di Montecitorio ⓳

**Map** 2 F3. **Palazzo di Montecitorio** ***Tel*** *06 676 01.* 🚌 *116.* ◯ *10am–6:30pm 1st Sun of month.*

The obelisk in the centre of Piazza Montecitorio formed the spine of a giant sundial brought back from Egypt by Augustus. It vanished in the 9th century, and was rediscovered under medieval houses during the reign of Julius II (1503–13).

The piazza is dominated by the rugged façade of Palazzo di Montecitorio, designed by Bernini and completed in 1697, after his death, by Carlo Fontana. It has been the seat of Italy's Chamber of Deputies since the late 19th century.

**La Maddalena's stuccoed façade**

## La Maddalena ⓴

Piazza della Maddalena. **Map** 2 F3. ***Tel*** *06 899 281.* 🚌 *116 & many other routes.* ◯ *8am–noon (from 9:30am Sat & Sun), 5–8pm daily.*

Situated in a small piazza near the Pantheon, the Maddalena's Rococo façade, built in 1735, epitomizes the love of light and movement of the late Baroque. The façade has been restored, despite the protests of Neo-Classicists who dismissed its painted stucco as icing sugar.

The diminutive dimensions of the church did not deter 17th- and 18th-century decorators from filling the interior with paintings and ornaments from the floor to the top of the elegant cupola.

# NORTHEAST ROME

This area stretches from the exclusive shopping streets around Piazza di Spagna to the Esquiline Hill, once bourgeois, but now a poor, often seedy area full of early Christian churches. The Piazza di Spagna and Piazza del Popolo district grew up in the 16th century, when the increase in the influx of pilgrims was such that a road was built to channel them as quickly as possible to the Vatican. About the same time, the Quirinal Hill became the site of a papal palace. When Rome became capital of Italy in 1870, Via Veneto became a lavish residential area, and the Esquiline was covered with apartments for the new civil servants.

Lion fountain in Piazza del Popolo

## SIGHTS AT A GLANCE

**Churches**
San Carlo alle Quattro Fontane 8
San Pietro in Vincoli 14
Sant'Andrea al Quirinale 7
Santa Maria della Concezione 10
Santa Maria della Vittoria 11
Santa Maria del Popolo 3
Santa Maria Maggiore 15
Santa Prassede 13

**Museums and Galleries**
Museo Nazionale Romano 12
Palazzo Barberini 9

**Ancient Sites and Buildings**
Ara Pacis 4
Mausoleum of Augustus 5

**Historic Buildings**
Villa Medici 2

**Piazzas and Fountains**
Piazza di Spagna and the Spanish Steps 1
Trevi Fountain 6

**GETTING THERE**
Metro stations Repubblica, Barberini and Spagna (line A) cover the area between Termini and Piazza del Popolo. Bus 16 runs from Termini to Santa Maria Maggiore and down Via Merulana.

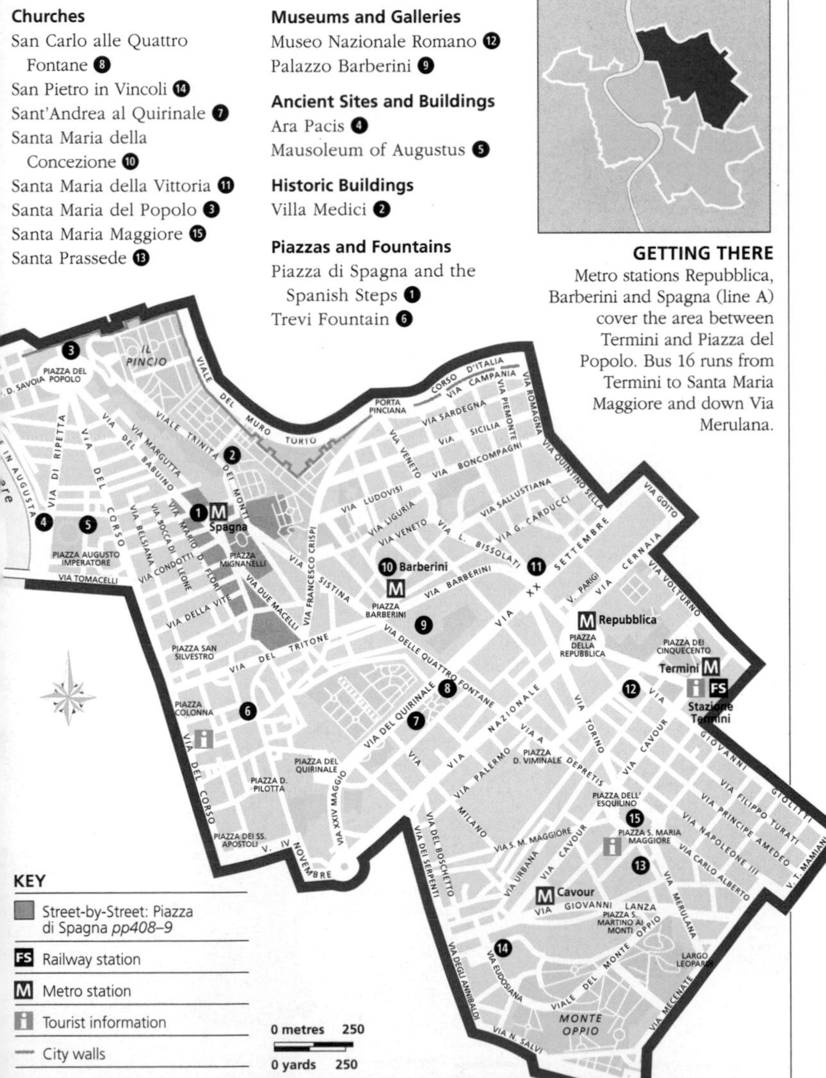


◁ The Spanish Steps with their spring display of azaleas

# Street-by-Street: Piazza di Spagna

The network of narrow streets around Piazza di Spagna forms one of the most exclusive areas in Rome, drawing droves of tourists and Romans to the elegant shops around Via Condotti. The square and its nearby coffee houses have long attracted those who want to see and be seen. In the 18th century the area was full of hotels for frivolous aristocrats doing the Grand Tour, as well as artists, writers and composers, who took the city's history and culture more seriously.

**Caffé Greco** is an 18th-century café once frequented by writers and musicians such as Keats, Goethe, Byron, Liszt and Wagner.

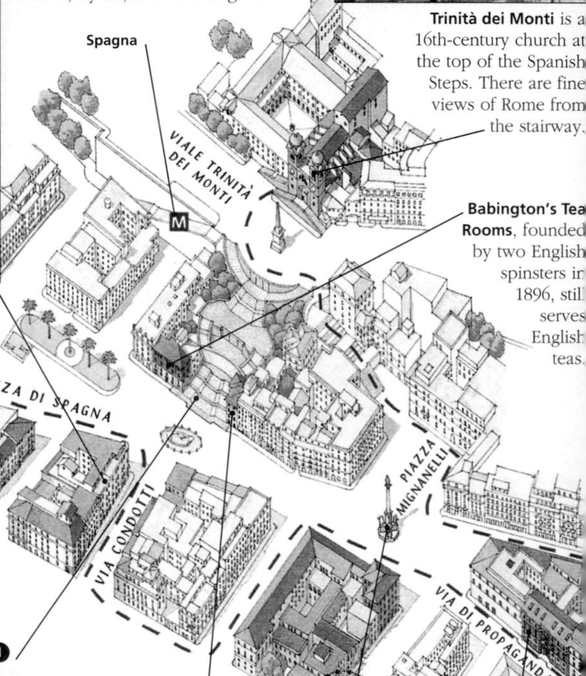

**Trinità dei Monti** is a 16th-century church at the top of the Spanish Steps. There are fine views of Rome from the stairway.

**Spagna**

VIALE TRINITÀ DEI MONTI

PIAZZA DI SPAGNA

VIA CONDOTTI

PIAZZA MIGNANELLI

VIA DI PROPAGANDA

**Babington's Tea Rooms**, founded by two English spinsters in 1896, still serves English teas.

**★ Piazza di Spagna and the Spanish Steps**
*These have been at the heart of tourist Rome since the 18th century* ❶

**The Keats-Shelley Memorial House**, where the poet Keats died in 1821, is now a museum honouring English Romantic poets.

**The Colonna dell' Immacolata**, erected in 1857, commemorates Pope Pius IX's doctrine of the Immaculate Conception.

**The Collegio di Propaganda Fide**, built for the Jesuits in 1662, has a superb façade designed by Francesco Borromini.

**KEY**

— — — Suggested route

0 metres 75

0 yards 75

**LOCATOR MAP**
*See Rome Street Finder map 3*

**Sant'Andrea delle Fratte** contains two angels by Bernini (1669) made for Ponte Sant'Angelo, which Pope Clement X thought too lovely to expose to the weather.

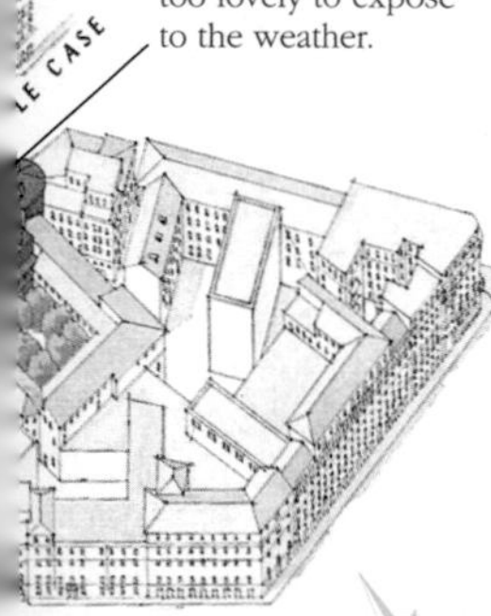


**STAR SIGHT**

★ Piazza di Spagna and the Spanish Steps

**The Fontana della Barcaccia at the foot of the Spanish Steps**

## Piazza di Spagna and the Spanish Steps ❶

**Map** 3 A2. 🚌 *116, 117.* Ⓜ *Spagna.*

Shaped like a crooked bow tie, and surrounded by muted, shuttered façades, Piazza di Spagna is crowded all day and (in summer) most of the night. The most famous square in Rome, it takes its name from the Palazzo di Spagna, built in the 17th century to house the Spanish Embassy to the Holy See.

The piazza has long been the haunt of foreign visitors and expatriates. In the 18th and 19th centuries the square stood at the heart of the city's main hotel district. Some of the travellers came in search of knowledge and inspiration, although most were more interested in collecting statues to adorn their family homes. When the Victorian novelist Charles Dickens visited, he reported that the Spanish Steps were crowded with models dressed as Madonnas, saints and emperors, hoping to attract the attention of foreign artists.

The steps were built in the 1720s to link the square with the French church of Trinità dei Monti above. The French wanted to place a statue of Louis XIV at the top, but the pope objected, and it was not until the 1720s that the Italian architect Francesco de Sanctis produced the voluptuous Rococo design which satisfied both camps. The Fontana Barcaccia, sunk into the paving at the foot of the steps due to low water pressure, was designed by Bernini's less famous father, Pietro.

## Villa Medici ❷

Accademia di Francia a Roma, Viale Trinità dei Monti 1. **Map** 3 A2. ***Tel*** *06 67 611.* 🚌 *117.* Ⓜ *Spagna.* ◯ *garden visits: 10:30am, 11:45am, 2pm, 3:15pm daily.* *only.*

Superbly positioned on the Pincio Hill, this 16th-century villa has retained the name that it assumed when Cardinal Ferdinando de' Medici bought it in 1576. It is now home to the French Academy, founded in 1666 to give artists the chance to study in Rome. From 1803 musicians were also allowed to study here: both Berlioz and Debussy were students.

The villa is only open for exhibitions, but the formal gardens, with a gorgeously frescoed pavilion, and copies of ancient statues, can be visited in certain months.

**19th-century engraving of the inner façade of the Villa Medici**

Pinturicchio's fresco of the *Delphic Sibyl* (1509) in Santa Maria del Popolo

## Santa Maria del Popolo ❸

Piazza del Popolo 12. **Map** 2 F1. ***Tel*** *06 361 08 36.* *95, 117, 119, 490, 495, 926.* *Flaminio.* *7:30am–noon, 4–7pm Mon–Sat; 7:30am–1:30pm, 4:30–7:30pm Sun.*

Santa Maria del Popolo was one of the first Renaissance churches in Rome, commissioned by Pope Sixtus IV della Rovere in 1472. Lavish endowments by Sixtus's descendants and other powerful families have made it one of Rome's greatest artistic treasures.

Shortly after Sixtus died in 1484, Pinturicchio and his pupils frescoed two chapels (first and third right) for the della Rovere family. On the altar of the first chapel there is a lovely *Nativity* from 1490 that depicts a stable at the foot of a Classical column.

In 1503 Sixtus IV's nephew Giuliano became Pope Julius II and had Bramante build a new apse. Pinturicchio was called in again to paint its vaults with Sibyls and Apostles framed in an intricate tracery of freakish beasts.

In 1513 Raphael created the Chigi chapel (second left) for the wealthy banker Agostino Chigi. The design is an audacious Renaissance fusion of the sacred and profane; there are pyramid-like tombs and a ceiling mosaic of God holding the signs of the zodiac describing Chigi's horoscope. Raphael died before the chapel was finished and it was completed by Bernini who added the dynamic statues of Daniel and Habakkuk. In the Cerasi chapel, left of the altar, there are two realistic works painted by Caravaggio in 1601: the *Conversion of St Paul* and the *Crucifixion of St Peter*. The artist uses daringly exaggerated lighting effects and foreshortening techniques to intensify the dramatic effect.

Detail of the Ara Pacis frieze

## Ara Pacis ❹

Lungotevere in Augusta. **Map** 2 F2. ***Tel*** *06 06 08.* *70, 81, 117, 119, 186, 628.* *9am–7pm Tue–Sun (last adm: 6pm).* **www**.arapacis.it

Painstakingly reconstructed over many years from scattered fragments, the exquisitely carved Ara Pacis (Altar of Peace) celebrates the peace created by Emperor Augustus throughout the Mediterranean. Commissioned by the Senate in 13 BC and completed four years later, the altar stands in a square enclosure of Carrara marble, carved with realistic reliefs of such quality that experts think the craftsmen may have been Greek.

The reliefs on the north and south walls depict a procession that took place on 4 July, 13 BC, in which the members of the emperor's family can be identified, including Augustus's grandson, Lucius, who is the toddler clutching at the skirts of his mother, Antonia. The site is now housed in a building by architect Richard Meier.

## Mausoleum of Augustus ❺

Piazza Augusto Imperatore. **Map** 2 F2. ***Tel*** *06 06 08.* *81, 117, 492, 628, 926.* *by appt only: permit needed.*

Now just a weedy mound ringed with cypresses and strewn with litter, this was once the most prestigious burial place in Rome. Augustus had the mausoleum built in 28 BC, the year before he became sole ruler, as a tomb for himself and his descendants. The circular building was 87 m (270 ft) in diameter with two obelisks (now in Piazza del Quirinale and Piazza dell' Esquilino) at the entrance. Inside were four concentric passageways linked by corridors where urns holding the ashes of the Imperial family were placed, including those of Augustus who died in AD 14.

## Trevi Fountain ❻

Piazza di Trevi. **Map** 3 B3. *116 & many other routes.*

Nicola Salvi's theatrical design for Rome's largest and most famous fountain was completed in 1762. The central figures are Neptune, flanked by two Tritons, one trying to

Rome's largest and most famous fountain, the Trevi

*For hotels and restaurants in this region see pp587–92 and pp636–41*

master an unruly sea-horse, the other leading a quieter beast, symbolizing the two contrasting moods of the sea.

The site originally marked the terminal of the Aqua Virgo aqueduct, built by Augustus' right-hand man and son-in-law, Agrippa, in 19 BC to channel water to Rome's new bath complexes. One of the reliefs on the first storey shows a young girl, Trivia, after whom the fountain may have been named. She is said to have first shown the spring, 22 km (14 miles) from the city, to thirsty Roman soldiers.

**Interior, Sant'Andrea al Quirinale**

## Sant'Andrea al Quirinale ❼

Via del Quirinale 29. **Map** 3 B3. ***Tel*** *06 474 48 72. 116, 117. 8:30am–noon, 3:30–7pm daily.*

Sant'Andrea was designed for the Jesuits by Bernini and executed by his assistants between 1658 and 1670. The site was wide but shallow, so Bernini took the radical step of pointing the long axis of his oval plan towards the sides, and leading the eye round to the altar by means of a strong horizontal cornice. At the altar he combined sculpture and painting to create a theatrical crucifixion of Sant'Andrea (St Andrew); the diagonally crucified saint on the altarpiece looks up at a stucco effigy of himself ascending to the lantern, where the Holy Spirit and cherubs await him in heaven.

**The dome of San Carlo alle Quattro Fontane, by Borromini**

## San Carlo alle Quattro Fontane ❽

Via del Quirinale 23. **Map** 3 B3. ***Tel*** *06 488 32 61. 116 & routes to Piazza Barberini. Barberini. 10am–1pm, 3–6pm daily (only am Sat & Sun).*

In 1638, Borromini was commissioned by the Trinitarians to design a church and convent on a tiny cramped site at the Quattro Fontane crossroads. The church, so small that it is said it would fit inside one of the piers of St Peter's, is designed with bold, fluid curves on both the façade and interior to give light and life to the diminutive building. The dome, with its concealed windows, illusionistic coffering and tiny lantern designed to make it look higher than it really is, is a cunning feature.

## Palazzo Barberini ❾

Via delle Quattro Fontane 13. **Map** 3 B3. ***Tel*** *06 482 4184. 52, 53, 61, 62, 63, 80, 95, 116, 175, 492, 590. Barberini. 8:30am–7pm Tue–Sun. public hols. (lift).* **www**.galleriaborghese.it

When Maffei Barberini became Pope Urban VIII in 1623, he decided to build a grand family palazzo. Designed by Carlo Maderno as a typical country villa on the fringes of the city, it now overlooks Piazza Barberini, where traffic hurtles around Bernini's Triton fountain. Maderno died shortly after the foundations had been laid, and Bernini and Borromini took over.

The most dazzling room is the Gran Salone, with an illusionistic ceiling frescoed by Pietro da Cortona in 1633–9. The palazzo also houses part of the Galleria Nazionale d'Arte Antica with works by Titian, Filippo Lippi, Caravaggio and Artemisia Gentileschi. The most famous is a portrait of a courtesan, reputedly Raphael's lover, *La Fornarina*, said to be a baker's daughter, although not painted by the artist himself.

**Ceiling fresco detail in Palazzo Barberini (1633)**

## Santa Maria della Concezione ❿

Via Veneto 27. **Map** 3 B2. ***Tel*** *06 487 11 85. 52, 53, 61, 62, 63, 80, 95, 116, 175. Barberini.* **Crypt** *9am–noon, 3–6pm daily.*

Below this unassuming church on Via Veneto is a crypt decked with the dismembered skeletons of 4,000 Capuchin monks. They form a macabre reminder of the transience of life, with vertebrae wired together to make sacred hearts and crowns of thorns, and, in one chapel, the poignant skeleton of a tiny Barberini princess.

## Santa Maria della Vittoria ⓫

Via XX Settembre 17. **Map** 3 C2. ***Tel*** *06 42 74 05 71.* *61, 62, 84, 175, 910.* *Repubblica.* *9am–noon Mon–Sat, 3:30–6:30pm daily.*

Santa Daria della Vittoria is an intimate Baroque church with a lavish, candlelit interior. Inside the Cornaro chapel is one of Bernini's most ambitious sculptures, the *Ecstasy of St Teresa* (1646). The physical nature of St Teresa's ecstasy is apparent as she appears collapsed on a cloud with her mouth half open and eyes closed, struck by the arrow of a smiling angel. Ecclesiastical members, past and present, of the Venetian Cornaro family, who commissioned the chapel, sit in boxes as if watching and discussing the scene being played out in front of them.

**Bernini's *Ecstasy of St Teresa* in Santa Maria della Vittoria**

## Museo Nazionale Romano ⓬

Palazzo Massimo, Largo di Villa Peretti 1 (1 of 5 sites). **Map** 4 D3. ***Tel*** *06 481 55 76.* *all routes to Termini.* *Repubblica.* *9am–7:45pm Tue–Sun.* *ticket valid for all sites.*

Founded in 1899, the Museo Nazionale Romano – one of the world's leading museums of Classical art – houses most of the antiquities found in Rome since 1870, as well as important older collections. During the 1990s it underwent a major reorganization and now has five branches: the Palazzo Altemps *(see p400)*; the Baths of Diocletian; the Aula Ottagona, the Crypta; Balbi, and the Palazzo Massimo. In the latter, exhibits dating from the 2nd century BC to the late 4th century AD are displayed in a series of rooms over three floors. Highlights include the *Quattro Aurighe* mosaics from a villa in northern Rome, the breathtaking series of frescoes from Livia's summer villa, and the famous statue of her husband, the Emperor Augustus.

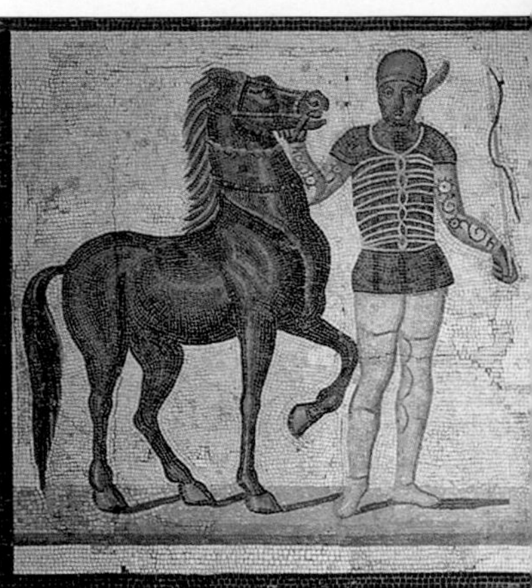

**One of the finely detailed Quattro Aurighe mosaics on display at the Museo Nazionale Romano**

## Santa Prassede ⓭

Via Santa Prassede 9a. **Map** 4 D4. ***Tel*** *06 488 24 56.* *16, 70, 71, 75, 714.* *Vittorio Emanuele.* *7:30am–noon, 4–6:30pm daily.*

The church was founded by Pope Paschal II in the 9th century and decorated by Byzantine artists with the most important, glittering mosaics in Rome. In the apse Christ stands between Santa Prassede and her sister, dressed as Byzantine empresses, among white-robed elders, lambs, feather-mop palms and bright red poppies. The Cappella di San Zeno is even lovelier, a jewel-box of a mausoleum, built by Pope Paschal II for his mother, Theodora. Her square halo shows that she was still alive when the mosaic was created.

**9th-century mosaic, Santa Prassede**

## San Pietro in Vincoli ⓮

Piazza di San Pietro in Vincoli. **Map** 3 C5. ***Tel*** *06 97 84 49 50.* *75, 84, 117.* *Colosseo.* *8am–12:30pm, 3–7pm daily (Oct–Mar: to 6pm).*

The church's name means St Peter in Chains, so called because it houses what are said to be the chains with which St Peter was shackled in the Mamertine Prison *(see p389)*. According to tradition, one set of chains was sent to Constantinople by Empress Eudoxia; when it was returned to Rome some years later it miraculously fused with its partner.

San Pietro is now best known for the Tomb of Julius II, commissioned from Michelangelo by the pope in 1505. Much to the artist's chagrin, Julius soon became more interested in the building of a new St Peter's and the tomb project was laid to one side. After the pope died in 1513, Michelangelo resumed work on the tomb, but had only completed the statues of the *Dying Slaves* (now found in Paris and Florence) and *Moses* when he was called away to paint the *Last Judgment* in the Sistine Chapel.

# Santa Maria Maggiore ⓯

A confident blend of architectural styles, ranging from Early Christian to late Baroque, Santa Maria is also famous for its superb mosaics. Founded in about AD 420, it retains the original colonnaded triple nave, lined with panels of rare 5th-century mosaics. The Cosmatesque marble floor and bell tower are medieval, as are the spectacular mosaics on the triumphal arch and in the loggia. The lavish coffered ceiling is Renaissance; the façades, domes and chapels Baroque.

**VISITORS' CHECKLIST**

Piazza di Santa Maria Maggiore.
**Map** 4 D4.
***Tel*** *06 69 88 68 00.*
*16, 70, 71, 714.* *14.*
*Termini, Cavour.*
*7am–6:45pm daily.*

**Coronation of the Virgin**
*This is one of the wonderful 13th-century mosaics in the apse by Jacopo Torriti.*

**Bell tower**

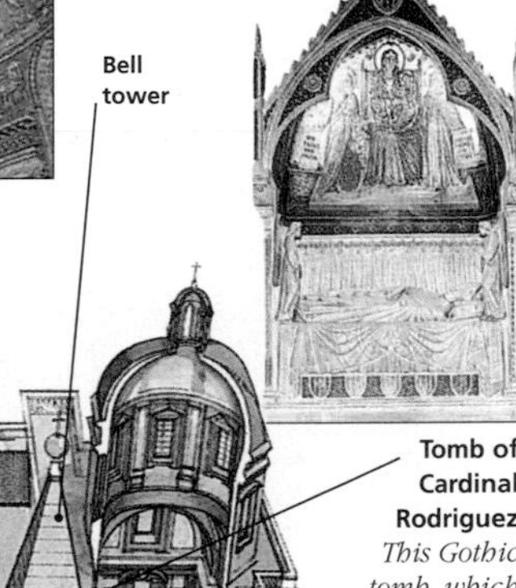

**Tomb of Cardinal Rodriguez**
*This Gothic tomb, which dates from 1299, contains magnificent marblework by the Cosmati.*

**5th-century mosaics**

**18th-century façade by Ferdinando Fuga**

**13th-century mosaics**

**Cappella Paolina**
*Flaminio Ponzio, architect of the Villa Borghese, designed this sumptuous chapel in 1611 for Pope Paul V who is buried here.*

**Column in Piazza Santa Maria Maggiore**
*In 1611 a bronze of the Virgin and Child was added to this ancient marble column which came from the Basilica of Constantine.*

**Cappella Sistina**
*This chapel was built for Pope Sixtus V (1584–7) by Domenico Fontana and was opulently covered with ancient marble. It houses the pope's tomb.*

MANVS PONT MAX AN MDCXII PONT VII

# THE VATICAN AND TRASTEVERE

Vatican City, the world capital of Catholicism, is the world's smallest state. It occupies 43 ha (106 acres) within high walls watched over by the Vatican guard. It was the site where St Peter was martyred (c.AD 64) and buried, and it became the residence of the popes who succeeded him. The papal palaces, next to the great basilica of St Peter's, are home to the Sistine Chapel and the eclectic collections of the Vatican Museums, as well as being the residence of the pope. Neighbouring Trastevere is quite different, a picturesque old quarter, whose inhabitants consider themselves to be the only true Romans. Sadly, the proletarian identity of the place is in danger of being destroyed by the proliferation of trendy restaurants, clubs and shops.

Pope Urban VIII's coat of arms in St Peter's

## SIGHTS AT A GLANCE

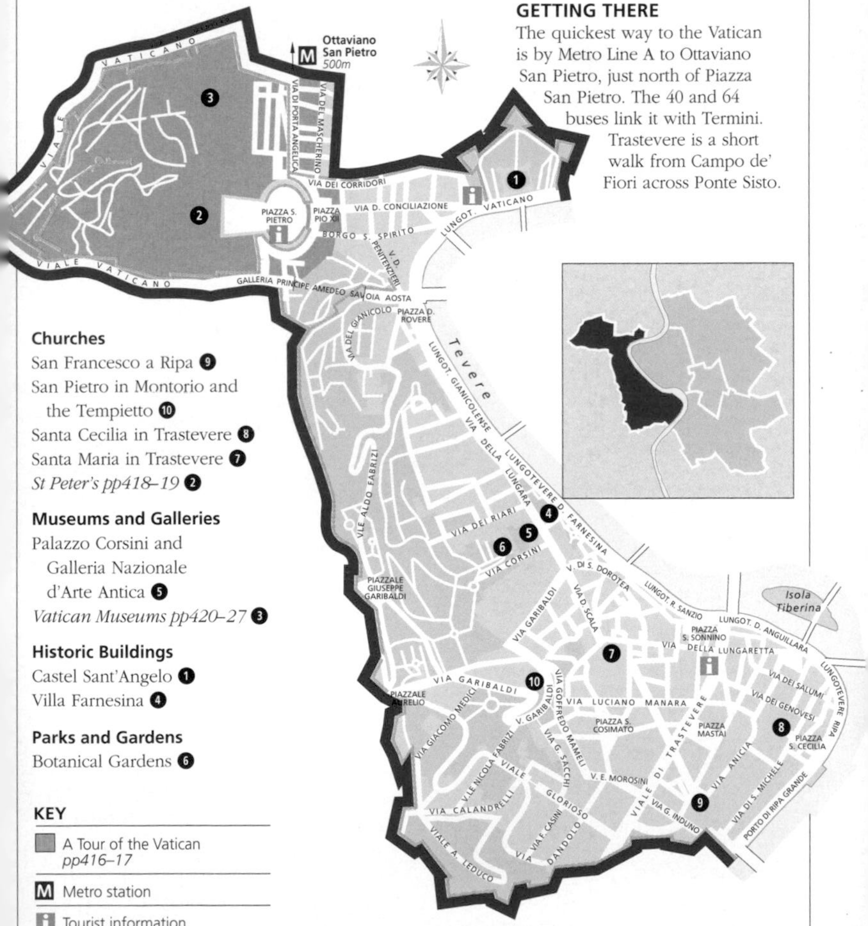

### GETTING THERE

The quickest way to the Vatican is by Metro Line A to Ottaviano San Pietro, just north of Piazza San Pietro. The 40 and 64 buses link it with Termini. Trastevere is a short walk from Campo de' Fiori across Ponte Sisto.

**Churches**
San Francesco a Ripa ⑨
San Pietro in Montorio and the Tempietto ⑩
Santa Cecilia in Trastevere ⑧
Santa Maria in Trastevere ⑦
*St Peter's pp418–19* ②

**Museums and Galleries**
Palazzo Corsini and Galleria Nazionale d'Arte Antica ⑤
*Vatican Museums pp420–27* ③

**Historic Buildings**
Castel Sant'Angelo ①
Villa Farnesina ④

**Parks and Gardens**
Botanical Gardens ⑥

**KEY**
A Tour of the Vatican *pp416–17*
Metro station
Tourist information
City walls

0 metres 250
0 yards 250

◁ **View of St Peter's with the Ponte Sant'Angelo in the foreground**

# A Tour of the Vatican

The Vatican, a sovereign state since February 1929, is ruled by the pope, Europe's only absolute monarch. About 500 people live here and, as well as accommodation for staff and ecclesiasts, the city has its own post office, banks, currency, judicial system, radio station, shops and a daily newspaper, *L'Osservatore Romano*.

Crucifix in the Vatican

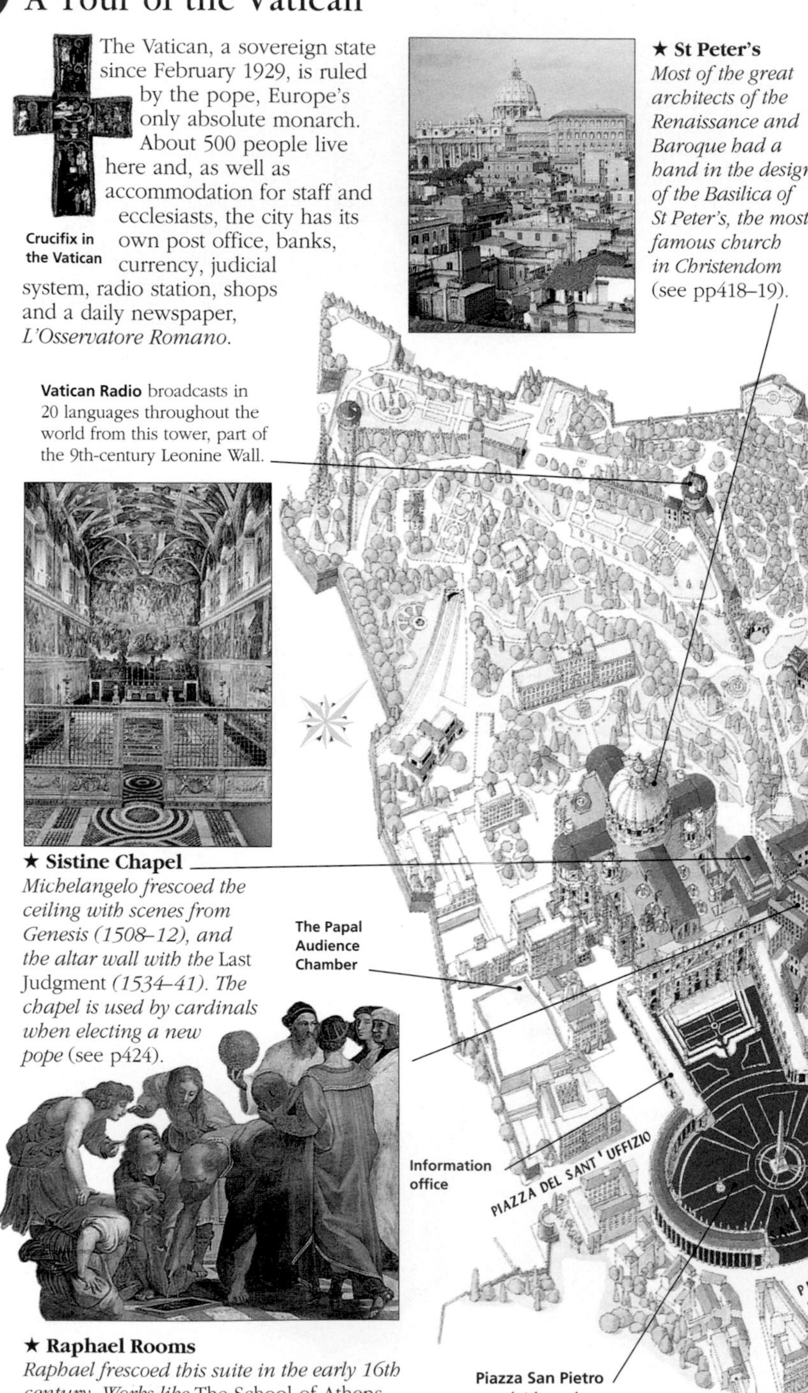


**★ St Peter's**
*Most of the great architects of the Renaissance and Baroque had a hand in the design of the Basilica of St Peter's, the most famous church in Christendom* (see pp418–19).

**Vatican Radio** broadcasts in 20 languages throughout the world from this tower, part of the 9th-century Leonine Wall.

**★ Sistine Chapel**
*Michelangelo frescoed the ceiling with scenes from Genesis (1508–12), and the altar wall with the* Last Judgment *(1534–41). The chapel is used by cardinals when electing a new pope* (see p424).

**The Papal Audience Chamber**

**Information office**

**★ Raphael Rooms**
*Raphael frescoed this suite in the early 16th century. Works like* The School of Athens *established his reputation, to equal that of his contemporary Michelangelo* (see p427).

**Piazza San Pietro** was laid out by Bernini between 1656 and 1667.

**To Via della Conciliazione**

**This staircase** leading down from the museums, designed in 1932 by Giuseppe Momo, is in the form of a double helix, consisting of two spirals: one to walk up and one to walk down.

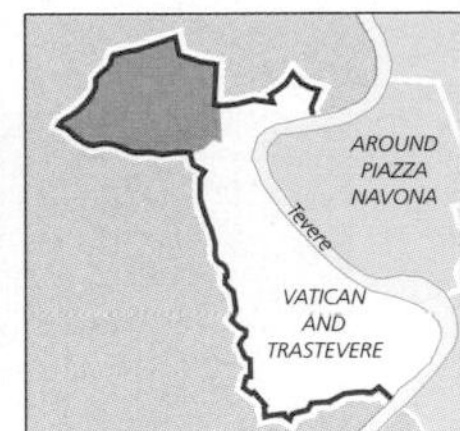


**LOCATOR MAP**

*See Rome Street Finder map 1*

**Entrance to Vatican Museums**

**★ Vatican Museums**

*The marble group of the* Laocoön *(AD 1) is one of many prestigious works of art in the Vatican* (see p422).

**The Cortile della Pigna** is named after a bronze pine cone from an ancient fountain.

VIA DI PORTA ANGELICA

**The Vatican Gardens**, open for guided tours, make up a third of the Vatican's territory.

**0 metres 75**

**0 yards 75**

**STAR SIGHTS**

- ★ Raphael Rooms
- ★ Sistine Chapel
- ★ St Peter's
- ★ Vatican Museums

## Castel Sant'Angelo ❶

Lungotevere Castello. **Map** 2 D3. ***Tel*** *06 681 91 11.* *23, 34, 280.* *9am–7pm Tue–Sun (last entry 6:30pm).* *1 Jan, 25 Dec.*

**www**.castelsantangelo.com

This massive fortress takes its name from the vision of the Archangel Michael by Pope Gregory the Great in the 6th century as he led a procession across the bridge, praying for the end of the plague.

The castle began life in AD 139 as the Emperor Hadrian's mausoleum. Since then it has been a bridgehead in the Emperor Aurelian's city wall, a medieval citadel and prison, and a place of safety for popes during times of political unrest. A corridor links it with the Vatican Palace, providing an escape route for the pope. From dank cells to fine apartments of Renaissance popes, the museums cover all aspects of the castle's history, including the Sala Paolina, with illusionistic frescoes (1546–8) by Pellegrino Tibaldi and Perin del Vaga and the Courtyard of Honour.

## St Peter's ❷

*See pp418–19.*

## Vatican Museums ❸

*See pp420–27.*

**View of Castel Sant'Angelo from the Ponte Sant'Angelo**

# St Peter's ❷

Catholicism's most sacred shrine, the sumptuous, marble-caked basilica of St Peter's draws pilgrims and tourists from all over the world. It holds hundreds of precious works of art, some salvaged from the original 4th-century basilica built by Constantine, others commissioned from Renaissance and Baroque artists. The dominant tone is set by Bernini, who created the baldacchino twisting up below Michelangelo's huge dome. He also created the Cathedra in the apse, with four saints supporting a throne that contains fragments once thought to be relics of the chair from which St Peter delivered his first sermon.

**Dome of St Peter's**
*The 136.5 m (448 ft) high dome, designed by Michelangelo, was not completed in his lifetime.*

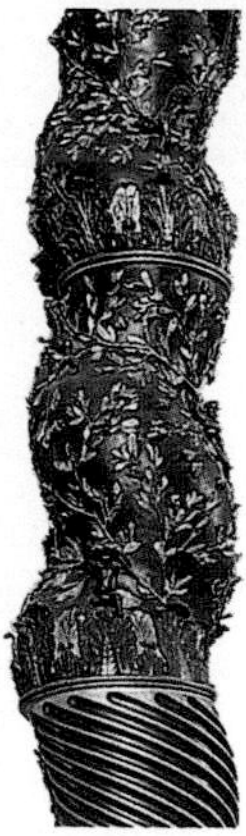

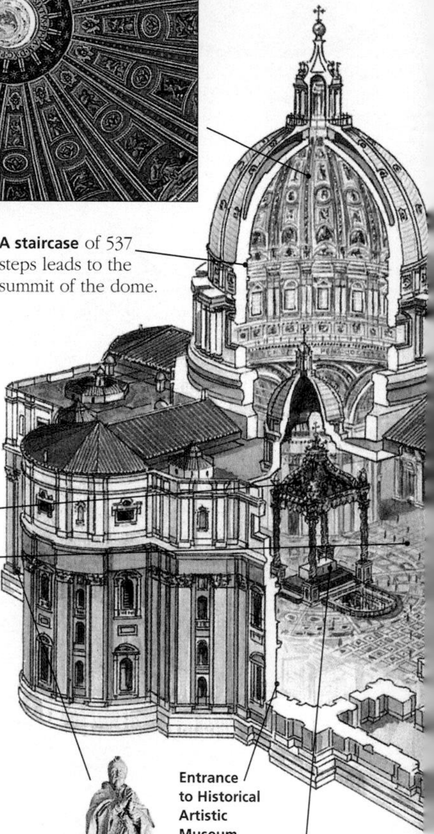

**A staircase** of 537 steps leads to the summit of the dome.

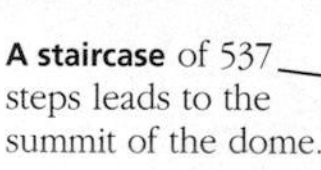

**Baldacchino**
*Commissioned by Pope Urban VIII in 1624, Bernini's extravagant Baroque canopy stands above St Peter's tomb.*

**The church** is 186 m (615 ft) long.

**Entrance to Historical Artistic Museum and Sacristy**

**The Papal Altar** stands over the crypt where St Peter is reputedly buried.

**Monument to Pope Alexander VII**
*Bernini's last work in St Peter's was finished in 1678 and shows the Chigi pope among the allegorical figures of Truth, Justice, Charity and Prudence.*

### HISTORICAL PLAN OF THE BASILICA OF ST PETER'S

St Peter was buried in AD 64 in a necropolis near the site of his crucifixion in the Circus of Nero. In AD 324 Constantine constructed a basilica over the tomb. The old church was rebuilt in the 15th century, and throughout the 16th and 17th centuries various architects developed the existing structure. The new church was inaugurated in 1626.

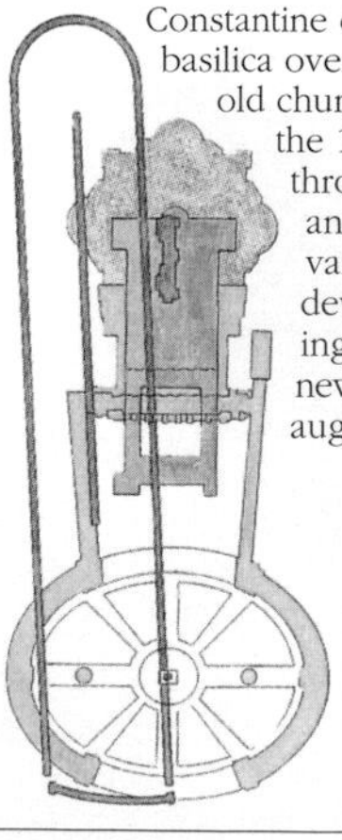

**KEY**

- Circus of Nero
- Constantinian
- Renaissance
- Baroque

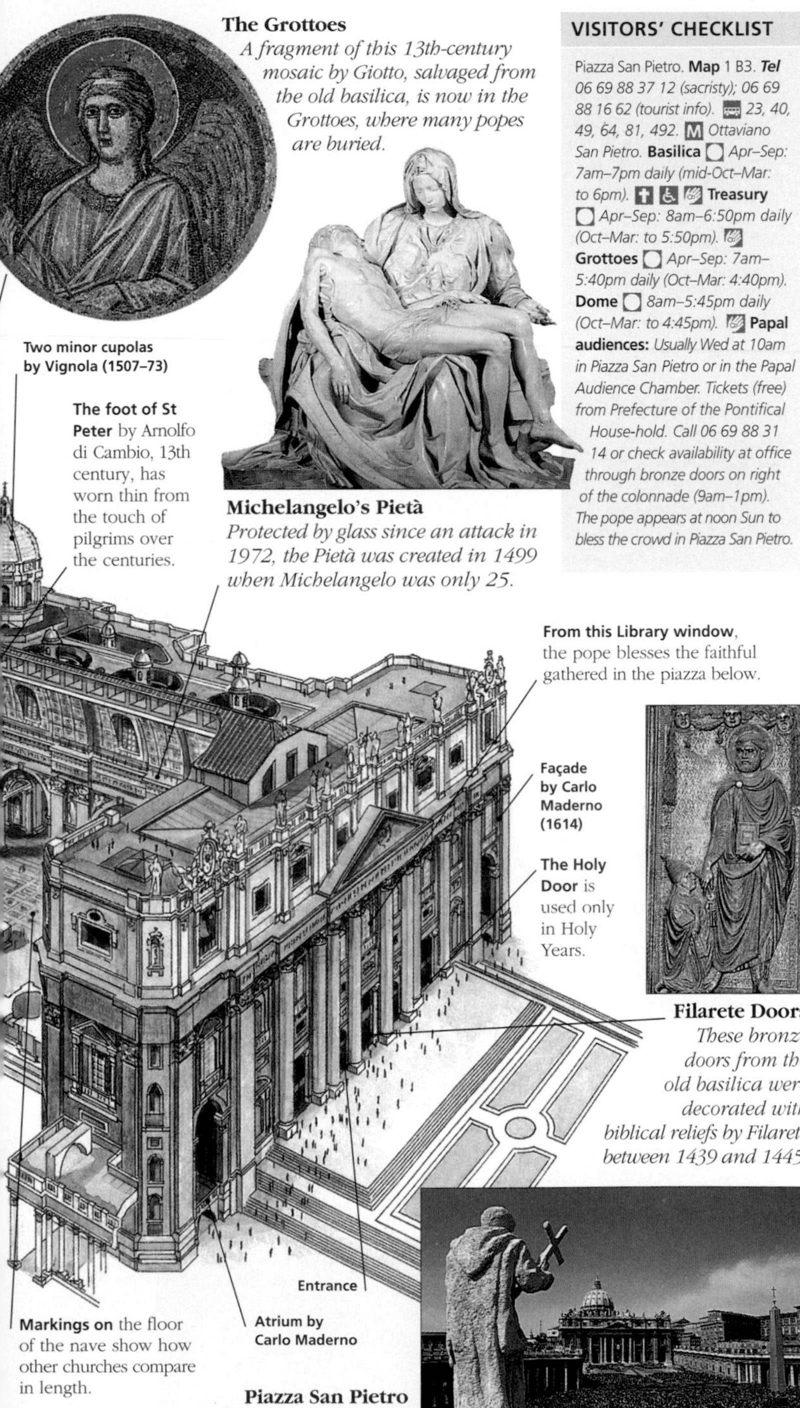

**The Grottoes**
*A fragment of this 13th-century mosaic by Giotto, salvaged from the old basilica, is now in the Grottoes, where many popes are buried.*

**Two minor cupolas by Vignola (1507–73)**

**The foot of St Peter** by Arnolfo di Cambio, 13th century, has worn thin from the touch of pilgrims over the centuries.

**Michelangelo's Pietà**
*Protected by glass since an attack in 1972, the Pietà was created in 1499 when Michelangelo was only 25.*

**From this Library window**, the pope blesses the faithful gathered in the piazza below.

**Façade by Carlo Maderno (1614)**

**The Holy Door** is used only in Holy Years.

**Filarete Doors**
*These bronze doors from the old basilica were decorated with biblical reliefs by Filarete between 1439 and 1445.*

**Entrance**

**Markings on** the floor of the nave show how other churches compare in length.

**Atrium by Carlo Maderno**

**Piazza San Pietro**
*On Sundays, religious festivals and special occasions such as canonizations, the pope blesses the crowds from a balcony.*

## VISITORS' CHECKLIST

Piazza San Pietro. **Map** 1 B3. ***Tel*** *06 69 88 37 12 (sacristy); 06 69 88 16 62 (tourist info).* *23, 40, 49, 64, 81, 492.* *Ottaviano San Pietro.* **Basilica** *Apr–Sep: 7am–7pm daily (mid-Oct–Mar: to 6pm).* **Treasury** *Apr–Sep: 8am–6:50pm daily (Oct–Mar: to 5:50pm).* **Grottoes** *Apr–Sep: 7am–5:40pm daily (Oct–Mar: 4:40pm).* **Dome** *8am–5:45pm daily (Oct–Mar: to 4:45pm).* **Papal audiences:** *Usually Wed at 10am in Piazza San Pietro or in the Papal Audience Chamber. Tickets (free) from Prefecture of the Pontifical House-hold. Call 06 69 88 31 14 or check availability at office through bronze doors on right of the colonnade (9am–1pm). The pope appears at noon Sun to bless the crowd in Piazza San Pietro.*

# Vatican Museums ❸

Home to the Sistine Chapel and Raphael Rooms as well as to one of the world's most important art collections, the Vatican Museums are housed in palaces originally built for Renaissance popes such as Julius II, Innocent VIII and Sixtus IV. Most of the later additions were made in the 18th century, when priceless works of art accumulated by earlier popes were first put on show.

**Etruscan Museum**
*The Etruscan collection includes a woman's gold clasp* (fibula) *from the 7th-century BC Regolini-Galassi tomb at Cerveteri, north of Rome.*

**Gallery of Maps**
*The* Siege of Malta *is one of 40 maps of the Church's territories, frescoed by the 16th-century cartographer Ignazio Danti on the gallery's walls.*

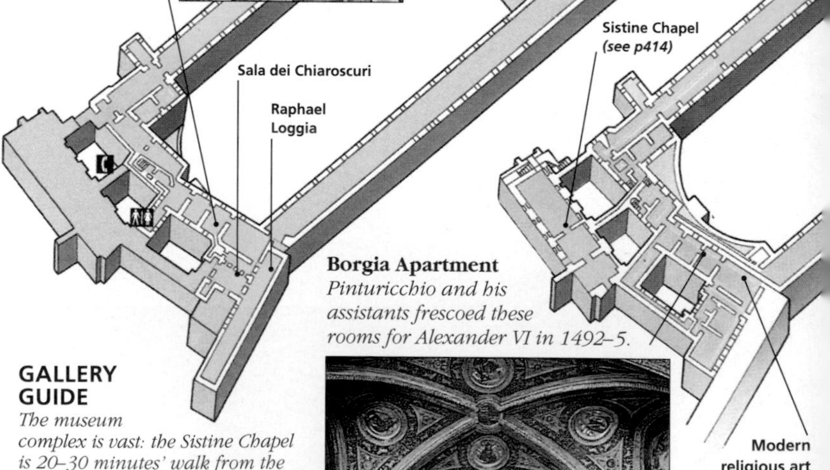

Gallery of the Candelabra

Gallery of Tapestries

Stairs down

Upper floor

**Raphael Rooms**
*This is a detail of the* Expulsion of Heliodorus from the Temple, *one of many frescoes painted by Raphael and his pupils for Julius II's private apartments* (see p427).

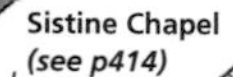


Sala dei Chiaroscuri

Raphael Loggia

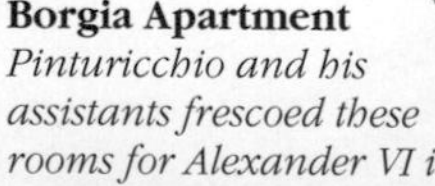

**Borgia Apartment**
*Pinturicchio and his assistants frescoed these rooms for Alexander VI in 1492–5.*

**Modern religious art** on view here was sent to the popes by artists worldwide, such as Bacon, Ernst and Carrà.

**GALLERY GUIDE**
*The museum complex is vast: the Sistine Chapel is 20–30 minutes' walk from the entrance, so allow plenty of time. There is a strict one-way system, and it is best to be selective or choose one of four colour-coded itineraries, which vary from 90 minutes to a five-hour marathon.*

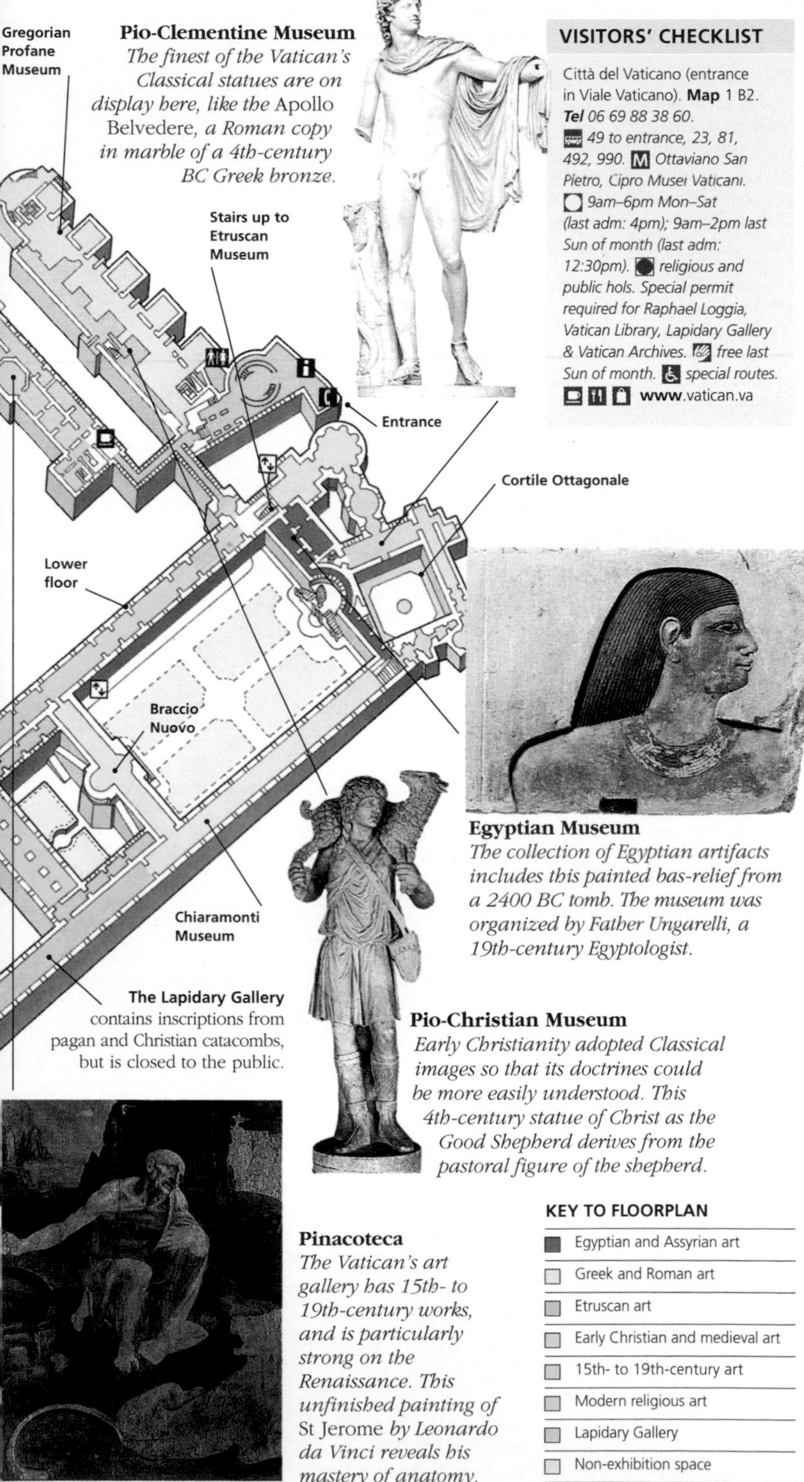


**Pio-Clementine Museum**
*The finest of the Vatican's Classical statues are on display here, like the* Apollo Belvedere, *a Roman copy in marble of a 4th-century BC Greek bronze.*

**Egyptian Museum**
*The collection of Egyptian artifacts includes this painted bas-relief from a 2400 BC tomb. The museum was organized by Father Ungarelli, a 19th-century Egyptologist.*

**The Lapidary Gallery** contains inscriptions from pagan and Christian catacombs, but is closed to the public.

**Pio-Christian Museum**
*Early Christianity adopted Classical images so that its doctrines could be more easily understood. This 4th-century statue of Christ as the Good Shepherd derives from the pastoral figure of the shepherd.*

**Pinacoteca**
*The Vatican's art gallery has 15th- to 19th-century works, and is particularly strong on the Renaissance. This unfinished painting of* St Jerome *by Leonardo da Vinci reveals his mastery of anatomy.*

## VISITORS' CHECKLIST

Città del Vaticano (entrance in Viale Vaticano). **Map** 1 B2. ***Tel*** *06 69 88 38 60.* *49 to entrance, 23, 81, 492, 990.* *Ottaviano San Pietro, Cipro Musei Vaticani.* *9am–6pm Mon–Sat (last adm: 4pm); 9am–2pm last Sun of month (last adm: 12:30pm).* *religious and public hols. Special permit required for Raphael Loggia, Vatican Library, Lapidary Gallery & Vatican Archives.* *free last Sun of month.* *special routes.* **www**.vatican.va

**KEY TO FLOORPLAN**

- Egyptian and Assyrian art
- Greek and Roman art
- Etruscan art
- Early Christian and medieval art
- 15th- to 19th-century art
- Modern religious art
- Lapidary Gallery
- Non-exhibition space

# Exploring the Vatican's Collections

The Vatican's greatest treasures are its superlative Greek and Roman antiquities, together with the magnificent artifacts excavated from Egyptian and Etruscan tombs during the 19th century. Some of Italy's greatest artists, such as Raphael, Michelangelo and Leonardo da Vinci, are represented in the Pinacoteca (art gallery) and parts of the former palaces, where they were employed by popes to decorate sumptuous apartments and galleries.

## EGYPTIAN AND ASSYRIAN ART

The Egyptian collection contains finds from 19th- and 20th-century excavations in Egypt, as well as statues that were brought to Rome in Imperial times. There are also Roman imitations of Egyptian art from Hadrian's Villa *(see p468)* and from temples in Rome devoted to Egyptian gods and goddesses, such as Isis and Serapis.

The genuine Egyptian works, displayed on the lower floor next to the Pio-Clementine Museum, include statues, mummies, mummy cases and a Book of the Dead. One of the main treasures is a colossal granite 13th-century statue of Queen Mutuy, the mother of Rameses II, which was found on the site of the Horti Sallustiani gardens near Via Veneto. Also noteworthy are the head of a statue of Montuhotep IV (20th century BC), the beautiful mummy case of Queen Hetepheres, and the tomb of Iri, who was the guardian of the Pyramid of Cheops. This dates back to the 22nd century BC.

## GREEK, ETRUSCAN AND ROMAN ART

The greater part of the Vatican Museums is dedicated to Greek and Roman art. However, the Etruscan Museum houses a superb collection of Etruscan *(see p44)* and pre-Roman artifacts from Etruria and the Greek colonies of southern Italy. Here, the most famous exhibits are the gold jewellery and bronze throne, bed and funeral cart, found in the 650 BC Regolini-Galassi tomb in Cerveteri *(see p466)*.

Prize Greek and Roman pieces form the nucleus of the Pio-Clementine Museum. These include high-quality Roman copies of 4th-century BC Greek statues, such as the *Apoxyomenos* (an athlete wiping his body after a race) and the *Apollo del Belvedere*. The splendid *Laocoön* (1st century AD), originally from Rhodes, was found in 1506 in the ruins of Nero's Golden House. Works such as these inspired Michelangelo and other Renaissance artists.

**Roman copy of the Greek *Doryphoros***

The much smaller Chiaramonti Museum is lined with ancient busts, and its extension, the Braccio Nuovo, has a 1st-century BC statue of Augustus from the villa of his wife Livia. It is based on the *Doryphoros* (spear-carrier) by the 5th-century BC Greek sculptor Polyclitus. There is also a Roman copy of this on display opposite. The Gregorian Profane Museum, housed in a separate wing, follows the evolution of Roman art from reliance on Greek models to a recognizably Roman style.

**Head of an athlete in mosaic from the Baths of Caracalla, AD 217**

In this museum, original Greek works include large marble fragments from the Parthenon in Athens. Among the Roman pieces are two reliefs, the *Rilievi della Cancelleria*, commissioned by Domitian in AD 81 to glorify the military parades of his father, Emperor Vespasian. There are also fine Roman floor mosaics, two from the Baths of Caracalla *(see p437)*, and one, in the Round Room, dated 3rd century AD, from the Baths of Otricoli in Umbria

In the Vatican Library is the 1st-century AD *Aldobrandini Wedding*, a beautiful Roman fresco depicting a bride being prepared for her marriage.

**Roman mosaic from the Baths of Otricoli, Umbria, in the Round Room**

***For hotels and restaurants in this region see pp587–92 and pp636–41***

## EARLY CHRISTIAN AND MEDIEVAL ART

The main collection of early Christian antiquities is in the Pio-Christian Museum, which contains inscriptions and sculpture from catacombs and early Christian basilicas. The sculpture consists chiefly of reliefs from sarcophagi, though the most striking work is a free-standing 4th-century statue of the *Good Shepherd*. The sculpture's chief interest lies in the way it blends Biblical episodes with pagan mythology. The idealized pastoral figure of the shepherd became Christ himself, while bearded philosophers turned into the Apostles.

The first two rooms of the Pinacoteca are dedicated to late medieval art, mostly wooden altarpieces painted in tempera. The outstanding work is Giotto's *Stefaneschi Triptych* of about 1300 which decorated the main altar of the old St Peter's.

The Vatican Library has a number of medieval treasures including reliquaries, textiles, enamels and icons.

**Detail of Giotto's *Stefaneschi Triptych* (1330) in the Pinacoteca**

## 15TH- TO 19TH-CENTURY ART

Many Renaissance popes were connoisseurs of the arts who considered it their duty to sponsor the leading painters, sculptors and goldsmiths of the age. The galleries around the Cortile del Belvedere were decorated by great artists between the 16th and the 19th centuries.

***Pietà* (c.1471–4) by the Venetian artist Giovanni Bellini in the Pinacoteca**

The Gallery of Tapestries is hung with tapestries woven in Brussels to designs by students of Raphael. The Apartment of Pope Pius V has beautiful 15th-century Flemish tapestries, and the Gallery of Maps is frescoed with 16th-century maps of ancient and contemporary Italy.

Alongside the Raphael Rooms *(see p427)* are the Room of the Chiaroscuri and Pope Nicholas V's private chapel. This was frescoed be tween 1447 and 1451 by Fra Angelico. Also worth seeing is the Borgia Apartment, decorated in the 1490s by Pinturicchio and his pupils for the Borgia pope, Alexander VI. Another set of fascinating frescoes can be found in the Loggia of Raphael, but a visit here requires special permission.

**Pinturicchio's *Adoration of the Magi* (1490), Borgia Apartment**

The Pinacoteca has many important Renaissance works. Highlights from the 15th century are a fine *Pietà* by Giovanni Bellini, part of his *Coronation of the Virgin* altar-piece in Pèsaro *(see p368)*; and Leonardo da Vinci's unfinished *St Jerome*, discovered, after being long lost, in two halves. One was being used as a coffer lid in an antique shop, the other as the seat of a stool in a shoemaker's. Exceptional pieces from the 16th century include eight tapestry cartoons, the *Transfiguration* and *Madonna of Foligno* by Raphael, in a room devoted to the artist; a *Deposition* by Caravaggio; an altarpiece by Titian; and *St Helen* by Veronese, which shows the saint as a gorgeously dressed aristocrat.

# Sistine Chapel: The Ceiling

Michelangelo frescoed the ceiling for Pope Julius II between 1508 and 1512, working on specially designed scaffolding. The main panels, which chart the Creation of the World and Fall of Man, are surrounded by subjects from the Old and New Testaments – except for the Classical Sibyls who are said to have foreseen the birth of Christ. In the 1980s the ceiling was restored revealing colours of an unsuspected vibrancy.

**Libyan Sibyl**
*The pagan prophete reaches for the Book of Knowledge. Like most female figures Michelangelo painted, the beautiful Libyan Sibyl was probably modelled on a man.*

Illusionistic architecture

**Creation of the Sun and Moon**
*Michelangelo depict God as a dynamic but terrifying figure commanding the sun to shed light on the earth.*

| 30 | 19 | 10 | 26 | 12 | 21 | 14 | 28 | 16 | 23 | 32 |
|---|---|---|---|---|---|---|---|---|---|---|
| 18 | 1 | 2 | 3 | 4 | 5 | 6 | 7 | 8 | 9 | 24 |
| 31 | 25 | 11 | 20 | 13 | 27 | 15 | 22 | 17 | 29 | 33 |

### KEY TO CEILING PANELS

**GENESIS: 1** God Dividing Light from Darkness; **2** Creation of the Sun and Moon; **3** Separating Waters from Land; **4** Creation of Adam; **5** Creation of Eve; **6** Original Sin; **7** Sacrifice of Noah; **8** The Deluge; **9** Drunkenness of Noah.

**ANCESTORS OF CHRIST: 10** Solomon with his Mother; **11** Parents of Jesse; **12** Rehoboam with Mother; **13** Asa with Parents; **14** Uzziah with Parents; **15** Hezekiah with Parents; **16** Zerubbabel with Parents; **17** Josiah with Parents.

**PROPHETS: 18** Jonah; **19** Jeremiah; **20** Daniel; **21** Ezekiel; **22** Isaiah; **23** Joel; **24** Zechariah.

**SIBYLS: 25** Libyan Sibyl; **26** Persian Sibyl; **27** Cumaean Sibyl; **28** Erythrean Sibyl; **29** Delphic Sibyl.

**OLD TESTAMENT SCENES OF SALVATION: 30** Punishment of Haman; **31** Moses and the Brazen Serpent; **32** David and Goliath; **33** Judith and Holofernes.

**Original Sin**
*This shows Adam and Eve tasting the forbidden fruit from the Tree of Knowledge, and their expulsion from Paradise. Michelangelo represents Satan as a snake with the body of a woman.*

**The Ignudi** are athletic male nudes whose significance is uncertain.

**The lunettes** are devoted to frescoes of the ancestors of Christ, like Hezekiah.

## RESTORATION OF THE SISTINE CEILING

A restorer cleaning the Libyan Sibyl

The restorers of the Sistine Chapel used computers, photography and spectrum technology to analyse the fresco before cleaning began. They separated Michelangelo's work from that of later restorers and discovered that the restorers had attempted to clean the ceiling with materials ranging from bread to retsina wine. The new restoration revealed the familiarly dusky, eggshell-cracked figures to have creamy skins, lustrous hair and to be dressed in brightly coloured, luscious robes: "a Benetton Michelangelo" mocked one critic, claiming that a layer of varnish that the artist had added to darken the colours had been removed. However, after examining the work, most experts agreed that the new colours probably matched those painted by Michelangelo.

# Sistine Chapel: The Walls

The massive walls of the Sistine Chapel, the main chapel in the Vatican Palace, were frescoed by some of the finest artists of the 15th and 16th centuries. The 12 paintings on the side walls, by artists including Perugino, Ghirlandaio, Botticelli and Signorelli, show parallel episodes from the life of Moses and of Christ. The decoration of the chapel walls was completed between 1534 and 1541 by Michelangelo, who added the great altar wall fresco, the *Last Judgment*.

**KEY TO THE FRESCOES: ARTISTS AND SUBJECTS**

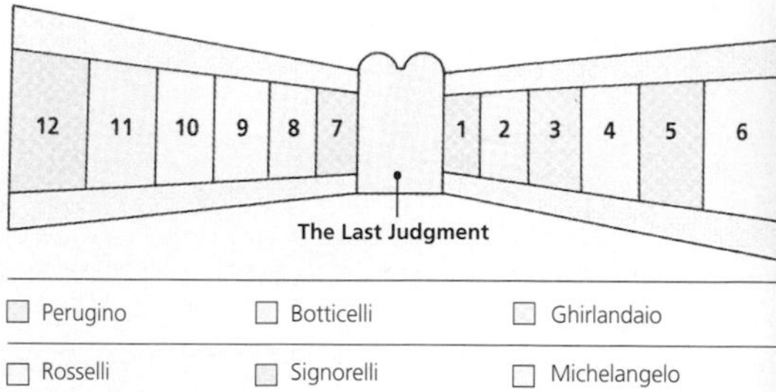


☐ Perugino ☐ Botticelli ☐ Ghirlandaio

☐ Rosselli ☐ Signorelli ☐ Michelangelo

**1** Baptism of Christ in the Jordan
**2** Temptations of Christ
**3** Calling of St Peter and St Andrew
**4** Sermon on the Mount
**5** Handing over the Keys to St Peter
**6** Last Supper
**7** Moses's Journey into Egypt
**8** Moses Receiving the Call
**9** Crossing of the Red Sea
**10** Adoration of the Golden Calf
**11** Punishment of the Rebels
**12** Last Days of Moses

## THE LAST JUDGMENT BY MICHELANGELO

Revealed in 1993 after a year's restoration, the *Last Judgment* is considered to be the masterpiece of Michelangelo's mature years. It was commissioned by Pope Paul III Farnese, and required the removal of some earlier frescoes and two windows over the altar. A new wall was erected which slanted inwards to stop dust settling on it. Michelangelo worked alone on the fresco for seven years, until its completion in 1541.

The painting depicts the souls of the dead rising up to face the wrath of God, a subject that is rarely used for an altar decoration. The pope chose it as a warning to Catholics to adhere to their faith in the turmoil of the Reformation. In fact the work conveys the artist's own tormented attitude to his faith. It offers neither the certainties of Christian orthodoxy, nor the ordered view of Classicism.

In a dynamic, emotional composition, the figures are caught in a vortex of motion. The dead are torn from their graves and hauled up to face Christ the Judge, whose athletic, muscular figure is the focus of all the painting's movement.

Christ shows little sympathy for the agitated saints around him, clutching the instruments of their martyrdom. Neither is any pity shown for the damned, hurled down to the demons in hell. Here Charon, pushing people off his boat into the depths of Hades, and the infernal judge Minos, are taken from Dante's *Inferno*. Minos has ass's ears, and is a portrait of courtier Biagio da Cesena, who had objected to the nude figures in the fresco. Michelangelo's self-portrait is on the skin held by the martyr St Bartholomew.

**Souls meeting the wrath of Christ in Michelangelo's *Last Judgment***

# Raphael Rooms

Pope Julius II's private apartments were built above those of his hated predecessor, Alexander VI, who died in 1503. Julius was impressed with Raphael's work and chose him to redecorate the four rooms *(stanze)*. Raphael and his pupils began in 1508, replacing works by better-known artists, including Raphael's teacher, Perugino. The new frescoes quickly established the young artist's reputation in Rome, but the project took 16 years to complete and he died before it was finished.

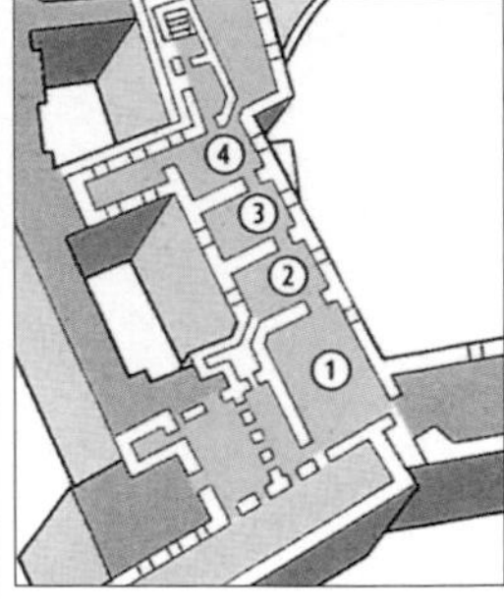


**KEY TO FLOORPLAN**

① Hall of Constantine

② Room of Heliodorus

③ Room of the Segnatura

④ Room of the Fire in the Borgo

**Detail from Raphael's *The Mass of Bolsena* (1512)**

## HALL OF CONSTANTINE

The frescoes in this room were started in 1517 and completed in 1525, five years after Raphael's death, and are largely the work of the artist's pupils. The theme of the decoration is the triumph of Christianity over paganism, and the four major frescoes show scenes from the life of Constantine, the first Christian emperor. These include the *Vision of the Cross* and the emperor's victory over his rival, Maxentius, at *The Battle of the Milvian Bridge*, for which Raphael had provided a preparatory sketch.

## ROOM OF HELIODORUS

Raphael decorated this private antechamber between 1512 and 1514. The main frescoes all contain thinly veiled references to the protective powers of the papacy. The room's name refers to the fresco on the right, *The Expulsion of Heliodorus from the Temple*, showing Heliodorus felled by a horseman as he tries to rob the Temple in Jerusalem. It alludes to Pope Julius II's victory over foreign armies in Italy. *The Mass of Bolsena* on the left wall refers to a miracle that occurred in 1263, in which a priest who doubted the doctrine of the Holy Host was said to have seen blood issue from it at the moment of sacrifice.

## ROOM OF THE SEGNATURA

Completed between 1508 and 1511, the frescoes here are the most harmonious in the series. The scheme followed by Raphael, dictated by Pope Julius II, reflected the Humanist belief that there could be perfect harmony between Classical culture and Christianity in the search for truth. The most famous work, *The School of Athens*, centres on the debate about truth between the Greek philosophers Plato and Aristotle. Raphael depicted some of his contemporaries as philosophers, including Leonardo da Vinci, Bramante and Michelangelo.

## ROOM OF THE FIRE IN THE BORGO

This was originally the dining room, but when the decoration was completed under Pope Leo X, it became a music room. All the frescoes exalt the reigning pope by depicting events in the lives of his 9th-century namesakes, Leo III and IV. The main frescoes were designed by Raphael, but finished by his assistants between 1514 and 1517. The most famous, *The Fire in the Borgo*, shows a miracle of 847, when Pope Leo IV put out a fire by making the sign of the cross. Raphael draws a parallel between this and the legendary flight of Aeneas from Troy, recounted by Virgil. Aeneas appears in the foreground, carrying his father Anchises on his back.

***The School of Athens* (1511) showing philosophers and scholars**

## Villa Farnesina ❹

Via della Lungara 230. **Map** 2 E5. ***Tel*** *06 68 02 72 68.* *23, 280.* *9am–1pm Mon–Sat.*

The fabulously wealthy Sienese banker Agostino Chigi commissioned this villa in 1508 from his fellow Sienese Baldassare Peruzzi. Chigi's main home was across the Tiber, and the villa was designed purely for lavish banquets. Artists, poets, cardinals, princes and the pope himself were entertained here in magnificent style. Chigi also used the villa for sojourns with the courtesan Imperia, who allegedly inspired one of the *Three Graces* painted by Raphael in the Loggia of Cupid and Psyche.

The simple, harmonious design of the Farnesina, with a central block and projecting wings, made it one of the first true villas of the Renaissance. Peruzzi decorated some of the interiors himself, such as the Sala della Prospettiva upstairs, in which the illusionistic frescoes create the impression of looking out over 16th-century Rome through a marble colonnade.

Other frescoes, by Sebastiano del Piombo and Raphael and his pupils, illustrate Classical myths, while the vault of the main hall, the Sala di Galatea, is adorned with astrological scenes showing the position of the stars at the time of Chigi's birth. After his death the business collapsed, and in 1577 the villa was sold off to the Farnese family.

**Raphael's *Three Graces* in the Villa Farnesina**

**Queen Christina of Sweden's bedroom in the Palazzo Corsini**

## Palazzo Corsini and Galleria Nazionale d'Arte Antica ❺

Via della Lungara 10. **Map** 2 D5. ***Tel*** *06 68 80 23 23.* *23, 280.* *8:30am–7pm Tue–Sun (call ahead).* *1 Jan, 1 May, 15 Aug, 25 Dec.* **www**.galleriaborghese.it

Built for Cardinal Domenico Riario in 1510–12, the Palazzo Corsini has numbered Bramante, the young Michelangelo, Erasmus and the mother of Napoleon among its guests. Queen Christina of Sweden died here in 1689. The palazzo was rebuilt by Ferdinando Fuga, who planned the façade to be viewed from an angle, as Via della Lungara is too narrow for a full frontal view.

When the palazzo was bought by the state in 1893, the Corsini family donated their collection of paintings, which formed the core of the national art collection, and was soon augmented. The collection is now split between Palazzo Barberini and Palazzo Corsini. Although the best works are in the Barberini, there are paintings by Van Dyck, Rubens, Murillo, and, notably, an androgynous *St John the Baptist* (c.1604) by Caravaggio and a *Salome* (1638) by Reni. The strangest work is a portrait of the rotund Queen Christina as the goddess Diana by J Van Egmont.

## Botanical Gardens ❻

Largo Cristina di Svezia 24. **Map** 2 D5. ***Tel*** *06 49 91 71 07.* *23, 280.* *9am–6:30pm (Oct–Mar: 5:30pm) Mon–Sat.* *public hols.*

Sequoias, palm trees, orchids and bromeliads are among the 7,000 plants from all over the world represented in the Botanical Gardens (Orto Botanico). Indigenous and exotic species are grouped to illustrate their botanical families and their adaptation to different climates and ecosystems. There are also some curious plants like the ginkgo that have survived almost unchanged from earlier eras.

**Palm trees in the Botanical Gardens, Trastevere**

## Santa Maria in Trastevere ❼

Piazza Santa Maria in Trastevere. **Map** 5 C1. ***Tel*** *06 581 48 02.* *H, 23, 280.* *7:30am–8pm daily.*

Santa Maria in Trastevere was probably the first Christian place of worship in Rome, founded by Pope Callixtus I in the 3rd century, when emperors were still pagan and Christianity a minority cult. According to legend, it was built on the site where a fountain of oil had miraculously sprung up on the day that Christ was born. The basilica became the focus of devotion to the Madonna, and although today's church, and its remarkable mosaics, date largely from the 12th and 13th centuries, images of the

Apse mosaic of the *Coronation of the Virgin*, Santa Maria in Trastevere

Virgin continue to dominate. The façade mosaics probably date from the 12th century, and show Mary, Christ and ten lamp-bearing women. Inside in the apse is a stylized 12th-century *Coronation of the Virgin*, and below, a series of realistic scenes from the life of the Virgin by the 13th-century artist Pietro Cavallini. The oldest image of the Virgin is a 7th-century icon, the *Madonna di Clemenza*, which depicts her as a Byzantine empress flanked by a guard of angels. It sits above the altar in the Cappella Altemps.

## Santa Cecilia in Trastevere 8

Piazza di Santa Cecilia. **Map** 6 D1. ***Tel*** *06 589 92 89.* *H, 23, 44, 280.* *9:30am–12:30pm, 4–6:30pm daily.* **Cavallini fresco** *10am–12:30pm Mon–Sat.*

St Cecilia, aristocrat and patron saint of music, was martyred here in AD 230. After an unsuccessful attempt to suffocate her by locking her in the hot steam bath of her house for three days, she was beheaded. A church was built, possibly in the 4th century, on the site of her house (still to be seen beneath the church, along with the remains of a tannery). Her body was lost, but it turned up again in the Catacombs of San Callisto *(see p442)*. In the 9th century it was reburied here by Pope Paschal I, who rebuilt the church.

A fine apse mosaic survives from this period. The altar canopy by Arnolfo di Cambio and the fresco of *The Last Judgment* by Pietro Cavallini can be reached through the adjoining convent; they date from the 13th century, one of the few periods when Rome had a distinctive artistic style.

In front of the altar is a delicate statue of St Cecilia by Stefano Maderno, which is based on sketches made of her perfectly preserved relics when they were briefly disinterred in 1599.

## San Francesco a Ripa 9

Piazza San Francesco d'Assisi 88. **Map** 5 C2. ***Tel*** *06 581 90 20.* *H, 23, 44, 75, 280.* *7am–noon, 4–7:30pm Mon–Sat; 7am–1pm, 4–7pm Sun.*

St Francis of Assisi lived here in a hospice when he visited Rome in 1219 and his stone pillow and crucifix are preserved in his cell. The church was built by a follower, a local nobleman called Rodolfo Anguillara, who is portrayed on his tombstone wearing the Franciscan habit.

Entirely rebuilt in the 1680s by Cardinal Pallavicini, the church is rich in 17th- and 18th-century sculptures. Not to be missed in the Altieri chapel (fourth left, along the nave) is Bernini's exquisite late work, the *Ecstasy of Beata Ludovica Albertoni* (1674).

Bernini's *Ecstasy of Beata Ludovica Albertoni*, San Francesco a Ripa

## San Pietro in Montorio and the Tempietto 10

P San Pietro in Montorio 2. **Map** 5 B1. ***Tel*** *06 581 39 40.* *44, 75, 100.* *8:30am–noon daily, 3–4pm Mon–Fri.* **Tempietto** *9:30am–12:30pm, 2–4:30pm (4–6pm in summer) Tue–Sat.*

Bramante's circular Tempietto at San Pietro in Montorio

The Tempietto, a diminutive masterpiece of Renaissance architecture completed by Bramante in 1502, stands in the courtyard of San Pietro in Montorio. The name means "little temple" and its circular shape echoes early Christian *martyria*, chapels built on the site of a saint's martyrdom. This was erroneously thought to be the spot in Nero's Circus where St Peter was crucified. Bramante ringed the chapel with Doric columns, a Classical frieze and fine balustrade.

# AVENTINE AND LATERAN

This is one of the greenest parts of the city, taking in the Celian and Aventine Hills, as well as the very congested area around San Giovanni in Laterano. The Celian, now scattered with churches, was a fashionable place to live in Imperial Rome. Some of the era's splendour is still apparent in the ruins of the Baths of Caracalla.

Mosaic fragment, Baths of Caracalla

Behind the Baths rises the Aventine Hill, a peaceful, leafy area, with the superb basilica of Santa Sabina, and lovely views across the river to Trastevere and St Peter's. In the valley below, cars and Vespas skim around the Circus Maximus, following the ancient charioteering track, while to the south lies Testaccio, a lively working-class district.

## SIGHTS AT A GLANCE

**Churches**

San Clemente ❻
San Giovanni in Laterano ❼
Santa Maria in Cosmedin ❷
Santa Maria in Domnica ❸
Santi Quattro Coronati ❺
Santa Sabina ⓫
Santo Stefano Rotondo ❹

**Ancient Sites and Buildings**

Baths of Caracalla ❽
Temples of the Forum Boarium ❶

**Monuments and Tombs**

Protestant Cemetery ❿
Pyramid of Caius Cestius ❾

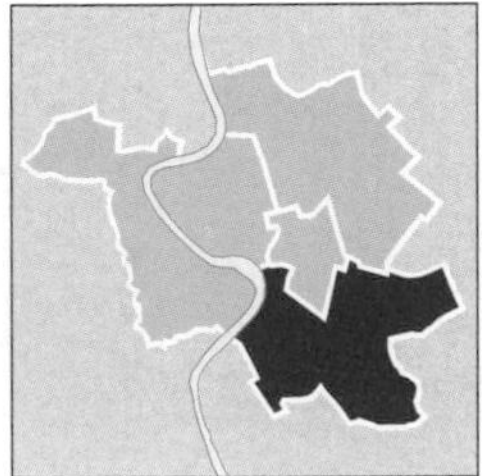

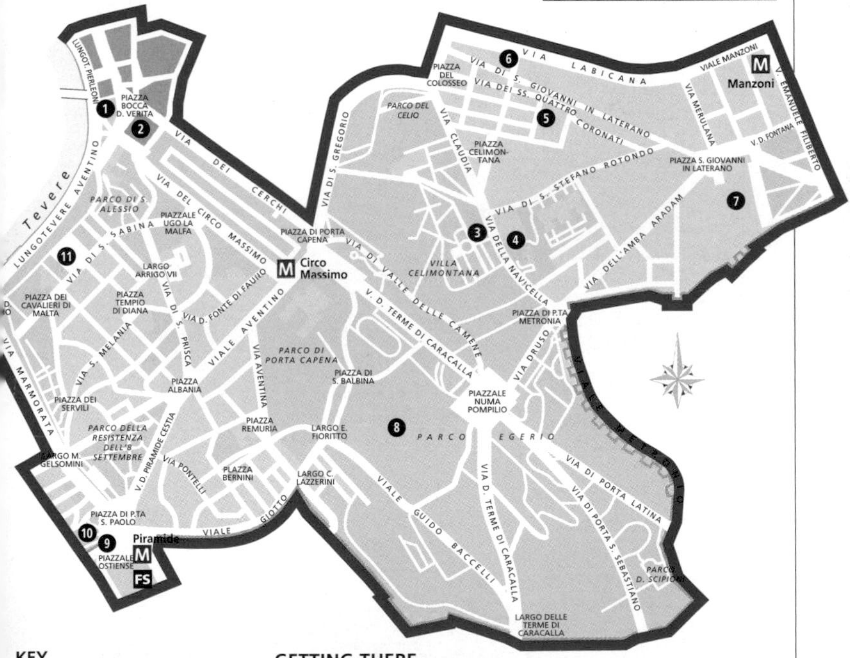

**KEY**

Street-by-Street: Piazza della Bocca della Verità *pp432–3*

FS Railway station

M Metro station

City walls

**GETTING THERE**

Bus 95 runs from Piramide to Piazza della Bocca della Verità. The Celian is near Metro Colosseo and Circo Massimo; tram 3 and buses 81, 160 and 715 are all good routes to the Aventine area.

0 metres 250

0 yards 250

◁ **Pines and orange trees in the Aventine's Parco Savelli, with the dome of St Peter's in the distance**

# Street-by-Street: Piazza della Bocca della Verità

The site of Rome's first port and its busy cattle market, this is an odd little corner of the city, stretching from the heavily trafficked road running along the Tiber to the southern spur of the Capitoline Hill, a place of execution from ancient times until the Middle Ages. Although best known for the Bocca della Verità (Mouth of Truth) in Santa Maria in Cosmedin, which is supposed to snap shut on the hands of liars, there are many other sites in the area, notably two temples from the Republican era. In the 6th century the area became home to a Greek community who founded the churches of San Giorgio in Velabro and Santa Maria in Cosmedin.

**The Casa dei Crescenzi**, studded with ancient fragments, incorporates the ruins of a 10th-century tower built by the powerful Crescenzi family to guard the river Tiber.

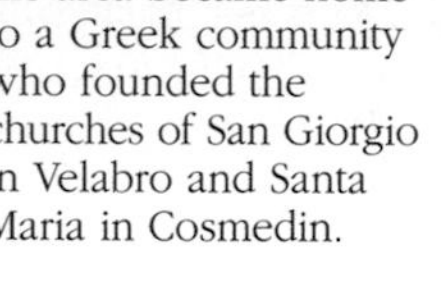

**★ Temples of the Forum Boarium**
*These two buildings are the best preserved of Rome's Republican temples* ❶

**Sant'Omobono** stands on an archaeological site where finds date back to the 6th century.

**Ponte Rotto**, as this forlorn ruined arch in the Tiber is called, simply means "broken bridge". Built in the 2nd century BC, its original name was the Pons Aemilius.

**The Fontana dei Tritoni**, built by Carlo Bizzaccheri in 1715, shows the strong influence of Bernini.

**★ Santa Maria in Cosmedin**
*The* Bocca della Verità, *a medieval drain cover, is set into the portico* ❷

**San Giovanni Decollato** belonged to a confraternity that encouraged condemned prisoners to repent.

**KEY**

 Suggested route

0 metres 75
0 yards 75

*For hotels and restaurants in this region see pp587–92 and pp636–41*

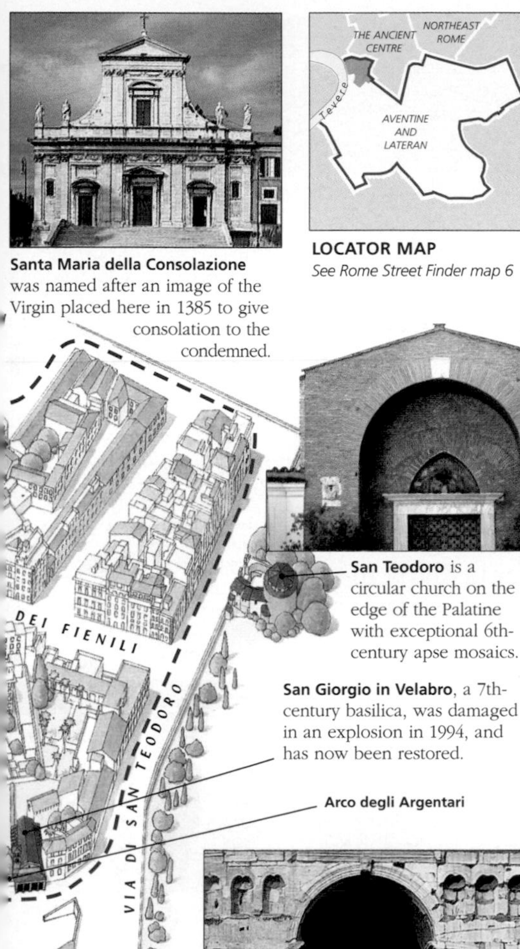


**Santa Maria della Consolazione** was named after an image of the Virgin placed here in 1385 to give consolation to the condemned.

**LOCATOR MAP**
*See Rome Street Finder map 6*

**San Teodoro** is a circular church on the edge of the Palatine with exceptional 6th-century apse mosaics.

**San Giorgio in Velabro**, a 7th-century basilica, was damaged in an explosion in 1994, and has now been restored.

**Arco degli Argentari**

**The 4th-century Arch of Janus**, a four-faced marble-plated arch at the edge of the Forum Boarium market, was an ideal place for merchants and customers to do business in the shade.

**STAR SIGHTS**

★ Santa Maria in Cosmedin

★ Temples of the Forum Boarium

# Temples of the Forum Boarium ❶

Piazza della Bocca della Verità.
**Map** 6 E1. 🚌 *23, 44, 81, 95, 160, 170, 280, 628, 715, 716.*

These wonderfully well-preserved Republican-era temples are at their best in moonlight, standing in their grassy enclave beside the Tiber sheltered by umbrella pines. During the day, they look less romantic, stranded in a sea of traffic. They date from the 2nd century BC, and were saved from ruin by being consecrated as Christian churches in the Middle Ages by the Greek community then living in the area. The rectangular temple, formerly known as the Temple of Fortuna Virilis, was probably dedicated to Portunus, the god of rivers and ports. Set on a podium it has four Ionic travertine columns fluted at the front and 12 half-columns embedded in the tufa wall of the *cella* – the room that housed the image of the god. In the 9th century the Temple was converted into the church of Santa Maria Egiziaca, after a 5th-century prostitute who reformed and became a hermit.

The smaller circular Temple, which is made of solid marble and surrounded by 20 fluted columns, was dedicated to Hercules, though it was long believed to be a Temple of Vesta because of its similarity to the one in the Forum.

**The Ionic façade of the Republican era Temple of Portunus**

Apse mosaic from the 9th century of the Virgin and Child in Santa Maria in Domnica

## Santa Maria in Cosmedin ❷

Piazza della Bocca della Verità. **Map** 6 E1. ***Tel*** *06 678 14 19.* *23, 44, 81, 95, 160, 170, 280, 628, 715, 716.* *9:30am–6pm daily (to 5pm in winter).*

This beautiful church was built in the 6th century on the site of the ancient city's food market. The Romanesque bell tower and portico were added during the 12th century. In the 19th century a Baroque façade was removed and the church restored to its original simplicity. It contains many fine examples of Cosmati work, in particular the mosaic pavement, the raised choir, the bishop's throne, and the canopy over the main altar.

Set into the wall of the portico is the Bocca della Verità (Mouth of Truth), a grotesque marble face, thought to have been an ancient drain cover. Medieval tradition had it that the jaws would snap shut on liars – a useful way of testing the faithfulness of spouses.

The nave of Santa Maria in Cosmedin with its Cosmati floor

## Santa Maria in Domnica ❸

Piazza della Navicella 12. **Map** 7 A2. ***Tel*** *06 772 02 685.* *81, 117, 673.* *Colosseo.* *9am–noon, 3:30–7pm daily (to 6pm in winter).*

Santa Maria in Domnica was probably founded in the 7th century, and renovated in the 9th century. By this time the Romans had lost the art of making mosaics, so Pope Paschal I imported mosaicists from Byzantium. They created an exquisite apse mosaic showing the Virgin, Child and angels in a delicate garden of paradise. Paschal I is kneeling at the Virgin's feet wearing a square halo, indicating that he was alive when it was made.

In 1513 Andrea Sansovino added a portico decorated with lions' heads, a punning homage to Pope Leo X.

## Santo Stefano Rotondo ❹

Via di Santo Stefano Rotondo 7. **Map** 7 B2. ***Tel*** *06 42 11 99.* ***Fax*** *06 42 11 91 25.* *81, 117, 673.* *by appointment via fax or email.* santo.stefano.rotondo@cgu.it

Santo Stefano Rotondo was built between 468 and 483 on a circular plan with four chapels in a cruciform shape. Its circular inner area is enclosed by two concentric corridors. A third, outer corridor was demolished on the orders of Leon Battista Alberti in 1453. In the 1500s Niccolò Pomarancio, Antonio Tempesta and others covered the walls with 34 frescoes detailing the martyrdoms of saints.

Cloister of Santi Quattro Coronati

## Santi Quattro Coronati ❺

Via dei Santi Quattro Coronati 20. **Map** 7 B1. ***Tel*** *06 70 47 54 27.* *85, 117, 850.* *3.* *6:30am–12:30pm, 3:30–7:45pm daily.* **Cloister & Chapel of St Sylvester** *10–11:45am, 4–5:45pm daily.*

This fortified convent was built in the 4th century to house the relics of four Persian stonemasons, martyred after they refused to make a statue of the pagan god Aesculapius. It was rebuilt after invading Normans set fire to it in 1084.

Highlights are a delightful garden cloister and the Chapel of St Sylvester, where 12th-century frescoes recount the legend of Emperor Constantine's conversion to Christianity.

# San Clemente ❻

In 1857 Father Mullooly, the Irish Dominican prior of San Clemente, began excavations beneath the existing 12th-century basilica. Directly underneath he and his successors discovered a 4th-century church, and below that a number of ancient Roman buildings. Both basilicas are dedicated to St Clement, the fourth pope. On the lowest level is a temple devoted to the cult of Mithras, a mystical all-male religion imported from Persia which rivalled Christianity for popularity.

**VISITORS' CHECKLIST**

Via di San Giovanni in Laterano. **Map** 7 B1. ***Tel*** *06 774 00 21.* *85, 87, 117, 186, 810, 850.* **M** *Colosseo.* *3.* *9am–12:30pm, 3–6pm Mon–Sat (from noon Sun & public hols). Last adm: 20 mins before closing.* *to excavations.*

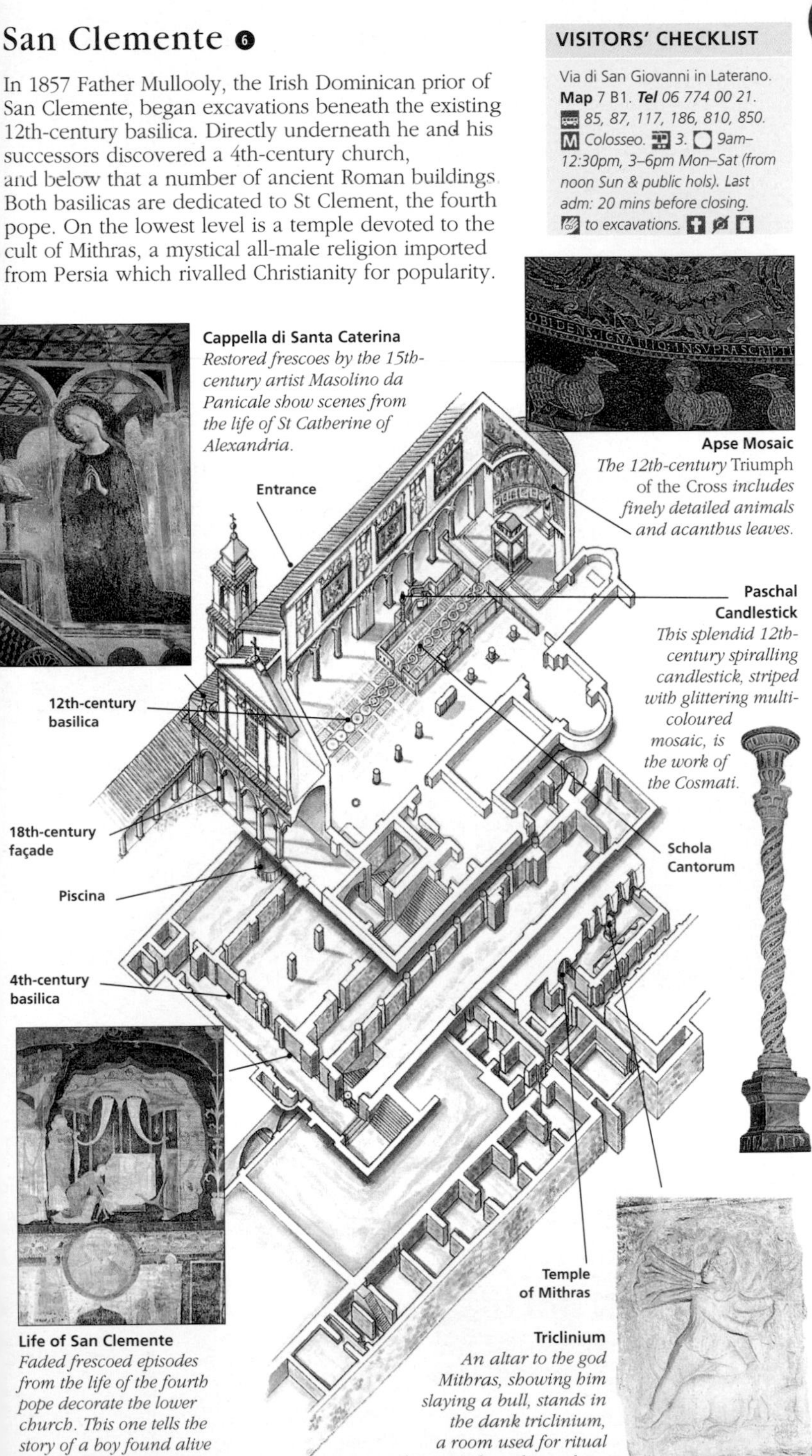


**Cappella di Santa Caterina**
*Restored frescoes by the 15th-century artist Masolino da Panicale show scenes from the life of St Catherine of Alexandria.*

**Apse Mosaic**
*The 12th-century* Triumph of the Cross *includes finely detailed animals and acanthus leaves.*

**Paschal Candlestick**
*This splendid 12th-century spiralling candlestick, striped with glittering multi-coloured mosaic, is the work of the Cosmati.*

**Life of San Clemente**
*Faded frescoed episodes from the life of the fourth pope decorate the lower church. This one tells the story of a boy found alive in his tomb under the sea.*

**Triclinium**
*An altar to the god Mithras, showing him slaying a bull, stands in the dank triclinium, a room used for ritual banquets by cult members.*

# San Giovanni in Laterano 7

San Giovanni, the cathedral of Rome, was founded by Emperor Constantine in the early 4th century. It has been rebuilt several times, notably in 1646 when Borromini restyled the interior, but retains its original basilica form. Before the papacy moved to Avignon in 1309, the adjoining Lateran Palace was the official papal residence. The present structure dates from 1589, but older parts survive, like the Scala Santa (Holy Staircase) which Christ is said to have climbed at his trial.

## VISITORS' CHECKLIST

Piazza di San Giovanni in Laterano. **Map** 8 D2. ***Tel*** *06 69 88 64 33.* *16, 81, 85, 87, 650.* *3.* *San Giovanni.* **Cathedral** *7am–6:30pm daily.* **Cloisters** *9am–6pm daily.* **Museum** *9am–1pm Mon–Sat (last admission noon).* **Baptistry** *8am–12:30pm, 4–7pm daily.*

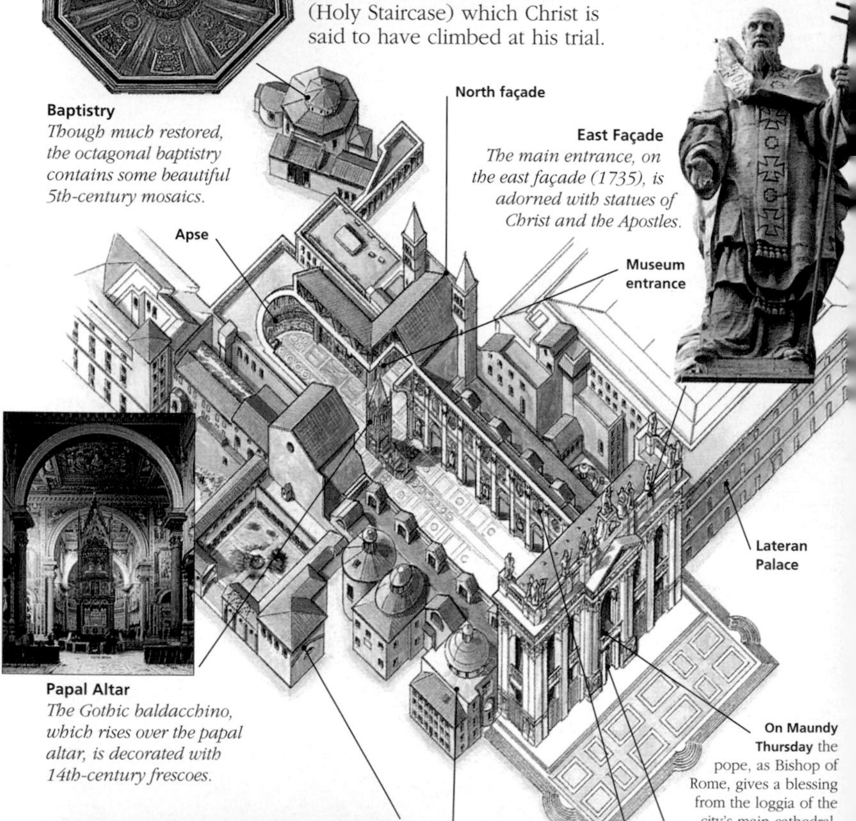

**Baptistry**
*Though much restored, the octagonal baptistry contains some beautiful 5th-century mosaics.*

North façade

**East Façade**
*The main entrance, on the east façade (1735), is adorned with statues of Christ and the Apostles.*

Apse

Museum entrance

Lateran Palace

**Papal Altar**
*The Gothic baldacchino, which rises over the papal altar, is decorated with 14th-century frescoes.*

**On Maundy Thursday** the pope, as Bishop of Rome, gives a blessing from the loggia of the city's main cathedral.

Main entrance

**The Corsini Chapel** was built in the 1730s for Pope Clement XII Corsini, who lies buried in a porphyry tomb from the Pantheon.

**Cloisters**
*Built by the Vassalletto family in about 1220, the cloisters are remarkable for their twisted columns and inlaid marble mosaics.*

**Boniface VIII Fresco**
*Possibly by Giotto, this fragment shows the pope announcing the Holy Year of 1300, which attracted around two million pilgrims.*

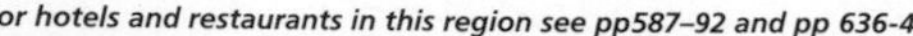

Part of one of the gymnasia in the Baths of Caracalla

## Baths of Caracalla ❽

Viale delle Terme di Caracalla 52. **Map** 7 A3. ***Tel*** *06 39 96 77 00.* *160, 628.* *3.* *9am–1 hr before sunset Tue–Sun, 9am–2pm Mon.* *1 Jan, 25 Dec.*

Rearing up at the foot of the Aventine Hill are the monolithic red-brick ruins of the Baths of Caracalla. Begun by Emperor Septimius Severus in AD 206, and completed by his son Caracalla in AD 217, they remained in use until the 6th century, when the Goths sabotaged the city's aqueducts.

Going for a bath was one of the social events of the day in ancient Rome. Large complexes such as Caracalla, with a capacity for 1,600 bathers, were not simply places to have a natter and get washed, but also areas which offered an impressive array of facilities: art galleries, gymnasia, gardens, libraries, conference rooms, lecture rooms and shops selling food and drink.

A Roman bath was a long and complicated business, beginning with a form of Turkish bath, followed by a spell in the *caldarium,* a large hot room with pools of water to moisten the atmosphere. Then came the lukewarm *tepidarium,* followed by a visit to the large central meeting place known as the *frigidarium,* and finally a plunge into the *natatio,* an open-air swimming pool. For the rich, this was followed by a rub-down with scented woollen cloth.

Most of the rich marble decorations of the baths were scavenged by the Farnese family in the 16th century to adorn the rooms of Palazzo Farnese *(see p401).* There are, however, statues and mosaics from the Baths in the Museo Nazionale Archeologico in Naples *(see pp490–91)* and in the Vatican's Gregorian Profane Museum *(see p422).*

So dramatic is the setting that it used to be the regular venue for the open-air opera season in August.

## Pyramid of Caius Cestius ❾

Piazzale Ostiense. **Map** 6 E4. *23, 95, 280.* *3.* *Piramide.*

Caius Cestius was a wealthy but unimportant 1st-century BC *praetor,* or senior magistrate. At the time, inspired by the Cleopatra scandals, there was a craze for all things Egyptian, and Caius decided to commission himself a pyramid as a tomb. Set into the Aurelian Wall near Porta San Paolo, it is built of brick and faced with white marble; according to an inscription, it took just 330 days to build in 12 BC.

The Pyramid of Caius Cestius on Piazzale Ostiense

## Protestant Cemetery ❿

Cimitero Acattolico, Via di Caio Cestio. **Map** 6 D4. ***Tel*** *06 574 19 00.* *23, 280.* *3.* *9am–5pm Mon–Sat, 9am–1pm Sun. Last adm: 30 mins before closing.* **Donation**.

Non-Catholics have been buried in this cemetery behind the Aurelian Wall since 1738. In the oldest part (on the left as you enter) is the grave of the poet John Keats, who died in 1821 in a house on Piazza di Spagna *(see p408).* He wrote his own epitaph: "Here lies one whose name was writ in water". Close by rest the ashes of Percy Bysshe Shelley, who drowned in 1822.

The interior of Santa Sabina

## Santa Sabina ⓫

Piazza Pietro d'Illiria 1. **Map** 6 D2. ***Tel*** *06 57 94 06 00.* *23, 44, 95, 170, 781.* *6:30am–12:45pm, 3–7pm daily (to 6pm in winter).*

High on the Aventine stands an early Christian basilica, founded by Peter of Illyria in AD 425 and later given to the Dominican order. It was restored to its original simplicity in the early 20th century. Light filters through 9th-century windows on to a nave framed by pale Corinthian columns. Above the main door is a blue and gold 5th-century mosaic inscription to Peter. In the side portico outside is a 5th-century panelled door carved with biblical scenes, notably one of the oldest images of the Crucifixion (top left-hand corner).

# Further Afield

It is well worth making the effort to see some of Rome's outlying sights. Highlights are the Villa Giulia, home to a magnificent Etruscan museum, and the Museo Borghese on the splendid Villa Borghese estate, with its extraordinary collection of virtuoso statues by Bernini. Other sights range from ancient churches and catacombs to the more modern suburb of EUR, a strange architectural medley begun by Mussolini in the 1930s.

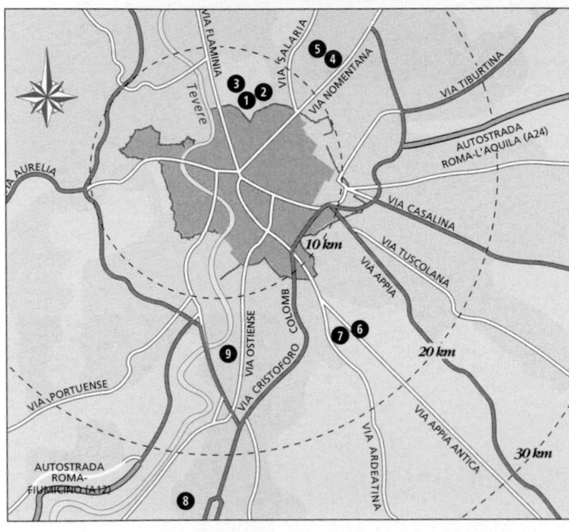


## SIGHTS AT A GLANCE

**Churches and Temples**
Sant'Agnese fuori le Mura 4
Santa Costanza 5
San Paolo fuori le Mura 9

**Museums and Galleries**
Museo e Galleria Borghese 2
Villa Giulia 3

**Parks and Gardens**
Villa Borghese 1

**Ancient Roads and Sites**
Via Appia Antica 6
Catacombs 7

**City Districts**
EUR 8

**KEY**

- Central Rome
- Suburbs
- Motorway
- Major road
- Minor road
- City walls

**10 km = 6 miles**

## Villa Borghese 1

**Map** 3 B1. *52, 53, 88, 95, 116, 490.* *3, 19.* **Park** *dawn–sunset daily.*

The villa and its park were designed in 1605 for Cardinal Scipione Borghese, the sybaritic nephew of Pope Paul V. An extravagant patron of the arts, he amassed one of Europe's finest collections of paintings, statues and antiquities, many of which are still displayed in the villa which he built especially to house his antique sculptures.

The **park** was one of the first of its kind in Rome, its formal gardens divided by avenues and graced with statues. It contained 400 newly planted trees, garden sculpture by Bernini's father, Pietro, along with many ingenious fountains, "secret" flower gardens, enclosures of exotic animals and birds, and even a grotto with artificial rain. There was also a speaking robot and a trick chair, which trapped anyone who sat in it. At first the grounds were open to the public, but after a visitor was shocked by the collection of erotic paintings, Paul V decided to keep the park private.

In 1773 work began on redesigning the park in the wilder, Romantic style made fashionable by landscape artists like Claude Lorrain and Poussin. Over the next few years mock-Classical temples, fountains and *casine* (summer-houses) were added. In 1901, the park and villa were acquired by the state, and in 1911 the area was chosen as the site for the International Exhibition. Pavilions were built by many of the world's nations, the most impressive of which is the **British School at Rome** by Edwin Lutyens. In the northeastern corner of the park lie the Museo Zoologico and a small redeveloped zoo, known as the Bioparco, where the emphasis is on conservation. Today the estates of the Villa Borghese, Villa Giulia and the Pincio gardens form one vast park, with the **Giardino del Lago**, at its centre, named after an artificial boating lake. Its main entrance is marked by an 18th-century copy of the Arch of Septimius Severus while on the lake's island is a fake Ionic temple to the Greek god of health, Aesculapius, designed by the 18th-century architect Antonis Aspurucci.

**Temple of Aesculapius, an 18th-century folly, at the Villa Borghese**

A circular Temple of Diana folly lies between the Porta Pinciana, at the top of Via Veneto, and Piazza di Siena, a grassy amphitheatre which hosts Rome's international horse show in May. Its umbrella pines inspired the composer Ottorino Respighi to write *The Pines of Rome* (1924). The open-air opera season is also held in the park.

To the northwest of the park is the Galleria Nazionale d'Arte Moderna, and the Orangery is now home to the Carlo Bilotti museum.

***Sacred and Profane Love* by Titian (1514), in the Galleria Borghese**

## Museo e Galleria Borghese ❷

Villa Borghese, Piazzale Scipione Borghese 5. ***Tel*** *06 328 10.* *52, 53, 116, 910.* *3, 19.* *9am–7pm Tue–Sun (reservations advised).* *public hols.* **www**.galleriaborghese.it

Cardinal Scipione Borghese's villa was designed in 1605 as a typical Roman country house, with its wings projecting into the surrounding gardens. It was built by Flaminio Ponzio, Pope Paul V's architect, and was used by Scipione for entertaining guests and for displaying his impressive collection of paintings and sculpture. Between 1801 and 1809 Prince Camillo Borghese, husband to Napoleon's sister Pauline, unfortunately sold many of the family paintings to his brother-in-law, and swapped 200 of Scipione's Classical statues for an estate in Piedmont. These statues are still in the Louvre and, as a consequence, the remaining antique Classical collection is less interesting than it might once have been. However, the hedonistic cardinal was an enthusiastic patron of the arts and the sculptures he commissioned from artists such as the young Bernini now rank among their most famous works.

The eight rooms of the ground floor of the Villa Borghese are set around a central hall, the Salone. The most famous statue is one of Bernini's finest works, *Apollo and Daphne* (1624) in room 3, which shows the nymph Daphne with bay leaves sprouting from her outstretched fingers, roots growing from her toes and rough bark enfolding her smooth body, as she begins to metamorphose into a laurel tree to escape being abducted by the god Apollo. Abduction is also the theme of *The Rape of Proserpina,* again by Bernini, in room 4. Depicting Pluto, the god of the underworld, carrying Proserpina, daughter of Ceres, off to be his bride, the sculpture is a virtuoso piece in which Bernini contrasts the taut musculature of Pluto with the soft yielding flesh of Proserpina, whose thigh dimples in his iron grip.

The third famous Bernini piece, which dates from 1623, is *David* in room 2. The artist captures the tensed, grimacing youth the moment before he releases the stone that slew Goliath. It is said that Pope Urban VIII held a mirror up to Bernini so that the sculptor could model David's face on his own. In the next alcove is the Villa Borghese's most infamous work – a sculpture, executed in 1805 by Canova, of Pauline Borghese as *Venus Victrix* (Venus the Conqueror). The semi-naked Pauline reclining on a chaise-longue shocked those who saw it and Pauline's husband kept the statue locked away, even denying Canova access to it.

**Bernini's *Apollo and Daphne* (1624)**

**Detail of *Rape of Proserpina* by Bernini (1622), Museo Borghese**

The next room holds a selection of antiquities, notably a Roman copy of a plump *Bacchus* by the 4th-century BC Greek sculptor Praxiteles, and fragments of a 3rd-century AD mosaic found on one of the Borghese estates in Torrenova, showing gladiators battling with wild animals.

The Galleria Borghese, on the upper floor, houses some magnificent Baroque and Renaissance paintings. Works on display include Raphael's masterpiece, the *Deposition,* various works by Caravaggio, the graceful *Danäe* by the 16th-century artist Correggio, as well as works by Pinturicchio, Barocci, Rubens and Titian.

# Villa Giulia ❸

This villa was built in 1550 as a country retreat for Pope Julius III. Designed by Vignola and Ammannati, with contributions by Michelangelo and Vasari, it was intended for entertaining guests of the Vatican, such as Queen Christina of Sweden, rather than as a permanent home. The gardens were planted with 36,000 trees and peppered with pavilions and fountains. Villa Giulia also used to house an outstanding collection of sculptures: 160 boats filled with statues and ornaments were sent to the Vatican after the death of Pope Julius III in 1555.

Since 1889 the villa has been home to the Museo Nazionale Etrusco, an impressive collection of pre-Roman antiquities from central Italy.

## VISITORS' CHECKLIST

Piazzale di Villa Giulia 9.
**Tel** *06 322 65 71.*
*52, 95.* *3, 19.*
*8:30am–7:30pm Tue–Sun.*
*1 Jan, 25 Dec.*
*with seven days' notice.*

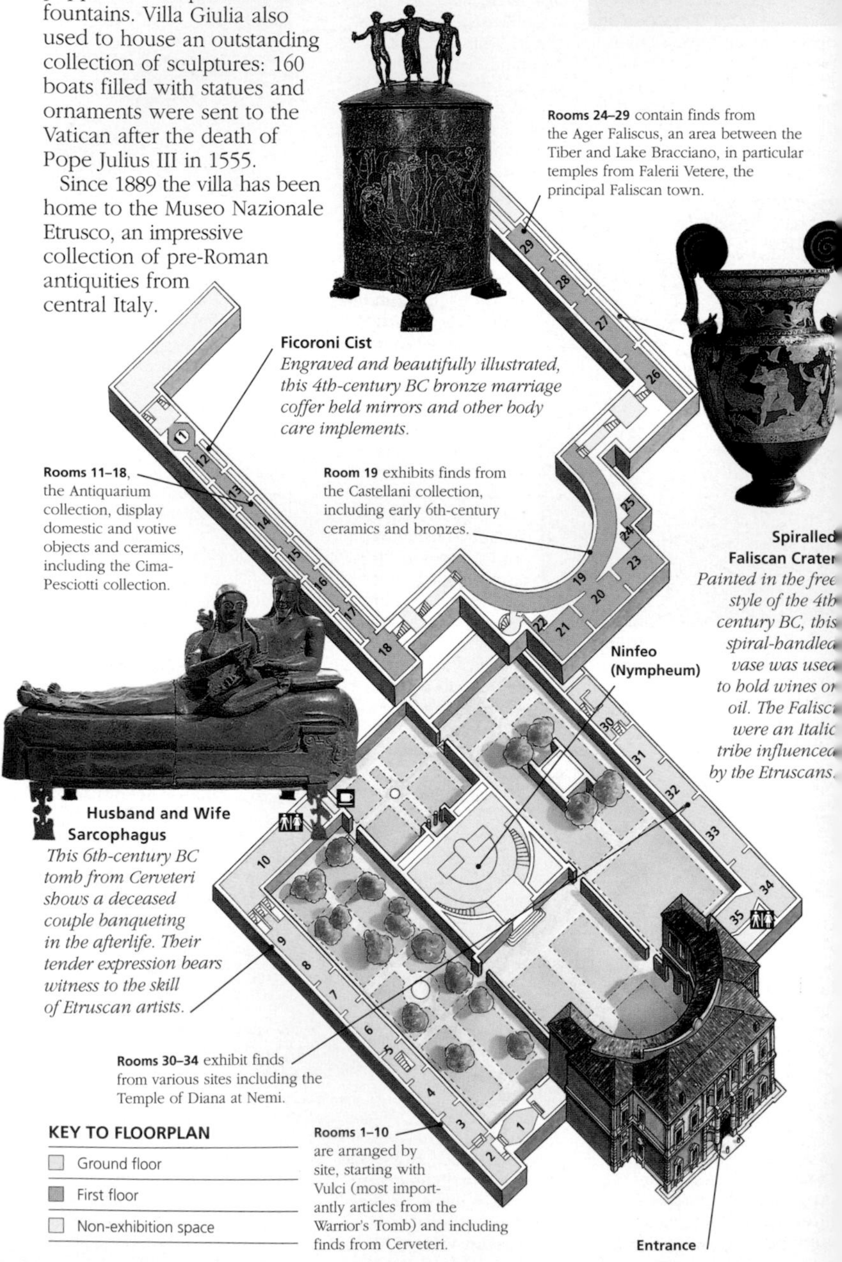

**Rooms 24–29** contain finds from the Ager Faliscus, an area between the Tiber and Lake Bracciano, in particular temples from Falerii Vetere, the principal Faliscan town.

**Ficoroni Cist**
*Engraved and beautifully illustrated, this 4th-century BC bronze marriage coffer held mirrors and other body care implements.*

**Spiralled Faliscan Crater**
*Painted in the free style of the 4th century BC, this spiral-handled vase was used to hold wines or oil. The Falisci were an Italic tribe influenced by the Etruscans.*

**Rooms 11–18**, the Antiquarium collection, display domestic and votive objects and ceramics, including the Cima-Pesciotti collection.

**Room 19** exhibits finds from the Castellani collection, including early 6th-century ceramics and bronzes.

**Ninfeo (Nympheum)**

**Husband and Wife Sarcophagus**
*This 6th-century BC tomb from Cerveteri shows a deceased couple banqueting in the afterlife. Their tender expression bears witness to the skill of Etruscan artists.*

**Rooms 30–34** exhibit finds from various sites including the Temple of Diana at Nemi.

**Rooms 1–10** are arranged by site, starting with Vulci (most importantly articles from the Warrior's Tomb) and including finds from Cerveteri.

**Entrance**



## KEY TO FLOORPLAN

- Ground floor
- First floor
- Non-exhibition space

*For hotels and restaurants in this region see pp587–92 and pp636–41*

Apse mosaic in Sant'Agnese, showing the saint flanked by two popes

## Sant'Agnese fuori le Mura ❹

Via Nomentana 349.
*Tel 06 861 08 40. 36, 60, 84, 90.*
*7:30am–noon, 4–7:45pm daily.*
*to catacombs.*

Sant'Agnese fuori le Mura was built in the 4th century above the crypt of the 13-year-old martyr St Agnes, and although much altered it retains the form of the original basilica. According to legend it was founded by Constantine's daughter Constantia, who was cured from leprosy after sleeping beside Agnes's tomb.

In the 7th-century apse mosaic, St Agnes appears as a bejewelled Byzantine empress in a stole of gold and a violet robe. Tradition has it that she appeared like this eight days after her death holding a white lamb. On 21 January two lambs are blessed in the church and a vestment called a *pallium* is woven from their wool, to be given to a new archbishop.

## Santa Costanza ❺

Via Nomentana 349. *Tel 06 861 08 40. 36, 60, 84, 90. 9am–noon, 4–6pm daily (Sun pm only).*

This circular church was built in the early 4th century as a mausoleum for Emperor Constantine's daughters, Constantia and Helena. The dome and its drum are supported by an arcade that rests on 12 magnificent pairs of granite columns, while the encircling ambulatory has a barrel-vaulted ceiling decorated with the world's earliest surviving Christian mosaics. Dating from the 4th century, they are thought to have been copied from a secular Roman floor and include flowers, animals and birds. There is even a charming scene of a Roman grape-harvest, though the wine is said by Christians to represent Christ's blood.

In a niche on the far side of the church is a replica of Constantia's ornate porphyry sarcophagus, carved with cherubs crushing grapes. The original was moved to the Vatican Museums in 1790.

Circular interior of the 4th-century church of Santa Costanza

The sanctity of Constantia is somewhat debatable. Described by the historian Marcellinus as a fury incarnate, constantly goading her equally unpleasant husband, Hannibalianus, to violence, her canonization was probably the result of some confusion with a saintly nun of the same name.

## Via Appia Antica ❻

*118, 218, 760.*

Cypresses lining the Via Appia

The first part of the Via Appia was built in 312 BC by Appius Claudius Caecus. In 190 BC, when it was extended to the ports of Taranto and Brindisi, the road became Rome's link with its empire in the East. It was the route taken by the funeral processions of the dictator Sulla (78 BC) and Emperor Augustus (AD 14), and it was along this road that St Paul was led as a prisoner to Rome in AD 56. The church of Domine Quo Vadis? marks the spot where St Peter is said to have met Christ when fleeing Rome.

The road is lined with ruined family tombs, decaying monuments, and collective burial places *(columbaria)*. Beneath the fields on either side lies a maze of catacombs, including those of San Callisto and San Sebastiano.

## Catacombs ❼

Via Appia Antica 126. 118, 218. **San Callisto** ***Tel*** *06 51 30 15 80.* *9am–noon, 2–5pm Thu–Tue.* *1 Jan, Feb, Easter Sun, 25 Dec.*

In burying their dead in underground cemeteries outside the city walls, the early Christians were simply obeying the laws of the time. They were not forced to use them because of persecution, as later popular myth has suggested. Many saints were buried here, and the catacombs later became shrines and places of pilgrimage.

Today several catacombs are open to the public. The vast Catacombs of San Callisto, hewn from volcanic tufa, contain niches, or *loculi*, which held two or three bodies, as well as the burial places of several early popes. Close by, walls in the Catacombs of San Sebastiano are covered in graffiti invoking St Peter and St Paul, whose remains may once have been moved here.

**Engraving of Christian ceremony in Catacombs of San Callisto (AD 50)**

## EUR ❽

*170, 671, 714.* *EUR Fermi, EUR Palasport.* **Museo della Civiltà Romana** *Piazza G Agnelli 10.* ***Tel*** *06 54 22 09 19.* *9am–2pm Tue–Sat (till 1:30pm Sun). Last adm 1 hr before closing.* *1 Jan, 1 May, 25 Dec.*

The Esposizione Universale di Roma (EUR), a suburb to the south of the city, was originally built for an international exhibition, a kind of "Work Olympics", that was planned for 1942, but never took place because of the outbreak of war. The architecture was intended to glorify Fascism, and as a result the bombastic style of the buildings can look overblown and rhetorical to modern eyes. Of all the buildings the best known is probably the Palazzo della Civiltà del Lavoro (the Palace of the Civilization of Work), an unmistakable landmark for people arriving from Fiumicino airport.

**EUR's Palazzo della Civiltà del Lavoro, the "Square Colosseum"**

The scheme was eventually completed in the 1950s. Despite the area's dubious architecture, EUR has been a planning success, and people are still keen to live here. As well as residential housing, the vast marble halls along the wide boulevards are also home to a number of government offices and museums. Best among the latter is the Museo della Civiltà Romana, famous for its casts of the reliefs from the Column of Trajan, and for a large scale model depicting 4th-century Rome with all the buildings which then stood within the Aurelian walls. The south of the suburb features a lake and shady park, and the huge domed Palazzo dello Sport, built for the 1960 Olympics.

## San Paolo fuori le Mura ❾

Via Ostiense 186. *23, 128, 170, 670, 761, 766, 769.* *San Paolo.* ***Tel*** *06 541 03 41.* *7am–6:30pm daily.* **Cloister** *9am–6pm daily.*

Today's church is a faithful if soulless reconstruction of the great 4th-century basilica destroyed by fire in 1823. Only a few fragments of the earlier church survived, most notably the cloister (1241), with its pairs of colourful inlaid columns, considered one of the most beautiful in Rome.

Elsewhere, the church's triumphal arch is decorated on one side with heavily restored 5th-century mosaics, and on the other with mosaics by Pietro Cavallini originally on the façade. The equally fine mosaics (1220) in the apse represent the figures of Christ with St Peter, St Andrew, St Paul and St Luke.

The single most outstanding work of art is the fine marble canopy over the high altar, the work of Arnolfo di Cambio (1285), with the possible assistance of Pietro Cavallini. Below the altar is the *confessio* where it is alleged St Paul was once buried. To its right is an impressive Paschal candlestick dating from the 12th century by Nicolò di Angelo and Pietro Vassalletto.

**19th-century mosaic on façade of San Paolo fuori le Mura**

# Shopping in Rome

Rome has always been a thriving centre for design and shopping. In ancient times, the finest craftsmen were drawn to the city, and artifacts and products of all kinds, including gold, furs and wine, were imported from far-flung corners of the Empire to satisfy the needs of the wealthy local population. Shopping in Rome today in many ways reflects this diverse tradition. Italian designers have a well-deserved reputation for their luxuriously chic style in fashion, knitwear and leather goods (especially shoes and handbags), as well as in interior design, fabrics, ceramics and glass. The artisan tradition is strong, and the love of good design filters through into the smallest items. Rome is not a city for bargains (although it is often better value than Florence or Milan), but the joys of window shopping here will offer plenty of compensation.

## FASHION

Italy is one of the leading lights in high fashion, or *alta moda*. Many famous designers may be based in Milan, but Rome is home to a cluster of sophisticated and internationally distinguished fashion houses. The most notable are probably **Fendi**, **Laura Biagiotti**, **Prada** and **Valentino**, whose studio dominates Piazza Mignanelli.

But even for those unable to splash out on genuine designer gear, much fun can be gained from a stroll down the streets that radiate out from the Piazza di Spagna: some of the window displays here are truly spectacular.

Rome is not a good place to buy everyday wear, since there is a distinct lack of mid-price shops bridging the gap between the dazzlingly priced *alta moda* designer exclusives and the ultra-cheap goods sold in markets. However, at **Discount dell'Alta Moda** you can find end-of-season designer labels at 50 per cent less than the boutique prices.

## BOOKS AND GIFTS

Rome offers huge scope for gift buying, both in the well-established tourist stores in the historic centre and in smaller shops located in less frequented parts of the city that might not feature in your holiday itinerary.

The central Via del Pellegrino is a street crammed with small specialist outlets, such as **Le Tre Ghinee**, which sells ceramics and glass objects. If you are more interested in contemporary design, visit the **Palazzo delle Esposizioni**, where a wide range of objects by famous designers is available.

The **Feltrinelli International** bookshop has an excellent range of foreign-language fiction, as well as non-fiction covering various subjects, including Italian art and architecture, cookery, travel and history. It also stocks some superb photographic, art and cinema posters. For cut-price deals on books try the second-hand stalls in Via delle Terme di Diocleziano and in Largo della Fontanella di Borghese.

Near the Pantheon, the Florentine **Il Papiro** sells a great range of illustrious paper-based products, including diaries, notebooks, envelopes and beautiful seal-and-wax sets that make ideal gifts.

Religious artifacts are readily available in bookshops near the main basilicas, such as the **Libreria Belardetti** near St Peter's. Other shops specialize in religious items for both the clergy and the layperson. Facing the Vatican gates, in Via di Porta Angelica, there are several shops, including **Al Pellegrino Cattolico**, that sell mementos to visiting pilgrims.

## FOOD AND DRINK

If you are tempted to take home some irresistible Italian delicacies, such as pecorino romano cheese, Parma ham, extra virgin olive oil, dried porcini mushrooms, sun-dried tomatoes, olives and grappa, as well as superb wines from Lazio and elsewhere then the traditional food stores, *alimentari,* are a great place to start. Try the well-stocked **Fratelli Fabbi**, near Piazza di Spagna, with its exceptional selection of delicious cold meats and cheeses from every corner of Italy, as well as quality wines and champagnes. A few doors down on the same street is **Focacci**, with its wonderful array of Italian delicacies. The historic but expensive **Volpetti** in Testaccio is synonymous with great service and uncompromising quality. Aside from specializing in unusual cheeses, olive oils, vinegars and a fabulous selection of food hampers, it also stocks a variety of Italian lard and caviar – you can even try before you buy.

In Pinciano, **Casa dei Latticini Micocci** sells a comprehensive range of cheeses from even the most remote regions of Italy, while in Trastevere, the family-run **Antica Caciara Trasteverina** has a vast assortment of local and regional dairy products, which include sheep's ricotta and the Piedmontese *toma del fen*. More local, reasonably priced cheeses are available at **Cisternino**.

If cakes and chocolate feature on your list, then there is plenty of opportunity to satisfy those cravings too. **Chocolat**, in the historic centre, sells brand-name and home-made chocolate and organizes occasional tastings and dinners for connoisseurs, while **Moriondo e Gariglio** specializes in chocolate delights made to traditional Piedmontese recipes. **La Deliziosa**, near Piazza Navona, offers a great range of Italian desserts and cakes; the ricotta-based variety deserves a special mention.

Bear in mind that customs restrictions can apply to certain foodstuffs.

## MARKETS

Rome's open-air markets are quintessential examples of the bubbling exuberance and earthiness for which Romans are renowned. They are wonderfully vivid experiences too, since Italian stallholders have raised the display of even the humblest vegetable to an art form.

The city is dotted with small local food markets, and there are several fascinating well-established markets near the centre. These include **Campo de' Fiori** for foodstuffs, the **Mercato delle Stampe** for old prints, books and magazines, and the **Nuovo Mercato Esquilino** for international foods.

Trastevere's famous flea market, **Porta Portese**, was established shortly after the end of World War II and is said to have grown out of the thriving black market that operated at Tor di Nona, opposite Castel Sant'Angelo, during those lean years. Anything and everything seems to be for sale, piled high on stalls in carefully arranged disorder – clothes, shoes, bags, linen, luggage, camping equipment, towels, pots, pans, kitchen utensils, plants, pets, cassettes and CDs, old LPs and 78s.

If you are looking for a traditional food market in the heart of the old city, Rome's most picturesque market is also its most historical. Its name, Campo de' Fiori *(see p401),* which translates as "field of flowers", sometimes misleads people into expecting a flower market. In fact, the name is said to derive from *Campus Florae* (Flora's square) – Flora being the lover of the great Roman general Pompey. A market has been held in this beautiful central piazza for many centuries. Every morning, except Sunday, the piazza is transformed by an array of stalls selling fruit and vegetables, meat, poultry and fish. One or two stalls also specialize in legumes, rice and dried fruits and nuts.

Throughout the year Rome also plays host to many street fairs. If they coincide with your visit, these are fun to go to, because they normally sell a good variety of local produce, handicrafts and clothes. Seasonal fairs also occur, especially around Christmas; among them is **Natale Oggi**, in the Fiera di Roma, where you can stock up on Italian specialities.

Be sure to keep your wits about you at markets: pickpockets work with lightning speed in the bustling crowds.

## DIRECTORY

### FASHION

**Discount dell'Alta Moda**
Via de Pretis 88.
**Map** 3 C4.
***Tel*** *06 47 82 56 72.*
Also:
Via di Gesù e Maria 14 & 16A.
**Map** 2 F2.
***Tel*** *06 361 37 96.*

**Fendi**
Largo Goldoni 419.
**Map** 10 E3.
***Tel*** *06 33 45 01.*

**Laura Biagiotti**
Via Borgognona 43–44.
**Map** 10 E1.
***Tel*** *06 679 12 05.*

**Prada**
Via Condotti 92–95.
**Map** 3 A2.
***Tel*** *06 679 08 97.*

**Valentino**
Via Bocca di Leone 15.
**Map** 3 A2.
***Tel*** *06 673 94 30.*

### BOOKS AND GIFTS

**Al Pellegrino Cattolico**
Via di Porta Angelica 83.
**Map** 1 C2.
***Tel*** *06 68 80 23 51.*

**Feltrinelli International**
Via VE Orlando 84–86.
**Map** 3 C3.
***Tel*** *06 482 78 78.*

**Libreria Belardetti**
Via della Conciliazione 4A.
**Map** 1 C3.
***Tel*** *06 686 55 02.*

**Palazzo delle Esposizioni**
Via Milano 15–17.
**Map** 3 B4.
***Tel*** *06 48 91 33 61.*

**Il Papiro**
Via del Pantheon 50 (leading to Via degli Orfani).
**Map** 10 D2.
***Tel*** *06 679 55 97.*

**Le Tre Ghinee**
Via del Pellegrino 90.
**Map** 2 E4.
***Tel*** *06 687 27 39.*

### FOOD AND DRINK

**Antica Caciara Trasteverina**
Via San Francesco a Ripa 140A/B. **Map** 5 C1.
***Tel*** *06 581 28 15.*

**Casa dei Latticini Micocci**
Via Collina 14.
**Map** 4 D2.
***Tel*** *06 474 17 84.*

**Chocolat**
Via del Teatro Valle 54.
**Map** 10 D3.
***Tel*** *06 68 13 55 45.*

**Cisternino**
Vicolo del Gallo 18–19.
**Map** 9 C4.
***Tel*** *06 687 28 75.*

**La Deliziosa**
Vicolo Savelli 50.
**Map** 9 B3.
***Tel*** *06 68 80 31 55.*

**Focacci**
Via della Croce 43.
**Map** 2 F2.
***Tel*** *06 679 12 28.*

**Fratelli Fabbi**
Via della Croce 28.
**Map** 2 F2.
***Tel*** *06 679 06 12.*

**Moriondo e Gariglio**
Via del Piè di Marmo 21.
**Map** 10 E3.
***Tel*** *06 699 08 56.*

**Volpetti**
Via Marmorata 47.
**Map** 6 D2.
***Tel*** *06 574 23 52.*

### MARKETS

**Campo de' Fiori**
Piazza Campo de' Fiori.
**Map** 2 E4 & 9 C4. 7am–1:30pm Mon–Sat.

**Mercato delle Stampe**
Largo della Fontanella di Borghese.
**Map** 2 F3 & 10 D1.
9am–1pm Mon–Sat.

**Natale Oggi**
Fiera di Roma, Portuense district.

**Nuovo Mercato Esquilino**
Via Principe Amedeo.
**Map** 4 E4.
9am–2pm Mon–Sat.

**Porta Portese**
Via Portuense & Via Ippolito Nievo.
**Map** 5 C3.
6:30am–2pm Sun.

# Entertainment in Rome

There's a particular excitement attached to entertainment in Rome. Football and opera, for example, are worth experiencing for sheer atmosphere alone, whether or not you are a fan. There is also a good jazz scene, with international stars appearing alongside local talent. Unexpectedly, given the general shutdown among shops and restaurants, the summer is Rome's liveliest time in terms of entertainment and cultural events, with the city's Renaissance squares, vast parks, villa gardens, Classical ruins and other open spaces hosting various arts festivals. Concerts and films take on an added dimension when performances take place beneath the stars in the many open-air arenas across the city. Rome also has plenty of nightclubs to choose from.

## PRACTICAL INFORMATION

Good sources of information about what's on are the listings magazine *Roma c'è* and *Trovaroma*, the weekly Thursday supplement to *La Repubblica* newspaper. Also worth getting hold of is *L'Evento,* available from the Rome Tourist Office (*see p665*), which gives details in English of cultural events in the city.

## BOOKING TICKETS

Among the ticket agencies that will book seats for some performances for you (for a small fee) are **Orbis** and **Box Office**. Many theatres do not accept telephone bookings – you have to visit the box office in person. They will charge you a *prevendita* supplement (about 10 per cent of the normal price) for any tickets sold in advance. The **Teatro dell'Opera** box office handles sales for both summer and winter seasons. Tickets for most big rock and jazz events can be bought at Orbis and at larger record shops, such as **Ricordi Media Store**. Look out for *due per uno* coupons in local bars – these allow two people entrance for the price of one.

## OPEN-AIR ENTERTAINMENT

Open-air opera, cinema, classical music and jazz concerts fill the Roman calendar from late June until the end of September. Both the **Cineporto**, a festival held along the Tiber, at the Ponte Milvio, and the **Festival di Massenzio**, at the Forum, offer films, live music, food and small exhibitions in July and August. The summer months also bring excellent open-air rock, jazz and world-music festivals, while Rome's main autumn performing-arts festival, **RomaEuropa**, has occasional performances in the grounds of the Villa Medici. Theatre also moves outside in the summer months, and some cinemas roll back their ceilings for open-air screenings.

More traditional is Trastevere's community festival, the **Festa de Noiantri** *(see p67),* with music, processions and fireworks. This religious festival begins on the Saturday after 16 July, and celebrations continue until the end of the month.

## CLASSICAL MUSIC AND DANCE

Classical concerts take place in a surprising number of venues. Tickets for opera premieres may be hard to find, but soloists, groups or orchestras playing in gardens, churches, villas or ancient ruins are more accessible.

World-renowned soloists and orchestras make appearances throughout the year in venues such as the Renzo Piano-designed **Parco della Musica** and the **Accademia Filarmonica Romana**. Past visitors have included Luciano Pavarotti and Placido Domingo, the Berlin Philharmonic and prima ballerina Sylvie Guillem. One of the most innovative programmes of classical and contemporary music is provided by the **Aula Magna dell'Università La Sapienza**. The opera season starts late at the **Teatro dell'Opera**, between November and January. The great ballet classics are also staged at this venue. The **Equilibrio Festival** in February brings contemporary dance to the city; performances take place mainly at the Parco della Musica.

## ROCK, JAZZ AND WORLD MUSIC

Rome's non-classical music scene is unpredictable and subject to vast seasonal changes. However, there is a huge variety of music at the many clubs and stadiums, such as the **Palalottomatica** and the **Stadio Olimpico**, which attract foreign and home-grown stars. The best jazz musicians play at the splendid **Casa del Jazz**, and **Alexanderplatz**. Trastevere's **Big Mama** is one of the city's legendary addresses for important jazz names, while world music is well served at the aptly named **Villaggio Globale**.

For smaller venues you might need to buy a monthly or annual membership card (between €2 and €11), which often includes the entrance fee for smaller bands.

## CINEMA AND THEATRE

Cinema-going is a popular pastime in Rome, with around 40 films on show on an average weekday. Most Roman cinemas are *prima visione* (first run) and show the latest international films in dubbed versions. The best cinemas for decor and comfort are the **Fiamma** (two screens) and the **Barberini** (three screens). Films in their original language are shown at the **Metropolitan** (daily) and at the **Nuovo Olimpia** (Mondays). Smaller art cinemas, such as the **Azzurro Scipioni**, are more likely to show subtitled versions of foreign films.

Theatre productions are performed in Italian whether the plays are national classics or by foreign playwrights. The main theatres – **Teatro Argentina**, **Teatro Quirino** and **Teatro Valle** – offer a selection by great Italian playwrights. There are also performances of traditional cabaret, dance and avant-garde theatre at the **Teatro India**. Theatre tickets cost between €8 and €50 and can generally be booked only in advance by visiting the theatre box office in person or through agencies such as Box Office.

## NIGHTLIFE

Rome's nightlife has never been as vibrant as it is today. Recent years have witnessed a sharp rise in the number of bars and clubs, all catering for an ever more demanding clientele. Once the choice was limited to a few well-established bars in the centre and the hugely popular clubs in Testaccio, such as the unashamedly commercial **Akab Cave** or the more cutting-edge **Locanda Atlantide**, which hosts a whole range of DJs from funk to reggae. Now, though, the capital offers a wide range of options designed to satisfy all tastes and budgets.

Head first to a stylish pre-clubbing venue such as **'Gusto**, where you can rub shoulders with out-on-the-town locals taking advantage of the range of facilities – on three sites there is a restaurant, a pizzeria, a wine bar and occasional live music. Alternatively, for a more leisurely start to your evening simply relax in a wine bar in one of the historic centre's breath-taking squares.

If you are looking for a gay venue, **Coming Out**, near the Colosseum, attracts both gay and straight drinkers, and **Alpheus** just off Via Ostiense regularly hosts gay nights.

For an alternative edge to Rome's vivacious nightlife, try out the *centri sociali,* illegally occupied buildings that have been converted into arts and entertainment centres. Top billing goes to **Brancaleone**, which features Italian and international DJs for the best in electronic and house tunes.

A night out in Rome can be expensive – you can be charged as much as €10 for a cocktail. For a cheaper alternative, visit one of the many bars in the area around San Lorenzo.

## DIRECTORY

### BOOKING TICKETS

**Box Office**
Galleria Alberto Sordi (inside Feltrinelli bookshop). **Map** 10 E2.
***Tel*** *06 679 49 57.*

**Orbis**
Piazza dell'Esquilino 37. **Map** 4 D4.
***Tel*** *06 474 47 76.*

**Ticketeria**
**www**.ticketeria.it

### CLASSICAL MUSIC AND DANCE

**Accademia Filarmonica Romana**
Via Flaminia 118.
***Tel*** *06 320 17 52.*
**www**.filarmonicaromana.org

**Aula Magna dell'Università La Sapienza**
Piazzale Aldo Moro 5. **Map** 4 F3. ***Tel*** *06 361 00 51.* **www**.concertiiuc.it

**Parco della Musica**
Viale de Coubertin 30.
***Tel*** *06 80 24 12 81* (info); *89 29 82* (credit card sales).
**www**.auditorium.com

**RomaEuropa**
Via dei Magazzini Generali 20a.
***Tel*** *06 45 55 30 00.*
**http**://romaeuropa.net

**Teatro dell'Opera**
Piazza Beniamino Gigli 1. **Map** 3 C3.
***Tel*** *06 48 16 02 55.*
**www**.operaroma.it

### ROCK, JAZZ AND WORLD MUSIC

**Alexanderplatz**
Via Ostia 9. **Map** 1 B1.
***Tel*** *06 58 33 57 81.*

**Big Mama**
Vicolo San Francesco a Ripa 18.
**Map** 5 C2.
***Tel*** *06 581 25 51.*

**Casa del Jazz**
Viale di Porta Ardeatina 55. **Map** 7 A4.
***Tel*** *06 70 47 31.*
**www**.casajazz.it

**Palalottomatica**
Piazzale dello Sport.
***Tel*** *199 128 800.*

**Stadio Olimpico**
Viale dei Gladiatori (north-west of city centre, across the Tiber by Monte Mario).

**Villaggio Globale**
Ex-Mattatoio, Lungotevere Testaccio 2. **Map** 6 D4.
***Tel*** *334 179 00 06.*

### CINEMA AND THEATRE

**Azzurro Scipioni**
Via degli Scipioni 82.
**Map** 1 C2.
***Tel*** *06 39 73 71 61.*

**Barberini**
Piazza Barberini 24.
**Map** 3 B3.
***Tel*** *06 482 10 82.*

**Fiamma**
Via Bissolati 47. **Map** 3 C2.
***Tel*** *06 48 55 26.*

**Metropolitan**
Via del Corso 7. **Map** 2 F1.
***Tel*** *06 320 09 33.*

**Nuovo Olimpia**
Via in Lucina 16.
**Map** 10 E1.
***Tel*** *06 686 10 68.*

**Teatro Argentina**
Largo Argentina 56.
**Map** 2 F4.
***Tel*** *06 684 000 311.*
**www**.teatrodiroma.net

**Teatro India**
Via L Pierantoni 6.
**Map** 5 C5.
***Tel*** *06 684 000 311.*

**Teatro Quirino**
Via delle Vergini 7.
**Map** 3 B3 & 10 F2.
***Tel*** *06 679 45 85.*
**www**.teatroquirino.it

**Teatro Valle**
Via del Teatro Valle 21.
**Map** 3 A4 & 10 D3.
***Tel*** *06 68 80 37 94.*
**www**.teatrovalle.it

### NIGHTLIFE

**Akab Cave**
Via di Monte Testaccio 69.
**Map** 6 D4.
***Tel*** *06 57 25 05 85.*

**Alpheus**
Via del Commercio 36–8.
**Map** 8 D5.
***Tel*** *06 574 78 26.*

**Brancaleone**
Via Levanna 13 (in Montesacro).
***Tel*** *06 82 00 43 82.*

**Coming Out**
Via San Giovanni in Laterano 8. **Map** 7 B1.
***Tel*** *06 700 98 71.*

**'Gusto**
Piazza Augusto Imperatore 9. **Map** 2 F2.
***Tel*** *06 322 62 73.*

**Locanda Atlantide**
Via dei Lucani 22b (San Lorenzo district).
***Tel*** *06 44 70 45 40.*

# ROME STREET FINDER

Map references given with sights described in the Rome chapters relate to the maps on the following pages. Map references are also given for hotels *(see pp587–92)* and restaurant listings *(see pp636–41)* and for useful addresses in the *Travellers' Needs* and *Survival Guide* sections at the back of the book. The first figure in the map reference tells you which Street Finder map to turn to, and the letter and number which follow refer to the grid reference on that map. The small map below shows the area of Rome covered by each of the eight maps and the corresponding map number is given in black. All the major sights are sketched out on the maps, and symbols, listed in the key below, are used to indicate the location of other important buildings.

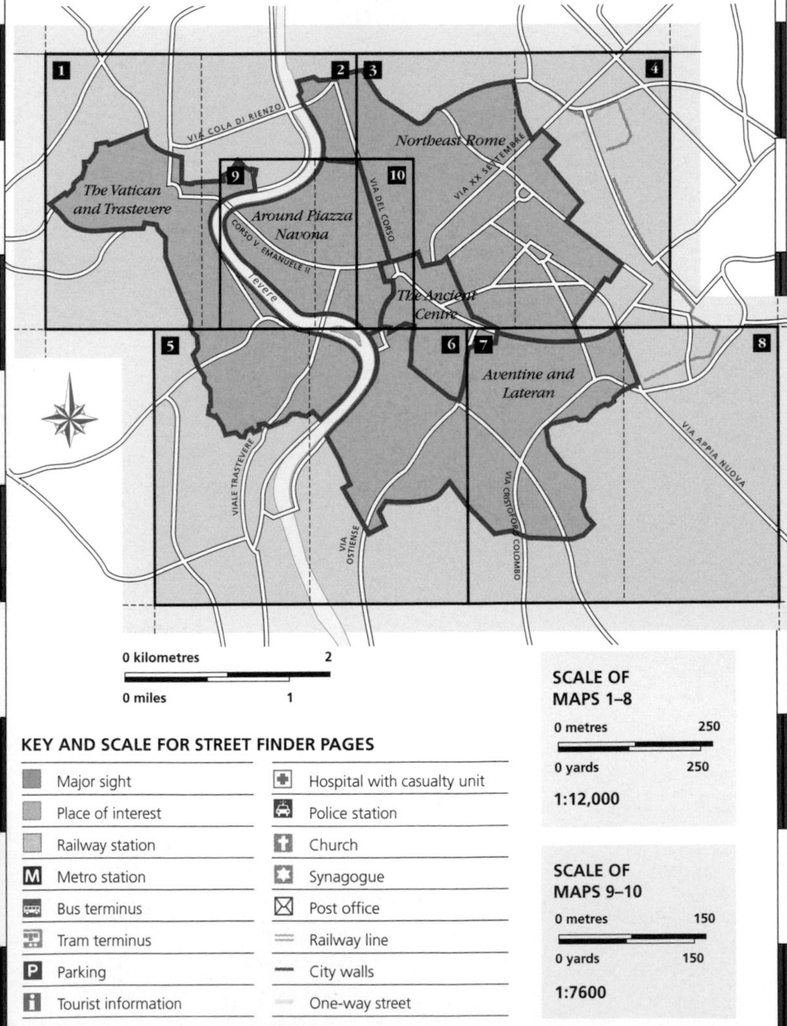


0 kilometres 2

0 miles 1

## KEY AND SCALE FOR STREET FINDER PAGES

| | |
|---|---|
| Major sight | Hospital with casualty unit |
| Place of interest | Police station |
| Railway station | Church |
| Metro station | Synagogue |
| Bus terminus | Post office |
| Tram terminus | Railway line |
| Parking | City walls |
| Tourist information | One-way street |

**SCALE OF MAPS 1–8**

0 metres 250

0 yards 250

**1:12,000**

**SCALE OF MAPS 9–10**

0 metres 150

0 yards 150

**1:7600**

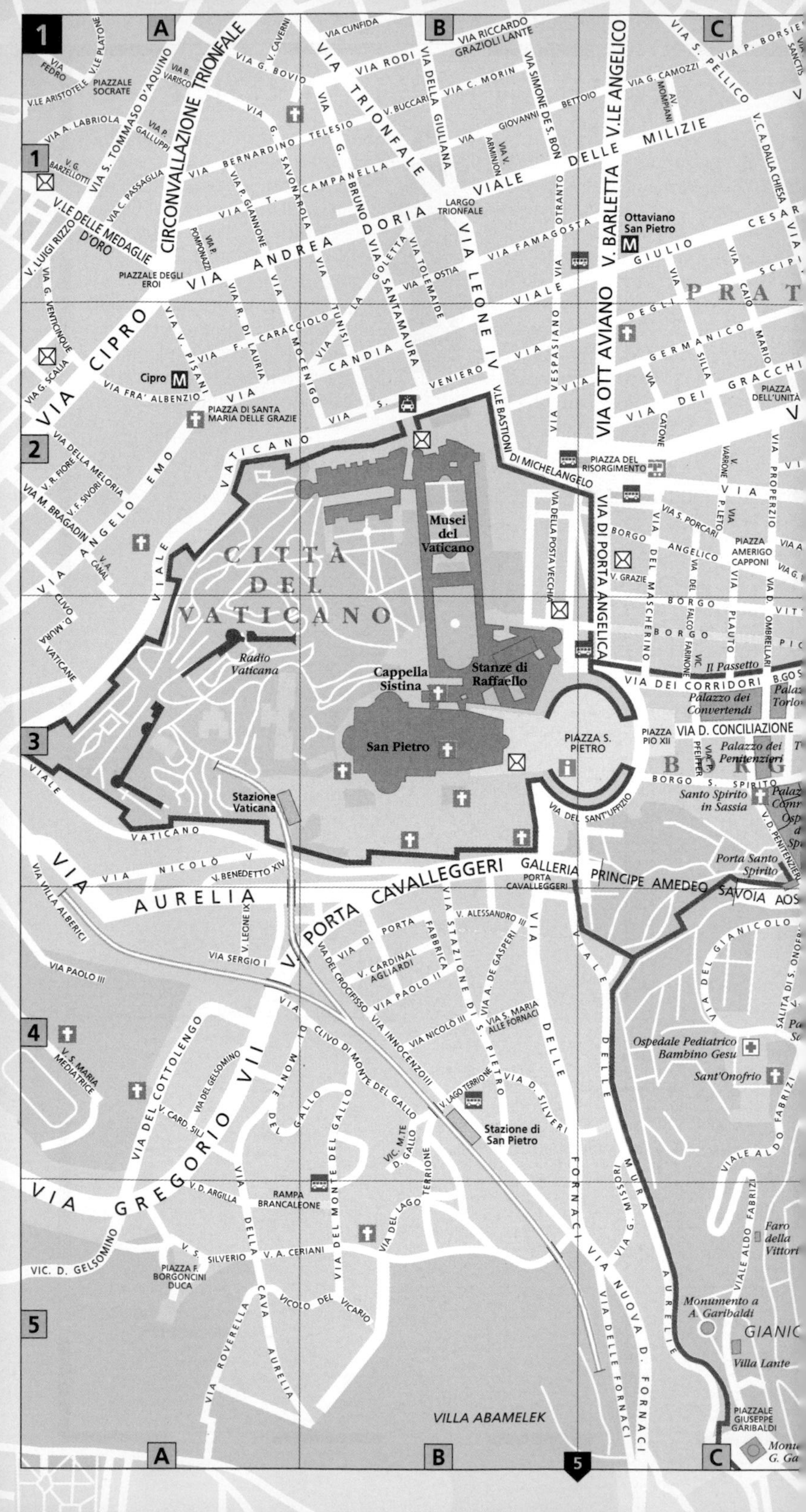
1
A
B
C
1
2
3
4
5
VIA FEDRO
V.LE PLATONE
PIAZZALE SOCRATE
V.LE ARISTOTELE
VIA A. LABRIOLA
VIA S. TOMMASO D'AQUINO
VIA B. VARISCO
VIA P. GALLUPPI
V. G. BARZELLOTTI
VIA C. PASSAGLIA
CIRCONVALLAZIONE TRIONFALE
V.LE DELLE MEDAGLIE D'ORO
V. LUIGI RIZZO
VIA G. VENTICINQUE
VIA G. SCALIA
VIA CIPRO
Cipro
VIA FRA' ALBENZIO
PIAZZALE DEGLI EROI
VIA ANDREA DORIA
VIA G. V. CAVERNI
VIA G. BOVIO
VIA CUNFIDA
VIA RODI
VIA TRIONFALE
VIA RICCARDO GRAZIOLI LANTE
VIA DELLA GIULIANA
VIA C. MORIN
V. BUCCARI
VIA SIMONE DE S. BON
VIA GIOVANNI BETTOLO
VIA G. CAMOZZI
AV. MOMPIANI
VIA S. PELLICO
VIA P. BORSIERI
V.LE ANGELICO
VIA BERNARDINO TELESIO
VIA T. CAMPANELLA
VIA P. GIANNONE
VIA G. SAVONAROLA
VIA G. BRUNO
VIA V. ARMINJON
VIALE DELLE MILIZIE
V.C.A. DALLA CHIESA
LARGO TRIONFALE
VIA P. POMPONAZZI
VIA LA GOLETTA
VIA SANTAMAURA
VIA TOLEMAIDE
VIA OSTIA
VIA LEONE IV
VIA FAMAGOSTA
VIA OTRANTO
V. BARLETTA
Ottaviano San Pietro
VIA GIULIO CESARE
VIA SCIPIONI
PRATI
VIA V. PISANI
VIA R. DI LAURIA
VIA F. CARACCIOLO
VIA TUNISI
VIA MOCENIGO
VIA CANDIA
VIA VENIERO
VIA VESPASIANO
VIA OTT AVIANO
VIA DEGLI
VIA GERMANICO
VIA SILLA
VIA CAIO MARIO
VIA DEI GRACCHI
PIAZZA DELL'UNITÀ
VIA CATONE
PIAZZA DI SANTA MARIA DELLE GRAZIE
VIA S.
VIALE VATICANO
V.LE BASTIONI DI MICHELANGELO
PIAZZA DEL RISORGIMENTO
VIA DELLA MELORIA
V. R. FIORE
V. F. SIVORI
VIA M. BRAGADIN
VIA ANGELO EMO
V. A. CANAL
CLIVO D. MURA VATICANE
CITTÀ DEL VATICANO
Musei del Vaticano
Radio Vaticana
Cappella Sistina
Stanze di Raffaello
San Pietro
Stazione Vaticana
VIA DELLA POSTA VECCHIA
VIA DI PORTA ANGELICA
VIA S. PORCARI
BORGO ANGELICO
V. GRAZIE
VIA DEL MASCHERINO
VIA DEL FALCO
VIC. FARINONE
VIA PLAUTO
BORGO VITTORIO
BORGO PIO
VIA D. OMBRELLARI
VIA V. VARRONE
VIA P. LETO
VIA PROPERZIO
PIAZZA AMERIGO CAPPONI
Il Passetto
VIA DEI CORRIDORI
B.GO S.
Palazzo dei Convertendi
Palazzo Torlonia
PIAZZA PIO XII
VIA D. CONCILIAZIONE
PIAZZA S. PIETRO
VIA PFEIFFER
Palazzo dei Penitenzieri
BORGO
BORGO S. SPIRITO
Santo Spirito in Sassia
V. D. PENITENZIERI
VIA DEL SANT'UFFIZIO
Porta Santo Spirito
VIALE VATICANO
VIA AURELIA
VIA NICOLÒ V
V. BENEDETTO XIV
VIA V. PORTA CAVALLEGGERI
PORTA CAVALLEGGERI
GALLERIA PRINCIPE AMEDEO SAVOIA AOSTA
VIA VILLA ALBERICI
VIA PAOLO III
V. LEONE IX
VIA SERGIO I
VIA DI PORTA FABBRICA
V. CARDINAL AGLIARDI
VIA PAOLO II
VIA DEL CROCIFISSO
V. ALESSANDRO III
VIA STAZIONE DI S. PIETRO
VIA A. DE GASPERI
VIA S. MARIA ALLE FORNACI
VIA NICOLÒ III
VIA INNOCENZO III
VIA CLIVO DI MONTE DEL GALLO
VIA DI MONTE DEL GALLO
V. LAGO TERRIONE
VIA D. SILVERI
Stazione di San Pietro
VIA DELLE FORNACI
VIALE DELLE MURA AURELIE
VIA DEL GIANICOLO
SALITA DI S. ONOFRIO
Ospedale Pediatrico Bambino Gesu
Sant'Onofrio
V. S. MARIA MEDIATRICE
VIA DEL COTTOLENGO
VIA DEL GELSOMINO
V. CARD. SILJ
VIA GREGORIO VII
V. D. ARGILLA
RAMPA BRANCALEONE
VIA DEL MONTE DEL GALLO
VIC. M.TE D. GALLO
VIA DEL LAGO TERRIONE
VIA G. MISSORI
VIA NUOVA D. FORNACI
VIA DELLA CAVA AURELIA
VIC. D. GELSOMINO
V. S. SILVERIO
V. A. CERIANI
PIAZZA F. BORGONCINI DUCA
VICOLO DEL VICARIO
VIA ROVERELLA
VIA DELLE FORNACI
VIALE ALDO FABRIZI
Faro della Vittoria
Monumento a A. Garibaldi
GIANICOLO
Villa Lante
PIAZZALE GIUSEPPE GARIBALDI
Monumento G. Garibaldi
VILLA ABAMELEK
5

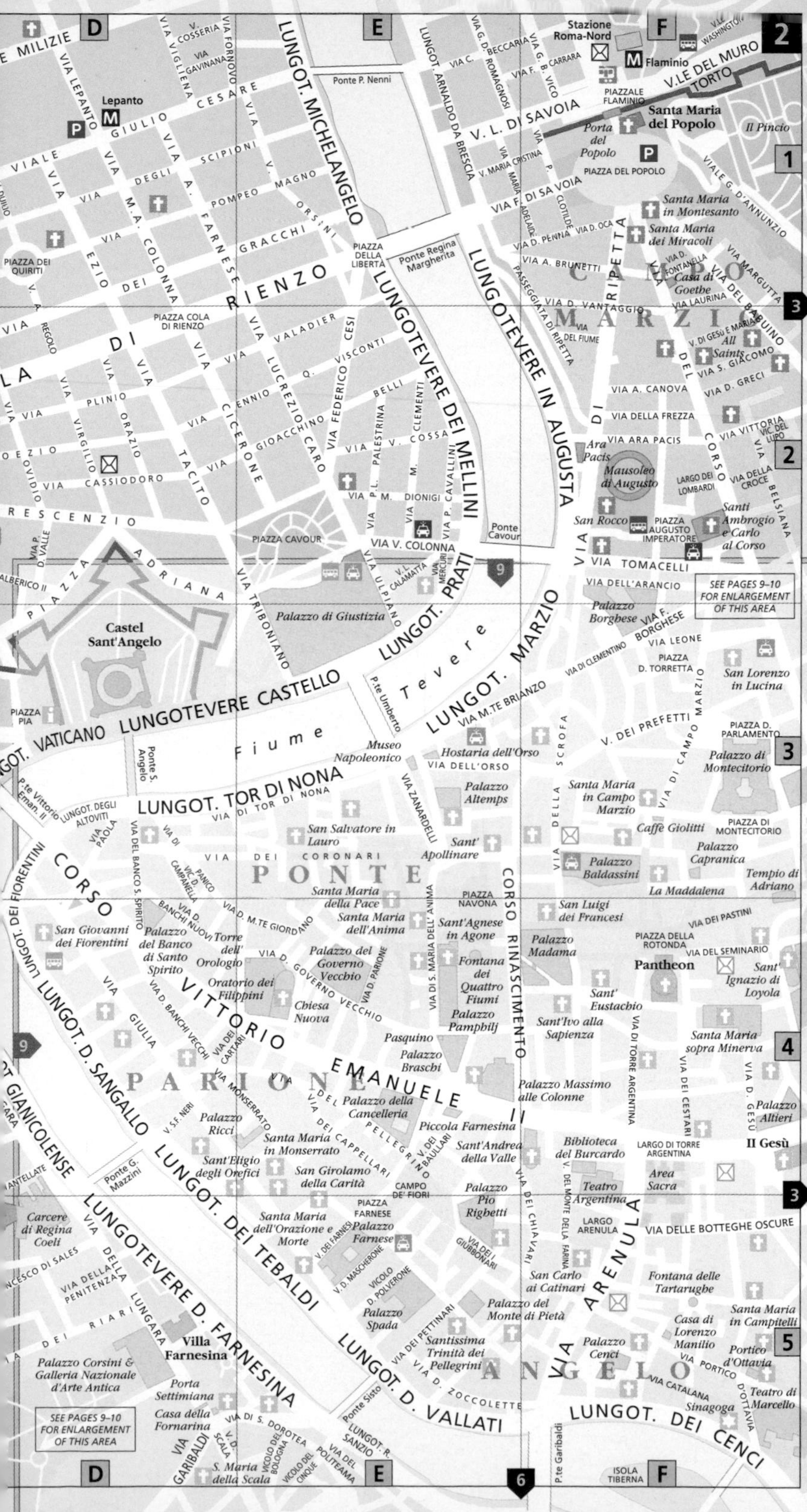

D
E
F
2
1
3
4
5
6
9
Stazione Roma-Nord
Flaminio
Lepanto
Santa Maria del Popolo
Porta del Popolo
Piazza del Popolo
Il Pincio
Santa Maria in Montesanto
Santa Maria dei Miracoli
Casa di Goethe
All Saints
Campo Marzio
Ara Pacis
Mausoleo di Augusto
San Rocco
Santi Ambrogio e Carlo al Corso
SEE PAGES 9–10 FOR ENLARGEMENT OF THIS AREA
Palazzo Borghese
San Lorenzo in Lucina
Castel Sant'Angelo
Palazzo di Giustizia
Piazza Cavour
Fiume Tevere
Museo Napoleonico
Hostaria dell'Orso
Palazzo Altemps
Palazzo di Montecitorio
Santa Maria in Campo Marzio
Caffè Giolitti
Palazzo Capranica
Tempio di Adriano
San Salvatore in Lauro
Sant' Apollinare
Palazzo Baldassini
La Maddalena
Ponte
Santa Maria della Pace
Santa Maria dell'Anima
Sant'Agnese in Agone
San Luigi dei Francesi
Palazzo Madama
Pantheon
Sant' Ignazio di Loyola
San Giovanni dei Fiorentini
Palazzo del Banco di Santo Spirito
Torre dell' Orologio
Palazzo del Governo Vecchio
Fontana dei Quattro Fiumi
Oratorio dei Filippini
Chiesa Nuova
Palazzo Pamphilj
Sant' Eustachio
Sant'Ivo alla Sapienza
Santa Maria sopra Minerva
Pasquino
Palazzo Braschi
Parione
Palazzo Massimo alle Colonne
Palazzo della Cancelleria
Piccola Farnesina
Palazzo Altieri
Palazzo Ricci
Santa Maria in Monserrato
Sant'Andrea della Valle
Biblioteca del Burcardo
Il Gesù
Sant'Eligio degli Orefici
San Girolamo della Carità
Campo de' Fiori
Palazzo Pio Righetti
Teatro Argentina
Area Sacra
Carcere di Regina Coeli
Santa Maria dell'Orazione e Morte
Palazzo Farnese
San Carlo ai Catinari
Fontana delle Tartarughe
Palazzo del Monte di Pietà
Palazzo Spada
Santa Maria in Campitelli
Casa di Lorenzo Manilio
Villa Farnesina
Santissima Trinità dei Pellegrini
Palazzo Cenci
Portico d'Ottavia
Palazzo Corsini & Galleria Nazionale d'Arte Antica
Porta Settimiana
Casa della Fornarina
Angelo
Sinagoga
Teatro di Marcello
S. Maria della Scala
Isola Tiberina
Corso Vittorio Emanuele II
Corso Rinascimento
Via Arenula
Lungotevere Castello
Lungot. Tor di Nona
Lungotevere dei Mellini
Lungotevere in Augusta
Lungot. Michelangelo
Lungot. dei Tebaldi
Lungotevere D. Farnesina
Lungot. D. Vallati
Lungot. dei Cenci

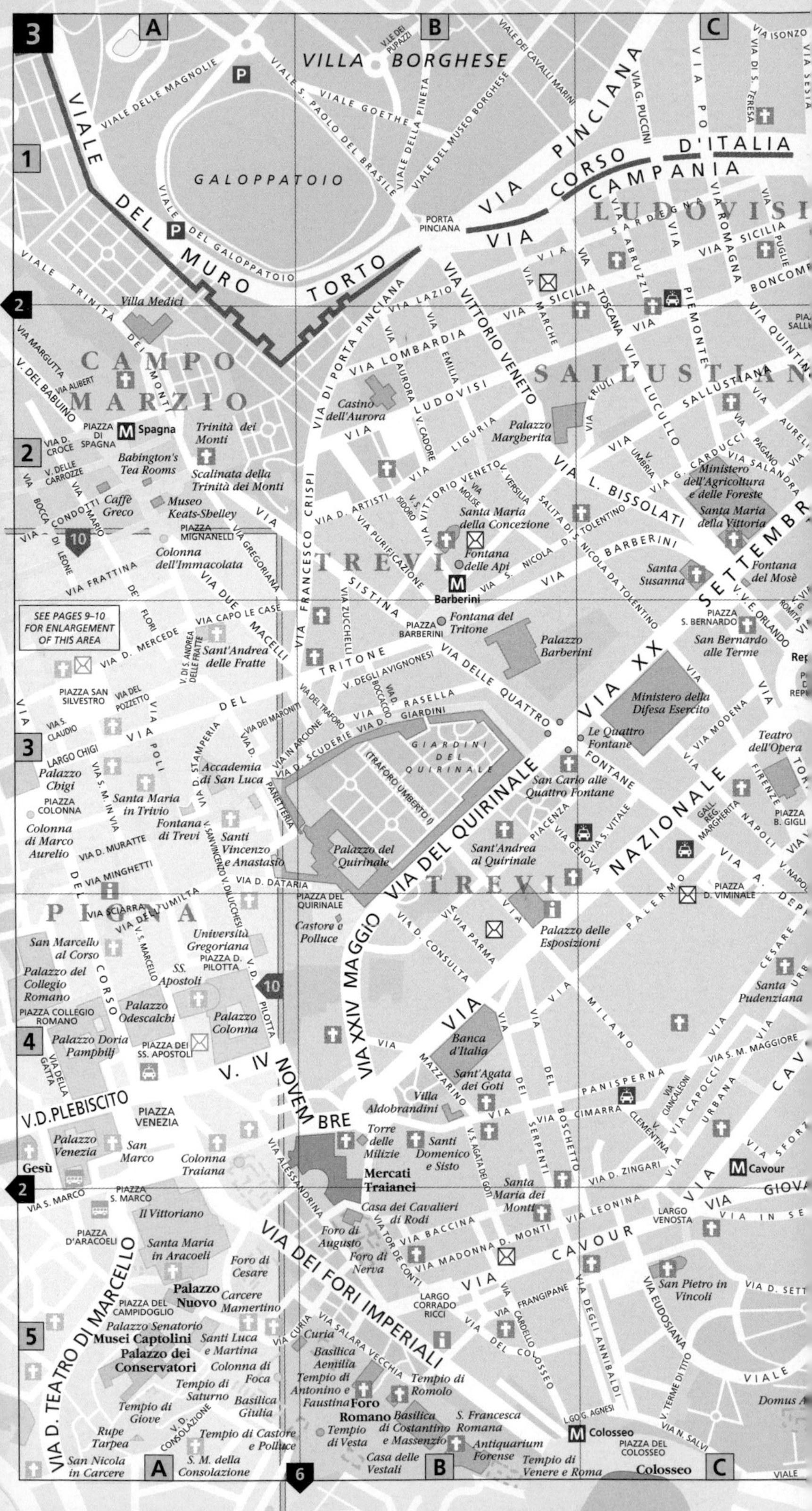
3
A
B
C
1
2
3
4
5
6
10
VILLA BORGHESE
V.LE DEI PUPAZZI
VIALE DEI CAVALLI MARINI
VIA ISONZO
VIA DI S. TERESA
VIA SESIA
VIALE DELLE MAGNOLIE
VIALE S. PAOLO DEL BRASILE
VIALE GOETHE
VIALE DELLA PINETA
VIALE DEL MUSEO BORGHESE
VIA G. PUCCINI
VIA PO
VIA PINCIANA
CORSO D'ITALIA
VIA CAMPANIA
GALOPPATOIO
VIALE DEL GALOPPATOIO
VIALE DEL MURO TORTO
PORTA PINCIANA
LUDOVISI
VIA SARDEGNA
VIA ABRUZZI
VIA ROMAGNA
VIA SICILIA
VIA PUGLIE
VIA BONCOMPAGNI
VIALE TRINITÀ DEI MONTI
Villa Medici
VIA LAZIO
VIA VITTORIO VENETO
VIA MARCHE
VIA TOSCANA
VIA PIEMONTE
VIA QUINTINO SELLA
VIA MARGUTTA
V. DEL BABUINO
VIA ALIBERT
CAMPO MARZIO
VIA DI PORTA PINCIANA
VIA LOMBARDIA
VIA AURORA
VIA EMILIA
SALLUSTIANO
VIA FRIULI
VIA LUCULLO
VIA SALLUSTIANA
VIA AURELIANA
Casino dell'Aurora
VIA LUDOVISI
Palazzo Margherita
PIAZZA DI SPAGNA
Spagna
Trinità dei Monti
VIA D. CROCE
V. DELLE CARROZZE
Babington's Tea Rooms
Scalinata della Trinità dei Monti
VIA V. CADORE
VIA LIGURIA
VIA UMBRIA
VIA L. BISSOLATI
VIA G. CARDUCCI
VIA PAGANO
VIA SALANDRA
Ministero dell'Agricoltura e delle Foreste
VIA BOCCA DI LEONE
VIA CONDOTTI
VIA MARIO DE' FIORI
Caffè Greco
Museo Keats-Shelley
VIA SISTINA
VIA CRISPI
VIA D. ARTISTI
VIA S. ISIDORO
VIA VITTORIO VENETO
VIA MOLISE
V. VERSILIA
SALITA DI S. NICOLA DA TOLENTINO
Santa Maria della Concezione
Santa Maria della Vittoria
PIAZZA MIGNANELLI
Colonna dell'Immacolata
VIA GREGORIANA
VIA FRANCESCO CRISPI
VIA PURIFICAZIONE
TREVI
Fontana delle Api
VIA BARBERINI
Santa Susanna
Fontana del Mosè
VIA XX SETTEMBRE
VIA FRATTINA
Barberini
VIA S. NICOLA DA TOLENTINO
SEE PAGES 9–10 FOR ENLARGEMENT OF THIS AREA
VIA CAPO LE CASE
VIA DUE MACELLI
VIA ZUCCHELLI
PIAZZA BARBERINI
Fontana del Tritone
PIAZZA S. BERNARDO
V. V. E. ORLANDO
San Bernardo alle Terme
VIA D. MERCEDE
V. DI S. ANDREA DELLE FRATTE
Sant'Andrea delle Fratte
VIA DEL TRITONE
V. DEGLI AVIGNONESI
VIA DELLE QUATTRO FONTANE
Palazzo Barberini
PIAZZA SAN SILVESTRO
VIA DEL POZZETTO
VIA DEL TRAFORO
VIA D. BOCCACCIO
VIA RASELLA
VIA D. GIARDINI
Ministero della Difesa Esercito
VIA S. CLAUDIO
VIA DEI MARONITI
VIA IN ARCIONE
VIA D. SCUDERIE
GIARDINI DEL QUIRINALE
Le Quattro Fontane
VIA MODENA
Teatro dell'Opera
LARGO CHIGI
Palazzo Chigi
VIA S. M. IN VIA
VIA POLI
VIA DELLA STAMPERIA
Accademia di San Luca
(TRAFORO UMBERTO I)
San Carlo alle Quattro Fontane
VIA FIRENZE
VIA TORINO
PIAZZA COLONNA
Santa Maria in Trivio
Fontana di Trevi
VIA DELLA PANETTERIA
VIA DEL QUIRINALE
VIA NAZIONALE
GALL. REG. MARGHERITA
VIA NAPOLI
PIAZZA B. GIGLI
Colonna di Marco Aurelio
VIA D. MURATTE
V. SAN VINCENZO
Santi Vincenzo e Anastasio
Palazzo del Quirinale
Sant'Andrea al Quirinale
VIA PIACENZA
VIA GENOVA
VIA S. VITALE
VIA D. MINGHETTI
VIA DEL CORSO
VIA D. DATARIA
VIA A. DEPRETIS
PIAZZA D. VIMINALE
VIA PALERMO
PIGNA
VIA SCIARRA
VIA DELL'UMILTÀ
V. DI LUCCHESI
PIAZZA DEL QUIRINALE
Castore e Polluce
VIA XXIV MAGGIO
VIA D. CONSULTA
VIA PARMA
Palazzo delle Esposizioni
San Marcello al Corso
VIA S. MARCELLO
Università Gregoriana
PIAZZA D. PILOTTA
VIA CESARE BALBO
Palazzo del Collegio Romano
SS. Apostoli
V.D. PILOTTA
Santa Pudenziana
VIA URBANA
PIAZZA COLLEGIO ROMANO
Palazzo Odescalchi
Palazzo Colonna
VIA MILANO
Banca d'Italia
Palazzo Doria Pamphilj
PIAZZA DEI SS. APOSTOLI
VIA S. M. MAGGIORE
VIA DELLA GATTA
V. IV NOVEMBRE
VIA MAZZARINO
Sant'Agata dei Goti
VIA DEI SERPENTI
VIA DEL BOSCHETTO
VIA PANISPERNA
VIA CIANCALEONI
VIA CAPOCCI
V.D. PLEBISCITO
PIAZZA VENEZIA
Villa Aldobrandini
VIA CIMARRA
V. CLEMENTINA
VIA CAVOUR
Palazzo Venezia
San Marco
Torre delle Milizie
Santi Domenico e Sisto
V.S. AGATA DEI GOTI
Gesù
Colonna Traiana
VIA ALESSANDRINA
Mercati Traianei
VIA D. ZINGARI
Cavour
VIA GIOVANNI LANZA
VIA S. MARCO
PIAZZA S. MARCO
Santa Maria dei Monti
Casa dei Cavalieri di Rodi
VIA LEONINA
LARGO VENOSTA
VIA IN SELCI
Il Vittoriano
PIAZZA D'ARACOELI
Santa Maria in Aracoeli
VIA DEI FORI IMPERIALI
Foro di Augusto
VIA TOR DE CONTI
VIA BACCINA
VIA MADONNA D. MONTI
Foro di Cesare
Foro di Nerva
San Pietro in Vincoli
VIA D. SETTE SALE
Palazzo Nuovo
Carcere Mamertino
LARGO CORRADO RICCI
VIA FRANGIPANE
VIA CARDELLO
VIA DEGLI ANNIBALDI
VIA EUDOSSIANA
VIA D. TEATRO DI MARCELLO
PIAZZA DEL CAMPIDOGLIO
Palazzo Senatorio
Musei Captolini
Santi Luca e Martina
VIA CURIA
VIA SALARA VECCHIA
Curia
VIA DEL COLOSSEO
Palazzo dei Conservatori
Colonna di Foca
Basilica Aemilia
Tempio di Antonino e Faustina
Tempio di Romolo
VIALE DEL MONTE OPPIO
Tempio di Saturno
Basilica Giulia
V. TERME DI TITO
Domus Aurea
V. D. CONSOLAZIONE
Tempio di Giove
Foro Romano
Basilica di Costantino e Massenzio
S. Francesca Romana
Rupe Tarpea
Tempio di Castore e Polluce
Tempio di Vesta
L.GO G. AGNESI
Colosseo
VIA N. SALVI
Antiquarium Forense
PIAZZA DEL COLOSSEO
San Nicola in Carcere
S. M. della Consolazione
Casa delle Vestali
Tempio di Venere e Roma
VIALE

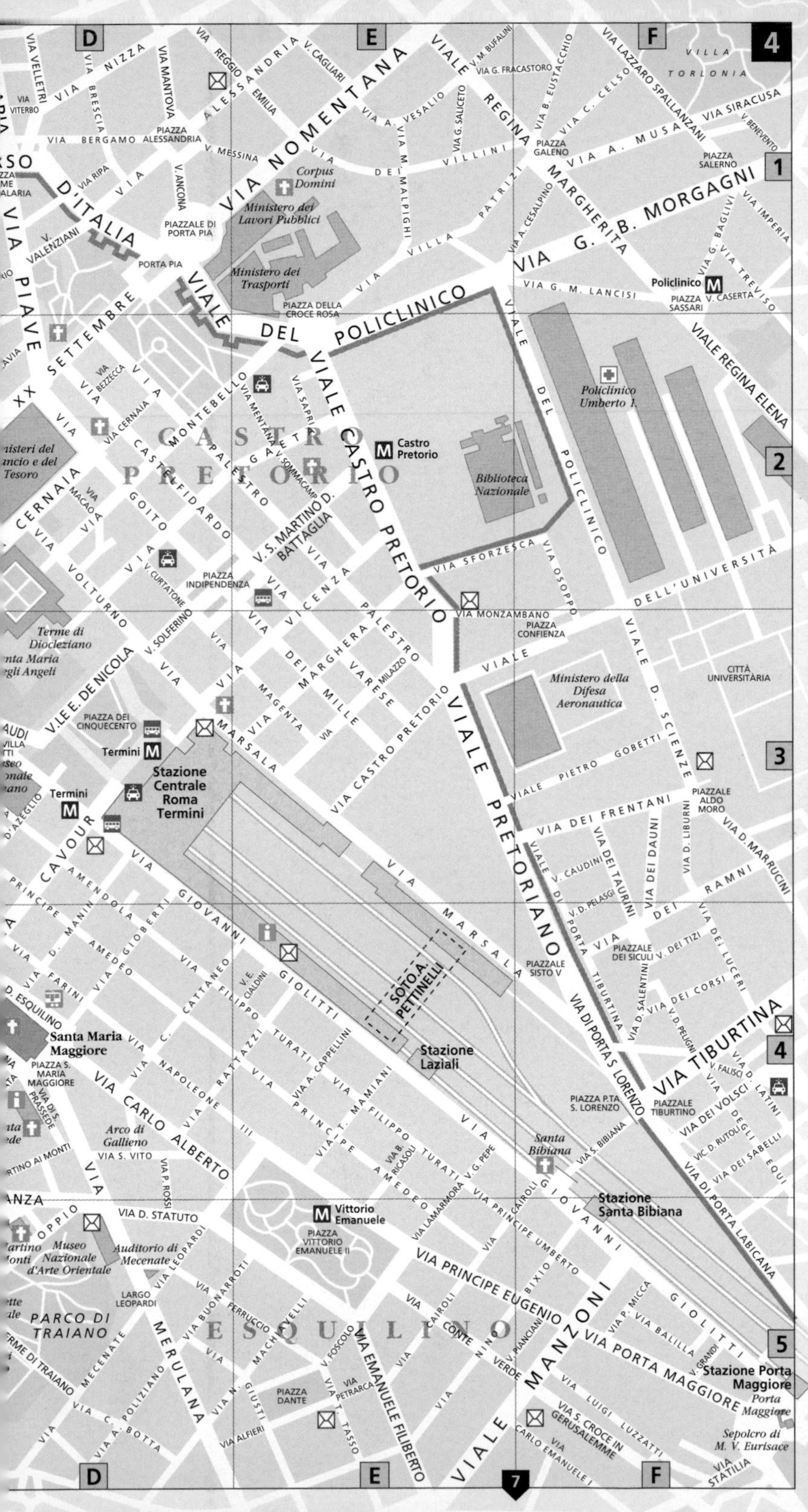

4
D
E
F
1
2
3
4
5
VILLA TORLONIA
VIA NOMENTANA
VIALE REGINA MARGHERITA
VIA G. B. MORGAGNI
VIA LAZZARO SPALLANZANI
VIA SIRACUSA
V. BENEVENTO
PIAZZA SALERNO
PIAZZA GALENO
VIA A. MUSA
VIA C. CELSO
VIA B. EUSTACCHIO
VIA G. FRACASTORO
V. M. BUFALINI
VIALE REGINA
VIA G. SALICETO
VIA A. VESALIO
VIA M. MALPIGHI
VIA DEI VILLINI
VIA CAGLIARI
VIA ALESSANDRIA
VIA REGGIO EMILIA
VIA NIZZA
VIA MANTOVA
VIA BRESCIA
VIA VELLETRI
VIA VITERBO
VIA BERGAMO
PIAZZA ALESSANDRIA
V. MESSINA
V. ANCONA
VIA RIPA
CORSO D'ITALIA
PIAZZA SALARIA
VIA PIAVE
V. VALENZIANI
PIAZZALE DI PORTA PIA
PORTA PIA
Corpus Domini
Ministero dei Lavori Pubblici
Ministero dei Trasporti
PIAZZA DELLA CROCE ROSA
VIA VILLA PATRIZI
VIA A. CESALPINO
VIA G. M. LANCISI
Policlinico
PIAZZA SASSARI
V. CASERTA
VIA G. B. BAGLIVI
VIA TREVISO
VIA IMPERIA
VIALE REGINA ELENA
VIALE DEL POLICLINICO
VIALE CASTRO PRETORIO
Policlinico Umberto I.
Castro Pretorio
CASTRO PRETORIO
Biblioteca Nazionale
VIA XX SETTEMBRE
VIA BEZZECCA
VIA CERNAIA
VIA MONTEBELLO
VIA MENTANA
VIA SAPRI
VIA GAETA
VIA SOMMACAMPAGNA
VIA PALESTRO
VIA CASTELFIDARDO
VIA GOITO
VIA MACAO
Ministeri del Bilancio e del Tesoro
V. S. MARTINO D. BATTAGLIA
VIA SFORZESCA
VIA OSOPPO
VIALE DELL'UNIVERSITÀ
V. CURTATONE
PIAZZA INDIPENDENZA
VIA VOLTURNO
VIA VICENZA
VIA MONZAMBANO
PIAZZA CONFIENZA
Terme di Diocleziano
Santa Maria degli Angeli
V. SOLFERINO
VIA MAGENTA
VIA DEI MILLE
VIA MARGHERA
VIA VARESE
VIA MILAZZO
VIALE D. SCIENZE
CITTÀ UNIVERSITÀRIA
Ministero della Difesa Aeronautica
V.LE E. DE NICOLA
PIAZZA DEI CINQUECENTO
VIA MARSALA
VIA CASTRO PRETORIO
VIALE PRETORIANO
VIALE PIETRO GOBETTI
Termini
Stazione Centrale Roma Termini
PIAZZALE ALDO MORO
VIA DEI FRENTANI
VIA D. LIBURNI
VIA D. MARRUCINI
VIA DEI DAUNI
VIA DEI RAMNI
VIA DEI TAURINI
V. CAUDINI
V. D. PELASGI
VIALE DI PORTA TIBURTINA
VIA CAVOUR
VIA AMENDOLA
VIA PRINCIPE AMEDEO
VIA D. MANIN
VIA GIOBERTI
VIA FARINI
VIA GIOVANNI GIOLITTI
VIA CATTANEO
VIA FILIPPO TURATI
V. E. CIALDINI
SOTO.A. PETTINELLI
PIAZZALE SISTO V
PIAZZALE DEI SICULI
V. DEI TIZI
VIA DEI LUCERI
VIA DEI CORSI
VIA D. SALENTINI
V. D. PELIGNI
VIA TIBURTINA
VIA DI PORTA S. LORENZO
Santa Maria Maggiore
PIAZZA S. MARIA MAGGIORE
VIA DI S. PRASSEDE
Stazione Laziali
VIA A. CAPPELLINI
VIA NAPOLEONE III
VIA RATTAZZI
VIA CARLO ALBERTO
VIA T. MAMIANI
VIA PRINCIPE
VIA FILIPPO TURATI
Arco di Gallieno
VIA S. VITO
VIA P. ROSSI
VIA B. RICASOLI
VIA G. PEPE
VIA LAMARMORA
VIA PRINCIPE UMBERTO
VIA CAIROLI
VIA GIOVANNI GIOLITTI
Santa Bibiana
VIA S. BIBIANA
PIAZZA P.TA S. LORENZO
PIAZZALE TIBURTINO
VIA DEI VOLSCI
V. FALISCI
VIA D. LATINI
VIA DEGLI EQUI
VIC. D. ROTULOI
VIA DEI SABELLI
VIA DI PORTA LABICANA
Stazione Santa Bibiana
Vittorio Emanuele
PIAZZA VITTORIO EMANUELE II
VIA D. STATUTO
VIA LEOPARDI
Museo Nazionale d'Arte Orientale
Auditorio di Mecenate
LARGO LEOPARDI
PARCO DI TRAIANO
VIA MERULANA
VIA MECENATE
VIA A. POLIZIANO
VIA C. BOTTA
VIA BUONARROTI
VIA FERRUCCIO
VIA MACHIAVELLI
ESQUILINO
VIA N. GIUSTI
PIAZZA DANTE
VIA ALFIERI
V. FOSCOLO
VIA PETRARCA
VIA T. TASSO
VIA EMANUELE FILIBERTO
VIA PRINCIPE EUGENIO
VIA CONTE VERDE
VIA NINO BIXIO
V. PIANCIANI
VIALE MANZONI
VIA PORTA MAGGIORE
VIA P. MICCA
VIA BALILLA
V. GRANDI
Stazione Porta Maggiore
Porta Maggiore
VIA LUIGI LUZZATTI
VIA S. CROCE IN GERUSALEMME
VIA CARLO EMANUELE I
Sepolcro di M. V. Eurisace
VIA STATILIA
7

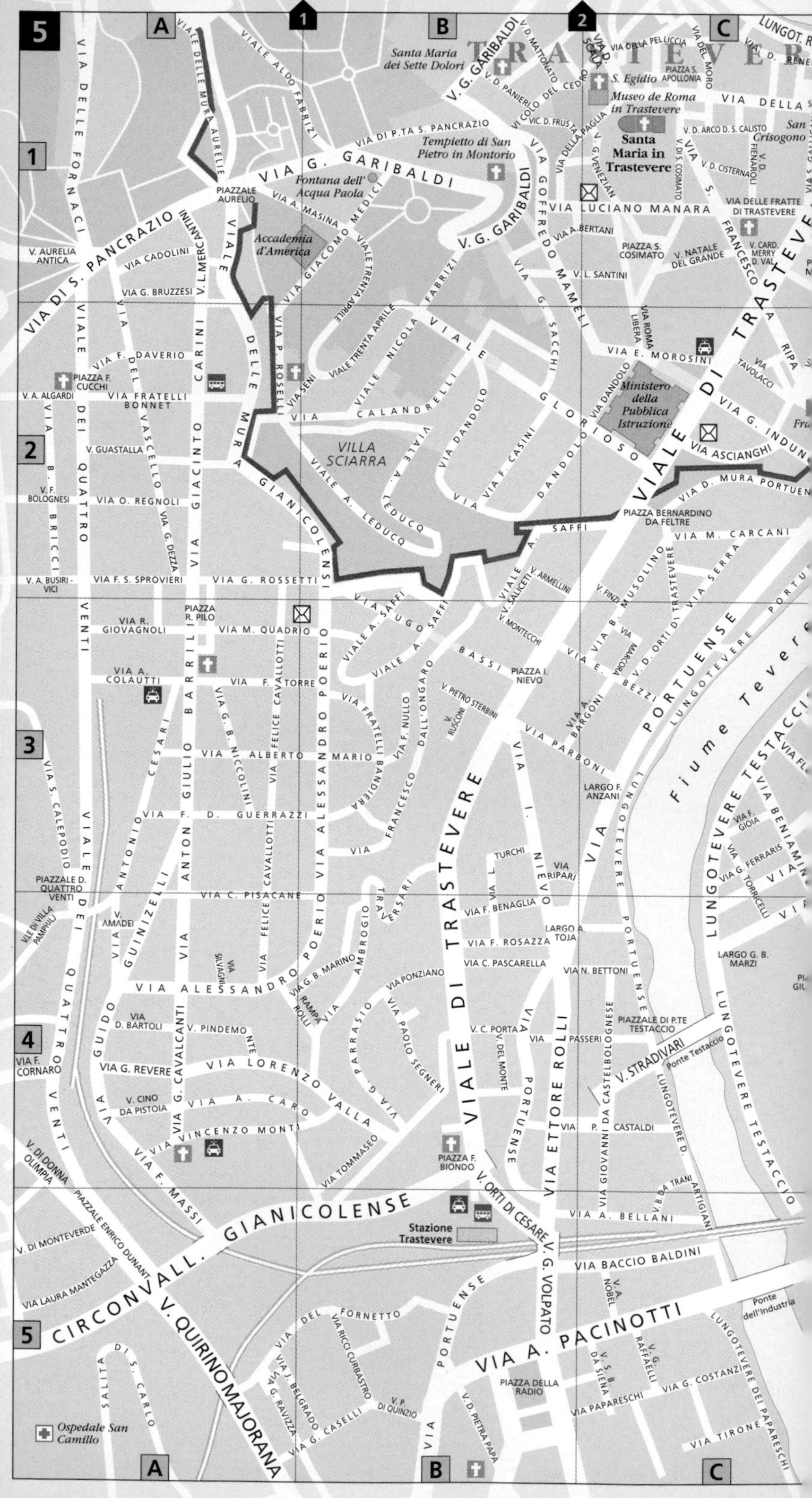
5
A
B
C
1
2
3
4
5
TRASTEVERE
Santa Maria dei Sette Dolori
S. Egidio
Museo de Roma in Trastevere
Santa Maria in Trastevere
San Crisogono
Tempietto di San Pietro in Montorio
Fontana dell' Acqua Paola
Accademia d'America
Villa Sciarra
Ministero della Pubblica Istruzione
Fiume Tevere
Ponte Testaccio
Ponte dell'Industria
Stazione Trastevere
Ospedale San Camillo
LUNGOT. R
VIA DELLA PELLICCIA
PIAZZA S. APOLLONIA
VIA DEL MORO
VIA DELLA S
V. G. GARIBALDI
V. D. MATTONATO
V. D. PANIERI
VICOLO DEL CEDRO
VIC. D. FRUSTA
VIA DELLA PAGLIA
VIA D. SCALA
V. D. ARCO D. S. CALISTO
V. D. FIENAROLI
V. D. CISTERNA
V. D'S. COSIMATO
VIA DI P.TA S. PANCRAZIO
VIA G. GARIBALDI
VIALE ALDO FABRIZI
VIALE DELLE MURA AURELIE
VIA DELLE FORNACI
PIAZZALE AURELIO
VIA A. MASINA
VIA GIACOMO MEDICI
VIALE TRENTA APRILE
VIA LUCIANO MANARA
VIA DELLE FRATTE DI TRASTEVERE
VIA A. BERTANI
PIAZZA S. COSIMATO
V. NATALE DEL GRANDE
V. CARD. MERRY D. VAL
V. L. SANTINI
VIA GOFFREDO MAMELI
VIA G. SACCHI
VIA S. FRANCESCO A RIPA
VIA DI S. PANCRAZIO
V. AURELIA ANTICA
VIA CADOLINI
V. L. MERCANTINI
VIA G. BRUZZESI
VIALE DELLE MURA GIANICOLENSI
VIALE NICOLA FABRIZI
VIA P. ROSELLI
VIA SENI
VIA CALANDRELLI
VIA DANDOLO
VIALE GLORIOSO
VIA ROMA LIBERA
VIA E. MOROSINI
VIA TAVOLACCI
VIA G. INDUNO
VIA ASCIANGHI
VIA D. MURA PORTUENSI
VIALE DI TRASTEVERE
VIA F. DAVERIO
PIAZZA F. CUCCHI
V. A. ALGARDI
VIA FRATELLI BONNET
VIA DEL VASCELLO
VIA GIACINTO CARINI
VIALE DEI QUATTRO VENTI
V. GUASTALLA
VIA B. BRICCI
V. F. BOLOGNESI
VIA O. REGNOLI
VIA G. DEZZA
VIALE A. LEDUCQ
VIA F. CASINI
VIA DANDOLO
PIAZZA BERNARDINO DA FELTRE
VIA A. SAFFI
VIA M. CARCANI
V. A. BUSIRI-VICI
VIA F. S. SPROVIERI
VIA G. ROSSETTI
VIALE UGO BASSI
V. ARMELLINI
V. SALICETI
V. MONTECCHI
V. FINZI
VIA B. MUSOLINO
VIA D. ORTI DI TRASTEVERE
VIA SERRA
PIAZZA R. PILO
VIA R. GIOVAGNOLI
VIA M. QUADRIO
VIA MARCORA
VIA E. BEZZI
PIAZZA I. NIEVO
VIA A. COLAUTTI
VIA F. TORRE
VIA ANTON GIULIO BARRILI
VIA G. B. NICCOLINI
VIA FELICE CAVALLOTTI
VIA ALESSANDRO POERIO
VIA FRATELLI BANDIERA
VIA F. NULLO
VIA DALL'ONGARO
V. PIETRO STERBINI
V. RUSCONI
VIA PARBONI
VIA A. BARGONI
VIA PORTUENSE
LUNGOTEVERE
VIA CESARI
VIA ALBERTO MARIO
VIA S. CALEPODIO
VIA ANTONIO GUINIZELLI
VIA F. D. GUERRAZZI
VIA FRANCESCO
LARGO F. ANZANI
LUNGOTEVERE PORTUENSE
LUNGOTEVERE TESTACCIO
VIA F. GIOIA
VIA BENIAMINO
VIA G. FERRARIS
VIA TORRICELLI
PIAZZALE D. QUATTRO VENTI
V.LE D. VILLA PAMPHILJ
VIA C. PISACANE
VIA L. TURCHI
VIA RIPARI
VIA I. NIEVO
V. AMADEI
VIA AMBROGIO TRAVERSARI
VIA F. BENAGLIA
LARGO A. TOJA
VIA F. ROSAZZA
VIA C. PASCARELLA
VIA N. BETTONI
LARGO G. B. MARZI
VIA SILVAGNI
VIA ALESSANDRO POERIO
VIA G. B. MARINO
VIA PONZIANO
RAMPA ROLLI
VIA PARRASIO
VIA PAOLO SEGNERI
VIA D. BARTOLI
V. PINDEMONTE
V. C. PORTA
VIA PASSERI
PIAZZALE DI P.TE TESTACCIO
VIA F. CORNARO
VIA GUIDO GUINIZELLI
VIA G. REVERE
VIA LORENZO VALLA
VIA G. CAVALCANTI
V. DEL MONTE
VIA PORTUENSE
VIA ETTORE ROLLI
VIA GIOVANNI DA CASTELBOLOGNESE
V. STRADIVARI
LUNGOTEVERE D. ARTIGIANI
V. CINO DA PISTOIA
VIA A. CARO
VIA P. CASTALDI
VIA VINCENZO MONTI
VIA F. MASSI
VIA TOMMASEO
PIAZZA F. BIONDO
V. ORTI DI CESARE
V. B. DA TRANI
V. DI DONNA OLIMPIA
PIAZZALE ENRICO DUNANT
VIA A. BELLANI
CIRCONVALL. GIANICOLENSE
V. DI MONTEVERDE
V. G. VOLPATO
VIA BACCIO BALDINI
V. A. NOBEL
VIA LAURA MANTEGAZZA
V. QUIRINO MAJORANA
VIA DEL FORNETTO
VIA RICCI CURBASTRO
VIA A. PACINOTTI
SALITA DI S. CARLO
VIA J. BELGRADO
VIA G. RAVIZZA
VIA G. CASELLI
V. P. DI QUINZIO
V. D. PIETRA PAPA
PIAZZA DELLA RADIO
V. S. B. DA SIENA
V. G. RAFFAELLI
VIA G. COSTANZI
VIA PAPARESCHI
LUNGOTEVERE DEI PAPARESCHI
VIA TIRONE

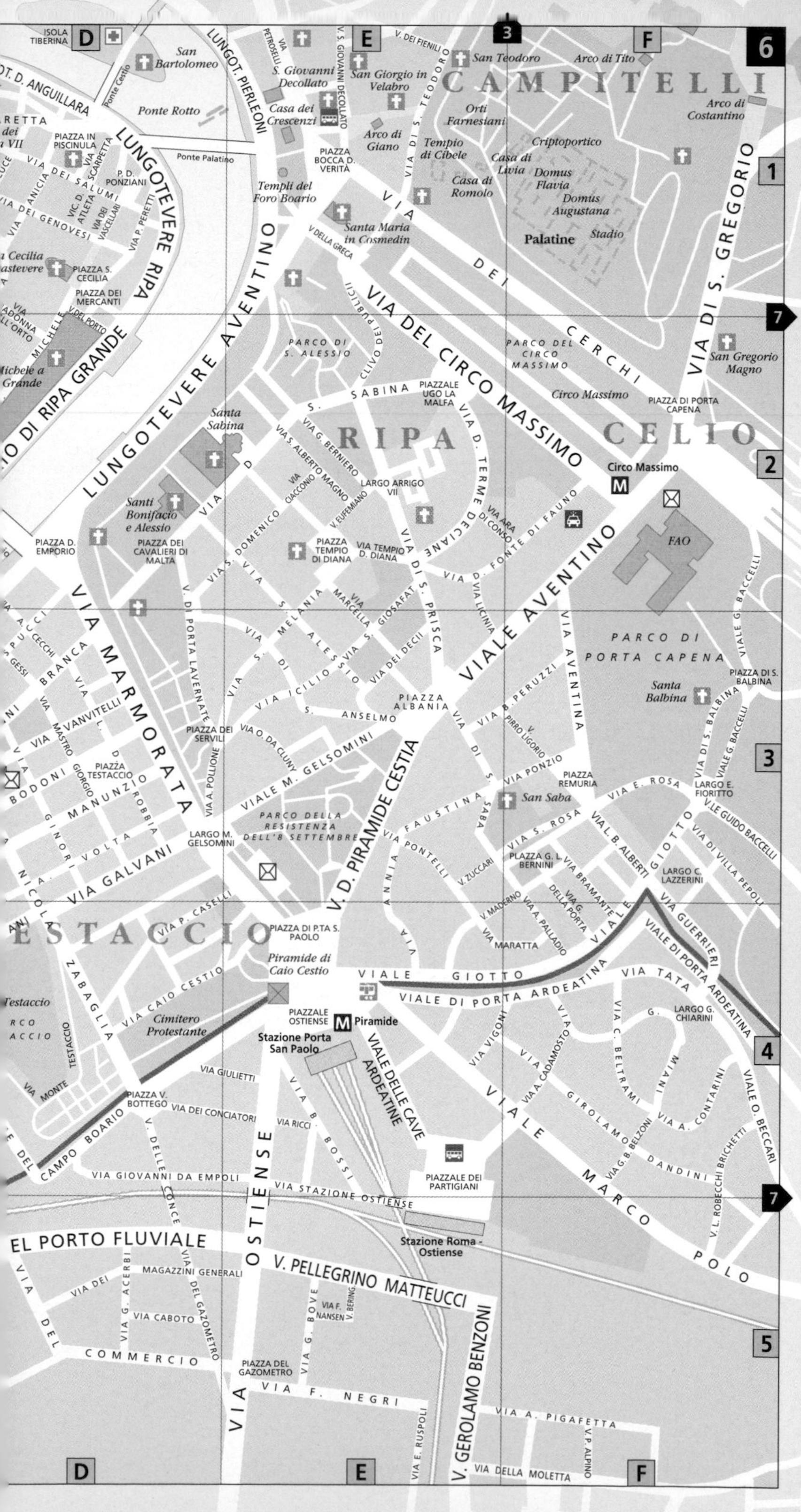
6
D
E
F
3
ISOLA TIBERINA
San Bartolomeo
Ponte Cestio
Ponte Rotto
Ponte Palatino
LUNGOT. D. ANGUILLARA
LUNGOT. PIERLEONI
LUNGOTEVERE RIPA
PIAZZA IN PISCINULA
VIA SCARPETTA
VIA DEI SALUMI
VIA ANICIA
P. D. PONZIANI
VIC. D. ATLETA
VIA DEI VASCELLARI
VIA P. PERETTI
VIA DEI GENOVESI
PIAZZA S. CECILIA
PIAZZA DEI MERCANTI
V. DEL PORTO
VIA MADONNA DELL'ORTO
VIA S. MICHELE
S. Giovanni Decollato
Casa dei Crescenzi
San Giorgio in Velabro
V. S. GIOVANNI DECOLLATO
V. DEI FIENILI
San Teodoro
Arco di Tito
CAMPITELLI
Arco di Costantino
Orti Farnesiani
Arco di Giano
PIAZZA BOCCA D. VERITÀ
VIA DI S. TEODORO
Tempio di Cibele
Criptoportico
Casa di Livia
Domus Flavia
Casa di Romolo
Domus Augustana
Templi del Foro Boario
Santa Maria in Cosmedin
V. DELLA GRECA
Palatine
Stadio
VIA DI S. GREGORIO
VIA DEI CERCHI
VIA DEL CIRCO MASSIMO
CLIVO DEI PUBBLICI
PARCO DI S. ALESSIO
PARCO DEL CIRCO MASSIMO
San Gregorio Magno
Circo Massimo
PIAZZA DI PORTA CAPENA
LUNGOTEVERE AVENTINO
VIA DI RIPA GRANDE
VIA S. SABINA
PIAZZALE UGO LA MALFA
Santa Sabina
RIPA
CELIO
VIA G. BERNIERO
VIA S. ALBERTO MAGNO
VIA D. TERME DECIANE
Circo Massimo
VIA CIACCONIO
LARGO ARRIGO VII
V. EUFEMIANO
VIA ARA DI CONSO
VIA D. FONTE DI FAUNO
Santi Bonifacio e Alessio
VIA S. DOMENICO
PIAZZA D. EMPORIO
PIAZZA DEI CAVALIERI DI MALTA
PIAZZA TEMPIO DI DIANA
VIA TEMPIO D. DIANA
VIA DI S. PRISCA
VIALE AVENTINO
FAO
VIA MARMORATA
V. DI PORTA LAVERNATE
VIA S. MELANIA
VIA MARCELLA
VIA S. GIOSAFAT
VIA D. LICINIA
VIA AVENTINA
PARCO DI PORTA CAPENA
VIALE G. BACCELLI
VIA A. CECCHI
VIA BRANCA
VIA GESSI
VIA VANVITELLI
VIA DI S. ALESSIO
VIA DEI DECII
VIA ICILIO
VIA DI S. ANSELMO
PIAZZA ALBANIA
VIA B. PERUZZI
PIAZZA DI S. BALBINA
Santa Balbina
VIA DI S. BALBINA
VIA MASTRO GIORGIO
PIAZZA DEI SERVILI
VIA O. DA CLUNY
V. PIRRO LIGORIO
VIA DI S. SABA
VIA A. POLLIONE
VIALE M. GELSOMINI
VIA PONZIO
PIAZZA REMURIA
VIA E. ROSA
LARGO E. FIORITTO
PIAZZA TESTACCIO
VIA BODONI
VIA MANUNZIO
VIA L. DELLA ROBBIA
VIA ANNIA FAUSTINA
San Saba
V.LE GUIDO BACCELLI
VIA S. ROSA
VIA DI VILLA PEPOLI
PARCO DELLA RESISTENZA DELL'8 SETTEMBRE
VIA GINORI
VIA VOLTA
LARGO M. GELSOMINI
VIA PONTELLI
V. ZUCCARI
PIAZZA G. L. BERNINI
VIA L. B. ALBERTI
VIALE GIOTTO
LARGO C. LAZZERINI
VIA GALVANI
V. D. PIRAMIDE CESTIA
VIA BRAMANTE
VIA G. DELLA PORTA
V. MADERNO
VIA A. PALLADIO
VIA MARATTA
VIA GUERRIERI
VIA N. ZABAGLIA
VIA P. CASELLI
TESTACCIO
PIAZZA DI P.TA S. PAOLO
Piramide di Caio Cestio
VIALE GIOTTO
VIALE DI PORTA ARDEATINA
VIA TATA
Testaccio
VIA CAIO CESTIO
Cimitero Protestante
PIAZZALE OSTIENSE
Piramide
LARGO G. CHIARINI
Stazione Porta San Paolo
VIALE DELLE CAVE ARDEATINE
VIA VIGONI
VIA A. CADAMOSTO
VIA C. BELTRAMI
VIA MIANI
VIA MONTE TESTACCIO
VIA GIULIETTI
VIA B. BOSSI
VIA GIROLAMO DANDINI
VIA A. CONTARINI
VIALE O. BECCARI
PIAZZA V. BOTTEGO
VIA DEI CONCIATORI
VIA RICCI
VIA G. B. BELZONI
V. L. ROBECCHI BRICHETTI
VIA DEL CAMPO BOARIO
V. DELLE CONCE
VIA OSTIENSE
VIALE MARCO POLO
VIA GIOVANNI DA EMPOLI
VIA STAZIONE OSTIENSE
PIAZZALE DEI PARTIGIANI
7
VIA DEL PORTO FLUVIALE
Stazione Roma - Ostiense
VIA DEI MAGAZZINI GENERALI
V. PELLEGRINO MATTEUCCI
VIA DEL
VIA G. ACERBI
VIA DEL GAZOMETRO
VIA CABOTO
VIA G. BOVE
VIA F. NANSEN
V. BERING
V. GEROLAMO BENZONI
VIA DEL COMMERCIO
PIAZZA DEL GAZOMETRO
VIA F. NEGRI
VIA A. PIGAFETTA
V. P. ALPINO
VIA E. RUSPOLI
VIA DELLA MOLETTA
1
2
3
4
5

7
A
B
C
4
6
1
2
3
4
5
Colosseo
Piazza del Colosseo
Via Labicana
Viale Manzoni
Manzoni
San Clemente
Via di S. Giovanni in Laterano
Santi Quattro Coronati
Via Merulana
Tempio di Claudio
Santi Giovanni e Paolo
Via Claudia
Piazza Celimontana
Ospedale del Celio
Ospedale di San Giovanni
Piazza S. Giovanni in Laterano
Palazzo Laterano
Scala Santa Sancta Sanctorum
Battistero
San Giovanni in Laterano
Clivo di Scauro
Arco di Dolabella
Sanatorio Umberto I
Ospizio d. Addolorata
Santa Maria in Domnica
Santo Stefano Rotondo
Via della Navicella
Via dell'Amba Aradam
Via dei Laterani
Villa Celimontana
Celio
Via D. Ferratella in Laterano
Piazza di P.ta Metronia
Piazzale Metronio
Viale Ipponio
V.D. Terme di Caracalla
Stadio delle Terme
Via Druso
San Sisto Vecchio
Santi Nereo e Achilleo
Terme di Caracalla
Piazzale Numa Pompilio
Parco Egerio
San Cesareo
Viale Metronio
Via Gallia
Piazza Epiro
Via di Porta Latina
San Giovanni a Porta Latina
Colombario di Pomponio Hylas
San Giovanni in Oleo
Tomba degli Scipioni
Parco D. Scipioni
Via di Porta S. Sebastiano
Viale Guido Baccelli
Via D. Terme di Caracalla
Bastione del Sangallo
Viale di Porta Ardeatina
Largo delle Terme di Caracalla
Arco di Druso
Porta San Sebastiano
Porta Ardeatina
Via delle Mura Latine
V. Cristoforo Colombo
Via Appia Antica
Viale Marco Polo
Via Cilicia
Via della Travicella
Viale O. Beccari
Via Capitan Bavastro

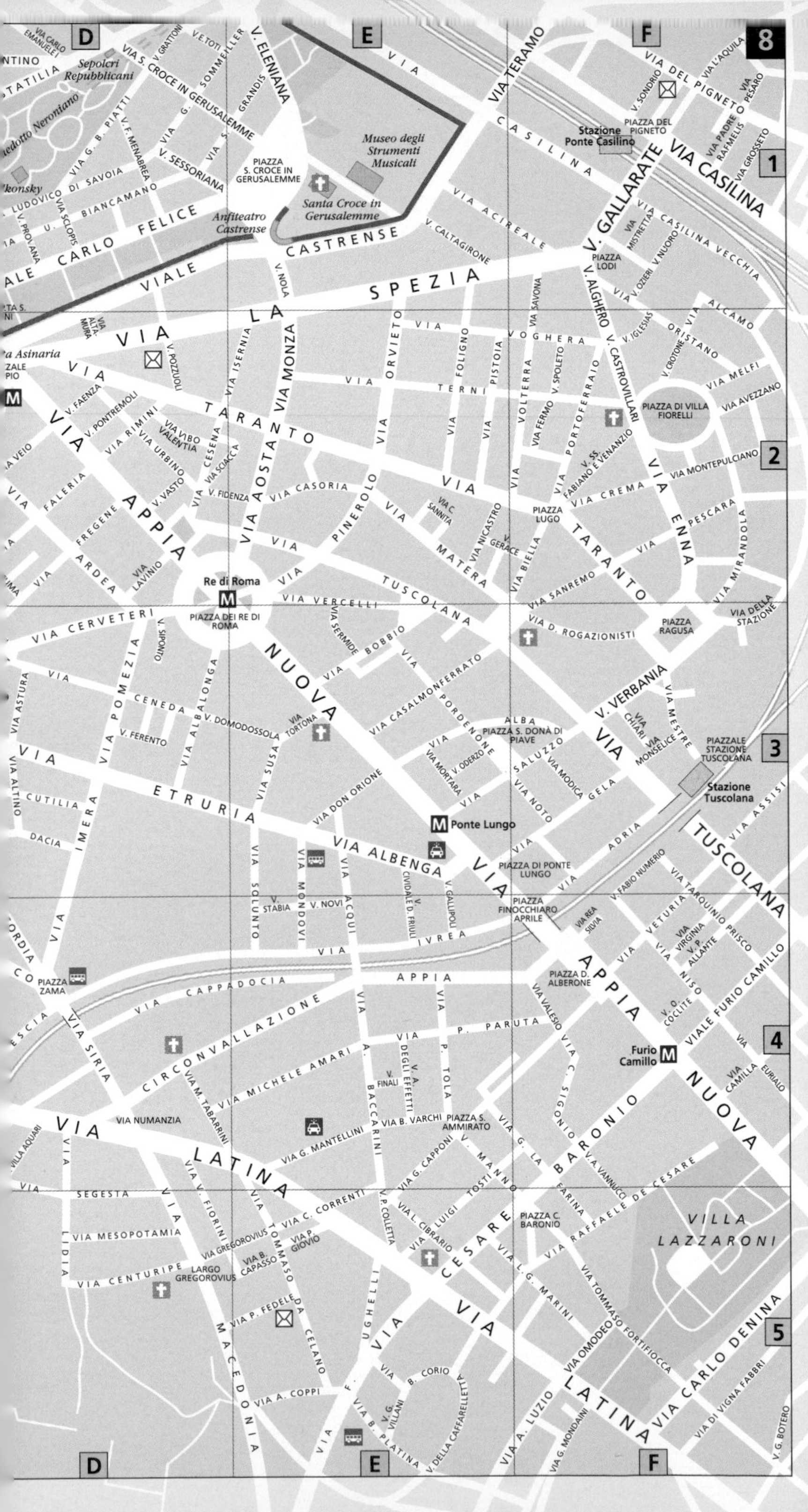

8
D
E
F
1
2
3
4
5
Sepolcri Repubblicani
Museo degli Strumenti Musicali
Santa Croce in Gerusalemme
Anfiteatro Castrense
PIAZZA S. CROCE IN GERUSALEMME
Stazione Ponte Casilino
PIAZZA DEL PIGNETO
VIA CASILINA
VIA TERAMO
V. GALLARATE
VIALE CARLO FELICE
VIALE CASTRENSE
VIA LA SPEZIA
PIAZZA LODI
PIAZZA DI VILLA FIORELLI
VIA TARANTO
VIA APPIA NUOVA
VIA AOSTA
VIA MONZA
VIA ENNA
PIAZZA LUGO
Re di Roma
PIAZZA DEI RE DI ROMA
VIA TUSCOLANA
PIAZZA RAGUSA
PIAZZA S. DONÀ DI PIAVE
PIAZZALE STAZIONE TUSCOLANA
Stazione Tuscolana
Ponte Lungo
PIAZZA DI PONTE LUNGO
PIAZZA FINOCCHIARO APRILE
VIA ETRURIA
VIA ALBENGA
PIAZZA ZAMA
VIA CIRCONVALLAZIONE APPIA
PIAZZA D. ALBERONE
Furio Camillo
VIALE FURIO CAMILLO
VIA LATINA
PIAZZA S. AMMIRATO
PIAZZA C. BARONIO
VIA CESARE BARONIO
LARGO GREGOROVIUS
VILLA LAZZARONI
VIA CARLO DENINA
VIA MACEDONIA

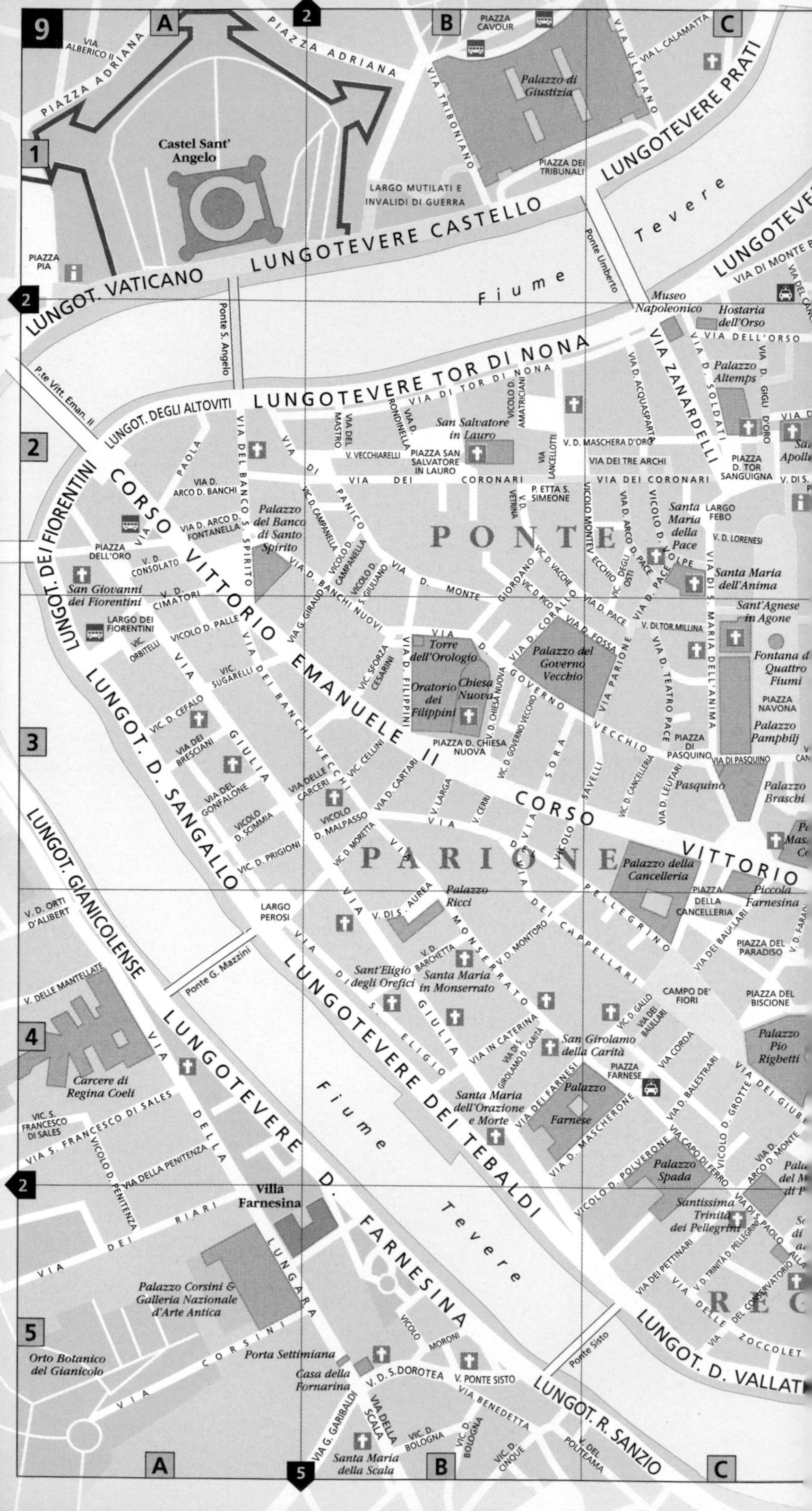
9
A
B
C
1
2
3
4
5
Piazza Adriana
Via Alberico II
Piazza Cavour
Palazzo di Giustizia
Via Ulpiano
Via L. Calamatta
Lungotevere Prati
Via Triboniano
Castel Sant' Angelo
Piazza dei Tribunali
Largo Mutilati e Invalidi di Guerra
Lungotevere Castello
Tevere
Fiume
Piazza Pia
Lungot. Vaticano
Ponte Umberto
Ponte S. Angelo
Museo Napoleonico
Hostaria dell'Orso
Via dell'Orso
Via di Monte Brianzo
Lungotevere Tor di Nona
Via di Tor di Nona
Via Zanardelli
Palazzo Altemps
Via d. Soldati
Via d. Gigli d'Oro
P.te Vitt. Eman. II
Lungot. degli Altoviti
Via del Mastro
Via d. Rondinella
Vicolo d. Amatriciani
Via d. Acquasparta
San Salvatore in Lauro
Piazza San Salvatore in Lauro
V. Vecchiarelli
Via Lancellotti
V. d. Maschera d'Oro
Via dei Tre Archi
Via dei Coronari
Piazza d. Tor Sanguigna
Sant'Apollinare
Via di Panico
Via d. Vetrina
P. etta S. Simeone
Vicolo Montevecchio
Via d. Arco d. Pace
Vicolo d. Volpe
Santa Maria della Pace
Largo Febo
V. d. Lorenesi
Lungot. dei Fiorentini
Corso Vittorio Emanuele II
Paola
Via d. Arco d. Banchi
Via d. Arco d. Fontanella
Via del Banco S. Spirito
Palazzo del Banco di Santo Spirito
Vic. d. Campanella
Vicolo d. Campanella
Vicolo d. S. Giuliano
Via d. Banchi Nuovi
Via d. Monte Giordano
PONTE
Vic. d. Vacche
Vic. d. Fico
Via d. Corallo
Vic. degli Osti
Via d. Pace
Santa Maria dell'Anima
Via di S. Maria dell'Anima
Piazza dell'Oro
V. d. Consolato
San Giovanni dei Fiorentini
V. d. Cimatori
Largo dei Fiorentini
Vicolo d. Palle
Vic. Orbitelli
Via G. Giraud
Via d. Governo Vecchio
Torre dell'Orologio
Oratorio dei Filippini
Chiesa Nuova
Via d. Filippini
Vic. Sforza Cesarini
V. d. Chiesa Nuova
Palazzo del Governo Vecchio
Via d. Fossa
V. di Tor Millina
Via Parione
Via d. Teatro Pace
Sant'Agnese in Agone
Fontana dei Quattro Fiumi
Piazza Navona
Palazzo Pamphilj
Vic. Sugarelli
Via dei Banchi Vecchi
Vic. d. Cefalo
Via dei Bresciani
Via Giulia
Via del Gonfalone
Vicolo d. Scimmia
Vic. d. Prigioni
Via delle Carceri
Vic. Cellini
Via d. Cartari
Vicolo d. Malpasso
Via d. Moretta
Piazza d. Chiesa Nuova
Vic. d. Governo Vecchio
Via della Sora
Vicolo Savelli
Vic. d. Cancelleria
Via d. Leutari
Piazza di Pasquino
Via di Pasquino
Pasquino
Palazzo Braschi
V. Larga
V. Cerri
Lungot. d. Sangallo
Lungot. Gianicolense
PARIONE
Corso Vittorio
Palazzo della Cancelleria
Piazza della Cancelleria
Piccola Farnesina
Palazzo Massimo alle Colonne
Palazzo Ricci
Largo Perosi
V. di S. Aurea
Via Monserrato
Via dei Cappellari
Via del Pellegrino
V. d. Orti d'Alibert
V. delle Mantellate
Ponte G. Mazzini
V. d. Barchetta
Sant'Eligio degli Orefici
Santa Maria in Monserrato
V. d. Montoro
Via dei Baullari
Piazza del Paradiso
Campo de' Fiori
Piazza del Biscione
Lungotevere dei Tebaldi
Via di S. Eligio
Via in Caterina
Via di S. Girolamo d. Carità
San Girolamo della Carità
Vic. d. Gallo
Via dei Baullari
Via Corda
Palazzo Pio Righetti
Carcere di Regina Coeli
Via della Lungara
Santa Maria dell'Orazione e Morte
Via dei Farnesi
Piazza Farnese
Palazzo Farnese
Via d. Mascherone
Via d. Balestrari
Vicolo d. Grotte
Via dei Giubbonari
Vic. S. Francesco di Sales
Via S. Francesco di Sales
Vicolo d. Penitenza
Via della Penitenza
Lungotevere d. Farnesina
Vicolo d. Polverone
Via Capo di Ferro
Palazzo Spada
Via d. Arco d. Monte
Palazzo del Monte di Pietà
Villa Farnesina
Santissima Trinità dei Pellegrini
Via di S. Paolo alla Regola
Via dei Riari
Lungara
Via dei Pettinari
V. d. Trinità d. Pellegrini
Via del Conservatorio
Palazzo Corsini & Galleria Nazionale d'Arte Antica
Via delle Zoccolette
REGOLA
Lungot. d. Vallati
Orto Botanico del Gianicolo
Via Corsini
Porta Settimiana
Vicolo Moroni
Ponte Sisto
Casa della Fornarina
V. d. S. Dorotea
V. Ponte Sisto
Via Benedetta
Lungot. R. Sanzio
Via G. Garibaldi
Via della Scala
Vic. d. Bologna
Vic. d. Cinque
V. del Politeama
Santa Maria della Scala

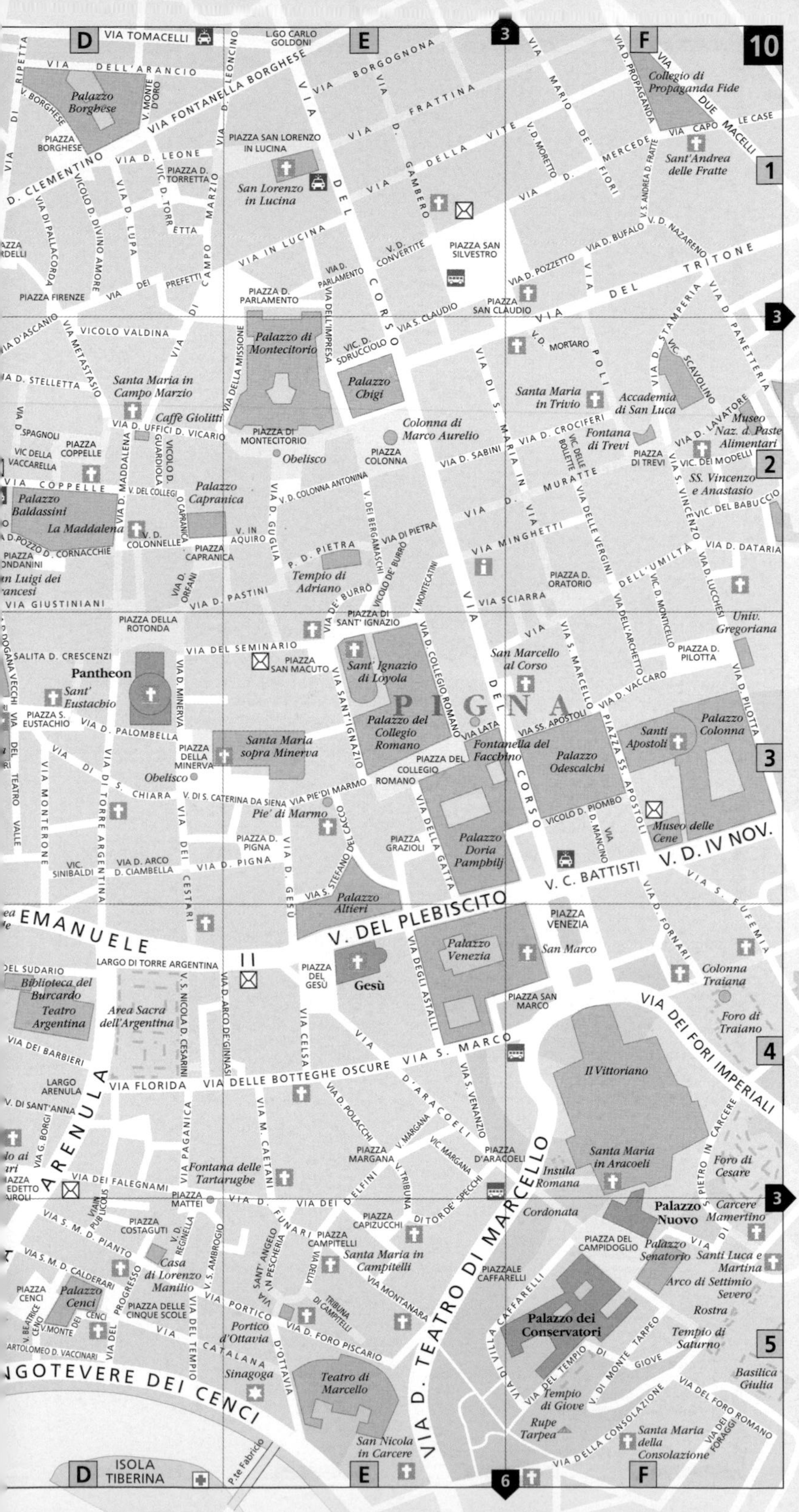

10
D
E
F
3
1
2
3
4
5
6
VIA TOMACELLI
L.GO CARLO GOLDONI
VIA DI RIPETTA
VIA DELL'ARANCIO
Palazzo Borghese
V. BORGHESE
V. MONTE D'ORO
VIA FONTANELLA BORGHESE
PIAZZA BORGHESE
VIA D. LEONCINO
VIA BORGOGNONA
VIA FRATTINA
VIA DELLA VITE
VIA MARIO DE' FIORI
VIA D. PROPAGANDA
Collegio di Propaganda Fide
VIA DUE MACELLI
LE CASE
VIA CAPO
Sant'Andrea delle Fratte
V.D. MERCEDE
V.D. MORETTO
VIA D. GAMBERO
PIAZZA SAN LORENZO IN LUCINA
San Lorenzo in Lucina
VIA D. CLEMENTINO
VIA D. LEONE
PIAZZA D. TORRETTA
VIC. D. TORRETTA
VICOLO D. DIVINO AMORE
VIA DI PALLACORDA
VIA D. LUPA
VIA DI CAMPO MARZIO
VIA IN LUCINA
V.D. CONVERTITE
PIAZZA SAN SILVESTRO
VIA D. POZZETTO
VIA D. BUFALO
V.S. ANDREA D. FRATTE
V.D. NAZARENO
VIA DEL TRITONE
PIAZZA FIRENZE
VIA DEI PREFETTI
VIA D. PARLAMENTO
PIAZZA D. PARLAMENTO
VIA DELL'IMPRESA
VIA DEL CORSO
VIA S. CLAUDIO
PIAZZA SAN CLAUDIO
VIA D. STAMPERIA
VIA D. PANETTERIA
VIA D'ASCANIO
VICOLO VALDINA
VIA METASTASIO
VIA D. STELLETTA
VIA DELLA MISSIONE
Palazzo di Montecitorio
VIC. D. SDRUCCIOLO
Palazzo Chigi
V.D. MORTARO
VIA POLI
VIC. SCAVOLINO
Santa Maria in Campo Marzio
Santa Maria in Trivio
Accademia di San Luca
Caffè Giolitti
VIA D. UFFICI D. VICARIO
PIAZZA DI MONTECITORIO
Colonna di Marco Aurelio
VIA D. CROCIFERI
Fontana di Trevi
VIA D. LAVATORE
Museo Naz. d. Paste Alimentari
V. D. SPAGNOLI
PIAZZA COPPELLE
VIC DELLA VACCARELLA
VIA D. MADDALENA
VICOLO D. GUARDIOLA
Obelisco
PIAZZA COLONNA
VIA D. SABINI
VIC. DELLE BOLLETTE
PIAZZA DI TREVI
VIC. DEI MODELLI
VIA COPPELLE
V. DEL COLLEGIO
Palazzo Capranica
V.D. COLONNA ANTONINA
VIA DI S. MARIA IN VIA
VIA D. MURATTE
SS. Vincenzo e Anastasio
Palazzo Baldassini
La Maddalena
VIA D. GUGLIA
V. DEI BERGAMASCHI
VIA DELLE VERGINI
VIA S. VINCENZO
VIC. DEL BABUCCIO
V.D. COLONNELLE
V. IN AQUIRO
VIA DI PIETRA
VIA MINGHETTI
VIA D. DATARIA
VIA D. POZZO D. CORNACCHIE
PIAZZA CAPRANICA
P. D. PIETRA
VICOLO DE' BURRÒ
VIA DELL'UMILTÀ
Tempio di Adriano
PIAZZA D. ORATORIO
VIA D. LUCCHESI
VIA D. ORFANI
VIA D. PASTINI
VIA DE' BURRÒ
V. MONTECATINI
VIA SCIARRA
VIC. D. MONTICELLO
VIA GIUSTINIANI
PIAZZA DELLA ROTONDA
PIAZZA DI SANT' IGNAZIO
VIA DELL'ARCHETTO
Univ. Gregoriana
SALITA D. CRESCENZI
VIA DEL SEMINARIO
PIAZZA SAN MACUTO
Sant' Ignazio di Loyola
VIA D. COLLEGIO ROMANO
San Marcello al Corso
VIA S. MARCELLO
PIAZZA D. PILOTTA
Pantheon
Sant' Eustachio
VIA D. MINERVA
VIA SANT'IGNAZIO
PIGNA
VIA D. VACCARO
VIA D. PILOTTA
PIAZZA S. EUSTACHIO
VIA D. PALOMBELLA
Palazzo del Collegio Romano
VIA LATA
VIA SS. APOSTOLI
PIAZZA SS. APOSTOLI
Santi Apostoli
Palazzo Colonna
Santa Maria sopra Minerva
PIAZZA DELLA MINERVA
Fontanella del Facchino
Palazzo Odescalchi
Obelisco
PIAZZA DEL COLLEGIO ROMANO
VIA DI S. CHIARA
V. DI S. CATERINA DA SIENA
VIA PIE' DI MARMO
VICOLO D. PIOMBO
VIA D. MANCINO
Museo delle Cere
VIA MONTERONE
VIA DI TORRE ARGENTINA
VIA DEL TEATRO VALLE
Pie' di Marmo
VIA DEI CESTARI
PIAZZA D. PIGNA
PIAZZA GRAZIOLI
VIA DELLA GATTA
Palazzo Doria Pamphilj
V. D. IV NOV.
VIC. SINIBALDI
VIA D. ARCO D. CIAMBELLA
VIA D. PIGNA
VIA D. GESÙ
VIA S. STEFANO DEL CACCO
V. C. BATTISTI
VIA S. EUFEMIA
Palazzo Altieri
V. DEL PLEBISCITO
PIAZZA VENEZIA
VIA D. FORNARI
EMANUELE
Palazzo Venezia
San Marco
Colonna Traiana
DEL SUDARIO
LARGO DI TORRE ARGENTINA
PIAZZA DEL GESÙ
Gesù
VIA DEGLI ASTALLI
Biblioteca del Burcardo
Teatro Argentina
Area Sacra dell'Argentina
V.S. NICOLA D. CESARINI
VIA D. ARCO DE'GINNASI
VIA CELSA
PIAZZA SAN MARCO
VIA DEI FORI IMPERIALI
Foro di Traiano
VIA DEI BARBIERI
VIA S. MARCO
Il Vittoriano
LARGO ARENULA
VIA FLORIDA
VIA DELLE BOTTEGHE OSCURE
VIA D'ARACOELI
VIA S. VENANZIO
V. DI SANT'ANNA
VIA ARENULA
VIA D. POLACCHI
VIA G. BORGI
VIA PAGANICA
VIA M. CAETANI
V. MARGANA
VIC. MARGANA
PIAZZA MARGANA
PIAZZA D'ARACOELI
Santa Maria in Aracoeli
VIA DI SAN PIETRO IN CARCERE
Foro di Cesare
Fontana delle Tartarughe
VIA DEI FALEGNAMI
V. TRIBUNA
VIA DEI DELFINI
Insula Romana
VIA DI TOR DE' SPECCHI
VIA DEL TEATRO DI MARCELLO
PIAZZA MATTEI
VIA D. FUNARI
Cordonata
Palazzo Nuovo
Carcere Mamertino
VIA IN PUBLICOLIS
VIA S. M. D. PIANTO
PIAZZA COSTAGUTI
V. D. REGINELLA
VIA S. AMBROGIO
PIAZZA CAPIZUCCHI
PIAZZA CAMPITELLI
PIAZZA DEL CAMPIDOGLIO
Palazzo Senatorio
Santi Luca e Martina
VIA S. M. D. CALDERARI
Casa di Lorenzo Manilio
VIA SANT' ANGELO IN PESCHERIA
VIA DELLA TRIBUNA
Santa Maria in Campitelli
VIA MONTANARA
PIAZZALE CAFFARELLI
Arco di Settimio Severo
PIAZZA CENCI
Palazzo Cenci
VIA DEL PROGRESSO
PIAZZA DELLE CINQUE SCOLE
VIA PORTICO D'OTTAVIA
TRIBUNA DI CAMPITELLI
VIA D. FORO PISCARIO
VIA DI VILLA CAFFARELLI
Palazzo dei Conservatori
Rostra
V. BEATRICE CENCI
V. MONTE DEI CENCI
Portico d'Ottavia
VIA CATALANA
VIA DEL TEMPIO
Tempio di Saturno
ARTOLOMEO D. VACCINARI
NGOTEVERE DEI CENCI
Sinagoga
Teatro di Marcello
VIA DEL TEMPIO DI GIOVE
V. DI MONTE TARPEO
Basilica Giulia
Tempio di Giove
VIA DEL FORO ROMANO
Rupe Tarpea
VIA DELLA CONSOLAZIONE
Santa Maria della Consolazione
VIA DEI FORAGGI
San Nicola in Carcere
ISOLA TIBERINA
P.te Fabricio

Rome Bus Routes
PRATI
Ottaviano
Lepanto
Flaminio
Stazione Roma-Viterbo
Villa Giulia
Santa Maria del Popolo
PIAZZA D. POPOLO
VIALE DELLE MILIZIE
VIA COLA DI RIENZO
VIA CRESCENZIO
VIA CICERONE
VIA D. RIPETTA
VIA DEL CORSO
VIA DEL BABUINO
VIA CONDOTTI
VIA TOMACELLI
P.ZA CAVOUR
Ponte Cavour
Ponte Umberto
Musei Vaticani
PIAZZA DEL RISORGIMENTO
VIA PORCARI
CITTÀ DEL VATICANO
Cappella Sistina
San Pietro
PIAZZA SAN PIETRO
BORGO S. ANGELO
V. D. CONCILIAZONE
BORGO
Castel Sant'Angelo
VIA D. PORTA CAVALLEGGERI
Ponte Pr. Amedeo
PONTE
CORSO VITTORIO EMANUELE II
CORSO D. RINASCIMENTO
Pantheon
PIAZZA D. ROTONDA
PARIONE
L.GO TORRE ARGENTINA
Gesù
Stazione di San Pietro
V. D. STAZIONE DI S. PIETRO
VIALE ALDO FABRIZI
Gianicolo
Ponte Mazzini
LT. TEBALDI
LT. D. FARNESINA
Villa Farnesina
Ponte Sisto
LT. D. VALLATI
VIA ARENULA
LT. D. CENCI
Ponte Garibaldi
LT.D.ANGUILLARA
Ponte Palatino
Santa Maria in Trastevere
TRASTEVERE
Villa Doria Pamphilj
V. DI TRASTEVERE
VIA DANDOLO
LUNGOTEVERE AVENTINO
Ponte Sublicio
Tevere
VIA MARMORATA
VIALE DI TRASTEVERE
VIA MANUZIO
VIA ZABAGLIA
TESTACCIO
Ponte Testaccio
Stazione Trastevere
KEY TO BUS MAP
62 Bus route
62 Start/end of bus route (capolinea)
Direction
19 Tram route
19 Start/end of tram route (capolinea)
Metro station
Railway station
Major sight
0 metres 500
0 yards 500

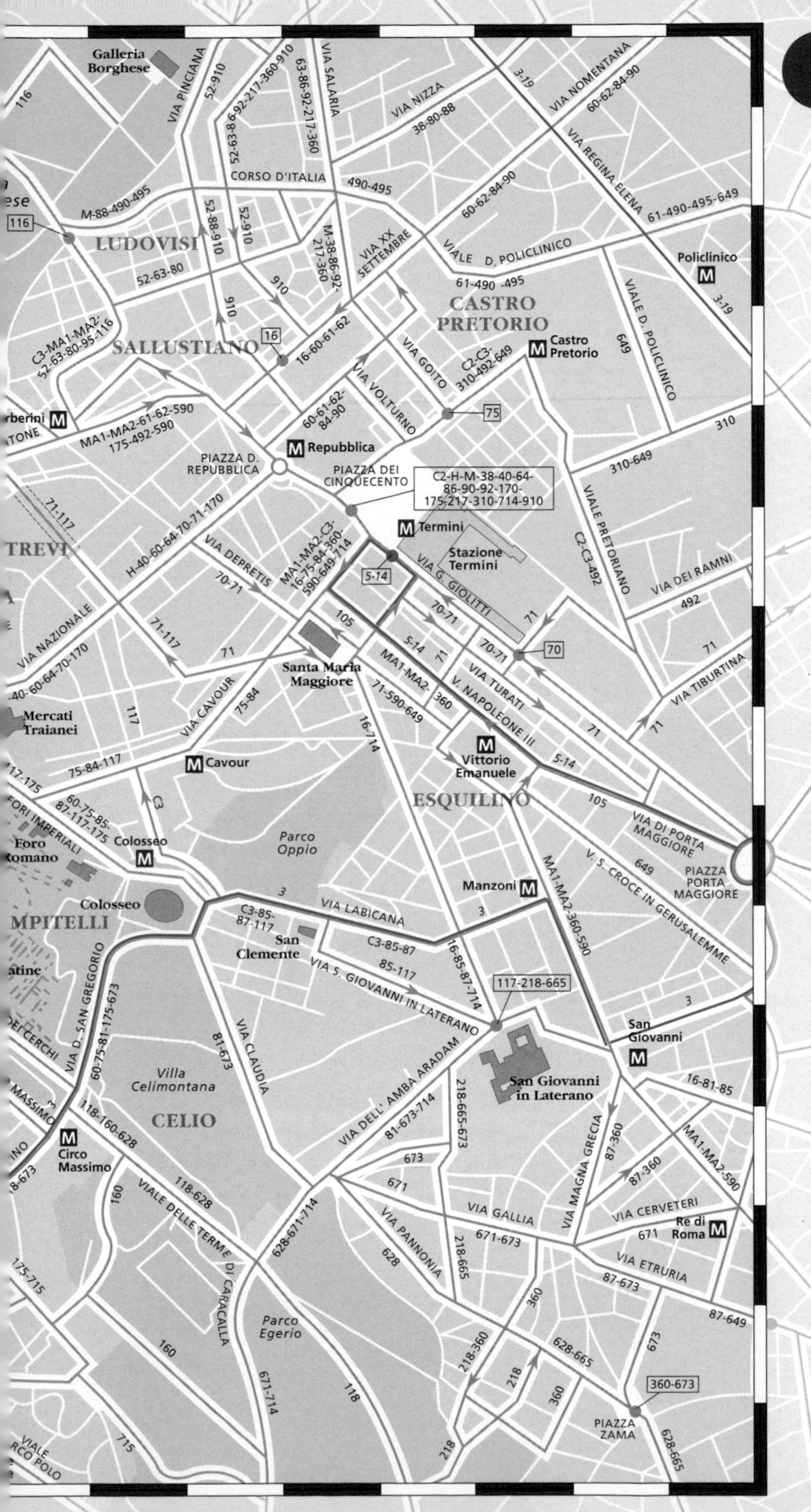

Galleria Borghese
VIA PINCIANA
VIA SALARIA
VIA NIZZA
VIA NOMENTANA
VIA REGINA ELENA
CORSO D'ITALIA
LUDOVISI
VIA XX SETTEMBRE
VIALE D. POLICLINICO
Policlinico
CASTRO PRETORIO
Castro Pretorio
SALLUSTIANO
VIA GOITO
VIA VOLTURNO
Repubblica
PIAZZA D. REPUBBLICA
PIAZZA DEI CINQUECENTO
Termini
Stazione Termini
VIA G. GIOLITTI
VIALE PRETORIANO
VIA DEI RAMNI
TREVI
VIA DEPRETIS
VIA NAZIONALE
Santa Maria Maggiore
VIA TURATI
V. NAPOLEONE III
VIA TIBURTINA
Mercati Traianei
VIA CAVOUR
Cavour
Vittorio Emanuele
ESQUILINO
FORI IMPERIALI
Foro Romano
Colosseo
Parco Oppio
VIA DI PORTA MAGGIORE
PIAZZA PORTA MAGGIORE
V. S. CROCE IN GERUSALEMME
Manzoni
VIA LABICANA
San Clemente
VIA S. GIOVANNI IN LATERANO
VIA D. SAN GREGORIO
VIA CLAUDIA
Villa Celimontana
CELIO
VIA DELL' AMBA ARADAM
San Giovanni in Laterano
San Giovanni
Circo Massimo
VIA MAGNA GRECIA
VIA GALLIA
VIA CERVETERI
Re di Roma
VIA PANNONIA
VIA ETRURIA
VIALE DELLE TERME DI CARACALLA
Parco Egerio
PIAZZA ZAMA

# LAZIO

*Lying between the Apennines and the Tyrrhenian Sea, Lazio is a varied region of volcanic lakes, mountains, ravines, vineyards and olive groves. Before the rise of Rome, it was populated by the Etruscans and various Italic tribes, including the Latins, after whom the region is named. Besides rich archaeological sites, Lazio also offers skiing and swimming and water sports in the lakes and sea.*

Lazio was inhabited at least 60,000 years ago, although the first signs of a substantial civilization date back to the 10th century BC. By the 7th century BC a flourishing Etruscan and Sabine civilization based on trade and agriculture existed in the north, while the region's southern margins were colonized by the Latins, Volsci and Hernici. History mingles with myth in the writings of Virgil, who describes how Aeneas landed in Lazio where he married the daughter of the king of the Latins. Romulus and Remus (legendary founders of Rome) were descendants of this alliance.

With the rise of Rome as a power, the Etruscan and Latin peoples were, in time, overwhelmed and the focus of the region turned to the city of Rome. Great roads and aqueducts extended out of the city like spokes of a wheel, and wealthy patricians built lavish villas in the surrounding countryside.

The early Middle Ages saw the rise of the Church's temporal power and, with the foundation of monasteries at Subiaco and Montecassino, Lazio became the cradle of western monasticism, and eventually part of the Papal States. In the 16th and 17th centuries, wealthy papal families competed with one another to build luxurious villas and gardens, hiring some of the best architects of the Renaissance and Baroque.

Throughout its history, however, Lazio has been eclipsed and neglected by Rome. The Pontine marshes were a malaria-ridden swamp until the 1920s, when Mussolini had them drained and brought new roads and agricultural improvements to the area.

Looking out over Caprarola during the early evening *passeggiata*

◁ Vignola's graceful Renaissance parterre gardens and fountains in Villa Lante, Viterbo

# Exploring Lazio

Much of Lazio's landscape was formed by the eruption of four volcanoes which showered the area with lava. Lakes formed in the craters, and the soil, rendered fertile by the lava, nourished vines, olives, fruit and nut trees. The volcanic activity also left Lazio with hot springs, notably around Tivoli, Viterbo and Fiuggi. Rome dominates the area, dividing the wooded hills of the north from the reclaimed Pontine marshes in the south. Swimming and sailing are possible in lakes Bracciano, Bolsena and Albano, while Lazio's best beaches lie between Gaeta and Sabaudia in the Parco Nazionale del Circeo.

## SIGHTS AT A GLANCE

- Anagni 15
- Bomarzo 4
- Caprarola 5
- Cerveteri 7
- Frascati and the Castelli Romani 10
- Gaeta 19
- Lake Bracciano 8
- Montecassino 14
- Montefiascone 3
- Ostia Antica 9
- Palestrina 12
- *ROME pp382–459*
- Sermoneta and Ninfa 16
- Sperlonga 18
- Subiaco 13
- Tarquinia 6
- Terracina 17
- Tivoli 11
- Tuscania 1
- Viterbo 2

### SEE ALSO


- ***Where to Stay*** pp592–3
- ***Where to Eat*** pp641–3

The Tolfa hills southwest of Lake Bracciano

**KEY**

- Motorway
- Motorway under construction
- Major road
- Secondary road
- Minor road
- Scenic route
- Main railway
- Minor railway
- Regional border
- Summit

**For additional map symbols** *see back flap*

The old quarter overlooking the beach at Sperlonga

## GETTING AROUND

Rome's two international airports at Fiumicino and Ciampino serve the region. The main motorways are the *Autostrada del Sole* Firenze–Roma (A1) and Roma–Napoli (A1–E45), and the Roma–L'Aquila (A24–E80). The ring road *(raccordo anulare)* around Rome connects the motorways and main roads.

The Lazio bus service, COTRAL, serves all the main towns with changeover points for the smaller locations in Rome and at Latina, Frosinone, Viterbo and Rieti. Train routes into the region from other Italian cities are efficient, although within Lazio the services are slower and less frequent.

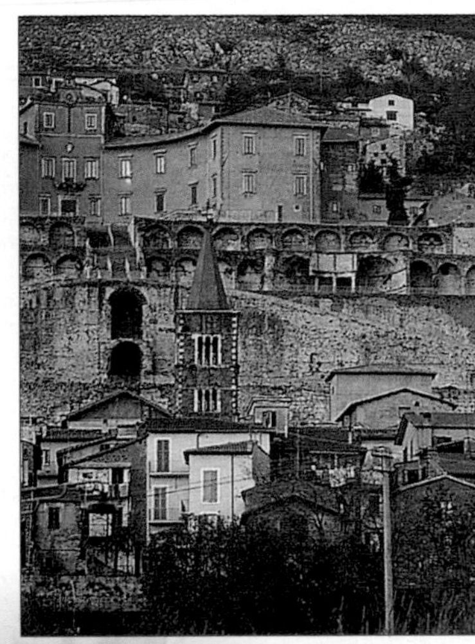

Palestrina's terraces climbing up the hill

Carved loggia of the Palazzo Papale, Viterbo

## Tuscania ❶

*Viterbo.* *7,500.* *Piazza Franco Basile 4.* *Fri am.*

Tuscania's trim walls and towers are visible from afar on the empty low-lying plains between Viterbo and Tarquinia. Although shaken by an earthquake in 1971, its medieval and Renaissance buildings have since been carefully reconstructed. Just outside the city walls, on the rocky Colle San Pietro, two remarkable churches dating from the Lombard-Romanesque period occupy the site of Tuscana, a major Etruscan centre conquered by Rome in 300 BC.

**Santa Maria Maggiore**, at the foot of the hill, has a typically Lombard-Romanesque asymmetric façade with blind arcades and a bold rose window. Over the central door lies a simple marble Madonna and Child, framed by abstract motifs and biblical scenes. Inside, a rare 12th-century full-immersion baptism font stands in the aisle.

The Lombard-Romanesque church of **San Pietro**, on top of the hill, is a striking building of ochre-hued tufa and white marble details. It stands on a grassy piazza, along with two medieval towers and a bishop's palace. The façade features an intricately inlaid rose window flanked by strange reliefs, including three-headed bearded demons. The interior is true to its 8th-century form, with squat columns, toothed arches, capitals carved with stylized plants and a Cosmati floor. Below the church lies a strange mosque-like crypt.

Façade of San Pietro, Tuscania

## Viterbo ❷

*63,000.* *FS* *Ex Porta Romana Station (0761 30 47 95).* *Sat.*

Viterbo was an important Etruscan centre before falling to the Romans in the 4th century BC. Its heyday, however, came in the 13th century when it briefly became the papal seat (1257–81). During World War II it was devastated, but the austere grey stone medieval core, still encircled by walls, and many of the town's churches, have been carefully restored.

In **San Pellegrino**, Viterbo's oldest and best preserved quarter, medieval houses with towers, arches and external staircases line narrow streets running between little piazzas decorated with fountains.

On Piazza San Lorenzo the 12th-century **Duomo** boasts an elegant black and white striped bell tower, a solemn 16th-century façade and a stark Romanesque interior. The adjacent 13th-century **Palazzo Papale**, with a finely carved loggia, was built for popes on their visits to the city.

The town's civic buildings border the main square, Piazza del Plebiscito. The most interesting is the 15th-century **Palazzo dei Priori**, frescoed inside by Baldassare Croce with scenes from the town's history and mythological past.

Outside the city walls, on Viale Capocci, the Romanesque **Santa Maria della Verità** has wonderful 15th-century frescoes by Lorenzo da Viterbo.

Villa Lante's small but splendid Renaissance gardens, considered Vignola's masterpiece

*For hotels and restaurants in this region see pp592–3 and pp641–3*

**Environs:** The **Villa Lante**, northeast of Viterbo, was begun in 1562 by Vignola for Cardinal Gambara. The main attractions are the outstanding Renaissance gardens and fountains. Be careful not to be a victim of a 16th-century practical joke: many of the fountains will sprinkle people without warning.

**Palazzo dei Priori**
Piazza Plebiscito. ***Tel*** *0761 34 82 41.* *daily.*

**Villa Lante**
Bagnaia. ***Tel*** *0761 28 80 08.*
*Tue–Sun.* *1 Jan, 1 May, 25 Dec.* *to gardens.*

## Montefiascone ❸

*Viterbo. 13,000. FS Largo Plebiscito 1 (0761 83 20 60). Wed.*

**Carved 11th-century capital in San Flaviano, Montefiascone**

This pretty town is perched on the edge of a defunct volcanic crater between the shores of Lake Bolsena, over which there are splendid views, and the Via Cassia. It is dominated by the octagonal bulk of its cathedral, **Santa Margherita**, whose dome, created in the 1670s by Carlo Fontana, is second only in size to St Peter's.

On the town's outskirts, along the Via Cassia towards Orvieto, lies **San Flaviano**, a lovely double-decker building with a 12th-century church oriented east over an 11th-century church pointing west. Inside are some fine 14th-century frescoes and freely carved capitals, thought to have been inspired by the traditions of Etruscan art.

**The main façade of the pentagonal Palazzo Farnese at Caprarola**

**Environs:** The popular lake-side beach resort of **Bolsena**, 15 km (9 miles) north on Lake Bolsena, has a medieval castle, as well as boats to the islands of Bisentina and Martana.

## Bomarzo ❹

*Parco dei Mostri, Bomarzo.*
***Tel*** *0761 92 40 29. FS to Viterbo.*
*from Viterbo (not Sun or public hols). 8:30am–sunset.*

The Sacro Bosco beneath the town of Bomarzo was created between 1522 and 1580 by Duke Vicino Orsini as a bizarre memorial to his late wife. Far from designing a meticulous Renaissance garden, Orsini embraced the artificiality and distortion of the Mannerist period by creating lop-sided buildings and sculpting huge boulders of stone into fantastic creatures and vast allegorical monsters.

**One of the bizarre stone monsters in Bomarzo's Sacro Bosco**

## Caprarola ❺

*Viterbo. 4,900. Via Filippo Nicolai 2 (0761 64 61 57). Tue.*

Perhaps the grandest of the country villas created during the 17th century by the wealthy families of Rome, **Palazzo Farnese** *(see p380)* is the focal point of the medieval village of Caprarola. Designed by Vignola, it was built between 1559 and 1575 and takes its star-shape from the foundations of a large pentagonal fortress designed by Antonio da Sangallo the Younger half a century earlier. On the main floor, reached by an elaborately stuccoed spiral staircase, the rooms were frescoed, largely by the Zuccari brothers in 1560, with scenes depicting heroic episodes from the life of Hercules and the Farnese family.

**Environs:** Created, according to legend, by the god Hercules ramming his club into the ground, **Lago di Vico**, 4 km (3 miles) west of Caprarola, in fact occupies the remnants of a volcanic crater. An idyllic enclave, the lake is encircled by the wooded slopes of the Cimini Hills (much of which is a nature reserve). A scenic road runs around the lake, and the best place for swimming is on the southeast shore.

**Palazzo Farnese**
Caprarola. ***Tel*** *0761 64 60 52.*
*Tue–Sun.* *1 Jan, 25 Dec.*

Etruscan tumulus tombs from the necropolis at Cerveteri

## Tarquinia 6

Viterbo. 15,000. FS *Piazza Cavour 23 (0766 84 92 82). Wed.*

Ancient Tarquinia (Tarxuna) was one of Etruria's most important centres. It occupied a strategic position to the north-east of the present town, on a ridge dominating the coastal plain, until the 4th century BC when it fell to Rome.

Tarquinia itself is worth a wander for its crumbling medieval churches and spacious main square, though the main reason to visit is the **Museo Archeologico e Necropoli**, which has one of Italy's better collections of Etruscan finds. Relaxed, reclining statues of the deceased adorn the sarcophagi on the ground floor, but the star attraction, on the mezzanine, is a group of terracotta winged horses dating from the 4th century BC.

On a hilltop 2 km (1 mile) southeast of town are the frescoed tombs of the **necropolis** dug into the soft volcanic tufa. There are almost 6,000 tombs but only about 15 can be visited at a time. The frescoes that decorate them, designed to remind the dead of life, range from frenetic dancing figures in the Tomba delle Leonesse to the diners reclining in the Tomba dei Leopardi.

Dancers from the 4th-century BC frescoed Tomba del Triclinio in the Museo Archeologico, Tarquinia

**Museo Archeologico e Necropoli**
Piazza Cavour. ***Tel*** *0766 85 60 36; 85 63 08 (necropolis). Tue–Sun. 1 Jan, 1 May, 25 Dec.*

## Cerveteri 7

Roma. 30,000. FS *P.za Risorgimento 19 (06 99 55 19 71). Fri.*

In the 6th century BC Cerveteri (ancient Kysry) was one of the most populated and culturally rich towns of the Mediterranean, trading with Greece and controlling a large area along the coast. The **necropolis**, a city of the dead 2 km (1 mile) outside town, is a network of streets lined with tombs dating from the 7th to the 1st century BC. Some of the larger tumulus tombs, like the Tomba degli Scudi e delle Sedie, are arranged like houses with rooms, doors and corridors. The Tomba dei Rilievi is decorated with plaster reliefs of tools, pets and mythological figures. Although the best finds from the necropolis are in museums such as the Vatican Museums, Villa Giulia and the British Museum in London, some can be seen in the small **Museo Nazionale Cerite** in the centre of town.

**Environs:** There are more traces of the Etruscans to be seen at **Norchia**, where the tombs are carved out of a rock face, and **Sutri**, whose amphitheatre is one of the few relics of the living Etruscans.

**Necropolis**
Via Necropoli. ***Tel*** *06 994 06 51. Tue–Sun. some pub hols.*

**Museo Nazionale Cerite**
Piazza Santa Maria. ***Tel*** *06 994 13 54. Tue–Sun. pub hols.*

## Lake Bracciano 8

Roma. FS *Bracciano. Piazza Mazzini 7, Bracciano (06 99 80 60 18).*

Medieval Anguillara on Lake Bracciano

Bracciano is a large lake famous for its fish, and popular for water sports and lakeside lunches.

Medieval **Anguillara**, to the south, is the prettiest of the lakeside towns with romantic views over the water. The main town, **Bracciano**, on the east shore, is dominated by the Orsini-Odescalchi fortress, a pentagonal 15th-century structure with frescoes by Antoniazzo Romano and other Tuscan and Umbrian artists.

**Castello Orsini-Odescalchi**
P.za Mazzini 14. ***Tel*** *06 99 80 23 79. Tue–Sun. 1 Jan, 25 Dec.*

## Ostia Antica 9

Viale dei Romagnoli 717, Ostia. ***Tel** 06 56 35 80 99.* M *Piramide, then* FS *from Porta San Paolo to Ostia Antica.* **Excavations & Museum** *8:30am–1 hr before sunset Tue–Sun.* *1 Jan, 25 Dec.*

For over 600 years Ostia was Rome's main port and a busy trading centre, until the 5th century AD when a disastrous combination of malaria and commercial competition brought the town into decline. Silt preserved its buildings and it now lies 5 km (3 miles) inland.

The ruins of Ostia give a vivid idea of life in Classical times. The main thoroughfare, the **Decumanus Maximus**, runs through the Forum, which houses Ostia's largest temple, the **Capitol**, and past the restored **theatre**, still used for open air concerts in summer. The road is lined with baths, shops and multi-storey buildings. There is even a **Thermopolium**, or bar, with a marble counter and paintings advertising food and drink.

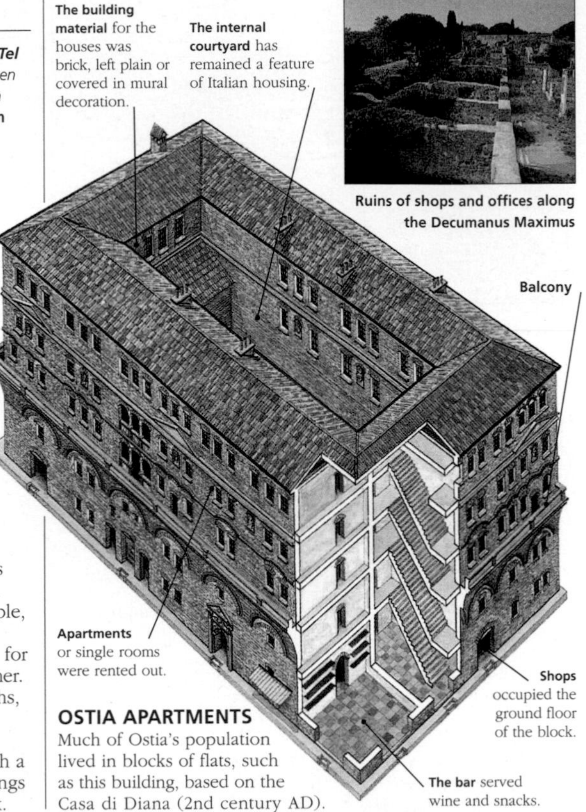


**Ruins of shops and offices along the Decumanus Maximus**

**OSTIA APARTMENTS**
Much of Ostia's population lived in blocks of flats, such as this building, based on the Casa di Diana (2nd century AD).

## Frascati and the Castelli Romani 10

Roma. FS *Frascati.* *06 94 18 42 56.* **Villa Aldobrandini Gardens** *Mon–Fri, call 06 9422 560 for permission a few days in advance.*

The Alban hills have long been a country retreat for Romans. In Classical times they were scattered with villas; in the Middle Ages with fortified castles (hence the name); and in the 16th and 17th centuries with luxurious residences and their spectacular parks. During World War II German defences were based in the Alban hills and many Castelli towns were damaged by Allied bombs. Although partly protected by a nature reserve, the hilltop towns are popular day-trip destinations as well as being famous for their white wine.

**Frascati**'s central piazza is a belvedere overlooked by the Villa Aldobrandini, a majestic 17th-century building set in a splendid park of secret grottoes, fountains and statues.

The fortified Abbazia di San Nilo in **Grottaferrata**, 3 km (2 miles) south, was founded in 1004 and contains some lovely 17th-century frescoes by Domenichino in the chapel.

Overlooking Lake Albano, 6 km (4 miles) south, **Castel Gandolfo** is the site of the pope's summer palace. When in residence the pope addresses the crowd from the balcony.

Gathered around a sturdy 9th-century castle, and famed for its strawberries, **Nemi**, 10 km (6 miles) southeast, looks down onto the glassy dark blue waters of Lake Nemi.

**The forested shores around the small, volcanic Lake Nemi**

Tivoli, a favourite place to escape the heat of the Roman summer

## Tivoli ⓫

Roma. 57,000. FS 0774 45 35 62. Wed.

Hill-town Tivoli, now probably the most popular excursion from Rome, was once a favoured resort of the ancient Romans, attracted by its fresh water and sulphur springs, and beautiful countryside. The temples that once covered Tivoli's hilltop are still visible in places. Some are half buried in medieval buildings, others, such as the Temples of Sibyl and Vesta, inside the gardens of the Sibilla restaurant (on Via Sibilla), are relatively intact.

Splendours from around the world reproduced in Hadrian's Villa

The town's most famous sight is the **Villa d'Este**, a sumptuous country residence created in the 16th century by Pirro Ligorio for Cardinal Ippolito d'Este from the shell of a Benedictine monastery. It is known primarily for its gardens, steeply raked on terraces, and studded with spectacular, if somewhat faded and moss-hung, fountains. Although suffering from reduced water-pressure and polluted water due to centuries of neglect, the gardens give a vivid impression of the frivolous luxury enjoyed by the papal families. Highlights include the Viale delle Cento Fontane and the Fontana dell'Organo Idraulico, which, thanks to a hydraulic system, can play music. At the other end of town, the **Villa Gregoriana**, now a hotel, is set in a lush wooded valley where paths wind down into a deep ravine.

**Environs:** About 5 km (3 miles) west of Tivoli are the ruins of **Hadrian's Villa**. Easily seen in conjunction with a visit to the town, this is one of the largest and most spectacular villas ever built in the Roman Empire (it once covered an area greater than the centre of Imperial Rome).

Hadrian was an inveterate traveller and his aim in creating the villa was to reproduce some of the wonders he had seen around the world. The Stoa Poikile, for example, a walkway around a rectangular pool and garden, recalls the painted colonnade of the Stoic philosophers in Athens, while the Canopus evokes the grand sanctuary of Serapis in Alexandria. There are also ruins of two bath complexes, a Latin and a Greek library, a Greek theatre, and a private study on a little island known as the Teatro Marittimo.

Today the rambling ruins, full of shady nooks and hidden corners, make a lovely place to relax, picnic or explore.

**Villa d'Este**
P.za Trento 1. **Tel** 0774 31 20 70. Tue–Sun. 1 Jan, 1 May, 25 Dec.

**Villa Gregoriana**
Largo Sant'Angelo. **Tel** 06 39 96 77 01. Tue–Sun. Dec–Feb.

**Hadrian's Villa**
**Tel** 0774 53 02 03. pub hols.

## Palestrina ⓬

Roma. 18,000. Piazza Santa Maria degli Angeli 2 (06 957 31 76).

Mosaic fragment of Nile in flood, Archaeological Museum, Palestrina

Medieval Palestrina grew up over the terraces of a huge temple dedicated to the goddess Fortuna Primigenia, the mother of all gods. The temple, founded in the 8th century BC and rebuilt in the 2nd century BC by Sulla, housed one of the most important oracles of ancient times. The terraces of the sanctuary, littered with fragments of columns and porticoes, lead up to the curved **Palazzo Barberini**. Built over the site of a circular temple, it now houses the **Museo Nazionale Archeologico**, best known for a 1st-century BC mosaic portraying the Nile in flood.

**Museo Nazionale Archeologico**
Via Barberini. **Tel** 06 953 81 00. daily. 1 Jan, 1 May, 25 Dec.

*For hotels and restaurants in this region see pp592–3 and pp641–3*

## Subiaco ⓭

*Roma. 9,000. Town Library, Via della Repubblica 26 (0774 82 28 00). Sat.*

In the 6th century, weary of the decadence of Rome, St Benedict left the city to become a hermit in a cave above Subiaco. Others joined him, and eventually there were 12 monasteries in the area.

Only two now survive: **Santa Scolastica**, dedicated to Benedict's sister, is organized around three cloisters, one Renaissance, one early Gothic and the third Cosmatesque. Higher up, the 12th-century **San Benedetto** is a more rewarding destination. Overhanging a deep gorge, it comprises two churches built on top of each other. The upper is decorated with 14th-century Sienese frescoes; the lower, built over several levels, incorporates the original cave where Benedict spent three years after fleeing Rome.

**Santa Scolastica**
3 km (2 miles) E of Subiaco.
***Tel** 0774 82 28 62. daily.*

**San Benedetto**
3 km (2 miles) E of Subiaco.
***Tel** 0774 81 98 00. daily. (upper church only).*

## Montecassino ⓮

Cassino. ***Tel** 0776 31 15 29.*
*Cassino then bus.*
*9am–12:30pm, 3:30–6:30pm daily (Nov–Mar: to 5pm).*

The Abbey of Montecassino, mother church of the Benedictine order and a centre of medieval art, was founded in 529 by St Benedict. By the 8th century it was an important centre of learning, and by the 11th century had become one of the richest monasteries in Europe.

In 1944 it was a German stronghold and a target for Allied bombs. Most of the complex was devastated, including the lavish Baroque church, but the walls remained intact and the abbey withstood for three months before falling to the Allies. The adjoining war cemeteries commemorate the 30,000 soldiers killed.

### THE MONASTERIES OF LAZIO

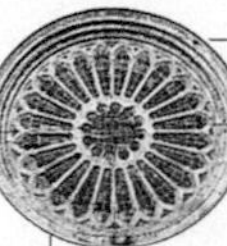

**Rose window, Fossanova**

St Benedict founded the Abbey of Montecassino around 529 and there wrote his famous Rule. Based on the principles of prayer, study and manual labour, this became the fundamental monastic code of western Europe. The Cistercian Order, an offshoot of the Benedictines, came to Italy from Burgundy in the 12th century. The Cistercians were followers of St Bernard, whose creed was based on austerity and self-sufficiency, qualities which were reflected in the simple, early Gothic architecture of their monasteries. Their first abbey was at Fossanova. Other Cistercian abbeys in Lazio include Valvisciolo (northeast of Sermoneta) and San Martino in Cimino (near Lago di Vico).

**The Abbey of Montecassino,** *destroyed during World War II, was rebuilt as a replica of its 17th-century predecessor.*

**The Abbey of San Benedetto,** *Subiaco, was founded in the 11th century over St Benedict's cave. A staircase carved in the rock leads to the grotto where he preached to shepherds.*

**The Abbey of Casamari,** *14 km (8 miles) east of Frosinone, was founded by Benedictine monks in 1035 and handed over to the Cistercians who rebuilt it in 1203.*

The abandoned medieval village of Ninfa, now a beautiful garden

## Anagni 15

*Frosinone. 20,000. FS Piazza Innocenzo III (0775 72 78 52). Wed.*

According to legend, Saturn founded five towns in southeast Lazio, including Anagni, Alatri and Arpino. This area is now known as La Ciociaria, from *ciocie*, the bark clogs worn in the area until about 30 years ago.

Before the Romans conquered this part of Lazio it was inhabited by several different tribes: the Volsci, the Sanniti, and the Hernici. Little is known of them, apart from the extraordinary walls with which they protected their settlements. In later years these were believed to have been built by the Cyclops, a mythical giant, which gave them their present name of Cyclopean walls.

**Anagni** was the most sacred Hernician centre until its destruction by the Romans in 306 BC. In the Middle Ages it was the birthplace and family seat of several popes, an era from which many buildings survive, most notably Boniface VIII's 13th-century mullion-windowed palace.

The beautiful Romanesque **Duomo**, Santa Maria, built over the ancient Hernician acropolis, boasts a fine Cosmati mosaic floor from the 13th century as well as 14th-century Sienese frescoes. The crypt of San Magno is frescoed with one of the most complete surviving cycles of the 12th and 13th centuries.

**Environs: Alatri**, perched on an olive-covered slope 28 km (17 miles) east of Anagni, was an important Hernician town. It preserves an impressive double set of Cyclopean walls, 2 km (1 mile) long and 3 m (10 ft) high, from its 7th-century BC acropolis. In the medieval town below the walls is the Romanesque church of Santa Maria Maggiore, greatly restored in the 13th century.

**Arpino**, 40 km (25 miles) east of Alatri, is a bustling town with a medieval core, and was the birthplace of the Roman orator, Cicero. About 3 km (2 miles) above Arpino, at the site of the ancient town of Civitavecchia, is a tremendous stretch of Cyclopean walls which includes a rare gateway with a pointed arch.

An unusual pointed arch in the Cyclopean walls at Arpino

## Sermoneta and Ninfa 16

*Latina. FS Latina Scalo. from Latina. Via Duca di Mare 19, Latina (0773 69 54 04).* ***Ninfa Tel*** *0773 63 39 35 (phone for group bookings). Apr–Oct: 1st Sat & Sun of the month (call for further dates).*

Sermoneta is a lovely hilltop town overlooking the Pontine Plains, with narrow cobbled streets winding around medieval houses, palaces and churches. The **Duomo** has a fine 15th-century panel by Benozzo Gozzoli showing the Virgin cradling Sermoneta in her hands. At the top of the town rises the moated fairy-tale Castello Caetani, frescoed with mythological scenes by a pupil of Pinturicchio.

In the valley below lies the abandoned medieval village of **Ninfa**, converted into lush gardens by the Caetani family in 1921. Streams and waterfalls punctuate the picturesque garden laid out among the crumbling buildings.

*For hotels and restaurants in this region see pp592–3 and pp641–3*

## Terracina ⓱

*Latina.* *40,000.* FS *Via Leopardi (0773 72 77 59).* *Thu.*

Roman Terracina was an important commercial centre on the Via Appia (the Appian Way). Today it is a popular seaside resort, with a fascinating collage of medieval buildings and Roman ruins in its historic centre, perched on the slopes of the Ausonian Hills. The more modern part of town by the sea is full of restaurants, bars and hotels.

Bombing during World War II uncovered many of the town's ancient structures, notably a stretch of the Appian Way and the original paving of the Roman Forum in Piazza del Municipio. The 11th-century **Duomo** was built in the shell of a Roman temple, and is still entered by the temple's steps. The medieval portico is adorned with a lovely 12th-century mosaic and the interior preserves the 13th-century mosaic pavement. Next door, the modern town hall houses the **Museo Archeologico**, devoted to local Greek and Roman finds.

**Duomo at Terracina with original Roman steps**

About 3 km (2 miles) above the town are the podium and foundations that once supported the Temple of Jove Anxur, dating back to the 1st century BC. This huge arcaded platform is illuminated at night and offers vertiginous views of Terracina and its bay.

**Museo Archeologico**
P Municipio. ***Tel*** *0773 70 72 77.* *Mon pm–Sun.* *some pub hols.*

## Sperlonga ⓲

*Latina.* *4,000.* *Corso San Leone 22 (0771 55 70 00).* *Sat.*

Sperlonga is a popular seaside resort surrounded by sandy beaches. The old town sits on a rocky promontory, a picturesque labyrinth of whitewashed buildings, narrow alleyways, piazzettas and balconies offering an occasional glimpse of the sea below. It is now full of bars, restaurants and boutiques. The modern part of town lies down on the seafront.

The area around Sperlonga was a favourite retreat for the ancient Romans during the hot summer months. They built villas along the coast, and converted the natural caves in the nearby cliffs into places to dine and relax.

In 1957 archaeologists excavating the huge complex of Tiberius's luxury villa, 1 km (half a mile) on the southern outskirts of town, found some marvellous 2nd-century BC Hellenistic sculptures in a large cave open to the sea. These sculptures, representing incidents from Homer's *Odyssey*, are thought to be by the same artists from Rhodes (where the Emperor Tiberius once lived) who were responsible for the Laocoön *(see p417)*. They are displayed, along with other local finds, in the **Museo Archeologico Nazionale** which is part of the archaeological zone.

**Stretches of sandy beach along the coast between Gaeta and Terracina**

**12th-century bell tower at Gaeta**

**Zona Archeologica**
Via Flacca. ***Tel*** *0771 54 80 28.* *daily.* *1 Jan, 25 Dec.*

## Gaeta ⓳

*Latina.* *22,000.* *Via Emanuele Filiberto 5 (0771 46 11 65).* *Wed.*

According to Virgil, Gaeta was named after Aeneas's wet nurse Caieta, who was allegedly buried here. The town sits on the southern headland of the gulf of Gaeta, under Monte Orlando. The historic centre is dominated by a mighty Aragonese castle and the pinnacles of mock-Gothic San Francesco. To the north, the modern quarter links Gaeta to the bay of Serapo, a picturesque beach resort.

Gaeta's most beautiful feature is the **Duomo**'s elegant late Romanesque bell tower, its lofty summit topped by a roof of coloured ceramic tiles. On the seafront lies the tiny 10th-century church of **San Giovanni a Mare**, with faded frescoes, a hemispherical dome and a sloping floor to let the sea flow out after flooding.

# SOUTHERN ITALY

# Southern Italy at a Glance

Visitors to southern Italy find a rich array of archaeological remains. Although those of the Romans at Pompeii are high on everyone's list, Greek ruins are found in Sicily and the southern coast and there are mysterious ancient structures, called *nuraghe*, in Sardinia. Campania, Puglia and Sicily are admired for their architecture, while across the south there are magnificent landscapes, abundant wildlife and endless opportunities for outdoor activities. The cuisine alone, with its eclectic heritage and diversity of tastes, provides the excuse to dawdle on the coast or in the mountain villages.

**The Parco Nazionale d'Abruzzo**, *a vast unspoilt wilderness, is home to wolves, bears and many species of birds* (see pp506–7).

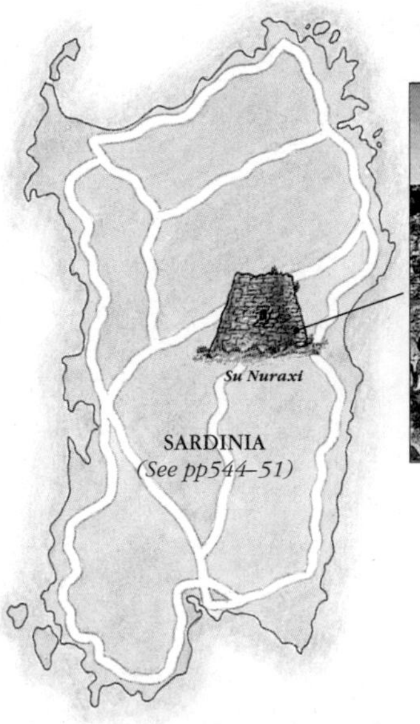

**Su Nuraxi at Barumini**, *built around 1500 BC, is the most celebrated of Sardinia's mysterious stone nuraghe sites* (see p549).

**The cloister decoration** *at Monreale cathedral is a legacy of Sicily's Arabic past, with elaborate columns adorned with fine mosaics and splendid sculpted capitals* (see pp530–31).

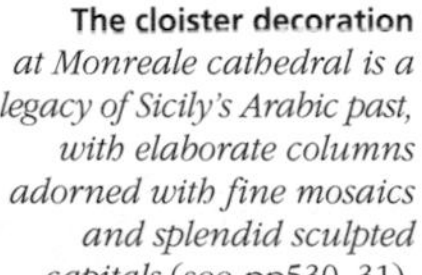

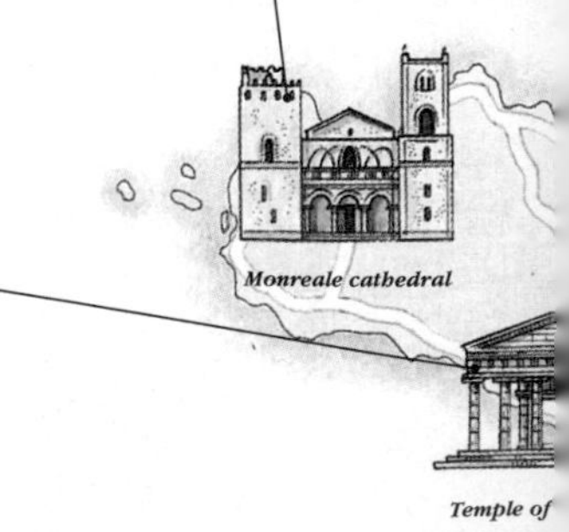

**Sicily's Valley of the Temples at Agrigento** *contains some of the best-preserved Greek ruins outside Greece. Mostly Doric in style, they date from the 5th and 6th centuries BC* (see p536).

0 kilometres 100

0 miles 50

◁ **Vines and citrus trees growing along Campania's scenic Amalfi Coast**

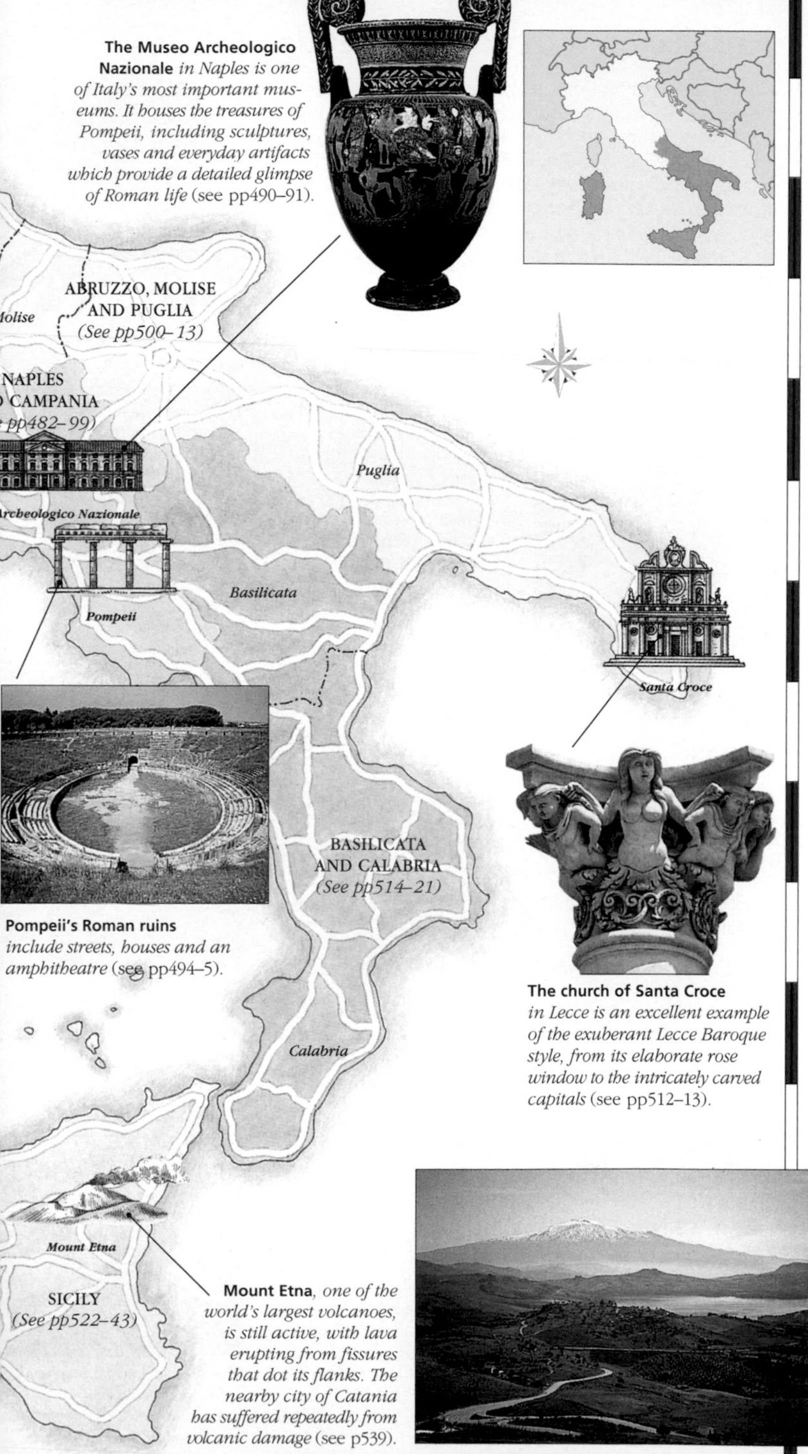


**The Museo Archeologico Nazionale** *in Naples is one of Italy's most important museums. It houses the treasures of Pompeii, including sculptures, vases and everyday artifacts which provide a detailed glimpse of Roman life* (see pp490–91).

**Pompeii's Roman ruins** *include streets, houses and an amphitheatre* (see pp494–5).

**The church of Santa Croce** *in Lecce is an excellent example of the exuberant Lecce Baroque style, from its elaborate rose window to the intricately carved capitals* (see pp512–13).

**Mount Etna**, *one of the world's largest volcanoes, is still active, with lava erupting from fissures that dot its flanks. The nearby city of Catania has suffered repeatedly from volcanic damage* (see p539).

# The Flavours of Southern Italy

The "land of the midday sun", the *Mezzogiorno* is majestic and fertile, yet in places barren and achingly poor. This is the land of the Mediterranean diet, which relies heavily on bright vegetables, fresh seafood, aromatic herbs and fruity olive oil. Puglia produces more grapes and olives than any other region in Italy, while the fertile volcanic soil around Vesuvius and Etna is ideal for growing plump vegetables, juicy fruits and vines. Naples is the birthplace of the pizza, and the region of Campania also produces the best buffalo mozzarella in the country.

Mixed herbs

Sicilian cheesemaker with a basket of fresh ricotta

## CAMPANIA

Naples is famous for pizza, but it's also the home of the tomato-based pasta sauce. Especially prized are the distinctive long, tapered tomatoes from San Marzano in Salerno. The tradition of combining mozzarella and tomato originates here. Pasta is generally tubular (in the north it tends to be ribbon-like). Other staple Campanian ingredients are olive oil, garlic, basil, chillies and lemons. Excellent seafood includes octopus and squid, anchovies, mussels and clams, most of which are simply prepared using lemon, garlic and pepper. Lamb, kid and buffalo are the most popular meats. There is also a long tradition of making pastries and ice cream.

## PUGLIA

This region is responsible for producing 80 per cent of Italy's pasta, as well as being the source of most of the country's fish. As in the rest of Southern Italy, meats such as poultry, pork and kid are often roasted over aromatic herbs. The distinctive local ear-shaped pasta, *orecchiette*, is popular, and fruits and vegetables,

Display of the superb seafood caught along the coastline of the south

### REGIONAL DISHES AND SPECIALITIES

Figs

Some of Italy's classic sauces originated in the South, such as the powerful *puttanesca* with tomatoes, anchovies, chilli, capers and olives. Along the Campanian coast, *zuppa di cozze* (mussels in hot pepper sauce) is a speciality. Octopus is particularly good served in dishes such as *polpo alla luciana*, where it is gently cooked in tomatoes and olive oil with parsley and garlic. *Orecchiette con cime di rapa* (ear-shaped pasta with turnip tops) is a signature dish from Puglia, as is *agnello allo squero* – lamb, spit-roasted over a fire scented with thyme and herbs. For those with a sweet tooth, mouthwatering *cassata Siciliana* is a rich sponge cake layered with ricotta cheese, liqueur, candied fruits and pistachio nuts.

**Maccheroncini con le sarde**
*Sicilian macaroni with sardines, fennel, pine nuts, raisins, breadcrumbs and saffron.*

Tresses of vine-ripened tomatoes hanging on a southern market stall

especially figs and quinces, are abundant.

A bounty of fish and shellfish is caught along the 400-km (250-mile) coastline. As well as mozzarella, other good cheeses include ricotta, goat's and smoked cheeses.

## SICILY

The island's long list of invasions is reflected in its varied cuisine. Greek colonists in the 8th century BC were amazed at the fertility of the volcanic soil. Rice was introduced to the area by the Arabs, while the influence of North African cuisine is shown in *cuscusu* (couscous) and other Arab flavours that appear in sweet and spicy dishes.

The lamb and pork raised in mountain pastures and oak forests is exceptional. Fish is excellent, especially sardines, tuna, anchovies and swordfish. Vegetables are plump and delicious and aubergines (eggplants) are a firm favourite. Sheep's milk ricotta cheese features in many delicious pastries and puddings, such as the sinfully rich Sicilian *cassata*.

Newly harvested olives, ready to be pressed into olive oil

## OTHER REGIONS

Mountainous Abruzzo and Molise are good sheep-rearing territory, so lamb is a speciality here, as is guitar-shaped pasta *(maccheroni alla chitarra)*. Food in Calabria and Basilicata is strong on spices, especially chilli peppers, which are considered a cure-all. Sardinia bakes wafer-thin unleavened bread – *carta da musica* (music paper). Honey, wild boar ham and thrushes are popular, as is *torrone*, a delicious almond nougat.

## ON THE MENU

**Arancini** Sicilian rice balls, usually stuffed with a meat, cheese or vegetable filling.

**Caciocavallo** Spun cow's milk cheese, especially good from Avellino in Campania.

**Insalata caprese** Salad from Campania with mozzarella, tomato, basil, olives and oregano.

**Maccheroni di fuoco** Pasta dish from Basilicata with large quantities of garlic and chilli.

**Seadas** A kind of doughnut from Sardinia, fried and covered with honey.

**Soppressata** A spicy, dry-cured salami from Calabria.

**Pizza Napoletana** *This thin-crusted pizza is topped simply with tomato, garlic, oregano, basil and anchovies.*

**Pesce spada** *In Campania, Puglia, Calabria and Sicily, swordfish steak is grilled with lemon and oregano.*

**Sfogliatella** *Paper-thin layers of pastry ooze with butter, sugar, cinnamon, orange peel and ricotta.*

# Understanding the Architecture of Southern Italy

The Romanesque style of southern Italy owes much to the Normans, who in the 11th century brought from France both form and style in architecture and sculpture. In the southeast, the style has hefty Byzantine overtones; in Sicily it is characterized by strong traditional Islamic motifs and a love of rich colour, pattern and ornamentation. These elements surface later in Sicily's Baroque style and are allied to a dynamism that originates in the Baroque of Rome – though in Sicily it is more vivacious. Neapolitan Baroque is more sophisticated and displays a greater interest in the creative use of space.

**Baroque carving on Bagheria's Villa Palagonia**

## BYZANTINE AND ROMANESQUE FEATURES

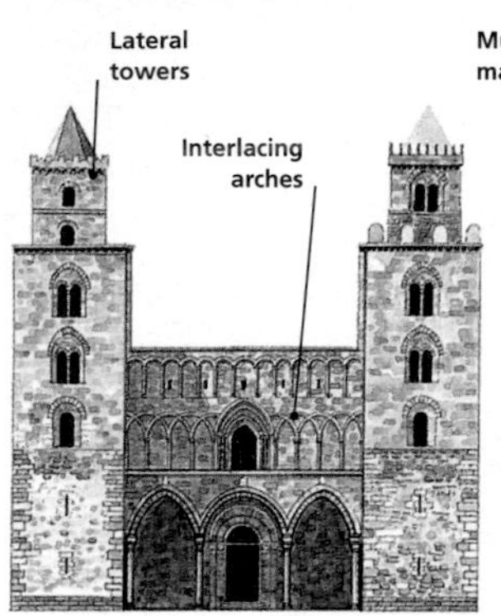


**Cefalù**, *begun in 1131 by Roger II, is one of Sicily's great Norman cathedrals* (see p535). *Its west front exhibits many northern Romanesque features, such as the massive towers.*

**Christ Pantocrator**, *a Byzantine apse mosaic (c.1132), adorns the Cappella Palatina* (see p526).

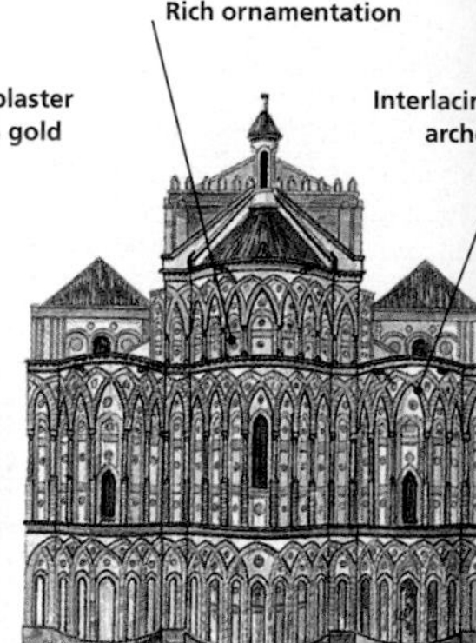


**The east end** *of the Norman cathedral of Monreale, founded in 1172 by William II, is built of multicoloured materials with interlacing arches* (see pp530–31).

## BAROQUE FEATURES

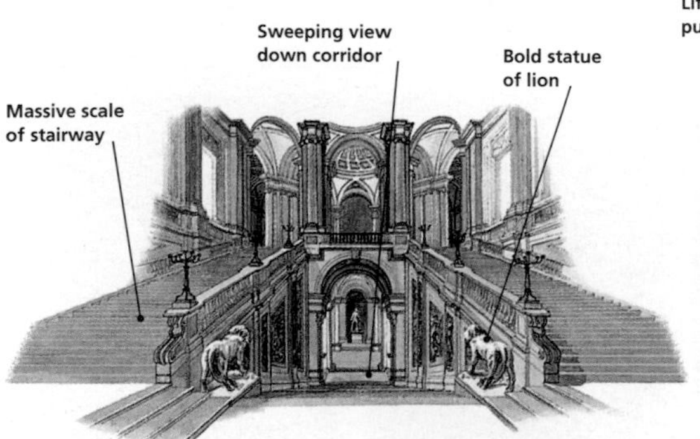


**Caserta's Palazzo Reale**, *a sumptuous royal palace begun by Charles III in 1752, is characterized by its monumental scale* (see p496). *The richly decorated interior is prefaced by several huge entrances and impressive staircases offering views. The enormous building was designed by Luigi Vanvitelli.*

**Giacomo Serpotta's** *stucco reliefs (c.1690) in Palermo's Oratorio di Santa Zita illustrate Sicilians' love of exuberant decoration* (see p529).

## WHERE TO SEE THE ARCHITECTURE

The best places to see Romanesque architecture are Puglia and the cathedral cities of northwestern Sicily. Puglia's best churches are those at Trani *(see p509)* and nearby Canosa, Molfetta and Bitonto; Ruvo di Puglia *(p510)*, San Leonardo di Siponto on the Gargano Peninsula and Martina Franca, near Alberobello. The Baroque style of the south is epitomized by the villas, palaces and churches of Naples and Sicily, and by the deeply encrusted ornamentation found on church façades in Lecce *(pp512–13)*, in Puglia. In Sicily, the Baroque of Palermo *(pp526–7)*, Bagheria *(p532)*, Noto, Modica and Ragusa *(p543)* and Siracusa *(pp542–3)* is well known. Less so are churches at Piazza Armerina *(p537)*, Trapani *(p532)*, Palazzolo Acreide, close to Siracusa, and Acireale, near Catania.

**The Duomo portal in Ruvo di Puglia**

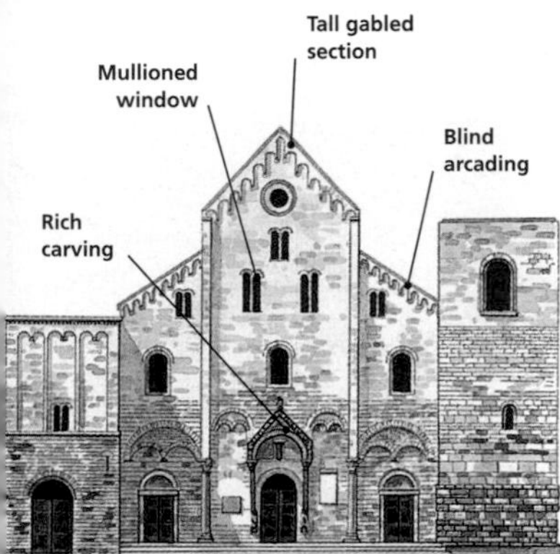


**Bari's Basilica di San Nicola** *(founded 1087) was the model for subsequent churches in Puglia* (see p510). *Based on Norman architecture, its façade is flanked by towers and divided vertically into three, reflecting the tripartite nature of its plan.*

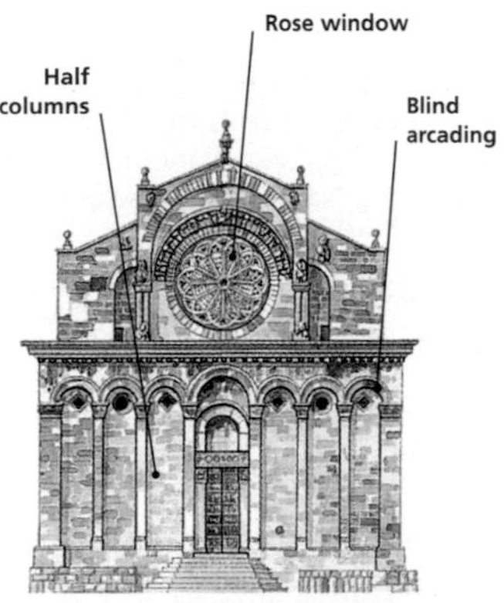


**The façade of Troia cathedral** *(1093–1125) owes its design to Pisan architecture and its rich ornamentation to Byzantine and Arab models* (see pp508–9).

**The façade** *of Siracusa's Duomo, begun in 1728 by Andrea Palma, is animated by broken or curved elements* (see pp542–3).

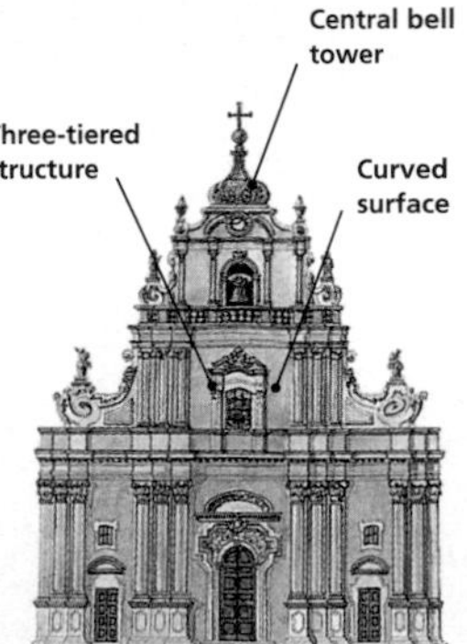


**San Giorgio in Ragusa** *(1744) has a façade by Gagliardi with layers of ornamentation culminating in the tower* (see p543).

**Lecce's Chiesa del Rosario** *(begun 1691) was built by Lo Zingarello of soft local sandstone in the Lecce Baroque style of profuse carving* (see pp512–13).

# The Ancient Greeks in Southern Italy

Some of the best ruins of the ancient Greek world are in Southern Italy. Syracuse, Selinunte, Segesta and Gela are among the better known Sicilian sites while those on the mainland include Crotone, Locri and Paestum. Magna Graecia is the collective name given to these scattered colonies of ancient Greece, the earliest of which were founded in the Naples area in the 11th century BC. Many great figures of the age – including Pythagoras, Archimedes and Aeschylus – lived in these far-flung settlements, and it was here that the ancient winemaker's art flourished. Artifacts from this age are exhibited in the excellent archaeological museums of Naples, Syracuse and Taranto.

KYME
Cuma
NEAPOLIS
Napoli
HERAK
Ercolan
POSEIDONIA
Paestum

**Ancient Herakleia** *(Herculaneum) was named after its patron deity, the mighty Hercules. It was buried by the eruption of Mount Vesuvius in AD 79* (see p495).

**Poseidonia** *(today's Paestum), was the city of Poseidon, God of the Sea. Its ruins, dating from the 6th century BC, include the bulks of two of the finest Doric temples in Europe* (see pp498–9).

**Mount Etna** *was believed to be the forge of Hephaistos (Vulcan) – God of Fire – and the Cyclops, the one-eyed giant* (see p539).

**Tyndaris** was one of the last Greek cities founded on Sicily.

LIPA
Lip
TYND
Ti
PANORMOS
Palermo
SOLUS
Solunto
HIMERA
Himera
ERYX
Erice
EGESTA
Segesta
Belice
SELINUS
Selinunte
Valley of the Temples
HENNA
Enna
Gela
MEGARA HYE
AKRAGAS
Agrigento
GELA
Gela

**Eryx**, founder of the town, was the son of Aphrodite and Poseidon.

**The legendary** founder of Agrigento was Daedalus, who created wings for himself and his son, Icarus, so they could fly.

**Egesta** *(built 426–416 BC) was colonized by the Elymians who may have originated at Troy. Among the ruins of this town are a half-completed temple and a theatre* (see p534). *Ancient Greeks used theatres for plays and cultural entertainment rather than combat.*

0 kilometres 100

0 miles 50

**Gela** was prosperous under the rule of Hippocrates in the 5th century BC.

**Aeschylus**, *the dramatist, died in Gela in 456. Considered the father of Greek tragedy, his plays include* Seven Against Thebes, Women of Aetna *and* Prometheus Bound.

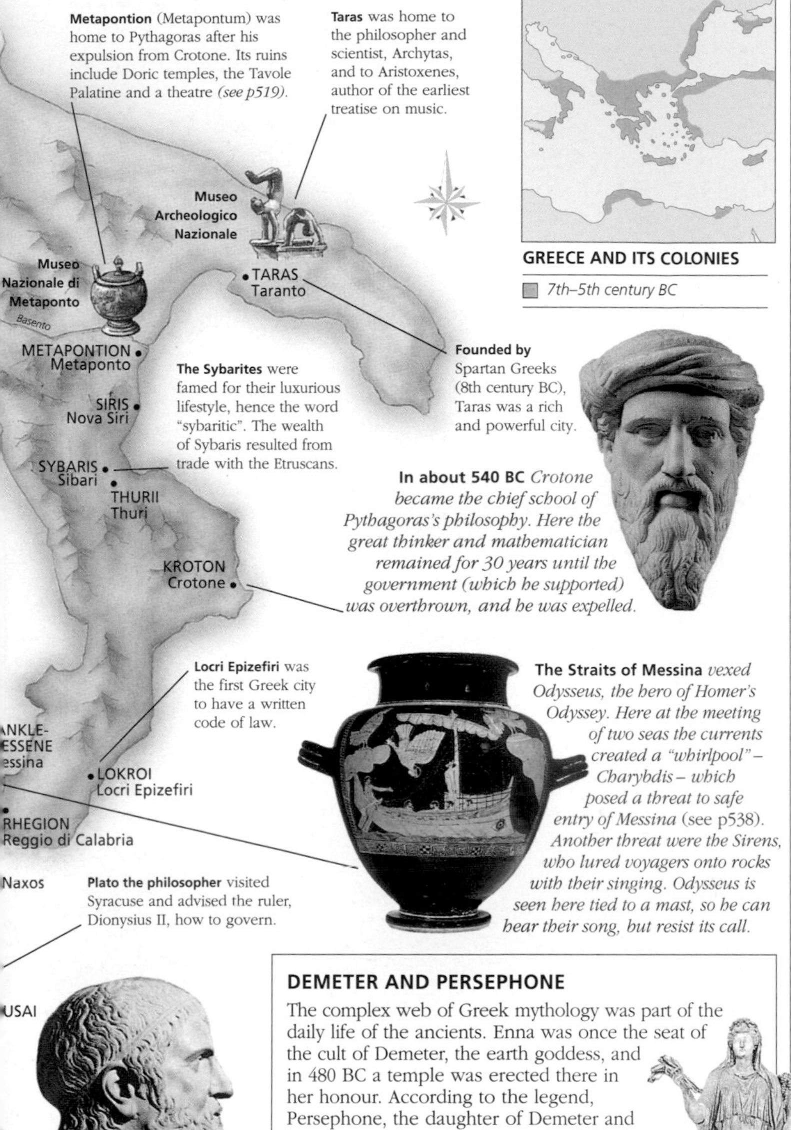


**Metapontion** (Metapontum) was home to Pythagoras after his expulsion from Crotone. Its ruins include Doric temples, the Tavole Palatine and a theatre *(see p519)*.

**Taras** was home to the philosopher and scientist, Archytas, and to Aristoxenes, author of the earliest treatise on music.

**GREECE AND ITS COLONIES**

*7th–5th century BC*

**Founded by** Spartan Greeks (8th century BC), Taras was a rich and powerful city.

**The Sybarites** were famed for their luxurious lifestyle, hence the word "sybaritic". The wealth of Sybaris resulted from trade with the Etruscans.

**In about 540 BC** *Crotone became the chief school of Pythagoras's philosophy. Here the great thinker and mathematician remained for 30 years until the government (which he supported) was overthrown, and he was expelled.*

**Locri Epizefiri** was the first Greek city to have a written code of law.

**The Straits of Messina** *vexed Odysseus, the hero of Homer's Odyssey. Here at the meeting of two seas the currents created a "whirlpool" – Charybdis – which posed a threat to safe entry of Messina* (see p538). *Another threat were the Sirens, who lured voyagers onto rocks with their singing. Odysseus is seen here tied to a mast, so he can hear their song, but resist its call.*

**Plato the philosopher** visited Syracuse and advised the ruler, Dionysius II, how to govern.

**The mathematician** *and inventor, Archimedes, was born in Syracuse c.287 BC. His inventions included the famous Archimedean screw, and various weapons to stave off the Romans* (see pp542–3).

## DEMETER AND PERSEPHONE

The complex web of Greek mythology was part of the daily life of the ancients. Enna was once the seat of the cult of Demeter, the earth goddess, and in 480 BC a temple was erected there in her honour. According to the legend, Persephone, the daughter of Demeter and Zeus, was abducted in the nearby fields by Hades who carried her off into the Underworld. Demeter then left Olympus and wandered the world searching in vain for her daughter. Discovering that Zeus had allowed the abduction to happen, Demeter put a blight on Sicily: it would remain barren until Persephone returned. Finally Hades allowed her return from the Underworld, but only for a few months of each year – from spring to autumn. Demeter, satisfied with the result, ensured that Sicily became the most fertile place on earth.

**Sculpture of Persephone**

SERENA

# NAPLES AND CAMPANIA

*The capital of Campania, Naples is one of the few European cities of the ancient world that has never been completely extinguished. Founded by Greeks, it was embellished and enlarged by the Romans and in subsequent centuries was the much-prized booty of foreign invaders and Imperialists – most prominently the Normans, Hohenstaufen, French and Spanish.*

Naples today is a chaotic yet spectacular metropolis sprawling noisily and dirtily around the edge of the Bay of Naples. To one side is Mount Vesuvius; facing from the sea are the islands of Capri, Ischia and Procida. Pompeii and Herculaneum, lying in the shadow of the volcano that destroyed them, contain the most revealing Roman ruins in Italy.

For centuries Naples dominated the Italian south, or *Mezzogiorno* (land of the midday sun). Unemployment, poverty and crime are a problem – the Camorra is as deep-seated here as the Mafia is in Sicily – but there is also an attractive, rude ebullience to the city.

The ancient history of Campania is linked to the Etruscans and the Greeks, whose massive ruins can be seen at Paestum. Next came a time of great prosperity under the Romans; archaeological evidence of this still exists at Benevento, Santa Maria Capua Vetere and Pozzuoli.

The hinterland, with its rich, well-cultivated plains, is eclipsed by the Amalfi coastline with its breathtaking views and the dramatic seaboard of the Cilento. The mountainous interior, remote and unvisited, contains small towns that were settled by the Greeks, developed by the Romans and often abandoned in the wake of malaria and Saracen attacks.

**A glimpse into the narrow streets of Naples' Quartieri Spagnoli (Spanish Quarter)**

◁ **The old fishing quarter on the island of Procida in the Bay of Naples**

# Exploring Naples and Campania

The main centre from which to explore Campania is the city of Naples (Napoli). To the north, verdant plains sweep down to Santa Maria Capua Vetere. To the east, the mountainous province of Benevento overlooks the valley, while earthquake-ravaged Avellino and its province lurk on a plain beyond Vesuvius. The Campi Flegrei area, west of Naples, is famous for the Roman ruins at Cuma. Further south is the splendid, rugged Amalfi Coast. Clean sandy beaches lie beyond the tip of the Sorrentine Peninsula and along the Cilento coast as well as on Capri, Ischia and Procida in the Gulf of Naples.

## SIGHTS AT A GLANCE

Amalfi Coast ❻
Benevento ❺
Capri ❾
Caserta ❹
Ischia and Procida ❿
*Naples (Napoli) pp486–93* ❶
Paestum ❽
*Pompeii pp494–5* ❷
Salerno ❼
Santa Maria Capua Vetere ❸

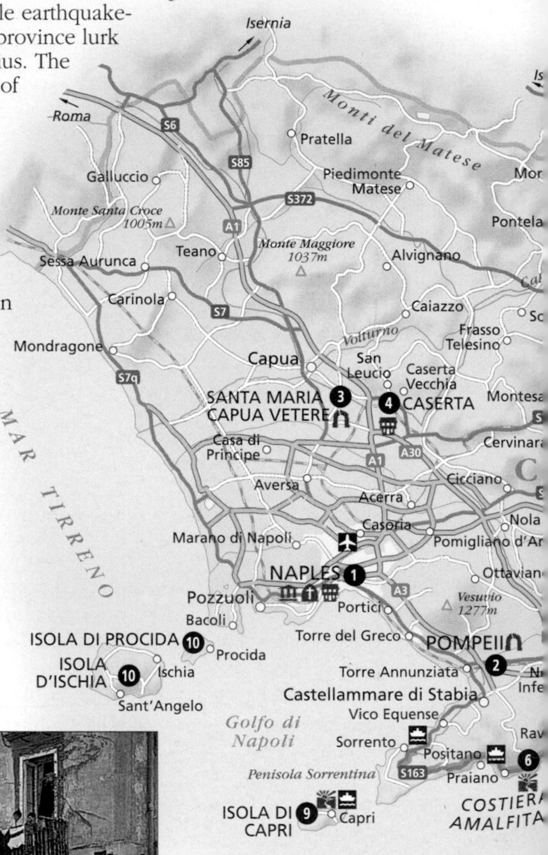


**KEY**

- Motorway
- Major road
- Secondary road
- Minor road
- Scenic route
- Main railway
- Minor railway
- Regional border
- △ Summit

0 kilometres 25

0 miles 20

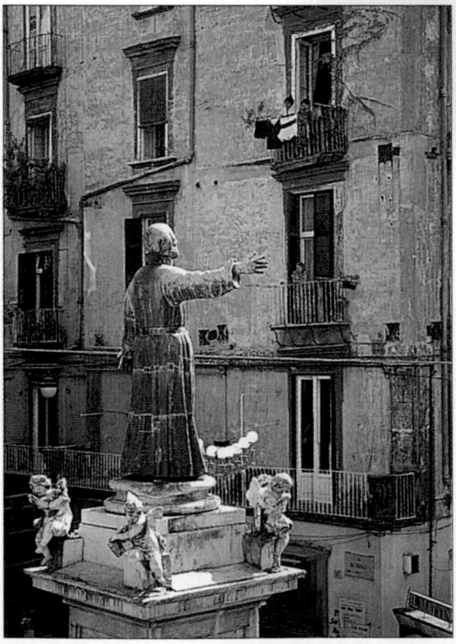

**Typical Naples street viewed from Santa Maria Maggiore**

**For additional map symbols** *see back flap*

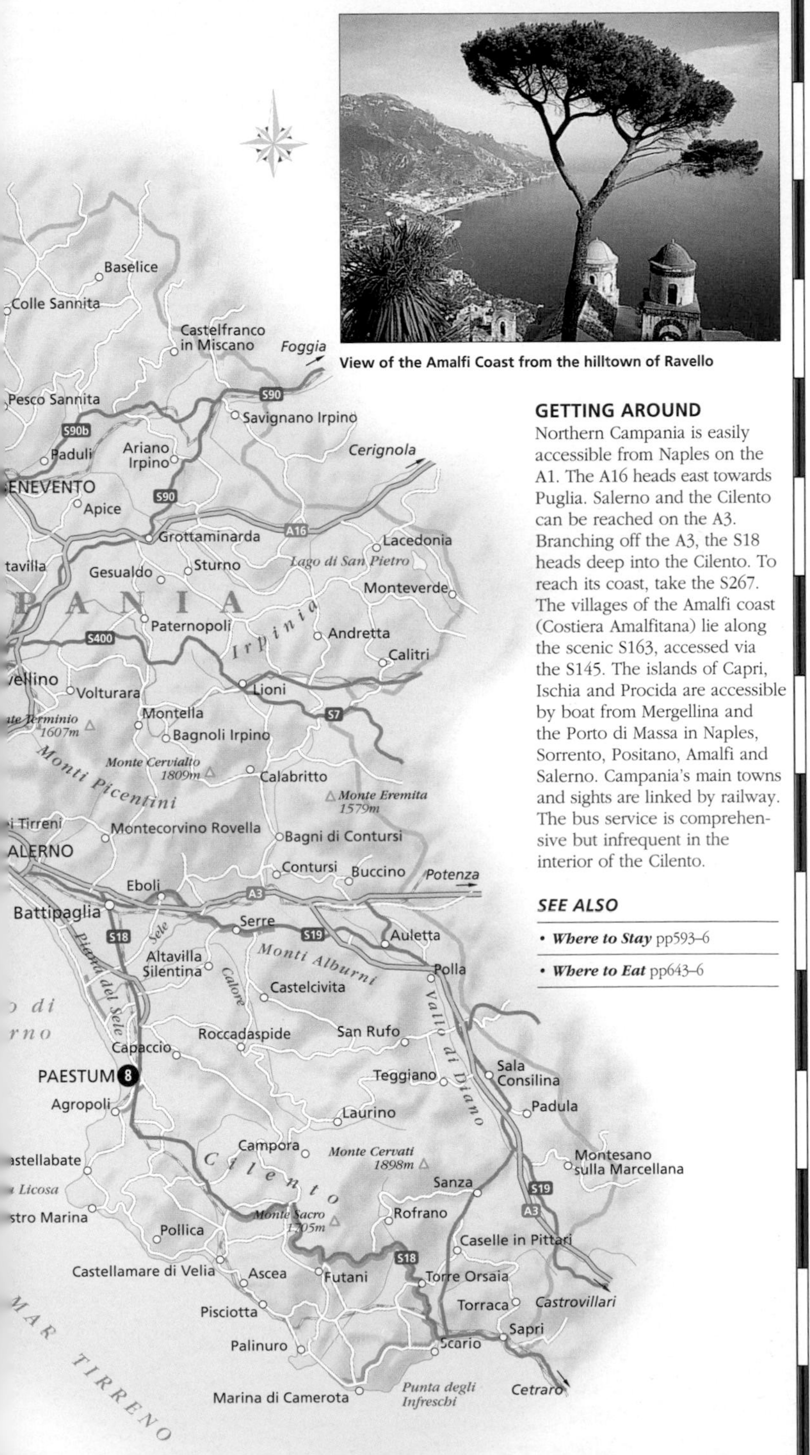


View of the Amalfi Coast from the hilltown of Ravello

## GETTING AROUND

Northern Campania is easily accessible from Naples on the A1. The A16 heads east towards Puglia. Salerno and the Cilento can be reached on the A3. Branching off the A3, the S18 heads deep into the Cilento. To reach its coast, take the S267. The villages of the Amalfi coast (Costiera Amalfitana) lie along the scenic S163, accessed via the S145. The islands of Capri, Ischia and Procida are accessible by boat from Mergellina and the Porto di Massa in Naples, Sorrento, Positano, Amalfi and Salerno. Campania's main towns and sights are linked by railway. The bus service is comprehensive but infrequent in the interior of the Cilento.

### *SEE ALSO*


- ***Where to Stay*** pp593–6
- ***Where to Eat*** pp643–6

# Naples ❶

San Gennaro, protector of Naples

The compact centre of Naples, filled with palaces, churches, convents and monasteries, revolves around just a few streets. From the Piazza del Plebiscito, Via Toledo (also called Via Roma) proceeds north towards Piazza Dante. To the east, narrow Via del "Tribunale and Via San Biagio dei Librai penetrate the historic and noisy heart of the city, the *Spaccanapoli* (split Naples). South of Palazzo Reale is the Santa Lucia district. To the west is the port of Mergellina and overlooking the city is the Vomero district.

View of the Bay of Naples and Mount Vesuvius

**Exploring Northeast Naples**

Much of the city's most interesting art and architecture can be found here, including the Museo Archeologico Nazionale and its Roman treasures from Herculaneum and Pompeii. The buildings provide a wide range of architectural styles from the French-Gothic of the Duomo to the Florentine-Renaissance style of the Porta Capuana.

### San Giovanni a Carbonara

Via Carbonara 5. ***Tel*** *081 29 58 73.*
*9am–1pm Mon–Sat.*

A great and rare success story in the annals of Neapolitan building restoration, San Giovanni a Carbonara (built 1343) is open again after suffering damage in 1943, long closure and pitiful neglect. Within are glorious medieval and Renaissance monuments, including Marco and Andrea da Firenze's masterpiece, the Tomb of Ladislas, located behind the church's high altar. Built to house the body of King Ladislas of Naples (1386–1414), who enlarged the church, the tomb is a three-storey confection of statues and arches topped by an equestrian figure.

Tomb of Ladislas, San Giovanni a Carbonara

The beautiful Renaissance gate of Porta Capuana

### Castel Capuano and Porta Capuana

Piazza Enrico de Nicola.

Begun by Norman King William I and completed by Frederick II, Castel Capuano was a royal palace until 1540, when it became the Court of Justice. Today it is a courthouse.

Nearby, between the Aragonese towers of the Capua Gate and facing a market, is a rare sculpture in the Florentine-Renaissance manner. Created by Giuliano da Maiano (and finished in 1490 by Luca Fancelli) as a defensive gate, Porta Capuana is perhaps Italy's finest Renaissance gateway.

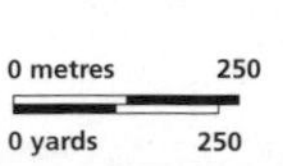

*For hotels and restaurants in this region see pp593–6 and pp643–6*

## SIGHTS AT A GLANCE

Cappella Sansevero ⑥
Castel Capuano and Porta Capuana ③
Castel Nuovo ⑮
Duomo ④
Galleria Umberto I and Teatro San Carlo ⑰
Gesù Nuovo ⑬
*Museo Archeologico Nazionale pp490–91* ①
Museo Filangieri ⑨

Palazzo Reale ⑱
Pio Monte di Misericordia ⑤
Quartieri Spagnoli ⑯
San Domenico Maggiore ⑪
San Giovanni a Carbonara ②
San Gregorio Armeno ⑧
San Lorenzo Maggiore ⑦
Sant'Angelo a Nilo ⑩
Sant'Anna e San Bartolomeo dei Lombardi ⑭
Santa Chiara ⑫

**Key to Symbols** *see back flap*

**Interior of the Duomo**

### Duomo

Via Duomo 147. ***Tel*** *081 44 90 97.* *8am–12:30pm, 4–7pm daily.*

Built between 1294 and 1323, the Cattedrale di Santa Maria Assunta, or Duomo, lies behind a mostly 19th-century façade. The nave is lined with ancient columns, and there is an array of monuments to past rulers, along with paintings by Lanfranco and Domenichino.

The Duomo houses the relics of San Gennaro, Naples' patron saint (martyred AD 305). The Cappella San Gennaro holds phials of his congealed blood, which miraculously liquefies three times a year (the Saturday before the first Sunday in May, 19 Sep and 16 Dec). The Cappella Carafa, a Renaissance masterpiece built from 1497 to 1506, contains the saint's tomb.

Accessible from the Duomo's north aisle is the Cappella di Santa Restituta, founded in the 4th century on the site of a former Temple of Apollo, and rebuilt in the 1300s. It has ceiling paintings by Luca Giordano (1632–1705) and a 5th-century baptistry. The nearby Museo del Tesoro di San Gennaro (Tel: 081 29 49 80) exhibits a fine range of gold, silverware, jewels, statues and art.

## VISITORS' CHECKLIST

*1,300,000.* *Capodichino 4 km (2.5 miles) NW.* *Centrale, P. Garibaldi.* *P. Garibaldi.* *Stazione Marittima, Molo Beverello & Mergellina.* *P. del Gesù Nuovo (081 551 27 01), Via San Carlo (081 40 23 94).* *daily.* *San Gennaro: 19 Sep.* **www**.inaples.it

### Pio Monte di Misericordia

Via dei Tribunali 253. ***Tel*** *081 44 69 44.* **Church & gallery** *9am–2pm Mon–Tue, Thu–Sun.* *public hols.* *Gallery only.* **www**.piomontedellamisericordia.it

The 17th-century octagonal church belonging to this charitable foundation houses Caravaggio's *Seven Acts of Mercy* (1607). The art gallery has paintings by the likes of Luca Giordano and Mattia Preti.

### Cappella Sansevero

Via F. de Santis 19. ***Tel*** *081 551 84 70.* *10am–5:40pm Wed–Mon (to 1:10pm Sun & public hols).* *(church).*

This tiny 16th-century chapel is the burial sepulchre of the Princes of Sangro di Sansevero. Featuring both Christian and Masonic symbolism, the chapel has an unusual character.

Remarkable 18th-century sculpture fills the chapel. Antonio Corradini's ironic *Modesty* is a voluptuous female, carefully veiled. *The Resurrection of the Prince*, by an unknown artist, is mirrored by that of Christ, above the altar. Giuseppe Sammartino's *The Dead Christ* is an alabaster figure beneath a marble veil, and is a work of breathtaking technical virtuosity.

Prince Raimondo, an 18th-century alchemist, is associated with the chapel. He performed gruesome experiments on human bodies, for which he was excommunicated. The results of some of his experiments can be seen in the crypt.

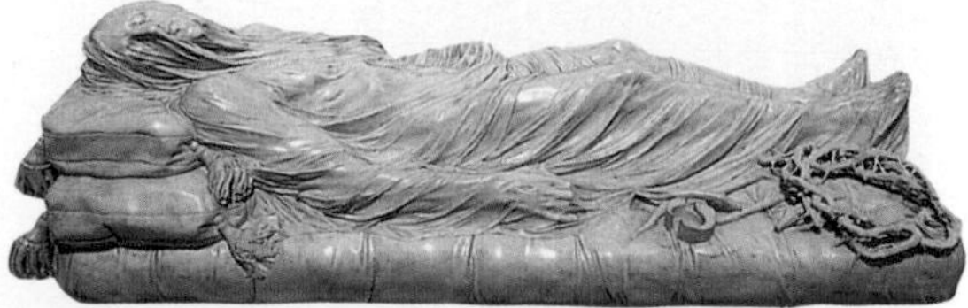

**Sammartino's *The Dead Christ* (1753) in the Cappella Sansevero**

# Exploring Central Naples

The part of Santa Lucia bordered by Via Duomo to the east, Via Tribunali to the north, Via Toledo (Roma) to the west and the water to the south, is the old heart of Naples. Especially rich in 14th- and 15th-century churches, the area offers visitors an abundance of sights.

Interior of San Gregorio Armeno

### San Lorenzo Maggiore

Via dei Tribunali 316. ***Tel*** *081 211 08 60.* **Church** *8am–1pm, 5–7pm daily.* **Excavations** *9:30am–5:30pm daily (to 1:30pm Sun).*

This mainly 14th-century Franciscan church (with an 18th-century façade) was built during the reign of Robert the Wise of Anjou. The storyteller Giovanni Boccaccio (1313–75) reputedly based the character Fiammetta on King Robert's daughter Maria, whom he saw here on Easter Eve, 1334. For Naples, San Lorenzo Maggiore is a rare Gothic edifice. Its nave and the apse ambulatory have a magnificent period simplicity. The church houses medieval tombs including the Gothic tomb of Catherine of Austria, who died in 1323, by a pupil of Giovanni Pisano. Excavations in the monastic cloister, where the lyric poet and scholar Petrarch *(see p159)* once stayed, have found the remains of a Roman basilica. There are also important Greek and medieval excavations.

The simple Gothic interior of San Lorenzo Maggiore, looking down the nave to the apse

### San Gregorio Armeno

Via San Gregorio Armeno 1. ***Tel*** *081 552 01 86.* *am daily.* *cloister.*

Benedictine nuns still preside over this church. The convent attached to it earned a reputation for luxury since the nuns, traditionally from noble families, were accustomed to lavish living, which continued here.

The sumptuous Baroque interior of the church sports frescoes by Luca Giordano. The cloister is a quiet haven in this noisy neighbourhood. Via San Gregorio Armeno is lined with the workshops of vendors of Nativity figures *(presepi)*.

### Museo Filangieri

Palazzo Cuomo, Via Duomo 288. ***Tel*** *081 20 31 75.* *for restoration until 2012.*

The 15th-century Renaissance Palazzo Cuomo houses the Museo Filangieri. Founded in 1881, the original museum collections put together by Prince Gaetano Filangieri were destroyed during World War II. The current collection contains interesting and varied objects, including porcelain, embroidery, manuscripts, Italian and Spanish arms, objects from local archaeological excavations and paintings by such artists as Luca Giordano, Ribera and Mattia Preti.

### Sant'Angelo a Nilo

Piazzetta Nilo. ***Tel*** *081 29 00 34.* *8am–1pm, 4:30–7:30pm daily.*

Renaissance tomb of Cardinal Brancaccio, Sant'Angelo a Nilo

This 14th-century church contains a fine work of Renaissance sculpture: the Tomb of Cardinal Rinaldo Brancaccio. Designed by Michelozzo, it was sculpted in Pisa, and then shipped to Naples upon completion in 1428. Donatello reputedly carved the right-hand angel drawing back the curtain, the shallow relief Assumption, and the cardinal's head.

### San Domenico Maggiore

Piazza San Domenico Maggiore. **Tel** *081 45 91 88.* *daily.* **Treasury** *daily.*

This Gothic church (1289–1324) contains some of the finest Renaissance monuments and sculpture in Naples. The tomb slab of John of Durazzo (died 1335), by Tino da Camaino, is in the south transept. In the sacristy are the *Apotheosis of Faith* ceiling frescoes by Solimena (18th century). The choir features a paschal candlestick (1585) supported by figures by da Camaino. The Cappellone del Crocifisso contains a medieval painting of the *Crucifixion*, which supposedly spoke to St Thomas Aquinas. The grand Brancaccio tomb by Jacopo della Pila (1492) is in the Chiesa Antica.

**Detail of the embossed façade of Gesù Nuovo**

### Santa Chiara

Via Benedetto Croce. **Church Tel** *081 552 62 09.* *7:30am–12:30pm, 4:30–7:30pm daily.* **Cloister Tel** *081 552 15 97.* *9:30am–5:30pm Mon–Sat, 10am–2:30pm Sun.*

This 14th-century church was bombed in World War II, but a reconstruction uncovered the original Provençal-Gothic structure. The tombs of the Angevin monarchs are housed here. The tomb of Robert the Wise (died 1343) is by Giovanni and Pacio Bertini; that of Robert's son, Charles of Calabria (died 1328), is by Tino da Camaino, and the tomb of Charles' wife, Mary of Valois (died 1331) is by da Camaino and his followers. Adjacent is a convent with an Angevin cloister designed by Vaccaro (1742) and adorned with fine majolica tiles. There is also a museum of medieval art and a Roman bath house (AD 1).

### Gesù Nuovo

Piazza del Gesù Nuovo 2. **Tel** *081 55 78 11.* *daily.*

The 16th-century Jesuit church was constructed by Valeriano (and later Fanzago and Fuga) from the Severini palace (15th century), of which only a façade survives. The ebullient decoration of the interior (1600s) is fully in accordance with the needs of the Jesuits, who used drama and direct appeal to the emotions to draw the faithful. It is resplendent with coloured marble and paintings, including works by Ribera and Solimena. In 1688 an earthquake destroyed the dome – the present one is 18th-century.

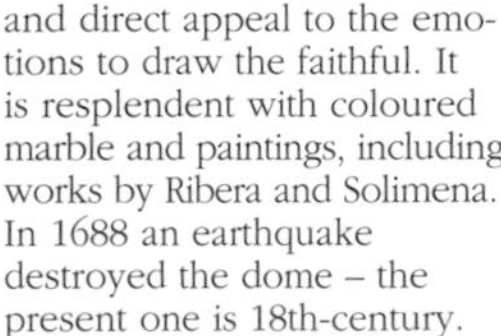

### Sant'Anna e San Bartolomeo dei Lombardi

Via Monteoliveto. **Tel** *081 551 33 33.* *9am–noon Tue–Sat.*

Also known as Santa Maria di Monteoliveto, this church was built in 1411 and restored after World War II. It is a repository of Renaissance art. Entering, past the tomb (1627) of Domenico Fontana (who completed the dome of St Peter's in Rome after Michelangelo's death), the richness of the interior unfolds.

The Cappella Mastrogiudice contains an *Annunciation* panel by Florentine sculptor Benedetto da Maiano (1489) and the Cappella Piccolomini contains Antonio Rossellino's monument (c.1475) to Maria d'Aragona (completed by da Maiano). The Cappella del Santo Sepolcro houses a *Pietà* by Guido Mazzoni (1492). Its eight terracotta figures are considered life-size portraits of the artist's contemporaries. The old Sacristy, frescoed by Vasari (1544), has inlaid stalls by Giovanni da Verona (1510).

**Mazzoni's *Pietà* (1492) in Sant'Anna e San Bartolomeo dei Lombardi**

**Majolica tiles decorated with scenes of rural life in the cloisters of Santa Chiara**

# Naples: Museo Archeologico Nazionale

This building, housing one of the world's most important archaeological museums, started life in the late 1500s as the home of the royal cavalry and was rebuilt in the early 17th century as the seat of Naples university. In 1777, when Ferdinand IV transferred the university to the former monastery of Gesù Vecchio, the building was again adapted to house the Real Museo Borbonico and library. In 1860 it became public property. The 1980 earthquake caused much damage to the collections. Major restoration and reorganization of exhibits continue but most areas of the museum are open on Sundays.

**Spring Fresco**
*The fresco removed from the Villa Stabia in the Varano plain is a masterpiece of grace and elegance; the female figure rendered with soft, delicate colours.*

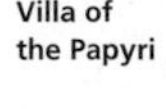

**Bust of "Seneca"**
*Found in the Villa dei Papiri in Herculaneum, this 1st-century BC bronze head was long thought to represent the philosopher Seneca the Elder (c.55 BC–AD 39). Today, however, its identity is less certain.*

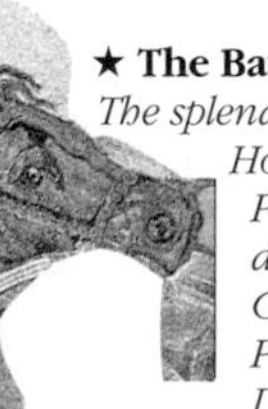

**★ The Battle of Alexander**
*The splendid mosaic from the House of the Faun in Pompeii* (see p494) *depicts Alexander the Great's victory over Persian emperor Darius III (333 BC).*

**KEY**

- Epigraphs
- Egyptian collection
- Engraved gems
- Sculptures
- Mosaics
- Numismatics
- Didactics
- Herculaneum & Pompeii
- Hall of the Sundial
- Prehistoric, Greek and Etruscan collections
- Non-exhibition space

**The Secret Cabinet**
*The erotic works from Pompeii and Herculaneum housed here caused embarrassment at the time of the Bourbons. Today, however, they are available for public viewing (book ahead).*

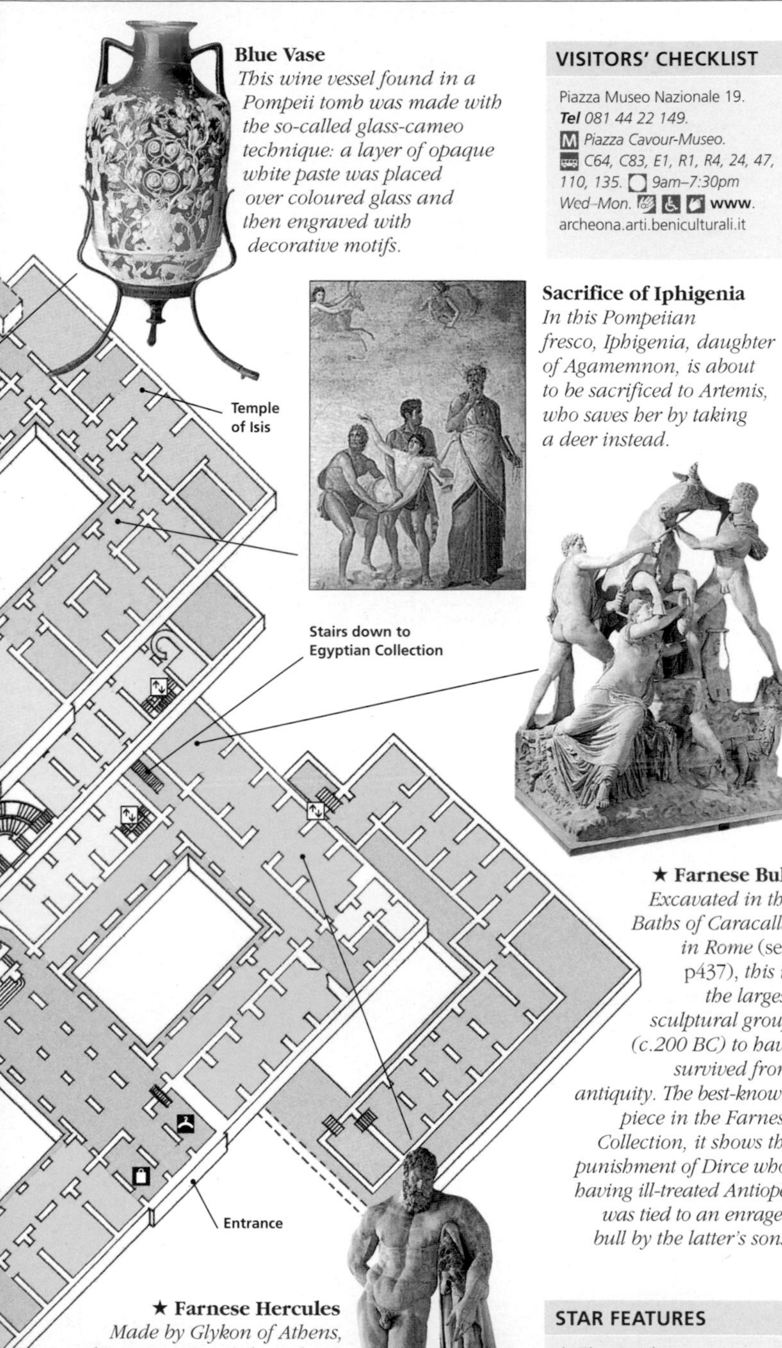


**Blue Vase**
*This wine vessel found in a Pompeii tomb was made with the so-called glass-cameo technique: a layer of opaque white paste was placed over coloured glass and then engraved with decorative motifs.*

**Sacrifice of Iphigenia**
*In this Pompeiian fresco, Iphigenia, daughter of Agamemnon, is about to be sacrificed to Artemis, who saves her by taking a deer instead.*

**★ Farnese Bull**
*Excavated in the Baths of Caracalla in Rome* (see p437), *this is the largest sculptural group (c.200 BC) to have survived from antiquity. The best-known piece in the Farnese Collection, it shows the punishment of Dirce who, having ill-treated Antiope, was tied to an enraged bull by the latter's sons.*

**★ Farnese Hercules**
*Made by Glykon of Athens, this statue is an enlarged copy of a sculpture by the Greek master Lysippus. Napoleon is said to have regretted leaving it behind when he removed his booty from Italy in 1797.*

## VISITORS' CHECKLIST

Piazza Museo Nazionale 19.
**Tel** *081 44 22 149.*
*Piazza Cavour-Museo.*
*C64, C83, E1, R1, R4, 24, 47, 110, 135.* *9am–7:30pm Wed–Mon.* **www.** archeona.arti.beniculturali.it

## STAR FEATURES

- ★ The Battle of Alexander
- ★ Farnese Bull
- ★ Farnese Hercules

# Exploring Southeast Naples

The area south of Via A Diaz is home to Naples' castles and royal palace as well as the densely populated Spanish Quarter. On the outskirts of the old town are a number of museums in historic buildings.

### Castel Nuovo

Piazza Municipio. **Tel** *081 795 20 03.* *9am–7pm Mon–Sat. Last adm: 6pm.* *some public hols.* **Museo Civico** *Mon–Sat.*
Also known as the Maschio Angioino, this Angevin fortress was built for Charles of Anjou in 1279–82. However, apart from the squat towers and the Cappella Palatina (with Francesco Laurana's *Madonna* of 1474 above the portal), most of the structure is Aragonese.

The castle was the main royal residence. In the Sala dei Baroni, Ferdinand I of Aragon brutally suppressed the ringleaders of the Baron's revolt of 1486. The Aragonese were capable of violence, but they were also patrons of the arts.

The triumphal arch of the castle's entrance (begun 1454) is theirs. Commemorating Alfonso of Aragon's entry to Naples in 1443, this ingenious application of the ancient triumphal arch design was worked on, at least in part, by Laurana. The original bronze doors by Guillaume le Moine (1468) are kept in the Palazzo Reale. Part of the building houses the **Museo Civico**.

The colourful and compact Quartieri Spagnoli

### Quartieri Spagnoli

Via Toledo (Roma) to Via Chiaia.
The Spanish Quarter – the neighbourhood west of Via Toledo, sloping up to San Martino and Vomero – is one of the city's most densely populated areas. It was named after the Spanish troops who laid out its grid of narrow streets in the 17th century. This is where the archetypal Neapolitan scene comes to life, in which laundry hung above the streets crowds out the sun. This area is lively by day, sinister by night.

### Museo Nazionale di San Martino

Largo di San Martino 5. **Tel** *081 578 17 69.* **Museo** *8:30am–7:30pm Thu–Tue.* **Castel Sant'Elmo** *8:30am–7:30pm Thu–Tue.*
High above Santa Lucia, the Baroque Certosa di San Martino, founded in the 1300s as a Carthusian monastery, has great views of the Bay of Naples. It houses a museum featuring a variety of *presepi*, Christmas cribs of Neapolitan tradition. The cloister was completed in 1623–9 by Cosimo Fanzago (the creator of Neapolitan Baroque) to the 16th-century designs of Dosio. The church and choir are other examples of his virtuosity.

Next to the Certosa, **Castel Sant'Elmo**, built from 1329–43 and rebuilt in the 1500s, offers stunning views over the bay.

### Museo Principe di Aragona Pignatelli Cortes

Riviera di Chiaia 200. **Tel** *081 66 96 75.* *9am–1:30pm Mon, Tue, Thu, Fri; 11am–7:30pm Sat & Sun.* *1 Jan, 1 May, 15 Aug.*
The Neo-Classical Villa Pignatelli, once home to the Rothschilds, houses this museum and its interesting collection of porcelain, period furniture, paintings and sculpture.

The bold Castel Nuovo, with the triumphal arch entrance

*For hotels and restaurants in this region see pp593–6 and pp643–6*

### Galleria Umberto I

Via Toledo. daily. **Teatro San Carlo** ***Tel*** *081 797 23 31.* *Aug, rehearsals and performances.* *9am–5:30pm daily (081 66 45 45 to book).* **www**.teatrosancarlo.it

Once a focus for fashionable Neapolitans, the handsome arcades of the Galleria Umberto I were built in 1887 and rebuilt after World War II. They face Italy's largest and oldest opera house: the **Teatro San Carlo**. Built for Charles of Bourbon in 1737, and later rebuilt, its fine auditorium once aroused envy in the courts of Europe.

***Danaë and the Shower of Gold*** **by Titian in the Museo di Capodimonte**

**Magnificent glass-roofed interior of the Galleria Umberto I**

### Palazzo Reale

Piazza Plebiscito. **Museo** ***Tel*** *081 40 05 47.* *9am–7pm Thur–Tue (last adm: 1 hr before closing).* *1 Jan, 1 May, 25 Dec.* **Biblioteca** ***Tel*** *081 781 92 31.* *8:30am–7:30pm Mon–Fri (to 1:30pm Sat). Bring ID.*

Begun by Domenico Fontana for the Spanish Viceroys in 1600, and expanded by subsequent residents, Naples' royal palace is a handsome edifice with great halls filled with furniture, tapestries, paintings and porcelain. The small private Teatro di Corte (1768) was built by Ferdinando Fuga. The building houses the riches of the Biblioteca Nazionale (library). The exterior of the palace has been partly restored – note the 19th-century statues representing the dynasties of Naples. The huge Piazza del Plebiscito facing it has been cleaned up. The great colonnades sweep towards 19th-century **San Francesco di Paola**, modelled on Rome's Pantheon.

**The façade of the Palazzo Reale, Naples' royal palace**

### Villa Floridiana

Via Cimarosa 77. ***Tel*** *081 229 21 10.* *8:30am–1:30pm Wed–Mon.* **Park** *daily.* *1 Jan, 1 May, 15 Aug, 25 Dec.*

Set in handsome gardens, this Neo-Classical villa houses the **Museo Nazionale della Ceramica Duca di Martina**, famous for its ceramics collection, including porcelain and majolica.

### Museo di Capodimonte

Parco di Capodimonte. ***Tel*** *081 749 91 11.* *8:30am–7:30pm Thu–Tue.* **www**.museo-capodimonte.it

Begun in 1738 by the Bourbon king Charles III as a hunting lodge, the **Palazzo Reale di Capodimonte** houses this museum and its magnificent collections of Italian paintings. Included are works by Titian, Botticelli, Raphael and Perugino, much of it originating in the Farnese family collections. There is also a gallery of 19th-century art, largely from southern Italy.

### Catacombs of San Gennaro

Via di Capodimonte 13. ***Tel*** *081 544 13 05.* *10am–5pm daily (to 1pm Sun).* *call to book visit.*

These catacombs – the original burial place of San Gennaro – are located near the church of San Gennaro in Moenia. The small church was founded in the 8th century, and is adjoined by a 17th-century workhouse. Two tiers of catacombs dating from the 2nd century penetrate the tufa, and there are mosaics and early Christian frescoes. Further along the street, the Catacombs of San Gaudioso commemorate the 5th-century saint who founded a monastery on the spot. Above is the 17th-century church of Santa Maria della Sanità.

### Castel dell'Ovo

Borgo Marinari. ***Tel*** *081 795 45 93.* *9am–5:30pm daily (to 2pm Sun & hols).* *for exhibitions.*

This castle, begun in 1154, occupies a small island facing, and joining, the Santa Lucia district – once the site of the city's shellfish market. A royal residence under the Normans and Hohenstaufen, today it belongs to the army. Interesting exhibitions are held here.

Beneath its ramparts, tiny Porta Santa Lucia is filled with seafood restaurants, and the Via Partenope running past it is a lovely promenade.

# Pompeii ❷

An earthquake in AD 62, which shook Pompeii and damaged many buildings, was merely a prelude to the tragic day in AD 79 when Mount Vesuvius erupted, burying the town in 6 m (20 ft) of pumice and ash. Although it was discovered in the 16th century, serious excavation began only in 1748, revealing a city petrified in time. In some buildings paintings and sculpture have survived, and graffiti is still visible on street walls.

**★ House of the Vettii**
*The villa of the wealthy merchants Aulus Vettius Conviva and Aulus Vettius Restitutus contains fresco* (see pp48–9). *It is currently closed for renovation.*

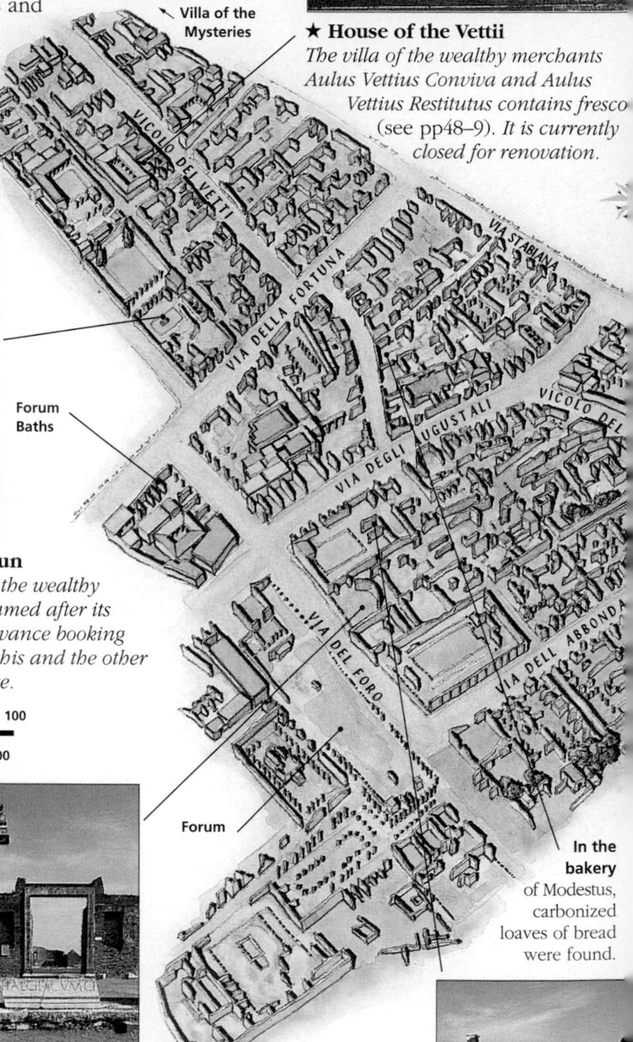

↖ Villa of the Mysteries

VICOLO DEL VETTI

VIA STABIANA

VIA DELLA FORTUNA

VICOLO DEL

VIA DEGLI AUGUSTALI

VIA DELL ABBONDANZA

VIA DEL FORO

Forum Baths

Forum

**★ House of the Faun**
*This famous villa of the wealthy patrician Casii is named after its bronze statuette. Advance booking is necessary to visit this and the other private houses on site.*

0 metres 100

0 yards 100

**In the bakery** of Modestus, carbonized loaves of bread were found.

**Sacrarium of the Lares**
*Close to the Temple of Vespasian, this building housed the statues of Pompeii's guardian deities, the Lares Publici.*

**STAR SIGHTS**

- ★ House of the Faun
- ★ House of the Vettii

**Macellum**
*Pompeii's market place was fronted by a portico with two money-changers' kiosks.*

*For hotels and restaurants in this region see pp593–6 and pp643–6*

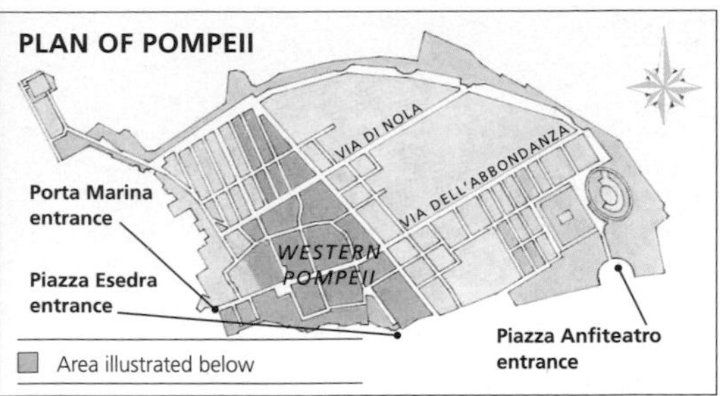


## VISITORS' CHECKLIST

Piazza Esedra 5. ***Tel** 081 857 53 47.* *FS Naples–Salerno: station Pompei Scavi; Circumvesuviana Naples–Sorrento: station Pompei Villa dei Misteri.* *8:30am–7:30pm daily (last adm: 6pm) (Nov–Mar: to 5pm, last adm: 3:30).* *1 Jan, 25 Dec.* **www**.pompeiisites.org **www**.arethusa.net *to book.*

## WESTERN POMPEII

This detailed illustration is of the western area, where the most impressive and intact Roman ruins are located. There are several large patrician villas in the eastern section, as wealthy residents built their homes outside the town centre.

However, much of eastern Pompeii awaits excavation.

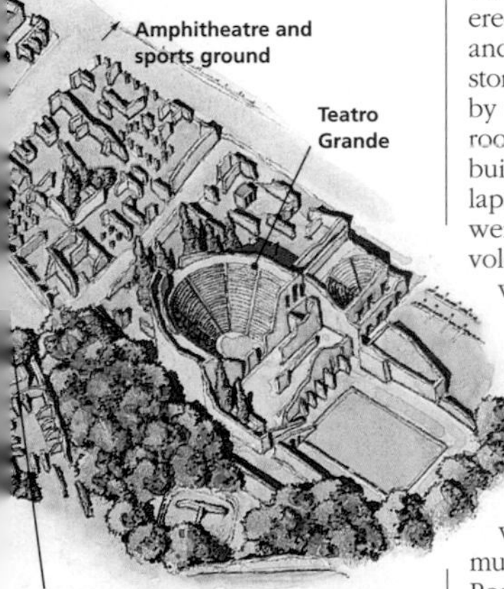

**Via dell'Abbondanza**
*This was one of the original and most important roads through ancient Pompeii. Many inns lined the route.*

## VESUVIUS AND THE CAMPANIAN TOWNS

Nearly 2,000 years after the eruption of Mount Vesuvius, the Roman towns in its shadow are still being released from the petrification that engulfed them. Both Pompeii and Stabiae (Castellammare di Stabia), to the southeast of Naples and the volcano, were smothered by hot ash and pumice-stone blown there by the wind. The roofs of the buildings collapsed under the weight of the volcanic debris. To the west, Herculaneum (Ercolano) vanished under a sea of mud. A large number of its buildings have survived, their roofs intact, and many domestic items were preserved by the mud. In all, about 2,000 Pompeiians perished but few, if any, of the residents of Herculaneum died.

In AD 79 Pliny the Elder, the Roman soldier, writer and naturalist, was the commander of a fleet stationed off Misenum (present-day Miseno, west of Naples) and with his nephew Pliny the Younger observed the impending eruption from afar. Eager to see this natural catastrophe closer to hand, Pliny the Elder proceeded to Stabiae, but was overcome by fumes and died. Based on reports by survivors, Pliny the Younger related the first hours of the eruption and his uncle's death in detail in two letters to the Roman historian Tacitus.

Much of our knowledge of the daily lives of the ancient Romans derives from the excavations of Pompeii and Herculaneum. Most of the artefacts from them as well as Stabiae are now in Naples' Museo Archeologico Nazionale *(see pp490–91)*, creating an outstanding collection.

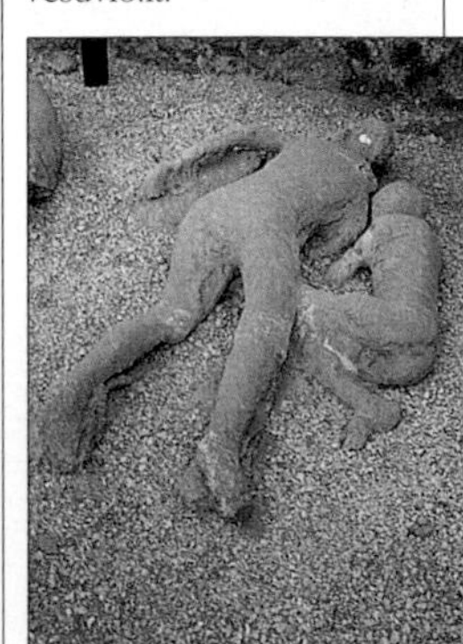

**Pompeiian vase in Museo Nazionale Archeologico**

Mount Vesuvius has not erupted since 1944, but occasional rumbles have caused minor earthquakes. Visitors can reach it by train to Castellammare di Stabia, or by car. A useful website is www.guidevesuvio.it.

**Casts of a dying mother and child seen at Pompeii**

## Santa Maria Capua Vetere ❸

Caserta. 34,000. FS
Palazzo Reale, Caserta (0823 32 22 33). Thu & Sun.

This town boasts a 1st-century AD Roman **amphitheatre**, once Italy's largest after the Colosseum, with well-preserved tunnels beneath it. The town occupies the site of ancient Capua, an Etruscan city and then a flourishing centre during the Roman Empire. It was the scene of the revolt of the gladiators, led by Spartacus in 73 BC. The on-site **Gladiator Museum** recreates the history of the gladiators. Nearby is a **Mithraeum** (2nd–3rd century) with well-preserved frescoes. Finds from the sites are shown in the **Museo Archeologico dell'Antica Capua** in Capua.

**Amphitheatre**
P.za 1 Ottobre. ***Tel*** *0823 84 42 06.*
*9am–1 hr before sunset Tue–Sun.*
*valid for* **Mithraeum**. *Tue–Sun.*

**Museo Archeologico dell'Antica Capua**
Via Roberto d'Angio 48, Capua.
***Tel*** *0823 84 42 06. 9am–7pm Tue–Sun.*

**Tunnels under the amphitheatre in Santa Maria Capua Vetere**

## Caserta ❹

66,000. FS Palazzo Reale (0823 32 22 33). Wed & Sat. **www**.casertaturismo.it

Magnificently opulent, the vast **Palazzo Reale** dominates Caserta. Built for the Bourbon King Charles III, Italy's largest royal palace boasts over 1,000 rooms, grand staircases and richly adorned apartments. It was designed by Luigi Vanvitelli and construction started in 1752. The surrounding park boasts fountains, ornamental waterworks, statuary and an English Garden. Sound and light shows, in English and Italian, take place in summer.

**A fountain in the gardens of the Palazzo Reale at Caserta**

**Environs:** The medieval town of **Caserta Vecchia** lies 10 km (6 miles) to the northeast. Its 12th-century cathedral is a fine example of southern Norman architecture. **San Leucio**, 3 km (2 miles) northwest of Caserta, is a model town built by Ferdinand IV, who also founded its silk industry.

**Palazzo Reale**
Piazza Carlo III. ***Tel*** *0823 45 62 13.*
*8:30am–7:30pm Wed–Mon.*
*1 Jan, 25 Dec.* **Park**
*8:30am–1 hr before sunset daily.*

## Benevento ❺

*62,000.* FS *Via Sala 31 (0824 31 99 11/38). Mon & Wed–Sat.* **www**.eptbenevento.it

Benevento, set in a lonely, mountainous province, is home to one of southern Italy's most interesting ancient Roman monuments: the **Arch of Trajan** on Via Traiano. The Roman city, Beneventum, was an important centre. It stood at the end of the first extension of the Via Appia from Capua, and the Arch was erected across the old road in honour of Trajan. Built from AD 114–166 of marble, it is extremely well preserved. The relief sculpture adorning it – scenes from the life of Trajan and mythological subjects – is in excellent condition.

Elsewhere, evidence of the Romans is to be found in the ruined **Roman theatre**, built during Hadrian's reign, and in the **Museo del Sannio**, which contains artifacts from the region, from ancient Greek finds to modern art.

During World War II, the city stood directly in the way of the Allied advance from the south. It was heavily bombed, hence its largely modern appearance today. The Duomo, a 13th-century building reconstructed after the war, has a sculpted façade that, though badly damaged, has since been restored. The remains of its Byzantine bronze doors are within. The town has centuries-old

**The ornate 2nd-century Roman arch in Benevento, built to honour Trajan**

*For hotels and restaurants in this region see pp593–6 and pp643–6*

associations with pagan worship, and a liqueur called *Strega* (witch) is made here.

**Roman Theatre**
Piazza Caio Ponzio Telesino. **Tel** *0824 47 213. 9am–1 hr before sunset daily. public hols.*

**Museo del Sannio**
Piazza Santa Sofia. **Tel** *0824 218 18. 9am–1pm Tue–Sun. 1 Jan, 25 Dec.*

## The Amalfi Coast 6

Salerno. *Amalfi. Corso delle Repubbliche Marinare 27, Amalfi (089 87 11 07).* **www**.amalfitouristoffice.it; **www**.ravellotime.it; **www**.aziendaturismopositano.it

The small town of Atrani on the Amalfi Coast

The most enchanting route in Campania is that skirting the southern flank of Sorrento's peninsula: the Amalfi Coast (Costiera Amalfitana). Popular pleasures here include dining on grilled fish and sipping Lacrima Christi from the vineyards on the slopes of Vesuvius, beach-hopping and trips to coastal summits to admire the breathtaking views.

From **Sorrento**, a well developed holiday resort, the road winds down to **Positano**, a village clambering down a vertiginous slope to the sea. A top spot for the jet set, it is nonetheless a good place to swim, or to catch the hydrofoil or ferry to Capri. Further on, **Praiano** is just as fashionable.

**Amalfi** is the coast's largest town and a popular resort. It was a maritime power before being subdued in 1131 by King Roger of Naples. The world's oldest maritime code, the *Tavole Amalfitane*, originated here. The 13th-century Chiostro del Paradiso flanks the Duomo, a magnificent 9th-century structure fronted by a rich 13th-century façade, and facing the town from the top of a long flight of steps. The style is Lombard-Norman, though the cloisters have a Saracenic-inspired appearance.

**Ravello** has the best views on this coast, the prime vantage points being the gardens of Villa Cimbrone and Villa Rufolo. Views from the latter provided inspiration for Wagner's *Parsifal*. The 11th-century Duomo has entrance doors by Barisano da Trani (1179) and an ornate 13th-century ambo (pulpit) held aloft by six spiral columns. The chapel of San Pantaleone contains the blood of its 4th-century namesake, which liquefies annually in May and August.

Beyond **Atrani**, the ruins of a Roman villa at **Minori** show that this coastline has always been a popular holiday spot.

A breathtaking view of the steep village of Positano on the Amalfi Coast

## Salerno ❼

Salerno. FS 🚌 ⛴ *Salerno.* ℹ *Piazza Ferrovia (089 23 14 32); Lungomare Trieste (089 22 47 44).*

Salerno is a big, busy port. Here the Allies landed in 1943, leaving in their wake a much-bombed city. Once famous for its School of Medicine (12th century), it is visited today for its **Duomo**, an 11th-century structure built on an earlier foundation. Its best feature is the Atrium, whose columns came from nearby Paestum. In the crypt is the Tomb of St Matthew, brought here in 954.

The **Museo Diocesano** is home to most of the cathedral treasures, including an 11th-century ivory altar-front called the Paliotto. Before wandering off down the bustling Corso Vittorio Emanuele, visit the **Museo Provinciale** for local archaeological finds.

**Environs:** The **Cilento** is a mountainous region south of Salerno with a remote interior and a lovely, quiet coastline that is only slightly more populous. Among the towns along the coast, **Agropoli** is a busy little seaside resort 42 km (25 miles) south of Salerno. Outside Castellammare di Velia, a further 28 km (17 miles) to the southeast, are the ruins of the Greek town of **Elea** (founded 6th century BC), once famous for its school of philosophy. It was much visited by the Romans – Cicero was here and Horace came on his doctor's orders to undergo a treatment of sea bathing. Excavations have revealed a magnificent 4th-century Roman gateway: the Porta Rosa, Roman baths, the foundations of a temple and the remains of the acropolis.

The busy port of Salerno

The Temple of Hera I (left) and the Temple of Neptune at Paestum

**Museo Diocesano**
Largo Plebiscito. ***Tel*** *089 23 91 26.* *9am–1pm daily (Sun also 3–7pm).*

**Museo Provinciale**
Via San Benedetto. ***Tel*** *089 23 11 35.* *8am–1:15pm, 2–3pm Tue–Sat.*

## Paestum ❽

Zona Archeologica. ℹ *Via Magna Grecia 887.* ***Tel*** *0828 81 10 16.* 🚌 *from Salerno.* FS *Paestum.* *9am – 1 hr before sunset daily.* **Museum** ***Tel*** *0828 81 10 23.* *9am–7pm daily (to 2pm Sun & hols).* *1st & 3rd Mon of month, 1 Jan, 25 Dec.*

This is the most important ancient Greek site south of Naples in Campania. The Greeks founded this city on

## Capri ❾

Napoli. ⛴ *Capri.* ℹ *Piazza Umberto I, Capri (081 837 06 86).* **Grotta Azzurra** ⛴ *from Marina Grande;* 🚌 *from Anacapri.* *in calm sea.* **Certosa** *Via Certosa, Capri.* ***Tel*** *081 837 62 18.* *9am–2pm Tue–Sun.* **Villa Jovis** Via Tiberio. *daily.* **www**.capritourism.com

Capri's reputation as a sybaritic paradise is nearly eclipsed by its notoriety as a tourist trap. However, the views are unmarred by the throng.

The home of emperors, seat of monasteries, place of exile, its fortunes changed during the 19th century when English and German expatriates discovered its charms. Today it barely has a "low season"; farmers run little hotels, and fishermen rent pleasure boats. Capri enjoys its well-deserved reputation as a Garden of Eden.

**The Grotta Azzurra**, or the Blue Grotto, is a cave bathed in iridescent blue light which can be reached by tour boat from Marina Grande.

**Anacapri** is Capri's second town.

*For hotels and restaurants in this region see pp593–6 and pp643–6*

the edge of the Piana del Sele in the 6th century BC and called it Poseidonia, the City of Poseidon. The Romans renamed it in 273 BC. It fell into decline and was abandoned in the 9th century due to malaria and a Saracen assault and rediscovered in the 18th century.

Paestum has three massive Doric temples in an excellent state of repair: the **Basilica** or **Temple of Hera I** (mid-6th century BC); the **Temple of Neptune** (5th century BC), the largest and most complete at Paestum; and the **Temple of Ceres**, thought to date between its two neighbours.

Excavations have revealed the remains of the ancient city, its public and religious buildings, roads and protective walls. A **museum** contains the extensive finds from the site, including tomb paintings, tomb treasures, some terracotta votive offerings, architectural fragments and sculpture.

**A view from the highest point of Procida, called Terra Murata**

## Ischia and Procida ⑩

Napoli. *Ischia & Procida.* *Via Sogliuzzo 72, Ischia (081 507 42 11); Via V. Emanuele 168 (081 810 19 68).* **La Mortella** ***Tel*** *081 98 62 20.* *Apr–Oct: 9am–7pm Tue, Thu, Sat–Sun.* **www**.infoischiaprocida.it

Ischia is the biggest island in the Bay of Naples and, with its beach resorts, thermal springs and therapeutic mud baths, it is nearly as popular as Capri. Ferries dock at **Ischia Porto**, the harbour and modern part of the main town, **Ischia. Ischia Ponte**, the older part, is a short walk away. The northern and western shores are developed; the southern flank of the island is the quietest. Here, the village of **Sant' Angelo** is dominated by a long-extinct volcano, **Monte Epomeo**, whose summit of 788 m (2,585 ft) offers terrific views across the bay. Also worth a visit are the gardens of **La Mortella** in Forio.

The tiny, picturesque island of Procida is less visited and very tranquil. The swimming is good at **Chiaiolella** and, as at Ischia, there are inexpensive places to stay. The main town, also called **Procida**, is home to the main ferry port – the **Marina Grande**.

**There are views** towards Vesuvius and the Bay of Naples from the north of the island.

**Capri** is the main town on the island.

**Marina Grande**
*This is Capri's main port of call for ferries from Naples and other ports on the Tyrrhenian coast. An array of colourful houses overlooks the harbour.*

**I Faraglioni**

**Marina Piccola** is reached by dramatic Via Krupp.

**Villa Jovis**
*Covering an enormous area, this was the Imperial villa from which Tiberius ruled the Roman Empire during his final years.*

**Certosa di San Giacomo**
*Founded in 1371 on the site of one of Tiberius's villas, this Carthusian monastery was suppressed in 1808 and is now in part a school. The distant rocks are I Faraglioni.*

# ABRUZZO, MOLISE AND PUGLIA

*Puglia is the "heel" of the Italian boot, the Gargano Peninsula is its "spur" and Abruzzo and Molise together form the "ankle". Hugging the southeastern seaboard of Italy and looking towards the Balkans, the mountainous regions of Abruzzo and Molise, united until 1963, differ considerably from Puglia, the richest of the three.*

Abruzzo and Molise are sparsely populated, quiet places where the wild landscape exerts a strong influence. Settled by various Apennine tribes in the Middle Bronze Age, the areas were later subdued by the Romans, united under the Normans in the 12th century and, thereafter, ruled by a succession of dynasties based in Naples. Abruzzo, dominated by the Apennines, is a brooding, introspective land of shepherds. Vertiginous drops preface the ascent to ramshackle hilltowns clinging to the sides of high mountains, semi-abandoned and poor. Molise's landscape is less dramatic. Legends of witches persist in both regions, as do strange fertility rites and rituals celebrating the changing seasons.

Puglia's advantage over its poverty-stricken neighbours is that it is nearly all flat and highly fertile. It produces the largest amount of olive oil in Italy, and its big cities – Lecce, Bari and Taranto – are lively commercial centres. The region experienced a long-lasting Greek influence, though the golden age of Puglia's past was under the rule of the Normans, followed by Frederick II who, between his return from Germany as emperor in 1220 and his death 30 years later, only spent four years away from here.

Puglia has glorious architecture, particularly in the churches and castles of the north. The curious *trulli* houses in central Puglia, the florid Baroque of Lecce and the Levantine atmosphere of its merchant cities complete the picture of an ancient land subject to more influences from outside the Italian peninsula than from within it.

**Traditional dress worn in the town of Scanno in Abruzzo**

◁ **The curious *trulli* buildings found in central Puglia, particularly around Alberobello and Locorotondo**

# Exploring Abruzzo, Molise and Puglia

Dominated by the Apennine mountain range, the hinterland of Abruzzo and Molise forms one of Italy's last wildernesses. At 2,912 m (9,554 ft), the highest peak is the Gran Sasso. Parts of Abruzzo are covered in tracts of forest, while Molise features high plains, gentle valleys and lonely peaks. The coastline of the Gargano Peninsula in Puglia (Apulia) is packed with cliffs, caves and islets. Reaching south is the fertile Tavoliere plain, and further south a series of upland plateaux (the Murge) descends towards the dry Salentine Peninsula and the Adriatic.

**The exotic *trulli* hou[ses of] Alberobello in central P[uglia]**

## GETTING AROUND

Northern Abruzzo is well served by the A24 and A25–E80, and the S17 traverses the interior of Abruzzo and Molise. The coastal highway (A14–E55) heads south through Abruzzo and Molise into Puglia. Beyond Foggia, it joins the S16 to Taranto. Brindisi, the main port for Greece, is accessible from Bari or Taranto. The roads throughout are good. Train and bus services go to the major centres, with buses only to more remote parts.

**The coast at Vieste on the beautiful Gargano Peninsula in Puglia**

**KEY**

- Motorway
- Major road
- Secondary road
- Road under construction
- Minor road
- Scenic route
- Main railway
- Minor railway
- Regional border
- Summit

**For additional map symbols** *see back flap*

## SIGHTS AT A GLANCE

**The high peaks of the Gran Sasso, north of L'Aquila in Abruzzo**

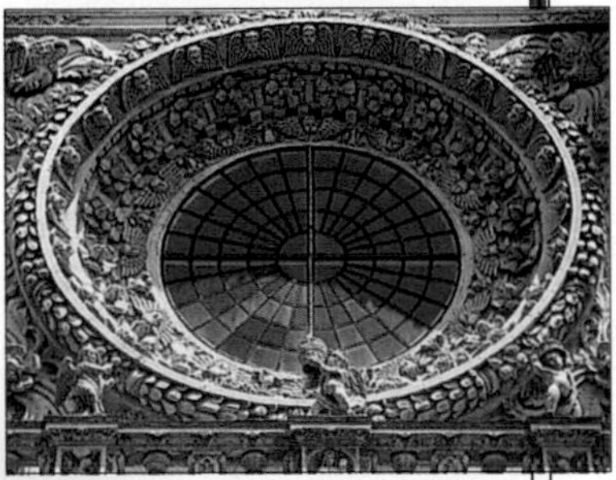

**Lecce's exuberant Baroque architecture, epitomized in Santa Croce's rose window**

### *SEE ALSO*


- ***Where to Stay*** pp597–8
- ***Where to Eat*** pp646–8

The pink and white stone façade of Santa Maria di Collemaggio in L'Aquila

## L'Aquila ❶

*70,000.* FS *Via XX Settembre 10 (0862 223 06).* *daily.* **www**.abruzzoturismo.it

Abruzzo's capital lies at the foot of the **Gran Sasso**, at 2,912 m (9,554 ft) the highest point of the Italian mainland south of the Alps (and good for skiing). Its ancient streets are peppered with churches. In April 2009 an earthquake, measuring 6.3 in magnitude, struck central Italy with the epicentre close to L'Aquila. Many of the historical churches and buildings described below have been seriously damaged by the quake. Restoration work is being carried out on many buildings so do check with the tourist office before visiting.

The domed **Santa Giusta** (1257), off Via Santa Giusta, has a rose window and a *Martyrdom of St Stephen* (1615) by Cavalier d'Arpino. **Santa Maria di Paganica**, off Via Paganica, has a 14th-century façade and a carved portal. The **Duomo** (1257) in Piazza del Duomo was rebuilt in the 18th century. The massive church of **Santa Maria di Collemaggio**, on Piazza di Collemaggio, has a façade of pink and white stone. It was built in the 13th century by Pietro dal Morrone, who later became Pope Celestine V.

Detail of Fontanelle delle Novantanove Cannelle in L'Aquila

**San Bernardino**, on Via di San Bernardino, houses the tomb (1505) of San Bernardino of Siena. The church (built 1454–1472), has a façade (1527) by Cola dell'Amatrice and an 18th-century carved ceiling by Ferdinando Mosca. The bell tower collapsed in the 2009 earthquake. The second chapel in the south aisle has an altarpiece by Andrea della Robbia, the Renaissance artist.

The medieval **Fontanelle delle Novantanove Cannelle** at the end of Via San Iacopo is a fountain commemorating the 99 villages that Frederick II supposedly united when he founded L'Aquila in 1240.

The **Museo Nazionale d'Abruzzo**, in the 16th-century castle, contains the remains of a prehistoric elephant, Roman artifacts and religious works.

**Museo Nazionale d'Abruzzo**
Castello Cinquecentesco. ***Tel*** *0862 63 32 29.* *8:30am–7:30pm Tue–Sun.* *1 May, 25 Dec.*

## Atri ❷

Teramo. *11,000.* *0861 24 42 22.* *Mon.* **www**. comune.atri.te.it

The prettiest in a series of small hill-towns in Abruzzo, Atri is a warren of stepped streets, alleys and passages bound by mostly brick and stone churches and houses. The 13th-century **Duomo** occupies the site of a Roman bath; the crypt was once a swimming pool, and fragments of the original mosaic floor are visible in the apse. Also in the apse is Andrea Delitio's beautiful 15th-century fresco cycle, in which he combined landscape and architecture in a variety of religious scenes from the Old and New Testaments. The cloister has views of the 15th-century brick campanile.

**Environs:** South of Atri is the hilltown of **Penne**, with its homogeneous buildings of reddish brick, which give it a wonderful, warm glow. East of Atri, **Loreto Aprutino** is known for the *Last Judgment* fresco (14th century) in Santa Maria in Piano.

Detail from 15th-century fresco by Andrea Delitio in Atri's Duomo

## Sulmona ❸

L'Aquila. *26,000.* FS *Corso Ovidio 208 (0864 532 76).* *Wed & Sat.* *Sep: International Exhibition of Contemporary Art.* **www**.comune.sulmona.aq.it

This town is famous as the home of both Ovid and *confetti* (sugared almonds). After a wedding celebration, guests are given *confetti* as a good luck token. Sulmona is filled with ancient buildings, especially along medieval **Via dell'Ospedale**. The **Palazzo dell'Annunziata** was founded in 1320 and combines Gothic and Renaissance styles. The **Museo Civico** holds a collection of local antiquities, costumes, paintings and the work of goldsmiths formerly housed in the palace. The adjacent church of the **Annunziata**, with a Baroque façade, was rebuilt in the 18th century. Behind the church are 1 BC–AD 2 ruins of a Roman house.

At the end of Viale Matteotti is the cathedral of **San Panfilo**, built over a Roman temple. **San Francesco della Scarpa**, in Piazza del Carmine, has a 13th-century portal. Winding past it to the **Fontana del Vecchio** (1474) is an aqueduct that once fuelled local industry.

**Environs:** East of Sulmona is the Maiella National Park, a massif of 61 peaks and forested valleys offering walking, bird-watching, climbing and skiing. To the west, Cocullo hosts the May Processione dei Serpari (Festival of Snakes) in which a statue of the patron saint, Domenico Abate, is draped with snakes and carried through the town. In the 11th century he is said to have rid the area of venomous snakes.

**Museo Civico**
Palazzo dell'Annunziata, Corso Ovidio. ***Tel*** *0864 21 02 16.* *Tue–Sun (Sun and pub hols am only).*

### OVID, THE LATIN POET

Born in 43 BC, Ovid (Publius Ovidius Naso) was Sulmona's most illustrious son. Not much survives here to remind you of his presence, however, apart from a **Corso Ovidio**, a 20th-century statue of him in Piazza XX Settembre and, just outside the town, a ruin traditionally known as **Ovid's Villa**. Known as one of the greatest poets of Classical Rome, his subjects included love *(Ars Amatoria)* and mythology *(Metamorphoses)*. In AD 8 he was banished into exile on the Black Sea, the far edge of the Roman Empire, after being implicated in a scandal of adultery with Julia, the granddaughter of Emperor Augustus *(see pp48–9)*. Ovid continued to write of his hardships, and died in exile in AD 17.

## Scanno ❹

L'Aquila. *2,400.* *Piazza Santa Maria della Valle 12 (0864 743 17).* *Tue.* **www**.scanno.org

Wonderfully well-preserved, this medieval hill-town set in beautiful, wild countryside is one of Abruzzo's most popular attractions. There are alleys and narrow flights of steps, oddly-shaped courtyards into which small churches have been pressed, and ancient mansions in whose windows women can be seen making lace or embroidering.

**Traditional costume still worn in Scanno**

In the shadow of Apennine peaks and beside lovely **Lago di Scanno**, the town is also a favoured stop on the way to the Parco Nazionale d'Abruzzo *(see pp506–7)*. The summer months are the busiest, with a variety of activities from riding, boating and camping by the lake, to the August classical music festival. During the January Festa di Sant' Antonio Abate, a large lasagna is cooked outside **Santa Maria della Valle**, which is built on the remains of a pagan temple. The food is doled out on a first-come, first-served basis.

**High Apennine peaks looming above the medieval hill-town of Scanno in Abruzzo**

# Parco Nazionale d'Abruzzo, Lazio e Molise ❺

This vast park, inaugurated in 1922, has a rich landscape of high peaks, rivers, lakes and forests, and is one of Europe's most important nature reserves. Part of a royal hunting reserve until 1877, today it provides refuge for 66 species of mammal, 52 types of reptile, amphibian and fish, and 230 species of bird, including the golden eagle and white-backed woodpecker, as well as over 2,000 varieties of flora. The park offers an extensive network of paths, and there are opportunities for riding, trekking and climbing.

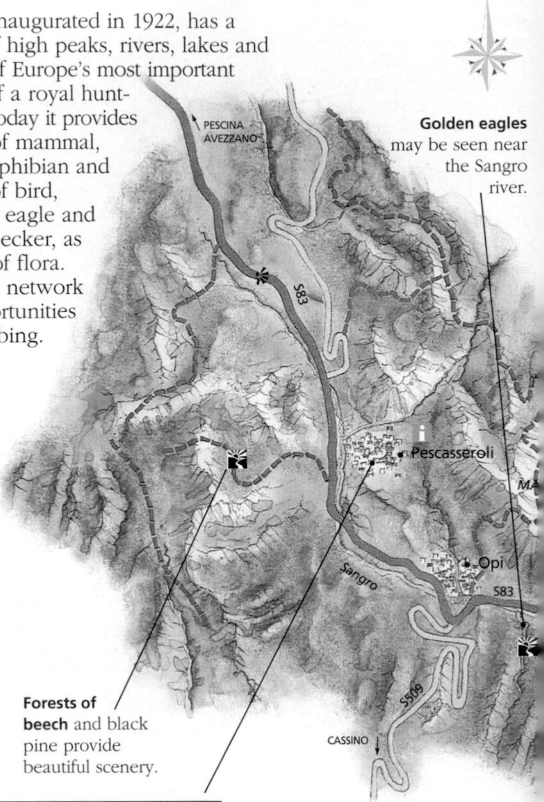

Iris

**Golden eagles** may be seen near the Sangro river.

**Young Chamois**
*Dense forests of beech and maple hide the Apennine chamois. There are also red and roe deer in the park.*

**Forests of beech** and black pine provide beautiful scenery.

**Pescasseroli**
*This town is a major centre for information on the area. It has good tourist facilities and a small zoological garden with animals living in the region, such as bears and wolves.*

**Apennine Wolves**
*The park guarantees protection for the Apennine wolf, and about 60 wolves survive here. The chances of seeing one, however, are fairly remote.*

**Marsican Brown Bear**
*Once hunted almost to extinction, between 80 and 100 brown bears now roam in the park.*

*For hotels and restaurants in this region see pp597–8 and pp646–8*

**VISITORS' CHECKLIST**

L'Aquila. FS *Avezzano or Castel di Sangro, then* bus *to Pescasseroli.* *Nature Centre: Pescasseroli (0863 911 32 21); visit the website for opening hours.* **www**.parcoabruzzo.it

**Horse Riding**

*Trekking is an excellent way to explore more remote areas of the park.*

**The Camosciara** is a spectacular area, home to many wild animals.

**Lake Barrea**

*Created by the artificial damming of the River Sangro, this lake is surrounded by valleys and forests offering walking and pony trekking.*

**Dense Forests**

*Beech and maple forests, dotted with black hornbeam, ash, hawthorn, cherry, wild apple and pear, protect the once persecuted bears and wolves.*

**KEY**

- Major road
- Minor road
- Walking path
- Viewpoint
- Tourist information

0 kilometres 5

0 miles 5

## Lanciano ❻

*Chieti.* *35,000.* FS *Piazza Plebiscito 50 (0872 71 78 10).* *Wed & Sat.* **www**.lanciano.it

Large parts of Lanciano's old nucleus remain from the Middle Ages. In the crumbling Civitanova quarter is the 13th-century church of **Santa Maria Maggiore**, with a magnificent 14th-century portal and a silver processional cross (1422). Also in this area is the now disused **San Biagio** (begun c.1059), near the 11th-century **Porta San Biagio** – a rare surviving town gate. The **Duomo** stands on the remains of a Roman bridge dating from the time of Diocletian. An underground passage links the bridge to the **Sanctuary of the Eucharistic Miracle**, where a host and wine that turned into live Flesh and Blood in the 8th century are kept.

The Ripa Sacca (Jewish ghetto) was a busy commercial centre in the Middle Ages – the period of Lanciano's greatest prosperity. The hefty walls of the **Torri Montanara** were built then by the Aragonese as a bulwark against attack.

## Isole Tremiti ❼

*Foggia.* *400.* *San Nicola.* *Via Perrone 17, Foggia (0881 72 31 41); Via Sant'Antonio Abate 21, Monte Sant'Angelo (0884 56 89 11).* **http://**tremiti.planetek.it

Off the Gargano coast, the Tremiti are the Italian islands least visited by foreigners. **San Domino** is the largest, with a sandy beach and coves. Julia, granddaughter of Augustus, was exiled here for adultery from AD 8 until her death in AD 28. The poet Ovid was allegedly involved *(see p505)*.

**Santa Maria a Mare**, in **San Nicola**, the administrative centre of the islands, is an abbey-fortress founded in the 8th century. It was turned into a prison in the late 1700s, a role it maintained until 1945.

Both islands are popular with Italians. The swimming is good, though the coastline of San Nicola is rocky.

The coast near Peschici on the Gargano Peninsula

## Gargano Peninsula 8

*Foggia.* FS *Piazza del Popolo 10, Manfredonia (0884 58 19 98); Via Sant'Antonio Abate 21, Monte Sant'Angelo (0884 56 89 11).* **www**.parcogargano.it

A rocky spur jutting into the Adriatic Sea, the Gargano is dotted with coves and cliffs. Its coastal towns of **Manfredonia**, **Rodi Garganico**, **Peschici** and **Vieste** are popular with holidaymakers. To the east lies the **Foresta Umbra**, a vast woodland of beech, oak, yew and pine, and to the north the salt lakes of **Lesina** and **Varano**, havens for waterfowl. Plunging through the Gargano is an old pilgrim route (S272) from **San Severo** in the west to the shrine at **Monte Sant'Angelo** in the east. The first stop is **San Marco in Lamis**, dominated by a huge 16th-century convent. Further along, **San Giovanni Rotondo** is a focus for pilgrims visiting the tomb of Padre Pio (1887–1968), a beatified miracle-worker. The last stop is **Monte Sant'Angelo** with its grotto where the Archangel Michael is said to have appeared to the Bishop of Sipontum in 493.

To the south of Manfredonia, beside the ruins of ancient Siponto, is the oriental-inspired 12th-century church of **Santa Maria di Siponto**.

Typical street scene in the town of Vieste on the Gargano Peninsula

## Lucera 9

*Foggia.* *35,000.* *Piazza Nocelli 6 (0881 52 27 62).* *Wed.* **www**.comune.lucera.fg.it

On the northeast edge of town, once a prosperous Roman colony, are the ruins of a Roman **amphitheatre** (closed for renovation). Lucera was rebuilt in the 13th century by Frederick II, who peopled it with 20,000 Sicilian Muslims. It became one of the strongest fortresses in southern Italy, and its **castle** is one of Puglia's most magnificent. Built in 1233 by Frederick II, and enlarged after 1269, its fortified wall of 900 m (2,953 ft) is interspersed with 24 towers. Of Frederick's original palace, only the base and some vaulting remains.

In 1300 Charles II, who killed most of Lucera's Muslim population, began the **Duomo** on the site of their main mosque. The high, soaring nave is filled with 15th- and 16th-century frescoes and carvings.

The **Museo Civico Fiorelli** has displays of episodes from throughout Lucera's history.

**Museo Civico Fiorelli**
Via de Nicastri 44. ***Tel*** *0881 54 70 41.* *for renovation (800 76 76 06).*

The remains of Lucera castle

## Troia 10

*Foggia.* *33,000.* *0881 97 82 41.* *1st & 3rd Sat of month.* **www**.comune.troia.fg.it

Founded in 1017 as a Byzantine fortress against the Lombards, Troia fell to the Normans in 1066. Until Frederick II destroyed it in 1229, the town had been ruled by a succession of powerful bishops who were responsible for producing many remarkable buildings, including Troia's **Duomo** *(see pp478–9)*.

Begun in 1093 and constructed over the following 30 years, it exhibits an extraordinary diversity of styles. It successfully blends elements of Lombard, Saracenic and Byzantine style with that of the Pisan-Romanesque.

Elegant blind arcading distinguishes the Duomo's lower storey. The upper sections are characterized by powerfully carved sculpture – projecting lions and bulls. The upper façade displays a rose window with Saracenic-style detailing.

The main entrance, with bronze doors by Oderisio da Beneventano (1119), is dominated by carved capitals and an architrave, both Byzantine in style. Within the Duomo is a Romanesque pulpit (1169).

## Trani ⓫

*Bari.* *55,000.* FS *Piazza Sacra Regia Udienza II (0883 58 88 30).* *Tue.* **www**.traniweb.it

During the Middle Ages this small, lively whitewashed port of Jewish origin bustled with mercantile activity and was filled with merchants and traders from Genoa, Amalfi and Pisa. It reached its peak of prosperity under Frederick II.

Today it is visited for its Norman **Duomo** in Piazza Duomo, built mainly from

**The façade of Trani's Duomo**

1159 to 1186 over an earlier church whose predecessor, the Ipogei di San Leucio, dates from the 7th century. It is dedicated to St Nicholas the Pilgrim, a little-remembered miracle worker (died 1094) who was canonized as an act of rivalry against the town of Bari, which possessed the bones of another, more memorable St Nicholas. The Duomo's most notable external features are its sculptures, particularly surrounding the rose window and the arched window below it, and the entrance portal with bronze doors (1175–9) by Barisano da Trani. The vigour of the interior has been revealed following restoration.

Next to the Duomo is the **castle** (1233–49) founded by Frederick II. Rebuilt in the 14th and 15th centuries, it is a well-preserved edifice with one wall dropping sheer into the sea.

The 15th-century Gothic-Renaissance **Palazzo Caccetta**, in Piazza Trieste, is a rare survival. Nearby, on Via **Ognissanti**, the 12th-century Romanesque church of the **Ognissanti**, the chapel of the Knights Templar erected in the courtyard of their hospital, is notable for its original portico. Other churches worth a visit are Santa Teresa and the monastery of La Colonna.

## Castel del Monte ⓬

*Località Andria, Bari.* *Beni Culturali (0883 56 99 97).* *9am–6pm daily.* *1 Jan, 25 Dec.* **www**.casteldelmonte.beniculturali.it

**Frederick II**

Remote in the endless plains near Ruvo di Puglia, Castel del Monte, built in the mid-13th century, outclasses every other castle associated with Frederick II. It is also one of the most sophisticated secular buildings of the Middle Ages. The emperor had broad intellectual interests, and he used his castles as hunting lodges where he could retire from court life with his falcons and books. Inside there are two floors, each with eight rib-vaulted rooms, some still lined with marble. This, and the marble mouldings on the entrance and the upper floor, as well as sophisticated lavatory arrangements, mark the castle as a palace.

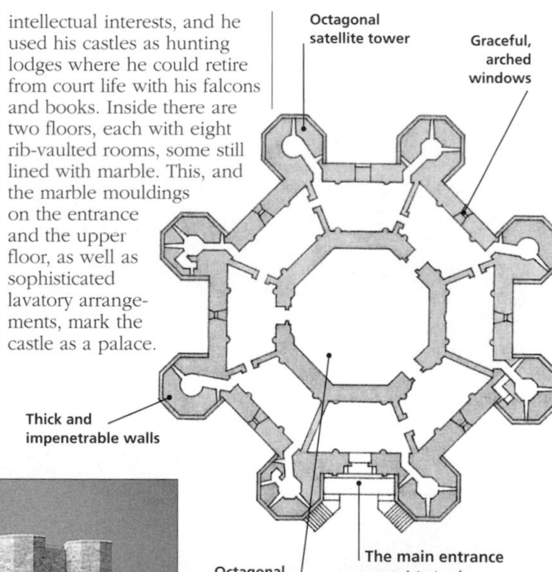


**FLOORPLAN OF THE CASTLE**

The building is a harmonious geometrical study with two storeys of eight rooms each. The reasons for such precise planning of this giant octagon remain a mystery to this day.

**The castle standing alone on the summit of a low hill**

## Ruvo di Puglia ⓭

Bari. 24,000. FS *Via Vittorio Veneto 48 (080 361 54 19). Sat.* **www**.ruvodipugliaweb.it

Once celebrated for its vases, Ruvo di Puglia's ceramics industry, producing "Apulian" ware, flourished until the 2nd century BC. The style was inspired by the striking red and black colours of Attic and Corinthian models. The **Museo Archeologico Nazionale Jatta** has a good overview.

The 13th-century **Cattedrale** is a bold example of the Apulian-Romanesque style with a portal that blends Byzantine, Saracenic and Classical motifs.

**Museo Archeologico Nazionale Jatta**

Piazza Bovio 35. ***Tel*** *080 361 28 48.* *8:30am–7:30pm daily (to 1:30pm Sun–Wed). 1 Jan, 1 May, 25 Dec.* **www**.palazzojatta.org

## Bari ⓮

*400,000.* FS *Piazza Aldo Moro 33a (080 524 23 61). daily.* **www**.comune.bari.it

Roman Barium was simply a commercial centre, but the city became the regional capital under the Saracens in 847, and was later the seat of the *catapan*, the Byzantine governor of southern Italy. Under the Normans, to whom it fell in 1071, Bari became a centre of maritime significance. Today it is Puglia's lively capital and an important port with ferries to and from Croatia and Greece.

Portal detail of Ruvo di Puglia's Duomo

The **Basilica di San Nicola**, one of Puglia's first great Norman churches (begun 1087), has a plain exterior with a tall gabled section flanked by towers. The Apulian-Romanesque portal has carving on the door jambs and arch in Arabic, Byzantine and Classical styles. Beyond the choir screen is a fine 12th-century altar canopy and an episcopal throne (c.11th century). The relics of St Nicholas – patron saint of the city (and also of Russia) – are buried in the crypt.

Sculpture at Bari castle

The late 12th-century Apulian-Romanesque **Cattedrale** is based on San Nicola, with a dome and one surviving tower (the other one collapsed in 1613). The Baroque portals on the façade incorporate 12th-century doorways. The interior has been restored to its medieval simplicity. The canopy over the high altar, the pulpit and the episcopal throne are reconstructions from fragments of the originals. The sacristy, built as a baptistry, is known as the *Trulla*. The crypt houses the remains of San Sabino, Bari's original patron saint.

The city's **castle**, founded by Roger II, was adapted by Frederick II in 1233–9. In the vaulted hall is a collection of plaster casts of sculpture and architectural fragments from various Romanesque monuments in the region.

Bari castle, in the old district known as Città Vecchia, where most of the town's sights are clustered

*For hotels and restaurants in this region see pp597–8 and pp646–8*

## Alberobello ⓯

Bari. *11,000.* FS *to Alberobello & Ostuni.* *Piazza Ferdinando IV (080 432 51 71).* *in English, French and German offered by Trulli e Natura (080 432 38 29).* *Oct/Nov: Frantoi Aperti (visits to the major olive-pressing factories).* **www**.alberobello.net

The parched landscape of the **Murge dei Trulli** features olive groves, vineyards and *trulli*. Strange circular buildings with conical roofs and domed within, *trulli* are built from local limestone stacked without using mortar. The walls and openings are generally whitewashed, while the stone roof tiles often have religious, pagan or magical symbols painted on them. The origins of *trulli* are obscure, though the name is traditionally applied to ancient round tombs found in the Roman countryside. Most *trulli* are souvenir shops.

**Alberobello** is a UNESCO World Heritage site and the *trulli* capital. Here the strange white buildings crowd the narrow streets, and there are *trulli* restaurants, shops and even a *trulli* cathedral.

Whitewashed and sun-baked *trulli* in Alberobello

**Environs:** The pretty whitewashed hilltown of **Locorotondo** is an important wine centre. The elegant streets of **Martina Franca** are enlivened by Rococo balconies. The spectacular **Grotte di Castellana** are caves estimated to be 50 million years old.

*Aphrodite* in museum in Taranto

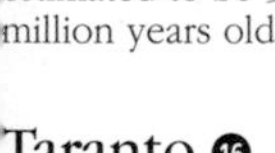

## Taranto ⓰

*220,000.* FS *Corso Umberto I (099 453 23 92).* *Wed, Fri & Sat.* **www**.comune.taranto.it

Little remains of the old city of Taras, founded by Spartans in 708 BC and at its most prosperous in the mid-4th century BC. The **Museo Archeologico Nazionale**, founded in 1887, has artifacts that shed light on the region's history. The museum has since been expanded to allow for a growing collection of historically significant pieces.

Taranto was heavily bombed in World War II and is garlanded by factories. The picturesque **Città Vecchia**, an island dividing the Mare Grande from the Mare Piccolo, was the site of the Roman citadel of Tarentum. A lively fish market offering the shellfish for which the city is famous, is housed in an Art Nouveau building. Here, too, is the **Duomo**. Founded in 1071, it has been the object of subsequent rebuilding. The most interesting features include the catacomb-like crypt, with its sarcophagi and fragmented frescoes, and the antique marble columns of the nave. Behind it is the 11th-century **San Domenico Maggiore**, which later gained a high double-approach Baroque staircase. The huge **castle** built by Frederick of Aragon (15th century) covers the eastern corner of the Città Vecchia. Now a military area, the castle is strictly off limits.

**Museo Archeologico Nazionale**
Via Cavour 10. ***Tel*** *0994 53 21 12.* *8:30am–7:30pm daily.*

### THE TARANTELLA

Italy's lively and graceful folk dance, the Tarantella, grew out of tarantism – the hysteria that appeared in 15th-to 17th-century Italy, and was prevalent in Galatina *(see p513)*. Alleged victims of the tarantula spider's bite could supposedly cure themselves through frenzied dancing which sweated out the poison. The dance is characterized by light, quick steps and a "teasing" flirt. The strange, private ritual takes place annually on 29 June at 6am at the celebrations for the Feast of Saints Peter and Paul in Galatina, the only place on the Salentine Peninsula where tarantism has survived.

# Street-by-Street: Lecce ⑰

Façade detail, Santa Croce

Lecce was the site of the Greek Messapi settlement. It became an important centre of the Roman Empire, and in the Middle Ages developed a strong tradition of scholarship. Much of the architecture is in the highly decorative Lecce Baroque style, which flourished in the 1600s and earned the city the name of Florence of the South. This style was possible due to the *pietra di Lecce*, an easily carved stone. Giuseppe Zimbalo (Lo Zingarello) was its greatest master. Lecce is also famed for its papier-mâché workshops.

**★ Palazzo Vescovile and Duomo**
*The bishop's palace (rebuilt in 1632), the adjoining Duomo by Lo Zingarello (after 1659) and a seminary (1709) enclose the Piazza Duomo.*

**Chiesa del Rosario**
*Said to be the finest work by Lo Zingarello (begun 1691), the exterior is ornate and idiosyncratic in its detail.*

**Porta Rudiae**
*This 18th-century city gate leads to the suburbs and to the ruins of Roman Rudiae.*

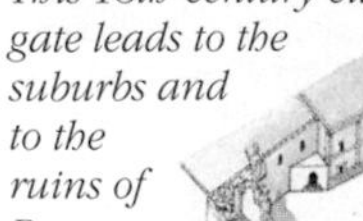

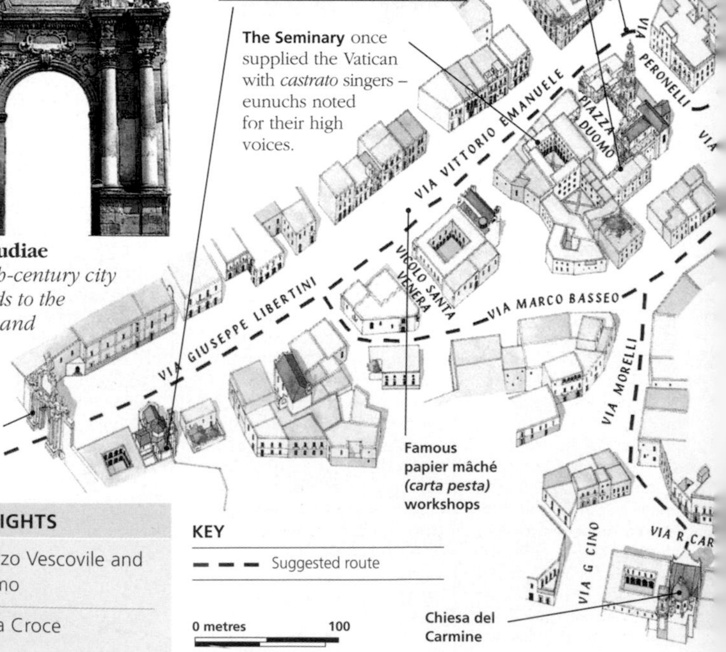

**The Seminary** once supplied the Vatican with *castrato* singers – eunuchs noted for their high voices.

**Famous papier mâché *(carta pesta)* workshops**

**Chiesa del Carmine**

## STAR SIGHTS

★ Palazzo Vescovile and Duomo

★ Santa Croce

**KEY**

– – – Suggested route

0 metres 100
0 yards 100

**★ Santa Croce**
*Built 1549–1679, this church was begun by Gabriele Riccardi; the rose window is by Lo Zingarello. Next door is the ex-convent of the Celestines.*

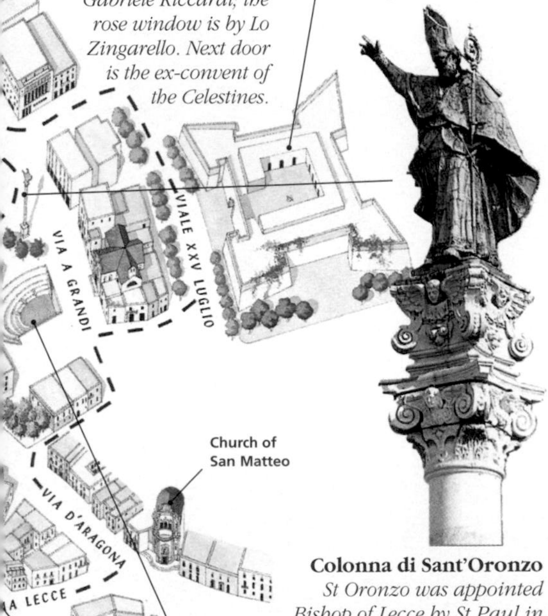

VIALE XXV LUGLIO

VIA A GRANDI

VIA D'ARAGONA

LECCE

**Church of San Matteo**

**A Roman theatre** was excavated virtually intact with its orchestra and seats.

## VISITORS' CHECKLIST

105,000. FS Viale Oronzo Quarta. Via Boito & Via Adua. Via Vittorio Emanuele 23 (0832 33 24 63). Mon & Fri. 24–26 Aug: Sant'Oronzo; 13–24 Dec: Fiera dei Pupi e Pastori. **www**.pugliaturismo.it

**The 16th-century Castello** lies between ancient city and modern suburbs. A 12th-century construction is enclosed by a wall built later by Charles V. Only one floor is open to the public.

**Colonna di Sant'Oronzo**
*St Oronzo was appointed Bishop of Lecce by St Paul in AD 57, and later martyred by the Roman emperor Nero. This bronze statue dates from 1739.*

**Roman Amphitheatre**
*Excavated in 1938, only part of this 1st-century BC amphitheatre is visible. Due to restoration, it is closed to the public.*

**Detail of a 15th-century fresco in Santa Caterina d'Alessandria**

## Galatina ⓲

Lecce. *28,000.* FS *Sala dell'Orologio (0836 56 99 84).* *Thu.* *29 Jun: Feast of Saints Peter & Paul.* **www**.comune.galatina.le.it

An important Greek colony in the Middle Ages, this *città d'arte* (city of art, a status given by the region) retains its Greek flavour. It is the centre of one of Puglia's chief wine-producing regions, although it is more famous for the ritual of tarantism *(see p511)*.

The Gothic church of **Santa Caterina d'Alessandria** (begun 1384) on Piazza Orsini contains early 15th-century frescoes with scenes from the Old and New Testaments that glorify the Orsini, who were feudal lords.

## Otranto ⓳

Lecce. *5,500.* FS *Piazza Castello (0836 84 14 36).* *Wed.* **www**.comune.otranto.le.it

Otranto was one of Republican Rome's leading ports for trade with Asia Minor and Greece, and under the Byzantines was an important toehold of the Eastern Empire in Italy. In 1070 it fell to the Normans. Turks attacked in 1480 and slaughtered its inhabitants. The 800 survivors were promised their lives if they renounced Christianity: all refused.

The Norman **Duomo** (founded 1080) on Via Duomo houses the bones of the martyrs. There is a 12th-century mosaic floor and a fine crypt.

A **castle** (1485–98) built by the Aragonese at the centre of town adds to Otranto's charm and there are some fine beaches close by.

# BASILICATA AND CALABRIA

*Remote and wild, Basilicata is one of the poorest regions in Italy. It is underdeveloped and undervisited, and rural areas remain unspoilt. Neighbouring Calabria has been immortalized in the drawings of Edward Lear who, travelling through on a donkey in 1847, was transfixed by the "horror and magnificence" of its savage landscape.*

Today these regions are distinctly separate, but they share a common history and, along with Sicily and Puglia, were part of Magna Graecia. Ancient Metaponto in Basilicata was an important centre, as were Crotone and Locri Epizephiri in Calabria. Their ruins evoke an illustrious past.

After the Greeks came the Romans, followed by Basilian monks. These were members of the Greek-Byzantine church who were fleeing their territories which had been invaded by Muslims. Their religious establishments make up a core of interesting monuments, such as the Cattolica at Stilo and Matera, where the monks took refuge in caves.

Many of the historic remains are Norman, but sporadic evidence of Swabian, Angevin, Aragonese and Spanish occupation still exists.

Centuries of rule by Naples led to the marginalization of Basilicata and Calabria. Nowadays Calabria has an infamous reputation due to the *'ndrangheta*, the ferocious first cousin to the Mafia, whose activities are a constant menace. Banditry exists, but the sensible traveller should have little to fear. Owing to emigration, Basilicata and Calabria are sparsely populated and have as much to offer in unspoilt countryside as in historic centres. The vast coastline boasts fine beaches, while the interior features the rugged Aspromonte and Sila mountain ranges.

The remote landscape has kept change at bay. Isolated Pentedattilo, for example, preserves customs of Byzantine origin while around San Giorgio Albanese there live close-knit communities of Albanians, descended from 15th-century refugees.

**Sparsely populated, rugged countryside surrounding Stilo in southern Calabria**

◁ **The silent Sassi district in Matera, where dwellings are scooped out of the rock**

# Exploring Basilicata and Calabria

Mostly upland country, Basilicata (or Lucania, as it is also known) is scattered with Greek ruins (like those at Metaponto), medieval abbeys and Norman castles (such as Melfi's). Matera, its most interesting city, stands amid an arid lunar landscape of denuded valleys. Calabria is often described as the land between two seas. The lovely beaches and virgin landscape between Tropea and Maratea attract many visitors. The Ionian coast's chief attractions are its Greek ruins, such as Locri Epizephiri, and the hill-towns, like Stilo and Gerace.

Repairing nets in the town of Pizzo, northeast of Tropea

## SIGHTS AT A GLANCE

Gerace ⑩
Lagopesole ③
Maratea ⑥
Matera ④
Melfi ①
Metaponto ⑤
Reggio di Calabria ⑪
Rossano ⑦
Stilo ⑨
Tropea ⑧
Venosa ②

## SEE ALSO

• ***Where to Stay*** pp598–9

• ***Where to Eat*** pp648–9

The picturesque hill-town of Rivello, north of Maratea in Basilicata

## KEY

- Motorway
- Major road
- Secondary road
- Minor road
- Scenic route
- Main railway
- Minor railway
- Regional border
- △ Summit

**For additional map symbols** *see back flap*

Bari
S99
La Martella
4 MATERA
S7
Montescaglioso
Ferrandina
Bernalda
Taranto
Craco
5 METAPONTO
Agri
Tursi
Scanzano
Sinni
Cavone
Rocca Imperiale
Oriolo
Montegiordano Marina
Amendolara
S106
Trebisacce
Cassano allo Ionio
Golfo di Taranto
Spezzano
Corigliano Calabro
Capo Trionto
7 ROSSANO
Acri
Cariati
Punta Fiume Nicà
Sila Grande
Campana
S106
Cirò Marina
Umbriatico
La Sila
San Giovanni in Fiore
Strongoli
Rogliano
S107
Monte Gariglione 1765m
Petilia Policastro
S19
Crotone
Capo Colonna
Taverna
Cutro
Nicastro
S106
S280
Catanzaro
Capo Rizzuto
Girifalco
Golfo di Squillace
Soverato
Davoli
Serra S. Bruno
9 STILO
Punta Stilo
Riace Marina
S106
MAR IONIO
0 kilometres 50
0 miles 25

The port of Maratea on the Tyrrhenian coast of Basilicata

## GETTING AROUND

Calabria's Tyrrhenian coast is well served by the A3–E45, a spur of which extends to Potenza in Basilicata. To reach the Ionian coast, it is best to skirt the Aspromonte via the S106–E90 from Reggio to Basilicata. Although the mountains can be crossed, namely on the S280–E848 to Catanzaro, the roads are narrow and pass through isolated countryside. Much of Basilicata is even less accessible, and Matera is more easily reached from Puglia. There are airports at Reggio di Calabria, Lamezia Terme (west of Catanzaro), Crotone, Bari and Brindisi (Puglia). Trains connect the bigger centres and country buses serve the small towns.

The countryside near Miglionico, south of Matera

**The impressive castle at Melfi, showing evidence of both Angevin and later construction**

## Melfi ❶

*Potenza. 16,600. FS Piazza Umberto I (0972 23 97 51). Wed & Sat.* **www**.aptbasilicata.it

A brooding and now almost deserted medieval town, Melfi is crowned by the **castle** where Pope Nicholas II conducted Robert Guiscard's investiture in 1059, thus legitimizing the Normans in the south. Melfi later became the Norman capital. Here Frederick II proclaimed his *Constitutiones Augustales* (1231), which unified his kingdom as a state. In the castle is the **Museo Nazionale del Melfese**, with its collection of Byzantine jewellery. The **Duomo**, off Via Vittorio Emanuele, was begun in 1155 by William the Bad but rebuilt in the 18th century. Only the campanile survives.

**Museo Archeologico Nazionale del Melfese**
Castello di Melfi, Via Castello. ***Tel*** *0972 23 87 26. 9am–8pm daily. Mon am, 1 Jan, 25 Dec. (Sat & Sun).*

## Venosa ❷

*Potenza. 12,200. FS Piazza Castello 47 (0972 316 09). 1st & 3rd Thu of month.* **www**.comune.venosa.pz.it

Venosa was one of the most important Roman colonies around 290 BC, and remains of **baths** and an **amphitheatre** survive in the archaeological zone along Via Vittorio Emanuele. It was also the birthplace of the Latin poet Horace (65–8 BC) and the site where the Roman general Marcellus died at the hands of Hannibal in 208 BC. Marcellus' reputed **tomb** is in Via Melfi. For more treasures, visit the **Museo Archeologico Nazionale**.

The **Duomo**, also on Via Vittorio Emanuele, and the huge **castle** in Piazza Umberto I date from the 16th century.

An abbey complex formed by an older, possibly early Christian (5th–6th century) church, **La Trinità** is backed by an unfinished 11th-century construction, in which Robert Guiscard (died 1085) was buried with his half-brothers and Alberada, his first wife. Only her tomb has survived.

**Museo Archeologico Nazionale**
P.za Castello. ***Tel*** *0972 360 95. 9am–8pm daily (only pm Tue).*

## Lagopesole ❸

*Potenza.* ***Tel*** *0971 860 83. FS to Lagopesole Scalo then bus to town. 9:30am–1pm, 4–7pm daily (3–5pm in winter).* **www**.aptbasilicata.it

Rising dramatically on a hill, Lagopesole's **castle** (1242–50) was the last castle built by Frederick II. The interesting carved heads above the portal of the keep are said to represent Frederick Barbarossa (grandfather of Frederick II) and Barbarossa's wife, Beatrice. Inside, the royal apartments and chapel can be visited.

## Matera ❹

*56,900. FS Via de Viti de Marco 9 (0835 33 19 83). 0835 31 94 58. Sat.* **www**.materaturismo.it

**The Sassi district of Matera**

Perched on the edge of a deep ravine, this town consists of the bustling upper district and the silent, lower **Sassi** (caves) district, divided into the Sasso Barisano and the more picturesque Sasso Caveoso. The people of Matera once lived here in dwellings scooped out of the rock. The two parts are odd neighbours, making Matera a truly fascinating city.

For the best overview, walk along the **Strada Panoramica dei Sassi** and look down into the caves. From the 8th to the 13th centuries, such caves probably provided refuge for monks from the Byzantine empire. Many chapels, gouged out of the rock, were taken over in the 15th century by peasants. Later, a cave-dwelling Matera evolved and by the 18th century some buildings fronting the caves had become fairly grand mansions and convents. By the 1950s and '60s the Sassi were overtaken by squalor and poverty, and the inhabitants forcibly rehoused. Carlo Levi (1912–75) drew attention to their living conditions in his book *Christ Stopped at Eboli*, comparing the Sassi to Dante's *Inferno*. The area was made a UNESCO World Heritage site in 1993.

Of the 120 *chiese rupestri* (rock-cut churches; www.parcomurgia.it) in the Sassi and the Agri district outside the town, **Santa Maria di Idris** in the Monte Errone area and **Santa Lucia alle Malve** in the Albanian quarter both contain 13th-century frescoes.

The **Museo della Tortura** (torture), in Via San Biagio, has exhibits dating back to the time of the Inquisition, while the **Museo Nazionale Ridola** provides a background to Matera and the Sassi. The artifacts from many Neolithic trench villages, necropolises and other ancient sites are displayed here.

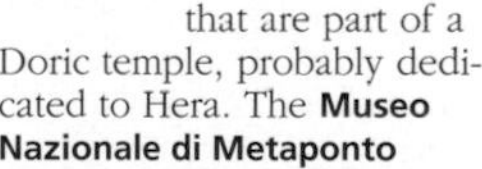

Church of San Francesco in Matera

The Apulian-Romanesque **Duomo** (13th century) in Piazza Duomo has interesting sculpture and a 12th-century painting of the *Madonna della Bruna*, the patroness of Matera. Via Duomo leads toward **San Francesco d'Assisi** (13th century with Baroque overlay). Other churches to visit are **San Domenico** and **San Giovanni Battista** on Via San Biagio (both 13th century), and the **Purgatorio** (1770) on Via Ridola.

Matera is where Mel Gibson's *The Passion of the Christ* (2004) was largely filmed.

**Museo Nazionale Ridola**
Via Ridola 24. ***Tel*** *0835 31 00 58.* *9am–8pm daily (from 2pm Mon).* *1 Jan, 25 Dec.*

The Tavole Palatine in Metaponto

## Metaponto 5

Metaponto Borgo. FS *to Metaponto.* *Via Apollo Licio (0835 74 52 20).* *9am–1 hr before sunset daily.* *Mon am, 1 Jan, Easter, 25 Dec.* **www**.aptbasilicata.it

Founded in the 7th century BC, ancient Metapontum was once the centre of a wealthy city-state with a philosophical tradition expounded by Pythagoras, who settled here after his expulsion from Croton. Its ruins include the **Tavole Palatine** (6th century BC) at the Bradano River bridge, 15 columns that are part of a Doric temple, probably dedicated to Hera. The **Museo Nazionale di Metaponto** displays artifacts from the site. The ruins of a theatre and the Doric **Temple of Apollo Lycius** (6th century BC) are in the **Archaeological Zone**. Further south, modern **Policoro** occupies the site of ancient Heracleia (founded 7th–5th century BC). Its **Museo Nazionale della Siritide** has finds from this and other sites.

**Museo Nazionale di Metaponto**
Via Aristea 21. ***Tel*** *0835 74 53 27.* *9am–8pm daily.* *Mon am, pub hols.* *includes Archaeological Zone.*

**Museo Nazionale della Siritide**
Via Colombo 8, Policoro. ***Tel*** *0835 97 21 54.* *9am–7pm daily.* *Tue am, 1 Jan, 1 May, 25 Dec.*

## Maratea 6

Potenza. *5,000.* FS
*Piazza del Gesù 32 (0973 87 69 08).* *1st & 3rd Sat of month.*

A tiny stretch of Basilicata meets the Tyrrhenian Sea in the Gulf of Policastro. This unblemished coast is home to Maratea. Its small port (Maratea Inferiore) is beneath the old centre (Maratea Superiore), which straddles the flank of a hill. From here the road climbs Monte Biagio to a summit with breathtaking views where a huge statue of the **Redeemer** stands.

**Environs:** Dramatically sited **Rivello**, 23 km (14 miles) to the north, once had a largely Greek population. Byzantine influences can be seen in the churches of **Santa Maria del Poggio** and **Santa Barbara**.

The small port of Marina di Maratea with fishing boats

A page from the precious *Codex Purpureus Rossanensis*

## Rossano ❼

Cosenza. 38,000. FS
Piazza Matteotti (0983 52 09 08).
2nd & 4th Fri of month.

This pretty hill-town was one of the main centres of Byzantine civilization in Calabria. It assumed power when Reggio di Calabria fell to the Saracens (9th–11th centuries). The **Museo Diocesano** houses the *Codex Purpureus Rossanensis*, a rare 6th-century Greek Gospel with silver lettering and splendidly detailed miniatures.

The Baroque **cathedral** contains the *Madonna Acheropita* fresco, a much venerated Byzantine relic of the 8th or 9th century.

**Environs:** On a hilltop to the southeast is the five-domed Greek church of **San Marco** (10th century). The 12th-century **Panaghia**, another Greek church, lies off Via Archivescovado. Both contain fragments of early frescoes.

**Santa Maria del Patirion**, on a hilltop 18 km (11 miles) to the west, is magnificently adorned with coloured brickwork, tile and stone. It offers great views over the Piana di Sibari (Plain of Sibari), the alleged location of the fabled city of Sybaris, destroyed in 510 BC. The church has remained virtually unaltered since it was built around 1095.

**Museo Diocesano**
Palazzo Arcivescovile, Via Arcivescovado 5. ***Tel*** *0983 52 02 82.* *Tue–Sun (Jul–Sep: also Mon).* *pub hols.*

## Tropea ❽

Vibo Valentia. *7,000.* FS
*Piazza Ercole (0963 614 75).*
*Sat.* **www**.tropea.biz

One of the most picturesque towns on Calabria's largely built-up Tyrrhenian coast, Tropea offers superb views of the sea and beaches. The old town hangs on to a cliffside facing a large rock, formerly an island. The rock is topped by **Santa Maria dell'Isola**, a former medieval Benedictine sanctuary. The **cathedral** at the end of Via Roma is of Norman origin, although it has been rebuilt several times. Inside is a 14th-century painting, the *Madonna di Romania*, by an unknown artist.

**Casa Trampo** (14th century) and **Palazzo Cesareo** (early 20th century) in Vicolo Manco are the most interesting of the small palaces in Tropea. The latter has a splendid balcony adorned with carvings.

Below the town are pretty beaches and a good choice of places to eat. Other seaside towns to visit are **Scilla** to the south and **Pizzo** to the north.

## Stilo ❾

Reggio di Calabria. *3,000.* *Town hall (0964 77 60 06).* *Tue.*

A short distance from the coast, Stilo is an earthquake-damaged town clamped to the side of Monte Consolino. Standing on a ledge looking out over the olive trees is the **Cattolica**, which has made Stilo a focus of pilgrimage for lovers of Byzantine architecture. Built in the 10th century by Basilian monks, the brick building with its terracotta-tiled roof is based on a Greek cross-in-a-square plan. Four antique, mismatched marble columns divide the interior into nine quadrants. The capitals are placed at the base of the columns, instead of on top, to indicate the triumph of Christianity over paganism. The frescoes within, discovered and restored in 1927, date from the 11th century.

The Cattolica dominates the town, but on Via Tommaso Campanella there is a medieval **Duomo** as well as the 17th-century ruins of the **Convent of San Domenico**, where the philosopher and Dominican friar Tommaso Campanella (1568–1639) lived. The church of **San Francesco**, built around 1400, has an ornate carved wooden altar and a lovely 16th-century painting of the *Madonna del Borgo* (unknown origin). Bivongi, northwest of Stilo, has two churches dedicated to St John: the Byzantine-Norman **San Giovanni Theresti**, and the Norman **San Giovanni Vecchio**.

**Cattolica**
2 km (1 mile) above Stilo on Via Cattolica. ***Tel*** *0965 81 22 56.* *Mon–Sat.*

The beautiful and unspoilt coastline at Tropea

The distinctive five-domed Cattolica in Stilo

## Gerace ⑩

Reggio di Calabria. 3,000.
Pro Loco, Via Regina Margherita 77, Locri (0964 23 27 60). www.comune.gerace.rc.it

Occupying an impregnable crag on the northeastern flank of the Aspromonte, this ancient place was founded by refugees from **Locri Epizephiri** who fled in the 9th century to escape Saracen attack. Its defensive character is reinforced by the medieval town walls and the remains of the castle.

Apart from the slow pace of life here – where you are as likely to meet a flock of sheep in an alley as a Fiat 500 – the main attraction is Calabria's grandest **Duomo**. This large structure indicates the significance of Gerace at least up to the time of the Normans. Constructed around the early 12th century, rebuilt in the 13th century and restored in the 18th century, the crypt is its chief treasure. Both crypt and church are simple, adorned by a series of antique coloured marble and granite columns probably stolen from the site of ancient Locri Epizephiri. At the end of Via Cavour is 12th-century **San Giovanello**, part Byzantine and part Norman. Nearby is the Gothic church of **San Francesco d'Assisi** which contains a Baroque marble altar (1615) and the Pisan-style tomb of Niccolò Ruffo (died 1372), a member of a prominent Calabrian family.

**Environs:** The vast site of **Locri Epizephiri**, the first Greek city to have a written code of law (660 BC), was a famous centre of the cult of Persephone. There are remains of **temples**, a **theatre** and Greek and Roman **tombs**. The **Museo** displays a ground plan of the site, as well as Greek and Roman votive statues, coins and sculptural fragments.

**Locri Epizephiri**
Southwest of Locri on the SS 106, Contrada Marasà. *9am–7pm Tue–Sun.*

**Museo Nazionale,** Contrada Marasà, SS 106. ***Tel*** *0964 39 00 23.* *Tue–Sun.* *1 May, 25 Dec.*

## Reggio di Calabria ⑪

*183,000.*
*Station (0965 271 20).* *Fri.*
**www**.prolocoreggiocalabria.it

One reason to visit Reggio di Calabria, which was heavily rebuilt after a major earthquake in 1908, is the **Museo Nazionale della Magna Grecia**. It houses a fine collection of artifacts from ancient Rhegion – a Greek city on the site of the present town – and from other Greek sites.

Chief among its treasures are the Greek bronzes, larger-than-life statues of warriors dredged from the sea off Riace Marina in 1972. Statue A (460 BC) is thought to be by Phidias, the Athenian sculptor and chief exponent of the idealizing, Classical style. If true, it is a rare survivor because his works, praised in the highest terms by ancient writers, were hitherto only known to us from Roman copies. Statue B (430 BC) has been attributed to Polyclitus. It is possible that the statues originated from an Athenian shrine at Delphi built as a momument to the victory of Marathon.

**Museo Nazionale della Magna Grecia**
Piazza de Nava 26. ***Tel*** *0965 81 22 55.* *for renovation.*
**www**.museonazionalerc.it

Riace Bronzes (6th and 5th century BC) in Reggio's Museo Nazionale

# SICILY

*On a crossroads in the Mediterranean, part of Europe and Africa, yet belonging to neither, Sicily was tramped across by half the ancient civilized world. As conquerors came and went, they left behind a rich and varied cultural deposit. This has resulted in a quirky mixture in almost every aspect of the local vernacular from language, customs and cooking to art and, most notably, the architecture of the island.*

During the 6th and 5th centuries BC, there cannot have been much difference between Athens and the Greek cities of Sicily. Their ruins are among the most spectacular of the ancient Greek world. The Romans took over in the 3rd century BC, followed by the Vandals, Ostrogoths and Byzantines. Not much that is tangible has survived from the days of the Arabs, who ruled from the 9th to 11th centuries, though Palermo's Vucciria is more souk than market. The Norman era, beginning in 1061, spawned brilliant artistic achievements, such as the cathedrals of Monreale and Cefalù, while the eclecticism of that period's architecture is best seen at Santi Pietro e Paolo outside Taormina.

The Sicilian Baroque of the 17th and 18th centuries is just as individual. The palaces and churches of Palermo, reflecting the elaborate ritual of the Spanish Viceregal court, tend towards extravagant display. At Noto, Ragusa, Modica, Siracusa and Catania the buildings are a useful vehicle for the Sicilians' love of ornamentation, itself a remnant from the island's early fling with the Arab world. The style is an expression of the nature of Sicilians, whose sense of pomp and pageantry is both magnificent and extreme.

Sicily is a curiosity, and the legacy of the past is redolent everywhere. The fact that it is an island has intensified the cultural impact of each successive occupier. They say that today there's less Italian blood in Sicilian veins than there is Phoenician, Greek, Arabic, Norman, Spanish or French. The resulting mixture – exotic, spicy and highly inflammable – has created a separate nation at the foot of Italy.

**Detail of a 12th-century mosaic from the Palazzo dei Normanni in Palermo**

◁ **The beautifully preserved doric Temple of Concord (c.430 BC) in the Valley of the Temples at Agrigento**

# Exploring Sicily

The vast coastline of Sicily (Sicilia) provides hundreds of vast, sandy beaches, particularly at Taormina and the Golfo di Castellammare by San Vito Lo Capo – part of a large nature reserve. Sicily's varied interior is characterized by remote hill towns and plains punctuated by mountain ranges known for spring flowers and wildlife. Among the most famous sights is Mount Etna, an active volcano whose lava flows over the centuries have fertilized the land, which supports an abundance of walnut trees, citrus groves and vineyards.

**Fishermen at work in their boats at Siracusa**

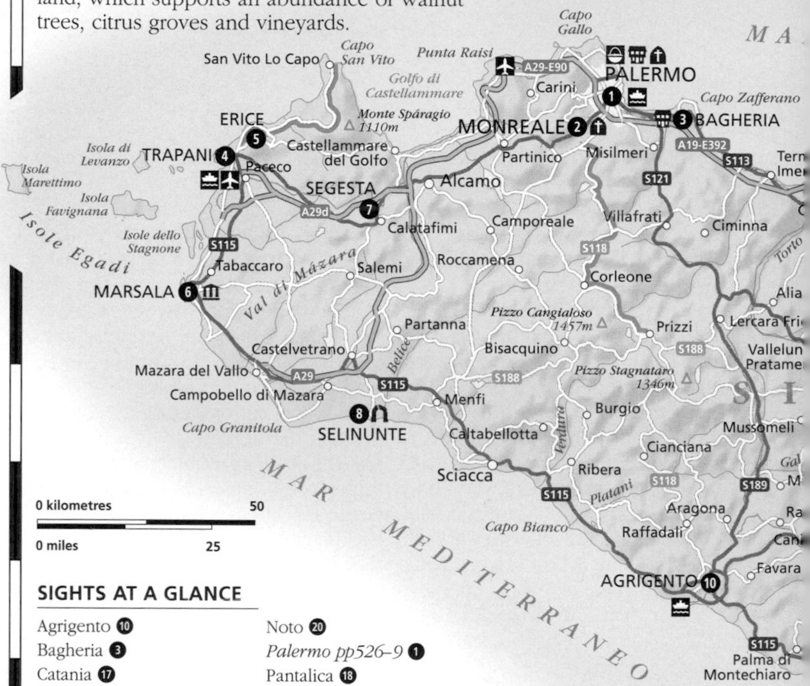

## SIGHTS AT A GLANCE

Agrigento 10
Bagheria 3
Catania 17
Cefalù 9
Enna 12
Erice 5
Marsala 6
Messina 14
*Monreale pp530–31* 2
Mount Etna 16
Noto 20
*Palermo pp526–9* 1
Pantalica 18
Piazza Armerina 11
Segesta 7
Selinunte 8
Siracusa 19
Taormina 15
Tindari 13
Trapani 4

**The magnificent temple at Segesta**

### GETTING AROUND

The A19–E932 links Palermo and Catania, the A18–E45 Catania and Messina, and the A20–E90 Palermo and Messina. The west is accessible from Palermo on the A29–E90. Ferry routes run from Messina to Reggio di Calabria, and from Palermo to Genoa or Naples. Between the larger towns, train services are efficient, but for smaller towns the buses are better. Catania, Palermo and Trapani have international airports.

**For additional map symbols** *see back flap*

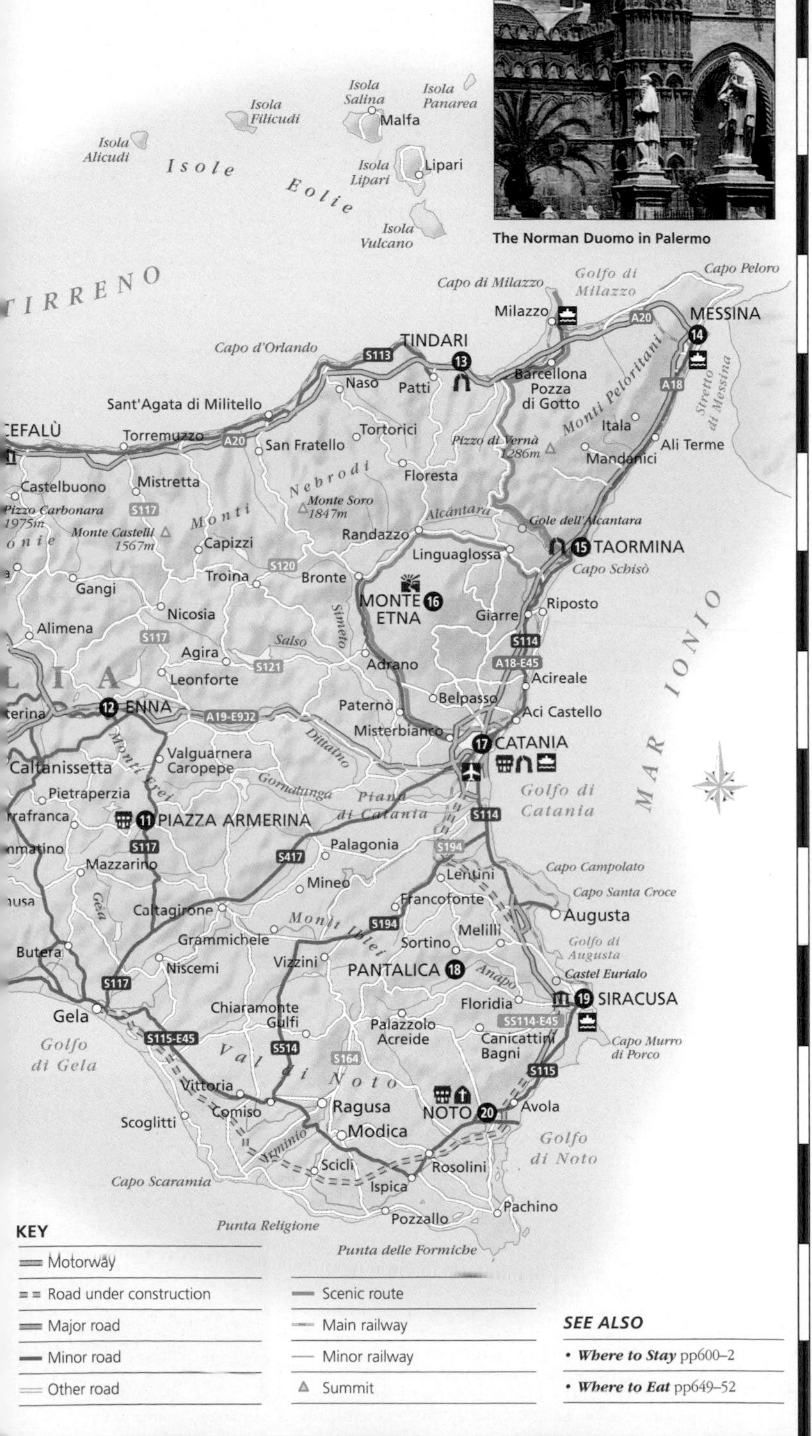


The Norman Duomo in Palermo

**SEE ALSO**


- ***Where to Stay*** pp600–2
- ***Where to Eat*** pp649–52

# Palermo 1

Mosaic detail from Cappella Palatina

Nestling on the protective flank of Monte Pellegrino with Monte Alfano to the east, Palermo lies in a natural amphitheatre called the Conca d'Oro (Golden Shell). The city is an eclectic mix of Oriental and old European influences, and it features architectural styles that range from Arabic to Norman, Baroque and Art Nouveau. This cultural infusion is unmatched in Italy, making this exotic city an exciting place to explore.

### Gesù

Piazza Casa Professa 21. ***Tel*** *091 607 62 23.* *7–11:30am, 5–6:30pm daily (to 12:30 Sun; Aug: 7–10am only).* *for mass.*

This Baroque church (1564–1633) is also known as the church of the Casa Professa. The interior is an example of the skill of Sicilian craftsmen in the treatment of marble carving and inlay. The oldest Jesuit church in Sicily, it was restored after World War II.

**Ruined cloister with the red domes of San Giovanni degli Eremiti behind**

### San Giovanni degli Eremiti

Via dei Benedettini. ***Tel*** *091 651 50 19.* *9am–5pm Tue–Sun.*

Reflecting Islamic architectural tradition with bulbous domes, corner arches and filigreed windows, this deconsecrated Norman church (1132–48) was built in the grounds of a mosque. Beyond church and mosque, a ruined cloister from a 13th-century monastery encloses a pretty garden.

### Palazzo Reale

P.za del Parlamento. ***Tel*** *091 626 28 33.* *8:15am–5:45pm daily (to 1pm Sun & hols). Last adm: 45 mins before closing.* **Cappella Palatina** *8:30am–noon, 2:30–5pm Mon–Sat; 8:30am–2pm Sun.* *for mass; Easter, 25 Apr, 1 May, 26 Dec.* *Sun.*

Also called the Palazzo dei Normanni, this site has been the focus of power since the days of Byzantine rule and is now home to Sicily's regional government. The nucleus of the present building was constructed by the Arabs, but after the Norman conquest of the city in 1072, it was enlarged for the Norman court. See the luxurious royal apartments, especially the Sala di Ruggero, and the splendid Cappella Palatina. Built by Roger II (1132–40), this dazzling chapel blends Byzantine, Islamic and Norman styles. It is lavishly adorned with fine mosaics and marble inlaid with gold. Next to the palace is the eccentrically decorated Porta Nuova (1535).

**Sumptuous interior of the Cappella Palatina, Palazzo Reale**

*For hotels and restaurants in this region see pp600–2 and pp649–52*

Duomo's exterior displaying a mixture of styles

## VISITORS' CHECKLIST

660,000. Punta Raisi 32 km (20 miles) W. FS Stazione Centrale, Piazza Giulio Cesare. Via Balsamo. Stazione Marittima, Molo Vittorio Veneto. P. Castelnuovo 35 (091 605 81 11). Mon–Sat. 10–15 Jul: U Festinu for the city's patron saint, Santa Rosalia; 4 Sep: Pilgrimage to Santa Rosalia's grotto; Easter: Byzantine Catholic celebrations in La Martorana. **www**.palermotourism.com

**Key to Symbols** *see back flap*

## SIGHTS AT A GLANCE

Duomo ④
Gesù ③
La Magione ⑭
La Martorana ⑥
Museo Archeologico Regionale ⑩
Oratorio del Rosario di San Domenico ⑧
Oratorio di San Lorenzo ⑫
Oratorio di Santa Zita ⑪
Palazzo Abatellis and Galleria Regionale di Sicilia ⑬
Palazzo Reale ②
San Domenico ⑨
San Giovanni degli Eremiti ①
Santa Caterina ⑤
Villa Giulia ⑮
Vucciria ⑦

### Duomo

Corso Vittorio Emanuele. ***Tel*** *091 33 43 73.* *7am–7pm Mon–Sat, 9am–5:30pm Sun & hols.* *during mass.* **Treasury** *9:30am–1:30pm, 2:30–5:30pm daily.* **www**.cattedrale.palermo.it

Founded in 1184, the Duomo displays many architectural styles. The exterior shows the development of the Gothic style from the 13th–14th centuries. The south porch (1453) is a masterpiece of the Catalan style, and at the apse end, sturdy Norman work can be seen through an Islamic-inspired overlay. The dome is 18th century. Within the much-altered interior are the tombs of Sicily's kings. Squeezed into an enclosure by the south porch are the remains of Emperor Frederick II; his wife, Constance of Aragon; his mother, Constance, daughter of Roger II (also entombed here); and his father, Henry VI. The Treasury houses the 12th-century Imperial Diadem of Constance of Aragon, which was removed from her tomb in the 18th century.

### Santa Caterina

Piazza Bellini. ***Tel*** *338 451 2011.* *9:30am–1pm daily (summer: also 5–7pm Mon–Sat).*

Although begun in 1566, most of the internal decoration of this unique church dates from the 17th and 18th centuries. A powerful example of the Palermitan Baroque, it boasts sculpture, marble inlay and illusionistic ceiling frescoes (18th century) – by Filippo Randazzo in the nave and by Vito d'Anna in the dome.

The church is flanked by Piazza Pretorio, which is dominated by the huge Mannerist Fontana Pretoria (1544).

Fontana Pretoria with Santa Caterina in the background

# Exploring Palermo

East of the Quattro Canti, where Via Maqueda and Corso Vittorio Emanuele meet, the city is sprinkled with ornate palaces and more churches. Squeezed behind them are labyrinthine medieval quarters where ancient buildings with crumbling fabric still survive.

### La Martorana

Piazza Bellini. **Tel** *091 616 16 92.* *8am–1pm, 3:30–5:30pm Mon–Sat; 8:30am–1pm Sun & hols (to 7pm in summer).*

Also called Santa Maria dell' Ammiraglio, this church was built around 1140 by George of Antioch, Roger II's admiral. The design derives from Norman and Islamic traditions with mosaics possibly by Greek artisans. In the right aisle, King Roger receives the Imperial Diadem from Christ; in the left aisle, George of Antioch is portrayed.

A nearby convent, founded by Eloisa Martorana in 1193, was the site where the Sicilian Parliament met in 1295 and decided to hand the crown of Sicily to Frederick of Aragon. The church was presented to the convent in 1433.

**Mosaic of Christ with Four Angels in the dome of La Martorana**

### Vucciria

Via Roma. *daily.*

Nowhere is Palermo's Arabic past more apparent than in this medieval casbah-style market which burrows through the ruinous Loggia district below Via Roma. Merchants, hawkers, shoppers and pick-pockets crowd an area once the haunt of artisans. The alleys all around are named after their professions, such as silversmiths, dyers and keymakers. This busy market, the largest in Palermo, offers the usual market ware from daily objects to junk, as well as a wide selection of fresh fruit, vegetables, fish and meat.

**Stuccoed interior of the Oratorio del Rosario di San Domenico**

### Oratorio del Rosario di San Domenico

Via Bambinai 2. **Tel** *091 609 03 08* to book. *9am–1pm daily.*

The interior of this tiny 16th-century chapel displays elegant Baroque decoration by the master of stucco, Giacomo Serpotta. Created around 1720–30, this was his latest and possibly his finest work. Serpotta's technical virtuosity, not to mention the sensory indulgence and whimsical fantasy in evidence here, is remarkable. The altarpiece is the famous *Madonna of the Rosary* (1624–8) by Anthony Van Dyck, and there are wall paintings by Luca Giordano and Pietro Novelli.

### San Domenico

P.za San Domenico. **Tel** *091 32 95 88.* *9–11:30am Tue–Sat (also 5–7pm Sat & Sun).* **Cloister** *call to check.* **Museo del Risorgimento** **Tel** *091 58 27 74.* *9am–1pm Mon, Wed & Fri.* *Aug.* **www**.storiapatria.it

Although the present building was begun in 1640, there has been a Dominican church on the site since the 14th century. Tommaso Maria Napoli, one of the masters of Sicilian Baroque, created the exuberant church façade (1726) and square in front (1724).

Within, the most interesting feature is Antonello Gagini's bas-relief of *Santa Caterina* (1528) in the third chapel on the left. Next to the church is a 14th-century cloister that gives access to the Museo del Risorgimento.

### Museo Archeologico Regionale

P.za Olivella 24. **Tel** *091 611 68 05.* *8:30am–1pm Mon, 8:30am–6:45pm Tue–Sat, 9am–1pm Sun & hols.*

Housed in a former monastery of the Filippini, Sicily's most important museum contains sculpture, architectural fragments and ceramics, bronzes, glassware, jewellery, weapons and terracottas. The collection is taken from the island's Phoenician, Greek and Roman sites of antiquity – Tindari, Termini Imerese, Agrigento, Siracusa, Selinunte and Mozia. The highlights are sculptures from the friezes of the ancient Greek temples at Selinunte.

**Palermo's noisy, bustling Vucciria market east of Via Roma**

## Oratorio del Rosario di Santa Cita

Via Valverde 3. **Tel** *091 33 27 79 or 091 609 03 08 (to book).* *9am–1pm Mon–Sat.*

This small chapel is dedicated to the Virgin of the Rosary after her miraculous intervention at the Battle of Lepanto *(see pp58–9)*. The stucco relief decoration is the work of Giacomo Serpotta (after 1688): the panel on the rear wall depicts the battle, and other reliefs show scenes from the New Testament. The neighbouring 16th-century church of Santa Zita, from which the oratory takes its name, is filled with sculptures (1517–27) by Antonello Gagini.

**Ornate interior of the Oratorio di Santa Cita**

## Oratorio di San Lorenzo

Via Immacolatella 5. **Tel** *091 611 81 68.* *10am–6pm daily.*

Lining the walls of this tiny oratory are incredible stucco scenes from the lives of St Francis and St Lawrence, and allegorical figures and putti by Giacomo Serpotta (1699–1706). These remarkable works exhibit the virtuosity of their creator in the handling of his medium. Caravaggio's *Nativity with St Francis and St Lawrence* (1609) was stolen from above the altar in 1969. The oratory lies hidden next to the 13th-century church of San Francesco d'Assisi, which brims with great sculpture. The highlight of the church is the triumphal arch (1468) by Pietro da Bonitate and Francesco Laurana in the Cappella Mastrantonio.

**The Palazzina Cinese (c.1799) set in the Parco della Favorita**

## Palazzo Abatellis and Galleria Regionale di Sicilia

Via Alloro 4. **Tel** *091 623 00 11.* *9:30am–1:30pm Tue–Sat, 9am–12:30pm Sun & hols (also 3–7:30pm Tue, Thu & Fri).*

Matteo Carnelivari built this palace combining Spanish late-Gothic and Italian Renaissance styles in the 15th century. It is home to the Galleria Regionale di Sicilia, which houses Antonello da Messina's *Vergine Annunziata* (1476) and Francesco Laurana's marble head of Eleanor of Aragon (15th century). Nearby, the 15th-century church of Santa Maria degli Angeli (or La Gancia) contains works by Antonello Gagini and Giacomo Serpotta.

***Vergine Annunziata* (1476) by da Messina in the Galleria Regionale**

## La Magione

Via Magione 44. **Tel** *091 617 05 96 or 339 377 41 37* (mobile). *8:45–11:45am, 3–6pm Mon–Sat; 8:45am–12:30pm Sun.*

Restorations have revealed the ancient structure of this church founded in 1191 by Roger II's chancellor, Matteo d'Aiello. A highlight of Norman architecture, it has a simple nave flanked by fine Gothic columns.

## Villa Giulia

Via Abramo Lincoln. *9am–5pm daily.* **Orto Botanico Tel** *800 90 36 31.* *Nov–Mar: 9am–5pm daily (to 2pm Sun); longer opening hours in the summer.* *pub hols.*

The villa's formal gardens were established in the 1700s. Once, with their statues and fountains, they evoked the antique world. Nowadays, their tropical flora and faded grandeur make them delightful for walks. There are splendid tropical plants in the adjacent Orto Botanico (botanical gardens), and plant specimens can be examined in Léon Dufourny's Neo-Classical Gymnasium (1789). Palermo's only central park,Villa Giulia has good children's facilities.

## Parco della Favorita

Entrance on Piazza Leoni & Piazza Generale Cascino. *daily.* **Museo Etnografico Siciliano Pitré,** Via Duca degli Abruzzi 1. **Tel** *091 740 48 90.* *8:30am–7:30pm Sat–Thu.* *pub hols.*

This park, laid out as a hunting ground in 1799 by the Bourbon Ferdinand IV, was surrounded by the nobles' summer villas. One of these, the Palazzina Cinese (c.1799), was built in a Chinese style for Ferdinand III and Maria Carolina, the sister of Marie Antoinette. The Museo Etnografico Siciliano Pitré, in the stables of the Palazzina Cinese, has a fine collection of Sicilian objects.

# Monreale ❷

Capital from cloister column

Magnificently adorned, and with a splendid view of the Conca d'Oro, the Duomo at Monreale is one of the great sights of Norman Sicily. Founded in 1172 by the Norman King William II, it flanks a monastery of the Benedictine Order. The interior of the cathedral glitters with mosaics carried out by Sicilian and Byzantine artists – the inspiration of a king who wanted to rival the power of the Archbishop of Palermo. Like Cefalù, and later Palermo, it was to serve as a royal sepulchre.

**★ Christ Pantocrator**
*The cathedral's Latin-cross plan focuses on the imposing mosaic of the all-powerful Christ (12th–13th century).*

**Apse Exterior**
*With their rich multi-coloured ornamentation in tufa and marble, the three apses represent the apogee of Norman decoration.*

**Nave and aisles separated by Roman columns**

**Magnificent gilded wood ceiling**

**Entrance to Cappella del Crocifisso and Treasury**

**Original Cosmati floor in choir**

**The royal tomb** of William II, in white marble, flanks the porphyry tomb of William I in the corner of the transept.

**Barisano da Trani's bronze door** (1179) on the north side is shielded by a portico designed by Gian Domenico and Fazio Gagini (1547–69).

**★ Mosaic Cycle**
*Completed in 1182, the rich mosaics show scenes from the Old Testament (nave), Teachings of Christ (aisles, choir and transepts), and the Gospels (side apses). The story of Noah's Ark is depicted here.*

*For hotels and restaurants in this region see pp600–2 and pp649–52*

★ **Cloisters**
*A masterpiece of Norman artistic expression from the time of William II, the columns – plain, carved or inlaid with richly lustred tiles – support elaborate capitals from which spring Saracenic-style arches.*

**VISITORS' CHECKLIST**

Piazza Duomo. *389, 809, 8/9 and many others going west.* **Church** ***Tel*** *091 640 44 13.* *May–Sep: 8am–6pm daily; Oct–Apr: 8am–12:30pm, 3:30–6pm daily.* **Cloister** ***Tel*** *091 640 44 03.* *9am–6:30pm Mon–Sat (to 1:30pm public hols).* **Treasury** *same as the church.*

**The south wall and cloisters** survive as elements from the Benedictine monastery.

**Small Oriental-inspired fountain**

**Column Detail**
*Craftsmen from Campania, Puglia, Lombardy and Sicily worked on the cloister columns. The detail here shows Adam and Eve.*

**The 18th-century porch** is surrounded by two squat towers.

**Bronze Door Panel**
*Bonanno da Pisa's fine bronze door (1185), signed by him, depicts 42 scenes from the Bible set within elaborate borders. The lion and griffin are symbols of the Norman kingdom.*

**STAR FEATURES**

- ★ Mosaic Cycle
- ★ Christ Pantocrator
- ★ Cloisters

## Bagheria ❸

Palermo. 50,000. FS *Corso Umberto I (091 90 90 20).* *Wed.* **www**.comune.bagheria.pa.it

Today Bagheria is almost a suburb of Palermo, though open countryside with olive and orange groves once separated them. In the 17th century Giuseppe Branciforte, Prince of Butera, built a summer retreat here, starting a fashion that was quickly followed by other Palermitan aristocrats. The town's core is sprinkled with their Baroque and Neo-Classical villas.

The **Villa Palagonia** was designed in 1705 by the architect Tommaso Maria Napoli for Ferdinando Gravina, the Prince of Palagonia. It has remarkable architectural qualities: a complex open-air staircase leads to the first floor, and the principal rooms, all with unusual shapes, are arranged around a curved axis. A later prince adorned the perimeter wall with the grotesque stone monsters which amused the 18th-century traveller Patrick Brydone, and horrified Goethe, who also travelled here and called this the "Palagonian madhouse". Across the piazza are **Villa Valguarnera** (begun in 1713 by Napoli), set in its own park, and **Villa Trabia** (mid-18th century), but neither is open to the public. **Villa Cattolica** (18th century) houses a modern art gallery.

Stone figure on Villa Palagonia

**Villa Palagonia**
Piazza Garibaldi 3. ***Tel*** *091 93 20 88.*
*daily (except during functions).*

**Villa Cattolica**
Via Consolare. ***Tel*** *091 94 39 02.*
*Tue–Sun.*

Fishing and pleasure boats moored in the harbour of Trapani

Open-air staircase of the eccentric Villa Palagonia in Bagheria

## Trapani ❹

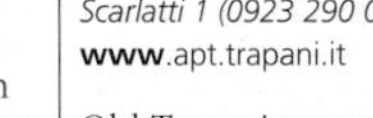

70,000. FS *Piazza Scarlatti 1 (0923 290 00).* *daily.* **www**.apt.trapani.it

Old Trapani occupies a narrow peninsula. The best buildings in this lively quarter are the churches, such as the **Cathedral of San Lorenzo** (1635) and the **Chiesa del Collegio dei Gesuiti** (c.1614–40). The façades of both, and that of the **Palazzo d'Ali** (17th century) on Via Garibaldi, display magnificently the ebullience of west Sicilian Baroque architecture.

The 17th-century **Purgatorio** on Via San Francesco d'Assisi contains 18th-century *Misteri* – realistic, life-sized wooden statues used annually in the Good Friday procession. **Santa Maria del Gesù** on Via Sant' Agostino should be visited for the *Madonna degli Angeli* by Andrea della Robbia (1435–1525) and Antonello Gagini's canopy (1521). In the Jewish quarter, west of Via XXX Gennaio, the **Palazzo della Giudecca** (16th century) has a strangely textured façade.

The **Museo Pepoli** has a collection of local antiquities. Of interest are the coral objects and the Christmas crib figures *(presepi)*, modern versions of which are made here. Next to the museum, the **Santuario di Maria Santissima Annunziata** contains the *Madonna di Trapani*, a statue revered by fishermen and sailors for its legendary miraculous powers.

**Museo Pepoli**
Via Conte Agostino Pepoli. ***Tel*** *0923 55 32 69.* *9am–1:30pm Mon–Sat, 9am–12:30pm Sun & hols (also 3–5:30pm Tue & Thu).*

## Erice ⑤

*Trapani.* 29,000. *Via Conte a Repoli 11 (0923 86 93 88).* *Mon.*

Poised on a crag overlooking Trapani, the medieval town of Erice was once the seat of the cult of the fertility goddess Venus Erycina. Her temple stood on the present site of the Norman castle **(Castello di Venere)**, beyond the **Villa Balio** public gardens. On a clear day, you can see all the way to Tunisia from the castle. The ancient town of Eryx was renamed Gebel-Hamed by the Arabs, Monte San Giuliano by the Normans and finally Erice in 1934 by Mussolini.

The **Duomo** (14th century) has a battlemented campanile and a 15th-century porch. Inside is a *Madonna and Child* (c.1469), attributed to either Francesco Laurana or Domenico Gagini. The deconsecrated 13th-century **San Giovanni Battista** on Viale Nunzio Nasi (now a hotel) contains Antonello Gagini's *St John the Evangelist* (1531) and Antonino Gagini's *St John the Baptist* (1539). **San Cataldo**, a plain 14th-century building on Via San Cataldo, houses a holy water stoup (c.1474) from Domenico Gagini's workshop. In the **Museo Cordici** are Antonello Gagini's *Annunciation* (1525), a variety of Classical remains and an old library.

### Museo Cordici

Piazza Umberto I. ***Tel*** *0923 86 91 72.* *8:30am–1:30pm, 2:30–5:30pm Mon & Thu; 8am–1:30pm Tue, Wed & Fri.*

**A typical medieval street in the small hill-town of Erice**

### SICILIAN ISLANDS

Surrounding Sicily are several island groups. The Isole Eolie (Aeolian Islands), to which Panarea, Lipari, Vulcano and Stromboli belong, are a mass of volcanoes (most of them nearly extinct) poking out of the sea off the coast of Milazzo. The Isole Egadi (Egadi Islands), off the coast of Trapani, have a distinctly Arabic flavour. They include Favignana, Levanzo (which has Palaeolithic and Neolithic paintings and drawings), and Marettimo – the smallest and most unspoilt. Ustica, renowned for its marine life and popular among divers, lies north of Palermo. To the south are the remarkably tourist-free Isole Pelagie (Pelagic Islands) – Lampedusa and Linosa, which are North African in character. Remote Pantelleria lies closer to Tunisia than to Sicily.

**The biggest and most popular** *of the Isole Eolie is Lipari, which has a pretty port and a good range of bars, restaurants and hotels. Nearby sulphur-smelling Vulcano offers hot mudbaths and black beaches.*

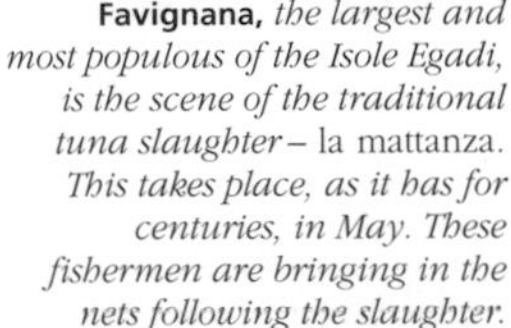

**Favignana,** *the largest and most populous of the Isole Egadi, is the scene of the traditional tuna slaughter –* la mattanza. *This takes place, as it has for centuries, in May. These fishermen are bringing in the nets following the slaughter.*

**Part of the Isole Pelagie,** *Lampedusa was once owned by the family of Giuseppe Tomasi di Lampedusa, author of* The Leopard, *Sicily's most famous novel. The island is nearer to Malta than Sicily and has limpid water and white beaches.*

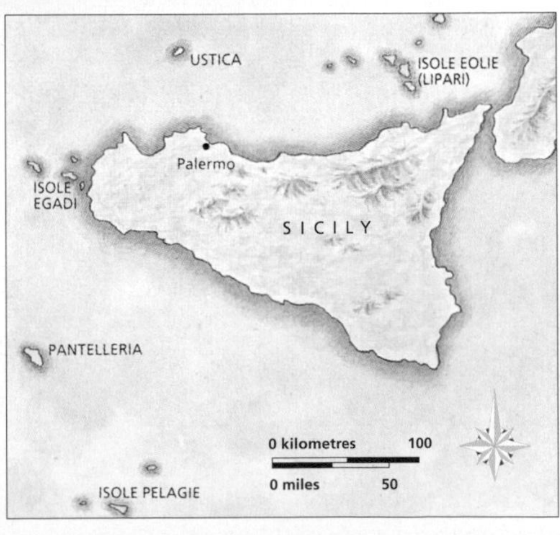

## Marsala ❻

Trapani. 78,000. FS *Via XI Maggio 100 (0923 71 40 97).* *Tue.* **www**.consorziovinomarsala.it

The port of Marsala is the home of a thick, strong, sweet wine that has been in production here since the 18th century. In 1798 Admiral Nelson ordered vast quantities of it following the Battle of the Nile. Its early manufacture was presided over by three British families living in Sicily. One of the old warehouses where the wine was produced is now the **Museo Archeologico di Baglio Anselmi**, housing important Phoenician artifacts.

The ruins of **Lilybaeum** are another attraction. Founded in 397 BC, this outpost of the Phoenician Empire was peopled by the survivors of the massacre by Dionysius I of Siracusa at Mozia (ancient Motya) – the island used by the Phoenicians as a commercial centre. Best of all are the reconstructed remains of a Punic ship thought to have been active in the First Punic War (263–241 BC). The **Museo di Mozia** in the Whitaker villa contains a remarkable early 5th-century BC statue of a Greek youth.

The excavations here are important; what we know of the Phoenicians today comes mostly from the Bible, and from Mozia. The **Duomo**, begun in the 17th century, was built on the site of an earlier church; both were dedicated to Marsala's patron saint, Thomas Becket of Canterbury. Its interior is full of sculptural works by members of the Gagini family. The small **Museo degli Arazzi**, behind the Duomo, contains several magnificent 16th-century Brussels tapestries.

**Statue of a Greek youth in Museo di Mozia**

**Museo Archeologico di Baglio Anselmi**
Via Lungomare. ***Tel*** *0923 95 25 35.* *9am–6pm daily.*

**Museo degli Arazzi**
Via Garaffa 57. ***Tel*** *0923 71 13 27.* *9am–1pm, 4–6pm Tue–Sun.*

**Museo di Mozia**
Isola di Mozia. ***Tel*** *0923 71 25 98.* *9am–1pm, 3–6pm daily.*

## Segesta ❼

Trapani. 7,500. *from Trapani & Palermo.* ***Tel*** *0924 95 58 41.* *9am–6pm daily (to 4pm in winter).*

According to legend, the ancient town of Segesta – still largely unexcavated – was founded by Trojan followers of Aeneas. It presents one of the most spectacular sights on the island: a massive unfinished **temple** stranded on a remote hillside. Its construction was started between 426 and 416 BC, and it was left incomplete following the devastation of Selinunte by the Carthaginians in 409 BC. Archaeologists regard the temple as a good example of "work in progress". Nearby, close to the summit of Monte Barbaro, the ruins of an ancient theatre (3rd century BC) can be visited. Summer concerts are now held here.

**The spectacularly situated, unfinished Doric temple at Segesta**

## Selinunte ❽

Trapani. ***Tel*** *0924 462 77.* FS *Castelvetrano then bus.* *9am–6pm daily (to 4pm in winter).* *Sun pm.*

Founded in 651 BC, Selinunte became one of the great cities of Magna Graecia – the part of southern Italy that was colonized by ancient Greece – and its toppled ruins are among Sicily's most important historic sites. Its ancient name, Selinus, derives from the wild celery that still grows here. The city was an important port, and its wall defences can still be seen around the Acropolis. The Carthaginians, under Hannibal, completely destroyed the city in 409 BC in a battle famous for its epic and spectacularly savage proportions.

While the city itself has virtually disappeared, eight of its temples are distinguishable, particularly the so-called **Eastern Temples** (E, F and G). Of these, the columns of huge Doric **Temple E** (490 – 480 BC) have been partially re-erected. **Temple F** (c.560–540 BC) is in ruins. **Temple G** (late 6th century BC), which had 17 massive side columns, was one of the greatest Greek temples ever built.

Higher on the Acropolis lie the remains of **Temples A, B, C, D** and **O**. Metope sculpture from **Temple C** (early 6th century), originally located on the frieze between the triglyphs, can be seen in the Museo Archeologico Regionale in Palermo *(see p528)*, along with ceramics, jewellery and other artifacts excavated here. A small **museum** on site houses less important finds, as does one in Castelvetrano, 14 km (8.5 miles) north of Selinunte. The ancient city is still being excavated; its **North Gate** entrance is well preserved and further north there is also a **necropolis**.

## Cefalù ❾

Palermo. 14,000. FS Corso Ruggero 77 (0921 42 10 50). *Sat.* **www**.cefalu.it

This pretty seaside town, with sandy beaches, restaurants and hotels, is dominated by a huge rock known as **La Rocca** – once the site of a Temple of Diana – and by one of the finest Norman cathedrals in Sicily. Begun in 1131 by Roger II, the **Duomo** was intended as the main religious seat in Sicily. Though it failed to fulfil this function, the building's magnificence has never been eclipsed. Its splendid mosaics (1148), which feature an image of Christ Pantocrator in the apse, are remarkable and often celebrated as purely Byzantine works of art on Sicilian soil.

The **Museo Mandralisca** houses a fine *Portrait of a Man* (c.1465) by Antonello da Messina and a collection of coins, ceramics, vases and minerals.

**Museo Mandralisca**
Via Mandralisca. ***Tel*** *0921 42 15 47.* *9am–1pm, 3–7pm daily (later in summer).* **www**.museomandralisca.it

The twin-towered façade of the Norman Duomo in Cefalù

The lavish apse of Cefalù's Duomo

## Agrigento ❿

57,000. FS *Via Empedocle 73 (0922 203 91); Piazzale Aldo Moro (0922 204 54).* *Fri.* **www**.comune.agrigento.it

Modern Agrigento occupies the site of Akragas, an important city of the ancient Greek world. Founded by Daedalus, according to legend, it was famed for the luxurious lifestyle of its inhabitants, and was a great power and rival to Siracusa. In 406 BC it fell to the Carthaginians, who sacked and burned it.

The historic core of the city, with its medieval streets, focuses on the Via Atenea. **Santo Spirito** (13th century) houses stuccoes by Giacomo Serpotta (1695). **Santa Maria dei Greci** was built on the remains of a 5th-century BC temple – see the flattened columns in the nave. The **Duomo**, founded in the 14th century and altered in the 16th and 17th centuries, exhibits a unique mixture of Arab, Norman and Catalan detailing.

**Environs:** The chief reason to visit Agrigento is to see the archaeological zone known as the Valley of the Temples *(see p536)*. The **Museo Regionale Archeologico** houses an interesting display of artifacts from the temples and the city, including a collection of vases, coins and Greek and Roman sculpture.

**Museo Regionale Archeologico**
Contrada San Nicola, Viale Panoramica. ***Tel*** *0922 40 15 65.* *9am–7pm daily (to 1:30pm Mon, Sun).*

### THE MAFIA

An international organization founded in Sicily, the Mafia developed as a result of the cruel State and severe poverty. By the late 19th century it had become a criminal organization thriving on property speculation and drug trafficking. Since the "singing" of Tommaso Buscetta and the capture of Toto Riina, the Mafia has been on the defensive against a State that has doubled its efforts against it. The "Boss of Bosses", Bernardo Provenzano, was arrested in 2006 after 43 years on the run. Violence is common in Sicily, but it is not directed at tourists.

Mafia assassination depicted in this scene from the film *The Godfather Part III* (1990)

# Valley of the Temples

Straddling a low ridge to the south of Agrigento, the Valley of the Temples (Valle dei Templi) is one of the most impressive complexes of ancient Greek buildings outside Greece. Its Doric temples, dating from the 5th century BC, were destroyed in part by the Carthaginians in 406 BC, and in part by Christians, who believed the temples to be pagan, in the 6th century. Earthquakes wreaked further havoc. Nine of the original ten temples are still visible, and the whole area can be covered in a day. To avoid crowds, visit early in the morning (some temples open as early as 8:30am) or late afternoon.

**Telamone from the Temple of Olympian Zeus**

**Temple of Hephaistos ①**
*Apart from a couple of incomplete columns still standing, very little remains of this temple, built c.430 BC. It is also called the Temple of Vulcan.*

**Sanctuary of the Chthonic Divinities ②**
*At this group of shrines, the forces of nature were worshipped.*

Via dei Templi
Hellenistic and Roman Quarter
San Biagio
Rock Sanctuary of Demeter
Strada Panoramica
(see p519)
Museo Regionale Archeologico
San Nicola
Catacombs
S115
Via Sacra
Temple of Asklepios

**Temple of Olympian Zeus ④**
*Begun c.480 BC, this was the biggest Doric temple ever built. Unfinished at the time of the Carthaginian attack, it is now a toppled ruin. Giant figures known as telamones were used in its construction.*

**Temple of Herakles ⑥**
*This is the oldest temple in the valley (late 6th century BC).*

**Temple of Juno ⑧**
*Built around 450 BC, this temple still has many intact columns.*

**Tomb of Theron ⑤**
*Here are the ruins of a Roman tomb (1st century AD).*

**Temple of Castor and Pollux ③**
*This is a controversial assemblage of pieces from other buildings, erected in the 19th century. Modern Agrigento (see p535) is in the background.*

**KEY**

- - Suggested route
P Parking
— Ancient walls

0 metres 500
0 yards 500

**Temple of Concord ⑦**
*This beautifully preserved temple (c.430 BC) was converted into a Christian church in the 4th century AD, thus saved from destruction.*

## Piazza Armerina ⓫

Enna. 21,000. Via Generale Muscara (0935 68 02 01). Thu. www.piazzaarmerina.org

This active town is half medieval and half Baroque. The 17th-century **Duomo**, at its highest point, is the most interesting of the Baroque buildings.

In August, the lively *Palio dei Normanni* festival attracts many visitors, but the real draw are the mosaics in the UNESCO-listed **Villa Romana del Casale**, 5 km (3 miles) southwest of the town. The mosaics were only excavated in the 20th century.

It is thought that this huge, once sumptuous villa with its public halls, private quarters, baths and courtyards, belonged to Maximianus Herculeus, Diocletian's co-emperor, from AD 286 to 305. His son and successor, Maxentius, probably continued its decoration, with Constantine taking over on Maxentius's death in 312.

Although little remains of the building fabric, the floors have some of the finest surviving mosaics from Roman antiquity. The hunting, mythological and domestic scenes, and exotic landscapes, all exhibit realistic attention to detail.

**Villa Romana del Casale**
Contrada Casale. ***Tel*** *0935 68 00 36.* *9am–4pm Fri–Sun.*

Roman *Girls in Bikinis* mosaic from the Villa Romana del Casale

## Enna ⓬

28,000. Piazza Colaianni 6 (0935 50 08 75). Tue. www.apt-enna.com

Impregnable on a crag above a fertile landscape where Persephone, mythological daughter of Demeter, once played, Sicily's highest town (942 m/3,090 ft) has been coveted by successive invaders since its earliest days. The venerated seat of the Cult of Demeter (goddess of fertility) was at Enna. Her temple stood on the **Rocca Cerere**, not far from the huge **Castello di Lombardia** (13th century) built by Frederick II.

Most of Enna's sights are clustered in the old town, among the ancient streets that open out of the Via Roma. The church of **San Francesco** has a 16th-century tower. **Piazza Crispi**, with its fine views to nearby Calascibetta, is dominated by a copy of Bernini's *Rape of Persephone*. The 14th-century **Duomo**, altered in later centuries, contains parts of Demeter's temple.

The **Museo Alessi** houses the Cathedral Treasury and an interesting coin collection. The **Museo Varisano** has exhibits on the area's history, from Neolithic to Roman. Away from the centre, the octagonal **Torre di Federico II** (13th century) is a former watchtower.

**Environs:** The ancient hill-town of **Nicosia**, northeast of Enna, was damaged in the 1967 earthquake, but still contains a smattering of churches. San Nicola, built in the 14th century, has a magnificent, carved entrance portal. Inside there is a much venerated wooden crucifix (17th century) by Fra Umile di Petralia. Santa Maria Maggiore houses a 16th-century marble polyptych by Antonello Gagini and a throne reputedly used by Charles V in 1535. Further east is **Troina**. It was captured in 1062 by the Normans, whose work survives in the Chiesa Matrice. Southeast of Enna, **Vizzini** commands fine views of the countryside.

A view from the hills overlooking Vizzini, southeast of Enna

**Museo Alessi**
Via Roma 475. ***Tel*** *0935 50 31 65.* *8am–8pm daily.*

**Museo Varisano**
Piazza Mazzini. ***Tel*** *0935 52 81 00.* *9am–6:30pm daily.*

Taormina's magnificently situated Greek theatre, with Mount Etna in the distance

## Tindari ⓭

Messina. *Tel 0941 24 11 36.* FS *Patti or Oliveri, then bus.* *9am–7pm daily (to 4pm in winter).*

Poised on the edge of a cliff overlooking the Golfo di Patti are the ruins of **Tyndaris**, one of the last Greek cities to have been founded in Sicily (395 BC). Apart from the city walls, the ruins are mostly Roman, including the **basilica** and **theatre**. An **antiquarium** houses artifacts from the site. A combined ticket allows entry at the massive 2nd-century **Villa Romana** in Patti Marina.

Tindari is also known for its shrine to a Byzantine icon, the **Black Madonna** on Piazzale Belvedere.

## Messina ⓮

*250,000.* FS *Piazza Cairoli 45 (090 293 52 92).* *daily.* **www**.azienturismomessina.it

Messina has been the victim of earthquakes and World War II bombing. The **Museo Regionale** houses treasures that include works by Antonello da Messina and Caravaggio. **Santissima Annunziata dei Catalani** in Piazza Catalani displays the eclecticism of 12th-century Norman architecture, with rich decoration. To visit the church, ask at the tourist office.

Outside, GA Montorsoli's **Fontana d'Orione** (1547) is the finest fountain of its kind from 16th-century Sicily. His **Fontana di Nettuno** (1557) celebrates Messina's foundation and position in the world as a principal commercial port.

**Museo Regionale**
Via Libertà 465. ***Tel*** *090 36 12 92.* *9am–1:30pm Thu–Tue (12:30pm Sun, hols; Tue, Thu & Sat also pm).*

Antonello da Messina's *Madonna and Child* (1473), Museo Regionale

## Taormina ⓯

Messina. *10,000.* FS *Palazzo Corvaja, Piazza Santa Caterina (0942 232 43).* *Wed.* **www**.gate2taormina.com

Splendidly situated, Taormina is Sicily's best-known resort. It retains an air of exclusivity while being on the tourist trail, with sandy beaches and a wide range of restaurants and hotels.

The most illustrious relic of the past is the **theatre**. Begun in the 3rd century BC by the Greeks, it was subsequently rebuilt by the Romans. Among other Classical remains are the ruins of the **odeon** (for musical performances) and the **naumachia** (an artificial lake for mock-battles). On Piazza Vittorio Emanuele (site of the Roman Forum), **Palazzo Corvaia** (14th century) was built using stone from a temple that once stood here. The 13th-century **Duomo** (renovated in 1636) is a fortress-like building.

**Environs:** Taormina's main beach, **Mazzarò**, boasts clear waters and is easily reached from the town. South of Taormina at **Capo Schisò** are the ruins of ancient **Naxos**. To the west is **Gole dell'Alcantara**, a 20-m (66-ft) deep gorge of basalt rock, a river and waterfalls.

*For hotels and restaurants in this region see pp600–2 and pp649–52*

## Mount Etna ⓰

*Catania.* FS *Linguaglossa or Randazzo; Circumetnea railway from Catania to Riposto.* 🚌 *to Nicolosi.* ℹ *Via G. Garibaldi 63, Nicolosi (095 91 15 05). To hire a guide: 095 791 47 55.* **www**.apt.catania.it/etna/index.html

Europe's highest (3,370 m/ 11,050 ft) and most active volcano, Mount Etna was thought by the Romans to have been the forge of Vulcan (god of fire). The climb to the summit should be made only with an experienced guide. The Circumetnea railway runs around the base, offering a good alternative to hiking and good views.

## Catania ⓱

*315,000.* ✈ FS 🚌 ℹ *Via Cimarosa 10 (095 73 06 211).* *Mon–Sat (general); Sun (antique & bric-a-brac).* **www**.apt.catania.it

Having been decimated by the earthquake of 1693, Catania was comprehensively rebuilt. While it is not immediately beautiful, it contains some of the most imaginative lava-built Baroque buildings in Sicily. **Piazza del Duomo**, featuring a lava elephant (Catania's symbol) carrying an Egyptian obelisk, offers a dramatic vista to Mount Etna. In 1736 the Norman **Duomo** was given a new façade by Vaccarini, who also worked on the **Municipio** (finished 1741), on the façade of **Sant'Agata** (1748), on the designs of **Collegio Cutelli**, built around 1779, and on **Palazzo Valle** (c.1740–50).

**The façade of Catania's Duomo**

Carrying on the Vaccarini tradition is Stefano Ittar's **San Placido** (around 1768). The frenzied stone carving on the **Palazzo Biscari** (early 18th century) is exceeded by Antonino Amato's unrestrained decoration of the vast Benedictine **convent** (1704) and the adjacent huge church of **San Niccolò** (1730)

On Via Vittorio Emanuele is the **Museo Belliniano**, birthplace of composer Vincenzo Bellini (1801–35). The lava ruins of the **Teatro Romano** (21 BC) are at Piazza Stesicono. **Verga's House**, home of the great Sicilian novelist Giovanni Verga (1840–1922), is on Via Sant' Anna. Via Crociferi is home to 18th-century churches **San Francesco Borgia, San Benedetto** and **San Giuliano**, whose interior is Vaccarini's masterpiece (1760). Further along Via Crociferi, the church of **Santo Carcere** contains the prison of St Agatha, who was martyred in AD 253.

### INFLUENCES ON TRADITIONAL SICILIAN CUISINE

Sicily has one of Italy's most varied cuisines. The island's unique location – marooned between North Africa, Europe and the eastern Mediterranean – and the invaders it attracted are responsible for this culinary diversity. The earliest Western cookbook, the now lost *Art of Cooking* (5th century BC), was written by Mithaecus, a Siracusan Greek. Sicily's fertility attracted Greek colonists, who exported oil, wheat, honey, cheese, fruit and vegetables to their homeland. The Arabs introduced oranges, lemons, aubergines and sugar cane. Their love of sweet confections inspired *granita*, a form of flavoured ice, and *cassata*, an elaborate sponge cake with ricotta and candied fruit. The Sicilians love to claim an Arabic origin for their ice cream, but the Greeks and Romans had created an earlier version by chilling their wine with snow from Mount Etna. Traditionally, the peasants existed on a subsistence diet while the aristocracy enjoyed extravagant fare, and one of the peculiarities of Sicilian food today is that it can be both frugal and handsomely ornate. All of the usual Italian dishes are available, but more interesting are the variations using local ingredients like swordfish, sardines, ricotta cheese, red chillies, aubergines, capers, olives and almond paste.

**A colourful selection of vegetables at a Sicilian market stall**

**Marzipan fruits made from almond paste**

Shorefront in Siracusa, one of the most beautiful cities of the ancient Greek world

## Pantalica ⓲

Siracusa. *from Siracusa to Sortino then 5-km (3-mile) walk to entrance (partial access), or bus from Siracusa to Ferla then 10-km (6-mile) walk to entrance.* **Necropolis** *Pro Loco, Ferla.* ***Tel*** *0931 87 01 36.*

Remote in the desolate Monti Iblei and overlooking the River Anapo is the prehistoric **necropolis** of Pantalica – a pleasant place to walk and picnic. The dead of a large, unexcavated village (occupied from 13th–8th century BC) were buried here in cave-like tombs cut into the rock. More than 5,000 of these tombs were arranged in tiers with a single flat stone sealing each opening.

The inhabitants of Pantalica are thought to have come from coastal **Thapsos**, which was abandoned after raids by warlike tribes from mainland Italy. The site was re-inhabited in the Byzantine period when some tombs were made into cave dwellings and chapels. Artifacts from the necropolis are displayed in Siracusa's Museo Archeologico Regionale.

Rock-cut tombs in the prehistoric necropolis of Pantalica

## Siracusa ⓳

*125,000.* FS *Via Maestranza (0931 46 42 55).* *Wed.*

Interior of Duomo in Siracusa

Siracusa (Syracuse) was the most important and powerful Greek city from the 5th to the 3rd centuries BC, and, according to the Roman consul Cicero, the most beautiful. The peninsula **Ortigia** is the hub of the old city. On the mainland, **Achradina, Tyche** and **Neapolis** have been occupied almost without a break since the expansion of the city in 480 BC. These were the years of Gelon, tyrant of Gela, when Siracusa was enriched with new temples, theatres and dockyards. The city was a powerful force until 211 BC, when it fell to the Romans in a battle that also killed the mathematician Archimedes, its most famous inhabitant.

The highlight of Ortigia is the extraordinary **Duomo**, begun in 1728 by architect Andrea Palma. Its Baroque façade masks the **Temple of Athena** (5th century BC), which has been absorbed into the Duomo. Facing the Ponte Nuovo are the ruins of Sicily's earliest Doric temple, the **Temple of Apollo**, which had monolithic columns.

Across from the Duomo is the **Palazzo Beneventano del Bosco** (1778–88), a bold example of Siracusan Baroque, as is **Santa Lucia alla Badia** (1695–1703). In the Municipio a small museum records the history of Ionic temples, and the coin collection of the Galleria Numismatica records Siracusa's past wealth. The delightful **Fonte Aretusa** is frequently referred to by Classical writers as the point where Aretusa emerged from the ground, having been changed into a spring by Artemis to help her escape her lover Alpheus.

At Ortigia's furthest point is the **Castello Maniace**, built by Frederick II around 1239. Here too is the **Gallerie Regionale di Palazzo Bellomo**, with sculpture and paintings including the *Burial of St Lucy* (1608) by Caravaggio.

The painting comes from the church of **Santa Lucia** in the Achradina quarter. This area was flattened during World War II, but the church survived.

It is mostly 17th century with a Norman campanile, and occupies the site where St Lucy, patron saint of Siracusa, was martyred in AD 304. Achradina is now the centre of modern Siracusa.

To the north, in Tyche, is the **Museo Archeologico Regionale Paolo Orsi**, with its important collection of artifacts from the Palaeolithic to the Byzantine era, taken from southeastern sites in Sicily. Included are vases, coins, bronzes, votive objects, busts, sculpture and fragments from Siracusan temples.

The Neapolis quarter and its **Parco Archeologico** feature the Teatro Romano, the Altar of Hieron II and the spectacular Teatro Greco, carved from the hillside. Beyond the Nymphaeum is the 2nd-century AD Roman amphitheatre and the stone quarries – the Latomia del Paradiso featuring the **Ear of Dionysius**. It is thought that 7,000 Athenians were incarcerated here and left to die after their calamitous defeat in 413 BC, in a battle described by Thucydides as "the greatest action in Hellenic history".

**Environs:** At **Epipolae**, 8 km (5 miles) north of Neapolis is the **Castle of Euryalus** – the most important ancient Greek fortification to have survived.

**Gallerie Regionale di Palazzo Bellomo**
Palazzo Bellomo, Via Capodieci 14. ***Tel*** *0931 695 11.* *9am–6:30pm Tue–Sun.*

**Museo Archeologico Regionale Paolo Orsi**
Viale Teocrito 66. ***Tel*** *0931 46 40 22.* *9am–7pm Tue–Sun (to 1pm Sun). Last adm: 1 hr before closing.*

## Noto 20

Siracusa. *24,000.* *Piazza XVI Maggio (0931 83 67 44).* *Mon & 1st & 3rd Tue of the month.* **www**.comune.noto.sr.it

Noto was built from scratch in the early 18th century to replace Noto Antica, which was devastated by an earthquake in 1693. The town was comprehensively designed in Baroque style, using the local white tufa, a limestone that has

**The façade of the Duomo in Noto rises above a huge staircase**

turned a honey-brown colour from the sun. Noto is a UNESCO World Heritage site, but unfortunately much of its beauty is behind scaffolding due to ongoing restoration.

The twin-towered **Duomo** (completed 1770s) that dominates Noto is by architect Rosario Gagliardi, who also designed the eccentric tower façade of the seminary of **San Salvatore** (18th century) in Piazza Municipio, the convex façade of **San Domenico** (1730s) in Piazza XVI Maggio, and the oval interior of **Santa Chiara** (1730) on Corso Vittorio Emanuele. The magnificent **Palazzo Trigona** (1781) stands on Via Cavour behind the Duomo. On Via Nicolaci, the **Palazzo Villadorata** (1730s) features a splendid façade adorned with elaborate stone carvings. At the north end of Via Nicolaci, the **Monastery of Montevergine** has a striking curved façade. In mid-May, Via Nicolaci is the site of the Infiorata flower festival. Gagliardi's church of the **Crocifisso** (1728) stands on the town's summit. It contains a sculpture of the Madonna by Francesco Laurana (1471). The **Municipio** (1740s), facing the Duomo, has a fine "billowing" ground floor design.

**Environs:** The earthquake of 1693 also devastated the towns of **Modica**, around 30 km (19 miles) to the west, and **Ragusa**, a short distance further. Like Noto, they were rebuilt in the region's rich Baroque style. Gagliardi worked on Modica's **San Giorgio** (early 18th century), on Ragusa's **San Giorgio** (begun around 1746, and one of his masterpieces) and **San Giuseppe** (mid-18th century).

**Boisterous carving on the façade of the Palazzo Villadorata in Noto**

# SARDINIA

*In his travelogue, Sea and Sardinia, DH Lawrence wrote that Sardinia was "left outside of time and history". Indeed, the march of time has been slow here, and traditions from ancient Europe have survived – the legacy of invasion by Phoenicians, Carthaginians, Romans, Arabs, Byzantines, Spaniards and Savoyards.*

These traditions are displayed in Sardinia's many festivals – some soberly Christian, others with pagan roots. Several different dialects and languages are spoken in Sardinia. Catalan can be heard in Alghero, and on the island of San Pietro, there is a Ligurian dialect. Even remnants of Phoenician survive. In the south, the traditional influences are Spanish, while pure native strains of people and language survive in the Gennargentu mountains. Peopled by shepherds in isolated communities, this region is so impenetrable that invaders have never bothered it.

Of particular interest are the prehistoric *nuraghe* castles, villages, temples and tombs dotted around the countryside – most notably around Barumini, north of Cagliari, and in the Valle dei Nuraghe, south of Sassari. The *nuraghe* were built by a people whose origins constitute one of the Mediterranean's great mysteries. In Cagliari, the capital of Sardinia, there is a museum with an excellent archaeological collection that offers insight into this enigmatic people.

Sassari, Oristano, Alghero and Olbia are all centres of areas marked by their individuality. Some remarkable Pisan-Romanesque churches are located around Sassari and here too dialects reveal close links with the languages of Tuscany. Olbia is a boom town made rich by tourism and the proximity of the jet-setting Costa Smeralda. Sober Nuoro with its province in the shadow of the Gennargentu mountains, by contrast, has little in common with the Sardinia of tourist brochures.

**Relaxing during the day in the tiny resort of Carloforte on the Isola di San Pietro, next to Sant'Antioco**

◁ **The Bay of Simius east of Cagliari in the southeast corner of Sardinia**

# Exploring Sardinia

This island, called Sardegna in Italian, is characterized by an interior of dramatic, rolling uplands covered in *macchia* – grassland mingled with myrtle, wild thyme, prickly pears and dwarf oaks – and a coastline of beguiling, translucent sea, isolated coves, long sandy beaches and caves. The Gennargentu mountains, with the highest peak at 1,834 m (6,017 ft), shield a nearly impenetrable area of rural villages. In the northeast, mountains fall away dramatically to the Costa Smeralda, Sardinia's most exclusive coastal area. Further south, the shoreline around the Golfo di Orosei is fairly unspoilt. Around Oristano in the west the land is flat, leading to the plain of Campidano where the island's corn, fruit and vegetables grow.

Prehistoric nuraghic remains at Su Nuraxi near Barumini

## SIGHTS AT A GLANCE

Alghero 3
Bosa 4
Cagliari 9
Cala Gonone 6
Costa Smeralda 1
Nuoro 5
Oristano 7
Sant'Antioco 8
Sassari 2

A typical scene of clothes hanging out to dry in Alghero

*SEE ALSO*


- ***Where to Stay*** pp602–3
- ***Where to Eat*** pp652–3


0 kilometres 50

0 miles 25

For additional map symbols *see back flap*

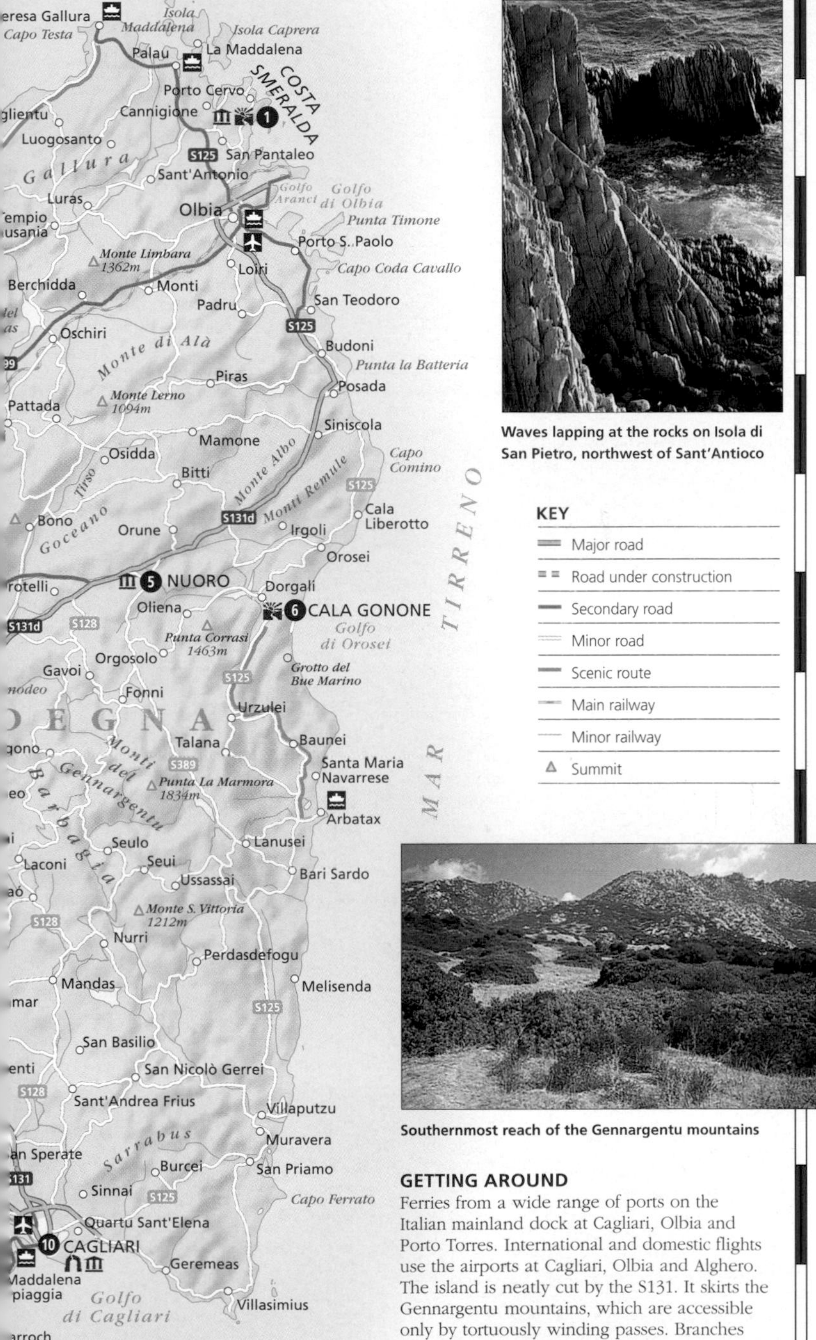


Waves lapping at the rocks on Isola di San Pietro, northwest of Sant'Antioco

Southernmost reach of the Gennargentu mountains

## GETTING AROUND

Ferries from a wide range of ports on the Italian mainland dock at Cagliari, Olbia and Porto Torres. International and domestic flights use the airports at Cagliari, Olbia and Alghero. The island is neatly cut by the S131. It skirts the Gennargentu mountains, which are accessible only by tortuously winding passes. Branches of the S131 reach Olbia and Nuoro. Express bus services connect the major cities, while the smaller towns are linked by slow and infrequent public transport.

**The extravagantly beautiful, *macchia*-scented Costa Smeralda**

## Costa Smeralda ❶

Sassari. FS *Olbia.* *Porto Cervo.* *AAST La Maddalena, Cava Civetta (0789 73 63 21); AAST Palau, Via Nazionale 94 (0789 70 95 70).* **www**.quicostasmeralda.it

Stretching from the Golfo di Cugnana to the Golfo di Arzachena, the Costa Smeralda was developed by a consortium of magnates in the 1950s. One of the world's most opulent holiday resorts, it is kept immaculate by strict controls.

In **Porto Cervo**, the main town, boutiques jostle with nightclubs, fine restaurants and luxury hotels. It caters for the seriously rich – billionaires, crowned heads and pop stars.

**Environs:** Head north to rural **Baia Sardinia** and **Cannigione**. From **Palau** ferries leave for **La Maddalena** and **Isola Caprera**, the home of Garibaldi and the **Museo Nazionale Garibaldino**.

**Museo Nazionale Garibaldino**
Frazione Caprera, La Maddalena. ***Tel*** *0789 72 71 62.*
*9am–1:30pm Tue–Sun.*
*1 Jan, 1 May, 25 Dec.*

## Sassari ❷

*130,000.* FS *Viale Caprera 36 (079 27 99 54).* *Mon.* **www**.comune.sassari.it

Founded by Genoese and Pisan merchants early in the 13th century, Sassari is known for its spectacular *Cavalcata Sarda* festival on Ascension Day, and for being the site of Sardinia's first university. There is a raucous, tight, church-filled medieval quarter around the **Duomo** (11th century, with later, mostly Baroque, additions), and to the north is the huge **Fonte Rosello**, a late-Renaissance fountain. The **Museo Archeologico Nazionale "GA Sanna"** is a good starting point for an investigation into the region's nuraghic history.

**Façade of Santissima Trinità di Saccargia**

**Environs:** To the southeast along the S131 is the Pisan-Romanesque church of **Santissima Trinità di Saccargia** (1116), with the only extant 13th-century fresco cycle in Sardinia. Further on is the 12th-century church of **San Michele di Salvenero**, and at **Ardara** the basalt-built Romanesque **Santa Maria del Regno**, or "Black Cathedral".

**Museo Archeologico Nazionale "GA Sanna"**
Via Roma 64. ***Tel*** *079 27 22 03.*
*9am–7:30pm Tue–Sun (to 7pm Sun).*

## Alghero ❸

Sassari. *41,000.* FS *Lungomare Dante 1 (079 97 59 96).* *Wed.* **www**.comune.alghero.ss.it

Founded on a peninsula facing the Bay of Alghero early in the 12th century, and taken from the Genoese Dorias by the Aragonese in 1353, Alghero was peopled by settlers from Barcelona and Valencia. Its original occupants – Ligurians and Sardinians – were expelled with such thoroughness that today the Catalan language and culture is enjoying a revival and the look of old Alghero is consistently Spanish.

Filled with labyrinthine alleys and cobbled streets, the lively port of old Alghero is flanked by battlemented walls and defensive towers on all but the landward section. Facing the Giardino Pubblico is the massive 16th-century **Torre di Porta Terra**, also known as the Jewish Tower after its builders. Around the periphery of the old town are more towers, including **Torre dell'Espero Reial** and **Torre San Giacomo** on Lungomare Colombo, and **Torre della Maddalena** on Piazza Porta Terra. The 16th-century **Duomo** at the bottom of Via Umberto is predominantly Catalan-Gothic with an Aragonese portal. Off Via Carlo Alberto, **San Francesco** (14th century)

**A typical house in Alghero**

***For hotels and restaurants in this region see pp602–3 and pp652–3***

The waterfront at Bosa

has a pretty cloister and octagonal campanile towering over Alghero, and Baroque **San Michele** has a bright tiled dome. In Via Principe Umberto is the **Casa Doria**, the house where the pre-Hispanic rulers of Alghero lived. It has a beautiful Renaissance portal and Gothic-arched window.

**Environs:** Take a boat or car trip (the latter involves much climbing down) to the spectacular **Grotta di Nettuno**, a deep natural cave round the point of Capo Caccia, or the nearby **Grotta Verde**.

## Bosa ❹

*Nuoro. 8,500. FS Pro Loco, Via Azuni 5 (0785 37 61 07). Tue.* **www**.comune.bosa.nu.it

Bosa is a small, picturesque seaside town at the mouth of Sardinia's only navigable river, the Temo. The historic **Sa Costa** district struggles up the side of a low hill capped by the **Castello di Serravalle**, built in 1122 by the Malaspina family. The narrow passages and alleys here have changed little since the Middle Ages. By the Temo are **Sas Conzas** – the former dyers' houses and workshops.

Languishing on the riverside, the cosmopolitan **Sa Piatta** district houses the Aragonese-Gothic **Duomo** (15th century) and Romanesque **San Pietro Extramuros** (11th century), with a Gothic façade added by Cistercian monks in the 13th century.

### NURAGHE IN SARDINIA

The dominant feature of Sardinia is the 7,000 or so *nuraghe* dotted around the island. Dating from 1800 to 300 BC, these strange, truncated cone structures were built without any bonding from huge basalt blocks taken from extinct volcanoes. To this day, little is known about the identity of the nuraghic people. They must have been well organized and possessed remarkable engineering skills, judging by their buildings, but appear to have left no written word. The mystery of these enigmatic people has intrigued Sardinians for years.

**The individual nuraghe** *are fairly small. A few were fortresses, equipped with wells and other defensive features.*

**Su Nuraxi at Barumini** *(above), Serra Orrios, near Dorgali, and Santu Antine at Torralba are among the most important* nuraghe *complexes. Houses, temples, tombs, and even a theatre have been identified.*

**This bronze figure** *of a hero with four eyes and four arms is among the many objects and statues discovered on nuraghic sites and associated with the nuraghic people.*

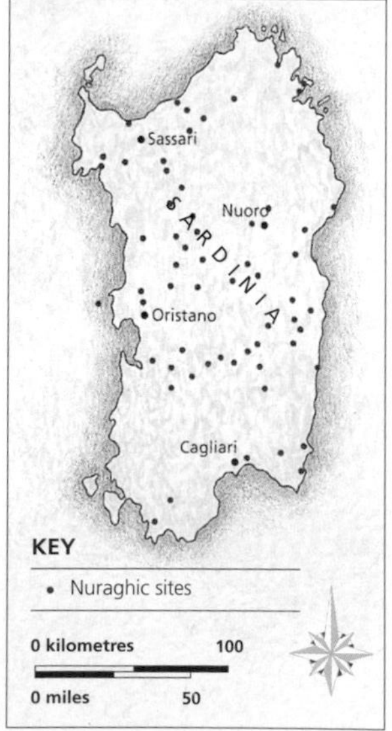

Nobel Prize-winning novelist Grazia Deledda from Nuoro

## Nuoro 5

38,000. FS Piazza d'Italia 19 (0784 300 83). Fri & Sat. 29 Aug: Sagra del Redentore. www.enteturismo.nuoro.it

This town, in a spectacular setting beneath Monte Ortobene and the dramatic Supramonte, was the home of Grazia Deledda, who won the Nobel Prize for Literature in 1926 for her portrayal of the power and passions in the primitive communities around her. A comprehensive collection of ethnic items, such as traditional Sardinian costumes and jewellery, can be seen in the excellent **Museo della Vita e delle Tradizioni Popolari Sarde**. Attending the *Sagra del Redentore* festival is the best way to witness the region's dancing and dialects.

**Environs:** Nuoro is on the edge of the Barbagia region, which has isolated villages of shepherds who have never experienced the hand of any overlord, so impenetrable are the **Gennargentu** mountains. This region was known to the Romans as Barbaria, an area they were never able to subdue. Traces of the traditional lawlessness of the Barbagia can be seen in **Orgosolo**, with its wall murals calling for Sardinia's independence. Rival clans were locked in bloody vendetta for almost 50 years, and the deeds of native bandits form part of local folklore.

In **Mamoiada**'s *Feast of the Mamuthones*, men in sinister masks and traditional costume perform a ritual dance ending with a symbolic "killing" of a scapegoat. The fervour of the event is indicative of the fierce folkloric tradition and deep resistance to change.

**Museo della Vita e delle Tradizioni Popolari Sarde**
Via Mereu 56. ***Tel*** *0784 24 29 00.*
*9am–1pm, 3–7pm daily.*

## Cala Gonone 6

*Nuoro. 800. Pro Loco, via Lamormara 108, Dorgali (0784 962 43). daily. from Dorgali to grottoes (Apr– mid-Oct).* ***Tel*** *0784 933 05.*

East of Nuoro, between the sea and the mountains, is the hamlet of Cala Gonone – a bustling seaside resort and fishing port, with magnificent beaches. Along the unspoilt coast are the isolated coves of **Cala Luna**, linked with Cala Gonone by a well-marked two-hour trail, and **Cala Sisine**. The famous **Grotta del Bue Marino**, adorned with weird rock formations, can only be reached by boat.

Entrance to the Grotta del Bue Marino, south of Cala Gonone

**Environs:** To the south, the villages of **Urzulei, Baunei** and **Santa Maria Navarrese**, along the spectacular SS125 road to Tortolì, feature breathtaking landscapes.

## Oristano 7

*Cagliari. 32,000. FS EPT, Piazza Eleonora 1 (0783 79 13 06); Pro Loco, Via Vittorio Emanuele 8 (0783 706 21). Tue & Fri.*

Ruins of Tharros near Oristano

The province of Oristano corresponds roughly with historical Arborea, over which Eleonora ruled *(see opposite)*. She is commemorated by an 18th-century statue in **Piazza Eleonora**. On Corso Vittorio Emanuele is the 16th-century **Casa di Eleonora**, and nearby the **Antiquarium Arborense**, which has Neolithic, nuraghic, Punic and Roman artifacts. The **Torre di San Cristoforo** (1291) in Piazza Roma once formed part of Oristano's fortifications. The **Duomo** (13th century) was later rebuilt in the Baroque style. More interesting are the churches of **Santa Chiara** (1343) on Via Garibaldi and 14th-century **San Martino** on Via Cagliari.

**Environs:** The 12th-century Pisan-Romanesque **Cathedral** at Santa Giusta has columns probably taken from Tharros,

**The tiny resort of Carloforte, the capital of Isola di San Pietro**

an 8th-century BC Punic settlement, 20 km (12 miles) west of Oristano on the Sinis peninsula.

**Antiquarium Arborense**
Palazzo Parpaglia. ***Tel*** *0783 79 12 62.* *9am–2pm, 5–8pm daily.*

## Sant'Antioco ❽

Cagliari. *Pro Loco, Piazza Repubblica 31a (0781 84 05 92).*

The main town on this unspoilt island off Sardinia's southern coast is **Sant'Antioco**, once a Phoenician port and an important Roman base. Proof of almost continuous occupation is clear from the **catacombs**, a Phoenician burial place later used by Christians, under the 12th-century basilica of **Sant'Antioco Martire**. The **Museo Archeologico** contains Phoenician artifacts. The Punic **Tophet** (sanctuary of the goddess Tanit) and the **necropolis** are nearby. The small **Isola di San Pietro** can be reached by ferry from Calasetta.

**Catacombs**
Piazza Parrocchia. ***Tel*** *0781 830 44.* *9am–noon, 3:30–6pm daily.* *only.*

**Museo Archeologico**
Via Regina Margherita 113. ***Tel*** *0783 744 33.* *9am–2pm, 3–8pm daily.* *1 Jan, Easter, 8, 25, 26 Dec.* *(& Tophet & necropolis).*

## Cagliari ❾

*165,000.* *Piazza Matteotti* *(070 66 92 55).* *daily; also Sun (flea) and 2nd Sun of month (antiques).* **www**.esit.net

The capital of Sardinia, this site was occupied by the Phoenicians, Carthaginians and Romans, and extensive ruins of the Phoenician city of Nora lie to the southwest of Cagliari. A 2nd-century **amphitheatre** survives from the Roman era, cut from rock. Discover the town's earlier history in the **Cittadella dei Musei**, the former royal arsenal. It houses several museums, including the **Museo Archeologico Nazionale**. The nuraghic items are the most interesting in the collection, especially the bronze votive statuettes. Also in the Cittadella dei Musei is the **Pinacoteca**, an art gallery.

The old core of Cagliari has an appealing North African character. In the high **Castello** district, the Romans and, later, Pisans built defences. The gracious **Bastione San Remy** on Piazza Costituzione offers magnificent views over the city and surrounding countryside. The **Duomo** is a 20th-century rehash of a Romanesque building. Flanking the entrance are two 12th-century pulpits originally destined for the cathedral in Pisa.

Nearby is the Pisan tower **Torre San Pancrazio** (14th century). From the partially ruined **Torre dell'Elefante** on Via dell'Università to the port lies the **Marina** quarter, which expanded from the old town in the 16th to 17th centuries. In Piazza San Cosimo, the 6th-century church of **San Saturnino** is a rare monument to Byzantine occupation.

**Amphitheatre**
Viale Sant'Ignazio. ***Tel*** *070 68 40 00.* *9am–5pm Tue–Sun (summer: 9am–1pm, 3:30–7:30pm).*

**Cittadella dei Musei**
Piazza Arsenale. ***Tel*** *070 68 40 00.*
**Museo Archeologico Nazionale** *9am–8pm Tue–Sun.*
**Pinacoteca** ***Tel*** *070 66 24 96.* *9am–8pm Tue–Sun.* *1 Jan, 1 May, 25 Dec.*

**The 6th-century church of San Saturnino in Cagliari, built on a Greek-cross plan**

### ELEONORA OF ARBOREA

A champion against rule from abroad, Eleonora was governing *giudicessa* (judge) of Arborea, one of four administrative divisions of Sardinia, from 1383–1404. Her marriage to Brancaleone Doria consolidated Genoese interests in Sardinia. She rallied the island to keep out Spanish invaders who tried to claim land that had been given to the Aragonese King James II. Her greatest legacy was the completion of the codifying of laws begun by her father. Written in Sardinian, they called for community of property in marriage and the right of women to seek redress from rape.

COCKTAIL BAR

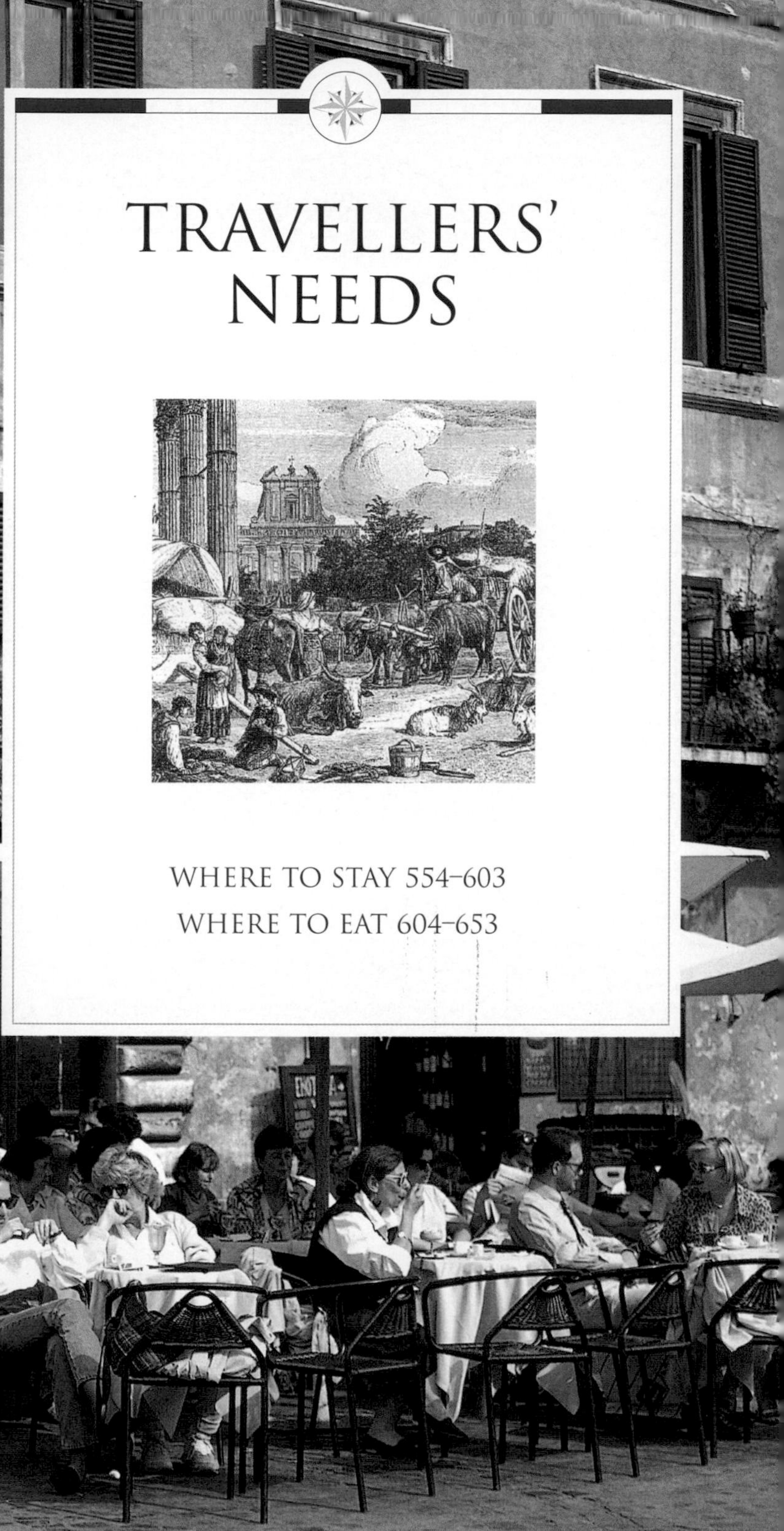

# TRAVELLERS' NEEDS

# WHERE TO STAY

People come from all over the world to visit Italy and most Italians spend their holidays here as well, particularly in the mountains or by the sea. This means that there is a dazzling range of accommodation options, from splendid hotels in old palazzi and historic residences, to simple family-run *pensioni* and hostels. Most major cities also offer up-market B&Bs. Those who want self-catering accommodation are also well served with everything from stately villas in Tuscany to purpose-built holiday flats in, or near, seaside resorts. Italian hotels are notorious for being expensive and short of services but you can still find excellent value in all price ranges. The hotels listed on pages 558–603 have been selected from every price category as among the best value in each area for style, comfort or location.

**Sign for a 3-star hotel**

**The Gritti Palace, one of Venice's historic palazzi *(see p91)***

## GRADINGS

Hotels in Italy are graded with one to five stars. Grading depends on facilities offered rather than atmosphere and each region awards stars according to slightly different criteria.

Sometimes a hotel has a lower rating than it deserves. This may be because the local tourist office has not upgraded it yet or the hotel itself has opted to stay in a lower category to avoid higher taxes.

## ALBERGHI

*Albergo* is Italian for hotel, but the term tends to refer to the upper categories. Room sizes vary considerably: in city centres even expensive hotels can have far smaller rooms than their counterparts in other countries, whereas outside the city your room may be more like a small suite. *Alberghi* will have private baths or showers in all rooms. Many top-range and boutique establishments also offer spa and fitness facilities.

## PENSIONI

Although the term *pensione* is no longer in official use, it still describes one- and two-star hotels, most of which are small and family run. On the whole you will meet immaculate standards of cleanliness and friendly, helpful service with basic, although perfectly functional, rooms. However, as *pensioni* are often in old buildings, historic charm may be paid for with noisy, erratic plumbing and dark rooms.

**Street sign showing the direction and location of hotels**

Many do not have public rooms other than a sparsely furnished breakfast room. Most will offer at least some rooms with a private shower although rarely a bath. If you intend being out late, check that you'll be able to get back into the *pensione*. Not all of them have night porters after midnight or 1am, but most will at least be able to provide a key to the main door.

A *locanda* was traditionally an inn, offering cheap food and a place to sleep for the traveller. The word is still in use, particularly in central and northern Italy, but is now synonymous with *pensione* and may be more of an affectation for the benefit of the tourist.

## CHAIN HOTELS

There are various Italian chain hotels at the upper end of the market, as well as the usual big internationals. **NH Hoteles** hotels appeal to the business traveller and there are one or two in most large cities; **Starwood Westin** and **Best Western** are more akin to international luxury chains, while **Notturno Italiano** cater for the more modest budget. **Relais et Châteaux** run charming hotels in historic castles, villas and monasteries with facilities to match.

## MEALS AND FACILITIES

Italian hotels tend to offer fewer special facilities than those in many other countries. In spite of the

◁ **Popular café in Piazza Navona, Rome**

Romantic Hotel Villa Pagoda in Nervi, Genoa *(see p573)*

hot summers, for example, air-conditioning is not always available and neither is 24-hour room service.

Some hotels may insist on full board *(pensione completa)* or half board *(mezza pensione)* in peak season. Avoid this if you can: unless the hotel is very isolated, there will almost certainly be a good range of places to eat nearby. Most hotel rates include breakfast, which in four- and five-star hotels will consist of a large buffet; the *pensioni* breakfast will probably consist of coffee and biscuits or brioches with butter and jam. A good alternative is to have breakfast at a local bar and take part in an enjoyable Italian institution.

For a double room, state if you want twin beds *(letti singoli)* or a double bed *(matrimoniale)*. Bathrooms in all but the most expensive hotels will have showers rather than baths.

## CHILDREN

Italians accept children as an ordinary part of life and, although there may not be many special facilities, they are always welcome.

Some of the cheaper hotels may not be able to provide cots. However, virtually all hotels, from the simplest to the grandest, will be happy to put a small bed or two into a double room for families travelling together. The price of this is usually an extra 30–40 per cent of the double room rate per bed. Note that most of the large hotels will also offer a babysitting service.

## PRICES

As a rule hotels in Italy are not cheap, although prices vary considerably between places and seasons. Increasingly, booking online secures a better rate, and hotel websites may offer special deals.

Prices, which include tax and service and are quoted per room, start from around €60 for a double room without a bathroom, and can rise to at least €80 with a bath, even for a very basic hotel. A single room will cost about two thirds of a double. Outside the big cities, €100 should get you something comfortable and often picturesque, although not particularly luxurious. For €210 and upwards you can expect a good range of facilities, a pleasant or central location and often a lot of local or historic charm. Hotels in the major cities and resorts are likely to be more expensive.

Hotel Sant'Anselmo's garden, Rome *(see p587)*

In larger hotels there is often a considerable difference in quality between standard and more luxurious rooms, and this is reflected in the price. Rooms with a view or a terrace are also more likely to command higher rates, though for those who prefer peaceful nights, it is generally best to avoid rooms facing the street in busy city centres.

By law hotels have to display their rates in every bedroom. Variation between high and low season can be as much as 100 per cent or more in resorts.

Also, beware of extra charges: the mini-bar can be very expensive as can charges for parking facilities, laundry or for making telephone calls directly from your hotel bedroom.

A traditional Florentine hotel interior

## BOOKING

Book as soon as possible, particularly if you have special requests such as a room with a view, off the street or with a bath. Two months should be ample, but be aware that, during the high season, popular hotels can be fully booked as early as six months in advance. August tends to be very busy at beach resorts and February at mountain resorts. The same goes for cities and towns depending on their particular cultural calendars *(see pp66–9)*.

You will be asked for a deposit when you book; this can usually be paid for by credit card (even in hotels that do not accept credit cards for final payment); otherwise by international money order, or via PayPal for online transactions.

Under Italian law the hotel must issue you with a receipt *(ricevuta fiscale)* for final payment which you must keep until you leave Italy.

Vaulted Art Nouveau entrance of a hotel in Florence

## CHECKING IN AND OUT

On arrival the management will take your passport to register you with the police. This is a mere formality, and it should be returned within an hour or two.

Checking-out time is usually before noon and may be earlier in small hotels. The room must be vacated, but most hotels will allow you to leave luggage in a safe place to be collected later in the day.

**Al Sole, Venice** ***(see p561)***

## SELF-CATERING AND AGRITURISMO

If you intend to be based in one area, self-catering accommodation often enjoys a marvellous location and is generally of a high standard.

Across rural Italy there are more than 2,000 farms, villas and mountain chalets offering reasonably priced self-catering or hotel-style accommodation as part of the **Agriturismo** scheme. Facilities range from those of a first-class hotel in beautifully kept villas or ancient castles to basic rooms with the family on a working farm. Some have excellent restaurants which serve farm and local produce, others can arrange riding, fishing or other activity holidays *(see p658)*. There may be a minimum stay requirement, especially in peak season. The booklet *Agriturist* can be found in the central office in Rome, in regional offices and in bookshops. Other self-catering options can be arranged through specialized agencies such as **Villas4you** and **Simply Travel** before you leave for Italy, but again, make sure you book in advance; they can be booked up for months.

There are also so-called *residenze*, found in the **ENIT** accommodation lists. These are halfway between a hotel and self-catering flats and often offer cooking facilities and some sort of restaurant service.

For stays of several months or more, accommodation agencies for apartments in the city centre as well as the nearby countryside can be found under *Immobiliari* in the *Pagine Gialle* (Yellow Pages).

## BUDGET ACCOMMODATION

As well as the International Youth Hostels Association (**AIG** in Italy), tourist offices in the major cities have lists of hostels. Prices, starting at around €12 per person per night, are much lower than even the cheapest *pensioni*. Accommodation may be in single- or mixed-sex dormitories, though many hostels also offer small private rooms. A room in a private house is another cheap option, offering often small but clean rooms. Bed-and-breakfast accommodation is increasing rapidly but is of variable quality, so only rely on trustworthy recommendation.

The **Centro Turistico Studentesco** can help students find rooms in university accommodation across Italy. This is not limited to students taking courses, particularly in the summer when resident students are on holiday.

A peaceful alternative is to stay in a convent or monastery with guest accommodation. The rooms are clean, if a little spartan, and they are usually in a secluded area or behind cloister walls. However, strict rules may be a price to pay: most have early curfews and many will not admit members of the opposite sex even when with their spouses. There is no central agency dealing with these but they are included in the **ENIT** accommodation lists for each region.

A boat carrying visitors' luggage to a hotel in Venice

## MOUNTAIN REFUGES AND CAMPSITES

Basic accommodation in huts and refuges is available in mountainous areas where there is hill-walking and hiking. Most of these huts are owned and run by the **Club Alpino Italiano** whose headquarters are in Milan.

Campsites abound in the mountains and around the coastal regions. Many of them offer basic accommodation in family-sized cabins *(bungalow)* as well as spaces for tents, caravans and trailers, with basic facilities such as water, electricity and washing. There is usually a restaurant and, especially in campsites by the sea, there may also be sports facilities such as swimming pools, boat and water sports equipment hire and tennis courts. The **Touring Club Italiano** publishes a good list of campsites with details of facilities for each one, as does **Federcampeggio**.

**A high-altitude refuge in the Valsesia Alps**

**Villa San Michele, a former monastery in Fiesole, Tuscany** ***(see p580)***

## DISABLED TRAVELLERS

Few hotels in Italy have special facilities for disabled travellers. Those that do are indicated with the appropriate symbol in the hotels listings on pages 558–603. In many cases, however, hotels without special facilities will do all they can to accommodate people in wheelchairs by giving them downstairs rooms (when available) and help with lifts or stairs.

## FURTHER INFORMATION

The Italian state tourist office (**ENIT**) has accommodation lists for every region. They are reprinted annually but may not be updated and prices may have changed. Rooms can also be booked at the local **APT** (Azienda Provinciale per il Turismo).

## DIRECTORY

### GENERAL

**ENIT (Ente Nazionale Italiano per il Turismo)**
Via Marghera 2–6, 00185 Rome. ***Tel*** *06 497 11.*
***Fax*** *06 446 33 79.*
**www**.enit.it

**Italian State Tourist Board**
1 Princes Street, London W1B 2AY. ***Tel*** *020 7408 1254.* ***Fax*** *020 7399 3567.*
**www**.italiantouristboard.co.uk

### CHAIN HOTELS

**Best Western Hotels**
***Tel*** *800 820 080.*
**www**.bestwestern.it

**NH Hoteles**
***Tel*** *800 017 703.*
**www**.nh-hotels.com

**Notturno Italiano**
***Tel*** *0578 31 118.*
***Fax*** *0578 31595.*
**www**.notturnoitaliano.it

**Relais & Châteaux**
***Tel*** *02 62 69 00 64.*
**www**.relaischateaux.com

**Starwood Westin**
***Tel*** *800 79 05 25.*
**www**.starwoodhotels.com

### SELF-CATERING

**Agriturismo**
Corso Vittorio Emanuele II 101, 00186 Rome.
***Tel*** *06 685 23 37.*
***Fax*** *06 685 24 24.*
**www**.agriturist.it

**Simply Travel**
***Tel*** *0871 231 40 50.*
***Fax*** *0207 391 0140.*
**www**.simplytravel.co.uk

**Villas4you**
Stoney Bank, Earby, Barnoldswick, Lancashire BB94 0AA.
***Tel*** *0845 604 3877.*
**www**.villas4you.co.uk

### MOUNTAIN REFUGES AND CAMPSITES

**Club Alpino Italiano**
Via E Petrella 19, Milan.
***Tel*** *02 205 72 31.*
**www**.cai.it

**Federcampeggio**
Via Vittorio Emanuele 11, 50041 Calenzano, Firenze.
***Tel*** *055 88 23 91.*
**www**.federcampeggio.it

**Touring Club Italiano**
Corso Italia 10, 20122 Milano. ***Tel*** *02 852 61.*
**www**.touringclub.it

### BUDGET ACCOMMODATION

**AIG (Associazione Italiana Alberghi per la Gioventù)**
Via Cavour 44, 00184 Rome.
***Tel*** *06 487 11 52.*
***Fax*** *06 488 04 92.*
**www**.aighostels.com

**Bed and Breakfast**
**www**.bed-and-breakfast.it

**Centro Turistico Studentesco**
Via Solferino 6A, 00185 Rome.
***Tel*** *06 462 04 31.*
***Fax*** *06 46 20 43 26.*
**www**.cts.it

# Choosing a Hotel

The hotels in this guide have been selected across a wide price range for their good value, exceptional location, comfort or style. The chart lists hotels by region, starting in the north and moving to the south. Map references refer to the Street Finders of Venice, Florence and Rome.

**PRICE CATEGORIES**
The following price ranges are for a double room per night, including breakfast, tax and service:

€ under €85
€€ €85–€150
€€€ €150–€250
€€€€ €250–€350
€€€€€ over €350

## VENICE

**CANNAREGIO Al Saor** €

*Calle Zotti 3904/A, 30125* ***Tel*** *041 296 06 54* ***Fax*** *041 71 32 87* ***Rooms*** *3* ***Map*** *3 A4*

This friendly guesthouse close to the Ca' D'Oro, is run by a local family who serve home-made cookies for breakfast. All guests have access to kitchen facilities, while a fully equipped apartment is available for self-catering families. Trips in the owners' rowing boat are offered. **www.alsaor.com**

**CANNAREGIO Al Gobbo** €€

*Campo S. Geremia 312, 30121* ***Tel*** *041 71 50 01* ***Fax*** *041 71 47 65* ***Rooms*** *10* ***Map*** *2 D4*

The Gobbo (or "hunchback") is a modest hotel with rooms overlooking the bustling thoroughfare of Campo San Geremia, a short walk from the railway station. The immaculately kept premises are comfortable; some rooms have air conditioning and continental breakfast is served in the rooms. Closed late Nov–Dec. **www.albergoalgobbo.it**

**CANNAREGIO Rossi** €€

*Lista di Spagna 262, 30121* ***Tel*** *041 71 51 64* ***Fax*** *041 71 77 84* ***Rooms*** *14* ***Map*** *2 D4*

Reserve well in advance for this excellent value and highly recommended family hotel. Just a five-minute stroll from the trains, it is conveniently located in a quiet alleyway off Lista di Spagna. The service is professional and the atmosphere is friendly and welcoming. **www.hotelrossi.ve.it**

**CANNAREGIO Giorgione** €€€

*Calle dei Proverbi 4587, 30125* ***Tel*** *041 522 58 10* ***Fax*** *041 523 90 92* ***Rooms*** *76* ***Map*** *3 B5*

This highly recommended hotel has been completely refurbished. The Giorgione is extremely comfortable and well situated – only a ten-minute walk from Piazza San Marco, and five minutes from the lively Rialto market. Several suites have terraces with wonderful views looking over the city's rooftops. **www.hotelgiorgione.com**

**CANNAREGIO Palazzo Abadessa** €€€

*Calle Priuli 4011, 30131* ***Tel*** *041 241 37 84* ***Fax*** *041 521 22 36* ***Rooms*** *15* ***Map*** *3 A4*

This charming 16th-century palace is tucked away in a quiet spot. The garden will delight summer visitors, who can relax there after a day of sightseeing. Water taxis draw up to the private entrance. Antiques and rich colours add to the relaxing ambience. Breakfast is served in a pretty boudoir in winter. Closed Jan. **www.abadessa.com**

**CANNAREGIO Ca' Sagredo** €€€€

*Campo Santa Sofia 4198, 30121* ***Tel*** *041 241 31 11* ***Fax*** *041 241 35 21* ***Rooms*** *42* ***Map*** *3 A5*

Located on the Grand Canal, across from the Rialto market, this magnificent 13th-century palazzo is steeped in history. It was renovated in the 1700s by the Sagredo family with decorations by Longhi and Tiepolo. Don't miss the stuccoed staircase, marble bathrooms and superb views. Excellent service. **www.casagredohotel.com**

**CASTELLO Locanda La Corte** €€

*Calle Bressana 6317, 30121* ***Tel*** *041 241 13 00* ***Fax*** *041 241 59 82* ***Rooms*** *16* ***Map*** *3 C5*

The inviting rooms in this converted 16th-century palace, the former residence of an ambassador, are tastefully furnished. In the summer, guests can enjoy breakfast in the charming courtyard. Water taxis can pull up at the entrance, otherwise public transport is close by at the Fondamente Nuove. **www.locandalacorte.it**

**CASTELLO Pensione Wildner** €€€

*Riva degli Schiavoni 4161, 30122* ***Tel*** *041 522 74 63* ***Fax*** *041 241 46 40* ***Rooms*** *16* ***Map*** *8 D2*

This small family-run hotel with immaculate rooms has a lovely roof terrace where guests can enjoy a leisurely buffet-style breakfast, along with wonderful views over St Mark's Basin to the island of San Giorgio. The novelist Henry James stayed here in 1881 while working on *The Portrait of a Lady*. **www.veneziahotels.com**

**CASTELLO Londra Palace** €€€€

*Riva degli Schiavoni 4171, 30122* ***Tel*** *041 520 05 33* ***Fax*** *041 522 50 32* ***Rooms*** *53* ***Map*** *8 D2*

Elegance, excellent service and spacious rooms characterize this top hotel. Located close to the monument to King Vittorio Emanuele on the broad bustling Riva a short stroll from the Piazza, it has splendid views over the water. It was here that Tchaikovsky composed his Fourth Symphony. **www.londrapalace.com**

**Key to Symbols** *see back cover flap*

**CASTELLO Metropole** €€€€

*Riva degli Schiavoni 4149, 30122* ***Tel*** *041 520 50 44* ***Fax*** *041 522 36 79* ***Rooms*** *67* ***Map*** *8 D2*

Luxurious rooms, sumptuous furnishings and antiques are found behind a rather nondescript exterior at this hotel on the waterfront near Piazza San Marco. Guests can enjoy the Michelin-starred restaurant (Met) and relax in the garden. Vivaldi is said to have composed his *Four Seasons* in the hotel's chapel. **www.hotelmetropole.com**

**DORSODURO Istituto Artigianelli** €€

*Rio Terrà Foscarini 909/A, 30123* ***Tel*** *041 522 40 77* ***Fax*** *041 528 62 14* ***Rooms*** *76* ***Map*** *6 E4*

This religious institution has bright, renovated rooms with en suite bathrooms. It is close to the sunny Zattere as well as the Accademia gallery. Winter guests share the premises with students. Reserving well in advance is highly recommended. **www.donorione-venezia.it**

**DORSODURO Locanda San Barnaba** €€

*Calle del Traghetto 2785–2786, 30123* ***Tel*** *041 241 12 33* ***Fax*** *041 241 38 12* ***Rooms*** *13* ***Map*** *6 D3*

A wonderful place to come back to after a hard day's sightseeing, this converted palace has a roomy foyer and pretty garden for summer guests. Only metres from the Ca' Rezzonico ferry stop. The spotless rooms are named after the plays of city son Carlo Goldoni. **www.locanda-sanbarnaba.com**

**DORSODURO Montin** €€

*Fondamenta Eremite 1147, 30123* ***Tel*** *041 522 71 51* ***Fax*** *041 520 02 55* ***Rooms*** *11* ***Map*** *6 D3*

Well off the beaten track, but only a matter of minutes from the lovely Zattere. The simply furnished rooms, most with en suites in a Venetian apartment situated above a renowned restaurant, overlook a typical canal and make for a pleasant stay. Breakfast is extra. **www.locandamontin.com**

**DORSODURO Pausania** €€

*Fondamenta Gherardini 2824, 30123* ***Tel*** *041 522 20 83* ***Fax*** *041 522 29 89* ***Rooms*** *24* ***Map*** *6 D3*

This hotel has elegant light-filled rooms with modern facilities, and a common Internet point is available. There is a delightful veranda for breakfast flanked by a spacious garden. Located on the Rio San Barnaba canal, the hotel is handy for Campo S. Margherita where nightlife is guaranteed. **www.hotelpausania.it**

**DORSODURO Agli Alboretti** €€€

*Rio Terrà Foscarini 884, 30123* ***Tel*** *041 523 00 58* ***Fax*** *041 521 01 58* ***Rooms*** *23* ***Map*** *6 E4*

Set in a peaceful spot handy for the Accademia and Zattere for *vaporetto* transport, this cosy hotel is popular with English-speaking tourists. The bedrooms are very attractive if a little small. A garden is available in the summer, and there's a good restaurant. Closed Jan. **www.aglialboretti.com**

**DORSODURO Locanda Ca' Zose** €€€

*Calle del Bastion 193/B, 30123* ***Tel*** *041 522 66 35* ***Fax*** *041 522 66 24* ***Rooms*** *12* ***Map*** *6 F4*

This guesthouse is run by two local sisters, and is just around the corner from the Guggenheim collection and La Salute *vaporetto* stop. The comfortable, well-equipped rooms are tastefully furnished and several have enchanting canal views. **www.hotelcazose.com**

**DORSODURO Pensione La Calcina** €€€

*Zattere ai Gesuati 780, 30123* ***Tel*** *041 520 64 66* ***Fax*** *041 522 70 45* ***Rooms*** *27* ***Map*** *6 E4*

Book well in advance for this marvellous guesthouse as it is justifiably popular. Everything is perfect here, starting from the waterside terrace, the pleasant breakfast room and the pretty rooms to the exquisite service. Sunsets over the Giudecca canal are memorable. Five apartments are available nearby. **www.lacalcina.com**

**DORSODURO Ca' Pisani** €€€€

*Rio Terrà Foscarini 979a, 30123* ***Tel*** *041 240 14 11* ***Fax*** *041 277 10 61* ***Rooms*** *29* ***Map*** *6 E4*

This converted 15th-century palace is very handily located for the Accademia galleries and the Peggy Guggenheim Collection. The atmosphere is compounded by stunning modern design, a roof terrace and a relaxing steam bath. **www.capisanihotel.it**

**GIUDECCA Cipriani** €€€€€

*Giudecca 10, 30133* ***Tel*** *041 520 77 44* ***Fax*** *041 520 39 30* ***Rooms*** *95* ***Map*** *7 C5*

A Venice institution, the Cipriani is served by a private shuttle from the Piazza San Marco waterfront. It offers a spa, an outdoor pool and a vast choice of restaurants. Linked to the Cipriani is the hotel, Palazzo Vendramin, offering exclusive suites, which come complete with butlers. A once-in-a-lifetime treat. Closed Nov–Mar. **www.hotelcipriani.com**

**LIDO DI VENEZIA Villa Mabapa** €€

*Riviera San Nicolò 16, 30126* ***Tel*** *041 526 05 90* ***Fax*** *041 526 94 41* ***Rooms*** *67*

This 1930s villa, originally built as a private residence, has been converted into a comfortable guesthouse. An attractive shady garden welcomes guests back from sightseeing expeditions. Close to the *vaporetto* landing stages, it stands on a promenade overlooking the lagoon. **www.villamabapa.com**

**LIDO DI VENEZIA Hotel des Bains** €€€€€

*Lungomare Marconi 17, 30126* ***Tel*** *041 526 59 21* ***Fax*** *041 526 01 13* ***Rooms*** *192*

Wonderful Art Deco ambience, cool arcades with plush armchairs and top-level service. The superb rooms have everything. Across the road from the beach, the Des Bains is open for guests from mid-Mar to Nov. Thomas Mann set his famous novel *Death in Venice* here. **www.ho10.net**

### SAN MARCO Al Gambero — €€€

*Calle dei Fabbri 4687, 30124* **Tel** *041 522 43 84* **Fax** *041 520 04 31* **Rooms** *30* — **Map** *7 B2*

Gondolas glide beneath the windows of this guesthouse, conveniently set halfway between bustling Rialto and Piazza San Marco. Traditionally styled rooms offer a full range of services. Good restaurants and shops abound in the neighbouring alleys. **www.locandaalgambero.com**

### SAN MARCO Flora — €€€

*Via XXII Marzo, Calle Bergamaschi 2283a, 30124* **Tel** *041 520 58 44* **Fax** *041 522 82 17* **Rooms** *43* — **Map** *7 A3*

This tiny hotel is squeezed in a narrow alley just off a major fashion shopping street, close to Piazza San Marco and the *vaporetto* landing stages. The rooms are a little cramped, but well equipped. A small but pleasant garden can be enjoyed when the weather is fine. It is advisable to reserve in advance. **www.hotelflora.it**

### SAN MARCO La Fenice & des Artistes — €€€

*Campiello Fenice 1936, 30124* **Tel** *041 523 23 33* **Fax** *041 520 37 21* **Rooms** *70* — **Map** *7 A2*

In a quiet square alongside the renowned opera house La Fenice, this pretty hotel is furnished with antiques and period-style fittings. The staff are very helpful. The premises consist of two buildings joined by a patio, and there is an atmospheric bar for that relaxing aperitif as the day draws to a close. **www.fenicehotels.com**

### SAN MARCO Concordia — €€€€

*Calle Larga San Marco 367, 30124* **Tel** *041 520 68 66* **Fax** *041 520 67 75* **Rooms** *53* — **Map** *7 B2*

Crammed in between the souvenir shops and near to the Piazza, this excellent family-managed hotel has many rooms with good views. It is furnished with impeccable period pieces. The top-notch restaurant specializes in seasonal produce. Book well in advance. **www.hotelconcordia.com**

### SAN MARCO Rialto — €€€€

*Riva di Ferro 5149, 30124* **Tel** *041 520 91 66* **Fax** *041 523 89 58* **Rooms** *79* — **Map** *7 A1*

This rambling establishment has good family rooms, excellent facilities and a canalside restaurant in the summer months. The marvellous position at the foot of the Rialto bridge ensures spectacular views from many of its rooms and the *vaporetto* is very convenient. **www.rialtohotel.com**

### SAN MARCO Saturnia and International — €€€€

*Via XXII Marzo 2398, 30124* **Tel** *041 520 83 77* **Fax** *041 520 71 31* **Rooms** *91* — **Map** *7 A3*

A luxury hotel with a friendly family feel, the Saturnia is on a main fashion shopping street only minutes from Piazza San Marco. Antique furniture is used throughout this 14th-century palace. Breakfast is buffet style. The ground floor houses one of the city's best restaurants, as well as a pretty courtyard. **www.hotelsaturnia.it**

### SAN MARCO Starhotel Splendid — €€€€

*Mercerie 760, 30100* **Tel** *041 520 07 55* **Fax** *041 528 64 98* **Rooms** *165* — **Map** *7 B7*

Only minutes away from Piazza San Marco, this discreet hotel exudes sparkling luxury. It is set on the city's prime shopping thoroughfare, the Mercerie. Guests can also glide up to the entrance by gondola or sleek water taxi. Le Maschere restaurant in the downstairs atrium is perfect for breakfast as well as other meals. **www.starhotels.it**

### SAN MARCO Bauer — €€€€€

*Campo San Moisè 1459, 30124* **Tel** *041 520 70 22* **Fax** *041 520 75 57* **Rooms** *117* — **Map** *7 A3*

This deluxe hotel is right in the heart of Venice amid top-name boutiques, and gondolas can be hired outside the front door. The Bauer also boasts wonderful Grand Canal views from many of its rooms, extending across to the Salute church. The waterfront restaurant does a gourmet buffet. **www.bauerhotels.com**

### SAN MARCO Europa & Regina — €€€€€

*Calle Larga XXII Marzo 2159, 30124* **Tel** *041 520 04 77* **Fax** *041 523 15 33* **Rooms** *185* — **Map** *7 A3*

This splendid establishment was the home of 18th-century artist Tiepolo. In an inspiring position on the Grand Canal, close to Piazza San Marco, it has beautifully decorated spacious rooms and sumptuous public areas. The excellent alfresco waterside restaurant is recommended. **www.westin.com/europaeregina**

### SAN MARCO Gritti Palace — €€€€€

*Santa Maria del Giglio 2467, 30124* **Tel** *041 79 46 11* **Fax** *041 520 09 42* **Rooms** *91* — **Map** *7 A3*

Ernest Hemingway described this as "the best hotel in a city of great hotels". Deluxe standards are combined with a superb setting on the magnificent Grand Canal for this sumptuous 15th-century palace. Service is meticulous and a meal at the waterside restaurant highly recommended. **www.luxurycollection.com/grittipalace**

### SAN MARCO Luna Hotel Baglioni — €€€€€

*Calle Larga dell'Ascension 1243, 30124* **Tel** *041 528 98 40* **Fax** *041 528 71 60* **Rooms** *104* — **Map** *7 B3*

Alongside Piazza San Marco, these sophisticated and surprisingly spacious premises once hosted knights en route to the Holy Land in the 12th century. Sparkling chandeliers and frescoes by pupils of Tiepolo now keep guests company at breakfast time. A welcome addition to the luxury hotel group. **www.baglionihotels.com**

### SAN MARCO San Clemente Palace — €€€€€

*Isola di San Clemente 1, 30124* **Tel** *041 244 50 01* **Fax** *041 244 58 00* **Rooms** *200*

A special haven away from the bustle of Venice, the luxury San Clemente has its own island, complete with [illegible] gardens, swimming pool, tennis courts, and conference and fitness centre. The superb [illegible] spacious and light-filled. A private launch ferries guests back and forth to San Marc[illegible] **www.sanclementepalacevenice.com**

**Key to Price Guide** [illegible] **Key to Symbols** *see back cover flap*

### SAN MARCO Santo Stefano €€€€€

*Campo Santo Stefano 2957, 30124* ***Tel*** *041 520 01 66* ***Fax*** *041 522 44 60* ***Rooms*** *11* ***Map*** *6 F3*

A charming establishment that occupies a tall narrow building overlooking Campo Santo Stefano – popular with children in the afternoon. The rooms are fully equipped, though several are quite small. The hotel is only a ten-minute walk to Piazza San Marco and the Rialto district. **www.hotelsantostefanovenezia.com**

### SAN POLO Al Campaniel €

*Calle del Campaniel 2889, 30125* ***Tel*** *041 275 07 49* ***Fax*** *041 275 07 49* ***Rooms*** *4* ***Map*** *6 E2*

Only metres from the San Tomà *vaporetto* stop, this cosy and spotless guesthouse in a quiet street is run by a Spanish-Venetian couple. Guests have tea- and coffee-making facilities in their rooms, otherwise a handy self-contained apartment is available for families who want self-catering. Closed Aug. **www.alcampaniel.com**

### SAN POLO Alex €

*Rio Terrà Frari 2606, 30125* ***Tel*** *041 523 13 41* ***Fax*** *041 523 13 41* ***Rooms*** *11* ***Map*** *6 E1*

Not all rooms have private bathroom facilities and there is no air conditioning, however, this friendly and simple family-run hotel is good value for money. Situated in the vicinity of the Frari church, it is also handy for the Rialto markets. The closest *vaporetto* stop is Piazzale Roma or San Tomà. **www.hotelalexinvenice.com**

### SAN POLO Hotel Marconi €€

*Riva del Vin 729, 30125* ***Tel*** *041 522 20 68* ***Fax*** *041 522 97 00* ***Rooms*** *26* ***Map*** *7 A1*

A popular hotel with English-speaking tourists, the Marconi has a wonderful street café on the lively Grand Canal next to the Rialto bridge. A refurbished 16th-century palace with an opulent reception area, its rooms are a little disappointing and cramped. It is essential to reserve in advance. **www.hotelmarconi.it**

### SAN POLO Oltre il Giardino €€€

*Fondamenta Contarini 2541, 30125* ***Tel*** *041 275 00 15* ***Fax*** *041 79 54 52* ***Rooms*** *6* ***Map*** *6 E1*

Just around the corner from the Frari church, a door leads into a peaceful garden and a small boutique hotel that offers home comforts rather than luxury. The spacious, light-filled rooms look on to the garden. It is wise to book well in advance – this place is becoming quite popular. Closed 6 Jan–6 Feb. **www.oltreilgiardino-venezia.com**

### SANTA CROCE Al Sole €€

*Fondamenta Minotto 136, 30135* ***Tel*** *041 244 03 28* ***Fax*** *041 72 22 87* ***Rooms*** *51* ***Map*** *5 C1*

Book well in advance to stay in this lovely 14th-century palace, with its marble-floored reception area and photogenic façade. Its courtyard is a blaze of scented blooms in summer. Handy for Piazzale Roma for buses and *vaporetti*. The inviting rooms have views over the canal or private garden. **www.alsolehotels.com**

### SANTA CROCE Hotel Falier €€

*Salizzada San Pantalon 130, 30135* ***Tel*** *041 71 08 82* ***Fax*** *041 520 65 54* ***Rooms*** *19* ***Map*** *5 C1*

A friendly establishment that boasts a wisteria-filled garden for summer visitors. The pleasant rooms are well equipped. A brief walk from the transport hub of Piazzale Roma, the Falier is close to San Rocco and other attractions. The staff are extremely friendly and helpful. Breakfast is included. **www.hotelfalier.com**

### TORCELLO Locanda Cipriani €€€

*Piazza Santa Fosca 29, 30012* ***Tel*** *041 73 01 50* ***Fax*** *041 73 54 33* ***Rooms*** *6*

Illustrious guests at this comfortable old-style *locanda* on the island of Torcello have included Hemingway and the British royal family. The rooms are comfortably furnished and a range of reading matter is on hand. It's advisable to book well in advance. Closed Jan. **www.locandacipriani.com**

## THE VENETO AND FRIULI

### ASOLO Hotel Duse €€

*Via R. Browning 190, 31011* ***Tel*** *0423 55 24 1* ***Fax*** *0423 95 04 04* ***Rooms*** *14*

Located right in the centre of Asolo, this charming small hotel represents good value for money. The rooms are attractively decorated although some of them are rather cramped as is the entrance hall. Most have views over the main square or over the rooftops. The staff are helpful and friendly. Closed mid-Jan–Feb. **www.hotelduse.com**

### ASOLO Hotel Al Sole €€€

*Via Collegio 33, 31011* ***Tel*** *0423 95 13 32* ***Fax*** *0423 95 10 07* ***Rooms*** *23*

The orange façade of this hotel is decorated with green shutters. Many of the rooms overlook the main square and the old town walls. The public rooms are slightly impersonal, but the bedrooms are spacious and well furnished. It has a lovely terrace ideal for a pre-dinner drink. Closed 2 wks Christmas–New Year. **www.albergoalsoleasolo.com**

### ASOLO Villa Cipriani €€€

*Via Canova 298, 31011* ***Tel*** *0423 52 34 11* ***Fax*** *0423 95 20 95* ***Rooms*** *31*

This superbly comfortable hotel is in a 16th-century villa where Robert Browning once lived. A popular feature is its beautiful garden which has a lovely view over the beautiful countryside. It also has a fine restaurant serving Venetian specialities and good wine list. A great base for exploring the area. **www.villaciprianiasolo.com**

### BASSANO DEL GRAPPA Victoria €

*Viale Diaz 33, 36061* **Tel** *0424 50 36 20* **Fax** *0424 50 31 30* **Rooms** *21*

Just outside the city walls, this pleasant hotel has comfortable, simply furnished rooms. It is a busy hotel that can occasionally be noisy. However, it is ideally placed for sightseeing, being a short walk from Palladio's bridge and the historic town centre. **www.hotelvictoria-bassano.com**

### BASSANO DEL GRAPPA Bonotto Hotel Belvedere €€

*Piazzale G Giardino 14, 36061* **Tel** *0424 52 98 45* **Fax** *0424 52 98 49* **Rooms** *83*

Standing in one of Bassano's main squares, this busy hotel is the best equipped in the area and is ideally situated for exploring the city. Rooms are comfortable and pretty. The hotel has a modern restaurant and spacious reception rooms and bar. Excellent service. **www.bonotto.it**

### BELLUNO Albergo Cappello e Cadore €

*Via Ricci 8, 32100* **Tel** *0437 94 02 46* **Fax** *0437 29 73 19* **Rooms** *31*

Centrally situated, Cappello e Cadore is popular with skiers in winter and walkers in summer. The rooms are comfortable, with independent heating and air conditioning. Most of the the rooms overlook the square but a few have panoramic views of the mountains. **www.albergocappello.com**

### CHIOGGIA Grande Italia €€

*Rione S. Andrea 597, 30015* **Tel** *041 40 05 15* **Fax** *041 40 01 85* **Rooms** *56*

This unpretentious old-fashioned hotel at the head of Chioggia's main street has a delightful Liberty-style façade. It has elegant, comfortable rooms, while offering an up-to-date well-being centre. The Grande Italia is conveniently situated for boats running to Venice. Closed mid-Sep–Nov. **www.hotelgrandeitalia.com**

### CIVIDALE DEL FRIULI Locanda Al Pomodoro €

*Piazzetta San Giovanni 20, 33043* **Tel** *0432 73 14 89* **Fax** *0432 70 12 57* **Rooms** *17*

Romantic hotel, painted a pretty shade of pink, in a former 12th-century inn. Tucked away in the corner of a quiet piazza in the historic centre, a short distance from the Duomo. The hotel's 17 rooms vary in size, but all have en suite facilities. **www.alpomodoro.com**

### CIVIDALE DEL FRIULI Locanda al Castello €€

*Via del Castello 12, 33043* **Tel** *0432 73 32 42* **Fax** *0432 70 09 01* **Rooms** *27*

This comfortable country inn was built in the 1800s as a summer retreat for Jesuits and is situated on the outskirts of Cividale. The 17 bedrooms are individually decorated and have views over the lovely Friuli countryside. A wellness centre, including sauna and spa, is also available to guests. **www.alcastello.net**

### CONEGLIANO Il Faè €

*Via Faè 1, San Pietro di Feletto, 31020* **Tel** *0438 78 71 17* **Fax** *0438 78 78 17* **Rooms** *8*

This comfortable guesthouse is in a converted farmhouse among hills and vineyards. It has good views over the foothills of the Alps and is a ten-minute drive from Conegliano. The hosts arrange activities for the guests including cookery classes. **www.ilfae.com**

### CORNO DI ROSAZZO Villa Butussi €

*Via San Martino 29, Visinale dello Judrio, 33040* **Tel** *0432 75 99 22* **Fax** *0432 75 31 12* **Rooms** *8*

This 17th-century villa has been tastefully converted into a six-room guesthouse plus two apartments. The rooms are spacious and very comfortable with views out over the surrounding vineyards. A well-manicured garden makes a pleasant place to relax. The rooms are charming and it represents great value for money. **www.butussi.it**

### CORTINA D'AMPEZZO Montana €€€

*Corso Italia 94, 32043* **Tel** *0436 86 04 98* **Fax** *0436 86 82 11* **Rooms** *31*

This hotel is conveniently situated in the town centre, close to the main shopping area. The area is pedestrianized, making the hotel quiet and a popular choice. Some of the rooms are rather small, but all are attractively decorated. There is a gluten-free breakfast on offer. Good value for money. Closed 3 wks Jun, Nov. **www.cortina-hotel.com**

### CORTINA D'AMPEZZO Hotel Cristallo €€€€€

*Via R Menardi 42, 32043* **Tel** *0436 88 11 11* **Fax** *0436 87 01 10* **Rooms** *74*

The only luxury hotel in Cortina, the Cristallo has a spa, state-of-the-art gym, indoor pool and nine-hole golf course, not to mention breathtaking views everywhere you look. Services ranging from a personal butler and babysitting to limousine transfer. Closed May, Jun, Oct, Nov. **www.cristallo.it**

### FOLLINA Villa Abbazia €€€

*Via Martiri della Liberta, 31051* **Tel** *0438 97 12 77* **Fax** *0438 97 00 01* **Rooms** *18*

This delightful 17th-century villa has been tastefully restored by the Zanon family. The spacious rooms are individually decorated in an English country house style. The small garden, with its Jacuzzi, is a wonderful place to relax or enjoy a drink. A wonderful base from which to explore the area. Closed Jan–early Mar. **www.villaabbazia.it**

### GARDA Locanda San Vigilio €€€€

*San Vigilio, 37016* **Tel** *045 725 66 88* **Fax** *045 627 81 82* **Rooms** *7*

One of the loveliest, most exclusive hotels on Lake Garda, exuding Old World charm. Set in tranquil grounds with a small church dedicated to San Vigilio. Comfort and service live up to all expectations and there is a private beach and free mooring for waterborne guests. Closed Dec–Mar. **www.punta-sanvigilio.it**

**Key to Price Guide** *see p558* **Key to Symbols** *see back cover flap*

### MALCESINE Sailing Center Hotel €€

*Via Gardesana 187, 37018* **Tel** *045 740 00 55* **Fax** *045 740 03 92* **Rooms** *32*

A modern hotel just outside town, away from the crowds. Rooms are cool and pleasant, and there is a tennis court and private beach. The hotel offers low-key service set in immaculate grounds. Its lakeside setting makes it an ideal base for guests keen on watersports. Closed mid-Oct–Mar. **www.hotelsailing.com**

### PADUA Augustus Terme €€

*Viale Stazione 150, Montegrotto Terme, 35036* **Tel** *049 79 32 00* **Fax** *049 79 35 18* **Rooms** *120*

A big, comfortable hotel with opulent rooms and a vast restaurant. It has spacious, welcoming public areas, as well as boasting tennis courts. However, its exceptional well-being and beauty centre and hot thermal springs are the focal point of this pleasant hotel complex. **www.hotelaugustus.com**

### PADUA Grand'Italia €€

*Corso del Popolo 81, 35131* **Tel** *049 876 11 11* **Fax** *049 875 08 50* **Rooms** *61*

Situated close to many of the city's main sights, this hotel is very good value for money. The comfortable rooms are clean and modern, and also act as a contrast to the stuccoed and gilded restaurant and main hall. All rooms have Wi-Fi and air conditioning. **www.hotelgranditalia.it**

### PADUA Donatello €€€

*Via del Santo 102, 35123* **Tel** *049 875 06 34* **Fax** *049 875 08 29* **Rooms** *44*

A modern hotel in an old building, the rooms are elegantly furnished and sunny. The hotel is named after the sculptor of the equestrian statue of Gattamelata in the square. Its central location means that many of the city's major sites can be reached on foot. Closed 8 Dec–7 Jan. **www.hoteldonatello.net**

### PADUA Plaza €€€

*Corso Milano 40, 35139* **Tel** *049 65 68 22* **Fax** *049 66 11 17* **Rooms** *139*

An established and efficiently run hotel with a deservedly good reputation. Though its 1970s exterior appears somewhat unattractive, inside it offers up-to-date technology and modern comforts. It provides a full range of services and a thoroughly warm welcome. **www.plazapadova.it**

### PESCHIERA DEL GARDA Peschiera €€€

*Via Parini 4, 37010* **Tel** *045 755 05 26* **Fax** *045 755 04 44* **Rooms** *26*

The hotel is set in its own verdant grounds and has lofty, cool bedrooms. There are fine lake views, though some of the rooms look out onto the equally pretty hills. There is a sun terrace and a private swimming pool. The hotel can arrange riding in the hills or golf at the new, nearby course. Closed Nov–Feb. **www.hotel-peschiera.com**

### PIEVE D'ALPAGO Albergo Dolada €€

*Via Dolada 21, 32010* **Tel** *0437 479 141* **Fax** *0437 478 068* **Rooms** *7*

A small, stylish hotel with an excellent restaurant much patronized by Venetians. Its bedrooms are modern and bright, each decorated with a colour of the rainbow. Most have good views over the surrounding countryside. The creative dishes are prepared following a seasonal menu. Closed Jan. **www.dolada.it**

### PORDENONE Palace Hotel Moderno €€

*Viale Martelli 1, 33170* **Tel** *0434 282 15* **Fax** *0434 52 03 15* **Rooms** *96*

A comfortable traditional hotel with a good range of facilities in all its bedrooms, the Palace Hotel Moderno is centrally located close to the station. The restaurant (which is under separate management) specializes in traditional cuisine, particularly fish dishes. **www.palacehotelmoderno.it**

### POVOLETTO La Faula €

*Via Faula 5, 33040* **Tel** *334 399 67 34* **Rooms** *9*

A traditional Friuli farmhouse which has been lovingly restored. The property is set amid vineyards and farmland. Spacious, well-furnished bedrooms and modern bathrooms complete the picture of a comfortable rural retreat. The bistro-style restaurant uses produce and wine from the farm. Open 1 Mar–1 Oct. **www.faula.com**

### SAN FLORIANO DEL COLLIO Golf Hotel Castello Formentini €€

*Via Oslavia 2, 34070* **Tel** *0481 88 40 51* **Fax** *0481 88 40 52* **Rooms** *14*

A lovely, 18th-century building furnished with antiques and set in its own well-kept grounds with a nine-hole golf course and tennis courts. A very good restaurant is located opposite the hotel. A wine museum attached to the hotel is worth a visit. Good base to explore the surrounding wine country. **www.golfhotelformentini.com**

### SARCEDO Casa Belmonte €€€

*Via Belmonte 2, 36030* **Tel** *0445 88 48 33* **Fax** *0445 88 41 34* **Rooms** *6*

A small hotel set on the top of a hill surrounded by vineyards and olive groves. The rooms are luxuriously decorated with antiques and rich drapes. Breakfast is served outside in the summer or in the conservatory. There is a large pool for the guests. A good base from which to explore the Palladian villas. **www.casabelmonte.com**

### TORRI DEL BENACO Hotel Gardesana €€

*Piazza Calderini 20, 37010* **Tel** *045 722 54 11* **Fax** *045 722 57 71* **Rooms** *34*

The 15th-century harbour master's house overlooking Lake Garda has been converted into a friendly, comfortable hotel. Its spectacular location means that there are views of the castle from the restaurant terrace, while rooms on the third floor have wonderful views of the lake. Closed Nov–Feb. **www.gardesana.eu**

**TREVISO Ca' del Galletto** €€

*Via Santa Bona Vecchia 30, 31100* **Tel** *0422 43 25 50* **Fax** *0422 43 25 10* **Rooms** *67*

Set in its own grounds and only a ten-minute walk from the city walls. The hotel's bedrooms are spacious and modern, though slightly lacking in charm. However, the friendly staff and excellent sports facilities, as well as the peaceful surroundings, make for a pleasant stay. **www.hotelcadelgalletto.it**

**TREVISO Il Focolare** €€

*Piazza Ancillotto 4, 31100* **Tel** *0422 566 01* **Fax** *0422 566 01* **Rooms** *14*

One of Treviso's best budget hotels, Il Focolare is clean and welcoming and situated in the heart of the historic centre. The rooms are rather small, as are the bathrooms, but the location makes up for it. There is an excellent restaurant opposite which serves Treviso dishes. **www.albergoilfocolare.net**

**TRIESTE Grand Hotel Duchi d'Aosta** €€€

*Piazza Unità d'Italia 2, 34121* **Tel** *040 760 00 11* **Fax** *040 36 60 92* **Rooms** *55*

A palace from a bygone era, this hotel has vast rooms fitted with all modern facilities, plus a swimming pool. It stands in the old part of town, with magnificent views of the square from its restaurant terrace. In summer, guests can use the hotel's private beach resort. **www.duchi.eu**

**TRIESTE NH** €€€

*Corso Cavour 7, 34132* **Tel** *040 760 00 55* **Fax** *040 36 26 99* **Rooms** *174*

A large, modern hotel aiming at business as well as holiday clientele. The well-equipped rooms are spacious, though rather impersonally decorated. Although somewhat lacking in character, it is centrally located and is very near the city's famous waterfront. **www.nh-hotels.com**

**UDINE Quo Vadis** €

*Piazzale Cella 28, 33100* **Tel** *0432 210 91* **Fax** *0432 210 92* **Rooms** *38*

A comfortable hotel on a tranquil, tree-lined street. It is fairly close to the centre of the city. The exterior is elegant while the decor of the interior is mixed, but there are plenty of plants. Though simply furnished, the rooms are clean and many overlook a private courtyard. Closed Christmas. **www.hotelquovadis.it**

**VALPOLICELLA Villa del Quar** €€€€€

*Via Quar 12, Pedemonte, 37029* **Tel** *045 680 06 81* **Fax** *045 680 06 04* **Rooms** *25*

Only a short drive from Verona, this hotel and its excellent restaurant occupy a listed historic villa surrounded by parkland. The comfortable rooms are beautifully furnished with exquisite fabrics, period furniture and marble bathrooms. Many have timber rafters on view. Closed Nov–mid-Mar. **www.hotelvilladelquar.it**

**VERONA Giulietta e Romeo** €€

*Vicolo Tre Marchetti 3, 37121* **Tel** *045 800 35 54* **Fax** *045 801 08 62* **Rooms** *41*

This prettily named hotel is situated in a quiet street just behind the Arena, which is just a few minutes' walk away. The city's main attractions are also nearby. The refurbished bedrooms are bright and comfortable with modern furnishings. Breakfast is served in the bar. The hotel also offers free bike hire. **www.giuliettaeromeo.com**

**VERONA Il Torcolo** €€

*Vicolo Listone 3, 37121* **Tel** *045 800 75 12* **Fax** *045 800 40 58* **Rooms** *19*

This small, family-run hotel is a mere stone's throw from the Arena, making it a popular destination during the opera season. Though some of the reception areas are rather cramped, the guest rooms are pretty and traditional. It has a breakfast terrace. Closed 3 weeks end Jan–mid-Feb. **www.hoteltorcolo.it**

**VERONA Byblos Art Hotel** €€€€

*Via Cedrare 78, Corrubbio di Negarine, 37020* **Tel** *045 685 55 55* **Fax** *045 685 55 00* **Rooms** *60*

Housed in a sumptuous 18th-century villa on the outskirts of Verona, this hotel can be reached by complimentary transfer. Works by contemporary artists add to the hotel's charm. Summer guests will enjoy the outdoor pool and vast park with marble fountains. Wine tastings and evenings at the opera can be arranged. **www.byblosarthotel.com**

**VERONA Due Torri Hotel Baglioni** €€€€

*Piazza Sant'Anastasia 4, 37121* **Tel** *045 595 04 44* **Fax** *045 800 41 30* **Rooms** *90*

Standing alongside a beautiful church in the heart of medieval Verona, this sumptuous 14th-century building is one of Italy's most eccentric hotels. Each bedroom is decorated and furnished in the style of a different era. The public areas are equally opulent in this unique hotel. **www.baglionihotels.com**

**VICENZA Casa San Raffaele** €

*Viale X Giugno 10, 36100* **Tel** *0444 54 57 67* **Fax** *0444 54 22 59* **Rooms** *29*

A tranquil hotel in charming surroundings with excellent views set on the slopes of Monte Berico. The comfortable rooms are all en suite. Friendly staff and simple style can be found at this central hotel. No high season means that this is one of the best budget choices in the area.

**VICENZA Albergo Due Mori** €€

*Contrà Do Rode 24, 36100* **Tel** *0444 32 18 86* **Fax** *0444 32 61 27* **Rooms** *53*

This is a welcoming, family-run hotel in Vicenza's central pedestrian zone, just off Piazza dei Signori. The spacious rooms have simple period furnishings and antiques. Please note that there are no TVs. Breakfast can be taken at the hotel or at any of the neighbourhood cafés. Closed late Jul–mid-Aug, 22 Dec–2 Jan. **www.hotelduemori.com**

**Key to Price Guide** *see p558* **Key to Symbols** *see back cover flap*

# TRENTINO-ALTO ADIGE

### ANTERSELVA DI SOTTO (ANTHOLZ NIEDERTAL) Bagni di Salomone €

*Anterselva di Sotto, 39030* **Tel** *0474 49 21 99* **Fax** *0474 49 23 78* **Rooms** *33*

This charming hotel is set in beautiful countryside, with a nature park nearby. The hotel contains a spa dating back to 1559, and guests can drink the restorative mineral water. Guests may also borrow a mountain bike or go fishing in the summer. In winter, skiing can be enjoyed close to the hotel. Closed May, Nov. **www.badsalomonsbrunn.com**

### BOLZANO (BOZEN) Cappello di Ferro €

*Via Bottai 21, 39100* **Tel** *0471 97 83 97* **Fax** *0471 31 20 70* **Rooms** *50*

Set in the historic centre of Bolzano, the restored Cappello di Ferro is a charming town hotel. In winter, the hotel organizes tours of local Christmas markets, skiing and snow-shoeing with a guide, while in summer you can hire mountain bikes or go hiking with a guide. The restaurant is excellent. **www.cappellodiferro.com**

### BOLZANO (BOZEN) Engel €€€

*Via San Valentino 3, Nova Levante, 39056* **Tel** *0471 61 31 31* **Fax** *0471 61 34 04* **Rooms** *70*

In a small town near Bolzano, the Engel is a good choice for families and the sporty, with hiking and skiing nearby. There is also a wellness centre which has a sauna and beauty farm. For those with children there is a children's club with outdoor play facilities. Summer activities include golf and riding. Closed Apr. **www.hotel-engel.com**

### BOLZANO (BOZEN) Luna-Mondschein €€€

*Via Piave 15, 39100* **Tel** *0471 97 56 42* **Fax** *0471 97 55 77* **Rooms** *77*

The Luna-Mondschein dates from 1798, although the buildings have been much added to since then. A pleasant garden allows for summer dining. It is one of the oldest hotels in Bolzano's historic centre, reconstructed after the war in 1946, and has since been refurbished. Some rooms have air conditioning. **www.hotel-luna.it**

### BRESSANONE (BRIXEN) Dominik €€

*Via Terzo di Sotto 13, 39042* **Tel** *0472 83 01 44* **Fax** *0472 83 65 54* **Rooms** *35*

The Dominik is furnished with antiques, although the buildings themselves date from the 1970s. It is set near the Rapp gardens in the oldest quarter of Bressanone close to the main square. The pool offers amazing views of the town and surrounding countryside. Closed 2 wks Jan, Nov. **www.hoteldominik.com**

### BRESSANONE (BRIXEN) Elephant €€€

*Via Rio Bianco 4, 39042* **Tel** *0472 83 27 50.* **Fax** *0472 83 65 79* **Rooms** *44*

A smart hotel named after an elephant sent from Goa to Genoa that stayed at the inn's stable in the 16th century. While offering all modern comforts (including a sauna), it has retained a strong traditional atmosphere. The hotel is surrounded by beautiful landscaped gardens with panoramic views. Closed Jan–22 Mar. **www.hotelelephant.com**

### BRUNICO (BRUNECK) Andreas Hofer €€

*Via Campo Tures 1, 39031* **Tel** *0474 55 14 69* **Fax** *0474 55 12 83* **Rooms** *48*

A family run chalet a short distance from the centre of Brunico, with wooden alpine-style furniture. The hotel is set in its own garden and some of the rooms have balconies. The restaurant serves Tyrolean specialities which can be enjoyed on the outdoor terrace in the summer. Closed mid-Apr–mid-May. **www.andreashofer.it**

### CALDARO (KALTERN) Leuchtenburg €€

*Campi al Lago 100, 39052* **Tel** *0471 96 00 93* **Fax** *0471 96 01 55* **Rooms** *11*

Set in a beautiful 16th-century farmhouse surrounded by vineyards, some of the simple bedrooms are furnished with traditional painted furniture. Close by there is a scenic lake to cool off in with a private beach and a terrace to enjoy the alpine atmosphere in the shade. Half-board only. Closed Nov–mid-Mar. **www.leuchtenburg.it**

### CANAZEI Dolomites Inn €€

*Via Antersies 3, Penia, 38032* **Tel** *0462 60 22 12* **Fax** *0462 60 24 74* **Rooms** *27*

British-Italian owners Bob and Lucia offer professional and friendly service at this hotel situated in one of the most beautiful parts of the Dolomites. Each room has a balcony offering breathtaking views. Excellent for mountain excursions; also has squash courts, a Jacuzzi and sauna. Closed after Easter–May, Oct–Nov. **www.dolomitesinn.com**

### CASTELROTTO (KASTELRUTH) Cavallino d'Oro €€

*Piazza Kraus 1, 39040* **Tel** *0471 70 63 37* **Fax** *0471 70 71 72* **Rooms** *23*

This charming hotel is set in a pretty village where traditional costume is still worn, 26 km (16 miles) from Bolzano. The hotel has a cosy, intimate feel with wood-lined communal rooms and Tyrolean-style furniture. The bar has a large selection of wines from the region. Some rooms have air conditioning. **www.cavallino.it**

### COLFOSCO Cappella Romantik Hotel €€€

*Strada Pecei 17, 39030* **Tel** *0471 83 61 83* **Fax** *0471 83 65 61* **Rooms** *46*

A chalet in the Dolomites, opened by the present owner's grandfather. The hotel also has an art gallery. There is lots of outdoor space providing impressive views of the Dolomites and a children's play area. There are a variety of styles of suites to choose from. Half-board available. Closed Apr–May, Oct–Nov. **www.hotelcappella.com**

**FIE ALLO SCILIAR Romantik Hotel Turm** €€€€

*Piazza della Chiesa 9, 39050* **Tel** *0471 72 50 14* **Fax** *0471 72 54 74* **Rooms** *40*

Hotel Turm comprises three houses and two towers, one of which dates from the 13th century. It also houses an amazing art collection which includes pieces by Beuys and Kokoschka. The art, and the hotel's restaurant (one of Italy's best), are the main attractions at this friendly hotel. Closed 3 wks Apr, Nov–Christmas. **www.hotelturm.it**

**LA VILLA Hotel La Villa** €€€

*Strada Boscdaplan 176, 39030* **Tel** *0471 84 70 35* **Fax** *0471 84 73 93* **Rooms** *31*

Set amid the splendid scenery of the Val Badia, this elegant hotel offers friendly hospitality all year round. It is attractively decorated with carved wood and rich fabrics. Many of the rooms have balconies, although some are a little small. An abundant buffet breakfast is served. Closed 1 Apr–20 Jun, 20 Sep–1 Dec. **www.hotel-lavilla.it**

**MADONNA DI CAMPIGLIO Albergo dello Sportivo** €€

*Via Pradalago 29, 38084* **Tel** *0465 44 11 01* **Fax** *0465 44 08 00* **Rooms** *11*

A small, family-owned pension in the heart of the village. Albergo dello Sportivo offers comfortable and modestly decorated rooms. Some have balconies although the singles are rather small. A good buffet breakfast is provided. Good value for money. The owners are welcoming. Closed May, 3 wks Jun, Oct–Nov. **www.dellosportivo.com**

**MADONNA DI CAMPIGLIO Grifone** €€

*Via Vallesinella 7, 38084* **Tel** *0465 44 20 02* **Fax** *0465 44 05 40* **Rooms** *40*

This spacious, alpine-style hotel offers a great range of facilities for summer- and winter-sports holidays. There are a variety of communal rooms including a piano bar, reading lounge and a children's games room. Some of the rooms have balconies. Half-board only. Closed after Easter–Jun, 10 Sep–early Dec. **www.hotelgrifone.it**

**MADONNA DI CAMPIGLIO Chalet Hermitage** €€€

*Via Casteletto 69, 38084* **Tel** *0465 44 15 58* **Fax** *0465 44 16 18* **Rooms** *25*

A "bio hotel", with the building and interior designed along environmental lines and to make the most of the magnificent scenery. The hotel is extremely comfortable and the rooms are spacious and well designed. Excellent restaurant that serves organic food. Good facilities. Closed after Easter–Jun, Oct–Nov. **www.biohotelhermitage.it**

**MALLES VENOSTA (MALS IM VINSCHGAU) Garberhof** €€

*Via Nazionale 25, 39024* **Tel** *0473 83 13 99* **Fax** *0473 83 19 50* **Rooms** *40*

Situated in the beautiful Vinschgau Valley, this modern, chalet-style hotel with extensive panoramic terraces has a good range of sports and leisure facilities. The restaurant serves traditional South Tyrolean cuisine with an international twist. Breakfast is buffet-style with a juice bar. Half-board available. Closed Nov–20 Dec. **www.garberhof.com**

**MERANO (MERAN) Der Pünthof** €€

*Via Steinach 25, Lagundo, 39022* **Tel** *0473 44 85 53* **Fax** *0473 44 99 19* **Rooms** *12*

Set in peaceful and attractive gardens, this farmhouse dates back to the Middle Ages and features a 13th-century fresco. The wooden floors and ceilings match the alpine furniture. Despite its apparent seclusion, the hotel is only five minutes from the town centre. A spa is also available to guests. Closed Nov–Mar. **www.puenthof.com**

**MERANO (MERAN) Castel Rundegg** €€€

*Via Scena 2, 39012* **Tel** *0473 23 41 00* **Fax** *0473 23 72 00* **Rooms** *30*

Parts of this fairytale castle date from the 12th century. Surrounded by extensive grounds giving wonderful views over Merano, inside the traditional atmosphere continues with wood furniture, beamed ceilings and parquet floors. In the summer guests can dine outdoors. **www.rundegg.com**

**MERANO (MERAN) Castello Labers** €€€€

*Via Labers 25, 39012* **Tel** *0473 23 44 84* **Fax** *0473 23 41 46* **Rooms** *35*

The 11th-century Castello Labers is the setting for this high-class country hotel. There are splendid views over the surrounding vineyards and woods. Guests can sample the wine produced by the estate, while home-made pasta, sweets and jam are specialities of the restaurant. There is also a chapel. Closed mid-Nov–mid-Apr. **www.castellolabers.it**

**MERANO (MERAN) Hotel Castel Fragsburg** €€€€

*Via Fragsburger Strasse 3, 39012* **Tel** *0473 24 40 71* **Fax** *0473 24 44 93* **Rooms** *16*

Built originally as a shooting lodge for local gentry, this beautifully situated hotel has fine views of the mountains and Merano in the valley below. Public rooms are light-filled and well decorated. The bedrooms are spacious and all quite different. The gardens are well maintained and a perfect place to relax. Closed mid-Nov–Mar. **www.fragsburg.com**

**ORTISEI Adler Dolomiti Spa & Sport Resort** €€€€

*Via Rezia 7, 39046* **Tel** *0471 77 50 01* **Fax** *0471 77 55 55* **Rooms** *110*

Superbly located, the Adler is suitable both in winter, for the skiing, and in summer, for the walking or just enjoying the outdoor pool and vast spa and fitness facilities. It is surrounded by large private parkland and offers a high level of service and comfort. Prices include half-board. Closed early Apr–mid-May. **www.adler-dolomiti.com**

**PERGINE VALSUGANA Castel Pergine** €€

*Via al Castello 10, 38057* **Tel** *0461 53 11 58* **Fax** *0461 53 13 29* **Rooms** *21*

A hotel since the beginning of the 20th century, Castel Pergine is a 13th-century castle with exquisite views over the countryside. The interior is simply decorated and has traditional wooden furnishings. The hotel also presents contemporary art exhibitions in its gardens and inner courtyard. Closed Nov–Mar. **www.castelpergine.it**

**Key to Price Guide** *see p558* **Key to Symbols** *see back cover flap*

### RENON Ploerr €

*Oberinn 45, 39050* ***Tel*** *0471 602 118* ***Rooms*** *11*

A guesthouse located on a working dairy farm in idyllic mountain scenery. The rooms are simple but very comfortable and decked out in pine, and most have balconies. Breakfast is plentiful to set you up for a day in the mountains. A perfect spot for a family holiday. You can expect a genuine welcome. Closed Jan. **www.ploerr.com**

### RIVA DEL GARDA Europa €€

*Piazza Catena 13, 38066* ***Tel*** *0464 55 54 33* ***Fax*** *0464 52 17 77* ***Rooms*** *63*

This traditional hotel in a colour-washed building overlooks the main square. Situated between the historic harbour and the Monte Oro near the bustling town centre. Many of the simply furnished yet comfortable bedrooms have views over the lake. The restaurant has a terrace by the water. Closed Nov–Feb. **www.hoteleuropariva.it**

### RIVA DEL GARDA Du Lac et Du Parc €€€

*Viale Rovereto 44, 38066* ***Tel*** *0464 56 66 00* ***Fax*** *0464 56 65 66* ***Rooms*** *159*

This hotel on the lake has its own private beach and sailing club. Make your choice of accommodation from the rooms in the main building, bungalows in the grounds or the elegant Murialdo suites. There is a vast array of beauty treatments and spa facilities available. Children are well catered for. Closed Nov–Mar. **www.dulacetduparc.com**

### SAN CASSIANO Rosa Alpina €€€€€

*Str Micura de Ru 20, 39030* ***Tel*** *0471 84 95 00* ***Fax*** *0471 84 93 77* ***Rooms*** *54*

This hotel is an oasis of luxury and comfort from which to explore the magnificent Dolomites. It has every facility that any guest could wish for, including four excellent restaurants. Well-manicured gardens, sauna, an indoor pool and beauty facilities are provided. The Pizzinini family are marvellous hosts. Closed Apr–Jun, Oct, Nov. **www.rosalpina.it**

### SAN PAOLO (ST PAULS) Schloss Korb €€

*Via Castel d'Appiano 5, Missiano, 39050* ***Tel*** *0471 63 60 00* ***Fax*** *0471 63 60 33* ***Rooms*** *50*

Partly set in a 13th-century castle, this prettily furnished hotel also has a modern annexe and tennis courts. An ideal hotel for an activity filled holiday with outdoor and indoor pools, nearby golf facilities and a children's play area. Guests can relax on the terrace overlooking the hotel's orchard. Closed Jan–Mar. **www.schloss-hotel-korb.com**

### SAN VIGILIO Hotel Monte Sella €€€

*Via Catarina Lanz 7, 39030* ***Tel*** *0474 50 10 34* ***Fax*** *0474 50 17 14* ***Rooms*** *35*

This lovely Art Deco hotel was built in 1901. Although the building has undergone renovation, it retains many of its original features. The public rooms are well furnished and designed to make the most of the magnificent view. Owner Norbert Cristofolini is a genial host. Closed after Easter–May, Oct, Nov. **www.monte-sella.com**

### SIUSI ALLO SCILIAR Albergo Tschoetscherhof €

*San Osvaldo 19, 39040* ***Tel*** *0471 70 60 13* ***Fax*** *0471 70 48 01* ***Rooms*** *11*

This is a lovely mountain hotel set amongst rolling green pastures. The guesthouse is quite simple, almost austere, with low ceilings, wooden floors and whitewashed walls. The rooms are modest but spotlessly clean and quite comfortable. Tranquillity reigns supreme and this is a perfect retreat. Closed Dec–Feb. **www.tschoetscherhof.com**

### TIRES (TIERS) Stefaner €€

*San Cipriano 65, 39050* ***Tel*** *0471 64 21 75* ***Fax*** *0471 64 23 02* ***Rooms*** *20*

A friendly chalet on the edge of the western Dolomites with amazing panoramas of the Tiers Valley. The bedrooms are spacious and the balconies decked with flowers. In the winter there is a large, traditional, tiled stove to gather round. Half-board only. Closed Nov–mid-Dec. **www.stefaner.com**

### TRENTO Accademia €€€

*Vicolo Colico 4–6, 38100* ***Tel*** *0461 23 36 00* ***Fax*** *0461 23 01 74* ***Rooms*** *42*

Set in a restored medieval building in the historic centre of Trento, close to Santa Maria Maggiore and Piazza Duomo. The interior of this relaxing hotel, although essentially modern, retains many original features, such as the inner courtyard and ancient vaults. Closed Christmas–6 Jan. **www.accademiahotel.it**

### VIPITENO Romantik Hotel Stafler €€

*Campo di Trens, Mules, 39040* ***Tel*** *0472 77 11 36* ***Fax*** *0472 77 10 94* ***Rooms*** *12*

Amid the mountains, just outside Vipiteno, this delightful family-run hotel offers four-star quality in a fabulous setting. It is ideal for winter- and summer-sports enthusiasts alike. For the less active, there is a luxurious wellness centre. In the restaurant, the Michelin-starred chef creates Italian dishes with an Alpine twist. **www.stafler.com**

## LOMBARDY

### BELLAGIO La Pergola €€

*Piazza del Porto 4, 22021* ***Tel*** *031 95 02 63* ***Fax*** *031 95 02 53* ***Rooms*** *11*

This renovated former convent dating back to 1500 has a peaceful lakeside location in a tiny fishing hamlet. Interesting features include vaulted ceilings, frescoes and antique furniture. Enjoy the lake views from the pretty terrace restaurant, which serves typical regional cuisine. Closed Dec–mid-Mar. **www.lapergolabellagio.it**

**BELLAGIO Hotel Florence** €€€

*Piazza Mazzini 46, 22021* ***Tel*** *031 95 03 42* ***Fax*** *031 95 17 22* ***Rooms*** *30*

A great location on the shores of Lake Como. This stylish hotel has elegant modern decor with canopy beds, roll-top baths, a charming bar and gourmet restaurant. A shady terrace offers guests wonderful views of the lake. Extra facilities include a spa with sauna, Turkish bath, Jacuzzi and massage. **www.hotelflorencebellagio.it**

**BORMIO Palace** €€

*Via Milano 54, 23032* ***Tel*** *0342 90 31 31* ***Fax*** *0342 90 33 66* ***Rooms*** *85*

Set within private gardens close to the centre of Bormio – famous since Roman times for its thermal springs. All the elegant cream rooms have private bathrooms. The restaurant offers Valtellina specialities and an extensive wine cellar. Wellness facilities include an indoor pool. Closed May–Nov. **www.palacebormio.it**

**BRATTO (BERGAMO) Hotel Milano** €€€€

*Via Silvio Pellico 3, Castione della Presolana, 24020* ***Tel*** *0346 312 11* ***Fax*** *0346 362 36* ***Rooms*** *67*

A large alpine resort hotel with plenty of comfort and style. Set amid stunning natural beauty it offers spa treatments and is a great base for the local mountains, watersports and golf. The restaurant, lounge bar and wine cellar guarantee relaxed evenings and fine regional cuisine. **www.hotelmilano.com**

**BRESCIA Park Hotel Cà Noa** €€

*Via Triumplina 66, 25123* ***Tel*** *030 39 87 62* ***Fax*** *030 39 87 64* ***Rooms*** *79*

The hotel is situated in a quiet park, northeast of the city. The functional, modernist exterior belies the elegant interior. Rooms feature dark wood furniture, cream walls and old paintings. Great views and an outdoor pool. Closed Christmas & New Year; 2 weeks Aug. **www.hotelcanoa.it**

**CERNOBBIO Villa d'Este** €€€€€

*Via Regina 40, 22012* ***Tel*** *031 34 81* ***Fax*** *031 34 88 73* ***Rooms*** *152*

A sumptuous, luxurious *grande dame* of a hotel set in 25 acres (10 ha) of parkland. Period furniture, fine paintings, chandeliers, marble fireplaces and Como silks add to the feeling of a princely villa. Excellent service and modern facilities, as well as superb views. Two villas on the grounds are available for weekly rentals. Closed mid-Nov–Feb. **www.villadeste.it**

**CERVESINA Hotel Castello di San Gaudenzio** €€€

*Via Mulino 1, Località San Gaudenzio, 27050* ***Tel*** *0383 33 31* ***Fax*** *0383 33 34 09* ***Rooms*** *45*

A glorious 15th-century castle boasting wonderful parkland, romantic rooms, a gym and pool, and a top-class restaurant. Explore the magnificent splendour of the fountains, follies, arboretum and cobbled courtyards, as well as the frescoes, old prints and period furniture within. The tower flat is a dream. **www.castellosangaudenzio.com**

**COLOGNE/FRANCIACORTA Cappuccini** €€€

*Via Cappuccini 54, 25033* ***Tel*** *030 715 72 54* ***Fax*** *030 715 72 57* ***Rooms*** *14*

This former monastery was built in 1569, and the monastic feel is echoed in the white rooms and long hallways. The magnificent surrounding countryside is peaceful. In addition to a relaxing terrace and gardens there is also a wellness centre with an outdoor pool. The restaurant serves local dishes such as risotto and polenta. **www.cappuccini.it**

**COMO In Riva al Lago** €

*Via Crespi 4, 22100* ***Tel*** *031 30 23 33* ***Fax*** *031 30 01 61* ***Rooms*** *10*

A basic but spotless hotel near the lake. Close to bus and train stations so rooms on the street side are noisier. A friendly, familiar atmosphere with a nearby pub for snacks and beer. Not all rooms have air conditioning or bathroom. Closed 2 weeks between Jan & Mar. **www.inrivaallago.com**

**COMO Hotel Firenze** €€

*Piazza Volta 16, 22100* ***Tel*** *031 30 03 33* ***Fax*** *031 30 01 01* ***Rooms*** *44*

This renovated Neo-Classical hotel sits in a pedestrianized square in the town centre. Rooms, all with bathrooms, are of a basic contemporary design. Some retain original beams or parquet flooring. Those looking on to the inner courtyard are quieter. A short walk from the lakeside. Closed Christmas. **www.albergofirenze.it**

**COMO Hotel Metropole Suisse** €€€

*Piazza Cavour 19, 22100* ***Tel*** *031 26 94 44* ***Fax*** *031 30 08 08* ***Rooms*** *71*

Located in the heart of Como on the waterfront, this hotel commands great views over the lake. The façade by famous architect Giuseppe Terragni dates back to 1892, with wrought-iron balconies for most of the rooms. Boat trips leave from the pier in front of the hotel. Closed 3 weeks Dec–Jan. **www.hotelmetropolesuisse.com**

**CREMONA Dellearti Design Hotel** €€

*Via Bonomelli 8, 26100* ***Tel*** *0372 231 31* ***Fax*** *0372 216 54* ***Rooms*** *33*

Cremona's only boutique hotel, the Dellearti, has a modern look. There is covered parking in the front of the hotel and the room service is swift and efficient. Close to the cathedral, medieval bell tower and the shops. Arty touches of burnished gold and bright colours warm the sleek, almost industrial design. **www.dellearti.com**

**CREMONA Hotel Impero** €€

*Piazza della Pace 21, 26100* ***Tel*** *0372 41 30 13* ***Rooms*** *53*

A small, friendly hotel with a great location, right in the centre of this historic town. The rooms are light, spacious and decorated in relaxing tones of blue, honey and cream; some have views of the cathedral. Public areas have both contemporary and antique furnishings. **www.hotelimpero.cr.it**

**DESENZANO DEL GARDA Piroscafo** €€

*Via Porto Vecchio 11, 25015* ***Tel*** *030 914 11 28* ***Fax*** *030 991 25 86* ***Rooms*** *32*

Located right on the old dock of the town in a historic building. The terrace on the ground floor is housed in an arched portico. Pick a room looking out on to the dock or watch the boats from the terrace. The rooms are simply decorated but are very comfortable. Parking close by. Closed Jan–Feb. **www.hotelpiroscafo.it**

**DESENZANO DEL GARDA Park Hotel** €€€

*Lungolago Cesare Battisti 19, 25015* ***Tel*** *030 914 34 94* ***Rooms*** *56*

An elegant hotel on the waterfront, close to the centre of town. Public areas feature luxurious fabrics, antiques and comfortable sofas. Bedrooms are classically furnished, with contemporary facilities. Some rooms have small balconies with lake views. A rooftop swimming pool adds a touch of glamour. **www.gardalake.com/park-hotel**

**GARDONE RIVIERA Villa del Sogno** €€

*Via Zanardelli 107, 25083* ***Tel*** *0365 29 01 81* ***Fax*** *0365 29 02 30* ***Rooms*** *33*

This splendid Neo-Classical villa has a peaceful panoramic position in its own grounds, close to the town centre. It is ideally located for exploring the surrounding countryside and towns. Facilities include tennis courts and a great outdoor pool. The villa's restaurant offers creative Italian cuisine. **www.villadelsogno.it**

**GARDONE RIVIERA Dimora Bolsone Bed & Breakfast** €€€

*Via Panoramica 23, 25083* ***Tel*** *0365 210 22* ***Fax*** *0365 29 30 42* ***Rooms*** *3*

Up on a hillside with magnificent views over Gardone Riviera from all of its period-styled rooms. The stone manor house abuts Il Vittoriale, the home of poet Gabriele d'Annunzio. However, it is not suitable for children under 12. Minimum stay two nights. Closed Dec–Feb. **www.dimorabolsone.it**

**GARDONE RIVIERA Villa Fiordaliso** €€€€

*Corso Zanardelli 132, 25083* ***Tel*** *0365 201 58* ***Fax*** *0365 29 00 11* ***Rooms*** *5*

This beautiful three-storey villa located ten minutes from the centre of Gardone, overlooking Lake Garda and with a lovely garden, has a flower theme throughout and the eclectic decor reflects the name. Try the Lombardy and Venetian specials in the restaurant. Closed Nov–Feb. **www.villafiordaliso.it**

**LIMONE SUL GARDA Capo Reamol** €€€

*Via IV Novembre 92, 25010* ***Tel*** *0365 95 40 40* ***Fax*** *0365 95 42 62* ***Rooms*** *58*

This lakeside hotel is 3 km (1.5 miles) from Limone (take the bus or use the hotel's bikes). Boasting a private beach and pool, balconies or terraces with lake views for all the rooms, plus an excellent surf school, it is a must for sporting families. Three-night minimum stay. Closed mid-Oct–mid-Apr. **www.hotelcaporeamol.it**

**LIVIGNO Hotel Capriolo** €€

*Via Borch 96, 23030* ***Tel*** *0342 99 67 23* ***Fax*** *0342 99 69 98* ***Rooms*** *12*

Located close to the shops, ski lifts, ski school, summer walks and restaurants in Livigno's quiet San Rocco district. A cosy and pleasant family-run residence full of basic rustic charm. A *bar-stube* with traditional Veltina cuisine, solarium and covered parking is offered. Closed May; Oct–end-Nov. **www.capriololivigno.com**

**LIVIGNO Hotel Intermonti** €€€

*Via Gerus 310, 23030* ***Tel*** *0342 97 21 00* ***Fax*** *0342 97 25 00* ***Rooms*** *160*

This large alpine hotel provides great amenities from ski-deposit and hire to sauna, solarium and pool. There is also a courtesy bus to the lifts and into Livigno town centre. Most rooms have views across the valley and some have balconies. Minimum stay three nights. Closed mid-Apr–mid-Jun; Sep–Nov. **www.hotelintermonti.it**

**MANTUA Antica Locanda Matilda B&B** €

*Via Rismondo 2, Castelletto Borgo, 46100* ***Tel*** *335 639 06 24 (mobile)* ***Fax*** *0376 30 24 18* ***Rooms*** *3*

A wonderful little guesthouse in an old manor house in the outskirts of Mantova with lovely gardens. The three rooms are decorated with antiques but the atmosphere is fresh, modern and familiar. Two rooms share a bathroom. Basic facilities at an affordable price with private parking. **www.locandamatilda.it**

**MANTUA Casa Poli** €€€

*Corso Giuseppe Garibaldi 32, 46100* ***Tel*** *0376 28 81 70* ***Rooms*** *27*

A boutique hotel that sits only a few moments' walk from the historic centre. Cosy rooms are warm-hued, elegant and minimalist, with contemporary furniture and parquet flooring. The hotel boasts an internal courtyard garden where guests can relax and enjoy a drink. **www.hotelcasapoli.it**

**MILAN Antica Locanda Leonardo** €€€

*Corso Magenta 78, 20123* ***Tel*** *0248 01 41 97* ***Fax*** *02 48 01 90 12* ***Rooms*** *14*

A chic family-run guesthouse with bar and dining room, and a wonderful terraced garden at the back. This 19th-century palazzo has antiques mixed with more contemporary decor, and is close to Leonardo da Vinci's *Last Supper*. Closed 1–6 Jan, 3 wks Aug. **www.anticalocandaleonardo.com**

**MILAN Gran Duca di York** €€€

*Via Moneta 1a, 20123* ***Tel*** *02 87 48 63* ***Fax*** *02 869 03 44* ***Rooms*** *33*

A very central location close to the Duomo and minutes from the designer shops. This hotel is in a renovated 18th-century palazzo; four rooms have their own terraces. The lobby is spacious, the bedrooms more compact. Parking available in a nearby garage. **www.ducadiyork.com**

### MILAN Spadari €€€

*Via Spadari 11, 20123* **Tel** *02 72 00 23 71* **Rooms** *39*

One of Milan's best-kept secrets, this discreet hotel is situated bang in the heart of the city, only a few streets away from the Duomo. Rooms vary in size, but all feature contemporary styling and facilities. The decor is restrained and tasteful. The breakfasts here are particularly notable. **www.spadarihotel.com**

### MILAN Antica Locanda Solferino €€€€

*Via Castelfidardo 2, 20121* **Tel** *02 657 01 29* **Fax** *02 657 13 61* **Rooms** *11*

The eclectic Old World charm throughout this guesthouse in the pretty bohemian Brera district mixes antiques with retro. Tiny wrought-iron balconies, creaky floorboards and narrow corridors. Most rooms overlook the street, which can be noisy. Closed 5–20 Aug. **www.anticalocandasolferino.it**

### MILAN Manzoni €€€€

*Via Santo Spirito 20, 20121* **Tel** *02 76 00 57 00* **Rooms** *45*

A beautiful hotel in a quiet yet central location near the fashion heart of the city. The interior features luxurious materials, including marble and inlaid parquet floors. The classically elegant rooms vary in size, and some have balconies. Discreet and with very friendly, attentive service. **www.hotelmanzoni.com**

### MILAN Straf €€€€

*Via San Raffaele 3, 20121* **Tel** *02 80 50 81* **Fax** *02 89 09 52 94* **Rooms** *64*

The Neo-Classical façade from 1883 disguises an ultra-modern interior. Luxurious raw natural materials set the minimal design tone. Five unique chromotherapy and aromatherapy rooms are available. Straf's lounge bar next door is very popular. Closed last 3 wks Aug. **www.straf.it**

### MILAN Exedra €€€€€

*Corso Giacomo Matteotti 4, 20121* **Tel** *02 77 67 96 11* **Rooms** *154*

Opened in 2009, this luxury design hotel is housed in a former bank from the 1920s. Public areas are ultra-contemporary, and rooms superbly stylish. The Exedra is centrally located and features all the amenities one would expect from a hotel of this class. **www.boscolohotels.com**

### MILAN Park Hyatt Milano €€€€€

*Via Tommaso Grossi 1, 20121* **Tel** *02 88 21 12 34* **Fax** *02 88 21 12 35* **Rooms** *117*

Housed in an old bank, this is an elegant modern addition to Milan's more traditional hotels. You can't get more central: from the front doors you step into the domed Galleria, Milan's central walkway of shops alongside the Duomo. Excellent bar and restaurant, facilities (including spa and gym) and service. **www.milan.park.hyatt.com**

### PAVIA Hotel Italia €

*Corso Partigiani 48, Certosa di Pavia, 27012* **Tel** *0382 92 56 56* **Rooms** *30*

A stone's throw from the splendid Certosa, this family-run hotel offers great value for money. Rooms are simply but tastefully decorated with whitewashed walls and antique country furniture. An added bonus is the presence of an excellent restaurant. The local bus from Pavia stops right outside the property. **www.italiacertosa.pavia.it**

### RANCO Il Sole di Ranco €€€€

*Piazza Venezia 5, 21020* **Tel** *0331 97 65 07* **Fax** *0331 97 66 20* **Rooms** *14*

Located in the village of Ranco, in its own grounds overooking the shores of Lake Maggiore. It boasts a private garden, panoramic views from the restaurant under a pergola in summer, secure parking and a helicopter landing area. New facilities include a pool, sauna and *hammam*. Closed mid-Dec–Jan. **www.ilsolediranco.it**

### RIVA DI SOLTO Albergo Ristorante Miranda €€

*Via Cornello 8, 24060* **Tel** *035 98 60 21* **Fax** *035 98 00 55* **Rooms** *25*

A peaceful panoramic setting on a hillside overlooking Lake Iseo. This simple family-run *pensione* offers comfortable rooms all with balconies. There is an outdoor pool in an olive grove, a play area for kids and two rooms have facilities for the disabled. Fresh fish dishes are offered in the terrace restaurant. **www.albergomiranda.it**

### RODIGO Hotel Villa dei Tigli €€€

*Via Cantarana 20, 46040* **Tel** *0376 65 06 91* **Fax** *0376 65 06 49* **Rooms** *30*

Once an aristocratic villa built at the turn of the 20th century, it lies some 15 km (9 miles) out of Mantova in the quiet countryside of Rodigo in acres of parkland. There are wellness and beauty facilities in addition to the high-class restaurant which serves organic, vegetarian and healthy traditional Mantuan food. **www.hotelvilladeitigli.it**

### SABBIONETA Al Duca €

*Via della Stamperia 18, 46018* **Tel** *0375 524 74* **Fax** *0375 22 00 21* **Rooms** *10*

This Renaissance building, tucked in a street near the Porta Imperiale in the town centre, is quiet and unpretentious. The impressive lobby has columns and pink marble, though the decor in the rooms is plain. The well-priced restaurant serves Mantuan food. Closed Jan–10 Feb.

### SALÒ Romantik Hotel Laurin €€€

*Viale Landi 9, 25087* **Tel** *0365 220 22* **Fax** *0365 223 82* **Rooms** *30*

A romantic lakeside villa sitting on a hillside overlooking Lake Garda with sweeping gardens, spacious bedrooms and an outdoor pool, plus a small beach and tennis courts nearby. Dine in the elegant, frescoed palm court-style restaurant or on the terrace under the stars. Closed mid-Nov–Feb. **www.laurinsalo.com**

### SIRMIONE SUL GARDA Villa Cortine Palace €€€€€

*Via Grotte 6, 25019* ***Tel*** *030 990 58 90* ***Fax*** *030 91 63 90* ***Rooms*** *54*

A vast luxurious Neo-Classical villa in a tranquil setting of lush immaculate gardens. Splendid meandering paths through parkland, ponds, fountains, a cypress grove by the lake, statues and a jetty with loungers. Enjoy lunch on the lakeside terrace in summer. Closed mid-Oct–Easter. **www.hotelvillacortine.com**

### TREMEZZO Hotel La Darsena €€€

*Via Regina 3, Lenno, 22016* ***Tel*** *0344 431 66* ***Rooms*** *13*

This restaurant with rooms is situated right by Lake Como and offers wonderful panoramic views over the water from each of the rooms' balconies. The restaurant is also highly recommended, especially the fixed-price menu. **www.centrohotelslagodicomo.it/darsena-tremezzo**

### TREMEZZO Tremezzo Palace Hotel €€€€€

*Via Regina 8, 22019* ***Tel*** *0344 424 91* ***Fax*** *0344 402 01* ***Rooms*** *94*

This prestigious lakeside hotel built in the Liberty style in 1910 is surrounded by gardens and terraces with lake views. The period feel is echoed in the ornate gilt and splendid antiques. The hotel also boasts a sauna, gym and tennis court, plus golf facilities nearby. Closed Dec–Feb. **www.tremezzopalace.com**

### VALSOLDA Stella d'Italia €€€

*Piazza Roma 1, 22010* ***Tel*** *0344 681 39* ***Fax*** *0344 687 29* ***Rooms*** *34*

This hotel sits in a lovely garden bordering Lake Lugano and has a shady terrace restaurant under a rose pergola. Guests have access to the private lido beach. Part of the hotel is in a renovated 18th-century villa. The restaurant offers Mediterranean cuisine and fish from the lake. Closed mid-Oct–Apr. **www.stelladitalia.com**

### VARENNA Hotel du Lac €€

*Via del Prestino 11, 23829* ***Tel*** *0341 83 02 38* ***Fax*** *0341 83 10 81* ***Rooms*** *16*

A peaceful hotel at the water's edge with enchanting views from the lake-facing rooms. Enjoy the terrace restaurant, looking out over the water. Charming features include marble columns, wrought-iron balustrades and floral names for every room. Tranquil and relaxing. Closed mid-Nov–end-Feb. **www.albergodulac.com**

## VALLE D'AOSTA AND PIEDMONT

### ACQUI TERME Roma Imperiale €€€

*Via Passeggiata dei Colli 1, 15011* ***Tel*** *0144 35 65 03* ***Rooms*** *26*

The Roma Imperiale is housed in an attractive 19th-century villa close to the centre of town and sitting in its own grounds. Rooms are spacious and furnished in a classic, elegant style with whitewashed walls, plaster ceilings, wooden beams and marble floors. A vaulted restaurant serves excellent food. **www.dimorestoriche.com**

### ALESSANDRIA Mercure Alessandria Alli Due Buoi Rossi €€

*Via Cavour 32, 15100* ***Tel*** *0131 51 71 71* ***Fax*** *0131 51 71 72* ***Rooms*** *48*

This hotel is very welcoming and friendly. As well as a free Internet point and a garage, it offers four rooms for guests with reduced mobility. The decor is simple and traditional. Since 1920 its trattoria has become an institution in Alessandria. Orson Welles once enjoyed a legendary feast here. **www.hotelalliduebuoirossi.com**

### AOSTA Albergo Mancuso €

*Via Voison 32, 11100* ***Tel*** *0165 345 26* ***Fax*** *0165 23 66 39* ***Rooms*** *12*

A well-positioned family-run residence near the cable car to the slopes and close to the town centre. It is basic and simple, but clean and very affordable. All rooms have twin beds and a bathroom. Parking is also available. **www.albergomancuso.com**

### AOSTA Hotel Milleluci €€

*Località Porossan-Roppoz 15, 11100* ***Tel*** *0165 23 52 78* ***Fax*** *0165 23 52 84* ***Rooms*** *31*

Set in a quiet area overlooking the lights of Aosta, hence the name of "a thousand lights". The farmhouse buildings have been renovated, and the hotel has a rustic charm with period furniture and exposed beams. There is also a pool, garden, garage parking and pretty terrace. **www.hotelmilleluci.com**

### ARONA Giardino €€€

*Corso Repubblica 1, 28041* ***Tel*** *0322 459 94* ***Fax*** *0322 24 94 01* ***Rooms*** *56*

The Giardino Hotel is located in the centre of the small town of Arona and affords splendid views across Lake Maggiore from its large terrace and ample grounds. It is comfortable but sparsely decorated, which lends it a light, airy feel. **www.giardinoarona.com**

### PINO TORINESE Hotel Aston €€

*Strada Traforo del Pino 23, 10025* ***Tel*** *011 899 87 33* ***Fax*** *011 898 94 72* ***Rooms*** *40*

Set in a peaceful park in the hills above Turin, dominated by Juvarra's splendid basilica, this hotel is a few minutes from the city centre. The contemporary, minimal decor incorporates a light marble reception hall-lobby, pale marble corridors and brown and cream bedrooms. Closed 2 weeks Aug. **www.astonhotel.it**

**TURIN Albergo Serenella** €

*Via Tarino 4, 10124* ***Tel*** *011 83 70 31* ***Fax*** *011 83 70 31* ***Rooms*** *7*

Offering unbeatable prices for the centre of the city, this simple little hotel is located in a street behind Palazzo Reale and the park, near the Mole Antonelliana. At this friendly hotel they serve home-made regional cuisine in its intimate restaurant. The rooms are clean and basic. Close to the shops and museums. **www.albergoserenella.com**

**TURIN Hotel Conte Biancamano** €€

*Corso Vittorio Emanuele 73, 10128* ***Tel*** *011 562 32 81* ***Fax*** *011 562 37 89* ***Rooms*** *24*

This is an intimate hotel on the third floor of a mansion in the heart of the city. The classic palazzo retains an old-fashioned charm, with hardwood floors, stucco work and crystal chandeliers. Very near Porta Nuova and Piazza Carlo Felice. Closed Aug; 25 Dec–1 Jan. **www.hotelcontebiancamano.it**

**TURIN Grand Hotel Sitea** €€€

*Via Carlo Alberto 35, 10123* ***Tel*** *011 517 01 71* ***Fax*** *011 54 80 90* ***Rooms*** *120*

Close to the central shopping area of Via Roma, the Grand Hotel Sitea sits proudly in its Neo-Classical palazzo in Turin's historic centre. Excellent service and the hotel is also renowned for its first-class restaurant, the Carignano. A must for lovers of tradition, Empire style and elegant suites. **www.sitea.thi.it**

**TURIN Hotel Victoria** €€€

*Via Nino Costa 4, 10123* ***Tel*** *011 561 19 09* ***Fax*** *011 561 18 06* ***Rooms*** *106*

Located in a quiet street overlooking a garden in the heart of downtown Turin, close to shops, restaurants, theatres and museums. Features include a full fitness centre, indoor pool and courtyard café. Great mountain views from top-floor terraced rooms. The decor is an eclectic English country house style. **www.hotelvictoria-torino.com**

**TURIN Villa Sassi** €€€

*Strada al Traforo di Pino 47, 10132* ***Tel*** *011 898 05 56* ***Fax*** *011 898 00 95* ***Rooms*** *15*

This luxurious 17th-century peach-coloured patrician villa still boasts many original features such as marble fireplaces and chandeliers. The rooms are elegant and the refined restaurant offers gourmet cuisine. Enjoy the terrace and surrounding beautiful gardens. Closed Aug; 25 Dec–31 Jan. **www.villasassi.com**

**TURIN Turin Golden Palace** €€€€

*Via dell'Arcivescovado 18, 10128* ***Tel*** *011 551 21 11* ***Fax*** *011 551 28 00* ***Rooms*** *195*

Impeccable service and traditional luxury can be expected in this hotel housed in a handsome palazzo dating back to 1872. The refined tranquil atmosphere also includes modern facilities. Centrally located for shopping, museums and sightseeing. **www.turinpalace.thi.it**

**VARALLO SESIA Albergo Sacro Monte** €€

*Località Sacro Monte 14, 13019* ***Tel*** *0163 542 54* ***Fax*** *0163 511 89* ***Rooms*** *24*

A charming hotel housed in an ancient 16th-century building at the entrance to the famous Sacro Monte. Restored to a comfortable small hotel with a private garden and lovely peaceful terrace. Rooms are simple and pretty, and the vaulted restaurant offers Valsesian specialities. Closed Dec–2 wks before Easter. **www.sacromontealbergo.it**

## LIGURIA

**CAMOGLI Cenobio dei Dogi** €€€

*Via Cuneo 34, 16032* ***Tel*** *0185 72 41* ***Fax*** *0185 77 27 96* ***Rooms*** *105*

On the shores of this fishing village, the villa built for the Doges of Genoa and frequented by priests and cardinals in the 17th century is now a vast luxury hotel. It has gorgeous sun terraces with views over the town and out to sea, palms and Mediterranean pines around the pool and comfortable rooms, each in its own style. **www.cenobio.it**

**CAMOGLI Hotel Portofino Kulm** €€€€

*Viale Bernardo Gaggini 23, 16030* ***Tel*** *0185 73 61* ***Fax*** *0185 77 66 22* ***Rooms*** *77*

This Art Nouveau jewel nestles in the verdant park on Mount Portofino, between Camogli and Santa Margherita. The elegant dining room has an outdoor terrace offering splendid sunset views over the bay. Facilities include indoor pool, Jacuzzi, beauty treatments and tennis. **www.portofinokulm.it**

**FINALE LIGURE Punta Est** €€€€

*Via Aurelia 1, 17024* ***Tel*** *019 60 06 11* ***Fax*** *019 60 06 11* ***Rooms*** *40*

An 18th-century villa houses this elegant hotel, which keeps the period charm in its furniture and exposed beams. Set among palms, pines and olives, it has majestic views across the Ligurian bay, as well as a small swimming pool. Paths, steps and shady terraces lead down to the sea. Closed mid-Oct–mid-Apr. **www.puntaest.com**

**GARLENDA La Meridiana** €€€

*Via ai Castelli, 17033* ***Tel*** *0182 58 02 71* ***Fax*** *0182 58 01 50* ***Rooms*** *28*

A relaxing country house style with wonderful gardens. In the heart of the Ligurian countryside, 4 km (2.5 miles) from the sea. Perfect for walking holidays and outdoor activities. The rooms and restaurant are elegantly decorated, and the service and facilities are excellent. Closed end-Oct–end-Mar. **www.lameridianaresort.com**

**Key to Price Guide** *see p558* **Key to Symbols** *see back cover flap*

**GENOA Best Western Metropoli** €€€

*Piazza Fontane Marose, 16123* ***Tel*** *010 246 88 88* ***Fax*** *010 246 86 86* ***Rooms*** *48*

Located in the heart of the city, in one of Genoa's prettiest piazzas, this hotel is close to museums, the Palazzo Ducale, opera, theatre and aquarium. Bus and metro stops are also nearby. The rooms are decorated in a modern style and provide comfort with basic facilities. **www.bestwestern.it/metropoli_ge**

**GENOA Hotel Bentley** €€€

*Via Corsica 4, 16128* ***Tel*** *010 531 51 11* ***Rooms*** *99*

The Bentley is a splendid hotel housed in an impressive Art Deco building in a residential district of the city. Offering contemporary style, high levels of design and great comfort, its rooms are beautifully furnished with quality fabrics and are decorated in subdued neutral and metallic tones. **www.thi.it**

**ISOLA PALMARIA Locanda Lorena** €€

*Via Cavour 4, 19025* ***Tel*** *0187 79 23 70* ***Fax*** *0187 76 60 77* ***Rooms*** *7*

A small beach hotel on Palmaria, the island facing Portovenere. Stylish Venetian motorboats shuttle guests to and fro. Lovely rooms with a simple, fresh style, bright colours and sea views. Watch the fishermen bring in the daily catch before it is served up for lunch. Closed Nov–mid-Feb. **www.locandalorena.com**

**MONTEROSSO AL MARE Porto Roca** €€€€

*Via Corone 1, 19016* ***Tel*** *0187 81 75 02* ***Fax*** *0187 81 76 92* ***Rooms*** *43*

Set amid the famed natural beauty of the area, this medium-sized hotel perches on a cliff with magnificent views just outside the fishing village in the Cinque Terre. It offers an oasis of calm, a lovely garden terrace, its own beach with shades and sun loungers in summer months, and a restaurant. Closed Nov–end-Mar. **www.portoroca.it**

**NERVI La Pagoda** €€€

*Via Capolungo 15, 16167* ***Tel*** *010 372 61 61* ***Fax*** *010 32 12 18* ***Rooms*** *17*

A very romantic hotel, once the villa of an 18th-century merchant who chose the Oriental style after falling in love with a Chinese girl. Marbled floors, chandeliers, antique screens, palms and terraces on different levels are some of the delightful touches. Closed Dec–end-Jan. **www.villapagoda.it**

**PORTOFINO Splendido** €€€€€

*Salita Baratta 16, 16034* ***Tel*** *0185 26 78 01* ***Fax*** *0185 26 78 06* ***Rooms*** *64*

Positioned on a series of terraces and housed in a former monastery overlooking the luxurious fishing village resort of Portofino, this is a truly magnificent place to stay. Service is impeccable and the views from all rooms are unforgettable. Closed mid-Nov–end-Mar. **www.hotelsplendido.com**

**PORTOFINO Splendido Mare** €€€€€

*Via Roma 2, 16034* ***Tel*** *0185 26 78 02* ***Fax*** *0185 26 78 07* ***Rooms*** *16*

A stylish hotel in the heart of Portofino's tiny harbour square, the Splendido Mare boasts well-appointed luxurious rooms, the coveted Ava Gardner suite on the top floor with private terrace and a superb garden terrace restaurant. Guests can dine here or at the Splendido, and can also use its facilities. Closed mid-Oct–end-Mar. **www.hotelsplendido.com**

**PORTOVENERE Genio** €€

*Piazza Bastreri 8, 19025* ***Tel*** *0187 79 06 11* ***Fax*** *0187 79 06 11* ***Rooms*** *7*

A cosy, simple but quaint, family-run hotel in a unique location built into the ivy-clad ancient castle wall. It is on several levels with little terraces and sea views. A hotel since 1813, it has plenty of character, near the old ramparts and church of St Peter. Closed mid-Jan–mid-Feb. **www.hotelgenioportovenere.com**

**RAPALLO Hotel Stella** €

*Via Aurelia Ponente 6, 16035* ***Tel*** *0185 503 67* ***Fax*** *0185 27 28 37* ***Rooms*** *28*

This small, pink hotel lies in the centre of Rapallo, close to the beach and seafront promenade. The rooms are bright and quaint. The hotel, which is housed in a turn-of-the-20th-century Genoese-style building, also has a sun terrace on the fifth floor, a small bar and a garage. Closed mid-Jan–end-Feb. **www.hotelstella-riviera.com**

**RAPALLO Hotel Italia e Lido** €€

*Lungomare Castello 1, 16035* ***Tel*** *0185 504 92* ***Fax*** *0185 504 94* ***Rooms*** *50*

A perfect spot between Portofino and the Cinque Terre, this hotel overlooks the promenade, old medieval castle and the Gulf of Tigullio. Bask in the sun on the terrace at the water's edge. Make sure that you book a room with a sea view. Closed Nov–Christmas. **www.italiaelido.com**

**SAN REMO Hotel Nazionale** €€

*Corso Matteotti 3, 18038* ***Tel*** *0184 5[illegible] 75 [illegible]* ***Rooms*** *[illegible]*

In the heart of San Remo and only minutes away from the sea, the shops and the casino, the Nazionale offers a high level of traditional service with a quality restaurant. Rooms are classically furnished; most feature a balcony and many have sea views. Staff are attentive and friendly. **www.hotelnazionalesanremo.com**

**SAN REMO Royal Hotel** €€€€

*Corso Imperatrice 80, 18038* ***Tel*** *0184 53 91* ***Fax*** *0184 661 445* ***Rooms*** *126*

This grand dame of a hotel on the seafront is renowned for its gardens and its three exceptional restaurants. It offers outstanding service and facilities, including Internet access, outdoor swimming pool, sunbeds at the lido, reading rooms, tennis courts, hairdressers and much more. Closed Nov–Feb. **www.royalhotelsanremo.com**

### SESTRI LEVANTE Grand Hotel dei Castelli €€€€

*Via Penisola di Levante 26, 16039* ***Tel*** *0185 48 70 20* ***Fax*** *0185 447 67* ***Rooms*** *50*

A truly beautiful hotel lovingly converted from an old castle. The old style rooms have modern decor and furniture, Moorish-style mosaics, marble and pillars. Set above the peninsula in a park, overlooking the bay, it has winding staircases, a private beach and a sun terrace on the roof. Closed mid-Oct–Mar. **www.hoteldeicastelli.com**

### VENTIMIGLIA La Riserva €€€

*Località Peidaigo 71, località Castel d'Appio, 18039* ***Tel*** *0184 22 95 33* ***Fax*** *0184 22 97 12* ***Rooms*** *19*

Located in a village above Ventimiglia, just 5 km (3 miles) from the French border, this hotel offers rooms and suites with panoramic views over both the Italian riviera and the Côte d'Azur. There is a pool, a small fitness centre, Wi-Fi throughout, and a shuttle bus into Ventimiglia. Closed Oct–Easter. **www.lariserva.it**

## EMILIA-ROMAGNA

### BOLOGNA Centrale €€

*Via della Zecca 2, 40121* ***Tel*** *051 225 114* ***Fax*** *051 235 162* ***Rooms*** *25*

On the third floor of a noble palazzo, on a side street minutes from the main square, this small, popular pensione-hotel has lovely clean rooms, some with charming views. Not all have en suite bathrooms or air conditioning, though all have satellite TV and telephone. A good central option. **www.albergocentralebologna.it**

### BOLOGNA Touring €€€

*Via De Mattuiani 1–2, 40124* ***Tel*** *051 584 305* ***Fax*** *051 334 763* ***Rooms*** *38*

A charming, well-run hotel in a quiet and picturesque area of the city. Public rooms are cheerful and welcoming, bedrooms are compact but smart, and some have views. The rooftop terrace, where breakfast is served in summer, has a little Jacuzzi set amidst flowerpots. Disabled access and bicycles available. **www.hoteltouring.it**

### BOLOGNA De Commercianti €€€€

*Via De'Pignattari 11, 40124* ***Tel*** *051 745 75 11* ***Fax*** *051 745 75 22* ***Rooms*** *36*

In the heart of the city, just off Piazza Maggiore, this historic building dates from the 12th century. Delightful bedrooms and suites, some with wooden beams or frescoes, others with a private terrace overlooking the church of San Petronio. Prices surge during the trade fairs. Bicycles and Internet access available. **www.bolognarthotels.it**

### COMACCHIO Hotel Gallia €

*Viale Leonardo da Vinci 45, Lido di Spina, 44024* ***Tel*** *0533 33 34 00* ***Fax*** *0533 33 35 00* ***Rooms*** *48*

Set in a beautiful pine wood a short walk from the beach, this modern hotel is the ideal place to enjoy the peace and tranquillity of the area. A good choice for families as the hotel has an indoor games room and a play area for children. Amex and Diners credit cards are not accepted. **www.hotelgallia.it**

### FAENZA Hotel Vittoria €€

*Corso G Garibaldi 23, 48018* ***Tel*** *0546 215 08* ***Fax*** *0546 291 36* ***Rooms*** *50*

In the centre of the town famed internationally for its ceramics ware, faience, the Vittoria has been a hotel since 1861. A Liberty-style building, elegant public rooms, frescoed ceilings, marble, tiles and antiques. Bedrooms and suites combine the old and the new. There is a garden and a good restaurant. **www.hotel-vittoria.com**

### FERRARA Europa €€€

*Corso Giovecca 49, 44100* ***Tel*** *0532 20 54 56* ***Fax*** *0532 21 21 20* ***Rooms*** *43*

A central position near the Castello Estense, Giuseppe Verdi was a regular guest at this charming hostelry. Rooms vary, some have frescoes and are furnished with antiques; others are plainer. There is a pretty patio garden and a beautiful frescoed drawing room. Disabled access rooms and apartments are available. **www.hoteleuropaferrara.com**

### FERRARA Ripagrande €€€

*Via Ripagrande 21, 44100* ***Tel*** *0532 76 52 50* ***Fax*** *0532 76 43 77* ***Rooms*** *40*

This converted 15th-century palazzo offers comfortable lodgings in the medieval heart of the city. Rooms are fairly spacious, traditionally decorated and with air conditioning, while the adjacent restaurant has a reputation for well-crafted local cuisine. Call ahead to reserve one of only four covered parking spaces. **www.ripagrandehotel.it**

### MODENA Hotel Cervetta 5 €€

*Via Cervetta 5, 41100* ***Tel*** *059 23 84 47* ***Fax*** *059 23 72 09* ***Rooms*** *22*

This central hotel is just a few steps from the cathedral. The use of white throughout gives it a clean, modern and spacious feel. Although the hotel doesn't have a designated garage, the staff can give you a pass to park nearby for free. The Wi-Fi connection is an added bonus. **www.hotelcervetta5.com**

### MODENA Canalgrande €€€

*Corso Canalgrande 6, 41100* ***Tel*** *059 21 71 60* ***Fax*** *059 22 16 74* ***Rooms*** *69*

A 16th-century patrician villa, set within a beautiful park just beyond the centre of town. The public areas have enchanting frescoes and Neo-Classical decor. The bedrooms are spacious, elegant and comfortable. The gardens are particularly pleasant for sunbathing or relaxing and the restaurant is highly regarded. **www.canalgrandehotel.it**

**Key to Price Guide** *see p558* **Key to Symbols** *see back cover flap*

### PARMA Brenta €

*Via GB Borghesi 12, 43100* ***Tel*** *0521 20 80 93* ***Fax*** *0521 20 80 94* ***Rooms*** *15*

A small, family hotel with friendly owners. Rooms are comfortable and en suite but without air conditioning – a good night's sleep is the priority. Double rooms face an internal courtyard, single rooms face a narrow street. Guide service and bicycles available. **www.hotelbrenta.it**

### PARMA Albergo Park Hotel Stendhal €€€

*Via GB Bodoni 3, 43100* ***Tel*** *0521 20 80 57* ***Fax*** *0521 28 56 55* ***Rooms*** *62*

In a very central position, a short walk from Piazza della Pilotta, this hotel is now part of the Italian Jolly chain. Public areas and bedrooms are very elegant, a mixture of the old and new, with wooden parquet floors. The hotel is popular with business travellers. **www.hotelstendhal.it**

### PIACENZA Ostello di Don Zermani €

*Via Zoni 38, 29100* ***Tel*** *0523 71 23 19* ***Fax*** *0523 71 23 19* ***Rooms*** *16*

A very pleasant hostel with beds available in private singles, doubles and family rooms, some with en suite bathrooms, as well as in shared dorms. Set in an oasis of green in the west of the city, it is popular with families. Breakfasts and evening meals served in the dining room. Excellent value. **www.ostellodipiacenza.it**

### PIACENZA Grande Albergo Roma €€€

*Via Cittadella 14, 29100* ***Tel*** *0523 32 32 01* ***Fax*** *0523 33 05 48* ***Rooms*** *76*

Located in the heart of old Piacenza, facing Piazza Cavalli, this is the city's grandest hotel. Public areas and bedrooms are spacious, and luxuriously decorated in *belle époque* style. Four apartments are available. Delightful terrace with bar, where breakfast is served, as well as a good restaurant. There are also bikes to rent. **www.grandealbergoroma.it**

### PORTICO DI ROMAGNA Al Vecchio Convento €

*Via Roma 7, 47010* ***Tel*** *054 396 70 53* ***Fax*** *054 396 71 57* ***Rooms*** *15*

On the Tuscan-Emilia Romagna border, this family owned hotel, in a 19th-century ex-convent, has an excellent restaurant and cooking school. The rooms have cherry or walnut furniture and wrought-iron beds. In summer, guests can eat breakfast in the lovely little garden. **www.vecchioconvento.it**

### RAVENNA Centrale Byron €€

*Via IV Novembre 14, 48100* ***Tel*** *0544 21 22 25* ***Fax*** *0544 341 14* ***Rooms*** *54*

This hotel is particularly popular with families. Economy or standard rooms are available – from doubles to quadruples. Although both types of room are equally comfortable, the standard rooms are bigger and with slightly nicer furnishing and decor. **www.hotelbyron.com**

### RAVENNA Hotel Diana €€

*Via Girolamo Rossi 47, 48100* ***Tel*** *0544 391 64* ***Fax*** *0544 300 01* ***Rooms*** *33*

A yellow-painted 18th-century villa with friendly service in an excellent, quiet location, near the tomb of Galla Placidia. Standard, superior or deluxe bedooms are available (the latter have broadband Internet access and minibar). The lobby is discreet and welcoming. Car park nearby. Bicycles are available. **www.hoteldiana.ra.it**

### RAVENNA Albergo Cappello €€€

*Via IV Novembre 41, 48100* ***Tel*** *0544 21 98 13* ***Fax*** *0544 21 98 14* ***Rooms*** *7*

Extremely central, on a pedestrianized street, this small boutique hotel is Ravenna's prettiest, though bedrooms are fairly small. Each bedroom has been individually styled and furnished with antiques. Renowned restaurant and wine bar. Non-smoking rooms/disabled access. **www.albergocappello.it**

### REGGIO EMILIA Hotel Posta €€

*Piazza del Monte 2, 42100* ***Tel*** *0522 43 29 44* ***Fax*** *0522 45 26 02* ***Rooms*** *38*

In the heart of old Reggio Emilia, the former Palazzo del Capitano del Popolo, and a hotel for over 500 years. Charming and family run, with professional staff. Standard double or superior rooms and one suite. The hotel's annexe, Albergo Reggio, has lower priced rooms with kitchenette. Bicycles are available. **www.hotelposta.re.it**

### RIMINI Esedra Hotel €

*Viale Caio Duilio 3, 47900* ***Tel*** *0541 234 21* ***Fax*** *0541 244 24* ***Rooms*** *47*

A charming Liberty style (Italian Art Nouveau) villa set in a pretty garden at Marina Centro, not far from Rimini's lively seafront. The hotel has a private beach and a small pool with a Jacuzzi. Bedrooms are simple but comfortable, with modern facilities. Apartments are also available, sleeping up to four people. **www.esedrahotel.com**

### RIMINI Hotel Card €€

*Via Dante Alighieri 50, 47900* ***Tel*** *0541 261 12* ***Fax*** *0541 543 74* ***Rooms*** *54*

A friendly little family-run hotel, extremely convenient for the railway station and exploring Rimini's lively old town. Bedrooms are very clean, with good, family-sized rooms available. No air conditioning (fans on request) and not all rooms en suite. A fine budget option. **www.hotelcard.it**

### RIMINI Le Meridien Rimini €€€

*Viale Lungomare Murri 13, 47900* ***Tel*** *0541 39 66 00* ***Fax*** *0541 39 66 01* ***Rooms*** *111*

A resort hotel designed by Italian architect Paolo Portoghesi. This stylish building is right on the beach, and is beautifully appointed with large, airy bedrooms – some interconnecting – perfect for families. Superior/deluxe rooms have sea views and terraces. Fashionable bar and fish restaurant. **www.lemeridien.com/rimini**

### SANTARCANGELO DI ROMAGNA Hotel della Porta €€

*Via Andrea Costa 85, 47822* **Tel** *0541 62 21 52* **Fax** *0541 62 21 68* **Rooms** *22*

In a medieval village inland from Rimini, this hotel has a little courtyard and garden with a terrace. Public rooms and bedrooms are charming, some with frescoes and antiques. Bedrooms have names such as Bluebell and Grapefruit. Non-smoking and disabled-access rooms available. The annexe rooms are more modern. **www.hoteldellaporta.com**

### SORAGNA Locanda del Lupo €€€

*Via Garibaldi 64, 43019* **Tel** *0524 59 71 00* **Fax** *0524 59 70 66* **Rooms** *45*

In a very quiet spot 30 km (18 miles) outside Parma, this small inn has a renowned restaurant with tables outside in a lovely courtyard during the summer. Public rooms have antiques, 18th-century fireplaces and wooden beams; bedrooms are equally charming. There is a relaxing sun terrace. **www.locandadellupo.com**

## FLORENCE

### Il Bargellino €

*Via Guelfa 87, 50129* **Tel** *055 238 26 58* **Fax** *055 21 21 90* **Rooms** *10* **Map** *1 C4*

This ten-room hotel has a vast plant-filled terrace on the first floor where guests can take breakfast in the summer. Just five minutes from the station, but a million light years away from the city bustle. Book early if you want one of the four rooms overlooking the terrace. **www.ilbargellino.com**

### Istituto Gould €

*Via dei Serragli 49, 50100* **Tel** *Tel: 055 21 25 76* **Fax** *055 28 02 74* **Rooms** *39* **Map** *3 B2*

The combination of unbelievably low rates with their contribution to a good cause (disadvantaged children), makes it easier to fully appreciate this sparsely furnished hostel-like outfit. The rooms are spotless, and the gardens make for a very attractive view. Ideal for those who want safety and comfort on a tight budget. **www.istitutogould.it**

### Locanda Orchidea €

*Via Borgo degli Albizzi 11, 50122* **Tel/Fax** *055 248 03 46* **Rooms** *7* **Map** *6 F3*

For those on a tight budget, this small, split-level *locanda* in a 12th-century palazzo in the centre of Florence is hard to beat. The English-speaking hosts are happy to direct you to Piazza della Signoria, Santa Croce or the Duomo – all are only a five-minute walk away. Rooms at the back are quieter. **www.hotelorchideaflorence.it**

### Cestelli €€

*Borgo Santi Apostoli 25, 50123* **Tel** *055 21 42 13* **Fax** *055 21 42 13* **Rooms** *8* **Map** *3 C1*

This eight-room hotel in a 15th-century building round the corner from Piazza Santa Trinità has been extensively refurbished, but the parquet floors in the three rooms that have a private bath are 17th-century originals. No breakfast, the hosts provide a list of their favourite local bars and cafés. **www.hotelcestelli.com**

### Dei Mori Bed & Breakfast €€

*Via D Alighieri 12, 50122* **Tel** *055 21 14 38* **Fax** *055 238 22 16* **Rooms** *5* **Map** *4 D1*

This well-appointed, clean and cosy guesthouse opened for business in 1996, and was the first in Florence. A dimly lit stairway leads to spacious, well-decorated rooms; all fittings in the (small) bathrooms are new. The rooms overlook a quiet courtyard. **www.deimori.com**

### Della Robbia €€

*Via dei Della Robbia 7/9, 50132* **Tel** *055 263 85 70* **Fax** *055 246 63 71* **Rooms** *24*

Just the other side of the *viale* (boulevard) that marks the edge of the old city, and housed in a restored late-19th-century building. Rooms are in the Italian Art Nouveau style called Liberty (a rarity in Florence). There are several suites and an annexe. Walk down Borgo Pinti and you are at Santa Croce. **www.hoteldellarobbia.it**

### Emma €€

*Via A. Pacinotti 20, 50131* **Tel** *055 57 59 01* **Fax** *Fax 055 504 89 14* **Rooms** *9*

There is a home-from-home feel about this nine-room hotel run by a Norwegian woman and her Italian husband. Worth the ten-minute bus ride from Piazza di San Marco. Two rooms overlook the street, the rest overlook the courtyard. There is a small terrace where breakfast can be taken in summer. **www.hotelemma.net**

### Hotel Casci €€

*Via Cavour 13, 50129* **Tel** *055 21 16 86* **Fax** *055 239 64 61* **Rooms** *29* **Map** *2 D4*

Located on the second floor of a 15th-century building in the bustling Via Cavour between the Duomo and San Lorenzo, this family-owned hotel offers large, clean, quiet rooms. The home of composer Gioacchino Rossini in the mid-1850s. Five non-smoking rooms. Free Internet access. **www.hotelcasci.com**

### Silla €€

*Via dè Renai 5, 50126* **Tel** *055 234 28 88* **Fax** *055 234 14 37* **Rooms** *35* **Map** *6 F5*

Located in a 16th-century building, this family-run hotel on the *Oltrarno* side of the river is reached through an elegant courtyard. A grand staircase leads to the entrance of this hotel (also lift). Breakfast is served on the terrace in the summer, overlooking the river and the city. **www.hotelsilla.it**

**Key to Price Guide** *see p558* **Key to Symbols** *see back cover flap*

**Alessandra** €€€

*Borgo Santi Apostoli 17, 50123* **Tel** *055 28 34 38* **Fax** *055 21 06 19* **Rooms** *27* **Map** *5 C3*

Located on second and third floors of a 16th-century building. Rooms overlooking the Arno are larger and cost more: the one suite, with balcony, offers good value for money. The other rooms have views on Piazzetta del Limbo and the church of the Santi Apostoli. **www.hotelalessandra.com**

**Firenze** €€€

*Piazza dei Donati 4 (Via del Corso), 50133* **Tel** *055 21 42 03* **Fax** *055 21 23 70* **Rooms** *57* **Map** *2 D5*

This 57-room hotel is an excellent budget option. The decor is fairly sparse but all the essentials are here. There are also several large rooms, accommodating up to four people. Quiet location in a tiny side street off the pedestrianized Via del Corso. **www.hotelfirenze-fi.it**

**Grand Hotel Minerva** €€€

*Piazza Santa Maria Novella 16, 50123* **Tel** *055 272 30* **Fax** *055 26 82 81* **Rooms** *102* **Map** *1 B5*

The only hotel in Florence to have a rooftop swimming pool. Watching the sunset from here or from the adjacent bar, is a totally memorable experience. This hotel has welcomed a long line of famous guests, including Henry James. Family suites have two bathrooms. **www.grandhotelminerva.com**

**Hermitage** €€€

*Vicolo Marzio 1, 50122* **Tel** *055 28 72 16* **Fax** *055 21 22 08* **Rooms** *28* **Map** *6 D4*

This hotel is on four floors of a medieval tower: the reception and common areas are on the fifth floor; the roof-garden on the sixth offers a panoramic view of the Vasari Corridor, the Ponte Vecchio, the Arno and beyond. Rooms facing the Duomo are quieter. **www.hermitagehotel.com**

**Hotel Botticelli** €€€

*Via Taddea 8, 50123* **Tel** *055 29 09 05* **Fax** *055 29 43 22* **Rooms** *34* **Map** *1 C4*

Located in a 16th-century building, the Botticelli boasts frescoed vaulted ceilings as well as a covered porch with spectacular views of the domes of the Duomo and San Lorenzo. Its location close to the San Lorenzo market, in the historic centre, is another bonus. **www.hotelbotticelli.it**

**Hotel Davanzati** €€€

*Via Porta Rossa 5, 50123* **Tel** *055 28 66 66* **Fax** *055 265 82 52* **Rooms** *21* **Map** *5 C3*

Five-star service on a three-star budget awaits at this restored Renaissance palazzo. The hotel is run by the Fuzier Cayla family, who take great care that their guests' every need is met. Rooms are sympathetically converted but still crisp and modern, and each comes with a free loan of a laptop and Internet access. **www.hoteldavanzati.it**

**Hotel Villa Belvedere** €€€

*Via Bernardo Castelli 3, 50124* **Tel** *055 22 25 01* **Fax** *055 22 31 63* **Rooms** *26* **Map** *3 A5*

Located at Poggio Imperiale, on the first hill outside the Porta Romana gate, to the south of the city, this spacious 1930s villa, with 1950s additions, is set in landscaped gardens. The views of the hills as well as of the city, are especially fine from the first-floor terraces. Elegantly furnished rooms. **www.villa-belvedere.com**

**Loggiato dei Serviti** €€€

*Via dei Servi 49 (Piazza Santissima Annunziata 3), 50122* **Tel** *055 28 95 92* **Fax** *055 28 95 95* **Rooms** *39* **Map** *2 D4*

Built in the 16th-century by the Padri Serviti order to house travelling prelates. A mirror-image of Brunelleschi's Spedale degli Innocenti across the square. All the rooms are different. Rooms overlook either the piazza or the garden of the Accademia delle Belle Arti. Advanced booking essential. **www.loggiatodeiservitihotel.it**

**Morandi alla Crocetta** €€€

*Via Laura 50, 50121* **Tel** *055 234 47 47* **Fax** *055 248 09 54* **Rooms** *10* **Map** *2 E4*

Just ten rooms and an established reputation mean that advanced reservations are essential. Stairs to the reception on the first floor where all the rooms are located. Three overlook the courtyard, the rest the street. Rooms are all furnished in different styles. No night porter; if you go out, you take the keys with you. **www.hotelmorandi.it**

**Orto dei Medici** €€€

*Via San Gallo 30, 50129* **Tel** *055 48 34 27* **Fax** *055 46 12 76* **Rooms** *42* **Map** *2 D4*

Ten minutes on foot from the Duomo, and five from Piazza San Marco and the Accademia, this mid-19th century building has large frescoed common rooms. A delightful flower-filled terrace overlooks San Marco. All rooms non-smoking. Four rooms on the fourth floor afford views of the Duomo and San Lorenzo. **www.ortodeimedici.it**

**Palazzo Benci** €€€

*Piazza Madonna Aldobrandini 3, Via Faenza 6/r, 50123* **Tel** *055 21 38 48* **Fax** *055 28 83 08* **Rooms** *35* **Map** *1 C5*

This 16th-century palazzo, with a beautiful courtyard garden, belongs to the Benci family. Contemporary furnishings set off the original features, carefully restored in 1989. All rooms are double-glazed, and those at the back overlook the Medici Chapels. Price includes breakfast. **www.palazzobenci.com**

**Pitti Palace** €€€

*Borgo San Jacopo 3, 50125* **Tel** *055 239 87 11* **Fax** *055 239 88 67* **Rooms** *72* **Map** *3 C1*

As close to the Ponte Vecchio as one can be, this modern hotel has two terraces (on the sixth floor) with splendid views over the city, especially into the Boboli Gardens. Small and functional but well priced for such a convenient location. Most of the rooms are on the first to the fifth floors, with one on the seventh. **www.vivahotels.com**

**Tourist House Ghiberti** €€€

*Via M Bufalini 1, 50122* ***Tel*** *055 28 48 58* ***Fax*** *055 26 41 70* ***Rooms*** *5* ***Map*** *6 E2*

Close to the Duomo this B&B has an airy, modern feel. Rooms are spacious and simply decorated with mosaics in the Florentine style. One of the communal areas includes a Jacuzzi and sauna for weary sightseers. Each room has an LCD TV and computer, and Wi-Fi is free throughout. **www.touristhouseghiberti.com**

**Roma** €€€€

*Piazza Santa Maria Novella 8, 50123* ***Tel*** *055 21 03 66* ***Fax*** *055 21 53 06* ***Rooms*** *57* ***Map*** *1 B5*

This large hotel features many elegant touches such as marble floors, wood panelling and intriguing stained-glass works by Galileo and Tito Chini. Rooms on five floors, four on each floor face the piazza. These rooms are larger but can be very noisy. **www.hotelromaflorence.com**

**Serristori Palace Residence** €€€€

*Lungarno Serristori 13, 50125* ***Tel*** *055 200 16 23* ***Fax*** *055 234 78 28* ***Rooms*** *12* ***Map*** *6 F5*

This is the perfect spot if you wish to stay in peaceful and stylishly furnished apartments a short hop from the centre of the city. It's set on a busy road but there are spectacular views from some apartments across the river to the Duomo. There's a relaxation room in the cellar with a bar and TV. **www.serristoripalace.com**

**Torre di Bellosguardo** €€€€

*2.5 km (1.5 miles) SW Florence. Via Roti Michelozzi 2, 50124* ***Tel*** *055 229 81 45* ***Fax*** *055 22 90 08* ***Rooms*** *16*

The views of the city from the beautiful gardens of this 14th-century villa, with 16th-century tower, are unparalleled. Indoors it is equally breathtaking with vast public areas and huge rooms; antique furniture and Persian carpets. There is a landscaped pool and fitness centre. **www.torrebellosguardo.com**

**Balestri** €€€€€

*Piazza Mentana 7, 50122* ***Tel*** *055 21 47 43* ***Fax*** *055 239 80 42* ***Rooms*** *51* ***Map*** *4 D1*

Located in a little piazza on the riverfront halfway between the Ponte Vecchio and Santa Croce, this hotel has been in business since 1888. Extensively renovated, rooms all have mini-bars. Thirty rooms face the Arno, the rest overlook a quiet courtyard. Close to the Museum of the History of Science. **www.hotel-balestri.it**

**Excelsior** €€€€€

*Piazza Ognissanti 3, 50123* ***Tel*** *055 271 51* ***Fax*** *055 21 02 78* ***Rooms*** *171* ***Map*** *5 A2*

The Excelsior is a wealth of marble floors and columns, grand staircases, stained-glass windows, statues and period paintings. The rooms are equally opulent, and the service impeccable. The restaurant Il Cestello serves Tuscan and international cuisine; the ground-floor terrace provides splendid views. **www.westin.com/excelsiorflorence**

**Four Seasons Hotel** €€€€€

*Borgo Pinti 99, 50121* ***Tel*** *055 262 62 50* ***Fax*** *055 262 65 00* ***Rooms*** *116* ***Map*** *2 E4*

Florence's biggest hotel opening in years followed a redevelopment that included the restoration of original 15th-century frescoes. Ultra-luxe rooms and suites, fine dining and an in-house spa have already established the Four Seasons as the city's number-one hotel. Business needs are catered for, too. **www.fourseasons.com/florence**

**Grand Hotel Villa Medici** €€€€€

*Via Il Prato 42, 50123* ***Tel*** *055 238 13 31* ***Fax*** *055 238 13 36* ***Rooms*** *100* ***Map*** *1 A4*

This 18th-century villa conversion is the only hotel within the city limits to have an open-air pool in its own gardens. Rooms furnished with antiques. A fitness club includes sauna and Turkish bath. Located by Porta al Prato, it is within walking distance of the centre of town. **www.villamedicihotel.com**

**Helvetia & Bristol** €€€€€

*Via dei Pescioni 2, 50123* ***Tel*** *055 266 51* ***Fax*** *055 28 83 53* ***Rooms*** *67* ***Map*** *5 C2*

If old-fashioned luxury is your thing, this sumptuous palazzo by Via de' Tornabuoni ticks all the boxes. Individually decorated rooms are embellished with period furniture. Liveried doormen, a winter garden and a refined restaurant complete the *belle époque* splendour. Check the website for occasional discounts. **www.royaldemeure.com**

**JK Place** €€€€€

*Piazza Santa Maria Novella 7, 50123* ***Tel*** *055 264 51 81* ***Fax*** *055 265 83 87* ***Rooms*** *20* ***Map*** *5 B2*

Neo-Classical inspiration, a modern yet aristocratic interior design and award-winning architecture make staying at JK Place an unforgettable experience. Rooms are warmer than the sleek monochrome public spaces would lead you to imagine, and they are equipped as you'd expect for a high-end hotel. **www.jkplace.com**

**Palazzo Niccolini al Duomo** €€€€€

*Via dei Servi 2, 50122* ***Tel*** *055 28 24 12* ***Fax*** *055 29 09 79* ***Rooms*** *10* ***Map*** *2 D5*

In a prime location directly facing the Duomo, this 16th-century palazzo is run by descendants of the original owners. Reception and rooms are on the second floor. Public rooms have paintings and antiques. Rooms have marble bathrooms. The living room of the suite has a unique view of Brunelleschi's dome. **www.niccolinidomepalace.com**

**Savoy** €€€€€

*Piazza della Repubblica 7, 50123* ***Tel*** *055 273 51/28 33 13* ***Fax*** *055 273 58 88* ***Rooms*** *102* ***Map*** *6 D3*

Architecturally magnificent, lavish interiors, elegantly appointed rooms with 14 suites (two of which have a *hammam*). The sixth-floor gym has spectacular views of the Duomo and Giotto's *campanile*. The L'Incontro bar on the piazza is a rendezvous point for the Florentines. **www.hotelsavoy.it**

**Key to Price Guide** *see p558* **Key to Symbols** *see back cover flap*

# TUSCANY

## AREZZO Hotel Il Patio €€€

*Via Cavour 23, 52100* ***Tel*** *0575 40 19 62* ***Fax*** *0575 274 18* ***Rooms*** *10*

Charismatic hotel in an 18th-century palazzo on Arezzo's antique shop-lined Via Cavour within just a few metres of the Chiesa di San Francesco. Each room is decorated to reflect the travels of author Bruce Chatwin (China, Australia, Morocco and so on). **www.hotelpatio.it**

## AREZZO Vogue €€€

*Via Guido Monaco 54, 52100* ***Tel*** *0575 243 61* ***Fax*** *0575 243 62* ***Rooms*** *26*

A lovely boutique hotel in walking distance from the church of San Francesco. Rooms aren't huge, but they come with designer fittings, luxurious bathrooms and modern conveniences such as mood lighting and flat-panel TVs. Pets are welcome. **www.voguehotel.it**

## ARTIMINO Hotel Paggeria Medicea €€€

*Via Papa Giovanni XXIII 1, 59015* ***Tel*** *0558 751 41* ***Fax*** *0558 75 14 70* ***Rooms*** *37*

In the converted servants' quarters of Artimino's famous Medici Villa "La Ferdinanda", this four-star hotel comes complete with original furnishings, wooden-beamed ceilings, terracotta floors and decorative frescoes. It has riding stables, well-reputed restaurant and a farm shop selling local wine and olive oil. **www.artimino.com**

## CASTELLINA IN CHIANTI Colle Etrusco Salivolpi €€

*Via Fiorentina 89, 53011* ***Tel*** *0577 74 04 84* ***Fax*** *0577 74 09 98* ***Rooms*** *19*

An elegant country-house hotel surrounded by vineyards, olive groves and cypress trees within walking distance of Castellina in Chianti. The rooms are warmly decorated with authentic Tuscan furniture with wrought-iron beds, terracotta floors and wooden beams. Large lounge room and garden. **www.hotelsalivolpi.com**

## CASTELLINA IN CHIANTI Tenuta di Ricavo €€€

*Loc. Scotoni, 53011* ***Tel*** *0577 74 02 21* ***Fax*** *0577 74 10 14* ***Rooms*** *22*

A charming resort hotel in a restored medieval hamlet in the middle of a natural park. The Tenuta di Ricavo offers a unique combination of history and nature. Bedrooms contain parts of the original furnishings, including stone, terracotta tiles and wooden beams. Gourmet restaurant the Pecora Nera. Closed Oct–Easter. **www.ricavo.com**

## CORTONA Hotel Italia €€

*Via Ghibellina 5–7, 52044* ***Tel*** *0575 63 02 54* ***Fax*** *0575 60 57 63* ***Rooms*** *26*

Just off the main square of medieval Cortona, this hotel is located in an old palace dating back to the 1600s. Though no longer a family-run establishment, the service is exceedingly personalized and friendly. The large room terrace has panoramic views over the Chiana valley and Lake Trasimeno. **www.planhotel.com**

## CORTONA Relais San Pietro in Polvano €€€

*Loc. Polvano 3, 52043, Castiglion Fiorentino* ***Tel*** *0575 65 01 00* ***Fax*** *0575 65 02 55* ***Rooms*** *10*

This delightful 17th-century farmhouse is in an idyllic hilltop position overlooking a valley. A family-run establishment, every detail is well thought out and it is the perfect place for those seeking a quiet retreat. Dinner is served on the terrace in summer months. Their breakfast of fresh fruits, cheeses and cakes is recommended. **www.polvano.com**

## CORTONA Villa Marsili €€€

*Viale Cesare Battisti 13, 52044* ***Tel*** *0575 60 52 52* ***Fax*** *0575 60 56 18* ***Rooms*** *27*

This 18th-century villa-turned-hotel enjoys endless views over the Valdichiana from its perch by Cortona's town gate. The interior decor is sophisticated and tasteful, in both public areas and the spacious, elegant guest rooms, and the terrace is a charming spot. Babysitting service available. **www.villamarsili.net**

## ELBA Hotel Montecristo €€

*Lungomare Nomelli 11, Campo nell'Elba, 57034* ***Tel*** *0565 97 68 61* ***Fax*** *0565 97 65 97* ***Rooms*** *43*

Simply furnished four-star hotel with stunning poolside terrace and views across the bay of Marina di Campo. Steps from the hotel lead down to the sandy beach and to the adjacent pine forest. Some rooms have sea views. Pool side restaurant and spa and wellbeing centre. **www.hotelmontecristo.it**

## ELBA Hotel Ilio €€€

*Via Sant'Andrea 5, Loc. S.Andrea, Marciana, 57030* ***Tel*** *0565 90 80 18* ***Fax*** *0565 90 80 87* ***Rooms*** *20*

Fabulous boutique hotel located on the edge of a natural park. Rooms are named after local flora such as oleander, geranium and pomegranate. The beach is a short walk away. The owners organize nature walks around the park. Restaurant serves Elban dishes, using local fish and vegetables. **www.ilio.it**

## ELBA Hotel Hermitage €€€€€

*Loc. La Biodola, Portoferraio, 57037* ***Tel*** *0565 97 40* ***Fax*** *0565 96 99 84* ***Rooms*** *130*

Elba's most luxurious hotel and in the island's most exclusive bay, the Hermitage has its own private beach of golden sand, three pools, three restaurants, a piano bar, a six-hole golf course and nine tennis courts. Accommodation is split between the main building and smaller cottages. Three-day minimum stay. **www.hotelhermitage.it**

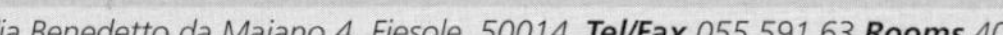

### FIESOLE Pensione Bencista' €€€

*Via Benedetto da Maiano 4, Fiesole, 50014* ***Tel/Fax*** *055 591 63* ***Rooms*** *40*

Recent additions to this 14th-century villa include a lift and some larger rooms. Although half-board is optional, the place is so welcoming and the views so lovely, that people are happy to stick around. Lots of return visitors, so it is advisable to book well in advance. **www.bencista.com**

### FIESOLE Villa San Michele €€€€€

*Via Doccia 4, Fiesole, 50014* ***Tel*** *055 567 82 00* ***Fax*** *055 567 82 50* ***Rooms*** *46*

Standing in its own grounds, Villa San Michele boasts spectacular views, the best being from the loggia, where dinner is served in summer. Ask for a room overlooking the city. The terrace of the upper-level suite is ideal for a candlelit dinner. The lower suite has a garden. Closed end-Nov–mid-Mar. **www.villasanmichele.orient-express.com**

### GAIOLE IN CHIANTI Residence San Sano €€

*Loc San Sano 21, 53100* ***Tel*** *0577 74 61 30* ***Fax*** *0577 74 68 91* ***Rooms*** *16*

A hotel-restaurant in a renovated 13th-century watch house. Up the ancient stairway, the rooms are charming with whitewashed walls and wooden-beamed ceilings. A three-course menu of Tuscan specialities is served under the restaurant's stone arches, with a garden terrace for the summer months. **www.sansanohotel.it**

### GAIOLE IN CHIANTI Castello di Spaltenna €€€

*Loc. Spaltenna, 53013* ***Tel*** *0577 74 94 83* ***Fax*** *0577 74 92 69* ***Rooms*** *30 rooms and 8 suites*

In an ancient feudal hamlet with splendid medieval church and belltower, this beautiful converted monastery has fabulous views over the vineyard-covered valley. Rooms are luxurious with four-poster beds, large lounge areas and Jacuzzis. Gourmet restaurant. Horse-riding by arrangement. **www.spaltenna.it**

### LUCCA Piccolo Hotel Puccini €€

*Via di Poggio 9, 55100* ***Tel*** *0583 554 21* ***Fax*** *0583 534 87* ***Rooms*** *14*

A small, friendly hotel in an attractive stone building in the very heart of Lucca, just over the road from the house in which Giacomo Puccini was born (now a museum) and the busy central square of San Michele. The rooms are small but well priced for the location. Courtesy car to airport and train station. **www.hotelpuccini.com**

### LUCCA Locanda L'Elisa €€€

*Via Nuova per Pisa 1952, Massa Pisana, 55050* ***Tel*** *0583 37 97 37* ***Fax*** *0583 37 90 19* ***Rooms*** *10*

Five-star accommodation in an 18th-century stately home, this elegant Relais & Châteaux hotel stands at the bottom of a range of hills close to Lucca. The luxury rooms are spacious with lounge areas full of antique furnishings, paintings and draperies. A popular choice for a romantic break. **www.locandalelisa.it**

### LUCCA Villa Romantica €€€

*Via Barbaranti 246, 55100* ***Tel*** *0583 49 68 72* ***Fax*** *0583 95 76 00* ***Rooms*** *6*

A quiet 1800s villa just outside Lucca's city walls. This small hotel has only four double rooms, one suite and one junior suite. Each furnished in a modern way sympathetic with the building's Liberty style. The suite has a four-poster bed and large living space. Large garden of mature trees. Tennis courts. **www.villaromantica.it**

### LUCCA San Luca Palace €€€€

*Via San Paolino 103, 55010* ***Tel*** *0583 31 74 46* ***Fax*** *0583 58 30 85* ***Rooms*** *26*

This beautiful Renaissance palazzo plays host to modern leisure lodgings and business facilities. The San Luca Palace has raised the level of comfort inside the town walls. Rooms (most of them suites) are spacious and come with modern conveniences such as air conditioning and flat-panel TVs. **www.sanlucapalace.com**

### MONTALCINO Porta Castellana €

*Via Santa Lucia, 53024* ***Tel/Fax*** *0577 83 90 01* ***Rooms*** *3*

This romantic B&B, housed inside a former mill and storehouse, is a short walk downhill from Montalcino's main drag. Immaculately converted large rooms retain their exposed brick vaults, and are enhanced by stylish modern furniture. There's a knockout terrace for summer breakfasts overlooking the Val d'Orcia. **www.portacastellana.it**

### PIENZA Chiostro di Pienza €€€

*Corso Rossellino 26, 53026* ***Tel*** *0578 74 84 00* ***Fax*** *0578 74 84 40* ***Rooms*** *37*

You could hardly sleep closer to Piazza Pio II than at this converted monastery in the heart of Pienza. Rooms are traditionally furnished (some with terracotta floors) and set round an atmospheric cloister. The pool, restaurant and garden are perched on a terrace at the back surveying the glorious Val d'Orcia. **www.relaisilchoistrodipienza.com**

### PISA Hotel Francesco €€

*Via Santa Maria 129, 56126* ***Tel*** *050 55 54 53* ***Fax*** *050 55 61 45* ***Rooms*** *13*

A small, welcoming hotel within walking distance of the Leaning Tower of Pisa, the terrace of this three-star hotel offers some beautiful views over the city. The rooms are clean, bright and minimally furnished; non-smoking rooms are available on request. It is also possible to rent scooters and bikes. **www.hotelfrancesco.com**

### PISA Novecento €€

*Via Roma 37, 56126* ***Tel*** *050 50 03 23* ***Fax*** *050 220 91 63* ***Rooms*** *10*

This shuttered colonial villa close to Pisa's botanical garden is a good-value, stylish addition to the city's hotel scene. The chaos of Piazza del Campo is just a few minutes' walk away, but you'd never know it in the quiet, air-conditioned (though mostly small) rooms ranged around a leafy courtyard. **www.hotelnovecento.pisa.it**

**Key to Price Guide** *see p558* **Key to Symbols** *see back cover flap*

**PISA Royal Victoria Hotel** €€

*Lungarno Pacinotti 12, 56126* ***Tel*** *050 94 01 11* ***Fax*** *050 94 01 80* ***Rooms*** *48*

In one of Pisa's most historic buildings, the Royal Victoria occupies a 10th-century tower built to house the Wine-maker's Guild. It became Pisa's first hotel in 1837, combining several medieval tower houses in the process. Run by the Piegaja family, the rooms are charming in size and decor. Bike rental and private garage. **www.royalvictoria.it**

**PISA Hotel Relais dell'Orologio** €€€€€

*Via della Faggiola 12/14, 56126* ***Tel*** *050 83 03 61* ***Fax*** *050 55 18 69* ***Rooms*** *21*

Five-star hotel in a renovated manor house with the remains of a 14th-century tower. Rooms are thoughtfully furnished with tartan rugs and curtains, antique furnishings and original fireplaces (some even have Jacuzzis). Breakfast is served in the manor garden and there is a good restaurant. **www.hotelrelaisorologio.com**

**PISTOIA Villa Cappugi** €€

*Via Collegigliato 45, 51100* ***Tel*** *0573 45 02 97* ***Fax*** *0573 45 10 09* ***Rooms*** *70*

Nestled between the town and the hills, this villa hotel with conference facilities makes a great base for touring the area. Rooms are light, spacious, and equipped with LCD TVs, air conditioning and large bathrooms. Bring your sports gear: there are tennis courts and football facilities, too. **www.hotelvillacappugi.com**

**PRATO Hotel Hermitage** €€

*Via Ginepraia 112, Loc. Poggio a Caiano, 59016* ***Tel*** *0558 772 44* ***Fax*** *0558 79 70 57* ***Rooms*** *59*

Located in a quiet residential area near the 15th-century Medicean Villa Ambra, this three-star hotel sits on a hilltop amid parkland. Rooms are simple, but comfortable, some with stunning views. The restaurant serves Tuscan food. A great spot for touring the nearby vineyards. Guests can hire mountain bikes. **www.hotelhermitageprato.it**

**RADDA IN CHIANTI La Locanda** €€€

*Loc. Montanino, 53017* ***Tel*** *0577 73 88 32/33* ***Fax*** *0577 73 92 63* ***Rooms*** *6 rooms and 1 suite*

A small, family-run hotel in a converted 16th-century farmhouse with breathtaking views over the Chianti countryside. A nearby stone building provides a cosy drawing room with bar and dining room. There is a large terrace beside the pool and a large garden. Minimum stay of two nights. **www.lalocanda.it**

**REGELLO I Bonsi** €€€

*Via I Bonsi 47, Località Sant'Agata, 50066* ***Tel*** *0577 28 73 42* ***Fax*** *0577 28 73 42* ***Rooms*** *6 apartments*

A tree-lined avenue leads to a turreted villa built in 1400 and set in parkland overlooking the Arno Valley. In the 17th century it was converted into a convent, but today it is used as a country residence and it is beautifully furnished throughout. Lovely walks in the surrounding area. Minimum stay three nights. **www.agriturismoibonsi.it**

**SAN GIMIGNANO La Cisterna** €€

*Piazza della Cisterna 23, 53037* ***Tel*** *0577 94 03 28* ***Fax*** *0577 94 20 80* ***Rooms*** *50*

In a 14th-century palazzo in the centre of town, La Cisterna has great views over both the main square and the surrounding countryside. Rooms are furnished in traditional Florentine style. The restaurant (open since 1918) is split into two parts – one of which, Loggia Rustica, has gloriously high wooden ceilings. **www.hotelcisterna.it**

**SAN GIMIGNANO La Collegiata** €€€€

*Loc. Strada 27, 53037* ***Tel*** *0577 94 32 01* ***Fax*** *0577 94 05 66* ***Rooms*** *21*

Exclusivity and serenity are the watchwords at this Relais & Châteaux retreat outside San Gimignano. Air-conditioned rooms in the converted 16th-century Capuchin monastery are individually furnished and decorated using traditional Tuscan materials and colours. The gourmet restaurant has a great reputation. Closed Nov–Feb. **www.lacollegiata.it**

**SIENA Antica Torre** €€

*Via di Fiera Vecchia 7, 53100* ***Tel*** *0577 22 22 55* ***Fax*** *0577 22 22 55* ***Rooms*** *8*

A small hotel in a stunning 16th-century tower along Siena's southeast walls. Quiet and romantic rooms are full of character with an old travertine stone staircase, wooden beams, stone arches and original brick vaults. The cosy breakfast room occupies a medieval potter's shop. Free parking. **www.anticatorresiena.it**

**SIENA Hotel Arcobaleno** €€

*Via Fiorentina 32/40, 53100* ***Tel*** *0577 27 10 92* ***Fax*** *0577 27 14 23* ***Rooms*** *19*

A peaceful country villa dating from the mid-1800s converted into a friendly hotel with a terrace and intimate rooms. Located at the city gates, the hotel is ten minutes' walk from Siena's historical centre. It has a romantic evening restaurant accessed via a charming winding stairway. Babysitting facilities. **www.hotelarcobaleno.com**

**SIENA Hotel Chiusarelli** €€

*Viale Curtatone 15, 53100* ***Tel*** *0577 28 05 62* ***Fax*** *0577 27 11 77* ***Rooms*** *48*

Close to Piazza del Campo, this tranquil villa is one of the oldest hotels in town. Built in 1870 by the Chiusarelli family, the rooms are furnished in Neo-Classical style and have views of the church of San Domenico. Ask for a room with a balcony. Generous buffet breakfast served on the veranda. Mountain-bike hire. **www.chiusarelli.com**

**SIENA Hotel Athena** €€€

*Via P Mascagni 55, 53100* ***Tel*** *0577 28 63 13* ***Fax*** *0577 481 53* ***Rooms*** *100*

A four-star modern hotel just a short hop from Siena Duomo, in the quiet, residential area around Porta S. Marco. It has a bar and terrace with views over Siena and beyond. The large rooms have either contemporary or classical decor. A fine restaurant offers local cuisine. **www.hotelathena.com**

**SIENA Pensione Palazzo Ravizza** €€€

*Pian dei Mantellini 34, 53100* ***Tel*** *0577 28 04 62* ***Fax*** *0577 22 15 97* ***Rooms*** *30*

A *pensione* in a quiet, Renaissance palace in the historical centre of Siena. Rooms come with original terracotta floors, frescoed ceilings, carved wooden doorways and antique furnishings. Suites have their own lounge areas. Gourmet evening restaurant and a garden terrace overlooking the Tuscan hills. **www.palazzoravizza.it**

**SIENA Hotel Certosa di Maggiano** €€€€€

*Strada di Certosa 82, 53100* ***Tel*** *0577 28 81 80* ***Fax*** *0577 28 81 89* ***Rooms*** *17*

Part of the Relais & Châteaux chain of luxury hotels, this converted monastery (built in 1314) lies in the countryside just outside Siena. The hotel is world renowned for its antique paintings and fine silk furnishings. The vast grounds include olive groves, vineyards and a helicopter landing pad. **www.certosadimaggiano.it**

**SINALUNGA Locanda dell'Amorosa** €€€€€

*Loc. L'Amorosa, 53048* ***Tel*** *0577 67 72 11* ***Fax*** *0577 63 20 01* ***Rooms*** *20*

Beautifully converted 14th-century villa in the rolling Sienese hills. Each room is individually decorated in typical Tuscan rustic style with antique furniture, prints and paintings. Visitors can enjoy the elegant restaurant, which now occupies the ancient stables, as well as the surrounding park, farm and vineyards. **www.amorosa.it**

**VIAREGGIO Hotel President** €€€€

*Viale Carducci 5, 55049* ***Tel*** *0584 96 27 12* ***Fax*** *0584 96 36 58* ***Rooms*** *39*

A well-reputed beachfront hotel, built in 1949 in Viareggio's typical Liberty style. Comfortable, modern rooms with a real seaside feel. The restaurant Gaudì serves a generous buffet breakfast and has an evening menu of Tuscan and international cuisine. Children's playground and bicycle rental. **www.hotelpresident.it**

**VOLTERRA Albergo Villa Nencini** €€

*Borgo Santo Stefano 55, 56048* ***Tel*** *0588 863 86* ***Fax*** *0588 806 01* ***Rooms*** *35*

This family-run country house hotel in a magnificent location just outside of town has views as far as the Tuscany Archipelago. Rooms are airy with light furnishings. The hotel *enoteca* in the converted stables serves a range of local wines. You can swim in the pool next to a garden of luxuriant oak trees. **www.villanencini.it**

**VOLTERRA Hotel San Lino** €€

*Via S. Lino 26, 56048* ***Tel*** *0588 852 50* ***Fax*** *0588 806 20* ***Rooms*** *43*

This former convent within the medieval walls of Volterra dating from the 1400s was converted into a four-star hotel in 1982. The rooms are modern, but in keeping with the building's past. Windows look out over the town's cobbled streets or into the hotel's small garden. It has a popular restaurant sitting up to 20 diners. **www.hotelsanlino.com**

## UMBRIA

**ASSISI Hotel Berti** €

*Piazza San Pietro, 06081* ***Tel*** *075 81 34 66* ***Fax*** *075 81 68 70* ***Rooms*** *10*

In a convenient central position at the bottom of a hill in old Assisi, not far from the bus stop linking the town with the railway station. A cosy, old-fashioned place with antique furniture, parquet floors and a sunny terrace restaurant. Bedrooms are a good size and smartly decorated. Good breakfasts. **www.hotelberti.it**

**ASSISI Fontebella** €€

*Via Fontebella 25, 06081* ***Tel*** *075 81 28 83* ***Fax*** *075 81 29 41* ***Rooms*** *46*

Inside an old oil mill, with seven storeys, this lovely ivy-covered stone house has tranquil gardens. The bedrooms are large, painted yellow and have modern bathrooms. Good family rooms; some rooms also have a private balcony with charming views. Elegant sitting room with a lovely fireplace and frescoed ceilings. **www.fontebella.com**

**ASSISI Hotel Alexander** €€

*Piazza Chiesa Nuova 6, 06081* ***Tel*** *075 81 61 90* ***Fax*** *075 81 61 90* ***Rooms*** *8*

This small hotel has been refurbished and is right in the heart of old Assisi. Wooden beams, antique furniture and high ceilings. The bedrooms are large and can accommodate extra beds, making it ideal for families. There is also a roof terrace with a lovely view. **www.assisi-hotel.com**

**ASSISI Hotel Umbra** €€

*Via degli Archi 6 (Piazza del Comune), 06081* ***Tel*** *075 81 22 40* ***Fax*** *075 81 36 53* ***Rooms*** *25*

Tucked away on a small street, not far from the town hall, this is a very popular little hotel and restaurant with a courtyard garden offering alfresco dining in summer. Quiet and family run, it has tiled floors and antiques throughout. Bedrooms are airy and elegantly decorated. **www.hotelumbra.it**

**ASSISI Hotel Le Silve** €€€

*Loc. Armenzano 82, 06081* ***Tel*** *075 801 90 00* ***Fax*** *075 801 90 05* ***Rooms*** *20*

In the Subasio national park, 10 km (6 miles) from Assisi, this charming 10th-century farmhouse is a tranquil hideaway. Situated in farmland, with sun terraces, pool and horse-riding. Bedrooms have lovely views, stone walls, terracotta floors, wooden beams, cosy fireplaces and antiques. Closed Nov–Mar. **www.lesilve.it**

**Key to Price Guide** *see p558* **Key to Symbols** *see back cover flap*

### CAMPELLO SUL CLITUNNO Il Vecchio Molino €€

*Via del Tempio 34, Località Pissignano, 06042* ***Tel*** *0743 52 11 22* ***Fax*** *0743 27 50 97* ***Rooms*** *13*

A 15th-century mill and ancient hostelry. The mill, which produced flour and olive oil, and was generated by the ancient waters of the Fonti del Clitunno, worked until recently. Bed and breakfast is offered in this lovely location beside the tumbling river. Rooms are simple, rustic and comfortable. Closed Nov–Mar. **www.vecchio-molino.it**

### CITTÀ DELLA PIEVE Hotel Piccolo Eden €€

*Via Santa Lucia 53, 06062* ***Tel*** *0578 29 70 65* ***Fax*** *0578 29 70 66* ***Rooms*** *36*

This welcoming hotel is a short walk from the historic walls of Città della Pieve. It is a delightful place to unwind, and it features a swimming pool and a terrace where, weather permitting, guests can enjoy their meals. A good base for visiting the local area, Lake Trasimeno and Tuscan cities like Siena and Arezzo. **www.hotelpiccoloeden.it**

### CITTÀ DI CASTELLO Hotel Tiferno €€€

*Piazza R Sanzio 13, 06012* ***Tel*** *075 855 03 31* ***Fax*** *075 852 11 96* ***Rooms*** *47*

In a former convent dating from the 11th century, this is one of Umbria's oldest hotels, in business since 1895. Located on a small square in the *centro storico*, the public areas are elegant with fireplaces and vaults and a collection of Alberto Burri's paintings. The rooms are modern and comfortable. **www.hoteltiferno.it**

### DERUTA Antica Fattoria del Colle €

*Str. Colle delle Forche 6, 06053* ***Tel/Fax*** *075 97 22 01* ***Rooms*** *7*

Outside Deruta, set in woodland on a hill surrounded by olive groves and vineyards, is this *agriturismo* owned by a charming couple from Rome. Two brick and stone farmhouses with antiques, terracotta floors, wooden beams and sunny terraces. Excellent homecooking and baking and delicious wine. **www.anticafattoriadelcolle.it**

### FONTIGNANA Villa Monte Solare €€€€

*Via Montali 7, Colle San Paolo, Panicale, 06064* ***Tel*** *075 83 23 76* ***Fax*** *075 835 54 62* ***Rooms*** *25*

A patrician villa in a panoramic oasis near Lake Trasimeno, with a wonderful restaurant serving local produce in a walled garden and orangerie. Public rooms have cornices, friezes, terracotta floors, antiques and a lovely old fireplace. Elegant dining room and belvedere roof bar. Also a tennis court. **www.villamontesolare.com**

### GUBBIO Grotta dell'Angelo €

*Via Gioia 47, 06024* ***Tel*** *075 927 17 47* ***Fax*** *075 927 34 38* ***Rooms*** *18*

In the heart of old Gubbio, this quietly located family hotel offers clean simple lodging in a small medieval house with whitewashed and stone walls, and a log fire in winter. Bedrooms are very clean and cheerful, all en suite. It has a garden and delightful restaurant under a pergola in summer. **www.grottadellangelo.it**

### GUBBIO Villa Montegranelli €€

*Località Monteluiano, 06024* ***Tel*** *075 922 01 85* ***Fax*** *075 927 33 72* ***Rooms*** *21*

An 18th-century/medieval structure 4 km (2.5 miles) from Gubbio, once owned by the counts Guidi di Romena e Montegranelli. Amidst an avenue of cypresses, the building is filled with stuccoes, frescoes and antiques. Bedrooms are luxurious, with lovely views over the valley. Good restaurant. **www.hotelvillamontegranelli.it**

### GUBBIO Relais Ducale €€€

*Via Galeotti 19, 06024* ***Tel*** *075 922 01 57* ***Fax*** *075 922 01 59* ***Rooms*** *30*

This stately building is on Gubbio's main square, the Piazza della Signoria. Furnished with antiques, with fine views over the city and surrounding hillsides, breakfast is served on a lovely terrace. Rooms vary in size and decor, but all are elegant, some with balconies and great views. **www.mencarelligroup.com**

### LAKE TRASIMENO, CASTIGLIONE DEL LAGO Hotel Trasimeno €

*Via Roma 174, 06061* ***Tel*** *075 965 24 94* ***Fax*** *075 952 52 58* ***Rooms*** *34*

A modern hotel on the shores of Lake Trasimeno, just a short hop from the historic town centre and within easy reach of ferries to visit the islands on the lake. Bikes are available in the summer, or you can enjoy activities such as tennis, golf, sailing and windsurfing. The hotel organizes excursions to nearby towns. **www.hotel-trasimeno.it**

### LAKE TRASIMENO, CASTIGLIONE DEL LAGO Miralago €€

*Piazza Mazzini 6, 06061* ***Tel*** *075 951 157* ***Fax*** *075 51924* ***Rooms*** *19*

In a central position in the lovely town of Castiglione del Lago, this charming red building on a square has comfortable old-fashioned rooms, each decorated individually. Views are either of the lake or of the square. The hotel garden faces Lake Trasimeno with alfresco dining in the summer months. **www.hotelmiralago.com**

### MONTEFALCO Albergo Ristorante Ringhiera Umbra €

*Corso Mameli 20, 06036* ***Tel*** *0742 37 91 00* ***Fax*** *0742 37 91 66* ***Rooms*** *13*

A charming family *locanda*, offering accommodation and good food in the heart of Montefalco and run by the same family since it opened in 1938. Bedrooms are single, double or triple (only triple rooms have en suite bathrooms). Rooms are simple but cosily furnished. The restaurant is very popular. **www.ringhieraumbra.com**

### MONTEFALCO Villa Pambuffetti €€€

*Viale della Vittoria 20, 06036* ***Tel*** *0742 37 94 17* ***Fax*** *0742 37 92 45* ***Rooms*** *15*

This is a lovely villa, where the charismatic Gabriele d'Annunzio stayed regularly, set inside a private park. Antiques abound. Rooms all face the landscaped gardens and many top-floor rooms have panoramic views, as far as Monte Subasio and Assisi. It has a good restaurant serving regional fare. **www.villapambuffetti.com**

**NORCIA Grotta Azzurra** €

*Via Alfieri 12, 06046* **Tel** *0743 81 65 13* **Fax** *0743 81 73 42* **Rooms** *45*

Close to the main square, this is one of several hotels owned by a local family. An inn dating from 1850, it has a lovely restaurant and a wide choice of rooms. The most basic are small and street-facing with little balconies; deluxe rooms are larger and grander with whirlpool bathtubs (two have frescoes). **www.bianconi.com**

**NORCIA Il Casale nel Parco** €€

*Località Fontevena 8, 06046* **Tel** *0743 81 64 81* **Fax** *0743 81 64 81* **Rooms** *12*

A delightful *agriturismo* just outside Norcia at the foot of the Monte Sibillini mountains. Inside a converted stone farmhouse and buildings, the rooms are cosy and charming, with wooden beams, wrought-iron beds and lovely garden views. Excellent picnics and dinners on request. **www.casalenelparco.com**

**ORVIETO Hotel Duomo** €€

*Vicolo di Maurizio 7, 05018* **Tel** *0763 34 18 87* **Fax** *0763 39 49 73* **Rooms** *18*

Centrally located, on a small road near the cathedral, the Duomo offers very clean, modern rooms with large bathrooms. Staff are friendly and helpful, and some of the rooms have balconies overlooking the cathedral. With a small garden, this hotel is very popular and perfect for a short stay. **www.orvietohotelduomo.com**

**ORVIETO La Pensiola** €€

*Loc. Lago di Corbara, SS448 Baschi, 05023* **Tel** *0744 95 05 21* **Fax** *0744 95 05 24* **Rooms** *19*

What this modern motel lacks in charm, it makes up for in friendliness, facilities and location. Simply furnished rooms come with either a terrace or a small private garden. There's tennis, a playground and a pool on-site, with watersports on the man-made lake close by. An ideal touring stopover. **www.albergolapensiola.it**

**ORVIETO Palazzo Piccolomini** €€€

*Piazza Ranieri 36, 05018* **Tel** *0763 34 17 43* **Fax** *0763 39 10 46* **Rooms** *34*

A 16th-century palazzo in a quiet part of town near the lift down to the public car park, this is Orvieto's grandest hotel. Public areas and bedrooms are elegant, with vaulted ceilings, whitewashed walls and wrought-iron candelabras. Rooms on the upper floors have panoramic views. **www.hotelpiccolomini.it**

**PERUGIA Hotel Sant'Ercolano** €

*Via del Bovaro 9, 06122* **Tel/Fax** *075 572 46 50* **Rooms** *15*

Near the church of Sant'Ercolano, in the *centro storico*, this economic hotel is in a 17th-century building. Two minutes from the bus station it is also very convenient as a base for exploring the region. The rooms are simple but comfortable, all en suite and with cooling fans in summer. Breakfast is extra. **www.santercolano.com**

**PERUGIA Albergo Lo Spedalicchio** €€

*Piazza Bruno Buozzi 3, 06080* **Tel** *075 801 03 23* **Fax** *075 801 03 23* **Rooms** *25*

A medieval fortress in a tiny hamlet midway between Assisi and Perugia, just off the main road. A latterday inn, used by travellers and pilgrims, it is a quiet enclave. Bedrooms are spacious and en suite, with wooden beams and antique furniture. Breakfast is extra. The restaurant serves fine regional fare. **www.lospedalicchio.it**

**PERUGIA Hotel La Fortuna** €€

*Via Luigi Bonazzi 19, 06123* **Tel** *075 572 28 45* **Fax** *075 573 50 40* **Rooms** *52*

A restored palazzo with a roof terrace, modern facilities and friendly, professional staff. There are frescoes in the restaurant and in some of the pricier rooms, many of which also have sitting rooms and terraces. Economy rooms are basic without air conditioning; standard rooms are larger and with air conditioning. **www.umbriahotels.com**

**PERUGIA Albergo Brufani Palace** €€€€€

*Piazza Italia 12, 06100* **Tel** *075 573 25 41* **Fax** *075 572 02 10* **Rooms** *94*

A four-storey luxury hotel on a hill in central Perugia with lovely views over the valleys below. High, frescoed ceilings, parquet floors, stone fireplaces, chandeliers and antiques abound; bedrooms are particularly sumptuous. The swimming pool has a glass floor above Etruscan ruins. Fine restaurant. **www.brufanipalace.com**

**SPELLO La Bastiglia** €€

*Piazza Vallegloria 7, 06038* **Tel** *0742 65 12 77* **Fax** *0742 30 11 59* **Rooms** *33*

A hotel with a Michelin-star restaurant on the slopes of Monte Subasio in an old mill surrounded by cypresses and olive trees. Junior suites have private terraces and whirlpool baths; deluxe rooms have private gardens; superior rooms have balconies, while standard rooms have window views. Heated pool. **www.labastiglia.com**

**SPELLO Palazzo Bocci** €€€

*Via Cavour 17, 06038* **Tel** *0742 30 10 21* **Fax** *0742 30 14 64* **Rooms** *23*

A beautifully restored hotel inside a 17th-century palazzo in the historical district of this lovely town. A warren of rooms and public areas, with terracotta floors, frescoes, fireplaces and wooden beams. Outside there's a fountain, hanging garden, palm trees and sunny terraces. **www.palazzobocci.com**

**SPOLETO Hotel Aurora** €

*Via Apollinaire 3, 06049* **Tel** *0743 22 03 15* **Fax** *0743 22 18 85* **Rooms** *23*

A small, family-run hotel in a very central position, near the stop for the bus that connects old Spoleto with the railway station. Set back from the road, the bedrooms are quiet, clean and comfortable, with views over the rooftops of the town. Guests can dine at special rates at the restaurant next door, the Apollinaire. **www.hotelauroraspoleto.it**

**Key to Price Guide** *see p558* **Key to Symbols** *see back cover flap*

**SPOLETO Palazzo Dragoni** €€

*Via del Duomo 13, 06049* **Tel** *0743 22 22 20* **Fax** *0743 22 22 25* **Rooms** *15*

A *residenza d'epoca* next to the cathedral. This 14th-century building has spacious bedrooms, tiled floors, wrought-iron beds, vaulted ceilings and antiques. Some rooms have French windows, opening on to views of the rooftops and valley; others have four-poster beds. Elegant dining room and small garden. **www.palazzodragoni.it**

**SPOLETO Hotel Gattapone** €€€

*Via del Ponte 6, 06049* **Tel** *0743 22 34 47* **Fax** *0743 22 34 48* **Rooms** *15*

In a romantic position beneath the Rocca Albornoziana, opposite the famous Ponte delle Torri. Named after the bridge's architect, this old villa has mainly standard rooms while a modern annexe has en suite accommodation. There is also a garden and terrace with views of the valley. **www.hotelgattapone.it**

**SPOLETO Hotel San Luca** €€€

*Via Interna delle Mura 21, 06049* **Tel** *0743 22 33 99* **Fax** *0743 22 38 00* **Rooms** *35*

A charming, family-run hotel in a converted tannery, dating from the 18th century, with gardens and a sunny courtyard where breakfast is served in summer. Bedrooms are large and soundproofed with gorgeous bathrooms, some with whirlpool tubs. A few have frescoed walls or a private balcony. **www.hotelsanluca.com**

**TODI San Lorenzo Tre** €€

*Via San Lorenzo 3, 06059* **Tel** *075 894 45 55* **Fax** *075 894 45 55* **Rooms** *6*

Staying in this little inn is like stepping back in time. It has an atmosphere from entirely another era. A family home with few modern conveniences, only antiques, paintings and an extensive library. All the bedrooms have lovely views over the rooftops and hills north of Todi – three have en suite bathrooms. **www.sanlorenzos.it**

**TODI Fontecesia** €€€

*Via Lorenzo Leonj 3, 06059* **Tel** *075 894 37 37* **Fax** *075 894 46 77* **Rooms** *37*

In the centre of Todi, this renovated 17th-century palazzo beside the former church of San Benedetto has large and comfortable standard rooms, while the five suites are truly sumptuous, each one quite different. Some bedrooms have views over the old town, others over the countryside. **www.fontecesia.it**

**TODI Relais Todini** €€€€

*Fraz. Collevalenza, 06050* **Tel** *075 88 75 21* **Fax** *075 88 71 82* **Rooms** *12*

One of Umbria's most celebrated retreats. This intimate hotel, housed inside a hilltop, 14th-century villa, is complemented by a famous restaurant and spa. Elegant rooms are stuffed with antique furniture, and the restaurant and pool command spectacular views across the vines to Todi. Pure class. **www.relaistodini.com**

**TORGIANO Le Tre Vaselle** €€€€

*Via Garibaldi 48, 06089* **Tel** *0759 88 04 47* **Fax** *0759 88 02 14* **Rooms** *60*

An enchanting 17th-century house hotel set amid vines, with extensive terraces and gardens, a spa centre and two pools. The rooms are elegant with handwoven fabrics and terracotta floors; suites have fireplaces. Excellent restaurant. There are apartments for rent on the grounds. A shuttle service is available to Perugia and Assisi. **www.3vaselle.it**

**TREVI Casa Giulia** €€

*Via Corciano 1, Bovara, 06039* **Tel** *0742 782 57* **Fax** *0742 38 16 32* **Rooms** *9*

Near to the Clitunno springs, this 17th-century home has been in the same family for generations. The rooms are furnished with antiques and have wooden beams, white walls and wrought-iron beds. A few have original frescoes depicting the countryside around the house. The pool is set amongst oleanders. **www.casagiulia.com**

## LE MARCHE

**ACQUAVIVA PICENA Hotel O'Viv** €

*Via Marziale 43, 63030* **Tel** *0735 76 46 49* **Fax** *0735 76 50 54* **Rooms** *12*

In a hilltop town with prime views of the beaches 6 km (4 miles) away in San Benedetto del Tronto and the mountains of the Sibillini, this charmingly restored house has a relaxing garden and restaurant. Cool and spacious, and filled with antiques, the rooms are beautifully frescoed. Entry to a private beach is provided. **www.oviv.it**

**AMANDOLA Affittacamere Il Palazzo** €

*Via Indipendenza 61, 63021* **Tel** *0736 84 70 82* **Fax** *0736 84 70 82* **Rooms** *8*

In a lovely medieval village, one of the gateways to the Monte Sibillini park, there is excellent walking nearby as well as delightful views. This 15th-century palazzo with terracotta flooring and a lovely fireplace in the sitting room, is cool in summer and cosy in winter. Bedrooms are charming, and all en suite. **www.palazzopecci.com**

**ANCONA Hotel Fortuna** €€

*Piazza Fratelli Rosselli 15, 60126* **Tel** *071 426 63* **Fax** *071 426 62* **Rooms** *56*

A good budget find opposite the railway station, the Fortuna has simple, clean and comfortable rooms and a welcoming air. Extremely convenient for transport to the centre and to the port, equally handy for exploring Ancona's *centro storico*. Two rooms have disabled access. **www.hotelfortuna.it**

**ANCONA Grand Hotel Palace** €€€

*Lungomare Vanvitelli, 60210* **Tel** *071 20 18 13* **Fax** *071 20 748 32* **Rooms** *40*

Central Ancona's grandest option within a converted palazzo, with a wonderful roof terrace overlooking the port and a view over the old city. Very central, within walking distance of all the sights. The rooms are elegant and very comfortable. There are also small apartments with sea views for weekly rental. **www.hotelancona.it**

**ASCOLI PICENO Palazzo Guiderocchi** €€

*Via Cesare Battisti 3, 63100* **Tel** *0736 24 40 11* **Fax** *0736 24 34 41* **Rooms** *32*

In the heart of old Ascoli, near the Palazzo del Popolo, a meticulously restored historic building, in the former home of a notorious tyrant noble. With beautiful, romantic rooms, grouped around two internal courtyards, deluxe rooms/suites have canopy beds and frescoes. Excellent restaurant. **www.palazzoguiderocchi.com**

**FABRIANO Hotel Relais Le Marchese del Grillo** €€€€

*Via Rochetta 73, 60044* **Tel** *0732 62 56 90* **Fax** *0732 62 79 58* **Rooms** *20*

A romantic restaurant and hotel in a rose-coloured villa in the lush countryside 5 km (3 miles) outside Fabriano – not far from the famous "Grotte di Frasassi". The bedrooms in the main villa are grand with original antiques, while the pretty annexe has more rustic rooms with stone walls and terracotta floors. **www.marchesedelgrillo.com**

**FANO Hotel Augustus** €€

*Via Puccini 2, 61032* **Tel** *0721 80 97 81* **Fax** *0721 82 55 17* **Rooms** *22*

A beach hotel just outside the city walls, not far from the medieval town or the seafront. Its modern exterior gives way to an old-fashioned oasis of calm, with charming public rooms filled with antiques. Bedrooms are spacious and bright, furnished stylishly with antiques and decorated in warm yellows. **www.hotelaugustus.it**

**JESI Albergo Mariani** €

*Via dell'Orfanatrofio 10, 60035* **Tel** *0731 20 72 86* **Fax** *0731 20 00 11* **Rooms** *33*

A central, family-run hotel, opened in 1951. Bedrooms are quiet and comfortable, with soundproofing and elegant decor. There are five mini suites, three of which have bathtubs instead of showers; some rooms have disabled access. There is a restaurant, Internet access and 24hr room service. **www.hotelmariani.com**

**MACERATA Hotel Lauri** €€

*Via Tommaso Lauri 6, 62100* **Tel & Fax** *0733 23 23 76* **Rooms** *28 + 6 apartments*

Right in the city centre, close to the university, the Hotel Lauri is in a charming 19th-century building. Offering double bedrooms, as well as mini apartments with a kitchen and sitting room, rooms vary in size. All are comfortably furnished in an old-fashioned style and with tiled floors. **www.albergolauri.it**

**MONTEMAGGIORE AL METAURO 2 Campanili Relais** €€€

*Via Panoramica 4, 61030* **Tel** *0721 89 23 01* **Fax** *0721 87 84 29* **Rooms** *35*

Based a little inland from Fano, the 35 rooms of this hotel are spread throughout the village in small brick houses on 15th-century alleyways, allowing guests to enjoy the luxury of a hotel combined with more direct contact with locals. The relaxing spa is surrounded by pine trees and each room is decorated in a different style. **www.duecampanili.it**

**PESARO Albergo Ristorante Villa Serena** €€€

*Via San Nicola 6/3, 61100* **Tel** *0721 552 11* **Fax** *0721 559 27* **Rooms** *8*

A palazzo hidden in the countryside between Pesaro and Fano, with elegant rooms and a prestigious restaurant set in beautiful grounds. Run by chef Count Renato Pinto and his son, Stefano, the cuisine is excellent and creative. Romantic candlelight dining, antiques, a sunny garden and sumptuous suites. **www.villa-serena.it**

**PESARO Hotel Vittoria** €€€€

*Piazzale della Libertà 2, 61100* **Tel** *0721 343 43* **Fax** *0721 652 04* **Rooms** *27*

A hotel since 1908, with a distinguished guest list. Located very centrally, with a terrace overlooking the sea and a small pool. Bedrooms are elegantly furnished, with antiques and marble bathrooms – many have balconies with sea views and whirlpool bathtubs. Staff are friendly and professional. **www.viphotels.it**

**PORTONOVO (CONERO PENINSULA) Fortino Napoleonico** €€€€€

*Via Poggio 166, 60020* **Tel** *071 80 14 50* **Fax** *071 80 14 54* **Rooms** *33*

Originally a Napoleonic fort built to keep the marauding English at bay, and now a hotel in a spectacular position with a private beach in a cove at the heart of the Conero Peninsula. Lovely gardens and terraces, an excellent restaurant and wine cellar and the sound of the waves at night to lull you to sleep. **www.hotelfortino.it**

**PORTONOVO (CONERO PENINSULA) Hotel Emilia** €€€€€

*Poggio di Portonovo, 60020* **Tel** *071 80 11 17* **Fax** *071 80 13 30* **Rooms** *30*

Nestled amongst holm-oaks, broom and lavender fields on a clifftop high over the sea, the Emilia is a lovely family-run hotel where antiques and contemporary art jostle for position. A shuttle bus takes guests to the private beach below. The lovely gardens play host to a summer jazz festival. **www.hotelemilia.com**

**SAN MARINO Hotel Ristorante Titano** €€€

*Contrada del Collegio 31, 47890* **Tel** *0549 99 10 06* **Fax** *0549 99 13 75* **Rooms** *48*

This hotel-restaurant dates from 1894 and is located in a quiet spot in the centre of the main *borgo* of Città di San Marino. The rooms and the dining room terrace share beautiful views over the Montefeltre plains below and on to the Apennines beyond. Half- or full-board options are available. **www.hoteltitano.com**

**Key to Price Guide** *see p558* **Key to Symbols** *see back cover flap*

**URBINO Albergo Italia** €€

*Corso Garibaldi 32, 61029* ***Tel*** *0722 27 01* ***Fax*** *0722 32 26 64* ***Rooms*** *43*

A hotel conveniently located in the historic centre of Urbino. Some rooms have a view of the cathedral and the Ducal Palace, while the Albornoz Fortress can be seen from the terrace where breakfast is served in the summer months. All mod cons can be found in this comfortable hotel. **www.albergo-italia-urbino.it**

**URBINO Albergo Raffaello** €€

*Vicolino S. Margherita 40, 61029* ***Tel*** *0722 47 84* ***Fax*** *0722 32 85 40* ***Rooms*** *14*

In the heart of the historical district, steps away from the birthplace of the painter Raphael, this hotel was a religious seminary. Simple, comfortable bedrooms, some have French windows and tiny balconies with views over the rooftops of the old town and on to the hills beyond. Run by a friendly family. **www.albergoraffaello.com**

**URBINO Hotel Bonconte** €€

*Via delle Mura 28, 61029* ***Tel*** *0722 24 63* ***Fax*** *0722 47 82* ***Rooms*** *23*

A short walk away from the *centro storico*, just within the city walls, this hotel has lovely views of the countryside around Urbino. This elegant old villa below the town is filled with antiques and set in a garden oasis, where breakfast is served in summer (not included in room rate). Good restaurant. **www.viphotels.it**

## ROME

**AVENTINE Domus Aventina** €€€

*Via di Santa Prisca 11b, 00153* ***Tel*** *06 574 61 35* ***Fax*** *06 57 30 00 44* ***Rooms*** *26* ***Map*** *6 E2*

Domus Aventina is an immaculate hotel, occupying a 14th-century convent at the foot of the Aventine Hill. Rooms are large and simply decorated in pastel tones. There are wonderful views of the Celian Hill from many of the rooms and from the huge terrace. **www.hoteldomusaventina.com**

**AVENTINE Sant'Anselmo** €€€

*Piazza di Sant'Anselmo 2, 00153* ***Tel*** *06 570 057* ***Fax*** *06 578 36 04* ***Rooms*** *34* ***Map*** *6 E3*

This pretty villa is on a peaceful square halfway up the Aventine Hill. Since refurbishment the rooms are all elegantly themed. The lounge looks onto the hotel's garden. Many of the rooms have terraces. The staff provide a warm service. **www.aventinohotels.com**

**AVENTINE FortySeven** €€€€

*Via Petroselli 47, 00186* ***Tel*** *06 678 78 16* ***Fax*** *06 69 19 07 26* ***Rooms*** *61* ***Map*** *6 E1*

FortySeven overlooks the temple of Hercules and the lovely church of Santa Maria in Cosmedin. Modern and very stylish with a wonderful roof terrace and bar. Rooms are spacious with lots of luxurious touches. Very friendly staff. **www.fortysevenhotel.com**

**AVENTINE Kolbe Hotel** €€€€€

*Via di San Teodoro 44, 00186* ***Tel*** *06 69 92 42 50* ***Fax*** *06 679 49 75* ***Rooms*** *72* ***Map*** *6 E1*

Perfectly placed for visiting the Palatine and the Forum, this former Franciscan monastery has been lavishly restored and elegantly furnished along clean, minimalist lines. Some rooms look onto the Palatine, though those facing the internal garden and cloisters are quieter. Charming outdoor area. **www.kolbehotelrome.com**

**CAMPO DE' FIORI Arenula** €€

*Via S Maria de' Calderari 47, 00186* ***Tel*** *06 687 94 54* ***Fax*** *06 689 61 88* ***Rooms*** *50* ***Map*** *10 D5*

With an excellent location, near the ruins at Largo Argentina, between Campo de' Fiori and Piazza Venezia and not far from Trastevere, this modest hotel offers very good value. Rooms are light and spacious, and the decor and furniture above average. All rooms are en suite with air conditioning. **www.hotelarenula.com**

**CAMPO DE' FIORI Smeraldo** €€

*Vicolo dei Chiodaroli 9, 00186* ***Tel*** *06 687 59 29* ***Fax*** *06 68 80 54 95* ***Rooms*** *50* ***Map*** *10 D4*

Smeraldo is located in a lovely spot, halfway between the Campo and Largo Argentina. The rooms are small but charming; one of them has facilities for the disabled. The rooftop terrace, though noisy, is a nice place for an alfresco drink (bring your own). Breakfasts are hearty and staff cordial. **www.smeraldoroma.com**

**CAMPO DE' FIORI Suore di Santa Brigida** €€€

*Piazza Farnese 96, 00186* ***Tel*** *06 68 89 25 96* ***Fax*** *06 68 89 15 73* ***Rooms*** *20* ***Map*** *2 E5, 9 C4*

The nuns at this discreetly appealing hotel offer en suite double rooms. B&B or half-board options are also available. Air conditioning, Internet points and access to the chapel and library are other pluses. Unlike many religious institutions, there is no curfew. Right on the prestigious Piazza Farnese. **www.brigidine.org**

**CAMPO DE' FIORI Teatro di Pompeo** €€€

*Largo del Pallaro 8, 00186* ***Tel*** *06 687 28 12* ***Fax*** *06 68 80 55 31* ***Rooms*** *12* ***Map*** *9 C4*

A lovely little hotel built on the remains of the ancient theatre of the same name, where Julius Caesar is said to have met his destiny. Rooms are large and comfortable with wooden beams and dark wooden furniture. Breakfast is served in the basement under a Roman vault. **www.hotelteatrodipompeo.it**

**CAMPO DE' FIORI Ponte Sisto** €€€€

*Via dei Pettinari 64, 00186* **Tel** *06 68 63 100* **Fax** *06 68 30 17 12* **Rooms** *103* **Map** *2 E5, 9 C5*

Ideally placed for both Campo de' Fiori and Trastevere, Ponte Sisto is particularly accessible for wheelchair users. A converted monastic complex, the hotel is modern in feel, with abundant terraces and a lovely cloister with restaurant and bar. The Belvedere suite on the top floor books up quickly. **www.hotelpontesisto.it**

**FORUM Paba** €€

*Via Cavour 266, 2nd Floor, 00184* **Tel** *06 47 82 49 02* **Fax** *06 47 88 12 25* **Rooms** *7* **Map** *3 B5*

Run by a charming lady, this tiny *pensione* is on the second floor of an elegant building, a short walk away from Piazza Venezia and the Forum. The clean, spacious, sound-proofed and nicely furnished rooms have parquet floors, Internet points, fridges and kettles for making hot drinks. **www.hotelpaba.com**

**FORUM Hotel Celio** €€€

*Via SS Quattro 35C, 00184* **Tel** *06 70 49 53 33* **Fax** *06 709 63 77* **Rooms** *20* **Map** *7 A1*

Hotel Celio has sumptuous decor, a great location and cordial staff. Bedrooms are furnished with flair, distinguished by frescoes in the style of Renaissance painters, such as Titian and Cellini. Upper-floor rooms have Jacuzzis and the suite has a private terrace with panoramic view. There's also a roof garden. **www.hotelcelio.com**

**FORUM Lancelot** €€€

*Via Capo d'Africa 47, 00184* **Tel** *06 70 45 06 15* **Fax** *06 70 45 06 40* **Rooms** *60* **Map** *7 A1*

A popular place to stay near the Colosseum with very friendly, helpful staff. Rooms are spacious and charming. Some have private terraces with views, and two are specially adapted for guests with disabilities. A half-board option is available and a hearty breakfast is served in the patio garden. **www.lancelothotel.com**

**PIAZZA DELLA ROTONDA Al Centro di Roma B&B** €€

*Piazza Sant'Andrea della Valle 3, 00186* **Tel** *06 68 13 59 46* **Rooms** *3* **Map** *2 F4*

Located on the top floor of a building with a charming courtyard near the Pantheon, Al Centro di Roma overlooks the church of Sant'Andrea della Valle, made famous by the opera *Tosca*. This small B&B has a great reputation for its service, cleanliness and value for money. **www.bbalcentrodiroma.com**

**PIAZZA DELLA ROTONDA Cesari** €€€

*Via di Pietra 89a, 00186* **Tel** *06 674 97 01* **Fax** *06 67 49 70 30* **Rooms** *47* **Map** *10 E2*

The historic Cesari is located on a lovely romantic square, steps away from the Pantheon beside the temple of Hadrian. First established as a hotel in 1787, it has been in the same family since 1899. A favourite of Stendhal's, rooms are elegant and spacious. Non-smoking floors, a roof terrace and free Internet access. **www.albergocesari.it**

**PIAZZA DELLA ROTONDA Santa Chiara** €€€

*Via di Santa Chiara 21, 00186* **Tel** *06 687 29 79* **Fax** *06 687 31 44* **Rooms** *96* **Map** *2 F4, 10 D3*

A substantial family-run hotel in an apricot-washed palazzo. Beyond the elegant marble lobby with glass chandeliers, bedrooms are comfortable, with parquet flooring and subdued, old-fashioned decor. Three of the upper rooms are small apartments with terraces. **www.albergosantachiara.com**

**PIAZZA DELLA ROTONDA Albergo del Senato** €€€€

*Piazza della Rotonda 73, 00186* **Tel** *06 678 43 43* **Fax** *06 69 94 02 97* **Rooms** *57* **Map** *2 F4, 10 D3*

A rather grand, noble old hotel with a side view of the Pantheon and the Piazza. Bedrooms are elegant and service is old-fashioned and reserved. Some rooms have a bath or private terrace, and the suite has a beautifully frescoed ceiling. Windows are soundproofed and there's a delightful roof garden. **www.albergodelsenato.it**

**PIAZZA DELLA ROTONDA Grand Hotel de la Minerve** €€€€€

*Piazza della Minerva 69, 00186* **Tel** *06 69 52 01* **Fax** *06 679 41 65* **Rooms** *135* **Map** *2 F4, 10 D3*

Favoured by Italy's first Grand Tourists, with generations following ever since, the charismatic Minerve is a fusion of Old World elegance and contemporary styling. Marble and chandeliers abound, as do wonderful frescoes, tastefully blended with cutting-edge design. Excellent rooftop bar and restaurant. **www.grandhoteldelaminerve.com**

**PIAZZA DI SPAGNA Panda** €€

*Via della Croce 35, 00187* **Tel** *06 678 01 79* **Fax** *06 69 94 21 51* **Rooms** *28* **Map** *3 A2*

Panda is an appealing little hotel with a faithful clientele, offering unpretentious, cheap accommodation in one of Rome's most expensive areas. Clean rooms with or without bathrooms, but all with air conditioning, telephone and Internet access. A couple of the rooms feature original 19th-century frescoes. **www.hotelpanda.it**

**PIAZZA DI SPAGNA Casa Howard** €€€

*Via Capo le Case 18, 00187* **Tel** *06 69 92 45 55* **Fax** *06 679 46 44* **Rooms** *5* **Map** *3 A3, 10 F1*

Close to the Spanish Steps, this extremely fashionable boutique hotel is English-owned and designed by Tommaso Ziffer. Rooms have dramatic individual themes, though small, and not all are en suite. There is an expert concierge. Extras are available, including use of a sauna and *hammam*. **www.casahoward.com**

**PIAZZA DI SPAGNA Hotel Art by the Spanish Steps** €€€

*Via Margutta 56, 00187* **Tel** *06 32 87 11* **Fax** *06 36 00 39 95* **Rooms** *46* **Map** *2 F1*

This sleek, modern luxury hotel near the Spanish Steps is located on Via Margutta, the "artists' street". The Hotel Art prides itself on being an excellent example of top design, with contemporary artwork adorning the lounge walls. Rooms are on the small side, but they have pretty much every amenity you could want. Service is friendly. **www.hotelart.it**

**Key to Price Guide** *see p558* **Key to Symbols** *see back cover flap*

### PIAZZA DI SPAGNA Locarno €€€

*Via della Penna 22, 00186* ***Tel*** *06 361 08 41* ***Fax*** *06 321 52 49* ***Rooms*** *66* ***Map*** *2 F1*

A gorgeous Art Deco hotel, with many original fittings in its public spaces and bedrooms. The Locarno is a step away from Piazza del Popolo. More than just a place to rest your head, this hotel has a pleasant sitting room with a log fire and a sunny flower-filled patio and roof garden. Bikes are available for guests' use. **www.hotellocarno.com**

### PIAZZA DI SPAGNA Parlamento €€€

*Via delle Convertite 5, 00187* ***Tel/Fax*** *06 69 92 10 00* ***Rooms*** *23* ***Map*** *10 E1*

This is a delightful hotel on the top floors of a building just off the bustling Corso. The affable, elegantly dressed owner runs a very tight ship, offering spacious, old-fashioned rooms with heavy wooden furniture and nicely appointed bathrooms. Air conditioning is available on request. Pleasant roof terrace. **www.hotelparlamento.it**

### PIAZZA DI SPAGNA San Carlo €€€

*Via delle Carozze 93, 00187* ***Tel*** *06 678 45 48* ***Fax*** *06 69 94 11 97* ***Rooms*** *50* ***Map*** *3 A2*

On a charming street just off the Corso and a short walk from the Spanish Steps, in the thick of Rome's shopping mecca, San Carlo is good value for its location, which can be a bit noisy for some. Rooms vary; superior rooms on the upper floors are of a higher standard, and some offer a terrace. **www.hotelsancarloroma.com**

### PIAZZA DI SPAGNA Hotel Piranesi €€€€

*Via del Babuino 196, 00187* ***Tel*** *06 32 80 41* ***Fax*** *06 361 05 97* ***Rooms*** *32* ***Map*** *2 F1*

Situated right beside Piazza del Popolo, in a restored historic palazzo built by Valadier, the Piranesi is a boutique hotel with a lovely roof terrace, gym and sauna. Rooms are large and luxuriously decorated in dark wood and muted gold fabric. **www.hotelpiranesi.com**

### PIAZZA DI SPAGNA Hassler €€€€€

*Piazza Trinità dei Monti 6, 00187* ***Tel*** *06 69 93 40* ***Fax*** *06 678 99 91* ***Rooms*** *95* ***Map*** *3 A2*

At the top of the Spanish Steps, this is the glitterati's choice and the *grande dame* of Rome's hotels. Service is impeccable and the public spaces are luxurious with marble, chandeliers and wood panelling. Bedrooms and suites are plush, styled individually and most have views. Legendary roof restaurant. **www.hotelhasslerroma.com**

### PIAZZA NAVONA Due Torri €€€

*Vicolo del Leonetto 23, 00186* ***Tel*** *06 687 69 83* ***Fax*** *06 686 54 42* ***Rooms*** *26* ***Map*** *2 E3, 9 C1*

Hidden away on a quiet, cobblestone road towards the river, Due Torri is decorated with red velvet and brocade against golden yellow walls, marble and parquet. Once the home of cardinals, it is cosy and friendly, with smallish rooms, some with private terraces, and some with lovely balconies with views. **www.hotelduetorriroma.com**

### PIAZZA NAVONA Teatro Pace €€€

*Via del Teatro Pace 33, 00186* ***Tel*** *06 687 90 75* ***Fax*** *06 68 19 23 64* ***Rooms*** *23* ***Map*** *9 C3*

Just around the corner from the piazza, the Teatro Pace opened in 2004. A beautiful ochre palazzo, lovingly restored, its original features – wooden beams, stucco and spiral stone staircase – are intact. Rooms vary but are all spacious and stylishly decorated. The suite has a tiny terrace. Good service. **www.hotelteatropace.com**

### PIAZZA NAVONA Raphael €€€€

*Largo Febo 2, 00186* ***Tel*** *06 68 28 31* ***Fax*** *06 687 89 93* ***Rooms*** *59* ***Map*** *9 C2*

A lovely burnt-sienna palazzo, strewn with ivy and fairy lights just off the piazza, Raphael is romantic and stylish. There are breathtaking views from its roof terrace, where meals are served in summer. Rooms are well appointed, if fairly small. The lobby is filled with art, including a Picasso porcelain collection. **www.raphaelhotelrome.com**

### QUIRINAL Giardino €€

*Via XXIV Maggio 51, 00187* ***Tel*** *06 679 49 97* ***Fax*** *06 679 51 55* ***Rooms*** *11* ***Map*** *3 B4*

A pleasant stroll from the Trevi Fountain and the Forum, Giardino shares a street with the Quirinal Palace, the residence of the president of Italy. Rooms are spacious and well furnished. Breakfast is served in a pretty room overlooking a little patio garden. **www.hotel-giardino-roma.com**

### QUIRINAL Fellini Inn €€€

*Via Rasella 55–56, 00187* ***Tel*** *06 42 74 27 32* ***Fax*** *06 42 39 16 48* ***Rooms*** *6* ***Map*** *3 B3*

The street next to this B&B is a bit loud, but that's the price you must pay for being literally two minutes away from the Trevi Fountain. The Fellini Inn offers clean, simple rooms with bathrooms and gorgeous views. Book the attic apartment for extra privacy and a pleasant rooftop area with chairs and table. Friendly service. **www.fellinibnb.com**

### QUIRINAL Tritone €€€

*Via del Tritone 210, 00187* ***Tel*** *06 69 92 25 75* ***Fax*** *06 678 26 24* ***Rooms*** *43* ***Map*** *3 A3, 10 F1*

Near Piazza Barberini and the Trevi Fountain, Tritone has comfortable rooms and fine decor. Superior rooms feature stylish wood-veneered walls, a flat-screen TV and MP3 player, and plush bathrooms with power showers. A roof terrace is used for breakfast in summer. **www.tritonehotel.com**

### QUIRINAL Fontana €€€€

*Piazza di Trevi 96, 00187* ***Tel*** *06 678 61 13* ***Fax*** *06 679 00 24* ***Rooms*** *25* ***Map*** *10 F2*

The fabulous Fontana stands opposite the Trevi Fountain. Before becoming a hotel in the 1700s, the building was a monastery and rooms reflect this: not all have air conditioning. It's old-fashioned with charismatic service and a lovely roof terrace. The crowds below may be noisy, but there are great views. **www.hotelfontana-trevi.com**

**TERMINI The Beehive** €

*Via Marghera 8, 00185* **Tel** *06 44 70 45 53* **Fax** *06 97 27 94 31* **Rooms** *7* **Map** *4 E3*

A small, boutique-style hotel run by an American couple. Rooms are simple – there's no TV or air conditioning, and bathrooms are shared – but decorated in a fun style. The hotel has a private garden, on-site café for breakfast (not included), and art exhibits. Three off-site self-catering apartments also available. **www.the-beehive.com**

**TERMINI Italy B&B** €€

*Via Palestro 49, 00185* **Tel** *06 445 26 29* **Fax** *06 445 74 16* **Rooms** *3* **Map** *4 E2*

Highly praised by former guests, the Sicilian Restivo family have moved house and opened a small guesthouse around the corner from their old *pensione*. Standards remain high with extremely clean, well-maintained rooms, with or without en suite bathrooms. **www.italybnb.it**

**TERMINI Piccolo Principe B&B** €€

*Via Giovanni Giolitti 255, 00185* **Tel** *06 99 31 10* **Fax** *06 97 99 99 62* **Rooms** *8* **Map** *4 E4*

This bed-and-breakfast offers many of the amenities of a large hotel. The rooms are decorated in vivid colours; some face on to the train station (with private balcony), while others look into the inner courtyard. A communal kitchen is available for guest use, and breakfast is self-service. **www.bebromatermini.it**

**TERMINI Canada** €€€

*Via Vicenza 58, 00185* **Tel** *06 445 77 70* **Fax** *06 445 07 49* **Rooms** *70* **Map** *4 E2*

Now a Best Western hotel, with lovely rooms and excellent service, Canada originally housed officers from the nearby barracks. Bedrooms vary in size but all have tiled floors and antique furniture and some have ceiling frescoes. Deluxe rooms are romantic with an eye for detail. Very convenient for the station. **www.hotelcanadaroma.com**

**TERMINI Hotel Columbia** €€€

*Via del Viminale 15, 00184* **Tel** *06 488 35 09* **Fax** *06 474 02 09* **Rooms** *43* **Map** *3 C3*

A quiet gem of a hotel in one of Rome's busiest neighbourhoods. Dark wood and light coloured fabrics give the rooms (some with balconies) an airy, Mediterranean feel. The extensive buffet breakfast can be enjoyed on the pretty roof terrace. **www.hotelcolumbia.com**

**TERMINI Oceania** €€€

*Via Firenze 38, 00184* **Tel** *06 482 46 96* **Fax** *06 488 5586* **Rooms** *9* **Map** *3 C3*

Small, yet very popular, Oceania has a nice location opposite Rome's opera house. Large, immaculate rooms are brightly decorated. All are en suite, with private heating and air conditioning. There is also a garage available to guests. The staff are very attentive. **www.hoteloceania.it**

**TERMINI Palladium Palace** €€€

*Via Gioberti 36, 00185* **Tel** *06 446 69 17* **Fax** *06 446 69 37* **Rooms** *81* **Map** *4 D4*

Conveniently placed for Termini and public transport, the Palladium is a short stroll away from Santa Maria Maggiore and the Esquiline Hill. Rooms are large and tastefully decorated. Superior rooms feature Jacuzzi bathtubs. There is also a roof terrace. Excellent staff. **www.hotelpalladiumpalace.it**

**TERMINI Residenza Cellini** €€€

*Via Modena 5, 00185* **Tel** *06 47 82 52 04* **Fax** *06 47 88 18 06* **Rooms** *6* **Map** *3 C3*

Close to Piazza della Repubblica, the Cellini is an absolute find, though it may look unpromising from the outside. Romantic and utterly endearing, this *pensione* has six bedrooms, each decorated with great care: antiques, fresh flowers and every detail you could ask for. Very helpful staff. **www.residenzacellini.it**

**TERMINI Radisson** €€€€

*Via Filippo Turati 171, 00185* **Tel** *06 44 48 41* **Fax** *06 44 34 13 96* **Rooms** *232* **Map** *4 E4*

The Radisson is a fabulous hotel, resplendent in glass, wood and steel, with multicoloured lighting at night. From its trendy rooftop bar and restaurant, beside an outdoor swimming pool (with gym and spa), it feels like an ocean liner. Modern rooms. Located beside Termini station. **www.radissonblu.com/eshotel-rome**

**TERMINI St Regis Grand Hotel** €€€€€

*Via Vittorio Emanuele Orlando 3, 00185* **Tel** *06 470 91* **Fax** *06 474 73 07* **Rooms** *161* **Map** *3 C3*

As grand as its name, this hotel was built in 1894 as the first deluxe hotel in Rome. Now completely restored, it is one of the world's finest hotels and attracts heads of state, celebrities, royalty and captains of industry. Its restaurant, Vivendo, is cited as Rome's finest. Sumptuous rooms and impeccable service. **www.starwoodhotels.com/stregis**

**TRASTEVERE Domus Tiberina** €€

*Via in Piscinula 37, 00153* **Tel/Fax** *06 580 30 33* **Rooms** *10* **Map** *6 D1*

Not far from the river and the Isola Tiberina, Domus Tiberina provides air conditioning, bathrooms and a 24-hour reception service in its ten flats. The rooms are cosy and richly decorated, with gold brocade bedspreads, warm yellow walls and original wooden beams in the ceiling. **www.hoteldomustiberina.it**

**TRASTEVERE San Francesco** €€€

*Via Jacopa de' Settesoli 7, 00153* **Tel** *06 58 30 00 51* **Fax** *06 58 33 34 13* **Rooms** *24* **Map** *5 C2*

A lovely little hotel, away from the crowds, with the perfect roof terrace. Very stylish, modern rooms in a converted Franciscan convent. Professional and friendly staff. A tiny shuttle bus on the adjacent square takes you to the heart of Trastevere and a tram takes you across the river to the centre. **www.hotelsanfrancesco.net**

**Key to Price Guide** *see p558* **Key to Symbols** *see back cover flap*

**TRASTEVERE Villa della Fonte** €€€

*Via della Fonte dell'Olio 8, 00153* ***Tel*** *06 580 37 97* ***Fax*** *06 580 37 96* ***Rooms*** *5* ***Map*** *5 C1*

A delightful guesthouse overseen by a charming owner, Villa della Fonte is a minute's walk from Piazza Santa Maria di Trastevere. Rooms are pretty with en suite bathrooms and air conditioning. Breakfast is served on a lovely flower-strewn patio, where guests can relax through the day. **www.villafonte.com**

**VATICAN Florida** €€

*Via Cola di Rienzo 243, 00192* ***Tel*** *06 324 18 72* ***Fax*** *06 324 18 57* ***Rooms*** *18* ***Map*** *1 C2*

A quiet place to rest your head, Florida is on the second floor of a residential building, very close to St Peter's. Comfortable decor at very good prices, especially off-season. Rooms with or without bathrooms are on offer. All en suite rooms have air conditioning but breakfast is not included. **www.hotelfloridaroma.it**

**VATICAN Bramante** €€€

*Vicolo delle Palline 24, 00192* ***Tel*** *06 68 80 64 26* ***Fax*** *06 68 13 33 39* ***Rooms*** *16* ***Map*** *1 C3*

Very conveniently placed for St Peter's and beating the queues at the Vatican, Bramante was the first hotel to open in the area, in the late 1870s. Housed in a lovely 16th-century building, its bedrooms are very comfortable and elegant, all with modern facilities. Located in a quiet street. **www.hotelbramante.com**

**VATICAN Farnese** €€€

*Via A Farnese 30, 00192* ***Tel*** *06 321 25 53* ***Fax*** *06 321 51 29* ***Rooms*** *23* ***Map*** *2 D1*

Conveniently placed for Lepanto metro station and a short walk from the Vatican, Farnese is a smart, small hotel with wooden parquet floors, custom-made walnut furniture and particularly nice bathrooms. A beautiful roof terrace offers unparalleled views of the dome of St Peter's. **www.hotelfarnese.com**

**VATICAN Orange Hotel** €€€

*Via Crescenzio 86, 00193* ***Tel*** *06 686 89 69* ***Fax*** *06 689 26 10* ***Rooms*** *26* ***Map*** *2 D2*

The "orange" concept is the main element of this boutique hotel's decor: everything here is orange-coloured – and scented, too. Conveniently located, the Orange is just a short walk from the Vatican. The rooms are comfortable and functional, and breakfast is served on the roof. Helpful staff. **www.orangehotelrome.com**

**VATICAN Palazzo Cardinal Cesi** €€€

*Via della Conciliazione 51, 00193* ***Tel*** *06 684 03 90* ***Fax*** *06 68 19 33 33* ***Rooms*** *30* ***Map*** *1 C3*

This former cardinal's palace is owned by a cultural association whose aim is to organize cultural events and provide lodging close to the basilica. An absolute gem, decorated in warm crimson and sienna with parquet flooring. Rooms have modern facilities. **www.palazzocesi.it**

**VATICAN Sant'Anna** €€€

*Borgo Pio 133, 00193* ***Tel*** *06 68 80 16 02* ***Fax*** *06 68 30 87 17* ***Rooms*** *20* ***Map*** *1 C3*

A burnt-orange, 15th-century building houses this lovely family hotel. Bedrooms are romantic and beautifully decorated, with pastel-toned *trompe l'oeil* and marble bathrooms. Upper rooms have terraces. Breakfast is served in a cellar with cheerful murals or on the delightful sunny patio. **www.hotelsantanna.com**

**VATICAN Spring House** €€€

*Via Mocenigo 7, 00192* ***Tel*** *06 39 72 09 48* ***Fax*** *06 39 72 10 47* ***Rooms*** *54* ***Map*** *1 A1*

The very modern Spring House is only a short walk from the Vatican Museums, and is ideally located for those wishing to beat the queues. Its public rooms are bright and cheerful, and its bedrooms have a simple decor in swathes of colour. Rooms partially adapted for the disabled are available. Good transport links. **www.springhousehotelrome.it**

**VATICAN Rome Cavalieri** €€€€€

*Via Cadlolo 101, 00136* ***Tel*** *06 35 09 20 31* ***Fax*** *06 35 09 22 41* ***Rooms*** *370*

Although a 15-minute drive from the centre of Rome, the Cavalieri is one of the city's top hotels, with the finest restaurant, La Pergola. Set in large, lush gardens, it has a huge pool and a sumptuous spa. Rooms are beautifully decorated and some have spectacular views over Rome. Extras are expensive. **www.romecavalieri.com**

**VIA VENETO Hotel Golden** €€

*Via Marche 84, 00187* ***Tel*** *06 482 16 59* ***Fax*** *06 482 16 60* ***Rooms*** *13* ***Map*** *3 B2*

On the first floor of a 19th-century palazzo, this cosy family-run hotel offers pleasant, elegantly furnished rooms with comfortable beds, and it is known for the extremely professional service and helpful staff. The park of Villa Borghese is across the street, and the surroundings are dotted with good restaurants and cafés. **www.hotelgoldenrome.com**

**VIA VENETO Lilium** €€€

*Via XX Settembre 50a, 00187* ***Tel*** *06 474 11 33* ***Fax*** *06 23 32 83 87* ***Rooms*** *14* ***Map*** *4 D2*

On the third floor of a residential building midway between Termini and Via Veneto, Lilium is a charming little hotel. Each of its small, beautifully decorated rooms is named after a flower and painted to match. The breakfast and sitting rooms are pretty with fresh flowers and colourful Australian songbirds. Excellent staff. **www.liliumhotel.it**

**VIA VENETO Oxford** €€€

*Via Boncompagni 89, 00187* ***Tel*** *06 420 36 01* ***Fax*** *06 42 81 53 49* ***Rooms*** *58* ***Map*** *3 C1*

Oxford is located on a quiet residential road off Piazza Fiume, and a short stroll from Via Veneto. The hotel also offers two apartments for brief or long stays. There's a good restaurant and a friendly bar. Bedrooms are comfortable. Stylish public rooms with sofas encourage relaxation. **www.hoteloxford.it**

**VIA VENETO Hotel Eden** €€€€€

*Via Ludovisi 49, 00187* ***Tel*** *06 47 81 21* ***Fax*** *06 482 15 84* ***Rooms*** *121* ***Map*** *3 B2*

One of Rome's historic hotels with an illustrious guestbook, the Eden is beautifully decorated and works like clockwork. Its rooms and suites gleam and the concierge service is impeccable. The roof garden has a wonderful view with an acclaimed Michelin-star restaurant. All at a very high price, however. **www.edenroma.com**

**VIA VENETO Westin Excelsior** €€€€€

*Via Veneto 125, 00187* ***Tel*** *06 470 81* ***Fax*** *06 482 62 05* ***Rooms*** *319* ***Map*** *3 B2*

Exotically sculpted balconies with caryatid figures announce the presence of this extravagant hotel on Via Veneto. Inside are boutiques, a wonderful spa with pool, excellent panoramic restaurants and bar and even a children's club. The rooms are classically sumptuous throughout. **excelsior.hotelinroma.com**

**VILLA BORGHESE Villa Borghese Resort** €

*Via Tevere 15, 00198* ***Tel*** *06 854 63 41* ***Fax*** *06 85 34 59 66* ***Rooms*** *7* ***Map*** *3 C1*

This hotel is ideal for those who want to stay away from the touristy areas – and the centre is a mere ten-minute bus ride away. Despite the name, it doesn't feel like a "resort", but the rooms are large and clean, and the atmosphere is pleasant. Staff are friendly and professional, though not everyone speaks English. **www.villaborgheseresort.it**

**VILLA BORGHESE Villa Mangili** €€€

*Via G Mangili 31, 00197* ***Tel*** *06 321 71 30* ***Fax*** *06 322 43 13* ***Rooms*** *12*

In a pleasant, quiet part of Parioli, Villa Mangili is close to the Villa Borghese park near the auditorium and the Villa Giulia. Although small, it has spacious and beautifully decorated rooms with wooden parquet floors. Breakfast is served in a lovely garden. The hotel exhibits and sells the works of new artists. **www.hotelvillamangili.it**

**VILLA BORGHESE Aldrovandi Palace** €€€€

*Via Aldrovandi 15, 00197* ***Tel*** *06 322 39 93* ***Fax*** *06 322 14 35* ***Rooms*** *108*

For those who prefer to stay away from the frenzy of central Rome, this relaxing luxurious hotel has a prime spot beside the Villa Borghese gardens. Rooms are elegantly decorated in subdued tones. However, the main attractions are its delightful swimming pool and its wonderful restaurant, Baby. **www.aldrovandi.com**

## LAZIO

**ANAGNI Villa La Floridiana** €€

*Via Casilina, km. 63.7, 03012* ***Tel*** *0775 76 95 82* ***Fax*** *0775 77 93 06* ***Rooms*** *13*

This charming 19th-century villa – with a faded pink façade and green shutters – features large, comfortable rooms filled with refined rustic furnishings of the 1800s. It is set in a little park 5 km (3 miles) from a medieval village. Regional dishes are served beneath frescoed ceilings in the restaurant. **www.villalafloridiana.com**

**GROTTAFERRATA Parkhotel Villa Grazioli** €€€€

*Via Umberto Pavoni 19, 00046* ***Tel*** *06 94 54 00* ***Fax*** *06 941 35 06* ***Rooms*** *62*

Set in a former cardinal's residence from the 16th century, this elegant hotel is located just up the road from the charming hill town of Frascati. Housed in three separate villas on the same grounds, rooms offer views of Rome, the sea, and nearby Tivoli. Facilities include meeting halls, banquet halls and golf course. **www.villagrazioli.com**

**ISOLA DI PONZA Grand Hotel Chiaia di Luna** €€€€

*Via Panoramica, 04027* ***Tel*** *0771 801 13* ***Fax*** *0771 80 98 21* ***Rooms*** *78*

Rooms in this four-star establishment are small and simple, but the location is the prime attraction here, since the hotel is nestled in a natural rock amphitheatre. Guests can relax on the terrace and enjoy the fabulous views of the sea while they order from the restaurant/bar, or swim in the seawater pool. **www.hotelchiaiadiluna.com**

**LADISPOLI La Posta Vecchia** €€€€€

*Località Palo Laziale, 00055* ***Tel*** *06 994 95 01* ***Fax*** *06 994 95 07* ***Rooms*** *19*

A magnificent 17th-century villa by the sea, this former home of John Paul Getty is one of Italy's most luxurious hotels. All rooms are exquisitely and individually decorated with antiques, such as gilded Renaissance furniture, Flemish tapestries and marble baths. Spa and ancient Roman museum on site. **www.lapostavecchia.com**

**PALESTRINA Anne's Place** €

*Via Loreto 220, 00036* ***Tel*** *06 957 35 54* ***Fax*** *06 60 51 36 12* ***Rooms*** *3*

This B&B offers simple but pleasant rooms with modern en-suite bathrooms. The rooms and the house's terraces overlook the hills of Palestrina, offering stunning views. A lounge room with satellite TV, DVD player and communal mini-bar is available. Service by the owners, Anne and David, gets rave reviews. **www.byanne.com**

**SABAUDIA Oasi di Kufra** €€€

*Lungomare di Sabaudia, km 29.8, 04016* ***Tel*** *0773 51 91* ***Fax*** *0773 519 88* ***Rooms*** *120*

A luminous hotel amid sandy dunes. Along with a private beach, spa and fitness centre, it offers balconies in most of the breezy, homely rooms. Suites overlooking the sea and several apartments with kitchenettes. From mid-Jun–late Aug, there is a minimum stay that varies from one to two weeks. **www.oasidikufra.it**

**Key to Price Guide** *see p558* **Key to Symbols** *see back cover flap*

### SAN FELICE CIRCEO Punta Rossa  €€€€

*Via delle Batterie 37, 04017* **Tel** *0773 54 80 85* **Fax** *0773 54 80 75* **Rooms** *33*

A charming hotel and spa set in a garden that leads down to the sea. The rooms – all of which have terraces and views of the sea and the Pontine Islands – are located in various buildings scattered about the verdant property. There are also private apartments in an old fishing village. **www.puntarossa.it**

### SUBIACO Foresteria Santa Scolastica €

*Monastero Santa Scolastica, 00028* **Tel** *0774 824 21* **Fax** *0774 82 28 62* **Rooms** *50*

Originally founded by St Benedict in the 6th century, the largely rebuilt monastery of Santa Scolastica provides lodgings for up to 100 visitors. The en-suite rooms have basic comforts and some come with good views of the town below. Special half-or full-board deals make staying with the monks a good budget option. **www.benedettini-subiaco.it**

### TARQUINIA Hotel Tarconte €€

*Via della Tuscia 19, 01016* **Tel** *0766 85 61 41* **Fax** *0766 85 65 85* **Rooms** *50*

Modern hotel with panoramic views to the coast. Rooms are decorated in a functional style, and public spaces have rather dated decor, but it is just five minutes from the National Etruscan Museum and there is an ancient tomb in the basement. The restaurant specializes in game. **www.hoteltarconte.it**

### TARQUINIA LIDO La Torraccia €

*Viale Mediterraneo 45, 01016* **Tel** *0766 86 43 75* **Fax** *0766 86 42 96* **Rooms** *18*

A modern, comfortable hotel set in pinewoods some 200 m (656 ft) from the sea. All rooms are decorated in bright primary colours (mostly red and yellow) with whitewashed walls, and each has a terrace. There's a garden terrace for breakfasts and a private beach just a short stroll away. **www.torraccia.it**

### TIVOLI Hotel Victoria Terme €€

*Via Tiburtina Valerio, Km 22,700, 00011* **Tel** *077 440 88* **Fax** *077 440 84 08* **Rooms** *130*

Situated inside the Acque Albule thermal park and surrounded by sulphureous hot springs, this modern hotel is just a few steps away from a popular thermal spa with four hot pools, a gym and a wellness centre. The rooms are simple but comfortable, and some even have a Jacuzzi and a balcony. **www.victoriatermehotel.it**

### TIVOLI Palazzo Maggiore €€

*Via Domenico Giuliani 89, 00019* **Tel** *393 104 49 37 (mobile)* **Rooms** *3*

In the historic heart of Tivoli, the 16th-century Palazzo Maggiore offers tastefully furnished rooms at budget rates. A two-room apartment sleeping up to six guests is also available. The continental breakfast can be enjoyed in the rooms, on the small terrace or in the owner's kitchen. Rome is just over an hour away by train. **www.palazzomaggiore.com**

### TIVOLI TERME Grand Hotel Duca d'Este €€

*Via Tiburtina Valeria 330, 00011* **Tel** *0774 38 83* **Fax** *0774 38 81 01* **Rooms** *184*

A modern and well-equipped hotel near Tivoli and the Villa Adriana and within easy reach of Rome by road or rail. Rooms are large, with nicely built functional units. Suites come with Jacuzzi tubs. There's a spa with sauna and an indoor pool, and tropical gardens hiding tennis courts and a pool. **www.ducadeste.com**

### TUSCANIA Al Gallo €€

*Via del Gallo 22, 01017* **Tel** *0761 44 33 88* **Fax** *0761 44 36 28* **Rooms** *13*

An old house in the historic centre of town. Antique furnishings, elaborate designs on the wallpaper, thick carpeting, dark woods, and heavy curtains give the well-maintained guest rooms a sumptuous look. There is also a very comfortable piano bar with live music at the weekends. **www.algallo.it**

### VITERBO Roma €

*Via della Cava 26, 01100* **Tel** *0761 22 64 74* **Fax** *0761 30 55 07* **Rooms** *67*

A very simple, and inexpensive, hotel right in the centre of town, halfway between the railway station and the Rocca fortress. The exterior is fabulous – a medieval palazzo – while the guest rooms are done in a modern, functional style. Good deals are arranged with local restaurants.

### VITERBO Hotel Mini Palace €€

*Via Santa Maria della Grotticella 2b, 01100* **Tel** *0761 30 97 42* **Fax** *0761 34 47 15* **Rooms** *40*

Located a short walk from Porta Romana and the historic centre, this hotel is perfect for visitors looking for a quiet stay. The rooms are large, cosy and elegantly furnished, and the staff are very friendly. The hotel restaurant, Le Chandelier, is worth a try as it serves local dishes and a selection of regional wines. **www.minipalacehotel.com**

## NAPLES AND CAMPANIA

### AMALFI Floridiana €€

*Via Brancia 1, 84011* **Tel** *089 873 63 73* **Fax** *089 87 39 07* **Rooms** *13*

This hotel is housed in a 12th-century palazzo near the Duomo, bus station and main beach. The breakfast buffet is served under sumptuous ceilings in a grand salon. Guest rooms are comfortable, marrying functional furniture with colourful tiled floors. The Junior Suite has a mezzanine with lounge and Jacuzzi. **www.hotelfloridiana.it**

### AMALFI Hotel Amalfi €€

*Via dei Pastai 3, 84011* **Tel** *089 87 24 40* **Fax** *089 87 22 50* **Rooms** *40*

A family-run hotel with a lovely terrace, patio and restaurant in a quiet spot in old Amalfi. Views of the Duomo across the rooftops, pretty geranium-covered balconies and a sense of peace, away from the crowds. The bedrooms are large and comfortable, most with air conditioning. Excellent value. **www.hamalfi.it**

### AMALFI Marina Riviera €€€

*Via P Comite 19, 84011* **Tel** *089 87 11 04* **Fax** *089 87 10 24* **Rooms** *34*

Grandstand views of Amalfi's main beach and skyline can be enjoyed from the breakfast terrace and from many of the rooms, which are decorated with cool hues, tiled floors and interesting artworks. Some have hydro-massage baths. There are suites and connecting rooms to suit families and groups. **www.marinariviera.it**

### AMALFI Hotel Santa Caterina €€€€€

*SS Amalfitana 9, 84011* **Tel** *089 87 10 12* **Fax** *089 87 13 51* **Rooms** *66*

Run by the same family since 1880, this luxury hotel is one of the Amalfi Coast's finest. Perched on a promontory tumbling down to the sea, it has extensive gardens and a private beach. Rooms and suites are lavish, all with antiques, majolica floor tiles and balconies or terraces. Spa and excellent restaurant. **www.hotelsantacaterina.it**

### BENEVENTO Hotel Villa Traiano €€

*Viale dei Rettori 9, 82100* **Tel** *0824 32 62 41* **Fax** *0824 32 61 96* **Rooms** *19*

This is a private villa built in Liberty style. It is situated in the heart of Benevento near the Arco Traiano, close to the railway station, shops and restaurants. Public areas and bedrooms are extremely elegant. The sunny roof terrace and courtyard offer a relaxing place to sit. **www.hotelvillatraiano.it**

### CAPRI Hotel Weber Ambassador €€

*Via Marina Piccola 118, 80073* **Tel** *081 837 01 41 or 800 84 26 23 (toll free)* **Fax** *081 837 88 66* **Rooms** *158*

Perched above Marina Piccola, Capri's best beach, with wonderful views over the famous Faraglioni Islands, is this yellow painted building with blue canopies and geraniums. There is also a lovely terrace where a generous breakfast is served and a roof garden. Sea-facing rooms and suites cost considerably more. **www.hotelweber.com**

### CAPRI Pensione Villa La Tosca €€

*Via D Birago 5, 80073* **Tel** *081 837 09 89* **Fax** *081 837 48 03* **Rooms** *11*

A cosy, old-fashioned *pensione* in Capri town, with white walls and ceramic tiled floors. Its terraces overlook the sea with the Faraglioni in the distance and the Certosa di San Giacomo below. Rooms are light, some with sea views and all en suite with air conditioning and phone. Closed Nov–Mar. **www.latoscahotel.com**

### CAPRI Hotel La Minerva €€€€

*Via Occhio Marino 8, 80073* **Tel** *081 837 03 74* **Fax** *081 837 70 67* **Rooms** *18*

A pretty five-storey hotel with flower-filled terraces, in a quiet, picturesque spot not far from the centre of Capri town. Majolica tile floors, antiques and sea views. Superior rooms have a terrace, deluxe rooms have whirlpool bathtubs and sea-facing terraces, while standard rooms are much cheaper. **www.laminervacapri.com**

### CAPRI JK Place €€€€€

*Via Prov Marina Grande 225, 80073* **Tel** *081 838 40 01* **Fax** *081 837 04 38* **Rooms** *22*

With its sea views and understated style, Capri's chicest hotel is the darling of lifestyle magazines. The boutique feel is achieved with classical statues, quirky objects, black-and-white photos and art books. Rooms mix luxurious fabrics with elegant furnishings. A spa and superb service complete the exclusive package. **www.jkcapri.com**

### CAPRI (ANACAPRI) Capri Palace Hotel & Spa €€€€€

*Via Capodimonte 14, Anacapri, 80071* **Tel** *081 978 01 11* **Fax** *081 837 31 91* **Rooms** *78*

This is one of Capri's most beautiful hotels, with a pool and spa and a Michelin-starred restaurant. Bedrooms are stylish: classic rooms have views over Monte Solare, others have sea views and balcony; suites have a private terrace, pool and garden. Art collection, hotel yacht and motorboat. Closed Nov–Mar. **www.capripalace.com**

### CASERTA Hotel Europa €€€

*Via Roma 19, 81100* **Tel** *0823 32 54 00* **Fax** *0823 21 66 23* **Rooms** *57*

Very close to the railway station and a short walk away from both the beautiful palace of Caserta and the city centre. Predominantly a business hotel, bedrooms are clean and smart – executive double rooms and suites have an adjoining sitting room. Guests can use a nearby gym and spa at a reduced rate. **www.hoteleuropacaserta.it**

### ERCOLANO Miglio d'Oro Park €€

*Corso Resina 296, 80056* **Tel** *081 739 99 99* **Fax** *081 777 70 49* **Rooms** *53*

A converted 18th-century pile named after the "Golden Mile" of Bourbon-era villas along the Vesuvian coastline. Cavernous rooms have contemporary furnishings; some look over the grounds and up to Vesuvius. A lounge is filled with quirky artworks. Superb buffet choice includes local mozzarella and pastries. **www.migliodoroparkhotel.it**

### ISCHIA Il Monastero €€

*Castello Aragonese, Ischia Ponte, 80070* **Tel** *081 99 24 35* **Fax** *081 99 18 49* **Rooms** *22*

A very distinguished and romantic address, high inside the castle at Ischia Ponte, inside a former convent. Bedrooms are former cells but are cool, comfortable and spacious, with modern bathrooms and most with spectacular views over the sea. Guests have free run of the beautiful castle grounds. Closed Nov–Apr. **www.albergoilmonastero.it**

**Key to Price Guide** *see p558* **Key to Symbols** *see back cover flap*

**ISCHIA Grand Albergo Mezza Torre** €€€€€

*Via Mezzatorre 23, Foriò d'Ischia, 80075* ***Tel*** *081 98 61 11* ***Fax*** *081 98 60 15* ***Rooms*** *57*

A luxury spa hotel pine forest on a bluff above the sea outside Foriò. Standard rooms have balconies overlooking the park; comfort rooms have balconies with sea views; superior rooms and suites are sumptuous, some within the Saracen Tower. Romantic restaurants, pool and private beach. **www.mezzatorre.it**

**NAPLES Cappella Vecchia** €€

*Vico Santa Maria a Cappella Vecchia 11, 81021* ***Tel*** *081 240 51 17* ***Fax*** *081 245 53 38* ***Rooms*** *6*

A small guesthouse in a charming area on a tiny street off the Piazza dei Martiri in Chiaia. Very convenient for exploring Naples, it is near a bus terminus and not far from the metro station at Piazza Amedeo. Its six bedrooms are cheerful and modern, with en suite bathrooms and air conditioning. **www.cappellavecchia11.it**

**NAPLES Donnalbina 7** €€

*Via Donnalbina 7, 80134* ***Tel*** *081 1956 7817* ***Fax*** *081 1956 7620* ***Rooms*** *6*

A good-value choice near Piazza Gesù Nuovo and all the sights, sounds and smells of Spaccanapoli. Rooms have a clean, unfussy feel with modern design pieces and vibrant artworks by Neapolitan artists. Welcome luxuries include free Wi-Fi and breakfast in bed up to 10:30am. **www.donnalbina7.it**

**NAPLES Hotel Chiaja de Charme** €€

*Via Chiaia 216, 81021* ***Tel*** *081 41 55 55* ***Fax*** *081 42 23 44* ***Rooms*** *27*

A lovely intimate hotel with reception on the first floor of a noble palazzo on the pedestrian street of Via Chiaia, two minutes' walk from Piazza Plebescito. All the rooms are soundproofed and individually furnished with antiques. Some of the bathrooms have whirlpool bathtubs. Charming, professional staff. **www.hotelchiaia.it**

**NAPLES Piazza Bellini** €€

*Via Santa Maria di Costantinopoli 101, 80138* ***Tel*** *081 45 17 32* ***Rooms*** *10*

This small hotel is on a leafy square famed for its cafés and boho hangouts. Rooms are whitewashed and feature vibrant artworks and stylish design flourishes. Overall, the Piazza Bellini offers good value for the location; however, parking restrictions make this hotel problematic for those with heavy luggage. **www.hotelpiazzabellini.com**

**NAPLES Costantinopoli 104** €€€

*Via Santa Maria di Costantinopoli 104, 80138* ***Tel*** *081 557 10 35* ***Fax*** *081 557 10 51* ***Rooms*** *19*

A Liberty style villa with beautiful stained glass set in a sunny courtyard and garden with palm trees, a sun terrace and a small pool. In the *centro storico*, five minutes' walk from the archaeological museum, on a street of antique dealers. Rooms and suites are available furnished with understated elegance. **www.costantinopoli104.it**

**NAPLES Micalò** €€€

*Riviera di Chiaia 88, 80122* ***Tel*** *081 761 71 31* ***Rooms*** *9*

Located opposite the Villa Comunale gardens, Micalò offers stone floors and curvy walls with intriguing Neapolitan artworks. Owner Michelle has added smart bathrooms and luxurious details to the cavernous Spanish-Aragonese-era rooms. The Art Bar is a relaxing place to enjoy cocktails by night and a bountiful breakfast. **www.micalo.it**

**NAPLES Romeo Hotel** €€€

*Via Cristoforo Colombo 45, 80133* ***Tel*** *081 017 50 08/9* ***Fax*** *081 017 59 99* ***Rooms*** *83*

This stunning conversion of a steel-and-glass office building opposite the ferry port features lighting wizardry, bold design and bathroom fittings designed by Philippe Stark. Artworks fill the lobby, sushi restaurant and cigar room. Spa treatments and a Jacuzzi complete the jet-set feel. Good deals are available. **www.romeohotel.it**

**NAPLES Hotel Vesuvio** €€€€

*Via Partenope 45, 81021* ***Tel*** *081 764 00 44* ***Fax*** *081 764 44 83* ***Rooms*** *143*

In Santa Lucia, the Vesuvio is unarguably Naples' most luxurious hotel, with a spectacular penthouse. All bedrooms and suites are extremely comfortable, furnished with antiques and have a terrace or balcony with sea or street views. Spa and gym, terrace restaurant, babysitting room and a hotel boat. **www.vesuvio.it**

**NAPLES Palazzo Turchini** €€€€

*Via Medina 21–22, 80133* ***Tel*** *081 551 06 06* ***Fax*** *081 552 14 73* ***Rooms*** *27*

Housed in the 16th-century former Royal Conservatory, this hotel is located near the Maschio Angioino castle and other sights. Interiors are sleek, with hardwood floors and a mix of modern and antique furnishings. Excellent roof-garden views. Email correspondence is unreliable, so it's best to phone them. **www.palazzoturchini.it**

**PAESTUM Agriturismo Seliano** €€

*Via Seliano, Capaccio, 84063* ***Tel*** *0828 72 36 34* ***Fax*** *0828 72 45 44* ***Rooms*** *14*

A farm and *agriturismo* owned by an aristocratic family. Rooms are dotted around the estate in cottages or in the main house. It is also possible to stay on the nearby buffalo farm and watch how mozzarella is made. Pretty gardens and pool. Excellent food and wine. **www.agriturismoseliano.it**

**POMPEII Hotel Amleto** €€

*Via Bartolo Longo 10, 80045* ***Tel*** *081 863 10 04* ***Fax*** *081 863 55 85* ***Rooms*** *26*

A comfortable and elegant modern hotel in central Pompeii, convenient for the Circumvesuviana train between Naples and Sorrento, and a short walk to the ruins of ancient Pompeii. Run by a family, the bedrooms are spacious and well furnished. The roof terrace is a pleasant place to relax and admire the views. **www.hotelamleto.it**

**POSITANO Palazzo Murat**  €€€€

*Via dei Mulini 23, 84017* **Tel** *089 87 51 77* **Fax** *089 81 14 19* **Rooms** *30*

Set in an enchanting courtyard with an excellent restaurant, this is the former summer residence of Napoleon's brother-in-law, Joachim Murat. The bedrooms are in the old 18th-century wing – complete with stucco, wooden beams and frescoes – or in the elegant modern annexe. Classical music concerts are held on the patio. **www.palazzomurat.it**

**PRAIANO (AMALFI COAST) Hotel Onda Verde** €€€

*Via Terramare 3, 84010* **Tel** *089 87 41 43* **Fax** *089 81 31 049* **Rooms** *25*

In a quiet town midway between Amalfi and Positano, this family-run hotel has sea views and a panoramic terrace with restaurant. Bedrooms, in five little villas clustered together on a clifftop, have a bath or shower and many have private balconies. Private lido, beside a small public sandy beach. **www.ondaverde.it**

**PROCIDA La Casa sul Mare** €€

*Via Salita Castello 13, Terra Murata Corricella 80079* **Tel/Fax** *081 896 87 99* **Rooms** *10*

A small hotel, high over the fishing harbour of Corricella, beside the abandoned Terra Murata (a fort and latterday prison). Breakfast is served in the charming sea-facing garden. There are elegant public areas and bedrooms (all with sea views and terraces). A summer boat service to the beach at La Chiaia. **www.lacasasulmare.it**

**RAVELLO Palazzo Sasso** €€€€

*Via San Giovanni del Toro 28, 84010* **Tel** *089 81 81 81* **Fax** *089 85 89 00* **Rooms** *44*

Breathtaking views of the Amalfi Coast make this a special place to stay. Luxurious facilities include a Michelin-starred restaurant (Rossellini), a sumptuous spa, exclusive access to seaside terraces and concierge service. Rooms vary from smart doubles to palatial suites with huge windows framing the coastal drama. **www.palazzosasso.com**

**RAVELLO Villa Cimbrone** €€€€€

*Via Santa Chiara 26, 84010* **Tel** *089 85 74 59* **Fax** *089 85 77 77* **Rooms** *19*

This 12th-century villa has world-famous romantic gardens, set in a citrus grove. Bought by an Englishman in 1904, it was a regular haunt of the Bloomsbury Set. Rooms have spectacular vaulting, frescoes, majolica tiles, fireplaces and antiques, as well as modern facilities. **www.villacimbrone.com**

**SALERNO Hotel Plaza** €€

*Piazza Vittorio Veneto 42 (Piazza Ferrovia), 84123* **Tel** *089 22 44 77* **Fax** *089 23 73 11* **Rooms** *42*

A very central hotel, opposite the train station and within easy walking distance of the port, the old quarter and buses for the Amalfi Coast. Bedrooms are large, modern, clean and comfortable with a choice of bath or shower. There is a bar and breakfast room. Parking available nearby. **www.plazasalerno.it**

**SANNIO (SANT'AGATA DEI GOTI) Agriturismo Mustilli** €

*Via dei Fiori 20, 82019* **Tel** *0823 71 81 42* **Fax** *0823 71 76 19* **Rooms** *6*

An *agriturismo* in the historical district of the lovely medieval town of Sant'Agata dei Goti in the lush Sannio area, famed for its wine and olive oil. In the same family since the 16th century, the palazzo has sunny terraces and gardens, and lovely reception rooms. Bedrooms are charming. Excellent food and wine. **www.mustilli.com**

**SANTA MARIA DI CASTELLABATE Villa Sirio** €€€

*Via Lungomare de Simone 15, Castellabate, 84072* **Tel** *0974 96 10 99* **Fax** *0974 96 05 07* **Rooms** *19*

A beautiful fishing town by the sea, in the heart of the Cilento. This palazzo dates from 1904 and is painted a handsome yellow with deep green wooden shutters and doors. Bedrooms face the sea or the lovely old town, and some have pretty balconies. Breakfast and dinner are served on the terrace in summer. Closed Nov–Mar. **www.villasirio.it**

**SAPRI Hotel Mediterraneo** €

*Via Verdi, 84073* **Tel** *0973 39 17 74* **Fax** *0973 39 20 33* **Rooms** *20*

A cheerful hotel in a prime location on the Gulf of Policastro near the national park of the Cilento. Surrounded by sea and countryside, this quiet hotel has a little garden, sun terrace and private beach. Bedrooms with sea views have private balconies. Children's play area and restaurant. Half-board only in July and August. **www.hotelmed.it**

**SORRENTO Hotel Mignon Meublé** €€

*Via A Sersale 9, 80067* **Tel** *081 807 38 24* **Fax** *081 877 43 48* **Rooms** *22*

In the historic centre, near the cathedral and the old walls, this charming *pensione* offers spacious rooms with old-fashioned furniture, tiled floors and smart bathrooms. Breakfast is served in the bedrooms; some of these have French windows and little balconies. Limited hotel parking. **www.sorrentohotelmignon.com**

**SORRENTO La Tonnarella** €€€

*Via Capo 31, 80067* **Tel** *081 878 11 53* **Fax** *081 878 21 69* **Rooms** *24*

On a clifftop outside Sorrento, this hotel is the former summer residence of a noble family. Lovely majolica floor tiles, vaulting and antiques throughout, with wonderful views over the bay. Room prices increase for a sea view, balcony or suite. There is a restaurant and a lift down to a private beach. Closed Nov–Mar. **www.latonnarella.it**

**SORRENTO Grand Hotel Cocumella** €€€€

*Via Cocumella 7, Sant'Agnello, 80065* **Tel** *081 878 29 33* **Fax** *081 878 37 12* **Rooms** *53*

A beautiful old hotel in a quiet suburb of Sorrento. A Jesuit monastery set in lush landscaped gardens. The suites have fabulous views over the Bay of Naples. A romantic restaurant, summer concerts, a tennis court and a boat for trips to Capri and Positano are some of the features. Many facilities close during low season. **www.cocumella.com**

**Key to Price Guide** *see p558* **Key to Symbols** *see back cover flap*

## ABRUZZO, MOLISE, PUGLIA

### ALBEROBELLO Hotel Ramapendula €€

*Via Locorotondo, 70011* ***Tel/Fax*** *080 432 60 69* ***Rooms*** *61*

Surrounded by olive groves and ideally suited for families with small children, this hotel features a *trulli*-style reception area and a modern, comfortable garden with a playground. More *trulli* can be seen in the conservation area a mere ten-minute stroll away. **www.hotelramapendula.it**

### ALBEROBELLO Masseria Montalbano €€€

*Contrada Montalbano Vecchio, 72017* ***Tel*** *0831 35 99 45* ***Fax*** *0831 35 99 71* ***Rooms*** *28*

A rustic farmstead turned into a chic retreat. Rooms have ornately carved furniture complementing the unfussy decor. Verdant grounds contain a large pool and ancient olive trees. Sandy beaches are 4 km (2.5 miles) away, and there are many opportunities for cycling and other activities in the surrounding countryside. **www.masseriamontalbano.it**

### BARI Hotel Adria €€

*Via Zuppetta 10, 70121* ***Tel*** *080 524 66 99* ***Fax*** *080 521 32 07* ***Rooms*** *38*

Conveniently located opposite the train station, this is a centrally placed, well-priced option. Bedrooms are spacious and comfortable, with Internet access and a choice of bath or shower. The roof garden with bar is a nice find. French beds or standard doubles. Pets welcome. **www.adriahotelbari.com**

### BARI Palace Hotel Bari €€€

*Via Lombardi 13, 70122* ***Tel*** *080 521 65 51* ***Fax*** *080 521 14 99* ***Rooms*** *195*

A smart hotel on the edge of the *centro storico*, close to the principal sights of old Bari. Rooms are spacious, furnished with antiques and unique, with special rooms for women, music lovers, children and pets. Award-winning breakfasts and excellent dining on the roof terrace. **www.palacehotelbari.it**

### FASANO Masseria Torre Maizza €€€€€

*Contrada Coccaro, 72015* ***Tel*** *080 482 78 38* ***Fax*** *080 441 40 59* ***Rooms*** *26*

This hotel is housed in a traditional Puglian farm building with a Moorish tower. The impressive choice of spacious rooms includes the wonderful tower Suite Palme, which comes with an enclosed private courtyard and a heated hydro-massage pool. The four restaurants on site use locally grown produce. **www.masseriatorremaizza.com**

### GARGANO PENINSULA-VIESTE Hotel degli Aranci €€

*Piazza S Maria delle Grazie 10, 71019* ***Tel*** *0884 70 85 57* ***Fax*** *0884 70 73 26* ***Rooms*** *121*

A modern resort hotel with friendly service and a lively atmosphere just outside Vieste. Bedrooms are cheerful and comfortable – most have a balcony and a choice of bath or shower. Ideal for families, there is a children's club and special menus. Swimming pool on site and a private beach nearby. Shuttle bus to town. **www.hotelaranci.it**

### L'AQUILA Hotel Duomo €€

*Via Dragonetti, 67100* ***Tel*** *0862 41 08 93* ***Fax*** *0862 41 30 58* ***Rooms*** *30*

In the heart of old L'Aquila, this small hotel is within an 18th-century palazzo, located on a side street with fine views over the main square. All rooms are elegant and clean, with wrought-iron beds and decorated in warm colours and cheerful fabrics. Generous breakfasts. **www.hotel-duomo.it**

### L'AQUILA Hotel San Michele €€

*Via dei Giardini 6, 67100* ***Tel*** *0862 42 02 60* ***Fax*** *0862 270 60* ***Rooms*** *32*

This business-orientated hotel near all of L'Aquila's main sights, including the Duomo, is a reliable, if unspectacular, choice in a town lacking quality accommodation. The smallish bedrooms have dark hardwood floors and functional furniture. Friendly staff have good local knowledge and can arrange excursions. **www.stmichelehotel.it**

### L'AQUILA/GRAN SASSO D'ITALIA Hotel Nido dell'Aquila €€

*Località Fonte Cerreto, Assergi, 67010* ***Tel*** *0862 60 68 40* ***Fax*** *0862 60 88 11* ***Rooms*** *23*

Located 20 km (12 miles) outside L'Aquila at the gateway to the noble Gran Sasso near the delightful medieval town of Assergi. A charming mountain chalet with rustic furnishing, a garden, sun terrace and play area for children. Excellent home cooking and Abruzzo wines. Near the ski runs of the Campo Imperatore. **www.nidodellaquila.it**

### LECCE B&B Prestige €

*Via S Maria del Paradiso 4, 73100* ***Tel*** *0832 24 33 53* ***Fax*** *0832 52 10 60* ***Rooms*** *4*

A lovely little guesthouse in a quiet part of old Lecce on a pedestrian street overlooking the basilica of San Giambattista. Each room has a little balcony with a view on to the street and Internet access. Breakfast is served in summer on the sunny terrace. Private bathrooms – not all en suite. **www.bbprestige-lecce.it**

### LECCE Risorgimento €€€

*Via Augusto Imperatore, 19, 73100* ***Tel*** *0832 24 63 11* ***Fax*** *0832 24 59 76* ***Rooms*** *47*

A smart boutique hotel housed in an 18th-century Lecce palazzo. Public areas include a rooftop garden terrace and a choice of elegant bars and restaurants. Beiges and dark wood dominate many of the standard rooms, while the swanky suites have contemporary furniture and design flourishes. Spa facilities. **www.vestashotels.it**

**LORETO APRUTINO (nr Pescara) Castello Chiola** €€

*Via degli Aquino 12, 65014* ***Tel*** *085 829 06 90* ***Fax*** *085 829 06 77* ***Rooms*** *36*

In the medieval town of Loreto Aprutino, this elegant and comfortable hotel is housed inside a lovely old castle dating from 864. Amid lush gardens, with sunny terraces and a pool, the restaurant serves particularly fine food and wine. Modern facilities and wonderful views from the rooms. **www.castellochiolahotel.com**

**MONOPOLI Melograno** €€€€

*Contrada Torricella 345, 70043* ***Tel*** *080 690 90 30* ***Fax*** *080 74 79 08* ***Rooms*** *38*

A Relais & Châteaux hotel set amid an olive grove in a 17th-century *masseria* (fortified farmhouse). Rooms are sumptuous, some have a private patio or whirlpool bathtubs. The owner, an antique dealer, has furnished the hotel beautifully. Free shuttle bus to a private beach and use of two sailing boats. **www.melograno.com**

**OTRANTO Hotel Rosa Antico** €€

*SS116. 16 snc, 73028* ***Tel*** *0836 80 15 63* ***Fax*** *0836 80 15 63* ***Rooms*** *27*

Just 800 m (870 yds) from the ancient city of Otranto, in a peaceful spot across the bay, this is a family palazzo from the 16th century, with a modern extension, both painted a lovely antique rose colour. Bright, cheerful bedrooms and a cool, vaulted breakfast bar. Surrounded by a lush garden. **www.hotelrosaantico.it**

**SCANNO Albergo Mille Pini** €

*Via Pescara 2, 67038* ***Tel/Fax*** *0864 743 87* ***Rooms*** *19*

Near the chairlift at Scanno, the starting point for walks and skiing on Monte Retondo. A lovely rustic hotel near the lake with stone walls, wooden floors, rugs and pine furniture. Bedrooms are warm and welcoming; the sitting room has a cosy fire in winter, and the restaurant serves good home cooking. Closed Oct & Nov. **www.millepiniscanno.it**

**SULMONA Hotel Rojan** €€

*Via degli Agghiacciati 15, 67039* ***Tel*** *0864 95 01 26* ***Fax*** *0864 95 01 29* ***Rooms*** *20*

Run by the Casaccia family, renowned for excellent customer service, this hotel is a conversion of an elegant palazzo on central Sulmona's cobbled streets. Many of the simply furnished, well-maintained rooms have superb views of the town and its tranquil courtyards. A good breakfast buffet adds to the superb value. **www.hotelrojan.it**

**TARANTO Hotel Europa** €€

*Via Roma 2, 74100* ***Tel/Fax*** *099 452 59 94* ***Rooms*** *42*

A converted 19th-century palazzo centrally located in modern Taranto, Hotel Europa overlooks the city's two seas, its old fishing port and famous bridge. Rooms and mansard suites are modern and stylishly furnished; some have kitchens and sea-facing balconies. **www.hoteleuropaonline.it**

**TERMOLI Hotel Mistral** €€

*Lungomare C Colombo 50, 86039* ***Tel*** *0875 70 52 46* ***Fax*** *0875 70 52 20* ***Rooms*** *66*

Termoli, a beach resort in southern Molise, has a lovely medieval harbour and regular ferries to the Tremiti Islands. This modern hotel, right on the beach, has a fine view of the coast and the old quarter. Bedrooms are spacious and comfortable: most have sea views. Lively terrace restaurant-bar and private beach. **www.hotelmistral.net**

**TRANI Hotel Regia** €€

*Piazza Monsignor R M Addazi 2, 70059* ***Tel*** *0883 58 44 44* ***Fax*** *0883 20 23 89* ***Rooms*** *10*

Right beside the harbour and opposite Trani's exquisite Norman cathedral, this old palazzo has stylish, airy bedrooms and a nice restaurant with a terrace in summer. Bedrooms have parquet floors and are elegantly furnished in cool whites and creams, with lovely views. Friendly management. **www.hotelregia.it**

## BASILICATA & CALABRIA

**COSENZA Hotel Royal** €€

*Via Molinella 24, 87100* ***Tel*** *0984 41 21 65* ***Fax*** *0984 41 24 61* ***Rooms*** *80*

In the heart of modern Cosenza and popular with business people and tourists. Although it has a slightly 1980s feel, with parquet floors, old-fashioned fittings and decor, it is comfortable and convenient. Bedrooms are spacious, with modern facilities. It has a good restaurant, La Caprice. **www.hotelroyalsas.it**

**GERACE La Casa di Gianna** €€

*Via Paolo Frascà 4, 89040* ***Tel*** *0964 35 50 24* ***Fax*** *0964 35 50 81* ***Rooms*** *10*

In the centre of Gerace, on a narrow medieval street, an old house with rooms around a sunny atrium. A charming restaurant, piano room and bar, and a sunny terrace in summer. Bedrooms are decorated with old-fashioned elegance and home comforts – the suite has a canopy bed and whirlpool bathtub. **www.lacasadigianna.it**

**MARATEA COASTLINE – CETRARO Grand Hotel Villa San Michele** €€€

*Località Bosco 8/9, 87022* ***Tel*** *0982 910 12* ***Fax*** *0982 914 30* ***Rooms*** *59*

Set on a clifftop above the sea, with views that stretch as far as the Aeolian Islands and Mount Etna. Sunny terraces scented with mimosa, broom and jasmine lead to a lift down to the private beach. Understated luxury set in an organic farm with a nine-hole golf course. A private residence is also available. **www.sanmichele.it**

**MATERA Hotel in Pietra** €€

*Via San Giovanni Vecchio 22, 75100* ***Tel*** *0835 34 40 40* ***Fax*** *0835 34 50 70* ***Rooms*** *8*

A boutique hotel hewn out of one of Matera's ancient cave dwellings, or *Sassi*. It offers minimalist design throughout, with unadorned stone walls and intriguing architectural features. Choose from hermit-style cells (with chic touches) or otherworldly suites with stone bath and bell tower terrace. The place for an unforgettable stay. **www.hotelinpietra.it**

**MATERA Palazzo Gattini** €€€

*Piazza Duomo 13, 75100* ***Tel*** *0835 33 43 58* ***Fax*** *0835 24 01 00* ***Rooms*** *20*

This 18th-century stone palazzo has been transformed by Italian *Architectural Design* magazine's editor into a stunning boutique hotel. Baroque flourishes are set against a contemporary glass entrance. Recessed lighting and ornate sculpture add to the drama. Rooftop pool, spa and elegant restaurant. **www.palazzogattini.it**

**METAPONTO (PISTICCI) Agriturismo San Teodoro** €€

*Contrada San Teodoro, Marconia, 75020* ***Tel/Fax*** *0835 47 00 42* ***Mob*** *338 569 81 16* ***Rooms*** *9*

An *agriturismo* in a romantic old farmhouse run by a noble family. It's just 5 km (3 miles) from the sea, among citrus and olive groves and grape vines. Excellent food and cooking courses. Bicycles, golf, tennis and riding are available, and there is a nearby health spa. **www.santeodoronuovo.com**

**REGGIO CALABRIA Hotel Palace Masoanri's** €€

*Via Vittorio Veneto 95, 89121* ***Tel*** *0965 264 33* ***Fax*** *0965 264 36* ***Rooms*** *65*

A modern hotel near the railway station, the old town and the archaeological museum. Bedrooms are large and comfortable, with modern facilities, including Internet, air conditioning and satellite TV. Many have balconies with views over the Straits of Messina. There is also a garage. **www.montesanohotels.it**

**ROCCELLA Parco dei Principi** €€

*Badessa, SS 106, 89047* ***Tel*** *0964 86 02 01* ***Fax*** *0964 860 26 20* ***Rooms*** *60*

At this modern resort with classical features and grand interiors, rooms have a functional feel. Among the facilities are two pools, a spa and gym, and five dining venues, including Il Laghetto, an intimate spot by a small lake. The hotel can get swamped with delegates and wedding guests, so book well in advance. **www.parcodeiprincipi-roccella.com**

**ROCCELLA JONICA Le Giare** €€

*SS106, km 111, 89047* ***Tel/Fax*** *0964 851 70* ***Rooms*** *10*

On the Jasmine Riviera, 4 km (2.5 miles) from Gioiosa Jonica, and 8 km (5 miles) from Locri, this *agriturismo* is set among citrus groves opposite a private beach. The apartments are simple but cheerful and the food is delicious, with all produce coming from the farm. Lots of activities for children. **www.agriclublegiare.it**

**ROSSANO Giardino d'Iti** €€

*Contrada Amica, 87068* ***Tel/Fax*** *0983 645 08* ***Rooms*** *11*

A lovely little *agriturismo* run by the Baroness Cherubini, set in an orange grove and surrounded by olive trees, 3 km (2 miles) from the Ionian Sea, yet close to the mountains. Comfortable bedrooms with rustic decor. Delicious food. Several courses on offer including cooking, weaving and plant therapy. **www.giardinoiti.it**

**STILO Casale Ceramida** €

*Contrada Cucudu, Stilo-Monasterace Marina, 89049* ***Tel*** *338 399 96 47* ***Rooms*** *3*

Set in a beautiful, quiet spot outside Stilo, this bed and breakfast offers two double rooms and one room with bunk beds, with two shared bathrooms. The rooms are pleasant and there is pretty decor throughout. The house has a homely and friendly atmosphere. Pets welcome. **www.casaleceramida.it**

**TROPEA Residenza Il Barone** €€€

*Largo Barone, 89861* ***Tel/Fax*** *0963 60 71 81* ***Rooms*** *6*

This tastefully renovated 18th-century residence overlooks Tropea's bustling Piazza Ercole. Rooms and suites are decorated in warm colours and have modern mosaic-covered bathrooms. A rooftop terrace provides stunning views of smoking Stromboli on the horizon – a special spot for breakfast or sunset aperitif. **www.residenzailbarone.it**

**TROPEA AREA – CAPO VATICANA Hostel Costa Azzurra** €

*Viale Giuseppe Berto, Ricadi, 89865* ***Tel*** *0963 66 31 09* ***Fax*** *0963 66 39 56* ***Rooms*** *30*

Near the train station of Ricadi, 9 km (6 miles) from Tropea at Capo Vaticano on the Costa degli Dei. Extensive gardens. Rooms are simple, clean and bright, and apartments are also available. Good Calabrian cuisine is served in the restaurant. Games for the children and rowboats available on the private beach. **www.hotelcostazzurra.com**

**TROPEA AREA – ZAMBRONE Casa Isabella** €

*SS522, km 24, Contrada Conturella, 89868* ***Tel*** *0963 39 28 91* ***Rooms*** *4*

A delightful *pensione* in the cool of the hills high above the Tropea coast, in a villa with gardens. Run by a German lady, who has lived in Tropea for over 30 years. Generous breakfasts are served on the patio. The bedrooms are cool and airy. Most rooms are en suite. **www.villaisabella.info**

**VENOSA Hotel Orazio** €

*Corso Vittorio Emanuele II 142, 85029* ***Tel*** *0972 311 35* ***Rooms*** *14*

A charming palazzo in the heart of the historical district, named after the Roman poet Horace, who was born in the town. The hotel offers modern facilities at a bargain with a lovely terrace looking out over the valley. Bedrooms have air conditioning, television and phone. **www.hotelorazio.it**

## SICILY

### AEOLIAN ISLANDS – LIPARI Villa Diana

€€

*Via Tufo 1, 98055* ***Tel*** *090 981 14 03* ***Fax*** *090 981 14 03* ***Rooms*** *17*

The home of Swiss painter Edwin Hunziker is set in a lovely garden of citrus and olive trees. The sunny terrace has views over Lipari town and the sea. All bedrooms overlook the garden in this cool, restful spot filled with antiques and the painter's family collection of art. Tennis court and a bowling green. Closed Nov–Mar. **www.villadiana.com**

### AEOLIAN ISLANDS – PANAREA Hotel Quartara

€€€€

*Via San Pietro 15, 98050* ***Tel*** *090 98 30 27* ***Fax*** *090 98 36 21* ***Rooms*** *13*

Teak wood furniture and vibrant tiles give this rustic retreat overlooking the port a homely feel. Guest rooms are themed, from minimalist Zen to colonial chic. Some have private balconies with sea vistas. There are great views from the Jacuzzi on the whitewashed terrace, and an excellent seafood restaurant, Broccia. **www.quartarahotel.com**

### AEOLIAN ISLANDS – STROMBOLI La Locanda del Barbablu

€€€

*Via Vittorio Emanuele 17-19, 98050* ***Tel*** *090 98 61 18* ***Fax*** *090 98 63 23* ***Rooms*** *5*

Small fishermen's dwellings, painted pastel colours and filled with antiques and *objets d'art*. The bedrooms are small but charming, all en suite. Bar and excellent restaurant with creative cuisine set in a green oasis and sun terrace, with a lovely view of Stromboli. Near to the beach at Fico Grande. Closed Nov–Mar. **www.barbablu.it**

### AGRIGENTO Fattoria Mosè

€€

*Via M Pascal 4, Villaggio Mosè, 92100* ***Tel*** *0922 60 61 15* ***Fax*** *0922 60 61 15* ***Rooms*** *10*

A delightful *agriturismo* 4 km (2.5 miles) from the Valley of the Temples and 3 km (2 miles) from the sea. Amid olive, citrus, pistachio and almond trees, this former hunting lodge and family farm has four rooms and six little apartments. Minimum stay two nights. Closed Nov–Mar. **www.fattoriamose.com**

### AGRIGENTO Hotel Colleverde

€€€

*Via Panoramica dei Templi, 92100* ***Tel*** *0922 295 55* ***Fax*** *0922 290 12* ***Rooms*** *53*

A modern hotel with views of the Valley of the Temples from its gardens. The bedrooms are comfortable and nicely furnished: deluxe rooms have wonderful views; some have a Jacuzzi tub. Close to Agrigento's centre and train station. The restaurant has a terrace. Two rooms have disabled facilities. Wi-Fi throughout. **www.colleverdehotel.it**

### CALTAGIRONE B&B La Pilozza Infiorata

€

*Via SS Salvatore 97, 95041* ***Tel/Fax*** *0933 221 62* ***Rooms*** *7*

A little guesthouse in the *centro storico* of Caltagirone, a city famed for its ceramics. Two minutes from the famous Santa Maria del Monte staircase, this late 19th-century building has charming rooms (not all en suite or with air conditioning) and apartments. Two terraces have views over the old city. **www.lapilozzainfiorata.com**

### CASTEL DI TUSA Hotel Atelier sul Mare

€€€

*Via Cesare Battisti 4, 98079* ***Tel*** *0921 33 42 95* ***Fax*** *0921 33 42 83* ***Rooms*** *40*

A lovely white building in a garden with a private beach in a fishing village 20 km (12 miles) east of Cefalù. Unique in concept, most rooms are standard doubles but 14 have been designed by international or Italian artists (these are more expensive). Some rooms have sea views. There is a sun terrace and restaurant. **www.ateliersulmare.it**

### CATANIA Residence La Ville

€€

*Via Monteverdi 15, 95131* ***Tel*** *095 746 52 30* ***Fax*** *095 746 51 89* ***Rooms*** *14*

Near Via Etnea and the delightful food market, this hotel is in a sunny yellow palazzo. Perfect for families, there are doubles, triples and quadruples on offer, as well as a suite, all beautifully furnished. Also, small apartments are available on a weekly basis. The staff are particularly helpful. **www.rhlaville.it**

### CATANIA Hotel Katane Palace

€€€

*Via Finocchiaro April 110, 95129* ***Tel*** *095 747 07 02* ***Fax*** *095 747 01 72* ***Rooms*** *58*

In a central position, convenient for the port, railway station and visiting the old quarter. Bedrooms are spacious, elegantly furnished and soundproofed; the en suite bathrooms are very smart. Cuciniere, the hotel's restaurant, is critically renowned and a series of music concerts is held here. Wi-Fi and Internet point. **www.katanepalace.it**

### CEFALÙ Hotel Kalura

€€

*Via Vincenzo Cavallaro 13, 90015* ***Tel*** *0921 42 13 54* ***Fax*** *0921 42 31 22* ***Rooms*** *72*

A family hotel perfect for watersports enthusiasts located in Caldura Bay, just east of Cefalù. It has a private beach and diving centre. Bedrooms are modern and spacious; most have sea views with balconies. There are many organized activities, a piano bar, aqua aerobics in the pool and massage. Closed Nov–Feb. **www.hotel-kalura.com**

### CEFALÙ Hotel Alberi del Paradiso

€€€€

*Via dei Mulini 18–20, 90015* ***Tel*** *0921 42 39 00* ***Fax*** *0921 42 39 90* ***Rooms*** *55*

Located amid orange and olive groves, this hotel offers rooms with rustic, vibrant tiles and simple fittings. Paying a little extra buys more space, a balcony and sea views. The top suite has a Jacuzzi and two private outside areas. Exclusive beach access nearby, pool, golf course, spa and tennis court. **www.alberidelparadiso.it**

**Key to Price Guide** *see p558* **Key to Symbols** *see back cover flap*

## EGADI – FAVIGNANA Albergo Ristorante Egadi €€

*Via Cristoforo Colombo 17, 91023* ***Tel*** *0923 92 12 32* ***Fax*** *0923 92 16 36* ***Rooms*** *12*

A yellow villa in the town centre, close to the seafront and the harbour. Bedrooms are in pastel tones and furnished with antiques. Two rooms on the top floor share a terrace – one has a whirlpool bathtub, the other a power shower. A family suite is available, as is a separate villa for four people called Casa Nenè. **www.albergoegadi.it**

## ENNA Hotel Sicilia €€

*Piazza N Colajanni 7, 94100* ***Tel*** *0935 50 08 50* ***Fax*** *0935 50 04 88* ***Rooms*** *60*

In the heart of Enna in central Sicily, this modern hotel is convenient for visiting many sights on the island. Bedrooms are compact but there's a lovely roof terrace and bar where breakfast is served in good weather. Elegant public rooms with antiques. Some rooms have views over the surrounding countryside. **www.hotelsiciliaenna.it**

## ERICE Hotel Moderno €€

*Via Vittoria Emanuele 63, 91016* ***Tel*** *0923 86 93 00* ***Fax*** *0923 86 91 39* ***Rooms*** *40*

A little hotel in the old quarter of Erice with a terrace looking out over the rooftops, where breakfast is served in the morning and aperitifs in the evening. Bedrooms are spacious, furnished with old-fashioned charm and fitted with modern conveniences. The restaurant is excellent. Pets welcome. **www.hotelmodernoerice.it**

## GIARDINI-NAXOS Hotel Arathena Rocks 

*Via Calcide Eubea 55, 98039* ***Tel*** *0942 513 49* ***Fax*** *0942 516 90* ***Rooms*** *49*

An elegant, modern hotel in a quiet part of Giardini-Naxos with a pool and sun terrace opening directly on to the sea over volcanic rocks. Comfortable and old-fashioned inside, most bedrooms have private patios and a sea view. Good restaurant, with alfresco dining in summer. Shuttle bus to Taormina. Pets welcome. **www.hotelarathena.it**

## MARSALA Baglio Oneto €€

*Contrada Baronazzo Amafi 55, 91025* ***Tel/Fax*** *0923 71 43 28* ***Rooms*** *48*

A fortified house set amid grapevines in the hills around Marsala, with a delightful pool and sun terrace with views towards the Egadi Islands. Bedrooms are lovely and spacious, each with its own balcony or terrace. The restaurant serves excellent regional fare and there is a fine wine bar. Closed Oct–Apr.

## MESSINA Green Manors Country Hotel €€€

*Via Porticato, Castroreale, 98053* ***Tel*** *090 974 65 15* ***Fax*** *090 974 65 07* ***Rooms*** *9*

A superb hotel surrounded by countryside. The library, dining room and guest rooms brim with interesting artifacts and artworks. Concerts and gastronomic events are held in the grounds. Relaxing areas outside include a palm-fringed pool. A large historic apartment is also available. Minimum stay two nights. **www.greenmanors.it**

## MILAZZO Petit Hotel €€

*Via Dei Mille 37, 98057* ***Tel*** *0909 28 67 84* ***Fax*** *0909 28 50 42* ***Rooms*** *9*

A pretty, yellow hotel opposite the port, extremely convenient for connections to the Aeolian Islands. Staff are very kind. Bedrooms are stylish with non-allergenic furnishings, de-ionizers, soundproofing and environmentally friendly heating and air conditioning. The charming roof terrace with majolica tiles is lovely. **www.petithotel.it**

## MODICA Hotel Relais €€

*Via Tommaso Campailla 99, 97015* ***Tel*** *0932 75 44 51* ***Fax*** *0932 75 44 51* ***Rooms*** *10*

A guesthouse in the heart of Modica Alta, near Teatro Garibaldi. The former home of a Sicilian count, a lovingly restored medieval building with wonderful views over the Baroque city from its terrace. The stylish bedrooms vary – some have balconies and wooden beams. Family rooms are available. **www.hotelrelaismodica.it**

## NOTO Masseria degli Ulivi €€

*Contrada Porcari, SS287, near Madonna della Scala, 96017* ***Tel*** *0931 81 30 19* ***Fax*** *0931 81 30 48* ***Rooms*** *34*

Eight km (5 miles) from old Noto and surrounded by carob trees and olive groves, this pretty villa dates from the late 1800s. Rooms feature terracotta floors, dark wood furniture, ceiling beams and shutters. An excellent restaurant and *enoteca*, with food served on the lovely terrace in summer. Closed Nov–late Mar. **www.masseriadegliulivi.com**

## PALERMO Giorgio's House €

*Via A Mongitore, 90100* ***Tel*** *091 52 50 57* ***Mob*** *347 221 48 23* ***Rooms*** *4*

A friendly guesthouse with an extremely hospitable owner, Giorgio. Located in the heart of the Albergheria area, between the station and the Palazzo Reale, it is also near the cathedral. Four bedrooms with two bathrooms, there is also a sitting room where guests can socialize. Organized excursions. **www.giorgioshouse.com**

## PALERMO Grand Hotel Garibaldi €

*Via Emerico Amari 146, 90139* ***Tel*** *091 601 70 11* ***Rooms*** *71*

A business-orientated hotel in the centre of Palermo, offering great value for cultural visitors too. Clean lines and understated decor throughout are enlivened with bold prints and fabrics. Public areas feel a little soulless. Traffic noise in some rooms – ask for a quiet room when booking. **http://hotel-garibaldi-palermo.h-rez.com**

## RAGUSA Eremo della Giubiliana €€€€

*Contrada Giubiliana, 97100* ***Tel*** *0932 66 91 19* ***Fax*** *0932 66 91 29* ***Rooms*** *23*

The Eremo has Sicily's only private landing strip, and private plane excursions are offered. A fortified feudal tenant farm for over 1,000 years, it is a beautiful oasis of calm amid sun-baked fields, with views to the sea and a private beach. Rooms and suites are truly splendid. Delicious food. Dogs welcome. **www.eremodellagiubiliana.com**

**SCIACCA Solaris B&B** €€

*Via Marco Polo 2/a, 92019* ***Tel/Fax*** *0925 99 30 32* ***Rooms*** *4*

Set in lush gardens, this friendly, family-run B&B with four apartments is a great value choice for families, groups and those wanting to cater for themselves. The decor is somewhat dated, and there are some intriguing 1970s furniture items. Outside areas for relaxation include a large terrace with sea views. **www.bbsolaris.com**

**SCICLI Hotel Novecento** €€

*Via Duprè 11, 97018* ***Tel*** *0932 84 38 17* ***Fax*** *0932 83 52 13* ***Rooms*** *7*

Modernism and original decorative touches combine at this restored palazzo. Guest rooms are simply furnished, with a relaxing feel. The gorgeous mosaic-tiled bathrooms are full of gleaming chrome. For those seeking period atmosphere, the grander suites have celestial scenes painted in the early 1900s on vaulted ceilings. **www.hotel900.it**

**SIRACUSA Algilà Ortigia Charme** €€€

*Via Vittorio Veneto 93, 96100* ***Tel*** *0931 46 51 86* ***Fax*** *0931 46 38 89* ***Rooms*** *30*

Deep in the throbbing heart of old Siracusa is this imposing Baroque palace with gorgeous sea views. It has been tastefully renovated to reveal beguiling architectural features. Guest rooms have ornate period-style furnishings, Moorish tiles and vibrant fabrics. The executive suite has a roof terrace with Jacuzzi and views. **www.algila.it**

**TAORMINA Hotel Condor** €€

*Via Dietro Cappuccini 25, 98039* ***Tel*** *0942 231 24* ***Fax*** *0942 62 57 26* ***Rooms*** *12*

A lovely bougainvillea-covered family villa five minutes from the centre of town with cool, old-fashioned public areas and a roof terrace with sunbeds. The bedrooms are simple and welcoming, many with a balcony. Economy rooms are smaller, without either balcony or sea view. One suite is available. Solarium. **www.condorhotel.com**

**TAORMINA Villa Belvedere** €€€

*Via Bagnoli Croce 79, 98039* ***Tel*** *0942 237 91* ***Fax*** *0942 62 58 30* ***Rooms*** *47*

A pretty, yellow Liberty style villa in a garden of orange and lemon trees surrounding a pool facing the sea. Five minutes from both the old quarter and the funicular down to the beach. Its public rooms are cool and welcoming and the bedrooms are generally airy and light, most with a balcony or terrace. **www.villabelvedere.it**

**TAORMINA Villa Ducale** €€€

*Via Leonardo da Vinci 60, 98039* ***Tel*** *0942 281 53* ***Fax*** *0942 287 10* ***Rooms*** *17*

One of Taormina's most romantic hotels, this villa is an oasis in the busy town. Beautiful terraces and garden with a Jacuzzi. Every bedroom has a balcony or veranda, with terracotta floor tiles, wrought-iron beds, frescoed walls and painted ceramics. There is a shuttle bus to the beach. A thermal spa is also available. **www.villaducale.com**

**TAORMINA Grand Hotel San Pietro** €€€€

*Via Pirandello 50, 98039* ***Tel*** *0942 62 07 11* ***Fax*** *0942 62 07 70* ***Rooms*** *63*

There are breathtaking views of the sea and Etna from this swanky hotel. Bedrooms and suites have artworks and colour schemes inspired by the local flora. There are three dining venues, including the enchanting Rotonda sul Mare: an intimate terrace above the waves that comes with your own waiter. **www.grandhotelsanpietro.net**

**TAORMINA Hotel Villa Carlotta** €€€€

*Via Pirandello 81, 98039* ***Tel*** *0942 62 60 58* ***Fax*** *0942 237 32* ***Rooms*** *23*

Built in 1860, this stone-clad boutique retreat combines Liberty-style grandeur with contemporary fittings. These themes continue in the tasteful bedrooms. Relaxing, well-tended grounds contain a pool and some Roman remains. Terraces give breathtaking views of the sea and Mount Etna. **www.hotelvillacarlottataormina.com**

**TRAPANI Tavernetta Ai Lumi** €

*Corso Vittorio Emanuele 71, 91100* ***Tel*** *0923 54 09 22* ***Fax*** *0923 54 77 20* ***Rooms*** *12*

A guesthouse above a taverna in central Trapani. Located inside the courtyard of a palazzo, the dining rooms are in the former stables. The rooms are cosy and charming, brightly coloured with old-fashioned furniture. All rooms are en suite, though not all have air conditioning. Apartments are also available. **www.ailumi.it**

**ZAFFARANA-ETNEA Hotel Airone** €€€

*Via Cassone 67, 95019* ***Tel*** *095 708 18 19* ***Fax*** *095 708 21 42* ***Rooms*** *62*

On the slopes of Mount Etna, in an area renowned for its honey, lies the medieval town of Zaffarana-Etnea. This family-run hotel has charming bedrooms, a garden with pool and restaurant and a popular spa. Unforgettable views over the blue Ionian Sea and the lava flows. Guided trips are organized. **www.hotel-airone.it**

## SARDINIA

**ALGHERO Hotel Angedras** €

*Via Frank 2, 07041* ***Tel*** *079 973 50 34* ***Fax*** *079 973 50 34* ***Rooms*** *31*

A stylish hotel ten minutes from Alghero Old Town in a quiet residential street. The decor combines traditional Sardinian features with modern elegance. Breakfast is a selection of typical Sardinian pastries made by the family bakery. Service is warm and friendly. There is a private beach and two disabled-adapted rooms. **www.angedras.it**

**Key to Price Guide** *see p558* **Key to Symbols** *see back cover flap*

**ALGHERO Villa Las Tronas** €€€€€

*Lungomare Valencia 1, 07041* ***Tel*** *079 98 18 18* ***Fax*** *079 98 10 44* ***Rooms*** *25*

A mustard-coloured 19th-century villa on a promontory overlooking Capo Caccia is the setting for this comfortable, elegantly decorated hotel. Public rooms are full of gilt and fine furniture, while the bedrooms are simpler but pretty. A garden and terraces overlook the sea. **www.hotelvillalastronas.it**

**ARBATAX Vecchio Mulino** €€€

*Via Parigi, 08041* ***Tel*** *0782 66 40 41* ***Fax*** *0782 66 43 80* ***Rooms*** *24*

Behind a rosy-hued exterior are suitably warm, stylish rooms with curvy walls and lots of quirky artworks and books. The wonderful owner's serene and generous nature shines through, and the home-baked goods are delicious. Boat trips to the Golfo di Orosei and other destinations can be arranged. **www.hotelilvecchiomulino.it**

**BOSA Hotel al Gabbiano** €€

*Viale Mediterraneo 5, 08013* ***Tel*** *0785 37 41 23* ***Fax*** *0785 37 41 09* ***Rooms*** *30*

Ideally positioned, this family-run hotel has scenic views over the bay. It has a private beach, and the staff will organize bike trips, diving and other excursions. Rooms are bright and airy. The restaurant specializes in local dishes. The hotel also has villas by the sea or in the countryside. Half-board in Aug. **www.hotelgabbiano.it**

**CAGLIARI Hotel Aurora** €

*Piazza Yenne, Salita Santa Chiara 19, 09124* ***Tel*** *070 65 86 25* ***Fax*** *070 64 05 050* ***Rooms*** *8*

A small, centrally located hotel in a 19th-century building off the busy Piazza Yenne. A couple of the rooms have been decorated with murals. Rooms at the front are noisier as the building opposite has a morning market. One of the cheaper hotels, it is very well positioned close to the major attractions. **www.hotelcagliariaurora.it**

**CAGLIARI T Hotel** €€

*Via Dei Giudicati 66, 09131* ***Tel*** *070 474 00* ***Fax*** *070 47 40 16* ***Rooms*** *207*

The stylish renovation of an unloved skyscraper has made the T Hotel an iconic symbol of the slowly emerging Parco della Musica, a new cultural hub in the Villanova area. The hotel's sleek lobby with stylish sunken bar hosts temporary exhibitions. Most rooms and suites have great city views. Superb, friendly staff. **www.thotel.com**

**CHIA Aquadulci** €€€€

*Località Capo Spartivento, Domus de Maria, 09010* ***Tel*** *070 923 05 55* ***Fax*** *070 923 05 16* ***Rooms*** *41*

The sand dunes of Chia are a fitting place for a hotel dedicated to simplicity and relaxation. Public areas and rooms have sculptural features and minimalist interiors, with light wood and splashes of colour. The grounds have a pool, a massage and spa treatments centre and a restaurant. Horse riding, sailing and other activities. **www.aquadulci.com**

**ISOLA DI SAN PIETRO Hotel Paola e Primo Maggio** €

*Località Tacca Rossa, 09014* ***Tel*** *0781 85 00 98* ***Fax*** *0781 85 01 04* ***Rooms*** *21*

A quiet, modern, family-run *pensione* surrounded by greenery and overlooking the sea. There is a shady terrace for outside dining at the restaurant, which prides itself on good quality Carloforte cooking. The rooms are simple but furnished with a homely feel. The main area is cosy and rustic. Closed Nov–Mar. **www.hotelpaolacarloforte.it**

**OLIENA Su Gologone** €€€

*Località Su Gologone, 08025* ***Tel*** *0784 28 75 12* ***Fax*** *0784 28 76 68* ***Rooms*** *68*

A rambling villa in the Sopramonte, the mountainous Barbagia region. Characteristic and delightfully peaceful with warm Sardinian hospitality. The stone buildings are in parkland and shaded by olives. The hotel has an excellent restaurant. It also offers a good range of sports, activities and excursions. **www.sugologone.it**

**PORTO CERVO Colonna Pevero** €€€€€

*Località Golfo del Pevero, 07020* ***Tel*** *0789 90 70 09* ***Fax*** *0789 920 64* ***Rooms*** *102*

Large luxury resort within rolling, lush grounds that run on to the idyllic coves and beaches of the Golfo del Pevero. There's tasteful minimalist decor throughout, from the relaxing public areas and dining spaces to the soothing suites. A selection of spa treatments and activities is available. **www.colonnapeverohotel.com**

**PORTO ROTONDO Sporting** €€€€

*Via Clelia Donadalle Rose 16, Porto Rotondo, 07020* ***Tel*** *0789 340 05* ***Fax*** *0789 343 83* ***Rooms*** *47*

An oasis of comfort on the Costa Smeralda. This hotel is a large complex with its own beach and a plethora of activities. The architecture and garden are typically Mediterranean. Rooms are airy and comfortable, with private, flower-filled terraces which open onto the beach. There is a piano bar. Closed Oct–Apr. **www.sportingportorotondo.it**

**SASSARI Vittorio Emanuele** €

*Corso Vittorio Emanuele 100–102, 07100* ***Tel*** *079 23 55 38* ***Fax*** *079 200 66 96* ***Rooms*** *80*

This early 1900s palazzo is a good choice near Sassari's main attractions. It offers unfussy modern decor throughout, with a surprise or three: a wine-tasting cellar with stone walls, a relaxing bar-lounge and panoramic terraces. Popular with business clients, and geared to the needs of disabled visitors too. **www.hotelvittorioemanuele.ss.it**

**VILLAGRANDE (NR LANUSEI) Orlando Village** €€

*Villagrande Strisaili, 08049* ***Tel*** *0782 328 23* ***Fax*** *0782 325 32* ***Rooms*** *30*

A rustic resort in the Santa Barbara forest, in the Sopramonte Mountains. Charming owner Pietrina Lecca organizes cultural and gastronomic events that attract a stimulating mix of locals and visitors. Simply furnished rooms and suites. Ogliastra's much-lauded centenarian-producing diet stars in the superb restaurant. **www.orlandovillage.it**

# WHERE TO EAT

Food is a serious subject in Italy. The Italians are justly proud of their fine cuisine and wines and many sociable hours are spent around the table. One of the great pleasures of travelling in Italy is exploring regional variations in pasta, breads and cheeses. Whether it is spinach-filled *tortelloni* from the north or stuffed sweet red peppers from the south, restaurants will rarely serve anything other than Italian specialities. You don't have to head to the most expensive places for good food; a simple *trattoria*, which has to answer to the local clientele, will often serve much better fare than the nearby international restaurant. However, whether it is a crowded *osteria* or a terrace with sea views, this introduction gives a few practical tips on types of restaurants, ordering and service to help you enjoy eating out in Italy.

Roman waiter with regional fare

## TYPES OF RESTAURANTS AND SNACK BARS

Traditionally a *trattoria* and an *osteria* are cheaper and more casual alternatives to the smarter *ristorante.*

A *pizzeria* is usually a cheap place to eat (as little as €12 with beer) and many serve pasta, meat and fish dishes as well as pizzas. *Pizzerie* are often open in the evening only, especially those with wood-fired ovens *(forno a legna).*

A *birreria* is another cheap option, serving pasta and snacks such as sausages and hamburgers. An *enoteca*, or *vineria*, is in fact a place to taste wine; however, as Italians will rarely drink without eating, there will normally be a range of light dishes on offer as well as a superb selection of wines. Prices vary and tend not to be cheap for the quantities served.

At lunch time and in the early evening, *rosticcerie* sell roast chicken, slices of pizza *(pizza al taglio)* and other snacks to take away. *Pizza al taglio*, with various different toppings, can also be bought straight from the baker. Bars have filled rolls *(panini)* and sandwiches *(tramezzini),* and some have a *tavola calda* counter with hot dishes for under €6.

Stop at a *gelateria* for ice cream, with a sometimes mesmerizing choice of different flavours, or a *pasticceria* for one of a dazzling variety of sweet and savoury pastries, cakes and biscuits.

A restaurant offering a cosy environment in a vaulted room

Villa Crespi in Piedmont, inspired by the Arabian Nights *(see p621)*

## EATING HOURS

Lunch is generally served between 12:30pm and 2:30pm and, particularly in the south, all other activity stops between these hours. Dinner is at about 7:30pm and goes on until 11pm or later (in the south eating hours tend to be later). It is not un-usual to see tables still full from lunch at 4pm or diners sipping *digestivi* well after midnight.

## RESERVATIONS

Good restaurants in Italy are likely to be popular, so book a table if you can. Otherwise, get there early to avoid having to queue. Many restaurants close one day a week and for a few weeks in either winter or the summer holiday season, so phone first if in doubt.

## THE MENU

Italian meals consist of three or four courses, and restaurants generally expect you to eat at least two, though you should not feel obliged to do so. The *antipasto* (starter), is followed by the *primo*, of pasta, rice or soup. The *secondo* is the main meat or fish course, with vegetables or salad (as *contorni*). Fruit, cheese or dessert follow, with coffee and a *digestivo* such as *grappa* or a bitter *amaro* to finish the meal.

Menus usually change with the season to make use of the freshest local produce, and the day's specials may be recited to you by the waiter rather than written down. Persevere, if you don't immediately understand, using the menu information at the beginning of each section *(see p720)*. Try to avoid restaurants that do not state prices on their menus.

## VEGETARIANS

While few places advertise specifically vegetarian meals, you are unlikely to have much trouble choosing from an Italian menu. Many pasta and *antipasto* dishes use no meat at all and for a main course you can ask for a selection of vegetables from the *contorni*. Vegetarians eat particularly well in spring when the first new vegetables come into the markets, and in autumn when wild mushrooms abound.

## WINE AND DRINKS

Many regions have their own *aperitivo* for before the meal and a *digestivo* for afterwards. Universal alternatives are *prosecco* (dry fizzy white wine) or an *analcolico* (non-alcoholic) aperitif, and *grappa* as a digestive. House wine (red or white) will be a simple local wine served by the litre or fraction thereof and will generally be perfectly palatable. In addition, all but the cheapest places have a range of other local and regional wines specially selected to accompany the food on the menu. For this reason, it is unusual to come across many non-Italian wines.

Tap water *(acqua del rubinetto)* is always drinkable and often very good, but Italy has a massive range of mineral waters. Fizzy ones *(frizzante)* may contain carbon dioxide, while *naturale* can mean still or naturally sparkling. If you particularly want a still water, ask for *non gassata*. Espresso bars usually charge more for table service.

**Diners enjoying a meal *al fresco* in Chianti, Tuscany**

## PAYING

Tax and service are usually included in the menu prices, but it is normal to leave a small tip (€1–€3). Note that, though no longer legal, many restaurants still charge for the *coperto*, an extra that covers bread (whether you eat it or not) and is charged per person.

Credit cards are not always accepted in Italy, particularly in smaller towns, and it is wise to check before you eat.

## DRESS

Italians generally tend to look smart but don't necessarily expect visitors to do the same. However, very scruffy or dirty clothes are unlikely to get you good or particularly friendly service.

## CHILDREN

Children are welcome in all but the smartest establishments and throughout Italy restaurants are likely to be filled with extensive Italian families for Sunday lunch. Facilities such as high-chairs or special menus are rare, but most places will provide cushions and small portions.

**Roman trattoria, Sora Lella, on Tiber Island *(see p637)***

## SMOKING

Smoking is still a popular pastime in Italy. However, smoking laws now mean that all restaurants in the country are non-smoking establishments. Unless a smokers' room is provided, you should step outside if you want to light up.

## WHEELCHAIR ACCESS

Few restaurants have special facilities for people in wheelchairs, but let them know you are coming in advance so they can reserve a suitable table and be ready to help if necessary when you arrive.

**La Marinella restaurant overlooking the Amalfi coast *(see p643)***

# Choosing a Restaurant

The restaurants in this guide have been selected across a wide price range for their exceptional food, good value and location. The chart lists restaurants by region, starting in the north and moving to the south. Map references refer to the Street Finders of Venice, Florence and Rome.

**PRICE CATEGORIES**
The following price ranges are for a three-course meal for one, including a half-bottle of house wine, cover charge, tax and service.
€ under €25
€€ €25–€35
€€€ €35–€45
€€€€ €45–€55
€€€€€ over €55

## VENICE

**BURANO Da Romano** €€€
*Piazza Galuppi 221, 30012* ***Tel*** *041 73 00 30*

It is advisable to book ahead to avoid disappointment since this is the leading restaurant on the island of Burano. A wide range of fish is served in traditional Venetian fashion, under the watchful eye of a descendant of the original 19th-century owner. Closed Sun dinner, Tue; mid-Dec–Jan.

**BURANO Ai Pescatori** €€€€
*Via Galuppi 371, 30012* ***Tel*** *041 73 06 50*

The menu at this welcoming establishment focuses on ancient Burano recipes, such as *broeddo* (fish soup), and fresh seafood such as crayfish or cuttlefish served in black sauce with *tagliolini* ribbon pasta, and accompanied by tiny, tasty local artichokes. Winter diners can also enjoy game dishes. Extensive wine list. Closed Tue; 2 wks Jan.

**CANNAREGIO Brek** €
*Lista di Spagna 124, 30121* ***Tel*** *041 244 01 58* ***Map*** *2 D4*

This vibrant self-service eatery close to the railway station serves freshly prepared fare all day long. It is handy for a quick sandwich or pastry, a coffee or a longer sit-down meal, and its reasonable prices make it accessible for all pockets. Tasty pasta and meat dishes are prepared while you wait.

**CANNAREGIO La Cantina** €€
*Strada Nuova 3689, 30121* ***Tel*** *041 522 82 58* ***Map*** *2 F4*

This jovial wine bar opens on to the bustling thoroughfare Strada Nuova. Mouthwatering snacks and substantial dishes are prepared on the spot with fresh seafood, roast meats, cheeses and cold cuts to accompany the excellent range of wines. Closed Sun; first 2 wks Jan, last wk Jul, first wk Aug.

**CANNAREGIO Trattoria da Gigio** €€
*Rio Terrà San Leonardo 1594, 30121* ***Tel*** *041 71 75 74* ***Map*** *2 D3*

During the week this busy trattoria is filled with the stallholders from the nearby produce market, which adds to the lively atmosphere. On the menu you will find fresh seafood dishes and huge fillet steaks. The friendly service is another pleasant plus. Closed Sun, Mon dinner.

**CANNAREGIO Osteria Giorgione** €€€
*Calle Larga dei Proverbi 4582A, 30121* ***Tel*** *041 522 17 25* ***Map*** *3 B4*

A cosy, sophisticated establishment with a good wine list. It serves seasonal fish specialities such as tuna carpaccio, while meat eaters will enjoy the *fegato alla veneziana*, Venetian-style liver with onions. Everyone should leave space for the scrumptious desserts, such as hot chocolate flan with ice cream. Closed Mon.

**CANNAREGIO Osteria l'Orto dei Mori** €€€
*Campo dei Mori 3386, 30121* ***Tel/Fax*** *041 524 36 77* ***Map*** *2 F3*

Off the beaten track, this inspiring *osteria* spreads into the adjacent square in the summer. It serves a refined take on local cuisine, following the seasons closely. A delicious antipasto is *insalata tiepida di carciofini e mazzancolle* (salad of warm artichokes and prawns). Excellent service and a good choice of wines. Closed Tue; 2 wks Jan.

**CANNAREGIO Fiaschetteria Toscana** €€€€
*Salizzada San Giovanni Grisostomo 5719, 30131* ***Tel*** *041 528 52 81* ***Fax*** *041 528 55 21* ***Map*** *3 B5*

Along with a superb wine list, the Busatto family serve fresh seafood such as a delicious warm salad of octopus, then turbot in caper sauce. Do book ahead – this is one of Venice's leading stylish restaurants. Closed Tue & Wed lunch; late Jul–Aug, 1 wk Dec.

**CANNAREGIO Vini Da Gigio** €€€€
*Fondamenta della Chiesa 3628A, 30121* ***Tel*** *041 528 51 40* ***Map*** *3 A4*

Elegant atmosphere and refined dishes that use seasonal produce. Risotto with prawns or grilled cuttlefish often feature on the menu, or delicious duck and local artichokes. There is also a vast wine list. Advance booking is advisable. Closed Mon, Tue; mid-Jan–first wk Feb, 3 wks Aug.

**Key to Symbols** *see back cover flap*

### CASTELLO Aciugheta €€

*Campo SS Filippo e Giacomo 4357, 30122* ***Tel*** *041 522 42 92* ***Fax*** *041 520 82 22* ***Map*** *7 C2*

Popular with the young local crowd for apéritifs, this place is busy until the early hours of the morning. Sleek and modern, it serves light salads and snacks for lunch, as well as excellent pasta dishes. The outdoor seating is a perfect way to watch the world go by. Only minutes from Piazza San Marco. Closed Jan.

### CASTELLO Trattoria Giorgione €€

*Via Garibaldi 1533, 30122* ***Tel*** *041 522 87 27*

A great neighbourhood trattoria serving flavoursome traditional-style fish meals (such as fish lasagne) and delicious risotto. The jovial owner entertains diners with Venetian folk songs and guitar music. Set on an animated avenue beyond the Arsenale. Closed Wed; 2 wks Nov.

### CASTELLO Da Remigio €€€€

*Salizzada dei Greci 3416, 30122* ***Tel*** *041 523 00 89* ***Map*** *8 D2*

Since this is a favourite with Venetians and seating is limited, you should book ahead. A memorable seafood meal is guaranteed, and should include the creamy *risotto ai frutti di mare* (seafood risotto). Conclude with a *sgroppino*, a lemon sorbet and prosecco delight. Closed Mon dinner, Tue; Christmas–20 Jan, 2 wks Jul–Aug.

### CASTELLO Al Coro €€€€€

*Campiello della Pescaria 3968, 30122* ***Tel*** *041 522 38 12* ***Map*** *8 E2*

This hidden gem tucked away behind the Arsenale boat strip is run by husband-and-wife team Cesare and Diane Benelli. Cesare is the chef and the focus is on fish dishes of the highest quality. Save room for one of Diane's desserts. Closed Wed, Thu; 2 wks Jan, 1 wk Aug.

### CASTELLO Osteria di Santa Marina €€€€€

*Campo Santa Marina 5911, 30122* ***Tel*** *041 528 52 39* ***Map*** *3 B5*

This elegant restaurant has built its reputation on its creative take on traditional local cuisine. Bean soup comes with spicy tomato confit, and black ravioli of sea bass are served with a seafood sauce. Kill-for desserts include *millefoglie di cioccolato croccante* (crispy chocolate pastry). Closed Mon lunch, Sun; 2 wks Jan, 2 wks Aug.

### DORSODURO Taverna San Trovaso €

*Fondamenta Priuli 1016, 30123* ***Tel*** *041 520 37 03* ***Fax*** *041 523 45 83* ***Map*** *6 E3*

This bustling restaurant just around the corner from the Accademia gallery is extremely popular with English-speaking tourists, so book a table in advance or be prepared to queue. Pizzas are on the menu, along with simple but flavoursome pasta, fish and meat dishes. Good range of desserts.

### DORSODURO La Rivista €€

*Rio Terrà Foscarini 979/A, 30123* ***Tel*** *041 240 14 25* ***Fax*** *041 277 10 61* ***Map*** *6 E4*

A modern, welcoming establishment close to the Accademia, La Rivista does light salads and cold platters for lunch. This attractive "wine and cheese bar" also serves divine desserts such as wild-berry cream. Unsurprisingly, there is an enviable wine list with labels from all over Italy, many of them by the glass. Closed Mon.

### DORSODURO Ai Gondolieri €€€€

*San Vio 366, 30123* ***Tel*** *041 528 63 96* ***Fax*** *041 521 00 75* ***Map*** *6 F4*

Close to the Guggenheim Collection, this restaurant is located in elegant wood-panelled premises where regional meat and vegetable specialities are served with flair. The stewed chicken with polenta and white truffles from Piedmont is especially recommended. Book ahead. Closed Tue; lunchtime Aug.

### DORSODURO L'Avogaria €€€€

*Calle dell'Avogaria 1629, 30123* ***Tel*** *041 296 04 91* ***Fax*** *041 520 57 41* ***Map*** *5 C3*

This modern stylish restaurant close to the Zattere is run by a young, creative crew. They specialize in fare from Puglia, such as delectable stuffed calamari and tasty *tiedda*, a summer dish made with rice, mussels and potatoes. Wines from all over Italy. L'Avogaria also has three rooms. Closed Tue; 1 wk Jan, 2 wks Jul–Aug.

### GIUDECCA Cipriani €€€€€

*Giudecca 10, 30122* ***Tel*** *041 520 77 44* ***Fax*** *041 529 39 30*

A courtesy launch ferries guests from the San Marco waterfront to this exclusive island hotel/restaurant for a unique meal. The food and service are impeccable and the views stunning. There are two restaurants, one formal and one more casual. Note that there is a dress code. Closed Nov–March.

### GIUDECCA Harry's Dolci €€€€€

*Fondamenta San Biagio 773, 30133* ***Tel*** *041 522 48 44* ***Fax*** *041 522 23 22*

A divine veranda on the Giudecca waterfront, far from the bustle of San Marco, gives diners a vast view of the craft plying the broad canal. Famous for its pastries and *gelati* (ice creams), this elegant restaurant also does superb meals. Booking recommended. Closed Mon dinner, Tue; Nov–Apr.

### MAZZORBO Ai Cacciatori €

*Mazzorbo 23, 30012* ***Tel*** *041 73 01 18*

A reasonably priced traditional trattoria on the island adjoining Burano, this establishment serves tasty dishes with fresh fish, such as gnocchi with crab. In the autumn months, duck and game also feature prominently on the menu. Only minutes from the ferry stop on Mazzorbo. Closed Mon; 8 Jan–early Feb.

**SAN MARCO Bar all'Angolo** €

*Campo Santo Stefano 3465, 30124* ***Tel*** *041 522 07 10* ***Map*** *6 F3*

Specializing in sandwiches of all kinds, this fun bar also offers light meals such as salads. It is a great place for relaxing with a spritzer after a few hours of sightseeing, and certainly one of the cheapest eateries in the square. If you manage to nab one of the outside tables, you can also indulge in a spot of people-watching. Closed Sun; Jan.

**SAN MARCO Da Raffaelle** €€€€

*Ponte delle Ostreghe 2347, 30124* ***Tel*** *041 523 23 17* ***Fax*** *041 241 65 46* ***Map*** *7 A3*

This well-established bustling restaurant offers a vast range of regional dishes in an especially romantic setting. Dishes worth trying include *granseola* (spider crab) as an antipasto, and risotto with scampi and turbot as a main course. Closed Thu (in winter); Dec–late Jan.

**SAN MARCO Antico Martini** €€€€€

*Campiello della Fenice 2007, 30124* ***Tel*** *041 522 41 21* ***Fax*** *041 528 98 57* ***Map*** *7 A2*

Alongside the Fenice theatre and the perfect destination for suppers, this smart restaurant boasts high-quality cuisine, a vast choice of wines and impeccable service. The lamb with balsamic sauce is just one of the many recommended dishes on the menu.

**SAN MARCO Harry's Bar** €€€€€

*Calle Vallaresso 1322, 30124* ***Tel*** *041 528 57 77* ***Fax*** *041 520 88 22* ***Map*** *7 B3*

Known the world over as Ernest Hemingway's favourite watering hole in Venice, Harry's Bar is a hallowed institution as well as a cosy café. Coffee and toasted sandwiches can be ordered, or a Bellini cocktail. The renowned food on the menu includes *carpaccio* (raw marinated beef), a dish invented by the owner.

**SAN MARCO La Caravella** €€€€€

*Calle Larga XXII Marzo 2397, 30124* ***Tel*** *041 520 89 01* ***Fax*** *041 520 58 58* ***Map*** *7 A3*

An outstanding restaurant with excellent service in the Hotel Saturnia, near Piazza San Marco, La Caravella is decorated to resemble the interior of a 16th-century Venetian galley. Fish soup or sea bass with toasted pine nuts, leeks and basil, are just two of the tempting dishes on the menu. High-standard wine list.

**SAN MARCO Ristorante La Colomba** €€€€€

*Piscina di Frezzeria 1665, 30124* ***Tel*** *041 522 11 75* ***Map*** *7 A2*

Sophisticated dining amid modern masterpieces by the likes of Picasso and De Chirico. Traditional fare is prepared with great flair. Try the *pasticcio di tagliolini gratinati con scampi e calamari alla Buranella* (Burano-style pasta with seafood), or the tiramisù with cookies and coffee sauce. Vast range of wines. Closed Wed; Jan, 2 wks Aug.

**SAN POLO Muro** €€€

*Rio Terà dei Frari, 30125* ***Tel*** *041 524 53 10* ***Map*** *6 E1*

A branch of the trendy Muro pizza restaurants, which are very popular with young locals. The pizza menu features buffalo mozzarella and exotic toppings such as walnuts and smoked tuna. There is also a vast choice of seafood, fresh fish and superb grilled-meat dishes. Wash them all down with Bavarian beer and Italian wines. Closed Thu.

**SAN POLO Trattoria alla Madonna** €€€

*Calle della Madonna 594, 30125* ***Tel*** *041 522 38 24* ***Fax*** *041 521 01 67* ***Map*** *7 A1*

In this well-known fish restaurant in the Rialto area, waiters dash around loaded with platters of traditional seafood, such as delicate *granceola* (spider crab) and *seppie in nero* (squid in black-ink sauce). Arrive early to avoid having to wait for a table. Closed Wed; end Dec–end Jan, 5–20 Aug.

**SAN POLO Poste Vecie** €€€€

*Rialto Pescheria 1608, 30125* ***Tel*** *041 72 18 22* ***Fax*** *041 72 10 37* ***Map*** *3 A5*

With its entrance from the fish market at Rialto, Poste Vecie claims to be the oldest restaurant in the city, and traces its history back to the 1500s. Fish such as baked turbot is excellent, as are the home-made ravioli and *tagliolini* (ribbon pasta). The wine list and the dessert trolley cannot fail to impress. Closed Tue.

**SAN POLO Da Fiore** €€€€€

*Calle del Scaleter 2202, 30125* ***Tel*** *041 72 13 08* ***Fax*** *041 72 13 43* ***Map*** *6 D1*

An exclusive establishment hidden behind Campo San Polo, Da Fiore is probably the city's best restaurant. Seasonal produce is the rule. Gourmet diners appreciate the sea bass with balsamic vinegar, tuna with rosemary, and *molecche* (soft-shelled crabs). Leave room for a delicate fruit sorbet. Closed Sun, Mon; 8–27 Jan, 3 wks Aug.

**SANTA CROCE Al Nono Risorto** €€

*Sottoportego di Sior Bettina 2338, 30135* ***Tel*** *041 524 11 69* ***Map*** *2 F5*

Going strong until late in the night, this busy pizzeria and modest restaurant has a pretty shady courtyard for summer dining. Located near the Rialto market area, it is popular with the locals, and booking is advisable at weekends. Closed Wed, Thu lunch; 3 wks Jan, 1 wk mid-Aug.

**SANTA CROCE Enoteca Al Prosecco** €€

*Campo San Giacomo dell'Orio 1503, 30135* ***Tel*** *041 524 02 22* ***Map*** *2 E3*

Enjoy light meals inside the simple premises or outside, in the tree-filled square. As the name suggests, sparkling Prosecco white wine from the Veneto is the signature drink here, accompanied by *cichetti*, or snacks of specialist cheeses, fragrant prosciutto or sausages flavoured with wild boar. Closed Sun; Jan, Aug.

**SANTA CROCE La Zucca** €€

*Calle del Megio 1762, 30135* ***Tel*** *041 524 15 70* ***Map*** *2 E5*

This pretty canalside restaurant is beloved of locals and tourists alike. With predominantly meat and vegetarian dishes, the menu focuses on traditional Veneto cuisine with some international variations. The pumpkin flan is famous and the puddings exquisite. Booking is advisable. Closed Sun.

**SANTA CROCE Il Réfolo** €€€

*Campo del Piovan 1459, 30135* ***Tel*** *041 524 00 16* ***Fax*** *041 72 13 43* ***Map*** *2 E5*

Set in a picturesque square on a canalside near San Giacomo dell'Orio, this modern establishment serves innovative gourmet pizzas and simple pasta meals. It belongs to the family who run the nearby Osteria da Fiore. Closed Mon, Tue lunch; mid-Dec–Jan.

**SANTA CROCE Antiche Carampane** €€€€€

*Rio Terà Carampane 1911, 30125* ***Tel*** *041 524 01 65* ***Map*** *2 F5*

Allow plenty of time to find this local favourite, which is hidden away in a maze of alleys. The menu is all about fresh fish, with dishes such as *bigoi cassapipa* (thick spaghetti with spicy seafood) and *rombo con arancio* (turbot with orange). Unforgettable desserts with lashings of chocolate. Closed Sun, Mon; 10 days Jan, 3 wks Aug.

**TORCELLO Locanda Cipriani** €€€€

*Piazza Santa Fosca 29, 30012* ***Tel*** *041 73 01 50* ***Fax*** *041 73 54 33*

A fisherman's inn in the 1930s, this charming exclusive island restaurant has a lovely shady courtyard where guests can enjoy dishes made with fresh produce from the kitchen garden. The risotto and seafood *fritto misto* (fried-fish platter) are both excellent. Closed Tue; Jan.

## THE VENETO AND FRIULI

**ASOLO Hostaria Ca Derton** €€

*Piazza D'Annunzio 11, 31011* ***Tel*** *042 352 96 48* ***Fax*** *042 352 03 08*

This attractive restaurant set in a medieval palace in the centre of Asolo offers a seasonal menu that changes regularly. It includes innovative interpretations of traditional dishes such as home-made brawn with balsamic vinegar, pasta with asparagus and roast goat with herbs. The dessert selection is luscious. Closed Sun dinner, Mon.

**ASOLO Villa Cipriani** €€€€€

*Via Canova 298, 31011* ***Tel*** *042 352 34 11* ***Fax*** *042 395 20 95*

Set in one of the grand hotels of the Veneto, this restaurant leads out on to the hotel gardens with breathtaking views of the verdant hills below. Local and seasonal ingredients are used in the creative cuisine, with dishes such as ricotta gnocchi with rosemary sauce.

**BASSANO DEL GRAPPA Alla Riviera** €

*Via San Giorgio 17, 36061* ***Tel/Fax*** *0424 50 37 00*

A traditional *osteria* serving typical Venetian dishes such as *pasta e fagioli*, a bean and pasta soup usually served tepid. *Baccalà* (cod) is served as an antipasto in the form of pâté and eaten with bread. Home-made desserts and a good selection of wine, including good local wine sold as *vino sfuso* (by the glass). Closed Sun dinner, Mon; 2 wks mid-Aug.

**BELLUNO Terracotta** €€

*Via Garibaldi 61, 32100* ***Tel*** *0437 94 26 44* ***Fax*** *0437 94 26 44*

Regional specialities in this friendly restaurant include pork wrapped in Parma ham with a grain mustard sauce, though the menu varies monthly. Views from the restaurant are limited, but there is a pretty wisteria-covered pergola. An extensive wine list suits all budgets. Closed Tue.

**BREGANZE Al Toresan** €€

*Via Zabarella 1, 36042* ***Tel*** *0445 87 32 60* ***Fax*** *0445 30 76 51*

In the autumn the locals flock here for the delicious wild-mushroom dishes. Mushrooms come in every shape and form: stuffed, as filling for ravioli, and grilled. The cooking is hearty and complemented by the local wines, of which the reds are particularly good. Closed Thu; 3 wks Aug.

**CAORLE Duilio** €€

*Via Strada Nuova 19, 30021* ***Tel*** *0421 810 87* ***Fax*** *0421 21 00 89*

A spacious restaurant with nautically inspired decor, where the fish-based regional cuisine is the house speciality: do not miss the *broeto alla Duilio*, a wine-drenched mixed fish soup. Less boozy is the grilled sole. In fact, wine and fish are the two major players here. Closed Mon in winter; early Jan–early Feb.

**CASTELFRANCO Barbesin** €€

*Via Circonvallazione Est 41, 31033* ***Tel*** *0423 49 04 46* ***Fax*** *0423 49 02 61*

A restaurant serving regional specialities, including risotto with asparagus or porcini mushrooms. However, it is the local radicchio that predominates. Other dishes include a generous mixed grilled and *baccalà alla vicentina* (cod prepared according to a local recipe). Closed Wed dinner, Thu; 1–15 Jan; 3 wks Aug.

### CHIOGGIA La Taverna €€€

*Via Felice Cavallotti 348, 30015* **Tel/Fax** *041 40 18 06*

Classic cooking based on seafood in an elegant setting. This restaurant, one of the oldest in town, is located next to a 14th-century bell tower, and the outdoor tables look out on to Chioggia's main square. Inside there are three dining rooms. Closed Wed; 2 wks Feb.

### CHIOGGIA Osteria Penzo €€€

*Calle Larga Bersaglio 526, 30015* **Tel/Fax** *041 40 09 92*

Located in the centre of Chioggia, this traditional trattoria serves a wide variety of fish dishes, including squid with peas, squid-ink noodles with prawns and tomato, and scallops with porcini mushrooms. Good local wine list and service. Closed 25 Dec–6 Jan: Mon dinner, Tue; summer: Tue.

### CIVIDALE DEL FRIULI Alla Speranza €

*Via Foro Giulio Cesare 15, 33043* **Tel** *0432 73 11 31*

Alla Speranza offers a cosy wood-panelled interior for winter dining, while the shady courtyard is a good place to enjoy a light lunch in the summer. The small menu is based on local ingredients and changes on a monthly basis. There is a limited but good wine selection, also by the glass. Popular with locals. Closed Tue; 1 wk Jan, end Sep.

### CIVIDALE DEL FRIULI Zorutti €

*Borgo di Ponte 9, 33043* **Tel** *0432 73 11 00* **Fax** *0432 73 11 00*

This family-run restaurant has developed a well-deserved reputation for good regional cuisine served in generous portions. The house speciality is *buzara*, a local dish of spaghetti with seafood, including giant prawns or lobster. There is also a good fixed-priced menu that changes seasonally. Closed Mon; 2 wks Jan.

### CONEGLIANO Al Salisa €€

*Via XX Settembre 4, 31015* **Tel** *0438 242 88*

An elegant restaurant set in a medieval house with a pretty veranda for eating outdoors. The traditional menu includes snails and home-made pasta served with a range of vegetarian sauces. The *guanciale di vitello* (veal), snails and the exemplary wine list guarantee a feast. Closed Tue dinner, Wed.

### CORMONS Trattoria al Cacciatore – La Subida €€€€

*Località Monte 22, 34071* **Tel** *0481 605 31*

The inventive Friulian and Slovenian menu here changes with the seasons. Try the *gnocchi con susine agrodolci* (dumplings with wild plums) in summer, and hearty *jota* soup (with cabbage and beans) in winter. The superb wines are mostly local and include Ribolla Gialla. Closed lunch Mon, Thu, Fri; Tue, Wed; 3 wks Feb, 1 wk Mar.

### CORTINA D'AMPEZZO Ristorante El Zoco €€

*Cademai 18, 32043* **Tel** *0436 86 00 41*

A small but cosy restaurant on the outskirts of trendy Cortina. As a first course, enjoy *canederli ai porcini*, delicate golf-ball-sized mushroom dumplings flavoured with chive sauce. Grilled meats and fresh seasonal vegetables also feature on the menu. The legendary wine cellar hosts many rare labels, exclusively Italian. Closed Mon; May, Nov.

### CORTINA D'AMPEZZO Baita Fraina €€€€

*Località Fraina 1, 32043* **Tel** *0436 36 34* **Fax** *0436 87 62 35*

This lovely wood-panelled mountain restaurant features a panoramic terrace and a massive play area for kids. The pasta dishes are good, as are the game dishes, which include *tagliata di cervo* (venison). There is an excellent wine list and a choice of over 100 types of grappa. Closed Mon low season; after Easter–Jun, Oct–Nov.

### DOLO Alla Posta €€€€

*Via Ca' Tron 33, 30031* **Tel** *041 41 07 40* **Fax** *041 41 07 40*

This superb fish restaurant in an old Venetian posthouse overlooking the town's main canal prepares regional specialities with fresh ingredients and well-blended flavours. On the menu you will find dishes such as mixed grilled fish platter and Venetian specialities. Closed Wed.

### GRADO Trattoria de Toni €€€

*Piazza Duca d'Aosta 37, 34073* **Tel** *0431 801 04* **Fax** *0431 87 78 58*

A beautiful trattoria in the historic centre. The house speciality here is *boreto alla gradese*, a delicious fish stew cooked in oil and vinegar. Though fans come for the superb fish and wine, the setting is also special, with transparent flooring in parts to show Roman remains beneath. Closed Wed; Dec–Feb.

### GRANCONA Isetta €€

*Via Pederiva 96, 36040* **Tel** *0444 88 99 92* **Fax** *0444 88 99 92*

This pretty little restaurant, just 15 minutes from Vicenza, serves regional food, with the emphasis on grilled meats and good puddings, based on recipes handed down by the owner's grandmother, Isetta. Set in the Berici Hills, the restaurant also offers accommodation in ten rooms. Closed Tue dinner, Wed; 2 wks Jan, 2 wks Aug.

### LAKE GARDA Antica Locanda Mincio €€

*Via Michelangelo Buonarroti 12, Valeggio sul Mincio, 37067* **Tel** *045 795 00 59* **Fax** *045 637 04 55*

Once a staging post, this is now a delightful restaurant, with frescoed walls and open fireplaces serving good regional food. The shady seating outside overlooks a river bubbling past. Specialities include trout and eels caught in the nearby Lake Garda. Closed Wed, Thu; 2 wks Feb, 2 wks Nov.

**Key to Price Guide** *see p606* **Key to Symbols** *see back cover flap*

### LAKE GARDA Locanda San Vigilio €€€€€

*Località San Vigilio, Garda, 37016* ***Tel*** *045 725 66 88* ***Fax*** *045 725 65 51*

This excellent restaurant overlooking Lake Garda has been offering wine and food for five centuries. Nowadays, it has an astounding range of freshwater fish and seafood dishes. The spacious garden has shady olive trees. Closed mid-Nov–mid-Mar.

### MIANE Da Gigetto €€€

*Via De Gaspari 5, 31050* ***Tel*** *043 896 00 20* ***Fax*** *043 896 01 11*

Traditional Venetian cuisine served with flair awaits at this restaurant. The menu is seasonal, and in the autumn the pumpkin and mushroom dishes are particularly good. Game dishes such as hare and deer are also served in the winter. The wine cellar is enormous and the service is very good. Closed Mon dinner, Tue; 2 wks Jan, 3 wks Aug.

### MONTECCHIO DI CROSARA Alpone €€€

*Località Pergola 17, 37030* ***Tel*** *045 617 53 87*

A refined restaurant offering a seasonal tasting menu. In the spring, try dishes based on mushrooms or cherries. The place also offers an à la carte menu with gnocchi, *crespelle* (pancakes) and grilled vegetables. End your meal with a plate of local cheeses served with a variety of chutneys and jams. Closed Sun dinner, Tue; 2 wks Jan, 2 wks Aug.

### MONTECCHIO DI CROSARA Baba Jaga €€€€

*Via Cabalao 12, 37030* ***Tel*** *045 745 02 22*

Black-truffle risotto is a good choice in this restaurant situated in the heart of the Soave wine-producing area. Other dishes in this friendly, informal setting include stuffed duck thigh in an Amarone wine sauce or tagliatelle with quail sauce. Closed Sun dinner, Mon; 3 wks Jan, 3 wks Aug.

### NOVENTA PADOVANA Boccadoro €€€€

*Via della Resistenza 49, 35027* ***Tel*** *049 62 50 29* ***Fax*** *049 62 57 82*

Good Paduan food is served in this family-run restaurant. The surroundings have an air of relaxed elegance and the service is exemplary. The *bigoli* pasta with goose sauce is well worth sampling, as is the guinea fowl with radicchio au gratin. Closed Tue dinner, Wed; 3 wks Aug, 27 Dec–6 Jan.

### ODERZO Dussin €

*Via Maggiore 60, Località Piavon, 31046* ***Tel*** *0422 75 21 30* ***Fax*** *0422 75 38 67*

Good-value traditional cuisine is served here. Fish is a speciality, with such dishes as seafood risotto and grilled tuna. However, the home-made desserts are not to be missed. The restaurant is situated just outside the town centre, in a tranquil setting. Closed Mon; 2 wks Aug.

### PADUA Osteria L'Anfora €

*Via dei Soncin 13, 35122* ***Tel*** *049 65 66 29*

Traditional Veneto cuisine, with elements originally brought by Renaissance merchants from far afield, is served in this lively restaurant in the heart of Padua. Local specialities are the fish stew and the perennial pasta and beans. Closed Sun; 1–7 Jan, 1 wk Aug.

### PADUA Antico Brolo €€

*Corso Milano 22, 35100* ***Tel*** *049 66 45 55* ***Fax*** *049 65 60 88*

This quietly chic restaurant delivers appropriately elegant food such as ravioli stuffed with courgette flowers. The veal's head cooked in vinegar and onion is the house's highlight. The menu includes a good wine list. Good for families and groups. Closed Mon lunch.

### PADUA San Pietro €€

*Via San Pietro 95, 35100* ***Tel*** *049 876 03 30*

The perfect place for regional dishes cooked with fresh, local ingredients. This traditional Paduan restaurant offers attentive, though not always friendly, service in an informal atmosphere. Many dishes come from the Lombardy region of Italy. Closed Sun; summer Sat and Sun; Jul.

### PADUA Zairo €€

*Prato della Valle 51, 35121* ***Tel*** *049 66 38 03*

Offering wonderful views of Padua's famous Prato, this lively restaurant has a dining room lavishly decorated with statuary, frescoes and Murano chandeliers. On the menu is a wide range of pasta, meat and fish dishes, in addition to a long list of pizzas. Staying open until late, Zairo is popular with the locals. Closed Mon.

### PORDENONE Vecia Osteria del Moro €€

*Via Castello 2, 33170* ***Tel*** *0434 206 58* ***Fax*** *0434 206 71*

A refined restaurant set in a beautifully restored 13th-century convent that provides a tranquil backdrop while you enjoy the regional food. The wine list is extensive, with many labels from the Friuli region. Daily specials include rabbit with polenta. Closed Sun.

### PREPOTTO Il Tinello di San Urbano €€

*Via XXIV Maggio 30, 33040* ***Tel/Fax*** *0432 71 30 80*

This handsome *agriturismo* is beautifully located among hills and vineyards, just a 10-minute drive from Cividale del Friuli. The chef uses ingredients fresh from the garden. Specialities include home-made pasta served with local sausages and leeks. Private rooms are also available. Open Friday to Sunday only. Closed Jan–Mar.

### REFRONTOLO Antica Osteria al Forno €€

*Via Degli Alpini 5, 31020* ***Tel*** *0438 89 44 96* ***Fax*** *0438 89 44 96*

This trattoria has been run by the Piol family for 150 years. The decor is rustic, with a large fireplace in the centre of the dining room. The pasta dishes are outstanding, and most of the vegetables are organic. The extensive wine list includes good local wine. There is also a shady courtyard for summer dining. Closed Mon, Tue; 2 wks Jan, Aug.

### STREGNA La Casa delle Rondini €€

*Frazione Dughe 2, 33040* ***Tel*** *0432 72 41 77*

Good home cooking prepared using mostly local ingredients can be enjoyed at this establishment, which also produces its own cheese and salami on the premises. Guests can dine on the panoramic terrace, while taking in the splendid views. Open Friday and Monday (dinner only) and all day Saturday and Sunday. Closed Jan–Feb.

### TREVISO Osteria all'Antica Torre €€€

*Via Inferiore 55, 31100* ***Tel*** *0422 58 36 94*

Exemplary wines accompany superb local cuisine. In season, radicchio is used in many ways, including in the making of the grappa. However, fish is the main contender on the menu, with imaginative dishes such as cuttlefish risotto. Art exhibitions are also held here. Closed Mon dinner, Sun; 3 wks Aug.

### TREVISO Ristorante Beccherie €€€

*Piazza Ancillotto 9, 31100* ***Tel*** *0422 54 08 71* ***Fax*** *0422 54 08 71*

Housed in a lovely building reminiscent of Venetian splendour. The name derives from local dialect, meaning "butcher's" and, indeed, meat is a speciality here. The guinea fowl in pepper sauce and roast goose with white celery are particular delicacies. Closed Sun dinner, Mon; last 2 wks Jul.

### TREVISO Toni del Spin €€€

*Via Inferiore 7, 31100* ***Tel*** *0422 54 38 29* ***Fax*** *0422 58 31 10*

A homely restaurant serving regional fare. Though busy serving office workers at lunchtime, this trattoria slows down in the evenings, offering a more intimate experience. House specialities include *pasta and fagioli* (beans), the ubiquitous *risotto al radicchio*, tripe and tiramisù. Closed Sun and Mon lunch; 20 Jun–20 Jul.

### TRIESTE All'Antica Ghiacceretta €€

*Via dei Fornelli 2, 34100* ***Tel*** *040 322 03 07* ***Fax*** *040 32 20 307*

Located in the centre of Trieste, this family-run trattoria serves local dishes such as *Jota* (cabbage and bean soup) and various fish dishes. Try the *baccalà con polenta* (salt cod) and other fresh local fish, usually served grilled. The good, hearty food at a reasonable price is matched by the good local wines on offer. Closed Sun; 1 wk Feb, 1 wk Nov.

### TRIESTE Al Bragozzo €€€

*Riva Nazario Sauro 22, 34124* ***Tel*** *040 31 41 11* ***Fax*** *040 31 41 11*

The seasonal menu changes from week to week, depending on the local produce available. However, fish is a staple ingredient, with both traditional and contemporary dishes on offer. A lively restaurant popular with the locals. Closed Mon.

### TRIESTE Harry's Grill €€€€

*Piazza Unità d'Italia 2, 34121* ***Tel*** *040 66 06 06* ***Fax*** *040 36 60 92*

This restaurant is distinguished by its central position and high-class cuisine. Try the ravioli with aubergine (eggplant) filling and crayfish sauce. More traditional truffle dishes also appear on the menu. The wine cellar holds an astounding 11,000 bottles, so there is something for all palates. Closed Sun.

### UDINE Da Raffaele €

*Via Cividale 11, 33100* ***Tel*** *0432 29 58 31*

This pizzeria offers a wide range of dishes. Pizzas and *calzoni* cooked in a wood-fired oven are the speciality, but the pasta and fish dishes are also good. There is beer on tap, as well as a good house wine. The informal atmosphere and friendly service make it a draw for the locals. Good value for money. Closed Thu dinner; 3 wks Jul–Aug.

### UDINE Agli Amici €€€€€

*Via Liguria 250, Località Godia, 33100* ***Tel*** *0432 56 54 11* ***Fax*** *0432 56 55 55*

Friulian dishes, such as *capesante all'aglio orsino* (scallops with wild garlic) and saddle of lamb with ginger, are cooked with flair here. The wine list is extensive and excellent, and the pretty pergola makes eating alfresco a very pleasant experience. Closed Sun dinner (all day in summer), Mon, Tue lunch in winter.

### VERONA Ristorante Greppia €€€

*Vicolo Samaritana 3, 37121* ***Tel*** *045 800 45 77*

Run by the Guizzardi family since 1975, this restaurant, named after the local word for a feeding trough, offers superb food. As well as delicious fresh-made pasta, there is a memorable *bollito misto* (boiled-meats platter): diners choose their meat from a trolley. Booking recommended. Closed Mon; 2 wks Jun.

### VERONA Arche €€€€€

*Via Arche Scaligere 6, 37121* ***Tel/Fax*** *045 800 74 15*

This long-established fish restaurant opened for business in 1879. It is perfectly situated next to Romeo's home, a location that only adds to its charm. On the menu: smoked oysters with horseradish and caviar, and marinated rock lobster. Closed Sun, Mon lunch; 3 wks Jan.

**Key to Price Guide** *see p606* **Key to Symbols** *see back cover flap*

**VERONA Il Desco** €€€€€

*Via Dietro San Sebastiano 5–7, 37121* ***Tel*** *045 59 53 58* ***Fax*** *045 59 02 36*

One of Italy's finest restaurants, set in a 16th-century palazzo, Il Desco boasts two Michelin stars. It is both romantic and understated. Dishes include pumpkin and Amarone wine risotto and aubergine (eggplant) ravioli. A gourmet menu offers a staggering seven courses. Closed Sun, Mon (except dinner Jul, Aug, Dec); 2 wks Jun, 2 wks Christmas.

**VICENZA Antica Casa della Malvasia** €€

*Contrà delle Morette 5, 36100* ***Tel*** *0444 54 37 04*

This traditional *osteria* in the shadow of the basilica has been around since the 13th century, when it was a favourite meeting point for wine merchants. Today it remains a great place to stop for lunch. The pasta dishes are highly recommended, as is the extensive wine list. Closed Sun, Mon.

**VICENZA Antica Trattoria Tre Visi** €€€

*Corso Palladio 25, 36100* ***Tel*** *0444 32 48 68* ***Fax*** *0444 32 03 15*

The building, conveniently situated in the historic centre of town, dates from 1483. Its outside courtyard is a pleasant place to dine alfresco in the warm summer months. Diners can see into the kitchen, where the excellent local dishes are prepared. Closed Sun dinner, Mon; 2 wks July.

**VICENZA Taverna Aeolia** €€€€

*Piazza Conte da Schio 1, Costozza di Longare, 36023* ***Tel*** *0444 55 50 36*

This restaurant is housed in an elegant villa with a beautiful frescoed ceiling. The menu specializes in creative meat dishes, with kangaroo, bison and frog all available. Vegetarians can enjoy the lemon risotto, and a children's menu is also available. Closed Tue; 1–15 Nov.

## TRENTINO-ALTO ADIGE

**ARCO Alla Lega** €

*Via Vergolano 8, 38062* ***Tel*** *0464 51 62 05* ***Fax*** *0464 51 08 96*

A lively, family-run restaurant housed in a rustically elegant 18th-century building with a beautiful courtyard. Some of the dining rooms have frescoed ceilings. The food is traditional, including such dishes as wild mushroom risotto, cured meats, trout with polenta and roast rabbit with livers. Closed Wed; end Jan–mid-Mar.

**BOLZANO (BOZEN) Castel Roncolo Osteria** €

*Sentiero Imperatore Francesco Giuseppe, 39100* ***Tel*** *0471 32 40 73*

A pleasant riverside stroll from the town, this tavern in the courtyard of a medieval castle is a great spot for lunch. On the menu is Tyrolean fare such as *Schlutzkrapfen* (fresh pasta parcels filled with spinach and ricotta cheese), roast meats and desserts such as vanilla ice cream with hot raspberries. Open only at lunch. Closed Mon; 2 wks Feb.

**BOLZANO (BOZEN) L'Aquila Rossa / Vogele** €

*Via Goethe 3, 39100* ***Tel*** *0471 97 39 38* ***Fax*** *0471 32 57 50*

This traditional restaurant is housed in one of the oldest buildings in Bolzano's historic centre. Try the *gnocchi tirolesi* (Tyrolean dumplings) and roast venison, and finish with one of the desserts made on the premises. The wine list is extensive, with a choice of over 200 local and international wines. Closed Sun.

**BOLZANO (BOZEN) Castel Flavon** €€€

*Via Castel Flavon 48, 39100* ***Tel*** *0471 40 21 30* ***Fax*** *0471 27 98 30*

Located in a castle dating back to the 12th century, this charming restaurant offers spectacular views in a historic setting. South Tyrolean dishes are served alongside more adventurous cuisine, such as tuna ragù with avocado and lime. Extensive range of local wine. Closed Sun dinner, Mon; 3 wks Jan, 2 wks Aug.

**BRESSANONE (BRIXEN) Fink** €€€

*Via Portici Minori 4, 39042* ***Tel*** *0472 83 48 83* ***Fax*** *0472 83 52 68*

The original owner's daughter-in-law is now the chef at Fink. Locals come here to sample immaculately prepared dishes such as black polenta, *canderli or knödel* (Tyrolean dumpling) or the pasta stuffed with oxtail. There is also a large selection of game dishes. The wine list includes many local offerings. Closed Tue dinner; Wed.

**BRESSANONE (BRIXEN) Oste Scuro-Finsterwirt** €€€

*Vicolo Duomo 3, 39042* ***Tel*** *0472 83 53 43* ***Fax*** *0472 83 56 24*

Housed in one of the oldest buildings in town, Finsterwirt specializes in imaginative regional cuisine. Dishes such as *carpaccio di salmone* (thin slices of raw salmon) or *speck* (smoked ham) served with regional breads and asparagus cream are served by the attentive staff. Closed Sun dinner; Mon; 2 wks Jan, 2 wks Jun–Jul.

**BRUNICO (BRUNECK) Agnello Bianco** €

*Via Stuck 5, 39031* ***Tel*** *0474 41 13 50*

The food here is typical of the South Tyrol region and served in large portions. The menu changes weekly, but *canederli* (dumplings) are always available, although the fillings vary with the season. In the autumn, try the mushrooms with polenta. The dessert omelette with red-berry jam is also typical. Closed Sun; 21 Apr–6 May, 3 wks Jun.

**BRUNICO (BRUNECK) Oberraut** €€

*Via Ameto 1, Località Amaten, 39031* ***Tel*** *0474 55 99 77* ***Fax*** *0474 55 99 97*

Set in woods, this Tyrolean-style restaurant specializes in game and seasonal dishes, such as pumpkin ravioli and delicious home-cured *speck* (smoked ham). The tantalizing dessert list includes favourites such as apple strudel, and there is an extensive wine list. The service is pleasant and the atmosphere relaxed. Closed Thu; 2 wks Jan.

**CALDARO Castel Ringberg** €€€

*San Giuseppe al Lago 1, 39045* ***Tel*** *0471 96 00 10* ***Fax*** *0471 96 08 03*

This stunning restaurant is housed in an atmospheric 17th-century castle set among vineyards from which the restaurant's own wine is produced. The terrace has panoramic views of the lake below. The excellent menu is updated monthly. The desserts are to die for. Closed Tue; Jan–mid-Feb.

**CARZANO Le Rose** €€

*Via XVIII Settembre 35, 38050* ***Tel*** *0461 76 61 77* ***Fax*** *0461 76 79 42*

This popular Valsugana restaurant concentrates on fish and seasonal produce. There is a mixed fresh-fish platter available, or try the *tortelli* (parcels) of fish with porcini mushrooms. The restaurant has a garden with lovely panoramic views for dining outdoors in the summer. Closed Mon.

**CASTELBELLO CIARDES Schlosswirt Juval** €

*Località Juval 2, 39021* ***Tel*** *0473 66 80 56*

This restaurant is set on a working farm, high in the mountains. Most of the food here is organic, as are the wines and grappa. Among the dishes worth trying are an excellent goulash, roast meats and trout. Also on offer are good mountain cheeses. Desserts include apple strudel and buckwheat cake. Closed Sun, Mon & Tue dinner, Wed; Nov–Mar.

**CAURIA Fichtenhof** €€

*Cauria 23, Salorno 39040* ***Tel*** *0471 88 90 28*

A family-run restaurant/hotel perched in a stunning position overlooking the Adige Valley. On the menu: home-grown vegetables and home-made jams, breads and cakes. Delicious meals include delicate *pasta con teroldego e ragù* (with wine and meat sauce). Closed Mon; 7 Nov–25 Dec.

**CAVALESE Costa Salici** €€

*Via Costa dei Salici 10, 38033* ***Tel*** *0462 34 01 40*

A popular restaurant with panoramic views of the Dolomites. Dishes include black ribbon pasta with calamari and fresh tomato, marinated venison, and, for dessert, a terrine of citrus fruits with ice cream and *limoncello* (lemon liqueur) sauce. It is advisable to book ahead. Closed Mon & Tue lunch (except Aug and Christmas).

**CIVEZZANO Maso Cantanghel** €€€

*Via della Madonnina 33, 38045* ***Tel/Fax*** *0461 85 87 14*

At this excellent restaurant outside Trento, the decor is cluttered and quaint, with pictures from customers hanging on the walls. The food changes with the seasons so that the produce is always at its best. Try the stuffed courgette flowers with tomato sauce, roasted meats, vegetable flans and pasta dishes. Closed Sat & Sun; 2 wks Aug, 1 wk Christmas.

**CORTACCIA Gasthaus Zur Rose** €€€

*Indergasse 2, 39040* ***Tel*** *0471 88 01 16*

A 200-year-old *osteria* offering typical Tyrolean dishes, fine wines and an attractive veranda for summer dining. Good *antipasti* include *speck* (smoked ham) with horseradish sauce and *grostl* (meat and potato cake flavoured with chives). The apple fritters with vanilla sauce are very good. Closed Mon lunch (except Sep–Oct), Sun; 1 wk Carnival, Jul.

**LEVICO TERME Boivin** €

*Via Garibaldi 9, 38056* ***Tel*** *0461 70 16 70*

This excellent trattoria, with its cosy and relaxing dining area, is one of the best places to taste authentic, local cuisine, such as potato polenta, *strangolapreti* (a type of dumplings) and apple and pear strudel. Emphasis is put on seasonal produce. Booking is recommended. Closed lunch (except Sun and Jul, Aug); Mon.

**MADONNA DI CAMPIGLIO Hermitage** €€€€€

*Via Castelletto Inferiore 63, 38084* ***Tel*** *0465 44 15 58* ***Fax*** *0465 44 16 18*

Hermitage is set in a private park at the foot of the Dolomites, offering incredible views of the mountains. The restaurant serves imaginative Trentino cuisine – fresh-flavoured, tasty dishes with a stress on organic, natural produce. There is also a well-researched and extensive wine list. Closed lunch; Mon; Apr–Jun, Oct–Nov.

**MALLES VENOSTA (MALS IM VINSCHGAU) Greif** €

*Via Generale Verdross 40a, 39024* ***Tel*** *0473 83 14 29* ***Fax*** *0473 83 19 06*

The resident chef here creates typical Tyrolean dishes using organic produce. Vegetarians will find a wide-ranging menu catering to their needs, while oenophiles are rewarded with a good selection of vintage wines. In the summer, guests can dine outside in the grounds. Closed Tue; 2 wks Nov.

**MERANO (MERAN) Rainer** €

*Via Portici 266, 39012* ***Tel*** *0473 236 149*

This attractive restaurant is located in the old part of the city, underneath the medieval portico. Three wood-panelled rooms are cosy for winter eating. On the menu are traditional dishes such as *bollito misto* (mixed boiled meats) served with a variety of sauces, and game. Home-made desserts and good service. Closed Sun; 3 wks Feb, 1 wk Jun.

**Key to Price Guide** *see p606* **Key to Symbols** *see back cover flap*

### MERANO (MERAN) Artemis €€

*Via Giuseppe Verdi 72, 39012* ***Tel*** *0473 44 62 82* ***Fax*** *0473 44 68 49*

Artemis overlooks a park with a lovely winter garden. Refined Italian and international cuisine using local and home-made and natural products is served here. The cellar has a large choice of wines chosen by owner and sommelier Carl de Franceschi. Live classical music occasionally. Closed mid-Nov–mid-Mar.

### MOENA Malga Panna €€€€

*Strada de Sort 64, 38035* ***Tel*** *0462 57 34 89*

Decorated in the typical style of the region, this romantic restaurant in a rustic setting about 1 km (half a mile) from the town centre has an inviting atmosphere. Mushroom and game dishes are served here. The cellar has a wide choice of around 700 local, national and international wines. Closed Mon (Dec–Apr); May, Jun, Oct, Nov.

### MOLVENO Antica Bosnia €€

*Via Paganella 7b, 38018* ***Tel*** *0461 58 61 23*

This rustic mountain restaurant offers good *antipasti* in the form of *speck* (smoked ham), smoked duck breast and home-made salami. For main course, try a pasta dish such as dumplings with mushroom sauce, or the *stinco di maiale* (pork shin). Fruit tarts and tiramisù for dessert. Good regional wine list. Closed Wed; Nov.

### ROVERETO Novecento €€

*Corso Rosmini 82d, 38068* ***Tel*** *0464 43 54 54*

The dining rooms of this refined restaurant, part of a hotel in the middle of Rovereto, are elegant, and the service is attentive and courteous. The carefully prepared local dishes include salmon marinated in dill, *strangolapreti alle ortiche* (nettle dumplings) and an excellent selection of home-made desserts. Closed Sun; 3 wks Jan, 3 wks Jul.

### SAN CASSIANO St Hubertus €€€€€

*Str Micura de Ru 20, 39030* ***Tel*** *0471 84 95 00* ***Fax*** *0471 84 93 77*

Chef Norbert Niederkofler creates imaginative cuisine using the freshest of local ingredients. The menu is varied, serving fish, meat and game dishes. The service is attentive and the surroundings elegant. The wine list is comprehensive, including national and international wines. One of Italy's best restaurants. Closed Tue; Apr–mid-Jun, Oct–Nov.

### TRENTO Osteria Alle Due Spade €€€€

*Via Don Rizzi 11, 38100* ***Tel*** *0461 23 43 43*

A welcoming cellar restaurant serving traditional cuisine, including game and freshwater fish. Try the *lasagnette* (small lasagne) with potato and freshwater prawns, or the herbed goat's cheese with mixed seasonal vegetables. For dessert, sample the pastries with apple and apricot jam. Closed Sun, Mon lunch; 1 wk Feb, 2 wks Jun.

### VAL DI VIZZE (PFITSCH) Pretzhof €€

*Località Tulve 259, 39040* ***Tel*** *0472 76 44 55*

Karl and Ulli Mair run this peaceful country inn, which is included in many gastro-guides. They use fresh produce from their own farm to create Tyrolean specialities. The menu is simple, with dishes such as game, cold cuts, and a large selection of local cheeses and breads. The wine list highlights local producers. Closed Mon, Tue (except public hols).

### VIPITENO (STERZING) Kleine Flamme €€€€

*Città Nuova 31, 39049* ***Tel*** *0472 76 60 65*

A high standard of creative cuisine is matched by good service and attention to detail at this chic restaurant in a 16th-century building. The chef has combined an unusual mix of Italian and Thai cuisine with much success. Typical dishes include roast prawns with tomato and pineapple sauce, although the menu changes daily. Closed Mon, Sun evening.

## LOMBARDY

### BELLAGIO Albergo Ristorante Silvio €€

*Via Carcano 12, 22021* ***Tel*** *031 95 03 22*

Silvio and Cristian Ponzini, the owner and his son, are the professional fishermen providing an abundant catch of freshwater fish for this restaurant-cum-hotel. Visitors can even arrange a fishing trip with them. The views over Lake Como are enchanting, especially from the vine-clad terrace. Closed mid-Nov–Feb (except 20 Dec–10 Jan).

### BELLAGIO La Busciona €€€

*Via Valassina 161, 22021* ***Tel*** *031 96 48 31*

Fish is the order of the day at La Busciona. This simple but pleasant restaurant has a friendly, familiar atmosphere and spectacular panoramic views of Lake Como over Bellagio. Try the *lavarello*, a small lake fish, grilled or sautéed in butter and sage. As well as a fine wine cellar, parking is available. Closed Tue.

### BERGAMO Vineria Cozzi €€

*Via Colleoni 22, 24100* ***Tel*** *035 23 88 36*

Vineria Cozzi is a wonderful old wine shop dating back to 1848. Part of the building has been kept intact and has a lovely courtyard at the back. The traditional fare served here perfectly complements the wines. Expect to find rich, traditional dishes using plenty of truffles and polenta. Closed Wed; 2 wks Jan, 2 wks Jul.

### BERGAMO Colleoni dell'Angelo €€€€€

*Piazza Vecchia 7, 24100* ***Tel*** *035 23 25 96*

Dominating a beautiful square in the heart of Bergamo Alta, this wonderful restaurant is loved by local business people, intellectuals and tourists alike. Service is excellent and the cuisine is an imaginative take on northern Italian fare, such as red tuna tartar on crisp young vegetables in a green curry sauce. Closed Mon; 2 wks Aug.

### BERGAMO Roof Garden €€€€€

*Hotel San Marco, Piazza della Repubblica 6, 24122* ***Tel*** *035 36 61 59*

Awarded a Michelin star in 2010, this restaurant on the eighth floor of the Hotel San Marco fuses world flavours and contemporary Mediterranean cuisine. Inventive dishes such as artichoke risotto with Tahitian vanilla sit alongside more traditional fare. There are stunning views across the city and beyond. Closed Sun; 10 days Aug.

### BORMIO Al Filò €€

*Via Dante 6, 23032* ***Tel*** *0342 90 17 32*

This restaurant on the Valtellina mushroom route offers local fare based on game, mushrooms and cured meats in a converted barn. Specials include stuffed venison with polenta, *bresaola* (cured beef) with mushroom salad, and buckwheat pasta baked with butter and vegetables. Closed Mon & Tue lunch; first 2 wks Jun, last 2 wks Nov.

### BRESCIA Trattoria Mezzeria €€

*Via Trieste 66, 25121* ***Tel*** *030 403 06*

Typical regional dishes such as hearty rabbit stews, cured meats and delicious home-made *gnocchi di zucca* (pumpkin dumplings) are on the menu here. Mezzeria is a busy little trattoria with a familiar atmosphere close to the centre of Brescia. Closed Sun; Aug.

### CASTELVECCANA Sant'Antonio €€

*Località Sant'Antonio, 21010* ***Tel*** *335 541 44 80*

A traditional restaurant with farm-like appeal: goats and cows roam on the hillside overlooking Lake Maggiore. In summer you can enjoy the views from the terrace, and in winter warm yourself by the fire. Typical fare includes polenta and recipes using local cheese and cured meats. Booking compulsory. Closed Mon dinner; mid-Dec–mid-Jan.

### COMO Al Giardino €€€

*Via Monte Grappa 52, 22100* ***Tel*** *031 26 50 16*

In a residential district of Como, this family-run restaurant serves local and regional specialities. The range of cured meats and cheeses is particularly fine. The fresh interior is a delight, and the service is friendly and relaxed. A garden makes this place family- and child-friendly. Book ahead. Closed Mon; 2 wks Jan, 2 wks Aug.

### COMO L'Angolo del Silenzio €€€

*Viale Lecco 25, 22100* ***Tel*** *031 337 21 57*

A locals' favourite, this attractive, elegant restaurant is situated in the heart of Como, just a few minutes from the cathedral. The menu is extensive, featuring regional and national cuisine, and it is evenly split between fish and meat dishes. Booking compulsory. Closed Mon and Tue lunch; 2 wks Jan, Aug.

### COMO Sant'Anna 1907 €€€€

*Via Turati 3, 22100* ***Tel*** *031 50 52 66*

Creative local cuisine is served up at this traditional restaurant near Piazza Camerlata. Typical fare includes veal in olive crust, fillet of red tuna cooked with chicory shoots and olives, and risotto of fish and saffron. Artichokes and polenta also feature heavily on the menu. Excellent wine selection. Closed Sat lunch, Sun.

### CREMONA Il Violino €€€€

*Via Sicardo 3, 26100* ***Tel*** *0372 46 10 10*

An elegant restaurant in the heart of Cremona's old town, with an arched columned entrance. The menu offers traditional local cuisine and international dishes. The rice with pumpkin, black stuffed pasta with sea bass, steak and fish dishes all come highly recommended. The desserts and wines are excellent too. Closed Mon dinner, Tue.

### GARGNANO DEL GARDA La Tortuga €€€€€

*Via XXIV Maggio 5, Porticciolo di Gargnano, 25084* ***Tel*** *0365 712 51*

Light, imaginative cuisine is offered at this refined and intimate family-run lakeside restaurant. There are two tasting menus, as well as an à la carte selection. Lake fish is a house speciality, and the wine list is superb. Guests travel here from miles around, and there are only 20 covers, so make sure you book ahead. Closed lunch; Tue; mid-Nov–Feb.

### LAKE COMO Locanda dell'Isola Comacina €€€€€

*Isola Comacina, 22010* ***Tel*** *0344 567 55*

A unique experience on this wonderful island, deserted except for this restaurant. The same set menu of fish has survived unchanged since 1947. The island is reached by boat from Sala Comacina (pay direct on board). Book ahead by phone or email (locanda@comacina.it). Closed Tue (except summer); Nov–Feb.

### LECCO Antica Osteria Casa di Lucia €€

*Via Lucia 27, località Acquate, 23900* ***Tel*** *0341 49 45 94*

A superb gourmet restaurant with a good reputation and a loyal clientele. Housed in a characteristic 17th-century house that is also a venue for photographic exhibitions. Herb linguine, lamb chops, roast rabbit and a delicious home-made chocolate tart are some of the dishes on the menu. Good wine list. Closed Sat lunch, Sun.

**Key to Price Guide** *see p606* **Key to Symbols** *see back cover flap*

### MANERBA DEL GARDA Capriccio €€€€

*Piazza S. Bernardo 6, Località Montinelle, 25080* **Tel** *0365 55 11 24*

This refined establishment with views of Lake Garda offers high-quality cuisine such as sea bass, scallops, or medallions of *ricciola* (greater amberjack fish) in fennel sauce. There are also three tasting menus, including a "no fish" menu that features ravioli with local Bagoss cheese. Closed Tue; Jan–Feb.

### MANTUA Antica Osteria Ai Ranari €€

*Via Trieste 11, 46100* **Tel** *0376 32 84 31*

The menu at this restaurant in the town centre follows seasonal produce and offers traditional Mantuan dishes. Among these are the famous local *tortelli di zucca* (pumpkin-filled pasta with nutmeg, butter and mustard sauce), house macaroni and slow-cooked rich sauces. Closed Mon; mid-Jul–mid-Aug.

### MANTUA L'Ochina Bianca €€

*Via Finzi 2, 46100* **Tel** *0376 32 70 77*

Pumpkin *tortelli* (stuffed pasta) and risotto *alla pilotta* (with sausage) are examples of regional dishes that are given a lighter, more contemporary touch here. Also try the *sbrisolona*, a classic hard Mantuan dessert that crumbles into pieces when cut. It is served with a wild-berry fruit sauce. Closed Sun dinner, Mon; last 3 wks Aug.

### MANTUA Il Cigno Trattoria dei Martini €€€€

*Piazza Carlo d'Arco 1, 46100* **Tel** *0376 32 71 01*

Il Cigno Trattoria dei Martini was a forerunner of the new Mantuan cuisine that simplified traditional heavy dishes. Its signature dish is *insalata di petto di cappone in agrodolce* (salad with sweet-and-sour capon breast). The fine fare is complemented by a good wine list. Closed Mon, Tue; first wk Jan, Aug.

### MILAN Geppo €

*Via GB Morgagni 37, 20100* **Tel** *02 29 51 48 62*

A fairly small classic pizzeria with over 50 varieties of pizza to choose from. A speciality is the local Milanese style, with rocket, saffron and porcini mushrooms. The convivial atmosphere makes this a good destination if you're on a budget. Parallel to Corso Buenos Aires, the busy shopping street. Closed Sun; 2 wks Aug.

### MILAN Premiata Pizzeria €

*Via Alzaia Naviglio Grande 2, 20144* **Tel** *02 89 40 06 48*

A great affordable pizzeria in a central location near the canals. Tables are available in a lovely courtyard at the back when the weather is warm. Service can be hurried and the seating is communal, at long tables. Good pizzas and pasta dishes or try the Parma ham focaccia or rocket salad.

### MILAN Be Bop Pizzeria €€

*Viale Col di Lana 4, 20136* **Tel** *02 837 69 72*

One of Milan's most popular pizza restaurants, this attractive and popular place is located close to the Navigli district. Diners looking for non-wheat or gluten-free, vegan and vegetarian pizzas are well catered for. In addition, Be Bop also serves Mediterranean-inspired fare. Open every day.

### MILAN Trattoria Aurora €€€

*Via Savona 23, 20144* **Tel** *02 89 40 49 78*

This upmarket brasserie just a short distance from the Navigli district offers hearty Piedmontese food. Try the *antipasti*, the great *agnolotti del plin* (stuffed ravioli tossed in butter and sage) or the slow-cooked, caramelized onion soup. Also a vast list of Piedmontese wines. Warm rustic atmosphere and a pretty veranda in summer. Closed Mon.

### MILAN Osteria di Via Pre €€€€

*Via Casale 4, 20144* **Tel** *366 159 7478*

A historic *osteria* serving Ligurian seafood specials with the delicate flavours of the coast. Try the stuffed vegetable *antipasti*, swordfish *carpaccio* (raw, thin slices), organic pesto from Albenga, *pansotti* with nut sauce (pasta filled with ricotta, lemon and herbs), or the fish ravioli. Closed Mon.

### MILAN Trattoria alle Langhe €€€€

*Corso Como 6, 20154* **Tel** *02 655 42 79*

Just a few doors down from the fabulous designer store 10 Corso Como, this restaurant has two rooms: the upstairs is for casual meals and the downstairs is ideal for more formal dining. Piedmont classics and wines, amazing Barolo risotto and *tomini alle erbe* (goat's cheese flavoured with herbs). Closed Sun; last 3 wks Aug.

### MILAN Da Giacomo €€€€€

*Via B Cellini, corner Via Sottocorno 6, 20129* **Tel** *02 76 02 33 13*

A peaceful and stylish family-run establishment and an insider address for the well-heeled and fashionable Milanese. The dining room is decorated with Art Deco lamps. House specialities include tartare of tuna *alla Giacomo*. The wine list offers a wide choice of quality vintages. Reservations recommended. Closed 2 wks Aug, 2 wks Christmas.

### MILAN Giglio Rosso €€€€€

*Piazza Luigi di Savoia 2, 20124* **Tel** *02 669 41 74*

A few steps from the main train station, this elegant place, decorated in contemporary neutral shades, is a firm favourite with the locals. It offers high-quality, Tuscan-inspired cuisine, with a menu of traditional and innovative pasta, fish and meat dishes. Vegetarians are also well looked after. Closed Sat and Sun lunch; Aug.

### MILAN Il Ristorante, Bulgari Hotel €€€€€

*Via Privata Fratelli Gabba 7b, 20122* **Tel** *02 805 80 51*

Join the fashionable set for a luxury dining experience, well worth the expense. The restaurant is located in a curvaceous space on two levels with an outdoor courtyard, at the edge of the Botanic Gardens. The lemon risotto with vanilla flowers has become a classic, and there is an excellent choice of wines.

### MILAN Rigolo €€€€€

*Largo Treves, corner Via Solferino 11, 20121* **Tel** *02 86 46 32 20*

Rigolo is located near Milan's bohemian district of Brera. It serves a predominantly Tuscan menu to the smart Milanese set. Pick from *pappardelle* (thick ribbon) pasta with wild boar, rich local sausages and steaming *bolliti* (boiled meats). The service is excellent. Closed Mon; Aug.

### MONTE ISOLA La Foresta €€€€

*Località Pescheria Maraglio 174, 25050* **Tel** *030 988 62 10*

What makes this a popular spot is the excellent menu, laden with fish from Lake Iseo. Good wines too, especially the Franciacorta champagne. Salted pressed fish, dried in the sun and marinated in olive oil, is a speciality, and you might even see them being prepared on the shore in front of the restaurant. Closed Wed; 20 Dec–1 Mar.

### PAVIA Locanda Vecchia Pavia al Mulino €€€€€

*Via al Monumento 5c, Località Certosa, 27012* **Tel** *0382 92 58 94*

This restaurant is atmospherically set in the grounds of the Certosa di Pavia. Typical dishes include *fiori di zucca* (courgette flowers fried with taleggio cheese and truffle) and *maialino da latte* (suckling pig baked in milk with apples, foie gras and truffles). Closed Mon, Tue lunch; first 3 wks Jan, last 3 wks Aug.

### SALÒ Alla Campagnola €€€

*Via Brunati 11, 25087* **Tel** *0365 221 53*

One of the oldest establishments around Lake Garda has become one of the best-known restaurants in the region thanks to Angelo del Bon, of Slow Food fame. He uses fresh ingredients to produce refined regional, national and international dishes. They also offer some 600 wines. Book well ahead. Closed: Mon, Tue lunch; Jan.

### SALÒ Antica Trattoria alle Rose €€€€

*Via Gasparo da Salò 33, 25087* **Tel** *0365 432 20*

This traditional trattoria offers local seasonal fresh produce from the market, lake fish and dishes such as *carpaccio* (wafer-thin slices) of raw beef with porcini mushrooms. All the pasta on offer is home-made: try the *tortelli al Bagoss* (pasta parcels stuffed with a local cheese filling). Closed Wed.

### SALÒ Osteria dell'Orologio €€€€

*Via Butturini 26, 25087* **Tel** *0365 29 01 58*

A laid-back place that prides itself on serving simple, traditional local cuisine, such as pasta dishes, grilled meats and fish. Delicious desserts include tiramisù, and chocolate and amaretti cream. Downstairs the vibe is more Old World, with Art Nouveau tiles and dark wood; upstairs it is more contemporary. Booking advisable. Closed Wed; Nov.

## VALLE D'AOSTA AND PIEDMONT

### ACQUI TERME La Schiavia €€€

*Vicolo della Schiavia, 15011* **Tel** *0144 559 39*

A welcoming, family-run restaurant in a renovated ancient palace near the cathedral. It serves a mixture of Piedmontese and Ligurian cooking comprising lots of imaginative fish and vegetable dishes. La Schiavia boasts a good wine list – about 350 types of Italian and French wines. Booking compulsory. Closed Sun, Tue; 3 wks Aug.

### ALBA Ristorante Madonna di Como €€€€

*Frazione Madonna di Como 31, 12051* **Tel** *335 534 91 53*

This homely restaurant in the hills east of Alba offers typical regional dishes. The highlight of the menu is the grilled-meat platter, and there are several truffle dishes available when in season. The panoramic terrace offering views over the surrounding countryside and the extensive wine selection complete the experience. Closed Tue.

### ALBA Piazza Duomo €€€€€

*Piazza Risorgimento 4, 12051* **Tel** *0173 36 61 67*

As well as an à la carte selection, Piazza Duomo offers three fixed menus: Traditional Piedmont (€90), Vegetarian (€100) and a tasting menu (€110). All show the best of chef Enrico Crippa's influences, from Japanese cuisine to Catalan star Ferran Adrià. Closed Sun dinner (except mid-Oct–mid-Nov), Sun (in Jul), Mon, 2 wks Jan, 2 wks Aug.

### ALESSANDRIA Il Grappolo €€€€

*Via Casale 28, 15100* **Tel** *0131 25 32 17*

Located in an ancient peachy-pink 17th-century palace, originally the City Hall of Alessandria, Il Grappolo is furbished in a rustic and elegant style. It has two dining halls, a winery and a summer patio. The food is typically Piedmontese with a modern flair and the wine list extensive. Closed Mon dinner, Tue.

### AOSTA Trattoria degli Artisti €€

*Via Maillet 5–7, 11100* ***Tel*** *0165 409 60*

Located in a cobbled street in the centre of town, the Trattoria degli Artisti offers a regional menu that changes weekly and includes gnocchi with nuts or herbs. There is also a wide range of cured meats and, for those with a sweet tooth, delectable home-made cakes and desserts. Closed Mon, Sun; 2 wks Jun, 2 wks Nov.

### AOSTA Grotta Azzurra €€€

*Via Croix de Ville 97, 11100* ***Tel*** *0165 26 24 74*

This reasonably priced pizzeria with informal surroundings in the centre of Aosta offers alfresco dining in the summer months. The traditional menu boasts a good variety of traditional dishes, pizzas, fish, risotto and pasta. Make sure to book ahead for the fabulous fish soup. Closed Wed; 3 wks Jul.

### AOSTA Vecchia Aosta €€€

*Piazza Porte Pretoriane 4, 11100* ***Tel*** *0165 36 11 86*

For a unique setting, head to the splendid Vecchia Aosta, atmospherically situated within the old Roman walls of the town. The food served is typical of the region, with favourites including ravioli, polenta and risotto with chicken livers. The atmosphere is relaxed and friendly. Closed Wed; 3 wks Nov.

### ARONA La Vecchia Arona €€€

*Lungolago Marconi 17, 28041* ***Tel*** *0322 24 24 69*

At this lakefront restaurant, Franco Carrera's à la carte menu shows a creative take on traditional dishes. Options range from home-made pasta to fish and excellent meat dishes, such as Piedmont lamb and beef; the aubergine (eggplant) terrine is a treat for vegetarians. Just 30 covers, so reservations are essential. Closed Fri.

### ASTI Osteria del Castello (ex Dirce) €€€

*Piazza Castello 1, Castel'Alfero, 14100* ***Tel*** *0141 20 41 15*

Located within an 18th-century castle known as "one of the five jewels of Piedmont", this restaurant offers excellent *maltagliati* (pasta), *bagna caöda* (a Piedmontese sauce of garlic, olive oil and anchovies, served with vegetables) and an unrivalled chocolate mousse. The dining terrace overlooks the hills of Monferrato. Closed Mon, Tue; Jan.

### ASTI Gener Neuv €€€€€

*Lungo Tanaro dei Pescatori 4, 14100* ***Tel*** *0141 55 72 70*

In a tranquil setting outside the centre, near the river, this family-run restaurant offers noble and local cuisine and a great wine list. Dishes include sweet and sour pigeon, roast veal *agnolotti* (pasta parcels), followed by marrons glacés glazed in chocolate. It has an open fire, beams and heraldic decor. Booking compulsory. Closed Sun dinner, Mon; Aug.

### BRA Battaglino €€

*Piazza Roma 18, 12042* ***Tel*** *0172 41 25 09*

This convivial restaurant in the heart of Bra, offers good home-made pastas such as gnocchi with local Castelmagno cheese sauce. Also good for hearty local dishes, especially its great *bollito misto*, a steaming dish of seven kinds of boiled meat, vegetables, and condiments. Closed Sun dinner, Mon; 1 wk Jan, 3 wks Aug.

### BRA Osteria Boccondivino €€

*Via della Mendicità Istruita 14, 12042* ***Tel*** *0172 425674*

This Slow Food restaurant offers 12 sorts of Piedmontese cheese and superb game and meat dishes, such as roast rabbit and beef braised in Barolo wine. Housed in an old townhouse full of rustic charm, with an arched entrance and iron balustrades, it boasts competent, knowledgeable service and good wines. Closed Mon, Sun.

### BREUIL-CERVINIA Al Solito Posto €€

*Via Meynet 11, 11021* ***Tel*** *0166 94 91 26*

Al Solito Posto is a charming simple restaurant with cuisine from the Aosta Valley and an interior of rustic elegance. The fixed-price menu includes delicious home-made pasta, polenta, lasagne and other filling mountain specials. Closed Thu (in low season); May, Oct.

### BREUIL-CERVINIA Les Neiges d'Antan €€

*Frazione Cret de Perrères 10, 11021* ***Tel*** *0166 94 87 75*

With the feel of an elegant log cabin, this restaurant-cum-hotel serves refined rustic and rich mountain fare, inspired by Italian and French cuisine and accompanied by great wines. Their *seuppa alla Valpellinentze* is legendary (regional soup with bread, cabbage, local fontina cheese and meat broth, cooked au gratin). Closed 1 May–1 Jul.

### CANNOBIO Osteria VinoDivino €€

*Strada Valle Cannobina 1, 28822* ***Tel*** *0321 719 19*

This youthful and cosy *osteria* is set in a converted 19th-century stable block. Specializing in cheese and wine, it has around 350 labels on its list. It also serves traditional dishes reinvented with a creative twist. When the weather permits, tables are set outside, in the pretty courtyard. Open March to December.

### CANNOBIO Del Lago €€€€€

*Via Nazionale 2, Località Carmine Inferiore, 28822* ***Tel*** *0323 705 95*

The refined Italian and international cuisine and the views of Lake Maggiore draw faithful followers to this restaurant. The freshest ingredients are used to produce imaginative simple dishes, such as lobster salad in a butter and orange sauce. There is a lovely summer terrace surrounded by verdant gardens. Closed Tue, Wed lunch; Nov–Feb.

**CASALE MONFERRATO La Torre** €€€€€

*Via Candiani d'Olivola 36, 15033* ***Tel*** *0142 702 95*

This restaurant is located in downtown Casale Monferrato. The creative regional cuisine privileges seasonal ingredients. Highlights include the range of cheeses served with an orange and onion compote. Alfresco dining is available in summer. Good wine list. Closed Tue dinner, Wed; 1 wk Jan, 3 wks Aug, 1 wk Dec.

**COGNE Lou Ressignon** €€

*Rue des Mines 22, 11012* ***Tel*** *0165 740 34*

This cosy mountain taverna has an ample wine list. Traditional Alpine and local recipes make hearty dishes featuring polenta, cured meats and salamis. The house special is *seupetta a la Cogneintze* (risotto with bread, fontina cheese, polenta and saddle of lamb baked in a red wine sauce). Closed Mon dinner (low season), Tue; last 2 wks May, Nov.

**COSSANO BELBO Trattoria della Posta** €€

*Corso Fratelli Negro 3* ***Tel*** *0141 881 26*

This friendly trattoria has been serving delicious Italian and international cuisine for more than a century, ever since its opening in 1875. Try the Piedmontese-style *fritto misto* (fried shellfish platter), seasonal specialities and the home-made pasta, served with a meat ragout. Closed Sun dinner, Mon; mid-Dec–mid-Jan, mid-Jul–mid-Aug.

**COSTIGLIOLE D'ASTI Cascina Collavini** €€

*Strada Traniera 24, 14037* ***Tel*** *0141 96 64 40*

This simple, elegant restaurant in an old farmhouse also offers accommodation. It has a warm, relaxed atmosphere and a menu comprising traditional Piedmont dishes using veal, lamb, mushrooms and seasonal vegetables. There is also a good choice of regional wines, especially the Barbera d'Asti. Closed Tue dinner, Wed; 3 wks Jan, 2 wks Aug.

**COSTIGLIOLE D'ASTI Sinoira** €€

*Piazza Umberto I 27, 14055* ***Tel*** *0141 96 60 12*

A two-floor restaurant and wine bar serving Piedmont specialities such as dishes with veal, rabbit, mushrooms and home-made pasta, all complemented by sublime wines from their extensive cellar. The *agnolotti* pasta in Barbera wine sauce is a favourite. Closed Mon, Tue.

**COURMAYEUR Du Tunnel** €

*Via Circonvallazione 80, 11013* ***Tel*** *0165 84 17 05*

In a busy part of town, this simple snack bar/pizzeria offers a good variety of huge and affordable wood-oven pizzas, as well as a convivial atmosphere. As an alternative to the maxi-pizzas, try one of the pasta dishes, *bresaola* (cured beef), steaks, desserts and cheeses, which are also on the menu. Closed Wed (off season); Jun.

**COURMAYEUR Cadran Solaire** €€€

*Via Roma 122, 11013* ***Tel*** *0165 84 46 09*

In a delightfully cosy setting, and boasting an interior of dark wood and stone, this restaurant serves hearty traditional local dishes that include *risotto alla Valdostana*, prepared with fontina cheese. Cadran Solaire is very popular with skiing visitors, who like to gather in its atmospheric bar before dinner. Closed Tue; May.

**CUNEO La Ciau del Tornavento** €€€

*Piazza Baracco 7, 12050* ***Tel*** *0173 63 83 33*

This restaurant looks a little austere from the outside, but the atmosphere inside is warm and welcoming. It is a good place for regional slow food: home-made pasta stuffed with meat, pumpkin ravioli, risotto and other creative dishes. There is also an outstanding selection of local cheeses. Outdoor seating available in summer. Closed Wed; Jan.

**CUNEO Osteria della Chiocciola** €€€

*Via Fossano 1, 12100* ***Tel*** *0171 662 77*

Renowned for its high-quality cuisine, this *osteria* has a cellar with a rich stock of vintage wines on the ground floor and dining rooms upstairs. It offers an informal atmosphere where the food plays the lead role. Excellent seasonal and regional dishes, including home-made ravioli, accompanied by good local red wines. Closed Sun; first 2 wks Jan.

**DOMODOSSOLA Piemonte da Sciolla** €€€

*Piazza della Convenzione 4, 28845* ***Tel*** *0324 24 26 33*

The regional food served here includes specials such as gnocchi made with rye and chestnuts or alpine fare from the Ossola Valley, with a heavy emphasis on hearty meat dishes with mushrooms and chestnuts. Tables outdoors for summer dining. Closed Wed; 10–21 Jan, mid-Aug–mid-Sep.

**IVREA Trattoria BoccondiVino** €€

*Via Aosta 47, 10015* ***Tel*** *0125 489 98*

A short distance from the Porta Aosta, in the historic centre of Ivrea, BoccondiVino is a small trattoria with a warm atmosphere serving traditional regional cuisine geared towards seasonal produce. The smoked fish is very good, and there is a fine selection of regional wines. Closed Thu; 1 wk Aug.

**NOVARA I Due Ladroni** €€€

*Corso Cavallotti 15, 28100* ***Tel*** *0321 62 45 81*

Located in a 16th-century palazzo in the heart of town, this restaurant specializes in traditional local cuisine. The menu changes regularly; examples include risotto with taleggio cheese, *zuppa vigezzina* (soup with spelt and cured ham) and *tapulon d'asino* (donkey meat slow-cooked in red wine). Excellent wine list. Closed Sat lunch, Sun; Aug.

**Key to Price Guide** *see p606* **Key to Symbols** *see back cover flap*

### NOVARA Osteria del Laghetto €€€€€

*Via Case Sparse 11, Località Veveri, 28100* ***Tel*** *0321 47 29 62*

This restaurant is set in its own beautiful grounds, and the dining rooms are filled with fragrant flowers. It serves regional cuisine using truffles and mushrooms, but the highlights on the menu are the fish specials. Enjoy the tables outdoors in the warm weather. Book ahead. Closed Sat lunch, Sun; 2 wks Aug, mid-Dec–mid-Jan.

### ORTA SAN GIULIO Villa Crespi €€€€€

*Via Fava, 18, 28016* ***Tel*** *0322 91 19 02*

A 19th-century folly restored to a beautiful eight-room hotel with charming decor from the Orient, inspired by *The Arabian Nights*. Creative Italian cuisine has won the restaurant two Michelin stars. This high level of gastronomy is matched by a list of more than 1,000 French and Italian wines. Closed Tue lunch; Mon; mid-Dec–mid-Feb.

### RIVOLI Combal.Zero €€€€€

*Il Castello, Piazza Mafalda di Savoia, 10098* ***Tel*** *011 956 52 25*

Located in the grounds of the lovely Castello di Rivoli, this restaurant offers a splendid creative Italian menu. Try the *raviole* filled with *burrata* (a milky mozzarella-type cheese), served with basil and a lime-tinged tomato sauce, followed by suckling pig with coconut and asparagus. Reservations essential. Closed Mon, Tue; Aug, Christmas.

### SAINT VINCENT Nuovo Batezar €€€

*Via Marconi 1, 11027* ***Tel*** *0166 51 31 64*

One of the best restaurants in the region, with an intimate atmosphere and typical antique local furniture. As a starter, the *sinfonia di pesce* (fish platter) is delicious, as are the *tajarin* (local home-made tagliatelle) in saffron or truffle sauce, and Alpine meat dishes. Make sure to book in advance. Closed Mon–Fri lunch; Wed; 3 wks Jun, 2 wks Nov.

### SESTRIERE Al Braciere del Possetto €€€

*Piazza Agnelli 2, 10058* ***Tel*** *0122 761 29*

Il Braciere is a medium-sized restaurant in the heart of Sestriere with a good reputation; it specializes in valley cuisine such as *raclette* (cheese fondue), *bourguignonne* (meat fondue), rich Piedmont specials and dishes using plenty of cheese from the region and all over Italy. Closed Wed; 3 wks May, 3 wks Oct.

### SORISO Al Sorriso €€€€€

*Via Roma 18, 28016* ***Tel*** *0322 98 32 28*

Famous throughout Italy for its high-quality creative cuisine using fresh, exquisite seasonal produce, this refined hotel/restaurant offers dishes such as risotto with apple, broccoli, walnuts and shrimp, and a range of seasonal specialities. Booking essential. Closed Mon, Tue; 2 wks Jan, 3 wks Aug.

### STRESA Il Piemontese €€€

*Via Mazzini 25, 28838* ***Tel*** *0323 302 35*

This intimate family-run restaurant in the centre of Stresa offers creative versions of traditional local cuisine. Enjoy the pretty alfresco terrace under vines in the summer. Set menus and an excellent selection of wines complete the picture. Closed Mon; 1 Dec–1 Feb.

### TORTONA Aurora Girarrosto €€€

*S.S. per Genova 13, Tortona, 15057* ***Tel*** *0131 86 30 33*

This restaurant, close to the little town of Tortona, is famed for its roasting jack, which gives it its name. The house speciality is barbecued meats. All meat comes from local organic farmers, including the T-bone steaks of Carru beef, an important Piedmontese breed. Extensive wine list. Closed Mon; 2 wks Aug.

### TURIN Birilli €€

*Strada Val San Martino 6, 10131* ***Tel*** *011 819 05 67*

Head here for a good variety of pasta dishes, grilled fish and meat skewers, risottos and seasonal vegetables. The Birilli brothers from Cuneo began a chain of restaurants in 1929, later opening others in Paris, Hollywood and New Delhi. A pretty garden courtyard is available for alfresco dining. Closed Sun (winter); Christmas hols.

### TURIN Dai Saletta €€

*Via Belfiore 37, 10126* ***Tel*** *011 668 78 67*

A typical trattoria with a warm, friendly atmosphere, checked tablecloths and a menu filled with Piedmontese classics. From *agnolotti* and *tajarin* (local varieties of pasta) to *bollito* (boiled meats), meat in Barolo wine and a great zabaglione. A good wine list, too. Closed Sun; Aug.

### TURIN Casa Vicina €€€€€

*Via Nizza 24, 10126* ***Tel*** *011 19 50 68 40*

Set on the lower level of the gastronomic store Eataly, this Michelin-starred gourmet restaurant has a very contemporary, almost minimalist vibe. Expect artfully presented classic dishes from Piedmont, such as stuffed *agnolotti* (pasta) and *bagna cauda* (warm anchovy dip). Closed Sun dinner, Mon; Aug, Christmas.

### TURIN Neuv Caval'd Brons €€€€€

*Piazza San Carlo 155, 10123* ***Tel*** *011 54 53 54*

This elegant, spacious restaurant in one of Turin's most beautiful squares offers a choice of three tasting menus, as well as an à la carte selection. The specialities are inspired by regional Piedmontese cuisine and prepared with an innovative, international twist. Closed Fri and Sat lunch; Aug.

### VERBANIA PALLANZA Osteria Dell'Angolo €€€

*Piazza Garibaldi 35, 28048* ***Tel*** *0323 55 63 62*

Located in a small square, Dell'Angolo is a typical regional taverna offering a variety of refined fish dishes, a mix of Piedmontese and Lombardy cuisine and good value for money. Tables are also available outside in the square in the summer. There is limited space so it's best to book ahead. Closed Mon; 1 wk Jan; Nov.

### VERBANIA PALLANZA Milano €€€€€

*Corso Zanitello 2, 28048* ***Tel*** *0323 55 68 16*

Milano is in a neo-Gothic building in the centre of Pallanza. It has a lovely terrace with views across Lake Maggiore. It serves great fish, including lake specialities such as *persico* (perch) and *salmerino* (char) accompanied by home-grown seasonal organic vegetables and great wines. Closed Mon dinner, Tue; Nov–Feb.

### VERCELLI Il Paiolo €€

*Viale Garibaldi 72, 13100* ***Tel*** *0161 25 05 77*

A relaxed trattoria in an old townhouse in the centre of Vercelli. Local cuisine is well represented here, and with Vercelli being the rice region of Italy, you simply must try the risottos and the *panisse* (Vercellese rice dish). Great wines accompany the seasonal menu. Closed Thu; mid-Jul–mid-Aug.

### VERCELLI Il Giardinetto €€€

*Via Sereno 3, 13100* ***Tel*** *0161 25 72 30*

This refined eight-room hotel with restaurant is part of a 19th-century villa. It looks out on to a lovely garden and serves a rich range of creative dishes using Piedmontese delicacies. Typical examples include risotto, truffles, mushrooms, home-made pasta, Parma ham, local cheeses and foie gras. Excellent wines. Closed Mon; 3 wks Aug.

### VILLARFOCCHIARDO La Giaconera €€€€

*Via Antica di Francia 1, 10050* ***Tel*** *011 964 50 00*

Housed in a stylish old staging inn with beams and chandeliers, La Giaconera offers regional fare with truffles, game and great locally grown vegetables. Specials include chestnut tagliatelle, veal medallions with truffles (in season; advance notice required), and mushrooms with crispy prawns. Excellent local wines. Closed Tue; 2 wks Aug.

## LIGURIA

### CAMOGLI La Cucina di Nonna Nina €€€

*Via Molfino 126, San Rocco di Camogli, 16032* ***Tel*** *0185 77 38 35*

Located 6 km (4 miles) from Camogli, on the other side of the Portofino promontory, this restaurant occupies two rooms in a rustic villa with stunning views. It serves delicious Ligurian dishes using local seafood and herbs. Try the stuffed cuttlefish or home-made pasta cooked with nettles and pesto. Closed Wed; last 2 wks Jan, Nov.

### CAMOGLI Rosa €€€€

*Via Ruffini 13, 16032* ***Tel*** *0185 77 34 11*

Housed in an Art Nouveau-style villa, this restaurant has a winter garden veranda and a summer terrace with views across the bay and of the old fishing harbour of Camogli. Typical seafood and pasta specials include tuna in a sweet and sour sauce, pasta in red mullet *(triglia)* sauce and stewed cuttlefish. Closed Tue, Wed lunch; Jan, last 2 wks Nov.

### CERVO San Giorgio €€€€€

*Via Volta 19, 18010* ***Tel*** *0183 40 01 75*

The owner of this charming place, nestled in a square in the city centre, blends local flavours and fresh, seasonal food. The results are creative simple dishes such as prawns with baby artichokes, and fish of the day with tiny olives and fresh marjoram. A tasting menu is available for €55. It is very popular, so book ahead. Closed Tue.

### GENOVA Da Genio €€

*Salita San Leonardo 61r, 16128* ***Tel*** *010 58 84 63*

One of Genoa's best-loved trattorias, with a loyal clientele, situated in the old quarter. The menu includes well-prepared fish dishes, such as fresh swordfish stuffed with anchovies and capers, but the famous starter is the traditional Ligurian dish *trenette al pesto* (pasta with pesto sauce). Closed Sun; 3 wks Aug.

### GENOVA Da O'Colla €€

*Via alla Chiesa di Murta 10, Località Bolzaneto, 16162* ***Tel*** *010 740 85 79*

Simple but excellent home-cooked Ligurian cuisine such as lasagne with a pesto sauce (instead of the more traditional meat sauce) and *minestrone genovese* (vegetable soup with pasta or rice and pesto). This trattoria is located 13 km (8 miles) from the city, but it is definitely worth the taxi fare. Closed Mon, Sun; 3 wks Jan, Aug.

### GENOVA Pintori €€

*Via San Bernardo 68r, 16123* ***Tel*** *010 275 75 07*

Loved by the locals for its affordable prices and stylish ambience, Pintori is run by a Sardinian family. The menu has both fish and meat dishes: try the feather-light *fritto misto* (fried seafood platter) or the grilled lamb. Two days' notice are required for the *maialino sardo* (Sardinian suckling pig). The desserts are also fine. Closed Mon, Sun.

**Key to Price Guide** *see p606* **Key to Symbols** *see back cover flap*

### GENOVA Cantine Squarciafico €€€

*Piazza Invrea 3, 16123* ***Tel*** *010 247 08 23*

Located just behind the cathedral, in a former patrician villa with frescoes on the façade and ancient pillars inside, this is a traditional Ligurian wine bar serving local specialities including *stracci*, a kind of lasagne, and a delicious chocolate tart. Wine bottles line the walls of the ancient vaulted dining room. Booking is advisable. Closed late Jul–early Aug.

### LEVANTO Due Lune €€

*Corso Roma 2, 19015* ***Tel*** *0187 80 87 67*

Located just behind the sea front, this pizzeria and restaurant is enormously popular with the locals for its good-quality fresh fish – it is particularly well regarded for its seafood dishes, and locals rave about the mussels and clams. Good value for money and friendly service, though it does get crowded. Booking advisable.

### LEVANTO Cavour €€€

*Piazza Cavour 1, 19015* ***Tel*** *0187 80 84 97*

Located between the station and the seafront, this typical trattoria with local cuisine specializes in fish. The original restaurant dates back to 1800. Dishes on the menu include *gattafin* (large fried ravioli filled with herbs, eggs, onion and cheese), anchovies in lemon and the local *trofiette* pasta with pesto sauce. Closed Mon; Dec–mid-Jan.

### MANAROLA La Scogliera €€€

*Via Birolli 101, 19017* ***Tel*** *0187 92 07 47*

A pretty family-run restaurant with exposed stone walls and country-style furniture, La Scogliera specializes in Ligurian cuisine, and it is particularly renowned for its fish and seafood specialities. The atmosphere is relaxed, though this is a very popular place in a busy village. It is wise to book ahead.

### NERVI Astor €€

*Via delle Palme 16–18, 16167* ***Tel*** *010 32 90 11*

This bright and unpretentious 41-room hotel/restaurant is just 50 metres from the seashore. It offers fine Ligurian cuisine and good wines in a simple, elegant setting. A house special is *pansotti al sugo di noci* (fresh pasta filled with ricotta cheese, served in a walnut sauce).

### PORTOFINO Da Puny €€€€€

*Piazza Martiri dell'Olivetta 5, 16034* ***Tel*** *0185 26 90 37*

Da Puny is one of the best restaurants lining Portofino's tiny harbour square. Among the house specialities are fresh fish, *pasta in pesto corto* (the rich basil, cheese and pine-nut sauce lifted with a dash of tomato) and *antipasti* – all are excellent. Booking is advisable. Closed Thu; mid-Dec–mid-Feb.

### PORTOFINO Da U Batti €€€€€

*Vico Nuovo 17, 16034* ***Tel*** *0185 26 93 79*

One of the finest fish restaurants in one of Liguria's most elegant spots. Set in a tiny square in the heart of the village, Da U Batti is a chic and intimate restaurant with exceptional fish cuisine and attentive service. It is popular with celebrities and foodies alike. Booking is highly recommended. Closed Mon.

### PORTOVENERE Da Iseo €€€€

*Calata Doria 9, 19025* ***Tel*** *0187 79 06 10*

A lovely little panoramic trattoria run by the eight-room Locanda Lorena hotel on Palmaria Island and located on the waterfront with views over the harbour and the Gulf of Poets. Typical fish dishes include Ligurian mussels stuffed with meat, anchovies in lemon sauce and seafood *antipasti*. Closed Wed; Nov.

### PORTOVENERE Le Bocche €€€€€

*Calata Doria 102, 19025* ***Tel*** *0187 79 06 22*

Perched on the promontory overlooking Portovenere, this restaurant is located below the church of St Peter, with great views. The minimalist design and wonderful shaded tables outdoors create the ideal background for the delicate flavours of the Ligurian fish dishes. Fine wine list too. Closed Mon; mid-Dec–mid-Feb.

### RAPALLO U' Giancu €€€

*Via San Massimo 28, Località San Massimo, 16035* ***Tel*** *0185 26 05 05*

In the hills northwest of Rapallo, among olive trees, this restaurant is the perfect destination for people who love both great food and cartoons. The owner is a prime mover of the annual Rapallo International Cartoon Festival. Vegetables from the garden complement typical Ligurian specialities. Closed lunch; Wed; mid-Dec–mid-Jan.

### SAN REMO Da Vittorio €€€€

*Piazza Bresca 16, 18038* ***Tel*** *0184 50 19 24*

A short distance from the shore, Da Vittorio is a traditional favourite specializing in fish. Try the home-made *tagliolini* pasta served with *gallinella*, a local sea fish, or the *burridda*, a fish soup with cuttlefish, served with artichokes when in season, or with peas. Closed 1 wk early Mar, 2 wks Nov.

### SAN REMO Da Paolo e Barbara €€€€€

*Via Roma 47, 18038* ***Tel*** *0184 53 16 53*

An exceptional restaurant with an international reputation. The menu mixes wonderful vegetables – courgettes, herbs and beans – with local fresh fish – mackerel tartar, San Remo shrimps. Barbara's expertise in patisserie is revealed with her ricotta-cheese cassata. Closed Wed, Thu; 1 wk Jan, 2 wks Jul, 2 wks Dec.

### VERNAZZA Gambero Rosso €€€

*Piazza Marconi 7, 19018* **Tel** *0187 81 22 65*

Creative modern interpretations of Ligurian seafood dishes are the specialities at the harbourside Gambero Rosso. The fish ravioli and the lemon risotto are particularly delicious, as are the original desserts. Diners can choose a tasting menu or from the à la carte selection. Closed Mon; Dec–Feb.

## EMILIA-ROMAGNA

### BOLOGNA Trattoria Fantoni €

*Via del Pratello 11/A, 40122* **Tel** *051 23 63 58*

One of the most popular simple *trattorie* on a street lined with eateries. The menu is very traditional, which means plenty of *cavallo* (horse meat), served as a steak, along with grilled sausages and delectable vegetable dishes such as *melanzane al forno* (baked aubergine/eggplant).

### BOLOGNA Antica Trattoria del Cacciatore €€

*Via Caduti di Casteldebole 25, 40132* **Tel** *051 56 42 03* **Fax** *051 56 71 28*

The "old hunter's trattoria" has for more than 200 years served traditional dishes in an old country inn, now by a park near the airport. As well as home-made pastas and breads, specialities include tortellini in broth, *capriolo alla boscaiola* (goat stewed with porcini) and ravioli in a cheese fondue with truffles.

### BOLOGNA Olindo Faccioli €€

*Via Altabella 15/B, 40126* **Tel** *051 22 31 71* **Fax** *051 44 09 68*

This tiny trattoria is justifiably proud of its wine list (more than 400 bottles line the two rooms); the daily menu is posted on a chalkboard. The cuisine is Bolognese, but with a light touch and lots of vegetarian options, including *crespellini* (cheese-filled pasta crêpes) and tagliatelle with home-made pesto.

### BOLOGNA Gigina €€€

*Via Stendhal 1, 40128* **Tel** *051 32 23 00*

Since opening in 1956, this place has become a firm favourite for a special dinner in a city renowned for the quality of its food. Fanatically local *primi* always include hand-crafted pasta dishes, such as *tortellini in brodo* (stuffed pasta in broth) and tagliatelle in the famous house *ragù*. Closed Aug.

### BOLOGNA Pappagallo €€€€

*Piazza Mercanzia 3c, 40125* **Tel** *051 23 28 07* **Fax** *051 23 28 07*

Since 1919, princes, artists, and actors have left signed photos to line the walls of this elegant restaurant housed in a 14th-century palazzo practically underneath Bologna's twin towers. The cuisine is traditional Bolognese, including tortellini (in broth or meat ragout), lasagne, and veal.

### CASTELL'ARQUATO Da Faccini €€

*Località Sant'Antonio, 29014* **Tel** *0523 89 63 40* **Fax** *0523 89 64 70*

This trattoria has been in the same family since 1932. There's no fixed menu; the chef just follows the seasons. You may find gnocchi with carrots, ravioli of duck and truffles, *agnellotti al culatello* (pasta stuffed with a typical local salami), or *faraona alla creta* (guinea fowl cooked in a terracotta container).

### CASTELL'ARQUATO Maps €€€

*Piazza Europa 3, 29014* **Tel** *0523 80 44 11*

This restructured medieval mill in the historic centre of town focuses on creative cuisine with international flair based on local ingredients. The menu changes daily, according to what is fresh at the market, and focuses around fish specialities (though the chef also works wonders with meat).

### FAENZA La Pavona €

*Via Santa Lucia 45, 48018* **Tel** *0546 310 75* **Fax** *0546 636 419*

Situated just outside Faenza in a very peaceful area, this rustic but elegant restaurant has a welcoming atmosphere and a multitude of traditional regional dishes to choose from. Recommended is *coniglio arrosto* (roast rabbit cooked in the wood-fired oven). Closed Tue, Sat lunch; Oct.

### FERRARA Antica Trattoria Il Cucco €€

*Via Voltacasotto 3, 44100* **Tel** *0532 76 00 26* **Fax** *0532 76 00 26*

In the historic centre near the cathedral, this lively restaurant has existed since the early 1800s. Try *Al burrodi di salvia* (pasta hats stuffed with pumpkin in a butter and sage sauce), complemented by a regional wine. There is a lovely garden where you can dine under a pergola in summer.

### FERRARA La Sgarbata €€

*Via Sgarbata 84, 44046* **Tel** *0532 71 21 10* **Fax** *0532 71 21 10*

This countryside trattoria on the outskirts of the city serves up tasty local dishes such as *cappellacci di zucca alla ferrarese* (Ferrara's signature pumpkin-stuffed pasta), as well as speciality fish dishes based on the catch of the day. Locals often make plans to meet here just for the tasty pizzas. Occasional live music in summer.

**Key to Price Guide** *see p606* **Key to Symbols** *see back cover flap*

## FERRARA Quel Fantastico Giovedì €€

*Via Castelnuovo 9, 44100* ***Tel*** *0532 76 05 70* ***Fax*** *0532 76 05 70*

This bright restaurant specializing in seafood dishes features a varied and creative menu that runs the gamut from the more traditional – such as the *risotto con vongole veraci* (rice with tiny clams) and braised *anguilla* (eel) – to the creative, including Japanese-style sushi of salmon. Book ahead.

## FERRARA L'Oca Giuliva €€€

*Via Boccacanale di Santo Stefano 38–40, 44100* ***Tel*** *0532 20 76 28*

In a town centre packed with budget eateries, this small, serene restaurant is the best place to sample refined local cooking. The daily changing menu might feature *faraona* (guinea hen), *anguilla arrostita* (roasted eel) or fillet of beef. The wine list is excellent. Closed Mon, Tue lunch.

## FIDENZA Il Duomo €

*Via Micheli 27, 43036* ***Tel*** *0524 52 42 68*

This restaurant serves a menu that includes such regional specialities as *tortelli alla ricotta* (cheese-stuffed pasta), *tagliatelle all'uovo con ragù* (egg noodles in meat sauce), *cappelletti in brodo* (pasta soup), and *trippa alla parmigiana* (tripe smothered in tomato sauce and grated cheese). Closed Wed.

## GORO Ferrari €€€

*Via Antonio Brugnoli 244, 44020* ***Tel*** *0533 99 64 48* ***Fax*** *0533 99 65 46*

A short stroll from the port and fish market, this restaurant has been family-run for 60 years. The market determines the daily menu at this purveyor of Po Delta specialities, though you can't go wrong with the *risotto di pesce* (fish risotto). There's also pizza on Fridays, Saturdays, and Sundays at dinner. Closed Wed.

## MODENA Al Boschetto da Loris €€

*Via Due Canali Nord 202, 41100* ***Tel*** *059 25 17 59*

Set in a vast park of century-old trees, Da Loris is installed in the Duke of Este's ancient hunting cabin. The menu is brief, but stuffed with the best of Modenese home-cooking, including tortellini in capon broth, *tagliatelle al ragù* (in a meat sauce), and meats, both spit-roasted and grilled. Summer seating in the garden. Closed Sun dinner; Wed.

## MODENA Fini €€€€€

*Rua Frati Minori 54, 41100* ***Tel*** *059 22 33 14* ***Fax*** *059 22 02 47*

A mainstay of local cuisine since 1912. Among the kitchen's exquisite dishes are such traditional specialities as *tortellini di cappone in brodo* (a soup of capon-stuffed pasta), *pasticcio di maccheroni* (a veal-based ragout folded in pasta crêpes), and an English-style *carrello* (cart) of boiled meats.

## MODENA Giusti €€€€€

*Vicolo Squallore 46/Via Farini 75, 41100* ***Tel*** *059 22 25 33* ***Fax*** *059 22 25 33*

Book ahead for one of the five tables at this bastion of Modenese cooking attached to a fine foods shop. The Galli (husband and wife proprietors) are fond of using capons in everything, from the tortellini soup to the crunchy salads, and the *stinco* (roasted joint) of veal or pork is excellent. Open lunch only (except Mon, Sun).

## PARMA Aldo €€

*Piazzale Inzani 15, 43100* ***Tel*** *0521 20 60 01* ***Fax*** *0521 20 60 01*

This trattoria in the city the very name of which makes up the foundation of Italian cuisine (this is the Parma of Parmesan cheese and Parma ham) serves up the classics with interesting touches: smoked roast beef, *tortellini al prosciutto* (ham-stuffed pasta), and guinea fowl with orange sauce. Closed Sun dinner, Mon.

## PARMA Le Viole €€

*Strada Nuova 60a, Località Castelnuovo Golese, 43100* ***Tel*** *0521 60 10 00* ***Fax*** *0521 60 16 73*

A delightful place in the suburbs of Parma run by two sisters from the Friuli/Slovenia border town of Gorizia. Their innovative touches and modern twists on local recipes result in such tasty titbits as *fagottini* (parcels) of turkey with vegetables. Excellent home-made desserts.

## PARMA La Greppia €€€€

*Strada Garibaldi 39A, 43100* ***Tel*** *0521 23 36 86* ***Fax*** *0521 22 13 15*

Top choice for a top-class meal in a city renowned for its cooking. Traditional choices abound – they make the best *stracotto* (braised beef) in Parma – as do innovative dishes. Try the veal kidneys with shaved truffles, the prosciutto-topped asparagus with herb-stuffed tortelli, and the veal *scaloppine* (escalope).

## PIACENZA Antica Osteria del Teatro €€€€€

*Via Verdi 16, 29100* ***Tel*** *0523 32 37 77* ***Fax*** *0523 30 49 34*

Set among the brick and plaster walls of a 15th-century palazzo, this elegant restaurant has an excellent wine list accompanying a seasonal menu of imaginative dishes prepared with the best of local produce. Look for *tortelli dei Farnesi* (ricotta and spinach pasta parcels in a butter and sage sauce). Closed Mon, Sun.

## RAVENNA Ca de Ven €

*Via C. Ricci 24, 48100* ***Tel/Fax*** *0544 301 63*

They say Dante lived in a boarding house on this site, now occupied by a 16th-century palazzo next to the poet's tomb. Its brick vaulted cellars are lined with wine bottles and host one of Ravenna's best trattorie. The speciality is *piadine*, the local flatbread, topped with meat, cheeses, or vegetables. Closed Mon.

### RAVENNA Villa Antica — €

*Via Faentina 136, 48100* **Tel** *0544 50 05 22*

Set in a 19th-century villa with a tent-link gazebo in the back garden. The menu changes seasonally and includes pastas, grilled or roasted meats and fish, as well as some unusual preparations like *garganelli all'indiana* (curried pasta). There is also game in season and pizza.

### RAVENNA Bella Venezia — €€€

*Via IV Novembre 16, 48100* **Tel** *0544 21 27 46*

A varied menu with something to suit everyone is available at this well-established central restaurant. Dishes are largely from the local Romagna tradition or Italian classics, and they include the house risotto or a choice of hand-made pastas, pork, veal and a selection of other grilled meats. Closed Sun; Jan.

### RIMINI Europa — €€€

*Via Roma 51, 47900* **Tel/Fax** *0541 287 61*

The Albani family's been serving some of Rimini's finest cooking for 70 years. Fish forms the basis of the menu here, with dishes including a salad of warm fish with radicchio, seafood spaghetti, and *strozzapreti ai crostaci* (pasta dumplings in a sauce of crustaceans). Closed Sun.

### RIMINI Osteria dë Börg — €€€

*Via Forzieri 12, 47921* **Tel** *0541 560 74*

Two successful decades have established Börg's reputation as the best place to eat meat in this fish-obsessed seaside town. A landlubber's menu could take in cured meats or pecorino cheese to start, followed by home-made pasta served any number of ways, and beef or lamb cooked on the open grill.

## FLORENCE

### Angiolino — €

*Via Santo Spirito 36r, 50125* **Tel** *055 239 89 76* **Map** 3 B1

Modernization has compromised the old-world atmosphere that used to prevail at this Oltrarno trattoria. Nonetheless, it retains a certain neighbourhood bustle, even if standards are not always consistent. Specialities on the menu include penne with porcini mushrooms and roast pork with garlicky spinach.

### Baldovino — €

*Via San Giuseppe 22r, 50122* **Tel** *055 24 17 73* **Map** 4 E1

Big, noisy and lively, Baldovino is one of those places where you can eat anything, from a salad or a plate of cheese to a full meal. In between there are excellent pizzas, good pasta dishes, a choice of fish or meat main courses and a number of vegetarian options. Puddings are particularly good and there's a long wine list.

### Boccadama — €

*Piazza Santa Croce 25–26r, 50122* **Tel** *055 24 36 40* **Map** 6 F4

This wine bar/restaurant enjoys a superb position on Piazza Santa Croce with a handful of outside tables; shelves of wine line the walls of the cosy interior. Wine can be ordered by the glass or the bottle from a long list. You can either nibble on a selection of cheese or cold meats or go for a full meal; the food is good and quite imaginative.

### Da Mario — €

*Via Rosina 2r, 50123* **Tel** *055 21 85 50* **Map** 1 C4

This lively trattoria is always packed with a mix of stall owners, business people and tourists, who come here for the good, traditional food at very reasonable prices. The daily handwritten menu is posted on the wall near the kitchen and features hearty soups, simple pasta and a number of meat and side dishes. Closed dinner; Sun.

### Da Sergio — €

*Piazza San Lorenzo 8r, 50129* **Tel** *055 28 19 41* **Fax** *055 28 19 41* **Map** 1 C4

A popular, family-run eatery, Sergio's trattoria is hidden behind the market stalls. Big tables (you may end up sharing) are laid with white cloths in two airy rooms. The food is Tuscan *cucina casalinga* (traditional cooking) and very good; there's always tripe on Mondays and Thursdays and fresh fish on Fridays. Closed Sun.

### Fuori Porta — €

*Via Monte alle Croci 10r, 50125* **Tel** *055 234 24 83* **Fax** *055 234 14 08* **Map** 4 E3

One of Florence's classic *enoteche*, this is a popular place where you can go for a glass of wine or something more substantial. Choose a wine from a list featuring over 600 labels. The *crostini* (toasted open sandwiches) make a particularly good accompaniment, but there are also good pastas and salads.

### Il Pizzaiuolo — €

*Via de' Macci 113r, 50122* **Tel** *055 24 11 71* **Map** 4 E1

Be sure to book a table: this lively pizzeria/restaurant is on the small side and it's always full. The pizzas come Neapolitan-style, with puffy bases and buffalo mozzarella. There's also a great selection of *antipasti* (grilled vegetables and seafood salad) and excellent pasta dishes from southern Italy.

**Key to Price Guide** *see p606* **Key to Symbols** *see back cover flap*

### Il Santo Bevitore €

*Via Santo Spirito 64/66r, 50125* **Tel** *055 21 12 64* **Map** *5 A4*

Housed in an ex-stable, this relaxed restaurant/wine bar features delicately flavoured innovative dishes. The menu changes seasonally, but there is always a selection of soups and home-made pastas, fish and grilled meat. Or you can choose from a selection of well-sourced cheese and cured meats. The wine list is interesting too.

### Il Vegetariano €

*Via delle Ruote 30r, 50129* **Tel** *055 47 50 30* **Map** *2 D3*

One of Florence's few vegetarian restaurants, this place has been around for a long time, but continues to be popular. The decor is rustic and the food wholesome and cheap; choose from the menu written on a blackboard, pay at the desk and take your receipt to the counter to collect your food. There's also a great salad bar.

### La Casalinga €

*Via del Michelozzo 9r, 50125* **Tel** *055 21 86 24* **Map** *5 B5*

In spite of the numbers of tourists that flock to this no-frills trattoria, it is still very much a neighbourhood affair, where the food is wholesome and plentiful. Go for the local dishes – *ribollita* (bread and vegetable soup), *arista* (roast pork) or *bollito misto* (mixed, boiled meats). For dessert, try the home-made tiramisù.

### Le Mossacce €

*Via del Proconsolo 55r, 50122* **Tel** *055 29 43 61* **Map** *4 D1*

It's not easy to find a genuine Florentine *trattoria* in the middle of town, but this place near the Bargello is as authentic as it gets. Cheap, top-quality Florentine dishes such as *ribollita* (bread and vegetable soup) and *spezzatino* (veal stew) are served in busy, noisy surrounds. Closed Sat, Sun; Aug.

### Nerbone €

*Stand 292, Mercato Centrale, Via dell'Ariento, 50123* **Map** *1 C4*

Don't be fooled by first impressions: insalubrious Nerbone's boiled-beef sandwich has made it into the world's finest food guides. This quintessential working lunch is supplemented by a value menu that includes Florentine classics like *pappa al pomodoro* (tomato and bread soup) and, of course, tripe. Lunch only; closed Sun.

### 4 Leoni €€

*Via dei Vellutini 1r, 50125* **Tel** *055 21 85 62* **Fax** *055 267 88 70* **Map** *5 B4*

This restaurant is conveniently situated five minutes from the city centre, near the Ponte Vecchio. In warm weather, tables are set out on the pretty Piazza della Passera, but the ambience inside is pleasant too. Though no longer the simple, traditional place it once was, the service is always friendly and the setting charming. Closed Wed lunch.

### Antico Fattore €€

*Via Lambertesca 1/3r, 50123* **Tel** *055 28 89 75* **Fax** *055 28 33 41* **Map** *6 D4*

This trattoria, a favoured haunt of the Florentine literati, was founded in 1908. Though it has lost some of its old charm, the food and service are still of a refreshingly old-fashioned kind. Try the pasta with wild boar and the *involtini* (meat wraps) with artichoke hearts. Closed Sun.

### Buca Mario €€

*Piazza degli Ottaviani 16r, 50123* **Tel** *055 21 41 79* **Fax** *055 264 73 36* **Map** *5 B2*

One of Florence's traditional cellar restaurants, Buca Mario is a staple among tourists. In spite of its popularity, it maintains its genuinely unpretentious Florentine atmosphere and offers local standards such as *ribollita* (vegetable soup), *osso buco* (veal shank), grilled meats and *arista* (roast pork).

### Cavolo Nero €€

*Via dell'Ardiglione 22, 50125* **Tel/Fax** *055 29 47 44* **Map** *3 B1*

This smart little Oltrarno restaurant, with elegant decor, is popular with an arty crowd who come for the sunny Tuscan cooking with the odd twist. Specialities include spaghetti with clams, roasted sea bass with aubergines (eggplant) and cherry tomatoes, and, for meat-eaters, pigeon stuffed with foie gras.

### Coquinaros €€

*Via delle Oche 15r, 50122* **Tel** *055 230 21 53* **Map** *6 E2*

A convenient, cosy little place, just behind the Duomo, where you can eat at almost any time of the day or evening. There are some delicious pasta dishes (try the ravioli with pecorino and pears). You can also order a salad, a plate of cheese or cured meats or a toasted open sandwich. There are good wines by the glass and bottle too.

### Frescobaldi Wine Bar €€

*Via dei Magazzini 2/4r, 50122* **Tel** *055 28 47 24* **Fax** *055 265 65 35* **Map** *6 E3*

This wine bar and restaurant is owned by one of Tuscany's foremost wine producers. Lunch is a casual affair, while dinner is more formal, with white tablecloths and gleaming crystal. Creative, elegant food is accompanied by some fine in-house wines; if you just want a snack and a glass, pop into Frescobaldino next door. Closed Sun, Mon lunch.

### Il Guscio €€

*Via dell'Orto 49, 50125* **Tel/Fax** *055 22 44 21* **Map** *3 A1*

This lively San Frediano restaurant is often full. The food is based on Tuscan traditions but is a little more refined than in your average trattoria and there is a good wine list too. First courses might include gnocchi with asparagus, and *crespelle* (thin pancakes), while the delicious mixed seafood *al guazzetto* (in tomato sauce) is a fixture.

### Ristorante Ricchi €€

*Piazza Santo Spirito 8r, 50125* ***Tel*** *055 21 58 64* ***Fax*** *055 28 08 30* ***Map*** *3 B2*

With elegant, modern decor and a lovely terrace, this small fish restaurant is situated on one of Florence's most beautiful squares. Oriental influences are evident in dishes such as pasta with shrimps and mint, swordfish with Sichuan pepper and salt cod in a spice crust. There's a limited choice for carnivores too.

### I Latini €€€

*Via dei Palchetti 6r, 50123* ***Tel*** *055 21 09 16* ***Map*** *5 B3*

There is always a crowd of both foreigners and locals clamouring for a table outside this large, noisy trattoria where huge hams hang from the ceiling. The food is traditional and the portions are enormous. Try the succulent grilled and roasted meats; *bistecca alla fiorentina* (broiled T-bone steak) is an experience.

### La Giostra €€€

*Via Borgo Pinti 12r, 50122* ***Tel*** *055 24 13 41* ***Map*** *2 E5, 6 F2*

A vaulted cellar-style dining area and traditional decor make this one of Florence's best spots for a romantic dinner. The quirky, Austrian-influenced menu includes dishes such as fillet of capon, roast pigeon, Chianina beef and *Wienerschnitzel*. Book ahead in summer if you want to claim one of the few street tables. Excellent fine wine list.

### Osteria del Caffè Italiano €€€

*V Isola delle Stinche 11/13r, 50122* ***Tel*** *055 28 93 68* ***Fax*** *055 28 89 50* ***Map*** *6 F3*

You can eat at any time of the day in this beautifully appointed restaurant; at mealtimes there is a full menu of mainly Tuscan dishes, but in between you can snack on excellent cheeses or cured meats and choose from a selection of Tuscan wines. The next-door pizzeria is under the same ownership.

### Osteria Santo Spirito €€€

*Piazza Santo Spirito 16r, 50125* ***Tel*** *055 238 23 83* ***Map*** *3 B2*

Attention to detail in both preparation and presentation is what places this stylish Oltrarno place a notch above its rivals in this square. Seafood, meat and vegetarian pasta dishes are prepared from scratch, and mains often include traditional ingredients such as *baccalà* (salt cod). The terrace is especially atmospheric on summer evenings.

### Cantinetta Antinori €€€€

*Piazza Antinori 3, 50123* ***Tel*** *055 235 98 27* ***Fax*** *055 235 98 77* ***Map*** *5 C2*

More than just a wine bar, yet not a full-blown restaurant, this room on the ground floor of one of Florence's finest Renaissance palaces makes a lovely place to eat. There are traditional Florentine dishes such as tripe and pasta with duck sauce and a fine selection of Antinori wines. Closed Sat, Sun.

### Garga €€€€

*Via del Moro 48r, 50123* ***Tel*** *055 239 88 98* ***Map*** *5 B2*

A Florentine classic presided over by Giuliano, one of the city's great characters, Garga is fun and often full. The walls are daubed in garish frescoes and you eat in one of a series of cosy rooms. Some dishes are better than others, but the *taglierini del Magnifico* (pasta with a creamy orange-and-mint flavoured sauce) is superb.

### Cibreo €€€€€

*V Andrea del Verrocchio 8r, 50122* ***Tel*** *055 234 11 00* ***Fax*** *055 24 49 66* ***Map*** *4 F1*

This restaurant offers superbly prepared traditional Tuscan dishes in an elegant and airy setting. There is no pasta, but an array of sublime soups and thoroughly Florentine dishes such as tripe, cockscomb and kidneys. Safer options include lamb with artichokes or stuffed pigeon. Fabulous desserts. Closed Mon, Sun.

### Enoteca Pinchiorri €€€€€

*Via Ghibellina 87, 50122* ***Tel*** *055 24 27 77* ***Fax*** *055 24 49 83* ***Map*** *4 E1*

Pinchiorri is frequently described as Italy's finest restaurant and it has one of Europe's best-stocked cellars, boasting over 80,000 bottles. On the ground floor of a 15th-century palazzo, the ambience is very special too, but the food (ultra-refined Tuscan/French) and the fussy service will not please all. Closed Mon, Sun.

### Fuor d'Acqua €€€€€

*Via Pisana 37r, 50143 (west of city centre)* ***Tel*** *055 22 22 99*

Many locals say that this is the best fish restaurant in Florence; it is also one of the most expensive. The fish is very fresh indeed, coming straight off the boats in Versilia and cooked with the minimum of fuss. Some crustaceans are served raw. Try the black thin pasta ribbons with calamari and sage. Closed Sun.

### Oliviero €€€€€

*Via delle Terme 51r, 50123* ***Tel*** *055 21 24 21* ***Map*** *5 C3*

A vaguely retro atmosphere prevails at this elegant restaurant in the centre of town, but the food is up-to-the-minute creative Tuscan, and delicious too. Choose between interesting fish and meat dishes – try galantine of rabbit or seared tuna steak with ginger and white beans. Service is professional and there's an excellent wine list. Closed Sun.

### Onice €€€€€

*Viale Michelangelo 78, 50125* ***Tel*** *055 68 16 31* ***Fax*** *055 658 25 44* ***Map*** *4 F3*

This award-winning and Michelin-starred restaurant is part of the smart Villa La Vedetta hotel, which overlooks the city from near Piazzale Michelangelo. The ambience is elegant and contemporary, while the food is superb and simply prepared. The menu changes with the season. Closed Mon.

### Ora d'Aria €€€€€

*Via dei Georgofili 9–11/r, 50125* **Tel** *055 200 16 99* **Map** 6 D4

Come to Ora d'Aria for modern Tuscan cuisine with Californian and French influences, served in stylish, design-savvy environs. The five-course seasonal tasting menu (€60) gives the best overview of celebrated local chef Marco Stabile's modern use of traditional local ingredients. Reservations are essential. Closed Sun; Aug.

### San Jacopo €€€€€

*Borgo San Jacopo 62r, 50125* **Tel** *055 28 16 61* **Fax** *055 29 11 14* **Map** 5 C4

One of the city's newer restaurants, San Jacopo enjoys a fabulous setting on the south bank of the Arno. Book ahead and ask for one of the tables on the tiny terrace. The chic and breezy atmosphere suits the unpretentious but beautifully served food very well. Fish fans should try the *brodetto* (fish soup), an Adriatic speciality. Closed Tue dinner.

## TUSCANY

### AREZZO Buca di San Francesco €

*Via San Francesco 1, 52100* **Tel** *0575 232 71*

Set alongside the church of San Francesco, in the historic centre, the Buca is ideal for those who have been sightseeing in the frescoed church. The restaurant is located in the basement of a 14th-century building. Here, you can sample the famous Tuscan *ribollita* (cabbage and bread soup), or try the Chianti beef stew.

### AREZZO Miseria e Nobiltà €€

*Piaggia San Bartolomeo 2, 52100* **Tel** *0575 212 45*

Sleek exposed brickwork and a soft jazz soundtrack signal right away that this establishment is a little different from the usual fare in this pretty hill town. The modern design is complemented by a menu of innovative flavour combinations. After dinner, the place turns into a cellar bar with late opening hours. Closed Mon, Tue lunch.

### ARTIMINO Da Delfina €€€

*Via della Chiesa 1, 59015* **Tel** *055 871 80 74* **Fax** *055 871 81 75*

Surrounded by vineyards and some interesting historic villas, this delightful restaurant is situated in a walled medieval village just 22 km (14 miles) from Florence. Owner Carlo Cioni renews the culinary traditions of his mother, Delfina. The rabbit galantine and macaroni with duck sauce are simply exquisite. Closed Tue lunch, Sun dinner; Mon.

### CAMALDOLI Il Cedro €€

*Via di Camaldoli 20, Località Moggiona, 52010* **Tel/Fax** *0575 55 60 80*

One of the most popular restaurants in the region. Camaldoli is known for its finely cooked specialities such as venison and boar, no doubt hunted in the thickly forested Casentino Mountains, which also provide breathtaking views. In spring and summer, go for delicate fried vegetables. Booking advised. Closed dinner (in winter); Mon.

### CASTELNUOVO BERARDENGA La Bottega del 30 €€€€

*Via Santa Caterina 2, Località Villa a Sesta, 53019* **Tel/Fax** *0577 35 92 26*

This is a serious, award-winning restaurant run by Franco Camelia and his French wife Hélène. The menu includes a renowned *petto di anatra con il finocchio selvatico* (breast of duck with wild fennel). Pasta dishes are cooked with a difference. There's also superb home-made spaghetti with nettles, wild mint and porcini. Fine wine list.

### COLLE VAL D'ELSA Arnolfo €€€€€

*Via XX Settembre 50/52A, 53034* **Tel** *0577 92 05 49*

French-trained chefs have earned this intimate restaurant one of Tuscany's few Michelin stars. The wines, food and service are all impeccable, though the reverential hush feels a bit odd for Italy. Typical dishes include a sublime *ribollita* (Tuscan bread soup with cabbage), and pigeon cooked with wine, prunes and pine nuts. Closed Tue, Wed.

### CORTONA Osteria del Teatro €€

*Via Maffei 2, 52044* **Tel** *0575 63 05 56*

This classic trattoria serves well-prepared traditional dishes. Apart from the excellent soups, try the risotto with porcini and saffron, or the *caramelle al radicchio rosso* (pasta stuffed with red chicory and ricotta). The guinea fowl with mushrooms is also good. There are some nice wines to wash it all down. Closed Wed.

### CORTONA Preludio €€

*Via Guelfa 11, 52044* **Tel** *0575 63 01 04* **Fax** *0575 63 16 82*

Cheese soufflé with pears and truffles: this unusual combination of flavours is typical of a restaurant that creatively mixes local ingredients to gratify the taste buds. Succulent meat dishes are based on Chianina beef, the renowned local breed. The menu also offers children-friendly dishes. Closed Mon (in winter).

### ELBA Osteria Libertaria €€

*Calata Matteotti 12, Portoferraio, 57037* **Tel** *0565 91 49 78*

At this informal eatery at the quiet end of Portoferraio's quayside the menu changes daily depending on the catch. Simple seafood, grilled over an open flame, is offered alongside traditional Elban stews. Crisp, local white wines make a fine accompaniment. Tables at the front have fine views over the harbour. Closed Dec–Mar.

### ELBA Publius €€

*Piazza del Castagneto, Località Poggio Marciana, 57030* **Tel** *0565 992 08* **Fax** *0565 90 41 74*

Food with a view. Not only does this historic trattoria have perhaps the best cellar on the island, but it also provides an alternative to the seafood that prevails elsewhere. In addition to fish, you can eat poultry, game, lamb roasted in herbs and a wide choice of cheeses. Closed Mon (in low season).

### GAIOLE IN CHIANTI Il Carlino D'Oro €

*Via Brolio, località San Regolo, 53013* **Tel** *0577 74 71 36* **Fax** *0577 35 70 77*

Eating here is a bit like being invited to Sunday lunch at the home of your Tuscan neighbours. *Crostini neri* (toast with black olive paste) will be followed by *panzanella* (bread salad) in summer, or a bean soup in winter. The ribbon pasta with hare sauce is also delicious. Leave room for fried chicken and rabbit, or calves' liver with sage.

### GAIOLE IN CHIANTI Castello di Spaltenna €€€€€

*Località Pieve di Spaltenna, 53013* **Tel** *0577 74 94 83* **Fax** *0577 74 92 69*

This lovely stone-walled, flower-filled restaurant forms part of a peaceful hotel in a castle just outside Gaiole in Chianti. Popular with expatriates, it offers refined versions of Tuscan classics such as pigeon cooked in Chianti, fresh porcini mushrooms, chickpea soup and, occasionally, more offbeat innovations.

### LIVORNO Da Galileo €€€

*Via della Campana 20, 57122* **Tel** *0586 88 90 09*

For two generations, the Piagneri family has been delighting diners with authentic local cuisine in this reassuringly simple restaurant. Even after five decades, Da Galileo's passion for gastronomy has not waned. Fish prevails, including various soups, seafood fettuccine, and salt cod cooked with onions, Livorno-style. Closed Sun dinner; Wed.

### LUCCA Da Giulio in Pelleria €

*Via delle Conce 47, 55100* **Tel** *0583 559 48*

You must book ahead and enter into the spirit of this bright, boisterous and extremely busy neighbourhood restaurant. This is the reign of hearty local dishes such as *zuppa di farro* (Tuscan white bean and spelt soup) and polenta, so expect no gastronomic surprises. The prices are remarkably reasonable.

### LUCCA Vecchia Trattoria Buralli €

*Piazza Sant'Agostino 10, 55100* **Tel** *0583 95 06 11*

This trattoria provides a complete vegetarian menu on Friday evenings. Try the vegetable-based *zuppa alla frantoiana*. For dessert, go for *buccellato di Lucca*, a warm pudding of fried bread, anise and raisins soaked in Vin Santo. The wine list features Luccan recipes and wines. Closed Wed.

### LUCCA Buca di Sant'Antonio €€

*Via della Cervia 3, 55100* **Tel** *0583 558 81* **Fax** *0583 31 21 99*

This duly restored 19th-century tavern, with an excellent location, serves classic local fare with the occasional innovative touch. The stuffed rabbit *en croute* with mushrooms is excellent. In winter, several dishes feature locally grown chestnuts. Try *buccellato*, the tasty local pudding. Interesting wines. Closed Sun dinner; Mon.

### MASSA MARITTIMA Taverna Vecchio Borgo €€€

*Via Norma Parenti 12, 58024* **Tel/Fax** *0566 90 39 50*

Ancient barrel-vaulted rooms with an enticingly well-stocked wine cellar. The menu usually features pasta stuffed with ricotta and dressed with a sauce of nuts and herbs, as well as *acquacotta* (bread soup). The wild boar cooked with olives and the pheasant breast done in Vin Santo are also recommended. Closed Mon.

### MONTALCINO Il Boccon Divino €€€

*Via Traversa dei Monti 202, 53024* **Tel** *0577 84 82 33*

Perfect for summer dining alfresco, this restaurant offers some interesting dishes and a magnificent view. The *carabaccia* (onion soup) is a must, and the *scottiglia di cinghiale* (wild boar stew) excellent. Not exclusively local, the cheese board is also interesting. Excellent wine list. Closed Tue.

### MONTECATINI TERME Ristorante Montaccolle €€

*Via Marlianese 27, 50016* **Tel** *0572 724 80*

Overlooking Montecatini and the valley below, this restaurant is a wonderful place to relax and enjoy a meal – the views are particularly wonderful from the outside tables, weather permitting. Exceptional hospitality and traditional Tuscan dishes, such as *spaghetti al Chianti*, are the speciality here. Closed Mon, lunch Tue–Sat, Sun, 10 days in Jul & Nov.

### MONTECATINI TERME Enoteca Giovanni €€€€€

*Via Garibaldi 27, 51016* **Tel** *0572 716 95*

Chef Giovanni Rotti's approach to local cuisine is both innovative and in keeping with the fine collection of wines in his cellar. This memorable dining experience is further enhanced by superb service. Try the pigeon with grapes and pine nuts, and seek Rotti's assistance in choosing what to drink with it. Closed Mon.

### MONTEPULCIANO Osteria Acquacheta €€

*Via del Teatro 22, 53045* **Tel** *0578 71 70 86*

This rustic Tuscan grill in the heart of Montepulciano is a meat lover's haven. As well as the famous *bistecca alla fiorentina* (T-bone steak), there's staples of local provenance, including hand-rolled *pici* pasta and pecorino cheese. It's small and always busy, so it is wise to book ahead. Closed Tue; mid-Jan–mid-Mar.

**Key to Price Guide** *see p606* **Key to Symbols** *see back cover flap*

**MONTEPULCIANO La Grotta** €€€€

*Località San Biagio 15, 53045* ***Tel/Fax*** *0578 75 76 07*

A restaurant for discerning diners, La Grotta is located opposite one of the foremost expressions of Renaissance architecture in Tuscany: Sangallo the Elder's Church of San Biagio. Specialities include *pici* (local pasta strings) with duck and saffron sauce. The fillet of Chianina beef with asparagus and truffles is also good. Closed Wed.

**MONTERIGGIONI Il Pozzo** €€€

*Piazza Roma 20, 53035* ***Tel*** *0577 30 41 27*

Occupying 13th-century stables, Il Pozzo is an ideal place for lunch. The food is rigorously Tuscan, essentially simple, but never banal. Try the truffle-fragrant *tortelli al cartoccio* (cooked in foil), which comes wrapped up like a packet to conserve the aromas. Equally delicious is the stuffed pigeon. Closed Sun dinner, Mon.

**ORBETELLO Osteria del Lupacante** €€

*Corso Italia 103, 58015* ***Tel*** *0564 86 76 18* ***Fax*** *0564 86 05 85*

This pleasant *osteria* sticks to old ways in a place increasingly overrun by affluent out-of-towners. Based on seafood, the cooking is light in touch and quite adventurous. The *zuppa di pesce* (fish soup) is excellent. Also good are the risotto with prawns and pine nuts, and the sole with almonds and onions. Closed Wed.

**PESCIA Cecco** €€

*Via Francesco Forti 96/98, 51017* ***Tel*** *0572 47 79 55*

This quiet, easy-going restaurant is the best place to sample Pescia's famous asparagus. Other examples of traditional fare include *pollo al mattone* (chicken cooked under a brick) and *fagioli al fiasco* (beans cooked in a flask). On cold days, try the pudding *cioncia*, a delicious house speciality.

**PIENZA Latte di Luna** €€

*Via San Carlo 2–4, 53026* ***Tel*** *0578 74 86 06*

A cute *trattoria* by Pienza's eastern gate, Latte di Luna offers reliable cooking in family-friendly environs. The menu generally sticks to Tuscan staples, like *pici al cinghiale* (rolled pasta with wild boar), and executes them well. For a local flavour, order *pecorino di Pienza*, the town's famed ewe's milk cheese. Closed Tue; Feb, Jul.

**PISA Osteria dei Cavalieri** €€

*Via San Frediano 16, 56126* ***Tel*** *050 58 08 58*

This friendly tavern occupies the ground floor of a medieval tower-house halfway between Pisa's two most prestigious centres of further education. It's common to find a scholarly looking crowd enjoying the special all-in-one lunch dishes. The menu expands in the evening. Try the beef with beans and mushrooms. Closed Sat lunch; Sun.

**PISA Porton Rosso** €€€

*Vicolo del Porton Rosso 11, 56126* ***Tel*** *050 58 05 66*

This restaurant in the warren of streets near Pisa's market has an enviable reputation for fish. A typical meal might include a mixed *antipasto di mare* (seafood starter) followed by *gnocchi al branzino* (dumplings with sea bass), then grilled *baccalà* (salt cod). There are many options for carnivores, too. Closed Sun; Aug.

**PISA Ristorante V. Beni** €€€

*Piazza Gambacorti Chiara 22, 56125* ***Tel*** *050 25 067*

In a building dating back to the 14th century, this restaurant is situated a 15-minute walk from the Leaning Tower of Pisa, meaning that it is relatively off the tourist trail. Even so, it is enormously popular with the locals, and it is best to book in advance. Fish-based dishes are a speciality. Closed Sun.

**PISTOIA La Bottegaia** €€

*Via del Lastrone 17, 51100* ***Tel*** *0573 36 56 02* ***Fax*** *0573 35 84 50*

Looking on to the old market square to one side and the cathedral to the other, this cheerful, unpretentious wine bar boasts 300 of Italy's best wines. The food menu features cheeses, cold cuts and other toothsome delicacies to go with the wines. Superb desserts. The service is friendly. Closed Sun lunch; Mon.

**PORTO ERCOLE Osteria dei Nobili Santi** €€€

*Via dell'Ospizio 8, 58018* ***Tel/Fax*** *0564 83 30 15*

There aren't many bargains to be had in Porto Ercole. Nonetheless, this little fish restaurant offers value for money and the food is delicious. The amazing *antipasti della casa* (the house starters) will leave you almost satiated. It's worth making an effort to leave some room for some of the delectable dishes and main courses. Closed lunch; Mon.

**PRATO Osteria Cibbè** €€

*Piazza Mercatale 49, 59100* ***Tel*** *0574 60 75 09*

Housed in a medieval building in the city centre, this cosy little family-run eatery serves good local cold cuts and *crostini* for antipasto, followed by classic Tuscan fare such as pappardelle with game sauce. The desserts are home-made too: try the apple and spelt tart. Interesting wine list. Closed Sun.

**SAN GIMIGNANO Osteria delle Catene** €€

*Via Mainardi 18, 53037* ***Tel/Fax*** *0577 94 19 66*

This small restaurant specializes in regional cooking enhanced with its own special touch. You could start off with cold cuts made from wild boar, then continue with a saffron soup made according to a medieval recipe. The hare cooked in local wine is also good, and the home-made desserts are worth leaving room for.

### SAN GIMIGNANO Dorandò €€€

*Vicolo dell'Oro 2, 53037* ***Tel/Fax*** *0577 94 18 62*

This restaurant is small and very select, so booking is advised. Impressive wine list, and dishes to go with it. The pasta with pigeon sauce on a bed of creamed mushrooms is delicious. There are various fish specialities, including angler fish in a nutty crust served with leeks. Take your time to enjoy it all. Closed Mon (in winter).

### SANSEPOLCRO Ristorante da Ventura €€

*Via Aggiunti 30, 52037* ***Tel/Fax*** *0575 74 25 60*

Run by the same family for over 50 years, this charming restaurant serves delectable *agnolotti al tartufo* (stuffed pasta with truffles). Another of their classic dishes is the veal cooked slowly in Chianti. Mushrooms often feature too. Even the *cantucci* biscuits for dipping in Vin Santo are home-made. Closed Sun dinner; Mon.

### SATURNIA Bacco e Cerere €€

*Via Mazzini 4, 58050* ***Tel/Fax*** *0564 60 12 35*

The wide range of starters at this small, friendly place is a great introduction to traditional Maremma cuisine. The *zuppa di ricotta* makes a delectable change from the traditional *acquacotta* (vegetable soup served over toast). The *enoteca* (wine bar) of the same name offers interesting bottles. Closed Wed.

### SIENA Enoteca I Terzi €€

*Via dei Termini 7, 53100* ***Tel/Fax*** *0577 443 29*

This restaurant has a nice vaulted space and a friendly atmosphere in which to enjoy a good bottle of wine accompanied by a wide range of premium cold cuts, *carpaccio*, smoked meats, steak tartare, and cheeses from all over Italy. In addition, each day there are three cooked dishes, which change with the seasons. Closed Sun.

### SIENA La Compagnia dei Vinattieri €€

*Via delle Terme 79, 53100* ***Tel*** *0577 23 65 68* ***Fax*** *0577 20 55 39*

An impressive underground, vaulted space with a magnificent wine cellar and some interesting food to go with it. You can sip by the glass, with a platter of cheese and salami, or enjoy a bottle with a hot meal featuring dishes such as a salt cod soup. Good desserts and unusual sweet wines. Only one table outside.

### SIENA La Taverna del Capitano €€

*Via del Capitano 6/8, 53100* ***Tel/Fax*** *0577 28 80 94*

Located up near the Duomo, this restaurant with vaulted ceilings and dark wood furnishings is quintessentially Sienese. The *ribollita* (vegetable soup); *pici* (traditional pasta) with pecorino and pepper, stewed rabbit and tasty beef platter all speak for unbroken traditions. The house wine is good too. Closed Tue (in winter).

### SIENA Osterie Le Logge €€€

*Via del Porrione 33, 53100* ***Tel*** *0577 480 13* ***Fax*** *0577 22 47 97*

Siena's prettiest, and often full, restaurant has a dark wood and marble interior. The tables are laid with crisp linen cloths and decorated with plants. Home-produced oils and Montalcino wines accompany dishes that wander slightly from mainstream Tuscan cooking. The stuffed guinea fowl is delicious. Closed Sun.

### SIENA Cane e Gatto €€€€€

*Via Pagliaresi 6, 53100* ***Tel*** *0577 28 75 45*

Traditional Sienese cooking features highly on the agenda at this intimate, family-run restaurant en route to the Porta Romana. There's no menu, just a fixed-price deal for *antipasto*, *primo*, *secondo* and dessert, all made with whatever ingredients are available at the morning market. Not a place to dine in a hurry. Closed lunch, Thu.

### VIAREGGIO Cabreo €€€

*Via Firenze 14, 55049* ***Tel*** *0584 546 43*

The main focus of this pleasant restaurant, located in a little side street, is seafood simply cooked and served in a way that best enhances its natural aromas. Specialities include spaghetti with clams, gnocchi with lobster sauce, and baked fish. It is advisable to leave enough room for the delicious home-made desserts. Closed Mon.

### VOLTERRA Etruria €

*Piazza dei Priory 6–8, 56048* ***Tel/Fax*** *0588 860 64*

Situated on Volterra's main square, Etruria has an interior decorated in a 19th-century style. In summer there are plenty of tables ouside to dine alfresco and soak up the ambience of this ancient town. Try the Etruria antipasti, truffles, or their speciality – sweet and sour wild boar. Closed Wed.

### VOLTERRA Osteria dei Poeti €€

*Via Matteotti 54, 56048* ***Tel*** *0588 860 29*

Located on one of the town's main thoroughfares, Poeti is a great place to sample quality local cooking. Dishes like *zuppa Volterrana* (bread and vegetable soup) and pasta with wild boar ragout arrive briskly. This is also a good choice for younger eaters: Poeti opens an hour earlier in the evening than most other establishments. Closed Thu.

### VOLTERRA Del Duca €€€

*Via di Castello 2, 56048* ***Tel*** *0588 815 10* ***Fax*** *0588 929 57*

A charming 16th-century palazzo houses this small restaurant with its ancient wine cellar and secret garden. Try the fried pumpkin flowers stuffed with ricotta and tomato. The pigeon breast cooked with locally grown saffron and olives is another speciality. There is also a good cheese platter. Closed Tue.

**Key to Price Guide** *see p606* **Key to Symbols** *see back cover flap*

## UMBRIA

### AMELIA Anita €

*Via Roma 31, 05022* **Tel** *0744 98 21 46* **Fax** *0744 98 30 79*

This simple restaurant and hotel just outside the city centre has been run by the Pernazza family since 1938. They offer no-frills Umbrian fare, such as *crostini* (toasted bread with various toppings), roasted meats, pasta with porcini mushrooms, and wild boar. The sweets are made in-house. Closed Mon.

### ASSISI La Fortezza €

*Vicolo della Fortezza/Piazza del Comune, 06081* **Tel** *075 81 29 93* **Fax** *075 819 80 35*

Family-run for more than 45 years, this restaurant is located halfway up a staircase-cum-street off the main piazza. Creative regional cooking at this level normally costs twice as much. Try the *cannelloni all'assisiana* (pasta sheets wrapped around a ragout of veal and baked under tomatoes and Parmesan).

### ASSISI Trattoria Pallotta €

*Vicolo della Volta Pinta 3, 06081* **Tel** *075 81 26 49* **Fax** *075 81 23 07*

A humble, homely place and one of the least expensive *trattorie* in the centre of town. The mixed antipasto platter is massive. Dine on such Assisian specialities as *torta al testo* (flatbread stuffed with a variety of vegetable or meat goodies) and *strangozzi* (hand-rolled spaghetti in an olive and mushroom pesto). Closed Tue.

### ASSISI Medioevo €€

*Via Arco dei Priori 4B, 06081* **Tel & Fax** *075 81 30 68*

An elegant restaurant set under the medieval stone vaults of an ancient palazzo in the centre of Assisi. Try the home-made pastas (featuring black truffles in season). Meat, such as *agnello al tartufo* (lamb with truffles), is cooked to traditional recipes and they work wonders with steak. Great home-made desserts.

### ASSISI Il Frantoio €€€

*Vicolo Illuminati 12, 06081* **Tel** *075 81 29 77* **Fax** *075 81 29 41*

A 17th-century olive press is the setting of this refined Umbrian restaurant, with a lovely garden terrace and a wine steward who is head of the Italian sommelier association. Sample the *stringozzi paesani* (thick ropes of hand-rolled spaghetti tossed with tomatoes, artichokes, and hot chilli flakes).

### BASCHI Vissani €€€€

*Strada Statale 448, km. 606, Todi-Baschi, 05020* **Tel** *0744 95 02 06* **Fax** *0744 95 01 86*

Gianfranco Vissani is famous throughout Italy for his balanced flavours and *haute cuisine* of game and meat, served in elegant surroundings. The recipes are inventive and original, but based around regional ingredients. For dessert, you move to a separate room as in an old-fashioned household.

### CAMPIELLO SUL CLITUNNO Trattoria Pettino €€

*Frazione Pettino 31, 06042* **Tel/Fax** *0743 27 60 21*

Occupying an old restored house in the middle of the mountains. The *bruschetta* (toasted bread with various toppings) is delicious as is, in season, the plethora of dishes made with truffles. Try the *stringozzi al tartufo* (thick, hand-rolled ropes of pasta dressed in black truffles) and the *agnello al tartufo* (lamb with truffles). Closed Tue.

### CITTÀ DEL CASTELLO Amici Miei €€

*Via del Monte 2, 06012* **Tel/Fax** *075 85 59 904*

Set in the brick-vaulted storerooms of a 16th-century palazzo in the historic centre, this restaurant offers a menu based on regional cuisine. Sample the *strangozzi con baccalà* (hand-rolled spaghetti with salt cod) and the *cinghiale in umido con fagioli* (a stew of wild boar chunks served with beans). Closed Wed.

### CITTÀ DEL CASTELLO Il Bersaglio €€

*Via Vittorio Emanuele Orlando 14, 06012* **Tel** *075 85 55 534* **Fax** *075 85 82 07 66*

A traditional Umbrian restaurant with specialities that vary seasonally. The chef is fond of using mushrooms and truffles as well as game. Sample the *gnocchetti* (little gnocchi) with truffles, or try a *degustazione* (tasting menu) of several different preparations of porcini.

### FOLIGNO Villa Roncalli €€€

*Via Roma 25, 06034* **Tel** *0742 39 10 91* **Fax** *0742 39 10 01*

This charming country inn of the 17th century is set in its own garden about one kilometre (half a mile) from Foligno. Regional specialities are well prepared using fresh ingredients. Try the ravioli or fettucine with truffles, braised lamb, wild asparagus, and châteaubriand with field herbs. Closed Mon.

### GUBBIO Taverna del Lupo €

*Via Ansidei 21, 06024* **Tel** *075 92 74 368* **Fax** *075 92 71 269*

Half the hotels and restaurants in Gubbio are run by the Mencarelli family, including this excellent, romantic set of medieval dining rooms in the centre. Plump for one of the exquisitely prepared tasting menus featuring a procession of traditional regional dishes. Closed Mon (except Aug, Sep).

**GUBBIO Locanda del Cantiniere** €€

*Via Dante 30, 06024* ***Tel*** *075 927 59 99*

Exposed brick and original wooden beams add to the rustic charm of this central Gubbio eatery. Ingredients for the classic Umbrian cuisine, including all the meats, are sourced locally. The bread is baked in their own oven, and pasta is handmade each morning. Great value for money. Closed Tue.

**MAGIONE Al Coccio** €€

*Via del Quadrifoglio 12a, 06063* ***Tel*** *075 84 18 29*

This established restaurant in the backstreets of Magione displays a near-fanatical devotion to local ingredients and recipes – even the chocolate is by Perugina, a well-known brand from the nearby Umbrian capital. Pasta is hand- and home-made, and mains always include traditional Umbrian meats like wild boar, rabbit and beef. Closed Mon.

**MONTEFALCO Coccorone** €€

*Largo Tempestivi, 06036* ***Tel*** *0742 37 95 35*

Impeccable service and a commitment to traditional ingredients are the hallmarks of this rustic restaurant in the "balcony of Umbria". Elegantly presented local specialities often include beef cooked in Sagrantino wine, pasta with porcini mushrooms (in season), and truffles with just about anything. Closed Wed (except in summer).

**NARNI Cavallino** €

*Via Flaminia Romana 220, Località Testaccio, 05035* ***Tel/Fax*** *0744 76 10 20*

Family atmosphere and home cooking in the Umbrian tradition, including interesting pastas such as *manfricoli* and *ciriole* (both of which are eggless pastas) served with tomato sauce, wild boar or porcini. They also do nice *scallopine al limone* (veal escalope in lemon sauce), grilled meats and pigeon. Closed Tue.

**NORCIA Dal Francese** €€

*Via Riguardati 16, 06046* ***TelFax*** *0743 81 62 90*

This country-style trattoria in the centre of Norcia offers a truffle-based *menú degustazione* (tasting menu) in season, as well as *pappardelle alla norcina* (wide noodles in a cream sauce with sausage) and *agnello scottadito* (lamb so succulent, the name says, that you'll "burn your fingers" in haste to eat it). Closed Fri.

**ORVIETO La Volpe e l'Uva** €

*Via Ripa Corsica 1, 05018* ***Tel/Fax*** *0763 34 16 12*

A popular and friendly trattoria in the centre of Orvieto, offering a variety of regional dishes at reasonable prices. Dishes change with the season, and the meat and game recipes are joined by a good selection of lake fish as well as lots of egg-based dishes (they make an effort to cater to vegetarians). Closed Mon, Tue.

**ORVIETO I Sette Consoli** €€€

*Piazza Sant'Angelo 1A, 05018* ***Tel/Fax*** *0763 34 39 11*

A comfortable, friendly restaurant installed in the sacristy of an old church, with a garden for summer dining. Try the *baccalà* (salt cod) marinated in apple vinegar with potato salad, stuffed rabbit, *ravioli di anatra* (duck-filled ravioli), and *zuppa di fave con finocchio* (bean soup with fennel). Closed Sun dinner; Wed.

**ORVIETO Le Grotte del Funaro** €€€

*Via Ripa Serancia 41, 05018* ***Tel*** *0763 34 32 76* ***Fax*** *0763 34 28 98*

Atmospheric series of cave-rooms carved from the tufa at the cliff's edge, once the workshop of a *funaro* (rope-maker) in the 12th century. The *ombrechelli del Funaro* are hand-made spaghetti with tomatoes, sausage, artichokes, and mushrooms. The mixed platter of grilled meats is tasty. Closed Mon.

**PASSIGNANO SUL TRASIMENO Cacciatori da Luciano** €€€€

*Via Lungolago 3, 06065* ***Tel*** *075 82 72 10*

The menu is based on both lake and sea fish – the restaurant is on the lake, and they make the trip from landlocked Umbria to a seaside seafood market three times a week – including a mixed-fish *carpaccio* (raw, thinly sliced fish), a risotto studded with different types of prawn and shrimp, and grilled sole. Closed Wed.

**PERUGIA Il Falchetto** €

*Via Bartolo 20, 06100* ***Tel*** *075 573 17 75* ***Fax*** *075 572 90 57*

Brilliantly prepared Perugino cooking in a 14th-century palazzo a few steps off the main square, with tables out on the piazza in summer. Whatever else you order, start with the *falchetti verdi* (a casserole of rich spinach and ricotta gnocchi baked in tomato sauce and cheese), followed by veal or lamb. Closed Mon.

**PERUGIA Giò Arte e Vini** €€

*Via Ruggero d'Andreotto 19, 06124* ***Tel/Fax*** *075 573 11 00*

This modern hotel and restaurant on the outskirts of town is famous for its spectacular selection of wines (some 1,200 choices), modern art on the walls, and well-chosen regional dishes prepared with special touches. The pumpkin ravioli and the *treccia di agnello* (lamb) are particularly good. Closed Sun dinner.

**PERUGIA La Taverna** €€

*Via delle Streghe 8, 06123* ***Tel*** *075 572 41 28* ***Fax*** *075 573 25 36*

The place in Perugia to go for a candlelit dinner with romantic music. First courses are classic Umbrian – tagliatelle in duck ragout, ravioli, fava-bean soup – while the chef gets more inventive with main courses. Try the *baccalà* (salt cod) with prunes, pine nuts, and raisins. Excellent desserts.

**Key to Price Guide** *see p606* **Key to Symbols** *see back cover flap*

**PERUGIA Osteria del Gambero** €€€€

*Via Baldeschi 8a, 01623* **Tel** *075 573 54 61*

Advanced booking is recommended at this highly regarded restaurant that spins innovative touches on traditional Umbrian dishes. For example, try the *pappardelle di crusca con lardo di colonnata* (wide noodles with salt-cured lard, chickpeaks, cantaloupe, and mint). Closed Mon.

**SPOLETO Il Panciolle** €€

*Vicolo degli Eroi 1, 06049* **Tel** *0743 22 12 41* **Fax** *0743 22 42 89*

A large terrace shaded by a spreading pine for summer dining, and a stone-walled inside room where the meat for main courses is grilled over an large open fire are the highlights of this restaurant. Try the *strangozzi alla montanara* (hand-rolled pasta strands with minced vegetables and chilli peppers). Closed Wed (usually).

**SPOLETO Il Tartufo** €€

*Piazza Garibaldi 24, 06049* **Tel** *0743 402 36*

The floor of the basement dining room of this restaurant specializing in truffles dates back to ancient Rome. The well-tried regional specialities include such delights as *zuppa di farro* (spelt soup), courgette flowers stuffed with cheese, aubergine and truffles, and duck in Sagrantino wine sauce. Closed Mon.

**SPOLETO Le Casaline** €€

*Località Poreta di Spoleto, Frazione Casaline, 06042* **Tel** *0743 52 11 13* **Fax** *0743 27 50 99*

An oasis of calm in a restored 18th-century mill. Try the gnocchi stuffed with mushrooms, *rigatoni alla norcina* (pasta tubes with mushrooms, peas, truffles, and sausage), or *cinghiale alla cacciatora* (wild boar in a wine and tomato sauce). Also, many peasant-inspired goose dishes. Closed Mon.

**TERNI Da Carlino** €

*Via Piemonte 1, 05100* **Tel** *0744 42 01 63*

Robust, rustic food in a historic building in town. Start off with the *crostini* (toasts) served alongside local salami, followed perhaps by tagliatelle with truffles, lamb, or a fish dish. The house speciality is *stracci* (home-made pasta tossed in a sauce of veal and fresh mozzarella). Closed Wed.

**TODI La Mulinella** €

*Località Pontenaia 29, 06059* **Tel** *075 894 47 79* **Fax** *075 894 82 35*

In the countryside about 2 km (1 mile) from Todi, this eatery serves simple, reliable dishes. The wood-fired breads and home-made pastas and desserts are excellent. Recommended are the *carni alle brace* (grilled meats) with seasonal vegetables, and the *pasta in ragù di anatra* (duck) or *oca* (goose). Closed Wed.

**TODI La Torre** €

*Via Cortesi 57, 06059* **Tel/Fax** *075 894 26 94*

In the picture-perfect hilltown of Todi, this restaurant serves up regional dishes of fish, meat and game (including hare, duck and lamb), often lacing dishes with truffles in season. The puddings, such as a *crema* (cream) topped with warm chocolate, are exquisite. Closed Sun.

**TREVI La Taverna del Pescatore** €€€

*Via Flaminia Vecchia 50, 06039* **Tel/Fax** *0742 78 09 20*

The freshest of local produce is combined and cooked in simple yet exquisite recipes based on Umbrian traditions and using fresh river fish. Try the *gamberi di fiume alle brace* or *all'arrabbiata* (crayfish grilled or served spicy hot). The atmosphere is relaxed with attentive service. Closed Sun dinner; Mon.

## LE MARCHE

**LORETO Andreina** €€

*Via Buffolareccia 14, 60025* **Tel** *071 97 01 24* **Fax** *071 750 10 51*

A grandmother-and-grandson team prepares traditional cuisine. Home-made pastas include *tagliatelle con ragù* (noodles in meat sauce), and, among the game dishes like quail, wild boar, and thrushes, *piccione allo spiedo* (spit-roasted pigeon), followed by tempting desserts. Closed Tue.

**MACERATA Osteria dei Fiori** €€

*Via Lauro Rossi 61, 62100* **Tel** *0733 26 01 42* **Fax** *0733 24 09 37*

The cooking at this popular place is regional and hearty – witness *coniglio in porchetta* (pork stuffed with rabbit) – and based on peasant traditions, none more so than the poverty-inspired *tagliulì pelusi al sugo finto* (noodles in a "fake sauce" that tastes like ragout but is made without costly meat). Closed Sun.

**MACERATA Da Secondo** €€€

*Via Pescheria Vecchia 26–28, 62100* **Tel/Fax** *0733 26 09 12*

An elegant atmosphere and well-prepared regional specialities contribute to this restaurant's popularity. Some of the dishes to try include *vincigrassi alla Macerata* (the local lasagne), *frittura mista* (batter-fried fish or meat and vegetables), and *maialino da latte allo spiedo* (spit-roasted suckling pig). Closed Mon.

### NUMANA La Costarella

€€€€

*Via IV Novembre 35, 60026* ***Tel/Fax*** *071 736 02 97*

This specialist fish restaurant is named after the stair-like street on which it sits, made of 150 steps. Try the *tagliatelle fatte a mano alle seppie* (home-made noodles, stained black with squid ink, in a cuttlefish-and-squidling ragout) and the fried fish with courgette flowers. Booking is advisable. Closed Tue (in winter).

### PESARO Da Gennaro

€€

*Via Santa Marina Alta 30, Località Santa Marina Alta, 61100* ***Tel*** *0721 273 21*

A bright spot of genuine cooking among the often banal eateries of this resort-filled coast. Located 7 km (4 miles) from the city centre, along a panoramic road up into the mountains, with great views of the coastline, Da Gennaro has for 40 years served rigorously traditional fish and fresh seafood dishes. Closed Mon.

### PESARO Da Alceo

€€€€€

*Via Panoramica Ardizio 121, 61100* ***Tel*** *0721 39 03 18* ***Fax*** *0721 39 17 82*

A famous fish restaurant with a spectacular panoramic terrace. Some dishes to sample include gnocchi or *tagliolini* (noodles) with shellfish, a fishy risotto, as well as simple *scampi del Conero al vapore* (steamed locally fished prawns). Desserts are home-made and tasty. Closed Mon.

### SENIGALLIA Uliassi

€€€€€

*Via Banchina di Levante 6, 60019* ***Tel*** *071 654 63* ***Fax*** *071 65 93 27*

This friendly restaurant run by the brother-and-sister team of Mauro and Catia Uliassi offers a high standard of cuisine. Try the speciality pasta with prawns and asparagus, the roasted sea bass with artichokes braised in soy sauce, and the *stoccafisso mantecato* (salt cod) served with a purée of leeks. Closed Mon.

### URBANIA Big Ben

€€

*Corso Vittorio Emanuele 61, 61049* ***Tel/Fax*** *0722 31 97 95*

Big Ben is an intimate restaurant set in a 17th-century palazzo in the city centre, with a lovely garden for dining. Among the regional Marchigiano specialities are *tagliolini* (thin noodles) with truffles, *lumache* (snails) with wild fennel and tomatoes, grilled lamb, good cheeses, and home-made desserts. Closed Wed.

### URBINO Taverna degli Artisti

€

*Via Bramante 52, 61029* ***Tel/Fax*** *0722 26 76*

The dining room, with its Renaissance-era frescoed ceiling and terracotta floor tiles, is as stupendous as the cooking is simple and good. The menu is based around hearty regional traditions, including home-made pastas, porcini mushrooms, grilled meats and delectable pizzas. Closed Tue.

### URBINO L'Angolo Divino

€€

*Via S. Andrea 14, 61029* ***Tel/Fax*** *0722 32 75 59*

A rustic basement joint of brick walls and wood beams in the heart of the historic centre, serving hearty regional cooking – half the menu is written in local dialect. Try *pasta nel sacco* (baked pasta casserole with cheese, eggs, and bread), and *costarelle alla gradella* (grilled pork chops). Closed Sun dinner; Mon.

### URBINO Cà Andreana

€€€

*Via Cà Andreana 2, 61029* ***Tel*** *0722 32 78 45*

For a taste of authentic local cooking, drive the short distance to this farmhouse 5 km (3 miles) from Urbino's walls. Many of the ingredients, including several cheeses and salami, are home-produced and organic. Pastas are handmade from scratch. Reservations essential. Dinner only Tue–Sat; lunch only Sun. Closed Jan, Feb.

### URBINO Vecchia Urbino

€€€

*Via dei Vasari 3–5, 61029* ***Tel/Fax*** *0722 44 47*

An elegantly rustic restaurant in a 16th-century structure serving simply prepared traditional dishes, including *vincigrassi* (the local lasagne of chicken, ham, and veal), *raviolone al tartufo* (a giant pasta parcel stuffed with ricotta and dressed in black truffles), rabbit, and polenta with mushrooms. Closed Tue.

## ROME

### AVENTINE Felice

€€€

*Via Mastro Giorgio 29, 00153* ***Tel*** *06 574 68 00* ***Map*** *5 C3*

A deservedly popular restaurant serving traditional Roman cuisine. The *spaghetti alla carbonara* or *cacio e pepe* (with cheese and pepper) make for excellent starters, while the *abbacchio arrosto* (roast lamb) and *torta di ricotta* (ricotta and candied peel cake) complete the feast. Booking ahead is always advisable. Closed Sun dinner.

### AVENTINE Checchino dal 1887

€€€€€

*Via di Monte Testaccio 30, 00153* ***Tel*** *06 574 38 16* ***Map*** *6 D4*

Checchino dal 1887 specializes in traditional *cucina romana*, using the *quinto quarto* (offal). Originally discarded in the slaughterhouses opposite, offal became a delicacy in working-class cuisine. The menu includes *rigatoni alla pajata* (calf intestines) and *coda alla vaccinara* (oxtail). Some good value set menus are also available.

**CAMPO DE' FIORI Ar Galletto** €€€

*Vicolo del Gallo, 00186* ***Tel*** *06 686 1714* ***Map*** *9 C4*

This popular trattoria serves straightforward Italian fare, though their *penne all'arrabbiata* (pasta with a spicy tomato sauce) deserves a special mention. However, Ar Galletto's main attraction is its location. In warmer months, dine out in a corner of the Piazza Farnese overlooking the fountains and the vast Farnese Palace. Closed Sun; 1 wk Aug.

**CAMPO DE' FIORI Ditirambo** €€€

*Piazza della Cancelleria 75, 00186* ***Tel*** *06 687 16 26* ***Map*** *2 E4*

This small restaurant, a cross between a French bistro and a Roman *osteria*, specializes in home-made bread, pasta dishes and desserts. It also offers one of the widest selections of wines and cheeses in the entire city. The cuisine is strictly Italian, but the inventive menu changes frequently. Service is friendly and relatively quick.

**CAMPO DE' FIORI Monserrato** €€€

*Via Monserrato 96, 00186* ***Tel*** *06 687 33 86* ***Map*** *2 D4, 9 B4*

Popular and well-located, with outdoor tables in summer, Monserrato is renowned for the quality of its fish and seafood. Service is impeccable and the fish arrives fresh every day. *Bigoli* (pasta) with prawns and asparagus and salted sea bass are excellent. Appetizing steaks and meat dishes are also available.

**CAMPO DE' FIORI Sora Lella** €€€€

*Via Ponte Quattro Capi 16, 00186* ***Tel*** *06 686 16 01* ***Map*** *6 D1*

In an enviable location, on the enchanting Isola Tiberina, Sora Lella was founded by the famous actress Lella Fabrizi in 1959. Excellent dishes include *tonnarelli alla cuccagna* (fresh pasta with sausage, ham and walnuts) and quiche of artichokes, potatoes and smoked cheese. There are also delicious vegetarian and fish menus. Friendly service.

**CAMPO DE' FIORI Camponeschi** €€€€€

*Piazza Farnese 50, 00186* ***Tel*** *06 687 49 27* ***Fax*** *06 686 52 44* ***Map*** *2 E5, 9 C4*

One of Rome's finest restaurants, Camponeschi offers wonderful views of the Piazza Farnese. Its cuisine, a creative fusion of Italian and Mediterranean flavours, is extremely refined. Superb fish and meat dishes. Its *cantina* contains over 400 wines, including its own prestigious label from the family vineyard. Open in evenings only.

**CAMPO DE' FIORI Piperno** €€€€€

*Via Monte de' Cenci 9, 00186* ***Tel*** *06 68 80 66 29* ***Map*** *2 F5, 10 D5*

A restaurant has been here since the mid-1800s, though the original Piperno has long gone. His name still carries great kudos, though as one of the finest in Roman-Jewish cooking. The pasta is handmade every day; the fish arrives daily. The house wine is a delicious Frascati. Don't miss the *carciofi alla giudia* (fried artichokes). Book ahead.

**CARACALLA Tramonti & Muffati** €€

*Via di Santa Maria Ausiliatrice 105, 00181* ***Tel*** *06 780 13 42*

This pleasant *enoteca* is located near the Via Appia and Furio Camillo metro station. Excellent wines complement a few daily specials and the meticulously researched *salumi* and cheeses. Creative use of local ingredients works exceedingly well. Open only in the evening. Booking is advised.

**ESQUILINE Scoglio di Frisio** €€

*Via Merulana 256, 00185* ***Tel*** *06 487 27 65* ***Map*** *7 C1*

This lively Neapolitan restaurant, popular with tourists, offers authentic cuisine and a lively atmosphere. Excellent pizzas and seafood. Try *spigola all'acqua pazza* (sea bass cooked in boiling water and herbs), served with wine from Campania, followed by delicious *babà* for dessert. Neapolitan singing in the evenings.

**ESQUILINE Monti** €€€

*Via di San Vito 13a, 00185* ***Tel*** *06 446 65 73* ***Map*** *4 D4*

Justly popular, this family-run trattoria offers seasonal cuisine from the Marche. Typical dishes are vegetable *lasagnette*, rabbit or chicken cooked with herbs and turkey in balsamic vinegar. The service is competent, the wine list excellent and the desserts delicious. Fish fresh from the Adriatic is served on Fridays. Booking is recommended.

**ESQUILINE Agata e Romeo** €€€€€

*Via Carlo Alberto 45, 00185* ***Tel*** *06 446 61 15* ***Map*** *4 D4*

Originally a trattoria, this is now an internationally renowned restaurant. The chef, Agata, uses the finest ingredients in an ever-innovative menu, based on Roman and southern Italian dishes. Her husband, Romeo, an expert sommelier, ensures the wines perfectly complement each dish. The taster menu is exceptional.

**JANICULUM Lo Scarpone** €€€

*Via San Pancrazio 15, 00152* ***Tel*** *06 581 40 94* ***Fax*** *06 58 33 27 02* ***Map*** *5 A1*

Halfway between town and country, from the top of the Janiculum Hill, this elegant, noble restaurant allows you to have the whole of Rome at your feet. The garden is very pleasant in summer. Inside, the decor is endearingly rustic. On the menu is good traditional food based on fish and grilled meats.

**LATERAN Hostaria Isidoro** €€

*Via di San Giovanni in Laterano 59a, 00184* ***Tel*** *06 700 82 66* ***Map*** *7 B1*

This restaurant located in an ex-convent from the 1600s, just up the road from the Colosseum, has been a Roman favourite for more than 50 years. Isidoro is famous for its *assaggini*, a sampler containing small portions of all the different vegetarian pasta dishes on the menu. The other house speciality is for meat-lovers: grilled steak.

**LATERAN I Clementini** €€

*Via San Giovanni in Laterano 106, 00184* **Tel** *06 45 42 63 95* **Map** *7 B1*

Popular with Irish trainee priests from nearby San Clemente, as well as locals, Il Clementini is a neighbourhood trattoria serving classic Roman cuisine. *Spaghetti alla carbonara, bucatini all'amatriciana* (a spicy tomato and bacon sauce), *carciofi alla romana* (artichokes with mint), and rabbit or lamb are typical dishes.

**LATERAN San Lollo** €€€

*Via dei Sabelli 51, 00185* **Tel** *06 494 07 26* **Map** *4 F4*

The owner of this Sicilian trattoria comes from Palermo and serves pizza, grilled meats and some classic dishes with a creative touch. Daily specials and staples feature *caponata* (ratatouille), *vermicelli con la mollica* (anchovies, orange rind and breadcrumbs) or *paccheri alla norma* (pasta with ricotta). Excellent desserts.

**LATERAN Primo** €€€€

*Via del Pigneto 46, 00176* **Tel** *06 701 38 27* **Map** *8 F1*

This minimal-chic restaurant serves gourmet dishes prepared with top-quality ingredients, such as the mini lasagna with asparagus, Castelmagno cheese and poached egg. The in-house sommeliers are always happy to advise guests on the best wine–food pairings. Book ahead. Closed Mon.

**PIAZZA DELLA ROTONDA Da Gino** €€

*Vicolo Rosini 4, 00186* **Tel** *06 687 34 34* **Map** *2 F3, 10 D1*

Da Gino is a friendly restaurant packed to the gills with politicians and journalists. The frescoed, old-fashioned interior opens on to a charming pergola in good weather. Classic Roman dishes include *spaghetti alla carbonara, abbacchio alla cacciatora* (a lamb dish), *seppie con piselli* (cuttlefish with peas), and rabbit.

**PIAZZA DELLA ROTONDA Grano** €€

*Piazza Rondanini 53, 00186* **Tel** *06 68 19 20 96* **Map** *10 D2*

Grano offers classic Mediterranean cuisine to a varied clientele. Large platters of local staples, such as *spaghetti alla carbonara* and *bucatini all'amatriciana* (a spicy bacon and tomato sauce) are served as first courses, followed by roast suckling pig. In warmer months, alfresco dining is available.

**PIAZZA DELLA ROTONDA Maccheroni** €€

*Piazza delle Coppelle 44, 00186* **Tel** *06 68 30 78 95* **Map** *2 F3*

This attractive restaurant adds modern cool to a retro *trattoria* base. The food is a similar blending of traditional Roman dishes (the *spaghetti alla carbonara* is very good) and some more unusual dishes, like *fettuccine al tartufo* (with truffles). The grilled meats are good choices for main courses. Great for alfresco dining, but book at weekends.

**PIAZZA DELLA ROTONDA Obika** €€€

*Piazza Firenze 28, 00186* **Tel** *06 683 26 30* **Map** *10 D1*

This ultra-modern place is Italy's equivalent of a sushi bar – minus the sushi, plus a large variety of mozzarellas served in myriad different ways: accompanied by prosciutto; as key ingredient for pasta recipes; grilled, smoked or plain. The wine list includes Southern Italian labels also served by the glass. Friendly service and great location.

**PIAZZA DELLA ROTONDA Clemente alla Maddalena** €€€€

*Piazza della Maddalena 4/5, 00186* **Tel** *06 683 36 33* **Map** *2 F3, 10 D2*

This 16th-century palazzo opposite the Maddalena church has wood-panelled dining rooms and a nice terrace in summer. Its creative cooking features anchovy, oregano and tomato tart; *paccheri pasta* with clams and turnip tops; spaghetti with wild chicory pesto and guinea fowl with polenta. Excellent wine list and attentive service.

**PIAZZA DELLA ROTONDA Riccioli Café** €€€€

*Via delle Coppelle 13, 00186* **Tel** *06 68 21 03 13* **Map** *2 F3*

This trendy hotspot features seafood galore. The owner and chef has created a fusion cuisine of Mediterranean classics, sushi and sashimi. Some good grilled fish and cheese dishes are also available, and diners can choose from an ample international wine list. There is an oyster bar, too. Also open for buffet lunch and happy hour.

**PIAZZA DELLA ROTONDA Da Fortunato al Pantheon** €€€€€

*Via del Pantheon 55, 00186* **Tel** *06 679 27 88* **Map** *2 F3*

Popular with Italian politicians and actors, the elegant Da Fortunato is famous among locals and tourists alike. The menu features fresh seafood – a favourite is baked turbot with potatoes – as well as other classic dishes of the Italian tradition. From October to mid-December, truffles from Alba steal the scene.

**PIAZZA DI SPAGNA Tad Café** €

*Via del Babuino 155a, 00187* **Tel** *06 95 06 14 82* **Map** *3 A2*

Perfectly located near Piazza del Popolo, this modern and stylish café with a picturesque patio garden serves daily specials and light meals. It is extremely popular after a morning's window-shopping by well-heeled Romans. The food combines Italian and Eastern inspiration. Recommended for lunches.

**PIAZZA DI SPAGNA Margutta Vegetariana** €€€

*Via Margutta 118, 00187* **Tel** *06 32 65 05 77* **Map** *2 F1*

A colourful, plant-filled dining room with modern art in profusion and a jazz soundtrack, this is Rome's first and finest vegetarian eatery. It also offers a special rate buffet lunch and an excellent value Sunday brunch. The adjacent restaurant prepares vegetarian meals with creative flair at much higher prices.

**Key to Price Guide** *see p606* **Key to Symbols** *see back cover flap*

**PIAZZA DI SPAGNA Le Sorelle** €€€€

*Via Belsiana 30, 00187* ***Tel*** *06 679 49 69* ***Map*** *2 F2*

Run by two sisters, Le Sorelle has attracted a loyal following, with a second branch in the Lateran. The atmosphere is cosy and the cuisine is creative Mediterranean. Typical dishes include scrambled egg with truffles, cream of porcini mushrooms in a pastry crust, and ravioli with gorgonzola and walnuts.

**PIAZZA DI SPAGNA Casina Valadier** €€€€€

*Piazza Bucarest, 00187* ***Tel*** *06 69 92 20 90* ***Fax*** *06 679 12 80* ***Map*** *2 F1*

This historic palace is housed within the Villa Borghese, a 10-minute walk from the top of the Spanish Steps. The food is creative Italian, served in the dining rooms on two floors. There's also a nice, spacious terrace with spectacular views over the city.

**PIAZZA DI SPAGNA Hassler-Roof Garden, Imagò** €€€€€

*Piazza Trinità dei Monti 6, 00187* ***Tel*** *06 69 93 40* ***Fax*** *06 69 93 47 26* ***Map*** *3 A2*

On the top floor of Hotel Hassler Roma, this restaurant overlooks the Spanish Steps, with a bird's-eye view of the roofs of old Rome. With impeccable service and delicious Italian food with a creative twist, it is ideal for a romantic meal or a moment of pure folly.

**PIAZZA DI SPAGNA Le Jardin de Russie** €€€€€

*Via del Babuino 9, 00187* ***Tel*** *06 32 88 88 70* ***Map*** *2 F1*

Surrounded by beautiful gardens, Le Jardin serves Italian food that does not disappoint. The changing menu offers tantalizing fare such as foie gras with tangerine chutney, fettuccine with porcini mushrooms, John Dory with truffle and endive, and honey with pears in red wine. There's also a children's menu.

**PIAZZA DI SPAGNA Porto Maltese** €€€€€

*Via San Sebastianello 6B, 00187* ***Tel*** *06 678 05 46* ***Map*** *3 A2*

Bustling and friendly by day and mesmerizing by night, Porto Maltese has a ramp entrance curving round a huge aquarium filled with lobster, giant prawns and fish. Dishes include *strozzapreti all'amatriciana di mare* (pasta with smoked fish and tomato), and prices are calculated according to portion weight.

**PIAZZA NAVONA Da Baffetto** €

*Via del Governo Vecchio 114, 00186* ***Tel*** *06 686 16 17* ***Map*** *9 B3*

The most popular pizzeria in town. They don't accept reservations, the queue is always long, and getting a table can be a challenge – when you do, expect to be seated right next to diners you don't know. The atmosphere is loud and lively, and the pizza is thin and light – the way the Romans like it.

**PIAZZA NAVONA Cul de Sac** €€

*Piazza Pasquino 73, 00186* ***Tel*** *06 68 80 10 94* ***Map*** *2 E4, 9 C3*

With 30 years of experience, Cul de Sac is Rome's oldest wine bar. While the wine list offers thousands of wines, from Italy and beyond, the food menu has an equally wide choice. The smoked swordfish, creamed red lentils, sundried tomatoes, chickpea sausages, cheese, *salumi* and patés make for a substantial meal.

**PIAZZA NAVONA Da Luigi** €€€

*Piazza Sforza Cesarini 24, 00186* ***Tel*** *06 686 5946* ***Map*** *9 B3*

Da Luigi's chef offers traditional Roman cooking. The restaurant's crowd-pleasing menu is extremely comprehensive. On offer are various salads and fish *carpaccio* (thin, raw slices), fresh oysters, pastas, grilled fish and meat dishes, in addition to Roman standards such as fried brains and baked lamb.

**PIAZZA NAVONA Il Cantuccio** €€€€

*Corso Rinascimento 71, 00186* ***Tel*** *06 68 80 29 82* ***Map*** *2 E3, 9 C2*

Dazzling at night with candlelight and mirrors, Il Cantuccio is celebrated by the rich and the famous. Try the pasta or the potato soup, flavoured with cod roe and pecorino cheese; continue with baked turbot in a potato and courgette crust; and end with home-made *profiteroles* or Vin Santo with *cantuccini* biscuits. Great service. Open late.

**QUIRINAL Antica Birreria Peroni** €

*Via di San Marcello 19, 00187* ***Tel*** *06 679 53 10* ***Map*** *3 A4, 10 F3*

Crowded at lunchtime, and popular with large groups, this conveniently located Art Nouveau beer house offers good food and generous portions. Cheese and *salumi* platters, salads, pasta, sausages, hamburgers and goulash are typical fare and the Peroni beer is excellent. Service is efficient.

**QUIRINAL Ristorante del Giglio** €€€

*Via Torino 137, 00184* ***Tel*** *06 488 16 06* ***Map*** *3 C3*

Near the Opera House and Via Nazionale, this old-time family restaurant is a local favourite due to the efficient service, good wines and classic cuisine. Try the *fettucine alla Tosca* (with ricotta and fresh tomato), or the delicious turbot, oven-baked with potato and tomato.

**QUIRINAL F.I.S.H.** €€€€

*Via dei Serpenti 16, 00184* ***Tel*** *06 47 82 49 62* ***Map*** *3 B4*

One of Rome's trendiest eateries, F.I.S.H. is run by two Italian brothers who spent several years in Australia. Decked out in black and red, L'Aqua Bar is a fine place for an apéritif with oysters. The Sushi Bar offers Japanese beer with sushi and sashimi and the Grill Lounge prepares temptingly fresh fish, cooked to perfection. Evenings only.

**QUIRINAL Al Presidente** €€€€€

*Via in Arcione 95, 00187* ***Tel*** *06 679 73 42* ***Map*** *3 A3*

One of the city's best restaurants, with wonderful, modern cuisine, elegant decor and fine wine – ideal for intimate chats. Only a short walk from the Trevi Fountain, it also has a great outdoor terrace. Ingredients are expertly researched, with the predominantly fish-inspired menu changing accordingly. Taster menus are available at dinner.

**TERMINI Da Vincenzo** €€€

*Via Castelfidardo 4/6, 00185* ***Tel*** *06 48 45 96* ***Map*** *4 D2*

Fish is the speciality at Da Vincenzo, a timeless neighbourhood restaurant near Termini. Start with the excellent seafood *antipasti* or smoked swordfish. For the pasta course, try *tonnarelli all'astice* (pasta with lobster) and baked sea bass or turbot with potatoes. For meat lovers, there's also roast lamb. Delicious home-made desserts.

**TERMINI Vivendo** €€€€€

*Via V Emanuele Orlando 3, 00185* ***Tel*** *06 47 09 27 36* ***Map*** *3 C3*

One of Rome's top restaurants, Vivendo is stylish, modern and unstuffy. The food is Italian and international – a delicious combination of traditional dishes with unusual ingredients. There is a tasting menu available and also a children's menu. Service is wonderful and the wine list extensive.

**TRASTEVERE Da Lucia** €€

*Vicolo del Mattonato 2b, 00153* ***Tel*** *06 580 3601* ***Map*** *5 B1*

A small family trattoria on one of Trastevere's loveliest alleys, Da Lucia has only a few tables and outside dining in summer. The cuisine is excellent, though with a limited choice of dishes each day. Typical fare includes *alici al limone* (anchovies in lemon juice); pasta with broccoli and stingray; rabbit, tripe or beef in onion.

**TRASTEVERE Ripa 12** €€€

*Via di San Francesco a Ripa 12, 00153* ***Tel*** *06 580 9093* ***Map*** *5 C2*

In southern Trastevere, far from the tourist trail, Ripa 12 serves excellent Mediterranean cuisine, with the focus firmly on fish. Marinated sea bass *carpaccio* (wafer-thin slices) is the house starter, followed by fresh fish of the day or a platter of fried seafood. Very much a locals' favourite.

**TRASTEVERE Antica Pesa** €€€€€

*Via Garibaldi 18, 00153* ***Tel*** *06 580 92 36* ***Map*** *2 D5, 5 B1, 9 B5*

Inside the 17th-century former customs house of the Papal State, Antica Pesa has a pretty patio garden, a popular bowling alley in the 19th century. The excellent cuisine is Mediterranean with a menu that changes according to the whim of the chef and the seasons. Extensive wine list. A delightful place to eat and relax.

**TRASTEVERE Enoteca Ferrara** €€€€€

*Via del Moro 1a, 00153* ***Tel*** *06 58 33 39 20* ***Map*** *2 E5, 9 B5*

Within a 17th-century palazzo, tucked behind Piazza Trilussa, Enoteca Ferrara is situated near Ponte Sisto. This wine bar, shop and restaurant offers an excellent, welcoming service in its five rooms. The cuisine is extremely good and creative, complemented by a wine list with over 1,000 labels.

**TRASTEVERE La Gensola** €€€€€

*Piazza della Gensola 15, 00153* ***Tel*** *06 581 63 12* ***Map*** *6 D1*

An important get-together for artists in the late 1800s, La Gensola is now a stronghold of Sicilian cuisine, based on fresh fish and Mediterranean fragrances. Husband and wife Claudio and Irene give the place an informal feel, and specials include a delicious tuna tartare with horseradish sauce. Well-stocked wine cellar and home-made desserts.

**VATICAN Osteria dell'Angelo** €€

*Via G Bettolo 24–32, 00195* ***Tel*** *06 372 94 70* ***Map*** *1 B1*

Timeless cuisine in an informal and bustling setting. On the menu: *spaghetti cacio e pepe* (pecorino and pepper) or *alla gricia* (pecorino and bacon), anchovy tart, *baccalà* (salt cod) and other staples from the Roman repertoire, followed by Vin Santo and biscuits. Excellent menu at a bargain price. Booking is essential.

**VATICAN Taverna Angelica** €€€

*Piazza A. Capponi 6, 00193* ***Tel*** *06 687 45 14* ***Map*** *1 C2*

Creative regional cuisine is served in this modern restaurant, with specialities including home-made pasta with prawns and pumpkin, potato gnocchi with a seafood sauce, and breast of goose or guinea fowl. Desserts such as citrus fruit cheesecake will tempt even the hardiest souls.

**VATICAN Dal Toscano** €€€€

*Via Germanico 58, 00192* ***Tel*** *06 39 72 57 17* ***Map*** *1 B2*

A popular and ever-reliable restaurant, Dal Toscano has outside tables in summer and a wood-panelled dining room. Expect exquisitely cooked meat dishes and excellent red wines. *Pappardelle sulla lepre* (pasta in a hare sauce), polenta and porcini mushrooms and *bistecca alla Fiorentina* (steak on the bone) are on the menu.

**VATICAN Da Benito e Gilberto** €€€€€

*Via del Falco 19, 00193* ***Tel*** *06 686 77 69* ***Map*** *1 C2*

A small, elegant restaurant with walls hung with paintings. The menu is very good, serving only the freshest of seafood and fish, displayed in a chilled cabinet. Dishes are simply but lovingly prepared, the wine list is good and the service is extremely cordial. Booking recommended. Closed Sun & Mon.

**Key to Price Guide** *see p606* **Key to Symbols** *see back cover flap*

**VATICAN La Pergola** €€€€€

*Via A Cadlolo 101, 00136* **Tel** *06 35 09 21 52* **Fax** *06 35 09 21 34*

A taxi ride away, in the hills above the Vatican, La Pergola is generally considered Rome's finest restaurant, run by celebrated German chef Heinz Beck. The superlative food, served on a wonderfully panoramic roof terrace, humbles even the sternest critics. There is an excellent tasting menu and the wines harmonize perfectly with the food.

**VIA VENETO Taverna Flavia** €€€

*Via Flavia 9, 00187* **Tel** *06 474 52 14* **Map** *3 C2*

Off Via XX Settembre, the old and celebrated Taverna Flavia evokes nostalgia, with autographed photos of American film stars covering its walls. Elizabeth Taylor and Richard Burton regularly ate here while filming *Cleopatra*. The food remains excellent and highly sought after, with dishes named after famous muses.

**VIA VENETO La Terrazza, Hotel Eden** €€€€€

*Via Ludovisi 49, 00187* **Tel** *06 47 81 27 52* **Fax** *06 481 44 73* **Map** *3 B2*

With a breathtaking view of the city, La Terrazza is undoubtedly one of Rome's most alluring restaurants and, to some people, worth the elevated prices. Service is top-notch and the young chef combines international cuisine with Mediterranean flair. There is also a tasting menu with wine included, available in the evenings.

**VIA VENETO Mirabelle** €€€€€

*Via di Porta Pinciana 14, 00187* **Tel** *06 42 16 88 38* **Map** *3 B1*

On the seventh floor of an elegant hotel, Mirabelle has a gorgeous panoramic terrace, a pleasing dining room and expert service. The well-compiled wine list complements memorable cuisine such as risotto with saffron and asparagus, duck with orange, or *spigola al vapore* (steamed sea bass). Book ahead.

**VILLA BORGHESE Caffè delle Arti** €€€

*Via A Gramsci 73, 00197* **Tel** *06 32 65 12 36*

A serene place to pause and rest a while, this café-restaurant is located in the grounds of the Museum of Modern Art, at the top of Villa Borghese. The delightful dining rooms and gardens are not only perfect for a coffee or an apéritif, they also have good light snacks and daily specials available all day. Good Sunday brunch.

**VILLA BORGHESE Duke's** €€€€

*Viale Parioli 200, 00197* **Tel** *06 8066 2455*

Attracting crowds of Rome's beautiful people every night, Duke's is a bar for an apéritif with nibbles and a late-night venue, as well as an excellent restaurant. The cooking is decidedly Californian fusion, with influences from the Orient, Mexico and the Mediterranean. Service is very professional and the outside terrace is arresting.

**VILLA BORGHESE Baby** €€€€€

*Via Ulisse Aldrovandi 15, 00197* **Tel** *06 321 61 26*

Baby is run by the renowned husband-and-wife team behind Don Alfonso (one of Italy's finest restaurants) on the Amalfi Coast. Outstanding Neapolitan-inspired cuisine is served in a delightful dining room and terrace at one of Rome's top hotels, the Hotel Aldrovandi Palace.

## LAZIO

**ALATRI La Rosetta** €

*Via del Duomo 39, 03011* **Tel** *0775 43 45 68*

A quiet restaurant near the 6th-century BC acropolis. The menu changes with the seasons, but rest assured all the pasta is made fresh daily on the premises. Try the house lasagne, or the speciality *maccheroni alla ciociara* (pasta in a sauce of wine, herbs, bacon and meat).

**AMATRICE Roma** €

*Via dei Bastioni 29, 02012* **Tel** *0746 82 57 77*

Since 1896, this hotel/restaurant has been producing perhaps the best rendition of this mountain town's famed signature dish: *spaghetti all'amatriciana* (spaghetti tossed with tomatoes, spicy red pepper and bacon). Terrace dining in the warmer months.

**BRACCIANO Vino e Camino** €€€

*Piazza Mazzini 11, 00062* **Tel** *06 99 80 34 33*

On the main square in town, with a view of the mighty Castello Odescalchi, from the outside tables, this restaurant offers a mix of regional and other Italian traditions. The chef makes good use of the adjacent lake for original dishes such as spelt risotto with perch and gorgonzola, though there are also many meat and vegetable dishes.

**CERVETERI Da Fiore** €€

*Via San Paolo 4, Località Procoio di Ceri, 00052* **Tel** *06 99 20 72 75*

A simple country trattoria where the specialities include home-cooked pastas with ragout, *penne al padellaccio* (pasta quills with sausage, Parma ham, sun-dried tomatoes, porcini and cheese), rabbit and grilled meats. The *bruschette* (toasted bread with various toppings) and pizzas are also good.

**FRASCATI Domus Park Hotel Taberna** €€€

*Via Tuscolana km. 18, 00044* ***Tel*** *06 940 85 87*

These bright, modern dining rooms surrounded by greenery are located on the road from Rome to Frascati. They provide a good choice of food and wines, including the local Frascati. The restaurant specializes in fish; classic seafood antipasti can be followed by *linguine riviera* (with a sauce of swordfish, sea bass and seasonal vegetables).

**FRASCATI Nuova Enoteca Frascati** €€€€

*Via Diaz 42, 00044* ***Tel*** *06 941 74 49*

More than 400 wines accompany an excellent range of seafood dishes at this wine bar/restaurant. The kitchen produces what it calls "new country", a mix of tradition and innovation resulting in an antipasto of assorted raw fish, and boiled *astice* (lobster) with tomatoes, potatoes and courgettes.

**GAETA Antico Vico** €€€€€

*Vico del Cavallo 2, 04024* ***Tel*** *0771 46 51 16*

What used to be a stable is now a fine fish restaurant serving classic dishes and inventive creations like the squid carpaccio or the ravioli filled with crustacean meat. The garden is perfect for hot summer nights, and the location is picturesque and convenient.

**NETTUNO Cacciatori dal 1896** €€€€

*Via Matteotti 27, 00048* ***Tel*** *06 988 03 30*

This large, rustically furnished restaurant is set in the storerooms of the 17th-century Colonna family palazzo, with a veranda overlooking the port and the sea. Fish is caught daily, and the dishes are taken from regional recipes of the early 1900s. Their signature dish is *minestra di pesce* (fish soup).

**OSTIA ANTICA Il Monumento** €€€

*Piazza Umberto I 8, 00119* ***Tel*** *06 565 00 21*

This restaurant at Rome's main beach resort, near its ancient port, features a fish-based menu. The house speciality, *spaghetti al Monumento*, is served in a seafood sauce. For a second course, the most popular dish is their patented *manzancolle al coccio*, a local breed of shrimp cooked in cognac.

**SPERLONGA Gli Archi** €€€€€

*Via Ottaviano 17, 04029* ***Tel*** *0771 54 83 00*

In a picturesque street in the heart of Sperlonga, this restaurant offers a romantic setting, especially when dining alfresco, with tables in a little square surrounded by arches. Gli Archi is a must for seafood lovers, with fresh fish specialities like home-made fusilli with courgettes (zucchini) and mixed seafood, or the classic spaghetti with clams.

**TIVOLI Villa Esedra** €€

*Via di Villa Adriana 51, 00010* ***Tel*** *0774 53 47 16*

The menu at this fish specialist is typical of the region, featuring fresh *antipasti* such as *insalata ai frutti di mare* (seafood salad), followed by *linguine all'astice vivo* (noodles with local lobster) or gnocchi with radicchio and walnuts, and grilled catch of the day. In the evening, and all day Sunday, they fire up a pizza oven.

**TIVOLI Adriano** €€€€

*Largo Yourcenar 2, 00010* ***Tel*** *0774 38 22 35* ***Fax*** *0774 53 51 22*

A charming restaurant set in a garden, perfectly placed for visits to the Villa Adriana and other Tivoli delights. The cuisine is traditional and wines are from local vineyards. Fettucine with aromatic herbs, *scrigno di venere* (oven-baked pasta with mushrooms and ragù) and filleted rabbit casserole are typical dishes. Booking is recommended.

**TIVOLI Avec 55** €€€€

*Via D Giuliani 55, 00019* ***Tel*** *0774 31 72 43*

Tradition revisited and modern interiors define this pleasant restaurant hidden away in Tivoli's historic centre. The menu features ethnic fusion dishes and a number of classics with creative twists. Careful ingredient selection is one of the main priorities. Desserts include a hot chocolate soufflé with vanilla from Madagascar. Superb wine list.

**TREVIGNANO La Grotta Azzurra** €€€

*Piazza Vittorio Emanuele 18, 00069* ***Tel*** *069 99 94 20*

Located in the central square of Trevignano, with spectacular views of the lake, this family-run restaurant serves delectable regional cuisine, featuring in particular freshwater fish prepared in a variety of ways. Outdoor tables in the garden make alfresco dining especially pleasant during the warm months.

**TUSCANIA Palazzo Ranucci** €€€

*Via della Torretta 8, 01017* ***Tel*** *0761 44 50 67*

Housed in a 15th-century building, this restaurant is renowned for its creative take on regional dishes. The speciality, *agnolotti di patate e manzo* (potato- and beef-filled ravioli), makes for a hearty starter; follow it with wild boar or fillet steak with rosemary. Great views from the terrace. Booking recommended. Closed Sat & Sun dinner.

**VITERBO Il Richiastro** €€

*Via della Marrocca 18, 01100* ***Tel*** *0761 22 80 09*

Set in a lovely 13th-century palazzo, Il Richiastro serves food based on medieval peasant recipes. Try the soup of *farro* (spelt), beans, mushrooms and endive, followed by sweet and sour meats, though the menu changes from week to week. Only open Friday through to lunch on Sunday; closed in the summer.

**Key to Price Guide** *see p606* **Key to Symbols** *see back cover flap*

**VITERBO Porta Romana** €€

*Via della Bontà 12, 01100* ***Tel*** *0761 30 71 18*

A simple trattoria with a wide range of classic dishes. The *ombrichelli all'amatriciana* (hand-rolled spaghetti in a bacon and tomato sauce) are excellent. In the winter, try *pignataccia*, a Viterbo speciality of mixed veal, beef and pork cooked on a slow fire with celery, carrots and potatoes.

## NAPLES AND CAMPANIA

**AGROPOLI Il Ceppo** €€€€

*Via Madonna del Carmine 31, 84043* ***Tel*** *0974 84 30 36*

A classic Mediterranean restaurant serving a wonderful range of local fish and home-made pastas and pizzas. The house speciality is *tagliolini* (noodles) with prawns, courgette flowers and clams, or try the spaghetti with seafood, prawns in lemon sauce or the *zuppa di pesce* (fish soup).

**AMALFI Il Tarì** €€

*Via Pietro Capuano 9–11, 84011* ***Tel*** *089 87 18 32*

Perennially popular, this crowded trattoria on Amalfi's main street serves fabulous pizzas such as the *pizza à la Tarì* (mozzarella, Parma ham, Parmesan cheese and rocket), good pasta dishes, and decent meat and seafood main courses, the best of which is *pesce al cartoccio* (the catch of the day baked in foil).

**AMALFI La Marinella** €€

*Via Lungomare dei Cavalieri 1, 84011* ***Tel*** *089 87 10 43*

A lively, friendly restaurant overlooking the Amalfi Coast just two metres from the sea. Much fish is served, as well as traditional local specialities such as *scialatelli ai frutti di mare* (home-made pasta with seafood and crustaceans). Open for lunch only, except in high season.

**AMALFI Eolo** €€€€

*Via Pantalone Comite 3, 84011* ***Tel*** *089 87 12 41*

Sited on the beach at the end of the seaside promenade, this restaurant's menu changes fortnightly to make use of seasonal ingredients. There are just ten tables, plus another three on the terrace, so booking is advisable. Try the *filetto di sarago* (smoked bluegill grilled with an herb sauce). Closed Jan, Feb.

**AMALFI La Caravella** €€€€€

*Via Matteo Camera 12, 84011* ***Tel*** *089 87 10 29*

Frequented by stars like Andy Warhol in its 1960s heyday, La Caravella offers intimate whitewashed spaces with colourful ceramics and painted ceilings. Pasta specialities share the menu with traditional and innovative seafood dishes. Superb wine list and cheese selection from the surrounding mountains. Closed Tue; early Jan–mid-Feb, Nov.

**AVELLINO La Maschera** €€€

*Rampa San Modestino 1, 83100* ***Tel*** *0825 376 03*

The red-and-white decor is peppered with literary quotes and striking artworks. The cuisine is based on seasonal produce from the surrounding mountains. Dishes include pasta with a sauce of salty *baccalà* (salt cod) and tender broccoli. Ask kindly, and they'll show you around the wondrous cheese and wine cellars. Closed 2 wks Jan.

**BENEVENTO Da Gino e Pina** €€€

*Via dell'Università 1, 82100* ***Tel*** *0824 249 47*

In the heart of the historic centre, this restaurant offers a menu evenly split between meat and fish dishes. Try the *cardone* (a type of thistle), the *pampanelle alla Gino e Pina* (asparagus and shellfish pasta), *filetto di maiale con patate* (pork fillet with potatoes), *zuppa di pesce* (fish soup), or a classic pizza. Excellent wine list.

**CAPRI La Savardina da Eduardo** €€€

*Via Lo Capo 8, 80073* ***Tel*** *081 837 63 00*

This is one of the most traditional restaurants on Capri, with an outdoor pergola, orange trees, sea views and tasty regional specialities such as *ravioli alla caprese* (cheese ravioli in a tomato and mozzarella sauce), *linguini all'Eduardo* (noodles with anchovies and capers) and stewed rabbit.

**CAPRI Da Gioia** €€€€

*Marina Piccola, 80073* ***Tel*** *081 837 7702*

This magical restaurant on a platform with lots of boardwalk tables over the lapping waves of Marina Piccola is perfect for a fishy lunch of the freshest *linguine ai frutti di mare* (thin pasta ribbons with shellfish and tomatoes) or *risotto alla pescatora* (seafood risotto). Check for the latest opening times – Da Gioia is often closed in winter.

**CAPRI La Pergola** €€€€

*Traversa Lo Palazzo 2, 80073* ***Tel*** *081 837 74 14*

A pleasant family atmosphere, large terrace with sweeping sea views, and delicious food bring many regular customers here. Lemons figure prominently, including in the *ravioli al limone* (pasta parcels stuffed with cheese, lemon and lemon-cream sauce) and the home-made lemon tart. Good fresh fish, too.

**CAPRI Quisi del Grand Hotel Quisisana**  €€€€€

*Via Camerelle 2, 80073* ***Tel*** *081 83 70 788* ***Fax*** *081 837 60 80*

The atmosphere is elegant at this restaurant ensconced in Capri's premiere hotel, and the seasonally changing menu is delightful. Try the succulent roast duck with peaches, the home-made pastas like spaghetti with seafood, turbot with lemongrass and dates, quail with peas and pistachios, or the *fritto misto* (mixed fried seafood platter).

**CAPRI (ANACAPRI) Il Solitario** €€€

*Via G Orlandi 96, 80071* ***Tel*** *081 837 13 82*

Laid-back charm can be enjoyed in this old tavern-turned-restaurant, with its rustic rooms and leafy pergola-covered garden strewn with colourful statues depicting the seasons. Simple delights like *pizza bianca* (white pizza) and *ravioli capresi* (cheesy pasta pockets) go down well with an international clientele. Closed Wed and in winter.

**CASERTA Le Colonne** €€€€

*Viale G Douhet 7, 81100* ***Tel*** *0823 46 74 94*

In an elegant house with gardens near the royal palace, this family-run restaurant serves typical regional cuisine with innovative touches. The meat, which is used for the tender-grilled steaks, comes not from cows, but from the local buffalo (which normally is reserved for making mozzarella milk). The best of Campania's produce is used.

**ISCHIA Da Peppina di Renato** €€€

*Via Montecorvo 42, Località Forio, 80075* ***Tel*** *081 99 83 12*

A simple, rustic trattoria on a hillside, with a large terrace offering candlelit panoramas of Citara Bay, serving simple fare such as *coniglio alla cacciatora* (hunters' style rabbit), *pasta e fagioli* (pasta and bean soup with sausage and lemon), grilled meats and fish, and pizzas cooked in a wood-burning oven.

**ISCHIA La Conchiglia** €€€

*Via N. Sauro 6/Via Chiaia delle Rose 3, Località Sant'Angelo, 80070* ***Tel*** *081 99 92 70*

A big, old pink building in the heart of a fishing village, with fresh seafood served under a barrel vault or out on a skinny patio six feet above the waves, with vistas down the coastline. The house specialities are *linguine ai frutti di mare* (noodles with seafood) and the *frittura* (fry-up) of squid and jumbo shrimp.

**ISCHIA Miramare** €€€€€

*Via Pontano 5, 80077* ***Tel*** *081 99 13 33*

A swanky hotel restaurant with outside terrace tables by the shore giving dramatic views of the Castello Aragonese. The cooking shows a lightness of touch and imaginative combinations of Ischian staples, including rabbit served *al pistacchio con polenta e paté di fegatini* (with a pistachio sauce, polenta and liver pâté). Closed Nov–Mar.

**ISCHIA Umberto a Mare** €€€€€

*Via Soccorso 2, Forio d'Ischia, 80075* ***Tel*** *081 99 71 71*

A historic restaurant on Forio's Soccorso promontory, affording stupendous sea views from the picture windows of the elegant dining room and the small terrace. Sophisticated creations include *ricciola* (amberjack) fish served with basil, artichokes and lemon. It's a wonderful dining spot at sunset – book early for the best table. Closed Nov–Mar.

**MONTEPERTUSO (NEAR POSITANO) La Tagliata** €€

*Via Tagliata 22, 84017* ***Tel*** *089 87 58 72*

True Amalfitan hospitality and a hearty menu can be found here. Picture windows are swung open in summer, with breathtaking views towards the Li Galli. Choose a tasting menu for lots of tapas-like plates of veg and meat, but be sure to save room for their *semifreddi* (creamy cakes). Phone in advance, and they'll pick you up from Positano.

**NAPLES Da Ettore** €

*Via Santa Lucia 56, 80132* ***Tel*** *081 76 404 98*

Unpretentious popular neighbourhood trattoria and pizzeria serving typical Neapolitan cuisine. Good pizzas and excellent seafood pasta with mussels or clams. Also sample the *parmigiana di melanzane* (a baked casserole of aubergines/eggplant, mozzarella and tomatoes). Excellent buffalo mozzarella antipasto.

**NAPLES Pizzeria Brandi** €

*Salita S. Anna di Palazzo 1–2/Via Chiaia, 80132* ***Tel*** *081 41 69 28*

This historic pizzeria (established 1780) lays claim to having invented the classic pizza Margherita in 1889 to honour a visit by Queen Margherita (the red tomatoes, white mozzarella and green basil representing the colours of the then-new Italian flag). Good pasta dishes as well.

**NAPLES Sorbillo** €

*Via dei Tribunali 32, 80138* ***Tel*** *081 44 66 43*

Opened in 1935, this family-run pizzeria does a brisk trade with groups, students and tourists. Disco lights spin around the walls – it can get raucous, but it is fun nevertheless. The superb pizzas are named after family members and spill over the large plates. Decent house wine and bottled beer are served in plastic cups. Closed Sun.

**NAPLES Amici Miei** €€€

*Via Monte di Dio 78, 80132* ***Tel*** *081 764 60 63*

A classic menu, though it concentrates mainly on meat dishes (a rarity in fish-oriented Naples). Excellent pasta with vegetables and pulses and main courses, especially the char-grilled meats and the *braciola di maiale al ragù* (pork chop smothered in sauce with pine nuts). Cosy atmosphere and an excellent wine list.

**Key to Price Guide** *see p606* **Key to Symbols** *see back cover flap*

**NAPLES Hosteria Toledo** €€€

*Vico Giardinetti a Toledo 78A, 80133* ***Tel*** *081 42 12 57*

This traditional Slow Food *osteria* in the heart of the downtown Quartieri Spagnoli district has been turning out classic Neapolitan meat and fish specialities since 1951. Try the *maccheroni al ragù, frittura di paranza* (fried seafood), and *zucchine alla scapece* (similar to gazpacho, but made with courgettes).

**NAPLES Umberto** €€€

*Via Alabardieri 30–31, 80121* ***Tel*** *081 41 85 55*

This venerable *pizzeria-ristorante* was opened in 1916 by the Di Porzio family; it is now run by the charming English-speaking descendant Massimo, president of the Associazione Verace Pizza Napoletana, which promotes the Neapolitan pizza. Delicious pizzas are served alongside classic pasta, meat and fish dishes and salads. Closed Mon.

**NAPLES La Cantinella** €€€€€

*Via Cuma 42, 80132* ***Tel*** *081 764 86 84* ***Fax*** *081 764 87 69*

One of Naples's most famous restaurants, this place has a distinctly colonial feel. Diners are attracted by the sea views, the impeccable service and a reputation for carefully and successfully prepared regional and international cuisine based around seafood and traditional dishes.

**NAPLES Rosiello** €€€€€

*Via Santo Strato 10, 80123* ***Tel*** *081 769 12 88*

Book a table on the terrace at this lofty perch in the leafy Posillipo district. Rosiello offers a special dining experience with views of the bay and Vesuvius. Classic Neapolitan fare includes *frittura di paranza* (fried seafood medley) and *salsiccia con friarelli* (sausage with tasty local brassica). Closed 2 wks Aug.

**NERANO Taverna del Capitano** €€€€€

*Piazza delle Sirene 10, Località Marina del Cantone 10, 80061* ***Tel*** *081 808 10 28*

In an old fisherman's house on the beach – with an outdoor terrace for better sea views – this restaurant serves excellent regional food with some creative touches. Sample the *cornetti di pasta con gamberi* (pasta filled with shrimp and covered in seafood sauce) and *millefeuille di San Pietro* (John Dory in filo). Closed early Jan–early Mar.

**PAESTUM La Pergola** €€

*Via Magna Grecia 51, Capaccio Scalo, 84047* ***Tel*** *0828 72 33 77*

Innovative regional cuisine that uses seasonal produce in a rustic restaurant 3 km (2 miles) from the ruins of Paestum. The house speciality is *susciello*, a soup of wild asparagus, wild onions, scrambled egg and aromatic herbs. Afterwards, try the fried fish with artichokes. Serves wonderful local buffalo mozzarella. Closed Mon (not in summer).

**POMPEII Il Principe** €€€€€

*Piazza B. Longo 1, 80045* ***Tel*** *081 850 55 66*

This airy, refined and elegant restaurant with a seasonally changing menu is close to the excavations. The cuisine is based on fish, including fish-filled ravioli and turbot with vegetables. Dishes may be inspired by 17th-century Neapolitan recipes, ancient Roman spices, or desserts pictured in Pompeii frescoes.

**POSITANO Lo Guarracino** €€

*Via Positanesi d'America 12, 84017* ***Tel*** *089 87 59 74*

A five-minute walk along a pathway hung off the cliffside leads to this restaurant's panoramic terrace overlooking a quiet bay and outlying islands. They bake excellent pizzas. Also try: *linguine ai ricci di mare* (noodles with sea urchin), grilled *pesce spada* (swordfish), and veal escalopes with lemon.

**POSITANO La Sponda** €€€€€

*Via Cristoforo Colombo 30, 84017* ***Tel*** *089 87 50 66*

A sumptuous restaurant in one of Italy's most elegant hotels, where guests are treated like wealthy family friends. A tempting range of modern and traditional dishes based on fresh fish and seasonal ingredients is on offer. Try *gragnano paccheri* (large pasta tubes with anchovies, roasted peppers and basil).

**PROCIDA Caracalè** €€€

*Via Marina Corricella 62, 80079* ***Tel*** *081 896 91 92*

The name of this seafood restaurant on the quayside of Procida's picturesque Corricella harbour derives from the Greek for "beautiful spot". Lots of fresh fish and vegetables are washed down with quality Campanian wines. Open weekends only in low season. Closed Tue; Nov–Christmas Day.

**RAVELLO Villa Maria** €€€€€

*Via Santa Chiara 2, 84010* ***Tel*** *089 85 72 55*

An elegant house converted into a hotel/restaurant. Book a table on the terrace overlooking the Dragon Valley and order the *trittico*, a sampler trio of the chef's daily specials, perhaps including *soffatini* (crêpes with cheese and spinach) or seafood-stuffed ravioli in a red clam sauce. Fresh fish and local game.

**SALERNO Pizzeria Vicolo della Neve** €

*Vicolo della Neve 24, 84121* ***Tel*** *089 22 57 05*

A pizzeria in the historic centre that – in addition to excellent pizzas and *calzoni* (folded pizzas) – also serves a range of dishes such as *pasta e fagioli* (pasta with beans), *baccalà* (salt cod) casserole, and sausages with broccoli. Like most traditional pizzerias, it's open for dinner only.

### SANT'AGATA SUI DUE GOLFI Don Alfonso 1890 €€€€€

*Corso Sant'Agata 11–13, 80064* ***Tel*** *081 87 80 026* ***Fax*** *081 53 30 226*

One of Italy's top Michelin-starred restaurants, set in elegant gardens. The modern Mediterranean dishes include seafood and fish specialities and delicious desserts. This place is so devoted to creating the best cuisine possible that the family bought a farm so they could grow their own fresh ingredients. Formal dress at dinner.

### SORRENTO Ristorante della Favorita O'Parrucchiano €€

*Corso Italia 71–73, 80067* ***Tel*** *081 878 13 21* ***Fax*** *081 532 40 35*

This century-old restaurant features an open-air terrace under a mass of vines, lemon and orange trees. It is popular with locals, tourists and celebrities alike, largely thanks to the excellent Sorrentino cooking: *scialatielli ai frutti di mare* (pasta with seafood) and steak with peppercorns are two of the highlights.

### SORRENTO Il Buco €€€€€

*Il Rampa Marina Piccola 5 (Piazza Sant'Antonino), 80067* ***Tel*** *081 878 23 54*

Pressed cotton tablecloths, fresh flowers and vaulted stone ceilings of the old *cantine* (cellars) make this a refined and atmospheric place. Alongside *pescato del giorno* (catch of the day), there are plates of lamb flavoured with thyme, and braised beef with tomatoes and oregano salsa. Closed Wed; Jan–mid-Feb.

## ABRUZZO, MOLISE, AND PUGLIA

### ALBEROBELLO La Cantina €€

*Vico Lippolis 9/Corso Vittorio Emanuele, 70011* ***Tel*** *080 432 34 73*

This small trattoria of just 32 place settings under stony vaults has occupied a basement room just off the main street since 1958. The dishes are rigorously traditional Apulian cuisine, such as the *orecchiette* ("little ear" pasta discs) served in a tomato sauce spiked with salty ricotta cheese and turnip greens.

### ALBEROBELLO Trullo d'Oro €€€

*Via Felice Cavallotti 27, 70011* ***Tel*** *080 432 18 20*

Dine inside a *trullo* (the typical pointy house of this area) on excellent regional cuisine. Sample three main courses with the *assaggini dello chef*, small servings of spaghetti with rocket and fresh tomatoes, *orecchiette in ragù* (pasta in a meat sauce topped with herbed bread balls) and fava bean purée with endive.

### ALBEROBELLO Il Poeta Contadino €€€€

*Via Indipendenza 21, 70011* ***Tel*** *080 432 19 17*

An elegant restaurant with stony walls and a piano in the corner. The excellent service matches the high standard of both food and wine. The cuisine makes imaginative use of fresh local ingredients, offering both fish and meat dishes on a menu that refers to the poetry of each course.

### BARI Terranima €€

*Via Putignani 213–215, 70123* ***Tel*** *080 521 97 25*

Popular trattoria serving a seasonal menu of typical Apulian fare that changes every two weeks and balances seafood and meat dishes. Try the *orecchiette* (pasta discs) with monkfish, or an *arista di maiale in salsa di agrumi* (roast pork flavoured with citrus). Friendly staff and pleasant setting.

### BARI Perbacco €€€

*Via Francesco Saverio Abbrescia 99, 70121* ***Tel*** *080 558 01 79*

Dark wood furniture and exposed stone walls lend this place a relaxed, rustic feel. Over 1,000 different wines are stacked in the cellar. Creative regional cooking includes ravioli filled with a tangy combo of *baccalà* (salt cod) and pink grapefruit, and an oh-so-sweet *torrone* (nougat) cake. Closed Sat lunch, Sun; between Jul–Aug.

### BARI Bacco €€€€€

*Corso Vittorio Emanuele II 126, 70122* ***Tel*** *080 527 58 71*

Bacco has a nationwide reputation for its modern twists on Puglian classics. Designer lighting, colourful artworks and an impressive wine cellar lend it an air of sophistication. Standouts include *orecchiette con cime di rapa* (pasta with brassica shoots), seafood *stuzzichini* (tapas bites) and Bari-style *tiella* (deep dish pie). Closed Sun dinner, Mon; Aug.

### GALLIPOLI Il Bastione €€€€€

*Via Sauro Nazario, 28, 73014* ***Tel*** *0833 26 38 36*

Twinkling lights from the lighthouse make this terrace restaurant on Gallipoli's fortifications an evocative dining venue. Large picture windows offer dramatic sea views. Well-crafted, traditional Gallipoli seafood dishes like *tubettini al sugo di pescatrice* (tube pasta with fishy sauce) can be found on the menu. Closed Mon; Jan.

### ISOLE TREMITI Al Gabbiano €€€

*Piazza Belvedere San Domino, 71040* ***Tel*** *0882 46 34 10*

The food at this island terrace restaurant is based on the best fish from the sea, just a few metres away. Try the traditional fish soup and fresh fish roasted in a case of salt. Also good are the *troccoli gabbiano al mare* (home-made pasta with mussels, shrimp, clams, calamari and prawns).

**Key to Price Guide** *see p606* **Key to Symbols** *see back cover flap*

**L'AQUILA Ernesto** €€

*Piazza Palazzo 22, 67100* ***Tel*** *0862 210 94*

A peaceful, sophisticated place with a courtyard for summer dinners. The menu is a tasty, creative mix based on typical Abruzzese mountain cuisine. Try the *sagnarelle alla pastora* (ricotta gnocchi tossed with ham, mushrooms, ricotta, truffles and pecorino cheese).

**LECCE Guido e Figli** €

*Via XXV Luglio 14, 73100* ***Tel*** *0832 30 58 68*

There are two choices for dining at this place just off Lecce's main square: in the restaurant, under stone vaults, or – paying half the price for the same Apulian dishes – at the *tavola calda* (self-service) branch in the back. You can take your food to an outdoor table and watch the evening parade of pedestrians stroll by.

**LECCE Alle Due Corti** €€

*Corte dei Giugni 1/Via Leonardo Prato 42, 73100* ***Tel*** *0832 24 22 23* ***Fax*** *0832 39 78 65*

The elegance of the dining rooms and service belie the low prices and excellent, traditional Salentino dishes. Try the *turcinieddhi* (toasted baby goat's heart, liver and lungs), *ciceri e tria* (flat pasta, half-fried/half-boiled, with chickpeas), and *pezzetti te cavallu* (chunks of horse meat in a spicy tomato sauce). Great for those with an adventurous palate.

**LOCOROTONDO Trattoria Centro Storico** €€€

*Via Eroi di Dogali 6, 70010* ***Tel*** *080 431 54 73*

Friendly restaurant in the centre of this whitewashed village. Their own-label wine goes well with the traditional Apulian dishes such as *pennette della casa* (pasta quills in a tomato sauce with spicy chilli peppers, onion and ham), and the *portafoglio* (lamb chop stuffed with cheese, parsley and herbs). Closed Wed.

**MANFREDONIA Coppolarossa** €€

*Via dei Celestini 13, 71043* ***Tel*** *0884 58 25 22*

Youthful atmosphere and old-fashioned decor (painted ceramic plates on stuccoed walls) at this restaurant serving traditional seafood dishes. Try the house speciality, *troccoli ai frutti di mare* (hand-rolled macaroni with seafood), or the *grigliata di pesce* (mixed grill of giant shrimp, fish and squid).

**MARTINA FRANCA Ritrovo degli Amici** €€€€

*Corso Messapia 8, 74015* ***Tel*** *080 483 92 49*

Understated, elegant decor is matched by expertly crafted dishes at this excellent restaurant. Locals and visitors often plump for the famous *crespelle* (savoury folded pancakes) served with tomatoes and aubergine. There's roast lamb for carnivores and delicious *dolci*, such as chocolate and orange cake. Closed Sun dinner, Mon; Jan–Feb.

**OSTUNI Osteria del Tempo Perso** €€€

*Via Gateano Tanzarella Vitale 47, 72017* ***Tel*** *0831 30 48 19*

In the heart of a stunningly whitewashed hilltown, this *osteria* has farm implements scattered over the walls of one room, while the other cave-like room is roughly carved from the bare rock. The cooking is regional, using the freshest of local ingredients, and the service is impeccable. Good local wine list.

**OTRANTO Vecchia Otranto** €€€€

*Corso Garibaldi 96, 73028* ***Tel*** *0836 80 15 75*

Good marine and other regional specialities in this traditional trattoria in the stony heart of town include *pasta with ricci di mare* (with sea urchin) and *zuppa di pesce all'otrantina* (a rich fish soup). Also try the rice with potatoes, the *cozze gratinate* (mussels au gratin) and the *anguilla allo spiedo* (spit-roasted eels).

**OVINDOLI Il Pozzo** €€

*Via Monumento dell'Alpino 5, 67046* ***Tel*** *0863 71 01 91*

Wonderful mountain setting for this atmospheric restaurant in the historic centre of town. The food is traditional and robust – though with a lighter, modern touch – and the dishes are made using local products, especially *zafferano* (saffron) and wild mushrooms. Closed Wed.

**POLIGNANO AL MARE Grotta Palazzese** €€€€€

*Via Narciso 59, 70044* ***Tel*** *080 424 06 77* ***Fax*** *080 424 07 67*

A massive cliffside cavern above the crashing waters of the Adriatic was turned into a formal dining room for tourists on the Grand Tour in the 1700s. It is a spectacular location. Although the menu concentrates on fish, there are plenty of meat choices available as well. Closed Nov–Apr.

**SULMONA Rigoletto** €€

*Via Stazione Introdacqua 46/Strada dei Confetti Pellino, 67039* ***Tel*** *0864 555 29*

A short walk from the centre of town. Home-made pastas are served with beans, *scamorza* (soft smoked cheese), rabbit and truffles. Particularly good are the *ravioli ripieni di scamorza e zafferano* (pasta parcels stuffed with cheese and saffron) and *agnello al forno* (oven-roasted lamb).

**TARANTO Da Mimmo** €€

*Via C. Giovinazzi 18, 74100* ***Tel*** *099 459 37 33*

Locals have been known to wait patiently for an outdoor table at Mimmo's place. The pizza chef is given to singing Elvis and Neapolitan folk songs while he works and his pizzas are small enough to leave room for a second course of fried seafood or meatballs or a veal roll stewed in tomato sauce.

### TARANTO Canale €€€

*Discesa Vasto, 74100* ***Tel*** *099 476 42 01*

Housed in bright modern rooms near the old fish market, Canale offers classic starters that include raw seafood salad and fried seasonal vegetables. Hop to the mains for the most satisfying briny bites, such as the catch of the day, which is often served with potatoes and artichokes. Small, excellent wine list. Closed Tue; 2 wks Nov.

### TARANTO Al Faro Masseria Saracena €€€€

*Via della Pineta 3/5, Strada Vicinale Fonte delle Citrezze 4000, 74100* ***Tel*** *099 471 44 44*

A whitewashed 18th-century farmhouse in the suburbs, with a grassy garden filled with tables and a view across the water to the city on the far side of the bay. The menu is fish-based, using locally caught fish and seafood for *antipasti*, soups, risotto and grills.

### TERMOLI Z' Bass €€€€

*Via Oberdan 8, 86039* ***Tel*** *0875 70 67 03*

This friendly, welcoming trattoria offers a high level of cuisine featuring fresh, seasonal ingredients and bread and desserts made on the premises. House specialities include a succulent *zuppa di pesce* (fish soup). There is an extensive wine list.

### TRANI Torrente Antico €€€€€

*Via Fusco 3, 70059* ***Tel*** *0883 48 79 11*

Exquisite, lightly prepared dishes based on traditional regional cuisine with modern touches. Try the *raviolo di pesce* (a giant pasta parcel stuffed with chopped sea bass and dressed with a mix of seafood and crustaceans). The wine list is also impressive.

### VIESTE Il Trabucco dell'Hotel Pizzomunno €€€€

*Lungomare Enrico Mattei, Km. 1, 71019* ***Tel*** *0884 70 87 41*

Surrounded by gardens and very close to the sea, this resort hotel has outside dining under bougainvillea by the pool and fine regional and Italian cuisine with some creative touches. The dishes are light and tasty. Try the *troccoli alla garganica* (pasta with shrimp, ricotta and courgettes).

### VILLETTA BARREA Trattoria del Pescatore €

*Via B. Virgilio 175, 67030* ***Tel*** *0864 891 52* ***Fax*** *0864 892 55*

A simple, family-run riverside trattoria in the Abruzzo National Park. Regional dishes include *trota al vino bianco* (trout in white wine), home-made *chitarrini ai gamberi di fiume* ("guitar string" pasta with crayfish), and *zuppa di orati e fagioli* (bean soup with a wild mountain green similar to spinach).

## BASILICATA & CALABRIA

### ACQUAFREDDA, MARATEA, BASILICATA Villa Cheta Elite €€€

*Via Timpone 46, località Acquafredda, 85046* ***Tel*** *0973 87 81 34* ***Fax*** *0973 87 81 35*

A romantic hotel/restaurant in an Art Nouveau-style villa on a sea-facing clifftop, with summer dining on a terrace. Fish dishes predominate, accompanied by excellent local wines from up-and-coming producers. *Involtini di sogliola* (stuffed rolled-up lemon sole) and spaghetti with sardines are some of the highlights. Delicious desserts.

### BIVONGI, CALABRIA La Vecchia Miniera €

*Contrada Perrocalli, 89040* ***Tel*** *0964 73 18 69* ***Fax*** *0964 73 18 69*

Just outside Bivongi, near the beautiful Cascate di Marmorico, this trattoria offers excellent local cuisine in a timeless setting. Specialities include local *salumi* (cured meats), handmade pasta with kid sauce or sardines, mountain trout or grilled pork, chicken and rabbit. Good house wine and tiramisù.

### CASTROVILLARI (PARCO POLLINO), CALABRIA La Locanda di Alia €€€€

*Contrada Letticelle 55, 87012* ***Tel/Fax*** *0981 463 70*

One of Calabria's finest restaurants, combining traditional recipes, creative flair and seasonal ingredients. Among the best dishes are the *panzerotti* (pastry parcels) with herbs, ricotta and aniseed, *carne n'cartate* (meat with honey and chilli peppers), swordfish with red onions, and potato tart. Excellent wine list and locally brewed beer.

### COSENZA, CALABRIA L'Arco Vecchio €€

*Piazza Archi di Ciaccio 21, 87100* ***Tel/Fax*** *0984 725 64*

Regional cuisine inside an elegant old palazzo with a beautiful pergola terrace. Try the *fiori di zucca* (fried courgette flowers), the *parmigiana di melanzane* (aubergine/eggplant flan) or the local *lagane* (pasta with chickpeas). Follow with pork chop with apple or roast kid with fried potatoes. Excellent wine list.

### GERACE, CALABRIA La Tavernetta €

*Strada Provinciale Locri-Antonimina 112, 89040* ***Tel*** *0964 35 60 20*

Located near the Terme di Antonimina, 4 km (2.5 miles) from the historic centre of Gerace, this restaurant has a cosy, pleasant interior, full of old-fashioned charm. Among the specialities are the *strozzapreti* (pasta) with sausage and wild fennel, and grilled lamb or boar meats. It is a popular place, so it is wise to book in advance.

**Key to Price Guide** *see p606* **Key to Symbols** *see back cover flap*

### MARATEA, BASILICATA Taverna Rovita €€€€

*Via Rovita 13, 85046* ***Tel/Fax*** *0973 876 588*

Down a pretty alleyway, this old-fashioned place with white walls and tiled floors serves home-made pastas, fresh fish, seafood and local meat dishes, prepared with seasonal vegetables and herbs. Try the pasta with chickpeas and mussels or the *bocconotto Rovita* (shortcrust pastry with sausage).

### MARINA DI GIOIOSA JONICA, CALABRIA Gambero Rosso €€€€

*Via Montezemolo 65, 89046* ***Tel*** *0964 41 58 06* ***Fax*** *0964 41 55 81*

This smart restaurant offers generous portions of the freshest fish and seafood, and a good wine list. Specialities include marinated fish *antipasti*, ricotta and vegetable or swordfish parcels, seafood pasta or risotto, *orecchiette* pasta baked in paper, and fried mixed fish, cod and langoustine. Set menus are also available.

### MATERA, BASILICATA Il Terrazzino sui Sassi €€

*Vicolo San Giuseppe 7, 75100* ***Tel/Fax*** *0835 33 25 03*

In the heart of the Sassi, with a wonderful panoramic terrace, this restaurant serves local cuisine, such as chickpea soup, grilled lamb, roast meat, lamb stew and *orecchiette al tegamino* (pasta with sausage, mozzarella and tomato baked in a terracotta dish). Try the *strazzate* for dessert. Good local wines.

### MATERA, BASILICATA Don Matteo €€€€

*Via San Biagio 12, 75100* ***Tel*** *0835 34 41 45*

Don Matteo is housed in atmospherically lit cave surroundings, with views of the Sassi, deep in the heart of Matera. Expect fancy creations like *millefoglie di melanzane* (aubergine and crunchy filo pastry) and pork with rich Malvasia wine and ginger salsa. The excellent *menu di degustazione* (tasting menu) is well worth considering. Closed Mon.

### MELFI, BASILICATA Novecento P €€€

*Via Pertini, 85025* ***Tel/Fax*** *0972 23 74 70*

An old-fashioned restaurant serving well-prepared regional cuisine, using the finest of local ingredients. Classic fare includes *agnello a cutturidde* (a local lamb dish), grilled meats and a *tegami* (terracotta dish) of baked vegetables and mushrooms. Delicious chocolate and chestnut mousse to finish. Superior wine list.

### REGGIO DI CALABRIA, CALABRIA Baylik €€€

*Vico Leone 1, 89100* ***Tel*** *0965 486 24* ***Fax*** *0965 455 25*

Turkish for "house of fish", the popular Baylik was established in 1950. The modern, minimalist decor is offset by the traditional hand in the kitchen. On the menu is a choice of seasonal starters and fresh fish. In season try the *carbonara di pesce* (fish carbonara) or swordfish and melon. Panoramic views over the Straits of Messina.

### ROSSANO, CALABRIA Paridò €€

*Via dei Normanni, 87067* ***Tel*** *0983 29 07 31*

Traditional local recipes reinterpreted with a creative twist make up the menu at this restaurant. Among the specialities are fish dishes such as cuttlefish stew, swordfish with red Tropea onions, fish soup and grilled fish with citrus fruits, as well as fried ricotta and aubergine "meat balls". Excellent selection of southern Italian wines.

### SCILLA, CALABRIA La Grotta Azzurra U'Bais €€€€

*Via Cristofero Colombo, 89058* ***Tel*** *0965 75 48 89* ***Fax*** *0965 70 42 98*

A wonderful setting on the beach where, according to legend, Ulysses came ashore. The freshest of fish and seafood is on offer here, cooked simply and to perfection. Pasta with shellfish or sea urchins; grilled swordfish, fillet of *agugliа imperiale* (a local fish) and fish rissoles in a tomato sauce. For dessert, try the lemon sorbet in prosecco.

### TROPEA, CALABRIA Pimm's €€€

*Corso Vittorio Emanuele 60, 88038* ***Tel*** *0963 66 61 05*

An elegant choice in the heart of the historic centre. Start with seafood *crostini* (toasted bread) or smoked swordfish; then move on to pasta with sea urchins or sardines, or the house speciality: prawns, tuna roe and Tropea's famous red onions. There is also delicious squid or swordfish with capers from Lipari.

### VENOSA, BASILICATA Il Grifo €€

*Via Fornaci 21, 85029* ***Tel/Fax*** *0972 353 46*

This charming trattoria beside the castle was established by a locally born chef after many years working in Rome. The decor is cool and romantic, with ancient stone walls, and there's a pleasant summer terrace. Traditional Lucanian cuisine includes fish and meat dishes, as well as pizzas, accompanied by an excellent Aglianico del Vulture wine.

## SICILY

### AEOLIAN ISLANDS – LIPARI Filippino €€€

*Piazza del Municipio, 98055* ***Tel*** *090 981 10 02*

Some of the best dining on Lipari since 1910. An essentially Sicilian, sea-based menu includes swordfish, home-made macaroni, and some excellent cassata Siciliana. Specialities include *trecette delle Eolie* (pasta with capers, tomatoes, basil, almonds, garlic, mint, anchovies and pecorino).

**AEOLIAN ISLANDS – LIPARI La Ginestra** €€€€€

*Via Stradale Pianoconte 10, Pianoconte, 98055* ***Tel*** *090 982 22 85*

Located on a hillside just outside town on the road from Lipari, this restaurant offers garden-terrace seating. It's wonderfully empty during lunch, when most people are in town or at the beach, but book ahead for dinner. Try the tagliolini with swordfish roe, lobster-stuffed ravioli, sweet-and-sour wild rabbit, or the grilled lamb.

**AEOLIAN ISLANDS – PANAREA Pina** €€€€€

*Via San Pietro 3, 98050* ***Tel*** *090 98 30 32*

Popular with visiting VIPs, Pina has white columns and exposed stone walls in the large dining rooms. Book a table near the large windows or on the leafy, covered terrace, and expect fresh seafood creations like *fritto misto di mare* (fried fishy bites) and delicious desserts like *cassata Siciliana*. Closed at various times during the winter months.

**AGRIGENTO Al Porticciolo** €€€

*Lungomare Falcone Borsellino 28, 92100* ***Tel*** *0922 42 36 31*

A popular seafood restaurant with a covered terrace along the seaside promenade. Traditional plates include *spaghetti bottarga e tonno* (with roe and tuna), *scampi grigliati* (grilled langoustine) and *risotto ai gamberoni e asparagi* (with prawn and asparagus). The superb wine list includes several regional favourites. Closed Tue.

**AGRIGENTO Kókalos** €€€

*Via Cavalieri Magazzeni 3, 92100* ***Tel*** *0922 60 64 27*

A friendly rustic trattoria with an extensive terrace facing the Temple of Juno. Try the fettuccine in orange sauce, fresh grilled fish, the *involtini valle dei templi* (thin sheets of veal wrapped around a mix of aubergine, cheese and sundried tomatoes), and the almond parfait; Sicily is famous for its almonds.

**BAGHERIA Don Ciccio** €€

*Via del Cavaliere 87c, 90011* ***Tel*** *091 93 24 42*

This town-centre trattoria concentrates on regional specialities and traditional Bagherese cooking. Look out for pasta served with sardines or in a *ragù di pesce spada* (swordfish sauce), grilled fish, *gamberi ripieni* (roasted stuffed shrimp), and *involtini di pesce spada* (swordfish rolls).

**CATANIA Osteria Antica Marina** €€

*Via Pardo 29, 95121* ***Tel*** *095 34 81 97*

Very popular trattoria in a corner of the daily fish market. Service is fast and furious, and the cooking – based on seafood, of course – is exquisite. Try the classic *spaghetti coi ricci* (with sea urchin) or *al nero di seppia* (stained black with cuttlefish ink). Booking is advisable.

**CATANIA Ambasciata del Mare** €€€

*Piazza Duomo 6, 92121* ***Tel*** *095 34 10 03*

Near the Duomo, in the heart of the *centro storico*, is this restaurant with uncluttered, elegant interiors, warm walls and immaculately made tables. Classic dishes with a dash of creativity include *frittura di paranza* (medley of lightly fried seafood with a wonderfully crispy batter) and *linguine ai ricci di mare* (with sea urchins). Closed Mon; Sep.

**CEFALÙ L'Antica Corte** €€€

*Ct Pepe 7, 90015* ***Tel*** *0921 42 32 28*

A trattoria-pizzeria in an old courtyard in the historic centre of town. The cuisine is local with influences from almost-forgotten Sicilian recipes. Try the *cous cous di pesce* (fish couscous), *involtini di pesce spada* (swordfish rolls), and home-made *pasta con le sarde* (with sardines). Pizza is available at dinner only.

**CEFALÙ La Brace** €€€

*Via 25 Novembre 10, 90015* ***Tel*** *0921 42 35 70*

The current owner of Cefalù's oldest restaurant is Dutch, which may explain the creative spin on Sicilian cuisine, including *involtini di melanzane* (aubergine/eggplant wrapped around tagliatelle and ricotta then baked in tomato sauce). Long waits (for a table and for service) are worth it for the wonderful desserts. Closed Mon dinner.

**ENNA Ariston** €€

*Via Roma 353, 94100* ***Tel*** *0935 260 38*

In the heart of Enna, this restaurant offers a selection of seafood dishes as well as non-fish specialities such as *cavatti* (a fresh, home-made pasta) tossed with tomatoes and hot chilli flakes, stuffed lamb, a soup of fava beans and peas, and fried stuffed olives, as well as pizzas. Closed Sun dinner.

**ERICE Monte San Giuliano** €€

*Vicolo San Rocco 7, 91016* ***Tel*** *0923 86 95 95*

Located on a quiet courtyard beyond a medieval gate in the centre of town. The menu is based on Sicilian traditions and includes *busati di San Giuliano* (a local speciality of fresh pasta with tomatoes, garlic, basil, almonds and olive oil), pasta with sardines, and couscous with fish.

**ERICE Osteria di Venere** €€€

*Via Roma 6, 91016* ***Tel*** *0923 86 93 62*

A delightful and refined restaurant in an attractive 17th-century building. The menu is basically Sicilian and Mediterranean, and stand-outs include *casarecce alla Venere* (fresh home-made pasta tossed with swordfish, tomatoes, aubergine and mint), as well as grilled catch of the day.

**Key to Price Guide** *see p606* **Key to Symbols** *see back cover flap*

**MARSALA Mothia** €

*Contrada Ettore Inversa 13, 91025* ***Tel*** *0923 74 52 55* ***Fax*** *3487 22 05 39*

Near the salt pans north of Marsala. The simple, delicious cooking balances fish and meat on set-price menus with home-made bread, pastas, pizzas, desserts and cakes. The tagliatelle with lobster sauce is particularly good, as is *la busiata alla trapanese* (pasta tossed with raw tomatoes and basil).

**MARSALA Garibaldi** €€

*Piazza Addolorata 36, 91025* ***Tel*** *0923 95 30 06*

Garibaldi offers four intimate colour-themed dining rooms with interesting prints and artworks, as well as alfresco dining. The menu has seafood staples (roasted, fried and grilled mullet and swordfish) and meaty options like veal cooked in Marsala wine. Seasonal fruits and *cassata* for dessert. Closed Sat lunch, Sun dinner; 2 wks in winter.

**MESSINA Piero** €€€€

*Via Ghibellina 121, 98123* ***Tel*** *090 640 93 54*

An old rustic *trattoria* turned elegant restaurant in central Messina. Check the display of the day's fresh *pescato* (catch) at the front to see what seafood delights are available. The *frittura di paranza* (crispy fried seafood with a wedge of lemon) is popular with the locals. Closed Sun; 1 wk Aug.

**PALERMO Trattoria Temptation** €€

*Via Torretta 94, Località Sferracavallo, 90148* ***Tel*** *091 691 11 04*

This trattoria with a sea view near one of Palermo's major beach resort areas (around the headland just north of the city), offers an all-inclusive menu of seafood, including a succulent array of starters The pasta with aubergines (eggplant) and fried fish is particularly recommended.

**PALERMO Antica Focacceria San Francesco** €€€

*Via Alessandro Paternostro 58/Piazza San Francesco d'Assisi, 90133* ***Tel*** *091 32 02 64*

The most historic, atmospheric and inexpensive spot in the city centre for a quick lunch. It has been open since 1834 and features an airy interior furnished in Art Nouveau style. Pastas and pizzas are available, but stick with the classic split focaccia flatbread stuffed with cheese, meat and vegetables, and have the classic *cannoli* for dessert.

**PALERMO Santandrea** €€€

*Piazza Sant'Andrea 4, 90133* ***Tel*** *091 33 49 99*

Elegant family-run restaurant of candlelit tables on a quiet little piazza in the heart of the city. The waiter recites whatever innovative Sicilian dishes the chef has come up with based on the morning market's bounty, perhaps spaghetti with lobster and fish roe, or sweet-and-sour tuna with mint and onions. Dinner only, closed Sun.

**PALERMO Trattoria Sympaty** €€€€

*Via Piano Gallo 18, Località Mondello, 90151* ***Tel*** *091 45 44 70*

The dining room has good views over the bay of Mondello – Palermo's most popular beach resort – and the menu is, appropriately, almost exclusively fish-based. Try the *fettuccini all'aragosta* (noodles with lobster), *spaghetti alle sarde* (with sardines), *ricci* (sea urchins), octopus or squid.

**PALERMO La Scuderia** €€€€€

*Viale del Fante 9, 90146* ***Tel*** *091 52 03 23* ***Fax*** *091 52 04 67*

This elegant restaurant set in the Parco della Favorita, on the north edge of Palermo, sticks to traditional Sicilian cuisine, carefully and deliciously prepared. Do not miss the *merluzzetti alla ghiotta* (whiting stewed with capers, potatoes, saffron and cherry tomatoes).

**RAGUSA La Ciotola** €€€

*Via Archimede 23, 97100* ***Tel*** *0932 22 89 44*

This elegant, modern restaurant in the city centre serves well-prepared Sicilian specialities like *maccheroni alla ciotola* (home-made pasta served with a sauce of aubergine, mushrooms and tomatoes). The chef is often invited to prepare local dishes at national culinary events.

**SCIACCA Hostaria del Vicolo** €€€€

*Vicolo Sammartino 10, 92019* ***Tel*** *0925 230 71*

In the centre of town. The menu is Sicilian with dishes such as *spaghetti alla bottarga* (with fish roe, mint and pine nuts), *casareccie con cacio, gamberi e ciliegino* (home-made pasta with sheep's cheese, shrimp and cherry tomatoes), and *coda di rospo con patate* (angler fish tail with potatoes).

**SIRACUSA Don Camillo** €€€€

*Via della Maestranza 96, 96100* ***Tel*** *0931 671 33*

Located in a 19th-century palazzo in picturesque Ortigia (the historic island centre of Siracusa), this seafood restaurant features swordfish in many of the specials, as well as simple tuna steaks. For a starter, try the *spaghetti della sirena* (spaghetti tossed with shrimp and fresh sea urchin).

**SIRACUSA Des Etrangers Et Miramare** €€€€€

*Passeggio Adorno 10–12, 96100* ***Tel*** *0931 31 91 00*

This swanky hotel restaurant has a large rooftop garden offering stunning views of Siracusa's port and beyond. Elaborate dishes combine fresh seafood and Sicilian produce with innovative twists. The quality wine list and refined atmosphere come at a price, though – this is the place for a special occasion or credit-card splurge.

### TAORMINA Al Duomo €€€

*Via degli Ebrei 11, 98039* ***Tel*** *0942 62 56 56*

A typical Sicilian restaurant with an outdoor terrace. Dishes make good use of Sicily's twin fish specialities: tuna and swordfish. But the chef's signature dish is *pasta ca 'nocca* (home-made macaroni with fresh anchovies, breadcrumbs and wild fennel), followed by grilled *agnello* (lamb).

### TAORMINA La Giara €€€€€

*Via La Floresta Livia 1, 98039* ***Tel*** *0942 233 60*

A pretty restaurant of columns and arches with beautiful views over the bay from tables out on the terrace. Try the lobster cocktail, the *petto d'oca affumicato* (smoked goose breast), ravioli with aubergine (eggplant), and *pesce alla eoliana* (baked grouper with potatoes, tomatoes and capers). It also has a piano bar/club. Closed lunch.

### TRAPANI Tra... Pani & Vini €

*Via Carolina 42, 91100* ***Tel*** *0923 276 25*

No-nonsense *trattoria* in a characterful area near Trapani's seafront. The amiable service and great-value food make it a real find. Start with a selection of Sicilian cheeses and cured meats, and perhaps the hearty *zuppa del giorno* (soup of the day). There is also a good choice of honestly priced wines and home-made desserts.

### TRAPANI Cantina Siciliana €€

*Via Giudecca, 32, 91100* ***Tel*** *0923 286 73*

In the bustling port area and old Jewish ghetto, this place attracts with the finest *cucina marinara* (seafood cooking). The menu depends on the day's catch, but expect crustaceans of various sizes, anchovies, red mullet, mackerel and swordfish, all served with seasonal vegetables, pasta and couscous side dishes.

## SARDINIA

### ALGHERO Al Tuguri €€€

*Via Maiorca 113, 07041* ***Tel*** *079 97 67 72*

A little gem of a restaurant with unpretentious decor and a cosy atmosphere. Excellent Mediterranean nouvelle cuisine combining Catalan and Sardinian recipes, like *crème catalan*. Recommended is the spaghetti with saffron and pecorino. Advance booking is a must, as the dining room is very small. Closed Dec–Feb.

### ALGHERO Il Pavone €€€

*Piazza Sulis 3–4, 07041* ***Tel*** *079 97 95 84*

A smart restaurant on the edge of the old town, overlooking the lively Piazza Sulis. Seasonal Mediterranean and innovative Sardinian cuisine: fresh figs with anchovies and chilli, squid ink pasta with smoked ricotta, lemon sorbet with spicy chocolate. Fish dishes are the speciality. Service is good.

### ALGHERO/FERTILIA Sa Mandra €€€

*Strada Aeroporto Civile 21–22, 07041* ***Tel*** *079 99 91 50*

A classic Sardinian *agriturismo*. The setting is rustic but the food is fit for a king. The fixed menu of traditional pastoral fare includes a selection of pecorino cheeses, hams and salamis, a variety of home-made pastas, roast suckling pig and lamb with fresh vegetables, followed by home-baked Sardinian sweets. The value is amazing.

### BOSA Mannu da Giancarlo e Rita €€€

*Viale Alghero 28, 08013* ***Tel*** *0785 375 07* ***Fax*** *0785 37 53 08*

A smart, modern restaurant in a family-run hotel, offering good local fish specialities. Bosa is famous for fresh lobster, which they serve here in a variety of sauces and styles. They also do meat dishes, roast suckling pig, and gnocchi with lamb. The restaurant prides itself on the freshness of the produce it uses.

### CAGLIARI Lillicu €€

*Via Sardegna 78, 09214* ***Tel*** *070 65 29 70*

Opened in the 1940s, this family-run restaurant is a Cagliari institution. Sit at one of the long refectory tables and let the amiable waiters bring heaped seafood plates of *frittura* (fried seafood) and *arselle* (tiny, sweet clams). Lillicu is a magical spot for chatting to locals and sharing a glass of superb house wine. Closed Sun.

### CAGLIARI Antica Hostaria €€€

*Via Cavour 60, 09124* ***Tel*** *070 66 58 70*

A comfortable, atmospheric restaurant in an old building on the backstreets of the Marina district. The cuisine is good, based on traditional and local produce. Seasonal specialities include risotto with radicchio and *pappardelle Antica Hostaria* (home-made pasta ribbons with shrimp and pesto). They have a good wine list.

### CAGLIARI Luigi Pomata €€€

*Viale Regina Margherita 18, 9214* ***Tel*** *070 67 20 58*

Sardinian chef Luigi brings Genoese influences to this sophisticated venture near the port. Enjoy fresh sushi as a starter, followed by handmade pasta dishes, and grilled meat and fish for *secondi*. Inventive twists include red tuna tartare with green apple, celery and lemon purée. There is a great-value two-course business lunch deal. Closed Sun.

**Key to Price Guide** *see p606* **Key to Symbols** *see back cover flap*

### CAGLIARI Dal Corsaro €€€€€

*Viale Regina Margherita 28, 09124* ***Tel*** *070 66 43 18* ***Fax*** *070 65 34 39*

An elegant restaurant with a pleasant atmosphere and refined service, in which to enjoy regional dishes such as fish ravioli, original creations (dentex with aubergine/eggplant and basil or fillet steak *all'Angelu Ruju*), and some Cagliari classics. Vegetarian dishes also available. A good wine list.

### CALASETTA Da Pasqualino €€€

*Via Regina Margherita 85, 09011* ***Tel/Fax*** *0781 884 73*

Delicious fish, particularly tuna-based, specialities are served in this simple and relaxed family trattoria in the old quarter of the town. The menu includes fish soups, *bottarga* (tuna roe), *musciame* (sun-dried tuna), spaghetti with fresh tuna, a local version of couscous, and lobster. The wines are local.

### CARLOFORTE Al Tonno di Corsa €€€€

*Via G Marconi 47, 09014* ***Tel*** *0781 85 51 06*

On a hill behind the seafront in the old town, this restaurant offers excellent local cuisine with some Tunisian influences, seafood *antipasti*, couscous and fresh pasta with basil and marjoram or seafood sauce, and a variety of tuna dishes, including tuna stomach with potatoes. The decor is characterful.

### OLBIA Gallura €€€€€

*Corso Umberto 145, 07126* ***Tel*** *0789 246 48*

Out of Gallura's wood-fired oven come the tastiest dishes made using only local, seasonal ingredients. Mussels and vegetable soup are menu mainstays. The *frue del Gennargentu* (fresh feta-like mountain goat's cheese) with tomatoes and *pane carasau* (Sardinian crisp bread) encapsulates Sardinia's simple pleasures. Closed Mon; Christmas.

### OLIENA CK €€€

*Corso M L King 2–4, 08025* ***Tel*** *0784 28 80 24*

This family-run restaurant (pronounced "chee kappa") in a pale pink villa in the historic town centre offers local cuisine and uses a wood oven. Home-made pasta (including *busa*, traditionally made using wire) with walnut sauce, roast meats, a fine selection of cheeses and wines.

### OLIENA Su Gologone €€€€

*Località Su Gologone, 08025* ***Tel*** *0784 28 75 12* ***Fax*** *0784 28 76 68*

Surrounded by greenery, top hotel Su Gologone is only 12 km (7 miles) from Nuoro. Its restaurant is known for its meat dishes (roast suckling pig, lamb and goat), *pane frattau* (Sardinian flatbread baked with stock, cheese, tomatoes and egg), ravioli, *malloredus* (Sardinian pasta often in a tomato sauce with sausage) and *seadas* (fried pastries).

### ORISTANO Craf da Banana €€€

*Via de Castro 34, 09170* ***Tel*** *0783 706 69*

A very popular restaurant in central Oristano, renowned for the best, locally-farmed meat on the island. It serves everything from ox to wild boar – or a selection from the grill if you have trouble deciding. Try the famous *sebadas* – cheese filled pastry, fried and topped with wildflower honey. Reservations recommended on weekends. Closed Sun.

### PORTO CERVO Gianni Pedrinelli €€€€€

*Località Piccolo Pevero, 07020* ***Tel*** *0789 924 36*

The regional menu here offers a wealth of fish dishes, such as lobster pasta and salt fish, but the house specialities are *porcettu allo spiedo* (spit-roast suckling pig) and the leg of lamb. The restaurant combines style and tradition in a large airy whitewashed room with arched doorway, wooden beamed ceilings and tiled floors. Closed Nov–Feb.

### PORTO ROTONDO Da Giovannino €€€€€

*Piazza Quadrata 1, 07026* ***Tel*** *0789 352 80*

A sophisticated restaurant decorated to the finest detail and with a lovely garden. It is popular with Italian politicians and media types, who dine on expensive but delicious Mediterranean specialities, such as scampi sushi with lemon juice, swordfish with tomatoes and capers, and grilled squid. Superb wine list.

### PORTOSCUSO La Ghinghetta €€€€€

*Via Cavour 26, Località Sa Caletta, 09010* ***Tel*** *0781 50 81 43*

Small and elegant, set in a charming fishing village facing the island of San Pietro. The almost exclusively fish-based menu adds a twist to local specialities. Fish and prawn tartare with quails' eggs and caviar, smoked fish, lobster terrine, ice cream with caramelized fruit all feature on the menu. Book ahead.

### SASSARI Il Cenacolo €€€

*Via Ozieri 2, 07100* ***Tel*** *079 23 62 31*

The traditional menu here offers the very best of sea and land regional specialities according to the season: there are mushrooms in autumn, seafood in summer and vegetables all year round. An elegant restaurant with a pleasant atmosphere in the centre of the city.

### SASSARI Liberty €€€€

*Piazza N Sauro 3 (corso Vittorio Emanuele), 07100* ***Tel/Fax*** *079 23 63 61*

Elegant and refined, this restaurant excels on all fronts. The food is fish-based. Start with the *antipasto Liberty*, a delicious array of fish and seafood, and follow with *gnocchetti camustia* (smoked ricotta and calamari dumplings), spaghetti with lobster, or oven-baked fish with potatoes and artichokes. Excellent wine list.

# SHOPPING IN ITALY

Italy is known for its quality designer goods, ranging from chic clothing and sleek cars to stylish household items. There is a strong tradition of craftsmanship, often from family-run businesses, and there are numerous markets selling regional specialities. Apart from the town markets, it is not a country for bargains, but the joys of window shopping will offer plenty of compensation. If you come from outside the European Union, you may be able to claim back the 10 per cent IVA tax (VAT). Make sure you leave time at your departure airport to fulfil all administrative requirements.

Fresh vegetables on display at a Venetian market stall

## OPENING HOURS

Opening times for shops are usually 9:30am–1pm and around 3:30–8pm, Tuesday to Saturday and Monday afternoons. However, shopkeepers are increasingly using more flexible hours. There are few department stores, but most large towns will have a Standa, Upim, Coin or Rinascente. These stores are often open non-stop *(orario continuato)* from 9am–8pm, Monday to Saturday. Music and bookshops sometimes stay open after 8pm and on Sundays.

## FOOD SHOPS

Even though there are supermarkets throughout Italy, the specialist shops, although more expensive, are still the most interesting way to shop. A *forno* has the best bread and a *macellaio* has the finest meat (go to a *norcineria* for pork products). Vegetables are freshest from market stalls or the *fruttivendolo*. You can buy cakes at the *pasticceria*, milk at the *latteria*, and pasta, ham, cheese and general foods at the often impressively stocked *alimentari*. Here you can also buy wine, but for a wider choice, head for the *enoteca*, *vineria* or *vinaio*, where you can sometimes taste the wine before purchasing.

## MARKETS

All towns have regional weekly markets. Large towns will have several small daily markets followed by a weekly flea market, usually on Sunday. In this guide the main market days are listed under each town. Traders set up at 5am and start to clear away at about 1:30pm. Food is sold by the *etto* (100 grams) and the *chilo* (kilo) *(see p665)*, or in numbers (two onions, etc). Food stalls selling seasonal products generally have fresher and cheaper produce than the shops. Bargaining is not usual when buying food, but it is worth asking for a discount *(sconto)* for clothes.

## SEASONAL PRODUCE

To make the most of Italian food, try to buy and eat what is in season. Grapes and mushrooms are best in autumn, whereas spring is the season for asparagus and strawberries. In winter, vegetables such as Roman artichokes, cauliflower and broccoli are at their best, as are lemons from Amalfi and Sicilian blood oranges. Summer is the time for plums, pears and cherries, as well as courgettes, aubergines, tomatoes and melon.

## CLOTHES AND DESIGNER SHOPS

Italy is renowned worldwide for its fashion industry. Milan is the fashion capital and Via Monte Napoleone, in the city centre, is lined with designer boutiques. All large towns will have a selection

Souvenir shop in Ostuni, near Brindisi, Puglia

of designer shops, usually situated near each other. Less expensive clothes are available in markets and many high-street shops, where the styles tend to be more conventional. Italy is also famous for leather shoes and bags, the prices of which tend to be reasonable.

Sales *(saldi)* are held in summer and winter. Second-hand shops can be expensive, but the quality and condition of the clothes are usually very good. Larger markets have stalls piled high with used clothes. Rummage through and you will often find bargains.

**Colourful shop display of leather handbags in Florence**

## JEWELLERY AND ANTIQUE SHOPS

Glitzy gold jewellery is very popular in Italy and every *gioielleria* (jewellery shop) will have a wide selection. For more unusual items, try the *bigiotteria* or artisan shops *(oreficeria)*. Antique stores like *Antichità* and *Antiquariato* sell furniture and ornaments of varying quality and prices. You will rarely find bargains in Italy, except perhaps at the *Fiere dell'Antiquariato* (antique fairs), held throughout the year all over the country.

## INTERIOR DESIGN AND HOUSEHOLD WARES

Interior design is another Italian sector where top names demand extravagant prices, with many shops concentrating on modern, high-tech styles.

**An elegant designer clothes boutique in Treviso**

There are household shops in cities and towns throughout the country. Italian kitchenware is particularly striking, with its stainless steel and copper pots, pans and utensils. For the lowest prices, avoid the tourist shops and, if possible, buy directly from the manufacturer. Less expensive items include the characteristic brown espresso and cappuccino cups sold in all markets.

## REGIONAL SPECIALITIES

Many of Italy's regional specialities are world famous: Parma ham, Chianti wine, olive oil and *grappa*. Regional sweets, including the Sienese *panforte* and Sicilian marzipan, are also well-known, as are cheeses such as Gorgonzola from Lombardy and Parmesan from Emilia-Romagna. Traditional crafts are still practised in Italy and range from delicate lacework and glassware in the Veneto to leatherwork, jewellery and marbled paper in Florence. Italian ceramics include elaborate Tuscan pottery, hand-painted dishes around Amalfi and De Simone's stylized designer plates from Sicily.

**Display of decorative glazed pottery from Tuscany**

## SIZE CHART

For Australian sizes follow the British and American conversions.

**Women's dresses, coats and skirts**

| | | | | | | | | |
|---|---|---|---|---|---|---|---|---|
| Italian | 38 | 40 | 42 | 44 | 46 | 48 | 50 | |
| British | 8 | 10 | 12 | 14 | 16 | 18 | 20 | |
| American | 6 | 8 | 10 | 12 | 14 | 16 | 18 | |

**Women's shoes**

| | | | | | | |
|---|---|---|---|---|---|---|
| Italian | 36 | 37 | 38 | 39 | 40 | 41 |
| British | 3 | 4 | 5 | 6 | 7 | 8 |
| American | 5 | 6 | 7 | 8 | 9 | 10 |

**Men's suits**

| | | | | | | | | |
|---|---|---|---|---|---|---|---|---|
| Italian | 44 | 46 | 48 | 50 | 52 | 54 | 56 | 58 (size) |
| British | 34 | 36 | 38 | 40 | 42 | 44 | 46 | 48 (inches) |
| American | 34 | 36 | 38 | 40 | 42 | 44 | 46 | 48 (inches) |

**Men's shirts** (collar size)

| | | | | | | | | |
|---|---|---|---|---|---|---|---|---|
| Italian | 36 | 38 | 39 | 41 | 42 | 43 | 44 | 45 (cm) |
| British | 14 | 15 | 15½ | 16 | 16½ | 17 | 17½ | 18 (inches) |
| American | 14 | 15 | 15½ | 16 | 16½ | 17 | 17½ | 18 (inches) |

**Men's shoes**

| | | | | | | | | |
|---|---|---|---|---|---|---|---|---|
| Italian | 39 | 40 | 41 | 42 | 43 | 44 | 45 | 46 |
| British | 6 | 7 | 7½ | 8 | 9 | 10 | 11 | 12 |
| American | 7 | 7½ | 8 | 8½ | 9½ | 10½ | 11 | 11½ |

# ENTERTAINMENT IN ITALY

Italians exude strong national pride and passion about every aspect of their cultural heritage. One of Europe's key centres of culture since Roman times, Italy was the cradle of the Renaissance, and it is known today as the home of opera and a mixed bag of regional styles of folk music. The country holds one of the most acclaimed international film festivals and every town boasts a *teatro*, an elaborate classical venue with mixed programmes incorporating every aspect of classic and traditional culture. Add to this the many street festivals and fairs, often in celebration of food, wine and the *dolce vita*, and you will never have a dull moment.

## PRACTICAL INFORMATION

Most venues have booking facilities online or a booking line to call. However, major events and most opera performances tend to sell out well in advance, so it is wise to book through specialist ticket companies such as **Liaisons Abroad** that may still have availability when the venue itself has sold out.

If you wish to find out what's on in Italy during your stay, check the Italian tourism website (www.italiantourism.com) or pick up a copy of *Dove*, a monthly publication about culture, travel and gastronomy that also highlights the month's events in Rome and Milan.

*Il Corriere della Sera*, Italy's oldest daily, contains sections on events and culture; its Vivimilano website (www.corriere.it/vivimilano) is a mine of information on events taking place in the fashion capital. Another website (www.romaturismo.it) offers an excellent service for Rome.

Tourist information offices *(see p665)* will also provide information on programmes, events and venues, as will the **Italian State Tourist Board**. Few Italian venues provide easy access for people with restricted mobility. The situation improves a little in the summer, when many events are held outside.

## OPERA AND CLASSICAL MUSIC

Italy has some of the world's most beautiful and historic opera houses. Venice's **La Fenice**, destroyed by fire in 1996, has been restored to its former splendour, and **Teatro alla Scala** *(see p193)* in Milan also underwent a major renovation. In addition to the original building, there is now an extra theatre, **Teatro degli Arcimboldi**, allowing the Scala to host more performances.

Verona hosts a summer season of opera and classical music in the outdoor **Arena di Verona** *(see p147)*, while Rome's venues include the open-air **Baths of Caracalla** *(see p437)*, the breathtaking Renzo Piano-designed auditorium **Parco della Musica** and the **Teatro dell'Opera**.

In May and June, Florence's **Maggio Musicale** *(see p66)* is packed with opera, ballet and classical performances.

The opera festival in Verona attracts huge crowds to the Roman arena

Poster advertising the Venice Film Festival

## ROCK, JAZZ AND CONTEMPORARY MUSIC

Large concerts tend to be held in classic theatres or in sports stadiums. The **Arena di Verona** hosts big names in summer, as does the **Stadio Olimpico** in Rome. In Milan, the **Forum di Assago** sports stadium is a popular venue. Tickets for concerts are sometimes sold in record shops.

World-class jazz performers gather annually in Perugia for the **Umbria Jazz** festival in July. The website provides booking details and information.

## THEATRE AND BALLET

Italy has the highest concentration of traditional theatres in Europe, offering a mixture of theatre, ballet and classical music all under one roof. All theatres also hold ballet performances, mainly by international touring troupes. The **Scala**'s ballet company has gained international renown. Both tradition and innovation can be seen at the international festival of ballet that takes place at Genoa's **Teatro Carlo Felice** in July.

## CINEMA

One of the highlights of the cinema year is the **Venice Film Festival** *(see p67),* which takes place in August to September. The Rome International Festival of Cinema *(see p68)* also draws major film stars. A smaller International Film Festival *(see p67)* is held in Taormina, Sicily, while Florence has the Festa dei Popoli *(see p68)* in winter.

**A thrilling moment in the Sienese Palio race held in Piazza del Campo**

## REGIONAL DANCE, MUSIC AND FESTIVALS

Seasonal festivals are either religious, relating to patron saints, or food-orientated. The best known is *Carnevale* (literally "farewell to meat") *(see p69),* which celebrates the end of winter and introduces Lent. Venice holds the most opulent and the oldest masquerade party, while Viareggio, in Tuscany, is famous for its lively themed floats.

Another festival highlight is the *Sienese Palio (see p67),* a bareback horse race that takes place twice a year in one of Italy's most beautiful squares. For further details on festivals throughout Italy, see pp66–69.

**An elaborate Carnival mask**

Every region in Italy has its own ancient music and dance, but the best known is the *tarantella*, a lively dance and rhythmic song from Puglia *(see p511)*. Legends trace the origins of the name to the tarantula spider, since victims of a tarantula bite would perform a frenzied dance to sweat out the poison.

## CULTURE

Spectating, whether at sporting events, rural festivals or even grand events, is what entertainment is all about. And part of this, of course, involves that very Italian pastime – seeing and being seen. You can witness this in daily life in the café culture – visit any of the large cities' popular squares, such as Piazza di Spagna or Piazza Navona in Rome, Piazza del Duomo in Milan or Piazza San Marco in Venice, and you will see people of all ages parading around in their best clothes. This is referred to as *la passeggiata*, a walk around that becomes a ritual at weekends, along the seafront and lakeside promenades in summer and in city and town centres.

Another aspect of daily life is *l'aperitivo*. This ritual of joining friends for an early evening drink after work or before going on to dinner or to a nightclub is back in fashion. Bars provide abundant finger-food buffets to accompany the drinks, which are generally priced higher than at other times of day. This trend has spawned new lounge clubs in the major cities.

## DIRECTORY

### PRACTICAL INFORMATION

**Italian State Tourist Board**
1 Princes Street, London W1B 2AY.
***Tel*** *020 7408 1254.*
**www**.italiantouristboard.co.uk

**Liaisons Abroad**
**www**.liaisonsabroad.com
***Tel*** *0870 421 4020.*

### OPERA AND CLASSICAL MUSIC

**Arena di Verona**
Piazza Brà, Verona.
***Tel*** *045 800 51 51.*
**www**.arena.it

**Baths of Caracalla**
Via delle Terme di Caracalla 52, Rome.
**Map** 7 A3.

**La Fenice**
Campo San Fantin, Venice.
**Map** 7 A2. ***Tel*** *041 24 24.*
**www**.teatrolafenice.it

**Maggio Musicale**
Florence. ***Tel*** *055 277 93 50.* **www**.maggiofiorentino.com

**Parco della Musica**
Viale de Coubertin 30, Rome. ***Tel*** *06 8024 12 81.* **www**.auditorium.com

**Teatro alla Scala**
Piazza della Scala, Milan.
***Tel*** *02 7200 3744.*
**www**.teatroallascala.org

**Teatro degli Arcimboldi**
Viale dell'Innovazione 20, Milan.
***Tel*** *02 641 142 212.*
**www**.teatroarcimboldi.it

**Teatro dell'Opera**
Piazza B Gigli 7, Rome.
**Map** 3 C3.
***Tel*** *06 481 60 255.*
**www**.operaroma.it

### ROCK, JAZZ AND CONTEMPORARY MUSIC

**Forum di Assago**
Via G Di Vittorio 6, Assago, Milan. ***Tel*** *199 128 800.*
**www**.forumnet.it

**Stadio Olimpico**
Viale dei Gladiatori, Rome.

**Umbria Jazz**
***Tel*** *075 573 24 32.*
**www**.umbriajazz.com

### THEATRE AND BALLET

**Teatro Carlo Felice**
Passo E Montale 4, Genova.
***Tel*** *010 53 811.*
**www**.carlofelice.it

### CINEMA

**Venice Film Festival**
***Tel*** *041 521 87 11.*
**www**.labiennale.org

# Specialist Holidays and Outdoor Activities

Exploring the countryside on horseback

Italy offers an amazing variety of cultural, sporting and leisure activities. However, many schools and groups require annual membership and short-term activities are often expensive and difficult to find. Information on current leisure and sporting events in a specific region is available from the tourist office listed for each town in this guide. For details on annual festivals, see *Italy Through the Year* on pages 66–9. The following suggestions include some of the most popular as well as some more unusual pursuits.

Cycling on the tree-lined flatlands of the Po Delta

## WALKING, CYCLING AND HORSE RIDING

Some Italian branches of the **World Wide Fund for Nature (WWF)** organize walks and treks. **Club Alpino Italiano (CAI)** runs trekking and climbing excursions and the **Italian Birds Protection League (LIPU)** arranges nature walks and bird-watching trips. The military *IGM* maps are the most detailed but unfortunately are only available from specialist map shops.

Cycling is popular despite Italy's mountainous landscape. Travel bookshops stock publications with suggested routes, such as the Po Delta, which has miles of scenic flatlands.

Many riding schools organize trips and outings, which are also advertised in the local press. For general information, contact the **Federazione Italiana Sport Equestri**.

## MOUNTAIN SPORTS

The most well-equipped and famous ski resorts are in the Dolomites, in the Italian Alps and around Turin, the city chosen to host the 2006 Winter Olympics. There are also smaller and less expensive resorts in the Apennines and in Sicily. Package ski holidays, arranged from outside Italy, offer the best deals. The **Federazione Arrampicata Sportiva Italiana** has a list of mountain climbing schools that arrange climbs for all levels.

Group hiking tour in the Dolomites of Trentino-Alto Adige *(see p78)*

Ski lift near the desolate Falzarego Pass, in the heart of the Dolomites

## ARCHAEOLOGICAL DIGS

The British monthly magazine *Archaeology Abroad*, available in the UK, gives a comprehensive list of archaeology groups and digs worldwide. In Italy, the **Gruppo Archeologico Romano** runs two-week digs in various regions. There are summer and winter digs, for both adults and children. The group has contacts with local archaeological organizations as well.

## ITALIAN LANGUAGE AND CULTURE

For a wide selection of material on courses and schools in Italy, contact the Italian consulate in your home country. The **Società Dante Alighieri** provides courses in the Italian language, history of art, literature and culture. There are both full- and part-time courses available, for every level. Language schools abound in Italy's main cities and are advertised in the Yellow Pages *(Pagine Gialle)* or foreign language bookshops and newspapers. For young students, **Intercultura** will organize weekly, monthly and year-long exchanges including language courses, accommodation with Italian families and enrolment in Italian schools.

A lesson in Italian cookery in Sicily

Cooking holidays run by English-speaking experts in Italian cooking have become very popular. **Tasting Places**, for example, does wine tours and week-long courses in Italian cuisine, and provides beautiful private accommodation. The course locations include the Veneto, Sicily, Tuscany and Umbria. Wine-tasting tours are organized by local tourist boards. The Università per Stranieri in Perugia runs courses on Italian culture, history and cooking.

## WATER SPORTS

Most lakes and many seaside resorts rent out sailing boats, canoes and windsurfing equipment. Lessons and courses are organized by clubs, which usually require membership. For a list of authorized associations contact the **Federazione Italiana Canoa Kayak** and the **Federazione Italiana Vela**. Weekend and weekly sailing holidays and courses are featured in the magazine *Avventure nel Mondo* and most travel agents have a selection of sailing holidays.

Swimming pools are expensive in Italy and many do not accept people on a daily basis. You often have to pay a membership fee and a monthly tariff. Some of the luxurious hotels open their pools to the public in summer, but at pricy rates. Water parks are popular and provide pools, slides, wave machines and games. Before diving into any lakes or rivers (and even the sea near main towns) it is best to check that the water is not polluted. The **Federazione Italiana di Attività Subacquee** runs underwater diving courses, and can give information on all local centres.

## AIR SPORTS

There are schools nationwide that offer hang-gliding and flying courses, but the minimum duration of each course is one month. For information and a list of schools contact the **AeroClub Italia**. You must be licensed before you can fly and all crafts must be registered with AeroClub.

## OTHER SPORTS

Golf is a popular sport in Italy and there are plenty of courses to choose from. Home membership and handicap are often required for daily access to a club.

Italian tennis clubs usually operate on a membership basis, unless you are invited as a member's guest. The national **Federazione Italiana di Tennis** has a list of all the tennis clubs in Italy.

The opportunity to watch a professional football game should not be missed. Seats can be scarce, so book tickets in advance from the stadium. Most Serie A matches are played on Sundays, with international games taking place on Tuesdays and Wednesdays.

Sailing in Italy, a popular leisure activity and competitive sport

## DIRECTORY

**AeroClub Italia**
Via Cesare Beccaria 35a, 00196 Rome. ***Tel*** *06 36 08 46 00.* **www**.aeci.it

**Club Alpino Italiano**
Via E Petrella 19, Milan. ***Tel*** *02 205 72 31.* **www**.cai.it

**Federazione Arrampicata Sportiva Italiana**
Via del Terrapieno 27, 40127 Bologna. ***Tel*** *051 601 48 90.* **www**.federclimb.it

**Federazione Italiana Attività Subacquee**
Via Flaminia Nuova 830, 00191 Rome. ***Tel*** *06 36 85 63 02.* **www**.fipsasroma.it

**Federazione Italiana Canoa Kayak**
Viale Tiziano 70, 00196 Rome. ***Tel*** *06 36 85 85 25.* **www**.federcanoa.it

**Federazione Italiana Sport Equestri**
Viale Tiziano 74, 00196 Rome. ***Tel*** *06 36 85 83 26.* **www**.fise.it

**Federazione Italiana di Tennis**
Stadio Olimpico, Rome. ***Tel*** *06 36 85 85 98.* **www**.federtennis.it

**Federazione Italiana Vela**
Piazza Borgo Pila 40, Genova. ***Tel*** *010 54 45 41.* **www**.federvela.it

**Gruppo Archeologico Romano**
Via Baldi degli Ubaldi 168, 00167 Rome. ***Tel*** *06 638 52 56.* **www**.gruppoarcheologico.it

**Intercultura**
Via Venezia 25, 00184 Rome. ***Tel*** *06 48 88 24 01.* **www**.intercultura.it

**Italian Birds Protection League (LIPU)**
Via Trento 49, 43100 Parma. ***Tel*** *0521 27 30 43.* **www**.lipu.it

**Società Dante Alighieri**
Via Gino Capponi 4, 50121 Florence. ***Tel*** *055 247 89 81.* **www**.dantealighieri.it

**Tasting Places Cookery and Wine Tours**
PO Box 38174, London W10 5ZP. ***Tel*** *020 8964 5333.* **www**.tastingplaces.com

**World Wide Fund for Nature**
Via Po 25c, 00198 Rome. ***Tel*** *06 84 49 71.* **www**.wwf.it

GELATERIA BA
CONFEZIONI ELY
BIANCHERIA
IL CAMPO

# SURVIVAL GUIDE

# PRACTICAL INFORMATION

Ask any Italian and they will almost certainly tell you that Italy is the most beautiful country in the world. They may not be far wrong. However, the charm and allure of Italy may help to veil some of her numerous practical problems. Getting information is rarely straightforward; public offices and banks are nearly always crippled by long queues and bureaucracy, and the postal service is renowned for its inefficiency. This section, together with some forward planning and a little patience, should help you cope with some of Italy's idiosyncrasies.

ITALIA
ENTE NAZIONALE ITALIANO PER IL TURISMO

Tourist board logo

Tourists crossing the Ponte della Paglia in Venice *(see p109)*

## WHEN TO VISIT

The northern part of Italy is generally more temperate than the south, which has a Mediterranean climate. From June to September the weather is hot throughout the country and, in peak summer, also humid. Seaside resorts tend to get very busy. Spring and autumn are ideal for visiting cities as temperatures are milder, making sightseeing much more comfortable, although you should be prepared for the odd downpour.

Italy's towns and historic sites are extremely popular attractions and it is worth considering this when planning your trip. Most sights are open all year, except on some public holidays *(see p69)*, and most close one day a week. Rome, Florence and Venice are all crowded from spring to October and it is advisable to book a hotel well in advance. In August the cities are generally slightly less busy, abandoned by their inhabitants for the summer holidays.

In February, Venice triples its population during Carnival *(see p69)* and at Easter, Rome is overrun by pilgrims and tourists. Winter can be bitterly cold, especially in the north, and December to March is the time of year for skiing in the high altitude resorts of the Italian Alps. *The Climate of Italy* on pages 72–3 takes a detailed look at the country's regional weather.

## VISAS AND PERMESSO DI SOGGIORNO

European Union nationals and citizens of the US, Canada, Australia and New Zealand do not need visas for stays of up to three months. Most European Union (EU) visitors need only a valid identity document including a photograph, but visitors from the UK, Ireland, Denmark and Sweden must have a passport.

All visitors should check requirements with the Italian embassy before travelling and, officially, declare themselves to the Italian police within eight days of arrival. If you are staying in a hotel or campsite, this will be done for you by the staff, otherwise contact the local *Questura* (police station).

Anyone wishing to stay in Italy for more than three months (or eight days for non-EU citizens) will have to obtain a *permesso di soggiorno* (permit to stay or residence permit). You can apply for a residence permit at any main police station, *Questura di Provincia*. In some cases you can obtain a kit containing the necessary application form from main post offices. You must apply for the correct permit, either a permit to work *(lavoro)* or a permit to study *(studio)*. The necessary documentation is listed on the *Questura* website *(see p665)*.

To apply for a study permit, it is necessary to get a letter from the relevant school or university at which you intend to study, giving details of your course. This then has to be sent to the Italian consulate in your own country of origin to obtain an official covering letter, or declaration.

You will also need some form of guarantee that your medical bills will be paid should you become ill or have an accident where you require medical treatment. A comprehensive insurance policy for the length of your stay *(see p667)* will usually be sufficient.

Rome's renowned Tazza d'Oro café, an ideal rest stop after sightseeing

beautiful Piazza del Campo in Siena, meeting place for visitors and locals

## CUSTOMS

On 30 June 1999, the intra-EU Duty and Tax Free Allowances, better known as Duty-free and mainly affecting such high-tax items as alcohol, perfumes and tobacco, were abolished. However, for EU residents the amount of these goods that can be imported for personal use has increased.

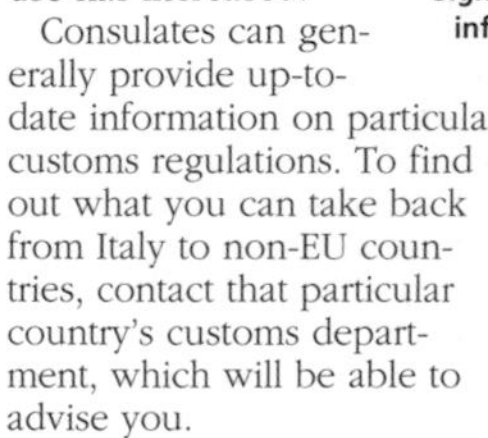

Sign for tourist information

Consulates can generally provide up-to-date information on particular customs regulations. To find out what you can take back from Italy to non-EU countries, contact that particular country's customs department, which will be able to advise you.

## TAX EXEMPTION

Value Added Tax (IVA in Italy) ranges from about 20 per cent, with a reduced rate of 4–10 per cent on some items. Non-European Union citizens making purchases in Italy can claim an IVA rebate, provided the total expenditure in the one shop is over €155. It is a long process, and it is easier to get a refund if you shop where you see the "Euro Free Tax" sign, rather than from a market stall. In this instance, show your passport to the shop assistant, complete a form, and the IVA will be deducted from your bill. Alternatively, present a customs officer with your purchases and their receipts on your departure from Italy. He or she will stamp the receipts, which you then send to the vendor. A refund should eventually be sent to you.

## TOURIST INFORMATION

The national tourist board, **ENIT**, has a good website as well as branches in capital cities worldwide, and offers general information on Italy. For specific requests, contact the local tourist offices. The addresses and telephone numbers are listed under each town or city, directly under the title, and they are plotted on the town and city maps.

An EPT *(Ente Provinciale di Turismo)* has information on its town and surrounding province, whereas an APT *(Azienda di Promozione Turistica)* deals exclusively with individual towns. Both offices help with practical information such as hotel bookings and tours. They also provide free maps and guidebooks in various languages. The EPT and APT can refer you to local tour guides and advise on trips and excursions.

Small towns will have a *Pro Loco*, a tourist office run by the local administration, which is sometimes open only during the tourist season. It is usually located in the town hall.

## TOURS

Many tour companies organize coach trips, with English-speaking guides, that include all the main tourist attractions in Italy. Companies such as the UK-based **Leger Holidays** offer coach tours that go all over the country. If you are looking for something a little more personal and off the beaten track, check the local pages of national newspapers for tour groups or organizations. Local tourist boards will also be able to advise you. Always employ official guides and be sure to establish the fee in advance. For information on specialist holidays, such as sporting or cultural activities, turn to pages 658–9.

A guided group tour through the streets of Florence

Daytime sightseeing on a tranquil canal in Venice

## SIGHTSEEING OPENING HOURS

Italian museums are gradually conforming to regulations, particularly in the northern and central regions of the country, opening from 9am–7pm daily, except for Mondays. In winter, however, many musuems revert to slightly earlier closing times, particularly on Sundays, but it is best to check.

Privately run and smaller museums set their own opening times, so it is advisable to phone in advance to avoid disappointment. Archaeological sites are generally open from 9am to one hour before sunset, Tuesday to Sunday. Churches are usually open from about 7am–12:30pm and 4–7pm. However, they often prefer not to let tourists in during services, so Sunday is not the best day to visit.

## ADMISSION CHARGES

Sightseeing fees range from €2 to €9. Churches are usually free, but some expect a donation, and you will need coins to illuminate works of art. Reductions for students are not always offered but many state-run museums and archaeological sites allow free entry for EU residents under 18 and over 60 years of age. Large groups are often entitled to a discount as well. If reductions are available, you will need to show a valid form of identification.

## ETIQUETTE AND TIPPING

People in Italy are friendly towards foreign visitors. On entering a shop or bar it is customary to greet people with a general *buon giorno* (good morning) or *buona sera* (good evening), and the same applies when leaving. They will also try to be helpful when asked directions in the street. If your Italian is slight, simply saying *scusi,* followed by the name of the place you wish to go to, will often suffice. *Grazie* (thank you) is replied to with *prego* (you're welcome).

Tipping in restaurants is expected when the 10–15 per cent service is not included. However, as much as 10 per cent would be considered generous and a tip is often not expected at all in family-run restaurants. Taxi drivers and hotel porters expect a few euros if they have been helpful. You could simply round the bill up to the nearest €2.

Italians are very dress-conscious and unusual clothes do get noticed. Be aware that in places of worship you should cover your torso and upper arms; shorts and skirts must reach below the knee.

Smoking is forbidden in all buildings open to the public (including offices, shops, bars and restaurants). However, it is tolerated in outdoor public places, whereas drunkenness is definitely frowned upon.

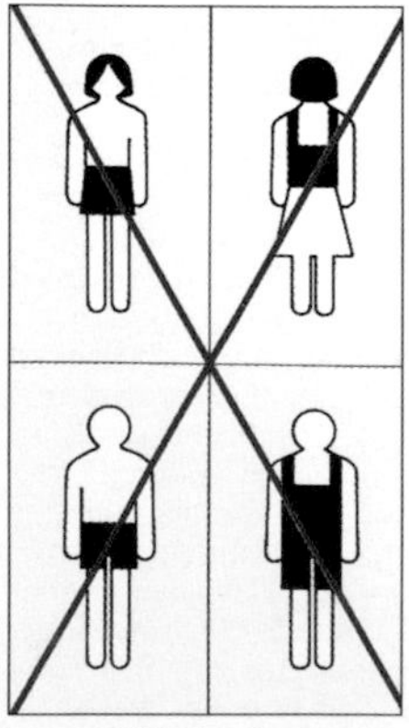

**Unacceptable dress in church: both sexes are required to cover torsos and upper arms**

**A student relaxing in the sun in Gaiole in Chianti**

## RELIGIOUS SERVICES

Around 35 per cent of the population is practising Catholic. Sunday mass is celebrated throughout the country, while in the principal churches, services are also held during the week. In major cities some churches, such as the church of Santa Susanna (Via XX Settembre 14) in Rome, offer services and confession in English. For some visitors, a trip to Rome will include an audience with the pope *(see p419)*.

With increasing numbers of foreigners making their home in Italy, all the main religious beliefs are also represented. For details contact the main centres in Rome.

## STUDENT INFORMATION

The national student travel organization, **CTS** (Centro Turistico Studentesco), has branches throughout Italy and Europe. They issue the International Student Identity Card (ISIC) and the Youth International Educational Exchange Card (YIEE). Both can be used, along with a passport, for discounts at museums and other tourist attractions. The ISIC card also gives access to a 24-hour telephone helpline that provides general advice and information. As well as issuing youth cards, CTS offers cut-price car hire and will organize holidays and courses. For details about youth hostels, contact the **Associazione Italiana Alberghi per la Gioventù** (the Italian YHA), providing that you are a current member.

**ISIC card**

## TRAVELLING WITH CHILDREN

On the whole, Italians love children, to an extent that sometimes seems over-indulgent. Most trattorias and pizzerias welcome them and there are no rules excluding children from bars; however, high chairs are unusual. Hotels also welcome children, but smaller establishments may have limited facilities. Some of the more up-market hotels offer a babysitting service. Very few museums, on the other hand, provide special child-orientated activities. It is common to see children playing outside fairly late at night, especially in summer. Most towns have city parks with playgrounds and many have summer funfairs. Regular stops for *gelato* are guaranteed to go down well with youngsters. For young swimmers, the calm Mediterranean is ideal, though care should always be taken.

## DISABLED TRAVELLERS

Awareness of the needs of the disabled is improving in Italy, especially in major cities, with ramps being added to museums and some churches. Trains and buses are also becoming more disabled-friendly. In Milan **AIAS** (Associazione Italiana Assistenza Spastici) and in Rome **CO.IN. Sociale** and **Roma per Tutti** provide information and general assistance. Train travellers with **Trenitalia** on both international and domestic routes receive help with special reservations and assistance at stations.

## PUBLIC CONVENIENCES

*Gabinetto* means public toilet, though signs often say WC. Tourist cities have well-signed public conveniences that charge around €1. Some have cleaning staff on hand and a tip may be left. Italian cafés usually have a toilet for their customers, though it is worth checking. Old-style "crouch" toilets are still common.

## ELECTRICAL ADAPTORS

The voltage in Italy is 220 volts, with two-pin round-pronged plugs, so it is advisable to bring a universal adaptor with you or buy one in the country. Most hotels with three or more stars have hair-driers and shaving points in all bedrooms, but check the voltage first, to be safe.

## ITALIAN TIME

Italy is one hour ahead of Greenwich Mean Time (GMT). The clocks are put forward one hour in March and back in October. For example: London is one hour behind Italy; Sydney is nine hours ahead; while Ottawa is six hours behind.

**The clock of San Giacomo di Rialto in Venice** ***(see p97)***

## RESPONSIBLE TRAVEL

Local attitudes towards environmental issues are developing rather slowly in Italy, despite the efforts of many concerned groups such as the Verdi political party. However, there are opportunities for low impact travel and alternative green options available.

Staying at family run guesthouses instead of international hotel chains helps support local economies. National and regional parks award eco labels to hotels and guesthouses that adhere to EU rules governing sustainable tourism, which cover issues such as energy and water saving, waste disposal and use of local products. The **National Association for Agritourism** and **Agriturismo** *(see p556)* offers countrywide farm stays. These are a great way of enjoying the countryside and experiencing local traditions, as well as helping supplement the income of small farm owners. Facilities vary and some farms offer visitors the opportunity to help out.

Farmers' markets and growers who sell their produce direct to the public are now more common, guaranteeing fresh, seasonal produce. Look for the label *biologico* when searching for organic produce.

## CONVERSION CHART

**Imperial to Metric**
1 inch = 2.54 centimetres
1 foot = 30 centimetres
1 mile = 1.6 kilometres
1 ounce = 28 grams
1 pound = 454 grams
1 pint = 0.57 litre
1 gallon = 4.6 litres

**Metric to Imperial**
1 centimetre = 0.4 inch
1 metre = 3 feet 3 inches
1 kilometre = 0.6 mile
1 gram = 0.04 ounce
1 kilogram = 2.2 pounds
1 litre = 1.8 pints

## DIRECTORY

### QUESTURA AND PERMITS

**www**.poliziadistato.it
**www**.portale immigrazione.it
**www**.esteri.it/visti

### ITALIAN CUSTOMS AND TAX

**www**.agenziadogane.it

### TOURIST INFORMATION AND TOURS

**APT Florence**
Via Cavour 1r. **Map** 2 D4.
***Tel*** *055 29 08 32.*
**www**.firenzeturismo.it

**APT Siena**
Piazza del Campo 56.
***Tel*** *0577 28 05 51.*
**www**.terresiena.it

**APT Venice**
Piazza San Marco 71f.
**Map** 7 B2.
***Tel*** *041 529 87 11.*
**www**.turismovenezia.it

**ENIT**
**www**.enit.it.

**IAT Milan**
Piazza Duomo 19a.
***Tel*** *02 72 52 43 01.*
**www**.turismo.milano.it

**Leger Holidays**
***Tel*** *0844 686 2424.*
**www**.leger.co.uk

**Rome Tourist Office**
Termini Station, Platform 24. **Map** 4 D3. ***Tel*** *06 06 08.* **www**.060608.it

### RELIGIOUS ORGANIZATIONS

**Catholic**
Ufficio Informazioni Vaticano, Piazza San Pietro, Vaticano, Rome.
**Map** 1 B3.
***Tel*** *06 69 88 16 62.*

**Jewish**
Unione delle Comunità Ebraiche Italiane, Lungotevere Sanzio 9, Rome. **Map** 6 D1. ***Tel*** *06 580 36 70.* **www**.ucei.it

**Muslim**
Centro Islamico Culturale d'Italia, Viale della Moschea 85, Rome.
***Tel*** *06 808 22 58.*

### STUDENT INFORMATION

**Associazione Italiana Alberghi per la Gioventù**
Via Cavour 44 (3rd floor), Rome. **Map** 3 C5.
***Tel*** *06 487 11 52.*
**www**.aighostels.com

**CTS**
Via Solferino 6A, Rome.
**Map** 4 D3. ***Tel*** *06 462 04 31.* **www**.cts.it

### DISABLED TOURS

**AIAS**
Via P Mantegazza 10, Milan.
***Tel*** *02 330 20 21.*
**www**.aiasmilano.it

**CO.IN.Sociale**
Via E Giglioli 54A, Rome.
**www**.coinsociale.it

**Roma per Tutti**
***Tel*** *06 57 17 70 94.*
**www**.romapertutti.it

### RESPONSIBLE TRAVEL

**National Association for Agritourism**
**www**.agriturist.it

# Personal Security and Health

Although Italy is generally a safe place for visitors, it is wise to keep a watchful eye on your personal belongings, especially in the larger towns and cities. There is a conspicuous police presence throughout the country, and in the event of an emergency or crime, any of the police officers described in this section will be able to assist you and tell you where to go to report an incident. If you fall ill, pharmacies are a good first stop where medically trained staff can give advice or tell you where to find further help. In an emergency, the Casualty Department *(Pronto Soccorso)* of any hospital will treat you and it is likely that you will encounter English-speaking staff, especially in large towns.

***Commissariato di Polizia*** **– a police station**

**Police car**

**Green Cross ambulance in Venice**

**Roman fire engine**

## PERSONAL PROPERTY

Petty theft such as pickpocketing, bag snatching and car theft is common in Italian cities. In the event of a theft you must report it within 24 hours to the nearest *questura* or *commissariato di polizia* (police station). If possible, show them some ID.

Avoid leaving anything visible in an unattended car, including a car radio. If you ave to leave luggage in a r, find a hotel that has pri- e parking. When making a hase, always check your ge and do not keep s in back pockets, lly on buses or in owded places. "Bum d money belts are a favourite target for pickpockets, so try to keep them hidden. When walking, hold bags and cameras in front of you and on the inside of the pavement so as not to tempt motorized snatchers, and do not show expensive cameras and video equipment in areas off tourist routes.

If attacked, never attempt to hang on to your things as you could be seriously injured and dragged along the street.

Avoid carrying large sums of money – take out only what you need for the day. It is advisable to get comprehensive travel insurance that covers theft of personal possessions in addition to covering cancellation/delay of flights, loss/damage of luggage, money and other valuables, as well as personal liability and accidents. It should include cover for legal assistance and advice.

If you do need to make an insurance claim for stolen or lost property, you must get a copy of the report *(denuncia)* from the police station when you report the incident. In case of lost passports, go to your embassy or consulate; for lost credit cards or travellers' cheques, contact the issuing company's nearest office.

If you do not have insurance cover, contact your embassy as soon as possible after an incident, such as an accident, occurs. The embassy can offer advice and should provide you with a list of English- and Italian-speaking lawyers who are knowledgeable about both the Italian and English legal systems.

## PERSONAL SECURITY

Although petty crime in cities is frequent, violent crime in Italy is rare. However, it is common for people to raise their voices aggressively during an argument. Usually, remaining calm and being polite will help to defuse the situation.

Always be wary of unofficial tour guides, taxi drivers or strangers who wish to assist you or advise you on accommodation, restaurants or shops as they may expect something in return. Decline their offers politely but firmly.

**A team of *carabinieri* in traffic police uniform**

## WOMEN TRAVELLERS

Women travelling on their own in Italy are likely to meet with a lot of attention. This is often more of an irritation than a danger, but it is best to keep away from lonely, unlit streets and areas near railway stations at night, and to carry an alarm or whistle and be equipped with the telephone numbers of your hotel and a local taxi service. Walking quickly and purposefully is a good way to avoid any unwanted attention. The staff at hotels and restaurants generally treat their single female guests and customers with extra care and attention.

## THE POLICE

There are several different police forces in Italy and each one fulfils a particular role. The state police, *la polizia*, wear blue uniforms and drive blue cars. They deal with most crimes.

The *carabinieri* are militarily trained and wear dark blue and black uniforms with red striped trousers. These officers deal with a variety of offences from organized crime to speeding and can also conduct random security checks.

The *guardia di finanza* are the financial police force (the fraud squad), and wear grey uniforms with yellow striped trousers. The *vigili urbani*, or the municipal traffic police, wear blue and white uniforms in winter and white during the summer.

**Municipal policeman**

Even though they are not official police officers, the *vigili urbani* can issue heavy fines for traffic and parking offences. They can usually be spotted patrolling the streets, enforcing laws or directing traffic. Officers from any of the forces will be able to help in an emergency.

**Outside a Florentine pharmacy with a green cross sign**

## MEDICAL TREATMENT

Emergency medical care in Italy is free for all EU and Australian citizens, thanks to reciprocal agreements. The EHIC European Health Insurance Card, which is available from the UK Department of Health offices, website or from a main post office, covers emergencies only; private medical insurance is needed for all other types of treatment. The card comes with a booklet that contains general health advice and information about how to claim free medical treatment when travelling abroad. You may find you have to pay and reclaim the money later. Australians need to apply to Medicare.

Non-EU citizens should try to arrive in Italy with comprehensive private medical insurance to cover all eventualities. If you do need emergency treatment, go to the *Pronto Soccorso* (Casualty Department) of the nearest hospital. If necessary, you will be referred to the appropriate specialist or department within the same structure. As an alternative, ask your hotel to call the night doctor – *guardia medica* – who can be consulted on the phone.

No inoculations are needed for Italy, but mosquito repellent is advisable in summer. Repellent creams and sprays are found in pharmacies, as are electrical repellers which burn pellets to deter the bugs.

## PHARMACIES

Various medical products, including homeopathic medicines, are available in any pharmacy *(farmacia)*, but a prescription is often required. Qualified staff will offer advice for minor ailments and common illnesses and provide appropriate medicines. Thanks to a night rota *(servizio notturno)*, there is always a pharmacy open in all cities and most towns. Those that are open at night are listed in the local pages of daily newspapers and on all pharmacy doors.

Pharmacies also sell toiletries and beauty items. Common non-prescription pharmaceutical products such as aspirin are also sold at lower prices in many large supermarkets.

## DIRECTORY

### EMBASSIES AND CONSULATES

**Australia**
Via A. Bosio 5, Rome.
***Tel*** *06 85 27 21.*
**www**.italy.embassy.gov.au

**Canada**
Via Zara 30, Rome. ***Tel*** *06 8544 429 11.* **www**.canada.it

**United Kingdom**
Via XX Settembre 80a, Rome.
**Map** 4 D2. ***Tel*** *06 42 20 00 01.*
**http**://ukinitaly.fco.gov.uk

**United States**
Via Veneto 119a, Rome.
**Map** 3 C1. ***Tel*** *06 467 41.*
**www**.usembassy.it

### EMERGENCY NUMBERS

**General Emergency**
***Tel*** *113.*

**Fire Service**
***Tel*** *115.*

**Medical Emergencies**
***Tel*** *118.*

**Police (Carabinieri)**
***Tel*** *112.*

### MEDICAL TREATMENT

**Medicare Australia**
Information for Individuals and Families
**www**.medicareaustralia.gov.au

**UK Department of Heal**
Information for Travellers
**www**.dh.gov.uk

# Banking and Local Currency

Virtually all Italian hotels, many shops, large restaurants and petrol stations accept major credit cards. Only in the more off-the-beaten-track locations will you have difficulties without euros, and some establishments will offer a discount for payments made in cash, especially in low season. When you pay with a credit card, you might be asked to show identification, such as your passport. Foreign currency can be changed in banks, although these are often crowded and service tends to be slow. All banks will cash travellers' cheques, and cashpoint machines *(bancomat)* will accept cards with a PIN number. Most machines also accept MasterCard, VISA and American Express cards. Although banks often have the best exchange rates, bureaux de change and foreign exchange machines can be more convenient.

**Cash dispenser, which also accepts VISA and MasterCard (Access)**

## CHANGING MONEY

Banking hours are somewhat restrictive and can also be slightly erratic so it is safest to acquire a small amount of local currency before you arrive in Italy. Exchange rates will vary from place to place.

Travellers' cheques are still a safe way to carry money, though commission charges can be hefty. Choose a well known name such as Thomas Cook or American Express. Once you arrive, the most convenient way to change money is to use the electronic exchange machines, which are located at all major air-ports, train stations and some anks. The machines have ltilingual instructions and exchange rate is clearly layed on the screen. Sim- ed in notes of the same n currency and you will euros in return.

Bureaux de change can be found in all main towns. Although they are easier to use, they usually have worse exchange rates and charge more commission than banks.

## REGIONAL DIFFERENCES IN COST OF LIVING

The north is generally more expensive than the south, but there are many exceptions. Restaurants and hotels off the beaten track are usually better value, and buying locally made produce is cost effective if you avoid obvious tourist traps.

## BANKING HOURS

Banks are usually open between 8:30am and 1:30pm, Monday to Friday. Most also open for an hour in the afternoon, from about 2:15pm to 3pm or 2:30pm until 3:30pm, depending on the bank. All banks close at weekends and for public holidays, and they also close early the day before a major holiday. Bureaux de change, however, are often open all day, and in some places they also stay open until late at night.

**Metal-detecting security doors found at most banks**

## USING BANKS

For security purposes, most banks have electronic double doors with metal detectors, allowing one person in at a time. Metal objects and bags should first be deposited in lockers situated in the foyer. Press the button to open the outer door, then wait for it to close behind you. The inner door then opens automatically. Do not be alarmed by the heavily armed guards that patrol most banks in Italy.

Changing money at a bank can be a frustrating process involving endless form-filling and queuing. First you have to go to the window that displays the *cambio* sign and then to the *cassa* to obtain your money. If in doubt, ask someone in order to avoid waiting in the wrong queue.

If you need to have money sent to you in Italy, banks at home can transfer money to an Italian bank, but it can take up to a week. American Express, Thomas Cook and Western Union all provide swifter money transfer services, with a charge to the sender.

## CASH MACHINES

Withdrawing cash from an ATM (automatic teller machine) with a credit card is a straightforward process. Choose your language on the screen and follow the instructions. You will need to type in your PIN number, so have it handy. Should your card be swallowed up by a cash machine for some reason (for example if you used an incorrect PIN number), it may be sent back to the issuing bank. However, if the bank is open do ask inside. Costs for cash withdrawals are set by your bank so check before you travel. It may be advisable to take out a largish amount of money in one go, but bear in mind that ATMs may run out of notes during weekends.

## THE EURO

The euro (€) is the common currency of the European Union. It came into general circulation on 1 January 2002, initially for twelve participating countries. Italy was one of those twelve countries taking the euro and the lire was phased out by March 2002.

EU members using the Euro as sole official currency are known as the Eurozone. Several EU members have opted out of joining this common currency. Euro notes are identical throughout the Eurozone countries, each one including designs of fictional architectural structures. The coins, however, have one side identical (the value side) and one side with an image unique to each country. Notes and coins are exchangeable in each participating country.

**Bank Notes**

*Euro bank notes have seven denominations. The €5 note (grey in colour) is the smallest, followed by the €10 note (pink), €20 note (blue), €50 note (orange), €100 note (green), €200 note (yellow) and €500 note (purple). All notes show the 12 stars of the European Union.*

5 euros

10 euros

20 euros

50 euros

100 euros

200 euros

500 euros

2 euro

1 euro

50 cents

20 cents

10 cents

**Coins**

*The euro has eight coin denominations: €1 and €2; 50 cents, 20 cents, 10 cents, 5 cents, 2 cents and 1 cent. The €2 and €1 coins are both silver and gold in colour. The 50-, 20- and 10-cent coins are gold. The 5-, 2- and 1-cent coins are bronze.*

5 cents

2 cents

1 cent

# Communications and Media

Although the Italian postal service is known for being very slow, Italy's other forms of communication, at least in the cities, are more efficient. Fax machines, courier services and telephones are all widespread, and Internet points are available throughout Italy. Foreign-language newspapers and magazines are on sale in all cities and most large towns. Both state-run and privately owned television stations exist, but only satellite television and radio stations broadcast foreign-language programmes.

Telephone company logo

## PUBLIC TELEPHONES

The Italian national telephone company is Telecom Italia. Coin-operated telephones have been phased out and replaced by card-operated machines. Most public telephones have instructions in five languages (Italian, English, French, Spanish and German). To select a language, push the top right-hand button. To use a public telephone you will need a Telecom Italia phone card. Phone cards (*carta* or *scheda telefonica*) can be purchased from bars, newspaper kiosks, post offices and *tabacchi* displaying the black-and-white T sign.

International phone cards, on sale at *tabacchi* and newsstands, are still a very cheap way to call abroad. Some cards offer as many as 3 hours of calls for about €10, depending on the country being called. Dial the toll-free number on the card and then enter the secret code found by scratching off the silver strip on the back of the card. You will be told the amount of credit available and then asked to dial the number you wish to call. Rates are slightly higher when calling from a mobile or public phone. Check with your hotel before using a card from your room as extra charges may be applied.

Telephone sign

## EMAIL AND INTERNET

Internet and email services are widely available throughout Italy, particularly in urban areas, so it should not be difficult to access email accounts or connect to the web. Telecom Italia, the Italian national phone company, has set up Internet services in the country's major train stations and public phone centres. Internet time can be purchased using a regular phone card.

Some major chains of Internet points sell magnetic cards with credit that can be used in any of their stores throughout Italy. **Internet Train**, with branches in almost 90 towns, is the most visible. Visit its website for a full list of stores. In addition, small Internet points are very common. These are usually clustered around train stations, cheap hotels and university areas and can range from the back room of a local grocery shop to a corner in a café or bar. Users can buy computer time in blocks as short as 15 minutes. There are usually student discounts available, and cost per minute decreases as the amount of time purchased increases.

Many hotels have Wi-Fi so travellers with their own laptop can have easy access. You'll probably need a plug adaptor too. Remember that with **Skype** or **Voip Stunt** installed it's possible to make phone calls over the Internet with the help of a small microphone. Calls are free between Skype users.

Using a public Telecom Italia telephone

## MOBILE PHONES

There are four main GSM frequencies (Global System for Mobile Communications) in use around the world, so to guarantee that your phone will work, make sure you have a quad-band phone. Tri-band phones from outside the US are also usually compatible but, because the US uses two frequency bands itself, a US tri-band phone may only have limited global coverage. Contact your service provider for clarification.

To use your mobile phone abroad you may need to get "permission" from your network operator, as often they need to enable "roaming" for your phone. At the moment, you are charged for the calls you receive as well as the calls you make, and you have to pay a substantial premium for the international leg of the call.

One popular option is to purchase a local SIM card – the electronic chip that links your phone to a particular network – that can be topped up with credit and uses the local mobile phone networks. You can only do this if your handset is "unlocked" – some operators lock their phones to specific networks.

It is worth checking your insurance policy in case your phone gets stolen. You should also keep your network operator's helpline number handy for emergencies.

## TV AND RADIO

Television channels in Italy include the state-owned RAI (Uno, Due and Tre) and Mediaset (Retequattro, Canale Cinque and Italia Uno). There are also many local channels. Most foreign programmes are dubbed into Italian, although satellite channels, such as BBC World News, Sky and CNN, show news and sports programmes in English. There are three national radio stations and hundreds of local stations.

**A selection of newspapers available at a newsstand**

## NEWSPAPERS

There are several national daily newspapers, including *La Stampa*, *Il Corriere della Sera* and *La Repubblica*. Papers with the most detailed news of Italy's major cities include *Il Mattino* for Naples, *Il Messaggero* for Rome, *La Nazione* for Florence and *Il Giornale* for Milan.

All newspapers will have local pages and listings for cinemas, theatres, main concerts and other cultural events. In Rome and Milan, *La Repubblica* also publishes regular "what's on and where to go" supplements called *TrovaRoma* and *ViviMilano* respectively. Florence's *Firenze Spettacolo* and Rome's *Roma C'è* are weekly entertainment listings magazines. The latter also has a useful restaurant section and a summary of listings in English at the back.

British and American papers, such as the *International Herald Tribune*, *International Guardian*, and *USA Today*, are readily available and tend to arrive in the main cities at around midday on the day of issue.

## POST OFFICE

Local post offices open from 8:25am–1:50pm weekdays, and from 8:25am–noon on Saturday. Main city post offices are open from 8:25am–7pm non-stop. Many tobacconists also sell stamps.

The Vatican City and the state of San Marino have their own postal systems and stamps. Bear in mind that letters bearing San Marino or Vatican stamps can only be posted in San Marino and Vatican post boxes.

The red post boxes (blue in the Vatican) usually have two slots labelled *per la città* (for the city only) and *tutte le altre destinazioni* (for all other destinations).

Italian post is notorious for its unreliability and letters can take between four days and two weeks to arrive.

For a faster service it is best to send letters by express post *(posta prioritaria)*. A more reliable option is recorded delivery *(raccomandata)*. Anything of value should be sent by insured post *(assicurata)*.

For urgent communications, try state couriers *Postacelere* and *Paccocelere*, which are based at all main post offices. They guarantee delivery within 24–72 hours and are far cheaper than private couriers.

**City letters** **Other destinations**

POSTE

**Italian post box**

## DIRECTORY

Remember to always use the full area code (including the first zero), even when phoning within a city.

### USEFUL NUMBERS

**Directory Enquiries**
***Tel*** *1254 (Option 1).*

**Multilingual Directory Enquiries**
***Tel*** *1254 (Option 2).*

**Operator Services**
***Tel*** *170* (also for reverse charge and calling card calls).

**American Operators**
***Tel*** *800 17 24 44 (AT&T).*
***Tel*** *800 17 24 01 (Verizon).*
***Tel*** *800 17 24 05 (Sprint).*

**Australian Operators**
***Tel*** *800 17 26 10 (Telstra).*
***Tel*** *800 17 26 11 (Optus).*

### COUNTRY CODES

To call Italy from these countries dial the code and then the full area code (including the 0) and the number.

***Tel*** *00 39 – UK*
***Tel*** *0 1139 – US & Canada*
***Tel*** *00 39 – Ireland*
***Tel*** *00 1139 – Australia*

### E-MAIL AND INTERNET

**Internet Train**
**www**.internettrain.it

**Skype**
**www**.skype.com

**Voip Stunt**
**www**.voipstunt.com

### POST AND COURIERS

**Italian Post Office**
**www**.poste.it

### PRIVATE COURIERS

**DHL**
***Tel*** *199 199 345.*
**www**.dhl.com

**Fedex**
***Tel*** *199 151 119.*
**www**.fedex.com

**UPS**
***Tel*** *02 30 30 30 39.*
**www**.ups.com

# TRAVEL INFORMATION

Italy has transport systems of varying efficiency, from the modern road, bus and rail networks of the north to the slower systems of the south. Numerous airlines operate flights to several of the country's major airports, while within Italy itself the national carrier Alitalia, and several smaller companies, provide an extensive network of internal flights. Connections by road to the rest of Europe are good, though Alpine roads can be adversely affected by the weather in winter. Motorways and other roads within the country are generally good, but can be busy at weekends and peak periods. Italy also has an efficient system of ferries connecting Sicily, Sardinia and many of the smaller off-shore islands. Many of these are car ferries, and are busy in summer.

Alitalia aircraft

### GREEN TRAVEL

Travelling in Italy without using high-impact flights or long car drives is straightforward, thanks to the excellent public transport network. Rail and bus systems both offer regular and reliable services and are reasonably priced. Connections with major European cities are good and travellers can often choose between day services on the Eurocity trains and overnight services on the EuroNight trains. There are also high speed trains, known as the *Alta Velocita* (*see pp676–7*).

Where only a few people use a service (such as to outlying hamlets in the Alps and Apennines), some authorities have set up a *servizio a chiamata* (demand-responsive service), whereby passengers phone a toll-free number to book a vehicle. This results in cost savings for the council and a reduction in carbon emissions, plus passengers get a personalized taxi for the price of a single bus ticket. Within cities, less polluting vehicles such as battery- or methane-powered buses and *vaporetti* have been introduced.

Bicycle tracks and cycle hire points are increasing in number, and many cities such as Milan and Rome have plenty of hire points and marked safe tracks. The Trentino-Alto Adige regions are especially well organized with long-distance cycle routes. For a small charge bicycles can be transported on many regional and international trains.

## Arriving by Air

Rome's Leonardo da Vinci (Fiumicino) and Milan's Malpensa are the key airports for long-haul flights into Italy. Milan's Linate airport handles some European flights, and most European airlines also fly to Venice, Turin, Naples and Pisa (for Florence). Many airlines are now flying regularly to smaller cities such as Florence, Genoa, Bologna, Verona and Bergamo, while charter flights serve summer destinations in peak season such as Catania, Olbia and Rimini.

Part of the extension to Fiumicino airport, Rome

### LONG-HAUL FLIGHTS

If you are flying from the United States, **Continental**, **Delta** and **United Airlines** operate regular direct scheduled flights to Rome and Milan, with services from New York, Philadelphia, Los Angeles, Boston and Chicago. **Air Canada** flies from Montreal and Toronto, and **Qantas** flies from Sydney and Melbourne.

A regular service between Rome and Milan and New York, Boston, Chicago, Miami and Toronto is also offered by the Italian state airline, **Alitalia**.

It may, however, be more convenient and cheaper for long-haul passengers to take a budget flight to London, Frankfurt, Paris, Athens or Amsterdam and then continue to Italy from there.

### EUROPEAN LOW-COST FLIGHTS

It has never been so easy to get to Italy by air. **British Airways** and **Alitalia** and its partners fly to major destinations in Italy from large European cities. However, low-cost, "no-frills" airlines offer many more destinations.

**Ryanair** flies to more than 20 airports (including Genoa, Rome-Ciampino, Turin and Venice-Treviso) from Stansted; while **easyJet**, from Gatwick or Stansted, serves Rome-Ciampino, Milan, Venice, Pisa, Palermo and Naples, and also Rome, Venice and Pisa from Bristol. **BMI British Midland** flies to Milan and Venice from Heathrow; **Meridiana** serves multiple destinations in Italy from Gatwick.

The entrance hall at Pisa airport

## TICKETS AND FARES

Fares vary enormously according to season and supply and demand. You can usually get the best deals by booking online well in advance.

Consult a good travel agent or check availability on the Internet. If you are based in the UK, it may be worthwhile to scour the small ads of newspapers for charter and discounted scheduled flights on major routes. Most charters leave from Gatwick or Luton, and may land at a city's second (and often less convenient) airport. Fares tend to vary greatly during the year, but the most expensive periods are during the summer months and over the Christmas and Easter holidays. Where possible, ask for available student discounts.

## PACKAGE HOLIDAYS

Package holidays to Italy are usually cheaper than travelling independently, unless you are travelling on a tight budget and are prepared to make use of youth hostels and campsites. Rome, Florence and Venice are often offered as separate or linked package deals, and many operators have packages to the Tuscan and Umbrian countryside, Sicily, the Italian Lakes, the Italian Riviera, Naples and the Amalfi coast. In winter, ski packages are available to many Alpine resorts. Specialist packages, such as cooking, walking and art tours are common.

In cities, different tour operators may use different hotels, so it is worth researching the most pleasant (and centrally located) accommodation options. Many operators include transfers from the airport to your hotel. Some include tour guides.

## DIRECTORY

### GREEN TRAVEL

**Cycling in Trentino**
www.trentino.to

### AIRLINES

**Air Canada**
www.aircanada.com

**Alitalia**
*Tel 06 22 22.* www.alitalia.com

**BMI British Midland**
www.flybmi.com

**British Airways**
*Tel 199 712 266.*
www.britishairways.com

**Delta** www.delta.com

**easyJet**
www.easyjet.com

**Meridiana**
www.meridiana.it

**Qantas**
www.qantas.com

**Ryanair**
www.ryanair.com

**United Airlines**
www.united.com

| AIRPORT | INFORMATION | DISTANCE TO CITY CENTRE | TAXI FARE TO CITY CENTRE | PUBLIC TRANSPORT TO CITY CENTRE |
|---|---|---|---|---|
| Rome (Fiumicino) | 06 659 51<br>www.adr.it | 35 km (22 miles) | €40 | FS 30 mins |
| Rome (Ciampino) | 06 659 51<br>www.adr.it | 15 km (9 miles) | €30 | M 45 mins |
| Milan (Linate) | 02 74 85 22 00<br>www.sea-aeroportimilano.it | 8 km (5 miles) | €15–€20 | 15 mins |
| Milan (Malpensa) | 02 74 85 22 00<br>www.sea-aeroportimilano.it | 50 km (31 miles) | €65–€75 | FS M 60 mins |
| Pisa (Galileo Galilei) | 050 84 91 11<br>www.pisa-airport.it | 2 km (1 mile) | €10 | FS to Pisa: 5 mins<br>FS to Florence: 80 mins |
| Venice (Marco Polo) | 041 260 92 60<br>www.veniceairport.it | 13 km (8 miles) | €35<br>(€90 water taxi) | 60 mins<br>20 mins |
| Venice (Treviso) | 0422 31 51 11<br>www.trevisoairport.it | 25 km (15 miles) | €70 to Venice | to Treviso: 20 mins<br>to Venice: 45 mins |
| Verona | 045 809 56 66<br>www.aeroportoverona.it | 12 km (7 miles) | €22 | 20 mins |
| Bergamo | 035 32 63 23<br>www.orioaeroporto.it | 5 km (3 miles) | €18 | 15 mins |
| Turin | 011 567 63 61<br>www.turin-airport.com | 15 km (9 miles) | €30 | 20 mins |
| Naples | 081 789 61 11<br>www.naples-airport.com | 7 km (4 miles) | €20 | 30 mins |
| Palermo | 091 702 02 73<br>www.gesap.it | 35 km (21 miles) | €40–€45 | 1 hr<br>1 hr |

# Arriving by Sea, Rail and Road

Orient-Express logo

Italy is served by an extensive network of roads, railways and international ferry lines. Road and rail links cross into the country from France, Switzerland, Austria and Slovenia, and there are through train services from as far afield as Budapest, London and Barcelona. Road connections into the country are generally of motorway standard, though delays can occur at some of the many Alpine passes and tunnels during bad weather or peak summer holiday periods.

Ticket windows at Florence's Santa Maria Novella station

## ARRIVING BY CAR

Most roads into Italy from the rest of Europe involve Alpine crossings by tunnel or mountain passes. The notable exceptions are the approach from Slovenia in the northeast (on the A4 motorway) and the route along the French Riviera that enters Italy as the A10 motorway at Ventimiglia.

The most popular route from Geneva and southeast France is via the Mont Blanc tunnel and A5 motorway, entering Italy close to Aosta and Turin. Another busy approach (from Switzerland) uses the St Bernard Pass and tunnel.

Further east, the main route from Austria and southern Germany crosses the Brenner Pass and goes down to Verona on the A22 motorway via Trento and the Adige valley. Weather conditions rarely close the passes, but snow and fog can make progress slow on the winding roads through the mountains. Most motorways are toll-roads; you pay as you leave the motorway.

## ARRIVING BY TRAIN

After air travel, arriving by train is the least painful way to reach Italy. Countless through services (including many sleepers) link Italian towns and cities with places as far afield as Brussels, Budapest and Barcelona. Connections from Paris (and London, via Eurostar) run to Turin, Milan, Venice, Bologna, Florence or along Italy's west coast, via Genoa and Pisa, to Rome and Naples. Services also operate from German, Swiss and other northern European cities to Milan, Turin, Venice and Verona. There are also direct services from Vienna, Spain and the south of France. Motorail connections exist from several centres in northern Europe and the Channel ports.

BINARIO 17

Platform sign

← uscita

Exit sign

The sleeping car on an international Eurocity train

Do-it-yourself help points with train information on screens

The popularity of low-cost airlines has forced international train travel to be a little more competitive – if booked online. Special discount fares, however, are often available for senior travellers and for people under 26.

Trains can be extremely busy during peak periods, particularly on Friday and Sunday evenings, and during the Christmas and Easter holiday periods. July and August can also be frantically busy, especially on routes from Germany and ports connecting with Greek ferries in the south. Reservations on most services are advisable.

## ARRIVING BY BOAT

Most people arriving in Italy by boat do so from Greece, using services from Corfu and Patras to Brindisi and other southeastern ports. Boats are crowded in summer, as are connecting train services from Brindisi to the rest of Italy.

Other international connections include ferries from Malta and North African ports to Palermo, Naples and various southern Italian ports. Boats also run from towns in the south of France to Genoa, Livorno and ports on the Italian Riviera, and from the Croatian coast across the Adriatic to Venice.

## ARRIVING BY COACH

Coach travel to Italy is relatively cheap, but long journey times make it one of the least comfortable ways to travel. The journey time from London to Milan is about 24 hours, and about 33 hours to Rome. A night on the road is thus unavoidable. **Eurolines** runs coaches from London's Victoria Coach Station to all of Italy's major cities as far as Rome and Naples. Buses travel via Dover, Calais, Paris and Dijon and it is useful to take some euros with you for the probable stops en route. Travel around Italy by long-distance coach is feasible with **SITA**.

SITA coach arriving at the station in Florence

# Travelling Around by Ferry

Italy's large number of off-shore islands mean that it has a large and well-developed network of ferries, as well as services to the rest of Europe and North Africa.

One of the Moby Lines car ferries that sail the Mediterranean

## FERRIES

Car ferries are a convenient link with the beautiful islands scattered off the Italian mainland. Boats for Sardinia leave from Civitavecchia (north of Rome), Livorno and Genoa, and depart for Sicily from Naples and Reggio di Calabria. Ferries run from the major Sicilian ports to the Egadi and the Aeolian archipelagoes, as well as to countless other small islands around Sicily (although be aware that ferries to the smaller islands do not always carry cars).

Boats also ply between Elba and Piombino, as well as the smaller islands of the Tuscan archipelago such as Capraia. Ferries run from ports close to Rome to Ponza and its surrounding islands, and from Naples to Capri and Ischia. On the east coast the Tremiti islands are linked to ports on the Gargano peninsula.

Hydrofoils are increasingly complementing conventional ferries, particularly on busy routes to Capri and Ischia. Hydrofoils, and ferries, also run on some of Italy's lakes, such as Como and Garda.

Queues for ferries are common in summer, so book well ahead if you wish to travel in July or August, especially if taking a vehicle. Ferry services are more frequent and reliable in summer than in winter.

Bookings can be made online, through travel agents or at a ferry line's agents in your own country. Ticket prices can vary according to the time of year but are generally reasonable. To check schedules and fares, visit the relevant website.

## DIRECTORY

### COACH COMPANIES

**Eurolines**
www.eurolines.co.uk

**SITA**
www.sitabus.it

### RAILWAYS

**Ferrovie dello Stato**
www.trenitalia.com

### FERRIES

**Corsica Sardinia Ferries**
*Tel* 199 400 500.
www.corsicaferries.com
Civitavecchia/Livorno – Golfo Aranci

**Grandi Navi Veloci**
*Tel* 010 209 45 91.
www.gnv.it
Genoa/Civitavecchia – Palermo
Genoa – Porto Torres/ Olbia

**Moby Lines**
*Tel* 199 303 040; 06 42 01 14 55.
www.mobylines.com
Piombino – Elba
Genoa/Livorno – Olbia

**SNAV**
*Tel* 081 428 55 55.
www.snav.it
Pescara – Hvat/Split
Naples – Capri/Ischia
Naples – Aeolian Islands/ Palermo

**Tirrenia**
*Tel* 892 123; 02 26 30 28 03. www.tirrenia.it
Bari – Durazzo
Genoa – Olbia
Civitavecchia – Golfo Aranci
Naples – Palermo/Cagliari
Cagliari – Palermo

**Venezia Lines**
*Tel* 041 272 26 47.
www.venezialines.com
Venice – Piran
Venice – Porec/Rovinj/Pula
Bari – Durazzo

# Travelling Around by Train

Trenitalia logo

Train travel is one of the best ways to explore Italy. Tickets are inexpensive, services frequent, and rolling stock some of the most modern in Europe. Services can be busy, but the days of rampant overcrowding are mostly over. Lines often run through lovely countryside, from mountain lakes to rolling plateaux, and they provide more convenient links between cities than roads or air travel. Only in the south, or deeply rural areas, are services slow and infrequent.

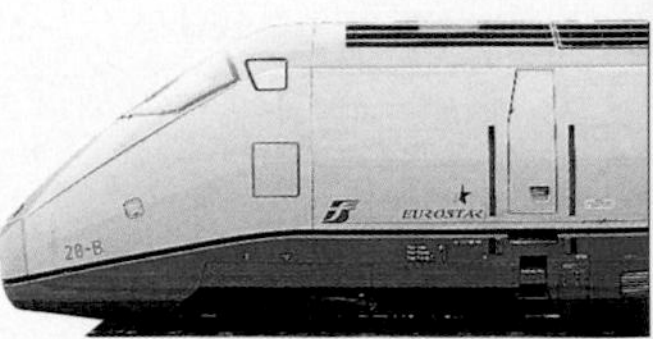

A Eurostar – one of Italy's fastest trains

The concourse at Stazione Termini, Rome

## THE NETWORK

The bulk of Italy's rail network is an integrated state-run system operated by Trenitalia of the Ferrovie dello Stato (FS), though the NTV consortium promises to introduce rival super-fast services in 2011. Smaller privately run lines also fill crucial gaps left by the FS, but through-tickets are generally available where travel involves both networks. State and private lines often (but not always) share the same main station *(stazione)*, and also charge similar fares.

## TRAINS

Trenitalia is in the process of changing the categories of trains, and has already constructed an *Alta Velocità* (AV) network between major cities in the north and southwards as far as Naples. These, the fast Eurostar (ES) and a handful of other special high-speed trains always require pre-booking of seats. Intercity (IC) trains and Eurocity (EC) trains only stop at major stations and require the payment of a supplement *(un supplemento)* on top of the standard ticket (supplements can be bought on the train, but are more expensive). *Regionali* and *Interregionali* trains make more stops and require no supplement.

All AV, ES, EC and Intercity trains are usually air-conditioned. Branch line carriages can still be ancient.

Facilities for the disabled, including assistance at stations, exist on all fast trains and international services. For assistance ask at the special *Sale Blu* (Blue Halls) in mainline stations.

## TICKETS AND FARES

Tickets *(biglietti)* are available as single *(andata)* or return *(andata e ritorno)* in first *(prima)* or second class *(seconda classe)*. They can be bought at some travel agents or at any station ticket office *(biglietteria)*.

Major stations have automatic ticket machines and you can also buy tickets for journeys of up to 250 km (155 miles) from newsstands or station tobacconists (such a ticket is called *biglietto a fascia chilometrica*). Be sure to validate all tickets on both outbound and return journeys, or you will be fined. A ticket's validity usually starts on the day of purchase, so be sure to specify the day of travel when buying tickets in advance. Booking and purchasing tickets online is handy and will often entail a discount.

Fares are calculated on a kilometric basis and are among the cheapest in western Europe. Many discounted fares are offered, including special family tickets.

Refunds involve a complicated process – enquire at the *Assistenza* counter at major stations. It is important, therefore, to buy the correct ticket before travelling.

## PASSES

The most useful pass for visitors is the **Interrail Pass**, which gives unlimited travel for consecutive or non-consecutive days over varying periods, with special rates for those under 26. It can be purchased online or at most mainline stations and various agencies outside Italy.

## TIMETABLES

If you plan to use trains often, it is a good idea to pick up an official Trenitalia timetable *(un orario)* at the railway station or newsstands. It is updated yearly. Alternatively, visit www.trenitalia.com for the online timetable.

## VALIDITY AND RESERVATIONS

Single or return tickets are valid for up to two months from the date of purchase. If a seat reservation is made with the ticket, however, the date you wish to travel will be stamped automatically on the ticket. Reservations are automatic on AV and Eurostar services, and they are a good idea on all trains on and around public holidays. Reservations can be made at most main stations or online.

## REDUCTIONS

The Smart Price deal offers discounts on international trains between Italy and various European countries. Single prices range from €15 to €49, though there are additions for couchettes and wagon-lits. Tickets can be bought at mainline stations or on the Trenitalia website, though only a fixed number are available so book ahead.

## LEFT LUGGAGE

Main city stations usually have left luggage facilities. Most are manned (but the smaller stations have self-service lockers), and you may need to present a passport or other form of identification when depositing or collecting bags. Fees are calculated per bag.

Left luggage logo

## SCENIC RAIL ROUTES

Italy's varied geography makes for some memorable train trips across the length and breadth of the country. The glacially shaped Adige valley between Bolzano and Verona in the north is thick with apple orchards and surrounded by soaring alpine peaks, with the pretty Trento-Male line branching off it. The Tuscan countryside south of Florence boasts views of hill towns and rolling wheat fields, while close by in Lazio the Roma Nord-Viterbo line winds its way through beautiful rural scenery. Further south, trains cross the Straits of Messina to Sicily on a special ferry, while a narrow gauge line circles Mount Etna.

For steam train enthusiasts there are trips run by the **FTI (Ferrovie Turistiche Italiane)** groups in the north through alpine foothills and past picturesque lakes, as well as in the countryside outside Siena.

## MACHINES FOR TRENITALIA RAIL TICKETS

These machines are easy to use, and most have instructions on screen in a choice of six languages. They accept coins, notes and credit cards.

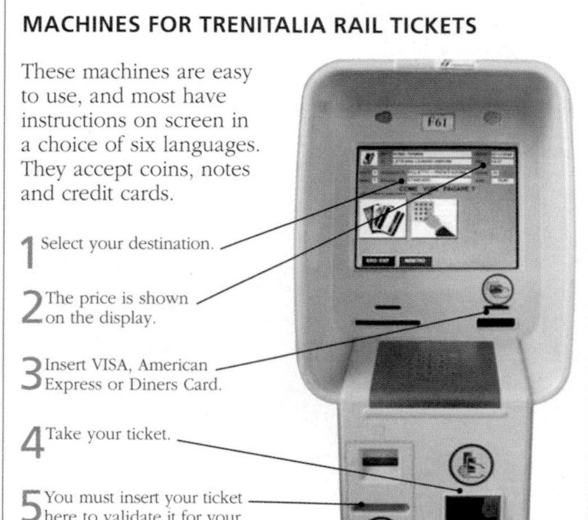


## ITALY'S PRINCIPAL FS NETWORK

The Italian state rail network operates various types of service. Check what is on offer before buying your ticket.

## DIRECTORY

### RAILWAY INFORMATION

**Italian State Railway Information Office**
Information for travel all over Italy.
***Tel*** *89 20 21.*
**www**.ferroviedellostato.it

**Interrail Pass**
**www**.interrailnet.com

**European Rail Ltd**
***Tel*** *020 7619 1083 (UK).*
**www**.europeanrail.com

**FTI (Ferrovie Turistiche Italiane)**
**www**.ferrovieturistiche.it

# Travelling Around by Car

The classic Fiat 500

A motoring tour is a practical way of exploring the country, though you should take into account high petrol prices, parking difficulties, driving restrictions in cities and the Italians' occasionally erratic approach to driving. A car is invaluable in the countryside and for extensive touring, but less useful in major towns and cities, due to congestion and the fact that most city centres are off-limits to non-residents' cars.

One-way street

Blue signs showing main roads and green signs showing motorways

Automatic tollbooths on the motorway outside Florence

## WHAT TO TAKE

Drivers from outside Italy bringing their own foreign-registered cars into the country must carry a Green Card (for insurance purposes), all the vehicle's registration documents, and a full, valid driving licence (*patente* in Italian). Any EU nationals who do not have the standard EU "pink" licence and are planning to stay for more than six months will need an Italian translation of their licence, obtainable from most motoring organizations or from the Italian state tourist office in your home country. A red warning triangle and fluorescent vests must also be carried at all times, for use in the event of a breakdown.

## PETROL

Petrol *(benzina)* in Italy is some of the most expensive in Europe (diesel, or *gasolio*, is a little cheaper). Although many petrol stations are now self-service, it is still common to be served by an attendant. Most petrol stations follow normal shop hours so make sure you have a full tank before lunchtime or public holidays. On motorways petrol stations tend to be open 24 hours a day. Credit cards are usually accepted.

## ROADS

Italy has a good network of motorways, though many have a total of only four lanes, often leading to congestion. Busy routes include the A1 from Bologna to Florence and between Bologna, Parma and Milan. Tolls are payable on most motorways *(autostrade)*, again leading to congestion at tollbooths *(Alt Stazione)* at busy periods. Payment is made at the end of the journey in cash, credit card or pre-paid magnetic VIA cards, available from tobacconists and the **ACI**. There is a congestion charge in Milan (7:30am–7:30pm Mon–Fri); phone 800 437 437 or visit www.comunemilano.it/ecopass before entering the city.

Secondary roads are known as *Nazionali* (N) or as *Strade Statali* (SS), and vary enormously in quality. Mountain roads are usually good, but distances can be deceptive. In winter, snow chains are obligatory on many higher routes. Some back roads (known as *strade bianche*, or "white roads") have only a gravel surface. These are slow, but usually passable to cars.

### Rules and Regulations

*Drive on the right and give way to traffic from the right. Seat belts are compulsory for all passengers. Heavy fines are levied for using a mobile phone while driving. Headlights must be turned on even during the day on motorways and outside built-up areas. The speed limit in urban areas is 50 km/h (30 mph); outside urban areas it is 110 km/h (70 mph) on dual carriageways and 90 km/h on other secondary roads. On motorways the limit is 130 km/h (80 mph) for vehicles over 1100cc, 110 km/h (70 mph) for those under 1100cc.*

No stopping

End of speed restriction

Pedestrianized street – no traffic

Give way to oncoming traffic

No parking

Danger (often with description)

Logo for international car hire company

## CAR HIRE

Car hire *(autonoleggio)* is expensive in Italy, and should be organized beforehand through fly-drive deals or pre-booked with firms who have branches in Italy. For on the spot hire Italian firms may be cheaper than big international names. Agencies are listed in Yellow Pages *(Pagine Gialle)* under Autonoleggio. Most airports conveniently have car hire offices on site.

To rent a car in Italy you must be over 21 (and sometimes older) and have held a valid driver's licence for at least a year. Visitors from outside the EU require an international licence, though in practice not all hire firms insist on this. Check the small print of the agreement for insurance cover.

## ACCIDENTS AND BREAKDOWNS

If you have an accident or a breakdown, switch on your hazard warning lights and place a warning triangle 50 m (164 ft) behind your car. Then (for breakdowns) call the **ACI** emergency number (803 116) or the emergency services (112 or 113). The ACI will tow any foreign-registered car free to the nearest ACI-affiliated garage. They also do free repairs for members of affiliated associations, such as the AA and RAC in Britain.

If you have an accident keep calm, and do not admit liability or make any statements that might incriminate you later. Simply swap car and insurance details, names and addresses.

## PARKING

Parking in most Italian cities and large towns is a problem. Many historic centres have restricted daytime access and baffling one-way systems. Other areas may be reserved for residents' parking (marked *riservato ai residenti*). Most towns have metered parking areas that charge an hourly fee paid with coins, cards or coupons bought from *tabacchi*. Cars can be towed away or clamped, especially in areas marked *zona rimozione*, particularly on street-cleaning days. Call the Municipal Police *(Vigili)* to retrieve your car.

Official parking area patrolled by attendant

## SAFETY

Car theft is rife in Italy. Never leave anything in your car, and (if possible) always remove radio-CD players. Leave your car in a guarded car park whenever you can. Be especially careful driving at night, when Italian driving is more cavalier than usual, and when many traffic lights switch to flashing amber. Hitching *(autostop)* is not a good idea (and is not common), certainly never for women on their own.

## DIRECTORY

### CAR HIRE

**Avis**
*Tel 06 481 43 73.*
www.avisautonoleggio.it

**Europcar**
*Tel 199 307 030.*
www.europcar.it

**Hertz**
*Tel 06 65 01 15 53 (Rome airport).*
www.hertz.com

**Maggiore**
*Tel 199 151 120.*
www.maggiore.it

**Sixt**
*Tel 06 65 21 11 (Rome).*
www.sixt.it

### EMERGENCIES

**ACI emergency**
*Tel 803 116.* www.aci.it

**Police**
*Tel 112 or 113.*

**Ambulance**
*Tel 118.*

## DISTANCE CHART

**10 Distance in kilometres**
10 Distance in miles

| | ROME | ANCONA | AOSTA | BOLOGNA | BOLZANO | FLORENCE | GENOA | LECCE | MILAN | NAPLES | TURIN |
|---|---|---|---|---|---|---|---|---|---|---|---|
| ANCONA | **286** 178 | | | | | | | | | | |
| AOSTA | **748** 465 | **617** 383 | | | | | | | | | |
| BOLOGNA | **383** 238 | **219** 136 | **401** 249 | | | | | | | | |
| BOLZANO | **645** 401 | **494** 307 | **449** 279 | **280** 174 | | | | | | | |
| FLORENCE | **278** 173 | **262** 163 | **470** 292 | **106** 66 | **367** 228 | | | | | | |
| GENOA | **510** 317 | **506** 315 | **245** 152 | **291** 101 | **422** 262 | **225** 140 | | | | | |
| LECCE | **601** 373 | **614** 382 | **1220** 758 | **822** 511 | **1097** 682 | **871** 541 | **1103** 685 | | | | |
| MILAN | **575** 357 | **426** 265 | **181** 113 | **210** 130 | **295** 183 | **299** 186 | **145** 90 | **1029** 639 | | | |
| NAPLES | **219** 136 | **409** 254 | **959** 596 | **594** 369 | **856** 532 | **489** 304 | **714** 444 | **393** 244 | **786** 488 | | |
| TURIN | **673** 418 | **547** 340 | **110** 68 | **332** 206 | **410** 255 | **395** 245 | **170** 106 | **1150** 715 | **138** 86 | **884** 549 | |
| VENICE | **530** 329 | **364** 226 | **442** 275 | **154** 96 | **214** 133 | **255** 158 | **397** 247 | **967** 601 | **273** 170 | **741** 460 | **402** 250 |

# Travelling within Cities

Pedestrian zone sign

The best ways of getting around Italian cities differ from place to place. In Rome buses are most useful, in Milan the metro is more efficient, and in Venice you will need to take a boat to get about. Trams still run in some cities, such as Milan and Rome. Cars are a liability almost everywhere, unlike walking, which in many cases is the easiest way to negotiate the tight historic cores of Italian towns and cities. Florence has a large limited-traffic zone, and most towns now have a pedestrian area in the centre.

A Roman bus in the red and grey livery of ATAC

One of the distinctive orange city buses, central Verona

## BUSES AND TRAMS

Virtually every Italian city and large town has a bus system. Most are cheap, comprehensive and as efficient as traffic and narrow streets will allow and vary only slightly from city to city. Bus stops are known as *fermate*, and increasingly (notably in Rome) list full details of the routes they serve. Buses *(autobus)* usually run from about 6am to midnight, and there are night buses *(servizio notturno)* in larger cities. If you arrive in a town by train, stations are invariably linked to the centre by shuttle buses from the station forecourt (tickets are usually available from the station bar or tobacconist).

## TICKETS

Tickets *(biglietti)* must be bought before boarding the bus from kiosks belonging to the bus company (ATAF in Florence, ATAC in Rome), bars, newsstands or tobacconists displaying the bus company's sticker. A few cities also have on-street vending machines around the main transport hubs. It is worth buying more than one ticket at a time, as outlets often close in the afternoon or early evening. Discounted tickets *(un blocchetto)*, or day- or week-long visitors' tickets and passes *(una tessera* or *tesserino)* are also available. In some cities tickets are valid for any number of journeys within a given time. The ATAC website has more details on buses in Rome.

**ATAC**
www.atac.roma.it

## USING BUSES AND TRAMS

Board buses via the front and rear doors, and exit via the central doors. Buses usually only have a driver and no conductor (though night buses may have a conductor from whom tickets can be bought). Tickets must be validated by

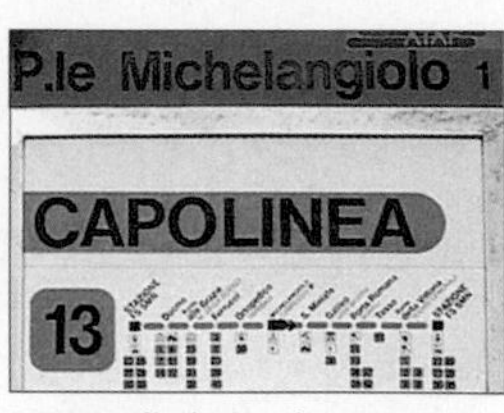


Bus stop displaying the route

punching them in machines at the front or rear of the bus. There are large on-the-spot fines if you are caught without a properly validated ticket. The front, low seats on buses are for people with children, the elderly and the disabled.

Most larger cities have transport information offices at the main train station or piazza which provide free maps, timetables and tickets.

The majority of city buses are painted bright orange and display the final destination *(capolinea)* on the front.

## METROPOLITANA

Underground systems, known as *metropolitana* (*la metro* for short), are found in Rome and Milan. Rome's network amounts to just two lines, A and B, which converge at Stazione Termini, the city's central railway station. Several stations are useful for key sights, and at peak times the lines provide the best way of crossing the city quickly. Stations are fairly dingy – though rarely dangerous – and train carriages can be stiflingly hot in summer. In Milan the network is more extensive, with three principal lines – MM1 (the red line), MM2 (green) and MM3 (yellow) – that meet at the hub stations of Stazione Centrale, Duomo, Cadorna and Lima. These three lines give easy access to the

M

Metro sign

Termini Metro station, Rome

Waiting for a fare at an official rank in Florence

majority of the city's main sights.

Metro tickets in both cities are available from the same sources as bus and tram tickets, and from machines and ticket offices in underground stations. Tickets in Rome are valid for one journey only, though the special *BIG* ticket offers a day's travel on bus, tram and metro. In Milan, by contrast, ordinary metro tickets are valid for 75 minutes for any number of journeys and can also be used on the buses and trams.

It is unwise to buy tickets from people outside stations, as they are invariably already used or otherwise invalid.

Stay on the pavement at all costs

Marginally less dangerous to cross

## WALKING

Walking can be a wonderful way to explore Italy's historic towns and cities, most of whose historic centres are smaller than you might expect. Traffic can be a curse, however, especially in narrow streets (Rome is worst in this respect), but many cities are introducing pedestrianized areas or cutting down on car access around key tourist sights. On certain Sundays *(Domenica a Piedi)*, entire town centres may be designated traffic-free zones.

Italian towns have plenty of shady squares and cafés to escape the heat of the summer sun, and churches and cathedrals also provide cool retreats from the rigours of sightseeing. Most sights are well signposted (churches, museums and other places of interest are often indicated by yellow signs). Always carry your valuables well out of sight. The best times to walk are in the cool of the morning, or in the early evening, when you can join in the pre-dinner stroll known as the *passeggiata*.

## TAXIS

Only accept rides in official taxis. Most drivers are honest but there are many supplements that can be legitimately levied. Generally an extra charge is made for each piece of luggage placed in the boot, for rides between 10pm and 7am, on Sundays and public holidays, and for journeys to and from airports.

In theory, taxis cannot be hailed. Take one at an official taxi stand (usually found at the station, main piazza or close to key tourist sights) or reserve one by phone. When you order a taxi by phone, take the driver's code name, eg Napoli 18. If you call a cab, the meter will run from your call.

## CYCLE HIRE

Many towns and cities, especially those popular with visitors, have stands and shops offering bikes and scooters for rent. You can usually rent hourly or by the day, and you may have to leave your passport with the shop as a deposit. Be very careful, however, if riding a bike in the busy traffic of the larger towns and cities.

**Roma Bikesharing** (www.atac-bikesharing.it, tel 06 570 03), in the capital, gives access to bikes at various places in the city centre. You pay a €10 deposit to enrol (this includes €5 for initial rides). You can top up your electronic "smartcard" while using the bikes. The current rate is €0.50 for every half hour of use.

## INTER-CITY TRANSPORT: COACHES

Long-haul buses *(pullman* or *corriere)* between towns operate in a similar way to local buses, though you can usually buy tickets on board, and services are often run by different companies in different-coloured buses (blue is the most common colour for *pullman*, orange for city buses). Coaches in some areas may be run by several companies (notably around Florence and in Tuscany), and not all operate from the same termini. Services often depart from outside railway stations, or from a town's main piazza. If in doubt, ask at local tourist offices. A reduced service may operate at weekends, when offices are shut.

Rome – Gubbio bus

**Rome**
COTRAL ***Tel*** *800 174 471.* **www**.cotralspa.it
Lazzi ***Tel*** *06 884 08 40.*
Appian ***Tel*** *06 48 78 66 04.* **www**.appianline.it

**Tuscany**
Lazzi ***Tel*** *055 512 82 86.* **www**.lazzi.it
Sita ***Tel*** *800 37 37 60.* **www**.sitabus.it
Tra-In ***Tel*** *0577 20 41 11.* **www**.trainspa.it

**National & International**
Eurolines ***Tel*** *0861 55 40 14.* **www**.eurolines.it

# Travelling Around Venice

For visitors to Venice, the *vaporetti* or waterbuses *(see pp136–7)* provide an entertaining form of public transport, although most journeys within the city can usually be covered more quickly on foot. The main route through the city for the *vaporetti* is the Grand Canal. Waterbuses also supply a useful service connecting outlying points on the periphery of Venice, and linking the city to the islands in the lagoon. The most important service from a visitor's point of view is the No. 1. This operates from one end of the Grand Canal to the other and travels slowly enough for you to admire the parade of palaces at the waterside *(see pp88–91)*.

A *vaporetto* or waterbus

The smaller, sleeker *motoscafo*

## THE BOATS

The original *vaporetti* were steam-powered (*vaporetto* means little steamer); today they are mostly diesel-run motor boats, with a handful of electric, battery-powered prototypes. Although all the boats tend to be called *vaporetti*, the word only really applies to the large wide boats used on slow routes, such as No. 1. These boats provide the best views. *Motoscafi* are the slimmer, smaller boats that look old but go at a fair pace, while *motonavi* are two-tier boats that run to the islands. To visit the islands of Murano, Burano or Torcello, take the LN Line, which departs from San Zaccaria and Fondamente Nuove.

## TYPES OF TICKET

If booths at landing stages are closed, single tickets can be purchased on board at no extra charge – the tickets are valid for 1 hour from purchase. A good way to save money, however, is by buying a travel card, available for 12, 24, 36, 48 or 72 hours. Such a card entitles the holder to unlimited travel on most lines. The Venice Card is a handy pass covering entry to the main sights as well as boats. It can be purchased in advance online (www.hellovenezia.com). Discounts on advance tickets are also available (www.veniceconnected.com).

If you are staying more than a few days, it is worth buying a weekly season ticket *(abbonamento)*, available from ticket offices, though non-residents are charged €50 for the privilege. Holders of Rolling Venice cards (with information packs and discounts for 14–29-year-olds) can buy a three-day youth pass. Tickets include transport for one piece of luggage, so be prepared to buy another ticket for extra items.

A two-tier *motonave* boat

*Vaporetto* stop at the Giardini Pubblici, Venice

## HOURS OF SERVICE

The main routes run every 10 to 20 minutes until the early evening. Services are reduced after midnight, but they run all night. From June to September the services are more frequent and certain routes are extended. Timetables are available at main landing stages. Be warned: from May to September the main routes and island boats are very crowded.

## VAPORETTO INFORMATION

**ACTV (Information Office)**
Piazzale Roma, Venice. **Map** 5 B1.
***Tel*** *041 2424.* **www**.actv.it

## TRAGHETTI

*Traghetti* are gondola ferries that cross the Grand Canal at seven different points, providing a useful service for pedestrians. Few tourists make use of this cheap (about 50 cents per trip), constant service. Points where *traghetti* cross the Grand Canal are marked on the Street Finder maps *(see pp126–35)*. A gondola on yellow street signs points to *traghetti* stops.

## GONDOLAS

Gondolas are a luxury form of transport used only by visitors and Venetians at weddings. Before boarding, check the official tariffs and agree a price with the gondolier. Official costs are around €80 for 40 minutes, rising to €100 after 7pm. During the low season, you may also be able to negotiate a lower fee, and a journey shorter than the usual 40 minutes.

## WATER TAXIS

For those with little time and sufficient funds, the fastest and most practical means of getting from A to B in Venice is by water taxi. The craft are sleek, white or polished wood motorboats, and all are equipped with a cabin.

They zip efficiently to and from the airport in only 20 minutes. There are 16 water taxi ranks, including one at the airport and one at the Lido. Beware of extra charges for transporting luggage, waiting, night service and for calling out a taxi. When the *vaporetti* go on strike, taxis are scarce.

A water taxi

Crossing the Grand Canal by *traghetto*

## WATER TAXI STANDS

**Radio Taxi (all of Venice)**
***Tel*** *041 240 67 12.*

**Piazzale Roma**
**Map** 5 B1.
***Tel*** *041 71 69 22.*

## THE MAIN ROUTES

① This is the slow boat down the Grand Canal, stopping at every landing stage. The route starts at Piazzale Roma, travels the length of the Grand Canal, then from San Marco it heads east to the Lido.

② The 2 is the faster route down the Grand Canal. With an extension to the Lido during the summer months, the route serves San Zaccaria, continuing westwards along the Giudecca Canal to Tronchetto and Piazzale Roma, then down the Grand Canal back to San Zaccaria.

㊶㊷(51)(52)(61)(62) These lines all extend as far as the Lido. The circular *Giracittà* routes 41-42 provide a scenic tour of Venice and Murano, while lines 51-52 and 61-62 also extend to the Lido.

(LN) This line departs from the Fondamente Nuove and runs to the main islands in the northern lagoon – Murano, Mazzorbo and Burano (with a connection to Torcello) – then loops via Punta Sabbioni and the Lido, before concluding at San Zaccaria.

## USING THE VAPORETTI

1 Tickets are available at most landing stages, some bars, shops and tobacconists displaying the ACTV sign. It is also possible to buy them on board. The price of a ticket remains the same whether you are going one stop or travelling the whole line.

2 Signs on the landing stage tell you the direction of the boats stopping there.

3 Imob electronic chip tickets are in use and should be validated before each journey at the electronic machines on the landing stages. Inspectors rarely board the boats and this makes it surprisingly easy to hop on and off the boats without a validated ticket. However, there are steep fines for any passengers caught without tickets.

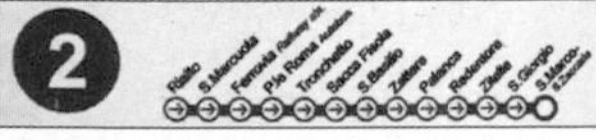


4 An indicator board at the front of each boat gives the line number and main stops. (Ignore the black numbers on the boat's side.)

5 Each landing stage has its name clearly marked on a board. Most stops have two landing stages and it is quite easy, particularly if it is crowded and you can't see which way the boat is facing, to board a boat travelling in the wrong direction. It is helpful to watch which direction the boat is approaching from; if in doubt, check with the boatman.

# General Index

Page numbers in **bold** type refer to main entries

## A

## B

## D

## G

## M

## P

## Q



## R

## T

## U



## V

# Acknowledgments

DORLING KINDERSLEY would like to thank the following people whose contributions and assistance have made the preparation of this book possible.

## Contributors

**Paul Duncan** is an expert on art and architectural history and has published a guide to Sicily as well as one on Italy's hill-towns.
**Tim Jepson**, formerly Rome correspondent for the *Sunday Telegraph*, has written guides to Tuscany, Umbria, Rome and Venice, a complete guide to Italy, *Italy by Train* and *Wild Italy*, a guide to Italy's nature reserves.
**Andrew Gumbel**, former Reuters correspondent in Rome, has written a number of guide books and is the correspondent for the *Independent* in Rome.
**Christopher Catling** has written guides to Florence and Tuscany, the Veneto and the Italian Lakes and is particularly interested in archaeology.
**Sam Cole** works for Reuters in Rome, where he has lived for some years, and contributes regularly to guidebooks on Rome and the Lazio region.

## Additional Contributors

Dominic Robertson, Mick Hamer, Richard Langham Smith, Gillian Price.

## Additional Photography

Francesco Allegretto, Giuseppe Carfagna & Associati, Peter Chadwick, Andy Crawford, Philip Dowell, Mike Dunning, Philip Enticknap, Steve Gorton, Dave King, Neil Mersh, Roger Moss, Poppy, Kim Sayer, James Stevenson, Clive Streeter, Jo-Ann Titmarsh, David Ward, Matthew Ward.

## Additional Illustrations

Andrea Corbella, Richard Draper, Kevin Jones Associates, Chris Orr and Associates, Robbie Polley, Simon Roulstone, Martin Woodward.

## Cartographic Research

Jane Hugill, Samantha James, Jennifer Skelley.

## Design and Editorial Assistance

Beverley Ager, Gillian Allan, Gaye Allen, Douglas Amrine, Emily Anderson, Peter Bently, Sonal Bhatt, Uma Bhattacharya, Tessa Bindloss, Hilary Bird, Sally-Ann Bloomfield, Samantha Borland, Isabel Boucher, Hugo Bowles, Reid Bramblett, Caroline Brooke, Nick Bruno, Paola Cacucciola, Stefano Cavedoni, Margaret Chang, Susi Cheshire, Elspeth Collier, Sherry Collins, Lucinda Cooke, Cooling Brown, Michelle Crane, Gary Cross, Felicity Crowe, Peter Douglas, Mandy Dredge, Stephanie Driver, Julia Dunn, Michael Ellis, Adele Evans, Mariana Evmolpidou, Danny Farnham, Karen Fitzpatrick, Anna Freiberger, Jackie Gordon, Angela-Marie Graham, Caroline Greene, Vanessa Hamilton, Amy Harrison, Sally-Ann Hibbard, Elinor Hodgson, Tim Hollis, Paul Jackson, Gail Jones, Roberta Kedzierski, Amy Knauff, Steve Knowlden, Suresh Kumar, Leonie Loudon, Siri Lowe, Carly Madden, Hayley Maher, Nicola Malone, Sarah Martin, Georgina Matthews, Ferdie McDonald, Sam Merrell, Ian Midson, Rebecca Milner, Adam Moore, Cherrye Moore, John Murphy, Cristina Murroni, Jennifer Mussett, Catherine Palmi, Helen Partington, Alok Pathak, Alice Peebles, Tamsin Pender, Marianne Petrou, Gillian Price, David Pugh, Rada Radojicic, Jake Reimann, Catherine Richards, David Roberts, Evelyn Robertson, Carolyn Ryden, Simon Ryder, Giuseppina Russo, Collette Sadler, Sands Publishing Solutions, Baishakhee Sengupta, Kunal Singh, Ellie Smith, Alison Stace, Solveig Steinhardt, Donald Strachan, Hugh Thompson, Jo-Ann Titmarsh, Conrad Van Dyk, Elaine Verweymeren, Ingrid Vienings, Karen Villabona, Stewart J Wild, Veronica Wood.

DORLING KINDERSLEY would also like to thank the following for their assistance: Azienda Autonoma di Soggiorno Cura e Turismo, Napoli; Azienda Promozione Turistica del Trentino, Trento; Osservatorio Geofisico dell'Università di Modena; Bell'Italia; Enotria Winecellars.

## Photography Permission

DORLING KINDERSLEY would like to thank the following for their assistance and kind permission to photograph at their establishments: Assessorato Beni Culturali Comune di Padova. Le Soprintendenze Archeologiche di Agrigento, di Enna, di Etruria Meridionale, per il Lazio, di Napoli, di Pompei, di Reggio Calabria e di Roma. Le Soprintendenze per i Beni Ambientali e Architettonici di Bolzano, di Napoli, di Potenza, della Provincia di Firenze e Pistoia, di Ravenna, di Roma, di Siena e di Urbino. Le Soprintendenze per i Beni Ambientali, Architettonici, Artistici e Storici di Caserta, di Cosenza, di Palermo, di Pisa, di Salerno e di Venezia. Le Soprintendenze per i Beni Artistici e Storici della Provincia di Firenze e Pistoia, di Milano e di Roma. Also all the other churches, museums, hotels, shops, restaurants, galleries and sights too numerous to thank individually.

## Picture Credits

t = top; tl = top left; tc = top centre; tr = top right; cla = centre left above; ca = centre above; cra = centre right above; cl = centre left; c = centre; cr = centre right; clb = centre left below; cb = centre below; crb = centre right below; bl = bottom left; b = bottom; bc = bottom centre; br = bottom right.

Works of art have been reproduced with the permission of the following copyright holders: © ADAGP, Paris and DACS, London 2006 *Bird in Space* by Constantin Brancusi 105cl; © DACS, 2006 *Mother and Son* by Carlo Carrà 199t.

DORLING KINDERSLEY would like to thank the following for their assistance: Eric Crighton: 83cra, FIAT: 220c, Gucci Ltd: 39cr, Prada, Milan: 39c, National Archaeological Museum, Naples:

495br, National Maritime Museum 40c, Royal Botanic Gardens, Kew: 83ca, Science Museum: 40cla, Telecom Italia: 670tc.

The publisher would like to thank the following individuals, companies and picture libraries for permission to reproduce their photographs: Accademia Italiana: Sue Bond 495c; Actv S.p.A: 682br; AFE, Rome: 38cb, 39tl; Giuseppe Carfagna 194b, 202b, 218tl, 218b, 221bl, 224b, 225t, 235t, Claudio Cerquetti 68t, 69bl, 69t; Enrico Martino 58clb, 66tr; Roberto Merlo 236b, 239t, 239b; Piero Servo 267t, 269b, Gustavo Tomsich 227t; Archivio APT Monregalese 229t; Action Plus: Mike Hewitt 70ca; Glyn Kirk 71tr; Alamy Images: Krys Bailey 666cl, CubolImages srl 11bl, /Adriano Bacchella 181tl, /Bluered 325tl; /Enrico Caracciolo 249c, gkphotography 79cl, Goodshoot 12tr, Steven May 682cla; Theodore Liasi 666cla, vario images GmbH & Co.KG/Ulrich Baumgarten 668cl, 670bl; Alitalia: 672t; Allsport: Mark Thompson: 71cl; Ancient Art and Architecture: 43t, 481br; Archiv für Kunst und Geschichte, London: 28bl, 34b, *Rossini* (1820), Camuccini, Museo Teatrale alla Scala, Milan 36br, 37bl, 41br, *Pope Sixtus IV Naming Platina Prefect of the Library,* Melozzo da Forlì (1477), Pinacoteca Vaticana, Rome 42, 44tl, *Statue of Augustus from Prima Porta* (1st century AD) 49tl, *The Gift of Constantine* (1246), Oratorio di San Silvestro, Rome 50cl, *Frederick I Barbarossa as a Crusader* (1188), Biblioteca Apostolica Vaticana, Rome 53bl, 56tl, *Giving the Keys to St Peter,* Perugino (1482), Sistine Chapel, Vatican, Rome 56cla, 56bl, *Machiavelli,* Santi di Tito, Palazzo Vecchio, Florence 57br, *Andrea Palladio*, Meyer 58cb, *Goethe in the Campagna*, Tischbein (1787), Stadelsches Kunstinstitut, Frankfurt 60cl, *Venetian Carnival in the Eighteenth Century*, Anon (19th century) 60clb, *Bonaparte Crossing the Alps*, David, Schloss Charlottenburg, Berlin 61cr, 61bl, 106t, 106b, 199b, 356–7, 466b, *Archimedes,* Museo Capitolino, Rome 481bl, 505t, 509cl; Stefan Diller *St Francis Appearing to the Brothers at Arles* (1295–1300), San Francesco, Assisi 53tl; Erich Lessing *Margrave Gualtieri of Saluzzo Chooses the Poor Farmer's Daughter, Griseldis, for his Wife,* di Stefano, Galleria dell'Accademia Carrara, Bergamo 34crb, *The Vision of St Augustine* (1502), Carpaccio, Chiesa di San Giorgio degli Schiavoni, Venice 57cr, 222b, 268b, 491b; Archivio IGDA, Milan: 204cl, 204bl, 205b, 521br; Emporio Armani: 24cl, 39tc; Artemide, GB Ltd: 39clb.

Mario Bettella 535clb, 542c; La Biennale di Venezia: 656cra; Frank Blackburn: 267c; Osvaldo Böhm, Venice: 89t, 94c, 111t; Bridgeman Art Library, London/New York: 46c, Ambrosiana, Milan 195tl; Bargello, Florence 279b, 283c; Bibliothèque Nationale, Paris: *Marco Polo with Elephants and Camels Arriving at Hormuz, Gulf of Persia, from India*, Livre des Merveilles Fr 2810 f.14v 41t; British Museum, London *Etruscan Vase Showing Boxers Fighting* 45tl, *Flask Decorated with Christian Symbols* 50tl, *Greek Attic Red-Figure Vase depicting Odysseus with the Sirens,* Stamnos 481cb; Galleria dell'Accademia Carrara, Bergamo 201tr; Galleria Borghese, Rome 439cl; Galleria degli Uffizi, Florence 26tc, 29tl, 29br, *Self-Portrait*, Raphael Sanzio of Urbino 57bl, 287b, 289b: K & B News Photo, Florence 276tl; Santa Maria Novella, Florence 297bl; Museo Civico, Prato 328bl; Louvre, Paris *Statuette of Herakles Brandishing his Club*, Classical Greek, Argive period 480t; Mausoleo di Galla Placidia, Ravenna 268tr; Museo di San Marco, Florence 297bl; Musée d'Orsay, Paris - Giraudon *Les Romains de la Decadence*, Thomas Couture 395tr; Museo delle Sinopie, Camposanto, Pisa 27clb; Palazzo dei Normanni, Palermo *Scene with Centaurs from the Room of King Ruggero* 523b; Pinacoteca di Brera, Milan 198c, 198b, 199t, Private Collection *Theodoric I* (455–526 AD) *Ostrogothic King of Italy* 50b; San Francesco, Arezzo 27tr; San Francesco, Assisi 355cb; San Sebastiano, Venice 29crb; San Zaccaria, Venice 33c, 33tr, 99c; Santa Croce, Florence 284bl, 285cb; Santa Maria Gloriosa dei Frari, Venice 28tr; Santa Maria Novella, Florence 27cla; Scrovegni (Arena) Chapel, Padua 27tr; Scuola di San Giorgio degli Schiavoni, Venice 120b; Staatliche Museen, Berlin *Septimius Severus and Family* 49b; Vatican Museums and Galleries, Rome 421bl; Walker Art Gallery, Liverpool *Aeschylus and Hygieia* 480b; British Museum, London: 46cl.

Capitoline Museum, Rome: 387cr; Demetrio Carrasco: 102br, 682tr; Cephas Picture Library Mick Rock: 2–3, 23t, 24t, 182tr, 183b, 183tr, 242–3, 251tl, 251tr, 472–3, 660–1; JL Charmet, Paris: 353br; Ciga Hotels: 91cb; Foto Elio e Stefano Ciol: 77cra, 164bc, 164br, 165bl, 165bc, 165br; Stephani Colasanti: 76bl; Comune di Asti: 68cl; Consorzio Motoscafi Venezia: 682clb; Corbis: Assignments Photographers/Bryn Colton 180cla; Dave Bartruff 476cla; Gerard Degeorge 11cra; Owen Franken 248cla, 249t, 477c; Michelle Garrett 477t; John Heseltine 378cla; Robert Holmes 79t; Reuters/Tony Gentile 379t; ML Sinibaldi 13br; Hubert Stadler 539crb; Joe Cornish: 22t, 82tr, 138, 160t, 244–5, 314, 364, 461b, 537b; Giancarlo Costa: 9c, 34t, 35cr, 35cra, 35tl, 75c, 177c, 182tl, 473c, 553c, 661c.

Il Dagherrotipo: 676cl; Archivio Arte 207t; Archivio Storico 35b, 206b, 261b; Salvatore Barba 506tl; Alberto Berni 225bl; Riccardo Catani 501b; Marco Cerruti 178cla, 213b, 215b, 216b; Antonio Cittadini 189tr, 192b, 202t ; Gianni Dolfini 550b; Riccardo d'Errico 70tr, 247t, 268c; Maurizio Fraschetti 496br; Diane Haines 173br, 659bc; Maurizio Leoni 67c; Marco Melodia 506clb, 506br, 507b, 547tl, 658tl, 658cl; Stefano Occhibelli 69c, 254, 401bl; Giorgio Oddi 247tc, 252t, 513tr; Donato Fierro Perez 533cb; Marco Ravasini 170t, 549c; Giovanni Rinaldi 25t, 66bl, 67tl, 179bl, 231b, 398c, 367t, 373t, 466c, 482, 499t, 507c, 533cr, 551t, 551c; Lorenzo Scaramella 468c; Stefania Servili 172t; James Darell: 348; CM Dixon: 421cb; Chris Donaghue The Oxford Photo Library: 117t.

ELECTA: 156c, 157c, 157t; EMPICS: 70ca, 70cbl; ET ARCHIVE: 36bc, 45c, 46tl, 49cr, 52–3c, 57tl, 59tl, 63b, 412tr, 481cra, 531b; MARY EVANS PICTURE LIBRARY: 34clb, 35cl, 41ca, 62b, 62crb, 63cr, 64cb, 80tr, 245c, 320cla, 326t, 391ca, 393bl, 409b, 442clb, 511cr, 511br, 550t.

FERRARI: 38b; ARCHIVIO STORICO FIAT, TURIN: 64tr; FIAT PRESS OFFICE: 220ca; APT FOLIGNATE E NOCERA UMBRA: 361t; by kind permission of FONDAZIONE ARENA DI VERONA: Gianfranco Fainello 656b; WERNER FORMAN ARCHIVE: 45br, 51tr, 435br; CONSORZIO FRASASSI: 372b.

STUDIO GAVIRATI, Gubbio: 352c; APT GENOVA: Roberto Merlo 238bl; GETTY IMAGES: Julian Finney 70bc; The Image Bank/Andrea Pistolesi 78cla; Maremagnum 671cl; Clive Mason 71bl, 71cb; Stone/Simone Huber 657t; GIRAUDON, Paris: *Aphrodite Persuading Helen to Follow Paris to Troy,* Museo Nazionale di Villa Giulia, Rome 45clb, *Pharmacy*, Museo della Civiltà Romana 48cb, *Grandes Chroniques de France; Coronation of Charlemagne in St Peter's by Leon III,* Musée Goya, Castres 51tl, *Taking of Constantinople,* Basilica of St John the Evangelist, Ravenna 53cr, *Dante's Hell with Commentary of Guiniforte delli Bargigi* (Ms2017 fol 245), Bibliothèque Nationale, Paris 54cb, *Portrait of St Ignatius of Loyola,* Rubens, Musée Brukenthal, Sibiu 59ca, *Charles III's Fleet at Naples 6th October 1759,* Joli de Dipi, Museo del Prado, Madrid 60tr, *Inauguration of the Naples-Portici Railway*, Fergola (1839), Museo Nazionale di San Martino, Naples 62clb, *Piedmontese and French at the Battle of San Martino in 1859* Anon, Museo Centrale del Risorgimento, Rome 63tl, 106clb, 107t, 199cr, 268tl; ALINARI-GIRAUDON: *St Mark Appearing to the Venetians Looking for His Body*, Tintoretto (1568), Brera Art Gallery, Milan 29tr, *Shrine*, House of the Vettii, Pompeii 49cb, *St Gregory in his Study* (Inv 285), Pinacoteca Nazionale, Bologna 51bl, *Portrait of Victor Emmanuel II*, Dugoni (1866), Galleria d'Arte Moderna, Palazzo Pitti, Florence 62tl, 107b, 199tl, *Louis II of Gonzaga and his Court*, Andrea Mantegna (1466–74), Museo di Palazzo Ducale, Mantova 208–209, 287tl-tc, *History of Pope Alexander III: Building of the City of Alexandria*, Aretino Spinello (1407), Palazzo Pubblico, Siena 55cr; ALINARI-SEAT-GIRAUDON: 227c; FLAMMARION-GIRAUDON: *Poem by Donizo in Honour of Queen Matilda,* Biblioteca Apostolica, Vatican 52ca; LAUROS-GIRAUDON: *Portrait of Francis Petrarch* 54b, *Liber notabilium Philippi Septimi, francorum regis a libris Galieni extractus* (Ms 334 569 fig17), Guy of Pavia (1345), Musée Condé, Chantilly 55b, *Gallery of Views of Ancient Rome*, Pannini (1758), Musée du Louvre, Paris 60–61c, *Portrait of the Artist*, Bernini, Private Collection 58tl, *Four Angels and Symbols of the Evangelists*, 32tr, 33tr; ORSI-BATTAGLINI-GIRAUDON: *Madonna of the Shadow*, Museum of San Marco, Florence 32c, *Supplice de Savonarola* Anon 56clb; THE RONALD GRANT ARCHIVE: 65b; Paramount *The God-father Part III* (1990) 535br; Riama *La Dolce Vita* (1960) 64cra;

TCF *Boccaccio '70* (1962) 23cl, *The Name of the Rose* (1986) 34cla; PALAZZO VENIER DEI LEONI, PEGGY GUGGENHEIM COLLECTION, VENICE: 91cla. PHOTO HALUPKA: 120t; ROBERT HARDING PICTURE LIBRARY: 1c, 70tl, 191b, 270, 390cl, 414, 419br, 658b; Dumrath 269c; Gavin Hellier 12crb; HP Merton 166, 658tr; Roy Rainford 499cr; JOHN HESELTINE: 467t; MICHAEL HOLFORD: 47ca; HOTEL PORTA ROSSA: 556t; HOTEL VILLA PAGODA: 555t; HSL: 679tl; THE HULTON DEUTSCH COLLECTION: 64br, 89cla, 90cla, 90br, 157br, 375c; Keystone 64ca.

THE IMAGE BANK, London: 334b; Marcella Pedone 187b; Andrea Pistolesi 255b; Guido Rossi 14b, 47cb; THE IMAGE BANK, Milan: 195b; IMPACT: 315b; INDEX, Florence: 282c, 327t, 327cr; ISTITUTO E MUSEO DI STORIA DELLA SCIENZA DI FIRENZE: Franca Principe 40b, 285c ISTOCKPHOTO.COM: Robert Caucino 396.
TIM JEPSON: 351t.

FRANK LANE PICTURE AGENCY: 216t, 217t, 217c, 217b; M Melodia/Panda 506cla.

MAGNUM, London: Abbas 64crb; THE MANSELL COLLECTION: 52clb, 393tl; MARCONI LTD 40t; MARKA: L Barbazza 97tr; E Cerretelli 121b; M Motta 667t; MASTERSTUDIO, Pescara: 504c; su concessione del MINISTERO PER I BENI CULTURALI E AMBIENTALI: *The Last Supper*; da Vinci, Leonardo 200b; MIRROR SYNDICATION INTERNATIONAL: 40clb; MOBY LINES: 675c; FOTO MODENA: 266t, 371c; TONY MOTT: 465b, 470t; MUSEO DIOCESANO DI ROSSANO 520t.

NHPA: Laurie Campbell 83crb; Gerard Lacz 83br; Silvestris Fotoservice 83cr; BY COURTESY OF THE NATIONAL PORTRAIT GALLERY, London: (detail) *Percy Bysshe Shelley,* Amelia Curran (1819) 60tl; GRAZIA NERI: 52tl; Roberta Krasnig 670bl; Marco Bruzzo 68br; Cameraphoto 108bl; Marcello Mencarini 88br; NEWIMAGE S.R.L: Rolando Fabriani 654cla; NIPPON TELEVISION NETWORK: 424c–425c, 424t, 424b–425bl, 425t, 425br, 426b; PETER NOBLE: 318t, 336–7, 341b, 666b.

L'OCCHIO DI CRISTALLO/STUDIO FOTOGRAFICO DI GIORGIO OLIVERO: 229b; APT ORVIETO: Massimo Roncella 358t; OXFORD SCIENTIFIC FILMS: Stan Osolinski 347cr.

PADOVA - MUSEI CIVICI - CAPPELLA SCROVEGNI: 77cr, 156t, 156cla, 156clb, 157cra, 157crb, 157bl; PADOVA - MUSEI CIVICI AGLI EREMITANI: 158t, 158c; LUCIANO PEDICINI - ARCHIVIO DELL'ARTE: 362b, 404t, 475t, 486tl, 490t, 490ca, 490cb, 491t, 491ca, 491cr, 493t, 530b; APT PESARO - LE MARCHE: 368cr; PICTURES COLOUR LIBRARY: 546b, 548l; ANDREA PISTOLESI: 20; PNALM ARCHIVE: in association with www.abruzzonatura.com 506bc; POLIS PHOTO LIBRARY, Milan: Eugenio Bersani 11t; POPPERFOTO: 64tl, 65tl, 65clb.

Sarah Quill, Venice: 90t, 94b, 100tl.

Retrograph Archive: 37c; Rex Features: 37t; Steve Wood 39tr; Reuters: Toru Hanai 70crb; Ferran Paredes 71tl.

Scala Group S.p.A: 26bl, 27b, 28br, 29ca, 29bl, 36tl, 49c; 252bl; 398cla, *Portrait of Claudio Monteverdi*, Domenico Feti, Accademia, Venice 36bl, *Portolan of Italy* (16th century), Loggia dei Lanzi, Firenze 291bl, Museo Correr, Venice 43b, *Etruscan Bronze Liver*, Museo Civico, Piacenza 44clb, *Earrings*, Museo Etrusco Guarnacci, Volterra 44br, 44r–45c, *Crater from Pescia Romana*, Museo Archeologico, Grosseto 45bc, *Terracotta Vase in the Shape of an Elephant*, Museo Nazionale, Naples 46cr, *Cicero denounces Catiline*, Palazzo Madama, Rome 47tl, 47bl, *Circus Scene Mosaic - Gladiator Fight,* Galleria Borghese, Rome 48t, 48br, *Theodolinda Melts the Gold for the New Church* (15th century), Famiglia Zavattari, Duomo, Monza 50clb, 50–51, 51br, *Tomb Relief depicting a School*, Matteo Gandoni, Museo Civico, Bologna 52b, *Detail from an Ambo of Frederick II* (13th century), Cattedrale, Bitonto 53cb, *Guidoriccio da Fogliano at the Siege of Note Massi*, Simone Martini, Palazzo Pubblico, Siena 54clb, 55tl, *Return of Gregory XI from Avignon* Giorgio Vasari, Sala Regia, Vatican 55cb, 56br, 56r–57c, 57crb, *Clement VII in Conversation with Charles V*, Giorgio Vasari, Palazzo Vecchio, Florence 58cla, *Portrait of Pierluigi da Palestrina*, Istituto dei Padri dell'Oratorio, Rome 58br, *Revolt at Masaniello,* Domenico Gargiulo, Museo di San Martino, Naples 59crb, 60br, 61tl, 61crb, 62cla, 62–63c, 63crb, 95cl, 100c, 118br, 146c, 222tr, 226b, 260tl, 263t, 265t, 269t, 274c, 274b, 275t, 276c, 276b, 277t, 277b, 280cl, 282t, 283tr, 283br, 286t, 286c, 286b, 287ca, 287cb, 288t, 288b, 289t, 289cl, 291bl, 292t, 292b, 293t, 293b, 294t, 294c, 295t, 296bl, 298–9 all, 301bl, 302tr, 302tl, 302c, 303t, 303cl, 303b, 325c, 325b, 330–331 all, 332t, 332b, 338b, 340t, 341cl, 344cla, 345b, 354t, 354c, 355bl, 358bl, 359c, 370t, 370b, 371t, 371bl, 377br, 384c, 400bl, 402tr, 404c, 411c, 416tl, 416c, 416b, 417t, 418b, 419t, 420t, 420cb, 421c, 423t, 423c, 423b, 427t, 427b, 490bc, 511c, 513tl, 529b, 530tr, 536t, 537t, 538b, 549b; Science Photo Library: 15t; Argonne National Laboratory 41cr; John Ferro Sims: 24b, 25b, 84, 176–7, 365b, 374–5, 460, 542b; Agenzia Sintesi, Rome: Antonella Girolamo 666clb; Mario Soster di Alagna: 557c; Frank Spooner Pictures: Diffidenti 548b; Gamma 65tr, 65tc; Sporting Pictures: 71cra; STA Travel Group: 664cb; Tony Stone Images: 83cla; Stephen Studd 31tr, 185cr; Agenzia Fotografica Stradella, Milan: Bersanetti 191tl; Lamberto Caenazzo 546c; Francesco Gavazzini 216c; F Giaccone 526c; Mozzati 370clb; Massimo Pacifico 507t; Ettore Re 499crb; Ghigo Roli 499b; Giulio Vegi 533t; Amedeo Vergani 210, 214b, 234t, 257t; SuperStock: age fotostock 379c; Sygma: 67tr.

Tasting Italy: Martin Brigdale 659t; Tate Gallery Publications: 64bl; APT dell'Alta Valle del Tevere: Museo del Duomo 54tl; Touring Club of Italy: 204br, Cresci 534t; Archivio Città di Torino Settore Turismo: 221t; Davide Bogliacino 213t; Fototeca APT del Trentino: Foto di Banal 174t; Foto di Faganello 173t, 175c.

Vela SpA: 683cr, 683crb; Venice Simplon-Orient-Express: 674tl; Villa Crespi: 604b.

Charlie Waite: 21b; Edizione White Star: Marcello Bertinetti 85b; Giulio Veggi 8–9, 74–5, 139b; Fiona Wild: 540–1; Peter Wilson: 5t, 92–3; World Pictures: 552–3.

Front Endpaper:
Joe Cornish: Lcrb, Rc, Rtcr; Il Dagherrotipo: Marco Melodia Lbl; Stefano Occhibelli Rtl; Giovanni Rinaldi Rbl; James Darell: Rcl; Robert Harding Picture Library: Lc, H.P. Merton Rtcl; John Ferro Sims: Ltr, Rbc; Agenzia Fotografica Stradella, Milan: Amadeo Vergani Ltl.

Back Endpaper:
Istockphoto.com: Roberto Caucino cl; Robert Harding Picture Library: Rolf Richardson tl.

JACKET
Front – Photolibrary: De Agostini Editore/C Sappa. Back – Dorling Kindersley: Demetrio Carrasco cla; Paul Harris and Anne Heslope t; John Heseltine bl; Linda Whitwam clb. Spine – Photolibrary: De Agostini Editore/C Sappa t.

# Phrase Book

## In Emergency

| | | |
|---|---|---|
| Help! | **Aiuto!** | eye-**yoo**-toh |
| Stop! | **Fermate!** | fair-**mah**-teh |
| Call a doctor. | **Chiama un medico** | kee-**ah**-mah oon **meh**-dee-koh |
| Call an ambulance. | **Chiama un' ambulanza** | kee-**ah**-mah oon am-boo-**lan**-tsa |
| Call the police. | **Chiama la polizia** | kee-**ah**-mah lah pol-ee-**tsee**-ah |
| Call the fire brigade. | **Chiama i pompieri** | kee-**ah**-mah ee pom-pee-**air**-ee |
| Where is the telephone? | **Dov'è il telefono?** | dov-**eh** eel teh-**leh**-foh-noh? |
| The nearest hospital? | **L'ospedale più vicino?** | loss-peh-**dah**-leh-pee-**oo** vee-**chee**-noh? |

## Communication Essentials

| | | |
|---|---|---|
| Yes/No | **Sì/No** | **see/noh** |
| Please | **Per favore** | pair fah-**vor**-eh |
| Thank you | **Grazie** | **grah**-tsee-eh |
| Excuse me | **Mi scusi** | mee **skoo**-zee |
| Hello | **Buon giorno** | bwon **jor**-noh |
| Goodbye | **Arrivederci** | ah-ree-veh-**dair**-chee |
| Good evening | **Buona sera** | **bwon**-ah **sair**-ah |
| morning | **la mattina** | lah mah-**tee**-nah |
| afternoon | **il pomeriggio** | eel poh-meh-**ree**-joh |
| Evening | **la sera** | lah **sair**-ah |
| yesterday | **ieri** | ee-**air**-ee |
| today | **oggi** | **oh**-jee |
| tomorrow | **domani** | doh-**mah**-nee |
| here | **qui** | **kwee** |
| there | **la** | **lah** |
| What? | **Quale?** | **kwah**-leh? |
| When? | **Quando?** | **kwan**-doh? |
| Why? | **Perchè?** | pair-**keh**? |
| Where? | **Dove?** | **doh**-veh? |

## Useful Phrases

| | | |
|---|---|---|
| How are you? | **Come sta?** | **koh**-meh stah? |
| Very well, thank you. | **Molto bene, grazie.** | **moll**-toh **beh**-neh **grah**-tsee-eh |
| Pleased to meet you. | **Piacere di conoscerla.** | pee-ah-**chair**-eh dee coh-**noh**-shair-lah |
| See you later. | **A più tardi.** | ah pee-**oo tar**-dee |
| That's fine. | **Va bene.** | va **beh**-neh |
| Where is/are …? | **Dov'è/Dove sono …?** | dov-**eh**/doveh **soh**-noh? |
| How long does it take to get to …? | **Quanto tempo ci vuole per andare a …?** | **kwan**-toh **tem**-poh chee voo-**oh**-leh pair an-**dar**-eh ah …? |
| How do I get to …? | **Come faccio per arrivare a …?** | koh-meh **fah**-choh pair arri-**var**-eh ah..? |
| Do you speak English? | **Parla inglese?** | **par**-lah een-**gleh** -zeh? |
| I don't understand. | **Non capisco.** | non ka-**pee**-skoh |
| Could you speak more slowly, please? | **Può parlare più lentamente, per favore?** | pwoh par-**lah**-reh pee-**oo** len-ta-**men**-teh pair fah-**vor**-eh? |
| I'm sorry. | **Mi dispiace.** | mee dee-spee-**ah**-heh |

## Useful Words

| | | |
|---|---|---|
| big | **grande** | **gran**-deh |
| small | **piccolo** | **pee**-koh-loh |
| hot | **caldo** | **kal**-doh |
| cold | **freddo** | **fred**-doh |
| good | **buono** | **bwoh**-noh |
| bad | **cattivo** | kat-**tee**-voh |
| enough | **basta** | **bas**-tah |
| well | **bene** | **beh**-neh |
| open | **aperto** | ah-**pair**-toh |
| closed | **chiuso** | kee-**oo**-zoh |
| left | **a sinistra** | ah see-**nee**-strah |
| right | **a destra** | ah **dess**-trah |
| straight on | **sempre dritto** | **sem**-preh **dree**-toh |
| near | **vicino** | vee-**chee**-noh |
| far | **lontano** | lon-**tah**-noh |
| up | **su** | **soo** |
| down | **giù** | **joo** |
| early | **presto** | **press**-toh |
| late | **tardi** | **tar**-dee |
| entrance | **entrata** | en-**trah**-tah |
| exit | **uscita** | oo-**shee**-ta |
| toilet | **il gabinetto** | eel gah-bee-**net**-toh |
| free, unoccupied | **libero** | **lee**-bair-oh |
| free, no charge | **gratuito** | grah-**too**-ee-toh |

## Making a Telephone Call

| | | |
|---|---|---|
| I'd like to place a long-distance call. | **Vorrei fare una interurbana.** | vor-**ray far**-eh oona in-tair-oor-**bah**-nah |
| I'd like to make a reverse-charge call. | **Vorrei fare una telefonata a carico del destinatario.** | vor-**ray far**-eh oona teh-leh-fon-**ah**-tah ah **kar**-ee-koh dell dess-tee-nah-**tar**-ree-oh |
| I'll try again later. | **Ritelefono più tardi.** | ree-teh-**leh**-foh-noh pee-oo **tar**-dee |
| Can I leave a message? | **Posso lasciare un messaggio?** | **poss**-oh lash-**ah**-reh oon mess-**sah**-joh? |
| Hold on. | **Un attimo, per favore** | oon **ah**-tee-moh, pair fah-**vor**-eh |
| Could you speak up a little please? | **Può parlare più forte, per favore?** | pwoh par-**lah**-reh pee-**oo for**-teh, pair fah-**vor**-eh? |
| local call | **telefonata locale** | te-leh-fon-**ah**-tah loh-cah-leh |

## Shopping

| | | |
|---|---|---|
| How much does this cost? | **Quant'è, per favore?** | kwan-**teh** pair fah-**vor**-eh? |
| I would like … | **Vorrei …** | vor-**ray** |
| Do you have …? | **Avete …?** | ah-**veh**-teh.. ? |
| I'm just looking. | **Sto soltanto guardando.** | stoh sol-**tan**-toh gwar-**dan**-doh |
| Do you take credit cards? | **Accettate carte di credito?** | ah-chet-**tah** -teh **kar**-teh dee **creh**-dee-toh? |
| What time do you open/close? | **A che ora apre/ chiude?** | ah keh **or**-ah **ah**-preh/kee-**oo**-deh? |
| this one | **questo** | **kweh**-stoh |
| that one | **quello** | **kwell**-oh |
| expensive | **caro** | **kar**-oh |
| cheap | **a buon prezzo** | ah bwon **pret**-soh |
| size, clothes | **la taglia** | lah **tah**-lee-ah |
| size, shoes | **il numero** | eel **noo**-mair-oh |
| white | **bianco** | bee-**ang**-koh |
| black | **nero** | **neh**-roh |
| red | **rosso** | **ross**-oh |
| yellow | **giallo** | **jal**-loh |
| green | **verde** | **vair**-deh |
| blue | **blu** | bloo |

## Types of Shop

| | | |
|---|---|---|
| antique dealer | **l'antiquario** | lan-tee-**kwah**-ree-oh |
| bakery | **il forno /il panificio** | eel **forn**-oh /eel pan-ee-**fee**-choh |
| bank | **la banca** | lah **bang**-kah |
| bookshop | **la libreria** | lah lee-breh-**ree**-ah |
| butcher | **la macelleria** | lah mah-chell-eh-**ree**-ah |
| cake shop | **la pasticceria** | lah pas-tee-chair-**ee**-ah |
| chemist | **la farmacia** | lah far-mah-**chee**-ah |
| delicatessen | **la salumeria** | lah sah-loo-meh-**ree**-ah |
| department store | **il grande magazzino** | eel **gran**-deh mag-gad-**zee**-noh |
| fishmonger | **il pescivendolo** | eel pesh-ee-**ven**-doh-loh |
| florist | **il fioraio** | eel fee-or-**eye**-oh |
| greengrocer | **il fruttivendolo** | eel froo-tee-**ven**-doh-loh |
| grocery | **alimentari** | ah-lee-men-**tah**-ree |
| hairdresser | **il parrucchiere** | eel par-oo-kee-**air**-eh |
| ice cream parlour | **la gelateria** | lah jel-lah-tair-**ree**-ah |
| market | **il mercato** | eel mair-**kah**-toh |
| newsstand | **l'edicola** | leh-**dee**-koh-lah |
| post office | **l'ufficio postale** | loo-**fee**-choh pos-**tah**-leh |
| shoe shop | **il negozio di scarpe** | eel neh-**goh**-tsioh dee **skar**-peh |
| supermarket | **il supermercato** | eel su-pair-mair-**kah**-toh |
| tobacconist | **il tabaccaio** | eel tah-bak-**eye**-oh |
| travel agency | **l'agenzia di viaggi** | lah-jen-**tsee**-ah dee vee-**ad**-jee |

## Sightseeing

| | | |
|---|---|---|
| art gallery | **la pinacoteca** | lah peena-koh-**teh**-kah |
| bus stop | **la fermata dell'autobus** | lah fair-**mah**-tah dell **ow**-toh-booss |
| church | **la chiesa** | lah kee-**eh**-zah |
| | **la basilica** | lah bah-**seel**-i-kah |
| closed for holidays | **chiuso per le ferie** | kee-**oo**-zoh pair leh **fair**-ee-eh |
| garden | **il giardino** | eel jar-**dee**-no |
| library | **la biblioteca** | lah beeb-lee-oh-**teh**-kah |
| museum | **il museo** | eel moo-**zeh**-oh |
| railway station | **la stazione** | lah stah-tsee-**oh**-neh |
| tourist information | **l'ufficio di turismo** | loo-**fee**-choh dee too-**ree**-smoh |

## Staying in a Hotel

| | | |
|---|---|---|
| Do you have any vacant rooms? | **Avete camere libere?** | ah-**veh**-teh **kah**-mair-eh **lee**-bair-eh? |
| double room | **una camera doppia** | oona **kah**-mair-ah **doh**-pee-ah |
| with double bed | **con letto matrimoniale** | kon **let**-toh mah-tree-moh-nee-**ah**-leh |
| twin room | **una camera con due letti** | oona **kah**-mair-ah kon **doo**-eh **let**-tee |
| single room | **una camera singola** | oona **kah**-mair-ah **sing**-goh-lah |
| room with a bath, shower | **una camera con bagno, con doccia** | oona **kah**-mair-ah kon **ban**-yoh, kon **dot**-chah |
| porter | **il facchino** | eel fah-**kee**-noh |
| key | **la chiave** | lah kee-**ah**-veh |
| I have a reservation. | **Ho fatto una prenotazione.** | oh **fat**-toh oona preh-noh-tah-tsee-**oh**-neh |

## Eating Out

| | | |
|---|---|---|
| Have you got a table for...? | **Avete una tavola per ... ?** | ah-**veh**-teh oona **tah**-voh-lah pair ...? |
| I'd like to reserve a table. | **Vorrei riservare una tavola.** | vor-**ray** ree-sair-**vah**-reh oona **tah**-voh-lah |
| breakfast | **colazione** | koh-lah-tsee-**oh**-neh |
| lunch | **pranzo** | **pran**-tsoh |
| dinner | **cena** | **cheh**-nah |
| The bill, please. | **Il conto, per favore.** | eel **kon**-toh pair fah-**vor**-eh |
| I am a vegetarian. | **Sono vegetariano/a.** | **soh**-noh **veh**-jeh-tar-ee-**ah**-noh/nah |
| waitress | **cameriera** | kah-mair-ee-**air**-ah |
| waiter | **cameriere** | kah-mair-ee-**air**-eh |
| fixed price menu | **il menù a prezzo fisso** | eel meh-**noo** ah **pret**-soh **fee**-soh |
| dish of the day | **piatto del giorno** | pee-**ah**-toh dell **jor**-no |
| starter | **antipasto** | an-tee-**pass**-toh |
| first course | **il primo** | eel **pree**-moh |
| main course | **il secondo** | eel seh-**kon**-doh |
| vegetables | **il contorno** | eel kon-**tor**-noh |
| dessert | **il dolce** | eel **doll**-cheh |
| cover charge | **il coperto** | eel koh-**pair**-toh |
| wine list | **la lista dei vini** | lah **lee**-stah day **vee**-nee |
| rare | **al sangue** | al **sang**-gweh |
| medium | **al puntino** | al poon-**tee**-noh |
| well done | **ben cotto** | ben **kot**-toh |
| glass | **il bicchiere** | eel bee-kee-**air**-eh |
| bottle | **la bottiglia** | lah bot-**teel**-yah |
| knife | **il coltello** | eel kol-**tell**-oh |
| fork | **la forchetta** | lah for-**ket**-tah |
| spoon | **il cucchiaio** | eel koo-kee-**eye**-oh |

## Menu Decoder

| | | |
|---|---|---|
| **l'acqua minerale gassata/naturale** | **lah**-kwah mee-nair-ah-leh gah-**zah**-tah/nah-too-rah-leh | mineral water fizzy/still |
| **agnello** | ah-**niell**-oh | lamb |
| **aceto** | ah-**cheh**-toh | vinegar |
| **aglio** | **al**-ee-oh | garlic |
| **al forno** | al **for**-noh | baked |
| **alla griglia** | ah-lah **greel**-yah | grilled |
| **l'aragosta** | lah-rah-**goss**-tah | lobster |
| **arrosto** | ar-**ross**-toh | roast |
| **la birra** | lah **beer**-rah | beer |
| **la bistecca** | lah bee-**stek**-kah | steak |
| **il brodo** | eel **broh**-doh | broth |
| **il burro** | eel **boor**-oh | butter |
| **il caffè** | eel kah-**feh** | coffee |
| **i calamari** | ee kah-lah-**mah**-ree | squid |
| **i carciofi** | ee kar-**choff**-ee | artichokes |
| **la carne** | la **kar**-neh | meat |
| **carne di maiale** | **kar**-neh dee mah-**yah**-leh | pork |
| **la cipolla** | la chip-**oh**-lah | onion |
| **i contorni** | ee kon-**tor**-nee | vegetables |
| **i fagioli** | ee fah-**joh**-lee | beans |
| **il fegato** | eel **fay**-gah-toh | liver |
| **il finocchio** | eel fee-**nok**-ee-oh | fennel |
| **il formaggio** | eel for-**mad**-joh | cheese |
| **le fragole** | leh **frah**-goh-leh | strawberries |
| **il fritto misto** | eel free-toh **mees**-toh | mixed fried dish |
| **la frutta** | la **froot**-tah | fruit |
| **frutti di mare** | **froo**-tee dee mah-reh | seafood |
| **i funghi** | ee **foon**-ghee | mushrooms |
| **i gamberi** | ee **gam**-bair-ee | prawns |
| **il gelato** | eel jel-**lah**-toh | ice cream |
| **l'insalata** | leen-sah-lah-tah | salad |
| **il latte** | eel **laht**-teh | milk |
| **lesso** | **less**-oh | boiled |
| **il manzo** | eel **man**-tsoh | beef |
| **la melanzana** | lah meh-lan-**tsah**-nah | aubergine |
| **la minestra** | lah mee-**ness**-trah | soup |
| **l'olio** | loh-lee-oh | oil |
| **il pane** | eel **pah**-neh | bread |
| **le patate** | leh pah-**tah**-teh | potatoes |
| **le patatine fritte** | leh pah-tah-**teen**-eh **free**-teh | chips |
| **il pepe** | eel **peh**-peh | pepper |
| **la pesca** | lah **pess**-kah | peach |
| **il pesce** | eel **pesh**-eh | fish |
| **il pollo** | eel **poll**-oh | chicken |
| **il pomodoro** | eel poh-moh-**dor**-oh | tomato |
| **il prosciutto cotto/crudo** | eel pro-**shoo**-toh **kot**-toh/**kroo**-doh | ham cooked/cured |
| **il riso** | eel **ree**-zoh | rice |
| **il sale** | eel **sah**-leh | salt |
| **la salsiccia** | lah sal-**see**-chah | sausage |
| **le seppie** | leh **sep**-pee-eh | cuttlefish |
| **secco** | **sek**-koh | dry |
| **la sogliola** | lah **soll**-yoh-lah | sole |
| **i spinaci** | ee spee-**nah**-chee | spinach |
| **succo d'arancia/ di limone** | **soo**-koh dah-**ran**-chah/ dee lee-**moh**-neh | orange/lemon juice |
| **il tè** | eel **teh** | tea |
| **la tisana** | lah tee-**zah**-nah | herbal tea |
| **il tonno** | eel **ton**-noh | tuna |
| **la torta** | lah **tor**-tah | cake/tart |
| **l'uovo** | loo-**oh**-voh | egg |
| **vino bianco** | **vee**-noh bee-**ang**-koh | white wine |
| **vino rosso** | **vee**-noh **ross**-oh | red wine |
| **il vitello** | eel vee-**tell**-oh | veal |
| **le vongole** | leh **von**-goh-leh | clams |
| **lo zucchero** | loh **zoo**-kair-oh | sugar |
| **gli zucchini** | lyee dzu-**kee**-nee | courgettes |
| **la zuppa** | lah **tsoo**-pah | soup |

## Numbers

| | | |
|---|---|---|
| 1 | **uno** | **oo**-noh |
| 2 | **due** | **doo**-eh |
| 3 | **tre** | treh |
| 4 | **quattro** | **kwat**-roh |
| 5 | **cinque** | **ching**-kweh |
| 6 | **sei** | **say**-ee |
| 7 | **sette** | **set**-teh |
| 8 | **otto** | **ot**-toh |
| 9 | **nove** | **noh**-veh |
| 10 | **dieci** | dee-**eh**-chee |
| 11 | **undici** | **oon**-dee-chee |
| 12 | **dodici** | **doh**-dee-chee |
| 13 | **tredici** | **tray**-dee-chee |
| 14 | **quattordici** | kwat-**tor**-dee-chee |
| 15 | **quindici** | **kwin**-dee-chee |
| 16 | **sedici** | **say**-dee-chee |
| 17 | **diciassette** | dee-chah-**set**-teh |
| 18 | **diciotto** | dee-**chot**-toh |
| 19 | **diciannove** | dee-chah-**noh**-veh |
| 20 | **venti** | **ven**-tee |
| 30 | **trenta** | **tren**-tah |
| 40 | **quaranta** | kwah-**ran**-tah |
| 50 | **cinquanta** | ching-**kwan**-tah |
| 60 | **sessanta** | sess-**an**-tah |
| 70 | **settanta** | set-**tan**-tah |
| 80 | **ottanta** | ot-**tan**-tah |
| 90 | **novanta** | noh-**van**-tah |
| 100 | **cento** | **chen**-toh |
| 1,000 | **mille** | **mee**-leh |
| 2,000 | **duemila** | **doo**-eh **mee**-lah |
| 5,000 | **cinquemila** | **ching**-kweh **mee**-lah |
| 1,000,000 | **un milione** | oon meel-**yoh**-neh |

## Time

| | | |
|---|---|---|
| one minute | **un minuto** | oon mee-**noo**-toh |
| one hour | **un'ora** | oon **or**-ah |
| half an hour | **mezz'ora** | medz-**or**-ah |
| a day | **un giorno** | oon **jor**-noh |
| a week | **una settimana** | oona set-tee-**mah**-nah |
| Monday | **lunedì** | loo-neh-**dee** |
| Tuesday | **martedì** | mar-teh-**dee** |
| Wednesday | **mercoledì** | mair-koh-leh-**dee** |
| Thursday | **giovedì** | joh-veh-**dee** |
| Friday | **venerdì** | ven-air-**dee** |
| Saturday | **sabato** | **sah**-bah-toh |
| Sunday | **domenica** | doh-**meh**-nee-kah |

# Central Rome

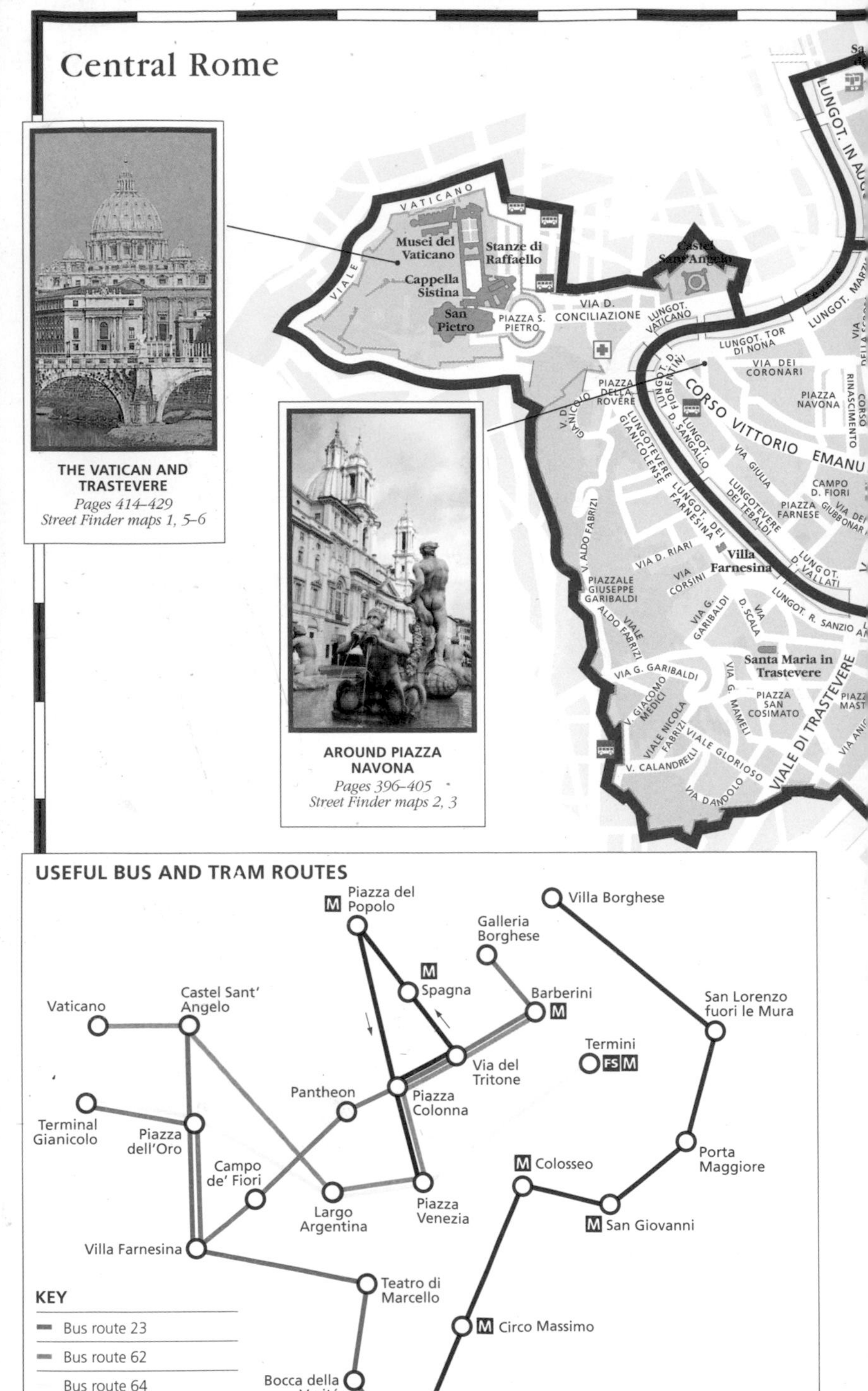


**THE VATICAN AND TRASTEVERE**
*Pages 414–429*
*Street Finder maps 1, 5–6*

**AROUND PIAZZA NAVONA**
*Pages 396–405*
*Street Finder maps 2, 3*

## USEFUL BUS AND TRAM ROUTES



**KEY**

- Bus route 23
- Bus route 62
- Bus route 64
- Bus route 116/116T
- Bus route 119
- Tram route 3